W9-AMX-870

Pathways for Exceptional Children: School, Home, and Culture

Paul Kaplan

Suffolk Community College and The State University of New York at Stony Brook

WEST PUBLISHING COMPANY

Minneapolis/St. Paul   New York   Los Angeles   San Francisco

TO MY NIECES AND NEPHEWS:

PENNY PLISKIN
MATTHEW PLISKIN

ALAN AND BARBARA KAPLAN AND SAMUEL
SHERRY AND JONAH COTTRELL
KELBY KAPLAN

Copyedit: Cheryl Wilms
Composition: American Composition & Graphics
Interior Design: Hespenheide Design
Art: Roslyn M. Stendahl, Dapper Design
Index: Amy Kaplan
Cover: Pierre Bonnard, *The Dance*, 1912. © ARS, NY, Pushkin Museum of Fine Arts, Moscow, Russia.

WEST'S COMMITMENT TO THE ENVIRONMENT

In 1906, West Publishing Company began recycling materials left over from the production of books. This began a tradition of efficient and responsible use of resources. Today, up to 95 percent of our legal bound volumes are printed on acid-free, recycled paper consisting of 50% new paper pulp and 50% paper that has undergone a de-inking process. We also use vegetable-based inks to print all of our books. West recycles nearly 22,650,000 pounds of scrap paper annually—the equivalent of 187,500 trees. Since the 1960s, West has devised ways to capture and recycle waste inks, solvents, oils, and vapors created in the printing process. We also recycle plastics of all kinds, wood, glass, corrugated cardboard and batteries, and have eliminated the use of Polystyrene book packaging. We at West are proud of the longevity and the scope of our commitment to the environment.

West pocket parts and advance sheets are printed on recyclable paper and can be collected and recycled with newspapers. Staples do not have to be removed. Bound volumes can be recycled after removing the covers.

Production, Prepress, Printing and Binding by West Publishing Company.

 TEXT IS PRINTED ON 10% POST CONSUMER RECYCLED PAPER  PRINTED WITH SOY INK

British Library Cataloguing-in-Publication Data. A catalogue record for this book is available from the British Library.

COPYRIGHT ©1996 By WEST PUBLISHING COMPANY
        610 Opperman Drive
        P.O. Box 64526
        St. Paul, MN 55164-0526

Library of Congress Cataloging-in-Publication Data

Kaplan, Paul S.
 Pathways for exceptional children: school, home, and culture / Paul S. Kaplan
  p. cm.
 Includes index.
 ISBN 0-314-04563-5 (hard: acid-free paper)
 1. Exceptional children--Education--United States. I. Title.
LC3981. K36 1996
371.9 0973--dc20
           94-49198 CIP

CONTENTS IN BRIEF

CONTENTS

CHAPTER 3

Early Intervention and Preschool Programs

PART TWO — High Incidence Exceptionalities

CHAPTER 4

Mental Retardation

PART THREE **Individual Differences and Children at Risk**

CHAPTER 8

Children at Risk

CHAPTER 9

Children from Minority Groups in Special Education

or spelling rules (Parette & Van Biervliet, 1991).

Assistive technology may be classified in many ways, but perhaps it is easiest to categorize it according to its major uses. For example, technology may be used to improve learning or instruction, communication, environmental control, and mobility. Specially written computer programs may assist the teacher in instruction. Assistive technology for communication would include all electronic communication devices, computers, and word processing programs for written communication, print translation devices for persons with limited vision, and assistive listening aids for people with auditory disabilities. Environmental control would include architectural adaptations for people with physical disabilities and devices, such as switch-operated appliances and voice activated controls for room temperature and lighting. Special mobility aids, such as powered wheelchairs, are used to improve mobility (Lewis, 1993).

Public Law 100-407, the Technology-Related Assistance for Individuals with Disabilities Act of 1988, provides funding to states, which allows them to plan and deliver assistive technology systems for people of all ages. The Individuals with Disabilities Education Act (IDEA) also further encourages the use of technology by adding services that evaluate the needs of an individual, purchases of such equipment, and the training of the individual with a disability to use these devices to the growing list of services to which people with disabilities are entitled.

In 1990, the federal government's Office of Special Education Programs ruled that children's needs for assistive technology should be evaluated on a case-by-case basis and included in the IEP. If the child requires an assistive device, it is to be provided at no cost to the family.

One portion of the Americans with Disabilities Act mandates that telephone companies provide relay services to people who use telecommunications devices.

In addition, some employers will need to modify equipment or provide special equipment for their workers in order to comply with this law.

Adapting technology to the needs of people with disabilities is a promising area of special education. The IEP team must analyze the individual's particular needs, analyze the technology available, fit the two together, and then give the child the training that is required for adequate use of the technological device. Such technological devices as closed circuit television, audio transmitters, powered wheelchairs, and computer touch screens can do much to help children with disabilities achieve and participate in classroom activities.

Choosing the appropriate technological device is not always easy. First, technology should be seen as a tool, not an end in itself. Sometimes, the technology overshadows the child and the purpose for which it is to be used because of a tendency to believe that the more sophisticated the technology the better. For example, a talking computer with a very colorful display is certainly an attention-getting tool, but perhaps a less sophisticated aid might do just as well (Lewis, 1993). Second, technology used for educational functions must be educationally valuable and appropriate. Computers need to be incorporated into the curriculum rather than used only to keep children busy. The standard of educational value should always be met. Last, thought should be given to the use of this technology after the child leaves school. Technology should increase independence and improve functioning across environments.

Technology has become so vital an area of concern that a specific feature will be devoted to its use in each chapter. The advent of such technology opens up new opportunities, provides more freedom of expression, and allows the child to more fully participate in activities both inside and outside the classroom.

PART FOUR   Gifted Students

CHAPTER 10

Intellectual Ability

CHAPTER 11

Creativity and Talent

Writing a text about children with exceptional needs involves keeping a balance and meeting a challenge. On one hand, each child is an individual, with strengths and limitations, abilities and weaknesses. This appreciation of individual differences is established in law. Unfortunately, most people speaking about children with disabilities emphasize the disability rather than the child. This may be understandable, since the child requires special services, but it does lead to overgeneralizing and the danger of forgetting the individual.

On the other hand, although every child with a learning disability has individual strengths and weaknesses, children with learning disabilities share the need for particular types of services and educational adaptations in order to achieve. These similarities permit a discussion of the general challenges teachers encounter when teaching children with a particular disability. A balance, then, must be maintained between appreciating the individuality of a child with a disability and understanding the general problems the child and others with similar disabilities may encounter as they mature.

The challenge of writing a text in this area is to encourage understanding and empathy, while presenting an objective evaluation—based on research—of the learning characteristics and requirements of the child in various environments. An empathetic understanding of the challenges that the child and the family encounter is a positive goal, but it must not be allowed to lead to an attitude in which children with disabilities are perceived as always needing others to make decisions for them. On the surface, such an attitude may seem positive because the attitudes expressed are ones of caring and interest. However, this attitude may interfere with the development of a sense of autonomy and independence in children with disabilities.

The field of special education is a dynamic and exciting one with a number of emerging trends that are reflected in this text. For example, special education, once connected with a place, be it the resource room or a special classroom, is presented now as a group of services and adaptations. This trend does not mean that arguments over placement are no longer valid; they remain a major source of disagreement in the field. However, the newer view emphasizes the nature of the services required by children with exceptionalities.

Another change is the growing focus on personal decision-making and independence. Many programs now foster independence and healthy functioning within society to the greatest extent possible. To reach this goal of independence, children with disabilities require not only extensive experience with their nondisabled peers but education and experience in decision-making. This text emphasizes the need to give children with disabilities opportunities to make their own personal choices and room to succeed *and* sometimes fail.

The effects of technology on the lives and education of children with special needs continue to be considerable. A number of technological advances enable children with particular disabilities to improve their functioning. Many of these technological improvements are discussed in the body of the text. In addition, the extensive use of computers for learning, leisure, and vocational pursuits presents a number of opportunities for children and their educators. The use of technology in education is so challenging that a special feature in each chapter, called **On-Line**, discusses possible uses of technology in the classroom.

This text, like other texts in the field, covers the basic information. However, professors and students indicated additional needs, including objective discussions of the issues in the field, the inclusion of material that encourages students to apply what they are learning to various situations in the classroom and home, and full coverage of areas often slighted, such as early intervention, children from minority groups in special education, parenting issues, and technology. Based upon the active input and feedback from professors and students, a number of distinct features appear in this book to make reading and using it a more meaningful experience.

Pedagogical Devices

Each chapter begins with an **Outline,** followed by a number of **True–False Statements**, which serve to focus the reader's attention on particular questions of interest. All **Key Terms** are found in bold print and the **Definitions of Key Terms** are provided in the page margins. A complete **Glossary** is found at the end of the text. Each chapter contains a **Summary** as well.

Special Features

Three special features deserve mention. Each chapter contains a number of cases called **Scenarios**. Each scenario describes a particular challenge and asks the reader to analyze it and respond with possible solutions and plans of action. A feature entitled **On-Line** discusses the use of technology in the education and daily lives of children with exceptional needs. In addition, a special feature called **In the Classroom** contains suggestions for teaching children with particular needs. Each suggestion is followed by a statement explaining reasons for its effectiveness.

Organization

This text presents a comprehensive view of the field based upon the research in each area. Where agreement is found in the literature it is noted, and where controversy occurs, which is quite frequent, that is also discussed.

The text is divided into five parts and generally organized from most to least prevalent exceptionalities. Part One contains three chapters that form the basis for understanding subsequent chapters. Chapter One reviews the basic concepts, philosophies, and major pieces of legislation affecting children with exceptional needs. It also contains an analysis of the types of classroom adaptations required.

Chapter Two discusses the social world of children and focuses on the changing nature of the parent-child, professional-child, and parent-professional relationships as the child matures. Chapter Three describes both early intervention and early childhood education, emphasizing programs and research on program effectiveness.

Part Two contains four chapters that cover the most prevalent exceptionalities: mental retardation, learning disabilities, communication disorders, and behavior disorders. Although not strictly in order of prevalence, these four categories of exceptionality comprise more than 90 percent of children who are considered to have disabilities.

Part Three looks at individual differences and the at-risk population. Chapter Eight discusses children who are at-risk including children who are abused, children who are homeless, and children who are exposed to drugs in utero. The concept of risk, programs that can help prevent disabilities, and finally, the effects of stress on children are central to the discussion. In Chapter Nine, the text addresses the important topics concerning children from minority groups with disabilities, particularly cultural differences, relationships between the school and the family, multicultural education for children with exceptional needs, and various issues in bilingual education.

Part Four offers two chapters on giftedness. Chapter Ten presents a broader definition of giftedness in its discussion of intellectual giftedness. Chapter Eleven expands the discussion of giftedness to the areas of talent and creativity and includes areas of giftedness that are often not covered in other texts, such as gifted children who underachieve, gifted children from minority groups, and gifted children who have disabilities.

Part Five describes the least prevalent exceptionalities—visual impairment, auditory impairment, orthopedic impairment and physical illness, autism, and severe and multiple disabilities—as well as the major issues and adaptations required for educating children with these disabilities.

A Word About Language

Particular ways of describing conditions and situations change as fields develop. This text follows current usage in most areas. In some areas, where newer terms have not yet completely replaced older terms, the decision has been made to stay with the older terms.

In a few cases, terms that may shortly become outdated are still useful. For instance, the new classification of mental retardation proposed by the American Association on Mental Retardation eliminates the classifications of mild, moderate, severe, and profound. Yet the new classification system, which involves a movement towards description in terms of types of support required, is not directly congruent with the older classifications. What was once considered mild retardation is not the same as intermittent in the new system. Literally thousands of research studies have used and many still use the older system. Therefore, the older classification provides greater clarity when discussing research, at least at the present time. All decisions concerning the use of terminology were made with sensitivity and care, but also with accuracy of meaning and effectiveness of communication in mind.

Writing a text is a team effort. Numerous people have been helpful and supportive in the writing of this book. First, I would like to thank the professionals at

West Publishing Company, including Peter Marshall, Holly Henjum, Jane Bass, and Angela Musey. They guided the project through the development and production processes to a successful conclusion. I would also like to thank the reviewers of the manuscript for their constructive criticism and encouragement: M. L. Anderegg, Kennesaw State College; Ann Candler-Lotven, Texas Tech University; Maggie Emery, Clemson University; Cheryl Grindol, Portland State University; James McAfee, Pennsylvania State University; Kathleen McCoy, Arizona State University; Phil Parette, Southeast Missouri State University; Joy Rogers, Loyola University; Marta Roth, Ohio University; Pamela Schutz, University of Maine; Jim Siders, University of Southern Mississippi; and Donna Tynan, Texas Women's University. Their suggestions were of enormous help in shaping a manuscript that meets the needs of their students. In addition, I owe a debt of gratitude to David Quinn and Joyce Gabrielle at the Suffolk Community College, Western Campus library, for their invaluable help in locating many references, and Nancy Sibilla of the Suffolk Bookstore for her help in obtaining some less accessible resources. Finally, I would like to thank my wife Leslie and daughters Stacey, Amy, Jodi, and Laurie, for their patience, understanding, and encouragement, without which this book could not have been written.

Foundations of Understanding

TRUE-FALSE STATEMENTS

See below for the correct answers.

1. Approximately one child in ten is considered to have a disability that requires special education services.
2. The largest number of children being served in special education programs are diagnosed as having learning disabilities.
3. Federal law requires special education for gifted pupils within their own school districts.
4. Schools must have adequate programs for students with disabilities, but may charge the families of these children something to offset the increased costs of their education.
5. A child may be tested for eligibility for special education services without parents' knowledge, but may not be placed in a special program without parents' permission.
6. The law requires that an individualized education program, which acts as a contract guaranteeing a particular amount of educational progress for the school year, be established for each child.
7. Most people with disabilities find full-time employment after attending high school.
8. The law requires every child with a disability to be educated in a regular classroom for at least part of the day.
9. Most children who are evaluated for eligibility for special education are accepted into special education programs.
10. Changing test conditions for a student with a disability, such as giving a student more time to complete a classroom test, is an acceptable procedure.

Answers to True-False Statements

1. True.
2. True.
3. False. See page 16.
4. False. See page 17.
5. False. See page 18.
6. False. See page 19.
7. False. See page 20.
8. False. See page 23.
9. True.
10. True.

3

An Individual's Experience

Have you ever thought what it would be like to be unable to see or hear, or to have difficulty learning? Most of us find it difficult to place ourselves in someone else's shoes, to understand what another person is experiencing. For example, Karen was almost a nonreader in the third grade. Her teachers thought her very slow. She was a pleasant child who kept to herself. She completed all her assignments, but disliked school intensely.

She was never popular. She played with a few children who lived on her block, but that was all. The children at school frequently snickered when she was asked to read aloud. Her lack of progress and the attitudes of the other children toward her took a toll. She did not want to interact much with other children, preferring to listen to music at home. Her parents tried to protect her, blaming others for her lack of friends, popularity, and achievement. She often was afraid of trying new things, and her social skills went relatively undeveloped.

In the third grade she was diagnosed as having a learning disability. With direct tutoring, she learned to read and was able to finish high school and college. She now reads well, but has difficulty writing and spelling. Still, she lacks self-confidence, hesitates to try new things, and is afraid to make mistakes.

If you asked Karen about the defining aspect of her childhood, she would tell you it was her learning disability. It affected every aspect of her life, including her academic achievement, social life, and her self-concept. Fortunately, Karen found ways to cope with her disability. She knows it takes her more time to process information so she allots more time to each task. She has improved her social skills and interacts quite well with people, although it is an effort. She is now a professional earning a good living, with a family and children, one of whom also has a learning disability. Despite her disability, Karen has built a satisfying, fulfilling life for herself by compensating for her disability.

Karen's story is not unique. Every person with a disability has his or her own personal tale of challenge, struggle, achievement, success, and failure. As we scientifically study people who have various disabilities, and seek a basic understanding of the nature of the disabilities and ways to help people fulfill their potential, we should not forget the individual's subjective experience.

Who Is the Child with Exceptional Needs?

The "average" child is a myth; every child has strengths and weaknesses. Every child is similar to the group, and yet is individually different. Of the following five children, who would you categorize as being a child with exceptional needs or having a disability?

1. Carlos has an IQ of 140 and seems to enjoy school.
2. Sarah has a severe hearing impairment and requires an interpreter in order to attend regular classes.

Children who are gifted or talented also have special needs and require different educational experiences if they are to develop their special abilities.

3. Tony is distractible, impulsive and hyperactive, and requires medication in order to function reasonably well in class.
4. Cheryl is mechanically inclined and would like to build her own engine.
5. Bill has not been able to walk since he was involved in a car accident and uses a wheelchair.

Children with exceptional needs include those whose intellectual, emotional, or physical performance differs significantly from the expected average within their peer and cultural group. The child with exceptional needs requires extra services in order to develop adequately or learn well. These services are most often educational, but may also be psychological or medical. For example, a child with a learning disability may need different educational services in order to learn how to read. On the other hand, a child with spina bifida, a condition in which the spine has not fused leading to medical problems, may require catheterization (a process whereby an instrument is inserted into the bladder to draw off urine when the natural discharge is stopped) within the school setting, but no change in educational curriculum except for physical education.

Two associated terms are commonly misused and need to be defined. The term **disability** refers to a total or partial behavioral, mental, physical, or sensory loss of functioning (Mandell & Fiscus, 1981), whereas the term **handicap** refers to the difficulty an individual has in adjusting to the environment. The term *handicap* is often used in connection with an environmental restriction that results from the exceptionality and usually depends on the situation. For example, Bill has not been able to walk since he was involved in a car accident. He travels to school in a specially designed bus and uses a wheelchair to get from place to place. Does he have a disability or a handicap? He has a disability, but his condition is only handicapping if the school does not have ramps, if the aisles of the classroom are too narrow, or if the bathrooms are not built to allow him to use them. He only has a handicap if the environment does not allow him to function to the fullest extent possible. Today, an emphasis on eliminating the barriers that prevent people with disabilities from participating in various activities, and the passage of some recently enacted laws, will lead to major improvements in this area.

But one need not have a disability to be considered as having exceptional needs. Children who are gifted or talented also have exceptional needs because they require a different educational experience in order to bring out their talents and skills. An individual may have a disability and be gifted at the same time.

Of the five children previously described, each could be considered as having exceptional needs and, with the exception of Carlos and Cheryl, has a disability. Whether Bill has a handicap depends upon the environment.

Children with exceptional needs: Children whose intellectual, emotional, or physical performance differs significantly from the average expected for their peer and cultural group so that special services are required for the child to develop adequately or learn well.

Disability: A total or partial behavioral, mental, physical, or sensorial loss of functioning.

Handicap: The difficulty an individual experiences in adjusting to the environment; the term used in connection with an environmental restriction.

Prevalence and Incidence

How many children are considered to have exceptional needs? The answer depends upon many factors, but most importantly on the definition of the various disabilities. For instance, mental retardation is defined *partially* in terms of an intelligence test score below a particular level. The choice of this level of intelligence will help to determine the number of children categorized as having mental retardation.

Definitions for certain exceptionalities such as learning disabilities and giftedness change, affecting the number of children placed in such categories. The number of children in any category may be expressed in terms of incidence or prevalence. **Incidence** refers to the number of new cases of a condition in a particular time period, usually a year. Incidence always refers to new cases discovered. **Prevalence** refers to the total number of cases that exist within a particular population at a given time. This population may be children in the world, in the United States, or in a specific age group such as five-year-olds in the United States. For example, when examining the number of children considered to have a learning disability, the incidence would refer to the number of new cases discovered in the past year, whereas the prevalence would show the total number of cases in the United States.

Caution is always required when analyzing incidence and prevalence figures because various factors can affect them greatly. If better ways of diagnosing a disorder are developed or the general public becomes more aware of the disorder, incidence figures will rise. For example, the number of complaints of child abuse has increased over the past 20 years, even adjusting for a growing population. Are more children being abused, or is the increase in reports due to better public understanding, a willingness to report child abuse, and new laws requiring the reporting of suspected child abuse?

Determining the exact factors responsible for an increase in incidence or prevalence is difficult. Both prevalence and incidence figures are affected by one's choice of population, definition used for the disability, criteria used for identification, and a host of other factors. In addition, prevalence figures (the total number of people in a population affected) are frequently discovered by researching a sample of people, be it 10,000 or 100,000, and noting the number of people in this sample who have the disability. A different population may yield somewhat different results, which explains why such figures taken from various studies may differ.

During the 1992–1993 school year, 4,663,674 children between the ages of 6 and 21 years received special education services (U.S. Department of Education, 1994). About half of these students were diagnosed as having learning disabilities, while about one million were considered to have a speech or language impairment. Figure 1.1 shows the changes in the distribution of children with specific disabilities served during the 1976–1977 school year and the 1992–1993 school year.

About 9.5 percent of all children between the ages of six and seventeen years receive special education services. This does not include children who are considered gifted, since education of gifted children is not mandated by federal law. If one uses the conservative figure of 3 percent of the population as gifted, approximately 12.5 percent of the children in the schools may be considered as having exceptional needs for educational purposes.

From these and other figures, a number of important trends stand out. For example:

1. The number of children diagnosed as having learning disabilities has increased dramatically since the 1970s.

Incidence:
The number of new cases of a condition within a particular time period, usually one year.

Prevalence:
The total number of cases that exist within a particular population at a given time.

THOUGHT QUESTION

1. *Has child abuse increased in our society, or is the increase in reports due to greater public knowledge and awareness?*

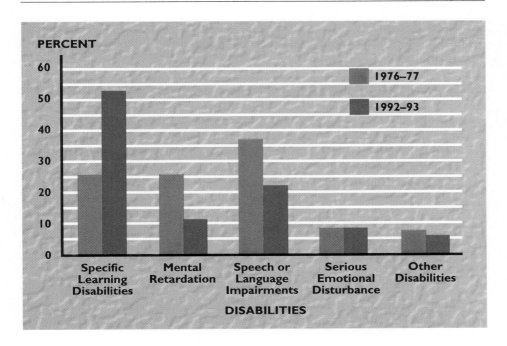

PERCENT

| | 1976–77 |
| | 1992–93 |

Specific Learning Disabilities | Mental Retardation | Speech or Language Impairments | Serious Emotional Disturbance | Other Disabilities

DISABILITIES

FIGURE 1.1 Changes in the Distribution of Specific Disabilities for Children Ages 6–21 Served Under IDEA, Part B: School Years 1976–77 and 1992–93

Source: U.S. Department of Education, Office of Special Education Programs, Data Analysis System (DANS).

2. The number of children diagnosed as having mental retardation has declined substantially since the 1970s.
3. Four exceptionalities comprise over 93 percent of all children receiving special educational services: specific learning disabilities, speech or language impairment, mental retardation, and serious emotional disturbance.
4. During the 1992–1993 school year, 460,119 children between the ages of 3 and 5 years and 76,449 infants and toddlers received special services. These children do not require a specific diagnosis. This new attempt at early intervention will be discussed in Chapter 3.
5. Many more boys than girls are considered to have disabilities. The ratio depends upon the disability, but about twice as many boys receive special education services.
6. About 90 percent of all children who have a disability are considered to have mild disabilities.

Classification

Some professionals place an emphasis on the diagnostic labels used to describe various disabilities. Labels such as mental retardation, visual impairment, and learning disability are constantly used. Psychologists and educators appear to be dealing with children in terms of group membership, in terms of these labels. The issue of labeling has been a vexing one for the field of special education since its inception. Labeling has its many pros and cons, and the controversy over labeling is ongoing.

Special ramps allow people with physical disabilities to participate in many activities.

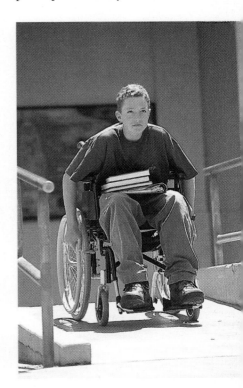

The Need for Labeling

Some educators and psychologists see labeling as necessary. They argue the following points:

1. Labeling allows us to analyze trends and understand whether the incidence or prevalence is increasing or decreasing.
2. Labeling gives us an opportunity to place our limited resources wherever they are most needed. If we know that more children have learning disabilities than visual impairments, we can allocate our resources fairly.
3. Labeling allows us to plan new facilities and programs according to the numbers of children in any category.
4. Labeling allows educators to place the child into the correct program. If a child has an auditory impairment, we know the nature of educational modifications that may be required, such as the need for sign language interpreters.
5. Labeling disabilities allows parents and advocate groups to join together to educate the public and obtain the necessary services for their children. Often, the public misunderstands the nature of a disability. Groups of interested people form associations which serve both to educate the public and advocate for the rights of children with various disabilities.

The Negative Side of Labeling

Those who emphasize the negative side of labeling often raise the following issues:

1. Labeling seriously stereotypes children. People often have a picture in their minds of children with various exceptionalities. Once we place a label on a child, people may use their stereotypes to evaluate the child. They may then deal with the child in a different, perhaps discriminatory manner. A person who believes that a child who has mental retardation cannot do anything is likely to treat the child in that manner. A person may believe that a child with a behavior disorder must be dangerous or that you cannot trust the child.
2. Labeling the child may lead to the child feeling different, and labeling stigmatizes the child (Winick, 1995; Lilly, 1992). Children with exceptional needs are different in that they require extra services, but labeling the child emphasizes the difference. The child may experience shame, isolation, or rejection due to the label.
3. Labeling the child may lead to the self-fulfilling prophesy. The child labeled as having a learning disability, mental retardation, or a behavior disorder may act in accordance with this label. Children labeled as having behavior disorders may pick up the subtle (or not-so-subtle) feelings of those around them and act in the manner expected of them. Children with learning disabilities may feel that they are not expected to do well in school.
4. Labeling children calls attention to their weaknesses rather than emphasizing their strengths.
5. Labeling the child often leads to the child receiving a curriculum that is less challenging.

6. Labeling may lead one to believe that a child cannot learn and runs counter to the idea that all children can learn.

Labeling: The Research

Undoubtedly, every situation has the potential for children to suffer adverse effects from labeling (Adelman, 1992). If a teacher acts as if the label describes the whole child, then the child will suffer because the teacher is reacting to a label rather than to a child with strengths and weaknesses.

Many of the difficulties described are *potential* problems, not inevitable problems. Researchers have expressed considerable doubt that labeling leads to a poor self-concept or stigmatization (MacMillan, Jones, & Olia, 1974). In fact, although stigmatization is certainly possible, it is doubtful how often it really occurs (Reschly & Lamprecht, 1979). In addition, the self-fulfilling prophecy, although certainly a potential problem, may be overstated. Research shows that teachers form their opinions based upon their own observations of the child's behavior and academic functioning. In other words, if a student demonstrates academic interest and ability, the teacher is likely to form a high opinion of the student. The student's actions in class, rather than the label, have a greater affect on the teacher (Kaplan, 1990). An increased awareness of the problems that can arise from labeling may reduce the negative effects as well.

The problems of stigmatization may be minimized through education and various new placement alternatives discussed later in the chapter, which reduce the chances of the child being isolated or receiving a less challenging curriculum. This does not make labeling desirable, but does demonstrate that it need not always lead to difficulties.

Although categorization tends to be stable, change does take place. In a study of approximately 600 students ranging from preschool through secondary school, more than one-third of the students receiving special services experienced a change in category, 21.9 percent by termination and 16.3 percent by reclassification into a different category (Halgren & Clarizio, 1993). In another two-year study, 71 percent of those children receiving special services continued in the same classification, 12 percent were reclassified, and 17 percent were no longer receiving special education services (Walker et al., 1988). Changes in classification do occur, and some students may no longer require special services after a time.

If we eliminated the use of these labels, how would we be able to provide services? One suggestion is to describe the child in terms of the child's needs and the services required, such as special reading help, environmental changes in the classroom, and so forth rather than use formal labels (Polloway & Smith, 1987). Although this represents an interesting alternative to the use of labels, at the present time classification is required by law.

From Paternalism to Self-Determination

When someone is labeled as having mental retardation or a learning disability, people may place that individual in a neat category and not allow the person's strengths to show and individuality to blossom. Lately, professionals have begun to focus on the strengths and individual functioning of the person rather than on

THOUGHT QUESTION

2. *Do the advantages of labeling outweigh the disadvantages?*

THOUGHT QUESTION

3. *Should a child who is diagnosed as having mental retardation and grows up to live an independent existence still be considered to have mental retardation?*

the disability itself. What a person can do is more important than the individual's limitations.

Once people with disabilities are viewed as individuals with strengths and weaknesses, a new attitude toward people with disabilities becomes possible. Today, society as a whole places more emphasis on the integration of people with disabilities into the mainstream of society. This change has come about due to the hard work of many groups including people with disabilities, parents, teachers, and others who have championed the cause. People with disabilities are now viewed as individuals with definite rights and the ability to achieve.

But the changes in attitudes do not stop at a belief that people with disabilities have a right to be included in society. One particularly important change is the shift from a paternalistic view to one in which people with disabilities are seen as capable of managing their own affairs and, at times, their own institutions. This process is called **self-determination** (Ward, 1993).

It is far too easy for people with a genuine concern for children with special needs to become paternalistic, overprotective, and not allow children with disabilities to make their own decisions. Children with disabilities have the right to try and may sometimes fail at reaching for a dream. Pity is not a desirable emotion when dealing with people with disabilities, nor is overprotection a desirable strategy. People who say they usually like people with disabilities because they find them kind, gentle, and pleasant are likely to be met with the cold shoulder or a nasty comment from people with disabilities who want to be accepted or rejected for who they are. The changes that are needed in the educational and physical environments are aimed at allowing the person with a disability to negotiate life on an equal basis, allowing strengths and weaknesses, abilities or lack of ability to determine success and failure.

Self-determination:
The ability to make one's own decisions and choices.

A recent philosophical advancement is the emphasis on self-determination, the ability to make one's own decisions and choices.

Defining the Field Through Law and Court Decisions

Today, most people take it for granted that children with disabilities will attend neighborhood schools, learn in regular classrooms, and have definite rights. We do not take a second look when we shop alongside people with disabilities or find that ramps are placed in front of buildings to enable people with physical disabilities to use the facilities.

This familiarity does not mean discrimination and prejudice against people with disabilities has been eliminated or that they easily negotiate their way through a caring society. Yet, when we focus on the problems and what yet must be done, we sometimes forget how far we have come and do not appreciate the progress we have made.

Societies have a long history of dealing with people who are different in an uncaring, sometimes brutal, manner. The experience of individuals with disabilities was frequently one of rejection, denial of rights, and cruelty. Even those professionals and average citizens who stood up for the needs of people with disabilities often were paternalistic, not seeing people with disabilities as having the ability to make their own decisions. Only recently have we accorded people with disabilities particular rights as well as emphasizing their ability to make their own decisions (Ward, 1993).

In the past 30 years, significant progress in the legal and educational areas has dramatically changed the lives of many people with disabilities. With each new law comes the necessity for interpretation, not only by the agency responsible for carrying out the law, but also for the courts that must interpret the law.

The first federal laws aimed at helping people with disabilities were passed in 1798, when the Congress authorized a Marine Hospital Service to provide medical care for sick and disabled seamen. In 1912, this service became the Public Health Service. Prior to World War II, few federal statutes existed that authorized benefits to people with disabilities, and those that did usually addressed the needs of injured veterans. Throughout most of American history, public schools were allowed to, and frequently did, exclude children with disabilities. Since 1960, though, a number of laws and various court decisions have afforded people with disabilities particular rights and the schools definite responsibilities.

Federal laws are labeled in a particular manner. They receive the abbreviation PL, which stands for Public Law, and then are followed by two sets of numbers. The first set indicates the session of Congress during which the law passed, and the second identifies its number in the sequence of all the laws passed during that session of Congress. PL 94-142, which is the most important law regarding the rights of children with disabilities in school, passed during the 94th session of Congress and was the 142nd law passed that session. Laws may also be given names. PL 94-142, the Education for All Handicapped Children Act of 1975, was amended in 1990 and its name changed to the Individuals with Disabilities Education Act (IDEA).

These laws, though, provide only a general framework. Once the law is passed, an administrative agency then writes detailed regulations based upon the law to guide in its implementation. These regulations are found in the Code of Federal Regulations (CFR). State agencies must comply with federal law, but frequently

TABLE 1.1   **Highlights of Legislation and Litigation Affecting the Education of Children with Disabilities**

1954 *Brown v. Board of Education*
Separate but equal is not equal. The Court held that separate facilities by race was unconstitutional. Although this case dealt with race, it set the stage for extending rights to people with disabilities.

1958 National Defense Education Act (PL 85-926)
Provided funds for training teachers for children with mental retardation.

1961 Special Education Act (PL 87-276)
Funded university-level program designed to train teachers of children who were deaf.

1963 Mental Retardation Facilities and Community Mental Health Centers Act (PL 88-164)
Provided financial backing to universities to train teachers for children with disabilities. Funds were also allocated for developing research projects to improve the educational experiences of children with disabilities.

1965 Elementary and Secondary Education Act (PL 89-10)
This law provided grants to states and localities to develop programs for disadvantaged and disabled children.

1966 Amendments to PL 89-10 (PL 89-313)
Provided funds for state-supported programs in various settings for children with disabilities.

1966 Amendments to the Elementary and Secondary Education Act (PL 89-750)
Provided grants to originate, expand, and improve programs specially designed for children with disabilities from preschool through secondary school.

1968 Handicapped Children's Early Education Assistance Act (PL 90-538)
Encouraged the development and establishment of experimental programs in early education for children with disabilities (birth through six years).

1970 *Diana v. State Board of Education*
A suit was brought on behalf of nine Mexican-American students placed in classes for children with mental retardation. These children were placed on the basis of intelligence tests given in English. When given the same tests in Spanish, these children scored high enough to become ineligible for such placement. It was argued that these children did not have mental retardation but were misclassified because of cultural differences. It was also charged that children had received poor education in these special classes and were "damaged" by the experience. In an agreement, the state of California agreed that testing

go beyond the federal mandates. Some states, for example, have broader definitions of children entitled to special education than are found in the federal mandate. In addition, these regulations and school districts' compliance with them may be challenged in court. In the history of special education, court decisions have frequently influenced the way the law is interpreted.

Table 1.1 describes some of the federal laws that are most important, along with a few of the court decisions. Four laws, though, are most important for our purposes and deserve some explanation.

Section 504 of the Rehabilitation Act of 1973

In 1973, Congress passed one of the most important bills in the history of the civil rights struggle of people with disabilities. PL 93-112, the Rehabilitation Act of

TABLE 1.1 *Continued*

would be conducted in the primary language, that Mexican-American children in special classes would be reevaluated, and that additional education would be provided for children who were misclassified. Steps were also to be taken to develop a more appropriate standardized intelligence test and procedures established for explaining to parents the special education process in their primary language.

1971 *Pennsylvania Association for Retarded Citizens (PARC) v. Commonwealth of Pennsylvania*

It had become common procedure to exclude children with severe mental retardation from attending public schools. PARC claimed that this exclusion denied children their equal rights and that these children were assigned to special programs without due process. In a consent agreement (signed in 1972), the state agreed to locate these children, provide medical and psychological evaluation for children excluded to determine the most appropriate placement, place them in a free appropriate public program, evaluate all children in special classes for children with mental retardation to determine proper placement, and submit a plan to assure all children an appropriate education.

1972 *Mills v. Board of Education of the District of Columbia*

This decision was similar to the PARC case, except that it involved children with a number of disabilities, including children who were categorized as showing hyperactivity, having an emotional disturbance, or having a physical disability. The court ordered all school-age children to receive an appropriate, free education regardless of disability and the severity of the disability. Lack of funds was not accepted as an excuse for not providing adequate services. In addition, the judge ordered the school to establish due-process hearings so a child could not be assigned or transferred to or from a special education program without a hearing. This decision caused school districts around the country to establish a formal set of guidelines and procedures for the placement of children with disabilities.

1972 *Larry P. v. Riles*

This case involved the testing and placement of six African-American pupils in San Francisco. It was charged that these children were misclassified as having mental retardation because testing procedures ignored the cultural backgrounds of these children and that the tests were based upon a middle-class culture. The court found that racial imbalance caused by inappropriate classification and testing occurred in classes for children with mental retardation. These tests could no longer be used for this purpose. (In response to the *Diana* and *Larry P.* cases, most state boards of education mandated the use of multiple sources of information and data for placement.)

1973, addresses discrimination against persons with disabilities. It focuses on a number of different areas of discrimination. In particular, Section 504, nondiscrimination under federal grants, provides individuals with disabilities with basic civil rights protection against discrimination in federal programs. The law states the following:

> No otherwise qualified handicapped individual in the United States shall, solely by reason of his (or her) handicap, be excluded from participation in, be denied the benefits of, or be subjected to discrimination under any program or activity receiving federal financial assistance.

This section covers only people with a disability who would otherwise be qualified to participate and benefit from a program. It assures equal access to pro-

TABLE 1.1   *Continued*

1973 Rehabilitation Act of 1973 (Section 504) (PL 93-112)
Prohibited discrimination on the basis of disability to all people qualified to attend a program receiving federal funds.

1974 Education of the Handicapped Amendments (PL 93-380)
This act amended the Elementary and Secondary Education Act of 1965. It presents a statement of policy on equality of educational opportunity. It stated, for the first time, that federal policy would reflect the commitment that children with disabilities are entitled to a free public education.

1975 Education for All Handicapped Children Act (PL 94-142)
This is the most important act guaranteeing children with disabilities educational opportunities. All children must be provided with a free, appropriate education. Due process must be observed, and all children are to be educated in the least restrictive environment.

1982 *Board of Education of Hendrick Hudson School District v. Rowley*
In this case, the parents of a child with a hearing impairment but good speechreading skills sued to gain the services of a sign language interpreter. The child was doing well in school and the school district denied the request after conducting hearings. The Supreme Court of the United States upheld the district's position, ruling that school districts did not have to maximize the student's potential (just as they do not have that requirement for students without disabilities). However, districts must provide services that allow children with disabilities to benefit from their educational experiences.

1983 *Irving Independent School District v. Tatro*
School districts must provide related services that will allow the child to remain in school during the day. In this case, the child was entitled to have clean intermittent catheterization performed by school personnel (the nurse) during the school day.

1984 *Burlington School Committee v. Department of Education*
Public school districts must, under certain circumstances, pay for private school placements if an appropriate educational experience is not provided by the school district.

1984 Perkins Act
Ten percent of all federal funding for vocational education must be used for students with disabilities. Such education is to be provided in the least restrictive environment. This law is noteworthy because it recognized the role of the secondary school and the importance of transition services to adulthood.

grams in schools and other public agencies receiving federal funds. If an agency persists in discrimination, it risks the loss of federal funds.

This act assures that programs will be accessible to everyone. For example, people with disabilities can no longer be told that they cannot attend a program receiving federal assistance because it is held on the twelfth floor of a college or public agency with no way for them to get to it. This law has improved access to many important programs and educational institutions for people with disabilities.

Americans with Disabilities Act

The Americans with Disabilities Act (PL 101-336), passed in 1990, guarantees equal opportunity for individuals with disabilities in employment, public accom-

TABLE 1.1 *Continued*

1986 *Alamo Heights Independent School District v. State Board of Education*
In this case, the court ruled that a child with a severe disability was entitled to summer programming in order to receive an appropriate education.

1986 Education of the Handicapped Act Amendments of 1986 (PL 99-457)
This law requires preschool services for children between the ages of 3 and 5 and creates incentives for states to develop early intervention programs for children birth to three years of age.

1988 *Honig v. Doe*
A child with a disability whose misbehavior is caused by that disability cannot be denied an education.

1989 *Timothy W. v. Rochester, New Hampshire, School District*
Timothy W. had brain damage, a seizure disorder, and many other disabilities. He could not make sounds and was quadriplegic and blind. The question was whether all children, regardless of the severity of disability were entitled to education or only children who would benefit from instruction. The court interpreted the law as indicating a "zero reject policy" and that an ability to benefit is not necessary for eligibility.

1990 Americans with Disabilities Act (PL 101-336)
Prohibits discrimination against people with disabilities in employment, access to services, public accommodations, transportation, and communications. Requires employers to make reasonable accommodations for workers with disabilities.

1990 Education of the Handicapped Amendments of 1990 (PL 101-476)
Changed the name of the Education for All Handicapped Children Act to the Individuals with Disabilities Education Act (IDEA), added autism and traumatic brain injury as new categories of disabilities, required statements of transition services no later than age 16 to be placed in individualized education programs, and expanded the nature of related services.

1993 *Oberti v. Board of Education of the Borough of Clementon School District*
The court decided that the school board violated federal special-education law when it failed to consider whether an eight-year-old child with mental retardation could be educated in a regular class if provided with special services. The school board's position was that the child's disabilities were quite severe and his behavior so disruptive that only education in a separate class was viable. The judge noted that the child did not have to earn a placement in a regular classroom and that inclusion was a right rather than a privilege.

modation, transportation, state and local government, and telecommunications (NARIC, 1993). This significant federal law assures full civil rights for individuals with disabilities and provides people with disabilities with new employment opportunities and access to public accommodations, such as transit systems and communication networks (Traver, 1990).

This law prohibits firms with more than 25 employees from discrimination in the hiring or promotion of workers with physical or mental impairments; it also outlaws tests that screen out job applicants who have disabilities (O'Keefe, 1995; Klimoski & Palmer, 1995). PL 101-336 requires employers to make reasonable accommodations for workers with disabilities, which means making facilities accessible and acquiring and modifying equipment so that people with disabilities can work there. Employers, of course, can inquire about the worker's ability to perform a job.

It also requires restaurants, stores, and other public accommodations to widen doorways and provide ramps for people in wheelchairs and makes inner city buses accessible to individuals with disabilities. This bill requires businesses to make new buildings and grounds conform to strict codes for access. Renovated or new hotels, retail stores, and restaurants will have to become accessible and barriers now existing must be removed if "readily achievable" (Berko, 1992). The law covers a full range of public accommodations, including lodging, restaurants, theaters, stores, rail depots, museums, parks, private schools, and health spas. The Americans with Disabilities Act will require car rental agencies to equip autos with hand controls for drivers who need them and telephone companies to provide operators to pass on messages from people who must use special phones with keyboards (*U.S. News and World Report*, June 4, 1990). Private clubs and religious entities are exempt from the law pertaining to accommodations.

Perhaps the most controversial provision of the act requires companies to make "reasonable accommodations" for employees with disabilities, such as providing readers for workers who are blind. The law also notes that these accommodations should not place an "undue burden" upon the employer. Although many large firms have been adapting their workplaces over the years, smaller firms fear the cost. The costs of most of these accommodations can be kept down. For example, wooden ramps are less expensive than concrete ramps, and attaching a buzzer on the front door, which would allow the owner to open the door, is probably legal. The cost of providing reasonable accommodations may not be great for many companies. Only about 22 percent of all employees with disabilities require any accommodations at the worksite at all. Of those who do require accommodations, in 31 percent of the cases these modifications will cost nothing, while in another 19 percent of the cases these changes will cost less than $50 (Eastern Paralyzed Veterans Association, 1992). Unfortunately, the language of the law is vague and phrases such as reasonable accommodations and undue burden will require interpretation by the courts (McKee, 1993).

Individuals with Disabilities Education Act (IDEA)

The most important law mandating educational services for children with disabilities is the Individuals with Disabilities Education Act (IDEA), which was formerly called the Education for All Handicapped Children Act, PL 94-142. This law does not cover the education of children who are gifted. Special education for the gifted is not required under federal statute, although many districts have instituted special programs for gifted children. This complicated law, first passed in 1975, has been amended a number of times. In 1990, PL 101-476 changed the terminology used from "handicapped children" to "children with disabilities," added two additional categories, autism (see Chapter 15) and traumatic brain injury (see Chapter 14), mandated transition services for children by age 16 years, and changed the name of the act, among other refinements. The major sections of this important law are as follows:

Identifying the Child with a Disability
School districts must make efforts to identify all children with a disability. The school must establish procedures for discovering which children need special help, and districtwide procedures for screening and referral must be in place.

A Free, Appropriate Public Education

A school can no longer claim that programs are unavailable for a child with a disability or that a child cannot be educated. The district is responsible for educating all children. This means that every child, no matter how severe the child's disability, is required to receive a free, appropriate public education. This is called the principle of zero reject. This education must be appropriate for the child and free of charge. The use of the term *appropriate* is not spelled out in the law and has led to a number of court cases that define the term.

The most important case was *Board of Education v. Rowley* argued before the Supreme Court. Amy Rowley was a student with minimal residual hearing, but excellent skills in speechreading. Amy was first placed in a regular kindergarten class to determine what additional services would be necessary. Some school officials attended a course in sign language, and a teletype machine was installed in the principal's office to facilitate communication with her parents who have severe hearing impairments. At the end of the trial period, it was determined that Amy should remain in class and be provided with an FM hearing aid that would amplify words spoken into a wireless transmitter by the teacher or fellow students. In the fall, Amy was provided with regular classroom instruction, the continued use of the hearing aid, instruction from a special tutor for one hour each day, and the services of a speech therapist.

Amy's parents agreed with all of these recommendations but also insisted that Amy receive a qualified sign language interpreter in all her academic classes. Such an interpreter had actually been in Amy's kindergarten class for a two-week experimental period, but the interpreter said that Amy did not need his services at that time. After a series of hearings, the school district decided that Amy was achieving educationally and socially without the interpreter and refused to provide this service. Amy's parents then brought the case to court claiming that the denial of the interpreter constituted a denial of a free, appropriate public education.

The Supreme Court decided that Amy was not entitled to an interpreter because the requirement that the state provide specialized educational services does not mean that the services must maximize each child's potential (Rothstein, 1995). Adequate special services, though, must be provided. Schools are therefore not held to a maximum benefit standard unless state law exceeds the "reasonable expectation of benefit," which is required by federal law. The Rowley standard is often quoted. It was criticized by some as meaning that children with disabilities need only to be given the bare minimum. However, the court specifically noted that children with disabilities were entitled to a number of services sufficient to allow them to benefit from education (Osborne, 1992). Health services, transportation, and physical therapy are required when necessary. An appropriate education is an education that has true value to the student.

The courts usually refrain from deciding which of two competing educational programs is most appropriate, leaving that decision most often to educators and administrators. In some cases in which the programs assigned to students were obviously inappropriate, however, the courts have stepped in and made the decision.

Due Process

The due process part of the law assures that parents will be involved throughout assessment and placement of the child. The school may not test children and

THOUGHT QUESTION

4. *How would you have ruled in the Amy Rowley case?*

place them in special classes on its own. Parents must be informed of the situation and of their rights. They have a right to refuse to allow their child to be tested and the right to a fair hearing if they disagree with the results of the testing or the placement that school personnel think is best.

PL 94-142 establishes particular procedures to be followed throughout the process, from evaluation through placement and programming. Parents are called in for hearings, and asked to consent to assessment, placement, and programming. Parents even have the right to seek an independent evaluation at public expense if they do not agree with the one provided through the school. If there are disagreements between parents and professionals, hearings are set for both sides to present their views and evidence is collected.

One of the most important features of this law is the promise of a partnership between parents and the school. This partnership requires parental approval and involvement in all areas of decision making. Most of the time, parents and educators can agree about eligibility, placement, and programming. Sometimes, though, there are disagreements. Some parents are reluctant to participate, either because they do not see themselves as qualified or else may feel their children do not require testing and evaluation. At other times, the history of the parent-school relationship is poor, and communication problems may arise. Some disagreements are due to honest differences in opinion as to what is best for the child.

Although parents today cannot say that they were completely unaware that their children were being tested or placed in particular settings, parents do not always understand what is going on nor can they always evaluate findings of professionals easily. This situation is most critical when poor, uneducated parents may be the ones involved in the process. Consider the parents who are given a long document to read and sign (in their own language) to permit testing, then are called in for conferences discussing the results of the testing and the placement alternatives. The parents may not understand the educational and psychological language, may not be able to stand up and make cogent arguments based upon test data, or understand the complicated arguments made for a particular placement. The parents have the right to representation but, again, may not know what is best for the child.

These problems are not the sole province of poor, uneducated parents. Imagine yourself walking into a room with a number of professionals with specialized backgrounds all evaluating tests and alternatives. Unless you are very well prepared, you may indeed be deferential, yielding to their arguments, and may not even know the right questions to ask.

The relationship between parents and professionals is not one of inevitable conflict, nor is it necessarily adversarial in nature. Often they are partners, coming to a unanimous agreement about what is best for the child.

Nondiscriminatory Evaluation

All testing must be nondiscriminatory. A Spanish-speaking child cannot be given an intelligence test written in English, nor can only one test be the sole basis for any decision. The evaluation process requires obtaining information from a variety of sources. As we shall see, evaluation often involves the use of standardized tests as well as interviews and observations. The usefulness of these evaluation procedures has been, and continues to be, a very controversial area.

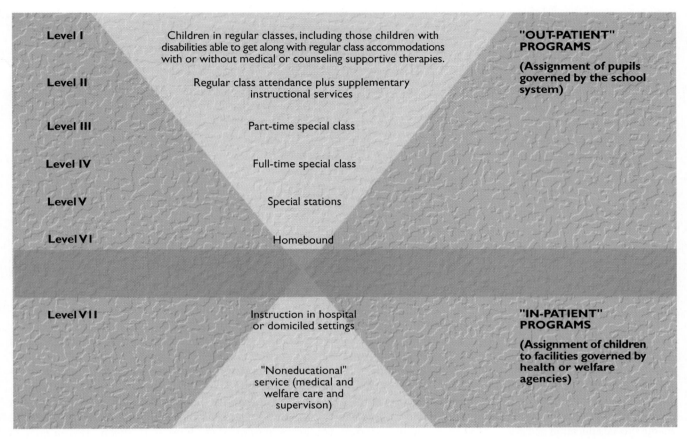

| Level I | Children in regular classes, including those children with disabilities able to get along with regular class accommodations with or without medical or counseling supportive therapies. | "OUT-PATIENT" PROGRAMS (Assignment of pupils governed by the school system) |

Level II — Regular class attendance plus supplementary instructional services

Level III — Part-time special class

Level IV — Full-time special class

Level V — Special stations

Level VI — Homebound

Level VII — Instruction in hospital or domiciled settings

"Noneducational" service (medical and welfare care and supervison)

"IN-PATIENT" PROGRAMS (Assignment of children to facilities governed by health or welfare agencies)

children with disabilities are educated in the regular classroom continues to be the source of controversy today.

In order to better understand this controversy, some terms must be defined. The term **mainstreaming** is used to describe the placement of children with disabilities in the regular classroom. About a decade ago, though, a movement called the **regular education initiative (REI)** arose, which argued that a merger should occur between special education and general education and that many more children, especially those with mild and moderate disabilities, be educated full time in regular classrooms (see Fuchs & Fuchs, 1994). Today, a relatively new term called **inclusion (full inclusion)** advocates all services for children with disabilities be delivered in the regular classroom. These last two movements can mean different things to different professionals, and their definitions are somewhat imprecise (Fuchs & Fuchs, 1994).

Mainstreaming

The most controversial provision of PL 94-142 mandates that the child be placed in the least restrictive environment. This has resulted in about two-thirds of children with disabilities being placed for either all or part of the day in the regular classroom. Mainstreaming, though, is not required by law; the law clearly uses the

FIGURE 1.3   The Cascade System of Special Education Services
The tapered design indicates the considerable difference in the numbers involved at the different levels and calls attention to the fact that the system serves as a diagnostic filter. The most specialized facilities are likely to be needed by the fewest children on a long term basis. This organizational model can be applied to development of special education services for all types of disability.

Source: "Instructional Alternatives for Exceptional Children," by E. Deno. Council for Exceptional Children, 1973. Reprinted with permission of the Council for Exceptional Children and the author.

FIGURE 1.4   Percentage of All Students with Disabilities Ages 6–21 Served in Six Educational Environments: School Year 1991–92

Notes: Separate school includes both public and private separate school facilities. Residential facility includes both public and private residential facilities.

Source: U.S. Department of Education, Office of Special Education Programs, Data Analysis System (DANS).

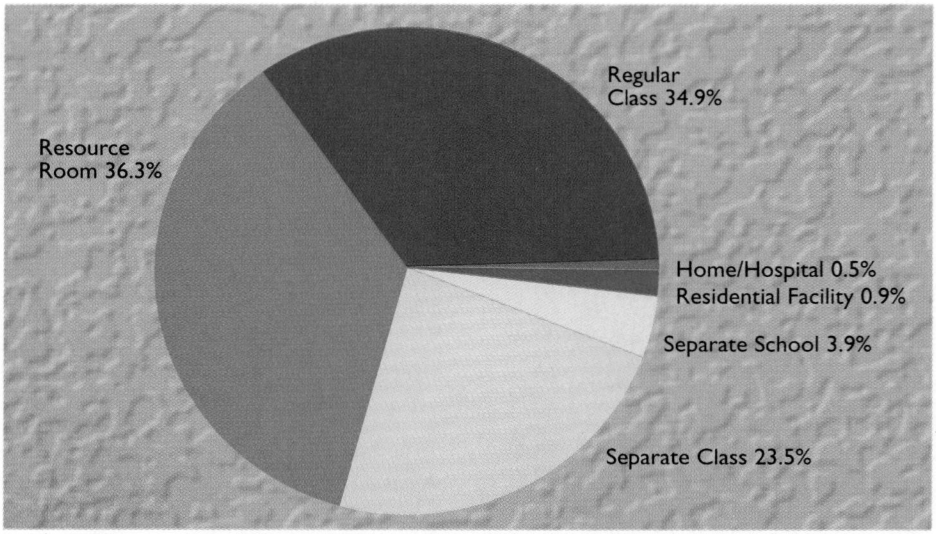

Regular Class 34.9%

Resource Room 36.3%

Home/Hospital 0.5%
Residential Facility 0.9%

Separate School 3.9%

Separate Class 23.5%

Mainstreaming:
The placement of children with disabilities in the regular classroom.

Regular Education Initiative (REI):
A movement in education to merge special education and general education.

Inclusion (full inclusion):
A movement advocating that all services for children with disabilities be delivered in the regular classroom.

phrase "least restrictive environment." About one-quarter of all students with disabilities are educated in separate classrooms within a regular school, a bit fewer than one in 25 are educated in special schools and about 1.5 percent are educated at home, hospital, or residential facility (see Figure 1.4).

Mainstreaming is considered important for three main reasons. First, it is impractical to expect children who are segregated from the mainstream to live in society without having adequate contact with people without disabilities. Such contact will improve social interactions and prepare students for living in mainstream society. Second, the achievement of students with disabilities in special classes generally has been unacceptable, and mainstreaming exposes students to a more challenging curriculum and, hopefully, improves academic achievement. Third, contact between children with and without disabilities will help to change the negative attitudes of some children toward their peers with disabilities. These negative attitudes are often fueled by fear and a lack of understanding.

The rationale for mainstreaming is easy to understand. If we want children with disabilities to grow up and take their places in society and if we wish people to respect the rights of their peers with disabilities, it makes sense to encourage the two groups to associate with one another as they grow up. Both children with and without disabilities benefit from being exposed to, and interacting with, one another. Children with disabilities learn to deal with a wide variety of challenges and gain the social skills necessary for independent living. Children without disabilities become more accepting of, and less prejudiced toward, individuals with disabilities. A strong case, then, can be made for mainstreaming from a social point of view.

Mainstreaming has not turned out to be a panacea, and problems have arisen. Teachers sometimes walk into classrooms to find they have children with disabilities to teach, but little or no training or information about how to meet the special needs of these children. One teacher found two children diagnosed as having behavior disorders in her elementary school classroom, but received little or no help in dealing with these children. Little, if any, time is included in the day to work with experts in special education, nor is the child with exceptional needs given much preparation for entering the mainstream.

Doubts about the reason some children are mainstreamed have also been raised. Many studies demonstrate that educating students all day in the regular classroom is much less expensive than educating students in a resource room setting, and it costs less than half of what placing students in special classes would cost (Viadero, 1988b). Some professionals and parents fear that students who should not be in regular classes will be placed in them and that some additional services, such as counseling and access to social workers, will be reduced. This may not be a violation of the law, but it would reduce the out-of-classroom services available to the students (Flax, 1988). In reality, if students with disabilities are placed in a regular classroom with *all* the appropriate supports necessary, regular classroom placement might not necessarily be less expensive. The appropriateness of the regular curriculum for some students is also a concern in the mainstreaming situation (Ohanian, 1990). Proponents sometimes believe that all children can work on the same subject but at different levels. However, what if some children need a qualitatively different program? Perhaps these children are cheated from learning what they need to know.

The evaluation of mainstreaming is difficult for many reasons. Some districts are more careful about mainstreaming than others. Some provide better support services. The question of which children do better in which environment is an important question whose answer is still unclear. Perhaps it is not the setting itself that makes as much difference as the type of teaching to which the student is exposed.

The academic effects of mainstreaming on children has been difficult to determine for a number of reasons. One such reason is that mainstreamed children often receive a different curriculum than students in a special classroom. For example, adolescents with auditory impairments who were mainstreamed took more academic classes compared to those in other settings (Kluwin, 1993). Differences between who is and is not mainstreamed are also important.

Mainstreaming has also been touted as a way of socially integrating students into the class and school. In this area, research supplies some answers. The evidence for improved social integration between children with and without disabilities in preschool programs is encouraging (Esposito & Reid, 1986). Successful mainstreaming during the school years remains a challenge. Unless considerable planning for including students into the social fabric of the class is done, children with disabilities tend to be isolated and rejected (Gresham, 1982; Fox, 1989). In other words, despite being part of the regular class, children with disabilities often are not effectively integrated into the social framework of the classroom.

Does this mean that mainstreaming or the concept of the least restrictive environment has failed? No! It means that we cannot merely place students with disabilities into regular classrooms and expect events to take their course. Proximity only gives us an opportunity to help; it does not ensure a better outcome. Strategies aimed at enhancing cooperation between children with and without disabilities are required, some of which will be discussed in Chapter 2. In addition, children with disabilities must be taught appropriate social skills, including conversation and listening skills, so that they can handle social situations (Wanat, 1983). Perhaps all children could use a dose of such training, but it is vital to the success of the child with a disability who may be negotiating a new situation at an initial disadvantage. The most successful mainstreaming programs have (1) continually evaluated the progress of the children, (2) promoted the use of adaptive techniques and materials, (3) individualized instruction, (4) taught students self-management strategies, (5) used cooperative learning arrangements, and (6) promoted communication among educators through a team approach (Wang, Andersen, & Baum, 1985).

Regular Education Initiative (REI) and Inclusion

Even when children are mainstreamed, most will receive services in other places such as the resource room. In other cases, children may spend only a small part of their day in the regular classroom, spending most of their time in a special classroom. Some professionals note that there are now two parallel educational establishments—a general educational establishment and one for special education—and advocate a merger between general and special education. They argue that the cascade of special education services caused the growth of two parallel systems; one for children without disabilities and one for children with disabilities (Pearman et al., 1992) and that this dual system is ineffective and costly (Lilly, 1986). The regular education initiative advocates the merger of general and special education.

Today, many educators would like to go beyond mainstreaming toward full inclusion. The full-inclusion movement maintains that all children with disabilities should be served in the regular classroom with the aid of various professionals and aides. The classroom teacher would have the primary responsibility for educating all children, but would also have the help of a support team. The entire educational system, the school and classroom would be adapted so that students with disabilities receive virtually all their education with their peers who do not have disabilities (Stainback & Stainback, 1984). Some advocates argue that this change will allow teachers to serve all children better, since all children will be included in the regular classroom (Will, 1986).

The aim of these movements is not to end services for students with disabilities, but rather to end the segregation of these children through pull-out programs, such as resource rooms and special classes. The services, as Madeleine Will (1986) notes, will be brought to the child in the classroom rather than the child brought to the services in a special classroom. Full inclusion will require a restructuring of the school and classroom. The environment will be changed by increasing instructional time for students who need to move through their work more slowly or who learn better in small groups. It will also require changes in educational materials and the organization of schoolwide support teams to assist the classroom teacher.

Arguments in Favor of Full Inclusion

Proponents of inclusion argue that, in most cases, the techniques used by regular and special education teachers are similar and that the classroom can be adapted to meet the needs of most children with disabilities. They argue that pull-out programs are so common and fragmented that the teacher rarely has an entire class to teach. Also, data clearly supporting the effectiveness of pull-out programs is lacking (Semmel et al., 1991). The resource room and other pull-out programs suffer from a lack of communication between special education specialists and the classroom teacher making coordination difficult (Gartner & Lipsky, 1987), and what the student learns in the resource room may not transfer well to the classroom (Anderson-Iman, 1987).

These advocates also emphasize the adverse effects of segregating children (Janney, Snell, Beers, & Raynes, 1995). Despite mainstreaming, some children are still segregated, and this segregation sends a strong signal that these children are so different that they cannot be involved in interaction with others (Davern & Schnorr, 1991). Full integration is also necessary to improve attitudes toward people with disabilities, encourage respect for individual differences, improve social interaction, and avoid the problems of segregation, including stigmatization and low self-esteem (Stainback & Stainback, 1991).

A civil rights argument, that separate but equal is unequal and that all children have the right to education with other children, is also part of the discussion. The regular classroom, currently, is designed to meet the needs of people *without* disabilities, which may be perceived as discriminatory (Stainback & Stainback, 1991). The idea, then, is to design integrated programs that include and educate all students within the regular classroom setting. The overall goal of inclusion is better integration of children and better coordination of programs.

People in favor of full inclusion further argue that the current system blames the victim, the student, holding him at fault. The school's responsibility is to adapt to the child's needs rather than requiring that the child adapt to the school's structure. While students are responsible for learning, the school is responsible for providing the environment that will allow children to learn (Lipsky & Gartner, 1991). In the past, students with disabilities were educated to conform to the limitations of the class, whereas a more enlightened approach would alter the classroom and the organization of the school to allow all children to gain an education (Stainback & Stainback, 1991).

Last, proponents of full inclusion argue that appropriate educational experiences can be provided within the regular classroom by the teacher with the aid of other professionals and paraprofessionals. The curriculum can be adapted as needed. For example, in one third grade science classroom, a unit on temperature was being taught. Most students learned to read and understand the Fahrenheit and Celsius temperature scales, while two students learned about molecular movement at different temperatures and one student learned to recognize and use appropriately items that were hot or cold (Stainback & Stainback, 1991). The classroom environment, these advocates claim, can be adapted to meet the needs of all students (Semmel et al., 1991). Effective teaching strategies are effective with all students, including students with disabilities (Raynes, Snell, & Sailor, 1991).

William Davis (1989) notes that "whereas the rallying cry of special education professional and advocacy groups during the 1960s and 1970s was 'greater access to the mainstream,' today it is being replaced by a much more complex rallying cry 'full access to a restructured mainstream'" (p. 440).

Arguments Raising Doubts about the Wisdom of Inclusion

You may notice that the subhead above does not read "arguments against inclusion." Many professionals who are skeptical do not oppose the idea of full integration, but are more cautious. They argue that full inclusion may harm the very students it hopes to help (Davis, 1989). They counter that the techniques used to teach children with disabilities are different, and if not treated differently, these children will not succeed (Lieberman, 1991). The relatively simple modifications made by classroom teachers may not be sufficient (Bryan, Bay, & Donahue, 1988). Regular classroom teachers may not be able to effectively educate these children. Even effective teachers may find themselves unable to accommodate the varied needs of some of these children (Kauffman, Gerber, & Semmel, 1988). After all, studies find that teachers who use very effective teaching techniques are often those who are the least accepting of the behavioral and cognitive differences that often characterize students with disabilities (Gersten, Walker, & Darch, 1988). The assumption, then, that effective teachers can adapt may not be correct.

The idea that labeling or pull-outs may stigmatize the student is countered by evidence showing that children may not be stigmatized because of their label but because of the way they act, which may not always be acceptable (Kauffman et al., 1988).

The discarding of the cascade of special education services is often singled out for criticism. This cascade gives educators and parents choices for the best placement. If it is eliminated, as some advocates desire, then there will be no choice for students. Shutting down all special services that are separate may not be in the best interests of children (Lieberman, 1991). An appropriate education may sometimes mean an education outside the regular classroom. The term *appropriate* does not refer to where the education occurs, but the type of instruction and program offered, and appropriate education is more important than the opportunities for social interactions with other children (Vergason & Anderegg, 1991). Although the present system is not perfect, it does work for some students and intensive work outside the regular classroom may sometimes be needed.

Many authorities are concerned about what they see as the inevitable reduction in services for the children whose interests they represent (Braaten et al.,

Will teachers be able to give students with disabilities the required individual attention if full inclusion occurs?

1988). For example, students with behavior disorders are identified on the basis of their behavior and labeled by others before entering the special education process. They are underserved, require highly specialized services, and may not receive such services in the regular classroom.

The extent of individualization possible is also a question. Will a regular classroom teacher with 30 students be able to give the individualized instruction necessary? If not, many children with disabilities may experience failure. Finally, the question arises as to where the teaching of highly specialized skills necessary for adequate functioning will take place. For example, no one believes that the regular classroom teacher can teach braille or provide orientation and mobility training for children who have visual impairments or teach a child with mental retardation the most basic procedures of self-care. When and where will such important services be delivered? Parents whose children require these specialized services have voiced fears that such services will be reduced (Hill, 1990).

The skeptics argue that integration is desirable, but that the child is best served in a variety of settings with programs that go well beyond what can be found in the regular classroom. The "one size fits all" approach may not be appropriate (Shanker, 1993). Teachers also question whether they will receive the necessary in-service training for such an ambitious program to succeed (Carnine & Kameneeui, 1990). The inclusion of all children may also affect the learning of others if the teacher must spend a great deal of time with one or two youngsters (Semmel et al., 1991). Last, many teachers fear that they will be left without the help necessary as soon as budget cuts are made in tough economic circumstances. Teachers question whether they will really receive the help they are promised (Silver, 1991). As resource rooms fade into oblivion, will the money saved be spent to help teachers who now will have the chief responsibility for the education of children with disabilities? If a significant reduction in staff occurs, special education professionals may find themselves with very high caseloads, which will not allow for individualized attention.

The Future of Inclusion

All of the arguments criticizing these movements can be answered by their advocates. For example, vigilance in resisting budgetary cuts and insisting on adequate classroom support would solve many of the problems discussed previously. The debate continues as parents and professionals argue the issues. Some parent groups have voiced doubts about whether their children will receive the necessary help if they are fully integrated. Parents of children with learning disabilities (Lieberman, 1992), and children with visual or auditory impairments in particular have raised such concerns (Sandberg & Michaelson, 1993). A policy statement of the National Joint Committee on Learning Disabilities (1993) stated that "The regular education classroom is one of many educational program options but is not a substitute for a full continuum necessary to assure the provision of an appropriate education for all students with learning disabilities" (p. 330). The Council for Children with Behavior Disorders has also voiced its concerns. On the other hand, parents of some children with mental retardation tend to support it. Historically, parents of children with learning disabilities and behavior disorders have fought for extra services, many provided outside the classroom, while parents of children with mental retardation have fought to have their children educated as much as possible within the mainstream (Lieberman, 1992). All parents want their chil-

THOUGHT QUESTION

5. *Which arguments made by proponents and opponents of inclusion sound most reasonable to you?*

dren treated as individuals and have their needs met, but some parents believe it can be done within the regular classroom and some do not.

The right of children to be educated in the regular classroom is now being test-ed in the courts. In one case, a child with Down syndrome and a measured intelli-gence of 59, whose parents objected to his placement in a special school, won the right to be educated in a regular classroom. The district was required to hire a spe-cial aide for his teacher. The parents explained that they believed their child was not gaining the social skills necessary by being placed in the special school. The court noted that the child had the right to be educated in a regular classroom rather than a more restrictive placement (*New York Times*, July 23, 1993).

No one can predict with certainty where these movements will lead. Will all students with disabilities be placed in regular classrooms and the cascade of ser-vices be relegated to history? Will there be some compromise and a hybrid system arise that would ensure that most students with disabilities are educated solely in the regular classroom and still keep the cascade of services for other students? No matter which alternative prevails, the implications for regular classroom teachers are important. First, many more children with disabilities will be placed full time and receive special services in the regular classroom. The regular classroom teacher will be required to be the primary educator for many more children, with the active assistance of the special educator for planning and other services. Sec-ond, if inclusion is to succeed, the classroom teacher must receive adequate support, including aides in the classroom, time to cooperate with the special edu-cator as well as specific training in ways to meet the needs of children with dis-abilities. Third, teachers, parents, and some advocates fear that this is merely a cost-cutting measure and that their children will not receive the necessary in-struction from experts. This fear is partially caused by the lack of teacher and par-ent involvement in the process of defining REI and inclusion (Sandberg & Michaelson, 1993). The debate has largely been held at the college and university level, and participation by local communities has been noticeably absent (Davis, 1989). Classroom teachers feel left out of the process (Kauffman et al., 1988).

How do teachers feel about REI and inclusion? Little research has been done on this subject. One study found that teachers did not mind pull-out programs and did not show much support for REI (Coates, 1989). Semmel and colleagues (1991) used a questionnaire to sample the attitudes of regular classroom teachers, special educators, administrators, and specialists such as speech-language spe-cialists and counselors from elementary schools in Illinois and California. Most favored the current practices rather than REI. Of course, this could be interpreted in terms of an innate conservatism, knowing what you have but being somewhat fearful of what might occur. When a questionnaire was sent out to various educa-tion personnel in a mid-sized Colorado school district in which inclusion was practiced, 70 percent of the respondents agreed or agreed strongly that inclusion worked well, but 49 percent doubted that inclusion was the best way to meet the needs of the students, and 28 percent thought it was detrimental to their educa-tion (Pearman et al., 1992). Ninety-one percent of the respondents did not believe adequate time was being provided for cooperative planning between the regular classroom teacher and special education teacher. Inclusion may work better in some communities than in others due to better planning and staff training. In some communities, a commitment to educate all students in the regular class-room seems to be succeeding (Forest & Lusthaus, 1990). However, comprehensive assessment of these changes is necessary before they are implemented on a national or statewide basis since they will have a profound effect upon the education of all students (McKenny & Hocutt, 1988).

Integrating the Child with Severe Disabilities

Most of the research and opinions on inclusion deals with children who have mild or moderate impairments—categories that include over 90 percent of the total of all children with disabilities. However, many advocates for full inclusion argue that children with severe disabilities should also be educated in the regular classroom (Fuchs & Fuchs, 1994). Such programs are now beginning to take shape. Giangreco and colleagues (1993) interviewed 19 general education teachers working in 10 Vermont schools from kindergarten through ninth grade who had children with severe disabilities placed in their classrooms. Most teachers reacted to the initial placement in a cautious or even negative manner. They were reluctant and often apprehensive. One teacher noted, "I didn't know much about how to deal with him and how to respond to him and interact with him. I was afraid" (p. 363).

For 17 of the 19 teachers a transformation occurred. They changed their initial expectations and increased their own responsibility for the education of the child. Their interactions increased greatly, as did their concern for the child's integration into the class. Their negative comments were replaced by more positive descriptions. The transformations were not abrupt, but rather progressive and gradual. The teachers began to view the child as a person, not a disability, and found that they did not have to make many changes. They developed a willingness to interact with the students, and the largest challenge was just to include these children in every activity possible, even if full participation was not possible. They used more group learning procedures, such as cooperative learning and group problem solving (see Chapter 2).

When questioned, these teachers noted the vital necessity of having a paraprofessional present on whom they could rely. The importance of a team approach, including the help of the special educator for consultation, was also noted.

Evaluations showed that these students became more aware of and responsive to their surroundings, and their communication and social skills improved. Most classmates accepted their presence without any fuss, while others actively sought these children out for interactions.

Other studies also show this increased rate of social responsiveness and social interaction (Janney et al., 1995; Staub & Hunt, 1993). In addition, this interaction enhances the sensitivity of students without disabilities toward students with differences (Biklen, Corrigan, & Quick, 1989). This is not just true in elementary school. When high school students without disabilities were questioned about their experiences with students with moderate to severe disabilities, the students showed a reduced fear of human differences and an increased tolerance for others (Peck, Donaldson, & Pezzoli, 1990).

Some parents of children who have severe disabilities want this integration while others do not. Even those who desire it express concerns about their children's safety, the attitudes of the staff and students toward their children, and the success and quality of the program. Others show concerns that their children's circles of friends with disabilities would be narrowed, that they would be deprived of role models who had disabilities, and wondered whether any real friendships would develop. None of the parents regretted the experience, and all noticed an enhancement in their children's social skills (Hanline & Halvorsen, 1989).

Many students with severe disabilities will not be able to participate in all facets of an activity. The principle of partial participation is often advanced to cover this difficulty, meaning that youngsters with severe impairments often have the skills to participate in some aspect of an activity (Baumgart et al., 1982). A child who cannot participate in a basketball game may still hold the ball or in some cases help keep score. Through direct and systematic instruction, children can learn to participate somewhat. This integration should begin at an early age.

It is difficult to predict how far this movement will progress. Children with severe disabilities require training in mobility and daily living skills. These skills must be specially taught and are not the province of the regular classroom teacher. Whether they can be taught in the classroom by specialists is still a question. Although the complete integration of these students is probably not going to occur in the near future, the movement toward partial integration may take hold.

The Process of Special Education

Most children with disabilities are not diagnosed in infancy or early childhood. They are referred and assessed during the middle years of childhood, in elementary school.

Screening

Schools have the responsibility to screen students to discover disabilities.

Schools have the obligation to discover which children have a disability that might adversely affect their achievement in school. Schools therefore perform vital screening functions. Visual and auditory screening for possible disabilities have been performed for many years. Developmental, psychological, and cognitive screening instruments are also used. If the child is identified through the screening process as possibly having a disability, the child will be referred for additional testing and evaluation.

The Referral Process

The first stage in determining the eligibility of the student for special services is referral. The regular classroom teacher is the source of referral for the overwhelming majority of children, which is only natural since the teacher sees these students every day, and the challenges of schoolwork often cause a disability, such as a learning disability, to become evident. Parents or physicians may also make referrals. Federal law requires that each school system have a referral system but does not mandate a specific referral procedure. Districts vary widely in their procedures and forms. One such referral form is found in Figure 1.5.

Referring Agent: _____

Child's Name: _____

Child's Age: _____

Child's Date of Birth: _____

1. Please describe, being brief but specific, academic and/or behavior problems evidenced by the child being referred.

2. Under what conditions does the problem exist?

3. What methods have you tried to solve the problem(s)?

4. What do you see as this particular child's strengths?

5. Additional information from school records and/or comments:

_____
Referring Agent, Signature

(This form is to be completed and returned to the committee chairperson.)

FIGURE 1.5 Sample Referral Form

Source: *Functions of the Placement Committee in Special Education*, 1976, by the National Association of State Directors of Special Education, p. 57. Reprinted by permission.

Most children who are referred for special education are evaluated and accepted. An often quoted study by Algozzine and colleagues (1982) found that 92 percent of children who are referred for special education consideration are evaluated, and of all those evaluated 73 percent are accepted into special education programs. Other studies find somewhat lower percentages (Furlong & Yanagida, 1985). Of all students referred for possibly having a learning disability in a sample of 12 suburban and rural school districts, 54 percent were found eligible (Fugate, Clarizio, & Phillips, 1993).

In many districts, prereferral programs exist in which teachers are asked to bring their observations to the attention of a committee of professionals who then suggest ways to help the child before referring the student for formal evaluation. This reduces the number of students who must proceed through the formal evaluation process. The results of such programs are quite positive (Kerr, Nelson, & Lambert, 1987).

Evaluation

When the parents agree that their child requires an evaluation, the next step is gathering relevant information. The evaluation/placement team may include a number of professionals as well as the child's parents and sometimes even the student. The team will look at the child's records and interview teachers. Sometimes, medical testing is conducted to determine if any sensory, motor, or physical difficulty is present. Standardized psychological testing is performed by a trained psychologist who tries to understand the child's functioning. Achievement and intelligence tests are administered. (It is in this area where so much controversy exists.) Standardized tests are often divided into two groups: norm-referenced tests and criterion-referenced tests.

Norm-Referenced Tests

Norm-referenced tests (NRTs) are those in which the score of the test taker is compared to the scores of other students who took the test when it was developed. The student's score is reported in terms of where the student stands in comparison with the national norm reference group. If a student scored in the 60th percentile in social studies, we could say that the student scored equal to or better than 60 percent of the people in the norm group.

The overwhelming majority of standardized tests are norm-referenced. Notice that in norm-referenced tests we can easily rank students; that is, we can say that if Paul scored in the 85th percentile on a biology test and Ed scored in the 75th percentile, Paul knows more biology than Ed, at least as measured by the test. NRTs do not tell us how much biology Paul or Ed knows, for they do not yield an absolute score. They only compare the student's score to those scores achieved by the standardized norm group. NRTs can provide information concerning student's achievement levels and can serve as tools to help in the selection of students for particular programs.

Norm-referenced tests are very useful, but a number of objections and cautions surround their use. The test's usefulness depends greatly on the characteristics of the group on which the test was standardized. Some authorities argue that the use of these tests with children who have disabilities is problematic. First, not all of these tests provide information as to whether the norm group contained children with disabilities and, even when they do, the extent and nature of the disabilities are rarely noted (Fuchs et al., 1987). Perhaps the most pressing question here is whether the norm group bears a relationship to the group being tested. Today, great care is taken in selecting and describing the norm group, yet each test is standardized on a different group of students. The nature of the norm group to which you compare your students makes all the difference. In addition, a child's disabilities may prevent that child from doing well on a test. For example, children with emotional difficulties may not do well because their ability to show what they can do is compromised by the disability. Children with learning disabilities may not do well if they require more time because they process material more slowly.

Another problem is that these tests may or may not reflect what is being taught in the classroom. Some authorities claim that curriculum-based assessment is necessary. That is, we should be certain that children are being tested on what they are learning since curricula across the country differs widely.

Criterion-Referenced Tests

Criterion-referenced tests (CRTs) compare a student's achievement level against some standard of proficiency in an area of content and are useful for implementing IEPs. With CRTs, if the student's score equals or surpasses a particular criteri-

Norm-referenced tests: Standardized tests in which the score of the test taker is compared to the scores of other students who took the test when it was developed.

Criterion-referenced tests: Tests in which student scores are compared to a particular criterion or absolute standard.

on, the student is said to be proficient or to have mastered the skill. If not, more work is required. Suppose Glenn takes a test on the addition of two numbers and answers correctly 18 of 25 questions. If the criterion for success is 20 correct, Glenn lacks proficiency or mastery of the skill.

On a different level, CRTs can tell teachers what students can and cannot do. A math test report of a CRT states the kinds of math operations the student can do and their difficulty level. The interpretation of a CRT is not dependent upon some comparison with the norm group, but rather is made in terms of the test's content meaning. When a teacher receives feedback about the class, the number and percentage mastering or not mastering a particular objective are noted, and the teacher can use this information to plan remediation. The skills that are measured are specific and detailed. For example, a language test may offer measurements of a child's specific skills in the areas of written composition, capitalization, punctuation, spelling, correct English usage, sentence structure, and proofreading (Houston et al., 1988). These areas can be broken down even further.

CRTs have their limitations, though. They are useful in areas where the domain of knowledge is well established, but there is doubt as to their usefulness in measuring more advanced levels of knowledge typified by critical thinking (Anastasi, 1988). Many CRTs do not offer appropriate data on how they were formulated. In addition, ground rules that determine whether a student has mastered an objective need to be established and understood. For example, why should the cutoff be 9 correct answers out of 11 questions: why not 8?

Many objections to standardized tests have been raised, but the most important of them is the possibility of a cultural bias in some of the tests, especially intelligence tests. The issues surrounding intelligence testing will be discussed in detail in Chapter 4.

Ecological Assessment

A particularly useful and appropriate method of collecting information about the student in all domains is called **ecological assessment**. This method involves looking closely at the environment where a particular activity typically takes place and determining through observation the steps involved in performing the activity and what changes in an environment are necessary in order to enable an individual to succeed. It emphasizes the importance of looking at the interactions of the child with the environment, not just looking at the child or the environment. In a school situation, we may look at the classroom's physical structure and the type of instruction given and then determine what changes must be made to facilitate learning. Perhaps wider aisles are necessary for a child with a physical disability, or the use of more small-group-oriented instruction for a child with a learning disability.

Such assessments are useful outside the classroom as well. For example, an instructor might go to a bus stop and observe in detail the steps involved in using a bus. The teacher might even ride the bus to check the list of steps and then describe each component skill in detail. Breaking down the task into the component parts in this manner is called **task analysis** (NICHCY, 1993). The student is then assessed on these skills and taught the needed skills, and when necessary, the environment is altered. Special considerations for people with disabilities, such as

Ecological assessment:
A type of assessment that seeks to understand the ongoing relationship between the child and the environment.

Task analysis:
The process of breaking down tasks into the smallest elements in their proper sequence.

special platforms for entering the bus, may be required. Ecological assessment is one of the most appropriate means of determining what skills and accommodations students require in the classroom and in the workplace (NICHCY, 1993).

Placement Decisions

After the assessment is made, the evaluation/placement team meets to discuss the case and determine the optimal placement. According to law, the child's teacher must be present at the IEP meeting, although which teacher—the regular classroom teacher or the special education teacher—is not stated. One of the special education teacher's duties is to make certain that the procedures match federal and state law. The regular classroom teacher's attendance at IEP meetings and conferences would represent a positive step since the success or failure of the educational program rests with the classroom teacher. Unfortunately, many elementary school teachers are minimally involved in the process. A student in secondary school may have many teachers, making direct involvement on the part of all teachers concerned even more difficult.

The special education team, including the student's parents, prepares the IEP, although too often parents are not as actively involved as would be desirable. The parents contribute to the process and may indicate their agreement to its contents by signing the IEP. Parents may seek to have the placement or other aspects of the IEP changed and do not have to agree to allow placement of their children in a particular environment. If they do not, an impartial hearing is held. During this time, no change in the child's placement can be made without approval of the parents.

Yearly evaluations as well as a major three-year evaluation are required, which allows all parties to note areas of progress and areas in which changes are required. The entire process emphasizes parental involvement.

Special Education as a Group of Services, Not a Place

One difficulty that often arises in any debate over where children with special needs ought to be educated is the over-identification of special education with special classes, the resource room, and other environmental settings. The debate over the regular education initiative and inclusion sometimes becomes a debate about place. This conception, though, is faulty. Special education is not a place, but a group of services tailored to the special needs of an individual student. It is important not to lose sight of the fact that what defines the child with exceptional needs is the requirement for special services and attention.

In order to accommodate the special needs of children with disabilities, teachers must be willing to adapt their lessons. Such adaptations are not difficult in many cases, and special educators and other experts can help the regular classroom teacher meet the special needs of children with disabilities.

Adapting Lessons to Accommodate Students with Disabilities

The key to educational success for students with disabilities in the regular classroom is the adaptation of the classroom so that all students may learn. There are a number of areas in which the classroom can be adapted to the special needs of students (Munson, 1986; 1987).

Instructional Materials and Equipment

Sometimes, students with disabilities require changes in the instructional materials and equipment being used. A student with a visual impairment may require large print books, while a student with mental retardation may need a more simplified version of an age-appropriate story.

Curriculum

Most students with disabilities can use the regular curriculum. When a curricular modification is made, such as using a text from a lower grade, it is noted on the IEP.

Format of Directions and Assignments

Sometimes, teachers must both repeat directions for those who require it or even break down the assignment into more manageable tasks. For example, children with learning disabilities may require a long-term assignment be broken down into a number of smaller assignments and each checked for successful completion. Extending the time limits for assignments may also be required for some

The key to educational success is adapting the classroom and its materials to allow children with disabilities to learn.

students. Students with visual impairments may be able to handle a smaller number of problems since they may read more slowly, but not require a reduction in the difficulty level of the problems.

Teacher Presentation Mode

A child with a learning disability may respond better to a multimodal presentation (one involving the use of many sense modalities). Children with various disabilities can benefit from a variety of presentation modes, such as the increased use of demonstration and hands-on activities.

Students Response Mode

Changing the way students respond—for example, permitting more verbal rather than written responses—can increase the effectiveness of a student's learning process.

Teaching Strategies

Some argue that an increased use of drill, questions that fill in gaps, or more frequent monitoring are required for students with disabilities. Other teaching strategies such as cooperative learning or peer tutoring may also be effective and are discussed in Chapter 2.

Individual Instruction

Individual instruction is necessary for all children who have difficulty with the material. Unfortunately, little individualized instruction takes place due to time constraints (Zigmond, Levin, & Laurie, 1985).

Instructional Grouping

Some grouping changes in the class may be helpful to students. The use of dyads (two students working together) or small group instruction may aid students with disabilities.

Testing Modifications

Changing the structure or circumstances of a test are among the most common modifications made for students with disabilities. Typical modifications involve giving students more time to finish an assignment or a test, changing the format of the test (from written to oral), or changing the format of the questions perhaps from multiple choice to something else. Consider the plight of students with visual impairments in school. These students cannot read the test, and if they are to be tested, someone must read it to them. It may not be possible to test these children's knowledge of graphs, except in the most general manner. A child with attention-deficit/hyperactivity disorder (ADHD) may not be able to sit still long enough to finish a unit test, and the child who cannot read but "knows his science" may also require alternative testing.

Alternative testing does not mean that a student is given easier tests. The student does not "get out of" doing anything. By changing the testing, a teacher simply recognizes the students' difficulties and, at the same time, ensures that the student's knowledge is measured in a valid way.

Two types of alternative testing techniques are commonly used. The first type involves modifications that alter the testing procedures but not the pupil skills

THOUGHT QUESTION

6. *How would you answer an objection from a student who could not finish the same test that you gave a student with a disability more time to finish?*

being tested. For example, some children need more time than teachers would typically give a class. Children with learning disabilities or who have attention-deficit/hyperactivity disorder may require more time. Since most tests are power tests (i.e., they are designed to measure how much the students know), rather than speed tests, which emphasize how quickly students answer questions, extending test time allotments should not be much of a problem. For other students, removal to another location for testing will allow them to perform better. Some students may not be able to use computer answer sheets and may require some other means of marking their answers.

The second type involves modifications to testing procedures so that the skills being tested are somewhat different than those imagined when the test was prepared. For example, some students may require the use of a calculator, while others may not be able to complete particular questions because of the item format, such as dictation in some spelling tests (New York State Department of Education, 1982).

Alternative testing requirements are listed on the IEP. Alternative testing procedures need not take much teacher time but may help children with disabilities show their knowledge in an appropriate manner.

 # Technology: The Promise

Technology has changed our lives both at home and at work. People use computers for personal entertainment, as a means of processing information, and to store large amounts of information. We use videocassette recorders to record our favorite shows and calculators to make our shopping and budgeting easier. Fax machines, sophisticated computer programs that help design machinery, and computers that are connected to each other have revolutionized the workplace, and will continue to do so in the future (Cook & Cohen, 1994).

Technology has also changed the lives of children and adults who have various disabilities. Children who have auditory impairments use many sophisticated devices designed to improve their ability to hear. Children with visual impairments may use calculators with raised numbers that announce the answers to a computation. Children who cannot speak may use talking computers on which they type their responses and an artificial voice vocalizes their thoughts. Children with physical disabilities may use powered wheelchairs and specially adapted computer keyboards.

Many children with disabilities are helped by assistive technology devices. Federal law defines an assistive technology device as "any item, piece of equipment or product system, whether acquired commercially off the shelf, modified, or customized, that is used to increase, maintain, or improve functional capabilities of individuals with disabilities" (see Lewis, 1993).

Such devices have two purposes. The first is to remediate or correct a specific impairment that the child may have. The use of glasses or magnifiers by children who cannot see well or of special positioning equipment that enables children to assume a particular posture are examples of these. The second purpose is to enable children to perform specific tasks or learn specific material. For example, a child with a learning disability may require a specific computer program for learning grammar

The use of computers and other technology has revolutionized the field of special education.

A New View

This text emphasizes an expanded view of people with exceptional needs. Older views emphasized the individual's difficulties and frequently fostered a pitiful and inadequate view of the person with a disability that saw him or her as basically incompetent and unable to make decisions. The emerging view focuses on the strengths of the individual rather than the disability, emphasizes self-determination and self-fulfillment, and looks at ways to remove barriers and encourage all people with disabilities to fulfill their potential. Changes in the classroom and in the social environment allow the child with a disability to participate, grow, and develop. The school has a responsibility to develop ways of adequately meeting the needs of children with disabilities. The school also has the responsibility to educate children without disabilities as to the nature of disabilities and the rights of people with disabilities, so that all children can fully develop their own personal and academic abilities.

SUMMARY

1. The terms *exceptional child* or *child with exceptional needs* refers to a child whose intellectual, emotional, or physical performance differs from the average expected for his or her peer or cultural group so much so that special services are required for the child to develop or learn. The term *disability* refers to a total or partial behavioral, mental, physical, or sensory loss of functioning.

2. Incidence refers to the number of new cases in a time period, usually one year. Prevalence refers to the total number of cases at a particular time in a particular group. About 9.5 percent of all students receive special education services for a disability and about 3 percent more are considered gifted. Four diagnostic categories comprise the vast majority of students with disabilities: learning disabilities, speech and language impairment, mental retardation, and behavior disorders.

3. There are many arguments both in favor and opposed to labeling. Although categorization may be necessary, it may potentially damage the student by stigmatizing and isolating the child.

4. Section 504 of the Rehabilitation Act of 1973 assures people with disabilities access to public programs. The Americans with Disabilities Act of 1990 forbids discrimination in employment, and requires employers to make reasonable accommodations for employees who have disabilities. It also requires access to public accommodations.

5. The Individuals with Disabilities Education Act (IDEA), formerly called the Education for All Handicapped Children Act, PL 94-142, requires schools to identify children with disabilities; to offer a free, appropriate public education, to assure due process; to provide nondiscriminatory evaluation and confidentiality of records; to formulate individualized education programs (IEP) stating the goals and placement for the student; to construct a transition plan at or before the student reaches 16 years of age; and to educate the student in the least restrictive environment.

6. PL 99-457 requires that states provide services to youngsters with disabilities ages three to five

years and encourages the states to begin infant and toddler programs.

7. Mainstreaming involves the integration of students with disabilities into the regular classroom environment either on a full- or part-time basis. The Regular Education Initiative (REI) advocates a merger between special education and general education. Inclusion or full inclusion involves the complete integration of children with exceptional needs into the regular classroom. The regular classroom teacher has the principal responsibility for the education of the child.

8. The integration of children with severe disabilities is also being accomplished in some school districts. Although some of these children cannot participate fully in all activities, they can participate in some way in most activities.

9. The first step in gaining aid for a student is to refer the student for evaluation. The evaluation process requires that a team look at many sources of information. Standardized testing is frequently used, although many questions remain about how these tests are used. Many districts have prereferral committees that try to help the regular classroom teacher and avoid unnecessary referrals for special education.

10. Special education is a group of services not a place. The regular classroom teacher may adapt the classroom to the needs of children with disabilities in a number of ways. These include changing instructional materials and equipment, curricular content, the format of directions and assignments, teacher input mode, student response mode, instructional strategies used, increasing the amount of individual instruction, and the use of alternative testing procedures.

The Child's Social World: Family and Society

THE CHILD'S SOCIAL WORLD: FAMILY AND SOCIETY

TRUE-FALSE STATEMENTS

See below for the correct answers.

1. Most children with disabilities are identified at birth or shortly after.
2. Most families raising children with disabilities adjust well to the challenge.
3. The oldest daughter in a family often finds that she has more responsibility caring for a sibling with a disability than any of her other brothers or sisters.
4. Teachers are more likely to accept children with sensory and physical impairments than children with cognitive impairments and behavioral difficulties.
5. Children in elementary school usually have a reasonably good knowledge of the nature of various disabilities.
6. Children with disabilities generally form friendships as easily as children without disabilities.
7. Children who have a learning disability or show attention-deficit/hyperactivity disorder are more likely to be actively rejected than are children with a sensory disability.
8. Placing children who have disabilities in close proximity to children without disabilities in the classroom usually improves the social status of children with disabilities as well as increasing social interaction.
9. If children without disabilities discover that children with disabilities have the same interests, interaction increases.
10. Adolescents with disabilities usually find interpersonal relationships during their teen years more difficult than during their elementary school years.

Answers to True-False Statements
1. False. See page 48.
2. True.
3. True.
4. True.
5. False. See page 58.
6. False. See page 61.
7. True.
8. False. See page 62.
9. True.
10. True.

The Child's Environment

Think of all the environmental influences that surround children as they grow up. Parents, siblings, grandparents, friends, the media, the school, the child's culture, and the neighborhood are just some of the more important factors that influence and mold a child. The child's environment consists of a complex group of factors that are always operating on the child, affecting every aspect of life. At times, environmental factors may be in conflict as when parents teach their child one thing and friends teach something else.

Teachers working with children with disabilities need to understand the child's social world for a number of reasons. First, the child's social development is, in itself, an important concern. The teacher must play an active role when integrating the child into the social fabric of the classroom. Second, the child's self-concept, behavior, and attitudes will be affected by the many social forces surrounding the child. Any attempt to improve the child's functioning requires an understanding of the child's social world. Third, teachers need to work with parents, and understanding parents' hopes, dreams, and concerns for a child can make parent-teacher cooperation a reality. This chapter focuses on the nature of the child's social environment, ways teachers can help improve the child's social integration into the class, and ways to improve communication with parents.

An Ecological View of the Child's World

Urie Bronfenbrenner (1979) argues that each individual is affected by the entire environment and that many facets of the environment are unappreciated. A number of systems operate and interact with each other. The *microsystem* involves immediate interactions within the family. The *mesosystem* involves the settings in which a family actively participates, such as their interactions with health-care workers, extended family, friends, neighbors, and professionals involved in early childhood or early intervention programs. The *exosystem* involves settings in which the family is not actively involved, at least at this time, but yet affect the family and child, such as the mass media, government support systems, and the educational system and schools. The *macrosystem* is composed of the ideology or belief system inherent in social institutions including the ethnic, cultural, and religious influences, as well as the economic and political systems that exist (Seligman, 1991a). An accurate understanding of the child's world must take into account these systems and the influence each has on the developing child.

Yet, to perceive the child as completely buffeted by environmental influences would be incorrect. Although one might be tempted to conclude that outside influences—parents, teachers, friends, and even psychologists—act upon a passive organism, as a potter does on clay, this conception has been discarded by psychologists as much too simplistic. It ignores the effect the child has on these people.

A newer view sees the child as affecting the environment, just as the environment affects the child (Clarke & Clarke, 1986). This conception, called **reciprocal interaction**, comes closer to an appreciation of the complexities of human interaction. It is sometimes called the transactional view. For instance, one child may react to a teacher's help with a smile and gratitude and become joyful at a success, which reinforces the teacher. Another child may resent the intrusion of the teacher and show frustration. The first child is more likely to find the teacher helpful in the future. One child reacts to another child's curiosity about a wheelchair with a smile and an engaging conversation, while another may interpret the peer's interest as singling him out and resent it. These differing reactions lead to different interactions in the future.

If we look at the interactions between parent and child, their reciprocal nature becomes obvious. Spend some time observing the interactions between a parent and an infant. Perhaps the parent hugs the baby, who responds with a smile. The parent then says something to the baby, who reacts with a vocalization. The baby's vocalization brings a stream of verbal praise from the parent. For years, psychologists have looked at the caregiver-child relationship in terms of what the mother or father did to the child, but the effect of the child on the parent was rarely considered. Today, child development specialists look at how each affects the other.

In the preceding example, the actions of both parties served as responses and stimuli, which prompted new actions. The baby's smile stimulated the parent to speak to the child, and this in turn stimulated the baby to vocalize. The interaction proceeded rapidly, with both parties affecting the behavior of the other. The system is bidirectional, with information flowing from one party to the other and back again (Bell, 1968; 1979).

But what if an infant or young child does not react to the signals given by parents in the usual manner or if parents do not understand the cues given by the child? In these cases, which are not uncommon with children who are slow to develop or have some sensory disability, the interactions may not promote growth and development. For instance, if the child who is developing more slowly does not meet the parents' attempts to communicate with him with a smile or some other emotional reaction easily recognized by the parent, the parent may then interact less with the child due to a misunderstanding about what the child can do and what the child is communicating.

This pattern may continue throughout childhood. A child may be slow in developing reading skills, leading the parents to react with impatience and criticism. These parental behaviors may cause the child to avoid any activities that remotely involve reading. The child's reduction in effort leads to further parental criticism. A knowledgeable professional may alert parents to the possibility that this scenario is occurring and suggest other ways for the parents to react to the child's progress. If a child elicits negative appraisals from others due to some behavior or developmental lag, the child may be at risk for developing later cognitive and behavioral problems (Meisels, 1989).

So we cannot simply view the child as adrift in an environment, being totally at the mercy of others. At the same time, while acknowledging the child as influential in the environment, we would be just as wrong to believe that the child can totally shape that environment. That would be giving too much power and influence to the child. Each element of the environment affects every other, making the system quite complex. As we look at various environmental influences, keep the concept of reciprocal interaction in mind.

Reciprocal interaction:
The process by which an organism constantly affects and is affected by the environment.

THOUGHT QUESTION

1. *The concept of reciprocal interaction is a great improvement over other conceptions of interpersonal interactions. Why has it taken so long to accept the concept of reciprocal interaction?*

Early identification of disabilities is advantageous as children can begin to receive extra help.

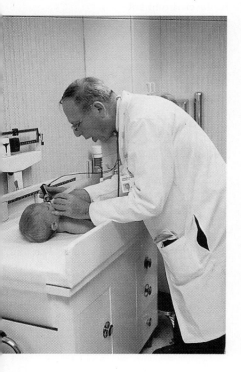

Parents and Children

Parents exert the greatest influence on their children. Parents of children with disabilities often find that their responsibilities go far beyond those of parents of children without disabilities. The general parenting requirements—love, attending to the child's physical needs, protection, and providing an atmosphere that allows the child to develop his or her intellectual abilities—are fundamentally the same. However, the parents of children with disabilities must often commit more of their resources in time and money, create an atmosphere that is more structured, and generally be more sophisticated observers of development (Darling, 1991a).

Looking at parental influences is complicated by the fact that most children with disabilities are not identified at birth, although more are being identified at earlier ages than ever before. Children with learning disabilities, communication disorders, behavior disorders, and the overwhelming number of children classified as having mental retardation, are *not* usually diagnosed at birth or even shortly after. Early identification is an advantage for many reasons. Besides allowing for early intervention it may lead to greater understanding of the child's behavior. A parent of a child with an undiagnosed hearing impairment may believe the child is intentionally ignoring the parent's call to dinner, which causes the parent to react with anger and a scolding. When the hearing impairment is discovered this situation will not occur. Early intervention programs will be described in detail in Chapter 3.

When Your Child Has a Disability

How would you react if a doctor told you that your infant or toddler has a disability? Some authorities argue that parents go through a series of stages in their acceptance of the condition (Berger, 1995; Seligman, 1985). First, there is denial, a refusal to believe the diagnosis. Parents are shocked. They may take the child to different doctors to get a more optimistic diagnosis and prognosis. This is followed by a stage of emotional disorganization in which parents experience a series of churning emotions including guilt, despair, anger, and hopelessness (Eden-Piercy, Blacher, & Eyman, 1986; Blacher, 1984). During this stage, the child's special needs for care become more obvious. Parents may find it difficult to learn to "read" the child when behaviors such as eye-to-eye contact and smiling may not be present, and social interactions may be affected (Wicks-Nelson & Israel, 1991). During the third stage, parents accept the disability and adjust to the needs of the child. Now, parents seek out the help that is available and create a more stable family environment.

Such stage theories are often criticized for a number of reasons. First, these stages are not always present (Allen & Affleck, 1985). Even if they are present, they are not necessarily sequential (Darling, 1991a). Finally, not all families adjust or accept the reality of a disability, although most do.

Some authorities do not reject the idea of stages; instead, they argue that many factors affect parents' reactions to the disability and their subsequent ability to cope with it. Some of these factors include socioeconomic status, available support services, the attitudes of physicians and other professionals, prior information, religion, culture, the child's physical appearance, and the nature of the disability and its severity (Seligman, 1991a; Schell, 1981). In theory, the more severe the disability, the more it affects the life of the family and the more difficult is the adjustment (Seligman, 1991a). A child with a severe disability is more likely to change the family's lifestyle than a child with a mild disability (McCubbin & Huang, 1989). Although the evidence is hardly universal, the stressors and demands on the family do increase with the severity of the impairment (McCubbin & Huang, 1989). On the other hand, if the disability is obvious, parents are more likely to accept the disability.

Parents whose children are diagnosed as having a mild disability are slower to recognize the problem and seek help for it because it is more easily overlooked or ignored. Parents may expect the child to catch up. Parental reaction to the news that their child has a mild disability varies greatly. For some, shock, disbelief, resentment, and stage-like sequence may occur. For others, the diagnosis may come as a relief to parents who now have an explanation for their child's difficulties (Fewell, 1991). The parents may then look back and see signs of the disability that they can now interpret in light of the diagnosis. The daily impact of a mild disability may be somewhat less than that of a severe disability, but it is still considerable. The parent of a child with a learning disability may have more responsibilities helping the child with homework and school-related problems, and a child with a medical problem may require a daily medical regimen or dietary changes (Fewell, 1991).

A Developmental Approach to Family Challenges

The challenges confronted by a family raising a child with a disability change with the child's age (see Table 2.1). Sometimes, professionals focus more on the parents' emotional reaction to the diagnosis rather than preparing them to deal with the ongoing nature of their concern. For example, Wikler and colleagues (1981) found that social workers tended to overestimate how upset parents were just after discovering that their child had mental retardation and underestimate the difficulties parents experienced later as the child developed.

In infancy, the challenges revolve about obtaining the right medical care for their children and finding ways to cope with their own emotions (Seligman, 1991a). Often, parents experience a feeling of powerlessness, a feeling that they have no control of the services they require (Darling, 1991a). They search for help and answers and begin their relationship with the medical establishment.

As the child enters early childhood, the nature of the disability becomes more evident. Parents may realize that their child is not progressing at the same rate as other children. Questions about the integration of children become more pressing.

During the elementary school years, the question of which placement is best becomes crucial. In many cases, the disability is just being discovered. Parents have less control over the child in elementary school. The child has to deal with an increasing number of peers and teachers and does not receive as much support. At the same time, the academic challenges increase.

In adolescence, children usually begin to separate from their parents and think about an independent future. After a period of acceptance and often reasonable success in middle childhood, a change may occur as transition problems take center stage and lack of peer acceptance becomes a greater problem (Seligman,

TABLE 2.1   **Possible Issues Encountered at Life Cycle Stages**

LIFE CYCLE STAGE	PARENTS	SIBLINGS
Early childhood, ages 0–5	Obtaining an accurate diagnosis Informing siblings and relatives Locating support services Clarifying a personal ideology to guide decisions Addressing issues of stigma Identifying positive contributions of exceptionality Setting great expectations	Less parental time and energy for sibling needs Feelings of jealousy over less attention Fears associated with misunderstanding of exceptionality
Elementary school, ages 6–12	Establishing routines to carry out family functions Adjusting emotionally to educational implications Clarifying issues of mainstreaming vs. special class placement Participating in IEP conferences Locating community resources Arranging for extracurricular activities Establishing positive working relationships with professionals Gathering information about educational services available to the family and the child Setting great expectations about the future for their child Understanding the different methods of instruction (community experiences, vocational training, integration)	Division of responsibility for any physical care needs Oldest female sibling may be at risk Limited family resources for recreation and leisure Informing friends and teachers Possible concern over younger sibling surpassing older Issues of "mainstreaming" into same school Need for basic information on exceptionality

1991a). These concerns add extra stress to the usual problems involved in raising any adolescent.

Stress

At one time, psychologists thought they understood the effect of raising a child with a disability on the family. A number of early studies emphasized the additional stress on the family. Mothers experienced higher levels of distress, depression, health problems, and isolation (see Fagan & Schur, 1993). Some researchers assumed that rearing a child with a disability was inherently stressful and that these families showed a higher level of marital problems and tension in the family (Shonkoff et al., 1992). After all, the endless series of medical, psychological, and therapy appointments, the additional financial responsibilities, the extra care needed for the child, and the endless questions from well-meaning people, all

TABLE 2.1 *Continued*

LIFE CYCLE STAGE	PARENTS	SIBLINGS
Adolescence, ages 12–21	Adjusting emotionally to possible chronicity of exceptionality	Dealing with possible stigma and embarrassment
	Identifying issues of emerging sexuality	Opportunity for sibling support groups
	Addressing possible peer isolation and rejection	
	Planning for career/vocational development	
	Arranging for leisure-time activities	
	Dealing with physical and emotional change of puberty	
	Planning for postsecondary education	
	Overidentification with sibling	
	Greater understanding of differences in people	
	Influence of exceptionality on career choice	
	Planning for the transition from school to adult life	
	Addressing issues of vocational training, community living, community participation (recreational and social)	
Adulthood ages 21 on	Planning for possible need for guardianship	Possible issues of responsibility for financial support
	Addressing the need for appropriate living situations	Addressing concerns regarding genetic implications
	Adjusting emotionally to any adult implications of dependency	Introducing new in-laws to exceptionality
	Addressing the need for socialization opportunities outside the family	Need for information on career/living options
	Initiating career choice or vocational program	Clarify role of sibling advocacy
	Adjusting to the changes that the adult life will have on the family (e.g., transition from full-time school to part-time work)	Possible issues of guardianship

Note: Adapted from *Families, Professionals, and Exceptionality: A Special Partnership* (pp. 134–135) by A. P. Turnbull and H. R. Turnbull, 1990. Columbus,OH: Merrill. Copyright 1990 by Merrill, an imprint of Macmillan Publishing Company. Adapted by permission.

add to the stress. The focus of the family may change when the emphasis turns toward obtaining the appropriate services and spending more time and effort than usual working with the child and caring for the child's needs (Cohen et al., 1989). Parents also experience the stress that comes from having to work through their own feelings. Parents of preschoolers with disabilities often report feelings of isolation and uneasiness around parents of children without disabilities (Blacher & Turnbull, 1983). No wonder that studies find increasing levels of stress-related problems in families with children with disabilities.

Although raising a child with a disability certainly presents special challenges, current thinking has backed away from the concept that raising a child with a dis-

Cohort effect:
The effect of living in a particular generation or historical time period.

THOUGHT QUESTION

2. What factors do you believe would increase or decrease the stress experienced by families raising children with disabilities?

ability is inherently stressful for a number of reasons. First, early studies conducted before current legislation designed to help families was passed may demonstrate a **cohort effect**, that is an effect dependent upon growing up in a particular generation (Shonkoff et al., 1992). Parents in the 1960s were basically alone and had few services available. Today, the situation is changing and more services exist for the child *and* the family. Earlier studies may not totally reflect the current experience of many families since so little help was available to previous generations.

Second, not all studies show that negative effects occur (Fagan & Schur, 1993). Some studies find no differences in psychosocial functioning between families raising children with disabilities and families with children without disabilities. Parenting stress is not invariably increased when comparing families of children with and without disabilities (Gowen et al., 1989). Many recent studies find that most families of children with disabilities demonstrate a positive adaptation to the situation (Noh et al., 1989). Just as in any other population, some families do better than others, and a wide variation is found. Today, research is directed toward discovering why some families seem to experience a negative impact while others do not.

These studies do not underestimate the potential for stress within the family, but take a more balanced approach that emphasizes the coping skills and variability within families of children with disabilities. For example, 28 percent of the parents raising children with chronic illnesses indicated that the child's disability had a directly stressful impact on the family's daily life, while 60 percent of those with multiple physical impairments identified stressful impacts. Yet many parents did not mention stress as a major factor at all (Palfrey et al., 1989). Although an interpretation of denial of the situation may be possible, it seems that many of these families have found ways of dealing with the child's disability. When 56 families raising children with disabilities were compared with 53 families raising children without disabilities, families with children with disabilities experienced somewhat more stress, but the adaptation was judged to be good in these families. Marital relationships in both groups were positive and strong, although mothers of children with disabilities were found to be somewhat more vulnerable than control group mothers to the negative effects of stress (Kazak & Marvin, 1984). Psychological support from the father was an important buffer in reducing maternal stress.

Teachers and other professionals are wrong, then, to assume that major family problems exist just because a child with a disability is present. Many families successfully cope with their challenges, and occasional stress is characteristic of all families (Longo & Bond, 1984).

The Importance of Social Support

Clearly, some families are more resilient and cope better than others. The search for factors that mediate between families that are more successful and those that are not has turned up a number of possible factors, beyond the severity of the disorder. The socioeconomic status of the family, the social support available, the strategies used to deal with family problems, and marital satisfaction are all important factors. People with higher income can more easily afford care for the child without the stress of trying to manage on a tight budget and having to do without things. In a strong marriage, each partner can serve as a support for the other and can sustain each other. Mothers who share good, strong, happy marriages report less psychological stress and show better adjustment than mothers in weak, unhappy marriages (Wallander et al., 1989). Parents who believe in themselves and have a positive perception of the situation cope better than parents who feel sorry for themselves and their child (Frey, Greenberg, & Fewell, 1989). A feeling of control is also helpful.

Lately, the critical nature of social support has been emphasized. The families of children with disabilities often must rely on an extensive network of social support (Marcenko & Meyers, 1991). Some support comes from the extended family, including aunts, uncles, and grandparents. Other support may include neighbors and service agencies, both public and private. Parents need both companionship and emotional support, which is especially true for the single parent who may be alone and lack family support. Immigrant families living in poverty may be faced with the double problem of being adrift in a new culture and trying to adapt to the needs of the child with a disability. The family must negotiate a strange obstacle course of governmental services and agencies beyond those typically used by their relatives (Lequerica, 1993).

Parents may obtain needed support from participating in group sessions in which parents can talk with each other about their feelings and problems and share ideas. They learn that they are not alone. Social support decreases the incidence of maternal depression and increases a sense of parental competence (Gowen et al., 1989). Since parenting stress is linked to a number of negative consequences, the finding that social support decreases perceived stress makes increasing social support for families with children with disabilities an important concern (Koeske & Koeske, 1990).

THOUGHT QUESTION

3. *How would feeling sorry for yourself or your child be related to poor adjustment?*

THOUGHT QUESTION

4. *How do social supports operate to reduce stress?*

Support from members of the family can help reduce stress.

What about Father?

Although both parents perceive the stress, the mother is often the one primarily involved in the caregiving and appears somewhat more vulnerable to stress. Most studies concentrate on the effects on the mother, probably because mother is usually the principal caregiver even if she is employed (Kaplan, 1993). However, we know that demands on any member of a family has reverberating effects on all other family members (see Shonkoff et al., 1992).

Although less research has been conducted concerning the effects of the child with a disability on the father, some argue that fathers are actually more at risk for psychological problems than mothers (Longo & Bond, 1984). Fathers are more likely to withdraw from the care of children and show emotional disturbance and stress than fathers of children who do not have any disabilities (see Palfrey et al., 1989). Fathers may become very involved in their work or community activities to avoid the home situation (Longo & Bond, 1984). Sometimes, fathers react differently to the news that their child has a disability than do mothers. Fathers may perceive the diagnosis in an instrumental manner, by looking at whether the child will be successful and independent, how the child will eventually become self-supporting, and what will be the cost of the treatments. Mothers may look at the care needed and the emotional strain on herself and the family (Lamb & Meyer, 1991). Fathers are also more likely to show extreme patterns of great involvement or withdrawal than mothers; these extreme patterns are found more often when sons rather than daughters have a disability (Lamb & Meyer, 1991).

Although the father may not be as involved as the mother in the care of the child, his help is vital. The demands on the mother may be partially reduced by increased paternal help. His emotional and behavioral support also reduces stress, making her more effective in dealing with the child's needs (Palfrey et al., 1989).

THOUGHT QUESTION

5. *Why is there so little effort to involve fathers in raising their children?*

Few programs aim at encouraging fathers to play a more prominent part in raising their children, but studies show that fathers can be very effective teachers and guides.

A great deal is said about parental involvement, but too often it means only maternal involvement (Carroad, 1993). Even among the nondisabled population, fathers are not as active as mothers in childrearing. Fathers are not as prepared for parenthood, know less about childhood development, and are not as sensitive to the needs of the child. Yet, when fathers are given simple training, such as a one-hour-a-week parent discussion group and one extra hour for play, fathers develop an increased sense of competence and become more comfortable with their paternal role (McBride, 1990).

Many programs do not encourage paternal participation. One program that does, the SEFAM (Support Extended Family Members: Father's Program) consists of peer support and the involvement of fathers with their children with disabilities every other Saturday morning. Those who participated showed less guilt, better satisfaction, less fatigue, less pessimism and stress, more satisfaction, a greater feeling of success relating to their child, and better decision-making abilities than did similar fathers of children with special needs who did not participate (Lamb & Meyer, 1991).

Sibling Effects

Siblings play an important role in the development of their brothers and sisters. Older siblings serve as teachers and models. They are playmates and confidants. They also serve a protective function; they may come to each other's aid when teased or verbally or physically assaulted by others (Kaplan, 1990).

Children often have many questions about their siblings' disability. Unfortunately, they may be told very little about the disability, which adds to their misperceptions and their fears. The concerns are age related. Early elementary school children are often interested in what their siblings with disabilities can and cannot do. Adolescents are interested in their chances of having a child with a disability or becoming disabled themselves (Murphy et al., 1976). While some children may ask questions, others may not, either because they fear the answers or do not want to raise the subject with their parents.

Siblings may experience a variety of emotions, including love for their brother or sister, anger at the extra time the parents must spend with the sibling, and guilt at the anger they experience. Many siblings have increased responsibilities. When 24 siblings of children with severe disabilities were interviewed, 84 percent had responsibilities for teaching, 79 percent for dressing, 71 percent for feeding, 71 percent for bathing, and 50 percent for discipline. Although they admitted extra stress and experienced some anger and guilt, most enjoyed playing with their siblings and showed considerable levels of kindness on a daily basis (Wilson, Blacher, & Baker, 1989).

Siblings may be forced to deal with increased parental requests or demands for help in meeting the needs of their sibling (Wilson et al., 1989). Older female siblings of less affluent families are most likely to be placed into a surrogate parent role. This situation is somewhat unfortunate, however, because when the responsibilities are more evenly divided everyone seems to benefit (Vadasy et al., 1984). The family, then, becomes stronger and more cohesive. If one sibling is asked to assume a greater share of the responsibilities, the sibling may grow to resent it.

In addition, some parents exhibit a tendency to expect the child without a disability to compensate for the limitations of the child with disabilities. This increased pressure is more likely placed on sons than daughters (Grossman, 1972). These two difficulties—an increase in caregiving responsibilities and compensation—are fairly well established today as major challenges (Dyson, Edgar, & Crnic, 1989).

The positive side of sharing a home with a child with a disability should not be overlooked (Bigner, 1994). When Grossman (1972) questioned 83 nondisabled college-aged students who had siblings with mild, moderate, or severe impairments, about 45 percent reported that they benefitted from having a sibling who had mental retardation. They felt they had more understanding of other people, more tolerance and compassion, and a greater appreciation of their own health and intelligence. Self-concept scores between siblings of children with and without disabilities showed no differences.

The experience of having a sibling with a disability, then, has a positive as well as a negative side. Although it is usual for the needs of the child with a disability to take precedence, parents must be careful to give their nondisabled children the attention they require (Vadasy et al., 1984). All children need attention and affection, and parents who are naturally most concerned with the special needs of their child with a disability must realize this simple fact. Parents are not always tuned into how well their nondisabled children are coping. Parents often perceive their nondisabled children as coping much better than the nondisabled children think they are (Wallinga, Paguio, & Skeen, 1987). New programs that help families cope with the special needs of children with disabilities may diminish this difficulty somewhat, as more help is offered to the child and the family as a whole (Wilson et al., 1989).

Siblings play an important role in the development of their sisters and brothers with disabilities.

It is important to understand and accept the feelings of the sibling. These feelings may be complicated and often ambivalent. Feelings of anger, guilt, love, and protectiveness may exist at the same time and are often not communicated (Seligman, 1991b).

SCENARIO

1 Jerry is a sixth grader whose third-grade sister has multiple disabilities. She requires a great deal of time, and the parents are constantly trying to get the best care possible for her. Jerry sometimes has to do things for her, but that does not bother him as much as the fact that his parents don't seem to have as much time for him. They also put a lot of pressure on him to do well—too much pressure as far as he is concerned.

Jerry's parents admit that they spend a great deal of time with Patricia but say that she needs more than Jerry. They take Jerry places he wants to go, but with Patricia. They try not to depend too much on him and make certain he gets to see his friends. They admit having high expectations for Jerry but ask what is wrong with that. They do not understand why Jerry is not doing well in school and want to know why he is somewhat resentful at home.

Peer Relationships in Childhood

As children proceed through the preschool and the elementary school years, their social world widens. They come into contact with many new people. Many children today attend nursery schools where they learn social skills and develop pre-academic skills (Kaplan, 1993). The middle years of childhood are dominated by children's school experiences. School-age children are expected to learn to read, write, and do mathematics proficiently. However, the school is not only a place of academic learning, it is the place where children meet their friends, learn to deal with hundreds of social situations, and begin to develop more personal autonomy as they move away from parents. A child's entrance into elementary school is an important step on the way to independence. Attendance is no longer optional, as it is during the preschool years, and more is expected of the child. Most children with disabilities are diagnosed during these years when increased academic and behavioral demands cause these disabilities to be identified. Most children with disabilities are educated on either a full- or part-time basis in the regular classroom, as noted in Chapter 1. One principle of inclusion is that children with and without disabilities must learn to live and work together. Whether true integration will occur depends upon the attitudes of the professionals involved and the attitudes and abilities of the children themselves.

Attitudes toward Children with Disabilities

The attitudes of teachers and children will partially determine the manner in which a child with a disability is greeted in class. These attitudes are shaped by many factors. For example, children learn from television, the movies, what happens at home, from the lessons taught by their teachers, and also through their own experience. People often make the mistake of meeting an individual who belongs to some group and then generalizing a stereotype from these one or two contacts. If a child meets another who is diagnosed as having mental retardation and gets along well with the individual, it is not unusual to then generalize the experience and develop a positive attitude. The opposite can also occur.

Society's attitude as demonstrated by its laws has changed drastically in the last 30 years (Lyon & Lyon, 1991). The progress is a reflection of our emerging philosophy that people with disabilities have rights to full access to social institutions and the right to create a life for themselves in society without discrimination, at least in law. Yet, many people still perceive the individual with a disability as incompetent, helpless, and deviant (Fewell, 1991). This view makes it more difficult for people with disabilities to achieve true "personhood" in society.

Teachers' attitudes toward having students with disabilities in their classrooms depend upon their experience and training with children who have special needs. Teachers may be nervous and worry about how much time will be required and how they will teach children with disabilities. Successful experiences certainly help (Janney et al., 1995).

Teachers have definite opinions about what types of disabilities they are most willing to accept (Margolis & McGettigan, 1988). They are less willing to accept children who show behavior disturbances and have cognitive difficulties than children who have sensory or physical disabilities (Johnson, 1987). The "less favored" disabilities are those that may cause more difficulty in the classroom or require more changes in curricula.

The attitudes of teachers are important to the integration of children into both the preschool and elementary school class (Madden & Slavin, 1983). The teacher's attitudes toward students may be reflected in such behaviors as avoiding the student or showing unhappiness with the student's presence in the classroom or with the student's disability. This posture will be communicated to the other students. On the other hand, feelings of pity and an attitude that the child is not competent will also have an impact. Sometimes, the teacher may bend over backwards and show favoritism, making the other students resentful, as in the case of a teacher who always allows a child with a disability to sit next to her during storytelling, a desired position for every child. Perhaps such behavior arises out of ignorance of how to teach children with a disability or out of guilt over one's feelings. This sort of behavior is often considered offensive by those who have a disability. Overprotectiveness is another problem (Schulz, Carpenter, & Turnbull, 1991). For example, teachers sometimes avoid asking questions of pupils who stutter since it takes longer for these students to answer. Although they might think they are protecting these children from embarrassment, they are employing a poor strategy to do so.

Almost all children in the classroom know when a teacher likes one student better than another or values one child's work over another child's efforts. Teachers may not be aware of their favoritism toward an attractive child or one whose work is superior, but it is present and can affect behavior. Bryan (1978) found that students with learning disabilities receive twice as much negative feedback and are twice as likely to be ignored by regular classroom teachers than children who do not have any learning disabilities.

The importance of a teacher's general attitude toward a disability can also be overemphasized. Whatever expectations a teacher may have for a child—and these may be decidedly negative or positive—are modified by the actual experience the teacher has with the child (Kaplan, 1991). The teacher's attitude toward a specific student is probably more important than the teacher's general attitude toward inclusion. Teachers reject students who disrupt class whether or not they have a disability and reinforce children for their correct responses whoever they are.

SCENARIO

2 You are a fourth grade teacher. It is the middle of November and a child with cerebral palsy will be placed in your class. The child uses a wheelchair for mobility. Her movements are not smooth, and her speech is somewhat slurred though easily understandable. How would you introduce her to the class? How would you encourage social interaction?

Improving Teacher Attitudes and Teaching Techniques

One way to improve teacher attitudes and teaching, generally, is to give teachers the training they require and desire. What if you were told that Linda, a child with a moderate physical disability, will be placed in your classroom? You might have many questions. What is the nature of her disability? How different will she act? How will her presence and behavior affect the other children? What skills does she have? What will I be expected to do? What adaptations are required to allow her to function in the classroom? What help will I be given? These are all valid questions. Unfortunately, teachers sometimes do not feel involved in the inclusion process. They may feel that some of the questions show a negative or nonaccepting attitude and therefore may not ask them. Yet, adequate information and support from other school personnel are both important.

Teachers want and require training in the use of techniques that will improve children's academic achievement. They also need help devising methods to promote the social integration of students. When Leyser and Gottlieb (1980) implemented a training program designed to increase teacher competency in promoting social integration, the results showed a significant improvement in social acceptance. The two-hour program included the presentation of a manual, consultation on how to improve social interaction during classroom activities and discussions of peer tutoring and other techniques to help improve the social status of children.

Social Acceptance and Rejection in School

Unfortunately, children with disabilities often find themselves less accepted by their peers (Stone & LaGreca, 1990). One common finding in studies looking at the social integration of students with disabilities into the regular classroom is that their mere physical presence is not sufficient to provide meaningful social interaction (Ferguson, Ferguson, & Bogdan, 1987). Some attention to the develop-

THOUGHT QUESTION

6. Why are so many children with disabilities ignored or rejected in class?

ment of interactions and friendships is necessary (Nietupski, McDonald, & Nietupski, 1992). Without some attention, children with disabilities are often isolated and ignored or rejected (Fox, 1989).

Children may be isolated and ignored for two major reasons. First, other children may not understand the nature of the child's disability. Second, they may not know how to interact with each other. For example, a child may not know how to play with a child in a wheelchair or how to communicate with a child who has a hearing impairment.

To some degree, acceptance of children with disabilities depends on the attitudes and knowledge that children without disabilities possess. If a child believes that a disability is communicable or that children with mental retardation cannot talk, the child's behavior will reflect these beliefs. In addition, the belief that children with disabilities want people to give them special attention or that they act very differently from other people might also affect how nondisabled children interact with their peers with disabilities.

Many children do not have much knowledge about disabilities, and their lack of knowledge affects their perceptions. Hazzard (1983) asked 411 students in grades three through six a number of questions measuring their experience with people with disabilities, their knowledge of disabilities, and their attitude toward people with disabilities. The children had little knowledge of disabilities, although knowledge increased with age. Attitudes were related to previous experience with people with disabilities. Children with more experience showed a greater willingness to interact with peers with a disability. Although this relationship was positive, it was weak, probably because the effects of such experience depend on many factors, for example, the nature of the contact. Age was not a factor, but gender was related to willingness to interact with children with disabilities. Girls were generally more willing to interact with children with disabilities than boys. Perhaps girls prize their nurturance more than boys. Perhaps the male stereotype is more challenged by the stereotype of disabled people, who may be viewed by some as weak and helpless. The relationship of knowledge to attitude was again positive but weak.

Looking at the children's answers to the questions on the knowledge scale, Hazzard noted that the major problem was their belief in the "pathetic stereotype of the disabled person" (1993, p. 137). Many subjects viewed people with disabilities as helpless, different, and deserving pity. Children were more accepting of children in school situations, such as eating in the cafeteria, than in more personal activities, such as sleeping over at their home.

The implications of this study are clear. Anyone seeking to successfully include children with disabilities will have to counter the stereotype of the "pathetic" disabled person. In addition, the positive but weak relationship between previous experience and attitude indicates that we must look at the type of experiences that produce positive attitude change. Some additional information about disabilities may help, but actively encouraging interaction is more important. For example, if children do not know how to communicate, then showing them how to do so and actively encouraging their interaction through structured activities, some of which will be suggested later in this chapter, may be effective.

Rejection differs from isolation and being ignored. It is more active and direct. The reasons for the active rejection of other children are similar for those with and without disabilities. Children are accepted if they can play cooperatively, give positive reinforcement, and stay on task, while children who are aggressive, disruptive, and engage in negative interactions are rejected (Coie & Dodge, 1988). Both teachers and peers in elementary school view academic ability and good behavior positively and relate them to social acceptance, while aggression and misbehavior are related to rejection. However, while this is generally true, the situation may be slightly different when children judge their peers with and without disabilities.

Roberts and Zubrick (1993) evaluated the social status of students with and without mild academic disabilities in integrated classrooms. Teacher perception of academic behavior, peer perceptions of academic behavior, and peer perceptions of disruptive behavior were related to social status for both groups of students. Teacher attitudes toward integration in general were not related to social rejection, but teacher ratings of behavior and academic work were related to social acceptance. The attitude of the teacher toward a particular student, then, is more important than the general attitude toward inclusion. Peer rejection of children with disabilities was based upon disruptive behavior, while peer rejection for children without disabilities was based upon academic problems. Interestingly, no differences were observed in disruptive behaviors between students with and without disabilities. Nondisabled students are more sensitive to the disruptiveness of children who have disabilities, but more forgiving of academic weaknesses, while the opposite is true for students who do not have disabilities.

Children with disabilities, then, may be rejected not because they are part of a rejected group but sometimes due to their own actions. That is why children who have physical disabilities or have a hearing or visual disability are more accepted than children whose behavior calls attention to itself in a negative manner. Much of the work on acceptance, unfortunately, is conducted with children whose disabilities are most accepted. These children may be ignored or isolated for other reasons, but are rarely rejected outright. Children with learning disabilities, behavior disorders, and mental retardation are more likely to be rejected, while children with physical, health, and sensory disabilities are frequently isolated (Sandberg, 1982; Gaylord-Ross & Haring, 1987; Horne & Ricciardo, 1988). Children who may act inappropriately, such as children with behavior disorders, attention deficit hyperactivity disorder, and some children with learning disabilities may find acceptance more difficult and rejection a constant problem. To counter the problem of rejection, some attention to social skills is needed.

SCENARIO

3 Two children with disabilities are placed in your class. Tina sits by herself and is ignored by the other students. She is withdrawn and gives one- or two-word answers to any questions you ask or her classmates ask. She does not do well in the class. Irene is different. None of the children want to be near her. She is always in trouble, talks loudly, is very bossy, and dominates every interaction. Her achievement is good, and when she is not misbehaving she has shown the ability to complete her work and be a good student. Most of the children reject her outright. What steps would you take to improve the social integration of these children?

Social Skills Training

Some students with disabilities may engage in behavior that offends their peers because they lack the social skills to interact positively. For example, a child who acts aggressively is likely to be rejected, and this rejection will occur well before the child is classified as having a behavior disorder. Some children with learning disabilities have social difficulties in communication and understanding the non-verbal behavior of others (Bender, 1995). Children with mental retardation often show social skill problems as well. If children with disabilities act inappropriately or do not communicate well, integration efforts will fail.

Some children require social skills training, and other children who are aggressive will require modification of their aggressive behavior (Erwin, 1994; Gresham, 1984). This point is often forgotten but should not be. It is in keeping with the entire concept of reciprocal interaction, the idea that children influence each other and that the child with a disability has the ability to influence other children in the environment. Social skills include the ability to follow instructions, accept criticism, disagree appropriately, greet someone, make a request, and reinforce and compliment others as well as using acceptable ways of getting attention (Kail, Downs, & Black, 1988). Nonverbal skills, such as looking at the listener when speaking, are also included.

The first step in improving social skills is to assess the extent to which particular skills are being used by an individual or a class (Keefe, 1988). A target skill is then identified and taught. Students learn such skills best when a number of examples are given. Stories and movies can be used to set the stage, and role playing is especially helpful (Manning, 1986). For example, a student may role play how to ask another student about homework. Special attention should be given to facial expressions, gestures, and intonations. Teachers can also model these techniques. A number of commercially prepared social skills training programs are available (Epstein & Cullinan, 1987). These programs cover both problems and opportunities for friendly interaction and focus on different ways to solve disputes using such tools as compromise, communication, cooperation, and support rather than power (Mergendoller & Marchman, 1987). Opportunities for rehearsal are important, and generalization should be encouraged (Gresham, 1982; 1984).

Techniques to Improve Interaction in the Classroom

THOUGHT QUESTION

7. What can a teacher do within the class to minimize the rejection and isolation of children with disabilities?

Just placing school-age children with and without disabilities in the same classroom usually does not lead to improved interpersonal relationships or increased interactions. Proximity is a factor, though. In some classrooms, children who have disabilities are seated in the back of the room or right in front of the teacher and may be isolated from other children. Whenever possible, children with a disability should be placed where they can interact with other children easily. But even when proximity is not a problem, little interaction may take place (Antonak, 1981). Teachers must, then, find ways to improve the interaction for children.

A number of different approaches can be taken to improve interaction. First, children without disabilities may be given information concerning various disabilities with the hope that their stereotypes and, especially for younger children, their fears will abate. For young children, a number of special programs, such as the "Kids on the Block," a group of puppets with disabilities who talk about their disabilities, are available. Programs that prepare children for such integration may be helpful. Adequate information, especially information that emphasizes the similarities between children with and without disabilities, is effective.

When novels and short stories present people with disabilities as major or minor characters, a discussion of the stereotyped or nonstereotyped behavior is possible. A caution is in order here. Sometimes, teachers believe that the characters with disabilities should always be portrayed as good and positive in order to reduce the stereotypes of the poor, unfortunate, or evil individual. The problem here is that this is also stereotyping, and many individuals with disabilities may not appreciate this stereotype either. Not all people with disabilities are good and likeable. Showing that individuals with disabilities are as capable and as varied in personality as everyone else is the primary goal.

Often, students without disabilities see their peers with disabilities as different. When children learn that children with disabilities have similar interests in sports or hobbies and share other mutual interests, they become more interested in interacting with them (Fox, 1989). Speakers, such as parents and children with disabilities, may also be effective. Instruction can also be helpful in teaching how to communicate and interact. For example, some children speak too quickly or scream at a child with a hearing impairment. A child in a wheelchair may not be at eye level, and young children may not know how to communicate.

A more active approach is to structure the classroom activities to encourage such interactions, which can be done in many different ways. Teachers may encourage the formation of peer groups that include children with disabilities and provide activities that lead to improved interpersonal relationships. Such activities may involve the use of group work in which small groups work on a project together (Reynolds & Birch, 1988). Becoming involved in extracurricular activities, clubs, and plays may be helpful as children with and without disabilities join together in social activities. A student who doesn't interact much with others can be paired with one or two other classmates to carry the lunch money to the office. Perhaps two students who do not know each other may be paired together and, after a few minutes of conversation, asked to write a paragraph about what each other likes.

Sometimes, a peer support committee of four or five students can be formed to help organize buddy systems and establish peer helpers and study partners. One such technique is called the friendship circle, which involves creating a group that welcomes new students and helps students who have not been included to become involved (Forest & Lusthaus, 1989). Verbal suggestions from teachers can help. For example, a teacher who sees two students building houses might suggest they build a house together. Working in teams can be reinforced. Teachers must also model good interpersonal relations by showing positive behaviors.

Two successful techniques that both improve academic achievement and encourage social interaction are cooperative learning and peer tutoring. Both techniques can be used throughout elementary and secondary school and have been extensively researched.

Cooperative Learning
Cooperative learning is a strategy that involves two or more students working together to reach some academic goal (Slavin, 1994). There are four basic elements involved in cooperative learning (Johnson & Johnson, 1981). First, group mem-

The Kids on the Block puppets can help inform young children about the nature of disabilities.

Cooperative learning:
Learning strategies that require two or more students to work together to reach some academic goal.

Group learning strategies have recently become popular. In cooperative learning, two or more students work together to reach some academic goal.

bers work together to accomplish a goal through division of labor, dividing materials or information among group members, and giving joint rewards. Second, face-to-face interaction is required. Third, students are held individually accountable for mastering the assigned material and contributing to the group's efforts. Finally, students are expected to use appropriate interpersonal and small group skills. Two cooperative learning strategies devised by Robert Slavin (1984; 1994) are STAD (Student Teams and Achievement Division) and TAI (Team Assisted Individualization). In STAD, the teacher presents a lesson, and then students study worksheets in teams comprising students of different ability levels. The students quiz each other, compare answers, and discuss problems within their groups. They then take individual quizzes; team scores are computed based upon the degree to which each student improved over his or her past records. The scores are recognized in the class newspaper. This strategy is similar to handicapping in golf in that low achievers score points while performing at a lower level while high achievers need to perform at a higher level (Weyant, 1986).

In TAI, students work in heterogeneous teams, but they work on individualized curriculum materials at their own levels and rates (Slavin, Madden, & Leavey, 1984). Students are encouraged to help each other and to check each other's work. Teams receive certificates based on the number of units completed and the accuracy of all team members' assignments. In a 24-week mathematics experiment using third, fourth, and fifth grade students, TAI students achieved significantly more than students taught using traditional mathematics instruction (Slavin et al., 1984). TAI is unique because TAI combines a cooperative structure and individualized instruction (Salend & Washin, 1988). Some research on TAI shows that it is successful in increasing academic performance, facilitating acceptance of students with disabilities, improving attitudes toward math and teachers' perceptions of students with disabilities.

Salend and Washin (1988) showed TAI's usefulness with a group of students with behavior disorders who were convicted for various felonies. First, baseline data was noted on each student's performance of academic and on-task behavior as well as rate of cooperative behavior, such as verbalized requests for assistance, verbalizations of friendship, and shows of concern. Students were placed into teams or groups of two or three members who were high, average, and low mathematics achievers. TAI was introduced. Individualized units of instruction, which contained a list of instructions, skill sheets, and answer sheets, were developed for each student. Team members exchanged answer sheets, worked on the skill sheets for their individualized units, and asked their teammates for assistance. When each team member completed a minimum of four problems from the skill sheet a teammate checked the answers using the answer sheet. If they were all completed successfully, the person went on to the next skill sheet. If any were wrong, the team member went back to the initial skill sheet until a minimum of four problems were answered correctly. After completing a unit and obtaining the consent of teammates, a team member could take a practice test that paralleled the skill sheets. Based upon the score on the practice test, the team determined if the member was ready to take the final test. If not, additional skill sheets were distributed. Each student also worked with the teacher for five to ten minutes to review difficult items and concepts.

When each team member had taken at least one final test, an average of the group's final test scores was computed. If the team's average was more than 85 percent, reinforcers were delivered, including computer time, free time, or a popcorn party. TAI resulted in increased on-task behavior and more cooperative behaviors. These students consistently favored TAI, preferring it to working independently.

A cooperative learning group can be composed of only two individuals. Some studies have paired a high-achieving student with a student of lower ability. The students are told to read a passage silently. The more accomplished student explains the passage while the other student listens for mistakes and omissions. The students are then instructed to discuss the material and to continue with the next selection. Under such a system, both low-ability and high-ability students learn more than in a traditional framework (Lambiotte et al., 1987). The system works because the lower-achieving students get more attention, while the higher-achieving students get an opportunity to verbalize their knowledge (Van Oudenhoven et al., 1987).

In a cooperative learning format, the success of one student contributes to the success of the group. This compares with a highly competitive environment where the success of one student requires that someone else be unsuccessful, or an individualistic environment where students are not concerned about the performance of others. Johnson and Johnson (1981) compared outcomes of cooperative and individualistic learning experiences for third grade students with and without disabilities. The instruction consisted of a daily 25-minute math lesson for 16 days. In the cooperative condition, students were divided into five small groups; four of the groups included one student with a disability. The groups were told to work together to complete assignment sheets. All students were expected to contribute ideas, and the teacher rewarded the group as a whole. In the individualistic condition, students worked alone and the teacher rewarded students on an individual basis. The researchers found that in the cooperative condition, students with and without disabilities asked each other for more suggestions, offered more suggestions, and provided more help. More interaction also occurred during free time after instruction.

Under a cooperative learning system, peer norms support achievement, and the perception by students that their classmates want them to excel has a strong positive effect on achievement. In addition, cooperative strategies can reduce intergroup antagonism and improve interpersonal relationships. Cooperative learning strategies can promote positive relationships among students of differing abilities as well as between students with and without disabilities (Waring et al., 1985).

The following guidelines can be helpful when designing cooperative learning activities (Knight, Peterson, & McGuire, 1982).

1. Specify the objective of the task.
2. Select the group size most appropriate for the lesson.
3. Cluster the groups.
4. Provide appropriate materials.
5. Explain the tasks and cooperative goal structure.
6. Observe student-student interactions.
7. Intervene and consult when necessary.
8. Evaluate the group product.

THOUGHT QUESTION

8. *Why is cooperative learning so effective with children who have a disability or are not achieving in class?*

In order for cooperative learning to work, children must be able to work together. Such skills as sharing materials and ideas, encouraging everyone to participate, saying at least one nice thing to everyone in the group, and checking to see if everyone understands and agrees with the answers are necessary for successful group work. Children may need instruction in such skills (Putnam et al., 1989).

Peer Tutoring

Another technique gaining popularity is peer tutoring (Soodak & Podell, 1994). In such tutoring, one student helps another to master some information or skill. The student who tutors sometimes has greater knowledge than the student who is being tutored. Sometimes, the tutoring can be structured such that any student can serve in the role of either the tutor or the tutee. For example, in one tutoring scheme, students were randomly chosen to be on teams that competed for the highest total points in social studies. The reward was a citation in the school weekly bulletin and bonus points on grades. Students were then randomly selected within teams to be either a tutor or a tutee. The tutoring required tutors to dictate study guide questions to the tutees, who then wrote the answer. The tutors said that the answer was either correct or incorrect, and then provided the tutees with the correct answer. The tutees then had to write the correct response three times. The process lasted 15 minutes, after which the tutoring pairs were reversed.

The research on the effectiveness of peer tutoring is quite impressive (Topping, 1987). Relatively simple tutoring procedures are successful and such tutoring shows great promise when applied both to students with mild disabilities and to low-achieving students (Maheady, Sacca, & Harper, 1988; Pickens & McNaughton, 1988). The evidence for its effectiveness with disadvantaged students is especially noteworthy (Shapiro, 1988; Greenwood et al., 1987). The effects are found for academic achievement in general and in reading and math in particular (Hedin, 1987).

Tutoring formats can be used in high school as well. Staub and Hunt (1993) trained high school students who were tutoring students with severe disabilities to use techniques that would promote social interactions. The training included techniques of sharing, behavior strategies, and self-confrontation exercises. It began with information to reduce negative attitudes, which identified ways people with disabilities are similar to and dissimilar to people without disabilities. Tutors were taught to recognize how certain behaviors of peers with severe disabilities might serve as socially oriented communications. This training resulted in higher amounts of social interactions between students. Interestingly, the students who had disabilities increased their social behaviors even though they had not received the training. They were being drawn out; their attempts at communication were rewarded, and perhaps they also imitated some of the social behaviors shown by their tutors.

Peer tutoring is an effective method to improve academic achievement.

Special Adolescent Concerns

Peer tutoring and cooperative learning are effective at every level. Adolescence, though, brings with it special challenges for all children, particularly for children with disabilities. At a time in which independence is a major issue, parents may remain overprotective, and an adolescent with a disability may require more help than an adolescent without a disability. Adolescents with learning disabilities may require a parent's help to understand the material, perhaps even to read it to them. The usual development of independence is often more difficult for children with disabilities.

Adolescence is also a time when social relationships take center stage. Many of these relationships are heterosexual, a change from the elementary school years. Parents are quite concerned about their adolescent's social acceptance (Darling, 1991a). Questions concerning sexual expression, dating, marriage, and many other adolescent issues come to the forefront and are somewhat more difficult for adolescents with disabilities to solve. Many children with disabilities may have made a reasonable number of friends and achieved social integration during middle childhood and yet be faced with more rejection during adolescence. Disabilities that were accepted in childhood may begin to isolate the individual in the more complex world of heterosexual relationships in adolescence. Peer acceptance determines the extent to which the child feels rejected and isolated, which increases the stress in the home (Seligman, 1991a).

There are no simple answers in overcoming the difficulties experienced by some adolescents with disabilities. One must realize, though, that adolescents without disabilities frequently experience social difficulties and rejection; not all the difficulties experienced by adolescents with disabilities are due to the disability. Still, one cannot dismiss the extra difficulties that may occur because of the disability.

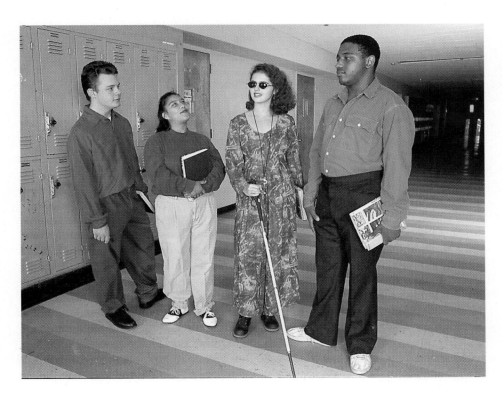

Adolescence is a time of considerable change and stress and adolescents with disabilities may experience additional challenges.

Some strategies of integration discussed earlier are valid for any age group. Encouraging involvement in out-of-school activities, group-oriented activities within school, and attention to social skills are possible ways of promoting interaction. Adolescents must find a group of friends they can relate to and with whom they share interests. The difficulties may be great, but the rewards of developing a group of friends, some of whom have disabilities and some who may not, are also great.

SCENARIO

4 Duncan has a severe learning disability. He has difficulty reading and following the material. Now that he is in high school, he finds that he is still dependent on his mother to read material to him and help him understand. Sometimes, both parents become frustrated and so does Duncan. He feels they are disappointed in him. His parents tell you, his high school biology teacher, that they do the best they can working with him. They understand his academic difficulties and try to tell him that they are proud of the fact that he does not give up. Lately, though, Duncan has refused their help, and his work has deteriorated. He is short with them and rejects all their suggestions. What action, if any, would you take?

Parent-Professional Relationships

So far, many of the influences on children's development, including parents, siblings, and peers of all ages have been highlighted. But children may also be affected by the parent-professional relationship. First, parents' attitudes toward the professionals in their children's lives may be voiced, which encourage a negative or positive attitude in the children. A parent may criticize a teacher or a therapist, which might affect the child's view. Second, parents may be asked to perform an activity with the child, such as reading or checking assignments.

Whenever I discuss the relationships between parents and professionals in my class, the unpleasantness of some of these contacts are raised. It seems that every parent has a story of disinterest, incorrect information, blame, and poor attitude as well as stories of teachers, therapists, and doctors who have served their families well. Some of these encounters, though, are uncomfortable, with feelings of disappointment and of distance.

Why are some encounters unsatisfying? One reason is the dominance of professionals in any relationship (Darling, 1991b). The helper is always stronger and in better control than the helped (Sonnenschein, 1981). Parents are often seen as clients to be aided and directed, rather than as people with whom a professional can share and maintain a partnership. This situation is somewhat less acute with teachers than other professionals, but is still present (Darling, 1991b). Professional training programs and societal attitudes about parent-professional relationships teach a dominance relationship. Teacher training programs and medical school curricula do not include much information about the role of the family in the educational or medical process (Donnellan & Mirenda, 1983).

Another problem is best described by the term *professional*, or *emotional, distance*. Often, parents complain of lack of empathy from the professionals they deal with during the year (Sonnenschein, 1981). Parents are often coping with great difficulties and would like professionals to show some warmth and understanding. Feelings of warmth are often not present as professionals are typically taught to keep a respectable emotional distance. This distance allows for objectivity, but may interfere with the establishment of a relationship. Professionals often see a child as one case among many with behavioral traits that can be understood in terms of some clinical syndrome. Parents are only concerned with one case—their child.

Many professionals see the ideal parent of a child with a disability as one who appropriately seeks out, understands, accepts, and rigorously follows professional prescriptions concerning the child's treatment and education. Parents who question, modify, or reject professional advice, or who persist in seeking services not usually available to them are negatively labeled (Donnellan & Mirenda, 1983). Professionals must examine their views of the ideal parent if they are to establish a relationship with parents of children with disabilities.

The first two problems described are, to some extent, the result of the different positions parents and professionals find themselves in during the interaction. Even professionals with children who have a disability may find themselves uncomfortable in the role of being helped rather than helper; and the issue of professional distance requires a delicate balance. Many professionals are objective and yet reflect a warmth and a concern that is transmitted to parents.

However, one professional behavior that is destructive and interferes with parent-professional relationships is the tendency to place blame on parents (Sonnenschein, 1981). In some cases, this is based upon poor information. For example, for many years it was incorrectly believed that poor parenting was partially responsible for autism, a condition in which children do not develop language and show an inability to relate to others. This belief was later proven to be unfounded but it certainly hurt many parents (Wenar, 1994; Donnellan & Mirenda, 1983). In other cases, a casual or sometimes a not-so-casual remark may be interpreted by parents as an attempt to blame them. Additional problems may be generated by the feelings of guilt that may exist in some parents of children with disabilities (even if they have no objective reason to feel that way). It does not take much to reinforce that guilt.

Professionals react more positively to parents of children who have mental retardation rather than to parents of children diagnosed as having a behavior disorder, because they consider parents of children with behavior disorders partially responsible for their children's problems (Wikler, Wasow, & Hatfield, 1981). This causes parents to feel guilty and act defensively. Defensiveness may lead parents to misinterpret neutral statements as accusatory and make any positive cooperation impossible.

Another difficulty is that parents are often made to feel that their opinions and impressions are unimportant or not useful (Sonnenschein, 1981). They feel they are considered less intelligent and their suggestions given little weight. Their ideas are not considered valuable. In good relationships, information, impressions, and evaluations are openly shared, and communication of feelings, needs, and priorities are conveyed without worrying about being labeled. Each person asks the other for help without being made to feel weak or incompetent, and each can admit that he or she does not know something without loss of respect. Efforts are made to avoid using jargon or any practice which makes the other person feel like an outsider (Sonnenschein, 1981).

Working with Parents

Many teachers complain that parents do not assume enough responsibility for helping children achieve. A parent may not participate as fully in this role as a teacher would desire for many reasons. A parent may be having difficulty making ends meet, may be working two jobs, or simply may be overwhelmed by parenting responsibilities (Clark, 1995). Some parents may not be aware of their children's behavior in school, may not be able to formulate questions, or may not have the background to help their children in school. In addition, many parents do not understand their role in the education of their children or see their children's education as solely the school's responsibility (Fredericks, 1984). Some parents may be uneducated or feel uncomfortable in the school environment and may not know how to join with teachers in a partnership. They may feel intimidated and unwelcome. Parents from some minority groups may especially feel this way and efforts must be made to overcome this problem (see Chapter 9). Anything the teacher can do to create a healthy parent-teacher partnership can help students' achievement.

Teachers are rather definite about the kind of relationship they want with parents. They see the ideal relationship with parents as one in which the parents support teacher practices, carry out teacher requests, and do not interfere with the teacher (Feinman-Nemser & Floden, 1986). You can see where some conflict may exist between a teacher and a more active parent who may want more input into the education of the child.

SCENARIO

5 You have been having some difficulties with Bart, a seventh grader with a moderate learning disability. Bart has not handed in a number of assignments and misbehaves in class. You have requested a parent-teacher conference with Bart's mother, who you know from other contacts is highly defensive and believes the school is not doing its job to educate her son. Specifically, how would you handle the situation and get something constructive out of the conference?

 **THE CLASSROOM**   **Communicating Effectively with Parents**

The teacher-parent relationship can be strengthened and improved with relatively little effort.

1. Keep in mind that communication with parents should be positive as well as informing parents of difficulties.	**Why?** Too often, the only letters or phone calls from teachers to parents are to complain about something or to tell the parent their child behaved poorly. A well-designed balanced regular communication is often appreciated.
2. Reinforce any interest parents show with a note of thanks or a phone call if practical. Fredericks (1984) suggests that a note of thanks for checking a homework paper is appropriate reinforcement. This is especially important if you asked the parent to do this.	**Why?** Parents require reinforcement for their efforts; a letter of thanks may maintain parent involvement.
3. Begin a positive dialogue. Parents may be afraid to ask about their child's progress because they are afraid the child is doing poorly. Ask parents about their goals for their child and pose such questions as: How do you feel about your child's progress so far? Do you feel good about what your child is doing?	**Why?** Such questions involve parents and also encourage a positive dialogue, which opens up communication.
4. The teacher must think through the possible responses the parent may give to any question and have a course of action and alternatives planned. Some of these suggestions may come from a consultation with a special education professional.	**Why?** Just outlining the problem without any solid suggestions is a hollow activity. The outcome of a parent-teacher conference should be an action-oriented plan.
5. Know what parents can do. Do not ask parents to do what they are incapable of doing.	**Why?** Most teachers want parents to monitor their children's work and support teachers' policies at home (Epstein & Becker, 1982). Teachers,

though, hold varied opinions about how involved parents should be in teaching their children, with some believing that parents might put too much pressure on their children, which might adversely affect parent-child relationships. The most popular formal program involves reading on a regular basis. Two-thirds of teachers ask parents to read with their children.

6. Parent-teacher conferences can be important sources of cooperation, and preparation is a key. This translates into having the child's work, hard data on tests, and examples of homework at one's fingertips. If the conference concerns conduct, having records of when and where the incidents occurred is necessary. One way to reduce defensiveness is to use a PNP, or a positive-negative-positive approach whenever possible, beginning with a positive statement. Using open-ended questions to encourage parents to talk and active listening are recommended.

Why? If the teacher asked for the conference, the teacher must provide the agenda. Parents should be accepted as equals in an effort to help the child (Chernow & Chernow, 1981). This reduces defensiveness and improves communication.

The Child's Social World in Perspective

This chapter focused on the child's social environment and the development of social relationships. The modern view of the child with a disability negotiating social interactions has changed in two ways.

First, instead of viewing the child as being acted upon passively by outside forces, we now see the child as both affecting and being affected by others. Second, the child is not seen as pitiable but as an individual with abilities, who must be taught to use individual strengths in social situations and who requires varied social experiences. Children with disabilities need to experience a wide range of social situations and be prepared to enter the social world of adulthood after childhood.

At the same time, their peers without disabilities must become comfortable in interacting with children with disabilities. This interaction is best when it is initiated early in life and continues during the school career through opportunities structured into the classroom. Success means easy and sustained interactions. We will know we are successful when children are free to like or not like each other, to interact or not interact with each other, based solely upon their individual personalities and interests rather than the presence or absence of a disability.

 **Parents, Children, and Technology**

You are on a team that is looking into the assistive technology support required for a child with a physical disability who has considerable difficulty using a keyboard. After some analysis, the committee decides that the use of a head pointer, a rod attached to a headband or helmet, is the best approach. The child, though, does not. He is not comfortable using it and believes the other children will think it odd. In fact, he flatly refuses to use it. Instead, he wants a keyguard, touch-screen, or light pen. What should be done?

In this case, the child has his own definite ideas about how acceptable a particular technology is to him. In other cases, parents may want one type of technology used, and the experts a different type. Parents and children have the right to participate in all aspects of planning and implementation of the IEP. This includes the choice of assistive technology.

Active parental and student participation is vital to the successful use of any technological aid. If parents do not favor the use of a hearing aid, a particular type of voice synthesizer or a particular type of magnifier, then the parent will neither participate in good faith in the training nor will the parent reinforce the child for correctly using it. If the child does not want it and won't accept the assistive device, even the most sophisticated assistive technological device will be ineffective.

Parental and student opinions about technology should always be taken seriously. The professionals who may think that one particular approach is superior should be able to discern from the parent or child what objections they have to the technological devices professionals think most appropriate. Sometimes, the objections may be reduced through explanation or minor changes, such as changing the size of the magnifying device. At other times, the lines may be drawn and little can be done to reduce the opposition of a parent or a child to a particular type of technology. The possibility exists, then, that the assistive device the child and parents select may not be the "most efficient" for that child. Rather, the child and his parents may use a standard that is somewhat different from the one a professional might use. How the child or parent views the technological device and how acceptable it is to others in the environment, especially peers, may enter the picture. The final choice of technology may be a compromise between what is best from a technical point of view and what the child and parents believe they can accept.

Professionals don't always accept compromises well and may find it difficult to see a child using something that is not the "most efficient" technology available. Technology, though, is a tool, and no tool can work if it is not being used.

A similar problem is found when using computer-aided instruction. Suppose a teacher finds an exceptional program that will help the child with a disability practice a particular skill, for example, mathematical computation or spelling. If the program is not interesting to the child, or if it is not age appropriate it will not be used. Although the final test of interest and usage remains an observation of the child, certain features of various pieces of software can be analyzed so as to predict acceptability and usefulness. For example, drill and practice programs that provide graphics and animation to support the skill or concept being practiced may improve interest (Okolo, 1993). On the other hand, if the graphics or animation is unrelated it may distract students and reduce practice time.

Although certain educational standards for drill and practice software guide its development, interest and willingness to use it are important considerations. For example, programs that provide high rates of response are most effective because they give feedback that helps students locate incorrect answers. Programs that offer options that allow individualization are also quite useful.

The use of technology allows teachers to build bridges with parents (Male, 1994). Parents may preview software and help their children use it. Teachers may find that if children have access to computers in their home, an involved parent may see to it that the program is used.

Some parents may also become so involved that they want to search for relevant software. The Alliance for Technology Access (ATA) is a network of computer resource centers working with technology vendors, parents, professionals, and various other interested parties to adapt technology to the needs of people with disabilities. More than forty resource centers in the United States provide advice, consultations, information on new products, telephone support, and demonstrations of new products.

Decisions concerning which technological devices and computer programs to use cannot be made in a vacuum. The parent and child must be involved, since the child will be using it and parents must support the use. The acceptability of the technological device for the parents and child and the interest and age appropriateness of the computer program are important aspects in the choice. Social and personal factors as well as educational considerations, then, must be taken into consideration if the technology is to have a major impact on the child's functioning.

S U M M A R Y

1. The world of the child includes parents, siblings, grandparents, peers, teachers, the media, cultural and religious factors, and a number of other influences. The most modern view of development emphasizes the importance of reciprocal interaction, the idea that people affect and are affected by their environment.

2. Most disabilities are not discovered at birth or in infancy or toddlerhood. The reaction of parents to the discovery that their child has a disability is shock, followed by a period of disorganization, followed by adjustment. Other factors, such as available support and socioeconomic influences must be taken into consideration if we are to understand the reactions of parents to the child's disability. Parental concerns change with the age and maturity of the child.

3. The presence of a child with a disability increases the level of stress in the family, but most families adjust well. Teachers should not assume that a serious adjustment problem exists in a family just because the child has a disability.

4. Siblings serve as models, teachers, and playmates for each other. Siblings may experience a number of ambivalent emotions, such as love, resentment over the time the parents spend with the child with a disability,

anger, and guilt over their anger. Older children, especially female siblings, may have extra responsibilities; and sons often feel pressure to compensate for the child with exceptional needs' limitations.

5. Many people perceive individuals with disabilities as incompetent, deviant, and helpless. Despite improvements in the law according people with disabilities rights, these perceptions make it difficult for them to achieve true personhood in society. Teachers' attitudes toward children with disabilities depend upon their training and experience, as well as the type of disability the child demonstrates. Teachers are more willing to accept children with sensory and physical impairments than children with behavioral and cognitive difficulties. Teachers' attitudes toward a specific child, though, are more important than their general attitudes toward a disability.

6. Children with disabilities may be isolated and ignored if children without disabilities do not know how to interact with them or have inadequate information. Children with disabilities may be rejected if they do not have the social skills necessary for good interpersonal interactions or if they act aggressively or inappropriately. Therefore, some children will need to improve their social skills and sometimes to reduce aggressive behavior.

7. Cooperative learning and peer tutoring are both effective methods of improving achievement and fostering social interaction.

8. Although some parent-professional relationships are good, they are sometimes strained because of the imbalance in the relationship, professional or emotional distance, the concept of the ideal parent as one who does not question much but accepts the professional's view, the tendency to blame the parents, and the fact that some professionals do not treat parental views and suggestions as important.

9. Attempts must be made to include parents as partners in the educational process rather than as adversaries. Building constructive relationships involves communicating positive comments not only complaints, listening to parents, and making them feel welcome.

Early Intervention and Preschool Programs

TRUE-FALSE STATEMENTS

See below for the correct answers.

1. The earlier the diagnosis and treatment of a disability, the greater are the developmental gains and the less the likelihood that later problems will develop.
2. Studies show that early intervention programs are cost effective—that is, they save taxpayers money in the long run.
3. In order to be eligible for intervention services, preschoolers must be classified as having a particular disability, such as a learning disability or mental retardation.
4. Most early intervention efforts focus on the child and ignore the importance of the family.

5. No formal screening instruments are available for use with infants and toddlers.
6. About one in every two mothers of infants and toddlers with disabilities is employed outside the home.
7. Evidence shows that early intervention programs produce short-term benefits for children, but little evidence exists that such programs produce significant long-term effects.
8. Children attending Project Head Start classes are less likely than their peers who did not attend the program to be held back a grade or require special education services during their school career.
9. Preschools have a right to refuse to admit a child with disabilities if they do not believe it is in the child's best interest to attend the preschool.
10. Historically, play has been considered an important learning activity for preschoolers with disabilities.

Answers to True-False Statements
1. True.
2. True.
3. False. See page 79.
4. False. See page 82.
5. False. See page 88.
6. True.
7. False. See page 97.
8. True.
9. False. See page 101.
10. False. See page 112.

How would you feel if you
discovered that your infant
had a disability?

A New Story

When Jaime was an infant, his parents realized his development was slow. He reached his developmental milestones, such as walking, much later than average. He didn't utter a word at the age of two years. After several consultations with their physician, Jaime was evaluated by a team of experts and a specially developed early intervention plan was formulated.

Jaime is now four years old, and his day is not much different than any other child's day. He interacts frequently with his mother, father, and two older siblings. He sees his grandparents once a week. He attends a preschool in which children who have disabilities attend with children without such disabilities. He enjoys playing with blocks and watching television.

Jaime's parents attend weekly meetings in which experts suggest ways to create a suitable environment for him. They also participate in a group session once a week, which helps them deal with their own feelings of frustration and concern. They hope, and expect, that Jaime will attend a regular kindergarten.

Jaime's mother had a difficult time with her pregnancy and her delivery was long and difficult. He was born a month prematurely, weighing only a little more than two pounds. He was also anoxic, which means he experienced a deprivation of oxygen. She believes Jaime's problems stem from this, but medical tests have not been able to determine the exact cause of his difficulties.

At first his parents did not want to accept the fact that something was "wrong" with him. They kept telling themselves that he would catch up. They brought Jaime to different doctors for either a more acceptable explanation or for a cure. His mother told a specialist working with Jaime that she was looking for a doctor who would either say that everything would be fine if given time or give them something to do that would enhance Jaime's development, allowing him to catch up. When this did not happen, they became angry and somewhat bitter, asking why it had happened to them. Gradually, they accepted the situation and, with help, learned ways to interact with Jaime, to create a stimulating environment for him, and to deal with their own feelings. They are hopeful that Jaime will improve, although they do not know what the future will bring.

Jaime and his family are part of a new group of families who are receiving specially designed early intervention. This help focuses on Jaime's entire family and takes a very broad perspective. This chapter will investigate the prospects of early intervention programs and preschool programs now being established across the country.

Early intervention:
A systematic effort to assist young children between the ages of birth and three years and their families. Programs attempt to enhance development, minimize potential developmental delays, remediate existing problems, and improve overall family functioning.

Rationale for Early Intervention

Early intervention involves a systematic effort to assist young children and their families between the ages of birth and three years. Among the goals of such intervention are enhancing development, minimizing potential developmental delays, remediating existing problems, and improving overall family functioning (Meisels, 1989).

Early intervention makes sense from a number of viewpoints. If the disability can be diagnosed early and treatment received, the effects of the disability may be reduced and further problems prevented. For example, if a child's hearing impairment is discovered early, it may be possible to fit a hearing aid or other device and improve the child's hearing. This may reduce the probability of a speech or language impairment. Early intervention, then, can sometimes reduce the detrimental effects of a disability.

In addition, early intervention may help to reduce parent-child difficulties and actually improve family relationships. Chapter 2 raised the possibility that some interactions between parents and their children may lead to problems. Perhaps if intervention takes place at the earliest possible moment, these problematic relationships may be altered or prevented. Parents may neither understand the reason for a child's behavior nor know how to provide a stimulating atmosphere for a child to grow. For instance, Jaime's parents had a difficult time dealing with their own feelings. Jaime's father had a tendency not to interact with the child, and his mother did not know what was necessary to help Jaime develop. Early intervention activities focus on the needs and concerns of the family and may improve the relationships within the family.

Early intervention may be more effective than later intervention. Psychologists use the term *plasticity* to refer to the extent to which an individual can be molded by environmental influence (Scarr, 1986). Although plasticity is present at every age, it decreases with age. Research demonstrates that the earlier the diagnosis of the disability or risk status and the earlier the intervention, the greater the developmental gains and the less likelihood of later problems (Bryant & Graham, 1993). The earlier intervention is started the higher the rate of educational attainment by children with disabilities (Bloom, 1991). For instance, we know that children develop much of their language abilities during the first five years of life. Early linguistic intervention can remediate the language problem or keep it from worsening. Although intervention at any age can be effective, the earlier we can make the necessary changes, the more effective it may be.

Early intervention is also cost effective. If early intervention prevents the effects of the disability from becoming worse and improves the child's functioning, it will save resources in the long run—the child may not require as much later help. If children exposed to cocaine in the womb are given the necessary early help, they may not develop the cognitive and behavioral difficulties that sometimes afflict these children (see Chapter 8). Numerous studies have demonstrated the cost effectiveness of early intervention efforts (Hall et al., 1993). For every one dollar society invests in high quality preschool programs, taxpayers receive about $1.50 in return by the time the child has reached the age of 20 years. Lifetime benefits are estimated to be as high as $5.73 for each dollar invested (Haskins, 1989). The savings include less need for intensive special education services, reduced welfare payments, reduced juvenile justice system costs, and tax payments by the person due to increased earnings capacity. The earlier the intervention is started, the greater the dollar savings (Bloom, 1991).

Plasticity:
The extent to which an individual can be molded by environmental influence.

THOUGHT QUESTION

1. Why is early intervention somewhat more effective than later intervention?

SCENARIO

1 You are at a school board meeting in which special early intervention and early childhood programs are being discussed. They are very expensive and some of the parents at the meeting as well as the board members are arguing that the programs just cost too much. The programs that are being debated are not required under federal law and would serve mostly children at risk. How could you make a case for including these programs in the district's offerings?

Early Intervention for Infants and Toddlers

In 1986, Congress passed PL 99-457, which amended PL 94-142. This law mandates services for children between birth and age five years who have special needs. Two important changes were enacted in PL 99-457. First, the age at which children were covered by the rights designated in PL 94-142 was lowered to age three years. Second, new programs were established to provide services for infants and toddlers and their families through Part H of the law (Hebbeler, Smith & Black, 1991).

The law requires interdisciplinary management of cases, improved early identification programs, individualized family service plans involving the entire family not just the child, and an interagency coordinating council on the state level to advise and assist in implementing the law (Bernstein & Morrison, 1992).

How Early Intervention Works

Under PL 99-457 each state decides which of its agencies will be the lead agency in charge of early intervention services for infants and toddlers with special needs. A parent may contact an early childhood specialist or someone in the lead agency of the state. An evaluation is arranged at no cost to the family. After the child is evaluated, and if found eligible for services, a service coordinator is chosen. The coordinator knows the state policies for intervention programs, what is available, and helps locate services in the community. The coordinator works with the family as long as the family receives early intervention services. At three years, the coordinator helps the family move on to special programs designed for that age group.

The family and the service coordinator work with a variety of other professionals to develop an **Individualized Family Service Plan (IFSP)**. This plan includes the following information:

Individualized Family Service Plan (IFSP):
A plan describing the child's developmental level, family functioning, major outcomes, services the child will receive, and transition support for young children with disabilities and their families.

1. A description of the child's developmental level, which is a basic understanding of how the child is functioning at the present time.
2. Family information, which describes, not only the demographic features of the family, but gives some information about how it operates.
3. The major achievements expected for the child and the family, which is a statement of goals for both the child and family.
4. The nature of the services the child will receive, and where and when the child will receive them.
5. Steps taken to support the transition to another program. Transition to other programs is an important area of concern, and finding programs after the child is three years is an integral part of the process.

The plan may also identify other services the family may be interested in, such as where to get information about financial matters (NICHCY, 1992).

Who Should Be Served?

The question of who should be served by these programs cannot be answered simply. Many of the classifications that are useful when discussing older children are inappropriate to use with infants and toddlers. For example, learning disabilities, mild forms of mental retardation, and emotional disturbance are much too definitive to use with such a young group of children. A specific diagnosis of a recognized disability is *not* necessary to be eligible for early intervention services (Bagnato, Neisworth, & Munson, 1993). Rather, eligibility is based upon developmental and behavioral criteria.

The states have considerable latitude for defining the populations to be served (Richmond & Ayoub, 1993). Children who are served by early intervention programs fall into three categories. First, infants who experience a delay in cognitive development, physical development, language and speech development, psychosocial development, sensory impairment, or deficits in self-help skills are eligible. These children are already showing delays. Second, infants and toddlers who are at risk for developmental problems due to medical conditions, such as low birth weight, are also eligible for services. Third, some children are raised under adverse social and environmental circumstances, such as children raised in abusive environments or by teenage parents in poverty. Services to this group are not required by federal statute, but are permitted under the law.

The extent to which services will be available to children in this last category is in doubt. This group is the most difficult to serve because criteria for eligibility has not been defined. At the same time, developmental outcomes for many established and biological risk conditions are not as severe as those that may result from multiple environmental risks (Benn, 1993). Children exposed to multiple environmental risks are in great need of services. The more risk factors in operation, the greater is the danger of developmental problems arising. When the impact of ten risk factors on verbal intelligence scores were investigated, including maternal anxiety, mental health, parental attitudes, mother-child interaction, maternal

THOUGHT QUESTION

2. *What are the arguments for and against the proposition that all infants and toddlers at risk because of environmental factors should receive early intervention services?*

Infants with low birthweight are eligible for special services, which can effectively reduce the probability that these children will develop a disability.

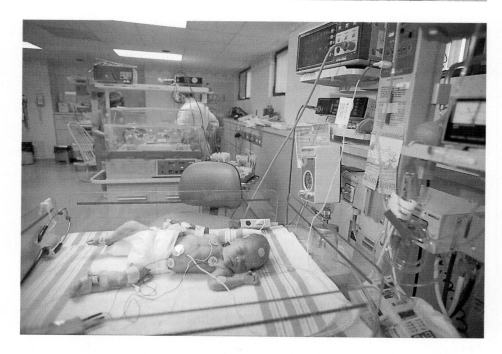

education, occupational level, minority group status, family support, family size, and stressful life events, the greater the number of risk factors present, the greater was the decrement in intelligence. This study did not include any information about the condition of the child at all (Sameroff et al., 1987). The prevalence of children at risk from these environmental factors is still questionable (Black, 1991). But there is no doubt about the importance of these factors, and authorities fear being overwhelmed by the demand for services.

The Emphasis on the Family

Two crucial points need to be made about early intervention programs. First, the services are truly multidisciplinary. Professionals from a variety of different backgrounds may be involved. Many disciplines are specifically mentioned in the law, including medicine and nursing, social work, nutrition, occupational therapy, physical therapy, psychology, social work, education, speech/language pathology, and audiology (Gallagher, 1993). The need for coordination is certainly great if an entire team is involved. As one parent noted, "By the time Janell was 2 years old, we had weekly contact with 14 doctors, 11 nurses, 2 home health agencies, 4 case managers, 4 state agencies, 3 therapists, 2 insurance companies, 2 pharmacies, 3 tertiary care centers, 2 durable medical equipment companies, and special education teachers" (Duwa, Wells, & Lalinde, 1993, p. 100). Although most families will not have to cope with such an extensive array of professionals, any multidisciplinary team requires coordination.

Second, the focus is on the family itself. Infants serviced in intervention programs are viewed not as isolated individuals with difficulties, but rather as members of a family and must be understood within a family context (Meisels, 1989). This emphasis makes sense from a transactional point of view. Social behaviors of

THOUGHT QUESTION

3. *What are the benefits and drawbacks of the family orientation found in PL 99-457?*

atypically developing infants may differ from other infants, making it more difficult for caregivers to read and respond to infant's attempts to communicate. Early intervention focuses not only on helping the child directly through exercises and activities, but also tries to assist caregivers to read and respond appropriately to the child's unique cues. The child and caregiver may then engage in more positive reciprocal interactions, which may in turn help the child develop social skills that will serve the child well as the child matures (Hanline & Hanson, 1989). The emphasis on the family goes beyond support and education. It also involves working together to solve those problems the family thinks are most pressing as well as improving decision-making skills (Duwa et al., 1993).

Screening, Evaluation, and Assessment

Part H of PL 99-457 distinguishes between screening, evaluation, and assessment. **Screening** refers to any activity used to identify children in need of further evaluation or assessment. For example, children may be screened for possible auditory or visual problems. **Evaluation** refers to the determination of the child's initial and continuing eligibility for help. Evaluation includes a determination of how the child is functioning in a number of developmental areas. **Assessment** refers to the ongoing procedures used to identify the child's unique needs, the family's concerns and priorities relating to the child's development, and the nature and extent of early intervention services required (Taylor, 1993). Evaluation, then, refers to the procedures used to determine whether the child is eligible for special services, while assessment is the gathering of information used to develop a plan of action. Under Part H of PL 99-457, five specific developmental areas must be assessed: cognitive, physical/motor, speech and language development, psychosocial functioning, and self-help skills (Taylor, 1993).

Screening During the Neonatal Period

General statements about the screening of infants and young children in the United States are not very useful. Screening procedures vary considerably from state to state and sometimes, from locality to locality. For instance, most states but not all require screening for some disorders at birth such as phenylketonuria, a genetic disorder in which the child cannot digest an amino acid called phenylalanine. If not discovered, the infant will develop mental retardation and other disabilities. When it is discovered, the child is placed on a special diet and many of the difficulties can be avoided or reduced (Whitney, Cataldo, & Rolfes, 1994). Some hospitals routinely screen for other conditions as well.

Hospitals have instituted specific procedures to measure the physical functioning and the capacity for independent survival of newborn infants. For example, newborn infants may be evaluated using a rating system called the **Apgar Scoring System**, which measures five physical characteristics: heart rate, respiration, reflex response, muscle tone, and color (see Table 3.1) (Apgar, 1953). The newborn is given a score of 0, 1, or 2 for each item according to a special criterion.

Screening:
Activities used to identify children in need of further evaluation or assessment.

Evaluation:
The determination of the child's eligibility for receiving special services.

Assessment:
The ongoing procedures used to gather information concerning the needs of the child and the services necessary. It requires gathering information about the present level of performance, identifying objectives, and measuring progress.

Apgar Scoring System:
A relatively simple system used on infants at birth that gives a gross measure of infant survivability.

TABLE 3.1   **The Apgar Scoring System**

The Apgar Scoring System is a relatively simple scale used to rate newborns on survivability. Each child is rated on each of the five behaviors listed below. Each behavior can have a score of 0, 1, or 2. (Highest possible total score is 10.) If the total score is greater than 7, no immediate threat to survival exists. Any score lower than 7 is cause for great concern. If the score is lower than 4, the infant is presently in critical condition.

AREA	SCORE		
	0	**1**	**2**
Heart rate	Absent	Slow (<100)	Rapid (>100)
Respiration	Absent	Irregular	Good, infant crying
Muscle tone	Flaccid	Weak	Strong, well flexed
Color	Blue, pale	Body pink, extremities blue	All pink
Reflex response			
Nasal tickle	No response	Grimace	Cough, sneeze
Heel prick	No response	Mild response	Foot withdrawal, cry

Source: Apgar, 1953.

For instance, if the newborn has a heart rate of 100 to 140 beats a minute, the infant receives a score of 2, for 100 beats a minute or below, the infant receives a score of 1; if there is no discernible heartbeat, a 0 is given (Apgar et al., 1958). Infants who receive a score of less than 7 need additional watching and care. The Apgar score can alert those responsible for the infant's care to a possible problem. Although the relationship of Apgar Score to infant mortality is significant, studies relating low Apgar scores to poor cognitive functioning or neurological abnormalities are mixed with some studies showing such a relationship and some failing to find significant relationships (Francis, Self, & Horowitz, 1987).

The doctors responsible for the care of the infant also serve a screening function. Their observations during physical examinations as well as observations of nurses and parents may be the first indications that additional testing of the infant is required.

In some states, screening may also consist of specific questionnaires that parents and sometimes professionals are asked to fill out. For example, the mother's behavior and experiences during pregnancy may place the child at risk and in need of evaluation. At other times, the parents' genetic background may cause concern for the child. Some states ask parents to fill out a questionnaire about their auditory abilities and the history of hearing problems in their families. If enough risk factors are present, an evaluation of the child's hearing can be made very early in infancy (see Chapter 12). If the condition of the infant is poor, a difficult delivery has taken place, or the mother took drugs during the pregnancy that may have affected the child, a more involved evaluation will be conducted.

THOUGHT QUESTION

4. What arguments can be made for and against a law mandating standardized comprehensive screening for all infants in the United States?

Screening in Infancy and Toddlerhood

Most screening in infancy and toddlerhood is developmental in scope. That is, parents, medical doctors, and other professionals may recognize that the child differs in development from other children. If a child's development is atypical, then further evaluation may be required. For example, most children develop grasping, walking, and communication skills during certain age ranges. If the child's progress is significantly slower or shows a qualitative decrement, further evaluation is required. This does not mean that every child who develops these skills more slowly is in need of help. Children show individual timetables for developing important skills and more than one pathway is possible (see Kaplan, 1990). Yet, significant deviations should at least be investigated. Developmental screening alerts parents and professionals to the possibility that a delay or learning problem exists. Screening focuses on one question: "Does a potential learning or behavior problem exist that requires further attention?" (Venn, 1994, p. 141).

Screening for delays should be a standard part of each child's well-baby checkup. These screening systems can act as a safety net for vulnerable children. For instance, children with severe visual and hearing impairments commonly are not diagnosed until the age of two or three years, which is unfortunate since early identification and service delivery are related to better outcomes (Bryant & Graham, 1993).

Some states have adopted specific screening procedures for infants and young children, which have identified many children in need of evaluation. In the first six months of Florida's Healthy Start Universal Prenatal and Infant Screening Program, 40 percent of the women screened were found to have risk factors that could adversely affect pregnancy outcome and 12 percent of the infants were found to be at risk and in need of either tracking or evaluation (Bryant & Graham, 1993).

Many states have systems that target specific populations, such as children exposed to drugs during the prenatal stage. Others focus on different areas of concern. Hawaii's Healthy Start program, which was originally designed primarily to prevent child abuse, provides universal screening during pregnancy, at birth, and when the child starts school. In North Carolina, the Child Service Coordination Program combines tracking high-risk children with targeted services and coordinates the two. It is administered through local health departments or hospitals. The staff completes an identification and referral form on every infant considered at risk at birth due to characteristics of the infant or family (Bryant & Graham, 1993).

Screening in Day-Care and Preschool

When the child enters a day-care or nursery school environment, screening procedures become more routine. Screening may involve standardized screening tests, screening checklists, observations of behavior, observations of samples of speech and language, various tests of vision and hearing, medical reports, and various records of parental interviews (Venn, 1994).

There is no substitute for people who come into professional contact with preschoolers being alert to the possible signs that a preschooler has a difficulty. A

TABLE 3.2　**Recognizing Possible Signs of Disabilities**

The following warning signs suggest the need for evaluation but do not automatically mean that a child has a disability.

Auditory Disabilities

Does the child:

- often ask the teacher to repeat?
- seem unable to hear when the teacher speaks directly to the child?
- seem inattentive or confused at group listening times?
- complain that the ears hurt?
- show difficulties in speech?
- appear not to pay attention?
- fail to turn his or her head when name is called?
- speak in a loud voice?
- fail to notice familiar sounds in the environment?
- seem not to hear verbal messages correctly?
- turn the head in the direction of the sound?

Visual Disabilities

Does the child:

- squint?
- frown?
- show redness of the eyes?
- frequently rub the eyes?
- stumble?
- hold the book too far or too close?
- appear to have difficulty focusing?
- seem not to be alert to the surroundings?
- tilt the head to see something?
- complain of headaches or dizziness?
- blink frequently?
- show problems judging distance when working with objects?
- show an inability to recognize familiar faces from a distance?
- show high sensitivity to light?

Motor Impairment

Does the child show:

- an uneven gait?
- jerky movements?
- rigidity?
- balance problems?
- shaking movements?
- poor muscle tone—stiff or flabby?
- motor regression—skills or strength decreases with age?
- frequent clumsiness?
- difficulty in running, climbing, or keeping body erect?

number of specific signs exist for each area of development and functioning and are found in Table 3.2 (Culpepper, 1993; 1992). These signs do not automatically mean that the child is in need of special services. However, they do offer a means of identifying which children require further attention.

TABLE 3.2   *Continued*

Impairment in Fine Motor Skills

Does the child show:

- lack of coordination in writing, drawing, or cutting?
- difficulty feeding self?
- difficulty working puzzles?
- difficulty turning pages of book?
- difficulty buttoning or zipping clothes?
- a tendency to pick up objects with the palm of the hand rather than the fingertips?

Language Disabilities

Does the child show:

- irregular articulation of language sounds?
- irregular rhythm of speech in forming sounds, words, or sentences?
- inappropriate pitch, volume, or voice quality for effective communication?
- delayed language?
- difficulty understanding speech of others?
- a refusal to speak?

Cognitive Disabilities

Does the child show:

- disorganized thinking?
- poor memory and recall?
- withdrawal from reality?
- extremely short attention span?
- poor verbal skills?
- a failure to learn developmental tasks (e.g., eating, dressing)?
- poor motor coordination?
- delayed speech and language development?
- frequent fascination with unimportant details?

Emotional and Behavioral Disabilities

Does the child:

- distance himself/herself from people or seem oblivious to others?
- seem out of touch and uninterested in what is going on?
- show inappropriate or no emotional response?
- repeat words, rather than respond to them?
- show no verbal communication?
- refuse to cuddle?
- show extreme distress when faced with change?
- demonstrate high aggressiveness and hostility?
- show extreme shyness?
- engage in temper tantrums?
- seem to have a highly negative self-concept?

Note: Many of these warning signs, such as temper tantrums and articulation problems, are commonly found in young children. A teacher who is aware of the developmental norms for young children may recognize behaviors that are more frequent or qualitatively differ from those of other children and suggest evaluation.

From: How to Recognize Handicaps in Preschoolers I by Susan Culpepper in *Day Care and Early Education*, 1992, copyright © 1992, and How to Recognize Handicaps in Preschoolers II by Susan Culpepper in *Day Care and Early Education*, 1993, copyright © 1993. Adapted by permission of Plenum Publishing and author.

Testing young children presents many difficulties because children may not cooperate during the process.

Formal Screening Instruments

A number of formal screening instruments are available, which can be used to alert professionals and parents to a possible difficulty. The results of screening with very young children, though, must be interpreted cautiously. Individual differences in development must be recognized. Sometimes, a possible early difference may predict a later problem. However, the predictive ability of these measuring instruments is often low or moderate. In addition, children develop quickly in these years and the rapid changes make prediction difficult (Venn, 1994). Last, young children may not cooperate with the person administering the screening instrument, making any finding difficult to interpret.

Two commonly used developmental screening tests are the Denver II and the Developmental Indicators for the Assessment of Learning, Revised (DIAL-R). The Denver II is a norm-referenced screening test used with children from birth to six years of age. It evaluates developmental progress in the personal-social area, such as dressing, eating, relating to others and imitation, fine motor-adaptive skills, language skills, and gross motor skills such as sitting up, standing, and manipulating objects (Frankenberg et al., 1991). The scores are used to determine if further evaluation should be conducted.

The DIAL-R assesses motor development, conceptual development, and language skills. It requires about twenty or thirty minutes to give. It is a norm-referenced test for children ages two to six years and is suitable for children with potential delays who need further evaluations. Screening teams frequently give the DIAL-R to all children in a particular site such as a day-care center, preschool, or Head Start program. Children below a cutoff level receive referral for a more complete evaluation.

Evaluation

Instruments used in evaluation are usually norm-referenced, allowing eligibility and placement decisions to be made (Venn, 1994). The most commonly used evaluation instrument for infants and toddlers is the Bayley Scales of Infant Development (Bayley, 1969). This evaluation tool has recently been updated (Psychological Corporation, 1993). The Bayley II is a norm-referenced, standardized, three-part evaluation. It includes the Mental Scale, which evaluates sensory/perceptual abilities, the ability to respond to various stimuli, memory, learning and problem solving, and the beginning of verbal communication. The Motor Scale assesses the degree of control of the body, coordination of muscles, and movement. The Behavior Rating Scale is a thirty-item rating of the child's test-taking behaviors, which provides information on attention, emotional regulation, and quality of motor control. The Bayley II can be used with children ranging from one to forty-two months of age.

The Battelle Developmental Inventory is a norm-referenced instrument measuring five domains including personal/social, adaptive, motor, communication, and cognitive skills in children between the ages of birth and eight years. It yields a detailed evaluation of these areas. A screening version includes fewer items in each domain.

Assessment Instruments

Assessment provides the information necessary for making educational decisions and providing the appropriate services for children. Assessment includes determining present levels of performance, identifying objectives, and measuring progress. Assessment is an ongoing process. If assessments are not accurate, teachers do not know how well a particular intervention is working or whether the child needs more of the same intervention or a different approach. It also documents when a particular skill has been learned.

While norm-referenced tests yield important information, many teachers and professionals claim that they do not offer specific programming suggestions for children (Bagnato & Neisworth, 1991). This limits the usefulness of these instruments. The most common assessment procedures are criterion-related; that is, they specifically measure whether the child has mastered a particular skill, rather than comparing the child to others. From an educational point of view, it may be more important to know just what skills the child does and does not have, than discovering how different the child is from others in the norm group.

Assessment instruments are used to establish educational objectives for infants and toddlers. Some assessment is based upon a measurement of a particular skill, such as whether the child is now using more words than a month ago or can now use a spoon.

Some formal developmental assessment instruments are available that are specifically designed to be used with infants and toddlers. The Early Learning Accomplishment Profile (E-LAP) is a criterion-referenced test assessing the development of children from birth to thirty-six months. The developmental sub-tests include gross motor, fine motor, cognitive, language, self-help, and social-emotional skill areas. It contains a set of 380 early learning activity cards. These sequenced cards contain learning activities and teaching techniques keyed to the E-LAP test items. Each card includes a written objective as well as procedures and suggestions for helping a child learn the skill. The E-lap does not measure sensory or neurological status and may not be as suitable for children with severe disabilities. It is most useful for those infants and toddlers with mild disabilities or those at risk (Venn, 1994). The E-LAP gives a detailed profile of strengths and weaknesses.

Curriculum-Based Assessment

Curriculum-based assessment (CBA):

Assessment of a student's progress which is tied directly to the curriculum used to teach the child.

Some authorities claim that assessment should be directly tied to the curriculum being used at the school or center. **Curriculum-based assessment (CBA)** is a procedure for determining instructional needs based upon students' ongoing performance in the existing curriculum (Gikling & Thompson, 1985). Children are assessed as to the degree to which they have mastered the content of the curriculum of the class, grade school, or district (Salend, 1994). The curricular objectives serve as the standards for identifying instructional targets and for assessment of progress (Bagnato & Neisworth, 1991).

Curriculum-based assessment provides an individualized, direct, and repeated measure of the student's progress in the curriculum. One great advantage of CBA is that it links testing, teaching, and evaluation. It is also sensitive to subtle changes over time.

In preschool settings, curriculum-based assessment focuses upon developmental progress in attaining milestones, such as using particular forms of language or being able to pay attention for a certain amount of time. These developmental milestones or skills may be used as goals or objectives and are organized into a hierarchy of tasks. Based on this hierarchy, a curriculum is then formed, which offers developmental objectives for teaching children who have developmental delays. Figure 3.1 shows developmental task analysis in the area of attention-task completion from the *Help for Special Preschoolers* curriculum. CBA can also be used in primary and secondary schools.

CBA allows teachers to determine where in the curriculum a child may enter. It also provides a plan of intervention and can be used to document the child's progress. Professionals using this model can easily communicate with each other. Two kinds of CBA instruments exist. Curriculum-referenced scales sample the types of skills found in most preschool curriculum but do not specify any particular curriculum, while curriculum-embedded scales are specifically formatted for a particular curriculum.

What Types of Services Are Provided?

Many possible services are provided to young children and their families depending upon their needs. Table 3.3 notes those services required by law, those that are optional, and those that are not required but may be desirable. The nature of the services provided, their intensity, and their length depend upon the specific needs of the child and family.

D.A.*	Developmental Task Analysis: ATTENTION-TASK COMPLETION
30–36 months	Starts task only with reminders and prompts
36–48 months	Completes 10% of task with little sustained attention
42–48 months	Attends to task for 5 minutes with no distractions
42–48 months	Remains on-task for 5 minutes with distractions
48–60 months	Starts with task with no reminders or prompts
46–50 months	Completes 25–50% of task with some prompts
48–60 months	Attends to task for 10 minutes with no supervision
48–60 months	Remains on-task for 10 minutes with distractions
60–66 months	Completes 50–75% of task with some prompts

*D.A. is developmental age.

FIGURE 3.1   Curriculum-Based Assessment Through Developmental Task Analysis.

© 1987 Santa Cruz County Office of Education. VORT Corp., Palo Alto, CA.

Service Delivery Models

Where are these services to children and their families delivered? Many models for service delivery exist. One way of categorizing systems is through the type of setting in which infants and toddlers are served. The intensity of the services required will partially determine the model of service delivery. For example, a surveillance or tracking system requires only a few visits by professionals or checkups, whereas a home visitation program may require weekly visits. A hospital-based program would require 24-hour care (Bryant & Graham, 1993). The continuum of early intervention service delivery options are shown in Table 3.4.

Tracking or Surveillance Programs

Tracking or surveillance programs are useful for children who may not be in need of formal services at the moment but show some vulnerability. These children may have been exposed to various risk factors. Tracking involves following these

TABLE 3.3   **Definition of Potential Services for Infants and Toddlers and Their Families**

PART H SERVICES (REQUIRED BY LAW)	OPTIONAL PART H SERVICES	OTHER SERVICES (NOT REQUIRED)
• Audiology • Assistive technology • Family training, counseling, and home visits • Family assessment • Health services (only in order to benefit from other intervention) • Intake—screening • Medical services (only for diagnostic or evaluation) • Multidisciplinary evaluation • Nursing services • Nutrition services • Psychological services • Service coordination • Service planning (IFSP, IEP) • Special instruction • Social work services • Therapy services (occupational, physical, and speech/language) • Transportation services • Vision services	• Developmental child care • Medical child care • Medical foster care • Therapeutic foster care/shelter care • Other health services • Family support (respite, homemaker, parent-to-parent) • Play/psychosocial therapy for children with emotional problems	• Housing • Educational opportunities and vocational training • Family planning • Family therapy • Culturally relevant special services • Family unification services • Environmental adaptations for special needs (i.e., wheelchair ramp) • Legal services • Comprehensive drug treatment • Medications • Dental services • After-school care • Training and professional support for early childhood, early intervention, and social support staff • Outreach programs that make extended effort to locate children and families

Source: Service Delivery and Design Study: Options for Delivery of Early Intervention Services: New Approach to Decision Making in Florida's Cost/Implementation Study for Public Law 99–457, Part H, Infants and Toddlers: Phase II Findings, © 1992, by M.A. Graham & L. Stone. Reprinted by permission.

children and closely monitoring their progress for signs that a problem may be developing. If a difficulty arises, the child can promptly receive the needed additional services.

Home-Based Programs

Home-based services have the advantage of delivering the services in an environment that is comfortable for the family. At the same time, professionals can gather vital information concerning the child's environment. A number of such programs exist today. *Family support services* may include information about child development and poverty programs, parent training, day-care services, and other programs tailored to the needs of the family. Family support programs tend to be cost effective and nonintrusive, but do not offer intensive services.

TABLE 3.4   **Continuum of Early Intervention Service Delivery Options**

Service intensity is greatest at the top of the table, and least at the bottom.

OUT-OF-HOME CARE

Therapeutic or Medical Foster Care	**Residential Medical Care**	**Hospital**
Out-of-home foster care for children whose special health needs cannot be met by family	Highly specialized developmental and health care for children not able to live at home	Full-time care in hospital (e.g., "boarder babies") for children with special health needs

COMBINATIONS

Home and Center-Based Programs
Combination programs that include center-based child care and a home visiting component

CENTER-BASED PROGRAMS

Parent-Child Centers	**Developmental Child Care**	**Reverse Mainstreaming**	**Traditional Specialized Intervention**	**Medical Child Care**
Group activities to provide consultation and training for parents and intervention services for child	Child spends the day in a developmentally appropriate classroom in a community day-care with many typically developing peers	A specialized early intervention classroom that includes some children without special needs	Specialized classrooms and interventions serving only children with developmental needs	Skilled nursing care in a group setting for children with complex health needs or children dependent on technology

HOME-BASED SERVICES AND SUPPORTS

Family Support	**Home Visiting**	**Family Day-Care Homes**
Range of support available, including materials, information, advice, instructions, and emotional support	In-home parent support and/or parent training; may include direct intervention with child	Child-care provider receives support and training to include child with special needs

SURVEILLANCE

Tracking	**Health Monitoring**
Regular monitoring of child's developmental status	Accessible and frequent health checkups

Source: Service Delivery and Design Study: Options for Delivery of Early Intervention Services: New Approach to Decision Making in Florida's Cost/Implementation Study for Public Law 99–457, Part H, Infants and Toddlers: Phase II Findings, © 1992, by M.A. Graham & L. Stone. Reprinted by permission.

Home visitation programs have been conducted with low birth weight infants, children with Down syndrome, and children with moderate and severe disabilities. Some visitation programs use paraprofessionals or Head Start parents, while others use professionals including nurses. The outcome of these programs are directly related to the intensity of the intervention with better results coming out of weekly programs than biweekly or monthly programs (Powell & Grantham-McGregor, 1989).

Home-based services are delivered in the environment that is most comfortable for the family.

The third type of home-based program is *family day-care homes*. A service provider looks after other people's young children in the provider's home. These programs are the most common nonrelative form of care for children under the age of three years (Bryant & Graham, 1993). The advantages include low costs, flexibility of hours, and a more home-like atmosphere. The disadvantages are that these homes often are run by less qualified providers and may not have adequate organization or materials.

Even with the doubts about the qualifications and overall quality of these programs, some states recognize the need to use family day-care for children with special needs. North Carolina funds the Partnership in Mainstreaming, which employs specialists to recruit, train, and support family day-care providers caring for children with special needs. With proper training, this type of care can be used to deliver some services. It cannot address family needs, though, so it should not be considered a model on its own (Bryant & Graham, 1993).

Center-Based Services

Service delivery often occurs within a special center. Services can be delivered from numerous out-of-home environments. Some of these centers are *parent-child centers* that aim to provide families with parent education, health, and social services. In these centers, parents are educated in a variety of ways to help their children grow. In addition, the parents' needs and problems are addressed. Andrews and colleagues (1982) studied three parent-child development centers and the programs they offer. Mothers spent between 6 and 20 hours a week at group meetings, child development classes, and workshops on community resources as well as interacting with their infants in the nursery. These mothers were more responsive and positive in their interactions with their children compared with a control group of mothers who did not receive the help. The level of parent involvement required was high, but so was the dropout rate.

Parent-child centers can also provide group intervention for infants and toddlers with disabilities. A skilled professional may lead group activities to show how to interact with infants. Groups may meet once or twice a week for an hour or two. The primary emphasis is on teaching parents as well as offering special intervention services for the child. Head Start has a number of parent-child centers in every state where parents from impoverished backgrounds can learn about parenting and child development. Although these centers may be effective in educating parents, they do not offer extensive child services. Children who require more intensive services need other types of center-based programs.

Another form of center-based program is called *developmental child care.* Children spend their days in developmentally appropriate environments being educated along with children without disabilities. Developmental child-care centers serve children from infancy and are run by nonprofit as well as profit-making institutions. How effective these centers are depends upon the quality of the care available in addition to the ability to obtain and use the special intervention and support services needed.

Numerous problems are involved in any day-care program, but the difficulties increase when caring for infants and toddlers and when these children present special needs. The services are costly, and it is not known how many of these centers provide adequate care. Staff turnover is high and salaries low.

The need is great for center-based day-care for children with special needs. Between 40 and 50 percent of mothers of infants with special needs are employed outside their homes (Klein & Sheehan, 1987). Parents of children with disabilities have the same and perhaps even a greater need for employment since the costs of raising a child with a disability are higher than the costs of raising a child without disabilities.

One of the advantages of such a program is that children are exposed to other children without disabilities (Hanline & Galant, 1993). These programs do not provide parenting education or support groups, so this model also does not address family needs.

Children with mild to moderate developmental and health needs are well served in this model. Special interventions and therapies can be provided in the setting either directly or through a consultant who trains the caregivers (Hueffner, 1988).

Some day-care programs for children with special needs use **reverse mainstreaming** in which a specialized day-care facility admits children who do not have disabilities in order to affect some integration. The teachers are trained in early childhood special education. This model provides the level of support services required for children with moderate and severe disabilities.

The *traditional specialized early intervention model* provides highly trained interventions for young children in segregated settings. Intensive therapies are provided and health services are available. The professionals are well trained and offer specialized intervention programs that provide a high level of support to families. Unfortunately, such programs do not provide opportunities to interact with nondisabled peers, and socialization opportunities are limited. The number of such programs is limited; many have waiting lists.

THOUGHT QUESTION

5. *What are the advantages and disadvantages of services delivered in the home or a center?*

Reverse mainstreaming: A program implemented in preschools for children with disabilities in which some children without disabilities are admitted in order to promote interaction between children with and without disabilities.

Finally, some children are served in *medical child care programs* that are specially designed to offer extensive medical services. These facilities sometimes serve as an intermediate placement between a hospital and another daytime environment. Such child care must be prescribed by a physician and is only for children who require nursing interventions, such as oxygen therapy, tracheotomy care, and intravenous feeding. They offer families a wide range of support services.

SCENARIO

2 Mrs. Dickens is a single parent of two children ages seven and two years. Her two-year-old child has a moderate physical disability and requires specially adapted materials. He attends a day-care program in which he is the only child with a disability. Despite her initial doubts about his acceptance by the other children, he is progressing well. Mrs. Dickens, though, is bothered by the idea that she is working full time. She believes the other parents in the school as well as a few of the teachers feel she ought to stay home and take care of her child with special needs. To date, no teacher has said anything, but one parent was truly surprised to find that she was employed full time, being that her child had such needs. Mrs. Dickens needs the money she makes at the job. She could "exist" without her job, working part time with the child support her ex-husband pays, but she feels she both wants to work and requires the extra money to provide a better life for the children and herself. Yet, the attitudes she senses in others distresses her, and she admits to feeling somewhat guilty. She asks you, a neighbor and friend, for your opinion. What would you say?

Combination Programs

Combination programs involve both center-based and home-based programs. Some of the most effective interventions occur when both center-based and home-based programs are combined. In the Milwaukee Project, families received many hours of home visits in the months after birth to help the mother with the newborn and to facilitate the transition into the center-based portion of the program (Garber, 1988; Garber & Heber, 1976). Forty women with IQ scores below 75 who had just given birth were divided into experimental and control groups. In the experimental group, the teacher, a trained community member, worked with infants five days a week. The curriculum was designed to encourage cognitive development, language development, and perceptual and motor skills. Mothers were given support when they needed it, shown how to stimulate their infants, and informed about how their children were doing in preschool. They were also given vocational counseling and help in homemaking skills. At age 3-1/2, children in the experimental group showed better language development. At 72 months, the mean intelligence of the children in the experimental group was more than 30 points higher than the intelligence scores of children in the control group (119 versus 87). When they progressed through elementary school, their intelligence scores were much higher than the scores of children in the control group (Garber & Heber, 1976). Fewer children in the experimental group repeated grades or required special education. However, the story is not all positive. Both children from the experimental and control groups tended not to do well in school, and the majority of both groups were below average in reading and mathematics by the fourth grade. Many children showed conduct problems in school.

Various technical concerns about the study's methodology have been voiced (Page & Grandon, 1981; Page, 1972). Overall, however, the project may be considered one piece of evidence that intensive combination programs are useful.

Another combination program, the Infant Health and Development Program involved a study of 985 infants born with low birth weight. Studies found that when intervention included home visits, participation in child developmental center programs, and parent discussion groups, children who received the intervention showed better cognitive development and fewer behavior problems compared with those who did not receive the intervention (Infant Health and Development Program, 1990).

How Effective Is Early Intervention?

Early intervention programs are effective. A survey of more than 30 studies of early intervention found that children who participated in these programs were superior to children who did not participate on measures of development, intelligence, motor skills, and language acquisition (Shonkoff & Hauser-Cram, 1987). Programs that adopt a joint focus on both the family and the child were the most effective. Children with mild disabilities who entered a program before the age of six months had significantly better outcomes; and those using a more structured curriculum were superior. For children with more severe disabilities, no effect for time of intervention within the early intervention program was found. These children showed a constant improvement no matter how early in their first three years they started the program. Programs that planned extensive parental involvement were also superior to those with less parental involvement. This involvement included volunteering for center-based activities, participating in planning and evaluation activities in the home, and implementing caregiving activities (Shonkoff & Hauser-Cram, 1987).

Various analyses of early intervention programs lead to five conclusions.

1. They are effective in producing benefits in a number of areas.
2. Programs that are structured are superior to those that are not.
3. Longer and more intense programs are somewhat more effective. A positive relationship exists between the intensity of services rendered and their impact on cognitive development (Reynolds, 1995; Black, 1991).
4. Earlier intervention seems to be an advantage (White, Bush, & Casto, 1986), although it may turn out to be more important for particular disabilities.
5. Programs that focus on both the child and the family are most effective (Duwa et al., 1993).

If services to children in this age group are to be successful, working with parents to some extent is necessary. Parents must at times act as co-therapists. If an exercise program is required twice a day, the parent must conduct it. Since parent-child interactions are so important, helping parents develop better parenting skills appears necessary.

However, it may not always be correct to state that the more parental intervention the better, or that the only successful way to intervene is through parents (Casto & Mastropieri, 1986). On the other hand, the desirability and effectiveness of parental involvement is well established (Strain & Smith, 1986).

Programs Aimed at Prevention

One of the purposes of early intervention programs is to prevent the development of more serious conditions. Programs to prevent disabilities may focus on the child, the parent, or both. Two types of programs can be identified, although it is not always possible to place a program neatly into one category or the other. One type of program aims to reduce the physical or medical problems that may lead to the birth of children with disabilities. These programs may include federal programs for nutritional supplements and prenatal care and programs to reduce teenage pregnancy. Since premature infants are more likely to develop disabilities, reducing the incidence of prematurity and helping infants who are born prematurely may prevent disability. If mothers who take drugs during their pregnancy are more likely to have children with serious disabilities, programs that reduce drug-taking behavior will prevent disabilities (Kogan et al., 1994). If teenagers are less likely to bear healthy children, programs that prevent teenage pregnancy will help prevent problems.

These prevention programs have a mixed record of success, with some programs, such as those dealing with premature infants, showing excellent results and others, such as those seeking to reduce drug use or teenage pregnancy, being generally less effective. Some sex education and drug prevention programs are compromised by arguments about which type of program is most effective and, to some extent, by society's refusal to take such problems as teenage pregnancy and the spread of AIDS as seriously as they should be taken. However, some programs dealing with these issues have been successful (Kaplan, 1993).

Other programs aim at preventing disabilities that arise out of environmental difficulties. Since children of mothers with low intelligence levels are more likely to have mental retardation, and children raised in poverty are more likely to experience developmental disability, providing services to these families should make it possible to prevent some disabilities. In this area, the results are most promising. For example, Ramey and Ramey (1992) analyzed the results of three major studies aimed at disability prevention finding that they were quite successful. In the Abecedarian Project, a group of children whose mothers had an intelligence quotient below 70 were selected and divided into two groups. Although both received supplementary medical, nutritional, and social services, only one group received special early education intervention services from birth through age three years. The early intervention group received five-day-a-week, 50-weeks-a-year, early education programs. All the children tested in the average range by age three years, while all but one of the children in the control group scored either borderline or in the range of mental retardation. Children in the early intervention group had, on the average, intelligence scores that were 20 points higher than the average child in the control condition! A follow-up of the program found that the intellectual gains persisted through seven years in school (Campbell & Ramey, 1994).

Early childhood programs are often based upon special programs that demonstrate success. The Perry Preschool Program showed the effectiveness of preschool programs with children at risk for failure (Schweinhart & Weikert, 1981). It has, in turn, influenced many other preschools (Harper, 1987). Children from families of low educational background, low occupational status, and whose parents had low intelligence scores, all areas that predict academic difficulties, were assigned to either an experimental or a control group. Children in the experimental group called the Perry Project attended a group preschool program for 12-1/2 hours a week for one school year. Home visits for an hour and a half each week were also conducted.

The differences between the two groups were impressive. The children attending the Perry Preschool began kindergarten with an intelligence score of 95 compared to 84 for the control group. Those who attended the preschool showed greater motivation in elementary school, had greater aspirations for college at age 15, and devoted more time to homework. They also achieved much more than the control group. They required fewer years of special education services. Only 19 percent of those attending the Perry Project received special education services for one year or more compared with 39 percent of the control group. Parents were more pleased with their child's performance and, as rated by elementary school teachers, these children were better behaved. At age 19 years, 67 percent of the graduates of the Perry Preschool had graduated high school compared with 49 percent of the control group. Thirty-eight percent of the graduates were in college or vocational training compared with 21 percent of the control group; only 31 percent of the graduates had ever been arrested compared with 51 percent of the control group (Berreuta-Clement et al., 1987; 1984). The reduction in juvenile delinquency and arrests is a finding of studies of other preschool programs as well (Zigler, Taussig, & Black, 1992). Although the exact reason for the decrease in juvenile arrests is not completely understood, perhaps the early success these children experienced carried over throughout their school years, reducing frustration and producing a more positive attitude toward school and life in general.

Head Start

Perhaps the most famous program directed at a more general population at risk is Project Head Start. Children from impoverished backgrounds who enter school behind their middle-class counterparts are likely to fall further behind as they progress through school. Perhaps if these children could attend a preschool program that would help compensate for their different experiences, this cycle could be stopped and such children would have a reasonable chance for academic success (Zigler & Berman, 1983).

Since its inception in 1964, millions of American children have taken part in the program. Project Head Start has both cognitive and noncognitive goals for participating children (Washington, 1985). Children learn to work and play independently, become able to accept help and direction from adults, gain competence and self-worth, sharpen and widen their language skills, be curious, and

THOUGHT QUESTION

6. *Why is there a reduction in arrests for juvenile delinquency for at-risk children who have attended preschools compared with those who have not attended a preschool program?*

Children who attend a Head Start program are less likely to be left back in school, and some studies show these children achieve more in school.

grow in ability to channel inner, destructive impulses. The program has health goals as well.

The first evaluations of Head Start were impressive, with studies showing sizable gains in cognitive abilities and self-esteem (Zigler & Berman, 1983). Soon, though, research found that the intelligence gains noted did not continue as the child progressed through second and third grade (Weinberg, 1979; Westinghouse Learning Corp, 1969). In other words, the gains in intelligence seemed temporary.

However, later research demonstrated the benefits of the Head Start experience. These studies looked at measures other than intelligence and reported that students who took part in Head Start were significantly less likely to be retained in grade or to require special education services. The results of studies on reading and mathematics achievement for children who attended a Head Start program were mixed, with some showing Head Start children achieving more in these areas (Lazar et al., 1982; Darlington et al., 1980). In fact, one study found that Head Start was superior to other preschool programs (Lee, Brooks-Gunn, & Schnur, 1988). Other advantages have been found, especially for such programs in which parental participation is encouraged. The children of parents who were very active in Head Start as board members and volunteers performed better on achievement tests (Washington, 1985). Participation in the program is often the first community involvement for many parents, and most authorities believe that more emphasis should be placed on involving parents (Sprigle & Schaefer, 1985). Parental involvement helped parents deal with younger siblings as well. Younger siblings of children who had taken part in Head Start had significantly higher intelligence scores perhaps because improved parental interactions carried over to other children (Gray & Klaus, 1970).

Other early intervention programs have also found benefits for younger siblings. In the Yale Child Welfare Program, special services given to the family including pediatric care, social work assistance, day-care, and home visitations by professionals led to better school adjustment and progress for the first-born child. When the younger siblings were examined, these children had better school attendance, were less likely to need supportive or remedial services, and were more likely to be making average school progress than a carefully chosen control group of siblings (Seitz & Apfel, 1994). Helping the family during the first child's infancy also provided benefits to later-born children.

Early Childhood Programs: Enhancing Social Competence

Social competence:
The ability of young children to successfully select and carry out their interpersonal goals.

One important lesson from the Head Start experience is the need to ask what changes should be expected. While some emphasize increased intelligence as an outcome, others seek a different outcome. One of the most promising is **social competence**, the ability of young children to "successfully select and carry out their interpersonal goals" (Guralnick, 1990, p. 4). The tasks involved in social competence include gaining entry into the peer group, resolving conflicts with parents and friends, acquiring a desired toy in a socially acceptable manner, and negotiating a new play situation.

Social competence is situational. Many children with mild disabilities appear socially competent when interacting in their own homes with parents and siblings, because these relatives are familiar with the children's signals and behavior and sometimes can anticipate the children's needs. When interacting with peers who are somewhat less forgiving, the circumstances change and deficits are frequently seen. Improving social competence increases social acceptance and improves peer group relationships, which are important factors in successful inclusion, and more generally, in life. Children with disabilities often have difficulties in social interactions, engaging in more solitary play and less group play (Guralnick & Bricker, 1987). They have more difficulty forming friendships. Young children with disabilities are somewhat delayed in developing social skills (Guralnick & Weinhouse, 1984).

Much effort is placed in improving social relationships between children who have disabilities and their nondisabled peers in preschool situations. Research on the effects of placing children together at this age revolves around two basic areas of interest: (1) comparing outcomes in segregated versus integrated schools and (2) focusing on the nature of the social interactions between children with and without disabilities.

In general, these studies indicate that children with and without disabilities benefit from integration. All children make progress, and children without disabilities develop at the expected rate in an integrated preschool (Hanline & Galant, 1993; Peck et al., 1989). Unfortunately, many preschools are not integrated. Recently, reverse mainstreaming has been used in which a preschool composed of children with disabilities is opened up to children without disabilities in order to give children a chance to interact (Bryant & Graham, 1993). Although this step is a positive one, better results will probably be obtained when children with and without disabilities are found in programs serving primarily nondisabled children (Hanline & Galant, 1993). A better situation for students and an easier one for teachers occurs when a few children with disabilities are integrated into a preschool setting with their peers without disabilities, allowing for more interaction between children who have a disability and those who do not. The Americans with Disabilities Act prohibits child-care centers and family child-care homes from discrimination in enrollment based on the child's disability (Hanline & Galant, 1993).

Success in integrating preschools depends upon satisfying the concerns of all groups involved. When parents, teachers, and administrators were questioned, three areas of concern arose: (1) preparation, (2) resources, and (3) the need to resolve possible conflicts (see Table 3.5). When each group's concerns are satisfied in these three areas, integration can be successfully implemented.

The benefits of such integration for the child with a disability are many. Placing young children together results in children with disabilities showing more advanced forms of social interaction and play (Guralnick & Groom, 1988). However, most studies show that children without disabilities interact less often with children with disabilities, so full social integration is not achieved simply by placing children together (Graham & Bryant, 1993; Hanline & Galant, 1993). Even preschoolers are aware of disabilities and differences, and react to them favoring their nondisabled peers (Brown, Ragland, & Fox, 1988).

THOUGHT QUESTION

7. *Why did children who attended Head Start Programs fail to sustain their increases in intelligence scores as they progressed through elementary school?*

TABLE 3.5   **Themes Reflected in Concerns Related to Integrated Programs**

PREPARATION	RESOURCES	CONFLICT
Parents		
Teacher attitude training	Staff/child ratios	Special education teachers seem unaware of impact of special needs children
Awareness of nonhandicapped children about disabilities	Adequate space for larger numbers of children	
Skills in individualizing instruction	Delivery of therapeutic services	Difficulties with parents of nonhandicapped children
		Easy for regular teachers not to be responsive to needs of children with disabilities
Teachers		
Sufficient planning of integrated program	Release time for daily planning and coordination	Difficulties in working with regular (or special) teachers
Training needs related to responding to special needs	Sufficient space for integrated groups of children	Competition between teachers and therapy staff for child's time
Clarification of responsibilities for team members	Adequate materials	Inconsistencies in educational philosophy between programs
	Consultant availability	
	Child/staff ratios	
Administrators		
Parent expectations may be unrealistic for child growth	Funding of nonhandicapped children	Liability for children in integrated programs
Teachers need training to change negative expectations	Finding and providing adequate class space	Increased parental expectations for the access to integrated programs (pre-school and K–12 programs)
Building parent awareness and support for integrated programs	Providing transportation to new program	
	Increased needs for teacher and aide time	Conflict between teachers in programs with different salary bases
	Increased needs for training related to integration	Conflicts between teachers holding different programmatic philosophies

Source: Charles A. Peck, Laurie Hayden, Mary Wandschneider, Karen Peterson, & Sherrill Richarz (1989). *Journal of Early Intervention* 13(4), p. 358.

Improving Social Interaction in Preschools

There are three ways to improve these interactions. First, a teacher may change the environmental arrangements. For example, designating special areas for play and engaging in actions that promote interpersonal relationships, such as supporting cooperative activities, are simple ways to alter a preschool environment. Forming small integrated groups for structured play promotes social interaction (Jenkins, Odom, & Speltz, 1989). Teachers must sometimes suggest ideas, such as playing together, and perhaps model such play. When this occurs, interactive play increases, and children with disabilities engage in less isolated play. More negative interaction also occurs, but at a very low rate. Perhaps such strategies simply increase the number of interactions, and when working with such young children, not all will be positive.

Second, child-specific interventions emphasize teaching social skills to children. Children must learn to greet each other and share. Third, attempts are sometimes made to teach peers how to initiate activities (Odom, McConnell, & Chandler, 1993). While all can be effective, some evidence indicates that providing integrated activities that are planned may be the most effective (Antia, Kreimeyer, & Eldredge, 1993; Antia & Kreimeyer, 1987).

Pointing to preschool programs that are successful in encouraging social competence and even to some that show tremendous success in follow-up studies is relatively easy. But a warning should be noted. Even programs with a history of success must be carefully monitored. Such programs easily become less effective without careful monitoring for quality. When these programs are cloned, care must be taken to ensure that children receive the benefits that pilot programs show they should. So constant monitoring is necessary.

THOUGHT QUESTION

8. Why is it necessary to structure play so that children with and without disabilities interact rather than just allowing social interactions to take their own course?

SCENARIO

3 The Playgroup Preschool has decided to enter into an agreement with a preschool that serves a population of preschoolers with disabilities. A number of children with disabilities will begin attending the preschool soon. You have the responsibility for planning the smooth integration of these children into the classes. The parents of children with and without disabilities are somewhat concerned. The parents of children with disabilities are concerned that their children will not be accepted and that they will not receive the attention they require. The parents of children without disabilities are concerned that their children will be adversely affected by the increased attention required by children with special needs. The teachers, who have little experience working with children with disabilities, have doubts about their ability to meet the challenges. How would you deal with the concerns of each group? How would you encourage the integration of the groups?

SCENARIO

4 Barry is a four-year-old child who shows delays in most of the important developmental areas, including language and motor skills. Barry is attending a regular preschool program but does not appear to be well accepted. He is not actively rejected as much as being ignored, and you believe it is due to his slowness and inability to express himself. When ignored, Barry plays by himself in the corner. What could you do to improve Barry's social involvement in the classroom?

Introducing the Child

The success of any preschool program will depend upon the attitudes of the teachers involved. In a recent national survey of various officials from preschool programs, nearly 60 percent of the survey respondents cited attitudes as a barrier to preschool inclusion (Rose & Smith, 1993). Sometimes, educators specifically trained to work with youngsters with special needs are not happy with the loss of control that often occurs when the child with special needs is placed in a community preschool. Regular preschool teachers may feel somewhat intimidated and uneasy if they have no experience in educating preschoolers with disabilities. Teachers need to explore their own feelings about children with disabilities and make an effort to address any negative feelings (Volk & Stahlman, 1994).

Children without disabilities must also be introduced to their new peers. The class can be prepared for the arrival of a child with special needs. Teachers may read stories about children with disabilities, and puppet shows or plays may be useful (Jambor, 1990). Information is important, but learning about disabilities should not be presented as a special unit; instead, it can be an ongoing process fitting naturally into the total curriculum (Buzzelli & File, 1991). Some preschoolers may experience anxiety with children who are different and these children need reassurance. As children interact with each other, they begin to accept children with disabilities and the barriers break down.

Simulation activities are sometimes used, such as being blindfolded for a short time to experience what a visual impairment is like. Although with older children these simulations may be appropriate, care should be taken about using them with very young children. Preschoolers may come away with more fear than knowledge. So teachers must carefully watch children's reactions to simulations (Buzzelli & File, 1991). On the other hand, children without disabilities may be encouraged to explore the adaptive equipment that children with disabilities use.

SCENARIO

5 For the first time, a child with a severe visual impairment will be placed in your preschool classroom. Latesha is three years old and has been blind since birth. You have spent some time with the child and her parents, showing them around the classroom and speaking with Latesha. You must introduce Latesha to the class as well as explain blindness to the other children. How would you do so?

The Curriculum of the Preschool

Early childhood programs often share goals in the areas of cognitive, language, social-emotional, and motor skill development. One preschool may emphasize social and personal growth, such as getting along with others and gaining a feeling of mastery over the environment. A different preschool may stress cognitive growth and preacademic skills. Most preschools, however, offer activities that cut across a number of domains and do not ignore any of these areas of interest.

Preschools, today, use usual daily routines in order to teach children developmentally appropriate skills (Leister, Koonce, & Nisbet, 1993). Taking turns is learned through game activities, and language is expanded as a natural part of play interaction. Maintaining a balance between teacher-directed activities and peer interactions is critical. Activities in preschools are fun, and active involvement is the key (Hochman, 1995). For example, a unit on growing things might involve observation and participation in planting and maintaining the plants.

Some preschoolers with disabilities may require direct instruction to learn particular skills or to remediate a difficulty. A child may be directly taught a self-help skill or a social skill like greeting others. In assessing whether a skill is one that a preschooler with disabilities needs to learn, the following questions should be answered:

- Is this skill one that the child will use across his or her lifespan?
- Will this activity set the child up to fail? Is it too difficult?
- What prerequisites are necessary for the child to perform this task?
- If the child is unable to complete this activity alone, how can it be changed so that the child can participate?
- Will this activity help the child interact with peers? (Leister et al., 1993, p. 100).

This need for specific instruction does not reduce the importance of the general curriculum of the preschool which fosters an attitude that learning itself is enjoyable and emphasizes social interaction and communication skills. Teachers will find it important to plan for success, especially with young children who may give up easily, and to encourage communication and social interaction among children. Most nursery school programs are characterized by a great deal of freedom, choice, and flexibility. Activities may include story time, listening to music, all types of artistic endeavors, trips within the neighborhood, growing plants and observing the environment, along with play-oriented activities. Children are encouraged to cooperate and share (Morrison, 1991). Teachers often create situations in which children can learn through self-discovery. Preacademic skills, such as learning letters and numbers, are also emphasized.

The same developmentally appropriate criteria may be used with children with disabilities who are integrated into preschools. Children with disabilities can participate in almost all preschool activities, although some will require adaptation. At the same time, these children's specific needs must be taken into account. For example, a child with poor motor skills may require much repetition to learn something. A child with a language impairment in which the child cannot speak in well-understood sentences may require opportunities to talk where the teacher may paraphrase rather than correct the child's statements (Morgan & York, 1981). With few exceptions, most activities in early childhood programs can be made appropriate for children with disabilities, if they are adapted properly (Morrison, 1991). Examples of such adaptations are found in Table 3.6. One major goal of early childhood programs is independence, which is also an appropriate goal for most children with disabilities.

TABLE 3.6   **Adapting to the Child with Special Needs**

IMPAIRMENT	CHARACTERISTICS	SPECIFIC TEACHING APPROACHES
Any disability		Accept the child
		Create real experiences to develop the sense of touch, taste, hearing, sight, or smell
		Adapt environment to accommodate needs
		Model appropriate behavior and language
		Encourage independence
		Allow ample time to complete tasks
		Facilitate participation in all class activities
		Remove hazards
		Apply same standards of behavior for all children, when possible
		Capitalize on children's talents, skills, interests
		Practice emergency procedures
		Confer frequently with child's therapist/ physician/parents
		Maintain accurate records of progress or observed changes
		Respond appropriately to other children's fears or questions about the disability
Language/speech	Use of single words and/or gestures	Describe ongoing activities
	Severe articulation problems, making it difficult to understand the child	Use phrases and short sentences
		Restate rather than correct
	Difficulty following directions	Provide abundant opportunities to talk
		Listen and respond to content of language
		Show interest; maintain eye contact
		Use speech rather than gestures
		Provide daily oral experience in
		singing and regular language activities
Mental	Few communication skills	Provide consistent, brief directions
	Poor motor skills	Plan for much repetition
	Lack of self-help skills	Reinforce successful efforts
	Learning at slower rate	Praise appropriate social behavior and participation
	Short attention span	Use multisensory experiences
	Limited communication skills (usually)	Break tasks into small components if necessary

TABLE 3.6   *Continued*

IMPAIRMENT	CHARACTERISTICS	SPECIFIC TEACHING APPROACHES
Hearing	Inability to understand others' speech and language May be learning hand signs in addition to speech reading and use of residual hearing	Learn child's hearing capacity Use child's name when directing speech to her/him Articulate clearly with moderate speech; avoid exaggeration, loud voice or mumbling Set child for good visibility of activity, teacher, or other children Learn to change hearing aid battery and/or cord (See language/speech section for additional suggestions)
Visual	May see shadow forms, colors, or even large pictures Peripheral vision may be best (turned-away face does not indicate inattentiveness	Orient child to classroom layout and materials locations Give directions related to child's body and orientation Describe objects and activities completely Give notice of change in activities Encourage other children to identify themselves and describe what is happening Acknowledge child when she/he enters room Provide activities to develop motor skills, listening skills, moving about, and use of senses
Physical	May use crutches or wheelchair Poor fine and/or large motor control and coordination May have speech delay Tenseness or stress may increase spasticity	Change child's position frequently (20–30 min.) Keep change of clothing available Determine child's most comfortable floor sitting position

From "Ideas for Mainstreaming Young Children" by D. Morgan and M.E. York, 1981, *Young Children* 36(2), pp. 22–23. Copyright © 1981 by the National Association for the Education of Young Children. Reprinted by permission.

A number of different preschool models are in use today. In a nationwide survey of preschools that serve children with learning disabilities, six common models were identified (Esterly & Griffin, 1987):

1. The *child development model* stresses self-initiated exploration of materials, dramatic play, field trips, and learning centers. It emphasizes socioemotional growth and attaining developmental milestones. The teacher

provides instruction at the appropriate developmental level. This setting is more or less a traditional nursery school.

2. The *psychoeducational model* emphasizes the development of the child's motivation and self-concept. The teacher serves as a model and a facilitator rather than an instructor.

3. The *behavioral model* is based upon learning theory. This model emphasizes the importance of environmental manipulation, the use of reinforcement, repetition, and measurable goals in terms of observable behaviors.

4. The *cognitive-developmental model* emphasizes the development of children's thinking skills. The focus is placed on creating an environment in which children can interact and learn things on their own. The teacher is an active guide.

5. The *diagnostic-prescriptive model* emphasizes matching the skills being taught with the developmental stage of the child. The teacher monitors children's progress in terms of developmental milestones. Tests are frequently administered to obtain data for designing individually appropriate programs.

6. The *perceptual motor model* emphasizes spontaneous learning in structured environments. The materials are sequenced to promote error-free learning in sensory, motor, and language skills. The teacher's role is to make certain that children have properly mastered skills before going on to more advanced levels.

 **A Is for Alligator**

Young children are fascinated by computers and enjoy using them immensely. After all, computer programs require active participation, can include bright colorful graphics, and can be made developmentally appropriate and entertaining. It is not surprising that children with and without disabilities look forward to using the computer in the preschool classroom.

Young children often prefer using the computer to other activities during free play or as alternatives to standard forms of instruction. Fazio and Rieth (1986) studied the free-play choices of preschoolers, finding that about seven of ten preschoolers with mental retardation chose computer activities even when a variety of other enjoyable activities were available. Both children with and without disabilities prefer software that gives them control over software that only requires a response, as in drill and practice programs. When preschool children with language impair-

ments were surveyed as to their preferences for similar computer-based or more traditionally based speech and language activities, 15 of 18 young children preferred the computer-based activities (Shriberg, Kwiatkowski, & Snyder, 1989).

The computer can serve a number of educational functions in early childhood classrooms, such as helping children learn their letters, numbers, colors, and parts of the body as well as providing experiences in problem solving. It can even increase social involvement. Although the computer is often thought of as a solitary activity, as when someone types individually on the keyboard, it can be used with others in pairs or even with larger groups. Two children can cooperate and pairing a child with a disability with a teammate without a disability is one way to increase interaction. Some programs can be specially designed for individual needs, so that a child with a particular difficulty may be taught specific skills. In addition, since computers are so important in our daily lives, early experience would seem appropriate.

Any number of computer programs designed for preschool children are used successfully by children with disabilities. Some use alternative keyboards that are simpler to use for preschoolers. The Muppet Learning Keys is a colorful keyboard containing letters, numbers, colors, and some command keys. Special software is required to use the keyboard and a number of packages are available. One is called Muppets on Stage in which children can type a letter and see an animal or object that begins with that letter, such as *A* for alligator (Lewis, 1993). The children can change the color and even the number of objects on the monitor. They can even make the objects move by pressing a command key "go." In another mode, the object is presented and the child must correctly type the letter it begins with.

PEAL (Programs for Early Acquisition of Language) software focuses on language development. This software promotes language learning by encouraging children to use language to describe play and daily routines. The child must touch color pictures overlayed on a keyboard. The computer verbalizes the vocabulary for a picture using synthesized speech, and a graphic appears on the monitor.

Research shows that computers can be an effective aid in the preschool classroom. Prinz and colleagues (1982) used a computer-based method for teaching preschoolers with severe hearing impairments to read before entering elementary school. These two- to six-year-old children were enrolled in the Pennsylvania School for the Deaf in Philadelphia. The children's language abilities were first analyzed, and then they were introduced to reading and language-oriented software fitted to their individual needs. The software included printed words and the graphic representation of the words. Graphics of manual signs and finger spelling were also included. Teachers could also interact by asking whether the child using the computer wanted to see the object in another size or by adding some information about the object. After six weeks of computer in-

Young children can learn much through carefully designed, age-appropriate computer programs.

struction, children showed a significant improvement in word recognition and identification.

Another desirable activity may be for children to learn to actually program a computer to make it do what they want it to do. One popular program that allows children to do so is LOGO, which can be used by children to write programs for computers and control and operate them. LOGO is best known for its graphics capabilities that allow students to create their own designs using the computer language. It does so by means of a turtle that leaves tracks on the computer screen when given specific, relatively simple commands. For example, the command FORWARD 30 means that the turtle moves forward thirty spaces. Children with disabilities may find control of the computer very satisfying (Grant & Semmes, 1983).

Preschool programs are bounded only by the originality and creativity of their authors. Many formats are used, including the popular concentration game format in which children must locate and match two objects.

Not everyone is thrilled by the prospect of computer use in preschools. Some preschool educators worry that computer-based programs will isolate children or be used to keep them quiet, and children may not be given adequate opportunity for the physical activity they need (Warren & Horn, 1987). Others fear that computers will replace valuable traditional experiences, such as playing with blocks and dramatic play. Perhaps the most sensitive question is whether children will be asked to do things that are not developmentally appropriate, such as early reading for those who are not ready (Haugland, 1993).

Certainly the use of a computer is not a substitute for good teaching, and what is being done on the computer must be integrated with curriculum goals in the classroom (Warren & Horn, 1987). The computer does not have to become the focus of attention to the detriment of all other activities. Any new item that is interesting begins with a flush of excitement but this typically weakens between two and six weeks after its introduction (Haugland, 1993; Shade, 1991).

The argument that computers do not lead to social interaction is patently false—if the computer is placed and used correctly. Young children will crowd around a computer being used by another child, helping the child and commenting on the program. A great deal of interaction takes place. Unfortunately, some teachers place the computer in a closet-like place or an isolated area of the classroom. This placement will isolate the child using the computer. The computer should be placed in a quiet but visible location where the child using the computer can see what else is going on and other children can see what the child is working with on the computer (Haugland, 1993).

The appropriateness of the computer programs depends upon the program itself. Some software is developmentally appropriate, and some is not. Previewing a program is a necessity as the teacher can see how it works, how easy or difficult it will be for children to use it independently, and then can determine its educational and entertainment value. Software evaluation guides, such as Developmental Evaluations of Software for Young Children and the Survey of Early Childhood Software, can also be of help (Haugland, 1993).

No advocate for computer use in preschools believes it should be the only activity available. Every child should be encouraged to participate in every aspect of the early childhood education program. The computer is only a tool; its use is not an end in itself. If the software is developmentally appropriate, the use of the computer can add much to the preschool program and help children both with and without disabilities gain the most from their preschool experiences.

Play in Early Childhood

People tend to overlook the contributions play makes to a child's development. The physical benefits of play are the most obvious. Children tossing a ball around are exercising their muscles and improving their eye-hand coordination. As they play, children refine their skills and become more self-confident and assured (McKimmey, 1993; Isenberg & Quisenberry, 1988).

In the psychosocial realm, play provides practice in socialization and social skills. It allows children to handle social situations, such as dominance, and teaches them to share power, space, and ideas (Rubin & Howe, 1986). Play also allows children to express their feelings and work through conflicts. Children can explore new ways of handling situations as they suspend reality, switch roles, and control a situation (Johnson & Yawkey, 1988). Role play encourages children to become less egocentric and provides them with practice in role taking. It also helps children develop a variety of social and group skills. In social play, children learn to negotiate and resolve conflict.

In the cognitive realm, play encourages children to improve their planning and problem-solving abilities. It provides a format that allows young children to integrate their experiences into a coherent structure. Preschoolers must learn what events happen and when they happen. During pretend play, children figure out the scripts that occur in various situations. While playing, preschoolers practice their newly acquired skills. Play also promotes creativity and flexibility, because it

Play makes a vital contribution to development. Unfortunately, the importance of play to the child with disabilities is now only beginning to be appreciated.

allows children to experiment without fear of consequences. There is no doubt, then, that play is an important developmental activity, and many of the child's interpersonal interactions occur in the context of play.

Although play is a developmentally important activity, the play of young children with disabilities has not received the attention it deserves (Guddemi, 1990). Despite the fact that play is an integral part of the preschool curriculum, this has not been true for the preschool programs for children with disabilities, which emphasize teaching specific skills, especially self-help skills (Jackson et al., 1991). Teachers of children with special needs often use direct instruction to remediate problems, and play, although certainly not discouraged, is not a priority. Although the need for direct instruction is great, play is now recognized as a powerful method by which children learn.

Unfortunately, many children with special needs do not receive the opportunity to engage in a wide variety of play situations both inside and outside of school for a number of reasons. First, the families of children with special needs may be too busy trying to get the necessary education and care for their young child to be concerned about play. Second, television is overused to keep children quiet. (This is true for children with and without disabilities.) Third, the need for more directive teaching of practical skills leads to less time and less emphasis on play (Guddemi, 1990).

In the past, children with disabilities were thought to have difficulties with play because they could not relate to their peers in social situations well or, in some cases, showed a lack of motivation to play with others. The actual reasons for the difficulties have less to do with the disability and lack of motivation and more to do with lack of opportunity and inappropriate play materials.

Since more children with special needs are being educated in regular preschools, opportunities for play should increase. This will only happen, as noted so often, if teachers encourage social interactions between children with and without disabilities. The role of the adult is to arrange the environment to support play by devoting different areas of the classroom to play and stocking these areas with the appropriate toys and other materials. A dress-up area and a block-playing area are examples of such arrangements. More sophisticated types of play may be encouraged by supporting role playing, dramatic play, game play, and sharing. Encouraging communication of needs, wishes, and feelings is also important.

Four areas of play are most important with young children with disabilities: exploratory play, social play, structured game play, and toy play (Beers & Wehman, 1985). Children learn by exploring the environment. Children with disabilities have the same exploratory needs as children without disabilities, but their disabilities may affect their ability to explore. A child with a hearing, visual, or physical impairment may have difficulty exploring the environment. Special adaptations, often using technology, are discussed in the appropriate chapters, but some environmental manipulations are possible. A child with a hearing impairment may need more visually attractive toys, and a child with a visual impairment needs toys that make noise.

Social play involves playing with others and helps children develop social and language skills. Children learn to interact with their peers, to share, and to compromise.

Structured game play helps children learn how to take turns and observe rules. Such game play is also social in nature. Last, toy play teaches much. Some toys, such as blocks, help children develop important visual spatial skills. Other toys may help children enrich their play. A toy village may encourage children to tell stories and use their imagination.

Toys and Children with Disabilities

The second possible reason that children with disabilities may not engage in developmentally appropriate play is difficulties with toys. Most children with disabilities relate to toys in the same way as children without disabilities. Yet, for some children, especially those with sensory, physical, or severe disabilities, standard toys may be difficult or impossible to use. When children play with toys, they learn about motion, sound, shape, color, and spatial concepts. Each of these areas is of fundamental importance for later academic learning. For example, motion, shape and spatial concepts are important pre-mathematical understandings. Spatial concepts and shape recognition and reproduction can lead to success in producing written symbols such as numbers and letters (Anderegg, 1995).

When children play with toys they learn about cooperation and sharing, and sometimes toys aid social play as when two children play with blocks. Toys may even enhance language development as children may share ideas about how to use the toy or talk with each other as they play with it. Although the overreliance on fancy, expensive toys can be criticized, toys can play a useful role in facilitating children's play.

Toys should be properly sized for ease in manipulation. Where severe physical disabilities limit manipulation, toys can be adapted for use. For example, a battery adapter and specially designed switch may permit children with physical limitations to make the car move or make sounds. The battery adapter is a device inserted inside the toy between the battery and metal contact. A wire with a jack for plugging into a switch is attached to the adapter. When the toy is turned on, the child presses the switch and the circuit activating the toy is completed (Lewis, 1993).

Some toys can be adapted easily for a cost of $7–$12, and others can be purchased with the adapter already inserted. Many types of switches can be used, depending upon the physical abilities of the child. For example, one switch stays down until released, while another is made to be activated by a turn of the head. A different type of companion switch used to activate a toy takes cooperation to activate two switches. Still another design requires a child with good motor skills to center the toy, perhaps some device that makes a design, and a child with a severe motor disability may push the switch activating the toy.

Toys should always be chosen with safety in mind. Toys which have sharp points or edges or multiple mouth-sized parts are not appropriate for young children. Toys can be expensive. Fortunately, there are places where children with special needs may borrow toys. The first center for lending specially adapted toys and games was established in Sweden in 1963. It was called a **lekotek** or play library. Often, photos of toys are available so that children and their parents can make choices. The toys range from stuffed animals to busy boxes to musical toys to action cars and trucks. Tape recorders and talking toys are also included.

Two basic types of toy libraries operate in the United States today. The first type models the Swedish lekotek and is generally staffed by professionals and funded by the local communities. In addition to lending toys, this type of toy library might teach play techniques, arrange family visitations, offer leadership training

Lekotek (play library):
A center in which children with disabilities can borrow specially adapted toys, games, and other material.

courses, and publish materials on play and computer use. The first of this type was opened in Illinois in the early 1980s, and other libraries have opened in a number of different states.

Another type of toy library based on the British system is staffed by volunteers and privately funded. These libraries not only serve children with disabilities but children at risk and children from poverty backgrounds. Many of the toy libraries in this category are associated with public libraries, such as the Learning Games Libraries in Illinois and the ToyBrary Project in Nebraska. Some have programs to deliver toys to children in shelters or hospitals (Jackson et al., 1991).

The Future of Early Education

Early education programs, both early intervention and preschool programs, will increase dramatically in the next decade, bringing with them an increased demand for the services of various experts in early intervention. Both national policy and demographic forces will increase the number of children entitled to and requiring early intervention. Our national policy of early identification and the increased public awareness of the importance of such intervention, added to a growing population, will translate into greater need.

But in the rush to provide the necessary programs some clouds are gathering on the horizon. With the institutionalization of preschool education programs may come a potential loss of creativity, traditionally a strength of preschool programs. Public education systems tend to be bureaucratic in the extreme and quite conservative. Will these programs become rigid? Funding is still another problem. Although funding has increased, such programs are expensive and it is necessary to search for ways of keeping costs down through more administrative flexibility and better use of available resources. Studies showing that these programs are cost effective help garner public and legislative support, but the financial resources available are limited and thought must be given to containing costs.

The most significant problem, though, is the possibility that early intervention and early childhood programs may be oversold to a public eager for answers. These programs may not meet society's expectations. Proponents must be very careful to explain what these programs will and will not accomplish (Odom & Warren, 1988).

Despite these potential difficulties, the studies on early intervention are very positive and encouraging. Such programs undoubtedly can and do help children and their families. The new focus on the entire family does not isolate the child and recognizes the importance of the entire family. The emphasis on multidisciplinary help is based on the real needs of the family in many areas. Good early intervention programs and early childhood programs are cost-effective means of helping children develop and their families deal with their concerns about their children. These programs represent a significant step forward in society's attempt to reduce the isolation of individuals with disabilities and their families and provide for their special needs as early as possible so that every child may have a chance to grow and learn.

SUMMARY

1. Early intervention aims at enhancing development, minimizing existing problems, and improving overall family functioning. Early intervention may be more effective than later intervention.

2. PL 99-457 amended PL 94-142, mandating services for children between birth and age five years who have special needs. The age at which children were covered by the rights designated in PL 94-142 was lowered to age three years and new programs were established for infants and toddlers and their families through Part H of the law. A definite diagnosis is not necessary to be eligible for help. Eligibility is based upon developmental and behavioral criteria. Services are interdisciplinary and emphasize a family perspective.

3. Children who are already showing developmental delay and children whose medical conditions indicate they are at risk for delay must receive services. States may provide services to children who are at risk due to environmental circumstances, such as abuse or poverty.

4. Infants are screened at birth during physical examinations and through the use of the Apgar Scoring System and blood tests. Some states screen for the risk of disabilities through the use of questionnaires alerting professionals to risk factors. If enough risk factors are operating the child is tested further. Most screening in infancy and toddlerhood is developmental in scope as parents, medical doctors and other professionals may recognize that the child differs in development from other children and more testing is required. Some norm-referenced tests for screening include the Denver II and the DIAL-R.

5. Evaluation instruments are norm-referenced and provide the basis for decisions concerning eligibility and placement. The Bayley Scales of Infant Development are most commonly used with very young children. The Battelle Developmental Inventory is also frequently used.

6. Assessment provides the information necessary for making educational decisions and suggesting appropriate services for children. Assessment includes determining present levels of performance, identifying objectives, and measuring progress. Assessment is an ongoing process. The Early Learning Accomplishment Profile (E-LAP) is a criterion-referenced test that assesses development in the gross motor, fine motor, cognitive, language, self-help, and social-emotional skill areas. Professionals sometimes advocate a curriculum-based assessment, which uses the goals of the curriculum as the basis for assessing the child's needs.

7. Services may be delivered at home, in a center, or in a combination of both places. Early intervention programs are successful and cost effective.

8. Children who attend Head Start are less likely to be left back in grade or to be diagnosed as needing special education assistance. Some studies show they read and do mathematics better than children who do not attend Head Start programs.

9. Social competence, the ability of young children to successfully select and carry out their interpersonal goals, is one goal of preschool programs related to positive outcomes later on. Social contact between children with and without disabilities brings benefits for both but must be structured into the preschool day.

10. Although preschools differ from each other, most have goals in the areas of cognitive, language, social-emotional, and motor development. Children with disabilities may participate in the regular curriculum of the preschool. They may also require direct instruction in some skills.

11. Play is an integral part of the regular preschool program but has not received much attention for children with disabilities. This oversight is unfortunate, for the social, cognitive, and physical benefits of play are well established. Toys may be adapted for the use of children with disabilities. The toy library or lekotek lends specially adapted toys to children with disabilities.

Mental Retardation

MENTAL RETARDATION

TRUE-FALSE STATEMENTS

See below for the correct answers.

1. Below average intellectual ability is the sole criterion for a diagnosis of mental retardation.
2. The concept of intelligence has no universally accepted definition.
3. The intelligence of an individual is fixed after five years of age.
4. The number of children diagnosed as having mental retardation has declined substantially since the late 1970s.
5. Many more males than females are considered to have mental retardation.
6. Most cases of mental retardation can be traced to known organic factors.
7. Most children with mental retardation do not look any different than their peers of average intelligence.
8. A teacher or parent acts inappropriately in offering a sixteen-year-old adolescent with mental retardation a story about dating written in simplified language.
9. Students with mental retardation have an especially difficult time using skills learned in one context in a different environment.
10. Employees with mental retardation can be paid less than the minimum wage, even if they work in regular jobs for large companies.
11. Employees with mental retardation tend to stay longer at their jobs than employees with average intelligence.
12. The attitude of most business executives toward hiring people with mental retardation is essentially negative.

Answers to True-False Statements
1. False. See page 118.
2. True.
3. False. See page 127.
4. True.
5. True.
6. False. See page 133.
7. True.
8. False. See page 138.
9. True.
10. True.
11. True.
12. False. See page 154.

Your neighbor approaches you to sign a petition. He tells you that a group home for people with mental retardation will be established in your neighborhood. Your neighbor tells you that these people will bring an "undesirable element" into the community and will depress home values. The most valuable asset you have is your home, which you have lived in for the past ten years and put quite a bit of money into remodeling. Would you sign the petition?

Such scenes are repeated in hundreds of communities around the nation. Community opposition appears even after data showing that property values will not suffer and that the neighborhood will not be adversely affected is presented (Landesman-Dwyer, 1981). Even with large-scale educational programs, the home is still not accepted. This issue is especially important at a time when community integration of people with mental retardation is being stressed. Why is the prejudice against people with mental retardation so great?

Would you sign a petition against the opening of a home for people with mental retardation or other disabilities? Across the United States, many such homes are opening, some with community opposition.

SCENARIO

1 You find that a community residence for people with mental retardation will be opening in the community. Some of your neighbors are upset because they were not told in advance. They claim that it will reduce property values and increase traffic. At a community meeting the state official not only quoted the law allowing the home to be placed where it is but stated that even when they have tried to gain community support, people still oppose the opening of such homes. As a result, they no longer give public notice until the last second. Should communities be prepared for group homes? If so, how should they be prepared?

The Definition of Mental Retardation

To understand this prejudice, we must look at just who is considered to have mental retardation. According to the American Association on Mental Retardation (AAMR), "**mental retardation** refers to substantial limitations in a person's present functioning. It is characterized by significantly subaverage intellectual functioning, existing concurrently with related limitations in two or more of the following applicable adaptive skill areas: communication, self-care, home living, social skills, community use, self-direction, health and safety, functional academics, leisure, and work. Mental retardation manifests before age 18" (AAMR, 1992, p. 1).

Mental retardation:
A term referring to subaverage intellectual functioning which exists with impairments in adaptive behavior and occurs before a person is 18 years of age.

General intellectual functioning is usually measured by some score on an individualized intelligence test. The scores on such intelligence tests must meet a particular criterion—for example, be below about 70 on the Wechsler Intelligence Scale for Children—to meet this criterion for mental retardation.

Adaptive behavior refers to a person's adjustment to the challenges of everyday life (NICHCY, 1993). These adaptive difficulties may show themselves in a number of areas, as stated in the definition. The requirement that mental retardation be shown before age 18 ensures that an adult who has had an automobile accident resulting in a brain injury causing difficulties in reasoning and judgment will not be considered to have mental retardation.

Problems in Defining Mental Retardation

A t first, this definition of mental retardation seems relatively straightforward, but this is not the case. The definition of mental retardation has been, and continues to be, the source of great controversy. The problems begin with the uncertainty over the definition of intelligence and the issue of how fair intelligence tests really are, and continue into the thorny question of defining adaptive behavior in an objective and measurable manner. In fact, although the AAMR's definitions, both this one and past ones, are accepted by most professionals, the education departments of some states have not adopted them (Utley, Lowitzer, & Baumeister, 1987).

What Is Intelligence?

If intelligence is a pivotal concept in determining mental retardation, then the nature of the tests and their fairness become matters of extreme importance. Despite improvements in the area, intelligence testing remains a controversial practice. Intelligence has been defined as the ability to profit from one's experiences, a cluster of cognitive abilities, the ability to do well in school, or whatever an intelligence test measures (Kaplan, 1990). Howard Gardner, a respected expert in this field, defines intelligence as "an ability to solve problems or to fashion a product which is valued in one or more cultural settings" (1987, p. 25). There is no universally accepted definition for intelligence.

Many theories of intelligence have been advanced, each with its strengths and weaknesses. Gardner (1983, 1987a, 1987b) developed the **Theory of Multiple Intelligences**, that is, the theory that a number of different types of intelligence exist (see Table 4.1), as follows:

* **Linguistic intelligence.** This is the ability to use and interpret words.
* **Logical-mathematical intelligence.** This involves scientific and mathematical ability. Both linguistic and mathematical intelligence are highly valued in society, and students who possess these types of intelligence will do well on intelligence tests and the SAT and ACT exams. However, whether students do well after they leave college may depend upon the other intelligences.

Theory of Multiple Intelligences: A conception of intelligence advanced by Howard Gardner, who argues that there are seven different types of intelligence.

TABLE 4.1   **Gardner's Conception of Intelligence**

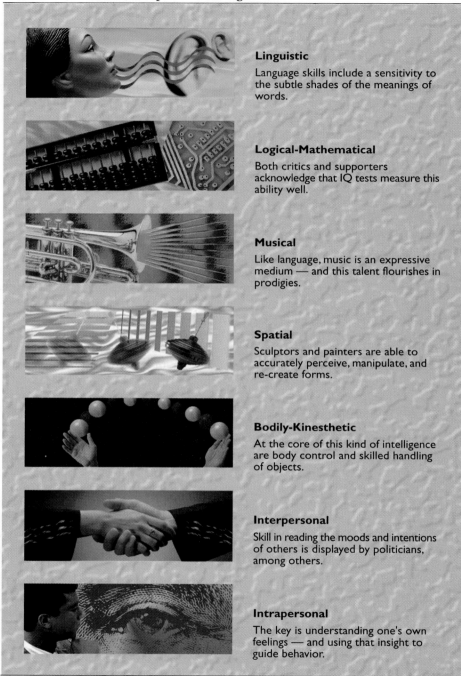

Linguistic

Language skills include a sensitivity to the subtle shades of the meanings of words.

Logical-Mathematical

Both critics and supporters acknowledge that IQ tests measure this ability well.

Musical

Like language, music is an expressive medium — and this talent flourishes in prodigies.

Spatial

Sculptors and painters are able to accurately perceive, manipulate, and re-create forms.

Bodily-Kinesthetic

At the core of this kind of intelligence are body control and skilled handling of objects.

Interpersonal

Skill in reading the moods and intentions of others is displayed by politicians, among others.

Intrapersonal

The key is understanding one's own feelings — and using that insight to guide behavior.

Source: Copyright, Nov. 23, 1987, U.S. News & World Report.

- **Musical intelligence**. Music is a method of expressing oneself, and Gardner considers it an intelligence on its own.
- **Spatial intelligence.** This is the ability "to form a mental model of a spatial world and to maneuver and operate using that model" (Gardner, 1987, p. 190). Sailors, engineers, surgeons, sculptors, and painters require this type of intelligence.
- **Bodily-kinesthetic intelligence.** This is the ability to solve problems or to fashion a product using one's body. Dancers, athletes, surgeons, and craftspeople exhibit this type of intelligence.
- **Interpersonal intelligence.** This is the ability to understand other people, how they work, what motivates them, and how to work with them. Salespeople, politicians, teachers, and religious leaders have, or should have, this type of intelligence.
- **Intrapersonal intelligence.** This is the ability to understand one's own feelings and then use this insight to guide behavior. Intrapersonal intelligence also includes one's knowledge of all the other intelligences.

Gardner thinks of the preceding as seven different intelligences people all possess to some extent, though not on equal levels. Most of the time, when people speak of intelligence, they are looking narrowly at what Gardner calls linguistic and logical-mathematical intelligence. These are the types of skills measured on most intelligence tests.

The Stanford-Binet, Wechsler Tests, and K-ABC

In the early 1900s, Alfred Binet created a test to identify students who supposedly could not benefit from traditional education. Binet used a series of tests that measured a sample of children's abilities at different age levels. At each level, some children performed better than others. Binet simply compared children's performance on these tests to those of others in the age group. If a child had less knowledge than the average child of the same age, that child was said to be less intelligent; if the child knew more, the child's intelligence was said to be higher. Binet used the term **mental age** to describe the age at which the child was functioning at that time (Kaplan, 1993).

The concept of mental age is often used when describing the mental functioning of children with mental retardation. Professionals find it fairly easy to communicate to parents or teachers that a child who is 12 years old has a mental age of 7. Mental age can serve as a ready reference point when understanding the child's reasoning abilities.

Using this concept of mental age has its drawbacks. It may lead to stereotyping a child and hampering that child's educational progress. A child's mental age also gives no information about specific strengths and weaknesses. In fact, two children with identical mental ages may have very different patterns of skills, strengths, and weaknesses (Drew, Logan, & Hardman, 1992). The mental functioning of an 11-year-old with a mental age of 7 is probably unlike that of an average 7-year-old. The 11-year-old is probably more similar to age peers in physical development and interests and may lag behind 7-year-olds in some qualities, appearing less curious, spontaneous, and creative (Baroff, 1986).

What type of intelligence is this child showing?

Mental age:
The age at which an individual is functioning.

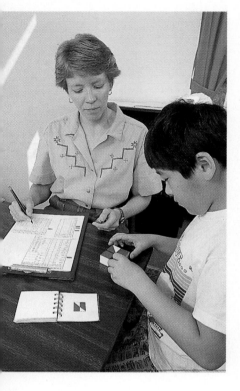

This child is taking the WISC, a very commonly used test of intelligence.

Later, another psychologist, William Stern, proposed the term *intelligence quotient*, or *IQ*, which is arrived at by taking the mental age of the child and dividing it by the child's chronological age (age since birth) and then multiplying by 100 to remove the decimal. The problem with the IQ is that it assumes a linear, or straight-line, relationship between age and intelligence. This is not the case, especially after age sixteen. Today, a more statistically sophisticated way of calculating the intelligence score, called a *deviation IQ* is used. The original Binet test has gone through a number of revisions and today is called the Stanford-Binet Intelligence Test (Fourth Edition).

Beginning in the late 1930s, David Wechsler began to develop another set of individualized intelligence tests. The Wechsler Intelligence Scale for Children (Third Edition), contains a number of subtests that can be divided into two categories, verbal and performance. The verbal subtests measure verbal skills such as information and similarities, while the performance subtests measure nonverbal skills such as completing pictures and putting puzzle pieces together. A composite or total intelligence score may also be obtained (Wechsler, 1991).

Another intelligence test of note is the Kaufman Assessment Battery for Children (K-ABC). This test uses a different conception of intelligence. It distinguishes between sequential and simultaneous mental processing, which are actually types of information processing. Sequential processing involves the "ability to solve problems by mentally arranging input in sequential or serial order" (Kaufman, Kamphaus, & Kaufman, 1985, p. 250). This occurs when one uses grammatical rules, understands the chronology of events, or makes associations between sounds and letters. Simultaneous processing refers to the child's "ability to synthesize information (from mental wholes) in order to solve the problem." It is the kind of processing used in determining the main idea of a text paragraph.

Suppose a person is using a map. Simultaneous processing would give an overall understanding of the configuration of the land, while sequential processing would allow a person to figure out when to make a right or left turn, thus getting the individual from point A to point B (Kaufman et al., 1985). Both styles are necessary for academic success. The K-ABC yields a Mental Processing Composite (MPC), a combination of the sequential and simultaneous processing scales. This mental processing ability is a measure of intelligence.

The K-ABC also contains subtests that measure achievement and a special nonverbal scale, which is useful for assessing intelligence of children with hearing impairments or children with limited proficiency in English, an important issue discussed in Chapter 9. This concept of intelligence is based upon some very modern cognitive research, but it remains to be seen whether this test will be used as extensively as the Wechsler test.

The Normal Curve

Normal curve:
A bell-shaped distribution in which scores occur symmetrically about the mean, and the mean and median are the same. It is very useful for understanding the distribution of many human traits.

If every eight-year-old child in the United States were to receive an intelligence test, how would you expect the distribution to look? Most scores would probably cluster around the middle, with fewer scores being found at each extreme. There are far fewer people who have mental retardation or qualify as geniuses than people of relatively average intelligence. In fact, such a distribution is called the **normal curve**. Many human characteristics are normally distributed; that is, they fit well on a normal curve. Very few people are really very tall or very short. Most

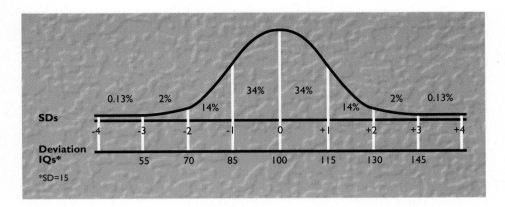

FIGURE 4.1 The Normal Curve

hover about the mean. If we plotted scores for a given characteristic and drew a curve, it would look like the one in Figure 4.1.

The normal curve has certain properties. It is centered at the mean or average score of the population. The right half of the curve represents all the scores above the mean, and the left half represents all the scores below the mean. A vital characteristic of the normal curve is that we know the percentage of scores that will fall between the mean and different places on the curve marked by standard deviations. A standard deviation is a measure of the variability of the scores on a specific test. For example, we know that about 34 percent of the scores will fall between the mean and one standard deviation above the mean and about 34 percent of all the scores will fall between the mean and one standard deviation below the mean. If the mean for an intelligence test is 100, we would place that at the center. Let's say that the standard deviation is 15 as it is on the Wechsler Intelligence Scale for Children (WISC-III) (Carvajal et al., 1993; Wechsler, 1991). Then 34 percent of the scores would fall between 100 plus 15, or 115. Therefore, 34 percent of the population has an intelligence between 100 and 115. We would find that most students score between one standard deviation above and one standard deviation below the mean. In other words, most students score between 100 + 15 = 115 and 100 − 15 = 85. In fact, we can predict that 68 (34 + 34) percent of the scores would fall between 85 and 115.

What percentage of the scores fall between plus and minus two standard deviations from the mean? We can calculate that 14 percent of the scores lie between one and two standard deviations above the mean, and the same percentage lies between one and two standard deviations below the mean. We can calculate that 96 (34 + 34 + 14 + 14) percent of the scores lie between plus and minus two deviations from the mean. On our intelligence test, 96 percent of the scores will fall between 130 (100 + 15 + 15 = 130) and 70 (100 − 15 − 15 = 70). Today, to meet the significantly subaverage intellectual functioning criterion found in most definitions of mental retardation, a child must score at least two standard deviations below the norm on the WISC or Stanford-Binet, a score of 70.

Problems in the Use of Intelligence Tests

In recent years, much controversy has arisen over the use of intelligence tests. The most important objection is directed at the issue of whether intelligence tests are culturally biased against children from minority groups (Hickson, Blackson, & Reis, 1995). In 1971, a group of parents of African-American children who were placed in classes for students with mental retardation sued in federal court claiming that the placements were discriminatory because they were based on intelligence tests that were culturally biased. Eight years later, the court ruled that IQ tests were indeed culturally biased. The famous decision, *Larry P. v. Riles* (see Chapter 1), meant that intelligence tests could no longer be used as the only basis for placing children in special classes (Rothstein, 1995).

Are the Tests Fair to Children from Minority Groups?

Opponents of the use of standardized intelligence tests often emphasize the negative social outcomes of testing, such as the overrepresentation of students from minority groups in special education. Children from minority groups may be unfairly stigmatized as less intelligent. Opponents blame biases in tests and testing procedures for these phenomena (Scarr, 1981).

Reasons for the poorer performance of children from some minority groups on intelligence tests are not difficult to find. One reason is the differing experiences of the minority group child. On an older version of a standardized intelligence test, a child is asked, "What would you do if you were sent to buy a loaf of bread and the grocer said he did not have any more?"

Professionals constructing the test thought the answer, "Go to another store," was reasonable, and it certainly is. Yet, more than a quarter of all children from minority groups said they would go home, a seemingly incorrect answer. When asked why they answered this way, the children simply told investigators that there were no other stores in the neighborhood (Hardy et al., 1976). We can see that experience determines how one answers questions. Many such examples show that the differential experiences of children from various minority groups affect the ways in which they answer questions on intelligence tests, leading some groups to argue that IQ tests discriminate against test-takers who don't fit the white middle-class profile.

The skills tested on standardized intelligence tests undoubtedly measure general cultural knowledge taught by middle-class parents (Scarr, 1981). Tests are formulated by middle-class psychologists and designed to predict achievement in schools that emphasize the dominant culture.

Vocabulary, too, can cause difficulties. In some cultures, words have a different meaning or a different connotation. In addition, children from the majority culture may be very comfortable with the testing setting, the format of the test, and the types of questions asked. Children from various minority cultures may not be as comfortable (Duran, 1989).

Finally, people from various cultures may organize information differently (Miller-Jones, 1989). If you were given a number of objects, you could classify them by type, placing vegetables and tools in their own categories. However, you could also classify them in a different way, by placing the knife with the vegetables, because the knife is used to cut the vegetables.

Along these lines, some argue that these tests are based on the reasoning style of the dominant group and do not take into consideration the possibility that children from various minority groups may reason differently and may have different cognitive styles (Helms, 1992). For example, tests are constructed so that each question has only one right answer that is determined by the normative majority group response. It is assumed that intelligent people will think in that particular manner. But perhaps people who grow up under different cultural beliefs, view the world differently, and possess different cognitive styles see alternative answers to a question. The alternative answers are considered incorrect by the test constructors (Helms, 1992).

A number of different ways of viewing the world and solving problems exist. For example, a person who is raised to believe that emotions and logic are equally important may have difficulty understanding a problem in which a person is reasoning about the best solution without any emotional input (Helms, 1992).

Opponents of testing frequently cite examples of questions that refer to experiences not common to all children, use words not as familiar to minority group youth, require test-taking skills not as well developed or different, and assume information-processing strategies that do not match those used by the minority culture. These opponents claim that eliminating these tests and using more culturally sensitive measures would make evaluation fairer and eliminate group differences on these tests.

Proponents of testing argue that the problem with intelligence and other testing devices is the way they are used, not their construction or what they indicate. They do predict, albeit not perfectly, academic success across ethnic groups (U.S. Department of Education, 1993). If some children both from the minority and dominant groups do not score well, intelligence tests would then predict poor achievement (which is too often the case). With current testing devices, 25–30 percent of all minority group youth test very well (Scarr, 1981).

In an attempt to free standardized tests of bias, culture-fair tests have been formulated that depend less on language abilities and speed of responding, and eliminate items that reflect differential cultural or social experiences. Such tests use matching, picture completion, copying, block designs, analogies, spatial relations, and ability to see relations between patterns (Brown, 1983). But a perfect culture-fair test has yet to be developed, and some argue that culture-fair tests are impossible (Cahan & Cohen, 1989). In addition, culture-fair tests do not predict school performance as well as our present standardized tests (Anastasi, 1988; U.S. Department of Education, 1993).

A major problem, a proponent of testing would argue, lies in the definition of intelligence used by the general public and some educators. The type of intelligence measured by intelligence tests relates to academic skills, but not what many people often regard as intelligence, such as "common sense" or being able to solve problems in the community or life. It does not really measure adaptation to life. In the manual for the administration of the Wechsler Intelligence Scale for Children (Third Edition), this is clearly brought out: "it cannot be presumed that the array of tasks, standardized and presented here as the WISC-III, can cover all aspects of an individual's intelligence" (Wechsler, 1991, p. 2).

If people would look at these tests as demonstrating past learning and understand they are not global measures of functioning, just narrow measures related to school achievement, the tests could be understood for what they are. These tests do not measure overall learning potential in every area, but do predict how well the child will do in the schools as they are now constructed (U.S. Department of Education, 1993). The tests could be improved so that questions with obvious cultural bias were removed and the test-taking procedures made more culture-friendly by giving children unfamiliar with such tests an opportunity to become familiar with the test format. Under this situation, if any child scored low on such tests, it would NOT be ascribed to some deficiency in ability but rather to a lack of particular skills necessary to negotiate schools the way they are now structured. Low scores indicate a need for action, rather than an indictment of the child.

The tests properly used would then become sources of diagnostic help for the teacher. Low scores indicate a need for different types of instruction. Test scores would only be part of an assessment, and other sources of information would be used to obtain a more complete picture of the child's functioning. No standardized tests can provide such a picture. Answers to questions of how a child functions outside the school, displays special abilities, processes information, and behaves, as well as other information, could then be used to complement test scores.

Some authorities, such as Sandra Scarr (1981), argue for culturally specific assessments. That is, specific assessments that discriminate between those who are more and less skillful in terms of their functioning within the community. These may not predict school-related achievement in the majority culture but would indicate strengths and styles of interaction and help teachers better understand the child's functioning. This information would also allow the educator to bridge the gap between school and community. We do not understand all the variations in competence in different cultures, but if we begin to research this area thoroughly it may help us capitalize on the child's strengths and begin to see differences in cognitive functioning as differences rather than deficits. Generally, then, proponents argue that the tests have been used incorrectly; with better education and some fine tuning, testing can help rather than injure a child.

Opponents, though, answer that no matter how these tests are improved or explained they are hopelessly flawed and should not be used. The tests just cannot overcome concerns about differences in experiences, vocabulary, motivation, and cognitive styles. No matter how well the tests are explained, their results will stigmatize children from minority groups.

Intelligence is not a new concept that can be carefully communicated to people. Intelligence tests have a history of abuse and misinterpretation. The general public misunderstands the concept. With such a legacy, can intelligence tests be used with children from minority groups?

The lines are drawn. Those who argue that these tests are inherently biased feel they should not be used. Others argue that, with the proper understanding and usage, these tests can be an aid to help students and do predict achievement.

A number of attempts have been made to reduce the problems characteristic of intelligence testing. One approach has been to factor socioeconomic status into the test scores and use a broader-based model to determine the existence of mental retardation. Since we know that many children from minority groups live in poverty, some have suggested the use of an equalizing factor.

One such system is called the System of Multicultural Pluralistic Assessment, or SOMPA, and makes allowances in intelligence scores by considering socioeconomic status (Mercer & Lewis, 1981). This system looks at medical factors, such as physical dexterity, weight by height, visual acuity, health history, and visual-motor ability. It takes into account adaptive behavior as well. The pluralistic model also uses an estimation of learning potential, which is derived from two scales, including one based on the child's comparison with others in the child's own ethnic group. All measures are scored and converted to percentiles (Drew, Logan, & Hardman, 1992). However, doubts are raised about this controversial procedure's assumptions and validity.

THOUGHT QUESTION

1. *Has the concept of intelligence outlived its usefulness? If you answer yes, what would you replace it with?*

Modifying Intelligence

Another problem in the interpretation of intelligence is that it is not a fixed quality etched in stone. Plenty of evidence indicates that changes in the environment can produce improvements in intelligence; one study conducted by Skeels (1966) stands out.

In the 1930s, Skeels was working in an orphanage, where the children received little attention and were subjected to a rigid schedule. The children had no toys, and the environment was depressing. Skeels took a special interest in two girls who rocked back and forth and spent most of their time in bed. These two girls were later transferred to a mental institution, where they came under the influence of an older woman with mental retardation who showered them with attention. Their behavior changed, and they became much more responsive.

Skeels decided to find out more about this phenomenon. A number of children were removed from the sterile setting of the orphanage and allowed to live in a better environment with older people who had mental retardation. The children's intelligence scores improved an average of 29 points, and one child's intelligence score actually rose by more than 50 points. The group that stayed in the depressing environment of the orphanage was found to have even lower intelligence scores than when the study had begun. Skeels' conclusion that a change in environment accounts for improvement in intelligence has been accepted by most psychologists today, although the methodology has been severely criticized (Longstreth, 1981).

The point of this discussion is not to remove the concept of intelligence from the definition of mental retardation. Both the American Association on Mental Retardation and most states use intelligence in their definitions of mental retardation. But, if it is to be used, the problem of cultural bias, the understanding of intelligence as a quality that can vary as an individual's experiences change, and some understanding of the nature of the construct are all important.

Adaptive Behavior

The idea that deficits in adaptive behavior are involved in the definition of mental retardation is challenging. Adaptive behavior refers to the impact that the mental retardation has on the individual's ability to adjust (Baroff, 1986). It covers many areas including social skills, communication, daily living skills, and meeting the standards of personal independence and social responsibility expected for someone of a particular age and membership in a cultural group (American Psychiatric Association, 1994). For example, people need to be able to care for themselves, understand monetary concepts, and travel by public transportation. Without these and many other skills, an individual cannot exist independently. Some researchers have noted that social competence is a vital part of adaptive behavior, involving the ability to enter into and sustain social relationships and to act appropriately in social settings (Siperstein, 1992).

Adaptation is age-related. In the preschool years, many children with mental retardation lag behind their peers in acquiring motor skills, language, and cognitive skills. During middle childhood, these children have difficulty achieving academically, and their responses to some social situations may be inappropriate. In adolescence, mental retardation may affect interpersonal relationships and sometimes results in isolation from peers. In adulthood, it may reduce an individ-

THOUGHT QUESTION

2. *Why is it necessary to use adaptive functioning as a criterion for mental retardation along with below average intellectual functioning?*

ual's ability to gain employment and to form and maintain adult interpersonal relationships (Baroff, 1986).

Measuring adaptation has always been a problem. Although a number of scales measure adaptive behavior, each has been criticized. One scale that has been used for many years is the Vineland Social Maturity Scale. It provides scores on four different adaptive behavior scales and one maladaptive scale (Sparrow, Balla, & Cichetti, 1984).

The Adaptive Behavior Scale (ABS) has also become a popular way of measuring adaptive behavior (Nihira et al., 1974). The first part consists of a developmental scale, which evaluates the person's skills and habits in ten behavioral domains considered necessary for independence and successful daily living. The second part measures maladaptive behavior related to personality and behavioral disorders and yields scores in many different areas. This scale covers the areas of independent functioning, physical development, economic activities, language, number and time concepts, vocational activity, self-direction, responsibility, and socialization.

One major problem with these scales is that if a child does not show a particular behavior we do not know whether it is due to a lack of opportunity to acquire the skill, the child's lack of interest, or a diminished ability in the area (Kessler, 1988). Another difficulty arising from these scales is that they do not always accurately predict a child's ability to function. Some children function somewhat better than the scales would indicate, while others do not do as well (Comer, 1995). These scales also have been criticized because they emphasize compliance with authority figures and socially accepted behavior (Kessler, 1988).

One additional scale should be mentioned. Mercer and Lewis (1981) developed the Adaptive Behavior Inventory for Children (ABIC), which is part of SOMPA (discussed earlier). This inventory looks at adaptation in terms of how well a child does in the child's own cultural surroundings, and uses information gleaned from parental interviews rather than from teachers, who are the source of information for most inventories. Sometimes, teachers and parents disagree for a number of reasons, not the least of which is that children may act very differently at home than at school (Kessler, 1988).

Defining Mental Retardation for the Teacher

Various descriptions can be used to define mental retardation. One definition suggested by Richard Dever (1989, 1990) emphasizes what mental retardation is from the standpoint of a teacher or a parent.

Dever argues that a common perception of mental retardation is that children need to be actively taught basic skills that others without the condition can learn without much instruction. These skills are placed into five categories including homemaking and community life skills, personal maintenance, developmental skills, vocational skills, and leisure and travel skills. With the exception of complex vocational skills, most children learn all the others without formal instruction. Dever argues that an instructional definition of mental retardation should refer to the need to teach skills in these areas. Mental retardation, then, refers to the "need for specific training of skills that most people acquire incidentally and that enable individuals to live in the community without supervision" (1990, p. 149).

THOUGHT QUESTION

3. Suppose a child with mental retardation develops into an adult who earns a living and lives independently. Should the adult still be considered to have mental retardation?

People with mental retardation are capable of learning; their need for instruction is central. The degree of mental retardation is defined by the amount and intensity of the instruction required to teach people to be independent. Dever also argues that people with mental retardation who can live without supervision in the community should no longer be considered as having mental retardation. The aim of instruction for all people is the same, that of independence, even though not every person with mental retardation will attain it. Independence involves more than just living on one's own, but also showing appropriate behavior in settings so that the individual is not seen by others as needing special help.

Dever places mental retardation in an educational perspective rather than a clinical one. However, this definition would easily fit many children who do not have mental retardation but have other disabilities. As such, it should not be seen as a replacement for the current definition, but as a different way of viewing mental retardation.

Classification of Mental Retardation: A New Approach

Years ago, people with mental retardation were classified into the categories of idiot, imbecile, and moron, which obviously have negative connotations. Then the terms *educable, trainable,* and *custodial* were introduced and are still sometimes used. The problem here is the connotation that children who are trainable cannot be educated. A great improvement was the American Association on Mental Retardation's four-level classification system using the terms *mild, moderate, severe,* and *profound.*

Children with mild mental retardation have an intelligence score between 50–55 and 70. Children with moderate mental retardation score between 35 and 50–55; children with severe mental retardation range between 25 and 35–40. Children diagnosed with profound mental retardation have intelligence scores below 20–25. Of course, concurrent deficits in adaptive behavior must be shown as well. About 85 percent of all children with mental retardation score in the range of mild mental retardation, about 10 percent in the range of moderate mental retardation, about 5 percent in the range of severe mental retardation and less than 1 percent of all children with mental retardation are considered to have profound mental retardation. Therefore, the majority of people with mental retardation are found in the upper ranges of mental retardation (Comer, 1995). Other figures increase the percentage of people with mild mental retardation to about 89 or 90 percent, and decrease the percentage of people diagnosed as having moderate mental retardation to 7 percent, those classified as having severe mental retardation to 3 percent, and those with profound mental retardation to about 1 percent (Grossman, 1983).

The most recent classification system advanced by the American Association on Mental Retardation (1992) shows a significant change. Under the old system, the classification of mental retardation as to mild, moderate, severe, and profound depended upon an intelligence test score. Under the new system, once a child is determined to have mental retardation, the emphasis shifts from the intelligence score to the intensity of support services required (Schalock et al., 1994).

TABLE 4.2   **Definition and Examples of Intensities of Support**

Intermittent

Support on an "as needed basis." Characterized by episodic nature, person does not always need the support(s), or needs only short-term support during life-span transitions (e.g., job loss or an acute medical crisis). Intermittent supports may be high or low intensity when provided.

Limited

An intensity of support characterized by consistency over time and time-limited but not of an intermittent nature, which may require fewer staff members and less cost than more intense levels of support (e.g., time-limited employment training or transitional supports during the school-to-adult period).

Extensive

Support characterized by regular involvement (e.g., daily) in at least some environments (such as work or home) and not time-limited (e.g., long-term support and long-term home living support).

Pervasive

Support characterized by constancy and high intensity; provided across environments with a potential life-sustaining nature. Pervasive supports typically involve more staff members and intrusiveness than do extensive or time-limited supports.

Source: *Mental Retardation: Definition, Classification, and Systems of Supports,* copyright © 1992 by the American Association on Mental Retardation. Reprinted by permission.

The AAMR recognizes four levels of support services: intermittent, limited, extensive, and pervasive, as shown in Table 4.2. These categories are more descriptive than previous categories and place the emphasis on the needs of the child and on the child's functioning rather than on the child's intelligence level. People with mental retardation need different levels of support to enhance their independence, productivity, and integration within the community.

This new classification method will result in a diagnosis of a person with "mental retardation who needs limited supports in communication and social skills" or "a person with mental retardation with extensive supports needed in the areas of social skills and self-direction."

The Three-Step Process for Diagnosis

The AAMR (1992) advocates a three-stage diagnostic process using four dimensions (see Table 4.3). In the first step, intellectual functioning and adaptive skills (dimension one) are measured. If the child meets the criteria for mental retardation, step two is carried out.

In step two, the strengths and weaknesses and the need for supports are investigated. These exist along three additional dimensions, psychological/emotional, physical/health/etiology, and environmental considerations.

In step three, using the profile obtained through the first two steps, the type and intensity of supports needed for each of the four dimensions are noted.

This change in classification procedures is a challenging one. It must be emphasized that the terms *intermittent, limited, extensive,* and *pervasive* do NOT simply replace *mild, moderate, severe,* and *profound.* It would be incorrect to say that mild mental retardation is now called intermittent. Rather, we can think of it as a complete shift in orientation in which classification is based on the supports required (Schalock et al., 1994).

In addition, note that the Diagnostic and Statistical Manual of the American Psychiatric Association (DSM-IV) uses the older mild, moderate, severe, and profound categories (APA, 1994). The question remains whether this manual, which is used by many mental health professionals for classifying disorders, will include the AAMR changes in the future.

Such important changes do not occur overnight. The older categories were used (and still are) to describe the nature of the population in thousands of research studies. For the sake of clarity and accuracy, the older classification system must sometimes be used in this chapter, especially when referring to a particular study.

TABLE 4.3   **The Three-Step Process: Diagnosis, Classification, and Systems of Supports**

	STEP 1. Diagnosis of mental retardation to determine eligibility for supports
	Mental retardation is diagnosed if:
Dimension I: Intellectual functioning and adaptive skills	**1.** The individual's intellectual functioning is approximately 70–75 or below. **2.** Significant disabilities are identified in two or more adaptive skill areas. **3.** The age of onset is less than 18.
	STEP 2. Classification and description and identification of strengths and weaknesses and the need for supports
Dimension II: Psychological/emotional considerations *Dimension III: Physical/ health/etiology considerations* *Dimension IV: Environmental considerations*	**1.** Describe the individual's strengths and weaknesses in reference to psychological/ emotional considerations. **2.** Describe the individual's overall physical health and indicate the condition's etiology. **3.** Describe the individual's current environmental placement and the optimal environment that would facilitate continued growth and development.
	STEP 3. Profile and intensities of needed supports
	Identify the kind and intensities of supports needed for each of the four dimensions.
	1. Dimension I: Intellectual functioning and adaptive skills **2.** Dimension II: Psychological/emotional considerations **3.** Dimension III: Physical health/etiology considerations **4.** Dimension IV: Environmental considerations

Source: *Mental Retardation: Definition, Classification, and Systems of Supports,* copyright © 1992 by the American Association on Mental Retardation. Reprinted by permission.

Prevalence and Incidence

The prevalence of mental retardation (the total number of cases in the total population) has been described at between 1 and 3 percent of the population (Wilson, O'Leary, & Nathan, 1992). The figure of 1 percent, however, shows up most often, which would mean that approximately 2.5 million Americans have mental retardation. The number of children with mental retardation has been decreasing steadily.

During the 1992–1993 school year, a total of 533,715 children diagnosed as having mental retardation received special education services. Since the 1976–1977 school year, the total number of children diagnosed as having mental retardation and receiving special education has declined by 39 percent or about 341,000 (U.S. Department of Education, 1993; 1994).

Contrast this with the numbers of children diagnosed with a learning disability. During that same period, the number of children classified as having a learning disability increased 183 percent, and since 1985 the number of students identified as learning disabled has increased about 2 to 3 percent annually. Approximately 11.5 percent of all children with disabilities are diagnosed as having mental retardation.

The incidence of mental retardation (number of new cases) depends greatly upon the age group discussed. It is less than 1 percent for children below the age of five but rises dramatically during the school years (ages five to eighteen) and then declines (Drew et al., 1992). Most children with mental retardation are identified during the elementary school years.

At first glance, both incidence and prevalence information seem confusing. Why the decrease in prevalence of the disorder, and why the difference between age groups? The decline in the number of children diagnosed as having mental retardation is due to a combination of reasons. These include changes in states' definitions and procedures for identifying mental retardation, greater care in identifying mental retardation among minority group children who have traditionally been overrepresented, improved medical diagnosis and treatment, and a preference on the part of many parents and school personnel to classify children as having a learning disability instead of mental retardation (U.S. Department of Education, 1993).

Many states have adopted stricter criteria for diagnosing mental retardation. By doing so, the number of children classified as having mental retardation has decreased. Professional concern about the disproportionate number of minority group children considered to have mental retardation has prompted attempts to reduce that number and to consider taking cultural factors into consideration. Perhaps the most important reason for the decreased prevalence though, is the tendency to categorize children, especially those on the borderline, as having a learning disability rather than mental retardation. Learning disability is a label that holds far less of a stigma than mental retardation.

The incidence data is easier to understand. Relatively few children before the age of five are diagnosed as having mental retardation because of the minimal demands placed on young children. Children diagnosed as having mental retardation during the first five years are likely to be in need of more intense supports and, as noted earlier, comprise a small percentage of people with mental retardation.

During the school years, the demands on the child increase, making difficulties in learning, judgment, and thinking more evident. When children in elementary school show poor achievement or social, or developmental difficulties, they are more likely to be identified and classified as having mental retardation.

When many of these children leave school they are able to live independently because they are no longer required to learn academic subjects and use abstract thinking. Therefore, the number of adults who are considered as having mental retardation is lower. This trend is so noticeable that a government study once called the population of children with mild mental retardation the "six-hour retarded child," referring to the number of hours most children spend in school. About 68.8 percent of all people with mental retardation are in the age group six through nineteen years (Munro, 1986).

Interesting prevalence data also occurs in the area of socioeconomic status. When the prevalence of the more severe levels of mental retardation across socioeconomic status is examined, no differences in rates of mental retardation are found. The child with moderate, severe, and profound mental retardation is just as likely to be found in the middle class as in lower socioeconomic groups. However, once the mildest form is examined, the differences become obvious, with many more children with mild mental retardation coming from lower socioeconomic level homes (Drew et al., 1992). Perhaps the more severe cases of mental retardation have biological causes that are spread evenly throughout the population, whereas the milder forms are more susceptible to environmental influences, such as lack of intellectual stimulation sometimes found in homes dominated by poverty.

Many more males are considered to have mental retardation than females. No one has a completely accepted answer to this, although part of the explanation may be that most cases of mental retardation are discovered during the school years. Boys and girls may not react to school problems in the same manner. A girl may be more likely to withdraw and a boy more likely to act out. The boy who acts out catches the attention of the teacher and is more likely to be referred for testing and diagnosis.

THOUGHT QUESTION

4. *Why are more male than female elementary school children diagnosed as having mental retardation?*

What Causes Mental Retardation?

The known causes of mental retardation are many, but they explain relatively few cases of mental retardation. Although that statement may seem unusual, it can be easily explained. The overwhelming majority of children with mental retardation are diagnosed with mild mental retardation. Within this group, the causes of mild mental retardation are usually unknown (Drews et al., 1995). As the level of intelligence decreases, many more definite causes of mental retardation can be found. Most of these are genetic and physiological. Even so, the cause of only 30–50 percent of all cases of severe mental retardation can be accurately determined (McClaren & Bryson, 1987).

The medical causes of mental retardation include infections, trauma, metabolic problems, gross brain damage caused by postnatal factors, various prenatal problems, and genetic and chromosomal disorders. For example, various prenatal problems, such as maternal alcohol consumption, and certain viruses, such as rubella, may cause mental retardation (Rosenthal, 1990). HIV, the virus that causes AIDS, can be transmitted either during the prenatal stage or at birth. Children with AIDS may show mental retardation (Diamond, 1989). Phenylketonuria (PKU), a rare genetic disease in which children cannot metabolize the amino acid, phenylalanine, may cause mental retardation if not treated. However, PKU can be diagnosed shortly after birth and with a special diet, mental retardation can be prevented.

Genetic and Chromosomal Factors

In a recent survey of the literature, a total of 503 genetic and chromosomal diseases resulted in disorders in which one of the symptoms was mental retardation (Wahlstrom, 1990). Most of these diseases are rare. The most common chromosomal condition causing mental retardation is Down syndrome.

Down Syndrome

Twenty years ago, the idea of a weekly television show about a child with a chromosomal abnormality would have been unthinkable, but the program "Life Goes

Christopher Burke, a teen with Down syndrome, played Corky on the television show "Life Goes On."

On," featuring Corky, a high school student with Down syndrome aired in the late 1980s. It signified a change in our attitude toward the disorder.

Down syndrome is the most common chromosomal cause of mental retardation. It occurs approximately once in every 1,000 births and is caused by the appearance of an extra chromosome on the twenty-first pair (Plomin, DeFries, & McClearn, 1990). The child has 47 chromosomes instead of the typical 46. The frequency of the disorder increases with the age of the mother as well as the age of the father. The risk for women under thirty is 1 in 1,250 births while those at age thirty-five have a 1-in-365 chance of bearing a child with Down syndrome. At age forty the chances are 1 in 110 births while at age forty-five it increases to 1 in 45 births (March of Dimes, 1987b). The disorder is also linked to the father in about 5 percent of all cases (Antonarakis, 1991). Each year in the United States, about 5,000 children are born with Down syndrome (Dullea, 1989).

There are three types of Down syndrome. In the most common type, called *trisomy*, an extra chromosome is found on the twenty-first pair of chromosomes. In the second type, called *mosaicism*, some of the cells show the extra chromosome while others do not. In the third type, called *translocation*, all or some part of the extra chromosome on the twenty-first pair becomes attached to another chromosome pair. These last two types of Down syndrome account for only about 5 percent of the entire number of cases.

Most children with Down syndrome are identified either at birth or shortly after by their physical appearance. Unusual physical features include folded eyes, short digits, flat face, protruding tongue, and harsh voice (Sue, Sue, & Sue, 1990). Mental retardation is associated with the disorder, but the degree of retardation varies greatly. Today, many children with Down syndrome are given special treatment including preschool programs, which have improved their cognitive functioning, and many score in the range of mild mental retardation on intelligence tests.

While years ago most children with this disorder were institutionalized immediately after birth, this is not the case today. Many of these children are now raised at home, which is usually beneficial to the child.

Children with Down syndrome show the same developmental milestones as other children, but at a delayed pace. This includes smiling and laughing, eye contact during play, self-recognition, some attachment behaviors, and symbolic play (Thompson et al., 1985). They often experience difficulties in a number of areas including coordination.

Not too long ago the life expectancy for Down syndrome children was ten years or less. Congenital heart problems are common and resistance to disease is low. However, medical advances have substantially increased the life expectancy of these children. Approximately 20 percent die during the first two years (Rondal, 1988). However, the majority who survive infancy live well into adulthood (Carr, 1994; Baird & Sadovnick, 1987). After the age of forty, people with Down syndrome appear to be more susceptible to diseases related to old age. By the time they reach forty, many have brain lesions that look like those resulting from Alzheimer's disease, and many show symptoms of senility (Kolata, 1989). The reason may be that genes associated with congenital heart defects, brain changes associated with familial Alzheimer's disease, and other disorders are also found on the twenty-first chromosome. Much research today is being conducted on the relationship between various genes on the twenty-first chromosome.

Down syndrome:
A chromosomal disorder leading to a distinct physical appearance and mental retardation of varying degree.

Not only has the health and life expectancy of these children improved, their entire life has changed. This is the first generation that with the help of early intervention programs has ventured forth into the world. Many attend public schools. As with any child with a disability, their placement is determined by their individual skills and needs. Some are presently educated in the regular classroom and more will be in the future as schools move toward inclusion. Unfortunately, many experience poor treatment from other children. In fact, approximately two-thirds face some harassment, ranging from name calling and teasing to physical aggression (Dullea, 1989). Despite this negative aspect, most parents and children rate the school experience quite positively, although forming friendships after school is frequently still a problem.

No one knows the extent to which children with Down syndrome can function in society if given the opportunities. Perhaps the best conclusion is offered by Diane Crutcher, who as director of the National Down Syndrome Congress noted, "We don't put limitations on our other kids and finally, finally, we're not putting limitations on kids with Down syndrome" (Dullea, 1989, p. 1).

Psychosocial Causation

The number of medical factors that can cause mental retardation is intimidating but, as noted, in the majority of cases, no recognizable physical cause for the mental retardation can be found (Polloway & Patton, 1990). This lack of physical explanation has led to a search for possible psychosocial causes of mental retardation.

Some evidence links low intellectual stimulation in the home to academic and intellectual problems (Comer, 1995). This supposition goes along well with the finding that prevalence of mild mental retardation is not uniform among socioeconomic groups—the poor have higher rates of such mental retardation.

Poor people have less access to quality medical care, are more likely to be malnourished, and are more likely to experience medical difficulties during the prenatal stage. These factors may increase a person's vulnerability to environmental stress. Poor people are also more likely to be raised in father-absent families, to be undereducated, underemployed, and highly stressed. Frequently, the level of intellectual stimulation as well as language usage is low.

Of course, not all children who have mental retardation without known physical causes come from poverty stricken families, but a disproportionate number do. Although environmental causes are only presumed at this point, the evidence does point to environmental influences as factors in mental retardation (Kramer, Allen, & Gergen, 1995; Drews et al., 1995).

The Characteristics of Children with Mental Retardation

A number of difficulties become obvious when discussing the characteristics of children diagnosed as having mental retardation. Evaluators may tend to overgeneralize, to list a number of characteristics, which leads to the incorrect assertion that all children diagnosed as having mental retardation function in the same manner. This assertion is not true. Children with the same intelligence scores function differently. Therefore, one can only assume that the child who is diagnosed as having mental retardation shows below average intellectual functioning and some adaptive problems as noted in the definition.

Physical Appearance

Most people with mental retardation do not look any different from their non-mentally retarded peers. As a rule, when the IQ level is below fifty, some physical differences in appearance are more probable (Erickson, 1992). These physical differences in children who have moderate, severe, and profound mental retardation may be traced to some medical problem, which caused their condition.

Those children who look different are laboring under an additional problem, since their different physical appearance may lead to rejection. All children need to be educated not to fear people who look different and not to reject others solely on the basis of their appearance.

Communication

Communication and language are central to human interaction (Warren & Abbeduto, 1992). Children with mental retardation often do not require extensive language training, but still show communication problems and reduced abilities. They may say inappropriate things that cause distress in people. This characteristic behavior may stem from their inability to read social situations adequately. Other communication problems include omitting important information and relevant details and voicing incomplete thoughts (Fraser & Rao, 1990). Such problems make it important for teachers to both encourage children with mental retardation to express their thoughts and to be more complete in their communication. Some children with mental retardation, though, especially those with other disabilities, may not be able to use speech effectively. These children may be taught to communicate using sign language or communication boards instead.

Social Skills

Social skill deficits can be marked in some children with mental retardation (Davison & Neale, 1994). These children may have difficulty making friends and acting appropriately. Some skills, such as initiating, interacting, and terminating interactions with others, receiving and responding to situational cues, recognizing feelings, and providing positive and negative feedback can be taught. Teaching social skills through coaching and modeling can be effective.

SCENARIO

2 A fourth grade student with mental retardation in your class often says inappropriate things and does not always greet people or pay attention to what others are saying. The other children in your fourth grade class ignore and sometimes reject this student. What strategies would you use to include the student in the class and improve the student's interpersonal relations?

Academic Skills

Academic achievement is the most obvious area in which mental retardation shows itself. It is a primary reason why a child might be referred for assessment. Such basic skills as reading, writing, and arithmetic are often difficult to learn, and delays in attaining these skills are common. Abstract reasoning is especially difficult for children with mental retardation.

The regular classroom teacher and the special educator dealing with students with mental retardation must recognize the tendency to treat these students as younger than they are because their academic skills are limited. This concern during these students' school years becomes more of a problem as children become older. A 15-year-old adolescent with mental retardation may not be reading well and may have many academic difficulties but is still 15 years old with the developmental interests of a 15-year-old. Whatever curricular modifications that are made should be appropriate to the student's mental abilities and developmental age. Asking a 15-year-old to read a story that is simplified for the student is certainly appropriate, but that story must also be age-appropriate and deal with something of interest to the student. Although most professionals subscribe to the idea of age appropriateness, little agreement has been reached on what activities, materials, and reinforcers are appropriate for children of different ages (Matson et al., 1993).

Sensorimotor Skills

Many children with mental retardation do not show any obvious deficits in motor skills. Some, though, may have a number of deficits in motor skills. Students who have other disabilities as well as mental retardation are more likely to experience motor skill deficits.

Self-Help Skills

Skills such as bathing, dressing, using the telephone, and eating with utensils are examples of self-help skills. Many children with mental retardation develop these skills with some support, while others may need considerable training to develop them.

Vocational Skills

Many children with mental retardation will function independently as adults and do not demonstrate mental retardation in adulthood when they are not faced with academic challenges. Their vocational skills are often somewhat limited to relatively simple work but considerable evidence suggests that some do well in the world of work. In the past, people with mental retardation were considered unable to work in competitive, industrial settings. However, this view has changed, and many people with mental retardation are employed in regular industrial and commercial settings.

Cognitive Abilities

Underlying these aspects of life are the child's problems in the cognitive sphere. For example, studies find that people with mental retardation often do not pay attention to the most important aspects of a situation. The most commonly discovered deficit is in the area of short-term memory, with long-term memory being average. Often people with mental retardation will not use rehearsal to remember something.

Children diagnosed as having mental retardation also take longer to process information. These children do not generalize from one situation to another similar one and show deficits in their knowledge of how to plan, monitor progress, solve problems, and check for accuracy. Effective instruction takes these cognitive differences into account.

Preventing Mental Retardation

The prevention of mental retardation has taken two different tracks. On the first track, the goal has been to reduce or eliminate the medical causes of mental retardation. On the second, attempts to improve the home environment of children at risk for mental retardation have increased.

Mental retardation caused by some medical disorders can be easily prevented. The development of a rubella vaccine and good prenatal care to reduce the risk of low birthweight and toxemia are relatively simple methods for preventing mental retardation. Sometimes, mental retardation can be prevented by intervening early in infancy. For example, phenylketonuria (PKU) is a recessive genetic disorder in

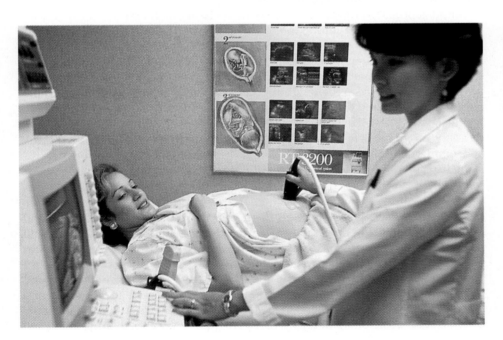

Good prenatal care can reduce the risk of low birthweight and toxemia, preventing some cases of mental retardation. This woman is receiving s sonogram, in which ultrasound is used to produce a picture of the fetus.

which the individual cannot digest a particular amino acid called phenylalanine which is found in all protein-rich foods including fish, meats, eggs, and milk. If not discovered and treated, mental retardation is the result. A blood test can determine if the child has PKU (Plomin et al., 1990). If the baby has PKU, the child is placed on a special diet and mental retardation is avoided.

Since so many cases of mental retardation do not involve known physical causes, focus must be placed on raising the level of intellectual stimulation in homes that appear to be at risk for producing children with mental retardation. For example, if the intelligence level of the home is low, the offspring may not have the opportunities necessary to develop their abilities. A number of early intervention projects have demonstrated that the intelligence level of children who are most at risk for mental retardation and other learning problems can be raised.

The Abecedarian Project, discussed in Chapter 3, tested whether mental retardation influenced by inadequate home environments could be prevented through intensive preschool programs together with medical and nutritional support (Ramey & Ramey, 1992). The program began between 6 and 12 weeks after birth. The treatment group, which received the special early education program, and the control group, which did not, both received medical and nutritional services and social services. By age three, all but one of the children in the control group with mothers with intelligence scores below 70 scored in the range of mild retardation (less than 70) or borderline range (70–85). This statistic is not surprising since the single strongest predictor of a child's intelligence is the mother's intelligence. Every child in the early intervention group who received the intensive help five days per week, fifty weeks per year, scored in the average range at age three. At six, the intelligence scores of the early intervention group children ranged from 7.9 to 20.1 points higher than control group children (Martin, Ramey & Ramey, 1990). However, no significant changes occurred in parental attitude or modifications in the home environment.

Another project, Project CARE, sought to change parental attitudes and the home environment. In addition to the day-care experience, Wasik and colleagues (1990) added a family support component. Over an eighteen-month period, 65 families whose children were judged to be at risk for delayed development due to social and educational factors participated in the study. One group received both preschool programs for the child and family education, the second group just family education, and the third did not receive either service, although nutrition, medical care, and social services were available to every family in the study. The day-care program included activities aimed at enriching the child's intellectual and emotional abilities, especially language usage. Family education was designed to foster cognitive and social development through a series of weekly home visits in which the trained visitors discussed goals of parenting and problem-solving strategies in raising children, including identifying problems, generating different ways of dealing with them, and making decisions. Home visitors also demonstrated and discussed day-care activities with the parents. The results showed improved intelligence scores for the education-plus-family group, but the home-based program alone was not sufficient to raise IQ scores. Perhaps, the home-based program itself was not intensive enough and a more involved program is needed to change parental attitudes (Ramey & Ramey, 1992). Apparently, a combination of professionally directed preschool experiences and family education can be successful, but an intensive program is required to bring about sufficient change in the home environment of these children.

THOUGHT QUESTION

5. *Why is the single greatest predictor of a child's intelligence the mother's intelligence?*

Early Intervention

Once a child is diagnosed as having mental retardation, early intervention can enhance development. Early intervention is most common with those children whose developmental lags and physical difficulties are most apparent, since they are most likely to be diagnosed at an early age (Epps & Krocker, 1995).

As noted in the discussion of early intervention programs in Chapter 2, early intervention programs focus on the family. An analysis of the child's strengths and weaknesses is conducted, and an individually designed program is instituted for the entire family. Parents are sometimes the primary teachers; they learn from experts special child care techniques, observational skills, and teaching strategies. Each activity is based upon the child's needs. For example, a special seat may be provided to support the baby and encourage the child to reach. Parents are taught ways to motivate the child. A number of specific exercises and activities help the child reach specific goals. This type of intervention requires a scheduled daily period of time, particular materials, and special methods. For example, special exercises for children with Down syndrome allow parents to help the children strengthen their abdominal muscles. These exercises are performed two or three times a day. Parents may also sit down with their children with blocks and a box and teach their child about shapes. The education for children with mental retardation is much more directive than is the case with children without disabilities (Goodman, 1994).

Placement Questions

During the 1991–1992 school year, 5.1 percent of all children with mental retardation were educated exclusively in regular classes, while 25.4 percent were helped in the resource room and spent part of their day in regular classes. A little more than 59 percent were found in separate classes within the school and included for art, music, or perhaps a few other subjects. Only 8.8 percent were educated in separate schools, 1.2 percent in residential facilities and 0.3 percent in homes or hospitals (U.S. Department of Education, 1994).

In Chapter 1, we discussed the issue of inclusion. The placement of children with mental retardation is moving toward increased inclusion. This tendency is not only for children once classified as having mild mental retardation but also, to some extent, for those classified as having moderate mental retardation (Saint-Laurent & Lessard, 1991).

Evidence shows that children with mental retardation benefit from being placed with classmates of average intelligence (Patton, Payne & Beirne-Smith, 1990). When children with mental retardation were integrated into a middle school environment and special support given to the teacher, the outcome was

THOUGHT QUESTION

6. *What are the arguments both in favor and opposed to integrating children with more severe forms of mental retardation into the regular classroom?*

positive but not troublefree. Teachers sometimes found it difficult to figure out ways to include these children in classroom activities. These children were accepted by their peers, and about 90 percent of the students thought it was a good idea that they be integrated. About two-thirds of the nondisabled students felt they had learned something about disabilities, and most felt that these students should be placed in nonacademic classes. Positive changes in social and communication skills were noted in the students with disabilities by the teachers, the other children, and special educators (York et al., 1992).

Although social acceptance is important, academic progress needs to be examined as well. Do children with mental retardation do better in regular classes or in their own classes? Most research shows that they learn fewer academic skills in self-contained classes than in mainstreamed classes, although sometimes no differences are found (Baroff, 1986). In the most recent studies, the differences have been less pronounced than in earlier studies (Pfeiffer, 1992). However, this analysis may be somewhat unfair. The traditional curriculum for the children in regular classrooms emphasizes academic skills, while the traditional special class for children with mental retardation emphasizes social and vocational areas rather than academic areas. In comparing them, we may not be comparing the same goals.

Reviews have consistently questioned the appropriateness of special classes. A number of problems with special class placement including failure to return to the mainstream, stigma, lack of peer social networks, and inadequacy of learning have been noted (Gartner & Lipsky, 1987; McDonnell & Hardman, 1989). A movement has arisen to keep students out of these classes. On the other hand, some students with mental retardation require such placement.

Again, as in any discussion of placement, we must remember that special education is a group of services not a place. Although much controversy in the area of placement exists, and research comparing different types of placement is certainly proper, we ought not lose sight of the overall importance of the quality of the services delivered, rather than simply where they are offered.

SCENARIO

3 You are a teacher of English in an elementary school. You are told that a child with mental retardation will be placed in your fifth grade class. As you expect, the child is slow and shows language difficulties but is pleasant to work with and willing to try. The child does, though, become frustrated rather easily when unable to understand. Specifically, what changes would you make to help this child succeed in class?

Curriculum and Teaching Strategies

What type of a curriculum is appropriate for students with mental retardation? What teaching strategies are most effective? These two vital questions should interest anyone working with children having mental retardation. Successful mainstreaming of children with mental retardation (as well as children with many other disabilities) involves individualization and support. Individualization is based upon the children's needs as identified in the individualized education programs (IEP), and the support includes providing necessary services so that children may develop their abilities as well as providing teachers with necessary aids to educate children in the regular classroom setting. The type of curriculum used depends upon individual ability and needs, and therefore generalizations are difficult. The nature of the child's school work will naturally be driven by the child's IEP.

Adaptations in instruction and curriculum are certainly required if students with mental retardation are to be successfully integrated into the regular classroom. Adaptation and integration require a great deal of teamwork. The many types of teams—the IEP team, building-based planning teams, planning teams organized around specific students, and collaborative teaching teams—consist of both regular and special educators (AAMR, 1992).

Depending on the child's age, IEP, and adaptive skills, different school activities with peers must be appropriately selected and adapted. During the preschool and early elementary grades, full inclusion will be more frequent. Curricular adaptations, such as easier but age-appropriate written materials, will be required to avoid frustration on the part of the child with mental retardation.

The older the student with mental retardation, the more likely the focus will be on developing job skills, functional academics, and independent living abilities. Students with mental retardation are more likely to be found in vocational courses rather than in college preparatory work.

One important aspect of schooling is promoting social integration. Peers are powerful models in language, behavior, and social skills. Children with mental retardation benefit when exposed to the usual peer interaction that takes place in regular classrooms but not in separate classes. As noted so often, social skills may have to be taught and social interactions structured so that children with and without disabilities interact with each other (see Chapter 2). This type of instruction is especially important for children with mental retardation who may, and often do, show adaptive difficulties in areas which will affect their social interactions.

When teaching children with mental retardation, a teacher should promote skill use in various environments used by the student including the home, school, leisure time activities, community, and work. Skills are more easily grasped when taught as an integral part of a functional routine, rather than in isolation, because of the problem of generalization. Teaching a skill in a concrete and useful context makes generalization more likely. Instead of being taught a basic motor skill or a particular language skill by itself, a student can be taught the skill as part of a regular activity.

For some children with mental retardation, the objectives of the curriculum are somewhat similar to those for regular students. They will learn basic skills such as reading, math, science, and social studies. The emphasis, though, is often on functional academics and functional skills. The term *functional academics* has two meanings. First, the academics and skills taught are specially designed to prepare the child for living and working in the community as an independent individual. For example, reading is taught for information and protection purposes, such as reading food labels and advertisements. Writing involves filling out employment applications and writing simple letters. Money handling is emphasized. In addition, job preparation skills, which include locating jobs and interview skills, are taught.

Second, these skills and academic areas are taught in a meaningful, practical context, rather than being taught in an abstract manner. For example, a math lesson may actually use a budget or a real problem in making change. Education must also deal with friendship, sexuality, interpersonal relations, and health concerns. Since these skills are to be functional, their choice must meet a criterion of usefulness.

Psychologists often note the difference between an internal and external locus of control. People with an **internal locus of control** believe they, themselves, are in control and can influence their future; people with an **external locus of control** believe that they are at the mercy of the outside world or luck. Children with mental retardation often have an external locus of control. In other words, they do not believe they have much control over their environment (Patton et al., 1990). When children learn skills that are functional, their confidence increases, leading to a more internal locus of control.

Another interesting change in teaching strategies for children with mental retardation is community-based instruction, which involves teaching a skill in the environment in which it will be used. If children are to be able to use money in purchasing items and understanding the concept of change, they should learn it in the context of a store. Learning how to use public transportation involves actually doing it. This type of learning accomplishes two important goals. First, the children learn important skills that are useful and obtain a feeling of accomplishment. Second, it overcomes the problem of lack of generalization that makes education of children with mental retardation more difficult.

Education must also help children learn how to make and express their choices (Houghton, Bronicki, & Guess, 1987). Making choices is a critical part of life. The child must also be able to express these choices so that they can be acted upon by others. If we are ordering food at a restaurant, we choose our food and must give the order. If we wish to go to the movies with someone, we must be able to express this desire to the other person. This skill is necessary for living a satisfying, independent life.

Some children with mental retardation must also learn daily living skills, including how to clean up, dress, and groom. These skills are often taught using task analysis.

Internal locus of control:
The belief that one is in control of one's own fate.

External locus of control:
The belief that one is at the mercy of other people or fate.

SCENARIO

4 A student with mental retardation in your math class has worked very hard but is not passing. The student's average test score is around 50, even though the student takes the tests in the resource room and receives extra time. You must give this student a grade. Using the test scores the student would fail, but you believe that this would cause the student to stop trying. What grade would you give, and why?

Task Analysis

If children with mental retardation are to succeed, they must learn adequate skills for living. They learn more slowly, though, and the material sometimes must be broken down into smaller pieces. One approach for teaching is to use **task analysis**. In task analysis the teacher breaks down a large skill, such as dressing or putting on a sweater, into its sequential behavioral components. For example, using the telephone involves recognizing numbers, matching numbers on paper to those on the dial, dialing the phone, speaking into the phone in an appropriate manner, and hanging up (Patton et al., 1990). How far a task must be broken down depends upon the learning ability of each child. Many tasks have already been task analyzed, and many curriculum guides, teaching manuals, and commercial teaching programs are available.

For example, how would you teach a child with mental retardation safety skills, such as cleaning up broken dishes and disposing of them? Remember that if children with mental retardation are to live a semi-independent existence certain safety skills are required. Winterling and colleagues (1992) first task analyzed a specific safety problem and then taught children to do so in three contexts (see Table 4.4). Specific safety precautions were used in this study. The students wore latex gloves and were not asked to perform the task with actual broken plastic materials until they were proficient at handling the simulated broken material perfectly. At each teaching session, the researcher told subjects why it was important to learn the tasks and then the investigator modeled each step of the task in sequence and provided a simple verbal description of each action. Students imitated each step as they received a prompt. The experimenter provided a cue to attend, a task request, and then waited five seconds for the student to make a response. If the student did not initiate the step within five seconds the investigator showed it again and the student imitated the investigator's behavior. Students were given verbal praise such as "Good, you used the fork to loosen the drain stopper." By using such a procedure, many children with moderate mental retardation can learn these important skills.

Task analysis:
The process of sequentially analyzing a skill into its teachable components.

SCENARIO

5 You are asked to teach a child with mental retardation to make a sandwich. It is a difficult task but you have read that task analysis can help. Briefly describe the steps necessary to task analyze this skill and what method you would use to teach it to this child.

IN THE CLASSROOM   Teaching Children with Mental Retardation

Teachers who have never taught students with mental retardation are often somewhat concerned. Indeed, these students learn at a slower rate, and their capacity to deal with more difficult abstract concepts is limited. Special attention

TABLE 4.4   **Task Analyses for Sink, Countertop, and Floor Tasks**

WET SINK	COUNTERTOP	FLOOR
1. Put gloves on.	1. Put gloves on.	1. Put gloves on.
2. Use utensil to dislodge drain stopper. Allow water to drain from sink.	2. Retrieve dust pan.	2. Get broom, dust pan, and brush.
3. Remove unbroken items, place to side out of sink.	3. Hold dust pan; place broken pieces from unbroken items into it. Place unbroken items in sink.	3. Tear small piece of paper towel and push any broken material on furniture into dust pan.
4. Rinse unbroken items in sink.	4. Tear piece of paper towel. Hold dust pan below counter surface; push broken pieces with paper towel into dust pan.	4. Empty dust pan into trash and throw away paper towel.
5. Bring trash can to sink area.		5. Move furniture out of area where broken material is on floor.
6. Grasp large pieces with hand and place in trash.	5. Empty dust pan into trash can. Use paper towel to wipe dust pan; throw paper towel into trash.	6. Use broom or dust brush to sweep the broken items into the dust pan
7. Remove drain stopper; empty contents in trash can.		

must always be given to their difficulty with generalization, which requires teachers to build opportunities for transfer into the teaching.

In addition, motivation can be a major problem. Sometimes, children with mental retardation have learned to fail. When given new tasks, children with mental retardation may desperately try to avoid failure, rather than to achieve success (Watson, 1977). Children with mental retardation do not trust their own skills and look for others to imitate. Because of their lack of confidence, acknowledging and pointing out progress is especially important. The use of task analysis can also help, and using reinforcement and encouragement is necessary.

When teaching students with mental retardation the following suggestions may be helpful:

1. Make social integration a goal and structure social interactions as much as possible through games and group work.	**Why?** These activities will encourage children with mental retardation to improve their verbal and social skills.
2. Watch closely for student rejection due to inappropriate behavior on the part of the child with mental retardation.	**Why?** Students with mental retardation are more often rejected for their inability to behave in an age-appropriate manner than for their slow acquisition of academic skills. Social skill instruction may be needed.

TABLE 4.4 *Continued*

WET SINK	COUNTERTOP	FLOOR
8. Replace drain stopper.	6. Rinse unbroken items in sink.	7. Empty dust pan in trash.
9. Tear small piece of paper towel; push small pieces of broken material into drain stopper with paper towel. Throw away paper towel.	7. Remove drain stopper; empty contents in trash can.	8. Replace furniture.
10. Remove drain stopper and empty contents into trash can. Replace drain stopper.	8. Replace drain stopper.	9. Return broom, dust pan, and brush to storage area.
11. Replace trash can.	9. Tear piece of paper towel; push pieces of broken material into drain stopper with paper towel. Throw away paper towel.	
12. Resume dishwashing activity.	10. Remove drain stopper; empty contents in trash can. Replace drain stopper.	
	11. Replace dust pan.	

Source: "Teaching Safety Skills to High School Students with Moderate Disabilities" by V. Winterling, D.L. Gast, M. Wolery, & J.A. Farmer, 1992, 25:217–227. *Journal of Applied Behavior Analysis*, copyright ©1992. Reprinted by permission of Journal of Applied Behavior Analysis and author.

3. Set reasonable goals and watch for signs that children are giving up.	**Why?** Many children with mental retardation do not have a history of success and may stop trying when faced with a challenge. Building success into a program is important and one way to do this is to set reasonable goals that children can attain.
4. Use peer tutoring and cooperative learning.	**Why?** Trained peer tutors are especially helpful in providing practice or drill. Cooperative learning uses rewards given on the basis of individual improvement within a group setting which helps the child who may not be able to compete on an individual basis learn.
5. Teach for transfer and generalization.	**Why?** A child with mental retardation might learn that three and three is six yet not understand that three toys and three toys equals six toys. Including multiple examples covering many areas encourages transfer.
6. Use frequent rewards and feedback.	**Why?** The use of reinforcers, consistent feedback, and appropriate prompts are educationally valuable. Success that is reinforced leads to a feeling of accomplishment.

7. Give the child a chance for verbal expression.	**Why?** Children with mental retardation should be required to answer appropriate questions in class and encouraged to verbalize their interests and needs.
8. Be sensitive to the special abilities of children with mental retardation.	**Why?** Children with mental retardation have strengths and weaknesses and areas of considerable ability and interest. Be on the lookout for these areas and use them to introduce new material.
9. Use age-appropriate materials.	**Why?** Simplifying reading material is certainly acceptable, but the material should be of interest to the student and age-appropriate.
10. Simplify directions.	**Why?** A student cannot complete a task if the student does not understand the directions.
11. Be concrete, not abstract.	**Why?** Children with mental retardation have difficulties with abstractions. Material should be taught in a concrete manner and presented so that no gaps are left.
12. Use frequent review.	**Why?** Students with mental retardation require review that should include examples of simple applications in the context of everyday life.
13. Reward initiative.	**Why?** Many children with mental retardation are outer-directed and wait for others to give direction or discover a problem and do not ask questions. Children must be rewarded when they show initiative.

The Teenager with Mental Retardation

Adolescents with mental retardation have the same social needs as their nondisabled peers. However, adolescents with mental retardation encounter more social problems than they experienced in earlier years. Most adolescents with mental retardation want to learn social skills and be like their peers as much as possible. They usually want to avoid any behavior that draws attention to limitations.

The difficulties increase as adolescents who may want to be socially included may act in inappropriate ways. They do not always know the difference between reality and what they have seen on television or heard, and may not be able to read the environment to determine what is acceptable. The problems associated with physiological changes are compounded during adolescence when persons with disabilities are rejected by nondisabled peers (Rowitz, 1988). Many teenagers with mental retardation are socially isolated and have few friends. Often their friends are younger children. Adolescents may see themselves as socially inept and may withdraw and act shy, or overcome anxiety in inappropriate ways, such as talking loud (Brier, 1986). Adolescents with mental retardation often experience difficulties separating from parents and attaining independence and establishing friendships (Brier, 1986).

Sex Education

Historically, people with mental retardation have been denied sexual expression and freedom. On the other hand, sometimes they were thought to be oversexed and dangerous. The sexual development of people with mental retardation is usually no different from their peers without mental retardation, although they have problems understanding and adapting to the physical changes that occur (Patton et al., 1990). Many are sheltered from sexual issues, and thousands have been sterilized. People with mental retardation often have limited and often incorrect sexual information (Branlinger, 1985). Adolescents have interest in sexual issues and require the information because their participation in society has increased their risk of unwanted pregnancy, venereal disease, and abuse (McCabe, 1993).

Although the need for sex education is obvious, questions concerning how much, when, and in what manner these children should be given such education must be answered (McCabe, 1993; Sundran & Stavis, 1994). How do teachers educate a young person with a mental age of 6 or 7 years and a chronological age of 15 years?

Children with mental retardation do not have as great an opportunity to acquire realistic understandings of sex; plus, they have an increased risk of sexual exploitation (Baroff, 1986). Along with sex education, generally, is a need for AIDS education. This education must be appropriate and presented simply. It may require somewhat more repetition, but should be given along with education about social relationships. Before any such educational attempts are made, parents' cooperation should be sought (Robertson, Bhate, & Bhate, 1991). The limited programs that exist in sex education often emphasize hygiene and morality and do not always cover sexual awareness, sexual behavior, and social development (Branlinger, 1988). Some new programs have been instituted which deal with anatomy, means of sexual expression, responsibility, interpersonal relationships, diseases, and values (Patton et al., 1990).

Sex education also includes the need to learn dating skills. Some success was found for a social skills training course using discussions and role playing (Mueser, Valenti-Hein, & Yarnold, 1987). Unfortunately, at the present time, data is lacking on the effectiveness of various materials and curricula in increasing knowledge or changing behavior (McCabe, 1993). What is clear is that just supplying information is not sufficient; these children need opportunities to develop a good self-concept, relationship-forming skills, and healthy attitudes toward sexuality.

SCENARIO

6 Mr. and Mrs. M. are parents of an adolescent with mental retardation. Their daughter lives with them and works in the community. She spends part of her day at work with people who do not have mental retardation and enjoys the company of others. Her mother has tried to explain sex and procreation to her, but her daughter does not seem to understand it. She likes boys and wants to date. Mr. and Mrs. M. are concerned that boys will take advantage of her, that she will not understand her sexuality and will become pregnant. If you were asked for your advice, what would you say?

The Transition between School and Work

The importance of the transition from school to the world of work has been emphasized by many authorities in the field (Rausch & Phelps, 1987; Knowlton & Clark, 1987). When special educators in secondary schools were questioned, the activities they considered most important were teaching social skills and job skills, involving parents, and matching skills to jobs (Morgan et al., 1992). This was true regardless of the severity of the mental retardation. These educators found some areas to be more important with children judged to need greater supports, such as the need for more coordination of services and transportation services.

Many special programs are available and more are on their way as we begin to realize that transition problems are common. According to law, all children receiving special services must have a transition plan by age 16 if not sooner, but some programs serve older students.

One demonstration program called STETS (Structured Training and Employment Transitional Services) targeted 18- to 24-year-old people with mental retardation for transitional help. It involved three phases. In phase one, initial training and support services were provided in a low-stress work environment, which could include up to 500 hours of paid employment. Phase two involved a period of on-the-job training in local firms and agencies, emphasizing both job performance and actual work stress. These jobs were designed as potentially permanent. Finally, in phase three, follow-up services were available. This program, implemented in five cities, was highly successful. When a total of 284 participants were compared to a control group who were not offered STETS services but could use any other services in the community, the results showed that those who received this help fared much better (Kerachsky & Halpern, 1987). After 22 months, 31 percent of those who were in the program were employed in regular jobs compared to only 19 percent of the control group.

Work-study options in high school are also possibilities. Such programs are most effective if training takes place in the projected place of employment.

Transition programs are vital to the success of the adolescent with mental retardation. Studies following adolescents with mental retardation after their
schooling ends find that they are much less likely than adolescents who do not
have mental retardation to be employed or living independently (Affleck et al.,
1990). Transition programs may improve this situation.

Employment

I f people with mental retardation are to be integrated into society, they must
successfully negotiate the world of work. Progress in this area has been quite
impressive, and the future looks bright.

Competitive Employment

Most adults with mental retardation who are employed work in competitive settings. These jobs, unfortunately, frequently do not pay very much, and often only
part-time work is available. Whether competitive employment is possible depends upon many factors including skills, personality, preparation, and the attitudes of the employer (Patton et al., 1990). The characteristics that predict job
success include positive attitude toward work, work-related behaviors including
promptness and pride, ability to get along with supervisors and co-workers, ability to communicate with more than one-word responses, physical attractiveness,
and fair motor coordination. Intelligence is not a good predictor for success since
so many lose jobs not because of their inability to perform the work but because
of a lack of social skills.

The placement of people with mental retardation into competitive employment has long been advocated by experts in the field (Levy et al., 1992). This
movement has accelerated for a number of reasons.

First, ample evidence points out that people with mental retardation can be
taught vocational skills, which is true for people with mild, moderate, and severe
mental retardation. Twenty years ago, Marc Gold (1973) formulated a training
program called "Try Another Way," which used behavioral strategies to teach vocational skills such as putting together bicycle brakes. Gold's method involved
very little if any verbal instruction, but asked people to perform certain behaviors
such as taking item A from bin 1 and item B from bin 2 and placing A on top of B,
then taking C and attaching it to the right place in A. These people were led
through the training exercise physically, and then slowly the guidance was faded.

The concept of **fading** is important. If the task has eight steps, the client with
mental retardation would be taken through each step with help and as the client
performed the task, the help would be faded or slowly taken away. Gold demonstrated that people with mental retardation could learn rather complex assembly
tasks. Others have also successfully demonstrated this. For example, Gaylord-
Ross and colleagues (1987) taught people with mental retardation to perform useful jobs such as conducting laboratory tests in a chemical lab.

Second, a number of studies report that people with mental retardation do better when they are trained in the actual atmosphere in which they will be working.

Fading:
The gradual removal of a prompt
or reinforcer.

Again, we see the need to take the generalization difficulty into account. If we want people to work in a regular environment, then we must do much of the training on the job. Finally, programs have shown that people with mental retardation can successfully work alongside nondisabled workers in such settings, although help in the form of coaching may be required.

Supported Employment

Matthew has Down syndrome and is employed by the Marriott Hotel chain for $3.60 an hour. He has been taught to scrub pots in a particular manner doing the bottom first, then the sides and then the rim, flipping it over and doing the same. Matthew has been working for a year. He is much like any other worker, as he has his likes and dislikes. He shares a single family house with five other people with mental retardation and a resident counselor. He commutes forty minutes using two buses to get to work and pays his own rent.

It took ten weeks of close daily guidance, being drilled on the routine, for Matthew to learn to wash pots. He has a job coach who is immediately available when necessary. This relatively new approach is called **supported employment** and assumes that the person with mental retardation may require continuous help managing the routines of living and working, so job coaches are offered at work and counselors at home. The amount of help required may be reduced in time, but some people will always need job coaches. For example, Matthew sometimes gets frustrated and wants to quit. Using a beeper he and his supervisor can immediately summon his job coach who helps him cope. Matthew will probably be paying income taxes this year and is being actively considered for a promotion to the mailroom, which entails a raise (Kilborn, 1990).

Supported employment:
A program emphasizing placement of individuals with disabilities in competitive employment with a job coach.

Supported employment in which a job coach is available is one possible way in which people with mental retardation may work in competitive employment settings.

Supported employment services contain three essential features: (1) opportunities for paid productive work with ongoing support, (2) training to assure continued employment, and (3) employment in a socially integrated environment (Sinnott-Oswald, Gliner, & Spencer, 1991). Under this plan people with mental retardation work in regular jobs but continue to be helped by coaches as they work. They may hold such jobs as food service workers, janitors, research laboratory assistants, developers of medical images in hospital darkrooms, and supply clerks.

A job has the same meaning to a person with mental retardation as it has to anyone else. It signifies independence, improves one's self-worth, provides interpersonal and social outlets, and generates money for spending. Employment also decreases support services and treatment costs and allows people with mental retardation to become tax-paying citizens.

The idea of people with mental retardation working in competitive industry is relatively new. Despite the fact that federal law prohibits discrimination in hiring and vocational training, everyone admits that it exists (Kessler, 1988). One special problem for people with mental retardation is that leaving one job and landing another is much harder. The goal for the overwhelming majority is independence, and that goal is possible but elusive.

Social and Vocational Skills

Everyone in the world of work requires two sets of interacting skills. First, they need job-related skills. For a person with mental retardation, it may mean the correct way to wash pots, make change, cook, sort, or whatever is necessary to perform the work. Second, they need adequate social and communication skills. Every worker must get to work on time, learn to deal with the public and co-workers, deal with job deadlines, and accept criticism and correction. People with mental retardation may experience more difficulty in gaining such personal skills. No matter how competent the worker is in work-related skills, if the worker cannot handle a customer's complaint and get along with a boss, that person will not succeed. In fact, one of the main reasons why people with mental retardation lose their jobs is interpersonal problems in relating to co-workers and supervisors (Herbert & Ishikawa, 1991). In one study, 42 percent of workers with mental retardation who lost their jobs did so because of problems in social skills including an inability to react appropriately to varying situations (Ford, Dineen, & Hall, 1984). Workers with good work records have better social judgment. Such skills cannot be learned in a vacuum, and so more on-the-job training using job coaches is being planned.

Different jobs require different levels of social skills. People must be matched to an appropriate atmosphere. An individual with mental retardation who has poor communication skills should be matched to an environment in which communication is not as important (Clark & Knowlton, 1987). On the other hand, the importance of positive attitudes on the part of the community and supportive services should not be minimized.

Success in the World of Work

Can people with mental retardation work in private industry either in supported or competitive employment? The answer is a definite yes. A chain of pizza restaurants hired over a thousand workers with disabilities, 73 percent of whom had mental retardation. These workers stayed four to five times longer than other employees, resulting in a substantial savings in recruitment and training costs. Federal law allows companies to pay less than the minimum wage in such cases because people in these programs may not be able to work as fast as the nondisabled workers. In this program, an employee who can work at 75 percent of the productivity of a nondisabled worker earns minimum wage. Some advocates for people with mental retardation argue that paying these workers less is exploitation and that their lack of speed is compensated for by their dependability. Others disagree claiming that often more than one worker will be needed for a particular job due to lack of speed, that it is an incentive for hiring people who employers have little experience hiring, and that when they prove themselves a raise often occurs.

A number of companies have found that people with mental retardation can work in competitive employment. When McDonald's restaurant trained people with mental retardation to work in their restaurants they found the turnover rate was about 40 percent for the workers with mental retardation, compared with 175 percent for other employees (Brickey & Campbell, 1981).

Attitudes of business executives toward hiring people with mental retardation are generally positive. Large firms are usually more positive than smaller companies. The results of a questionnaire sent to *Fortune* 500 executives showed that these employers saw the advantages for the individual who has a disability, and the lack of disadvantages for others in the work setting. The predictors of positive attitude were hiring people with disabilities in the past three years, previous employment experience with persons with disabilities, and positive evaluation of the experience. Having a disability or contact with disabilities in a family context did not predict more favorable attitudes. Therefore, positive contact at work itself determines attitudes toward employing people with mental retardation.

Sheltered Workshops

Not every individual with mental retardation can succeed in the competitive world. Sheltered work programs provide long-term support in a controlled and protected work environment and offer work experiences for those who cannot work in competitive environments.

Sheltered workshops offer an environment that is noncompetitive and friendly (Rusalem & Malikin, 1976). The individual receives specific instructions and is closely supervised. The jobs may include sorting and packaging. For example, one workshop might require workers to take one item from three or four piles and place them in a bag, which is then brought to another worker who seals it. Such labor gives workers a sense of satisfaction and feelings of productivity, along with a few extra dollars for enjoyment. However, some parents report that their adolescents are bored on such jobs (Hirst, 1983).

The sheltered workshop model is often criticized. With the advent of supported employment, there is less need for these services. Productivity is low and the workers make very little money. The tasks are not challenging, and the workplace is segregated with little movement to the next level.

Although these claims contain some truth, the fact cannot be ignored that some people will not be able to work in a more competitive environment and will require the constant support available in these workshops.

Living in the Community

Some people with mental retardation live relatively independent lives. Others live with their parents or other relatives. Living at home has some advantages; the person usually receives love and care, protection, and understanding (Seltzer et al., 1991).

The disadvantages should not be overlooked, though. The individual with mental retardation is not independent and may have fewer interpersonal relationships, and aging parents or siblings with responsibilities of their own may have difficulty continuing the care.

Apartment Living

Some individuals with mental retardation live in apartments in which the degree of supervision and support depends upon personal needs. Some routinely receive help in money management, household, and other support services, while others receive support only in times of crises.

Community Residences

Community residences are very popular. Most group homes have fifteen or fewer residents and an in-house staff. Some offer services such as a nurse on duty, while others do not. Some of these community residences house only people with mental retardation while others provide housing for people with other disabilities as well. Usually, supervisory personnel are present all the time. The houses vary in size, location, and staffing patterns.

The 1980s saw a great expansion in community living alternatives. Those who enter these residences are often specially chosen for their ability to deal with the stresses and strains of group living. Even when placed in residential situations within a community, they are often not integrated into the community and remain separate (Crapps, Langone, & Swaim, 1985). Studies most often find much more personal growth in community living when compared to institutional living (Hickson, Blackson, & Reis, 1995; Conroy & Bradley, 1985).

What skills are required to live in the community successfully? Richard Dever (1989) surveyed a number of experts in the field of mental retardation and formulated the taxonomy of community living skills (see Figure 4.2). The three sides of the triangle include those skills that must be exhibited in community settings. In the center are skills that people must learn in order to care for themselves, and finally travel connects the people with the community. The taxonomy for each domain is found in Table 4.5.

Many communities oppose the opening of community residences. They argue that housing prices will decline, that traffic will increase, that some areas are already saturated. Although evidence does not show that housing prices are adversely affected, community opposition remains. Efforts to educate the community usually end up increasing community opposition, and so many residences adopt a low profile, do not announce their entrance, and simply begin operations without much fanfare (Seltzer, 1984).

FIGURE 4.2   Organization of the Taxonomy

Source: *Community Living Skills: A Taxonomy* by R.B. Dever, copyright © 1988 by the American Association on Mental Retardation. Reprinted by permission.

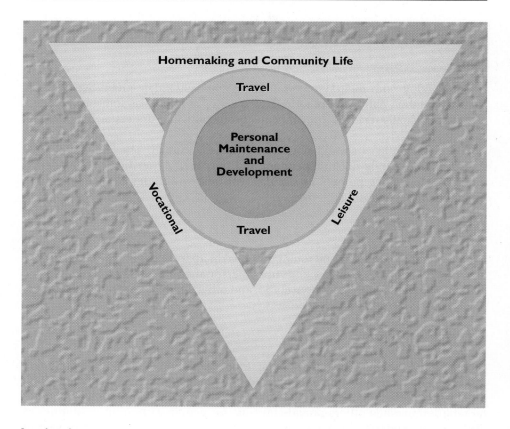

Institutions

Fewer people with mental retardation live in institutions today than years ago. The regimen of an institution is restrictive, allowing for fewer opportunities for personal growth. Some institutions today have attempted to create a more family-like, dormitory-type atmosphere with special facilities and private or semi-private bedrooms.

About 94,000 people with mental retardation currently reside in such state institutions. A high percentage of severe behavior disorders and psychiatric impairments are found among these patients. Psychiatric illness is more common among people with mental retardation than among the general population (Bodfish, 1992).

Sometimes people are so strongly opposed to institutionalization that they want everyone to live in a community residence. However, a need for institutionalization may continue for those who have major psychiatric problems in addition to mental retardation.

The Future

Certain trends described in this chapter are likely to continue into the future. Currently, a powerful movement towards normalization and integration both

TABLE 4.5   **List of Major Goals**

DOMAIN P
PERSONAL MAINTENANCE AND DEVELOPMENT

1. The learner will follow routine body maintenance procedures.
   a. Maintain personal cleanliness
   b. Groom self
   c. Dress appropriately
   d. Follow appropriate sleep patterns
   e. Maintain nutrition
   f. Exercise regularly
   g. Maintain substance control
2. The learner will treat illnesses.
   a. Use first aid and illness treatment procedures
   b. Obtain medical advice when necessary
   c. Follow required medication schedules

3. The learner will establish and maintain personal relationships.
   a. Interact appropriately with family
   b. Make friends
   c. Interact appropriately with friends
   d. Cope with inappropriate conduct of family and friends
   e. Respond to sexual needs
   f. Obtain assistance in maintaining personal relationships
4. The learner will handle personal "glitches"
   a. Cope with changes in daily schedule
   b. Cope with equipment breakdowns and material depletions

DOMAIN H
HOMEMAKING AND COMMUNITY LIFE

1. The learner will obtain living quarters.
   a. Find appropriate living quarters
   b. Rent/buy living quarters
   c. Set up living quarters
2. The learner will follow community routines.
   a. Keep living quarters neat and clean
   b. Keep fabrics neat and clean
   c. Maintain interior living quarters
   d. Maintain exterior of living quarters
   e. Respond to seasonal changes
   f. Follow home safety procedures
   g. Follow accident/emergency procedures
   h. Maintain foodstock
   i. Prepare and serve meals
   j. Budget money appropriately
   k. Pay bills

3. The learner will coexist in a neighborhood and community.
   a. Interact appropriately with community members
   b. Cope with inappropriate conduct of others
   c. Observe requirements of the law
   d. Carry out civic duties
4. The learner will handle "glitches" in the home.
   a. Cope with equipment breakdowns
   b. Cope with depletions of household supplies
   c. Cope with unexpected depletions of funds
   d. Cope with disruptions in routine
   e. Cope with sudden changes in the weather

DOMAIN V
VOCATIONAL

1. The learner will obtain work.
   a. Seek employment
   b. Accept employment
   c. Use unemployment services
2. The learner will perform the work routine.
   a. Perform the job routine

   b. Follow work-related daily schedule
   c. Maintain work station
   d. Follow employer rules and regulations
   e. Use facilities appropriately
   f. Follow job safety procedures
   g. Follow accident and emergency procedures

Continued on next page

TABLE 4.5   *Continued*

DOMAIN V
VOCATIONAL

3. The learner will coexist with others on the job.
   a. Interact appropriately with others on the job
   b. Cope with inappropriate conduct of others on the job

4. The learner will handle "glitches" on the job.
   a. Cope with changes in work routine
   b. Cope with work problems
   c. Cope with supply depletions and equipment breakdowns.

DOMAIN L
LEISURE

1. The learner will develop leisure activities.
   a. Find new leisure activities
   b. Acquire skills for leisure activities

2. The learner will follow leisure activity routines.
   a. Perform leisure activities
   b. Maintain leisure equipment
   c. Follow leisure safety procedures
   d. Follow accident and emergency procedures

3. The learner will coexist with others during leisure.
   a. Interact appropriately with others in a leisure setting
   b. Respond to the inappropriate conduct of others

4. The learner will handle "glitches" during leisure.
   a. Cope with changes in leisure routine
   b. Cope with equipment breakdowns and material depletions

DOMAIN T
TRAVEL

1. The learner will travel routes in the community.
   a. Form mental maps of frequented buildings
   b. Form mental maps of the community

2. The learner will use conveyances.
   a. Follow usage procedures
   b. Make decisions preparatory to travel
   c. Follow travel safety procedures
   d. Follow accident and emergency procedures

3. The learner will coexist with others while traveling.
   a. Interact appropriately with others while traveling
   b. Respond to the inappropriate conduct of others while traveling

4. The learner will handle "glitches"
   a. Cope with changes in travel schedule
   b. Cope with equipment breakdowns
   c. Cope with being lost

Source: *Community Living Skills: A Taxonomy*, by R.B. Dever, copyright © 1988 by the American Association on Mental Retardation. Reprinted by permission.

at work and in the community is taking place. New programs, such as supportive employment and the use of group homes, are radically changing the field. Although the goal of unsupervised independent living may not be realistic for all, living and working in the community with the help of a counselor and job coach is already a reality for many.

But with this integration comes difficulties and challenges. People with mental retardation will live and work in a more competitive, less supportive environment and must deal with increased social and vocational pressures. These problems, though, as difficult as they may be, are the result of success and of progress, which will continue as more people with mental retardation take their places in society.

 **Using Technology That Matches the Needs and Abilities of Children with Mental Retardation**

Teachers often note the importance of adapting teaching materials and strategies to the characteristics of their students. Because children do not all learn in the same way, different strategies succeed with different children.

Consider children with mental retardation who are required to learn various skills. Although each child has strengths and weaknesses, research has identified some learning characteristics shared by many children with mental retardation. Children with mental retardation learn at a slower pace than children who do not have mental retardation. They are frequently behind their classmates in acquiring academic skills (Okolo, 1993). They often show problems of attention, being distractible or not paying attention to the most important aspects of a problem or task. They take longer to process information and frequently show memory difficulties. Children with mental retardation often have not experienced success in learning and may expect to fail and therefore may resist new challenges. Motivation may be a significant problem.

The key question, then, is how to adapt materials and strategies to make them more consistent with the learning characteristics of these children. One area of interest in answering this question is computer-aided instruction, which can be specially designed to match the learning needs of children with mental retardation as well as other disabilities. For instance, computer programs can present material slowly in small steps and repeat material as needed. The individualization possible using the computer is a definite advantage. The computer can be programmed to go slower or faster and allow students to proceed at their own pace. Teachers often become impatient and have difficulty adapting to the lack of speed shown by children with mental retardation. The computer, on the other hand, gives children with mental retardation the time required to answer without showing impatience or disappointment. Frequently, children with mental retardation do not use strategies, such as rehearsal, which are needed to learn and remember material. The computer can be programmed to allow adequate repetition and practice or rehearsal.

Computer-aided instruction can be especially useful with children who have difficulty reading. Such innovations as talking computers using speech synthesizers allow oral presentation of material rather than using only written text (Iocono & Miller, 1989). The computer may also be used to teach reading skills. For example, students ranging in age from 9 to 22 years were given the task of learning to read specific words (Conners & Detterman, 1987). In the task, four words were presented on the screen. The students could have any of the words pronounced by moving a pointer in the figure of a person to the word. When they thought they knew the words they could move the pointer to the bottom of the screen and be tested by having the computer present the words in a different order. The computer orally presented a word, which the students then had to identify.

Word learning is dependent upon a number of skills, such as the ability to discriminate stimuli and hold material in memory. It is possible to isolate these necessary skills and individualize the programs to help students with difficulties in these skills succeed. For instance, students with poor stimulus discrimination abilities were given words that at first looked very different from each other, making discrimination easier. Students with better discrimination started with words that looked more alike. Students with memory problems were given increased drill. The computer program capitalized on the strengths and weaknesses of each student.

The motivational value of computer-aided instruction is well supported by research and computers can be used to improve student motivation (Iocono & Miller, 1989). The computer program can use a game format through which students receive immediate feedback for correct responses and corrective feedback for incorrect responses. After an incorrect response, the student may be channeled into a loop that explains the mistake and gives additional practice.

Computer-aided instruction often leads to a feeling of success and satisfaction as students begin to answer questions correctly and receive positive feedback. The creative use of graphics and game strategies overcome motivational problems. In fact, improved motivation is one of the most commonly found reactions to computer-aided instruction (Lewis, 1993). When students with mental retardation between the ages of 13 and 22 years were interviewed about their attitudes toward using computers in school settings, almost all students liked using computers because they were either fun or students felt suc-

cessful when using them (Gardner & Bates, 1991). Most students also believed they were learning more when they used computers. Their main complaint was that many programs did not tell students why their answers were incorrect, so some additional attention to corrective feedback is required. Most students, however, wanted to use the computer more often.

If motivation is better, one would expect and find that attention improves (Iocono & Miller, 1989). Studies show that children with attention problems often find the computer visually stimulating and stay on task for a longer amount of time (Turkel & Podell, 1984).

The use of computers to help educate children with mental retardation goes beyond drill and practice software. The computer can also be used to teach problem-solving skills (Turkel & Podell, 1984). Some programs also allow students to draw and explore using computer graphics programs.

Finally, computers allow students to improve their communication and writing skills. Children with mental retardation often have difficulty with handwriting and their grammar and spelling may be poor. Using computerized simplified word-processing programs, these problems can be minimized.

Technology may be useful for mastering math as well. Children with mental retardation often have difficulties with automatization. For example, knowing basic addition and multiplication facts in such a way that they are readily available with little effort allows people to concentrate fully on the problem rather than the calculation. It takes much longer for children with mental retardation to master these tables. Computerized drill and practice may be successful because they can be individualized, repeated, and programmed to provide immediate reinforcement (Podell, Tournaki-Rein, & Lin, 1992). In addition, the use of electronic calculators can help children with mental retardation by making calculations less difficult and allowing the teacher to focus on the solving of practical daily problems. Junior high school students taught to solve math problems using calculators performed at a higher level than those who used pencil and paper strategies (Horton, Lovitt, & White, 1992). Students with mental retardation can be taught to use calculators to make purchases in stores, which allows them to pay more attention to other aspects of making purchases or shopping (Frederick-Dougan, Test, & Varn, 1991).

One additional area of interest is the use of interactive videodisc technology to help students learn social skills (Iocono & Miller, 1989). A videodisc with computer control can be used to present simulations to students in social and vocational areas. At the appropriate times, students may be asked what they should do in such situations. Discussions may take place or students may be asked to role play their responses. Improvements in social skill knowledge in such areas as problem solving and asking for help have been found (Browning et al., 1986).

Two points stand out in using technology to help children with mental retardation.

First, computers and other technological aids can be useful adjuncts to instruction. They should not usually be thought of as alternatives to traditional instruction. Second, technology is most useful when it is adapted to the learning characteristics of the students, i.e., through programs written specifically for children with mental retardation as well as other disabilities. Technology is most effective when it enhances the individual's learning strengths and compensates for any weaknesses.

At this point, the use of technology to help children learn is well established. What is now needed is a better understanding of which types of computer-aided instruction are best for teaching particular skills. For example, drill and practice software may be helpful in teaching vocabulary but simulations and other problem-solving software are required for teaching social skills. In the future, more programs will be specifically designed with the flexibility to match the learning characteristics of children with particular disabilities and will be of even greater assistance to the teacher in helping children learn.

S U M M A R Y

1. Mental retardation is characterized by significantly below-average intellectual functioning, existing concurrently with related limitations in adaptive skills. Mental retardation manifests before age 18.

2. The Stanford-Binet and Wechsler Intelligence Scale for Children are two individual intelligence tests often used to measure intelligence in children. To be considered to have mental retardation a child must score at least two standard deviations below the norm on an individualized intelligence test. Some authorities claim that the tests are culturally biased. Some have tried to develop culture-fair tests, while others factor socioeconomic status into the equation. The System of Multicultural Pluralistic Assessment, or SOMPA, makes allowances in intelligence scores by taking into consideration socioeconomic status. Strong evidence that intelligence can change has also been presented.

3. Adaptive behavior refers to the individual's social skills, communication, and daily living skills. The Vineland Social Maturity Scale and the Adaptive Behavior Scale are often used to measure adaptive behavior.

4. In an older system of classification, children with mental retardation were categorized as having mild, moderate, severe, and profound mental retardation, depending on their

intelligence scores. The newer classification system is based upon the types of support required: intermittent, limited, extensive, or pervasive. Diagnosis is a three-stage process. First the child's intellectual and adaptive functioning is measured, which determines whether the diagnosis of mental retardation is appropriate. In the second stage, the child is assessed on three additional dimensions: psychological/emotional, physical/health/etiology, and environmental considerations. Finally, the type and intensity of supports are noted.

5. The prevalence of mental retardation is estimated to be 1 to 3 percent of the population. The incidence is less than 1 percent below the age of five and then rises dramatically during the school years. The number of children with mental retardation has been decreasing steadily; more children are classified as having a learning disability who might previously have been considered to have had mental retardation. Also, greater care is taken in identifying minority group children. Changes in states' definitions of mental retardation have occurred as well.

6. Biological causes for mental retardation include prenatal difficulties, genetic and chromosomal disorders, certain infections, metabolic problems, and brain injuries. However, these physical causes explain relatively few cases. The cause of most cases of mental retardation is unknown. Psychosocial factors may also play a role in the causation of mental retardation.

7. Most children with mental retardation do not look any different from their peers without mental retardation. Children with mental retardation may show communication difficulties and academic problems. They may show poor social judgment and social skills. Short-term memory problems are common, as are slower processing speeds and difficulties monitoring their own progress.

8. Prevention of mental retardation involves reducing the possible medical causes of mental retardation as well as improving the level of intellectual stimulation in the home through parenting programs and preschool education.

9. Most children with mental retardation are educated in self-contained classes within the neighborhood school. They may be included for some nonacademic subjects. Only about 30 percent are educated in regular classrooms or regular classrooms with resource room help. The movement toward inclusion will greatly affect the number of children with mental retardation who are educated in regular classrooms. Research shows better academic progress for students educated in the regular classrooms, but the aims of regular and special classes may differ somewhat.

10. The curriculum used to educate a student with mental retardation depends upon the child's abilities and needs as reflected in the child's IEP. Children with mental retardation are often taught functional academics, the learning of academic skills that will be needed to live in the community and taught in the context of daily experience. Some instruction is community based.

11. People working with children with mental retardation must be careful not to treat those children as younger than they are. Motivation is also a key since many children with mental retardation have failed in the past. Often, skills are taught through task analysis in which the skill is broken down into its component tasks, and each is taught to the child.

12. Adolescents with mental retardation may have a greater difficulty fitting in to teenage society. They have a great need for sex education.

13. More attention must be given to the transition between schooling and the world of work. Studies show that people with mental retardation can do well in competitive employment. A relatively new concept of supported employment allows people with mental retardation to work in industrial and commercial establishments with the continuous aid of specially trained job coaches. Some people with mental retardation who

experience greater social and personal problems may work in sheltered workshops that offer a supportive and noncompetitive climate.

14. Some people with mental retardation live well on their own, and some live with their parents, while others live in apartments where they receive help with their money or interpersonal problems, depending upon their needs. Many live in special community residences with other people with mental retardation or other disabilities and are supervised by an in-house staff. Fewer people with mental retardation live in institutions today than in years past.

Learning Disabilities

TRUE-FALSE STATEMENTS

See below for the correct answers.

1. A student must show a significant discrepancy between ability and performance in order to be diagnosed as having a learning disability.
2. More children receiving special education services are diagnosed as having learning disabilities than any other type of disorder.
3. The percentage of children considered to have a learning disability has remained stable for the past twenty years.
4. The majority of children with learning disabilities show hyperactivity.
5. Children with attention-deficit hyperactivity/ disorder (ADHD) treated with stimulants become more attentive, less distractible, and less hyperactive.

6. Hyperactivity can be reduced in most children through the use of a diet that eliminates food additives, such as artificial colorings and flavorings.
7. Most children with learning disabilities have excellent social skills which allow them to become popular with their classmates despite their poor academic records.
8. Most children with learning disabilities show definite lesions in the brain leading to the diagnosis of brain injury.
9. More than three-quarters of all students with learning disabilities are educated in regular classrooms for at least part of the day.
10. The school attendance of adolescents with learning disabilities is usually much better than the attendance of students without learning disabilities.
11. Adults with learning disabilities claim that their problems have faded and deny that they have any lasting effects from having a learning disability.

Answers to True-False Statements
1. True.
2. True.
3. False. See page 168.
4. False. See page 170.
5. True.
6. False. See page 171.
7. False. See page 174.
8. False. See page 176.
9. True.
10. False. See page 201.
11. False. See page 203.

Questions, Questions, Questions

How is it that she could read all these words yesterday, and can't get a single one correct today?

Can't he see the difference between *b* and *d* or *saw* and *was*?

If she can talk about so many complicated things, why can't she add 24 and 36?

Why does he always seem to say the wrong thing at the wrong time?

She's so quiet and tries hard, but she can't seem to remember anything.

Why won't he keep still for a few minutes so that he can learn something?

Consider how you would feel if any of these statements described your child. Perhaps your third grader has had a difficult time learning to read, despite having average intelligence. The child is frustrated, and the lack of progress has affected the child's social relationships and self-concept. After much testing, you are told that your child has a learning disability. What questions would enter your mind? What is a learning disability? What causes it? How is it remedied?

More children receive special education services for learning disabilities than for any other classification.

What Is a Learning Disability?

The definition of a learning disability is long and involved and, like everything else in this field, it is a matter of dispute. The federal government defines a learning disability as

a disorder in one or more of the basic psychological processes involved in understanding or in using language, spoken or written, which may manifest itself in an imperfect ability to listen, think, speak, read, write, spell or to do mathematical calculations. The term includes such conditions as perceptual handicaps, brain injury, minimal brain dysfunction, dyslexia, and developmental aphasia. The term does not include children who have learning problems which are primarily the result of visual, hearing, or motor handicaps, or mental retardation, or emotional disturbance, or of environmental, cultural, or economic disadvantage (*Federal Register*, December 29, 1977, p. 65083).

When diagnosing a learning disability, three factors stand out: (1) there are significant academic difficulties; (2) there is a discrepancy between ability and performance; and (3) the problems are not the result of the exclusions previously noted (mental retardation, emotional disturbance, etc.).

Many aspects of this definition have been criticized. The use of the term *basic psychological processes* is vague. In addition, the definition specifically excludes children with other disabilities, as long as the learning problem is believed to emanate from these. It is difficult to determine whether a child's visual impairment is the primary cause of a learning problem. Even the use of the term *children* is a problem, since the definition is seen as excluding adolescents and adults (Adelman & Taylor, 1993). Still another controversy arises from the discrepancy criterion (Stanovich, 1994). How much of a discrepancy is necessary to be diagnosed as having a learning disability? Finally, a vexing issue is whether every student with a large discrepancy between ability and performance, and not covered by the exclusions, can be considered to have a learning disability? A bright student may do poorly for many reasons, such as lack of motivation, which are not covered by the exclusions.

After a great deal of study, the National Joint Committee for Learning Disabilities (NJCLD) formulated a definition that deals with some of these problems. It defines learning disabilities as

> A general term that refers to a heterogeneous group of disorders manifested by significant difficulties in the acquisition and use of listening, speaking, reading, writing, reasoning, or mathematical abilities. These disorders are intrinsic to the individual, presumed to be due to central nervous system dysfunction, and may occur across the life span. Problems in self-regulatory behaviors, social perception, and social interactions may exist with learning disabilities, but do not by themselves constitute a learning disability. Although learning disabilities may occur concomitantly with other handicapping conditions (for example, sensory impairment, mental retardation, serious emotional disturbance), or with extrinsic influences such as cultural differences, insufficient or inappropriate instruction, they are not the result of those conditions or influences (1988, p. 1).

Absent from this definition is the reference to basic psychological processes. The definition does refer to the co-occurrence of learning disabilities with other disorders, and presents a life-span perspective by adding adolescents and adults. This definition has also been criticized because it still refers to the presumed cause as being central nervous system dysfunction. Today, some argue, there is less need to tie the definition to some central nervous system difficulty in functioning (Adelman & Taylor, 1993).

These are not the only definitions of learning disabilities. In a review of 11 proposed definitions, Hammill (1990) found similarities as well as differences among them and analyzed the trends. All the definitions consider the student with a learning disability an underachiever, and most definitions imply that learning disabilities can be present throughout life. While some definitions note central nervous system involvement, others do not state a cause. Some definitions refer to a deficit in psychological processes underlying school achievement, some do not refer to these processes. Some definitions specifically mention that listening and speaking problems can be considered learning disabilities, others do not. Some focus on academic problems or thinking and reasoning skills as prime concerns, while others do not. Some mention social skills and motor abilities, while others do not. Finally, some clearly allow learning disabilities to coexist with other disabilities, some exclude the coexistence, while others are silent on the matter. Hammill argues that the NJCLD definition is, at this point, the most promising.

THOUGHT QUESTION

1. Why has it been so difficult to formulate an adequate definition for learning disabilities?

THOUGHT QUESTION

2. In your opinion, do all children with average intelligence who are achieving poorly (and do not have any other disability) have a learning disability? If so, why? If not, why not?

SCENARIO

1 A third grader has just been diagnosed as having a learning disability. You have been asked to sit in on a conference in which the child's parents will be present. The family immigrated to the United States five years ago. Although they speak English well, they have had little experience with the school system and have never heard of a learning disability. The situation is not adversarial; both the mother and father understand that their child is having difficulties in school. How would you explain the nature of a learning disability to this family?

Prevalence

During the 1992–1993 school year, 2,369,385 students with the diagnosis of learning disabilities received special education services in the United States. A bit more than half of all children being served in special education programs have learning disabilities (51.1 percent), and about 5 percent of all children enrolled in schools are considered to have learning disabilities (U.S. Department of Education, 1993; 1994). The increase in the number of students diagnosed as having a learning disability has been enormous. In 1976–1977, 796,000 students were considered as having a learning disability which comprised 21.6 percent of the students receiving special education services. This was 1.8 percent of all students enrolled in the schools. The greatest increase, approximately 14 percent per year, occurred between 1977 and 1983. Since the 1983–1984 school year, the increase has been about 2.5 percent per year (Frankenberger & Fronzaglio, 1991). The increase has been uneven, with some states showing as much as an 863 percent increase and others showing an increase of about 32 percent. Since the passage of PL 94-142, there has been a 152 percent increase nationally in the number of children identified as having learning disabilities.

Why this tremendous increase? When asked that question, state directors of special education identified five reasons for the growing number of students considered as having a learning disability. They include

THOUGHT QUESTION

3. In your opinion, is the diagnosis of learning disabilities being overused? If it is, why is the diagnosis being made in so many cases?

1. Improvements in both the identification and assessment procedures.
2. Liberal eligibility standards used by some local districts.
3. Diminishing instructional options other than special education for children with learning problems.
4. Greater social acceptance and preference for being classified as having a learning disability as opposed to having mental retardation.
5. Judicially sponsored changes that altered the identification procedures for children thought to have mental retardation (Lovitt, 1989).

Many more males than females are identified as having a learning disability. The ratio ranges from 2:1 to 4:1 (Smith, 1991). The reasons for this disparity are not definitely known. Perhaps males are more biologically vulnerable to the neurological deficits assumed to be the cause. On the other hand, this may be partially a function of who is identified. Boys identified as having a learning disability differ from girls so diagnosed (Vogel, 1990). Females diagnosed as having learning disabilities have lower intelligence scores, have more severe academic deficits in reading and math, and are better in visual motor abilities, spelling, and writing than males diagnosed as having learning disabilities. Males with learning disabilities are much more likely to show attentional deficits and behavior problems and, as a result, boys may be referred for evaluation more quickly and more often. Perhaps boys with less severe impairments act out more, making them stand out. Perhaps girls with a milder degree of impairment react by withdrawing. As a result, only girls who have more serious impairments are recognized.

A number of studies have examined the ratio of minority group members diagnosed as having a learning disability, but these studies have contradicted each other. Some note a representative percentage of African-American, Hispanic, and Caucasian students diagnosed as having learning disabilities (Chinn & Hughes, 1987), while others have reported either an underrepresentation or an overrepresentation of students, especially in special classes (see McLeskey, Waldron, & Wornoff, 1990).

Characteristics of Children with Learning Disabilities

What types of behavior are demonstrated by children who have learning disabilities? It is easy to describe many characteristics that are found in this population, but not all of them will be exhibited by any one child. So, while reading descriptions of these characteristics keep in mind that a child with a learning disability may or may not exhibit a particular characteristic and still be considered to have a learning disability.

THOUGHT QUESTION

4. When you are told that a person has a learning disability, what characteristics do you ascribe to that person?

Academic Difficulties

The academic performance of children with learning disabilities is generally poor. After all, doing poorly in school, especially in the basic skills of reading and writing and, to a lesser extent, in mathematics, is the primary reason for being referred for assessment (Feagans, 1987). Generally, these children show considerable difficulty in acquiring these basic skills (Wicks-Nelson & Israel, 1991). They also make many more errors in learning the basic skills than children without learning disabilities (Houck & Billingsley, 1989). Achievement in some subjects may be average, but achievement in others is poor and well below what would be expected based on their intelligence scores and grade level (Erickson, 1992). This lack of achievement is found in secondary school as well as elementary school (Algozzine et al., 1988). In one large study, Gregory, Shanahan, and Walberg (1985) found that tenth graders with learning disabilities performed at a lower level in mathematics, science, social studies, vocabulary, reading, and writing when compared to their peers without learning disabilities. Children diagnosed as having learning disabilities are also more likely to have been retained in grade. In fact, a retention in grade often precedes being diagnosed as having a learning disability (McLeskey & Grizzle, 1992).

Cognitive Processing

In order to read, students must be able to pay attention, perceive letters and numbers accurately, process and use language, remember what has been taught, use effective learning strategies to solve problems, and monitor how they are doing. A deficit in any of these processes can affect children's learning. Studies show that children with learning disabilities have difficulties in these areas (Bender, 1995).

Attention and Hyperactivity Problems

A relationship exists between attentional and hyperactivity problems and learning disabilities, but figures vary widely on the percentage of children with learning disabilities who also show attentional problems (Stanford & Hynd, 1994). It is estimated that between 15 and 20 percent of children and adolescents with learning disabilities have **attention-deficit/hyperactivity disorder (ADHD)** (Silver, 1990). In other words, most children with learning disabilities will not be considered to have an attention or hyperactivity problem. It is estimated that between 3 and 5 percent of all children have ADHD (Fowler, 1991). Other studies find a somewhat lower incidence of ADHD (Viadero, 1993).

Children with ADHD show inattentiveness, impulsivity, and in many cases, hyperactivity (Fowler, 1991). ADHD is not the same as a learning disability, although both may lead to problems in learning.

Originally, psychologists focused on the hyperactivity problems of these children. Today, the attentional problems and impulsivity as well as the hyperactivity are emphasized. The *Diagnostic and Statistical Manual of Mental Disorders* (DSM-IV), published by the American Psychiatric Association, which defines and describes disorders, recognizes three specific types of ADHD: one in which inattention predominates, another in which hyperactivity-impulsivity is most noticeable, and a third type in which all three major symptoms exist (American Psychiatric Association, 1994).

Attention-deficit/hyperactivity disorder (ADHD):
A diagnostic classification in the DSM-IV system involving a number of symptoms including inattention, impulsivity, and hyperactivity.

Many children diagnosed as having attention-deficit/hyperactivity disorder are given Ritalin to reduce the symptoms of the disorder. Placing any child on a medication for a long period of time, though, is a controversial practice.

Children with ADHD are impulsive, easily distracted, inattentive, and show a great deal of inappropriate behavior (Barkley, 1990). These children have difficulty in school, and their relationships with their teachers are often strained. About 40 percent show conduct difficulties, including fighting, disobedience, and rule breaking (Weiss, 1990). They are considered aggressive and annoying, and are not well accepted by their peers. Their parents find them less compliant and less responsive to their questions, and parents report many more conduct problems than they do for their other children who do not have ADHD (Tarver-Behring, Barkley & Karlsson, 1985). As these children mature, between 30 and 50 percent carry some of the symptoms of the disorder into adulthood. They do not fidget as much, but they are likely to be impulsive and to have difficulty forming relationships.

Three basic approaches are used to treat ADHD. These children are often treated with stimulant medications, most commonly Ritalin, to reduce the symptoms of the disorder. Under such medication, the children become calmer and more attentive (Forness & Kavale, 1988), and the number of aversive and disruptive acts declines. Evidence indicates that parents and teachers interact more positively when the children show less disruptive and impulsive behavior (Barkley et al., 1984). Evidence of the medication's effects on academic performance is more equivocal due to methodological problems, but some studies report about 60 percent of children given medication show cognitive improvements and, therefore, as many as 40 percent may not (see Swanson et al., 1991). A clear answer, though, is not possible at the present time. Some, but not all, evidence indicates that their social status improves as the disruptive behavior decreases, but peer appraisals of these children still are not as positive as for children who do not have ADHD (Whalen et al., 1989).

The use of medication is widely criticized because the medicine treats only the symptoms, not the underlying cause, and may produce unpleasant side effects. In addition, although medication is effective in reducing the symptoms in the short run, it may not be effective in the long run unless other treatments are inaugurated, probably because no substitute behaviors to the aggression and antisocial behavior are being taught (Weiss, 1990). Others have criticized the overuse of drugs.

No one claims that the use of medication will improve intelligence or even school work, only that it reduces the symptoms. Therefore, the use of medication is not always the treatment of choice. The very idea of a child taking medication for a long period of time should be approached with caution. Some authorities claim that such treatment should be used only as a last resort, and then always in combination with another type of treatment.

One nondrug treatment is the Feingold diet, named after the physician who developed it. Feingold (1975) noted that hyperactivity was related to the consumption of food additives, such as preservatives and artificial colors and flavors. He claimed that if hyperactive children were put on a diet free of these compounds, a significant number would improve.

Some clinical support for the Feingold diet does exist (Burlton-Bennet & Robinson, 1987). Controlled experimental studies, however, have not supported its effectiveness (Barkley, 1990; Silver, 1987). A relatively small group of young children may show hyperactive responses to artificial food additives, but generally the negative effects do not seem as widespread as formerly claimed (Smith, 1991). The success rate with the diet is also lower than has been asserted by its supporters (Johnson, 1981). Though the diet may be effective for some children, it will not be the answer for the majority of children with ADHD.

The third approach to treating ADHD, which may be used in combination with medication, involves manipulating the environment and its reinforcers. For example, providing structure and solid routines and using positive reinforcers can be helpful (Walden & Thompson, 1981). Often, short reprimands given in a calm, firm, consistent manner with eye contact are effective in increasing on-task behavior (Abramowitz & O'Leary, 1991). More involved behavioral programs, such as token economies and home-school cooperation show promise. In some home-school programs, teachers complete a brief checklist that indicates whether the child has met specific behavioral goals for the day. The checklist is sent home, signed by the parent and returned to the school. The parents provide appropriate reinforcers at home that have been carefully designed for the child. If the child has not met the criteria for success, some privilege is forfeited. Although such programs may be effective, they are not easy to implement. The selection of consequences, both positive for meeting the standards and sometimes negative for failure to meet standards is critical to the success of the program and not always easy to find. A great deal of teacher time is needed to implement such a program, as well as some parent training. Most importantly, some parents will react too harshly or even abusively to a poor report (Abramowitz & O'Leary, 1991). More involved behavioral interventions require teacher training and perhaps the help of a school psychologist.

SCENARIO

2 Your child has been diagnosed as having attention-deficit hyperactivity disorder, which does not come as a surprise to you. The child is distractible, impulsive, and hyperactive, although at home the problem is hardly as acute as in school where the child cannot sit still. After a number of conferences, a suggestion has been made that your child be placed on the medication, Ritalin, in order to counter the effects of the ADHD. You have been told that it improves the situation by countering the symptoms, but have doubts about placing your child on medication. What would be your feelings about placing your child on the medication?

Perceptual Problems

Since reading problems are so common among children with learning disabilities, early researchers naturally emphasized the perceptual problems of this population (Lovitt, 1989). Individuals with learning disabilities sometimes show visual, auditory, tactual, movement, and coordination problems (Kaplan, 1991). For instance, they may have difficulty perceiving the letters, and discriminating a *p* from a *b*, or they may not perceive the position of the stimuli correctly, reversing letters or words, and reading *saw* for *was*. These problems are common in young children, but they persist in children with learning disabilities. Some children might have difficulty discriminating between spoken words that sound similarly (phonological problems). Others may have difficulty putting puzzles together, seeing and remembering forms in designs, and remembering the sequence and order of what they see (Lerner, 1988). Some children show poor auditory discrimination, auditory memory, auditory sequencing and auditory blending, the ability to blend single phonic elements into a complete word such as c-a-t to cat (Lerner, 1988).

Memory and Executive Functions

A good memory is certainly an aid to learning. Students must remember information in order to use it at a later time. Children also must use strategies to learn new material. Suppose Carmella must learn the state capitals. She might organize them on cards and rehearse them. Finally, Carmella needs to use some executive ability, exert some control of the entire process of learning. This executive function allows the student to monitor progress and know if a change in strategy is necessary. For example, Carmella might realize that just rehearsing these capitals is not working and switch to categorizing these capitals by region. Carmella would also have to understand what she knows and what she does not know. This knowledge of one's own memory processes is known as **metamemory**, and knowledge of all cognitive processes **metacognition**.

Metamemory:
People's knowledge of their own memory processes.

Children with learning disabilities often show memory problems. Children with learning disabilities have difficulties both in short-term memory and working memory. They have difficulties holding things in memory for a brief time (short-term memory) as well as holding something in memory while carrying out some other operation (working memory) (Swanson, 1994). Children with learning disabilities have difficulty remembering what things looked like (visual memory) or sounded like (auditory memory) (Lerner, 1988). If one cannot remember explanations, words, or directions, learning becomes inefficient and difficult.

Metacognition:
The conscious monitoring and regulation of the way people approach and solve a problem or challenge.

The better one knows something, the more automatic it becomes, and the fewer cognitive resources it takes. Children with learning disabilities often show problems in automatization. In successful reading, rapid recognition of words is needed. Children with learning disabilities have difficulty quickly processing material.

Children with learning disabilities also have difficulty in the areas of metacognition and metamemory. They do not monitor what they are doing well. They do not use efficient learning strategies and do not change these strategies when they should (Lerner, 1988). Children who are good readers and learners often ask themselves questions and actively organize their experience. Children with learning disabilities do not seem to know how to control and direct their own thinking. They do not use efficient strategies such as self-questioning, rehearsal, and review, nor do they effectively organize material and monitor their strategy use (Lerner, 1988; Smith, 1991).

Linguistic Weaknesses

Many children with learning disabilities have difficulties in listening, comprehension, and speech. Gibbs and Cooper (1989) analyzed communication disorders in

Many, but not all, children with learning disabilities experience social difficulties.

242 children between eight and twelve years of age with learning disabilities. Language impairments were found in 90.5 percent, articulation problems in 23.5 percent, voice disorders in 12 percent, and 1.2 percent showed fluency disorders. Hearing impairments were found in about 20 percent of the children. Only 6 percent of these children were receiving the services of a speech-language pathologist. Other studies confirm that as many as 90 percent of children with learning disabilities show developmental language disorders. These involve problems in expression, vocabulary, and sentence structure. Many of these children show difficulties in phonological awareness, that is, they have difficulty understanding the sounds of the letters (Hatcher, Hulme, & Ellis, 1994). Some of these children may also show comprehension problems.

This list of cognitive and academic difficulties is impressive, but one must keep in mind that children diagnosed as having a learning disability will have strengths and weaknesses. They will also differ greatly from each other in their learning characteristics. For example, one child may have considerably more difficulty with memory than another child.

Social Relationships

Social interactions are often difficult for children with learning disabilities (Tur-Kaspa & Bryan, 1995). They are more likely than children without learning disabilities to be rejected or ignored by peers and to have difficulties making and keeping friendships (McIntosh, Vaughn, & Zaragoza, 1991; Gresham & Elliott, 1989). The experience of rejection and being ignored may be the result of different behavior patterns shown by these children (Stone & La Greca, 1990). Children who are rejected are more likely to show aggressive and disruptive behaviors, while children who are neglected are more likely to be withdrawn and socially anxious. These problems begin as early as kindergarten as measured by children's statements, but teachers do not perceive students with learning disabilities as deficient in social skills that early (Vaughn et al., 1990). Children with learning disabilities have a poorer social status and are generally not as popular in their classes (Stone & La Greca, 1990).

They also show social skills deficits (Haager & Vaughn, 1995). They are more likely to show poor social problem solving, have difficulty interpreting social cues, show a poor ability to adjust their communication to what is being said, and have difficulty responding to the thoughts and feelings of others (Vaughn et al., 1993).

The research on social deficits is so strong that the U.S. Interagency Commission on Learning Disabilities (ICLD) recommended that social skills deficit should be added to the definition of learning disabilities (Conte & Andrews, 1993). This inclusion will probably not occur, because it would require a change in the federal law, cause assessment problems, and might increase the number of children eligible for services (Hammill, 1990).

Why do children with learning disabilities experience such social problems? First, some show more maladaptive and inappropriate behavior than their peers without disabilities (Toro et al., 1990). They are more easily frustrated, and show more overall classroom behavior problems, including acting-out behaviors. They are also less task oriented, spending less time on task (Bender & Smith, 1990). Perhaps these behaviors lead to rejection. Second, a relationship exists between lan-

THOUGHT QUESTION

5. *In your opinion, should social skills deficits be added to the formal definition of learning disabilities? If so, why? If not, why not?*

guage related problems (shown by many children with learning disabilities) and lack of social skills. Perhaps some children are rejected because of their inability to use language properly. They may not stay on the topic, may miss the point of jokes, or have difficulty appreciating the point of view of the listener (Conte & Andrews, 1993). A third possibility is that children with learning disabilities have a disorder in social perception that hinders their ability to understand the social environment. Simply stated, they do not read other people in social situations well. For example, Holder and Kirkpatrick (1991) suggest that a smirk and a smile may be similar in appearance, but being able to distinguish between the two is essential to social interaction. When children were shown pictures of various people exhibiting a number of emotions, such as fear, sadness, surprise, anger, happiness, and disgust, 8–15-year-old children diagnosed as having learning disabilities were much less accurate in their interpretation of facial expressions (Axelrod, 1982). Underlying the communication and perceptual problems may be neurological differences between children with and without learning disabilities (see Spafford & Grosser, 1993).

A fourth possibility is that the rejection may stem from their poor achievement in school. Students who do not achieve, whether or not they have a learning disability, are frequently less popular. Vaughn and colleagues (1990; 1993) compared children diagnosed as having a learning disability to groups of average/high-achieving children and children who were poor achievers but not considered to have a learning disability. Children were followed for four years, from kindergarten through third grade. Students with learning disabilities did not differ significantly from their low-achieving peers, while the average/high-achieving group showed better social skills. In addition, both the group of children with learning disabilities and the low achievers without learning disabilities showed more inappropriate and problem behavior in class than the average/high-achieving students, but did not differ much from each other.

Other studies have also failed to find significant differences in behavior patterns and classroom behaviors when comparing groups of slow learners, groups of students with mild mental retardation, or children with other developmental disabilities (Vaughn et al., 1992; Oakland, Shermis, & Coleman, 1990). This comparison suggests that the pattern of social and behavioral problems shown by young children with learning disabilities may be part of a general pattern seen among low-achieving children, whether or not they are considered as having a learning disability.

Not all children with a learning disability experience extensive social problems (Stone & La Greca, 1990). When the social status of fourth, fifth, and sixth grade students was studied, 54 percent of the children with learning disabilities could be placed into one of the low-status categories as measured by peer opinions (28 percent were rejected and 26 percent were neglected). But 17 percent of the students fell into the popular or average group. About one-third could not be classified. The findings were supported by other studies (see Gresham & Elliott, 1989). Some students with learning disabilities have good friends, show an ability to cope with conflict, and are cooperative (Smith, 1991). Children with learning disabilities comprise a heterogeneous group and not every child shows serious problems. Still, any comprehensive program to help children with learning disabilities should address these social skills problems.

SCENARIO

3 Kevin is a fourth grader with a severe learning disability. His reading is poor and his progress slow. He is usually ignored by the rest of the class, although he has a few friends in the class. His social skills appear reasonably good. He is somewhat shy, but no more than a few other children in his class without disabilities. Your problem is that when asked to read or answer a question, the class becomes somewhat unpleasant, and an undercurrent of whispers making fun of Kevin persist. Sometimes, the word *dummy* is heard. As the teacher you are upset at this. Not only does it show a lack of tolerance but it also upsets Kevin, who is making any excuse not to have to read or answer questions out loud. What would you do in this case to change the behavior of the class?

What Causes a Learning Disability?

The long-standing assumption has been that some type of brain dysfunction underlies a learning disability, and many modern definitions mention central nervous system dysfunction. Other factors, though, may also be involved.

Neurological Explanations

Most people have their language functions based in their left cerebral hemisphere. Almost all right-handed people and more than half of left-handed people show such asymmetry. One possible cause of learning disabilities is the lack of hemispheric asymmetry. In other words, if the typical asymmetry does not develop, children are at risk for developing a learning disability (Lovitt, 1989). Indeed, some studies of people with learning disabilities find no obvious defects and lesions in the brain but sometimes find a lack of asymmetry (Hynd, Marshall, & Gonzalez, 1991). The evidence for this lack of asymmetry is greatest for reading disorders, but since learning disabilities is such a heterogeneous group of disorders it may not be true for all types of learning disabilities (Hynd et al., 1991).

Perhaps the most challenging neurological theory has been advanced by Galaburda and colleagues (1989; Galaburda et al., 1978; 1985). When conducting postmortem examinations on the brains of people with learning disabilities, microscopic changes consisting of abnormal collections of cells in the area of the left hemisphere implicated in language were found. These changes were attributed to difficulties arising during the second trimester of prenatal development. Researchers also found alterations in the pattern of asymmetry affecting language areas. These researchers, then, find important abnormalities in the language areas of the brain that might arise during the prenatal period. When findings of neurological studies are considered as a whole, a small but increasing number of studies point to some neurological abnormalities as a cause of learning disabilities (Hynd & Semrud-Clikeman, 1989).

Although some evidence for neurological differences exist, a single pattern does not for many reasons. First, a number of different neurological abnormalities may underlie the disorder, and a number of mechanisms of expression exist (see Rosenberger, 1992). This explanation would be expected from the research showing that people with learning disabilities comprise a heterogeneous population with some children showing some characteristics and others showing different patterns of behavior, which would lead to the suggestion of the existence of various subtypes (see Flynn et al., 1992). The approach using subtypes is promising (Arfa, Fitzhugh-Bell & Black, 1989; Shafrir & Siegel, 1994). On the basis of comprehensive neuropsychological assessment, different clusters of difficulties can be identified. Unfortunately, researchers do not agree on the nature of such subtypes of clusters at the present time.

Some studies have examined children who have brain damage, and many of these children do show learning disorders. However, these children may be demonstrating only one mechanism by which a brain dysfunction may affect learning. The vast majority of children with learning disabilities do not have such brain injuries. In fact, the neurological differences found in some children with learning disabilities are also found in some children who are not considered to have a learning disability.

Second, neurological dysfunction may only increase the child's vulnerability, and other environmental factors interact with it to cause the learning disability. Third, the state of our neurological knowledge may not yet be capable of finding such problems. Just because researchers have not been able to pinpoint the exact neural differences does not mean they do not exist. This possibility leads to an obvious fourth explanation. Even though some learning disabilities may be caused by neurological problems, other cases may be caused by something else, perhaps an environmental problem, a controversial view that will be discussed shortly.

What might cause such neurological differences? Evidence for genetic involvement exists (Segal, 1990; Decker & DeVries, 1980), with some authorities arguing that the genetic abnormality is found on chromosome 15 (Herbert, 1993). However, the mechanism for transmission is still a question (Wenar, 1994). Also, the strength of genetic influence is not known at the present time (Wicks-Nelson & Israel, 1991).

Other biological factors that may be implicated as possible causes of learning disabilities include deficiencies in the mother's diet, exposure to diseases, exposure to radiation, use of certain drugs, and cigarette smoking during pregnancy. A relationship has been demonstrated between prematurity and many disabilities, including learning disabilities. Many agents may lead to central nervous system problems, including anoxia at birth, accidents, and lead poisoning (Adelman & Taylor, 1993).

Another theory, although neurological, does not posit a dysfunction but rather a maturational or developmental lag. Perhaps children with learning disabilities are not ready for the school tasks they are exposed to and do not profit from the instruction that is appropriate for other children. In such a case, the mismatch is the problem rather than the lag. The assumption is made that children are ready for this instruction, but a child who is not able to profit from the school experience will fall further behind as the teacher moves from one lesson to another. The child then misses the opportunity to develop vital academic skills (Adelman & Taylor, 1993).

Social Factors

A number of social factors may be involved in the development of learning disabilities. Socioeconomic status, cultural factors, family interactions, parental attitudes toward learning, and motivation may each affect learning ability (Wicks-Nelson & Israel, 1991). Poor teaching and an inappropriate curricula may also be tied to it. These factors are often not stressed, but if some neurological difference increases vulnerability, then environmental factors may be significant and act as triggers.

The most controversial challenge to the idea that a learning disability is caused by neurological dysfunction comes from Gerald Coles (1987; 1989a and b). Coles claims that the neurological evidence has been overinterpreted, and differences that are found are not dysfunctions. Coles admits that neurological dysfunctions cause a relatively small number of learning disabilities. However, Coles argues that the cause of most cases are not to be found in neurological differences.

Coles suggests that the important reasons for school failure should be viewed in broad social terms. Learning disabilities can be explained by numerous complex activities and interactions which create, maintain, or even prevent learning problems. The school's structure, attitudes, and teacher-child relationships may cause the problems. According to the basic ideas he develops in his interactivity theory, systematic economic, social, and cultural conditions are the main influences contributing to learning failure. Coles attempts to broaden causation to include curricula difficulties, poor administrator and teacher expectations, poor school climates, poor organization, community values, and teacher factors. Some argue that such a reorientation from the child to the school is necessary if progress towards reducing learning problems is to occur (Bartoli, 1989; Sigmon, 1989). They reason that if the problem is seen as emanating from within the child and not the school and society, there will be no impetus for change.

Such a theory as advanced by Coles was certain to generate opposition and controversy. Some have noted that it is more an explanation for general poor reading and achievement than for the subset of such learners diagnosed as having learning disabilities (Stanovich, 1989). Coles also does not explain how a child might have problems with reading, but still have an average intelligence score (Stavonich, 1989). Why would not all the cognitive functions be poor? Rourke (1989) argues that looking at learning disabilities in social and political terms ignores the fact that other societies with different social systems, many of which have firmer social welfare traditions than our own, have students with learning disabilities, and often these children are educated in special schools. Even in the United States, many middle-class and privileged children have learning disabilities. Also difficult to explain is why so many children who experience the same political, social, and economic problems and receive the same instruction learn while this subset of children experiences so much difficulty.

The most controversial consideration is that poor teaching may contribute to the development and maintenance of learning disabilities. This factor may involve an inappropriate match between the curriculum and the children's abilities, teacher difficulties in dealing with children who show differences in cognitive functioning, and motivational difficulties (Smith, 1991). Others point to the problems of poverty, claiming that impoverished students are at risk for academic failure and language problems.

There are problems with the poor teaching and environmental explanations of learning disabilities. First, separating students with learning disabilities from other poorly achieving students continues to prove difficult. Many of the poor teaching explanations do not differentiate between the effect of poor teaching practices on those who have learning disabilities and those who are poor achievers but do not have a learning disability. Second, whereas the biological argument is criticized for assuming the problem lies within the child, the environmental argument refuses to take into consideration within-child differences, emphasizing that everything is caused by external agents. Finally, it does not answer the question of why so many children exposed to the same teaching practices do learn and succeed.

At this point in time, the definitive cause of learning disabilities is not known. Perhaps some vulnerability exists in children with learning disabilities, and when taught in the usual fashion, they show these learning problems. Perhaps many different factors cause learning disabilities; and, perhaps, different types of learning disabilities are caused by different mechanisms.

SCENARIO

4 You are attending a lecture in which the speaker notes the astounding increase in the number of students with learning disabilities in the past 30 years. She argues that the term is being used indiscriminately and that it is merely a label used to transfer the blame for lack of learning caused by poor teaching, poor school administration, and a poor curriculum. She continues to argue that if a child cannot learn from a particular teacher, the child is labeled "learning disabled," which serves to absolve the school system from responsibility. Since you are known as a person with an interest in the area of learning disabilities, the group asks to hear your response. How would you respond?

Evaluation and Assessment

The evaluation and assessment of children with learning disabilities is a great responsibility, especially considering the problems in definition and criteria (Adelman, 1989). Assessment, though, means more than seeking a diagnosis. It refers to the constant monitoring of the child's ongoing progress.

The identification of learning disabilities is based upon extensive testing, but there is a lack of uniformity in the tests selected. In addition, various states and localities may use different operational definitions for the disability, meaning that a child might qualify in one state and not another (McLeskey & Waldron, 1991). For

Children suspected of having a learning disability take a great many diagnostic tests.

example, the most common way to determine eligibility for learning disabilities is the use of the discrepancy criteria, that is a discrepancy between intelligence (potential) and academic achievement. The sole use of some discrepancy formula is criticized by the Council for Learning Disabilities because it focuses on a single aspect and creates a false sense of objectivity and precision (Council for Learning Disabilities, 1986). Finally, the question of how large the discrepancy must be to be considered as having a learning disability must be answered. The size of the discrepancy is often not found in state regulations but left to the community.

The assessment process collects and analyzes information to guide planning and implementation of special services to help the child with learning disabilities achieve. Lerner (1988) suggests that the entire evaluation and assessment process must answer the following questions:

1. *What are the student's present levels of educational performance?* This is discovered by collecting information from many sources, including norm-referenced, criterion-referenced, and curriculum-based measures.
2. *What additional information about the student can be gathered from reviewing the data collected by the team?* Evaluators need to go beyond norm-referenced tests and include information based upon observations of behavior and data concerning health and attendance, as well as other useful information gleaned from many sources.
3. *Does information point to a discrepancy between achievement and intellectual ability?* Although the discrepancy model has been harshly criticized, the overwhelming majority of states still use it (Mercer, King-Sears, & Mercer, 1990). In order to use a discrepancy measure, some measure of ability level must be found, usually through an intelligence test.

4. *Does the student have a learning disability?* The determination of whether a child has a learning disability depends upon the specific criteria of the state and school district.

5. *What annual goals, including short-term instructional objectives, should be set for the student?* These goals note the priorities for each subject area. They should be as specific as possible, such as being able to multiply two digits by one digit with a particular level of accuracy.

6. *What specific special education and related services are to be offered? Where will the services be offered?* This involves a decision concerning the nature of the services to be provided and the placement of the student.

7. *How will the student's progress be monitored and measured?* Continuous assessment of the student's progress is the key to educational progress. If progress is measured frequently, teachers and parents can determine if the child is making significant progress or if changes in the approach are needed.

8. *What teaching plan is appropriate for this student?* Developing a plan for teaching is necessary for each student, including a determination of what adaptations will be used. This plan must take into account the student's strengths and weaknesses, skills, age, interests, and attitudes.

The Use of Formal Testing

Many standardized tests are used to evaluate whether a child who shows academic problems has a learning disability. At the very least, an individualized test of intelligence and achievement tests are required. Other tests may also be given depending upon the psychologist's orientation, the student's difficulties, and the district's policies.

Intelligence Tests

A number of intelligence tests are used to test children for learning disabilities. The Stanford-Binet (fourth edition), Kaufman Assessment Battery for Children, and the System of Multicultural Pluralistic Assessment (SOMPA) may be used. The most popular, though, is the Wechsler Intelligence Scale for Children or WISC, now in a new edition called the WISC-III (Lyon, 1995). The WISC-III contains a number of subtests that can be divided into two categories—verbal and performance. The five verbal subtests are information, similarities, arithmetic, vocabulary, and comprehension. The five performance subtests are picture completion (pointing out what is missing in the picture), picture arrangement (arranging a group of pictures in sequential order), block design (copying a pattern with blocks), object assembly (putting together puzzle pieces), and coding (a test in which people are asked to translate one set of symbols into another). Three additional subtests, one verbal and two performance, are sometimes used: digit span (a test of immediate recall in which the test taker is asked to repeat random series of digits, sometimes in forward order and sometimes in reverse order), mazes, and symbol search. A composite or total intelligence score can also be obtained.

The WISC's various subtests offer useful diagnostic information, although IQ tests cannot be considered primarily diagnostic. Petti (1987; 1988) suggests that performance on each of the subtests of the WISC has a number of educational implications. For example, a teacher may assume that a student knows certain facts. However, if this student scores low on the WISC subtest of information, the teacher will now understand that the student lacks the knowledge base, and the teacher can respond accordingly. If a student does poorly on digit span, it might indicate a short-term memory problem, and the student may have difficulty in remembering what has just been heard and in following directions. A student who is weak in finding missing details in pictures may overlook arithmetic signs and punctuation marks. Therefore, at times, an individual intelligence test may point to specific strengths and weaknesses in addition to measuring intellectual ability.

Yet, we must be careful not to overgeneralize. No single pattern on intelligence tests is always found among students with learning disabilities. One such proposed pattern was great variability on the subtests, with performance scores much higher than verbal scores. However, Kavale and Forness (1984) evaluated more than 90 studies assessing the pattern of scores of students diagnosed as having a learning disability on the WISC and found that these students, as a group, do not show greater discrepancies between performance and verbal scores than students without learning disabilities. Kline and colleagues (1993) found that the variability of scores on the Kaufman Assessment Battery for Children and the fourth edition of the Stanford-Binet intelligence test was not useful as a diagnostic indicator for children. Children with learning disabilities do not show any unique patterns on subtests of intelligence tests.

Achievement Tests

A number of achievement tests may be administered to students in an attempt to measure how well a child reads or does math. These formal tests are norm-referenced and compare the student's scores to those of the norm group, which took the test at an earlier time. In order for a test to be useful, it must be valid—that is, measure what it is supposed to measure and yield reliable, consistent scores. The norms must also be based on an appropriate comparison group (e.g., children from similar socioeconomic, ethnic, and educational backgrounds) and the administration standardized.

Many norm-referenced tests are available. Some measure a wide range of areas, while others measure only a single area, such as reading. The Woodcock-Johnson Psycho-Educational Battery-Revised is a comprehensive test measuring many areas that can be useful in evaluation. It contains many different subtests, all or only some of which may be administered. Part One tests long-term memory, short-term memory, processing speed, auditory processing, visual processing, comprehension, knowledge, and fluid reasoning. Part Two tests achievement in reading, mathematics, written language, knowledge, and skills (Sweetland & Keyser, 1991). The Peabody Individual Achievement Test-Revised (PIAT-R) is another test battery that examines a number of areas such as general information, reading recognition, reading comprehension, mathematics, and spelling as well as written expression. It is especially useful as a starting point in the evaluation, indicating which areas need further assessment (Venn, 1994). The Kaufman Test of Educational Achievement (K-TEA) is both a screening and a diagnostic test of student achievement. It offers both a brief screening form and a more comprehensive form that provides an in-depth description of achievement across many basic skills, including reading, mathematics, and spelling. Another test battery, the Iowa Tests of Basic Skills is frequently given at specific times to students in the course of their studies.

A number of specific tests of reading and mathematical achievement are available. These single-purpose tests vary widely on the nature of the information provided. Some permit a specific analysis of the child's strengths and weaknesses in reading or mathematics and recommend specific remedial procedures. For example, the Gates-MacGinitie Reading Tests, the Durrell Analysis of Reading Difficulty, and the Woodcock Reading Mastery Tests-Revised are specifically oriented toward measuring reading skills.

When choosing which achievement tests to use, the validity, reliability, and the nature of the norm group used should be evaluated. The content of the test should match what the student has been learning in the classroom. In addition, the achievement test should measure the material in a way that is similar to the way it is measured in the classroom. For instance, as Smith (1991) notes, spelling may be tested in a number of ways perhaps by having a child write the word from dictation or underline which of four words presented is spelled correctly. The child should be tested in the same manner on the standardized test as in the classroom.

Other standardized tests are also administered. Language difficulties are often present in children with learning disabilities and a number of tests are available which measure specific aspects of language. The Clinical Evaluation of Language Functions Screening Tests (CELF) measures various aspects of language comprehension and expression. It consists of two screening tests, one for grades kindergarten through five; and the advanced test for grades five through twelve. The elementary screening test uses a "Simon Says" format, while the advanced screening test uses playing cards to elicit verbal responses. The Diagnostic Battery of the CELF employs a number of subtests evaluating linguistic abilities (Sweetland & Keyser, 1993).

The Peabody Picture Vocabulary Test-Revised (PPVT-R) evaluates a child's knowledge of receptive vocabulary. The test administrator verbalizes a word and the child is asked to point to one of four pictures which corresponds to the vocalized word. The words become progressively more difficult (Lovitt, 1989). The test also yields an estimate of verbal ability and is often used with students for whom English is a second language (Sweetland & Keyser, 1993).

Process Testing

In the past, many students who were tested for learning disabilities were given process tests. These tests measured various perceptual and motor processes thought to underlie the learning disability. Frostig and colleagues developed the visual perceptual assessment measure called the Developmental Test of Visual Perception (DTVP) (Frostig, 1972; Frostig et al., 1963). Frostig argued that children with neurological impairments have deficits in the area of visual perception. The DTVP included subtests of eye-motor coordination, figure-ground detection, form constancy, and spatial constancy. Another process test, the Illinois Test of Psycholinguistic Abilities (ITPA) taps psychological and linguistic abilities assumed to contribute to academic achievement (Kirk, McCarthy, & Kirk, 1968). Once information concerning how a child processed information was discovered, it was assumed that the teacher could find a suitable method of instruction (Lovitt, 1989).

Process testing led to a number of attempts to either improve areas of perceptual deficits or design classroom strategies aimed at allowing visual learners to learn according to their preferred pattern. Attempts to improve such perceptual processes were ineffective and did not result in reading improvements (Farnham-Diggory, 1992; Larson & Hammill, 1975). The reliability and validity of these tests were also questioned. Many of these tests were based upon the idea that processes could be separated from each other, and today we know that the situation is more complicated and that a mental process never exists alone (Farnham-Diggory, 1992). Actually, one of the problems of the process approach was the overestimation of what such treatment, even if successful, could accomplish. Some people mistakenly thought it would do more than facilitate some skills, but would by itself lead to improvements in all sorts of cognitive abilities, including reading. This was really never the case and reading instruction was always needed (Smith, 1991).

Criterion-Referenced Tests

Criterion-referenced tests provide more information than norm-referenced tests on just what should be taught. They are especially useful for writing IEPs and evaluating pupil progress when items match what is actually taught in school. Criterion-referenced tests describe rather than compare and give information about mastery levels rather than grade levels (Lerner, 1988). A number of commercially produced criterion-referenced tests are available, such as the Prescriptive Reading Inventory/Reading Systems (Anastasi, 1988), the Test of Reading Comprehension (TORC) and Test of Written Language (TOWL) (Sweetland & Keyser, 1993). The Brigance Inventory of Early Development–Revised is a criterion-referenced test that measures many different skill sequences in a number of domains, such as the psychomotor, self-help, speech, and language areas. Criterion-referenced tests do not emphasize how the child is different than other children, but rather yield information concerning where children are in developing a skill.

Curriculum-Based Assessment

One difficulty in using formal evaluation instruments, such as achievement tests, is that they may cover some areas of the school's curriculum, emphasize others that are only touched on by the curriculum, and completely omit others. Students may be tested on areas they have not yet been taught. In one district, most of the students did very poorly on the map skills portion of an achievement test. The district sent a letter home telling parents that map skills were taught in the following year in the district. The students could not be expected to do well on this portion of the test because they were not taught the material. In fact, students will score better or worse on various achievement tests depending upon the degree to which the test items on the standardized tests match the curriculum (Good & Salvia, 1988).

An interpretation of what skills or knowledge a child has or does not have is only accurate to the extent that the child has had an opportunity to learn the material tested (Shriner & Salvia, 1988). Unfortunately, studies show that many tests may not reflect what is being taught in the classroom. When Shriner and Salvia (1988) compared two elementary school mathematics curricula and two standardized arithmetic achievement tests in grades one through three, a consistent lack of correspondence was found. Shapiro and Derr (1987) found that after the second grade, agreement on vocabulary between the students' basic readers and standardized tests was poor (Shapiro & Derr, 1987). This discrepancy reduces the usefulness of these tests.

Another problem with some achievement tests is that teachers find it difficult to link the test results to instruction (Blankenship, 1985). Because the tests are also given infrequently, they are less useful as guides for teachers. Teachers do not use standardized achievement tests much in their everyday teaching.

An alternative that solves many of the problems just described is to use curriculum-based assessment (CBA), which involves "using the material to be learned as the basis for assessing the degree to which it has been learned" (Tucker, 1985, p. 199). Curriculum-based assessment means that the child is evaluated on the exact areas stressed in the school's curriculum. This format eliminates the problem of using standardized tests for assessment that are not linked to what is being taught or whose norm group does not match the demographic characteristics of the students in the classroom. The teacher receives specific information on the areas in which the student needs work. For example, if the curriculum of the child's grade requires the student to multiply two numbers by two numbers, to write sentences of a particular length and accuracy, and to read at a particular level, this would be reflected in the assessment process (Lovitt, 1989). The advantage of CBA is that it directly links assessment and instruction by evaluating students in the areas they will be expected to learn (Deno, 1985).

Actually, curriculum-based assessment has two meanings. First, it is the approach in which the student is assessed on the areas being taught. Second, the term *curriculum-based assessment* is used to refer to the measuring instrument itself. The instrument, which offers a measure of performance on various relevant skills, can be used as a basis for making instructional decisions. A CBA can be developed for almost any area and separate ones are developed for different areas. The steps required to construct a CBA and then to use it for instructional decisions include:

1. Listing the skills presented in the material selected.
2. Examining the list to see if all important skills are presented.
3. Deciding if the resulting, edited list has skills in a logical order.
4. Writing an objective for each skill on the list.
5. Preparing items to test each listed objective.
6. Preparing testing material for student use which presents the items.
7. Planning how the CBA will be given.
8. Giving the CBA immediately prior to beginning instruction on a topic.
9. Studying the results to determine which students have mastered the skills, which are ready to begin instruction, and which require other instruction first.
10. Readministering the CBA after instruction to determine success and the need for modification of teaching strategies.
11. Readministering the CBA periodically throughout the year to assess long-term retention (Blankenship, 1985).

When CBA is used, students are assessed frequently, and the results may be charted or graphed as shown in Figure 5.1. This figure shows the improvement in oral reading as measured by the number of words read correctly in a one-minute reading sample for a child over a three-week period. The first period is a base line

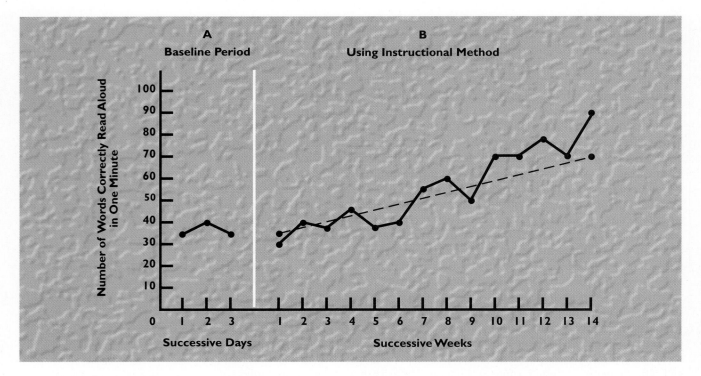

FIGURE 5.1 A Curriculum-Based Assessment Chart Monitoring an Individual Student's Progress

Janet W. Lerner, *Learning Disabilities: Theories, Diagnosis, and Teaching Strategies*, Sixth Edition. Copyright © 1993 by Houghton Mifflin Company. Reprinted with permission.

in which the child's original skills were charted over three days. Period B shows the progress after the instructional program is begun as measured weekly for 14 weeks. The dashed line shows the IEP objective which, in this case, is reading 70 words per minute (Lerner, 1988).

CBA has decided advantages over more traditional norm-referenced measures. It links assessment to what is being taught and to instruction. If a child is not progressing, the teacher can see it and change instructional technique. Teachers frequently overestimate what students have learned and consequently do not give sufficient practice. CBA reduces this problem by showing teachers what students know and do not know relative to what they are being taught (Deno, 1985).

Teachers who use CBA make more instructional modifications than those who do not CBA (Fuchs, Fuchs, & Stecker, 1989). It is most effective when direct instructional recommendations are received by the teacher and designed into the program (Fuchs et al., 1994).

Tests devised by districts based upon their own curriculum must meet the same standards of validity and reliability met by other methods of assessment. Standards for CBA should be kept high and studies show that they are generally reliable and valid (Deno, 1985). CBA can be used to differentiate between children who learn slowly and those with a learning disability. Those students with learning disabilities show much slower rates of learning (see Smith, 1991). The use of CBA seems to increase a teacher's accuracy in referral as well. When CBA is implemented, it significantly reduces the referrals for testing (Marston & Magnusson, 1985). CBA is implemented much more often at the elementary level where the skills being taught are easier to define than at the secondary school level.

Direct Daily Measurement

Since frequent assessment is so important, continuous, even daily measurement is sometimes advocated. For instance, if a teacher were teaching math, under direct daily measurement that teacher would measure the progress of the student and chart it. Such a chart allows the teacher to see graphically how the child is progressing, assess the child's progress, and change teaching methods if necessary.

This concept of daily monitoring is used in some particular methods of teaching. **Precision teaching** is a technique based on behavioral concepts which is especially useful with students with disabilities who are attending regular classes for the first time. In this system, the teacher first finds a target behavior the student must master, and then charts the student's progress in learning that single skill. Perhaps the skill is to know how to use a particular number of vocabulary words or to be able to read at a particular rate. The student's mastery of the targeted behavior is tested, usually on a daily basis, and the number of correct and incorrect responses given in a specified time period (sometimes one minute) is charted. These tests are called probes (Raybould, 1984). Mastery is defined in terms of a certain rate of correct responses, i.e., reading 100 to 140 words per minute with two or fewer errors.

Precision teachers record the daily performance of each student and chart the results. The value of the daily charting lies in the fact that it offers a direct, continuous, and precise measurement system. Teaching in this model is direct and simple. It can involve a number of materials and methods, including commercially prepared materials, drill sheets, flash cards, and games. The results have been impressive (Mercer, 1986).

Precision teaching:
A systematic procedure using continuous and direct recording of behavior.

Ecological Assessment

Recently, there has been a movement to take a more comprehensive view of student functioning into account. Ecological assessment takes both the student and the environment into consideration (see Chapter 2). Such factors as classroom seating, the size of the room, the patterns of movement, transitions, personal interactions, learning styles, and expectancies are considered (Lovitt, 1989). The curriculum, the presence and absence of praise, time schedules, and many other factors are examined. The ecological model requires a look at the adaptive fit between the individual's behavior and the particular setting. For example, a child might achieve more in a small group setting than a larger classroom. The ecological model leads educators to examine the individual's functioning and the immediate environment and find ways to improve the fit between them. Using this approach, professionals learn a great deal more about the child and the environment, the student's functioning, and the child's strengths and weaknesses.

Medical Examination

Sometimes, neurological examinations consisting of a number of tests, including an electroencephalogram (EEG) and various brain scanning techniques are given. Sometimes, neuropsychological test batteries are used. These batteries measure sensory-perceptual, motor, psychomotor, linguistic, and cognitive skills that reflect brain functions. These tests are interpreted with respect to brain functioning and the nature of the information processing involved. One such battery successfully differentiated between children with learning disabilities who did and did not show attention-deficit/hyperactivity disorder, demonstrating that children with ADHD had difficulties in control while children with learning disabilities showed problems in phonological awareness and verbal memory among other areas (Korkman & Pesonen, 1994). Their validity for educational planning is now being researched (Smith, 1991). Physical examinations are also often used, since any physical and sensory impairments must be found. These examinations are especially important since the federal definition of learning disabilities excludes children whose learning problems arise primarily because of some other disability.

Other Assessment Instruments

Rating scales and checklists provide important information. Teachers may be asked to rate students on some task, for example, how well they decode words or pay attention in class. The use of rating scales as screening instruments reduces referrals for evaluation (Salvesen & Undheim, 1994). Some referrals are based upon the teacher's global impression of the child, and students who may bother the teacher may be referred. These more broad-based referrals are less likely to occur when rating systems, which focus the attention on relevant variables, are employed. Rating scales and checklists, though, provide only a small amount of information. Case studies, interviews, and observations may also be used to supplement information available. In addition, some informal reading tests are available to pinpoint some of the child's difficulties. The important factor to remember is that professionals want to collect as much specific information as possible about children's knowledge and skills for both evaluation and assessment purposes.

Early Identification

Early identification of children with learning disabilities would certainly be an advantage. If professionals could predict who will have difficulty learning to read, children could receive the proper help before they fell too far behind.

Early identification of children with the potential for developing learning problems is possible. For example, children who show risk factors involved in birth difficulties, early medical problems, trauma, as well as family factors such as abuse or neglect, may be helped before a possible problem shows itself in school. Other early identification possibilities involve giving specific tests to young children, who may demonstrate some developmental delay related to the possibility of poor learning later on. Some of the instruments frequently used include the Brigance Diagnostic Inventory of Early Development, the Denver Developmental Screening Test-Revised, the Learning Accomplishments Profile, and the DIAL (see Chapter 3). Young children can be screened for vision, hearing, language, motor, cognitive, and self-help skills.

The search continues for ways of predicting who will and will not have a learning problem. For example, a test of phonological processing which taps sound discrimination and phonemic segmentation, in which a child after repeating a word given by the evaluator must say the word without some consonant, such as saying the word *bug* without the *b*, shows promise. Results of this test given early in the first grade predicted reading achievement two years later. It also differentiated children who were poor readers from children who had learning disabilities (Hurford et al., 1994).

It is important to remember that very young children do not require a specific diagnosis to receive help. A finding of a developmental delay is sufficient. The academic disability has not yet occurred, so programs attempt to prevent a learning problem from arising.

Many programs can be helpful in this regard. Rothenberg (1990) notes the success of a program in which children at risk for school failure as indicated on a screening test administered upon entrance into kindergarten were given intensive help. Each activity in the kindergarten curriculum was task analyzed—that is, broken down into small, discrete steps—and these students' specific learning problems were identified. The students were taught how to proceed through more difficult activities. Special education teachers and classroom teachers worked together, charting students' progress carefully. Over an eight-year period, standardized achievement measures were collected for these children and compared to those of a control group. Throughout the eight years, those students who received the special help were achieving at or above national averages and demonstrated superiority in achievement compared with a control group not given the help. Studies, discussed in detail in Chapter 3, demonstrate that prevention and remediation are definitely possible throughout early childhood, and many programs can reduce the possibility that a child will develop a learning problem.

Placement

If the initial assessment shows that a diagnosis of learning disability is proper, the question of placement is then raised. The overwhelming majority of students—about 79 percent—are educated in a regular classroom setting for at least part of the day. The majority of students with learning disabilities—54.2 percent—receive instruction both in the regular classroom and in the resource room, while 24.7 percent are educated solely in the regular classroom. Twenty percent are educated in separate classes, 0.9 percent in a separate school and 0.1 percent in a residential facility, while another 0.1 percent receive home instruction (U.S. Department of Education, 1994).

Special Classes for Students with Learning Disabilities

Special class placement for children with disabilities has generally not fared well, but the situation is not as clear with children with learning disabilities. Instead, the research is mixed. Some studies show that children with learning disabilities in special classes make greater gains both academically and perhaps even socially than when placed in regular classrooms. Students in special classes are more confident and have better academic self-concepts than students with learning disabilities in regular classes (Butler & Marinow-Glassman, 1994; Battle & Blowers, 1982). Some students with learning disabilities in these classes seem to experience some benefits (Carlberg & Kavale, 1980; Yauman, 1980). Other studies doubt the effectiveness of placing children with mild disabilities in special classes (Madden & Slavin, 1983). The problems of such placement, including the isolation of students and the possible stigma, remain.

The evidence suggests two possible conclusions. First, some children with learning disabilities may do better in special classes; so special classes may remain a placement option for a minority of students. Second, we need to discover which students do better in such placements. The factors that may lead to success for some students need identification so that, if possible, they can be imitated in the regular classroom. Although certain students benefit from highly structured programs, an emerging consensus among professionals is that students with learning disabilities should be provided with services in regular classrooms (McLeskey & Pacchiano, 1994).

Resource Rooms

Resource rooms are the primary source of alternative help for children with learning disabilities. The amount of time children spend in these rooms varies greatly. Some evidence has been shown for the effectiveness of such intervention. When Rust and Miller (1978) tested second through sixth graders who had been randomly assigned to either a resource room or had remained in regular classes, those in the resource room gained in total reading and word knowledge, although the differences were relatively small. Marston (1987–1988) found evidence for considerably greater academic progress for children in resource room placements compared to those who attended only regular classrooms. These gains are aca-

Many children with learning disabilities are helped in the resource room. However, questions concerning the transfer of what is learned to the regular classroom and the articulation between the regular classroom teacher and resource room specialist remain to be answered.

demic and do not occur in the social or personal realms (Sindelar & Deno, 1978). In addition, these academic gains may not transfer directly to better achievement in the classroom, raising the need for better articulation between the regular classroom teacher and the resource room specialist (Anderson-Inman, 1986).

There are problems with resource room services. These problems include missing classroom work, scheduling difficulties, and the lack of coordination between the regular classroom and the resource room. A personal variable may also come into play; sometimes children prefer to be in a regular class and do not want to be taken out (Jenkins & Heinen, 1989). At the same time, studies do not find a reduction in peer acceptance or a decrease in self-concept due to resource room attendance (see Smith, 1991).

Teaching Strategies

A bewildering number of programs are aimed at helping students with learning disabilities achieve. The techniques advocated depend upon the theoretical orientation of the professionals and the services available (Erickson, 1992).

Today, the attempts to help these children focus on three areas. First, skill training, usually achieved through the direct instruction of skills, is stressed. Second, there is a movement to teach students learning strategies and improve their self-monitoring abilities. Third, since so many children have difficulty with social skills, some training program in this area is needed.

Skill Training

The skill training approach assumes that the child requires extra attention and a more carefully programmed presentation to learn some skill not previously learned. Today, **direct instruction** is often used to accomplish this purpose. Direct instruction conveys to students either a body of information or a particular skill (Borich, 1988). The basic components of direct instruction are setting clear goals and communicating them to students, presenting a sequence of well-organized assignments, giving students clear and concise explanations and illustrations of the subject matter, asking frequent questions to ascertain student understanding, and giving students frequent practice in what they have learned (Judy et al., 1988; U.S. Department of Education, 1987a).

A lesson might begin with some review of the previous day's work, including homework and reteaching if necessary. An overview of the new material is given, with the material so structured that it is taught in small steps at a rapid pace. A great deal of interaction takes place between students and teachers, much of it involving questions asked by teachers. Guided practice and applications are included with corrections and reteaching. Finally, independent seatwork is assigned when students know the material, and students receive weekly and monthly reviews. Evaluation is conducted through classroom achievement tests (Womack, 1989).

Many students first react to this description of direct instruction, saying "That's the way we learned when I was in school. It's boring and repetitive." Studies find,

Direct instruction:
A type of instructional method especially useful for teaching a body of information that includes setting clear goals, presenting a sequence of well-organized assignments, explaining material to students, presenting examples, asking frequent questions, and giving frequent practice in what the students have learned.

TABLE 5.1   **Instructional Functions**

Direct instruction follows a logical sequence. As you can see, it is anything but straight lecture.

1. **Daily review, checking previous day's work, and reteaching (if necessary)**
    Checking homework
    Reteaching areas where there were student errors

2. **Presenting new content/skills**
    Providing overview
    Proceeding in small steps (if necessary), but at a rapid pace
    If necessary, giving detailed or redundant instructions and explanations
    Phasing in new skills while old skills are being mastered

3. **Initial student practice**
    Allowing high frequency of questions and overt student practice (from teacher and materials)
    Providing prompts during initial learning (when appropriate)
    Providing all students with a chance to respond and receive feedback
    Checking for understanding by evaluating student responses
    Continuing practice until students are firm
    Maintaining a success rate of 80% or higher during initial learning

4. **Feedback and correctives (and recycling of instruction, if necessary)**
    Giving feedback to students, particularly when they are correct but hesitant
    Allowing student errors to provide feedback to the teacher that corrections or reteaching is necessary
    Making corrections by simplifying question, giving clues, explaining or reviewing steps, or reteaching last steps
    When necessary, reteaching using smaller steps

5. **Independent practice so that students' responses are firm and automatic**
    Using seatwork
    Teaching unitization and automaticity (practice to overlearning)
    Allowing a need for procedure to ensure student engagement during seatwork (i.e., teacher or aide monitoring)
    Maintaining 95% correct or higher

6. **Weekly and monthly reviews**
    Reteaching, if necessary

Note: With older, more mature learners (1) the size of steps in the presentation is larger, (2) student practice is more covert, and (3) the practice involves covert rehearsal, restating, and reviewing (i.e., deep processing or "whirling").

Adapted from "Teacher Functions in Instructional Programs" by B. Rosenshine. In *Elementary School Journal* 83:4, 338–351 (1983). Copyright © 1983 University of Chicago Press.

though, that direct instruction is not used very much (Gaskins, 1988). Students are rarely told what they are going to do or why, how and when to apply the skill. A careful review of Table 5.1 may be enough to convince you that direct instruction is rarely practiced. This low incidence is unfortunate, because direct instruction can be effective when the aim is to transmit a body of information or skills to students (Shapiro, 1988). It is particularly effective when teaching new material to students who are disadvantaged, young, or have learning disabilities (U.S. Department of Education, 1987b; Duffelmeyer & Baum, 1987).

Direct instruction is a challenge for the teacher, not because the techniques are so difficult, but because it is so easy to fall into bad habits and simply lecture. For some, such a teacher-dominated scheme is something to be avoided entirely. However, too much research demonstrates the effectiveness of direct instruction for transmitting information and skills to simply push it aside.

Direct instruction is not a panacea for everything that is wrong with education, nor is it the deadening, cold, dry type of instruction some of its detractors claim it to be. It can be used effectively to transmit to students information and skills if it is well paced, if the teacher interacts well with the class, and if the students are given enough feedback and experience success.

Teaching Learning Strategies

A second approach focuses on the difficulties students with learning disabilities have in knowing how to approach learning tasks (Lovett et al., 1994). Children with learning disabilities have a difficult time choosing the correct strategy and monitoring their progress (Palincsar & Klenk, 1992; Butler, 1995). Teaching specific strategies to students makes sense. As noted earlier, many children with learning disabilities have phonological problems. Lovett and colleagues (1994) found that when children with learning disabilities were taught four decoding strategies, they were better able to transfer what they learned in their reading lessons to new words.

Some students are aware of the strategies they use when reading, while others are not. It is one factor that separates good from poor readers. Metacognition as it applies to reading involves "knowing that," "knowing how," and "knowing when and why." "Knowing that," called declarative knowledge, involves knowing the different ways to read. Procedural knowledge involves knowing how to read the material and includes the strategies the reader has available, such as skimming and outlining. Conditional knowledge involves using these strategies in different contexts (knowing when and why). Good and poor readers differ on these dimensions, with good readers knowing more about reading strategies, correcting errors more often, and having better recall (Paris & Myers, 1981). Knowing when and knowing why to use strategies are keys to the transfer of skills as well (Paris & Oka, 1986).

A number of teaching approaches are available to improve metacognition. One is called Informed Strategies for Learning or ISL. This program emphasizes the awareness of reading strategies and provides practice in these skills, including dialogues that stimulate students to think and share their ideas. The package includes twenty modules arranged in groups of five aimed at planning and preparing to read, identifying meaning, reasoning about text content, and comprehending material. Strategies include elaboration, creation of inferences and summaries, and comprehension monitoring (rereading, self-questioning, checking consistencies, and paraphrasing). Instruction is faded; that is, children slowly take on more and more responsibility from the teacher. Results from the use of ISL are quite positive (Cross & Paris, 1988).

Another promising approach is called **reciprocal teaching**, which involves students and teachers in a dialogue for discovering the meaning of a written passage (Palincsar, 1986, Palincsar & Brown, 1984; Palincsar & Klenk, 1992). The approach uses four activities: summarizing, question generating, clarifying, and predicting. Each day, before beginning the dialogue, the students review the strategies they are learning and the context in which the strategies are to be used. The students

Reciprocal teaching:
An approach to teaching reading strategies that involves summarizing, question generating, clarifying, and predicting, and requires students and teacher to enter into a dialogue for discussing the meaning of a written passage.

are then presented with the title of the text. They are encouraged to make use of all the background information they have about the topic under discussion and to make predictions about what they will learn and what they would like to learn about the topic. A teacher is appointed from the students, and all the students read the material. The student teacher then asks a question which is answered by the other students, summarizes the answers, asks for elaborations on the summary, and leads a discussion aimed at clarifying the meaning of the passage. The group finally discusses predictions about what might happen next and a new teacher is appointed.

In the initial days, the adult teacher is responsible for keeping the dialogue moving as well as modeling and providing instruction in the four strategies. As the process continues, the teacher tries to give more and more responsibility to the student teachers while providing feedback and coaching. An example of such a dialogue is found in Figure 5.2. The results have been quite favorable, and studies show the benefits of reciprocal teaching to children with difficulties learning in both the elementary and secondary school environments (Kaplan, 1991).

Cognitive and metacognitive strategy can also be used to help students learn mathematics (Montague, 1992; Montague & Bos, 1986). As students become more aware of what they are doing and how they are doing it, they become more autonomous learners and better able to function when faced with an unfamiliar

---

FIGURE 5.2 Sample Reciprocal Teaching Dialogue

This sample dialogue demonstrates how students and teachers can become involved in discovering the meaning of written work by using summarizing, question generating, clarifying, and predicting.

From "Metacognitive Strategy Instruction" by A.S. Palincsar, *Exceptional Children*, 53, 1986, p. 120. Copyright © 1986 by The Council for Exceptional Children. Reprinted with permission.

Text from which students are working:

Crows have another gift. They are great mimics. They can learn to talk and imitate animal sounds. Some have been known to learn one hundred words, and even whole phrases. They can imitate the squeak of a chicken, the whine of a dog, or the meow of a cat.

Games have a certain fascination to crows. In a game of hide-and-seek, a crow hides in the hollow of a tree and then sounds a distress caw. The others rush to the spot, look around, then flap away. This may be done over and over, after which the young crow pops out of its hiding place and caws gleefully. Far from being annoyed at this, the flock bursts into loud cawing themselves. They seem to like the trick that played on them.

T   Chantel, you're our teacher, right? Why don't you summarize first? Remember, just tell me the most important parts.

S1 Crows have a hundred words they can learn by imitation. They can imitate chickens, the whine of a dog, and cats.

T   Okay. We can shorten that summary a bit.

S2 You could say they can imitate other animals.

T   Oh! Good one! There's a list there, Chantel, did you notice that? It says they can imitate the squawk of a chicken, the whine of a dog or the meow of a cat; and you could call that "animal sounds." Can you ask us a question?

S1 Ain't no questions here.

S3 The words (sic.) that need to be clarified are (sic.) "mimics."

S4 That means imitate, right?

T   Right. How did you figure that out, Shirley?

S4 The paragraph.

T   Show us how somebody could figure out what "mimic" means.

S5 They are great mimics. They can learn to talk and imitate animal sounds.

task. So far, the results of strategy training have been encouraging, but more research is required (Ryan, Short, & Weed, 1986).

Teaching the Student with Learning Disabilities

To effectively teach a child with a learning disability, the regular classroom teacher must be acquainted with the child's specific strengths and weaknesses. It is this determination that defines the most effective way to present the material (Moskowitz, 1988). For example, the teacher must help students who have organizational deficits to organize their work perhaps by teaching them list-making techniques and how to identify the most important points, checking their progress on long-term assignments, and teaching them how to organize a notebook. If a child has difficulty with following directions given orally, preparing the material visually may be in order, for example, providing outlines as well as asking students to repeat the question before answering it. If the child has difficulty with word meanings, it may be necessary to explain idioms and vocabulary before beginning a chapter and have the student repeat directions in his or her own words. The classroom teacher can find ways to present the material that allows this student to learn. Students appreciate it when their teachers make changes in instructional technique to allow for individual needs (Vaughn, Schumm, & Kouzekanani, 1993).

T Yes, so the next sentence tells you what it means. Very good. Anything else need to be clarified?

All No.

T What about that question we need to ask? (pause) What is the second paragraph about, Chantel?

S1 The games they play.

S3 They do things like people do.

S4 What kinds of games do crows play?

S3 Hide and seek. Over and over again.

T You know what, Larry? That was a real good comparison. One excellent question could be, "How are crows like people?"

S4 They play hide and seek.

T Good. Any other questions there?

S2 How come the crows don't get annoyed?

S5 What does annoyed mean?

T Irritated, bothered.

S5 Because they like it, they have fun. If I had a crow, I'd tell him he was it and see what he'd do.

T Let's summarize now and have some predictions.

S1 This was about how they play around in games.

T Good for you. That's it. Predictions anyone?

S2 Maybe more tricks they play.

S4 Other games.

T Maybe. So far, they have told us several ways that crows are very smart; they can communicate with one another, they can imitate many sounds, and they play games. Maybe we will read about another way in which they are smart. Who will be the next teacher?

THE CLASSROOM   Teaching Children with Learning Disabilities

Teaching children with learning disabilities is a challenging task because the population is so heterogeneous.

1. Use a multimedia approach when possible.	**Why?** Students achieve more when a number of different modalities are used, so tapes, films, and outside readings may help.
2. Use an outline if lecturing.	**Why?** An outline may serve as an organizer for the lesson and students with learning disabilities have difficulties with organization.
3. Give students practice using many different formats, for example, take-home projects and group assignments.	**Why?** Using different formats may bring out the student's strengths rather than weaknesses and aid in generalization.
4. Offer different evaluation methods when required.	**Why?** It is useless to give students with learning disabilities a written test that they cannot read and to infer from that examination that they do not know their science or social studies. Oral examinations, projects, and numerous other types of graded assignments can be used. Give more time when necessary as well.
5. Try to avoid distractions.	**Why?** Many children with learning disabilities are easily distracted, and minimizing distractions by having them sit farther from the windows may be advisable.
6. Avoid criticizing these students as much as possible.	**Why?** These students are used to criticism and need the encouragement of praise when they show initiative or perform up to standard. Bringing attention to their strengths can encourage them to work harder.
7. Use peer tutoring.	**Why?** Peer tutoring is effective in improving academic achievement (Keller & Hallahan, 1987). It should be highly structured and tutors must

	be trained for their role (see Chapter 2).
8. Implement cooperative learning strategies.	**Why?** Cooperative learning strategies are effective in improving academic achievement and social interactions of children with learning disabilities (Slavin, 1994).
9. Analyze material whenever possible.	**Why?** A student may not complete an assignment due to a difficulty with only one or two of the ten steps required. Breaking assignments down into easy-to-understand steps makes it easier for the student. Specific steps in drawing a map of a country may be to go to the library, find an atlas, find the page with the map by looking at the index, and trace the map. Each step is outlined.
10. Be aware of pacing.	**Why?** Sometimes students cannot perform a task because the material is presented too fast. Some children with learning disabilities process material more slowly.
11. Encourage students with learning disabilities to express their thoughts.	**Why?** Students with learning disabilities often have language problems including difficulties with word ordering, word endings, word meanings, and language rules. They benefit from a rich language environment and the opportunity to talk about things of interest to them (Dudley-Marling & Searle, 1988).
12. Closely monitor student progress.	**Why?** Children with learning disabilities, even when receiving special services, often fall progressively behind their classmates in reading comprehension (McKinney & Fegans, 1984). Constant assessment of student progress allows the teacher to change strategies when necessary.

13. Help students develop metacognitive abilities.	**Why?** Many students with learning disabilities have difficulty with the metacognitive aspects of reading. Techniques such as reciprocal teaching and teaching the student self-questioning methods can help (Keller & Hallahan, 1987).
14. Use direct instruction with considerable opportunities for practice.	**Why?** Research shows that direct instruction is an effective method for teaching new concepts to students with learning disabilities (Lawrence, 1988).
15. Assign seatwork, workbook assignments, and other types of independent work only after the students show they understand the material.	**Why?** Many students say they understand the material but really do not. Independent practice should be assigned after the student gets at least 80 percent of the material in the practice exercises correct (Lawrence, 1988).

Social Skills Training

The social problems of students with learning disabilities need attention as well. Schumaker and Hazel (1984) argue that social skills problems fall into three categories. Some children simply do not have an adequate repertoire of social skills; some children possess the skills but do not use them at appropriate times; and some children have a self-control problem.

There are many approaches to building social skills in children who have learning disabilities. For example, peer tutoring and cooperative learning bring together both friendship and academics (Smith, 1991). Teachers may observe a student's inability to act in an appropriate manner and suggest changes. Social skills training may involve a number of techniques, including coaching specific social skills, modeling these skills, reinforcing their use, teaching self-monitoring techniques, as well as cooperative interventions, such as arranging situations in which students must work together for a common goal (Madden & Slavin, 1983). For example, the teacher may observe that a student has difficulty with a particular skill, such as responding appropriately to criticism or giving compliments. After targeting the skill, the teacher may discuss the importance of the skill with the student, coach the individual in what to do or say, and model the response. The teacher may use role-play situations and give the student feedback, and have students try out the new skills in appropriate situations. Students may also be taught to analyze interpersonal difficulties in a new way, by analyzing the situation, generating alternatives to solve the problem and then to make a selection of an alternative to solve the difficulty (McIntosh, Vaughn, & Zaragoza, 1991).

Children with learning disabilities are helped when different methods of evaluation are used so they can show what they know.

A number of commercial social skills programs are also available. For example, the DUSO program (Developing Understanding of Self and Others) aims at increasing ability to express feelings and learning to act appropriately (Dinkmeyer & Dinkmeyer, 1982). The eight units cover many areas, including understanding of one's feelings, goals, choices and consequences, resourcefulness, and emotional maturity.

The Skillstreaming series is another program aimed at improving prosocial and interpersonal skills in the early childhood, elementary school and adolescent years. Many age-related skills are emphasized. For example, in elementary school, classroom survival skills such as following instructions, asking questions, and friendship-making skills, and skills for dealing with feelings, dealing with aggression, and coping with stress are taught. The program uses a structured learning approach emphasizing modeling, role playing, feedback, and opportunities for transfer of what children are learning. Each skill is broken down into parts and children are shown examples of the skill. Students then rehearse the skills (role playing) and receive feedback from others. Last, procedures are used to enhance transfer (McGinnis & Goldstein, 1984; 1990).

In an analysis of social skills programs, Young (1987) suggests that such programs ought to be organized in ways that integrate students with and without learning disabilities, provide students with opportunities to practice these skills, involve peers both in training and in the practice of the skills, and extend the skills into the home and community.

SCENARIO

Peter is a sixth grader who is quite unpopular in class. He has a learning disability; however, in this case, it does not seem to be his lack of academic progress that is hindering his social interactions but rather his own conduct. Peter does not seem to know how to interact. For example, if a group of students are talking, Peter pushes his way in and makes a comment off the topic in a forceful manner. He does not greet people in the class and does not listen to the desires of others, always concentrating on what he wants to do. Peter is not physically aggressive. He seems to realize that he is rejected, and this causes him to become more insistent and his manner becomes more forceful. His parents ask you, his teacher, what they can do, and would like you to help design a plan to teach him particular social skills. How would you go about creating and using such a plan?

The Adolescent with Learning Disabilities

Some of the emotional, social, and academic difficulties experienced by adolescents with learning disabilities are similar to the problems faced by teenagers who do not have learning disabilities. Adolescence is a time of increasing doubt, of various anxieties, of academic challenges, and of asking questions about one's self. Most studies find that compared to other adolescents, teens with learning disabilities experience these problems to a greater extent.

Research evidence indicates that adolescents with learning disabilities are at risk for emotional difficulties. They are more likely to experience depression. One study found that about 20 percent of the males and 32 percent of the female junior high school students with learning disabilities were severely depressed, as were 17 percent of the male and 18 percent of the female high school students (Maag & Behrens, 1989). Although, unfortunately, no control group students without learning disabilities was used, the figures are quite high. They are also more likely to commit suicide (Huntington & Bender, 1993). They experience more anxiety and sleep-related disorders (Dollinger, Horn, & Boarini, 1988). The anxiety is related to making mistakes, being teased, getting poor grades, and being criticized. Adolescents with learning disabilities are frequently overwhelmed and disorganized and have a fear of failure. Sometimes they have feelings of letting their parents down or anger (Smith, 1988). They are also very critical of themselves.

When adolescents with and without learning disabilities are compared, adolescents with learning disabilities score lower on some aspects of self-concept, but not others (Montgomery, 1994; Raviv & Stone, 1991). Although global measures do not show differences, academic self-concept is a problem (Chapman, 1988). Another problem is body self-image (Kistner et al., 1987).

Continuity is the most common pattern in social skills development. Those adolescents with good social skills continue to function well; some even compensate for perceived deficiencies in other areas by using their social skills. Those who have had difficulty in the social area continue to experience hardship. They continue to adapt slowly, to overreact, and to be distractible. Teens with learning disabilities are less able to understand subtle communication and less accurate in interpreting social interactions and emotions. These students may become isolated. Some turn to music, cars, or athletics, while others may use food or drugs as a method of escape. In the early years of childhood, parents can actively organize the child's social life making certain that other children are invited to the home, but now that they are adolescents, they must do so on their own.

Teenagers with learning disabilities are more likely to believe good luck is more important than hard work for success, that every time they get ahead something or somebody stops them, that planning only makes a person unhappy since plans rarely work out, and that people who accept their condition in life are happier than those who try to change it (Gregory, Shanahan, & Walberg, 1986).

The Secondary School

The focus of programs designed to help adolescents with learning disabilities changes as students enter secondary school. Although teaching basic skills may continue, there is more of an emphasis in secondary school in the areas of planning and organization and in help in summarizing, asking questions, and solving problems (Smith, 1988). Although younger children with learning disabilities require such instruction, the emphasis in adolescence is on preparing adolescents to enter the world of adulthood where success often requires these skills.

The focus in the later years of high school changes from an emphasis on remediation to how to live with the disability (Lieberman, 1981). Ways of compensating for weaknesses and building learning strategies to cope are more important.

Whereas elementary school teachers may actively organize work for their younger students, in secondary school (especially high school) students are expected to do so themselves. And whereas things are planned out for younger children, older children are expected to do their own planning.

There are many ways to help students organize. For example, helping students break down a task into small parts and making lists can be helpful. Adolescents with learning disabilities may be given opportunities to plan by being required to make a video, run a dance, or operate a school store. Often, these students have not been given much responsibility in these areas because of their planning and organizational weaknesses, but they require the experience.

Secondary school teachers are willing to make changes to help junior high school and high school students with learning disabilities as long as the teachers see these modifications as reasonable. These changes include providing students with support and extra instructional cues, enhancing classroom behavior management procedures, simplifying instruction, and using supplemental resources (Ellett, 1993). Basically, secondary school teachers are willing to use strategies they feel they can implement in their own classrooms, can apply to all students, and require little time.

THOUGHT QUESTION

6. *Why is there a shift in emphasis in high school away from remediation and toward learning to cope with the learning disability?*

Should a student who cannot pass a minimum competency test due to a learning disability but achieves well in school be granted a regular diploma?

One definite problem in secondary school for students with learning disabilities is school attendance (Lovitt, 1989). The attendance of students with learning disabilities is poor. More students with learning disabilities fail regular courses because of attendance than for any other reason. Motivation seems to be a key.

One controversial secondary school issue is minimum competency testing. States have instituted policies aimed at making sure students have certain skills when they graduate. One way of doing this is to give a test that students must pass to receive a high school diploma. Many adolescents with learning disabilities cannot pass such examinations and may be denied diplomas on this basis alone. This can affect their vocational futures. The Council for Exceptional Children has taken issue with these standards and advocates a more flexible criteria based on individually determined curricula (Cain et al., 1984).

Some states allow the tests to be read aloud and students to respond orally, while others allow unlimited time. Some allow reordering items from least to most difficult, allowing bigger margins to help guide the eye while reading, placing answer bubbles next to multiple choice questions to avoid having answer sheets, having reading comprehension passages set off within shaded boxes from other test items, and using arrows to indicate continuation of material or stop signs to indicate the end (Beattie, Grise, & Algozzine, 1983). Some may administer only a few sections at a time. These are relatively simple changes that do not adversely affect the validity of the exam. The state of the students' knowledge is still being systematically examined, and this gives students the best chance to show what they know.

Some states allow the awarding of high school diplomas if the requirements of the IEP are met, and still other states require the IEP to state how minimum competency test standards will be met. Some students with learning disabilities obtain modified high school diplomas, certifying school attendance and that they have met the requirements of the IEP.

Vocational preparation is also necessary. Matthews, Whang, and Fawcett (1982) simulated a number of scenarios measuring different skills necessary for successfully meeting the challenges of the world of work. Students were asked to act out these scenarios. The students without learning disabilities were significantly better in job interviews, accepting criticism, providing constructive criticism, explaining a problem to a supervisor, writing a letter to request an interview, writing a letter following a job interview, and completing income tax forms. The non-learning-disabled youth were better, but not significantly so, in getting a job lead from a friend and telephoning a potential employer to arrange an interview, while the groups were the same in accepting suggestions from an employer. Students with learning disabilities were better in complimenting a co-worker on a job well done and accepting a compliment.

Students with learning disabilities need help in learning to fill out job applications. Employers receive many applications for a single position. The student may never obtain an interview for a job if the application is missing information or data is written in the wrong places. Nelson and colleagues (1994) used a learning strategies approach to teach adolescents to fill out applications. The approach used a six-step strategy called SELECT. The stages included *Surveying* the job application and looking for the *Emphasized* words to indicate the type of information requested. Students were taught to ask themselves questions throughout the process such as "What information do I have to have to complete the application?" Then, the student was taught to *Locate* cues that indicate where the requested information is to be entered (line immediately below), and ask questions such as "Where does the information go?" Next, the student *Enters* the information and after completing the application, *Checks* it, and finally *Turns* it in to the appropriate individual. Students receiving strategy instruction made fewer errors of omission or location (placing the information in the wrong space) and their applications were neater than students who received more traditional instruction involving discussion and modeling of how to fill out the application with some practice.

Some high schools offer work-study options, which may be appropriate for some students with severe learning disabilities. These programs are designed to teach students vocational and personal decision-making skills.

More college students have learning disabilities than any other disability on campus (see Morris & Levenberger, 1990). It is estimated that 1 percent of all college students have learning disabilities. These students can succeed if modifications are made that allow them to do so. Such relatively simple modifications as extending time periods for taking examinations, allowing tape recordings, and sometimes providing alternative examinations may help. This does not excuse the college student with a learning disability from demonstrating knowledge in some acceptable way. However, a student can show mastery of the work in many ways. Another area of importance is the need for academic survival skills training (Human Resources Center, 1988). Although many students require help in budgeting time and money, long-range planning, and organizing their work, help for students with learning disabilities who frequently have specific deficits in these areas is vital. With assistance, many students with learning disabilities can succeed in college.

SCENARIO

6 Ellen's problem is obvious and has been for a long time. Her father, with whom she lives, and her teachers are careful not to be overly critical of her grades. However, they are now losing their patience with her "lack of effort." In a word, her motivation is poor. She does not do her assignments, often does not pay attention to her work in school, daydreams instead of staying on task, and does not appear interested in any of her work. She does not act out in class, and her social skills appear good. Although the other girls in her high school class may not seek out her company, they do not reject her either. She enjoys watching mysteries on television and going to the movies as well as playing sports, especially baseball. How would you deal with her lack of motivation?

Adulthood

A learning disability does not just fade into oblivion with the ending of high school or college. It persists into adulthood (Polloway, Schewel, & Patton, 1992). Such characteristics as slow information processing, distractibility, self-concept problems, and lack of organization continue.

Gerber and colleagues (1990) asked 133 adults with learning disabilities, ranging in age from 23 to 71 with a mean age of about 42 years, to rate themselves presently and during the school years on a number of characteristics. These adults with learning disabilities were characterized as either moderately successful or highly successful, according to an assessment of a number of factors including job satisfaction, occupational status, income, and education level. (The instrument was also administered to a group of adults without disabilities.) The group of adults with learning disabilities saw themselves as having a greater number of problems and more severe problems than the nonlearning-disabled group (see Table 5.2). For example, 51 percent of the highly achieving sample claimed their reading problem was worse and 54 percent of the moderately successful said the same. Because this is a sample of moderately and highly achieving adults, no definitive statement can be made about those who have not achieved. However, there is no doubt that these people see their disabilities as not having appreciably improved. Adults with learning disabilities routinely report problems in reading, spelling, arithmetic, written expression, and in the social, personal, and vocational domains (Hoffman et al., 1987).

Most adults with learning disabilities, then, do not outgrow their problems. Their success lies in developing coping strategies that help them meet the challenging world of adulthood. Successful adults are aware of their strengths and weaknesses, capitalize on their strengths and find ways of coping with their weaknesses. For example, a bank manager noted, "I depend on my computer a lot. I make a lot of lists or I'm dead in the water. I keep lists on my computer. I've developed a computer environment that handles all of my memorization" (Polloway et al., 1992, p. 521). A deputy sheriff solves his problem of spelling poorly by keeping two dictionaries in his squad car. "This way I am able to write my reports without

TABLE 5.2   **Percentage of Adults Reporting Persistent Problems from School Age to the Present**

Item	HIGH GROUP (n = 49)								MODERATE GROUP (n = 84)							
	Never a Problem		Remained Stable		Got Better		Got Worse		Never a Problem		Remained Stable		Got Better		Got Worse	
	n	%	n	%	n	%	n	%	n	%	n	%	n	%	n	%
Listen	21	43	16	33	1	2	11	22	19	23	16	19	8	9	41	49
Speak	20	41	9	18	4	8	16	33	37	44	7	8	3	4	37	44
Read	6	12	17	35	1	2	25	51	13	15	22	26	4	5	45	54
Write	7	14	19	39	0	0	23	47	10	12	34	41	2	2	38	45
Spell	4	8	27	55	1	2	17	35	14	17	40	48	2	2	28	33
Math	12	24	22	45	2	4	13	27	19	23	33	39	5	6	27	32
Visual Perception	20	41	16	33	3	6	10	20	20	24	23	27	11	13	32	36
Auditory Perception	16	33	20	41	3	6	10	20	20	24	23	27	9	11	32	38
Coordination	29	60	11	22	2	4	7	14	27	32	24	29	5	6	28	33
Impulsive	17	35	13	26	0	0	19	39	18	21	25	30	9	11	32	38
Distractible	12	24	15	31	1	2	21	43	8	10	28	33	9	11	39	46
Hyperactive	23	47	10	20	2	4	14	29	29	35	27	32	5	6	23	27
Attention Span	18	37	12	24	0	0	19	39	17	20	26	31	4	5	37	44

Source: "Persisting Problems of Adults with Learning Disabilities: Self-Reported Comparisons from Their School-Age and Adult Years," by P.J. Gerber, C.A. Schnieders, L.V. Paradise, H.B. Reiff, R.J. Ginsberg, & P.A. Popp, 1990, *Journal of Learning Disabilities*, 23, pp. 570–573. Copyright © 1990 by PRO-ED, Inc. Reprinted by permission.

errors." Most adults with learning disabilities adjust to the complex demands of adulthood, but a disproportionate number, especially those with more severe problems, do not (Patton & Polloway, 1992).

Studies of vocational achievement of adults with learning disabilities show a mixed picture. The rates of employment are high, but often the jobs are relatively low paying (Zigmond & Thornton, 1985). Adults with learning disabilities also express more dissatisfaction with their jobs (Gajar, 1992). In one study, three-quarters of all graduates from regular classes in high school earned only minimum wage (Edgar, 1987).

Certain factors predict employment. When 175 individuals with learning disabilities were contacted four years after leaving school, people with high math ability, those employed during high school, and those whose parents were actively involved in their education were most likely to experience employment success after high school (Fourquerean et al., 1991). In this sample, 86 percent were employed either full or part time. Other important factors in job success include social acceptance, a work ethic, family support, the availability of programs and services, as well as a willingness to seek additional training in order to meet the requirements of the job (Siegel & Gaylord-Ross, 1991).

Still another factor is a sense of control. Gerber and colleagues (1992) found that control was a key to success for adults with learning disabilities. This control meant making conscious decisions to take charge of one's life and adapting oneself to the environment in order to move ahead. Adults with learning disabilities who were successful spent time deciding how to control their lives. Even though they had experienced years of failure, they were able to move forward.

The research on learning disabilities in adulthood is fragmented. Studies show that many people adjust well, take command of their lives, and develop ways of coping. At the same time, their problems in the areas of learning and social perception persist across time. Those who have found ways to cope and compensate have been successful, while others have experienced less success. One important caveat to remember is that adults with learning disabilities in their forties have had a very different educational background than young adults with learning disabilities in their twenties, and future adult generations will probably gain much from changes in education and vocational preparation.

The Future

The entire field of learning disabilities is in transition. Every part of the field, from its definition to its diagnostic criteria to its treatment methods, is controversial. This controversy, though, is healthy and has led to progress.

Despite problems in identifying the cause, a group of children exists who do not learn well through regular classroom methods even though other children exposed to the same educational practices achieve. This group of children requires changes in the educational experience and, if preliminary research on adolescents and adults with learning disabilities is confirmed, may require continuing help to reach their potential.

People with learning disabilities must find ways to use their strengths. Unfortunately, they often do not receive much empathy from others. Despite the many academic and social problems they face, many succeed by developing ways of effectively adapting and coping with their disabilities. In the future, more will succeed as newer methods of teaching, which hold so much promise, are developed and used more extensively. There is every reason to expect progress in the scientific understanding of learning disabilities to continue. The combination of scientific, psychological, and educational progress means that the future will be much brighter for the present generation of children with learning disabilities, and more of these children than ever before will develop their potential to the greatest extent possible.

 **Teaching Verbal Skills to Children with Learning Disabilities**

Erik Erikson (1963) argued that during the elementary school years children need to develop a sense of industry, a belief that their own work is valued. This belief leads to self-confidence. On the other hand, children whose work compares poorly may develop a sense of inferiority and lack self-confidence. An important part of school work is the development of verbal skills such as reading and writing. A child who reads and writes reasonably well can meet the challenges in many school subjects, such as science, English, and social studies. The child who cannot read and write may find it embarrassing and avoid situations in which reading and writing are required. A vicious cycle may ensue in which avoidance of reading leads to lack of development of reading skills leading to a lack of progress. The child with reading and writing problems falls further and further behind.

If teachers and parents are to break this unending cycle of failure and avoidance, they must devote considerable attention to developing children's academic skills. But since children with learning disabilities avoid reading and writing, they are frequently unmotivated to attend to the lessons. One parent decided that a way to encourage her child with a learning disability to read was to inaugurate a family reading hour. Each evening the entire family would sit in the living room and read. Snacks were served and the telephone was taken off the hook. Each member of the family could read anything he or she desired. Unfortunately, the parents found that the child for whom this program was designed found almost any excuse to avoid the silent reading. He would sit for a few minutes then go to the bathroom, then sit again for a minute then find something else to do. The parents ended up chastising the child, something they definitely did not want to do. What had begun as a pleasant way to encourage reading ended up as a tension-filled and unpleasant situation.

The use of computer programs to help children with learning disabilities develop their skills has a number of advantages. The computer is a nonjudgmental, value-free tutor that gives off no negative body language (Galloway, 1990). Mistakes are not followed by scowls or signs of impatience. The computer does not become tired and angry at wrong responses. The student working on a computer program is not publicly embarrassed if the student answers slowly or gives the incorrect answer (Larson & Roberts, 1986). The computer also requires active participation and gives students some control over their environment (Higgins & Boone, 1990). Computer programs may also improve motivation and time on task (Cosden et al., 1987).

From a teaching standpoint, computer programs can be especially helpful in delivering drill and practice, tutorial, and improving problem-solving skills. Students with learning disabilities often do not receive enough practice. Computer programs allow for individualization as programs can be specifically designed to deliver practice at many difficulty levels. The programs also provide immediate feedback, can offer a choice of speed, and measure student responses easily (Smith, 1991). The computer is also a tool for writing, which is particularly useful for children with learning disabilities.

All programs designed to help teach reading skills must be age-appropriate. Often, the child with a learning disability may be reading at a lower level and some programs are too juvenile. If the programs are inappropriate, the child may resist using the computer. Second, the programs must be inventive enough to keep the interest of children who have not had much success in more traditional teaching environments. If they are not interesting, then again the student will not use them. Third, all programs should be based upon what we know about the reading (and writing) process and about instruction.

Some computer programs concentrate on word attack skills and word recognition, and studies show that computer programs can be especially helpful in these areas (Goldman & Pellegrino, 1987). Jones and colleagues (1987) used a program called Hint and Hunt I to improve the decoding skills of elementary school children with learning disabilities. This program provides practice on a number of vowel sounds. There are ten levels, each presented on a separate disk. In the Hint portion of the program, the vowel sounds are introduced using synthesized speech in an instructional manner that does not emphasize speed. During the Hunt phase, a game-like format is used to provide practice in recognizing words and nonsense syllables that contain the vowel sounds introduced during the Hint phase. The game can be played at four different speed levels. Students with learn-

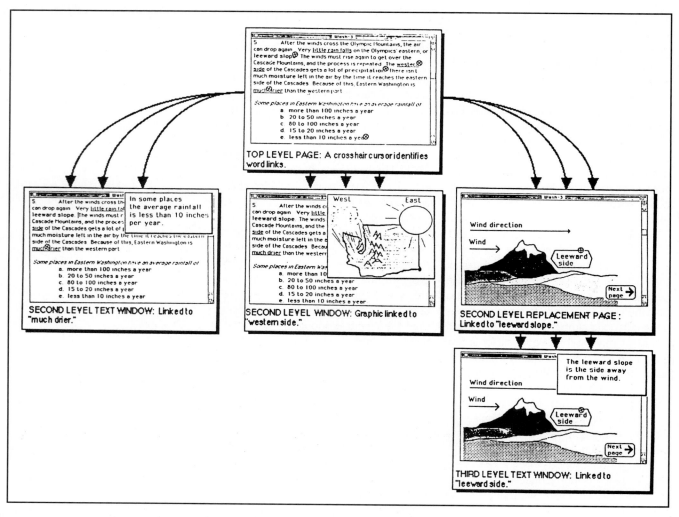

FIGURE 5.3 Hypertext Flow Chart Showing Multiple Text Levels.

Source: "Hypertext Computer Study Guides and the Social Studies Achievement of Students with Learning Disabilities, Remedial Students, and Regular Education Students," by K. Higgins & R. Boone, 1990, Journal of Learning Disabilities, 23(9), pp. 529–540. Copyright © by PRO-ED, Inc. Reprinted by permission.

ing disabilities using this program improve their decoding skills substantially.

One of the most modern applications of technology to help students achieve in a number of subjects is the use of hypertext. According to Higgins and Boone (1990), hypertext is best understood as a group of several transparencies overlaying one another. The top layer contains text to be read but also serves as a menu for accessing additional information found at different levels. The student positions the cursor on a specific area and selects additional information found on the other layers. Figure 5.3 shows a hypertext flow chart with its multiple text levels. Higgins and Boone (1990) created a study guide on state his-

tory from a text. Students could access other portions of the program using three functions. The note function consisted of short explanatory information and was available whenever a word was underlined. The replacement function allowed students to replace the main text with a clarifying text or a graphic. The replacement function was signified through the use of **boldface**. Last, the inquiry function controlled student movement through multiple choice questions; students could not move on to the next screen of text until they answered questions correctly (see Figure 5.4). An incorrect answer rerouted the student back to the appropriate text. The hypertext computer study guide was effective, and

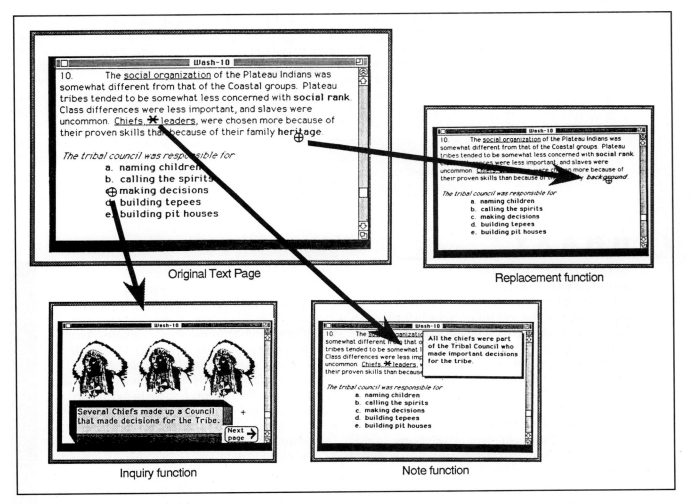

Original Text Page

Replacement function

Inquiry function

Note function

more children with learning disabilities using the hypertext than other methods of instruction passed examinations. Hypertext can be effectively used for students who miss a lecture or need repetition of all or part of the material covered in class.

Other software programs are available, which attempt to teach strategies associated with effective reading comprehension, including asking questions about the text, making predictions about what will happen next, and monitoring outcomes (Okolo, 1993).

Writing can be significantly improved using word-processing programs. They allow students with learning disabilities to check spelling mistakes and to edit more effectively (MacArthur & Schneiderman,

1986). Some word processors allow the computer to talk aloud so the students can hear what they've written. A word-processing program allows students to produce very neat-looking work, a boon to students with poor handwriting. Some programs help students through the entire writing process, including planning, organizing, and editing (Okolo, 1993). These programs can show errors in syntax or sentence structure and suggest alternatives. The Bank Street Writer, for example, is a program that aids students in developing many different writing skills. It presents students with reminders at the top of the screen to tell writers how to proceed. The program has modes for writing, editing, and transfer or printing.

FIGURE 5.4 Hypertext Functions Used in the Study Guides

Source: "Hypertext Computer Study Guides and the Social Studies Achievement of Students with Learning Disabilities, Remedial Students, and Regular Education Students," by K. Higgins & R. Boone, 1990, Journal of Learning Disabilities, 23(9), pp. 529–540. Copyright © by PRO-ED, Inc. Reprinted by permission.

Computer programs can certainly help students learn to read, spell, and write. The use of multimedia and hypertext allows new instructional options. Many programs are inventive, combining important skill practice with an entertaining format. Word-processing programs allow students with learning disabilities to write more efficiently and effectively. The unique attributes of the computer seem well fitted to the needs of many children with learning disabilities. But no one should oversell the usefulness of computer programs to help students with learning disabilities learn to read and write. These programs are not a magic cure for the difficulties that so many of these students have in the language area. Many programs can, however, be useful supplements to instruction allowing students to gain skills in a nonthreatening, sometimes game-like environment and encouraging students to practice their skills.

SUMMARY

1. There are many definitions for the term *learning disability*. Usually, three criteria are used to diagnose the condition: significant academic difficulties; a discrepancy between ability and performance; and the problems are not the result of visual, hearing, or motor disabilities, mental retardation, emotional disturbance, or of environmental, cultural, or economic disadvantage.

2. Children with learning disabilities comprise the largest proportion of children presently receiving special education services.

3. Children with learning disabilities have academic problems and may show difficulties in a number of cognitive processes including attention, memory, and executive functions such as self-monitoring. They often show perceptual problems. Children diagnosed as having a learning disability often experience difficulties in choosing learning strategies and in self-monitoring, as well as in listening and language.

4. Between 15 and 20 percent of all children with learning disabilities have attention-deficit/hyperactivity disorder (ADHD). Children with ADHD show inattentiveness, impulsiveness, and hyperactivity. Children with ADHD are often treated with stimulant medications—most commonly with Ritalin, which reduces many of the symptoms. Cognitive improvements in about 60 percent of the cases are found. Behavior modification is useful as well.

5. Children with learning disabilities are often rejected or ignored for a number of possible reasons, including their lack of social skills, their inability to read body language in social situations, their inappropriate behavior, or because they are not doing well in school.

6. The exact cause of learning disabilities is not known. Although children who have neurological problems such as brain lesions are more likely to have learning problems, most children with learning disabilities do not show such obvious physical signs. Research seems to indicate subtle differences between children with and without learning disabilities in central nervous system functioning. Any agent that potentially causes a neurological problem can cause a learning disability. Some believe environmental factors such as poverty, poor schooling practices, and poor curricula also may contribute to learning disabilities.

7. Children suspected of having a learning disability are given batteries of tests including intelligence and achievement tests. Curriculum-based assessment uses the goals of the curriculum to assess the child's progress. In addition, ecological assessment is becoming more popular. In an ecological assessment, the

entire environment of the child is taken into consideration. The progress of children with learning disabilities should be assessed frequently. In precision teaching, the child's progress is graphed daily.

8. About three-quarters of students with learning disabilities are educated in regular classrooms. Most receive some instruction in resource rooms.

9. Today, three different areas of teaching are being emphasized. First, students are taught specific skills through techniques such as direct instruction, which involves a series of carefully planned steps leading to mastery of the material. Second, students are taught learning strategies so that they may know how to learn, for example, how to summarize. In addition, since many children with learning disabilities do not monitor their own understanding and progress, they are taught self-questioning techniques. Third, since many children with learning disabilities have social skills problems, they may receive social skills training.

10. Adolescents with learning disabilities are at a greater risk for anxiety, depression, and suicide. They experience the typical problems of adolescents, but their academic and social problems become somewhat more acute. In the secondary school, direct teaching of skills may continue, but the emphasis is on learning how to cope with one's problems and on learning strategies, including organizing and summarizing. Attendance and motivation are frequent problems. Many students learn how to compensate for their problems and use their strengths and succeed.

11. Studies show that some difficulties continue into adulthood. The most successful adults learn to cope with their disability by using personally developed techniques. These successful adults have also made the decision to take charge of their own lives. Rates of employment are high, but a disproportionate number are working at jobs that pay little. However, many adults with learning disabilities have managed to succeed and with improvements in education many more will succeed in the future.

Communication
Disorders

COMMUNICATION DISORDERS

Never the Star of the Game
What Are Language and Speech?
How Do Children Develop Language?
Speech
Speech Disorders
Language Disorders

On-Line: Using Computers in Context
Parents, Teachers, and Speech Disorders
In the Classroom: Helping Children with
Communication Disorders Succeed
Parents, Teachers, and Language Development
Children with Communication Impairments in
Adulthood
Summing Up
Summary

TRUE-FALSE STATEMENTS

See below for the correct answers.

1. Children understand the babbling of infants, but for some reason, adults do not.
2. A two-year-old child whose speech leaves out words such as "the," "to," and "for" is in need of language therapy.
3. Most children with speech disorders are educated in regular classes.
4. Although speech disorders negatively affect the social relationships of preschool children, speech disorders do not have much of an effect on the social relationships of elementary school children.
5. A person with a distinct regional accent has a speech disorder.
6. The majority of young children with articulation problems (who mispronounce words) recover without the need for therapy.
7. A person with a very squeaky voice who can be understood may still be diagnosed as having a speech disorder.
8. The most common cause of stuttering is an auditory problem that was not discovered in early childhood.
9. Telling a child with a speech disorder to relax, speak more slowly, and speak distinctly is counterproductive.
10. An accident can cause children who have already developed language to lose some or all language abilities.

Answers to True-False Statements
1. False. See page 216.
2. False. See page 217.
3. True.
4. False. See page 221.
5. False. See page 225.
6. True.
7. True.
8. False. See page 231.
9. True.
10. True.

213

Never the Star of the Game

Bob Love played professional basketball in the National Basketball Association for twelve years. He was one of the top basketball players in the NBA and led his team in scoring for seven straight years. Yet, players on the bench made more money than Bob Love. Love never got any endorsements or made the extra money professional athletes do. No matter how well he did on the court, the star of the game would always be someone else; in fact anyone else except Bob Love (Spivey, 1992). Why this seeming unfairness? Bob Love stuttered terribly. Reporters told him that they would like to talk with him but did not have the time.

Despite the fact that Bob Love had a degree in nutrition, he could not find a decent job after he retired from basketball. As he puts it, "No one wanted to hire someone who couldn't communicate." He found a job bussing tables and washing dishes, then was promoted to making sandwiches and salads. He remembers that he was the only person in the restaurant system who had a degree in nutrition. He was told that his supervisors wanted to promote him to management but he had to do something about the stuttering. The company sent him to a speech-language therapist, and his speech vastly improved. He is now in management.

In 1987, the proudest moment of his life occurred. The Northern Illinois High School Awards committee asked him to give a speech at one of their banquets about how his stuttering affected his life. He gave an impressive speech under pressure in front of 700 high school students and received a standing ovation. Before receiving speech therapy he could hardly speak to another person without

Bob Love, a star in the National Basketball Association for twelve years, learned to control his stuttering, changing his life.

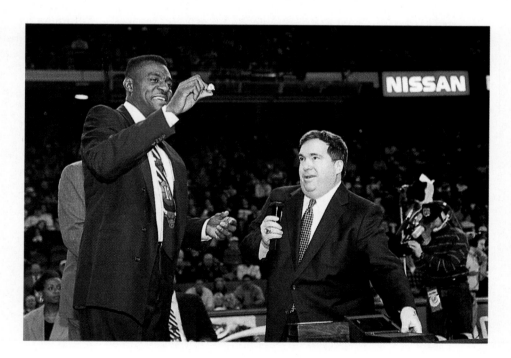

stuttering. He still has some difficulty speaking, especially when he is not relaxed, and visits his therapist on occasion, but he has essentially mastered his problem.

Few of us consider what it is like to be unable to communicate easily. Have you ever had laryngitis and could not speak? Did you find the day frustrating? People with communication problems experience similar frustrations, but instead of the condition passing quickly, it is always with them.

Think of the effect a communication difficulty has on the student in the school environment. Learning, language, and communication in general are intimately related. Teaching and learning require communication competence. Reading, writing, speaking, and listening are all vital skills necessary for learning. Children with speech impairments may not participate in class and may be embarrassed at their speech, which affect both academic work and interpersonal relationships. Children with language impairments may find the difficulties in communication overwhelming and poor learning may result.

What Are Language and Speech?

Before examining speech and language impairments it is appropriate to define communication, language, and speech, and look at how they develop. Language and communication are not the same. Language is only one part of **communication**, which is the process of sharing information including facts, desires, and feelings. Communication entails a sender, a receiver, and a message. **Language** involves arbitrary symbols with agreed-upon meanings (Shatz, 1983). Most of the time it is verbal, but it need not be. American Sign Language is a manual language used by many people with severe hearing impairments in the United States. It is a recognized language with a grammar of its own, even though it is not verbal.

Just what do children learn when they acquire language? Language has a number of subsystems. These include phonology, morphology, syntax, and semantics, as well as the rules for social language use, sometimes called pragmatics. **Phonology** includes the sounds of a language, the rules for combining them to make words, and the stress and intonation patterns (Gleason, 1985). For example, the sound /cl/ occurs in English, but not /kx/.

Children must also learn how to construct words. The morpheme is the smallest unit of meaning in a language. Some morphemes such as *dog* and *little,* can stand by themselves, while others, such as *ed* and *ing,* must be added to another word. The rules of **morphology** make certain that some sequences (such as *walked*) will occur, and that others (such as *walkness*) will not.

Every language also has its own rules for combining words to make sentences, called its **syntax**. For instance, "Johnny hit Mary" conveys a meaning quite different from "Mary hit John." The child must also acquire a vocabulary and understand the meaning behind the words. This area is called **semantics**. The general term, **grammar**, is used to refer to our total linguistic knowledge of phonology, morphology, syntax, and semantics (Best, 1986).

The child must also be able to use language appropriately, to express ideas efficiently and to get things done. This ability is called **pragmatics**. For example, chil-

---

Communication:
The process of sharing information including facts, desires, and feelings.

Language:
Any system of arbitrary symbols with agreed-upon meanings.

Phonology:
The study of the sounds of language, the rules for combining the sounds to make words, and the stress and intonation patterns of the language.

Morphology:
The study of the patterns of word formation in a particular language.

Syntax:
The rules for combining words to make sentences.

Semantics:
The study of the meaning of words.

Grammar:
A general term that refers to the total linguistic knowledge of phonology, morphology, syntax, and semantics.

Pragmatics:
The study of how people use language in various contexts.

American Sign Language is a manual language with a grammar of its own.

dren must learn the proper way to ask for something and how to use language in social situations. Each language has its own rules, and each culture has its own idea of how language should be used.

In order to communicate with each other, people must both understand what others are communicating, which is called comprehension, and also produce meaning through language or gestures. People can comprehend many more words than they themselves produce, and this imbalance remains throughout life.

How Do Children Develop Language?

If experts are to correctly diagnose language and speech impairments, they must understand how children develop language. Under typical circumstances, every human child in every culture proceeds through similar steps in reaching linguistic competence.

Prelanguage Communication

Communication between infants and their caregivers does not require language. Smiles, cries, gestures, and eye contact all form a basis for later communication. The nonlanguage interaction between parent and infant approximates a conversation. Although very young infants cannot understand words, they do respond to the caregiver's language (Fernald & Simon, 1984). Some linguistic abilities are present almost from birth. One-day-old infants respond to speech sounds by moving their bodies in rhythm to them (Condon & Sander, 1974). One-month-old infants are able to discriminate between certain vowels, such as /-u/ from /i-a/, and /pa/ from /pi/ (Trehub, 1973).

Infants produce single-syllable sounds called cooing. Vowel sounds are often led by a consonant, resulting in a sound like "moo." Infants enjoy listening to themselves vocalize, but these early noncrying vocalizations are not meant to be formal communication.

Babbling:
Verbal production of vowel and consonant sounds strung together and often repeated.

The next step in language development is **babbling**. Babbling involves both vowel and consonant sounds strung together and often repeated. Babbling may begin as early as three months, and it gradually increases until about 9 to 12 months of age. Then it decreases as the child begins to use words (de Villiers & de Villiers, 1978). Most infants are babbling by the age of six months (Silverman, 1995). No one has been able to decipher the meaning of any of the babbles of infants. Although babbling begins as a relatively uncoordinated activity, social stimulation does affect the amount of babbling children produce (Hegde, 1995).

The First Word

Holophrase:
One word used to stand for an entire thought.

Children usually utter their first word any time between 10 and 15 months, but there is considerable individual variation. Words are used at first in isolation and then gradually generalized to similar situations. Babbling continues during this one-word stage. Psychologists call this one-word utterance a **holophrase**, meaning a single word that stands for a complete thought (Carroll, 1994). For instance, a child says "Up" and means "Pick me up," or the child says "Wet" and wants to be changed. Parents must go beyond the word and use the context in order to interpret the child's ideas.

Toddlers use particular rules of word order. For example, to show possession children use the possessor and then the item, such as "baby, doll."

Toddler's Language

By 18 months the child is using up to 20 words, and names familiar objects and uses gestures easily. Words such as "no," "mine," and "hot" are common, although word usage is inconsistent; that is, a word may be used at one time in the day and not in another. A marked increase in word learning occurs in the second half of the child's second year. Right before the child knows about 50 words, an acceleration in vocabulary is found. It could be called a naming explosion, because about three-quarters of these new words are nouns. Perhaps this explosion occurs because children begin to understand that everything can and ought to be placed in categories (Gopnick & Meltzoff, 1987). Some children, however, learn their words at a more gradual pace and maintain a balance of nouns and other kinds of words especially verbs (Goldfield & Reznick, 1989). This may mean that no single "correct" strategy exists, and more roads to linguistic competence may be available than first thought.

By two years of age the child is using up to 270 words. Two- or three-word sentences are spoken and the first pronouns such as *I* appear. Some simple adjectives and adverbs are present. By 30 months the child is using up to 425 words. The child uses more adjectives and adverbs and often demands repetition from others. The child begins to announce intentions before acting and asks questions (Weiss & Lillywhite, 1976).

The two-word stage is well organized. The child's use of these words is governed by rules that make the meaning of the communication easier to understand. The meaning depends upon specific word orders (Owens, 1994). For example, when expressing ownership, toddlers use a word to stand for the possessor and another for the item, as in "mommy ball" or "baby doll." When something has happened or the toddler wants something to happen again, the child will use a recurrent word such as "more" or "nuther" and then the object such as "nuther cookie" (Owens, 1992). A number of these semantic rules are found in toddler language. When about half the child's utterances contain two words, the child begins to use three words. However, these sentences are still governed by specific rules.

The child's early speech leaves out small words, such as "a," "to," or "from," and concentrates on the more important words. This is called **telegraphic speech**, because it is similar to the language found in telegrams where the sender includes only the words absolutely necessary for communication (for example, "Mommy go store" or "baby take toy"). These important words are commonly stressed by other speakers in the environment, which makes them easier to imitate and learn (Brown, 1973). Parents still must interpret the child's meaning according to the context of the remark, but the thoughts are communicated more precisely at this stage.

Telegraphic speech: Sentences in which only the basic words necessary to communicate meaning are used, which leaves out helping words such as "a" or "to."

Language Development in Early Childhood

From ages three through six years, the child's language ability increases in vocabulary and the average number of words in a sentence. The child's style of speech also improves. These advancements are shown in Table 6.1. For example, by three years of age, the child is using up to 900 words, while by age six years, 2,500 words are being used. At three years of age, preschoolers' sentences average 3–4 words, while by age six years they are averaging 7 words per sentence. At three years of age, the child's sentences are well formed but very simple. By six years, the child is using all parts of speech and can use language in a much more efficient and effective manner. By the end of the preschool stage, the child is making fewer grammatical errors, can sustain a conversation longer, has more focused conversations, and can attend longer to one topic of conversation.

TABLE 6.1   **Linguistic Advancements During the Preschool Stage**

During the preschool stage, the child shows great progress in language acquisition.

AGE	NO. OF WORDS USED	NO. OF WORDS PER SENTENCE	NEW DEVELOPMENTS
3	900	3–4	Sentences show subject and verb but are simple; uses present tense; uses words such as *when, time, today*; begins to use plurals and some prepositions; uses commands.
3-1/2	1,200	4–5	Rate of speech increases; asks permission (*may I?*); uses *couldn't* and *if* as conjunctions.
4	1,500	5–5-1/2	Demands reasons why and how; rhymes; questions a great deal; uses words such as *even, almost, like*, and *but*; understands most questions; has difficulty with how and why.
4-1/2	1,800	5-1/2–6	Does not command or use demands as often; most sentences complete.
5	2,200	6	Asks meanings of a particular word; asks function of items, and how they work; uses many types of clauses; discusses feelings; understands *before* and *after*.
5-1/2	2,300	6-1/2	Fewer grammatical errors; sentences become more sophisticated.
6	2,500	7	Uses all parts of speech to some extent; can define by function.

Adapted from Weiss & Lillywhite, 1976; Owens, 1992; Kaplan, 1991.

Language Development in Middle Childhood

During middle childhood, the child improves in every subsystem of language. In the area of syntax, the child uses more elaborate phrasing and uses the passive voice as in "was sad" or "got lost" or "was chased." The child now knows that a verb can be made into a noun by adding *er*. For example hunt is a verb, and if you add an *er* it is hunter. After seven years, the child understands the adverb "ly" and verb agreement with irregular nouns, such as the "The sheep is eating," improves greatly. The child begins to use past participles, such as "eaten," and perfect tenses, such as "has been." These tenses develop slowly and, even though some forms are produced early in this stage, their use may be uneven until later in the period. This gradual development is common in this period. For example, the prepositions "if," "so," and "because" are used much earlier, but their full development does not occur until later in the period. Some forms, such as "although" and "therefore," may not be used until late elementary school or early adolescence.

Pragmatically, one of their great advancements is school-age children's ability to use language more subtly. Children's ability to get what they want now improves because in their middle years of childhood they begin to understand things from other people's point of view. This gives the child the ability to ask for things indirectly as in "Gee, that cowboy hat looks great." Most parents understand that this is an indirect request. The school-age child can gain attention in a more socially acceptable manner, ask for things giving a rationalization, and more easily direct the actions of others. The child can now introduce a topic into the conversation, keep the conversation going for awhile, and close the conversation less abruptly than preschoolers.

Speech

When we communicate our thoughts to others, the mechanism of communication is most often speech. We are rarely aware of the fine movements that must be made in order to pronounce words correctly. A number of different brain and body parts are involved when we pronounce words. Speech begins as air coming from the lungs is expelled and passes through the vocal folds located in the larynx, or voice box. The air vibrates these vocal folds in the process called phonation, which produces a low-pitched buzz or tone. The vocal fold's size and tension contribute to voice pitch. The vocal tract consisting of the throat, oral cavity, tongue, nasal cavity, and lips modifies the sound (Owens, 1992). The sound is resonated in the vocal tract (Massachusetts Eye and Ear Infirmary, 1992).

Speech has four components: phonation, articulation, resonance, and rhythm. **Phonation** is the utterance of vocal sounds themselves, in other words, the voice as produced in the larynx or voice box. **Articulation** is the ability to produce specific sounds such as the /w/ in *water* or the /t/ in *tin*. **Resonance** is the modification of the voice after it leaves the voice box, which gives the voice its quality. **Rhythm** involves the rate and timing of speech (USDHHS, 1988). Speech requires excellent coordination among the brain; the respiratory system; the vocal apparatus, including voice box, lips, teeth, mouth, and throat; and the auditory system.

Phonation:
The ability to vocalize sounds.

Articulation:
The ability to utter specific sounds required for communication.

Resonance:
The quality of the voice.

Rhythm:
The rate and timing of speech.

It is easy to forget the sophisticated coordination required when we speak to other people.

Speech disorders:
Difficulties involving the physical reproduction of speech.

Language disorders:
Difficulties involving poor grammar, delayed language, or the proper use of words.

The brain's involvement is central to language and speech. Most people have their language systems in the left hemisphere of the brain. If the left hemisphere is injured in young children the right hemisphere can sometimes take over. This compensation is less likely in adolescents and young adults.

Children develop their ability to produce sounds at will in a particular order. Certain sounds are easier to produce than others. As a rule, vowels are acquired before consonants in English. Sander (1972) found that most three-year-olds have mastered vowel sounds and consonants /p/, /m/, /h/, /n/, /w/, /b/, /k/, /g/, and /d/. At least 50 percent of three-year-olds can also use /t/, /n/, /f/, /j/, /r/, /l/, and /s/. Some consonant clusters and blends are pronounced as early as age four years, while others do not appear until seven or eight (Owens, 1992). The time at which children master these sounds varies considerably, making it somewhat difficult to tell whether a particular child will experience a pronunciation problem later on. For instance, consider the child who cannot pronounce the /p/ sound at three years. Although most children can do so, many children will typically not be able to do so at this age, but one cannot usually predict from this who does and does not need special early help.

What Are Communication Disorders?

Communication disorders can be divided into two general categories: speech disorders and language disorders. **Speech disorders** involve problems in the physical reproduction of speech. The three categories of speech disorders include (1) articulation or phonological disorders that occur when people mispronounce words; (2) voice disorders that involve difficulties in voice quality (e.g., the child with a hoarse or a very squeaky voice), and (3) disfluencies, including stuttering and stammering. The second category of communication disorders is **language disorders**, which involve difficulties with the proper use of words, poor grammar, and delayed language (see Hegde, 1995).

Although the physical appearance of children with communication disorders is most often similar to children without disorders, their impairment cannot be hidden. Their speech and language usage betrays them. Since almost all children with these disorders are educated in the regular classroom, teachers can expect to encounter these students on a regular basis.

The Prevalence of Communication Disorders

The prevalence of communication disorders changes with age. Communication disorders are most prevalent in childhood; the number of people with such disorders declines during adolescence and young adulthood. Then an increase occurs after age 40 (Culton, 1986). Many adult speech and language disorders occur because of stroke and other conditions more often affecting the elderly.

Speech and language disorders comprise the second most common exceptionality. During the 1992–1993 school year, more than one million children were diagnosed as having speech or language impairments and received special services. This figure does not include children who experience language impairments secondary to other conditions such as deafness, mental retardation, or cerebral palsy who also require speech and language help (NICHCY, 1991). Children with speech and language impairments account for 21.6 percent of all children receiving such services (U.S. Department of Education, 1994). This represents a decrease of 14 percent since the 1976–1977 school year when students with speech and language impairments represented 35.6 percent of the total student population receiving special education services.

The decline is due to three factors. First, more accurate identification and assessment procedures are being used. Second, the trend is to identify students with language disorders as having specific learning disabilities rather than speech or language impairments. As we noted in Chapter 5, learning disabilities and difficulties in language are intimately related. Third, many children are receiving speech and language services within the regular education system (U.S. Department of Education, 1993). That is, many children with mild speech and language impairments are being served without need for them to enter the formal service delivery system created for special education. A child with an articulation disorder and no other disability in many instances will be helped outside of the special education structure.

About 2.4 percent of the school population are considered to have a speech disorder. Using data collected over a thirteen-year period, Culton (1986) discovered that 1.37 percent of school-aged children showed articulation disorders, 0.75 percent voice disorders, and 0.30 percent fluency disorders. Language disorders affect about 2–3 percent of preschool children and about 1 percent of the school-age population. About two-thirds of all children with communication disorders are male (USDHHS, 1988).

Public Perception of Children with Communication Disorders

People often perceive children with speech impairments as less intelligent, even though this is not the case. When more than one hundred second graders listened to videotape recordings of a seven-year-old girl speaking with a lisp and no lisp condition, both male and female listeners rated the lisping speaker as less intelligent and less friendly (Madison & Gerlitz, 1991). Both elementary school and high school students tend to perceive classmates who have articulation problems in a more negative light (Hall, 1991; Silverman & Paulus, 1989; Gies-Zaborowski & Silverman, 1986).

Even in children's books, children who stutter are very rarely portrayed as strong, attractive, and personable but most often as characters who are timid, shy, and withdrawn, or sullen, unattractive, self-serving, and having some emotional disturbance (Bushey & Martin, 1988). In a series of informal interviews with employers, many misconceptions regarding stuttering were found, including the ideas that stuttering is associated with low intelligence and personality problems and that people who stutter cannot work in social situations, cannot handle emergencies, work more slowly, or require special attention and emotional support (Schloss et al., 1987).

One last point is important. Various cultural groups may view communication disorders differently. Some cultures are more tolerant of such disorders as stuttering than others. For example, some Pacific Island cultures do not seem to react negatively to people who stutter, while other cultures are very intolerant of stuttering and language differences. Bebout and Arthur (1992) administered a questionnaire concerning attitudes towards speech disorders to a group of university

THOUGHT QUESTION

1. *Why are people who have speech disorders often considered less intelligent than other people, even when they have average or even above-average intelligence?*

students and found some significant differences between North American-born students and students from other cultures who were not born in North America— Chinese, Japanese, Spanish, Vietnamese, and British students. Students from Southeast Asia, China, and Hong Kong were more likely than members of other groups to believe that people with speech impairments could do better if they just tried.

Speech and language disorders can affect social interactions even in early childhood. Rice and colleagues (1991) divided preschool children into four groups: children who were developing language and speech in an average manner, children with specific language impairments, children whose speech was impaired, and children for whom English was a second language. The researchers found that those children developing language and speech in a typical manner initiated more interactions with other average-developing peers and preferred to listen to other average-developing peers as well as giving these children longer responses. Children with more limited communication skills were more likely to initiate communication with adults, to shorten their responses, and to use nonverbal responses. Children as young as three years of age are sensitive to communication skills. Although children with language differences or difficulties had many opportunities to initiate verbal interactions with their peers, they often chose not to. Research also shows that children with language disorders are at risk for long-term academic problems (Bashir & Scavuzzo, 1992).

All communication disorders can potentially isolate the affected individual from others. Negative appraisals from others are internalized until the individual with a speech or language disorder anticipates these appraisals and develops anxiety attached to communication and avoids communication with others. Babyish language is cute when uttered by small children, but when language is greatly delayed or the speech pattern of older children remains childish, it affects every aspect of the child's social and interpersonal life. Since speech and language impairments can lead to social and academic difficulties, therapy needs to begin early.

SCENARIO

1 You are an employer in search of an employee who will greet people as they come into your establishment. A young man (seventeen-years-old) answers the advertisement, and you are impressed by his demeanor and appearance. As he begins to answer your questions, you notice that he has a stutter. The stutter is noticeable but you easily understand the applicant. Would you hire the person?

When Does a Child Need Speech Therapy?

On the surface, early intervention would seem relatively uncontroversial and desirable. Since children learn language so quickly during the first five years of life, early intervention makes sense. Serious problems arise, though, with early intervention for children with speech and language impairments not necessarily found when discussing early intervention in other contexts.

First, the acquisition of language and speech is variable, with some children well ahead of others. Second, many children with particular speech problems, especially articulation problems, improve greatly on their own without the aid of therapy. One difficulty in analyzing communication disorders compared to other disorders is trying to determine which children require speech help and which children will "grow out" of these problems. Indeed, disfluencies and articulation problems are not unusual in young children. No definitive test can determine who will recover and who will not. Third, no single standard of language is acceptable; many forms and styles are "proper," and individual preferences rather than scientific criteria may enter into the picture. Speech and language use are not perfectly standardized in each society. Many people have accents, and people from various subcultures may differ in style or grammar and still be understood. Most people show disfluencies such as "uh" in their speech. American English has many acceptable forms; having only one standardized, correct form does not conform to typical social usage.

With these three problems in mind, how can one tell who needs and who does not require speech and language help? The American Speech-Language-Hearing Association (ASHA) suggests that four main questions can differentiate those with speech/language problems from those who do not have such problems.

1. Is the individual's speech and/or language so different from others of the same age, gender, or ethnic group that it attracts unfavorable attention?
2. Is the individual's speech and/or language difficult to understand?
3. Does the individual appear to have difficulty hearing or understanding speech?
4. Does a person avoid communicating with others because the person is self-conscious about speech, hearing and/or language ability? (ASHA, 1992).

THOUGHT QUESTION

2. *Why is it often difficult to predict which children who have articulation or stuttering problems will recover without therapy?*

THOUGHT QUESTION

3. *Is a foreign-born person with a recognizable accent that is difficult to understand in need of speech therapy?*

SCENARIO

2 Your four-year-old child stutters a bit. You know that many young children stutter but you are not sure that she will grow out of it. You speak to two of your friends whose opinions you respect. One of your friends believes that early intervention is important and that you should seek out a good therapist. The other argues that any attempt to correct it will simply draw attention to the speech problem reinforcing the stuttering. What would you do?

Recognizing Communication Disorders

If the answer is "yes" to any of the questions above, an evaluation by a speech-language pathologist and an audiologist may be necessary. Two observations are important here. First, notice that language differences are accepted based upon subculture, and these differences are only considered a disability if the speech and language patterns differ from people of the same age, gender, or ethnic group. Tolerance for subgroup differences is found.

Second, notice that sometimes whether an individual is considered to have a problem depends not only on how others view the speech, but how the individual views it (see question four). A person who has a mild disorder or difference but is bothered by it may seek the help of speech or language therapy, despite the fact that others may not be bothered by the person's speech.

Language and Cultural Group

Have you ever travelled to a different part of the United States and had difficulty understanding all the words spoken by the people who live there? People in different parts of the country speak differently with various accents and sometimes use different phrasing and grammatical constructions. In addition, some groups within our society may use a different dialect of English. It is important to understand that these differences in language usage are not deficits or impairments. It often takes a specialist who has experience with children from various regions and cultural groups to separate dialectical differences from true impairments.

Because they may not have experience working with students from various cultural groups, many teachers at the beginning of their careers will "over-refer" students for speech testing. This is understandable, and as the teacher gains experience, the number of such referrals will decline. Remember that only if children's speech differs appreciably from other children of their age, cultural group, or gender will the child be considered to have a speech or language impairment.

Assessment

School districts use various screening procedures to identify students who might be in need of help. Such screenings may involve a short developmental history to alert a speech-language pathologist to any factor in the child's background that may increase the risk of a speech or language impairment. For example, a child who had a cleft palate or has recurrent bouts of otitis media (middle ear infections) would be at a significant risk for developing a communication problem. In addition, children with some disabilities such as cerebral palsy may have speech and language difficulties. Communication disabilities are referred to as primary if they exist without any other disabilities or secondary if they occur with other disabilities.

As part of a screening, the speech-language pathologist may request the child to participate in specific tasks, such as counting, and generally converse with the child. The activities and questions are specially designed to encourage the child to use a variety of speech sounds and linguistic constructions. Depending upon the child's age, a number of specific screening tests may be used. For example, the Bankson Language Screening Test measures word knowledge, morphology, syntax, and visual and auditory perception (Wiig, 1990).

If a referral is received from a teacher or parent or if preliminary screening shows a need for a more involved assessment, both formal and informal methods are used. The child's hearing will be checked routinely for a hearing loss that may be a cause of the difficulty. The child's case history including developmental, academic performance, problems in learning, and dialectical and linguistic background are investigated. Since the existence of speech-language disorders is based upon one's age and group status, a formal evaluation of intelligence and language ability as well as knowledge of cultural group differences are necessary. Children suspected of having a communication disorder are commonly given an intelligence test, but since many of these tests depend upon verbal abilities, they must be supplemented with nonverbal tests of intelligence. In addition, the speech-language therapist must be aware of group differences in pronunciation, which occur when someone's primary language is not English. A child whose primary language is Spanish may show some pronunciation differences. The child may also require some help, but a speech-language specialist will realize that the child does not need to enter the special education system. Bilingual programs and other services may be available for such children.

The analysis of the speech and language usage of the child will cover all linguistic subsystems, including phonology, morphology, syntax, semantics, and pragmatics. The teacher's referral is most helpful if it is specific, noting vocabulary problems or difficulties in syntax and under what circumstances these occur.

During the diagnostic interview, the child will be asked to produce words under various circumstances. Both production and comprehension will be analyzed. The child may be asked to name things found in the environment in order to be certain the child can pronounce particular sounds. Also, some measurement of the child's conversational ability will be elicited through spontaneous interactions.

The child may also receive standardized comprehension tests, which include both word and sentence comprehension. These tests may focus on word knowledge or knowledge of various grammatical rules. They are not context related, though, so they only yield a small part of the overall linguistic picture (Wiig, 1990). In order to further understand the child's comprehension abilities, the therapist may show the child pictures and ask the child to identify them or give the child age-appropriate directions for doing something—perhaps making a design—and see whether the child can understand the communication.

Standardized tests that measure the child's ability to articulate and measure fluency are also used. For example, an articulation test may require students to pronounce words containing various sounds in the beginning, middle, and end of the word shown in pictures. Although these tests are useful in noting the differences between the student and the norm group, they do not measure all the possible variations, so they must be supplemented with other measures. Such tests do not provide sufficient information for planning individualized education programs, but again add to our information about the student's communication abilities. In addition, many of these standardized tests only have a few items measuring each area, and so interview procedures are necessary to evaluate the child's abilities in greater depth (Leonard, 1994).

A speech-language therapist may also obtain a sample of a child's language usage through an audiotape of a conversation. The advantage is that the language sample obtained is found within the context of a conversation. These conversations involve topics of interest on which the student can easily converse. Analyzing these taped conversations allows for a greater appreciation of the child's difficulties.

The child's ability to communicate with and receive communication from other children in the child's own environment is another important aspect to evaluate. A difficulty in pragmatics may be discovered through observation and discussion between the classroom teacher or parent and the speech-language specialist. For example, a child may have difficulty forming a question or expressing a statement. Sometimes, videotapes may be made of interactions and then analyzed.

In evaluating these audiotapes or videotapes, both quantitative and qualitative scoring systems may be used. The number of times the child pronounces a particular sound correctly and incorrectly may be calculated and the circumstances under which the child pronounces or mispronounces the word may be noted.

Observations are also possible. The teacher and speech-language specialist may observe the child during interactions with other children to see whether the child is understood by other children, how the child responds to questions from adults and children, and how the child interacts with others. This observation may be attempted during a game, so such verbal abilities as expressions of intent may be noted (Wiig, 1990).

Three important points should be kept in mind. First, communication is a functional skill. People communicate for particular reasons—for example, to request something, warn someone of a danger, or answer a question. Although information obtained about how a child uses a speech sound, word, or a grammatical construction in isolation can be useful, it is most important to discover how the child uses language in the everyday contexts that are natural for a child of a particular age.

Second, when obtaining samples of a child's language, a number of samples should be used, not just one. This permits analysis of more varied situations as well as making certain that the sample of speech obtained is representative of the child's usage of language.

Third, building a rapport with the child being assessed is always important and is crucial to the successful evaluation of a child's communication abilities. After all, the child must produce the required sounds, words, and sentences if the speech-language specialist is to receive a representative sample of the child's linguistic abilities (Leonard, 1990). A one-word answer to the speech-language specialist's questions or refusal to participate in a conversation will not permit a valid and reliable analysis of the child's communication competencies. This cooperation is a general consideration with all children, but one which is most acute with younger children.

Are the Child's Language and Speech Impaired or Delayed?

When categorizing speech and language impairments, therapists ask whether the disorder is expressive, receptive, or a mixture of both. They must also decide whether the child is simply delayed in speech or language development, or whether the child is not only delayed but deficient in speech and language as these skills develop.

Some children with language impairments have *expressive* or speaking disorders; others have *receptive* disorders or problems understanding speech, while still others have both. Consider the following conversation between Becky, a six-year-old girl, and a clinician.

Clinician: What is your favorite game?
Becky: Doctor.
Clinician: How many can play that game?
Becky: Two four.
Clinician: Two or four?
Becky: Or three.
Clinician: How do you play doctor?

Becky: One has to be doctor.
Clinician: Anything else?
Becky: One operation man.
Clinician: Anything else?
Becky: No.
Clinician: What do you want to be?
Becky: A nurse.
Clinician: Oh, you need a nurse?
Becky: No you don't.

Six-year-old Becky understands quite well but does not produce complete sentences. She does not use verbs or conjunctions either. She has a good vocabulary but cannot connect words. Her patterns of speech are similar to those of a much younger child (USDHHS, 1988, p. 16).

Other children may have receptive disorders in which they do not understand language. Receptive language problems rarely occur alone but are usually accompanied by some expressive language deficit. Some of these children are misdiagnosed as having behavior problems or hearing problems, but standardized language tests can differentiate between language problems and other conditions.

Professionals do not yet agree whether children with language impairments acquire language in a typical fashion but more slowly or if they develop language in an unconventional manner. Perhaps both are correct. Some children may develop language much more slowly but in the usual fashion, while others may show not only delayed but incorrect speech and language.

Speech Disorders

The average speaker produces about three words a second, from a fund of many thousands of words. Incredibly, only about one word per million is selected or pronounced incorrectly (Kosslyn & Koenig, 1992). This accomplishment is indeed impressive, especially when we realize that a number of cognitive abilities are necessary in order to use language and speak. People use language so often and so easily that people who have difficulties stand out. Many muscles are required, and excellent coordination is necessary (Shames, 1990). The whole process is very complicated. Lenneberg (1967) argues that 140,000 neural events are required for each second of motor speech production.

Articulation Disorders (or Phonological Disorders)

The most common speech problem, as well as the easiest to treat, is an **articulation disorder** (sometimes called a phonological disorder) (Schwartz, 1994). Some children make omissions such as saying "sow" instead of "slow" or "at" for "hat." Some make substitutions such as saying "tar" instead of "car" or "wabbit" for "rabbit." Others distort, such as an initial lisping sound; some use additions that involve adding an irrelevant sound like "washish the doggog" instead of "wash the dog."

Articulation (phonological) disorder:
A speech disorder in which speech sounds are mispronounced.

Articulation difficulties sometimes sound like baby talk because many young children do mispronounce sounds, syllables, or entire words. Frequently, a four-year-old child says "pinano" instead of "piano" or "aminal" instead of "animal." However, when these words are mispronounced by older children it may interfere with communication (ASHA, 1992).

Another type of phonological impairment is called *verbal dyspraxia*. This involves the inability to produce the sequential, rapid, and precise movements required for speech. Nothing is wrong with the child's vocal apparatus but the child's brain cannot give the correct instructions for the motor movements required for speech. These children show many sound omissions, halting speech with many false starts and stops before the right sounds are produced (USDHHS, 1988).

Another such disorder is called *dysarthria*. In this disorder the problem lies in the lack of muscle control. This most commonly occurs when there is some nervous system disorder such as cerebral palsy or a stroke or other disabling disorder (USDHHS, 1988).

About 2 percent of all elementary school children have severe pronunciation problems, and many other children show milder problems. Some of these children fail to hear the difference between how they produce the sounds and how others do, while other children know the difference, but have difficulty producing the proper sounds because they have not learned to move their tongue or use their lips in a correct manner (Barach, 1983).

Phonological problems may result from physical disabilities, such as cerebral palsy or cleft palate or even dental problems. Hearing disorders may also cause such problems. Children learn language and speech through a complex interaction of listening and participating in conversation. This process is adversely affected by a hearing problem. A test of the child's hearing ability is often required to discover the nature of the difficulty. Even mild hearing loss can cause difficulties in language acquisition and speech, but one cannot say that the more severe the hearing impairment the more severe the language impairment, at least not for mild and moderate disorders (Davis et al., 1986).

Sometimes these hearing problems are caused by recurring bouts of otitis media, or middle ear infections. These infections are common in young children and may lead a child to mishear adult speech and produce it incorrectly. Children who experience recurrent bouts of otitis media at an early age may show evidence of phonological problems (Paden, Novak, & Beiter, 1987).

Most of the time the exact cause of articulation problems is unknown (ASHA, 1992). Many theories have been proposed, however. Some argue that it is caused by the faulty learning of speech sounds. For some unknown reason, a child pays attention to one aspect of the word but not another. Others argue that poor auditory discrimination may play some part, although this is a controversial theory. At the present time, we do not understand why some children who do not show any physical problems develop articulation disorders while their peers do not.

Some of the issues discussed earlier are especially important to the diagnosis and treatment of a child with an articulation disorder. First, at what point should a child be considered to have an articulation problem? No specific criteria is available that can tell a teacher or speech-language pathologist exactly when a child has a problem that requires treatment. Suppose a child has difficulty enunciating an /s/ but nothing else. Does that child need help? When speech-language therapists conduct evaluations they use their experience to determine whether border-line cases require help.

The second issue surrounds the rate of spontaneous recovery. Unlike so many other disorders, articulation disorders are subject to a substantial recovery rate even without intervention. In other words, many children who show this disorder recover by themselves. Some suggest the figure as 50 percent; others as high as 75 percent. Unfortunately, no reliable test is available to help determine whether a child will "grow out" of such a difficulty, especially if the disorder is mild or moderate. Since speech therapy is expensive and resources are limited, evaluators must differentiate between who really needs the help and who does not. The judgment of an experienced therapist is often required for this purpose.

SCENARIO

3 Deena is a bright ten-year-old who has an articulation problem. She has been going to therapy for about a year and has improved somewhat. Unfortunately, the other children tend to imitate her and make fun of the way she talks. She has run out of the class twice. You are her parent and notice the adverse effect this is having on her. What would you do to help your child?

Voice Disorders

Have you ever found yourself listening to the voice of another individual speaking rather than to what the person is saying? Perhaps the person's voice is so hoarse or so high pitched that it calls attention to itself. Perhaps it is too nasal or lacks resonance (ASHA, 1992). A person may have a **voice disorder** if listening to that person causes a listener distress or discomfort.

Some voice disorders are due to hyperfunctioning, which involves excessive pressure and excess tension in the voice mechanism. A person with a harsh voice often sounds like a drill sergeant with new recruits (Rieber, 1981). Some people have a problem with voice quality itself, perhaps their voice is hoarse and repeatedly breaks and requires constant throat clearing. Sometimes the pitch is unusual, either too high or too low and has a strained, tense quality to it. Hypofunctional voice disorders involve breathiness or an exceedingly weak voice. Still other problems involve too much nasality or even sometimes too little nasal resonance.

Traditionally such disorders have been considered either organic or functional (not organic). However, ample reasons throw doubt on the usefulness of this division. Continuous misuse of the vocal mechanism can lead to organic voice disorders, and organic disorders such as continuous laryngitis can lead to functional problems in speaking even after the organic problem has disappeared (Rieber, 1981). Sometimes a temporary situation can lead to a voice disorder, such as cheering loudly at a baseball game. Physical problems such as paralysis, injury, tumors, cysts, nerve damage, or edema (swelling) can also cause voice problems (Moore, 1990). Vocal nodules referred to as singer's nodes or screamer's nodes are a type of polyp or benign tumor often found in people who use their voices extensively (Moore & Wicks, 1994).

Voice disorder:
A speech disorder involving the quality of the vocalizations.

Sometimes, temporary situations such as screaming on the playground can lead to voice disorders, but for others it is a continuous problem.

Recently, more attention has been paid to voice disorders, especially for people such as teachers, politicians, and singers who use their voices a great deal. The most common reason people see an otolaryngologist (specialist on voice problems) is hoarseness. It has many causes ranging from misuse to colds to cancer. A person should see a doctor if hoarseness persists for two weeks and especially if the person smokes (Massachusetts Eye and Ear Infirmary, 1992). Conditions that may cause frequent coughing or throat clearing, such as bronchitis, may also cause voice problems. Excessive smoking can damage the vocal cords as can various injuries.

SCENARIO

James is a seventeen-year-old whose voice is very strident and loud. His voice is unpleasant to listeners. When a teacher suggested to James that he might want to avail himself of speech therapy, he told the teacher that nothing was wrong with his voice and not to bring it up again. Unfortunately, James is being ostracized by the other students in school because he is overly loud and demanding even when he probably does not mean to be. As an adult who cares, how could you help James become more receptive to therapy?

Disfluencies

Everyone occasionally stammers and some disfluencies are certainly acceptable in everyday speech. People repeat words or syllables, and no person's speech is totally smooth (Ainsworth & Fraser, 1986). People are sometimes astounded when they hear themselves speak after being recorded. They may use more than an occasional "uh" or stumble on some tongue twisters. A young child trying to coordinate thought, language, and speech may understandably stumble more than an older child or adult. In addition, when someone is under stress more disfluencies are found. It is sometimes difficult to conclude that the child has a stuttering problem since the behaviors themselves are common. However, when these disfluencies get in the way of effective communication they become part of a disfluency disorder. A number of disfluencies have been identified. However, the most common and troublesome is stuttering, which is the type of communication disorder that affected Bob Love.

Children who stutter may repeat sounds or words or prolong sounds (Shames, 1990). There are secondary symptoms as well such as eye blinking, head jerking, and facial grimaces. Some show a great deal of muscular tension. Many children who stutter become quite good at substituting for words that they cannot pronounce (Kaplan, 1990). Some have given incorrect names when asked or ordered a different food because they could not say what they wanted without stuttering (Shames, 1990).

More than three million or about 1 percent of the American population stutters (SFA, 1992). However, a much higher percentage of young children (about 25 percent) go through a temporary period in which they stutter. About 4 percent of all children stutter for six months or more. Most children who stutter begin to do so at ages three to five years. Rarely does a person begin to stutter after this age (Andrews, Neilson, & Curlee, 1988). Most children do not develop a stuttering problem, but unfortunately some do.

As in articulation disorders, some disagreement exists concerning the percentage of children who stutter who recover spontaneously. Some argue that as few as 36 percent or as many as 80 percent recover spontaneously (Seider, Gladstein, & Kidd, 1983). Studies, however, have failed to differentiate between those whose stuttering will disappear and those who will continue to have problems in this area into adulthood. Generally, females recover at a higher rate than do males. About four boys stutter for every girl. The reason for this disparity in gender is not known.

The cause of stuttering is largely unknown. Genetics may play a part. The risk of a first-degree relative of a person who stutters also doing so is three times the risk for the general population (Andrews et al., 1991). When identical and fraternal twins were investigated, the concordance rate (the rate at which both twins have a particular condition) for stuttering ranged from 32 to 63 percent for identical twins (who share the same genes), and from 4 to 23 percent for fraternal twins (Andrews et al., 1988). Although this certainly demonstrates genetic involvement, these figures also show that identical twin pairs exist in which only one child stutters. Other factors must be involved (Hegde, 1995).

Some argue that neurological factors are important. Children with neurological impairments have an increased risk of stuttering as do adults with cerebral damage (Andrews et al., 1988). Although neurological factors may be involved, sufficient research is not yet available to demonstrate that they are the cause in most cases (Bloodstein, 1987). In a related theory, some believe that children have problems with the fine coordination needed for speech. This lack of coordination causes disfluencies in much the same way as poor coordination may cause stumbling while walking (Ainsworth & Fraser, 1986). In many cases, as the child learns to control speech muscles the problem fades away, while in others it does not.

Learning theorists argue that people learn to stutter. They may be classically conditioned because they have linked anxiety-provoking circumstances to speaking. In addition, stuttering can be increased or decreased by various reinforcers. The importance of other people's reactions has been emphasized for quite some time. As parents become concerned about disfluencies, they may create an atmosphere in which stuttering occurs by responding to the child's disfluencies in inappropriate ways. However, while some parents may indeed call attention to disfluencies or create tension when speaking to the child, significant questions remain as to whether these behaviors cause the disorder in most cases. In addition, this analysis causes the parents to experience guilt even though evidence to demonstrate that they are at fault is lacking. Professionals dealing with parents of children who stutter should not act in an accusatory manner or assume that parents are the cause of the stutter. No single factor appears to be the cause of stuttering (Erickson, 1992).

Speech Therapy

A speech-language pathologist prevents, diagnoses, and treats speech and language disorders. These professionals hold a Certificate of Clinical Competence (CCC) from the American Speech-Language-Hearing Association and have a state license to practice (Silverman, 1995).

Speech-language pathologists tailor their treatment to the individual's particular difficulty. Therapy for phonological problems might include making the client aware of the correct sound for the /s/ or /th/, modeling these sounds, showing the client how to make the sound, and the use of various practice techniques. If the condition is due to some physical problem, such as dental problems or cleft palate, the physical problem must also be identified and treated.

Treatment of voice disorders is somewhat more controversial than treatment of other speech disorders. Some theorists advocate aggressive treatment (Kahane & Mayo, 1989), while others argue that it is not called for (Sander, 1989). But all agree that any decision as to what to do should be made after a physical examination. Children suspected of having a voice problem must see a medical doctor as soon as possible in order to discover possible physical causes for the problem (Pannbacker, 1992). When a medical cause is found, a treatment can be pursued. In the case of nodules, they are often removed surgically but may return unless the abuse stops. Recent developments in microsurgery using lasers has eliminated the need for incisions.

Treatment of voice problems also centers on reducing the vocal abuse and determining under what circumstances it occurs (Pannbacker, 1992). For example, if the child screams too much, this abuse of the vocal chords may have to be stopped. People with voice problems are often told to keep hydrated and to avoid alcohol and caffeinated beverages, which cause dehydration, as well as to avoid smoke-filled rooms and eliminate their own smoking.

If the problem arises from improper speaking habits, the individuals must learn the proper way to use their voices, not an easy task, especially for an adolescent or an adult.

For a number of years, therapy for stuttering did not emphasize direct treatment of the stuttering itself. Therapists assumed that direct work on the stuttering act itself would be harmful because it would make the young child even more aware of the disfluency and increase the problem (Shames, 1990). Some children who stuttered were given psychotherapy, hypnosis, or medication, which proved ineffective since there is little evidence that emotional problems cause the disorder (Andrews et al., 1988). Others emphasized the importance of working with the adults in a child's environment to be certain that they were not reinforcing the stuttering or causing the child embarrassment. These interventions emphasized reducing stress in the parent-child communication, not interrupting the child, paying attention when the child isn't stuttering, allowing the child to complete thoughts, maintaining natural eye contact, and finding ways to show that the child is valued (Schwartzberg, 1991). Telling children to talk slowly, relax, and take a deep breath will not help. Asking the child to repeat what the child has just said does not help the problem either. Loud orders to stop that or hard looks and punishment are counterproductive.

Although some environmental changes are still advocated today, direct therapy aimed at both reducing or eliminating the stuttering and dealing with the muscular tension or anxiety surrounding interpersonal communication is conducted. Most therapy programs for both adults and children involve three general features. First, a method is used that reduces or eliminates the stuttering under very controlled conditions. Second, the child is helped to transfer the improvement to other situations beyond the therapy session; and finally, strategies for maintaining the improvement are pursued. Stuttering can be controlled in the therapy setting using a number of different techniques called fluency-shaping or fluency-inducing therapies (Shames, 1990). Breathing and vocalization exercises are often used (Erickson, 1992). These techniques control the rate and reduce the frequency of stuttering (Onslow & Ingham, 1987). The amount of training received is a good predictor of the final outcome (Andrews et al., 1993). The program often begins with the child speaking simple sentences without stuttering and then increasing the complexity of the communication. Behavioral programs using reinforcers for fluent speech are also extensively used (Ryan & Van Kirk, 1974).

Transfer is accomplished by systematically introducing the child who stutters to increasingly demanding speaking situations. Maintenance may include continuing contact with the speech therapist on a reduced basis. However, questions remain concerning the best maintenance procedures (Ingham, 1990). Research indicates that many different programs can be successful with people who stutter (Andrews et al., 1988). Even in later childhood and adolescence, intensive speech therapy can often be successful.

The child's interpersonal skills and anxiety over the communication process is an area that needs attention. Many times people who stutter have developed poor interpersonal skills. Lack of competence in communication and fears of stuttering may interfere with such important activities as job interviews and interpersonal interactions. Role play and behavioral rehearsal are important in the treatment of children who stutter. In role play, a particular situation, such as a job interview, is simulated, and the person who stutters is given practice in desirable behaviors. This practice not only develops good interpersonal skills but may also desensitize the individual to anxieties associated with speech.

THOUGHT QUESTION

4. *Why have the advances made in speech and language therapy been so difficult to maintain outside of the therapy situation?*

Language Disorders

Billy's mother phoned the clinic when he was two-and-a-half years of age. He only said four words, about the same number as his one-year-old brother. Billy didn't seem to have any other problems, and the pediatrician had told her not to worry, but she worried nonetheless. Was it normal for a two-year-old not to be talking? Would he grow out of it, or should she get him some sort of therapy? Why wasn't he talking, and was there anything she could do at home that would be helpful? (after Whitehurst et al., 1991).

Eliza, age two and a half, toddles around her nursery school classroom, the straps of her purple overalls slipping off her shoulders. She watches and smiles, and generally she follows directions, but Eliza is silent. The only words she utters are "dog" to describe a wooden plaything and "bus" when it's time to go home.

Ben is older, nearly five, but uses words sparingly in two-word phrases, and these are all but unintelligible to a stranger. Ben wants to join in the activities of his class, but he cannot understand his teacher's instructions about putting a beanbag on his head, on his shoe, on his shoulder. He simply holds onto the beanbag and smiles, waiting to imitate the other children's responses (USDHHS, 1988).

All three of these children have language disorders. Billy is being treated at a clinic for delayed language. Eliza has a brain dysfunction and is delayed primarily in her ability to translate thoughts into language, even though she understands almost everything that a child her age is expected to comprehend. Ben has both speech and language problems. His problems involve the neurological motor skills that produce speech as well as the brain function of understanding language.

Language disorders involve some difficulty in the acquisition or use of language itself. Some children do not develop language, others may show it but at a very delayed rate, and still others show abnormalities in their ability to use and understand language. They show improper use of words and their meanings, inability to express ideas, inappropriate grammatical patterns, reduced vocabulary, or inability to follow directions (NICHCY, 1991). Leonard (1990) argues that children have a language disorder whenever their language abilities are below those expected of their age and their level of functioning. Such disorders may be expressive (i.e., being able to express oneself) receptive (i.e., being able to understand language), or both.

Speech-language pathologists generally identify children as having a language disorder if they lag significantly behind their peers in reaching certain speech and language milestones. The significance of the lag is determined by professional assessment. The ages at which children develop particular linguistic abilities is variable, and it takes a skilled practitioner to distinguish between a child who is slow and will catch up and a child with a true delay (USDHHS, 1988).

Language impairments show themselves in any or all of the subsystems of language. Form errors involve the inability to use the rules of grammar as when a child says "we go pool," instead of "we are going to the pool." Content errors involve difficulties with semantics. The child may use inaccurate words or the words may not make sense to the average listener. The child may have a limited vocabulary or fail to understand that one word can have different meanings. For example, some children with language disorders have difficulty giving names to objects and using these names to formulate ideas. They cannot seem to learn that a toy they are playing with is called a car and that a toy car of another color is also called a car. Sometimes, the difficulty is in pragmatics as children may not know when to talk, how to request information, or how to take turns. The child may not be able to ask for help (USDHHS, 1988).

Although language disorders may be classified in many ways, three main categories are most often used. Isolated developmental dysphasias involve either delayed and deviant language in the absence of hearing disabilities, mental retardation, or other disabilities. The second category is acquired language disorders called aphasias, which refers to loss of previously acquired language due to brain damage. The third category includes developmental language disorders due to or associated with hearing impairment, mental retardation, or autism (Resnick & Rapin, 1991). Some people with hearing impediments and other sensory or mental disabilities show language and speech-related problems. Since the communication problem in these cases is often an outgrowth of the main disability, it is usually considered secondary to the other disorder. However, many children with mental retardation speak well, and many individuals with hearing impairments have good language skills.

Isolated Developmental Dysphasias

Children with **isolated developmental dysphasias** show either delayed or deviant language in the absence of hearing disabilities, mental retardation, or other disabilities. They are often categorized according to the nature of the deficit, for example, as developmental receptive language disorders or developmental expressive language disorders (Resnick & Rapin, 1991). In the child's early years, all disorders of language acquisition affect verbal expression; a young child rarely has a receptive problem but no expressive problem. Any problem in comprehension at this age adversely affects speech production, which is not the case in adults. An older adult may not understand language in some contexts and still speak very well. On the other hand, a child may have impaired expression but reasonable comprehension.

Some children show a developmental delay in language acquisition. They acquire features of language in the same sequence but much more slowly. Sometimes the child may catch up, but more often, without help, the child continues to lag behind (Leonard, 1990). Table 6.2 shows the major language milestones and the nature of delayed language development.

Children with mixed expressive-receptive disorders, the most prevalent developmental dysphasia, speak late and are not fluent. Their speech is distorted and contains faulty syntax. Comprehension is deficient but equal to or superior to ex-

Isolated developmental dysphasias:
Language disorders involving delayed or deviant language in the absence of any other disability.

TABLE 6.2   **Pattern of Development Shown by a Child with a Language Disorder and a Child Developing Language in an Average Manner**

CHILD WITH A LANGUAGE DISORDER			CHILD DEVELOPING LANGUAGE IN AN AVERAGE MANNER		
AGE	ATTAINMENT	EXAMPLE	AGE	ATTAINMENT	EXAMPLE
27 months	First words	this, mama, bye bye, doggie	13 months	First words	here, mama, bye bye, kitty
38 months	50–word vocabulary		17 months	50–word vocabulary	
40 months	First two-word combinations	this doggie more apple this mama more play	18 months	First two-word combinations	more juice here ball more T.V. here kitty
48 months	Later two-word combinations	Mimi purse Daddy coat block chair dolly table	22 months	Later two-word combinations	Andy shoe Mommy ring cup floor keys chair
52 months	Mean sentence length of 2.0 words		24 months	Mean sentence length of 2.0 words	
55 months	First appearance of -ing	Mommy eating		First appearance of -ing	Andy sleeping
63 months	Mean sentence length of 3.1 words		30 months	Mean sentence length 3.1 words	
66 months	First appearance of 's	The doggie's mad		First appearance of "is"	My car's gone!
73 months	Mean sentence length of 4.1 words		37 months	Mean sentence length 4.1 words	
				First appearance of indirect requests	Can I have some cookies?
79 months	Mean sentence length of 4.5 words		40 months	Mean sentence length of 4.5 words	
	First appearance of indirect requests	Can I get the ball?			

Source: Reprinted with the permission of Simon & Schuster from the Macmillan College text *Human Communication Disorders 4/E* by George Shames, Elisabeth Wiig, and Wayne Secord. Copyright © 1994 by Macmillan College Publishing Company, Inc.

pression. Some of these children show delayed motor milestones, and some have learning disabilities. These children often show improvements by school age and show less severe comprehension deficits.

Language disorders may be found in any of the subsystems of language. Children with semantic pragmatic deficit disorder speak very clearly in well-formed sentences but show impaired pragmatic skills and speak too much. They cannot take turns, constantly chatter on narrow topics, and repeat themselves often. Verbal expression is often superior to comprehension. They do not comprehend open-ended questions having to do with why, when, or how. They may simply repeat the question although they may know the answer. They cannot read the facial expressions nor understand the tone of voice of others.

Children with lexical syntactic deficit disorder have adequate pragmatic abilities but cannot retell stories or retrieve the correct word in conversation. They do not comprehend language or open-ended questions well but can answer concrete questions.

The cause of these disorders is still controversial. It is tempting to attribute them to brain dysfunctions and probably some processing difficulty at some level (Kosslyn & Koenig, 1992). Some argue that difficulties during the prenatal stage create the problem. During the middle of gestation, nerve cells migrate from areas where cells are produced, called germinal zones, to regions of the brain in which they will reside. This brain cell migration begins at about the sixteenth week and ends by the twenty-fourth week. Some errors in migration could lead to language disorders. Despite much research, finding reasons for such deficits is not always possible. When these types of language disorders are found with hearing disorders, neurological impairment, or mental retardation, the cause is easier to understand, but often, no cause can be discovered. Other specialists believe that some damage to the left hemisphere may be the reason, but the evidence is not convincing in many cases (Leonard, 1991). However, with new ways of investigating the brain now being used, evidence may be found more quickly.

What Is Aphasia?

Aphasia involves a loss of language or disruption of language due to brain injury (Williams, 1987; Silverman, 1995). Sometimes, children just fail to develop language; other times, language development ceases due to an accident or catastrophic illness. When the term *aphasia* is applied to children it must be differentiated between acquired or developmental aphasia. Developmental aphasia is the inability to develop language at all and is most common in children with autism. Acquired aphasia involves language loss resulting from some brain injury after some language has been developed (Cooper & Flowers, 1987). Head injuries, especially from motor vehicle accidents, and diseases like encephalitis are the most common causes for aphasia in children, while stroke is the most common cause of aphasia in adults (Holland, Swindell, & Reinmuth, 1990). Children who have experienced head trauma often show excellent understanding of language when they recover consciousness but their speech may lag far behind. (The challenge of educating children with traumatic brain injury is discussed in Chapter 14.) Sometimes even reading ability may return before speech. Aphasia can be found in many specific areas of language, for example, articulation, loss of gram-

Aphasia:
A loss of language or disruption of language due to brain injury.

mar, syntax, or fluency. At times, a person may lose one linguistic function and not another such as losing speech but not reading and writing (Swindell, Holland, & Reinmuth, 1994). Sometimes, but rarely, it is accompanied by inability to comprehend.

More than 100 years ago, Paul Broca discovered that damage to the left side of the brain in a region on the side of the frontal lobe led to an inability to speak clearly. The speech when it does occur is labored and slow, and articulation is poor. It is sometimes called nonfluent aphasia because these people have problems finding words, particularly uncommon ones; have difficulty naming objects; and have poor syntax. These people speak hesitantly and are aware of how the speech sounds.

About the same time, Karl Wernicke discovered that damage to a part of the temporal lobe led to speech that sounds reasonable but does not make sense. In Wernicke's or fluent aphasia, the patient emits words but the speech is meaningless, and the person may be unaware of poor communication (Williams, 1987). In Wernicke's aphasia, comprehension, reading, and writing are affected.

Aphasia is a complicated disorder, and it is not easy to predict who will recover. The extent of the damage is naturally important but so is age. Children under eight years often make excellent recoveries from such aphasias (Zemlin, 1990). Certainly the recovery of children is more extensive and rapid than adults. Perhaps children's brains show more plasticity and flexibility and develop alternative routes for the transmission of neural messages. Even with children, though, some subtle learning deficits may remain. Often children with aphasia show continuing language problems even ten years after the accident or illness even though some recovery is evident (Cooper & Flowers, 1987). The problems are diverse, though, and no one pattern has been found.

THOUGHT QUESTION

5. *Why do young children who have accidents that affect their language abilities seem to recover some of these abilities more quickly and more extensively than older adults?*

Treatment for Language Disorders

Comprehensive treatment for language disorders is a recent development (Schery, 1985). In the past, educational programs for children with language impairments meant either no treatment at all or placement into classes for children who learn very slowly. Children with good intelligence and good health improve much more than children with lower intelligence and a number of medical problems, such as major neurological problems.

In the 1970s, children with language delays were taught to repeat sentences through imitation. The problem was that these children showed no flexibility in their use of words. Today, the emphasis is less on imitation than on grasping the context of language. Children play with toys and are taught to translate their activities into words—a mode of learning more meaningful for them—which gives them the tools to construct their own sentences. This addresses the important issue of whether a child who is taught a particular verbal skill in one situation will generalize that skill to another. Often, these programs use reinforcement procedures to improve the grammar, syntax, and pragmatics of the child with a language impairment. Although some evidence for generalizability has been offered (Warren & Kaiser, 1986), more research is needed.

Speech-language therapists use a number of special techniques while working with children.

ON-LINE   Using Computers in Context

Suppose you are a teacher who wants to help students with language impairments develop a more varied vocabulary and improve the ability to express themselves. Perhaps you find that motivation is a problem. The students don't seem to want to participate in discussions, and more traditional methods have not worked well. Research demonstrates that the use of computers can improve motivation (Shriberg, Kwiatkowski, & Snyder, 1989). So, you decide to try computers. How can they be used?

One way is to use the computer as a teacher. For example, perhaps a computer is programmed to ask various questions about a scene, such as "Which of these animals is brown?" and the student responds.

The computer then praises the student for the correct response and goes on to the next question. Such programs have a number of different variations that teach verbs, sentence structure, and so on. Children can certainly improve their scores on these exercises, but a question still arises as to whether these children really improve their communication abilities. Their knowledge of verbs and adverbs may improve but this may not translate into use in their everyday communication. In fact, little data exists showing that such programs improve children's communication abilities in the real world (Nippold, Schwarz, & Lewis, 1992). These programs may be useful when a particular linguistic target, such as improving reading comprehension, sight words, spelling, or grammatical knowledge, is involved (see Cochran & Bull, 1993). However, computers do not seem very helpful in the area of oral language. Although many reasons may account for this lack of success, the fact that these exercises are isolated, somewhat artificial, and lack a meaningful context are probably most important.

Communication is functional and always takes place within a context. A recent development in the use of the computer with children with language impairment is to use the software to provide a context for fostering language development. Something the teacher, therapist, or child can do on the computer becomes the context for communication (Cochran & Bull, 1993). Software must be flexible and allow for control by the user. Perhaps the child is able to draw a person and, together with the aid of the teacher, learns the parts of the body and discusses them. Perhaps the child's figure on the screen performs a number of actions; the teacher or therapist may then use this "screen activity" as a source of conversation. The computer is not instructional but provides the context for the session. The computer software provides the examples that the teacher or therapist thinks necessary and serves as the context for the lesson. Studies show that such learner-based software programs can promote speech and language progress (Steiner & Larson, 1991). The computer used in this way also provides a motivational boost for students.

To provide a meaningful context, however, the program must allow the participants to vary material to create new contexts as well as provide interesting graphics capable of motivating language use. O'Connor and Schery (1986) presented vocabulary items to young children with little or no language. Six mechanical toys were presented along with computer graphic representations of these toys. The additional six vocabulary items represented actions that could be carried out using the toys. The action items were also pictured on the computer monitor using color graphics. Another context used a purse and five objects that could be manipulated and placed into it. The additional six vocabulary items were actions that could be applied to the purse and objects. Children pressed a picture on the keyboard and a large matching color graphic came up on the monitor as the child heard the corresponding word. The therapist sat beside the child and identical toys were displayed out of reach on top of the monitor. When the child pressed a key and the representation was shown on the computer, the therapist handed the toy to the child for a play period. Verbal praise and questions were used. The children improved their communication abilities, and such an interactive model facilitated language growth in these toddlers with multiple disabilities.

Computer technology is also being used in an attempt to help students with speech impairments. Instruments are available that can convert sound from voice into a graphic that allows the individual with a speech disorder to see the changes in pitch or loudness. Immediate feedback is available, and as the student changes the loudness or pitch the progress is visualized allowing for practice and change. Many computer-based speech and language systems are available and are proving successful (Volin, 1991).

The computer does not replace the teacher or therapist in any of these areas. It simply provides a more flexible way to help children develop their speech and language abilities. The sophisticated computer with voice synthesizer and superior graphics capabilities can serve as a vehicle for practice and as a focus for conversation and teaching. Future research will be directed at improving the software available and discovering which students seem to gain most through a computer-based approach.

Parents, Teachers, and Speech Disorders

Whatever the cause of the speech or language disorder, how parents and teachers react to the child is an important factor in determining how the child will react to the problem. Parents and teachers sometimes make problems worse by either embarrassing children who do not speak correctly or giving them extra attention focused on the speech impediment. A comment such as "speak slowly and distinctly" to a child who stutters is counterproductive, as is a parent's habit of always correcting a child's mispronunciation of certain words.

Teachers and parents have the responsibility for recognizing the possibility of a speech or language disorder. Teachers may refer children with a speech or language impairment if they believe that the child's communication patterns are not age-appropriate and differ from the speech and language usage of children from their cultural group. For example, disfluencies are common in preschoolers but should become less so in early elementary school. If the pattern continues, a referral should be made. Voice disorders are rather obvious, and a referral is made if the poor quality continues. Children whose language is inappropriate and immature for their age should also be referred for evaluation. However, teachers should understand that accents and dialects are not considered disorders (Taylor & Payne, 1994).

Many children with speech problems find it embarrassing to talk. Since in the past these children may have been ridiculed, they begin to withdraw (Kaplan, 1990). Providing an accepting atmosphere for these students in which they can be involved in class discussions and question-and-answer sessions is important.

Children with communication impairments will spend almost all their school day in the regular classroom as long as speech or language is the primary disability. In fact, 85.5 percent are educated in regular classrooms all the time, while another 9.1 percent are helped in the resource room for part of the day. Only 3.9 percent are educated in special classes, 1.4 percent in separate schools, and 0.2 percent in residential facilities, hospitals, or home (U.S. Department of Education, 1994). When the impairment is connected to a different disorder, such as cerebral palsy or mental retardation, these statistics may not hold. For suggestions for working with children with communication disorders, see the In the Classroom section.

Three main concepts stand out when helping the child with a speech or language disability. First, close collaboration between the speech-language therapist and the regular classroom teacher is a necessity. The therapist can tell the teacher what areas are being targeted and suggest ways to reinforce the skills being taught. If the teacher is covering a particular book and an oral report is required, the speech-language therapist may use this as a starting point for the therapy.

Second, the teacher must accept and help others to accept the child. Some children with speech or language impairments are used to being quiet or being ignored and may not have their communications accepted. This tendency is unfortunate and can lead to both academic and social problems. Involving this child by accepting and valuing the child's ideas as well as helping to improve the child's social world through group activities are important.

Third, the child with a speech-language impairment will be helped by general activities in the classroom that aim at fostering language development. Some of these activities include language games, encouraging students to create original stories, and having children use pictures from magazines as a focus for a discussion.

 **THE CLASSROOM**   **Helping Children with Communication Disorders Succeed**

1. Actively listen to children with speech impairments, even if it takes longer for the child to get the statement out.	**Why?** Students with speech-language impairments need to be encouraged to participate in conversations. Active listening is the first step.
2. Do not criticize speech errors.	**Why?** Drawing attention to a speech error may increase the child's anxiety. The teacher and parent may demonstrate the correct speech, but not criticize the error. For example, if a child says, "A rabbit is an aminal," the teacher or parent may say, "That's right, a rabbit is an animal."
3. Seat students with speech impairments in the middle of the classroom next to other students.	**Why?** Since these children are often reluctant to communicate, placing them near other children encourages communication.
4. Provide opportunities for verbal practice.	**Why?** Although practice is important for all students, it is critical to the linguistic development of children with speech or language disorders. Such opportunities include participation in all aspects of the class activities.
5. Adjust language to the level of the child's comprehension ability.	**Why?** If a child's language abilities are not age-consistent, the child must be spoken to with words and structure consistent with the child's ability level.
6. Paraphrase what the child is saying.	**Why?** If the teacher understands the child's statements but the other students do not, paraphrasing is acceptable.

7. Praise children for their use of new skills.	**Why?** The teacher is in an excellent position to quietly praise the child and reinforce the student for new communication skills.
8. Use these new skills in the classroom.	**Why?** Integrating the skills into the classroom academic study and social activities allows the child to practice new skills in a meaningful context.
9. The teacher and speech-language therapist must collaborate and the teacher receive instructions on what to do and what *not* to do.	**Why?** The classroom teacher and the speech language therapist must translate clinical goals into educational goals and strategies for meeting these goals.
10. Model good language usage.	**Why?** Children learn from what they experience. If adults do not finish their sentences or use poor grammar, children may imitate.
11. Encourage oral communication.	**Why?** Often, one or two children in a class monopolize conversations or discussions. Attempts should be made to encourage everyone to participate, especially the child with communication difficulties.
12. Use role playing and active participation.	**Why?** Teachers can design oral communication into classroom activities. A discussion question that can be answered by everyone is one way of doing this.
13. React to the child's speech and language without impatience or criticism.	**Why?** Reacting inappropriately may set the child's progress back. Teachers may be tempted to say "take a breath" or "relax" or to finish the child's sentences. These remarks are simplistic and demeaning.
14. Maintain eye contact and wait, use a relatively slow and relaxed rate of speech but a natural one in your conversation and convey to students that their communication is important (SFA, 1992).	**Why?** These behaviors communicate acceptance and do not increase the child's anxiety level.

15. Call on these children early in the session.	**Why?** This reduces the child's anxiety level (SFA, 1992). Children with speech or language impairments, though, should be required to answer questions just as any other student in the class is required to do so.

Parents, Teachers, and Language Development

The language development program for students with communication disorders is an outgrowth of the total classroom language experience, though certainly tailored to meet the individual needs of particular students. The school and home both share responsibilities in the area of language development, and home-school partnerships are possible.

Before discussing some particular strategies and activities that encourage language development, the importance of the teacher's use of language should be noted. The teacher models language and has a direct effect on the classroom. If the teacher uses well-formed sentences with a rich but understandable vocabulary then students will be influenced by it. If the teacher communicates in an unhurried and clear manner, communication will be enhanced. The teacher also creates an atmosphere in which children either feel free to communicate or not. The teacher may do this by showing an appreciation for student opinions and questions and by being an active listener. Active listening involves answering questions asked, responding both verbally and nonverbally, and showing acceptance and appreciation for communication.

Many techniques encourage the use of language and the development of rich language. Language skill development can be tied to other classroom activities and should not be seen as isolated from a meaningful context.

Reinforcement can be very useful. Nonverbal reinforcers such as a nod or a smile can be used to encourage communication. Communication that is understood and acted upon by another individual is reinforcing in itself. When a child asks for something, such as a pen, and receives it, the child is reinforced for the communication.

Imitation may also be used but not in the traditional sense. Just having students repeat a phrase is not effective, but modeling the correct grammar and then, in an appropriate manner, requiring students to use it can be effective. For example, a teacher may hold a picture and note that the boy is riding a bicycle and ask the student what the child in the next picture is doing. The child is learning through imitation the "ing" ending for a word (Mandell & Gold, 1984). In a similar manner, if a teacher requires students to ask for things using please, the children will hear it often enough and perhaps begin to use it when appropriate as well.

Another technique, expansion, involves both acknowledging that the student has communicated something and also extending or modifying the child's statement. For example, if a child says "Ball fall," the teacher or parent may say "Yes, the ball fell" (Penner, 1987). Parents sometimes do this, as when a child says "That are a giraffe," the parent says, "Yes, that is a giraffe." Parents also respond with expansions in which adults reproduce major parts of the child's statement but add something (Bohannon & Stanowicz, 1988). Parents may also ask the child to clarify the meaning of the entire statement or some part of the statement. Children with language impairments are often not specific enough to give the listener a real understanding of what they are speaking about, leading to frustration. For example, overusing such terms as "thing," "that one," and "it" is a frequent problem (Mandell & Gold, 1984). It is appropriate for the teacher to ask for a clarification as in "When you said, that thing, did you mean the pencil sharpener by my book?"

Teachers can also give information by labeling what is going on within the context of an activity. For example, the teacher may comment on a child's drawing or action, giving some information the child may not know. Although labeling is useful, one should not provide too many labels at one time.

Since listening is part of the communication process, practice in active listening is important. Students often require some help in developing good listening skills. For example, a teacher may give clear directions once and then ask questions of the students that show whether the children understood the directions. When a child does not understand, the teacher can analyze why and help the child learn to listen carefully to such directions. Other activities include rhyming words, identifying the words that do not belong on a list, and asking how things are alike or different.

Students can be encouraged to listen to each other as they speak in class. Students typically listen to the teacher but not to each other when a question is answered. Teachers should beware of simply repeating every statement a student makes since this can encourage students not to listen to each other. In some cases, of course, paraphrasing is necessary to clarify a student response. Students can be encouraged to listen to each other by accepting another student's communication, commenting on it, and if necessary, asking the student to repeat it for the class.

Teachers can help students become good listeners and make comprehension easier for children with language impairments by simplifying sentences when necessary, making certain they complete their sentences, avoiding use of the passive form (was ridden), and giving contextual cues. Sometimes, modifying the rate of speech and using nonverbal cues are helpful.

Asking and answering questions is an important communication ability. Teachers ask questions for a variety of reasons, including eliciting information from students that demonstrates their level of understanding, providing opportunities for students to become involved, and encouraging students to think. Unfortunately, teacher questions are sometimes poorly formulated. A question such as "What about these angles?" may give rise to the student response "I don't like them." Such questions are called elliptical or ambiguous questions (Fairbairn, 1987). Asking multiple questions—such as "Who fought the Civil War, and in which state did most of the battles take place?"—called an overlaid or multiple question, also creates difficulties for students. Other questions that are not really questions, such as "Don't you agree?" should not be used. Sometimes, questions can be formulated at the beginning of an activity, which helps students focus on the important aspects of the written work or film.

One problem often seen in classrooms is that teachers don't wait long enough after asking a question (Rowe, 1986). In fact, when elementary school teachers increased their wait time from the usual 1 second to at least 3 to 5 seconds, students increased the length of their responses, student-to-student exchanges became more common, the number of times students failed to respond decreased, and the number of student questions increased, as did the number of students participating in discussion (Swift & Gooding, 1983). These improvements were prompted by simply counting from one to three before choosing a student (Morine-Dershimer & Beyerbach, 1987).

Parents can become partners in fostering their children's language development. Parents of children with language impairments can provide valuable practice for their children. Many schools send home suggestions for helping students develop their language skills. These suggestions may involve techniques of reading to children and ways of encouraging children to talk to parents using fuller sentences rather than simply using "yes" and "no" answers. In addition, the school, in cooperation with parents, may teach children how to use and practice language in a variety of situations, for example, asking for information from a store, ordering from a menu, or expressing feelings in an appropriate manner. However, any home program must begin with parents understanding that the experiences must be pleasurable and incorporated into the daily activities rather than being associated with a set time and place, and remembering that language is fostered within a context. Parents do not always interact in a fashion that promotes language development. Some parents only ask for one-word answers; others do not use an appropriate vocabulary or grammar. Others repeat their statement when a child does not understand it rather than paraphrasing and changing it to foster understanding. Active listening is also important. In one family with seven children, the youngest would never get an opportunity to talk at the dinner table where conversation was monopolized by older children. To demonstrate active listening, parents can comment on subjects such as the weather and react with understanding to the child's verbalizations. Helping the child associate words with objects, actions, and experiences, and using descriptions of the environment are additional ways of promoting communication.

Promoting language development is a general goal for all students, but is certainly vital to the development of children with language impairments. Activities that promote language growth should be part of all basic classroom and home activities. For communication to be functional, it must be encouraged within meaningful contexts. The tendency, though, may be to ignore the child with a language impairment who, in actuality, requires more practice and encouragement. Although the level of the communication may have to be modified and special care taken to involve this child in the language life of the classroom, the classroom teacher and the parent can do much to promote language learning in a child with a communication disability.

SCENARIO

5 Jonathan is a seven-year-old whose language development is impaired. He appears to be about one-and-a-half years behind. One of the problems is that he does not talk much and when he does, he rarely uses full sentences, although he is capable of doing so. You are his teacher and want to increase the frequency of his verbal communication. How would you go about this?

Children with Communication Impairments in Adulthood

Many, but certainly not all, children with speech impairments improve significantly so that they do not carry serious speech impairments into adulthood. Some children grow out of their problems, while others are helped through therapy. This success is rarely the case with language disorders. Language disorders are more likely to persist into adolescence and cause problems in the understanding and production of language in adulthood. For example, when 18 children with speech disorders and 18 children with language disorders were followed into adulthood, 9 of the children with language disorders still had communication and learning difficulties in adulthood compared with only 1 child in the group of children with speech disorders.

Summing Up

People with speech and language impairments are often keenly aware of them. Children may be teased and considered less intelligent. Adults often find that people do not listen to what they say, just how they are saying it. Every utterance may cause anxiety. In recent years, progress has been reported in the treatment of communication disorders. Although much progress is still needed, especially in the treatment of language disorders, many people with communication impairments can now be helped to do something that most of us take for granted every day: to communicate effectively with others in our environment.

S U M M A R Y

1. Communication is the process of sharing information including facts, desires, and feelings. Language involves arbitrary symbols with agreed-upon meanings. It consists of a number of subsystems including phonology, morphology, syntax, semantics, and pragmatics.

2. Infants communicate with the people around them by smiling, crying, and gesturing. Babbling, which involves verbalization of vowel and consonant sounds, begins as early as three months. Children utter their first word anytime between ten and fifteen months of age. Some psychologists argue that children use one word, called a holophrase, to stand for an entire thought. The child's early sentences are called telegraphic because they contain only words absolutely necessary for communicating meaning to other people.

3. The four components of speech are articulation, phonation, resonance, and rhythm. Speech requires coordination between the brain, respiratory system, larynx, and oral tract. Some sounds are easier for children to pronounce than others, and some sounds are produced before others.

4. Communication disorders fall into one of two categories. Speech disorders include

articulation disorders (involving the inability to pronounce words correctly), voice disorders (involving problems with the quality of the voice), and fluency disorders (involving a disturbance in rate). The category of language disorders involves problems in the acquisition, use, or comprehension of language. Children with communication disorders comprise the second largest category of children receiving special education services. Many children with mild speech disorders are helped outside the special education framework.

5. The public holds a somewhat negative picture of people with language and speech impairments, often believing them to be less intelligent and experiencing emotional problems.

6. Early intervention is necessary for children who have speech and language problems but it is complicated by the variability in the acquisition of speech and language. Many children with speech problems will recover without therapy.

7. An individual requires therapy if the individual's speech and/or language is so different from others of the same age, gender, or ethnic group that it attracts unfavorable attention, if the individual's speech and/or language is difficult to understand, if the individual appears to have difficulty hearing or understanding speech, or if the individual avoids communicating with others because of a self-consciousness about speech, hearing, and/or language ability. People who speak with an accent or show subcultural differences in language usage or grammar are not considered to have communication disorders as long as they can be understood.

8. Articulation or phonological disorders are the most common speech impairment and involve problems in pronunciation. Many children's articulation problems eventually correct themselves.

9. Voice disorders involve problems in voice quality. Often voice disorders are caused by physical problems, such as polyps or small growths, and sometimes from misuse of the voice, such as straining the voice through yelling.

10. Disfluency disorders involve problems with rate, rhythm, and speed of speech. The most common is stuttering, which is a condition in which words or sounds are repeated or prolonged. Many young children go through a period in which they stutter, but the recovery rate without therapy is relatively high.

11. Speech-language pathologists are licensed by the various states and have a certificate of clinical competence. Therapy for articulation disorders consists of helping children become more aware of their pronunciation, modeling the correct sounds, and practice. Therapy for voice disorders involves correction of physical problems that often cause the disorder and sometimes help in reducing vocal strain and avoiding misuse of the voice. Therapy for stuttering usually consists of adopting a method that reduces or eliminates the stuttering under controlled conditions, and helping the client to transfer the improvement to other situations beyond the therapy interview.

12. Language disorders involve an impairment or deviant development of comprehension and/or use of spoken, written, and/or other symbol system. The disorder may involve the form of language (problems in phonology, morphology, or syntax), the content of language, semantics and the function of language (pragmatics), or any combination of these systems. Some children show a delay in language acquisition, others show abnormalities in their use of language, while some others do not develop language at all. Some language disorders are receptive; some are expressive, while others are both.

13. Language disorders are often grouped into three categories. Isolated developmental dysphasias involve either delayed or deviant language in the absence of hearing problems, mental retardation, or other disability. Aphasia refers to loss of language or disruption of

language due to brain injury. The third category includes developmental language disorders due to or associated with hearing impairment, mental retardation, or autism.

14. Children with language disorders are treated by being taught to translate their activities into words. Often these programs use reinforcement procedures such as shaping and fading to train grammar, syntax, and pragmatics.

15. Classroom teachers can do much to foster the linguistic development of all children, including children with language disorders by being active listeners, modeling good language usage, creating an atmosphere of acceptance, and using such techniques as reinforcement, labeling, and expansion.

Behavior Disorders

TRUE-FALSE STATEMENTS

See below for the correct answers.

1. According to law, only children who show serious behavior disorders rather than mild or moderate ones may be classified as having an emotional disturbance.
2. Most children diagnosed as having a behavior disorder score in or near the gifted range on intelligence tests.
3. Boys are diagnosed as having a behavior disorder more often than girls.
4. Children who act very aggressively have no friends.
5. Children who are aggressive usually have parents who rarely, if ever, punish them for their misbehavior.
6. Delinquents do not show high levels of aggression towards people they know, only toward strangers.
7. Aggression is a mostly stable trait.
8. Children who are depressed tend to see the world and interpret their own experience in a realistic manner.
9. Adolescents who talk the most about suicide are the ones least likely to make a suicide attempt.
10. Mothers of children who show school phobia often agree with their children's complaints about school and want to protect their children from all discomfort.

Answers to True-False Statements
1. True.
2. False. See page 255.
3. True.
4. False. See page 261.
5. False. See page 262.
6. False. See page 267.
7. True.
8. False. See page 272.
9. False. See page 277.
10. True.

An Uneasy Feeling

Think back on your days in elementary and secondary school. Do you remember students who acted aggressively, were very anxious, or seemed constantly unhappy and withdrawn? Students who are always hitting others, are always nervous or upset, or who are depressed and do not speak to anyone are found in every school. These students are certainly not popular with either their teachers or their peers (Konopasek, 1990). Many are rejected, ignored, teased, and criticized.

Teachers often feel uncomfortable about having these students in class. They frequently have difficulty differentiating the child who has a behavior disorder from the child who is simply misbehaving in class at the present time or is experiencing some transient problem. In fact, although learning disabilities is the most common exceptionality according to educational statistics, if we judge by teacher's estimates, the most common would be behavior disorders (Kaplan, 1986). Rubin and Balow (1978) asked teachers to identify those students they considered to have a behavior disorder. An incredible 48 percent of all students were identified as having a behavior disorder by at least one teacher over a three-year period, and 7 percent of all students were cited by every teacher over this period of time.

The Legal Definition of Behavior Disorder

Public Law 94-142 defines serious emotional disturbance as "a condition exhibiting one or more of the following characteristics over a long period of time and to a marked degree, which adversely affects educational performance:

1. An inability to learn, which cannot be explained by intellectual, sensory, or health factors.
2. An inability to build or maintain satisfactory interpersonal relationships with peers and teachers.
3. A general pervasive mood of unhappiness or depression; or a tendency to develop physical symptoms or fears associated with personal or school problems" (*Federal Register*, April 1977).

The definition specifically includes children who have schizophrenia, but excludes children who are socially maladjusted, unless it is determined that they have a severe emotional disturbance (*Federal Register*, 1981). The terms *emotional disturbance* and *behavior disorder* are often used interchangeably by psychologists. Although behavior disorder has become more the term of choice over the years, the law still uses the term *emotional disturbance*.

The PL 94-142 definition, although long, is conceptually easy to understand. Children are experiencing a serious emotional disturbance if they do not establish or maintain reasonable interpersonal relationships, show inappropriate behavior, or develop psychological symptoms, such as depression or fears, which interfere with school achievement. These difficulties cannot be caused by sensory, intellectual, or health problems. They must also be shown for a long period of time and to a marked degree.

Problems with the Definition

This definition contains some terms and phrases that are not easily defined in a way that allows for accurate and unbiased measurement. For example, what does "a long time" and "to a marked extent" mean? In addition, "inappropriate behavior" and "reasonable interpersonal relationships" are subjective evaluations. Certainly, we might all agree that some behaviors demonstrate emotional disturbance—such as a child who rages at everyone indiscriminately or a child who experiences hallucinations—but many behaviors defy consensus. A considerable amount of subjectivity exists in this definition. In addition, a behavior disorder is the only exceptionality in which the law uses the term "serious." Children who show moderate or mild disturbances are specifically excluded from consideration. The puzzling exclusion of children who are socially maladjusted tops off the list of problems with the definition.

The Case of Social Maladjustment

The greatest question surrounding the definition involves the exclusion of social maladjustment. Social maladjustment refers to behaviors that are aggressive, show no respect for the rights of others, and are antisocial. Coleman (1992) suggests that children showing these behaviors are often diagnosed as "conduct disordered" by mental health clinicians, "socially maladjusted" by the educational establishment, and "delinquent" by the legal system. The exclusion of these children by definition has been a constant source of controversy, and many states have ignored this exclusion (Nelson et al., 1991a and b).

Part of the reason social maladjustment is never defined in the law is because the framers of the law wanted to exclude those children from various subcultures who may be socialized into deviant and antisocial behavior. Their behavior and attitudes, shaped by the standards of their own subculture, are simply different from those of the majority. Since the behavior of these children and adolescents is in accordance with their subgroup's standards, they are not considered to have a behavior disorder. The law did not intend to minimize their problems or accept their behavior, much of which is dangerous to others, just to exclude them from receiving special education services.

Although the understanding of subgroup differences may be a lofty ideal, separating these students from those who should be classified as having a behavior disorder has proven difficult if not impossible. And even though these students may or may not have a behavior disorder under this definition, they undoubtedly need help (Maag & Howell, 1991).

A New, Improved Definition

The problems with the federal definition are significant enough that various groups have tried to change it. The Council for Exceptional Children suggests that "emotional or behavioral disorders (EBD) refer to a condition in which the behav-

THOUGHT QUESTION

1. Why is the term "serious" considered necessary when diagnosing children with behavior disorders?

THOUGHT QUESTION

2. Should children and adolescents who are delinquent automatically be considered to have an emotional disorder?

One commonly used method of classification uses the American Psychiatric Association's Diagnostic and Statistical Manual of Mental Disorders, now in its fourth edition.

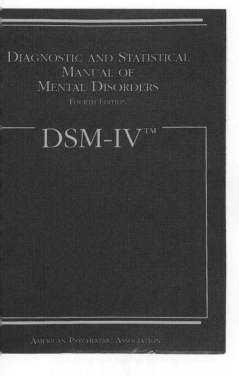

ioral or emotional responses of an individual in school are so different from his/her generally accepted, age appropriate, ethnic or cultural norms that they adversely affect educational performance in such areas as self-care, social relationships, personal adjustment, academic progress, classroom behavior or work adjustment. These behaviors are long lasting, and the decision on any diagnosis should be based upon multiple sources of information and the behavior must be shown in at least two settings, one which must be school related. Emotional or behavioral disturbance can co-exist with other handicapping conditions and includes youths with schizophrenia, affective disorders or other sustained disturbances of conduct, attention or adjustment" (1991, p. 10). This definition has some advantages over the federal definition in that it deals with social maladjustment in a different manner, uses standards of the group, and requires the use of multiple sources for assessment.

Classification

Two major methods are used to classify behavior disorders. The first uses a number of systems devised by clinicians based upon their experience and is best typified by *The American Psychiatric Association's Diagnostic and Statistical Manual of Mental Disorders* (DSM-IV). The DSM-IV offers a number of categories for disorders that affect mostly children and adolescents. In addition to these categories, children may be diagnosed as having almost any disorder that adults experience. For example, substance use disorders, anxiety disorders, schizophrenia, and mood disorders can be applied to children and adolescents as well as adults.

The second approach is more empirical, or statistical, and attempts to identify patterns of behavior that are related to each other. In this procedure, a person rating a child's behavior indicates whether some specific behavior is present or absent and to what degree. A statistical technique is then used to indicate which behaviors go together, and this cluster of behaviors is known as a **syndrome**. A number of these rating instruments exist and the results of these studies are consistent (Quay, 1986). Two general syndromes that always appear are labeled externalizing and internalizing. **Externalizing**, also called undercontrolled, includes the behaviors of fighting, temper tantrums, disobedience, and destructiveness. **Internalizing**, also called overcontrolled, includes such behaviors as anxiety, withdrawal, and depression.

Describing Behaviors

How do we know that any particular behavior is a sign of a behavior disorder? A specific behavior can be described and analyzed using the following components.

- *Form:* The form or the shape of the behavior involves a description of the behavior itself. Some behaviors, by their very nature, such as children biting themselves, would be considered a cause for concern.

Syndrome:
A collection of symptoms that are found together.

Externalizing behaviors:
A collection of behaviors that includes fighting, disobedience, and destructiveness.

Internalizing behaviors:
A collection of behaviors that includes anxiety, withdrawal, and depression.

- *Chronicity:* Many children show short periods of anxiety or withdrawal. However, if these behaviors last a long period of time, they may be considered a sign of a behavior disorder.
- *Frequency:* The temper tantrums of a child may be considered a sign of a behavior disorder if they occur far more often than is usual (Coleman, 1992).
- *Severity:* The severity of the symptom is important. Some children show mild depression, others are more severely depressed. Some children's aggressive behavior may not be as extreme as others.
- *Setting Events:* Knowing what activities or events preceded the child's behavior is also useful. A child's aggressive actions, for example, may only be shown when asked to comply with someone else's wishes. Such information can help in devising treatment plans.

How Do Children with Behavior Disorders Achieve in School?

The majority of children classified as having a behavior disorder have average intelligence, averaging about 90 to 95 (Coleman, 1992). Even so, studies find that these children are underachieving. They are doing more poorly in many subjects including the basic skills of reading and math than one would expect from children with their intelligence scores (Lewis & Doorlag, 1987). No one knows whether poor school skills set in motion some difficulty in self-esteem leading to behavioral difficulties, or whether the behavior problems interfere with school achievement (Wenar, 1994). Perhaps both are true. Either way, these findings have a great deal of significance.

If children who show behavior disorders do not do well in school, a program to help these children should contain an academic element. Children who are not doing well, whether or not they show behavior disorders, will experience a loss of self-respect and self-esteem and may avoid anything that shows them to be incompetent. Improving the child's academic skills will improve the child's self-concept and may reduce some of the problems. Keeping students on task also reduces some disruptive behavior. Unfortunately, with the emphasis on the child's behavior, the student's academic problems are often forgotten. Later in the chapter, when discussing strategies for helping these children, some behavioral interventions aimed at increasing time on task and improving academic work will be noted.

THOUGHT QUESTION

3. *Why don't children with behavior disorders do well in school?*

Models of Analysis

The cause of behavior disorders can be viewed in a number of ways. In fact, every school of psychology discusses the possible reasons a child might develop a behavior disorder.

- *The Biophysical Model:* Explanations from this model focus on the possible physiological causes of the disorder, which may include structural abnormalities in the central nervous system, biochemical difficulties, or genetic factors. Although biological factors may be involved in some disorders, they frequently interact with environmental factors.

- *The Psychoanalytic Model:* The psychoanalytic or Freudian approach looks for the cause of a behavior disorder in the early parent-child relationship. The problems lie within the child and with unconscious attempts to cope with emotional difficulties that arise during the early stages of development. Children are viewed as having difficulties when they experience conflicts between their unconscious desires and societal constraints.

- *The Behavior Model:* This model claims that the behaviors reflecting behavior disorders are learned, just as any other behavior is learned. The same processes by which a child learns to act in a socially accepted manner can explain antisocial and overly anxious patterns of behavior. These learning processes include classical conditioning, operant conditioning, and imitation.

- *The Cognitive Model:* The cognitive model considers behavior disorders the result of difficulties in thinking, reasoning, and problem solving. A child who interprets other people's actions and statements as hostile will react in an aggressive manner.

- *The Humanistic Model:* The humanistic perspective views behavior disorders as the unique ways in which an individual adjusts and copes with environmental challenges. The importance of the individual's self-concept is stressed. Each individual has a unique potential, is responsible for personal behavior, and can rise above poor environmental influences.

- *The Ecological Perspective:* In this perspective, behavior disorders are viewed as a complex interaction between children and their environments. Examining only the environment or the child is insufficient. What must be analyzed are the interactions of the two. In addition, although the family is undoubtedly the primary influence, the child's world also includes the school, media, neighborhood, culture, and many other important forces, which must be taken into account in understanding the child's behavior.

These models or any of the many other existing models that one chooses encourage certain questions and lead to particular interventions. For example, a person adhering to the cognitive perspective would investigate the reasoning processes of the child and try to alter them. An individual embracing the behavioral model would search for the forces that reinforce the troublesome behavior and seek to change these reinforcers.

THOUGHT QUESTION

4. *Which psychological models of behavior disorders are of the greatest use for teachers?*

Prevalence of Behavior Disorders

Prevalence figures for behavior disorders vary widely, depending upon the definition used. Remember that the federal definition focuses only on those students with severe disorders, and various prevalence studies use different criteria. After a review of the research, Cotler (1986) suggested that in middle childhood (elementary school), about 7 percent of the children have severe or moderate behavior disorders, and 15 percent show mild behavior disabilities. Coleman (1992) suggests that 2 percent of the school-aged children show severe behavior disorders and another 7–10 percent show disorders that are serious enough to require intervention. The U.S. Department of Education suggests the prevalence is lower, between 1.2 and 2 percent (see Kauffman, 1989). In the 1992–1993 school year, 402,668 children diagnosed as having behavior disorders were entitled to special educational services (U.S. Department of Education, 1994).

The population of children diagnosed as having a behavior disorder represents less than 1 percent of the entire school population. So, regardless of the fact that teachers believe so many children show such disorders, and conservative estimates of prevalence rates are at least 2 percent, as many as half of the children who show behavior disorders are not being served (Kauffman, 1989).

A number of reasons explain this phenomenon. A stigma is attached to the classification of behavior disorder or emotional disturbance, which may make parental cooperation in the special education process difficult. Evaluators find placing the child in a different classification far easier and more socially acceptable. Second, the definition with its subjectivity, its emphasis on the term *severe*, and its exclusion of social maladjustment may make it difficult to use this category.

Significant gender differences can also be noted in prevalence. Boys are much more commonly diagnosed with behavior disorders than girls, by an 8:1 or 9:1 ratio, depending upon the disorder (Coleman, 1992). Boys' behavior disorders are more likely to be disruptive, such as acting out in class thereby calling attention to themselves, whereas many of the disorders shown by girls in school may go unnoticed. Cultural differences also enter into the picture. Some cultures are more tolerant of withdrawal or aggressive behavior than others, and gender differences are prominent in such subcultural tolerances.

> **THOUGHT QUESTION**
>
> **5.** *Why are boys diagnosed as having behavior disorders so much more often than girls?*

Assessment

A ssessing the behavior and properly diagnosing the child's disorder are certainly vital to providing effective intervention. The evaluation and assessment of children thought to have a behavior disorder, though, are more of a challenge than with other disabilities. Part of the challenge lies in obtaining parental cooperation in such a situation. When children have a sensory impairment or a learning disability, parents may not see the disability as reflecting on them. However, parents, whose children show aggressive behavior or are withdrawn or overly anxious, may be defensive. Children may also choose not to participate in the process of evaluation or in any treatment. Children told to see a psychologist may not like it and not cooperate. Young children may be fearful of a psychologist, and older children may think that seeing a psychologist means that they are "crazy." Unlike the situation with adults who visit psychologists, children are referred by adults for help and do not often appear because they want to (Wenar, 1994).

As always, the initial referral acts as a starting point, since it contains information about the topography, duration, onset, effects on others, and efforts to counter the problem. The most useful referrals are those that provide the most descriptive behavioral information without interpretation or labeling.

Information about behavior disorders is gathered in many ways. The evaluation depends, to some extent, on the theoretical orientation of the clinician. For example, a behaviorist may use somewhat different techniques than a psychoanalytically oriented psychologist.

SCENARIO

1 Kristin is a student in your sixth-grade class. She is disruptive, rarely finishes her work, and frequently day dreams. Her parents are having difficulties with her at home as well, since she often lies about finishing her work and does not appear to be happy. They would like her to visit the guidance counselor or the school psychologist, but Kristin adamantly refuses. She claims she does not need the help and is not "disturbed." What, if anything, can you or her parents do to encourage Kristin to accept the help?

The Clinical Interview

The most common tool for assessment is the clinical interview. This process involves the psychologist directly asking questions of the child (and others) about the behavior, the child's relationships, and any other subject that is deemed appropriate. There are two types of clinical interviews. In an unstructured interview, the clinician asks pertinent questions concerning the child's feelings, attitudes, and expectations. Some of these questions may be planned, but others may be suggested to the clinician as the interview unfolds. Because these questions are not standardized, the clinician might ask the next child very different questions. Flexibility is certainly present; however, the question of reliability is less clear. Would another clinician asking different questions come to a different diagnosis? This issue can be especially important when a clinician must determine which of two similar diagnoses is the correct one.

The structured interview contains a number of questions concerning the child's behavior, which are asked in a standardized way. These questions are based on the DSM-IV definitions of disorders and are always asked in the same way by all clinicians. The manner in which the child answers is recorded according to a particular method as well (Gutterman, O'Brien, & Young, 1987). Reliability is certainly greater, but flexibility is reduced in structured interviews. Semistructured interviews are also available in which the features of a standardized interview are combined with some additional discretion on the part of the therapist.

Observation

Observation is also used in an evaluation. A psychologist might observe a child in class, in a day-care situation, or even on the playground. A psychologist may be interested in observing aggressive behaviors or the nature of interpersonal interactions. Sometimes, the observations are quite structured with the number of such actions in a 10-minute segment counted, and sometimes a more unstructured observation may occur.

Teachers tend to overestimate the number of children who have behavior disorders, often assuming that students who misbehave have serious behavior disorders.

Rating Scales

In the past decade or so, rating scales have become popular assessment instruments. For example, the Child Behavior Checklist (CBCL) contains a listing of many behaviors rated on a number of domains and severity by parents, teachers, and the children themselves (Achenbach & Edelbrock, 1981; Chang et al., 1995). Many other checklists are available. These rating scales allow the clinician to gather information about the child more objectively.

Personality Tests

There are two types of personality tests. The first is an inventory in which people answer questions concerning their attitudes, behaviors, or preferences. Their answers are then compared to those of groups of people who show a particular behavior pattern or show some syndrome. For example, the California Psychological Inventory (CPI) includes scales measuring responsibility, sociability, and many other qualities.

The second type consists of projective personality tests. These involve giving children some ambiguous stimulus and asking them to make up a story, interpret what they are viewing, or even asking them to draw something. The theory, which follows a Freudian perspective, is that people will provide valuable information to the psychologist as they project their unconscious problems and conflicts into their explanations of the ambiguous stimuli.

The most famous projective personality test is the Rorschach Inkblot test, which asks people what they see in a particular ink blot (Rosenhan & Seligman, 1995). Items in the test have common answers but no correct answers. The psychologist administering the Thematic Apperception Test (TAT) shows the client

Special class placement is more common for children with behavior disorders than for children with other disabilities. Full inclusion would mean more changes for these children than for children in some other classifications.

THOUGHT QUESTION

6. *What criteria would you use to decide whether a child with a behavior disorder should be educated in a regular classroom?*

an ambiguous picture and asks the client to tell what is happening, what led up to it, and what is going to happen. The TAT is considered applicable to children as young as four years of age, but the Children's Apperception Test (CAT), which uses pictures of animals rather than human beings, is designed especially for use between ages three and ten years (Bellak, 1986). Children from first grade on may be given the CAT-H, a test specifically designed for children using human figures.

The interpretation of projective personality tests is subjective, and they should never be used as the sole basis for personality testing (Blau, 1991). They can, though, sometimes add information about the child.

Other Sources of Information

During the evaluation process, the psychologist may see the need for various intelligence and achievement tests (Blau, 1991). Along with these source of information, a general medical and sometimes a neurological examination may also be required.

Placement

Special class placement is more common for children with behavior disorders than for children with other disabilities. Fewer than half of these children are educated either solely in the regular classroom or in the regular classroom with resource room help (15.8 percent in the regular class, 27.8 percent in the resource room). The majority are not found in the regular classroom: 36.9 percent are educated in separate classes, 13.9 percent in a separate school, 4.0 percent in a residential facility, and 1.5 percent in a hospital or home (U.S. Department of Education, 1994).

The inclusion movement is certainly controversial when considering the problems of this population. A decision to foster inclusion would mean a great deal of change in the placement of children with behavior disorders. If these children are excluded from the regular classroom, then they will probably be educated with other children with similar disturbances and learn new ways to aggress or imitate poor behavior. On the other hand, questions—such as, Can this population be adequately served in the regular classroom? and Will the behavior of these children adversely affect the learning environment of others?—make inclusion in this area a particular challenge.

Most teachers are less interested in clinical diagnoses than in particular behavior patterns shown by children and what they can do to help the child succeed. Based upon these concerns, behavior disorders will be discussed in terms of symptoms of aggression, depression, and anxiety. Both the long-term intervention programs available and what the individual teacher can do to help the child learn will also be noted. At the end of the chapter, a number of specific techniques that may be used to increase time on task and reduce behavior that interferes with learning will be described.

Aggression

M ost teachers occasionally face the challenge of a child who acts aggressively. Aggression, though, has become more than an individual problem. Today, as never before, the shocking violence and aggression found in our society and especially in the schools have become a rallying cry for change. A recent study by the National School Board Association found significant increases in student assaults, fistfights, knifings, and shootings in 82 percent of the districts sampled (Henry, 1994).

Many children who act aggressively have long histories of meeting frustration or challenge with aggression, and of using aggressive means to get what they want, often without regard for the rights of others. They often seem out of control. Teachers find these children difficult to work with, because they often disrupt the class and create an undesirable atmosphere in the classroom. Aggression in the classroom is a serious problem and the aggressive-disruptive behavior pattern is one of the most common problems presented in mental health facilities (Cullinan & Epstein, 1982).

Children who show a great deal of aggression are rejected by other children (Kaplan, 1991). Even so, aggressive children do have friends. They usually play with other aggressive children (Cairns et al., 1989). In fact, aggressive children are often members of solid peer clusters throughout elementary school and beyond. These children may be generally rejected by the majority of children, but they do find other children with whom they can share a relationship, and their relationships are no less meaningful to them.

Most children occasionally show defiance, verbal or physical aggression, or throw tantrums. These behaviors are not unusual in children, but when they occur more frequently or are qualitatively different than found in the age and cultural group, these children are considered to have a difficulty with aggression.

THOUGHT QUESTION

7. *Why has the problem of aggression in schools and in society generally become worse? What, in your opinion, can be done about it?*

SCENARIO

2 Jeremy is an excitable second grader who likes to get his own way. He frequently yells and takes things away from others. Sometimes, he is cooperative, but often he acts aggressively. The other students do not want to play with him. If you were his teacher, what would you do to reduce the aggressive behavior?

Causes of Aggressive Behavior

Consider children who watch their parents argue violently, are hit hard and often, or discover that they get what they want by being aggressive toward others. One would predict that these children are more likely to act aggressively, and research confirms this hypothesis (Parke & Slaby, 1983). Evidence showing that children can learn to aggress, both through operant conditioning (the use of rewards) and through observation learning (watching aggressive models) is plentiful (Becker et al., 1994). For instance, if the child takes things away from other children and is allowed to keep them, the child learns that the consequences are positive and that when the child wants something the child should just take it. Aggression becomes a characteristic method of dealing with wants and frustrations.

Children can also learn to be aggressive by watching aggressive models. Children who witness violence in the home or an acceptance of violence on the part of parents as a way to settle disputes may learn that it is acceptable (Comer, 1995). Often, parents of violent children have created an atmosphere of conflict and hostility. In a series of studies, children were frustrated and then exposed to live or filmed models acting aggressively or playing constructively with toys. They were then given the opportunity to play. Usually, the children imitated whatever they saw. If exposed to aggressive actions, they acted aggressively; if shown constructive actions, they imitated those actions (Bandura, 1986; Bandura, Ross, & Ross, 1961).

A number of parenting styles can lead to aggressive children. One style involves a combination of permissiveness and punitiveness (Sears, Maccoby, & Levin, 1957). Parents who are very permissive tend to raise aggressive children. In addition, the more punishing the parents are, the more aggressive their children. The combination of permissiveness and punitiveness leads to the most aggressive children. If parents allow their children to vent their aggressive impulses, children think it is acceptable. They are then harshly punished for it, which causes frustration and anger, leading to further aggression. One might think that parents of children who are aggressive never punish their children, however this assumption is false. In fact, the most common pattern of parenting with very aggressive children is strong and frequent punishment for misbehavior. Parents of such children are very punitive and often both cold and rejecting. These children are often physically abused. This aggressiveness does not remain confined to the home. In a sample of third graders, parental use of physical punishment was related to the child's ag-

Research shows that children can learn to behave aggressively by watching models.

gressiveness at school (Eron, Walder, & Lefkowitz, 1971). Lack of monitoring and inconsistent discipline is another pattern often found with children who show a great deal of aggression (Kazdin, 1994).

The process by which some highly aggressive patterns of behavior may develop was described by Patterson (1986). He noted that any criticism from the parent brings an immediate aggressive response from the child, which causes the parent to withdraw from the interaction. The child, then, is reinforced for the aggressive response. Patterson argues that a lack of parental monitoring, inconsistent discipline, and failure to use positive management techniques or teach social skills are important factors in establishing and maintaining aggression.

Peer groups also influence aggressive behavior (Parke & Slaby, 1983). Such influence may occur in three ways. First, children may model themselves after a violent individual, especially if the model gains something of value through violence. Second, the peer group may reinforce the violent deeds. Although aggressive individuals are often rejected by the majority of children, as noted earlier, they often find a group in which this behavior is acceptable. This leads to the third point, the social norms of the peer group. Some groups reject violence more than others.

Other influences on aggression include the neighborhood, the media, and the culture. Some cultures and subcultures are more accepting of violence. If aggressiveness is modeled and rewarded by society, it is thought to be the proper way to deal with problems. Our own society seems to have a love-hate relationship with violence. On one hand, violence is condemned and punished (sometimes violently). On the other hand, our heroes use violence freely, sometimes without regard for the law, and children see violence, often being rewarded, all around them. In some neighborhoods violence is, unfortunately, a way of life; the response to any real or imagined insult or challenge is violence. This same pattern is found in schools. Any disagreement or presumed slight is met with a violent answer.

In addition, the influence of the media should not be forgotten (see the On-Line feature). Although blaming violent television and the movies for children's violence is untenable, we can still consider them important factors (Liebert & Sprafkin, 1988). The media may influence aggression in three ways. First, some children may directly imitate what they see. Obviously other factors are involved, because most children do not imitate such behavior. Aggressive children, though, may learn different ways to aggress by watching violence. Second, televised violence disinhibits aggression. People have certain inhibitions against violence, which may be reduced by witnessing aggression. Third, television violence may lead to antisocial attitudes and encourage children to accept violence as a way of dealing with problems. Desensitization to violence occurs, and people may not take it seriously. As some people get used to violence on television, they come to accept it as a normal part of life (Donnerstein, Slaby, & Eron, 1994).

 **LINE**

Television Viewing and Children with Behavior Disorders

The influence of television on children's behavior is an ongoing concern for both : professionals and parents. Questions surround the effects of viewing violent programs on children's subsequent behavior, the influence of advertising on consumption habits, and television's potential as both an academic learning and a therapeutic tool. Many studies, probably numbering more than a thousand, have investigated various issues relating to television and its effects on children. The influence of television on children with exceptional needs, though, has not been studied extensively. Of the research that does exist, much focuses on children with behavior disorders.

Studies consistently find that children with exceptional needs, especially those with learning disabilities or behavior disorders, watch more television than children who do not have disabilities (Sprafkin, Gadow, & Abelman, 1992). Children with behavior disorders are heavy viewers of crime dramas, adventure shows, and cartoons, especially those with high levels of violence (Sprafkin, Watkins, & Gadow, 1990).

Why do children with behavior disorders watch so much television? Perhaps watching television is a substitute for playing with others, since children with behavior disorders are more likely to be rejected because of their behavior. It is one activity in which they do not receive negative appraisals from others, since they are not bothering anyone. They also identify with characters more often than other children and are more likely to view their own behavior as similar to that of their favorite television characters (Sprafkin et al., 1992). Children with behavior disorders are twice as likely to report pretending to be their favorite television characters than other children (Sprafkin & Gadow, 1986).

Children with behavior disorders have more difficulty separating reality from fiction. Most children of school age know that television heroes are not real, that fistfights and shoot-outs are faked, and that superhuman feats cannot really be performed. Children with behavior disorders are less likely to understand these facts.

They are more likely than children without behavior disorders to believe that what they see on television is real and to have difficulty discriminating the actor from the role being played (Sprafkin, Gadow, & Dussault, 1986). Many children with behavior disorders believe that superhuman feats shown on television, such as flying or making things disappear, are realistic and possible (Sprafkin, Kelly, & Gadow, 1987). Forty percent of children with behavior disorders believed that people could fly just as a television character could if they wore the same shoes. Fifty-three percent of children with behavior disorders believed that filmed violence, such as the bullets used in shoot-outs, are unreal, compared to 86 percent of the other children (Sprafkin et al., 1987).

Children with behavior disorders are influenced by the television programs they watch (Sprafkin et al., 1992). However, the relationship between the degree of violence of the shows watched, the amount of viewing hours, and the previous aggressive behavior of the child is complicated, and simple explanations do not fit the facts. For example, although laboratory studies show that the more aggressive the shows, the greater the effect they have on behavior, the results from field studies are inconsistent (Sprafkin et al., 1992). Children who watch a great deal of violent television believe that aggression is even more common than it really is and develop a view of the world as being filled with people likely to hurt them. They may then read the behavior and verbal statements of others as being provocative and react in a more aggressive manner (Sprafkin et al., 1992).

Parents of children with behavior disorders believe that their children are adversely affected by the violent programs they watch, but parents do little to counter the effects of the programs. They do not intervene frequently, and when they do, it is to use loss of television viewing time as a punishment (Sprafkin et al., 1992).

Much has been written about the negative effects of television on children; however, children can also be exposed to shows demonstrating positive behaviors. Programs showing prosocial behavior can sometimes encourage children to act in a more socially responsible manner and engage in less name calling and teasing (Sprafkin & Rubinstein, 1982).

Televised programs may be an effective medium for reducing problem behavior and useful in treating behavior disorders. Elias (1983) divided a sample of more than 100 boys aged 7 through 15 years who were residents of a treatment center for children with behavior disorders into two groups. Fifty-two boys in the experimental group viewed a series of videotapes depicting children, ages 8 to 12 years, from different racial and ethnic groups being confronted with, and working through, common situations. These situations involved dealing with teasing and bullying, coping with peer pressure, learning how to express feelings in an appropriate manner, and managing oneself in new and unfamiliar social situations. The tapes ran for 15 minutes and were developed and evaluated by a consortium of 33 educational and broadcasting agencies in the United States and Canada, managed by the Agency for Instructional Television. The tapes were designed to be meaningful to the students and to encourage discussion and expression of feeling. Teachers were given orientation sessions in which their roles as guide were stressed. They were to ask questions, encourage discussion, and summarize important points. The tapes were shown twice a week for five weeks followed by a 15-minute discussion. Both groups received the intensive therapy available at the center, including individual and group psychotherapy, casework, cottage meetings, and other therapies, but only the experimental group received this extra help. Children in the experimental group showed meaningful changes in behavior that continued for at least two months after the program stopped. Children showed improvements in emotional control, peer acceptance, and social behavior. They showed more prosocial behavior as well. Teachers noted the improved social and work-related behaviors.

The research on the effects of television on children with behavior disorders leads to the following conclusions. Children with behavior disorders spend more time watching television than children without disabilities. They watch more violent programs, especially crime dramas and cartoons, and tend to identify with and pretend to be these characters. They are affected by the shows they see. They have more difficulty separating fiction from reality and have less understanding of the way television programs and commercials represent reality, often believing that the superhuman feats performed on television are real.

Teachers and parents can do much to counter the negative effects of television and use television programs to promote prosocial behavior. Children must be educated as to the realities of television. A number of curricula have been developed, but one that has been used with children with behavior disorders is called the Curriculum Enhancing Social Skills Through Media Awareness (CESSMA). This curriculum was specially developed to help children with learning disabilities and behavior disorders better understand the realities of television (Sprafkin, Watkins, & Gadow, 1990). It consists of 14 lessons organized around brief taped segments of popular programs. Its main theme is to help students differentiate what is real from what is shown on television by looking at storytelling, special effects, and the nature of commercials. When children are exposed to this curriculum, their knowledge increases and students with behavior disorders identify less with aggressive television characters.

Parents and teachers can also help students understand the nature of television by rewarding children for finding inaccuracies in programs and commercials. In addition, many families have more than one television set, with the additional set for the children, and do not know what their children are watching. Parents should always be aware of what their children are watching and how many hours they have been seated in front of the television.

Another suggestion is that television viewing be limited. This is a sensible suggestion; however, the time taken from viewing television must be replaced by some positive activity. Other suggestions include encouraging critical viewing by discussing the program on television, not using the television set as a babysitter, and not allowing children to just watch television because they have "nothing else to do." On the positive side, parents should be aware of television programs that may be vehicles for educational and social growth (Kaplan, 1986).

The point of this analysis is not to demonize television. It is rather to understand how some children with behavior disorders are interpreting what they see on television and to counter these misperceptions. Parents and teachers must formulate ways to reduce the possible injurious effects of television and use the powerful medium in a positive manner.

The DSM-IV View: Conduct Disorders

Oppositional defiant disorder:
A disorder in which children defy rules, show anger and resentment, and often lose their tempers, but show limited aggressiveness and do not usually violate the rights of others.

Conduct disorder:
A disorder marked by aggressive behavior and continuous violation of the basic rights of others.

Two specific disorders involving aggression are found in the DSM-IV. The first is called an **oppositional defiant disorder** in which children argue repeatedly with authority figures, show resentment, and often throw temper tantrums. These children defy adult rules and blame others for their mistakes. However, they do not usually violate the rights of others, and their aggressiveness is limited.

This limited aggressiveness is not true of children in the second group, those with conduct disorders. Children with **conduct disorders** show a "repetitive and persistent pattern of behavior in which the basic rights of others or major age-appropriate societal norms or rules are violated" (American Psychiatric Association, 1994, p. 85). This pattern manifests itself everywhere: at school, at home, with peers, and in the community. These children are physically and verbally aggressive, destroy the property of others, and may treat animals cruelly. Lying, cheating, and stealing are relatively common behaviors. Children with conduct disorders often break the law and may show histories of mugging and assault. They do not experience guilt over what they have done. If this behavior continues past the age of 18 years, it is diagnosed as an antisocial personality (Wilson, O'Leary, & Nathan, 1992).

Children with conduct disorders often commit offenses that result in them being labeled "delinquent" by the legal establishment. Although delinquent behavior is not considered necessary to have a conduct disorder, it frequently does occur; conversely, many (but certainly not all) delinquents meet the standards for being considered to have a conduct disorder. Unfortunately, these aggressive behaviors are relatively stable. These children may not grow out of the problem, and often problems in criminality, antisocial behavior, as well as marital and job problems are found in adulthood (Kazdin, 1989).

SCENARIO

3 When your friend, Herb, was told that Len would be a member of his sixth-grade class, he was so upset that he ran down to the principal's office to complain. Len is a child who has a behavior disorder. He acts out in class, is discourteous, gets into arguments with other students, and generally makes it difficult to teach. Although Herb has not had Len previously in his class, Len's reputation precedes him. Len's home life is terrible, with an alcoholic father and a mother who can't handle the problems and works full-time at a job she hates. His siblings have been in trouble with the law, and he spends most of his time being cared for by an elderly grandmother who is not up to it. The principal told Herb that the boy is receiving help from a therapist and that, although bothersome, the boy has never done anything so dangerous as to make him a safety problem in the classroom. He told Herb to "make the best of it." With no other choice, Herb must find some way of dealing with Len. If he asked you to suggest an approach that will work, what would you tell him?

Delinquency

Concern about youth crime or delinquency is certainly not new, and statistics show that it is a serious ongoing problem. According to the Uniform Crime Report of 1993, 30 percent of all persons arrested in 1993 were under 21 years of age, and 43 percent of all serious crimes were committed by persons under the age of 21 and 29 percent by people under 18. In 1993, 2,014,472 adolescents under 18 were arrested (FBI, 1994). The expense of vandalism and other crimes is hard to calculate, as is the effect that the threat of violence has on people's lives. Males comprise 81 percent of all arrests and 87 percent of the arrests for violent crimes. Of course, most delinquent actions are not as serious as murder and rape. The most frequent complaints against boys involve joyriding, drunken driving, burglary, malicious mischief, auto theft, and illegal drug use. Girls are most likely to be reported for running away and for illicit sexual behavior.

These adolescents as a group are impulsive, resentful, socially assertive, defiant, suspicious, and lack self-control. They often feel inadequate and see themselves as lazy or bad (Conger & Petersen, 1984). They view social problems in hostile terms, do not seek explanations, generate few solutions, anticipate few consequences for aggression, and see violence as a legitimate way to solve problems (Guerra & Slaby, 1990).

Adolescents who are delinquent usually have poor relationships with their parents. In many of the homes that yield delinquents, the family lacks routine, provides inconsistent discipline in which parents yell, threaten, and nag, but do not follow through, and shows an inability to deal with family problems (Wilson & Herrnstein, 1985). The family relations of delinquents are characterized by rigidity, lack of cohesion, and little positive communication, and delinquents' peer relations are often characterized by high levels of aggression (Blaske et al., 1989). Parent-child interactions lack warmth and intimacy and are characterized by rejection and indifference.

Lack of supervision may be a key factor, especially in single-parent families. Mothers of single-parent families often have more difficulty controlling their teenagers. Adolescents in these mother-only households are more likely to make decisions without direct parental input, lack parental supervision, and exhibit deviant behavior when compared with two-parent or extended families controlled for socioeconomic status (Dornbusch et al., 1985). Youths who believe their parents know what they are doing and whom they are with are less likely to engage in criminal acts than are unsupervised youths. Many parents of children considered beyond control set rules inconsistently, are not very likely to praise, show less interest in their children, and exhibit high levels of hostile detachment (Siegel & Senna, 1988).

Some authorities consider the involvement of genetic or biophysical factors a possibility (Eysenck, 1975). Many of these children have parents who showed such patterns of behavior, but this correlation does not demonstrate genetic input since the behavior could have been learned (Wilson et al., 1992). Others claim that perhaps some people are more easily aroused and, perhaps, neurological factors are involved (see Wicks-Nelson & Israel, 1991). However, at this point, the question of genetic involvement is a controversial question, and even if genetics were found to play some part, the environment is certainly extremely important.

Programs for Aggressive Youth

Aggression is a stable trait. It is wishful thinking to believe that the aggressive child will simply grow out of it (Cullinan & Epstein, 1982; Olweus, 1982). When more than 600 children were followed from ages 8 through 30 years, the more aggressive 8-year-olds developed into the more aggressive 30-year-olds (Huesman, Lagerspetz, & Eron, 1984). Early conduct-disordered behavior is related to later aggression and antisocial behavior and to many psychological problems later in life, especially for boys (Caspi, Elder, & Bem, 1987).

Some people do break the cycle of aggression. People with higher intelligence and women are more likely to break the violence cycle. Although the outlook for children with conduct disorders may not be very positive, some people who show aggressive behavior do manage to change and improve. Although adult criminals have a history of juvenile delinquency, most adolescents who have delinquency problems do not go on to lives of crime (Moffitt, 1990). Not all delinquents are violent, and adolescents who have done property damage may not continue to demonstrate such behavior. Others may learn that the consequences of aggression are negative and control their aggression.

No simple answers exist to the problems of delinquency, conduct disorder, and aggressive behavior in general. Some community-based programs have had some success in dealing with behavior problems, especially those that provide recreational activities, work directly both with gangs and with individuals, and include campaigns for community improvement (Clarizio & McCoy, 1983). Community involvement seems to be one key. In the educational realm, alternative schools offer some hope.

In addition, some family interventions are successful. For instance, delinquents usually have negative interpersonal relationships with others, including family members, often because of their social behavior and the reactions people

Lack of supervision is a key factor in delinquent behavior.

have to it. Some programs hope to reduce negative interpersonal interactions by teaching these individuals better ways to interact (Guerra, Tolan, & Hammand, 1994; Henggeler et al., 1986). Others have looked at the possibility of altering some of the cognitive and social skills of these troubled youth. One 12-session program teaches social problem-solving skills and involves identifying the problem; stopping and thinking; answering the questions Why is there a conflict? and What do I want?; thinking of solutions; looking at the consequences, doing something; and evaluating the consequences (Guerra & Slaby, 1990). This program increased skills in solving social problems, reduced the youth's endorsement of aggression as a way of solving problems, and reduced aggressive behavior. However, these changes did not endure over time, possibly because the environment to which these youths returned did not support the changes. Changing the conditions that mediate aggressive behavior may be possible but ways must be found to encourage youths to continue using what they have learned.

One of the most surprising and positive prevention programs seems to be early childhood preschool programs. These preschool programs were certainly not designed to prevent delinquency; rather they were designed to improve the general functioning of children at risk for developmental disorders (see Chapter 3). These programs often use an ecological model, emphasizing not only the family interactions but relationships with others including the family's relationships with social services and the school. For instance, the Perry Preschool Project was designed for preschoolers deemed at risk for poor intellectual functioning and eventual school failure. Low-income children were randomly assigned to an experimental preschool condition or a control group. Those who attended the preschool re-

In some schools, programs to reduce violence use students specifically trained in conflict management.

ceived high-quality cognitively oriented early childhood education. Teachers made home visits to keep parents informed of their children's activities and to encourage participation, and monthly small group meetings allowed parents to exchange views. Studies showed lower rates of grade retention and fewer placements in special education, as well as improved reading skills. Follow-up studies also showed fewer arrests or charges for crimes. Fifty-one percent of the control group was arrested or charged with a crime while 31 percent of the experimental group was arrested or charged. Other studies have also found a reduction in criminality, sometimes to an even greater extent. Some parent education programs also reduce future delinquent behavior (Zigler, Taussig, & Black, 1992).

Perhaps these programs reduce risk factors. These children experience success and feelings of competence in these programs, and this success may cause more success and greater competence. Improved child-rearing strategies may also partially be responsible. Whatever the mechanism involved, preschool programs that emphasize improving general functioning seem to reduce delinquency.

Today, many schools are initiating programs aimed at reducing violence in the schools. Some of these programs use a peer mediation model, where students take disputes to other, specially trained student counselors for help. Other programs take a view that teaching children alternatives to violence as a means of responding is the best way to handle the problem. Still others aim at teaching students the consequences of violence and have victims of violence talk to students. These schoolwide programs are valuable, and some show promising results, although better evaluations are still needed (Guerra et al., 1994).

Teachers and parents can help reduce the level of violence by supporting such schoolwide programs. Children who tend to use aggressive means to further their aims must be told exactly what types of behavior will and will not be tolerated, and the classroom must be structured so that their behavior can be monitored continuously.

Trying to build a supportive relationship by speaking with these students when they have not been aggressive or disruptive can help. Emphasizing the positive things or behaviors they have engaged in is also important. These students rarely see any progress, which makes showing them how they have improved all the more appropriate. The problems of verbal outbursts and aggressiveness may be best handled by behavioral and cognitive means, some of which will be discussed at the end of the chapter.

SCENARIO

4 You are presently teaching at a junior high school in which violence is common. Guns are brought to school and fights are common in the halls or outside. You find that in your classroom students react to even slight problems with threats of force, verbal insults, and sometimes with physical aggression. The parent-teacher association is also concerned, as is the administration. You are serving on a joint committee to plan a program to meet this challenge. What suggestions would you make?

Depression

Everyone—adults, adolescents, and children—experiences times in their lives during which they are unhappy. A child in third grade who studied but failed the science test, the child who struck out with a runner on third and two out in the last inning to lose the game, or a child who had a fight with a good friend may all feel dejected. On a different plane, the child who feels unloved or unlovable, who feels alone, or whose parents are divorcing may show signs of sadness and depression.

The federal definition of serious emotional disturbance includes children who have "a general pervasive mood of unhappiness or depression." Today, depression in childhood and adolescence is recognized as a critical problem and is receiving more attention.

Symptoms of Depression

Depression is not just a feeling. Cognitive, motivational, and physical symptoms go along with it.

- *Emotional symptoms:* The most common symptom is naturally a mood of unhappiness and dejection, as well as an inability to find any pleasure in activities that the child usually enjoys.
- *Cognitive symptoms:* Many depressed people also show guilt, hopelessness, and a negative attitude toward themselves. They evaluate most situations negatively and commonly engage in self-blame (Seligman et al., 1984). Children also find it very difficult to concentrate on school work. More than half show academic difficulties (Kaslow, Rehm, & Siegel, 1983).
- *Motivational symptoms:* Children who are depressed tend to withdraw and avoid interpersonal relationships. They show a lack of initiative. They may also think about suicide.
- *Physical symptoms:* Children who are depressed show chronic fatigue and loss of energy. Sleep disorders are relatively common, and somatic complaints, such as headaches and stomach aches, may be present. Changes in appetite and psychomotor agitation may occur.

Some evidence shows that depression coexists with conduct disorders, eating disorders, substance use, and anxiety disorders (Coleman, 1992). In one study of juvenile offenders, major depression was found in 18 percent of these youths (Kashani et al., 1982).

Causes of Depression

The causes of depression are many and varied. Each school of psychology has its own view of the cause, and each may be helpful in explaining some cases of depression.

Childhood depression has only recently become the focus of a great deal of research.

Biological Explanations

Increased interest has recently been shown in the biological factors in depression. Some evidence indicates neurotransmitter difficulties, which involve norepinephrine and serotonin, two neurotransmitters responsible for the transmission of neural impulses from neuron to neuron. Perhaps low levels of norepinephrine cause a reduced level of neural firing. Unfortunately, demonstrating whether neurotransmitter differences cause or are the effect of depression is a difficult task.

Other evidence indicates a genetic influence on depression (Plomin, DeFries, & McClearn, 1990). However, less research has been conducted on children and adolescents than on adults. Although the biological explanation for depression may be part of the answer, it does not appear to be the full answer; psychological causes must be considered.

Separation and Loss

The most common reason for a depressed mood is separation or loss. A death of a parent, the loss of some loved object, or separation can cause depression. In fact, psychoanalytically oriented psychologists consider these to be major factors in depression. This analysis may be extended to mean loss of one's reputation or experiencing some negative changes in life. For example, if a child's parents divorce, the child may experience depression, caused by a loss of the family's cohesion.

Some psychoanalytically oriented authorities believe that anger—when it is turned inward toward oneself—causes depression. Teachers may see this. Perhaps a child gets a low grade and first tries to blame it on the test or the teacher. As the student comes to the realization that the student's own efforts or knowledge were insufficient, the student turns the anger in on the self and becomes depressed.

Lack of Reinforcement

Behaviorally oriented psychologists often look at depression as caused by a lack of positive reinforcement and pleasant events (Lewinsohn, 1974). Children who are depressed do not receive positive reinforcement from others and receive more criticism. An absence of pleasant events may set in motion a downward spiral in some cases. The fewer pleasant events someone enjoys, the more depressed that person may feel and the less inclined to take the initiative to partake in other activities (Lewinsohn & Graf, 1973; Lewinsohn & Libet, 1972). On the other hand, the child's poor interactive skills may lead to a loss of reinforcement from parents and peer groups (Patterson & Capaldi, 1990). These children are often unpopular, and rejected and isolated children are at risk for depression.

Cognitive Explanations of Depression

Cognitive explanations of depression have become more and more popular in the last two decades. The discovery that many depressed people think differently than nondepressed people has led to a number of such explanations. Two such explanations, Seligman's theory of learned helplessness and Beck's theory of depression, are most often quoted.

Learned Helplessness: There Is Nothing I Can Do to Help

Learned helplessness is the belief that any action is futile, so one might as well give up trying to make things better (Seligman, 1975). When people believe it

Learned helplessness: The learned inability to overcome obstacles that involves the belief that one cannot do anything to improve one's lot.

makes no difference how or whether they respond to a situation, they stop trying. Students who quit studying because they don't believe they can pass the course, or children who believe that they cannot succeed with friends no matter what they do, are typical of this kind of self-entrapment. People showing learned helplessness see no relationship between what they do and the consequences of their actions (Miller, 1986). If they later have an opportunity to exercise control, they behave as if they were helpless (Phares, 1988). Learned helplessness results from the personal belief that any action is futile, so the person might as well give up. One of the frustrating elements of this situation is that the escape is often obvious to an outsider but not to the depressed person. Symptoms of depression are commonly found in people who give up, who believe that there is nothing they can do.

The concept of learned helplessness is readily applied to the classroom. Teachers often describe poor readers in terms of passivity, lack of persistence, negative self-attitudes about intellectual performance, and low self-esteem—symptoms that match descriptions of people with learned helplessness.

Beck's Theory of Depression

One of the most outstanding characteristics of people who show depression is a self-defeating, pessimistic attitude and thought pattern. The child rejects compliments and shrugs them off. If the child is shown proof of success at a job, the child responds by repeating the one criticism that the teacher or a parent stated a week ago. Instead of seeing the positive the student concentrates on the negative aspects of life, overgeneralizing from one less than perfect situation to all others (Beck, 1967).

Beck (1974) argues that depression is caused by the way people interpret events, and by the negative way people view themselves, the world, and the future. Depressed people show certain errors of thinking that distort reality. They devalue themselves, see the environment in negative terms, see the future as hopeless, and interpret everything in these terms. Depressed people show cognitive distortion in which they fail to process positive events.

Studies find evidence that children's thought patterns as described by Seligman and Beck exist. Depressed children hold negative expectations of the future (Haley et al., 1985). They also exhibit a systematic bias in processing negative events, which predicts depression (Rush, Weisenburger, & Eaves, 1986). Nolen-Hoeksema and colleagues (1992) conducted a longitudinal five-year study of children beginning in third grade. A developmental change was noted among children. Early childhood negative events but not explanatory style were related to depressive symptoms, while later in childhood negative explanatory style was a significant predictor of depressive symptoms both by itself and with negative events. The pessimistic style remained long after the depression subsided and placed these children at risk for more depression. They showed helpless behaviors in both school and social life. In early childhood, then, the thinking style is not yet established, but as the child matures, a pessimistic style of thinking seems to lead to depression.

Competence and Depression

David Cole (1990; 1991) argues that understanding children's depression requires an appreciation of the feedback children receive in a number of areas of life, including academic performance and relationships. Lack of academic competence is related to depression (Leon, Kendall, & Garber, 1980). The same holds true in the social domain. Cole argues that, after the age of seven years, children realize that they are good at some things and bad at others. But children who are regarded as incompetent in several areas may overgeneralize and believe they are poor in everything, which leads to both a depressive style of reasoning and depression when faced with negative experiences. Cole found that depressive symptoms strongly correlate with social and academic competence.

Cole obtained self-reports and peer nominations of competence in five important domains of childhood, including academic, social, physical attractiveness, conduct, and sports, from more than 1,000 elementary school children. Those who were seen as incompetent in various domains were more likely to be depressed. Being nominated in one or more domains led to lower depression scores. The relationship was cumulative, with incompetence in many domains more related to depression than incompetence in one domain.

SCENARIO

5 Celia's parents are getting a divorce. She is a shy child who is withdrawn. Her best friend moved away last week. She has a few girls who call her but no close friends. She feels isolated and appears apathetic. If you were one of her seventh-grade teachers, what could you do to help Celia?

Help for Children Who Are Depressed and Withdrawn

One of the most important things a teacher can do is to recognize children who may be depressed. These children do not stand out. They may go unnoticed because they do not disturb the class. Their work may be acceptable, though they never volunteer and may even refuse to answer questions in class.

Professional help is available and frequently successful. Sometimes, medication is used with depressed adolescents. Psychotherapy, based upon a number of different theories, is also successful (Puig-Antioch & Weston, 1983). For example, in cognitive behavioral therapy, children are taught to correct their thinking and monitor themselves. In one study, moderately to severely depressed 9- to 12-year-olds were taught self-management skills, such as self-monitoring and self-reinforcement. These children were taught to monitor pleasant events and social behavior was reinforced. These strategies were superior to a no-treatment group in reducing depression (Stark, Reynolds, & Kaslow, 1987).

Much work has centered on the child's lack of social skills and withdrawal (Cullinan & Epstein, 1982). Certain activities and educational programs, such as participating in peer tutoring, social skills training, as well as rehearsing social skills with these children, can successfully reduce withdrawal (Ladd, 1981; Rosenberg et al., 1992).

Depressed students do not try to interact much with others, and if they are rebuffed, they may say to themselves, "You see, it doesn't work. I can't make friends." These children may have interpersonal successes and a few failures but will emphasize the failures over the successes. The teacher may help the child value the successes and place the failures in perspective.

Many withdrawn students do not volunteer in class. A trusted teacher may rehearse an answer with a child and then, when appropriate, call on that child. Such children require patience and should not be expected to do too much too soon. Many such children are afraid of rejection and failure, and may have to practice their conversation skills.

Working with children who show learned helplessness is a difficult task, since these students stop trying. They often have low expectations for their own performance, make self-deprecating remarks, are quick to link failure to ability, and constantly think of causes for their failure rather than concentrating on finding effective ways to deal with their problems (Diener & Dweck, 1978). Sowa and Burks (1983) describe a three-phase cognitive restructuring program for children who show learned helplessness. In the educational phase, students receive an explanation of the relationship between cognitions and behavior and how such a relationship affects performance in mathematics. A list of negative or self-defeating statements related to attributions to ability are given to students, who are asked to list their own self-defeating statements. Finally, a list of positive self-statements is generated that contradicts these negative ones. For instance, a student who says, "I can't do the work because I'm stupid," might generate, "I couldn't do the work because I have to work harder." In the rehearsal phase, negative self-attributions about ability are contradicted aloud by positive statements. In the application phase, students are asked to substitute positive self-statements in actual stress situations in the absence of the trainer. To help students do this they are asked to practice while working on math homework or solving problems in math class. These students have much more positive attitudes toward math and perform quite well.

Teachers who identify children with a learned helplessness orientation might try a similar strategy of helping students restructure their cognitions through the following steps:

1. Teach children the relationship between thoughts and performance.
2. Find out the negative self-statements that children make and counter them with other, more positive ones.
3. Help students rehearse the positive statements.
4. Write the statements on cards and encourage students to use them when they encounter a difficult assignment.

Another important way teachers can help these children is to teach them to interpret failure as feedback, which tells them that they need more information.

SCENARIO

6 Jackson is a courteous second grader who appears to have good friends and a good relationship with his parents. The problem is that whenever he makes a mistake or finds the work difficult, he simply gives up, puts his paper and pencil down, and sits there dejectedly. Whenever he encounters the first obstacle, he gives up and says, "I can't do it." Although Jackson is maintaining a passing grade, the trend is a disturbing

one since the difficulty of work is increasing and Jackson's "giving up" is occurring more often. What could you do to help Jackson?

Suicide

Suicide is the third leading cause of death among people between 15 and 24 years of age (accidents and homicide are first and second) (Worsnop, 1991). Each year, more than half a million young people attempt suicide; unfortunately, more than 5,000 succeed (Neiger & Hopkins, 1988). Males complete suicide four times as often as females, but females try three times more often than males. The difference is probably due to the more lethal methods of suicide (often firearms) used by males. Whites have higher suicide rates than African Americans, but the highest suicide rates are among Native Americans. A Gallup Poll national survey of 1,152 teens between the ages 13 and 19 showed the extent of the problem. Sixty percent of the teens personally knew other teens who have attempted suicide, and 15 percent had admitted to considering it. Six percent have attempted suicide (Ackerman, 1993).

The most common cause of suicide is depression (Gispert et al., 1985). Children with exceptional needs are more often vulnerable to the emotional trauma that leads to stress, low self-esteem, and suicidal behavior. Children with learning problems are more likely to be at risk for depression and suicidal behavior (Pfeifer, 1986). A sense of hopelessness seems to pervade these children (Farberow, 1985). When psychological autopsies (analyses of why suicides occur after they have already taken place) are performed, certain factors appear, which include drug and alcohol use; prior suicide attempts; depression, antisocial, or aggressive behavior; and family histories of suicidal behavior (Garland & Zigler, 1993).

The best predictor of a future suicide attempt is a previous suicide attempt; about 40 percent of all successful suicide victims have tried before. Suicides most often have a precipitating event, such as a humiliating experience, an arrest, a perceived or actual family rejection, being fired from work, or a romantic conflict. In a study of 229 youth suicides, an argument with a boyfriend, girlfriend, or parents was the precipitating factor in 19 percent of the cases, while school-related problems were the precipitating event in 14 percent (Hoberman & Garfinkel, 1988).

Most adolescents who attempt suicide experienced a large number of stressful events in childhood, with a marked increase in stress in the year preceding the attempt. Having someone in the family who talks about, has attempted, or actually did commit suicide also increases the risk (Lawton, 1991).

Whenever a suicide occurs in a community, people start looking for answers and clues. Indeed, in a majority of cases, clues are found. About 80 percent of the adolescents communicate their feelings and intentions to other people before attempting suicide (Shafii et al., 1985). Research provides some clues to predict the possibility of suicide, but unfortunately people do not always pay attention to them. For instance, many people believe that individuals who talk about suicide never actually do it. However, people who talk about suicide are actually *more* likely to attempt it. Other warning signs include giving things away and talking about "ending it." A previous attempt at suicide is also a warning that a future attempt might be made if the predisposing factors are not controlled or adequately dealt with (Colt, 1983). When a child experiences situations that cause extreme anxiety, depression, and hopelessness, those people around the child should be aware that suicide may be contemplated (Schneidman, Farberow, & Litman, 1970). Familial determinants include divorce, poor communication, conflict, unavailable parents, high parental expectations, mental illness, job loss, suicide of a family member, and alcoholism (Allen, 1987; Butler et al., 1994). Some of the warning signs for teachers to watch for are found in Table 7.1.

Some schools offer classes in which students are taught how to recognize the warning signs and help their troubled friends. Such classes also introduce students to the community resources that are available. Some report positive results, including gains in understanding suicide prevention techniques (Nelson, 1987). One interesting outcome is that most of the teens questioned after the program reported that they were more likely to use a hotline to help themselves (Viadero, 1987).

Some authorities, however, are concerned by the possible negative effect such programs might have on already troubled students and doubt their effectiveness. A review of 300 prevention programs found that the most effective programs were based upon sound empirical knowledge, including a clear understanding of risk, and collected evaluative data (Price et al., 1989). Most suicide prevention programs, though, fail on both accounts. Many programs are not based upon the research about suicide. In an attempt to destigmatize suicide, the programs often deny that suicide victims experience mental disturbance. Additionally, suicide is

THOUGHT QUESTION

8. *Should units on suicide prevention be mandated in high schools?*

TABLE 7.1   **Warning Signs of a Potential Suicide Attempt**

1. Preoccupation with themes of death or expressing suicidal thoughts.
2. Giving away prized possessions or making a will or other "final arrangements."
3. Changes in sleeping patterns—too much or too little.
4. Sudden and extreme changes in eating habits or losing or gaining weight.
5. Withdrawal from friends and family or major behavioral changes.
6. Changes in school performance, lowered grades, cutting classes, dropping out of activities.
7. Personality changes, such as nervousness, outbursts of anger, or apathy about appearance and health.
8. Use of drugs or alcohol.
9. Recent suicide of a friend or relative.
10. Previous suicide attempts.
11. Feelings of hopelessness and depression.
12. Recent loss of people who are close to them.

sometimes incorrectly portrayed as a reaction to common stress. The incidence of suicide is also exaggerated in many cases. Deemphasizing the link between emotional disturbances and suicide does not do a service to anyone, and many students only remember the link between stress and suicide.

Many prevention programs fail to reach the populations at greatest risk, which include dropouts, runaways, and youths who are arrested and incarcerated (Garland & Zigler, 1993). When students are asked what the schools should do about suicide, they want special programs for troubled teenagers, programs for parents on how to be better parents, and information about hotlines and drop-in groups (Lawton, 1991).

One promising preventive approach is to help students improve their problem-solving skills and feelings of efficacy, or belief that they can influence the situation (Cole, 1990). Finally, reducing the availability of firearms and targeting education of at-risk populations, such as friends of people who have committed suicide and runaway youths, may also be effective in preventing suicide (Garland & Zigler, 1993).

Anxiety

Fear and anxiety are sometimes adaptive responses to threats in the environment. People avoid objects they fear; and when an individual experiences anxiety, the person becomes wary and alerted to the possibility of danger. A problem arises, though, if the fear and anxiety are either out of proportion to the stimulus, are attached to many objects, or lead to inappropriate behavior.

Both fear and anxiety have physiological, motoric, and experiential (subjective) components. Physiological responses include an increase in autonomic nervous system functioning, for example, increased heart rate, sweating, and muscle tension. Motor responses include crying, nail biting, clenching of the jaw, and hand trembling. Subjective responses include thoughts of being frightened or hurt, fear of bodily injury, or fear of losing control (Wicks-Nelson & Israel, 1991). Fear and anxiety are experienced in the same manner, as unpleasant emotions. The two emotions are not quite the same, though. Fear is directed toward a specific focus, whereas the object of anxiety is often vague, undifferentiated, and uncertain. A second distinction is that of time orientation. Anxiety is directed toward events that haven't yet occurred; it is futuristic. Fear, in contrast, is immediate.

Classification

The DSM-IV lists three specific anxiety disorders for children. *Separation anxiety disorder* involves excessive anxiety on separation from major attachment figures. The DSM-IV recognizes the fact that in early childhood some degree of separation anxiety is a typical phenomenon, and clinical judgment is necessary for proper diagnosis. Later in childhood, one of the possible symptoms is persistent refusal to go to school and complaints of physical symptoms on school days. The second disorder, called *avoidant disorder of childhood or adolescence*, is a persistent and excessive avoidance of strangers so severe that it interferes with social functioning. The third disorder is *overanxious disorder* in which the essential feature is excessive worrying and fearful behavior not focused on specific situations or objects. In addition, almost all of the anxiety disorders that are diagnosed in adults may be diagnosed in children. These include phobic disorders, panic disorders, obsessive-compulsive disorders, and posttraumatic stress disorder. A *phobic disorder* is one in which a child experiences a persistent and irrational fear of an object or situation. *Panic disorders* are characterized by recurrent attacks of terror. An *obsessive-compulsive disorder* is one in which a child who experiences a persistent thought (obsession) engages in a ritualized action (compulsion) that reduces the anxiety in the short term. Finally, *posttraumatic stress disorder* involves fear and related symptoms experienced long after a traumatic event. A child who has experienced some unusual and terrible event, such as being a victim of a violent crime or being involved in a natural catastrophe (hurricane, earthquake, etc.), may relive the event and become hypersensitive to stimuli in the environment.

Overanxious Children

Overanxious children experience an excessive amount of anxiety directed at many things. The anxiety is, objectively speaking, unrealistic. These children excessively worry about the future and often have somatic complaints. They develop nervous habits, such as nail biting, as well. Frequently, they exhibit excessive or unrealistic concern about competence in some area of importance, be it athletic, academic, or social. They cannot relax. These children worry about a wide variety of future problems.

Most overanxious children are not failing, nor are they doing poorly in school or in any other sphere of life. Yet, these students' anxiety interferes with their school functioning, their interpersonal relations, and their enjoyment of life. Teachers may notice that these children are anxious no matter how well they do and may require constant reassurance (Coleman, 1992). These children may also have separation anxiety disorders.

Phobias

A **phobia** is a persistent and irrational fear of a specific object, activity, or situation (Comer, 1995). The fear may also be simply out of proportion to the danger or situation. For example, some wariness of snakes, especially if the person has not had much experience with them, might be understandable, but if the individual screams at the sight, avoids camping, or even taking walks this fear may be viewed differently.

People may develop a phobia to almost anything. They may fear darkness, being in an enclosed place, heights, or animals. People with phobias avoid the feared stimulus. Phobias are found more often in girls than in boys (Erickson, 1992). Duration and intensity are two factors that differentiate usual fears from phobias (Graziano, DeGiovanni, & Garcia, 1979). When an individual is confronted by the object of the anxiety, physical reactions and feelings of panic may also occur.

School Phobia (School Refusal)
Perhaps the most researched anxiety disorder in children is school phobia or school refusal (Wicks-Nelson & Israel, 1991). Actually, researchers have difficulty separating the data concerning school phobia and separation anxiety disorder. It

Some children experience a great deal of anxiety, affecting their behavior and achievement.

Phobia:
A persistent and irrational fear of a specific object, activity, or situation.

is not common, with a prevalence of 0.4 to 1.7 percent (Erickson, 1992). These children show an unwillingness to go to school, often combined with symptoms such as headaches or stomach aches. They may put up fights to stay out of school. The disorder is found equally across intelligence levels and is no more prominent in children with learning disabilities or learning problems (Coleman, 1992). Lack of ability or demonstrated failure do not cause the problem.

Some authorities divide school phobias into two distinct problems: separation anxiety and actual school phobia (Last et al., 1987). The idea is that some cases of school phobia may be based upon separation problems from the home, while still others may be based upon something that has occurred in school. School phobia is differentiated from separation anxiety disorder because the child with school phobia fears the school situation whether or not the child is accompanied by a parent. But in practice this distinction is never checked, and parents rarely come to school (Kessler, 1988).

Mothers of children who have school phobia do show a pattern. They often reflect their children's complaints about school giving them credence. They also tend to be overprotective and have tried to be certain that their children experience no discomfort at all (Erickson, 1992). Sometimes the parents are ill, and the child takes on complete responsibility in the home. At other times, a child simply refuses to separate from parents.

On the other hand, perhaps something aversive has happened in the school, and the school is now linked with this punishing condition causing fear or anxiety. This fear may be reinforced by parents who allow the child to avoid school.

Treatment for school phobia has been successful in many cases and is based upon getting the child back to school as soon as possible (King & Ollendick, 1989). Parents are taught not to reinforce the children's behavior. If physical symptoms exist in the child, a pediatrician is consulted after school. Sometimes desensitization and relaxation are used to reduce the anxiety, and positive reinforcement is given for going to school and any reinforcement for not attending is eliminated. A program of ignoring the fear, enlisting the cooperation of everyone in the environment and helping parents attend to positive behaviors has been very successful (see Last, 1992).

Causes of Anxiety Problems

What causes excessive anxiety in children? Some psychoanalytic explanations of anxiety surround difficulties in separation. In addition, according to Freud, people try to control their unacceptable impulses by using defense mechanisms. If these defense mechanisms do not perform well, anxiety occurs (Allen, 1994).

Behavioral interpretations are based upon both classical and operant conditioning. If a stimulus that does not cause fear is paired with a stimulus that does elicit fear, the result may be a conditioned fear response. For instance, if a child is in an elevator and something calamitous occurs, the child experiences a fear response. The child may possibly react with fear when placed in a similar environment. In addition, the child may now not only fear elevators but all small enclosures. Extinction of the fear may not take place because the fear-producing stimulus is avoided.

Children may also learn fears through reinforcement. Perhaps parents give children social reinforcement in the form of attention for their fears and anxieties.

For example, children who show school phobia or a fear may be allowed to stay with their mother who then plays with them.

Children may also learn to fear something or some situation by observing someone showing anxiety in the situation (Bandura, 1986). Imagine a parent who is afraid of spiders and shows this fear as the child is watching. A child who watches as another child is bitten by a dog may also experience a fear of dogs.

Beck (1976) provides a cognitive theory of anxiety. Anxiety comes from unrealistic perceptions of dangers. One or more cognitive errors—including, overestimating the probability or the severity of the feared event or underestimating what one can do about it or what others can do to help—affect the development of anxiety. For example, people with anxiety disorders hold unrealistic assumptions, believing that any strange situation should be regarded as dangerous, assuming the worst, and not trusting others.

Some evidence also points to neurological mechanisms as the source of anxiety reactions (Comer, 1994). A significant genetic contribution may be present as well (Rose & Ditto, 1983). However, more research is required in these areas.

Helping Children with Anxiety Disorders

The most common clinical method of treating many anxiety disorders, especially phobias, is through **systematic desensitization**, which involves progressive relaxation and the gradual presentation of the feared stimulus either through imagination or in reality. For example, a person afraid of spiders may first be placed into a relaxed state and then presented with, or asked to imagine, a spider twenty feet away. Slowly the spider is brought closer. The relaxation inhibits the anxiety response. Although systematic desensitization is certainly one of the more effective techniques with adults, its value for children and adolescents is not well established (Morris & Kratochwill, 1987). Although this method has shown some evidence for success, more research is needed.

Modeling procedures have become a popular treatment. A child watches a model interact with the feared object. The child is then encouraged to do the same. The more involvement on the part of the client the more effective it is (Strauss, 1987).

Cognitive techniques have been used as well. For example, children may be taught self-statements in order to counter fear. Kindergarten children afraid of the dark were taught self-statements such as, "I am a brave boy/girl," "I can take care of myself," and "The dark is a fun place to be." This group showed much less fear than a group taught neutral statements (Mary had a little lamb) or no self-statements at all (Kanfer, Karoly, & Newman, 1975). These techniques are used by therapists as part of the program to reduce the anxiety reactions.

Teachers can help the child experiencing a great deal of anxiety by reducing the pressure on the child. Sometimes working with parents can be helpful. Certain classroom activities, such as taking tests and giving speeches in front of the class, tend to increase anxiety. In such situations, trying to ensure success is important. Whenever possible, the student should be introduced gradually to a potentially stressful situation.

Consider the teacher's problems when dealing with a student experiencing great anxiety from the requirement of giving a speech in front of the class. Asking the student to answer a question while seated in class would serve as a good intro-

Systematic desensitization: A behavioral technique for reducing anxiety, which involves progressive relaxation followed by the gradual introduction of the feared stimulus.

THOUGHT QUESTION

9. *How would you help a student who shows so much test anxiety that it interferes with the student's performance on examinations?*

duction to speaking before the class. The student may then be asked to stand up at the student's seat and say a few words, then perhaps write the answer to a question on the blackboard and explain it while standing in front of the classroom. These and other activities might gradually lead up to the student's giving a speech. In addition, positive support can be most helpful. The teacher can give gentle encouragement, which may enable a student to approach these potentially anxiety-producing situations with more confidence.

SCENARIO

7 Tanya is a nervous fifth grader. She looks tense, and sometimes you can see the anxiety as she twists in her seat during an exam or becomes tense during question time. Everyone is giving oral reports on some area of interest. Tanya asks to be excluded and given a different assignment because she fears giving the speech in class. Would you grant her request? If not, how could you help Tanya?

Children with Behavior Disorders in the Classroom

Even though teachers are not therapists, a teacher faced with a student showing a behavior disorder can devise various useful strategies for helping the child. The fundamental principle is to deal with the behavior disorder so that the child can learn, as well as help the student deal with any difficulties the student faces. When dealing with children who show the types of problems previously discussed, the teacher (or parent) will want to either encourage a particular behavior (for example, participating in social activities for a child who withdraws) or discourage a particular behavior (for example, showing aggression against another child). At times a teacher or parent may want to do both. Certain techniques are quite effective in this regard and may be used by classroom teachers, sometimes with the help of the special education teacher, the school psychologist, guidance counselor, or other professionals in the school who may have more experience and training in these specific techniques.

Four important points should be kept in mind regarding instituting a program to change behavior. First, if the child is seeing a therapist, communication between the teacher (and parent) and therapist is important. The therapist may have specific ideas what the teacher can do or should not do. If the child is taking medication, the teacher will know whether the child is too drowsy and some dosage restriction is necessary. Second, any program instituted by the teacher or any responsible individual will be more successful if the relationship between the teacher and the student is good. When the student and teacher get along and have good communication, the student will be more willing to participate in programs designed to help change behavior. Third, some of these procedures should be used to improve the school work of the student, not just focus on conduct. As noted earlier, many of these children are not doing well in school and improving their academic achievement helps these children feel more confident, more successful, and more competent.

Finally, no procedure will turn a withdrawn child into an highly socially active child, an anxious child into a calm one, or an aggressive child into one who will never again commit an aggressive act. Instead, what can be offered is a group of techniques to improve the behavior of the student, which allows the student to do class work. A child who shows five aggressive acts in a class may improve after treatment to showing only one aggressive act, which is an obvious improvement, but may not be sufficient for the teacher.

Most programs to modify behavior take a behavioral or a cognitive-behavioral perspective. That is, they attempt to modify the child's behavior or to modify the child's thought patterns. The use of behavioral principles to change behavior is called **behavior modification**. All procedures must be ethically sound and in consonance with education law.

Behavior modification:
The use of the principles of learning theory to change behavior.

THE CLASSROOM   Designing a Behavior Modification Program

How does a teacher go about designing a program to modify behavior? It involves the following procedures:

1. *Target the behavior.* The first step is to specify the behavior that the teacher wants to change. Although this task may seem simple, it is not. Such statements as "I want the child to act better," "I want the child to work harder," or "I want the child to act more maturely," may make sense, but they do nothing to target the behavior. Examples of specific targeted behaviors would include reducing the child's calling out to once (or perhaps not at all) per period or having a student participate at least twice a period in class. Teachers can observe and measure these specific behaviors.

2. *Obtain a baseline.* Suppose the teacher wants to encourage Jimmy to raise his hand more often instead of shouting out. To see any improvement, the teacher must have some idea of what was happening before the behavior modification program was introduced. If good records are not kept, the success of the program cannot be adequately evaluated.

   Sometimes charts are kept and the frequency of behavior graphed. Figure 7.1 on the next page shows a child's talk-outs counted during a half-hour each day. The solid line shows the number of talk-outs for a child while the dotted line shows the teacher's self-count of verbal praises given to any child in the class during another class period. The first section, entitled baseline, provides a basis for comparing the student's behavior before and after the procedures designed to reduce talk-outs are implemented. In this case, you may notice that in the last two days of the baseline, the teacher's praise increased and the student's calling out decreased. Such changes occur because baseline activities force the teacher to become aware not only of the student's behavior but also of the teacher's own behavior, and sometimes the teacher alters the behavior. This may cause the baseline to change and should be considered when evaluating the effectiveness of the program.

3. *Choose a procedure.* Now the teacher is ready to change the environment in some way. The procedure must be worked out carefully while being practical. The criteria for giving the reinforcer(s) must be precise and communicated clearly to the student. The reinforcement procedure must require a response that the student can attain.

In the figure, the teacher decided to use the reinforcer of teacher praise. The response the teacher wanted, the child's raising the child's hand instead of calling out, was a response the child could perform. During the change procedure #1, verbal praise was increased for designated behaviors, not only for this student but for the entire class, and talk-outs were ignored. Notice the praise rate rising quickly and talk-outs decreasing rather slowly each day. Also notice that keeping a chart makes it easier at the very beginning to note changes.

FIGURE 7.1   Graph of Child's Talk-Outs

In this graph, notice the pattern of both the student's talk-outs and the teacher's use of two strategies, praise and ignore and praise and self-count, over the course of about two weeks.

Source: Adapted from *Behavior Modification*, Second Edition, by Robert J. Presbie and Paul L. Brown. Copyright 1985. Washington, D.C.: National Education Association. Reprinted by permission of the NEA Professional Library.

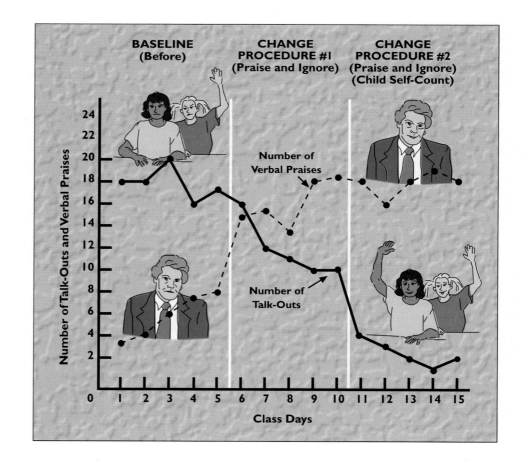

Because the decrease was somewhat slow, the teacher decided to add another procedure in which the child kept a record on an index card of every time the child talked out. The teacher continued to ignore the talk-outs and praise other behaviors. The talk-outs decreased markedly under this procedure.

4. *Analyze and try something else if necessary.* The last step is to evaluate the program and see if it is working. Is the behavior being modified? If it is, the teacher may want to continue the program or use a maintenance procedure. If not, the teacher may want to try something else. This process was demonstrated in the attempt to reduce talk-outs shown in Figure 7.1. When the praise-and-ignore procedure was not working to the teacher's satisfaction, another approach was tried, which proved more effective. Most teachers first want to try the least intrusive method, and only if it does not work will they use a more involved procedure. The aim is to not take up too much classtime. However, if something doesn't work, teachers should be prepared to try something else that might be more involved but may have a greater chance of success. Another teacher or the school psychologist who is more experienced in this area may also be consulted for help in improving the procedures and suggesting alternatives.

Reinforcement Techniques

A full explanation of the many reinforcement techniques available to teachers and parents would take up an entire book. A **reinforcer** is any event that increases the likelihood the behavior that preceded it will reoccur. For reinforcers to be effective, they must be contingent upon a specific desired behavior, which means that before the reinforcer is given the desired behavior must be exhibited. It should also be delivered as soon after the desired behavior occurs as possible. Various types of reinforcers can be used. Some are social, as in the case of praise or attention, while some involve allowing a child to participate in an enjoyable activity and are called activity reinforcers. For example, a child may be allowed a few extra minutes of play time for behavior that matches criterion. Others, especially for young children, may be consumables involving food or stickers.

Reinforcer:
Any event that increases the likelihood the behavior that preceded it will reoccur.

Token Reinforcement

The students in the class have been told that each time they finish an assignment with a predetermined level of accuracy, they will be given a star. In this type of system, called a **token economy** or **token reinforcement system**, a star or some other symbol can be used immediately to purchase reinforcers—such as free time, reduced or no homework, or other privileges—or saved up to purchase larger reinforcers, called backup reinforcers.

Tokens can include chips, stars, play money, stamps, points, or check marks (Forman, 1987). Token economies have been used successfully for a variety of purposes, including improving reading and writing skills, encouraging cooperation, and finishing work on time (Presbie & Brown, 1985). In one study, a number of fifth-grade boys who exhibited discipline problems were identified. The teacher

Token economy (token reinforcement system):
A system of reinforcement in which students receive a token (such as a star) for performing the desired behavior and can either use it immediately or save it and add it to previously earned tokens to "purchase" reinforcers.

TABLE 7.2   **Backup Reinforcers**

POINTS EARNING CRITERIA FOR FIFTH-GRADE READING CLASS	
1. 80% correct on workbook assignments	= 2 points
2. 100% correct on workbook assignments	= 5 points

BACKUP REINFORCERS	
Daily	
1. Access to game room (15 minutes)	2 points
2. Extra recess time (10 minutes)	2 points
3. Buy a ditto master	2 points
4. Have ditto copies run off (per copy)	1 point
5. Review grades in teacher's book	5 points
6. Reduce detention (10 minutes)	10 points
7. Change cafeteria table	15 points
8. Have the lowest test grade removed	20 points
9. Become an assistant teacher	Auction
Weekly	
1. See a movie	6 points
2. Have a good work letter sent to parents	15 points
3. Become the classroom helper for one week	Auction
4. Become the ball captain for one week	Auction
5. Do bulletin board (will remain up for three weeks)	Auction

Source: "Eliminating Discipline Problems by Strengthening Academic Performance" by T. Ayllon and M.D. Roberts, *Journal of Applied Behavior Analysis.* Copyright © 1974. Reprinted by permission of *Journal of Applied Behavior Analyses* and author.

observed the students for some time to discover the boys' average level of disruption (a baseline procedure). A token reinforcement procedure was applied to reading performance, which was measured by the percentage of correct answers in daily performance sessions of 15 minutes each. The students were required to produce written answers to test material selected daily by the reading teacher for which they were awarded points. Table 7.2 shows the point system and lists the backup reinforcers. Such a system improved academic performance, but even more interesting is that it greatly reduced classroom disruptions (Ayllon & Roberts, 1974). In another study, third-grade boys with attention-deficit/hyperactivity disorder received tokens—to be exchanged for fifteen minutes of play on video games—which they earned by completing academic assignments and other tasks. Task completion improved dramatically with the use of tokens (Robinson, Newby, & Ganzeli, 1981).

To establish such a program, the teacher first must specify the behavior to be performed (e.g., students must finish the mathematics assignment in 20 minutes with either one error or no errors). The teacher then determines the number of tokens a student obtains for correctly doing the behavior and formulates a list of reinforcers that the tokens can buy. For example, 5 tokens might entitle the student to 15 minutes of free time, while 10 tokens might entitle the student to a homework-free night.

Self-Reinforcement

Another approach to reinforcement is to teach students to reinforce themselves. **Self-reinforcement** is the process by which people increase and maintain their behavior using rewards that they control whenever they attain a standard (Dickerson & Creedon, 1981). The key to this process is that the students themselves are agents of their own reinforcement (Goldiamond, 1976). A self-reinforcement process has many advantages. It teaches the student responsibility and independence and demands less teacher time. In addition, teacher-administered programs normally require teachers to notice each time a certain behavior is exhibited, which is not always possible. A teacher may simply be unaware of one student's time spent on a task if the instructor is working with another student.

Self-reinforcement procedures involve teaching students to monitor their own behavior, record it, and reinforce themselves when appropriate. Students can monitor, for example, the number of times they raise their hands and give themselves reinforcers, such as free time. Self-monitoring by itself leads to small improvements, probably because students learn how often they are engaging in a specific behavior. For example, students who fail to finish their work may not be aware of how often this happens. If they monitor themselves, they may begin to appreciate the problem. However, awareness usually results in only a temporary improvement.

Self-reinforcement is certainly not appropriate for every student and does present certain problems. Recording is more likely to be reliable if the behavior is clearly defined, and the teacher must periodically check for accuracy.

Extinction Procedures

Extinction involves withholding the reinforcer that is maintaining some behavior (Nelson, 1987). It requires teachers to identify the reinforcer and control it. It is used only when teachers realize that they are reinforcing the poor behavior, perhaps by giving attention to poor work. Let's say that when Jenny doesn't do her work, she receives a great deal of attention and coaxing. The attention, itself, may be a reinforcer. Instead, the teacher may choose to ignore the poor work itself and use positive reinforcement to increase the accuracy and amount of Jenny's work. For this to work, the teacher must be certain that the act is being reinforced by the teacher's own attention. For instance, if talk-outs in class are reinforced not only by teacher attention but also by student attention, extinction procedures will not work.

Extinction procedures are not as useful in the classroom as are other behavioral procedures. Ignoring talking and aggression will not lead to extinction, because their reinforcement is not under the teacher's direct control. Extinction procedures should *only* be used if the reinforcer is under the control of the teacher. When an extinction procedure is first being used, the frequency of the undesirable response may increase somewhat. This occurrence is known as **extinction burst**. Parents or teachers may have difficulty tolerating this increase in inappropriate responding and inadvertently deliver a positive reinforcer such as attention, which sustains the poor behavior. For example, a child's tantrums may become worse as they are ignored, and the parents may give in and provide

Self-reinforcement:
A process in which students reinforce themselves for desired behaviors.

Extinction:
Withholding a reinforcer that is maintaining a particular behavior.

Extinction burst:
The increase in the frequency of the undesirable behavior that sometimes occurs when extinction procedures are initially implemented.

attention for the tantrums, increasing the probability of more severe tantrums since the reinforcer was provided when the tantrums were so intense (Kazdin, 1994). This temporary increase in the problem behavior does not necessarily mean that the procedure is failing. In fact, the effects of the extinction procedure may be just beginning.

Response Cost

Response cost:
A punishment procedure in which a positive reinforcer is lost if an undesirable behavior is exhibited.

Response cost involves taking away a reinforcer, often points or tokens, if the un-desired behavior is exhibited. For example, suppose a student receives two points for completing math practice sheets with only one mistake per sheet. However, if there are more than four mistakes, the student loses a point. In this type of sys-tem, the student receives points when the desired behavior is exhibited and loses points when the student is careless. If two or three errors are made, the student does not gain or lose. A student might receive tokens for each time homework is done according to criteria and be penalized when the student does not do the homework. In one study, Rapport and colleagues (1978) used response cost to re-duce off-task behavior. Each time an incident of off-task behavior occurred, the teacher removed 1 minute of a possible 30 minutes of free time that students were allowed.

Response cost can be administered in various ways. Students can be given re-inforcers for desired behaviors and lose them for undesirable behavior. For exam-ple, a student may receive points for doing work correctly during class and lose a point for a well-publicized infraction. Response cost systems can work, but only if the criteria and scoring system are reasonable. If it is very difficult to gain rein-forcers but easy to lose them, the situation becomes frustrating. In addition, if er-rors are to be the reason for losing tokens, students must know the work and be able to do it accurately. This is not a procedure to be used when students are just learning the material and mistakes can be expected.

Time Out for Misbehavior

Time-out:
A punishment procedure in which access to positive reinforcement is withdrawn for a brief time period if a serious behavior infraction occurs.

One method of dealing with aggressive behavior is to use a **time-out** procedure. Time-out involves placing a student in a less reinforcing environment for a short period of time following misbehavior (Kazdin, 1994; Axelrod, 1983). Sending a child who is misbehaving to sit in a more isolated area of the classroom is an ex-ample of such a procedure. Time-out periods should be short—no more than five minutes.

A number of forms of time-out exist which are usually grouped into two cate-gories: nonexclusionary and exclusionary time-out. In non-exclusionary time-out, a student remains in the immediate setting but is removed to another part of the classroom. Perhaps the child is required to sit in a nearby chair and can ob-serve but not participate in a classroom activity. In exclusionary time-out, the per-son is excluded from the immediate setting, for example, by being placed in another room for a very short amount of time (Malott, Whaley, & Malott, 1993).

Time-out is one of the most controversial tactics used because of its misuse and misapplication (Smith, 1989). Many children are escape-oriented and do not mind spending some time on their own. In addition, it is often imposed only after severe behavioral difficulties are shown, such as violent outbursts or fights, re-quiring the teacher to intervene at a particularly dangerous and sometimes emo-tionally laden time. This situation holds the potential for confrontation.

A number of legal and practical problems are involved in the use of time-out, especially exclusionary time-out, and some precautions are required (Rosenberg et al., 1992). First, an appropriate and safe place where the student can be continually monitored is necessary. If one is not available, then a different intervention should be used. The school principal and specialists should be consulted and their agreement noted. Parental consent is also required. Time-out procedures should be stated explicitly on the IEP of any student who is diagnosed as having a behavior disorder (Abromowitz & O'Leary, 1990). Once a procedure such as time-out is begun, detailed records should be kept on the number of times it is used and the amount of time the student spends in time-out (Smith, 1989). In addition, since it has a negative focus, it should be used with positive reinforcers for correct behavior. The use of exclusionary time-out raises potential legal problems, such as the issue of unlawful restraint. Although under certain well-defined conditions, time-out may be useful, the practical, ethical, and legal difficulties make it a less attractive alternative. Other less intrusive procedures should be implemented before considering time-out.

Alternate Response Training

Alternate response training is a self-control procedure that has become increasingly popular. It involves training a child to perform an alternative behavior in place of an undesirable behavior. This alternative behavior may either interfere with or replace the undesirable behavior. To be successful, the student must recognize the circumstances in which a troublesome response occurs. Robin (1976) developed the turtle technique, which uses as its model the image of a turtle withdrawing into its shell when reacting to something in the environment. Young children are taught to react to their aggressive impulses by imagining that they are turtles withdrawing into their shells and actually pull their arms close to their bodies, put their heads down, and close their eyes. They are also taught to use problem-solving strategies to generate other responses. The problem solving involves role-playing and discussions in which children are offered alternative strategies for coping with problems. Peers are also taught to support the use of the turtle technique. In Robin's study, six children whose behavior was frequently aggressive were taught how to emit the turtle response when they believed that an aggressive interchange was about to occur. If a teacher noticed that the child was about to throw a tantrum the teacher called out, "Turtle!" Results showed a significant decrease in aggressive behavior.

Alternate response training: A self-control procedure in which students are taught to use responses that either interfere with or replace an undesirable response.

Cognitive Behavior Modification: Self-Statements

When you are trying to perform some intricate maneuver, do you ever talk to yourself out loud? In self-instruction training, a student is taught to control behavior by making suggestions and comments that guide behavior as if the student were being instructed by someone else.

In a famous study, Meichenbaum and Goodman (1971) succeeded in altering the impulsive behavior of children. The experimenters asked teachers to model performance carefully on such tasks as solving classwork problems. The teachers then talked out loud, verbalizing questions about the task, answers to those questions, and self-instructions, such as to "go slow." They finally used self-reinforcement. The children were asked to do this the same way the teachers had. They learned first to whisper the instructions and finally to say them privately without lip movements. Using this technique, a significant reduction in impulsive behavior occurred.

In another study, Bornstein and Quevillon (1976) trained preschoolers who were highly disruptive to ask themselves, "What does the teacher want me to do?" and to answer the questions and give themselves praise. For example, the answer might be, "I'm supposed to copy the picture." First, the children were taught to say it out loud, then in a whisper, and finally to themselves. Again, behavior was significantly improved.

Social Skills Training

Children who act out, show depressed affect, or are anxious often have poor social skills. In addition, if some behavioral strategy is being used to reduce the frequency of a behavior, a reasonable question is what to replace the behavior with. Social skills training should be used to teach youngsters with behavior problems socially acceptable ways to meet their needs. For example, social skills training may include how to ask for things or how to give and receive compliments, as well as focus on special areas of need, such as how to deal with wanting something that doesn't belong to them. After a child learns the skills, practice and feedback are necessary; some opportunities for generalizing these skills outside the training situation are also beneficial.

Teachers and parents are not usually experts in behavior modification and social skills training. They do not have to be. Frequently, school psychologists and other mental health personnel have a great deal of experience with these programs and may serve as valuable resource people. The central idea is to try different methods that are ethically sound until one is found that works.

The Child with a Behavior Disorder

Different strategies are required to help children who act aggressively, are overly anxious or depressed, or exhibit withdrawal function in the classroom. All children with behavior disorders need teachers to pay attention to their academic successes and help them develop social skills. It is especially important for these children to receive positive feedback when they achieve or show behavioral improvement, since many children with behavior disorders receive only criticism for their work and actions. Both teachers and parents can work together with mental health personnel to reduce the symptoms of the behavior and help children with behavior disorders function and achieve in the classroom and the world outside the classroom.

SUMMARY

1. According to law, children are experiencing a serious emotional disturbance if they fail to establish or maintain reasonable interpersonal relationships, show inappropriate behavior, or develop psychological symptoms, such as depression or fears, which interfere with school achievement. These difficulties cannot be caused by sensory, intellectual or health problems, or social maladjustment. The behaviors must be exhibited for a long period of time and to a marked degree. This definition is criticized for being vague and for excluding social maladjustment. Other definitions have been considered for acceptance.

2. Behavior disorders can be classified in two major ways. One involves a classification used by clinicians, e.g., the Diagnostic and Statistical Manual of Mental Disorders of the American Psychiatric Association (DSM-IV). The second approach is statistical and places behaviors that go together into basic behavior patterns. Two such patterns commonly found are externalizing (involving aggression and disobedience) and internalizing (involving anxiety, withdrawal, and depression).

3. Behavior can be described and analyzed as to its shape and form, chronicity, frequency, severity, and the setting events.

4. The majority of children diagnosed as having a behavior disorder have an average intelligence score, but do not do well in school. Programs to help children with behavior disorders should contain academic elements as well.

5. A number of psychological models are useful for examining behavior disorders, including the psychoanalytic, behavioral, cognitive, humanistic, and ecological perspectives.

6. About 1 percent of the school population is diagnosed as having behavior disorders, and evidence exists that more children have such disorders than are diagnosed and served.

7. The most common ways of gathering information about behavior disorders are through clinical interviews, observation, rating scales, and personality testing. Intelligence tests and medical tests are also given.

8. Less than half of all children with a diagnosis of a behavior disorder are educated in the regular classroom and/or in resource rooms. The others are educated in special classes, special schools, or residential facilities.

9. Children learn to aggress by being reinforced for aggressive behavior. They also learn through observing aggressive models who get results from aggression. Parental inconsistency in discipline, a combination of permissiveness and punitiveness, and laxness in monitoring may lead to aggression. Peer groups may also encourage and maintain aggressive behavior in their members. The neighborhood, culture, and the media are factors in encouraging or inhibiting aggression.

10. Children showing oppositional defiant disorders argue constantly and defy authority but are generally not violent. Children who show conduct disorders are violent and do not respect other people's rights or property. Adolescents with conduct disorders frequently are labeled delinquent. They interpret social problems in hostile ways and are impulsive. Poor family relationships are the rule with these children. Some community-based programs, family intervention programs, and mediation programs have had some success. Studies indicate that preschool programs may prevent delinquency.

11. Depression is a feeling of dejection. Cognitive, motivational, and physical symptoms frequently accompany the emotion. Some biological theories emphasize the role of neurotransmitters within the brain. Behavioral psychologists view depression as a lack of positive reinforcement. One cognitive theory advanced by Seligman notes that some people are depressed due to learned helplessness, the belief that their actions do not influence the outcome. Beck argues that depressed people have a pessimistic attitude, seeing only the

negative, interpreting the world, their self, and the future in negative terms. Children who think of themselves as incompetent in many areas tend to be depressed.

12. Depressed children and adolescents are sometimes treated with medication and psychotherapy. Building a relationship with a student who shows withdrawal and helping to improve the student's social skills can also help.

13. The most common cause of suicide is depression and hopelessness. Teachers must learn to recognize the warning signs given by a person contemplating suicide. Hotlines have had some success.

14. Excessive anxiety and fear can interfere with school work and cause subjective discomfort. Behaviorists explain anxiety as a learned response, and cognitive psychologists argue it is due to faulty information processing because people have unrealistic perceptions of danger. Clinicians use systematic desensitization in which an anxiety-provoking stimulus is gradually presented to a relaxed subject, thereby reducing the anxiety response. Another method is modeling in which a person watches another cope with the feared stimulus. The use of self-statements is also possible.

15. Teachers can use behavior modification and cognitive behavior modification to help improve the child's behavior and allow the child to succeed in class. The procedure for behavior modification includes targeting a specific behavior, obtaining a baseline, choosing a procedure, and evaluating the results. Reinforcement techniques include token reinforcement and self-reinforcement. Behavioral techniques, such as response cost and time-out, may reduce a behavior but must be used carefully. Children may also be given alternate response training. Social skills training is also important.

Children at Risk

CHILDREN AT RISK

TRUE-FALSE STATEMENTS

See below for the correct answers.

1. The percentage of American children living below the poverty line is higher today than fifteen years ago.
2. The infants of women who smoke during pregnancy weigh about one-half pound more than the infants of mothers who do not smoke.
3. Although fetuses exposed to cocaine are more likely to suffer prematurity and even fetal death, those who survive show no distinguishable behavioral characteristics as compared with fetuses not exposed to cocaine.
4. Premature infants are at increased risk for developmental problems, compared to infants born at full term.
5. Unusual as it may seem, parents who physically abuse their children often believe that physical punishment is wrong.
6. A majority of abused children grow up to abuse their own children.
7. After a divorce, the custodial parent typically becomes stricter, while the other parent becomes more permissive.
8. Teenage mothers are more patient and sensitive to the needs of their infants than mothers in their twenties.
9. Most homeless children do not go to elementary school.
10. Children who experience a great deal of stress and still thrive often take care of their younger siblings and are socially outgoing and flexible.

Answers to True-False Statements

1. True.
2. False. See page 301.
3. False. See page 302.
4. True.
5. False. See page 310.
6. False. See page 311.
7. True.
8. False. See page 318.
9. False. See page 324.
10. True.

Does Everyone Have an Equal Chance?

Let's suppose that you chose a random sample of 1,000 American children in 1995. Would all of these children have an equal chance of developing in a healthy manner? If scientists followed these children as they grew up, could they predict who would develop a disability or demonstrate psychopathology?

Consider the following cases:

Donna was born in 1990 at a hospital in a large urban center. She tested positive for cocaine. Her mother is a crack addict and has tried to kick the habit twice before.

Ellis is a six-year-old who has been homeless for four months. He and his mother live in a city shelter.

Tanya's father calls her all sorts of names whenever she does anything wrong. He berates her at the slightest mischief and sometimes threatens to throw her out of the house.

All of these children have something in common. They are at risk for developmental and behavioral problems. Not all children have an equal risk of developing a disability; some children are more likely to experience a developmental problem or show poor academic achievement than others. Although most people would like to believe that every child has an equal chance of developing in a healthy manner and succeeding, it is not the case. This chapter is about risk, the factors that create increased risk, the prevention of risk, and the possibility of reducing a risk factor once it is present.

What Is Risk?

When a child is considered "at risk," it means that the child has an increased probability of developing some sort of developmental difficulty. The risk factor may be exposure to an agent such as cocaine or a social condition such as poverty. Risk, then, is basically a statistical concept. Scientists who conduct research on risk must identify the agent or situation, specify the effect, and then estimate the probability that they are associated. Research is more helpful if it identifies the population that is at risk, notes the factors that increase or decrease the risk, and establishes the time frame for the causal link.

If a child is at a particular risk for developmental delay, it does not mean that such a child will definitely develop a disability. For example, psychologists know that a particular percentage of children who are physically or emotionally abused will experience developmental difficulties. The percentage, though, will not be 100 percent. This means that some children who are victims of poor treatment will grow up to be average or even superior adults. However, if these abused children are compared to those who are not abused, the abused children are *more likely* to show these problems. At-risk status does not indicate that a particular child will definitely develop a disability.

Second, even though a population is at increased risk, a majority of that population may develop in an average manner. For example, many people will flatly state that abused children grow up to abuse their own children, but research has shown that this is a gross overstatement. Anywhere between 25 and 33 percent of all children who are abused grow up and abuse their own children (Wisdom, 1989). That means that between 67 and 75 percent of all children who are abused —the majority—will not grow up to abuse their own children. However, since about 3 percent of the population at large abuses their children, the 25–33 percent figure means that the risk of abuse is about 10 times greater if a parent has been abused as a child. Increased risk does not have to mean that a majority of affected children will develop problems, only that compared to the general population the probability is significantly greater.

Third, at times risk factors may exist together, and their effects may be additive or even multiplicative. Many children who test positive for cocaine after birth are raised in poverty-stricken homes by parents who have many problems. Although cocaine is no doubt a risk factor, the environment in which the child is raised is also important. So the child is exposed to two risk factors: cocaine and a poor environment. Separating out each factor independently is not always easy.

Fourth, if professionals are aware that a particular condition increases risk, they can take action to prevent that condition or to remediate it so as to reduce its adverse effects (Vickers, 1994). Many programs aim at either preventing a risk factor from occurring or reducing the effects after it has already developed. For example, programs that prevent drug use or child abuse will improve the chances of infants developing in a healthy manner, and programs to meet the needs of these children once exposed to the risk factor can successfully help these children develop as well.

Finally, the concept of risk forces us to consider the reasons why two children with the same risk factors may differ in developmental outcome. Almost everyone knows people who have experienced some trauma in their childhoods, whether divorce or poverty or other negative experience. Some succeed and overcome their adversity while others do not. This question of why some children seem to be able to cope with trauma well while others do not is discussed at the end of the chapter and is a relatively new area of research in psychology.

The Teacher and Children at Risk

You might be asking why the concept of risk is important in a book devoted to children with exceptional needs. This chapter has been included in the text for a number of reasons. First, if educators and psychologists know that particular risk factors are present, they can sometimes intervene to prevent a child from developing a disability. Teachers, as well as other professionals, will be involved in both designing these programs and carrying them out. Second, teachers will often be faced with children exposed to risk factors who have special needs, and teachers must take the needs of these children *and* the risk factors into consideration during their teaching. Third, teachers may be able to help parents deal with their children who are at risk for developing disabilities.

As noted in Chapter 2, states offer help through early intervention programs to children who are considered at risk, but the eligibility requirements differ from state to state. Although at-risk children are eligible for special educational services in elementary school only when diagnosed with a disability, more and more schools are searching for ways to reduce the incidence of disability and provide services short of special education for children at risk.

Poverty as a Risk Factor

Poverty is one of the greatest risk factors in the lives of children (Bradley et al., 1994; Duncan, Brooks-Gunn, & Klebanov, 1994). Poor children are at greater risk for almost every developmental and intellectual difficulty. More children from impoverished backgrounds are considered to have mental retardation, a behavior disorder, or other disabling conditions, ranging from visual and auditory impairments to learning disabilities, than children from more economically secure backgrounds. This increased incidence is because poverty is not just a lack of spendable income. It affects every aspect of life, from where people live to their vocational aspirations.

People living in poverty tend to live in areas where children are exposed to violence and criminality (McLoyd & Wilson, 1991). Poor children are more likely to be born premature, to experience more illness and disabilities, and to die young (Klerman, 1991b).

Poverty is a great risk factor for children, and more children than adults live in poverty in the United States.

Without adequate financial resources, medical care for low-income families is often substandard and bills cannot be paid. When questioned about their children's health, fewer parents with family incomes under $10,000 considered their children in excellent health than parents of children whose family incomes were $35,000 or more. For children under five years of age from poverty backgrounds, 38.9 percent were viewed as excellent in health compared with 63.8 for middle-class children. For children aged 5 to 17, 35.4 percent of the children were considered in excellent health compared to 64.1 percent of the middle-class children (Adams & Benson, 1990). These children from low-income families are also much more likely to have poor dental health and to experience psychosocial and psychosomatic problems (Zill & Schoeborn, 1990). They live unhealthier lifestyles, tend to have their children younger, and lack good housing. Often their homes are overcrowded (Klerman, 1991b). Illegal drug use and legal drug use such as cigarette smoking are more prevalent among the poor. These have a negative effect on both parents and children and also reduce the parents' ability to care for children. Poverty is correlated with many problems such as homelessness, prematurity, inadequate nutrition, and lack of intellectual stimulation in the home.

Although many families remain in poverty for generations, other families do break the cycle of poverty. Many people in poverty do manage to escape through hard work and make a better life for themselves and their children. Still, poverty remains a major risk factor in children's lives.

About 22 percent of all American children live in poverty (Statistical Abstract, 1994). This figure is up from 15 percent in 1970, and children are much more likely to live in poverty than are young adults, middle aged or elderly people (Larson, 1992; Huston, 1991; Zigler, 1995). The poverty rate had declined between the 1950s and the early 1970s. Beginning in the later part of that decade, however, an increase in the poverty rate occurred and continued throughout the 1980s (Huston, 1991). The poverty rate, though, was quite a bit higher just after World War II. In 1949, an estimated one out of every two children was growing up in poverty, and seven of eight African-American children were poor (Duncan, 1991).

Why the increase in poverty over the last two decades? First, the number of single-parent families has increased greatly, and the poverty rate among female-headed families is much greater than the poverty rate among married couples (Duncan, 1991). In 1990, 45 percent of all female headed households with children aged 18 or younger fell below the poverty line as compared with just 8 percent of two parent families (Larson, 1992). Most single mothers come from one of two groups—divorced mothers and never-married mothers.

The number of divorces had increased until leveling off recently. Still, a large number of single mothers with custody find themselves living in poverty. Some fall into poverty because of lack of child support and others because they were poverty stricken or on the borderline when they were married and living with their husbands. In the year prior to a divorce, about 12 percent of the children and 7 percent of all of the women live in families classified as poor. In the year following a divorce or separation, these figures double to 27 percent for children and 13 percent for women.

Only about half the women due child support receive full payment and one-quarter receive nothing at all. An old observation states that after a divorce, women and children's standard of living declines, and men's standard of living increases. This is not so. The standard of living of women with custody of children declines by about 40 percent while divorced men's standard of living declines by

The number of single parents who are unmarried has increased dramatically and many live in poverty.

about 15 percent (Duncan, 1991). Many men recover but many fewer women with young children do.

Second, the number of single parents who are unmarried has increased dramatically. One-quarter of all births in the United States now take place out of wedlock, compared with 11 percent in 1970 (American Demographics, 1992). Many of these women are undereducated and do not have employable skills. Becoming a parent in adolescence is related to poverty (Klerman, 1991a). This was not always the case as many women, especially in the 1950s, gave birth in their teens. The difference is that most teenagers in the 1950s giving birth were married while the overwhelming majority of teenage births today are to unmarried teens. Today about four in ten females will become pregnant before their 20th birthday. About 87 percent of all pregnancies among never-married adolescents are unintended (Morris, Warren, & Aral, 1993). About half give birth, about 40 percent have abortions, and the rest have miscarriages. Almost all those who give birth keep their children. Presently, more than 65 percent of all women giving birth between the ages of 15 and 19 are unmarried (Klerman, 1991a; Glazer, 1993). Other reasons for the increase in the number of children living in poverty are the loss of blue-collar well-paying jobs and the inability of federal poverty programs to keep up with the need throughout the 1980s (Huston, McLoyd, & Coll, 1994).

Poverty and People

Poverty can be classified in many ways. First, not all poverty lasts throughout childhood (see Schmidt, 1995). Many more children experience poverty for a year or so than are poor throughout their childhoods (Huston, 1991). Many children's families experience bouts of unemployment followed by times that are relatively good, and conditions for the entire family improve. One startling finding, though, is that African American children are at greater risk for chronic poverty. About one-third of all African American children are chronically poor (Duncan, 1991). Transitory poverty has somewhat less social and developmental risk attached to it than chronic poverty, but it still affects children by creating a great deal of stress (Duncan et al., 1994).

In addition, when people think of poverty they usually picture the stereotype of an urban ghetto with large numbers of people belonging to minority groups living in poor conditions. Indeed, much urban poverty is found in clusters or ghettos. Poor families tend to be isolated, because those who have been successful flee these areas for better housing and schools, leaving those with fewer resources in these problem-filled communities. But poverty also exists in rural areas.

Rural poverty is often forgotten. During the 1960s, pictures of poverty from the rural areas of Appalachia were commonly shown on television. The poverty is still there, but urban poverty is reported more frequently. Urban and rural poverty differ in significant ways. Poor people living in rural areas are more likely to be married, have a man as head of the family, have fewer children, and receive many fewer benefits. Single women and children in small towns and rural areas are often employed in lower-level jobs than people in the urban and suburban areas, and their poverty is often due to low wages (Huston, 1991).

Many of the risk factors that will be discussed in this chapter are related to poverty. That does not mean that these factors cannot or are not present in some middle-class homes, only that statistically they are more likely to be found in poverty-stricken homes. Many of these risk factors coexist with each other, adding or even multiplying the risk of developing a disability.

Prenatal Factors

The evidence that children who are exposed to a variety of drugs and diseases in utero experience damage is well established. For example, diseases that are usually transmitted during sexual intercourse, such as AIDS, syphilis, and chlamydia, pose significant dangers to the developing fetus. Legal drugs such as alcohol and nicotine as well as illegal drugs such as cocaine can also damage the fetus. The National Institute on Drug Abuse estimates that 375,000 to 739,000 drug-exposed children are born each year—about 18 percent of all newborns in the United States. Of these children, 73 percent are exposed to alcohol, 17 percent to marijuana, and about 5 percent to cocaine. Many of these children have been exposed to multiple drugs (Sautter, 1992). Sometimes the damage is obvious; such is the case with **fetal alcohol syndrome**, which is related to slower, less efficient information processing, mental retardation, and growth defects (Jacobson et al., 1993; Sampson et al., 1994). Sometimes exposure to alcohol results in other alcohol-related birth defects that are less obvious, called **fetal alcohol effect**. Alcohol consumption during pregnancy is considered the leading preventable cause of birth defects in the United States; each year 5,000 infants are born with fetal alcohol syndrome and another 50,000 with fetal alcohol effect (Orgain, 1993).

A substance that causes a birth defect is called a **teratogen**. The most famous case of a teratogen causing birth defects involved the drug thalidomide, which was widely used in Europe as a treatment for morning sickness. A significant number of infants—estimated at over 10,000—were born without limbs or with extremities that were grossly underdeveloped. Relatively few American women took the drug because it was never approved by the U.S. Food and Drug Administration.

Many teratogens, though, do not always produce a particular defect. Sometimes, the presence of a teratogen may increase the risk of a child developing some birth defect or a later disability. For example, about 25 percent of all American pregnant women smoke (March of Dimes, 1990). Smokers are twice as likely as nonsmokers to have low birthweight babies (Fielding, 1985). The infants of smokers weigh an average of 200 grams (about 0.5 pound) less than infants of nonsmokers (Vorhees & Mollnow, 1987). In addition, infants of mothers who smoke are shorter; have smaller head, chest, arm, and thigh circumferences; and have lower neurological scores than infants of nonsmokers (Metcoff et al., 1989).

Injurious long-term effects from maternal smoking have also been found. Deficits in achievement scores in spelling and reading as well as in attention span were found in a large group of seven-year-old children whose mothers smoked heavily during pregnancy compared to children whose mothers had not smoked (Naeye & Peters, 1984). Other studies have found positive correlations between smoking during pregnancy and hyperactivity, low achievement, poor attention, and minimal neurological dysfunction (Streissguth et al., 1984; Landesman-Dwyer & Emanuel, 1979).

Fetal alcohol syndrome:
A number of characteristics—including mental retardation, facial abnormalities, growth defects, and poor coordination—caused by maternal alcohol consumption during pregnancy.

Fetal alcohol effect:
An umbrella term used to describe injury to the child caused by the mother's alcohol consumption during pregnancy, which is somewhat less pronounced than fetal alcohol syndrome.

Teratogen:
Any agent that causes birth defects.

THOUGHT QUESTION

1. Why is it so difficult to get pregnant women to stop smoking?

Women who smoke when they are pregnant are more likely to give birth to low-birthweight babies.

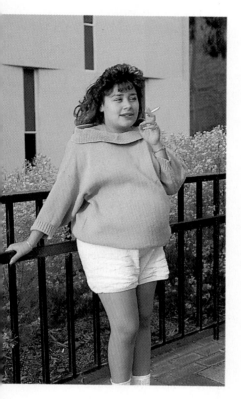

If every smoker gave birth to a child with an obvious disability, the public would cry out for action. But even though smoking and many other teratogens often act to increase risk, they do not automatically cause birth defects. Other factors, many of which scientists do not understand well, including genetics, the presence of other teratogens, and general health of the mother and child may combine with smoking to cause these problems.

Many illegal drugs, such as marijuana and heroin, cause injuries to the child. Infants whose mothers smoke marijuana are more likely to show poor fetal growth (Zuckerman et al., 1989). Also, the infants of regular marijuana smokers show abnormal cries that reflect possible neurological problems (Lester & Dreher, 1989). Babies of heroin addicts are born addicted to heroin and must go through withdrawal. They often show disturbances in activity level, attention span, and sleep patterns (Householder et al., 1982). Because these infants are frequently premature and very small, their withdrawal is sometimes a life-or-death situation.

A surprising number of pregnant women use cocaine (Chasnoff, 1987). The use of cocaine during pregnancy is related to infant mortality, low birth weight, and a number of medical problems including neurological damage and malformed heart, lung, and digestive systems (Scherling, 1994; Besharov, 1989). These infants are also very irritable and often do not respond to the human voice or face (Berger et al., 1990). They show more stress-related behavior and seem unable to interact with others (Chasnoff et al., 1985; Chasnoff, 1987). About one-third are seriously damaged by exposure to the drug (Treaster, 1993). However, between 60 and 80 percent of babies exposed to cocaine prenatally experience some disturbance. In one study of 39 newborns of women who used cocaine in various forms throughout their pregnancy, 34 babies showed neurological abnormalities (Doberczak et al., 1988). Many infants are jittery and show an abnormally high-pitched cry. They are overwhelmed by sensations, and some stiffen while being touched. Some cry when they hear music or voices or are brought into bright lights, while others simply tune out and go to sleep. They show developmental delays in walking and talking and some throw tantrums.

In school, some children exposed to cocaine in utero race around classrooms and show poor behavioral control. Other symptoms include language delays, emotional difficulties, impulsivity, low frustration tolerance, and attention problems (Scherling, 1994). The National Association for Perinatal Addiction Research and Education estimates that more than 500,000 babies have been exposed to cocaine and other drugs, and perhaps 300,000 have suffered damage. Less than 10 percent have received treatment, leaving the problems for schools. Precisely why cocaine affects some infants more than others, why damage is great in some cases but less so in others is not clear. But certainly the care that they receive after birth is one of the great deciding factors.

Initial difficulties are compounded by the fact that these troubled infants may not receive the care they require. If the infant is taken away after birth by welfare agencies, their lot may be a string of foster homes. Sometimes the babies are even abandoned in the hospital or raised by a grandparent who may or may not be capable of dealing with infants who show behavioral and physical difficulties. If they go home with their mothers, often they are subjected to an environment of poverty and inadequate parenting, which increases the risk of poor intellectual development. The parents often continue to use cocaine, which exposes the infants to extreme poverty, since the parent uses all the family resources to buy the drug (Wrightman, 1991). The lifestyle of these parents is chaotic, and the rate of neglect and physical abuse is high (Besharov, 1989). The parenting techniques used by cocaine-addicted mothers are usually substandard. The mothers are rigid and show a lack of enjoyment and pleasure in relating to their infants, are not responsive to their infants, and show very little emotional involvement with them (Burns et al., 1991).

The child's initial problems in relating to others are compounded by the parent's own difficulties, and the child often develops various cognitive and behavioral problems involving either withdrawal or aggressiveness (Rist, 1990). These infants experience both congenital problems due to prenatal exposure and subsequent damage due to the poor parenting and deficient environment in which they are raised during their early years.

The research is clear, then, that infants prenatally exposed to cocaine are at risk (Lester et al., 1991). The substandard home environment and parenting practices of cocaine-using parents are likely to lead to many problems and intensify the already serious problems experienced by infants exposed prenatally to cocaine. Children exposed prenatally to the drug and those who are exposed to the drug environment after birth make up a population of children who are at risk for many serious behavioral and developmental problems.

Although the problems are certainly real enough, some experts argue that the media has sensationalized the problem, often presenting the worst-case scenario as the norm. Daniel Griffith (1992), a prominent researcher in the field, notes that if we were to believe the media we would incorrectly think that all cocaine-exposed children were severely affected, that little can be done for them, and that all medical, behavioral, and learning problems shown by these children are caused directly by their exposure to cocaine. In reality, great individual differences exist in the behavior of children exposed to cocaine in utero. Many of the problems, especially the oversensitivity to stimuli and difficulty in self-regulation, are caused by both the exposure to cocaine and other drugs in utero and the deficient environment experienced by so many of these infants.

Perhaps, though, the most damaging belief is that nothing can be done for these children. This is simply not true, and society should not give up on these children (Mayes et al., 1992). Growing evidence exists that early treatment to eliminate drug use in pregnant mothers, along with prenatal care and follow-up examinations can improve the long-term behavioral competence of these cocaine-exposed infants (Chasnoff et al., 1992). For example, infant stretching exercises are often used to help these children develop. At age two or three, these children have difficulties grasping small toys; exercises that require them to pick up a series of smaller and smaller balls improve fine motor coordination. Five- and six-year-olds who stumble and bump into things may be helped to improve their balance through exercises on a small trampoline. They also may receive speech therapy since delays in speech development are often present. In addition, teaching parents how to soothe their irritable infants may also help.

When pregnant women who abused cocaine and other drugs received prenatal care, nutritional counseling, and drug treatment, the majority of infants were carried to full term, with premature infants born less than a month early. These children showed many classical signs of drug exposure. Since these infants showed a deficiency in the quiet-alert state, a state during which infants are best able to process information, caregivers were taught comforting techniques including swaddling, using pacifiers, and vertical rocking. The parents were taught how to maintain an appropriate low-stimulus environment to keep the child below the threshold of overstimulation, as well as how to recognize when the child was approaching overstimulation. The majority of these children showed little difference at 3, 6, 12, 18, and 24 months from a group of nonexposed infants (Griffith, 1992). Still some differences were shown; one-third showed delays in language development and problems in attention and self-regulation. Although this program had a number of advantages not enjoyed by others, especially early identification before birth, it does show what can be accomplished.

Children who are exposed to drugs in utero and show developmental delays are eligible for services under PL 99-457, Part H, although those who are simply at risk may not necessarily receive appropriate intervention (Sautter, 1992). This lack of intervention is unfortunate for these children require aid from early infancy through the preschool period.

A number of programs are available. For example, the Harlem Hospital Program, formed in 1991, offers a therapeutic preschool nursery for two- to four-year-olds who were exposed to drugs. Seven children are placed in each class, along with two special education teachers, a speech-language pathologist, and a play therapist. In Project DAISY (Developing Appropriate Intervention Strategies for Young Children), which operates in Washington, D.C., children identified as prenatally exposed to drugs are educated in a standard early education classroom with a regular classroom teacher who is given support by a multidisciplinary consultation team including a clinical psychologist, clinical social worker, speech/language pathologist, and a nutrition specialist. The team provides home support and tracks intervention strategies. The children go on to regular kindergarten. Children enrolled in this program are offered a number of choices as to what activities they want to pursue; once the choice is made experts intervene, designing the appropriate content for the child. For example, if a child chooses to work in the dramatic play area, a clinical social worker might help the child work through the difficulties the child faces. If a child is involved in prewriting activities or literacy activities, the speech-language pathologist would become active. Supports are also offered to the family through this program (Gregorchik, 1992).

Cocaine exposure increases risk for developmental disability but early childhood programs can be of benefit to the child (Neuspiel & Hamel, 1991). Early intervention both to stop the drug taking and to improve the environment can benefit these children (Zuckerman & Frank, 1992).

SCENARIO

1 Ms. D. has just given birth to a baby who has tested positive for cocaine. The mother has been on crack for some years and has tried to break the habit twice by entering drug treatment programs. The baby was born very early but will survive. The question is what is best for the child. Ms. D. is willing to enter drug treatment and says that with the child present she has an extra motivation to succeed. The child welfare bureau is not so certain and points out that Ms. D. has been through treatment unsuccessfully and cannot at the present time provide a good environment for the child. The alternative is foster care, which Ms. D. does not believe is healthy for the child. If you were the judge in this case, what would you do?

Prenatal Risk Factors and the Teacher

Teachers become involved in three ways in helping children who are at risk due to exposure to drugs in utero. First, education becomes a factor in the prevention of drug abuse on the part of the parents. People may not be aware of the effects of particular drugs on the developing fetus. Clinics routinely disseminate information to their patients in a number of languages about particular dangers, and the March of Dimes publishes many useful booklets. Educational programs in the schools dealing with the effects of drugs on the fetus may at least give the information to the students. In addition, this information should be coupled with a list of agencies where people can receive help within the community.

Second, so often premature conclusions may unfairly compromise the future of a particular at-risk population, and teachers should be aware of their stereotypes. Just a few years ago educators were bracing for an avalanche of children who were exposed to crack and who would have such serious problems that teachers would find them difficult to deal with effectively. While no one doubts the risk factors involved in prenatal exposure to cocaine, the inevitability of disability has been disproved and the importance of postnatal environment emphasized. A teacher who believes that a child exposed to crack *must* develop some disability is not only mistaken but may well expect less from the child. The stereotype of the inevitability of disaster must be put to rest.

Third, since some children exposed to drugs in utero will demonstrate problems, educators must be aware of their needs. Sometimes, social and work-related behaviors, such as cooperation and perseverance, may be lacking, and modeling and direct teaching may be required. Class size should be limited to allow for greater individual instruction. Multidisciplinary teams are often necessary since the needs of these children are so great, and regular classroom teachers require support. Finally, home-school partnerships need to be established (see Chapter 3).

No one is minimizing the risk factors involved in exposure to drugs before birth, but taking too pessimistic an attitude becomes a self-defeating strategy. With help, especially early intervention, many of these children can improve greatly, and teachers in elementary school must be wary of taking the worst-case scenario for the average scenario.

Child Abuse

Not all risks are medical. Some risks are found in parent-child relationships in which abuse occurs. **Child abuse** occurs when parents intentionally injure their children. **Neglect** refers to a situation in which the physical care and supervision of the child is inadequate or inappropriate, for example a child who comes to school each day dressed inadequately for bitterly cold weather. All states now require professionals such as doctors, nurses, and teachers to report suspected cases of child abuse or neglect. In 1993, 2,998,000 children were reported to child protective agencies as suspected victims of child abuse or neglect (NCPCA, 1994). Since 1985, child abuse reports have increased more than 40 percent. Between 35

Child abuse:
A general term used to denote an injury intentionally perpetrated on a child.

Child neglect:
A term used to describe a situation in which the care and supervision of a child is insufficient or improper.

and 40 percent of all reports are substantiated after investigation, which means that conservatively about 1 million children are victims of child abuse each year (Clark, 1993). In 1993, 1,299 children died from abuse or neglect (NCPCA, 1994).

The results of child abuse are serious. They include language delays, poor self-concept, aggression, social and emotional withdrawal, and poor social relationships with peers (Hennessy et al., 1994; Mason, 1993; Salzinger et al., 1993). Children who are abused have lower intelligence scores and are at an increased risk for depression, suicide, and drug problems (Wisdom, 1989).

Sexual Abuse

One type of child abuse—sexual abuse—has been the subject of much discussion in the media. Sexual abuse can involve forcible rape, statutory rape, sodomy, incest, or "indecent liberties," such as genital exhibition and physical advances (Sarafino, 1979). Sexual abuse is the least reported type of abuse and is generally considered to be grossly underreported, partly because it is often not recognized as abuse. Sexual abuse accounts for about 15 percent of all abuse cases (Clark, 1993).

According to reported incidents, sexual abusers are mostly men, and girls constitute the majority of victims (Canavan, 1981). Sexual abuse is most likely to occur between people who are related, but a child may also be victimized by a stranger. The consequences of sexual abuse can be both physical—such as venereal disease and pregnancy—and emotional. Long-term effects include depression, self-destructive behavior, anxiety, feelings of isolation and stigma, poor self-esteem, difficulty trusting others, substance abuse, and sexual maladjustment (Clark, 1993; Browne & Finkelhor, 1986). One-fifth of all victims of sexual abuse develop serious long-term psychological problems (AMA, 1992).

Parents often ask what they can do to prevent sexual abuse. Knowing where their children are, what they are doing, and who they are with are obvious precautions, but parents cannot foresee every circumstance. For instance, one six-year-old boy was abused by an older boy when he went to the bathroom of a supermarket while his mother waited in the checkout line (DeVine, 1980).

Parents should remind their children not to accept money or favors from strangers or accept a ride to go anywhere with someone they do not know. Children should be told that if they think they are in danger, it's okay to make a scene by running away and screaming for help. Because the sexual abuser may be someone they know and trust, children should be told that they do not have to agree to demands for physical closeness—even from relatives. Finally, children should be encouraged to report any instances of people touching them in intimate places or asking them to do the same.

The increase in publicity surrounding sexual abuse has led to frank public discussion of the problem. This offers some hope that the incidence of sexual abuse can be reduced through prevention, and its consequences through early discovery and treatment.

Emotional Abuse

Not all child abuse is physical. Consider the parent who constantly yells at and berates a child. Imagine a four-year-old child who has just spilled some juice hearing a parent shout, "You're a stupid, rotten kid. If I had any sense, I'd give you away!"

Defining emotional abuse, sometimes called psychological maltreatment, is difficult (Baumrind, 1994; Rosenberg, 1987). Certain parental actions can lead to a loss of self-esteem in the child and interfere with the child's emotional development, but defining these actions and describing remedial steps is not a simple matter. Conceptually, such parental behaviors as rejecting, isolating, terrorizing, ignoring, and corrupting constitute psychological maltreatment (Garbarino, Guttman, & Seeley, 1986). These forms of abuse produce emotional and behavioral problems in children (Hart & Brassard, 1987). An objective definition of the behaviors that constitute such abuse that would allow mandatory intervention to reduce such abuse remain somewhat elusive (Melton & Davidson, 1987). In the absence of such specific guidelines, the courts have taken a hands-off attitude toward everything but the most extreme forms. Perhaps in the future, the more obvious cases will be identified, and some help for both parents and children will be forthcoming.

Not all abuse is physical. Sometimes, parental actions may lead to a constant loss of self-esteem defined as emotional or psychological abuse.

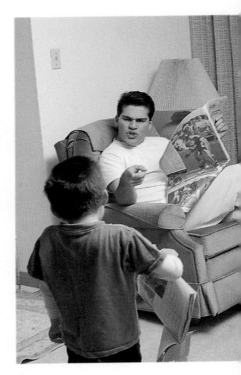

SCENARIO

2 Mr. and Mrs. L. do not physically abuse their seven-year-old son, Hank, but they constantly scream at him. Hank is a disappointment to his parents. His mother constantly berates him because he is clumsy and often "misbehaves." She considers this misbehavior intentional and often tells him how bad he is and that if he is not good she will leave him. His father believes that he is a "sissy" since he does not play sports well and refused to put his face in water when learning to swim. He believes that by shaming the child, Hank will learn to overcome his fears. Hank's teacher has noticed that he has a low self-image, and discussions with Hank's parents show that they will continue to act in this way. What should Hank's teacher do to improve the situation?

Signs of Physical Child Abuse and Neglect

The range of symptoms that indicate child abuse is wide, and often these symptoms are suggestive, not absolute. Many children have bruises or broken bones or may come to school inappropriately dressed once in a while because they run out the door before their parents can check to see if they are wearing a coat in cold weather. However, repeated injuries, new injuries before previous ones have healed, welts, evidence of lack of nutrition, and burns on the palms of the hands are definite causes for concern and investigation. Table 8.1 lists physical and behavioral indicators of abuse, neglect, and emotional maltreatment. Teachers should ask children who arrive with a physical injury how the injury occurred. For example, children are often innocently injured on their knees, forehead, or hands when they attempt to break a fall. A teacher can often determine whether the injuries were sustained in the way the child suggests.

Source: *How Schools Can Help Combat Child Abuse and Neglect,* Second Edition, by Cynthia Crosson Tower. Copyright 1987. Washington, D.C.: National Education Association. Reprinted by permission of the NEA Professional Library.

TABLE 8.1   **Physical and Behavioral Indicators of Child Abuse and Neglect**

TYPE OF CHILD ABUSE/NEGLECT	PHYSICAL INDICATORS	BEHAVIORAL INDICATORS
Physical Abuse	Unexplained bruises and welts: —on face, lips, mouth —on torso, back, buttocks, thighs —in various stages of healing —clustered, forming regular patterns —reflecting shape of article used to inflict (electric cord, belt buckle) —on several different surface areas —regularly appear after absence, weekend, or vacation —human bite marks —bald spots Unexplained burns: —cigar, cigarette burns, especially on soles, palms, back, or buttocks —immersion burns (sock-like, glove-like, doughnut-shaped on buttocks or genitalia) —patterned like electric burner, iron, etc. —rope burns on arms, legs, neck, or torso Unexplained fractures: —to skull, nose, facial structure —in various stages of healing —multiple or spiral fractures Unexplained lacerations or abrasions: —to mouth, lips, gums, eyes —to external genitalia	Wary of adult contacts Apprehensive when other children cry Behavioral extremes: —aggressiveness —withdrawal —overly compliant Afraid to go home Reports injury by parents Exhibits anxiety about normal activities, e.g., napping Complains of soreness and moves awkwardly Destructive to self and others Early to school or stays late as if afraid to go home Accident prone Wears clothing that covers body when not appropriate Chronic runaway (especially adolescents) Cannot tolerate physical contact or touch
Physical Neglect	Consistent hunger, poor hygiene, inappropriate dress Consistent lack of supervision, especially in dangerous activities or long periods Unattended physical problems or medical needs	Begging, stealing food Constant fatigue, listlessness or falling asleep States there is no caretaker at home Frequent school absence or tardiness

TABLE 8.1   *Continued*

TYPE OF CHILD ABUSE/NEGLECT	PHYSICAL INDICATORS	BEHAVIORAL INDICATORS
Physical Neglect	Abandonment Lice Distended stomach, emaciated	Destructive, pugnacious School dropout (adolescents) Early emancipation from family (adolescents)
Sexual Abuse	Difficulty in walking or sitting Torn, stained, or bloody underclothing Pain or itching in genital area Bruises or bleeding in external genitalia, vaginal, or anal areas Venereal disease Frequent urinary or yeast infections Frequent unexplained sore throats	Unwilling to participate in certain physical activities Sudden drop in school performance Withdrawal, fantasy or unusually infantile behavior Crying with no provocation Bizarre, sophisticated, or unusual behavior Anorexia (especially adolescents) Sexual behavior or knowledge Sexually provocative Poor peer relationships Reports sexual assault by caretaker Fear of or seductiveness toward males Suicide attempts (especially adolescents) Chronic runaway Early pregnancies
Emotional Maltreatment	Speech disorders Lags in physical development Failure to thrive (especially in infants) Asthma, severe allergies, ulcers Substance abuse	Habit disorders (sucking, biting, rocking, etc.) Conduct disorders (antisocial, destructive, etc.) Neurotic traits (sleep disorders, inhibition of play) Behavioral extremes: —compliant, passive —aggressive, demanding Overly adaptive behavior: —inappropriately adult —inappropriately infantile Developmental lags (mental, emotional) Delinquent behavior (especially adolescents)

Reporting Child Abuse

In every state, educators are required to report suspected cases of child abuse. In most states, teachers can make a report orally to a governmental agency such as social services. However, many school districts encourage or require teachers to report to the principal, who then notifies the authorities. Many states require the oral report to be followed by a written report, and school officials may then become involved. Teachers need to know the procedure to follow within their schools and districts in reporting child abuse cases. Some districts have clear rules, but some don't. Some districts also have a school team composed of counselors, nurses, administrators, and teachers who discuss the potential report. Such a system partially relieves the teacher of the pressure and offers support in reporting abuse cases, since the teacher is one of the individuals legally responsible to report suspected child abuse (Tower, 1987).

Physical Child Abuse

Most cases of child abuse involve the physical injury of the child. To understand the causes of child abuse, the characteristics of the parents, the child, and the situation must be taken into consideration.

The Abusive Parent

THOUGHT QUESTION

2. Is striking a child ever appropriate?

As a group, parents who physically abuse their children are impulsive, have unmet dependency needs, have a poor self-concept and a poor sense of identity, are defensive, and project their problems onto their children (Green, Gaines, & Sandgrund, 1974). They believe in the value of physical punishment, and, indeed, two-thirds of all incidents of child abuse can be related to parental attempts to discipline and control their children's behavior (Gil, 1970). They are frequently afraid of spoiling their children and have difficulty empathizing with their offspring (Martin, 1978). The picture that emerges of abusive parents is that they derive little enjoyment from parenting or from life in general, show little satisfaction with their child, or express little affection for the child. They are isolated from the community and do not encourage autonomy or independence, yet they still hold high standards of achievement for their children (Trickett et al., 1991).

These characteristics are general ones. Many parents who are impulsive and isolated, for example, do not physically abuse their children, which has led many professionals to deny that there is any definite "abusive" personality (Green et al., 1974). A personality profile of a parent is not an accurate predictor of abuse.

Some studies have attempted to compare abusive and nonabusive parents' child-rearing practices. Trickett and Kuczynski (1986) found that physically abusive parents did not report using physical punishment any more than parents in a control group did, but were more likely to report more severe forms of punishment, such as striking the child's face, hitting the child with an object, or pulling the child's hair. Abusive parents are distinguished more by the quality rather than the quantity of their punishment.

Many—between 25 and 33 percent—of the parents who were physically abused as children abuse their own children (Kauffman & Zigler, 1987). This statistic means that the general statement that abusive children grow up to abuse their own children is greatly overstated (Wisdom, 1989). Although children who are abused are certainly at a greater risk of abusing their own children compared with the general population, most children who are abused do not abuse their own children.

Why would some children who have been abused or neglected perpetuate similar patterns of behavior in adulthood? Perhaps repeated exposure to aggressive parents provides children with a model of what a parent is, and such children use this model in their own parenting, with little thought of the alternatives or concern with why they are doing it (Simons et al., 1991). If this is true, how do we explain the majority of abused and neglected children who do not abuse their own children? Those people who break the cycle of abuse tend to have received emotional support from a nonabusive adult during childhood, participated in therapy during some time in their life, or had a nonabusive, more emotionally stable mate with whom they could share a satisfying relationship. Those who continue the cycle of abuse experience significantly more life stress and anxiety and are more dependent, immature, and depressed (Egeland, Jacobovitz, & Sroufe, 1988). Therefore, the presence and influence of other supportive and nonabusing adults and/or a helpful counseling relationship are two factors that may reduce the potential for abusiveness. Since those who continue the cycle experience more stress, teaching stress reduction and problem-solving skills may also help.

The Abused Child

Certain characteristics of a child may predispose that child to being a victim of abuse. This statement causes some people to feel uneasy. Any suggestion that the child contributes to the problem is usually met with hostility. The reaction is understandable. It is easier to see a child as a helpless victim of a vicious adult than to look at the characteristics of a child that may bring out the worst in a parent. No one is excusing an abuser's behavior or blaming an innocent victim. However, a child's personality or physical and intellectual characteristics, in combination with an inadequate parent may cause problems (Parke & Collmer, 1975). For instance, children who are premature, who have physical disabilities, or who have mental retardation are abused more often than children who do not have these conditions (Friedrich & Boriskin, 1976). Children with disabilities, then, are at an increased risk of being abused. The common characteristic in all these groups is the need for special care. The child whose needs are greater is at risk for abuse.

Abusing parents often hold unreasonable expectations for their children and distorted perceptions of what their children can do (Martin, 1978). Children with physical, emotional, or mental disabilities often cannot meet their parents' expectations and are more likely to be abused. Consider the premature baby, who requires a great deal of care. The demand may be more than an impulsive, unrealistic parent can handle, and the parent may resort to violence to quiet the child. As the child grows, the pattern is reinforced; physical violence keeps the child in line until the behavior becomes well established and continues throughout childhood. These abused children often justify the parent's actions on the basis of their own behavior, believing themselves to be generally bad (Dean et al., 1986). The child whose needs are greater, who engenders anger in a parent, or who is difficult to care for is more likely to set in motion abusive parental responses that may become the standard parent-child interaction.

The Situation

Any situation that raises the level of tension and stress can promote abuse. For instance, neglect and abuse increase when economic problems within the community increase (Steinberg, Catalano, & Dooley, 1981). Unemployment and underemployment cause stress. Parents may displace—that is, transfer their feelings from one person or object to another. Thus, the child may become the object of a parent's anger toward the boss or the life situation in general.

Programs to Prevent and Deal with Child Abuse

Programs to deal with child abuse have focused on both prevention and treatment. Programs aimed at preventing abuse enroll parents in educational programs, have professionals visit the homes, and offer courses on child development in high schools. In such courses, students are taught child-care techniques, given information concerning children's nutritional and emotional needs, and told where parents can turn for help. Other programs include giving information at health fairs and promoting drop-in centers where parents can talk with other parents, social workers, or counselors (McCauley, 1992).

Many approaches have been used to treat child abusers. Social work, individual and family therapy, self-help groups such as Parents Anonymous that provide emotional support, and group treatment can all claim some success. Generally, about half the parents involved in abusive situations can be helped at least to stop physically abusing their children. This means that in most cases, children will stay within the family and school environment.

The victims of abuse need help. Abused children show many behavioral disturbances that affect learning and development. Many improve even when only a mild to moderate improvement occurs in the home situation. Early identification is one factor in successful treatment.

Many schools have programs that teach young children about sexual abuse. They teach students that they do not have to allow anyone to touch them if they do not want to be touched, they shouldn't take candy from strangers, they do not have to agree to demands for physical closeness even from relatives, and they should report instances of people touching them in intimate areas or asking them to do the same to them. One concern of sexual abuse prevention programs is that they might have a negative effect on children by making children frightened of strangers or uncomfortable about physical affection. Studies generally show that this does not occur (Wurtele & Mill-Perin, 1987a; 1987b). These programs should be included in the school's regular health curriculum. Programs are also available to help students recognize other types of abuse; and some filmstrips are available.

Identifying possible cases of child abuse is definitely part of a teacher's job both legally and morally. Being alert to the possible signs of abuse is of primary importance, but teachers must also be familiar with the school's policies and procedures. As awareness of the negative affects of abuse increases, more districts will become involved in setting up programs and committees to help teachers in this difficult area of concern. Child abuse is a significant problem and early identification and intervention can make an important difference in the lives of these children.

Single-Parent Families

The American family today is a far cry from what it was even thirty years ago. The number of single-parent families has increased substantially from 2.3–2.5 million in 1960 to 10.9 million in 1993 (Statistical Abstract, 1994). In 1993, about 17.9 million children lived with only one parent, and the number has almost doubled since 1970 (American Demographics, 1994). If trends continue, 61 percent of all American children will spend some time in a single-parent household before their 18th birthday.

As noted earlier, two major causes increase the number of single-parent families: divorce and teenage parenting. The divorce rate has increased greatly over the past 35 years (Kaplan, 1993). About one million children are affected by divorce each year. Divorce is responsible for 46 percent of single-parent households, with marital separation accounting for another 21 percent. The second reason is the increase in the number of unwed mothers. Twenty-six percent of all single-parent families are the result of single mothers giving birth. The least common cause, the death of the spouse, is responsible for 7 percent of single-parent households.

Are children of single parents at risk for future problems? The research shows that they are, but care should be taken not to overestimate the risk (see Bronstein et al., 1994). Children who are from divorced families or have a never-married parent are less likely to complete high school and more likely to have low earnings as adults than offspring of intact families. Evidence also shows that living with a single mother is related to the teenage children giving birth, teen marriage, and divorce or separation (McLanahan, Astone, & Marks, 1991). Children from one-parent families do not differ in academic ability or intelligence, but they are absent from school more often, are more disruptive, have lower grades, and are viewed by teachers as less motivated (Minuchin & Shapiro, 1983). As noted earlier, the single-parent status is associated with poverty, and disentangling the effects of the two variables is frequently difficult. Again, this discussion simply describes risk status; many children from single-parent families do well. Researchers must discover why some do well while others do not.

The Experience of Divorce

Divorce is an experience that affects the entire family forever. Five and ten years later, a divorce remains the central event in the childhood years and casts a "long shadow" over those years (Wallerstein, 1983, p. 233). Divorce itself brings many changes. The child's world is torn asunder, and the child's entire lifestyle may be

THOUGHT QUESTION

3. *Why has the divorce rate increased dramatically over the past thirty years?*

THOUGHT QUESTION

4. *Why are children of single parents at risk for poor educational achievement?*

disrupted. Financial problems may force the family to move to a new neighborhood, altering the child's daily routine. Most children do not see such changes in a positive light, even years after the divorce (Wallerstein, Corbin, & Lewis, 1988).

Immediate Reactions to Divorce

Almost all children find their parents' divorce a painful experience. The early symptoms may differ, but they include anger, depression, and guilt (Berger, 1995; Hetherington, 1979). Children often show such behavioral changes as regression, sleep disturbances, and fear (Wallerstein, 1983). Children may grieve for the absent parent and may respond with aggression or noncompliance (Hetherington, Stanley-Hagan, & Anderson, 1989). Parent-child relationships also change. The custodial parent, usually the mother, becomes stricter and more controlling, while the other parent becomes permissive and understanding though less accessible. Both parents make fewer demands on children to mature, become less consistent in their discipline, and have more difficulty communicating with the children (Hetherington, Cox, & Cox, 1976). Parents' discipline practices become poorer (Forgatch, Patterson, & Skinner, 1988) and conduct problems are not uncommon (Brody & Forehand, 1988).

After the initial period some children show a remarkable ability to recover, while others do not. Some adapt well in the early stages, and some show delayed effects. How quickly children recover from the initial shock depends on whether a stable environment is created after the divorce and on the social supports available to the child (Kurdek, 1981). Often, however, such supports are not available. Parents are confused and must rearrange their own lives. Relatives are often judgmental and their relationships with both parents and with the child may change. Peer relationships may suffer, as some children feel guilty about what is happening. Family friends may be forced to take sides and maintain contact with only one parent. The main social supports are not available.

Long-Term Effects of Divorce

Many of the initial reactions either become less severe or disappear by the end of the first year to 18 months (Portes et al., 1992; Hetherington, 1979). The long-term effects of divorce on children, however, can be severe. In one study of children whose parents divorced in their middle childhood years, the functioning of half had improved, while about one-fourth of the subjects had become significantly worse (Kelly & Wallerstein, 1976).

When children whose parents were divorced when they were in middle childhood were followed, Wallerstein (1987) found feelings of sadness, neediness, and an increased sense of vulnerability expressed by a majority of these children. Even though it had been ten years since the divorce, the children spoke sadly of their loss of the intact family and especially of the lack of contact with their noncustodial parent. They expressed a great concern of being betrayed in relationships, and anxiety about personal commitments was high. Half of the boys and one-fourth of the girls were considered poorly adjusted and at high risk at this ten year

Children whose parents are divorced are somewhat at risk but there is much the parents can do to prevent difficulties.

follow-up. Children from divorced families, then, experience a greater number of social, academic, and personal adjustment problems than children from nondivorced families, and the transition following separation and divorce is highly stressful for most children (Doherty & Needle, 1991).

The long-term effects of divorce are dependent on a number of factors. For example, if parents continue to quarrel after the divorce whenever they talk to each other children will suffer (Berger, 1995; Wallerstein, 1983). Children have a much more difficult time coping with stress when a great deal of conflict between parents occurs (Portes, Haas, & Brown, 1991). Unfortunately, many parents, about 50 percent according to one study, continue to argue after the divorce is final (Stark, 1986). Postdivorce adjustment is much better if parents can cooperate after divorcing (Bronstein et al., 1994; Camara & Resnick, 1989).

The nature of the relationship between parents and children after the divorce is also important. Children do better when their parents maintain a warm relationship with them (Hess & Camara, 1979). When adolescents were divided into three groups—divorce/good relationships with parents, divorce/poor relationships with parents, and intact/good relationship with parents—those who were from the divorced/good relationship with parents group showed no more cognitive or behavioral problems than those in the intact/good relationship group. These good relationships buffered the child against the problems of divorce (Wierson et al., 1989). Last, adjustment difficulties will be less severe if financial problems and parental conflict are minimized and if social supports exist (Kurdek, 1981). Unfortunately, parents' difficulties involving finances, loneliness, anxiety about the future, and the loss of social supports reduce their ability to give their children what the children need to soften the blow.

Divorce and the Age of the Child

Children at different ages experience divorce somewhat differently. Preschoolers react quite negatively, often showing regressive behavior and separation anxiety, although most do recover from the initial shock after a year or so (Allison & Fursteinberg, 1989; Wallerstein & Kelly, 1979). Continued deterioration after 1 year is linked to continuing family disorder. The preschooler does not understand what is going on, and parents don't explain much to preschoolers. They are not as able to understand the divorce and may blame themselves and fear abandonment by their parents (Wallerstein et al., 1988). School-age children experience loyalty problems, including feelings that they must choose between their parents. Children in elementary school feel powerless and frightened and frequently are angry at one or both parents. They may support one parent against the other. About one-half show severe drops in achievement during the first year (Wallerstein et al., 1988).

Adolescents have a difficult time coping with anger, often showing acute depression, acting-out behaviors, emotional and social withdrawal, and anxiety about their future. They are often disturbed by the fact that the family's financial problems no longer allow them to buy things they formerly could buy.

Does Divorce Affect Boys and Girls Differently?

One generally accepted, but not unanimous, research finding is that the long-term effects of divorce are greater for boys than for girls (Doherty & Needle, 1991). Boys are much more likely to show psychological, social, and academic problems and act out than are girls (Hetherington et al., 1989). The reasons for this are not definitely known. In the majority of cases, mothers gain custody, and perhaps the absence of the male authority figure may have an especially injurious effect on boys (Huston, 1983).

On the other hand, perhaps girls are affected as much, but they react differently. Psychologists now appreciate the influence fathers have on their daughters' development. Girls raised by their mother have more difficulty relating to men later on. Hetherington (1972) found that girls from divorced families were more flirtatious, sexually precocious, and seductive, while girls raised in widowed families were more withdrawn. Therefore, paternal absence affects daughters as well as sons.

Family Discord and Behavior Problems

Studies that compare children from divorced families with children from intact families often conclude that children in divorced families have significantly more problems (Allison & Furstenberg, 1989). However, the differences may not be due to divorce itself but to family problems that existed long before the divorce took place. Family turmoil—whether it ends in divorce or not—creates problems for children (Emery, 1982). The more open and intense the hostility, the more serious are the children's problems. Marital turmoil is also related to underachievement in school. In one interesting longitudinal study, the personalities of children from intact families were assessed. A number of these families later experienced divorce. The behavior of the boys prior to divorce was affected negatively by the stress in the family. Such problems as uncontrolled impulsiveness and aggressiveness were common. The behavior of girls was found to be less affected than that of boys. The researchers conclude that some of the problems considered to be consequences of divorce may be present prior to divorce (Block, Block, & Gjerde, 1986).

Helping Children of Divorce

For divorced, single parents, the first step is to be certain that they receive the child support they are entitled to. However, it is wrong to believe that just getting fathers who can pay to do so would end the problem. Although improved child support collection policies are undoubtedly important, they will have only limited success if the father is poor, unemployed, or even lower middle class (Salt, 1991). A father in poverty may not be able to pay enough to prevent poverty, even if he pays what the court requires. Single parents also need adequate day-care so the single mother can seek employment. In addition, mediation that allows the divorced couple to settle their disputes out of court may also help to reduce the tension.

The research points to ways that children can be helped through the difficult time of divorce. First, parents must make it clear that the child is not the reason for the divorce and that both parents still love the child. Second, they must try to get along after the divorce, not an easy thing to do. Continued discord, which is common, makes it more difficult for the child to recover. Third, the custodial parent must try to build a new life with the child that is bounded by a secure routine. Divorced families in which mutual support, nurturance, and some reasonable routines are established and maintained minimize the chances of maladjustment in children (Portes et al., 1991). Unfortunately after a divorce, the custodial parent burdened with so much responsibility and enduring a personal crisis becomes stricter but somewhat less organized. Fourth, frequent contact with the noncustodial parent is important for the child. Children must realize that they have not lost a parent.

SCENARIO

3 The Thomases had been quarreling for a number of years and finally agreed to a divorce. They have two children, ages 5 and 7. Now with the divorce final, Mrs. Thomas finds that she and her former husband constantly argue when they see each other. Each blames the other for the divorce. Mr. Thomas resents the money he pays each month, while Mrs. Thomas complains that it is not enough. The children seem to be suffering. Mrs. Thomas has had to increase her hours at her job, and Mr. Thomas believes she is neglecting the children for her active social life. Mrs. Thomas resents the fact that Mr. Thomas is giving the children anything they want on weekends when they visit him, and both criticize the other in front of the children. In simple terms, they can no longer stand each other. If you were their friend and they both asked you for advice, what would you tell them and why?

The Teen Parent

The second reason for the increase in single-parent families is unwed mother-hood. In 1993, there were 532,000 births to women under the age of 20 years. Of these births, 357,000 were to unmarried women between the ages of 15 and 19, and 11,000 were to women under the age of 15 years (Statistical Abstract, 1994). These single mothers usually opt to keep their infants; of those who give birth, 94 percent keep their babies.

The pregnant teenager belongs to the highest risk group both for birth complications and for fetal abnormalities (Fogel, 1984). Adolescent mothers experience the greatest number of prenatal and postnatal problems. This high rate of complications may be explained by the relationship between adolescent pregnancy and such factors as low socioeconomic status, poor education, and poor health care (Ventura, 1994). Teenage mothers are likely to have repeat pregnancies. They are at increased risk for delivering prematurely and for these children to have birth defects (Seitz & Apfel, 1994; Strobino, 1987). Out of fear, ignorance, or the desire to deny the pregnancy, many teens do not seek prenatal care until the last minute. Other behaviors, including poor compliance with medical recommendations when medical services are obtained, and poor nutritional habits also contribute to the increased rate of premature births. Early pregnancy hinders achievement in school as well.

A large difference exists between teenage mothers and those in their twenties. In a study that compared the two age groups, Culp and colleagues (1988) found that pregnant adolescents were generally less happy about being pregnant and had less social support from both their family and the child's father than did women in their twenties. Adolescent mothers also spoke less to their infants. However, feelings among the adolescent group varied greatly, with some being very unhappy about their situation and others being happy. Therefore, care should be exercised in making generalizations.

The combination of youth, poverty, lack of knowledge, poor nutritional habits, poor health care, and lack of motivation to act on warnings about drugs is difficult to combat. Teenage pregnancy is part of a larger social and economic problem that must be approached educationally and medically.

The young mother does not seem to be ready for her role. Most of the children of single, unwed mothers will spend their time in homes where the father is not present and are likely to live in poverty. In fact, of all the families with children younger than six years headed by mothers who gave birth as teens, two-thirds live below the poverty level (American Home Economics Association, 1986). Adolescent mothers tend to be impatient, insensitive, and prone to punish their children. Their behavior is characterized as highly physical and less verbal than that of more adult mothers (see Garcia-Co, Hoffman, & Oh, 1987). The rates of child abuse are higher in young families as well (Astone & Upchurch, 1994).

The adolescent mother's style of parenting is not conducive to the child's optimal development. Children born to adolescent mothers lag behind their peers in cognitive, social, and school performance, and are at greater risk than their peers for maladjustment (Dubow & Luster, 1990). These teenage parents often reach out for help and require it. If they are to raise their children successfully, they must receive a special type of parenting education.

Prevention and Help

Preventing unwanted teenage pregnancies is a vital concern (Lee & Stewart, 1995). Comprehensive sex education programs may help. These programs combine information with access to high quality contraceptive services. One interesting experimental program was conducted in Baltimore in which junior and senior high school students received not only sex education but also information presented by social workers in their homerooms dealing with the services offered at a clinic. For several hours each day, staff members assigned to each school made themselves available for individual counseling. After school, a special clinic across the street or a few blocks away offered open group discussion and group counseling that emphasized personal responsibility, goal setting, parental communication, and health care, including contraception. The results showed better knowledge of contraception and sex as well as a delay in the age of first intercourse. Students attended the clinic sooner after initiating sexual activity, and there was an increased use of contraception among those who were sexually active. This behavior was especially noticeable among the younger teens who usually show less responsible sexual behavior. The program altered behavior partially because access to high-quality free services, including professional counseling, was assured (Zabin et al., 1986).

Some programs try to help teenagers during their pregnancy. For example, the Polly T. McCabe Center is a public school operated by the New Haven Board of Education, which serves a population of pregnant teenagers. The school follows the regular district calendar, curriculum, and schedule, but also offers comprehensive social and medical services. Counseling is provided for the prospective parent to promote planning and decision making in such areas as day-care arrangements, educational planning, delaying subsequent childbearing, coping with familial conflict, and finding housing. The goal is to realistically plan for self-sufficiency. Information is also given on childbirth and child care. When medical and school records were reviewed for 230 adolescent mothers, a reduction in premature deliveries was found. The earlier in the pregnancy students began attending the school, the better the outcomes (Seitz & Apfel, 1994).

THOUGHT QUESTION

5. *Why do sex education classes in schools cause such a controversy?*

SCENARIO

4 The parents in the school seem to be split down the middle. One group of parents is in favor of giving out condoms in the high school. They claim that, although it would be best for students to wait to experience sex, the fact is that many, perhaps even most are sexually active in high school. These parents believe that if students are going to have sex, they should be encouraged to use protection. Prevention of venereal disease and pregnancy is most important. The other group of parents disagrees and claims if you give out condoms you are encouraging and approving premarital sex. They claim that abstinence should be discussed and encouraged and that the school should not be in the business of promoting sexuality. If you were asked to speak, which side would you agree with and why?

Services for the Young Mother

Once the infants are born, the parent requires assistance. Grandparents help out in many cases. The parents may require help in learning to take care of their child since studies have shown them often to be less than optimal parents. When teenage mothers (16 years old and younger) were given weekly classes covering such areas as ways to stimulate their infants, nutrition and family planning, and a number of supportive services, significant improvements were found both in the mothers and in the infants (Badger, Burns, & Vietze, 1981). The infants showed higher scores on infant intelligence tests than a control group, and the mothers were more physically and emotionally responsive to their infants. Many other parent education programs also show success (Kaplan, 1991).

These young mothers require counseling services from the schools in two specific areas: child care and vocational planning. High school teachers may find that sometimes these students are involved in child-care responsibilities and unable to meet particular deadlines on assignments. Although excellence may be expected as with any other student, some flexibility regarding deadlines may be required.

 **THE CLASSROOM**   **Helping the Child from a Single-Parent Family Achieve**

The experience of many youngsters today is different than it was years ago. The changes are great, and no doubt the educational experience of the child is affected by the home situation. Yet, before we make any wild suppositions about divorce or single-parent families causing children's difficulties, we must look at the research and put prejudices aside.

The modern family is more varied, and teachers may be dealing with children who face a number of challenges at home. Yet, these children can and do succeed. The teacher can play a positive role not only teaching academic skills, but also in helping children with their adjustment to their new family situation, improving their self-esteem and their interpersonal relationships. The following suggestions might be helpful in dealing with some of the challenges these families face.

1. Become aware of your attitude toward single-parent families, day-care, and other alternatives to the traditional child-care setup.	**Why?** Teachers sometimes possess negative stereotypes of the nontraditional family or the child whose parents divorce. Attitudes may influence one's dealings with both students and parents.
2. Use the parent/guardian or family on forms.	**Why?** Don't assume all children live in two-parent traditional families.

3. Make appointments and communicate with parents when it is practical and convenient for all parties.	**Why?** Working parents are not always able to get a day off. Although not always possible, some teachers advocate evening conferences (Barney & Koford, 1987). Still, telephone calls and regular communication channels can be established.
4. Consider how families are portrayed in stories and textbooks.	**Why?** Many texts still emphasize a working father, a homemaker mother, and two children, but most children do not live in this traditional family. Stories that deal with nontraditional families in a positive manner can boost self-esteem and lead to greater understanding and acceptance of diverse family settings.
5. Be aware of changes in student conduct, work habits, or grades that may signify a deterioration of the home situation.	**Why?** Teachers often do not know that a divorce is occurring in the home and do not understand that behavioral changes may be due to the family breakup. If the child's behavior or academic work shows a precipitous change, contact the parents immediately.
6. Be sensitive to the child's reaction to divorce.	**Why?** Children going through a parental divorce often show symptoms, especially withdrawal. The child may need support, and cooperative activities can keep the child involved.
7. When dealing with parents going through a divorce, encourage the parents to keep communication with their children open.	**Why?** Children experiencing a parental divorce often show a decrease in academic performance, but a good relationship with at least one parent can prevent some school-related problems (Forehand, Middleton & Long, 1987). Parents need to reassure the children that they are loved and that the divorce was not their fault, as well as to create a stable environment for them.

8. Be ready to refer the student to counseling if necessary.	**Why?** A student going through a parental divorce or having difficulties in the home may require counseling. Sometimes the child will feel more comfortable talking to a teacher, but a teacher may not feel confident about providing the counseling necessary. Some referral to the guidance counselor may be in order.
9. Involve the noncustodial parent when appropriate.	**Why?** Many noncustodial parents are eager to learn about their children's progress (Carlson, 1987). However, regular channels of communication may not be open. The district's policies in this area should be checked, and when appropriate, noncustodial parents should receive progress reports if they want them.
10. Communication with the home should not always be critical of the student.	**Why?** When a parent receives letters or telephone calls from the school it is normally a complaint about the child. Sometimes a teacher must be critical of a student, but the teacher needs to balance criticism with positive feedback about the student's progress whenever possible.

Homeless Families

One family situation in the news today is homelessness (Jones, Levine, & Rosenberg, 1991). Most homeless people are single adults, and studies disagree sharply concerning the number of homeless families in the United States (Toro & Warren, 1991). The best estimate to date is that about 600,000 people—including at least 68,000 to 100,000 children under the age of 16—are homeless (Rosenberg, Solarz, & Bailey, 1991; Kondratas, 1991). Other figures are much higher, often including those who are homeless for a brief period of time (Heflin & Rudy, 1991). The fastest growing segment of the homeless population is families with children (Anderson & Koblinsky, 1995). The number of poor people who may become homeless in the near future is increasing because many poor families are either sharing apartments with other families or spending a very high percentage of their income—sometime upwards of 70 percent—for housing (Foscarinis, 1991; Milburn & D'Ercole, 1991).

Becoming homeless is a process that often begins with a family's being forced to leave an apartment because of an event such as nonpayment of rent or fire (Gewirtzman & Fodor, 1987). The next step is often doubling or tripling up with other families (Foscarinis, 1991). This sharing continues until the family is asked to leave, possibly because of the constant tension of overcrowding. Having little or no income and nowhere to go, these families then become homeless.

The homeless family is most likely to be headed by the mother. In fact, more than nine of ten homeless families are headed by women, and most families have histories of not living in a single place for a long time (Anderson & Koblinsky, 1995; Bassuk, Rubin, & Lauriat, 1986). About half of the mothers have completed high school, but only one-third have worked for longer than one month (Bassuk & Rosenberg, 1988).

Research generally shows that homeless families are more similar to than different from other poor families but that homeless parents have experienced more disruptions in their early life than other poor people (Milburn & D'Ercole, 1991). One-third of the mothers heading homeless families report having been abused during childhood, and two-thirds have experienced major family disruptions, such as divorce in their early life. Homeless mothers are more likely than poor single mothers who have housing to report an early experience that includes being in a foster home, running away for a week or more, living on the street for a time, or being physically or sexually abused (Bassuk & Rosenberg, 1988). The frequency of alcohol and other drug abuse and serious psychiatric problems is also greater among homeless mothers than among poor, housed mothers (Bassuk & Rosenberg, 1988; Robertson, 1991). Homeless mothers, then, seem to be an emotionally vulnerable group with histories of childhood disruptions. With the scarcity of affordable housing, the most vulnerable segment of society becomes homeless first (Bassuk, Rubin, & Lauriat, 1986).

A popular view of homeless mothers is that they do not have any family contact and have been abandoned by family and friends, but this view is actually only half true. Although these families presently have no one to turn to and are isolated, often it is because they have already used up their social supports. Shinn and colleagues (1991) found that homeless women were more likely than poor, housed mothers to have had recent contact with parents and friends. Homeless women, though, could not receive any support from these people, because they were likely to have stayed with these family members or friends in the past.

Homeless families may live in hotels or in temporary shelters. In these shelters, families sleep on cots in an open room that lacks both privacy and cooking facilities. Young children may run through the facility or simply lie on cots. Many shelters have few toys and no play area (Gewirtzman & Fodor, 1987).

How do children who are homeless compare to children who are poor but housed? Studies—comparing homeless children raised by single mothers to housed children who are very poor and also raised by single mothers—demonstrate that homeless children are at a greater risk for medical, developmental, and educational problems (Hausman & Hammer, 1993). For example, homeless children experience a greater number of both acute and chronic health problems than other poor children (Rafferty & Shinn, 1991). When Alperstein and colleagues (1988) compared homeless children younger than age five to other poor children, homeless children were more likely to have delayed immunization, elevated blood lead levels, and higher rates of abuse and neglect. When Chavkin and colleagues (1987) compared homeless women living in welfare motels in New York City with women living in public housing, 16 percent of the homeless women compared with 11 percent of the women in public housing had given birth to low birthweight babies. Only 60 percent of the homeless women received any prenatal care compared to 85 percent in the public housing. The infant mortality was also much higher among homeless families. Evidence also indicates that more homeless children have iron deficiencies and are at risk for delayed or stunted growth (Molnar, Rath, & Klein, 1990).

Homeless children are more likely to show developmental problems than poor but housed children (Molnar et al., 1990). The most common problem is a lag in language development (Whitman et al., 1990; Rafferty & Shinn, 1991). Other problems in visual motor development are also found (Rescorla, Parker, & Stolley, 1991). Studies by Bassuk and colleagues (1986; 1987; Bassuk & Rosenberg, 1988) found that half the preschoolers in a shelter exhibited at least one serious impairment in language, social skills, or motor development compared with 16 percent of the low income, housed preschoolers. For such children at risk, early education programs could help. Yet, significantly fewer homeless children are enrolled in preschool programs than poor housed children (Rescorla et al., 1991).

Homeless children are also more likely to show such psychological problems as depression and anxiety (Bassuk et al., 1986). Sleep problems, withdrawal, and aggression are also relatively common (Bassuk & Rubin, 1987).

Most homeless children do attend public school (Gewirtzman & Fodor, 1987), but their attendance is poor (Molnar et al., 1990). Between 15 and 30 percent of all homeless children do not attend school regularly, but other figures are much higher. Children who are homeless are also more likely to drop out (Molnar et al., 1990). The importance of attendance was shown in a study by Rescorla and colleagues (1991). The outcomes for homeless school-aged children were similar to the outcomes for housed children of similar socioeconomic status if the children who were homeless attended school on a regular basis.

Homeless children are more likely to read and do mathematics below grade level and to be retained in grade (Rafferty & Shinn, 1991). The relatively poor achievement is caused often by poor school attendance and lack of adequate educational services, inadequate shelter materials and instability. Bassuk & Rubin (1987) found that 40 percent of the students who were homeless were failing or performing below-average work, 25 percent were placed in special classes, and 43 percent had repeated one grade. Russell and Williams (1988) found that a significant percentage of the population of homeless children have disabilities. The most common disabilities were learning disabilities, followed by speech impairments, mental retardation, and behavior disorders. Homeless children also show more difficulties interacting positively with other children and often do not have a healthy self-concept (Stonge & Tenhouse, 1990).

Although the long-term effects of homelessness on children are not yet known, this population is clearly not only at risk but currently experiencing physical, emotional, and psychological damage. What can be done? Obviously, affordable, permanent housing is needed. If temporary shelters are required, such shelters must provide children with day-care, Head Start programs, medical care, and space for physical activity. Homeless families also have special needs for job training, and intensive social and psychological services for both parents and children must be provided (Anderson & Koblinsky, 1995).

Homelessness is a definite risk factor and most shelters are not designed to foster the adequate development of young children.

Children who are homeless have specific problems that affect their school attendance and academic progress. The transience of the family creates such problems as a lack of school records, transportation difficulties, and lack of clothing and supplies. The school experience is crucial, not only because of the general importance of learning but because it may be the only stable situation homeless children experience. Homeless children often require remedial educational services to address specific academic problems, preschool services to help prevent failure, psychological support services and some sensitivity to avoid stigmatization (Rafferty & Shinn, 1991).

The most important law aimed at helping homeless people is the Stewart B. McKinney Homeless Assistance Act (PL 100-77), passed in 1987. It created 20 new programs that allocate federal funds to states and local governments and nonprofit organizations. Most of the programs are emergency in nature. Shelter programs provide funds for acquisition, rehabilitation, and operation of emergency shelters and transitional housing with some funding for permanent housing for single homeless adults (Weinreb & Buckner, 1993).

Another group of programs provide funds for physical and mental health care for persons in shelters and on the streets, including mobile vans and outreach teams (Foscarinis, 1991). The law recognized that the needs of the homeless population go beyond housing. The act includes programs run by seven different federal departments that provide not only housing assistance but also health and mental health care, food assistance, substance abuse treatment education, and job training (Kondratas, 1991).

One section of the law, which is especially important for educators, is Subtitle VII-B administered by the U.S. Department of Education. This guarantees homeless children access to elementary and secondary education. It requires that states revise their residency, guardianship, and other criteria for enrollment that in the past have prevented homeless children from attending school in their districts. State education agencies receive grants to be used to hire a coordinator for the education of homeless children. States identify the needs of the children, compile data about the degree of homelessness, document school access, and develop educational plans. Such plans include the formation of programs for homeless children with disabilities, including services for gifted and talented students, programs for students whose native language is not English, and vocational educational programs.

This law did not end the barriers that made access to school for children who are homeless difficult, so later amendments contained provisions aimed at improving the coordination, development, and delivery of services to homeless children. The activities of the state coordinator were expanded to include coordination and provision of comprehensive services, to provide information concerning the rights and services available to homeless families, and to develop and institute strategies to ensure that homeless children and youth receive services for which they are eligible, including nutrition and before- and after-school services. Funding was also included for programs that would serve as examples for other districts as well as for state and local education agencies to provide such educational services as tutoring and remedial education. It required districts to allow a child who became homeless during the summer to remain in the same school the child received services in during the previous academic year. In addition, homelessness was not considered a reason by itself for segregating children in special classes, and states were to develop programs to make certain the children were not isolated or stigmatized (Heflin & Rudy, 1991).

Children who are homeless face a number of problems directly and indirectly relating to their education. They often move around making it impossible to attend a particular school, transportation is difficult, and they may be absent quite often. They may be embarrassed because of their clothing. They may have had little opportunity to interact with their peers and lack a sense of stability or of anything being their own. Those who require evaluation for special education services may be frequently absent or attend the school for only a short while, making the process of evaluation and assessment more difficult. These children may require remediation of their academic difficulties, tutoring, and counseling. Attention to their health and nutritional needs is also required (Heflin & Rudy, 1991).

Some of these problems require a team effort, including community networks of professionals to coordinate the many services needed by these families. The school staff and administration must also look at how they are serving these children. This includes an awareness of their own attitudes toward homeless families as well as an appreciation of the difficulties these families face and their special needs. School professionals can do much to help. They can make certain that any necessary evaluations are conducted in an accelerated time period, and that after- and before-school activities are available for these children. Transportation problems must be solved, and the records must be sent to other schools in a timely manner when the child changes schools. Since absenteeism is a definite problem, some method of helping children catch up is important. These children also require their own spaces such as lockers and materials such as books in school since they often do not have a concept of personal belonging. They may also lack social competence and have difficulties in social interactions. Some attention to social skills training and directly involving children who are homeless in the peer interaction during classroom activities is necessary (Heflin & Rudy, 1991).

SCENARIO

5 Gerald is a sixth-grade student in your class who is homeless. He lives with his mother who moves around quite a bit. He is frequently absent. His attendance is good for some weeks and then there may be a two-week stretch in which he is absent. He and his mother spend time in shelters, friend's homes, other emergency housing, and sometimes on the street. He is embarrassed about his situation and reads and writes poorly. He is behind in most of his work. His clothing is worn and tattered and often not clean, and he is often shunned by the other children in the class, although they do not often pick on him or tease him. He tries to do his work when he is in class, but is often in a position of having to try to catch up. What could you do to help Gerald succeed in class?

Stress-Resilient Children

One common thread throughout this chapter has been the problem of stress. Children of divorce, children in single-parent families, homeless children, and children of poor families face great amounts of stress. Yet, assuming that entire groups do not succeed is absolutely wrong. Despite many problems and challenges, most children do grow up to be independent, well-functioning adults (see Herrenkohl, Herrenkohl & Egolf, 1994). Why do some children exposed to tremendous amounts of stress develop some difficulty while others seem to do well?

Research has demonstrated the relationship of stress to a number of problems. Earlier we noted how changing family circumstances sometimes lead to poor adjustment and emotional difficulties. Positive correlations can be shown between children's stress and anxiety, depression, behavior problems, delinquency, physi-

The most significant buffer against stress is the establishment of a good parent-child relationship.

cal illness, and accident proneness (Clapp, 1988). Stress also adversely affects intellectual functioning.

As many as 35 percent of all American children are estimated to experience stress-related health problems (*U.S. News and World Report*, 1986). Yet many children who are exposed to a great deal of stress do not develop such problems. Consider the case of Michael. Born to teenage parents, he was a premature infant who spent his first three weeks in the hospital. Immediately after his birth his father went to Southeast Asia for two years with the U.S. Army. By the time Michael was eight, he had three younger siblings and his parents were divorced. His mother left the area and had no further contact with the children. By age 18, though, Michael had high self-esteem and good values, was liked by his peers, and was successful in school (Werner, 1984).

Children like Michael used to be called invulnerable, since they did not seem to be very affected in the long term by great amounts of stress. Today, this term is not used as often because it does not correctly describe the child. Since no child is invulnerable to stress, the more modern term is **stress-resistant or resilient children** (Rutter, 1985; Herrenkohl, Herrenkohl, & Egolf, 1994). Some children seem to bounce back and can cope with pressures that seem at times to be too much for any child. These children are not uncommon, and in the past decade or so, psychologists, such as Norman Garmezy (1982), have searched for factors that differentiate stress-resistant children from others. These factors can be grouped under the headings of protective factors within the child, within the family, and outside the family.

Resilient children show a strong social orientation as well as autonomy, even during the preschool period (Werner, 1984). They seem to lack fear and are self-reliant. Sociability and independence are characteristics that mark these children and make them more resistant to problems (Garmezy, 1985; Anthony, 1974). The child's temperament is another factor, as the more flexible, adaptable, and easy-

Stress resistant (resilient) children:

Children who do not appear to be negatively affected by stress and are able to cope with stressful environments. The adjustment of these children during adolescence and adulthood is surprisingly good.

going child is more likely to cope better with stress than the less adaptable child (Wertlieb et al., 1987). The more adaptable child also receives more positive responses from others, which reduce the stress (Rutter, 1985). Many of these children have something about them that is special and allows them to garner whatever emotional resources the family has to offer (Radke-Yarrow & Sherman, 1991). For example, one such child was the only healthy child in the family, while another had some musical talent.

Stress-resistant children often find hobbies and outside interests as a refuge from the problems of the family. They also tend to be active in after-school activities that allow them to be away from the poor home environment. These children also use better problem-solving strategies and are less likely to catastrophize, that is, make a mountain out of a molehill. They do not focus on the negative aspects of a situation (Brown et al., 1986). A study of resilient abused and neglected adolescents found that those who were able to rise above their environments and achieve had developed a positive self-image and an internal locus of control, which are expressed in goal-setting and planning behavior (Herrenkohl, Herrenkohl, & Egolf, 1994).

The relationship with parents is the greatest buffer or protective device for children (Clapp, 1988). Children who have a good relationship with at least one parent tend to do better than those who do not (Rutter, 1991). But the positive relationship with an adult does not have to be with a parent. Sometimes an older sibling, a grandparent, or another adult—perhaps a teacher—can serve as a role model and confidant. In fact, stress-resistant children seem to be very active in finding these adults (Werner, 1984). When third and fifth graders were rated on problem-solving skills, social support, resistance to stress, and behavior problems, children who were competent problem solvers had higher levels of social support and showed fewer behavioral problems (Dubow & Tisak, 1989). Social support moderates the effects of stress (Wertlieb, Weigel, & Felstein, 1989).

Children who are resilient are frequently involved in taking care of others, most commonly younger siblings. This concept is called required helpfulness. When children living in terrible family circumstances were observed, Werner and Smith (1982) found that many of the stress-resistant children had assumed responsibility for their younger siblings. Helping others may increase their coping skills and morale and generally give them a sense of purpose.

Promoting Resilience

This emphasis on stress-resistant children is refreshing. Instead of looking only at the factors that cause behavioral problems, psychologists are looking at why some children are able to transcend or cope with these stressors. This knowledge can be used to help children who find themselves under a great deal of stress. First, psychologists and educators know that once the child is exposed to a particular stressor, the child then requires time to adjust before going on to cope with the next stressor. Therefore, buffering the child from multiple stressors is a good idea (Rutter, 1980). Second, children who have warm relationships with their parents, a single parent, or adults outside the nuclear family do best, so building relationships is important.

Finally, since resilient children have hobbies and interests outside the home, encouraging participation in extracurricular activities is desirable. Such participation allows the child to focus attention elsewhere and obtain a sense of self-esteem from such activities. The school can provide some after-school programs, and teachers can encourage children to participate in these programs. Resilient children also have a sense of responsibility and caring for others, and encouraging these children to become involved in meaningful helping activities can bring self-respect and a sense of purpose. Again, the school may run programs to help other children, perhaps children who have learning problems and require tutoring, and children under stress may find participating in these programs meaningful. Resilient children also tend to be sociable, and helping children develop friendships with others is another possibility.

SCENARIO

6 Kendra is a ten-year-old who is under great stress. Kendra's parents are divorced, and she lives with her mother who is an alcoholic. When the mother is drunk, she berates Kendra and her younger brother, Kurt. Kendra's father abandoned the family, and Kendra has not seen him for years. Kendra tries to shield Kurt from his mother's anger, but is not always successful. Teachers claim that Kendra is a bright student and is doing surprisingly well, although she could do even better. She is respectful and rarely gets into trouble. You are her guidance counselor and aware of the situation. How can you help Kendra continue to develop and achieve well?

Retrospect

How does the concept of risk affect the child with special needs? First, prevention of disabling conditions is certainly an important aspect of the field. Since some of the conditions that increase risk are known, reducing the risk is possible through reducing the cause, be it prenatal drug usage or teenage pregnancy. Second, the concept of risk helps teachers and other professionals to design programs to temper the seriousness of the disability and pathology, even if it cannot be prevented. Third, the concept of risk alerts professionals to certain groups of children faced with particular situations who are vulnerable to developing disabilities and where to best place their available resources. Last, looking at why some children succeed despite the presence of risk factors may yield some idea of how to help those who are exposed to such factors. The research can help to create an environment in which children are more likely to be able to deal with their problems.

This chapter discussed just a few of the risk factors that are relatively common. Clearly, risk does not imply some immutable destiny. Society can and sometimes has provided the programs necessary to reduce the risk and prevent problems from arising. Success cannot be guaranteed, but our experience with programs that prevent problems and help reduce the severity of problems once they occur has shown us that they can be both psychologically and medically beneficial as well as cost effective.

 **Catching Up**

Children who can be placed in at-risk categories differ from each other in many ways. However, all are at risk for poor academic achievement. The reasons are many. Some at-risk children are absent from school for medical or familial reasons, missing a great deal of work. Other at-risk children enter school behind their peers and need special help if they are to catch up. For still others, their rate of learning is somewhat slower, and they may be lost in class and fall further behind. Teachers certainly cannot solve the societal and familial problems that affect these children. But teachers can do much to address the academic difficulties these children experience. This teacher intervention requires the use of techniques that will help children catch up and work at their own pace.

The most popular use of computers as tools of instruction is to provide drill and practice. Computer drills can be similar to flashcards, or they can be much more involved. In the simplest drills, a computer might generate mathematics questions concerning basic facts; the student responds, and the computer gives immediate feedback. The questions that are answered incorrectly can be placed in a file and presented after all the other examples are tendered to the student. This process is similar to the strategy one might use with flashcards. Drill and practice are useful in mathematics, social studies, and foreign language; although we may argue that the procedure can be overused, it certainly has its place.

A reasonable question to ask is why computerized practice is more effective than the teacher simply drilling a student or having parents do it. Individual drill takes a considerable amount of time and is labor intensive. Teachers may not have the time to give individual drill. When drill is given in a group situation, the drill presented may not match the speed or need of certain students. Parents may not have the time to drill their children and may be impatient with them. Children may not be able to drill themselves either. The seemingly simple strategies of retesting those items that a student gets wrong may not be understood by some younger students, and computerized drill is very effective for students who may lack these self-learning strategies (Salisbury, 1988). In addition, computerized drill and practice software can be designed as an arcade game to keep students motivated.

The ability to program practice activities goes beyond simple strategies, however. Some drill and practice activities have been written so that they make better use of the computer's capabilities. One is the corrective feedback paradigm (CFP) (Siegel & Misselt, 1984). Several features are added to the familiar flashcard drill to improve it. First, the kind of feedback offered depends upon the type of mistake made. For instance, consider a drill involving the elements of the periodic table. What if the computer shows "Mg" and the student types in "metal." If the student response is not the answer to another drill question, the computer gives the correct answer "magnesium." However, if the student types "manganese," the computer provides feedback explaining that Mg is magnesium and Mn is manganese. The computer tells the student the question the student responded to as well as the correct answer to the original question.

Students can also be given discrimination training, where the item missed and the confused item are presented simultaneously so that the students can see the items' similarities and differences. For instance, if the student answered with magnesium for Mg and Mn, they would be presented together and the student made aware of the differences between them. The student would then need to correctly respond to both items before the drill continued.

In addition, in the normal flashcard procedure, an error is placed at the end of the pile and then presented again after the student has answered all the other questions. By that time, the student may have forgotten the correct answer. The problem is avoided using what is called increased ratio review. In this more complicated drill, if the student makes a mistake and receives feedback and possibly discrimination training, the missed items reappear according to a spaced review schedule determined by the teacher before the drill begins. The missed item may appear after three more items. If it is answered correctly, it appears after six more and then finally after ten more items. An incorrect response indicates a need for more review. This is similar to placing the error into the middle of the deck of flashcards according to a prearranged schedule, which is difficult to do by hand, but easily done by a computer.

The teacher may also decide on the number of times an item is to be answered correctly before it is no longer asked. The rule is called a retirement criterion. For example, the teacher may decide that if the item is answered correctly twice, it can be dropped from the drill. The teacher may decide five correct answers are necessary. Of course, the computer has no difficulty counting how many times the item has been presented and answered correctly, whereas teachers would find such bookkeeping rather difficult.

Computer drills can be used in a number of areas, including biology, spelling, arithmetic, foreign language, social studies, and English as a second language. These techniques are superior to the more traditional methods of review (Siegel & Misselt, 1984). One caution is necessary, however. Computerized drill and practice are meant for review purposes and as a way of perhaps increasing response speed. They are

not meant as a way to introduce students to new material. If students do not have a basic knowledge of the material, they will find the drill program frustrating.

Unlike practice and drill, tutorials are designed to introduce students to new material. The computer acts as a tutor, with the student directly interacting with the computer to learn new material. The computer is programmed to present material and to react to student responses and questions with prearranged questions and responses (Percival & Ellington, 1988). Tutorials present information by setting up a dialogue. A program might print a few sentences of text and some graphic illustration to give information and then ask questions. Based upon the student's input, the program repeats the material or branches into other material. The tutorial must anticipate types of errors the student may make and be able to help students correct these errors (Wiebe, 1993). Tutorials have the advantage of being easily tailored to meet the needs of an individual learner. The timing of the presentation of any new material is contingent upon student responses to tutorial questions. Tutorials are interactive, requiring active participation, and provide immediate feedback for the student (Lepper & Gurtner, 1989). They are especially effective in helping students who have missed several days to catch up.

Newer tutorial programs are more complex and flexible. They provide further instructional assistance based upon student inquiries and use graphics to demonstrate a point. In addition, the branching programs used are more involved. The computer not only notes that an answer is wrong, but also depending upon the type of incorrect answer, directs the student to a different remedial subprogram. Just as in the area of drill, computerized tutorials now use more flexible and effective strategies.

Drill and practice software and tutorials are especially useful since they allow students to proceed at their own pace, provide flexibility, and can be designed to be entertaining and interesting. These programs provide one method of helping students keep up with their work and catch up if they are behind.

S U M M A R Y

1. Risk involves the probability that a child will develop psychopathology or a disability. A population may possibly be at increased risk if a greater percentage of that population than the general population develops a disability. A population may be at risk even though a majority of that population develops in an average manner. Risk factors may be additive or multiplicative.

2. Poverty is a significant risk factor for the development of disabilities. About 21 percent of all American children live in poverty. Single parents with young children are statistically more likely to live in poverty than children of two-parent families. Divorced and never-married teenage mothers are very likely to live in poverty.

3. Risk factors before birth include drug usage by the pregnant woman or fetal exposure to disease. Mothers who smoke are more likely to give birth to lower-weight infants, and the children of smokers are more likely to develop disabilities. Drugs such as marijuana and heroin are also related to disabilities. Pregnant women who use cocaine are more likely to give birth to low birthweight infants, and many of these infants have medical problems. They are frequently more irritable and do not respond to the human voice or face. The care these infants receive after birth is crucial to whether they will improve. Often the parents continue taking the drug, and the child is exposed to extreme poverty, poor parenting practices, and a chaotic home situation.

4. Child abuse is a major societal problem. To understand abuse, the characteristics of the parents, child, and situation must be taken into account. Sexual abuse is the least-reported type of abuse. Psychological or emotional abuse involves various actions, including those of rejecting, isolating, terrorizing, ignoring, and corrupting. Many parents who physically abuse their children can be helped to stop abusing them.

5. The percentage of single-parent families has increased greatly in the past thirty years. Children of single-parent families are at greater risk for developmental difficulties and are less likely to complete high school.

6. Children's immediate reaction to divorce involves anger, depression, and guilt. Normally, children recover from the initial shock after a year or so, but the long-term effects of divorce can be serious if parents continue to argue, if serious financial problems exist, and if social supports are unavailable.

7. Teenage pregnancy is a widespread problem for everyone concerned. Infants born to teenage mothers have more health problems, and teen mothers are more likely to drop out of school. Teenage mothers do not tend to engage in behaviors that would optimize the child's development.

8. Most homeless families are headed by mothers, many of whom have experienced serious disruptions in their early lives. Homeless children experience many more health problems, developmental problems such as lags in language development, and psychological problems such as depression and anxiety, compared with children who are poor but housed. The Stewart B. McKinney Homeless Assistance Act is an important federal law creating programs to help people who are homeless. Homeless families need permanent, affordable housing and intensive psychological and social services.

9. Children often cope well with a single stressor, but when exposed to multiple stressors they develop stress-related problems. Some children

are stress-resistant or resilient. These resilient children show a strong social orientation and are flexible and more adaptable. They tend to be active in after-school activities and use better problem-solving strategies than other children. Many of these children have a particular ability that allows them to get attention for positive behavior. A good parent-child relationship can be a buffer against the negative consequences of stress. Children who take care of others are more resilient as well.

Children from Minority Groups in Special Education

CHILDREN FROM MINORITY GROUPS IN SPECIAL EDUCATION

TRUE-FALSE STATEMENTS

See below for the correct answers.

1. African-Americans form the largest minority group at the present time.
2. Generally, African-American, Hispanic-American, and Native American youth are overrepresented in special education programs for children with mental retardation and behavior disorders.
3. The consensus is that after a child whose primary language is not English has lived in the United States for five years or more, the child may be tested in English.
4. Determining whether the academic difficulty experienced by a child with limited English proficiency is due to a learning disability or to the child's language abilities is relatively easy.
5. Familiarity with the test examiner (person administering the test) is more important for children from minority groups than for children from the majority culture.
6. The percentage of children of migrant workers who receive special education services is much greater than the percentage of children in the general population receiving such services.
7. Multicultural education has one meaning that is both recognized and accepted by educators across the country.
8. Although multicultural education is an important concern for general educators, it has little meaning for educators who work mostly with children with disabilities.
9. Fewer parents from minority group backgrounds attend IEP conferences than parents from the majority culture.
10. Bilingualism leads to cognitive difficulties and academic problems.

Answers to True-False Statements
1. True.
2. True.
3. False. See page 341.
4. False. See page 342.
5. True.
6. False. See page 354.
7. False. See page 360.
8. False. See page 362.
9. True.
10. False. See page 369.

The Changing Racial and Ethnic Scene

Today, one in every four Americans is a member of a minority group (Bradley, 1991; Statistical Abstract, 1994). African-Americans form the largest minority group, accounting for about 12 percent of the population. However, the Hispanic population grew by 53 percent during the 1980s and now comprises 9 percent of the nation. By the year 2000, Hispanic-Americans will be the largest ethnic minority as well as the youngest ethnic minority group (Fracasso & Busch-Rossnagel, 1992). African-American and Hispanic-American youth now constitute about 27 percent of the current child population but will comprise about 33 percent of the child population in the year 2010 (SRCD, 1991).

The number of Asians and Pacific Islanders in the United States doubled in the 1980s. In 1950, less than 1 percent of the country was counted by the census as something other than white or black. In 1990, the count was more than 7 percent (*Newsday*, 1991).

The population of the United States will change dramatically in the first half of the next century. A much higher percentage of people in the United States will be members of minority groups, especially African-American, Hispanic-American, and Asian-American.

Minority Group Status and Special Education

This chapter is devoted to children from minority groups with special needs for a number of reasons. First, a disproportionate number of minority group children are diagnosed as having a disability (U.S. Department of Education, 1993). This fact raises important questions concerning assessment and placement practices (Benavides, 1988).

Second, if teachers and other professionals working with minority group students and their parents are to be effective, they must have a solid understanding of the cultural background of the children they are teaching. Without that cultural appreciation many misunderstandings take place. Ford (1992) suggests that teachers working with children with special needs from minority groups have to explore their own attitudes toward various cultures. Teachers also require accurate information regarding the values, communication patterns, and parental attitudes toward disabilities and schooling of the families they are working with. Teachers must acquire an appreciation of the differences both between and within cultural groups, understand which interactions are effective, and apply multicultural perspectives to special educational concerns.

Third, both Hispanic-American and Asian-American children often speak a primary language other than English. The difficulties in assessment and instruction when a student does not speak English well continues to be a source of challenge. These children have to negotiate not only a difficult school environment, but also an environment in which a not-so-familiar language is spoken.

Finally, educators need to develop ways of teaching all children, including children in special education, about the cultural traditions of the many groups that comprise America in the 1990s. Unfortunately, this multicultural education is the source of much controversy today.

This chapter will focus on five specific areas of interest: assessment; the need to understand the cultural background of minority group families; the importance of multicultural education to the child with special needs; particular challenges in working with parents from minority groups; and issues relating to bilingual education.

Overrepresentation of Minority Groups in Special Education

Evidence points to the overrepresentation of children from minority groups in many programs for children with disabilities (Ramirez, 1988). As will be discussed in detail in Chapter 11, they are also underrepresented in programs for the gifted. Many studies confirm a general numerical imbalance in the percentage of minority group youth diagnosed as having mental retardation or manifesting a behavior disorder (Ortiz & Polyzoi, 1988; Antiles & Trent, 1995).

Listing the possible reasons for this phenomenon is easy, but ranking them in importance is difficult. Children from minority groups are much more likely to be raised in poverty, have poor health, be raised in crowded and sometimes crime-ridden environments, and be raised in young single-parent families, which may place them at risk for developing mild disabilities (see Knitzer & Aber, 1995; Kramer, LaRue, & Gergen, 1995).

In addition, children who belong to some minority groups have a long history of discrimination and powerlessness. Their relationships with the dominant group are less than satisfying. They are also more likely to have a culture that does not match the values, structure, and instructional techniques used in schools. Their differences in expression, behavior, culture, and language are often seen as deficits rather than differences, creating an atmosphere that sometimes lacks respect (Poplin & Wright, 1983). Many immigrants find themselves in an alien culture whose values and procedures are different from those they remember in their native land. Adjusting to these changes is very difficult.

Assessment Issues

Accurate evaluation and assessment are necessary if students with special needs are to be served adequately. The issues surrounding assessment and culture are very complicated. Some are essentially psychometric and involve the interpretation of data on the validity and reliability of various tests. Other issues are more conceptual and relate to just how to evaluate children from a different culture in an equitable manner.

Each exceptionality, such as learning disabilities, hearing impairment, mental retardation, and giftedness, has its own assessment difficulties. Yet, all assessment and evaluation procedures become more complicated and create more concerns when the child being assessed has a different cultural background and perhaps speaks a different language.

The Uses and Abuses of Standardized Tests

While assessment is supposed to be a wide search for information from many sources, it frequently—some would argue too frequently—focuses on standardized testing (Figueroa, 1989). Most decisions about eligibility and placement are supported by the results of standardized tests. A general argument is made that when a child is referred and tested, psychologists are concerned about finding something wrong with the child that explains the child's lack of performance (Cummins, 1989). That is, little or no consideration is given for the possibility that the lack of performance might result from a difficulty in the school environment or the interactions between the school personnel and the student. For some, this means that if a student does not fit into the school, then the student must change. The student, not the school, has a difficulty that requires remediation.

Some believe this search for factors within the child allows the school to continue to function without making necessary changes in instruction and structure. In some cases, the cause of a difficulty may indeed be found within the teacher-student relationship and the structure of the school, rather than emanating from the child (Duran, 1989).

To what extent should standardized testing be used? If the system of evaluation is to be changed, more attention to other sources of information is necessary. Pre-referral committees are sometimes effective because they require an investigation into what is being done to help the child and issue suggestions for changes in the classroom.

While such a widening of the assessment process is certainly welcome, and in the case of cultural minorities absolutely necessary, not all difficulties arise from the classroom itself. Some children in all cultures require special education, and a system that always looks at the problem as emanating from within the child should not be replaced with one that completely excludes factors within the child. An ecological view that looks at the interactions between child and environment and takes internal, external, and interactional factors into account may improve the system of assessment (see Chapter 2).

Finally, standardized tests are easily criticized. Historically, they have been abused, and their weaknesses are often discussed. What is sometimes lost in the criticism is that the use of alternative sources of information gleaned from parents and informal means are often quite subjective and subject to bias.

Testing and Minority Group Youth

The argument concerning tests used in evaluations and whether they discriminate against children from minority groups has a long and bitter history. The use of intelligence tests with minority group youth and especially consideration of the issues of differential experience and cultural bias were discussed in Chapter 4. Here, other issues in testing, which relate to all standardized tests, not just intelligence tests, will be discussed.

Language and Testing

Many children from minority groups speak a primary language other than English. At the present time, a majority of Hispanic-American children come from homes in which the primary language is Spanish (Duran, 1989). Many Asian-

American immigrants also speak a language other than English. These children are both culturally and linguistically different.

The principle that children have to be tested in their native language as well as English, and that nonverbal intelligence scores can be used in assessment, was first enunciated in the 1970 case of *Diana v. State Board of Education* discussed in Chapter 1 (Figueroa, 1989). The case did not, unfortunately, resolve all the difficulties relating to language and testing.

Language and testing are intimately related. Most tests require verbal skills, either written or oral, and expression and comprehension of language are necessary for educational progress. Poor comprehension, limited vocabulary, and poor syntax may indicate a learning disability in some students, but for others they may simply indicate a lack of proficiency in English (Ortiz & Polyzoi, 1988).

A strong argument can be made that, in many cases, lack of language proficiency interferes with the assessment process and sometimes leads to incorrect assessment (Ortiz & Garcia, 1988). Numerous referrals are made for minority group students' speech and language differences, which may not reflect a need for special education (Poplin & Wright, 1983). Children who speak a language other than English may incorrectly be identified as having a disability because of their limited English proficiency (Benavides, 1988).

Consider this situation. Estella came to the United States from Mexico three years ago. Her progress is very slow, and the teacher refers her for evaluation, thinking that the child may have a learning disability. An intelligence test is considered as are tests of her achievement in math and reading. Should these tests be given in English or Spanish?

If you said English, how would you know if the child's scores actually measure her achievement or her language proficiency? If you said Spanish, at what point should a child be expected to be tested in English? If the child had lived in the United States for five years or ten years, would that have made a difference in your decision? When should the changeover be made?

The seemingly simple question of when a changeover to testing in English should take place has never been a major concern to school psychologists (Figueroa, 1989). One simple answer is to assess language proficiency before testing in English, but tests of language proficiency have their own technical problems and evidence indicates that one's primary language has a lasting impact on test scores. In addition, the difference between acquisition of social language, such as a conversation between two people on the street, and the more difficult acquisition of academic language, the language of learning and academic functioning, is notable. Too often, educators do not realize the extent to which second language learning affects achievement and test results.

Many children with limited English who are tested cannot show their abilities because their difficulties in English interfere with their performance. These tests become linguistic tasks rather than tasks of intelligence or achievement (Figueroa, 1989). Despite these findings, most children with limited English proficiency are tested predominantly in English (Ortiz, 1986).

Testing in the Primary Language

So why not test Estella in her primary language? This option also presents problems. For example, how would you do this? Should a test in English be translated, should interpreters be used, or should norm-referenced tests devised originally in

Mexico or in another Spanish-speaking country for Spanish-speaking youngsters be used? None of these alternatives have been shown to work well.

Translation is relatively easy, but the results are often poor. Years ago, when an earlier version of the Weschler Intelligence Scale for Children (the WISC-R) was translated into Spanish, some of the vocabulary took on a different difficulty level (Figueroa, 1989). A word in English may be more or less difficult than its equivalent in Spanish. In addition, a construct in one language may have a different connotative meaning in another language.

The use of an interpreter is certainly possible, but interpreters differ in skills and must receive proper training if they are to help administer assessment instruments. In addition, no rules have been devised for determining what the bounds of interpretation may be. Tests are very delicate instruments meant to be given in a particular manner. Explanations that might seem reasonable for a child with limited English proficiency may alter the test's validity.

Finding tests normed for Spanish-speaking children is not difficult. The testing market is worldwide. Such tests, though, are created for monolingual children in a Spanish-speaking culture, not children who have immigrated to America and now have two cultures and use two languages.

Testing children with limited English proficiency is very difficult. A problem arises as to whether students are experiencing difficulties caused by a learning disability or mental retardation, or because they have limited comprehension of English or are experiencing difficulties in negotiating two cultures with two languages (Gerstein & Woodward, 1994). Teachers most often refer Hispanic-American youngsters for attention/behavior problems, poor academic progress in general, poor progress in reading, and problems related to language. When a closer inspection is made, most referrals are related to limited English proficiency (Ortiz & Yates, 1988). Some of these difficulties are symptomatic of children who are second language learners.

Ortiz and Yates (1988) argue that before any other tests are given, some assessment of the child's language, both native and English, should be made. Unfortunately, few standardized tests are available for students with limited English proficiency (LEP), and some adaptations to the testing situation must be made if our most commonly used tests are to be administered. Adaptation is frequently done for many children from minority groups. Seventy percent of the intelligence tests given to Native American children are administered in a nonstandard manner because of language difficulties (Ramirez & Johnson, 1988). Any adaptation must be placed in the student's records; but as noted previously, these changes have a questionable effect on the validity of the test scores. Due to language difficulties, any score obtained should be considered minimal rather than maximal. Assessment should also be made with the help of personnel fluent in the dominant language and more frequent follow-up assessments are needed to follow the child's progress.

Most children who are referred and assessed are found eligible for special education. Yet, if language makes evaluation so difficult, evaluators need to be certain that only those who need special education services receive them. The prereferral process suggested by Ortiz and Garcia (1988) and shown in Figure 9.1 graphically illustrates the steps that can be used to make certain that the child actually requires referral. Questions to answer include those related to the curriculum, validation of the difficulty, efforts made to find the source of the difficulty, corrective measures taken, and program alternatives.

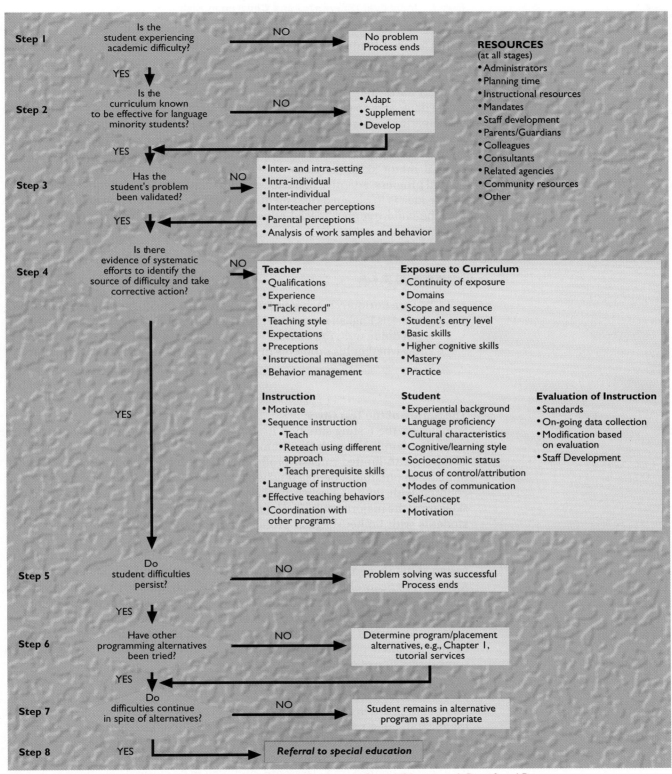

Step 1 — Is the student experiencing academic difficulty? → **NO** → No problem Process ends

YES ↓

Step 2 — Is the curriculum known to be effective for language minority students? → **NO** → • Adapt • Supplement • Develop

YES ↓

Step 3 — Has the student's problem been validated? → **NO** →
• Inter- and intra-setting
• Intra-individual
• Inter-individual
• Inter-teacher perceptions
• Parental perceptions
• Analysis of work samples and behavior

YES ↓

Step 4 — Is there evidence of systematic efforts to identify the source of difficulty and take corrective action? → **NO** →

Teacher
• Qualifications
• Experience
• "Track record"
• Teaching style
• Expectations
• Preceptions
• Instructional management
• Behavior management

Exposure to Curriculum
• Continuity of exposure
• Domains
• Scope and sequence
• Student's entry level
• Basic skills
• Higher cognitive skills
• Mastery
• Practice

Instruction
• Motivate
• Sequence instruction
   • Teach
      • Reteach using different approach
      • Teach prerequisite skills
• Language of instruction
• Effective teaching behaviors
• Coordination with other programs

Student
• Experiential background
• Language proficiency
• Cultural characteristics
• Cognitive/learning style
• Socioeconomic status
• Locus of control/attribution
• Modes of communication
• Self-concept
• Motivation

Evaluation of Instruction
• Standards
• On-going data collection
• Modification based on evaluation
• Staff Development

YES ↓

Step 5 — Do student difficulties persist? → **NO** → Problem solving was successful Process ends

YES ↓

Step 6 — Have other programming alternatives been tried? → **NO** → Determine program/placement alternatives, e.g., Chapter 1, tutorial services

YES ↓

Step 7 — Do difficulties continue in spite of alternatives? → **NO** → Student remains in alternative program as appropriate

Step 8 — **YES** → *Referral to special education*

RESOURCES
(at all stages)
• Administrators
• Planning time
• Instructional resources
• Mandates
• Staff development
• Parents/Guardians
• Colleagues
• Consultants
• Related agencies
• Community resources
• Other

FIGURE 9.1   Preventing Inappropriate Placements of Hispanic Students in Special Education: A Prereferral Process

Source: "A Prereferral Process for Preventing Inappropriate Placements of Culturally Diverse Students in Special Education" by A.A. Ortiz and S.B. Garcia, in *School and the Culturally Diverse Exceptional Student: Promising Practices and Future Directions* (p. 9) by A.A. Ortiz and B.A. Ramirez (Eds.), 1988, Council for Exceptional Children. Reprinted by permission.

If a referral is made and an assessment is required, a complete assessment must include input from parents, teachers, a school administrative representative, and other interested individuals. Baca and Cervantes (1989) suggest that such an assessment include data about classroom performance, primary language data, and observation and interview data assessing peer dynamics, group participation, classroom structure and organization, learning environments, and teacher-student interaction. A determination of whether alternative educational approaches are possible should also be made. Data should be obtained on perceptual motor skills, language proficiency, educational achievement, developmental progress, adaptive behavior, medical concerns, and cognitive functioning.

The idea is to obtain a total picture of the child's functioning and to be certain that the child requires special educational services and will receive the proper services.

SCENARIO

1 You are Enrique's teacher in third grade. His English is poor, and he is not doing well. You do not know whether his problems in class are due to his limited English proficiency or due to a learning disability. What steps would you take to determine whether a referral is necessary?

The Nature of the Test Giver

Sometimes, the testing situation itself may be cause for concern. Evidence indicates that familiarity with the examiner is a definite factor in test performance. Children with limited English proficiency score higher when tested by familiar rather than unfamiliar people (Fuchs et al., 1985). Familiarity is a greater factor for children with limited English proficiency than for children with good English skills from the majority culture. Unfamiliar examiners depress the performance of students with limited English proficiency but not students from the dominant culture.

This same pattern holds for African-American students as well. While Caucasian students performed equally well with familiar and unfamiliar examiners, African-American children scored significantly higher with familiar examiners (Fuchs & Fuchs, 1989). At least one hour of examiner-student interaction is required to overcome the familiarity factor and obtain reliable data. While familiarity is an important factor, unfortunately it is a double-edged sword. Familiar examiners often overestimate the child's performance when scoring tests, so some discussion of objectivity may be necessary.

The Meaning of Behavior

Another problem in assessment, especially of behavior disorders, revolves around the meaning of a particular behavior. Children are referred for assessment for a possible behavior disorder when teachers consider children's behavior unusual or disruptive to the educational process. However, these behaviors are shown in a very narrow context, the classroom, and may have cultural significance. For example, children in some cultures are socialized to be more active or less active, to talk more or less, and to self-disclose to different degrees (Dana, 1993). Misinterpretation of these behaviors can lead to serious misunderstandings. For example, when Native Americans reportedly took things off the teacher's desk, this behavior was sometimes interpreted as stealing. In some Native American cultures, though, people in authority are expected to share and provide for other people. Without this cultural understanding, a misinterpretation of the behavior results (Lewis & Ho, 1979). When assessing an individual for a possible behavior disorder, the assessment requires a determination of whether the behavior differs significantly from that shown by children in the same cultural group (Sugai, 1988).

A broad view of the total behavior of the child inside and outside the school is also necessary. For example, some difficulty in the teacher-student interaction might cause the behavior problem.

Assessment Reconsidered

Clearly, extra care must be taken when assessing children from different cultural backgrounds. The following suggestions outline steps to assure an accurate assessment:

1. *Be aware of the possible difficulties.* Being aware of the problems involved is the first step to better evaluation. Understanding the controversies and the weaknesses of various evaluation instruments leads to a more cautious assessment.
2. *Gather information from many different sources.* This most common suggestion can increase the validity of the assessment. A number of sources including parent and teacher interviews, as well as observations should be used to augment information from standardized instruments. This information should be taken seriously, not just gathered and left in the file.
3. *Look for possible reasons for a difficulty.* In an attempt to limit referrals, a look at the classroom context, the nature of the teacher-student relationship, the language sophistication of the child, and the functioning of the child in all classrooms should be undertaken. One difficulty often faced is the lack of any alternative programs available for poorly achieving children who do not have a disability. Prereferral committees can help identify problems at this stage and suggest alternatives.
4. *Obtain information useful for teachers.* Assessment should yield information that is not only useful for eligibility decisions but which helps teachers in their quest to provide better instruction. Assessments should offer information relevant to the teaching process.
5. *Make certain familiarity is taken seriously.* The nature of the testing situation is a concern. Children should be familiar with the types of questions to be asked and with the examiner.
6. *Counter bias in evaluation.* Be aware of the differences in the way children from various cultures act. Judging a child by the standards of the teacher's or administrator's ethnic or cultural group can lead to a narrow and biased approach.

Accurate evaluation and assessment are vital to the success of the special education process. If it is fair, unbiased, and based upon what is known about the cul-

THOUGHT QUESTION

2. If you had test results that say one thing and reports from parents and others that say another, which source of information would you be more comfortable relying on?

tural group, assessment can help everyone provide a better education for the child. Only when assessment contains information about the total functioning of the child can informed decisions about placement and changes in instruction be made, and evaluation work in the best interests of the child.

Understanding the Child's Culture: Caution Ahead

Having some knowledge of a child's cultural background is necessary if professionals are to educate children of various cultural backgrounds. This knowledge is needed in the assessment area, the teaching area, and when working with families. At first glance, learning about the culture of others and using this knowledge to improve instruction and build good working relationships with parents would appear to be easy. However, looking at a culture often means making generalizations; and the emphasis on culture, even if divorced from political implications, has many pitfalls attached to it.

Mistake Number One: Defining a Person by Group Membership

If you were told that someone was an African-American, Hispanic-American, or Native American, how much would you really know about the person? People's tendency to define others in terms of their culture and forget the individual creates many problems. Although understanding culture is important to appreciating the behavior and values of the person, one should not forget the individual.

When I attended graduate school, instructors and course material stressed the importance of treating an individual as a unique person, rather than as a member of a particular group. By appreciating the individuality of the child rather than reflecting on the child's racial or ethnic membership, many thought children would experience greater success in realizing their potential. Perhaps this assumption ignored the importance of group identification. Today, with the emphasis on group membership, people tend to group others by culture and to forget the individual. While some individuals identify closely with their racial and ethnic groups, not all do.

It would be truly unfortunate if the new appreciation of culture led to increased stereotyping. People usually think of stereotyping in terms of negative images, such as the stereotyping of Native Americans in the older movies. Yet, today when we try to understand a culture, we may be in danger of stereotyping everyone belonging to a particular group and overemphasizing group affiliation. For instance, if certain minority group cultures emphasize sharing, this emphasis does not mean that every person in the group does so. People then stereotype the individual as someone who should share because they believe the culture values this behavior.

The possible loss of an appreciation for individuality was noted by Smith (1977) when writing about culture and individuality with respect to the counseling process. Smith noted, "The recognition of cultural differences in the counseling of

THOUGHT QUESTION

3. *Is the emphasis on culture interfering with the appreciation of the child's individuality?*

Although an appreciation of culture is important, one should not forget the importance of the individual. Some people in minority groups identify strongly with their groups while others do not.

Blacks is one thing, but the stereotyping of these differences is quite another. When cultural, psychological and sociological characteristics are applied indiscriminately to all members of any one particular group, there is the potential danger that the promise of counseling will not be obtained—the promise that says that people will be seen as individuals first and secondarily as a member of any specific group" (1977, p. 391).

Mistake Number Two: Treating Minority Groups as Single, Unified Entities

People often view minorities as unified, monolithic wholes rather than as fragmented entities (Ryan, 1994). At times, the differences between subgroups in the minority culture are misunderstood. For example, Hispanic-Americans do not all belong to the same group. People from Cuba, Mexico, and Puerto Rico differ greatly. They often consider themselves to be Mexican, Puerto Rican, or Cuban rather than Hispanic.

Hispanic-Americans may share some elements of culture and attitudes, but they are certainly not identical. Various Asian groups such as Japanese, Vietnamese, and Chinese also differ greatly in attitudes, language, and background. This realization stresses the importance of understanding the varied nature of different cultures.

Mistake Number Three: Ignoring Acculturation

No pure forms of minority culture exist. Whenever a minority group comes into contact with the majority culture some change occurs. The change may take a few

Acculturation:
The transfer of culture from one ethnic group to another.

generations, but it is inevitable. This process is called **acculturation** (Birman, 1994). Acculturation occurs when contact between cultures affects the cultural patterns of one or both groups (Hernandez, 1989).

Acculturation has always occurred in the United States and certainly throughout the world. Since people from different minority groups live in the United States, their culture affects the dominant culture, while the minority group's culture has also changed.

Japanese parents living in the United States for some years were interviewed about their attitudes toward compliance and assertiveness and compared to American families (Kobayashi-Winata & Power, 1989). The children ranged in age from four through seven years. Parents were asked about the types of child behaviors that they were currently encouraging and discouraging in the areas of self-care skills, responsibilities, manners, politeness, and prosocial behaviors. The children's teachers were also surveyed.

Important differences were apparent in child rearing practices. Japanese parents were less likely to report the use of external punishments, such as sending the child to the child's room or using physical punishment. American parents were more likely to report using praise, whereas Japanese parents were more likely to report repeating commands and scolding their children. Japanese parents relied mostly on verbal commands, reprimands, and explanations to achieve compliance, while American parents were more likely to report supplementing these techniques with external punishments. However, the longer the Japanese parents lived in the United States the less they reported using verbal techniques to achieve compliance and the greater the tendency to use external punishments. Furthermore, American parents viewed assertiveness and compliance as positively related and believed that both indicated good behavior while Japanese parents did not. Japanese parents viewed assertiveness as a characteristic of a poorly behaved child. The longer the Japanese parents were in the United States, the more verbally assertive their children were rated by teachers and the less compliant and emotionally mature they were rated by their fathers (Kobayashi-Winata & Power, 1989).

Consider the Japanese parent and child in the United States surrounded by a culture that values individuality and sometimes nonconformity and does not emphasize dependence on others as much as traditional Japanese culture. The longer the child remains in the United States the more likely that some of this individuality and assertiveness will be learned by the child, which may cause some difficulty with parents who may value a different type of behavior.

Mistake Number Four: Assuming All Minority Group Members Are Poor

Painting a picture of all members of minority groups as being poverty stricken is quite inaccurate. About 40 percent of all Asian and Pacific Islanders have incomes of more than $50,000 per year. The African-American and Hispanic-American middle class is growing in number and many live in the suburbs, rather than the central city (O'Hare & Frey, 1992). Just as ignoring those who live in poverty would be wrong, educators would be just as incorrect to ignore the substantial numbers of minority group families who are not living in poverty.

It is a mistake to believe that all people from minority groups are poor.

At the same time, the influence of poverty and lack of education on child rearing and educational achievement should not be minimized. However, sometimes studies that deal with particular minority group members do not differentiate the effects of poverty and culture. Many studies find that parents who lack education do not create an optimal environment for promoting children's cognitive development, which is true across all ethnic groups. Therefore, researchers and evaluators must differentiate socioeconomic status from minority group status.

Mistake Number Five: Idealizing the Minority Group's Culture

Finally, no one should hold an idealized picture of one culture and denigrate another culture in the process. One culture should not be portrayed as pristine and pure, fighting against some bad dominating culture. If American culture values individuality more than some other cultures, this does not make American culture better or worse than any other culture. Differences have to be understood and appreciated. While the new appreciation of the importance of culture is to be applauded, we must be wary of the tendency of steeping cultures in myths and half-truths and adopting simplistic notions about the goodness or badness of a particular culture.

When speaking about different cultures, some generalizations are inevitable. The purpose of an explanation of culture is not to stereotype families, but to become aware of a set of attitudes, values, and beliefs that may be considered when interacting with people of a particular group (Salend & Taylor, 1993). In dealing with various groups, educators need to appreciate the situation in which that group now finds itself and to understand the group's history.

Focus on Minority Groups

The United States has many different minority groups. The largest groups and, therefore, the ones receiving the most frequent attention are African-Americans, Hispanic-Americans, Asian-Americans, and Native Americans. As some aspects of the cultures of these groups are discussed, keep in mind the cautions offered in the preceding sections.

African-Americans

African-American youth face a combination of social and environmental problems. A disproportionate number of African-American children live in poverty, poor housing, and crime-ridden areas (Edelman, 1985). Unemployment is high (Prater, 1992). Many children are born into single-parent families. These children are especially vulnerable to school failure, since they are more likely to live in poverty, their health is poorer, and their mothers are less likely to promote optimal development and are under more stress (Comer, 1985). Programs designed to overcome these problems are helpful, especially if they emphasize parental involvement (Comer, 1985). Many schools in primarily African-American neighborhoods experience funding problems and lack a safe and orderly environment.

The culture of African-Americans in the United States is influenced by three different group experiences. First, African-Americans share a common African heritage. They also share a heritage of living in the American society as slaves and then in segregated communities. Finally, many experience the influence of racism and poverty (Slonim, 1991).

No minority group family structure has been subjected to more analysis and as much criticism as the African-American family. Many of these criticisms have not been fair to black families. Actually, African-American families tend to be characterized as having one of three structures. A large number of basically middle-class or working class families which do not differ greatly in structure from majority families make up one group. Another group is poor African-Americans with a stable family structure and potential for economic and social mobility. The third is an African-American group of families with unstable structures, composed of people with poor job skills and insufficient education.

The multigenerational family structure, with grandmothers playing very important roles, is more common in African-American families than in most other cultural groups. Older children often help take care of their younger siblings and often have after-school child-care responsibilities. A strong work ethic can be found in African-American families. Adolescents often enter the work force before their Caucasian cohorts and help the family with their income.

Child-rearing practices also differ. Often, the emphasis is placed on a people orientation rather than an object orientation. For example, when African-American children reach for an object or surface, their attention is often redirected to the person holding them. The interaction between mother and child tends to be a rhythmic volley of speak and respond. Many African-American children assume responsibilities in the family early and are accustomed to a high-energy, fast-paced home with a great deal of concurrent stimulation. This environment

Grandparents play an important part in raising grandchildren in many minority groups, but it is most common among African-Americans.

sharply contrasts with the less personal, low energy classroom, which is not very stimulating.

Franklin (1992) suggests that affectively oriented teachers who use a more interpersonal and cooperative structure may be most effective. Cooperative learning, in which teams of students learn together, and peer and cross-age tutoring are often successful (see Chapter 2). Verbal interplay and stimulus variability are more in keeping with the culture. Using a combination of oral, visual, and more verbal expressiveness, focusing on real work and person-to-person interaction, is more in keeping with the cultural experience of many African-Americans (Franklin, 1992).

Education and academic achievement are valued in African-American families, but often the learning process is compromised by the effects of poverty and the historic lack of job opportunities available for African-Americans. When Stevenson and colleagues (1990) investigated both school achievement and attitudes toward achievement in African-American, Hispanic-American, and Caucasian families in Chicago, they found that African-American and Hispanic-American families placed a greater emphasis on and showed more concern about education than the Caucasian families they examined. African-American and Hispanic-American parents evaluated the children's academic abilities highly and held high expectations for their children. So the old idea that parents from minority groups just do not care as much about education is simply not true.

The family situation, though, cannot be isolated from the social context. Authorities, such as cultural anthropologist John Ogbu (1992; 1981; 1978), argue that understanding African-Americans in the school environment requires an appreciation of the historical relationship between African-Americans and the dominant society.

Ogbu argues that African-Americans have a long history of discrimination and lack of opportunity. African-Americans were excluded from almost all higher-paying jobs. The majority and some minority groups who have achieved view school as the gateway to these higher-paying jobs. But with the black community's history of negative experiences, the question becomes, "Why study if it will not lead anywhere?" Ogbu sees difficulties in achievement as caused by prior negative experience and a history of discrimination which now pervades the culture. Some African-American and Hispanic-American youngsters perceive the opportunities available in a different manner than both Caucasian and Asian-American students. Black and Hispanic youth often believe they will face a labor market that will not offer the rewards equal to the effort they put in and the educational credentials they may attain. A lack of motivation shown may then be a response to the belief that educational effort may not pay off.

Also, Ogbu claims that African-Americans growing up in the ghetto have found alternative strategies for becoming successful within the ghetto community where conventional ways have not led to success in the past. "Child-rearing techniques are functional, even though they differ from middle class techniques, and engender self-reliance, resourcefulness, the ability to manipulate people and situations, mistrust of people in authority, and the ability to 'fight back' or 'ward off' attacks" (1982, p. 425).

In addition, African-American youth may view school as a place where they are being asked to give up their culture and history; success in school may be related to giving up one's identity. Peers, in such an environment, frequently do not support achievement and may isolate and criticize such achievement.

Ogbu's ideas have generated quite a bit of discussion, but little empirical investigation. For instance, many argue that lack of motivation and effort is not the province of any minority group and is often considered a problem by teachers for many students who are not members of minority groups. Additionally, changes have occurred, and many students from minority groups are succeeding, though cultural attitudes change very slowly. Ogbu suggests that, to change perceptions, job opportunities within the general society must be opened up for minority group members so they can see for themselves the value of schooling.

In one study that relates to Ogbu's ideas, Steinberg and colleagues (1992) surveyed 15,000 adolescents, about one-third of whom were from various minority groups, asking two questions.

- *Question 1*: Suppose you do get a good education in high school. How likely is it that you will end up with the kind of job you hope to get?
- *Question 2*: Suppose you don't get a good education in high school. How likely is it that you will still end up with the kind of job you hope to get?

They found that students and parents from all the groups valued education. Students who believed that doing well in school pays off reported putting in more effort, and the effort led to better academic performance. The researchers found no significant differences, though, across ethnic groups in this belief. Adolescents in all groups believed that getting a good education enhanced their chances for success.

The researchers found definite group differences in the answers to the second question, however. Asian-American and Caucasian adolescents were much more likely than Hispanic-American and African-American students to believe that they were unlikely to get a good job if they received a bad education. What distinguished Asian-American and Caucasian students from Hispanic-American and African-American adolescents in this study was not their stronger belief that education is rewarded, but their stronger feeling that failure had negative consequences. Based on the results of this study, one would conclude that students who believe they can succeed without doing well in school will devote less energy to schooling, while those who believe in the negative consequences may put in more effort. The researchers found that the extent to which students believed negative consequences followed school failure was a better predictor of their school performance and effort than the extent to which they believed positive consequences came from school success.

Steinberg and colleagues also found that the peer group is a potent daily influence on behavior in school. Across all ethnic groups, youngsters whose friends support achievement perform better in school. For both white middle class students and Asian-American students, parent encouragement and peer encouragement converged. But for many African-American and Hispanic-American students, parents supported achievement, but their peer groups did not. African-American and Hispanic-American teens may be caught in a conflict between performing well in school and being popular with peers (Fordham & Ogbu, 1986). In this counter-school culture in some low-income African-American and Hispanic-

American communities, academic success is devalued by peers and education is not seen as a means of improving one's life (Steinberg et al., 1992; Slonim, 1991).

Not all studies find that the peer culture devalues educational achievement. In a recent study of African-American and Hispanic-American youth in Indiana, 85 percent of the students surveyed believed that their friends valued getting good grades in school (Schmidt, 1994). It is difficult to determine just how widespread any peer devaluation of educational achievement may be, but where it exists, these attitudes must be countered if educational achievement is to be maximized.

THOUGHT QUESTION

4. How can the effects of a peer group that does not value academic achievement be countered?

Hispanic-Americans

Hispanic or Latino (Hispanic is the English word, and Latino is the Spanish word) is a generic label for all people who are of Spanish origin. The majority of Hispanic-Americans are from Mexico, but many come from Puerto Rico, Central and South America, and Cuba. They share a common language, although some expressions used in one country may not be used in another. Most also share a common religion, Catholicism, although about 20 percent of Hispanic-Americans are Evangelical Protestants (Slonim, 1991).

Certain attitudes and family features are fairly common in Hispanic-American families. They emphasize sharing and cooperation rather than competition. Often the individualism and competition of American schools are in conflict with the child's learning at home (Delgado-Gaitan & Trueba, 1985). In addition, Hispanic-American families nurture a sense of family pride. Their time orientation is usually present tense, and they tend to believe in destiny, which often shows itself in a fatalistic attitude toward life. This tendency may translate into a view of disability as God's will.

The traditional role expectations demand that men be virile, somewhat aggressive, and protective of women—the well-known machismo attitude (see Bigner, 1994). Machismo has often been criticized, but it actually refers more to the male's responsibility in the family. Family loyalty often supersedes individual interests. Frequently, Hispanic-American mothers differentiate between the roles of mother and teachers, emphasizing the maternal role. Therefore, many Latino children do not get as much cognitive stimulation in their younger years. Consequently, although professionals emphasize the teacher role for parents of young children, it may not be readily accepted.

In the past, multigenerational family structure was typical, but this arrangement is somewhat less common today. The roles of mother and father are often clearly defined, with the fathers being more authoritarian and the mothers more involved in the child rearing. Generally, parents are more concerned with physical well-being and behavior than with the development of cognitive skills. Eldest children are frequently expected to assume child-care responsibilities.

The Hispanic-American community is buffeted by a number of problems. Obesity, diabetes, cigarette smoking, and alcohol abuse are more prevalent among Latinos than among Caucasian or African-American teenagers (Public Health Service, 1993). The clash of cultures may be one reason for these problems. Hispanic-American parents often feel less able to help their children at school than do African-American and Caucasian-Americans (Stevenson et al., 1990).

The greatest challenge in teaching Hispanic-American students with special needs is the understanding of how language affects every aspect of the special education process (Fradd & Correa, 1989). Individuals without disabilities may experience difficulty learning another language which is the dominant language of the adopted culture, but the presence of a disability creates an even more challenging situation. Earlier, the role of language in assessment was discussed and later in the chapter issues relating to bilingual instruction will be investigated.

Many Hispanic-American parents do not have much schooling themselves (Gerstein & Woodward, 1994). Some parents read to their children and discuss children's books with them, many others may not feel comfortable in this activity, and therefore the children do not have these experiences (Ruiz, 1989). The more contact Hispanic-American children and adolescents have outside the home and school with social groups, churches, scouting, and the business community, the greater their ability to use school-related language (Ruiz, 1989).

To help Hispanic-American children with learning disabilities, one curriculum, called the Ole Curriculum, suggests oral language activities that involve children interacting with peers to jointly solve problems, such as figuring out how to build a crystal rock garden. Programs are most effective if they use peer-oriented structures, focus on problem-solving activities that require language, and encourage children to use precise language as they clarify meanings and messages needed for successful completion of activities (Ruiz, 1989).

One group that requires special attention is migrant workers, most of whom are Hispanic. Children of migrant workers are at risk for developmental disabilities due to their high mobility, poverty, poor health and nutrition, poor housing, and cultural and linguistic differences (Baca & Harris, 1988). Statistics show that these children are under-served. About 1 percent of all children of migrant workers receive special education, far below the percentage of children served by special education in the general population (Salend, 1990).

One possible reason for this lack of service is the difficulties evaluating and serving children who move about as often as migrant-worker families. School attendance is frequently poor. Even when children are referred, they may not remain in the same school long enough to complete the evaluation process. The IEP may even be developed but may not follow the children to their new schools.

In 1969, the Migrant Student Record Transfer System was created to facilitate the transfer of student educational records from school to school. The National Commission on Migrant Education in 1991 criticized the system for being underused, slow, expensive, and missing information. Congress acted in 1994 to end funding for this system. Although states are still required to transfer records, no national system is now in place for doing so. The law leaves it up to the states to decide how to fill the need using available federal funds (Schnaiberg, 1995). Many states have systems that operate within that particular state, but a national system is required, and will need to be worked out in the near future.

Children of migrant workers often have gaps and discontinuities in their education. After all, a fourth-grade class in one school is probably not doing the exact same work as a fourth-grade class in another school. Migrant students entering the school may be isolated, and involving these students in the class is a challenge. Salend (1990) suggests that migrant students and their parents discuss their experiences and where they lived and map the family's migrations. Teachers can establish pen-pal systems and discuss the importance of migrant workers to the economy.

Educating migrant workers' children who have disabilities raises special issues as their mobility makes program management a challenge.

Migrant workers work long hours, and special programs must be instituted to involve parents of children with exceptional needs. Some programs train bilingual family members as educational paraprofessionals, teaching them general instructional skills that enable them to help develop the children's basic skills (McConnell, 1981).

Migrant workers should be encouraged to inform the school in advance of their next move. In addition, if a migrant student is suspected of having a disability, assessment must be carried out in an accelerated manner. Immediate consultations and, when appropriate, evaluations should take place. This acceleration increases the chance that the entire process will be completed before the child moves on to another school. Educators from different schools also need to cooperate with one another and discuss the IEP. Parents should be given materials to take to the new school (Baca & Harris, 1988). Because the education of migrant-worker children with disabilities presents many challenges, a greater amount of cooperation and coordination among professionals is necessary and active attempts must be made to include parents in the educational planning.

Asian-Americans

Immigrants from Asian countries are often used as examples of the traditional American success story and in many ways they are. Asian students are very well represented at the highest levels of achievement (Sue & Okazai, 1990). Males from all Asian countries are equal to or above the percentage of white males graduating from high school (Kitano & Daniels, 1988). Asian-American females don't fare as well, with the exception of Japanese and Filipino Americans, but some evidence notes change and improvement here.

In 1970, only three Asian-American groups were highly visible in the United States—the Japanese, Chinese, and the Filipino. In the last twenty years, Koreans, Pacific Islanders (Guam and Samoa), and Vietnamese have become more numerous (Huang, 1989).

About 13 percent of Asian-Americans live at or below the poverty level, somewhat greater than Caucasians but only slightly so. Some immigrants are well-educated middle or upper class professionals, while others have little education, are very poor, and speak little English.

The stereotypes of the Asian-American are mostly positive, but living up to the stereotype may be particularly difficult for those Asian-Americans who find standards difficult to attain. Just as in any other group, some Asian-American students do well in school, some do average work, and some do not achieve as well.

Asian-American students come from many different countries. The cultures of people from China, Korea, Japan, Cambodia, Laos, Viet Nam, India, and Pakistan differ. The differences in culture, including language, customs, and traditions, between two neighboring countries can be significant.

In one incident, Marianne Felice, a physician, asked a Vietnamese interpreter to talk to a Laotian youth. The Vietnamese interpreter "indignantly" announced that he was Vietnamese and "stormed away." Later the physician was told that if she had asked the Vietnamese interpreter to translate for a Cambodian patient it would have been worse, because these two countries have been at war for centuries (Felice, 1986; Olness, 1986).

The stereotype of the successful Asian student is positive but just as with any other group, some children achieve well, some average, and some poorly.

Appreciating the differences between these groups is crucial to understanding the behavior of people who come from diverse cultures. For example, in Thailand, when a person is angry at another person, the angry individual does not show it directly. Instead, the person may turn toward another object or person and scold it or the other individual. A teacher or doctor must then understand that the angry words directed toward a dog or a child may actually be directed at the teacher or doctor.

Many Asian-American children experience a very different child-rearing regimen compared to most other Americans. For instance, most non–Asian-American children sleep by themselves and have their own toys. American parents foster self-reliance, assertiveness, and speaking one's own mind. But Asian-American children, especially from the Pacific Rim, are taught to view their role within the society and the family in terms of obligations. Asian-American children are taught to think of the family first and to subjugate their own desires and concerns. For many Asian-Americans, individual behavior reflects either shame or pride on the family (Morrow, 1987).

Asian-American families stress the individual as secondary to the family. Anger and displeasure are to be avoided, and social customs demand strict adherence. Communication is often indirect, and outward displays of emotion are not encouraged, except with infants (Slonim, 1991). Touching, especially on the head, is considered highly inappropriate. Child-rearing practices in infancy and early childhood are indulgent, but become formal and demanding after five years. They encourage a commitment to hard work and education. Rote learning is common, and creative individual abilities are not always fostered.

Most Asian-American children are accustomed to a fairly structured environment and formal setting. They may not be familiar with open classrooms, the lack of structure in playgrounds, and even the friendliness of the teacher, which may lead to a variety of behaviors, including withdrawal or overexcitement due to a lack of understanding of the limits (Olion & Gillis-Olion, 1984).

Asian-Americans often show limited English proficiency, which may prevent them from completely entering mainstream American life. Working with the Asian-American child with special needs may be difficult because some communities view the disability in terms of family shame and do not want assistance from the outside world (Morrow, 1987). Disabilities such as severe emotional disturbances, mental retardation, or physical and sensory disabilities are sometimes seen in terms of a stigma and may be considered a punishment for sins. This attitude may prevent the delivery of services to the Asian-American child with special needs.

SCENARIO

2 A student in your class has just been diagnosed as having a learning disability. The child comes from Southeast Asia and is having a great deal of difficulty in class. You attend a meeting at which the team discusses ways of talking with the student's mother, who does not speak much English, about her child's academic difficulties. They ask you for advice since you have extensive dealings with the family. What would you do to prepare for the parent's arrival? How would you inform the parent of her child's learning disability?

Native Americans

More than 500 Native American tribal units are recognized by the federal government, and 200 distinct tribal languages are actively spoken (Brown, 1993). Although the Navaho tribe numbers about 165,000 and the Cherokee about 95,000, most tribes are much smaller, many averaging about 500 people (Brown, 1993). As with so many other minority groups, the average age of Native Americans is young, 20 years compared to 30 years for all other U.S. citizens (LaFramboise & Low, 1989). The category of Native American includes Alaskan Natives and Aleuts. The term "Native Americans" is replacing the term "Indians," but Native Americans often prefer tribal designations, for example, Lakota or Navaho.

Native Americans are often stereotyped by the news media and by movies that either show them in the old cowboys-and-Indian motif or idealize the Native American culture. American policy has waffled between warring against Native Americans until their numbers bordered on extinction and acculturating them with paternalistic policies (Lewis & Ho, 1979).

With so many tribes, a general Native American culture is difficult to define, but some commonalities do exist. Often, the familial and cultural ideals run counter to the dominant culture, perhaps to a greater extent than for any other minority group discussed.

For example, sharing is an important value that is learned very early, as it is in some other cultures. However, people in authority are supposed to share what they have (Lewis & Ho, 1979). Saving for the future, an ideal among the dominant culture (although not always practiced), is relatively unimportant. One's worth is measured by one's willingness and ability to share; therefore, the accumulation of wealth is not as respected (Slonim, 1991). Strong extended-family structures are common, although not as prevalent as years ago.

In many Native American cultures, the concept of time is less exacting and may involve morning or evening and not a specific hour. If a Native American is on the way to a meeting and a friend wanders past, the conversation may take precedence; sharing experiences is more important than punctuality.

Patience is a virtue that many Native American tribes teach. Sometimes, Native American children who have been taught to be patient may not seem competitive in the dominant society or even seem lazy since they have been taught to wait patiently for their turn that will come without having to be assertive.

Another frequent difference is eye contact. In some tribes and among some other minority groups, looking at someone directly, especially an authority figure, is a sign of rudeness. This behavior can be misinterpreted as a lack of attention by a teacher who does not understand.

Native American children are also frequently given choices, and teachers may be better off following this cultural practice and allowing children to have choices. Children often participate in adult activities (Pepper, 1976).

Native American children are also very sensitive to nonverbal communication, and if a teacher or counselor gives the impression of being busy, communication will not occur because they would be impolite to interrupt. Finally, interference in the affairs of others is not permitted (Youngman & Sadongei, 1974).

Native American and some Asian-American children may not ask questions or even respond, because they may consider it impolite or unnatural to set oneself apart from the group. Being part of the group and blending in are more important, even if it means denying knowledge (Nazarro, 1981). In fact, direct questions and personal information are shared only if others are willing to share. Anonymity and submissiveness are preferable to asserting one's individuality (Sattler, 1988).

Native Americans have many difficulties. One particular problem concerns health. Native Americans have a low life expectancy, and many die before age 45. Alcoholism is probably the greatest health problem and an estimated one out of three Native American deaths is caused by alcohol (*CQ Researcher*, 1992). Cirrhosis of the liver, due to excessive alcohol consumption, is three times more prevalent than in the rest of the U.S. population. One-fifth of all deaths among Native Americans results from injuries sustained in motor vehicles and other accidents, and alcohol is implicated in three-quarters of these accidents. Alcoholism is seven times as prevalent as in the general population. It is also a factor in homicide and suicide rates, which are much higher than in the general population (*The Economist*, 1993). (Suicide rates are double the national average.) Fetal alcohol syndrome is much more common than among the general population (Rosenthal, 1990). Native Americans are also more likely to smoke (Public Health Service, 1993). They also have the lowest standard of living of any ethnic group, high teen pregnancy rates, and the highest dropout rate of any ethnic group (LaFramboise & Low, 1989).

Another problem is high unemployment. The jobless rate approaches 30 percent on most reservations. Native American and Alaskan natives who are 25 years of age or older average 9.6 years of formal education, the lowest rate of any major ethnic group (Brod & McQuiston, 1983).

A cultural renaissance is taking place today with more people identifying with their Native American roots.

Today, interesting changes are taking place in the Native American community. A cultural renaissance is occurring, with many more people today claiming some connection to their Native American ancestors than in the past. Tribal bonds remain strong. In addition, a growing belief sees only economic improvement in the form of jobs as the solution to the problems experienced by Native Americans. The number of businesses owned by Native Americans increased 64 percent between 1982 and 1987, compared with a 14 percent general rise. Gambling and tourism are major businesses, but other industries such as crafts have been growing. Some major corporations have begun to buy products from Native American tribal industries. For example, Laguna Industries is a tribal-owned manufacturing firm that employs 350 people and markets its products to a number of major corporations. Laguna Industries built a communications shelter used by U.S. forces in the Gulf War (Fost, 1991). These accomplishments are just a beginning, however, and much remains to be done to improve the lives of Native Americans.

Cultural Pluralism: Multicultural Education

In the last decade or so, the way in which some educators and social scientists perceive American society has changed. At one point, the concept of the melting pot was popular, that is, minority groups melted into American society as they took on the values of the dominant culture. Today, because the melting pot seems not to explain our society anymore (if it ever did), many look at a culturally pluralistic society, one in which a number of cultural groups exist side by side. This

Multicultural education:
A general term referring to a multidisciplinary approach to education aimed at teaching students about the cultural heritage of various groups and the many contributions each group makes to society.

change in emphasis implies that educational practice should be modified by the new demographic and cultural realities in the United States (Hilliard, 1980).

One of these modifications is the provision of what is called **multicultural education** to students, including students receiving special education services. Multicultural education means different things to different people (Ryan, 1994). Some see it as a way of providing more information about the contributions of minority groups. Still others emphasize the importance of reinterpreting history and the American experience in terms of how it affects different groups, while another group sees it in terms of encouraging a wider, global view of society. Finally, the multicultural perspective has a political dimension as a movement that seeks to empower minorities. Although everyone wants to include some material about culture and ethnic diversity in the curriculum, no agreement has been reached on how this should be accomplished.

Sleeter (1993) suggests five possible approaches to multicultural education. The first approach, called *teaching the exceptional and culturally different*, aims at helping students in minority groups to "make it" in society as it currently exists. Culturally relevant materials are used, and programs are instituted to bring students up to grade level. The emphasis is on changing the educational opportunities for minority students with less emphasis on the majority student.

The *human relations approach* fosters positive interpersonal relationships among members of diverse groups in the classroom and strengthens the self-concept and self-esteem of children. Advocates of this approach are concerned with how children feel about one another and how they relate to each other (Winter, 1994/1995). Teaching about cultural differences and similarities, avoiding stereotyping, and noting how every group contributes to American society are in-

What does multicultural education mean to you? One problem is that the term has so many meanings and connotations. Defining specifically what it means is the first step in any discussion of these programs.

corporated into the curriculum. Cooperative learning is often used to promote student relationships. Often, ethnic fairs and special celebrations are held to introduce culture to students. The emphasis is on attitudes and feelings. Those who use this approach see intergroup problems in terms of stereotyping and misunderstandings and view positive contact and information as necessary.

Single-group studies focus on particular groups, such as women or people with disabilities. They raise consciousness about how each group experiences history, its culture, its contributions, and how it relates to the dominant society. This approach requires an in-depth study of a particular group or culture.

The approach Sleeter actually calls *multicultural* reconstructs the entire educational process to promote cultural pluralism. Curriculum content is reorganized around knowledge of various cultures. Students are actively encouraged to analyze life situations and encouraged to use their native language, and multilingual acquisition is fostered for all students. Students debate issues from the point of view of different groups. The academic emphasis is on achievement, and the entire curriculum is rewritten to emphasize multicultural understandings, often drawing on content developed through the single group and human relations perspectives.

The last approach, the *multicultural/social reconstructionist approach*, combines the multicultural approach with an activist component. It emphasizes everything in the multicultural approach, but also focuses on social action. Because of its emphasis on social action, it contains a political facet.

These programs certainly differ in their emphases. However, no program is completely pure, and programs labeled as using one of these approaches may borrow from other approaches.

Educators have voiced some concerns about multicultural education. To some educators, multicultural perspectives seem to dwell solely on the negative societal experiences of minority groups and especially their school experiences (Garcia & Pugh, 1992). Others fear that it will serve to fragment American society (Krauthammer, 1990; Schlesinger, 1994). Still others, even some who are excited at the prospect of multiculturalism, fear that indignation and anger rather than rigorous academic criticism will be taught (Winkler, 1990). Sometimes, the tendency is to go from a denial of the role of minorities to a belief that everything can be traced to the minority experience, and some tempering of the rhetoric on both sides would be welcome (Price, 1992). Indeed, sometimes in the rhetoric, the purposes of multiculturalism are lost.

The emphasis on cultural pluralism has led to changes in curriculum. A greater emphasis has been placed on showing how history has affected each group. For instance, Columbus was an explorer but the meaning of Columbus to Native Americans is quite different than to other groups. A person of European ancestry may see Columbus as the explorer who opened up the New World to settlement by Europeans eventually leading to the establishment of the United States and other countries in the Western Hemisphere. Native Americans may see Columbus as the explorer whose voyages ushered in the era of European encroachment on Native American lands and the wars that would bring many tribes to the brink of extinction. A recent movement to read books written by authors from minority groups emphasizes the minority experience in America and fosters appreciation for the accomplishments of scientists and business and community leaders from minority groups.

THOUGHT QUESTION

5. *Which approach to multicultural education, if any, would you prefer?*

A greater appreciation of different cultural practices and beliefs has also been emphasized. This change is certainly welcome, but *all* cultures must be studied and appreciated, not just the culture within the school. For example, students in heavily Hispanic-American areas who study Hispanic culture are learning to appreciate it and be proud of their heritage. However, to be truly multicultural, these students should also be exposed to African-American, Native American, Asian, Jewish, and a number of other cultures as well as the dominant culture. If one of the goals is to encourage students to learn to communicate and interact with people of different cultural backgrounds, then education must be truly multicultural and emphasize that children learn similarities as well as differences between cultures (Hernandez, 1989).

Multicultural education is often thought of in terms of the education of children in urban areas. However, it is necessary for all children. Students in rural areas or communities in which the children may not come into contact with other children from one or more of the principal minority groups also need some multicultural education. These students require an understanding of the cultures of the citizens in other parts of the country so that they may better understand the world outlook and challenges faced by children from various minority group cultures. Such education minimizes stereotypes and also paves the way for children to accept others when they do come into contact with children from various minority groups. The lack of opportunity to meet students from different cultures is a problem faced by children who live in urban areas as well, who, for example, may never have met a Native American.

SCENARIO

3 You teach at a school whose student body is one-third African-American, one-third Hispanic-American, and one-third Caucasian. Tensions run high between the three groups who tend to stay separate. Both between and within each group a great deal of racial and ethnic name calling takes place. One professional suggests that the school adopt a multicultural program, but does not offer much in the way of specifics. You are asked to develop such a program. Briefly describe the kind of program you would develop.

Multicultural Education and the Student in Special Education

Multicultural education in all its varied forms is influencing what children receiving special education services are learning. Children with learning disabilities, hearing impairments, or orthopedic disabilities have the same need to understand their own culture and that of others. Children with disabilities must learn to live in a pluralistic culture. The materials may have to be reworked so they are appropriate for children with various disabilities, though. For example, children with mental retardation may require easier, but still age-appropriate materials.

Some argue that students in special education first need to focus on activities that help them develop a more positive understanding of their own heritage. Ford and Jones (1990) observed a class of students who had developmental disabilities. Most of these students were African-American and showed negative attitudes about themselves. They sometimes teased and baited each other using racially-oriented name calling.

The researchers provided students with information about the historical experiences of and contributions made by African-Americans. A number of activities allowed students to get involved, such as drawings concerning the voyage of slaves to the Western Hemisphere and role-playing various scenes. All written materials were developmentally appropriate and interesting. Students actively worked on a book of feelings that included information and student reactions and interpretations of their studies. Working on this project promoted a sense of unity. The book was laminated and each child was given a copy. The authors note that the incidence of name calling was greatly reduced, and some of these students chided their nondisabled peers when they heard such statements made in the halls or classrooms.

While concentrating on the question of multicultural education for students, multicultural education and awareness for teachers ought not be forgotten (Pang, 1994). For instance, some people question whether teachers who work with African-American students understand the interests, dialect differences, and values of African-American students (Ford, 1992). Teachers' attitudes toward their students are partially shaped by the stereotypes and misconceptions they may hold of the children's cultural group, so exploring one's own attitudes is important. If teachers do not believe that Hispanic-American or African-American parents value education or believe that students from particular groups have little interest in education, then their behavior will show this, and teachers will not expect or receive high achievement from their students. Understanding the history and differences both within and between groups leads to a clearer understanding of the cultural environment in which students find themselves. Such education also encourages the incorporation of multicultural perspectives into the curriculum, and may decrease student-teacher misunderstandings and encourage effective student-teacher interaction (Ford, 1992).

Working with Parents

Parents are an integral part of the entire special education process from evaluation to placement to the formulation of the IEP. Two roles belong specifically to parents. The first is giving or withholding consent, while the second is collaborating with the teacher in formulating the IEP. Regulations require parents to be invited to attend a conference for this purpose. Parental attendance, though, leaves much to be desired; parents from minority group children attend IEP conferences less often than parents from the majority culture (Harry, 1992b).

The issue of parent participation is more acute for minority group parents of children with special needs. Parents from many minority group cultures are not comfortable when dealing with the schools or other governmental institutions (Harry, 1992a). Minority group parents tend to be less knowledgeable about and less involved in their children's special education (Lynch & Stein, 1987). Many parents have little reason to trust the institutions, since their experiences have not been especially positive. In addition, poverty and the parents' lack of education may compound the problem.

In the best of circumstances, the parent-school partnership might be one-sided. As noted in Chapter 2, the general problems of an unequal relationship and the unfortunate situation of blaming the parents are problems that require some attention for all parents, regardless of whether the parent is a member of a minority group.

Many people, especially those belonging to the majority culture, have had a good relationship with the school. They feel involved, understand the nature of the classifications used, and generally have the ability to take advantage of the services offered. Unfortunately, many minority group parents do not feel comfortable in the school and may feel intimidated.

Most strategies and programs used to encourage parental involvement are designed to serve families who are familiar with English, are basically middle class, and possess a cultural perspective that makes it easier for them to participate in the programs (Lynch & Stein, 1987). For many minority group parents these qualifications hardly apply. Some Hispanic-American parents come from countries in which the roles of parents and schools are sharply divided. Some parents come from countries in which schools provide no special services, maintain no complex records, and offer no identification and assessment procedures. Consequently, these procedures seem strange and new to them (Lynch & Stein, 1987). Some lower-income Hispanic-American parents view the school system as an impersonal bureaucracy run by professionals whom they do not have the right to question (Inger, 1993). Some parents from minority groups have had negative experiences with schools during their youth and maintain resentments into adulthood (Petersen & Warnsby, 1993).

Parents with limited English skills face other difficulties. Consider the plight of parents with limited English whose child is being evaluated for eligibility to receive special education services. The parents are given information in their native language but may be intimidated by the experts that surround them and the technical jargon used. Often, Hispanic-American parents show less familiarity with schools than parents of other minority groups (Stevenson et al., 1990). These parents may experience difficulty in dealing with the special education process and feeling like they are a part of it.

Yet another challenge involves the inability to translate concepts from English into another language. A particular term may have a different connotation in their native language. For example, such terms as learning disability, instructional strategies, and advisory committee may defy translation and complicate school-parent communication (Lynch & Stein, 1987). Some Asian and Native American languages may not even have a written form of language, and some people may not be literate in their own language.

Parents of various cultures often see disabilities somewhat differently. A study of Puerto Rican parents' understanding of various disabilities found constant linguistic confusion (Harry, 1992b). For example, mental retardation has the connotation of mental derangement (being crazy) among some Puerto Rican parents, and the term *handicap* would apply only to people whose competence is severely impaired.

This demonstrates the importance of understanding how parents might perceive a particular diagnosis. Some terms must be differentiated from others and explained carefully. The parents of many of the children in Harry's study did not see their children as having mental retardation, especially since their child was in the fifth grade and they never finished the third grade. The term *learning disability* was more accepted and parents understood it, but as a difficulty not a disability.

Some parents may see a disability as a reflection on the family or the family's character, as a stigma, and try to hide it. Understanding how people from different cultures view disabilities can help teachers explain terms in a manner more compatible with the cultural understanding of the disability.

Some African-American parents may not trust the schools and feel that African-American children are overrepresented in special education programs. African-American parents may disagree with the classification of their children. They may be aware of the possibilities of bias in assessment and may not consider their children slow.

Sometimes, parents who do not seem to be involved are considered apathetic. However, research shows repeatedly that parents of all groups are interested in their children. What teachers see as disinterest or apathy is often a mask for parental mistrust and withdrawal from participation (Harry, 1992a). In other cases, parents are simply overwhelmed by their problems (Harry, 1992b).

Some rather practical problems can also be responsible for lack of participation. For example, among African-American and Hispanic-American parents, fundamental difficulties with scheduling, transportation, and child care were cited as reasons why they could not attend conferences (Harry, 1992b; Lynch & Stein, 1987). In addition, poor knowledge of their rights and the process itself caused confusion.

In other cases, the formality of the process, which was instituted for the protection of the children, can backfire. The impersonal, legal communication with its emphasis on formal written documents may alienate people from some ethnic groups, such as Hispanic-Americans (Harry, 1992a). When paraprofessionals framed the child's difficulties in more personal terms and in a more informal situation, communication between school and family improved. The use of technical language, the greater acceptance given the formal conveyance of information from a higher-ranking person, and the tendency for teachers and professionals to totally set the agenda potentially cause a lack of active participation.

SCENARIO

4 You are a teacher in a largely minority community. As in any school, some of the children have special needs and require special education services. Yet, the number of parents who attend IEP conferences and other meetings is small, and most parents do not seem as involved as most professionals believe they need to be. You head a committee whose purpose is to improve the participation of all parents but especially those whose children have special needs in the school. What steps could be taken to increase the involvement of parents in their children's school?

THE CLASSROOM

Making the School and Classroom User-Friendly for Parents from Minority Group Cultures

Teachers can do much to make the school and their classrooms more friendly and to encourage participation by minority group parents. The following are some suggestions for encouraging parental involvement.

1. Listen to what parents say about their children and seriously consider the importance of such information.	**Why?** PL 94-142 intended parents to be involved, and a thorough assessment should include a social history given by the parents. Parents may offer information that is unexpected, revealing the talents and general functioning of their children. In addition, parents from minority groups may not believe the school is interested in their perspective of the child and with their difficulties. Asking parents questions designed to elicit positive statements about their children as well as noting their problems can increase a parent's confidence that educators are interested in the child's progress.
2. Encourage parents to act as teachers' aides.	**Why?** When parents become teachers' aides they feel more connected to the school (Harry, 1992b).
3. Establish parent advisory committees.	**Why?** Such committees may serve as mediators between the school and the community as well as a source of information. Parents can elect their own representatives. These committees may follow up parent contacts, provide support for conferences, and boost parental participation.
4. Conduct studies of parental attitudes and concerns to determine the needs within the community.	**Why?** Developing informational and training programs based upon what parents identify as their difficulties can help to minimize the challenges of the school-parent relationship and to provide the most effective education possible for the child.

5. Provide inservice education to school personnel describing cultural and linguistic differences, and sensitizing teachers to the values and beliefs of the families they serve (Lynch & Stein, 1987).	**Why?** A thorough understanding of the cultural and linguistic differences can help school personnel better appreciate the students whom they serve.
6. Encourage successful teachers to share some of their ideas with their colleagues.	**Why?** Some teachers are especially successful in teaching children from particular groups. These teachers may help their colleagues by sharing their techniques and understandings.
7. Invite community leaders and people involved in cultural groups and community organizations to participate in school activities and planning.	**Why?** Community leaders may be helpful in developing strategies for involving parents, and their backing may improve attendance at programs. Their understandings of community needs are especially helpful in planning appropriate programs as well as increasing acceptance of such programs.
8. Disseminate information about the special education services through community organizations such as churches and business establishments (Lynch & Stein, 1987).	**Why?** The school's usual methods of communication may be ineffective. Other ways to communicate with the community must be found.
9. Involve the extended family in the special education process when appropriate.	**Why?** Some cultural groups may have extended family systems which make grandparents, older siblings, and other relations integral parts of the family (Inger, 1993). These people may act as interpreters or help students with their work.
10. Investigate the possibility of home visits.	**Why?** A home visit is sometimes an effective, although a time-consuming, way to evaluate a child's level of functioning and factors that may influence various behaviors. School personnel may learn which families need babysitting, transportation, or other services in this way.

11. Arrange personal face-to-face conversations when possible.	**Why?** Impersonal flyers, announcements, or even radio broadcasts may be ineffective even if they are in the language of the people to be served. People usually respond more positively to a personal conversation.
12. Make the school and classroom less intimidating. For instance, posting welcome signs in many languages, having interpreters available, and meeting with parents in a less formal atmosphere, perhaps during celebrations, may encourage parental involvement.	**Why?** Some parents of children from minority groups may be intimidated by the school and the teacher. A more open atmosphere might stimulate parental communication and involvement.
13. Provide the practical help necessary for parents to be involved. If parents cannot attend meetings during the day, schedule evening meetings. If parents need transportation, have the school provide it.	**Why?** Research evidence shows that many minority group parents simply cannot attend important meetings because of practical reasons that can be addressed by the school.

The parent from a minority group with a child in special education faces a number of challenges. The culture and history of the group may increase a parent's suspicions, and the intimidating nature of the school may decrease parental willingness to attend meetings. But actions can be taken and services provided by the school to reduce these problems, to actively encourage parents to help create an effective parent-school partnership, and to make it more convenient and thereby more likely that parents will attend meetings and programs.

The Bilingual Puzzle

When discussing Hispanic-American and Asian-American children, one area of great concern is learning English. Children with disabilities often experience even greater difficulty in learning English as a second language. Children who have limited English proficiency (LEP) may also not be identified as gifted as often as they should be. Their language differences may interfere with accurate identification.

No one knows the precise number of children who have LEP, but the estimate is 1.9 million (U.S. Department of Education, 1993). About 78 percent of all LEP students are Spanish speaking, and about 9 percent speak an Asian language. If we hypothesize that the same percentage of LEP children have a disability as are found in the general population, then about 200,000 LEP students require such services.

The issue of second language learning is important both for children with and without disabilities. A person with a heavy accent or nonfluent English may need help in order to be able to participate fully in vocational and social activities, but this characteristic cannot be considered a language or speech disorder. Yet, children must learn to use English if they are to succeed in American society. Children with disabilities have the same need to learn English, and so the questions surrounding bilingualism and second language learning are important issues in educating these children.

An estimated 91 percent of all LEP elementary school children come from impoverished backgrounds (U.S. Department of Education, 1993). Their success in climbing out of poverty depends on their academic success and partly on learning standard English.

At first glance, knowing more than one language seems like a great advantage. However, research in the 1950s indicated that bilingual children did poorly in school and experienced poor language development in both languages (Segalowitz, 1981). These studies have been criticized for their poor methodology and the questionable testing devices used. Often, they did not control for economic status, and what they actually found was *not* that bilingual children had more difficulties but that children in poverty situations found school more difficult. In other words, many of these early studies confused poverty and bilingualism.

A substantial change has occurred on the issue of bilingualism. In one review of the literature, McLaughlin (1978; 1977) found no clear evidence that bilingualism leads to intellectual or cognitive problems in school. Some of the difficulties encountered by bilingual students are not due to their bilingual nature but to poverty, poor housing, lack of intellectual stimulation, and other socioeconomic variables (Diaz, 1985). In fact, when the effects of socioeconomic status are controlled, evidence shows that bilingual children score well on verbal and nonverbal intelligence tests and demonstrate more cognitive flexibility (Segalowitz, 1981). These children enjoy advantages in concept formation and creativity as well (Padilla et al., 1991). Some argue that this is so only in a balanced bilingual situation in which both languages are encouraged and taught and the child is allowed to develop full competence in both languages (see Padilla et al., 1991). However, bilingual students are often not given any opportunity to continue studying their native language, and their knowledge of it may be relatively poor (Crawford, 1987). This situation is unfortunate, because some authorities believe that continuing study in the child's native language is necessary for the child to adequately learn English (Collier, 1989).

What conclusions can be made, then, concerning the bilingual child? First, bilingualism, itself, does not cause any difficulties, and some evidence even indicates that bilingual children have certain advantages over their monolingual peers. Second, poverty and bilingualism are often confused. Many minority groups in the United States who speak a language other than English suffer from the degradations of poverty, including poor self-concept, disillusionment, discrimination, poor opportunity, and so forth. Perhaps the clash of cultures and the effects of poverty rather than bilingualism actually causes many of the problems cited by teachers in the public schools.

Although old ideas about the psychological consequences of bilingualism have been reevaluated, children also need to learn English. If children leave school knowing mathematics, science, and social studies but functioning poorly in such language-related areas as reading, writing, and speaking, their prospects for educational advancement and jobs will be limited. Many programs have been instituted to teach English to children whose primary language is something other than English.

Two Approaches to Bilingual Education

Many people do not understand the differences between the experience immigrant groups face now and what immigrants faced at the beginning of the century. In fact, a number of people point to the success many immigrant groups have had in learning English and argue that special programs are not needed for these children.

This attitude is unfortunate, because times have changed. Although discrimination has always existed, the need for advanced education and training has not. Fifty years ago, an advanced education was not required and the importance of academic advancement could be minimized. Most immigrants took low-paying jobs, their children may have taken a step up but still may not have had much advanced training. By the third generation, these families were routinely sending children to college.

Children do not have this luxury, today. Few jobs that do not require education permit a reasonable standard of living. Today, the educational goal for children with poor English skills is not just to teach them the basic six hundred words of English, but rather to help them gain the necessary academic skills to succeed in high school and perhaps beyond.

Every child who spends a great deal of time in the United States will eventually learn enough English to function in the community. However, the type of English used in advanced schooling differs. It is more abstract, technically more exacting, and uses a higher vocabulary level. A child learns the type of social English necessary for conversation within three years, but the more academic school-related language takes much longer (U.S. Department of Education, 1993). Only recently have educators been asked to accomplish this feat and teach advanced language skills not in a matter of generations but in a relatively few years.

How can this be accomplished? A number of programs are being used in communities across the country. Generally, these programs can be viewed as a continuum between the active encouragement and use of the primary language on one side, sometimes called native language emphasis, and the increased focus on English, called sheltered English or structured immersion on the other (Gerstein & Woodward, 1994).

Some educators propose that a bilingual program be introduced in the school, and that subjects such as math and social studies be taught to Spanish-speaking students in Spanish until the children gain sufficient ability in English to function effectively in English. At the same time, these children would receive instruction in standard English. These educators reason that if children learn to read in their native language, the switch to English will become easier. Complex subjects, such as reading and social studies taught in English cannot be understood by these children, and they receive little benefit from their schooling.

Advocates of such an approach, such as Cummins (1989), argue that the use of the native language empowers these students and reinforces their cultural identi-

Should bilingual children be taught subjects other than English in their native language or in English?

ty. He argues that when children learn to read in Spanish, they do not have to learn to read all over again. They transfer what they have learned. Under this system, students are encouraged to use their native language around the school, signs are provided in different languages, people who can tutor in the native language are recruited, books in the native language are read, and writing in the student's native language is assigned.

The structured immersion or sheltered English approach assumes that proficiency in English can be best attained through well-designed content instruction where English is used, but at a level that is constantly modified and expanded as the child's abilities increase. Teachers control their classroom vocabulary, use concrete objects and gestures to enhance understanding, and use many instructional strategies so students understand the academic material. In some cases, students receive native language instruction for 30–90 minutes each day at school. However, English is used during the majority of the teaching day.

In some of these programs, students are taught in English by teachers who know the child's native language but use it only to help students who do not understand the material. Students are encouraged to use English, but also to ask questions in their native language when necessary (*U.S. News & World Report*, 1986).

Students in this type of program learn English while they are developing basic academic abilities and skills. This approach is used successfully in Quebec, Canada, with English-speaking students, with Southeast Asian immigrants in elementary schools, and to a somewhat more limited but increasing extent with Hispanic-American youth at the secondary level (Gerstein & Woodward, 1994).

Research to date has not generally shown much difference in achievement between children taught with either emphasis (Ramirez, 1992). In a longitudinal study of 500 mostly Mexican American low-income immigrants, no significant differences in achievement or academic engagement was found among students taught using any of three different bilingual approaches, two of which were structured immersion and native language emphasis (see Ramirez, 1992). Admittedly, research is difficult in this area due to discrepancies in program emphasis and differences between how the program is designed to operate and the reality of the services provided. A supposed native language program may feature more English than planned, and a structured immersion program more of the primary language.

Evaluations of bilingual programs generally are mixed, but tend to be positive. Some evidence shows that the programs have helped students achieve scholastically (Crawford, 1987; Willig, 1985). Other researchers disagree, noting that these programs have not been as successful as hoped (Porter, 1990; Baker & de Kanter, 1981). Other detractors focus on how difficult it is to recruit effective bilingual teachers, and that there are problems involved when more than one foreign language is used by children in the class.

Bilingual students have several demands placed upon them. Mastering a new language as well as traditional subject matter is a daunting task, and teachers may sometimes request assistance for the students from special educators and other professionals. Not every student with LEP who is having difficulty has a learning disability, but differentiating between who does and who does not have one is sometimes quite difficult.

The debate over the best way to teach children whose primary language is not English is ongoing (August, 1986). The models described differ in the ratio of native-to-English language instruction offered. No matter what techniques are used, educators and parents must understand that the goals have changed. The goals involve more than teaching children enough English so they can get along in society. The pressure now is to teach bilingual children sufficient English so they can succeed in advanced schooling. What is obviously needed is a relatively quick way of accomplishing this task. Although a practical way of doing it has not yet emerged, more research can be expected in this area in the future. Any successful strategy requires a complex balance between use of native language and the language to be acquired (Gerstein & Woodward, 1994). It is to be hoped that researchers will provide educators with clues that may answer this challenge in the near future.

THOUGHT QUESTION

6. *Do you believe the native language emphasis or structured English is the best way to teach bilingual students English?*

SCENARIO

5 Roberto is a first grade student. He has been in the United States for about three years and can speak some "social English" but does not do well in school. His "academic English" is poor. The question is how he should be taught. One teacher suggests teaching him in Spanish and having English enter the program gradually. Another teacher suggests that the child be immersed in structured English and not Spanish, while a third professional suggests continuous teaching of both English and Spanish but with math, science, and social studies taught in English. Which program, in your opinion, would be best for Roberto?

Two Paths to Travel

This chapter focused on five areas of interest that directly concern the child from a minority group with special needs. Assessment issues, the need to be familiar with the cultural background of the child, the need for multicultural programs for children receiving special education services, challenges relating to working with parents, and finally bilingual programs were discussed. Many controversial questions arise from these areas, and heated debate is common.

The challenges of educating minority group youth with disabilities in special education can be viewed two ways. The first calls for some changes in the evaluation process to make it fairer, a better understanding of the cultures of people being served, helping students to understand their own culture and that of others, and implementing programs that encourage achievement and parental participation. Advocates of this approach believe the school and special education services as now constructed can make the changes necessary to serve students of all cultures.

Others, though, call for a more radical approach. They argue that the overrepresentation of minority group students in programs for children with disabilities is a symptom of a school system that needs fundamental change. They believe that professionals should stop looking for answers within the child and look within the system itself. They aim at wholesale changes in the system of assessment, teaching, and curriculum, not just reform of the present system.

Whether the changes are made within the present context of the school system or a more radical alteration is undertaken, educators within the system need to be more culturally sensitive and more culturally aware without losing sight of the individuality of the student. By paying more attention to the cultural roots of the family, by encouraging parental inclusion in the process, and by truly incorporating a multicultural perspective that emphasizes tolerance and understanding of all cultures, teachers can make the school experience for the child with exceptional needs from a minority group a more rewarding one.

 **Students Learning English as a Second Language**

Consider students who may come to school with a limited knowledge of English. They do not hear much English spoken in the home. In school, English is spoken quickly. The students understand some of it but much is incomprehensible. When a film is shown, students have difficulty comprehending much of it. Books written in English require great effort to read and children become frustrated looking up words they do not understand. Under such circumstances, motivation to learn may be reduced.

The individual differences students show compound these general problems. Some students will learn English faster than others. Some will need more repetition and more reinforcement than others. Some students will experience significant difficulties.

The teacher faces a number of challenges in promoting English language skills.

Research demonstrates that children learning a second language benefit when the linguistic input is meaningful and children are willing to risk making mistakes, since they will be using an unfamiliar vocabulary in their new language (Lalas & Wilson, 1993). Students need to feel in control and involved. They require repetition and immediate feedback and reinforcement (Lewis, 1991). Finally, children need to be motivated and be able to learn at their own pace.

How can teachers provide this feeling of control, adequate feedback and reinforcement, and meet the individual pacing and level of difficulty needs of their students? In recent years, schools have turned to sophisticated technology as a tool for meeting this challenge (Durrer, 1992).

The use of technology with children who have limited English proficiency is varied. Technological innovations allow students to learn at their own pace, to control the program, to hear English as well as see it on the screen, and to make frequent inquiries into the system to receive more explanation when necessary.

One possible way of helping students is through using interactive video, which is basically the marriage of a video cassette recorder or videodisc player and the computer. The aim of the combination is to provide interactive teaching programs through the computer and the best visual and sound characteristics through the video cassette recorder or videodisc. Interactive video merges graphics and sound with computer-generated text. The videodisc player will probably be used more than the video cassette recorder because it allows for easier access to specific parts of the program. Discs are more durable than tapes, can store more material, and can store both motion pictures and slides. Also, the quality of the videodisc is better than that of tapes, and the videodisc permits precise computer control (Schneider & Bennion, 1981). In the past, videodiscs have been used mostly for high-

quality music recordings, but they can also store color graphics, images, and animation (Mandell & Mandell, 1989). The interactive process involves the user responding to computer-generated questions and making inquiries into the system.

The interactive video using a videodisc allows access to any part of the program within seconds. Therefore, if a student needs to repeat a phrase or a sentence, the student can do so. A teacher who may be presenting a book on videodisc can repeat a scene as many times as necessary. Besides movies and books, encyclopedias, paintings and sculptures from art galleries, and even National Geographic specials can be found on videodisc. The quality sound, specific explanations of difficult concepts, and excellent graphics allow for interesting and meaningful presentations (Lewis, 1991).

CD-ROM is another useful technology. A child may sit at an interactive computer workstation, load the CD-ROM into the computer, put on the headphones, and listen to a children's book. The text and synchronized pronunciation of the words appear on the screen in the student's native language, in English, or both. The text can flow at a speed determined by the student or the teacher. The child can also have any unfamiliar words defined in both languages (Lalas & Wilson, 1993).

A number of interactive programs that help students learn English as a second language are available. One program called the Principles of Alphabet Literacy Program (PALS) is designed to teach adolescents to read and write English. It uses a story, presented in cartoon format, that tells students how sounds make letters and then words. Another program, English Express, is a multimedia presentation that involves listening, reading, speaking, and writing.

Sophisticated technology allows students to work at their own pace. In one school, an integrated learning system computer lab was established in which children have access to lessons in reading, language arts, and mathematics. These lessons vary in difficulty level and speed at which they are delivered (Cataldo, 1989). The student or the teacher can therefore individualize lessons. The software has a speech component so children hear well-articulated English while reading from the screen. Students, who were usually reluctant to participate in reading activities, suddenly began to show a willingness to do so.

Writing is another skill that is necessary for academic success. Many teachers experience difficulty motivating students to write. Word-processing programs with spelling checkers and sometimes grammar checkers are useful. Writing, though, is not just an exercise. As with any other form of communication, it must have a purpose. Creating one's own written stories with graphics can be motivating. A computer pals program in which children write to other children around the world through an electronic mail system has been successfully established (Clark, 1989).

Computer technology has also made electronic translation equipment possible. Students commonly request permission to use such hand-held instruments during examinations. Students may type an English word into the computer, which is then translated into the students' native lan-

guage. Students can also reverse the process and type a word in their native language and have it translated into English. These translation devices allow students to look up words much more quickly than conventional dictionaries. The use of such translation devices occasionally may be inappropriate, such as when the vocabulary itself is being tested. However, the translation device is quite useful for students who may experience difficulties with general vocabulary. It avoids the situation in which students continually ask the teacher questions throughout the test on the meaning of particular words.

The use of various technologies to promote English language linguistic skills among children for whom English is a second language is an exciting advancement. Interactive programs motivate students, allow them to feel in control, and provide the practice, feedback, and reinforcement they need. Such programs allow students to work at their own level and at their own pace. With some interactive programs, two or more students are able to work on a program together, which encourages social interaction. The future looks bright, and technology can make an important contribution to the promotion of English skills among children who have limited proficiency in English.

S U M M A R Y

1. Demographics in the United States are changing rapidly. A large percentage of American youth in the beginning of the next century will belong to minority groups, principally African-American, Hispanic-American, and Asian-American.

2. More African-Americans, Hispanic-Americans, and Native Americans are identified as having disabilities than their proportion of the population would indicate.

3. One difficulty in assessment is the tendency to search for factors within the child to explain poor achievement rather than to take a more ecological point of view and look at teacher-student interactions and the structure of the school.

4. Testing a child from a different language background is difficult, and evaluation is complicated by the lack of English proficiency. Lack of familiarity with the test examiner is a

factor affecting test results for minority group students. Assessing behavior is also difficult, because particular behaviors may have different meanings in various cultures.

5. Teachers should avoid defining a person by group membership; treating minority groups as single, monolithic entities; ignoring acculturation; believing that all minority group members are poor; and idealizing minority group cultures.

6. A disproportionate number of African-Americans live in poverty-filled environments and are raised in single-parent households. Multigenerational families are common, and helping out is expected. Older children often have child-care responsibilities. African-American families demonstrate more of a people-centered than object-centered orientation, a faster-paced interaction with others, and varied stimulation. Historically, African-Americans have been victims of discrimination and, in the past, have had little reason to view school as the vehicle to a better life.

7. Hispanic-American families are Spanish-speaking, emphasize sharing and cooperation, have a fatalistic attitude and a present-time orientation. Gender roles are well defined.

8. Asian-American children differ greatly from each other in culture. Many cultural traditions are not well known to outsiders. Asian-American children often see their role in terms of obligations to the family and strict adherence to social customs. They demonstrate language differences and are often bilingual.

9. Native American tribes differ in language and culture. People in authority positions are expected to share; strong extended families are common; time orientation is less exacting; and patience is stressed. Being part of the group is particularly important. Alcoholism is a critical problem among Native Americans. Unemployment is high, especially on reservations.

10. An appreciation of their own culture and the culture of other groups in the United States is important for children with and without disabilities. The meaning of multicultural education differs, but generally it involves an appreciation and understanding of various cultures, and enhancing cooperation between people.

11. Although parents are supposed to be partners in the special education experience, parental participation, especially among minority group parents, is low. Many feel intimidated by the school, may not feel connected positively with the school, and may not understand their role. Limited English proficiency (LEP) may be another reason for lack of participation.

12. A great deal of controversy surrounds bilingual programs. Some programs emphasize native language instruction with classes taught in the native language, while others emphasize using an appropriate level of English as the major mode of communication. More research concerning the best way to educate bilingual children is necessary. Every child needs to learn standard English so that the child may be successful in advanced schooling.

Intellectual Ability

INTELLECTUAL ABILITY

Would You Choose to Have a Gifted Child?
Defining Giftedness
What Gifted Children and Adolescents Are Really Like
What About the Geniuses Among Us?
Do Intellectually Gifted Students Need Special Programs?

Identifying Gifted Students
Services for Gifted Students
■ In the Classroom: Enriching the Curriculum
Delivering Services to Gifted Students
Special Academic Ability
Gifted Children in Adulthood
The Future
■ On-Line: Stretching the Limits
Summary

- -

TRUE-FALSE STATEMENTS

See below for the correct answers.

1. The public generally views academically gifted children and adolescents as socially advanced as well and intellectually superior.
2. Children who have great leadership ability are considered gifted.
3. A child who is an excellent athlete is defined as gifted under the federal government's definition.
4. Intellectually gifted children tend to be quick learners and attribute their success in school to their ability.

5. Gifted children are generally well adjusted and have good social skills.
6. Gifted children often believe their siblings' and peers' attitudes toward their giftedness are more negative than they really are.
7. The majority of students who drop out of school are actually bored, gifted children.
8. The federal government requires states to set up comprehensive programs to foster the education of gifted children.
9. Children who are accelerated, that is who skip grades, often find themselves socially isolated and unpopular.
10. Substituting one assignment for another so that gifted children can be more challenged is appropriate.

Answers to True-False Statements

1. False. See page 380.
2. True.
3. False. See page 381
4. True.
5. True.
6. True.
7. False. See page 388.
8. False. See page 389.
9. False. See page 396.
10. True.

379

How do you perceive the gifted child? While some people do not see giftedness as advantageous, research shows these children to be socially adept and healthy.

Would You Choose to Have a Gifted Child?

Imagine that you're an expectant parent who has learned that a certain safe treatment will ensure that your child will have an IQ of 160. Would you seek out this treatment?

I often ask my students this question and, after assuring them that safety is not an issue, the stereotypes begin to unfold. "He would be a misfit," one student told me. "She would be socially backward," noted another. The stereotypes of gifted children are probably as great as for any other exceptionality.

Indeed, many people believe gifted children are socially backward, have little or no common sense, and look down on other people (Richert, 1981). Another stereotype is of the bright person as a "nerd" with little or no social skill. These stereotypes are sometimes perpetuated by movies and especially by television programs, which rarely show gifted individuals as socially adept and well adjusted. These beliefs run counter to research that, as will be discussed later in the chapter, demonstrates that most gifted children do indeed have good social skills and are well adjusted.

Teachers also do not always have the most positive attitudes toward gifted children (Tuttle, Becker, & Sousa, 1988). These attitudes often change with education. When teachers are given specialized training in teaching gifted children, their attitudes and teaching strategies improve greatly (Hanson & Feldhusen, 1994; Reis & Westberg, 1994). Most principals, however, continue to believe that gifted children should remain in the same classes and at the same grade level as their nongifted peers in order to make certain their social adjustment is good (Dettmer, 1981).

Two points stand out. First, the general public does not have a very positive or accurate view of gifted children; and second, if educators are given some training in teaching gifted children their attitudes do change, although concern for social adjustment remains high. If negative stereotypes of gifted children are communicated to these children, gifted children may actively try to hide the fact that they are gifted especially in adolescence when the desire to fit in is so great and their achievement may not match their abilities (Kaplan, 1990).

Defining Giftedness

- Leslie scored 145 on a standardized test of intelligence, but has an academic average of 80.
- Shu Lin creates beautiful sculptures in art, but is barely passing her academic subjects.
- Peter shows great musical talent on the oboe and other wind instruments and is doing B+ work in school.
- Tanisha is a whiz at math but does not do well in English and social studies.
- Robert has always been a leader. In fact, everyone seems to look to him for guidance and advice.

If you were asked which of these children is gifted, how would you reply? At first glance, defining giftedness would seem to be an easy task. Gifted children, most people think, are those who have a high level of intelligence. Children who score notably above average in intelligence are indeed gifted, but is that all there is to it? What of the child who is artistically gifted, creative, or shows leadership ability?

Older definitions considered giftedness only in terms of IQ, but newer definitions have expanded the concept greatly. In 1972, the U.S. Office of Education issued a definition of giftedness that has had an enormous impact on the field (Marland, 1972). The federal government defined a gifted child as any child who either has demonstrated or seems to have the potential for high capabilities in general intellectual ability, specific academic aptitude, creative or productive thinking, leadership ability, the visual and performing arts, or psychomotor ability. In 1978, the definition was changed to eliminate psychomotor ability (Gifted and Talented Children's Act of 1978). The psychomotor abilities required in dancing and the arts were classified under these categories, and athletically gifted children were well provided for in special athletic programs already thriving (Davis & Rimm, 1989). Gifted children require services that are not ordinarily provided by the school in order to fully develop these abilities (Education and Consolidation Act of 1981). Under this definition, each of the children noted previously would be considered gifted.

Unfortunately, most services for gifted children are directed only at children with an above average IQ. However, children who demonstrate other abilities also require special services if their abilities are to be developed adequately.

A child may be gifted in one area and not another. A gifted musician may be a poor social studies student, and someone who can lead others may not be intellectually gifted. In addition, a student who has a specific ability in a particular subject, such as mathematics or English, may not be a great all-around student. Finally, the relationship between creativity and intellectual achievement is not as strong as people generally believe. If giftedness is defined simply in terms of an intelligence score in the top 20 percent—a very liberal criterion—then about 75 percent of these children who score very high on tests of creativity would not be identified as gifted (Torrance, 1962).

The point of this discussion is simply to show that while children who score very high on intelligence tests are considered gifted, so are many other children who do not. In order to do justice to the many categories of giftedness, the coverage of gifted children is divided into two chapters. This chapter will deal with intellectual giftedness and those students who have exceptional ability in a particular academic area. Chapter 11 will focus on other forms of giftedness as well as investigating particular groups of students such as gifted underachievers, gifted children with disabilities, children from minority groups who are gifted, and gifted women, groups that have been underrepresented in various programs for gifted students.

The Nature of Intelligence

The general concept of intelligence was discussed in Chapter 4, which introduced Howard Gardner's expansive Theory of Multiple Intelligences (Gardner, 1993; 1987a; 1983). Gardner argued for the existence of seven different types of intelli-

THOUGHT QUESTION

1. *How could a school use Gardner's conception of intelligence in planning curricula and special programs?*

gence including linguistic intelligence, logical-mathematical intelligence, musical intelligence, spatial intelligence, bodily-kinesthetic intelligence, interpersonal intelligence, and intrapersonal intelligence (see pages 119-121). According to Gardner, all people possess each of these seven different intelligences to some extent though not on equal levels. One of the responsibilities of the school is to assess students' individual abilities and then to find ways to enrich the students' education by challenging all their talents. Although Gardner's theory does not represent the only way to view intelligence, his theory fits in well with the broad definition of giftedness offered by the federal government, extending giftedness beyond those who score high on intelligence tests.

What Gifted Children and Adolescents Are Really Like

A number of studies have investigated the personal attributes of gifted youth. From a historical point of view, such studies have been both popular and beneficial, starting with a series of important studies conducted by Lewis Terman.

Would you take a book away from a three-year-old child who wants to learn to read because being too advanced would cause personality problems? Would you refuse to allow a child to play with an older brother's puzzle because you were concerned that a child who developed too quickly would be maladjusted? You would probably answer "no" to these questions, but they were part of the prevailing conventional wisdom early in this century. People believed that gifted children were maladjusted, socially isolated, and tended toward emotional instability.

In this environment, Lewis Terman began his study of gifted children. This most important of all studies on gifted children followed about 1,500 children through their childhood, adolescence, and adulthood (Goleman, 1995). Terman's data continues to be used to test out certain hypotheses: for example, how younger gifted children in Terman's sample achieved compared to older gifted children. The participants in Terman's study were given the name "termites," and quite a bit of pride goes along with this label (see Friedman et al., 1995).

The results of Terman's studies, which comprise a five-volume work and the subsequent follow-ups (Terman, 1925; Terman & Oden, 1947), served to break down the prejudice against gifted children. The majority of the children in his study had intelligence scores greater than 140; so again, a narrow definition was used to identify giftedness.

Terman found that these gifted children became leaders and achieved very well in adulthood. They were quite popular with classmates and mentally and physically healthy. They showed less psychopathology than the general population and a lower mortality rate (Terman & Oden, 1947). A great many went on to higher levels of education, something that only a small proportion of the population did at that time, and they received many honors and awards. Only 12 of the 1,528 subjects did not graduate from high school. The overwhelming majority graduated from college, whereas at that time in California only about 8 percent of all students graduated from college. They were socially well adjusted and made impor-

Historically, the most important studies on the nature of giftedness were performed by Lewis Terman.

tant contributions to society. So, gifted people in Terman's sample did well socially, academically, and in their careers.

Despite the great value of Terman's work, a number of caveats should be kept in mind. First, these children were generally from a high socioeconomic group and already privileged. They had the resources to do well, giving them a head start in life.

Second, Terman's studies were begun in the 1920s, and he dutifully followed his subjects through their adult lives which meant through the Great Depression of the 1930s and World War II. Every generation is deeply affected by the historical context in which it lives; and Terman's subjects were affected by these events, just as later generations were affected by experiences such as the Viet Nam War and the 20 percent inflation rate in 1980. The effect of being brought up in a particular generation is called the **cohort effect**. Each cohort has common experiences. If such a study was begun today with elementary school students, the results may or may not be the same. For instance, the role of women is much different today than in the 1920s, and many more people go on to higher education than in years past. The cohort effect should always be kept in mind.

Third, Terman's effect on his subjects should be considered. Although most of the people in Terman's sample did not think that being "termites" affected their lives, some evidence indicates that they were not even aware of his influence. When Terman died and his papers were read, researchers noted the tremendous volume of individual correspondence with the parents of these gifted children. Clearly, he had a personal relationship with many of them and often helped the families solve problems. He advised them on many issues, including college choice. Not surprisingly many decided to enroll in Stanford University, where Terman taught (Feldman, 1984). Although Terman's data is accepted and his

Cohort effect:
The effect of living in a particular generation or historical period.

As long as children are developmentally ready and have the motivation to accomplish something, they should be encouraged to do so.

THOUGHT QUESTION

2. Why do some people believe that children who are very bright will be social misfits?

contribution to the reduction in the stereotypes of gifted youth is secure, his personal involvement with his sample can be questioned.

Terman's research exploded many of the myths concerning the nature of gifted people. Since Terman's work, many research studies have focused on various attributes of the gifted youth. These studies generally show that gifted children are quick learners. They score higher than their nongifted peers in such attributes as self-sufficiency, dominance, independence, originality, nonconformity, and self-confidence (Lehman & Erdwins, 1981). They believe they are in control of their own destiny, that is, they have an internal locus of control.

Gifted elementary school children tend to be well accepted by other nongifted children and rather popular (Cohen, Duncan, & Cohen, 1994; Schneider et al., 1989). Whether they are well accepted in junior and senior high school is more of a question, especially for gifted girls (Cornell, 1990). Gifted youth are generally not socially isolated. In fact, their interpersonal relationships are generally quite good (Austin & Draper, 1981). Gifted students tend to be interested in school and also energetic, physically healthy, intuitive, perceptive, and a bit rebellious (MacKinnon, 1978). Intellectually gifted children show superior concentration skills, persistence, and are active in their own learning experiences (Scott, 1988). They do not tend to accept superficial answers or statements and understand general principles. They see relationships among diverse ideas and are curious (Tuttle et al., 1988). They are developmentally advanced in both language and thought (Davis & Rimm, 1994). They have good memories, read at an earlier age, and show superior reasoning abilities (Bjorklund, 1994; Schulz, Carpenter, & Turnbull, 1991). Of course, not all gifted children will show all these characteristics, and some will show them at a later age than others.

At first glance, all of these would seem to be positive traits. However, they may lead to difficulties in the classroom, especially one not designed to meet their needs. Children who are not satisfied with simple answers may be seen as pestering the teacher. If children challenge the teacher, they may find themselves being considered disruptive. Gifted children may be bored to tears if they can move at a faster rate through mathematics or social studies but are not permitted to do so. In fact, in such a case children may not even do very well on tests, since they are not being challenged.

Any portrait of the population of gifted children, however, must be drawn with care. Gifted children do not comprise a homogeneous population (Juntune, 1982). Some overgeneralizations can be harmful. For example, although most gifted children are quick learners, being smart should not be equated with being fast (Sternberg, 1982). Some very intelligent people may spend more time planning how they are going to solve a problem instead of merely jumping into a solution.

What About the Geniuses Among Us?

The "average" gifted child is well adjusted, but what of the geniuses among us? The term *genius* has real problems attached to it since no one has yet formed an accepted definition. If genius is defined in terms of an intelligence score on an individual intelligence test, what cutoff should be used: 140, 160, or 180? Second, other attributes may define genius, including extreme precocity, doing everything very early. A recent trend is to use the term *prodigy* to define the child, most often younger than 10 years old, who can function in an area at the level of a highly trained adult (Feldman, 1993). The fields that have produced the most prodigies are music and chess (Feldman, 1993). Prodigies tend to be very focused and highly motivated but are not exceptionally advanced in other areas or in their emotional or social development.

Throughout the ages, geniuses have been considered somewhat odd, even perhaps maladjusted. It is easy to see why. A person with extreme ability may not be very patient and may not fit in well, especially with a peer group, and even be considered unstable by some. Indeed, some psychologists have suggested that this instability is the case, arguing that these children are prone to social and emotional problems (Hollingworth, 1942; Roedell, 1984). However, such studies are fraught with problems because researchers often do not use appropriate control or comparison groups, and defining genius and adjustment is often difficult.

Most studies have not found these children to be unstable. In fact, many studies show just the opposite. For example, Terman did not divide his sample between those who had over 160 intelligence scores and those whose scores lay between 140 and 160. However, his data does allow for such a comparison. Feldman (1984) reviewed follow-up data on 26 subjects in Terman's sample who scored above 180 and compared them to 26 subjects chosen at random with lower but still gifted intelligence. The comparison group had an average IQ of 150. He found very few differences between the groups in adjustment. Although the "geniuses" were certainly successful, they were really no more successful than the other gifted children in the comparison group. From this data, the idea of instability cannot be supported. When Grossberg and Cornell (1988) compared gifted students with intelligence levels between 120 and 168, they found that intelligence was actually positively related to adjustment. Children with higher levels of intelligence were less anxious and nervous and less likely to show physical, cognitive, or disciplinary problems. As would be expected, some of the children in all categories of giftedness showed some adjustment problems. As the researchers note, intelligence does not make an individual invulnerable to adjustment problems. Generally, then, little evidence supports the idea that above some level of intelligence people become unstable or more prone to emotional disturbance. However, since few children fall in the highest IQ category, if even one shows some problem, that behavior is more obvious because these children tend to stand out.

Some studies do find some difficulties in the social aspects of life for precocious children. Extremely precocious children were found in one study to see themselves as less popular, less socially adept, more inhibited, and to have a lower social standing than a group of more modestly gifted students (Dauber & Benbow, 1990).

Without a doubt, though, children who are extremely gifted need specialized educational experiences. Very precocious children may find themselves not really interacting with same-age peers. Their intellectual abilities certainly require types of experiences that can be difficult to provide in a regular neighborhood school environment, even for schools that have good programs for gifted students. Because so few children are considered prodigies, their needs may be met by special university programs, early admission to appropriate programs, and summer institutes in which they can use their distinct gifts to the best advantage.

THOUGHT QUESTION

3. *How would you define "genius"?*

Sometimes, gifted children are not satisfied with simple answers and may want more explanation. Although many teachers enjoy this type of questioning, some do not.

How Do Gifted Children See Themselves?

Your self-concept is the picture you have of yourself. Some psychologists have considered it in a global manner, while others argue that self-concept has different parts: a physical self-concept, an academic self-concept, a social self-concept, and a number of others. Some professionals may even incorporate both ways of viewing self-concept. With age, children are better able to separate various parts of the self-concept from each other (Harter, 1986).

Studies of the self-concepts of gifted children have yielded mixed results. Some studies find that the self-concept of gifted children is significantly higher than that of their nongifted peers, while other studies show little difference (Schneider et al., 1989). Most gifted children have positive self-concepts (Maddox, Scheiber, & Bass, 1982). Some evidence indicates a gender difference. In elementary school, gifted girls have a more positive self-concept than nongifted girls (Loeb & Jay, 1987). But in adolescence this balance shifts; gifted adolescent boys have better self-concepts than nongifted adolescent boys, and differences can no longer be found in self-concepts between gifted and nongifted girls (Kelly & Colangelo, 1984).

When self-concept is divided into some of its components, a definite pattern is found. Perceived academic competence is an important factor in the global self-worth of gifted children from grade four through grade eight (Hoge & McSheffrey, 1991). This pattern is especially so for girls. The scores for both athletic and social self-concepts are somewhat lower but not significantly so. However, a discrepan-

THOUGHT QUESTION

4. Why do the self-concepts of gifted girls in adolescence seem to drop while the self-concepts of gifted boys seem to improve?

cy between academic and social self-concepts occurs; gifted children have a much more positive academic self-concept (Ross & Parker, 1980). This discrepancy may reflect a realistic view of themselves as particularly good at school-related subject matter and good but not necessarily superior in the social aspects of life.

Gifted children often have a mixed and perhaps a confused attitude towards their own talents. They may not like to stand out, and they may be teased for how well they do in school (Clark, 1988). They often are proud of being considered gifted both in elementary and high school from an academic point of view, but are concerned about what they see as the negative views of others (Kerr, Colangelo, & Gaeth, 1988; Colangelo & Kerr, 1983). They see the advantages in terms of personal growth and development, but worry about negative appraisals from others (Manaster et al., 1994). Some, but not all, gifted students in high school consider it a social handicap (Coleman & Cross, 1988). Gifted girls show more concerns for the possible negative social implications than gifted boys, although they too recognize some definite advantages of being labeled gifted. In fact, girls are both more likely to see both the advantages and the disadvantages of being considered gifted than boys are.

Are the attitudes of other students so negative toward gifted children? The answer is "not as much as gifted children believe." Many gifted students perceive the attitudes of others as being negative toward them. However, a neutral rather than a negative attitude is most commonly found on the part of peers (Colangelo & Kelly, 1983). The same misperception is found in studies of siblings and parents. Siblings and parents show considerably more positive attitudes toward their gifted family members than gifted youngsters believe (Colangelo & Brower, 1987). The reason for this misperception is not known at the present time.

SCENARIO

1 Gina is a fifth grade student with a high intelligence score. She is doing well in elementary school, and the teacher has suggested that she enter a gifted program which involves special classes. Her parents are not certain. She is shy and has few friends, even though she enjoys school. They believe that if she were placed in a gifted program she would have less contact with other children and not develop her social skills. They are also afraid that she will be picked on and teased since even now she is called "teacher's pet." If Gina's parents asked you for your opinion about her placement, what would you say?

Do Intellectually Gifted Students Need Special Programs?

When people argue for special services to meet the needs of children who have mental retardation or visual impairments, we do not question these children's special needs. This consensus is not so when the needs of gifted children are discussed.

Real community opposition to special services for gifted children is not uncommon within a school district. Many people do not consider it a necessity. The main points of their argument include:

1. Gifted students will make it on their own and do not require much extra help. Teachers can easily adapt their lessons to meet the needs of gifted youth.
2. Gifted children will be separated from others and will feel elite and look down on others.
3. It costs a great deal of money, which could be spent on the education of the "average" child.

None of these points are correct. Certainly, many gifted students do well in school. That fact would be impossible to deny. However, evidence shows that gifted students are underachieving greatly. The National Commission on Excellence in Education (1983) noted that about one-half of all gifted children do not perform up to potential. This is an astounding figure, even leaving room for definition and measurement problems. It also exposes the myth that gifted children achieve just because they are gifted (Maker, 1986). Many gifted children are bored and unchallenged in school (Tuttle et al., 1988). Some evidence even indicates that a number of gifted students drop out. Between 10 and 20 percent of all dropouts can be considered gifted (Whitmore, 1980; Lajoie & Shore, 1981). Osborne and Byrnes (1990) found that about 8 percent of students in an alternative high school for students who were disruptive and alienated could be considered gifted. Therefore, one cannot make the assumption that gifted children will succeed, and certainly many will not work up to their potential.

In addition, many teachers are forced by circumstances to teach to the average student and have little or no training in enriching their classes for gifted children. Suggesting to classroom teachers that they are solely responsible for providing enrichment for gifted children in their classes puts an added burden on teachers that many may not want.

No evidence shows that gifted children have an elitist attitude or look down on others. Most likely, gifted children want to fit in socially. It is in their area of giftedness where they require some additional help if they are to achieve.

The last question speaks of the cost. Most districts do not spend much money on the education of gifted students, but many services for gifted youth need not be costly. The evidence indicates that gifted children may not develop their talents and abilities without help. Gifted students need faster-paced, more intensive lessons with more advanced content (Clark, 1992).

The points that have just been refuted are commonly read in the popular press and heard in community discussions of providing special educational services for gifted children. However, some resistance for providing special educational services outside the classroom comes from people who argue that it runs counter to the spirit of the inclusive classroom (Sapon-Shevin, 1992). Just as the inclusion movement seeks to have children with disabilities receive their services in the regular classroom, it is argued that gifted children belong there also. The inclusive classroom, with a wide range of ability levels present, would encompass gifted students. Whatever special needs these children may possess can be met by the regular classroom teacher just as the classroom teacher meets the needs of the other students in the classroom.

The claim is also sometimes made that labeling children as gifted may lead to unreasonable expectations and a feeling of isolation from others, and children who are not considered gifted may feel that they have less to offer. In addition, some services to gifted children are in the form of formalized programs which track students rigidly, not allowing other children to enter. Finally, although some teachers may feel positively toward pull-out programs that take gifted students out of their classes, others may feel that this implies that they are inadequate for the task and may also cause teachers to see these students as more different than they really are.

The debate on the needs of gifted children continues. While some argue that special services are not required, others argue that without them, many gifted children will not develop their talents. Some claim that gifted children's needs can be met by the regular classroom teacher, but others believe educational services that are above and beyond what is available in the regular classroom are required. And some believe that labeling children as gifted is unnecessary, while others feel that it is vital to providing the needed services.

SCENARIO

2 You are a parent of a gifted child and have been asked by other parents to present a case for gifted education to the school board of your local district. The board of education is under great financial strain at this point and is concerned about starting any new programs. Some of the members argue that the gifted do very well in regular classes and need nothing else. They are also afraid of providing an elitist atmosphere for the children and, of course, the financial problems are paramount in their mind. How would you present your case for a program for gifted children?

Support for Programs for Gifted Children

When discussing children with exceptional needs it is usually necessary to comment on the legal rights of the individuals involved, and knowledge of the Individuals with Disabilities Education Act and various court cases is indispensable. Not so when writing about the education of gifted students. States do not have to accept the federal definition, although most do. Many states have laws promoting programs for gifted and talented students, but these laws vary widely. Gifted and talented students are not included in the federal laws requiring free and appropriate education. Although Congress, in the Omnibus Education Bill of 1987, did provide some financial support for research and programs for gifted children, the states themselves or various localities have to shoulder most of the cost burden.

Federal support for the education of gifted children has been spotty at best and characterized by fits and starts. Following the launching of Sputnik by the Soviet Union, Congress enacted a law to allocate funds for developing potential in math, science, and foreign language. Other acts since that time studied the state of education for gifted children and even allocated some money for the development of model gifted programs. In 1973–1974, the Office of Gifted and Talented was established in the U.S. Office of Education, and money was appropriated for training, research, and demonstration projects. Since then, between $2.5 million in 1975 to about $7.9 million in the late 1980s has been spent annually by the federal government on various aspects of gifted education (Reis, 1989). This figure is not a very large one.

Most states have adopted some policy on the education of gifted children. Almost every state, plus Guam and Puerto Rico, has passed legislation concerning the education of gifted students and assigned professional staff to positions in this area. Only about one-half of all states require programs for gifted students (Delisle, 1992). Most services remain fragmented with few districts having programs that run from elementary through high school. Unlike children with disabilities whose rights are protected by federal law and court decisions, many state laws are vague on just what must be provided for children considered gifted. Most programs also focus only on academically gifted children; few programs for children who show other aspects of giftedness exist.

Providing special services for gifted students may be even more controversial today. With many education budgets stretched, programs for gifted students often are among the first to lose funding during hard economic times. One district hit by reductions in state aid cut many of their programs for gifted children. These included many advanced placement and special courses. Some gifted students graduated early (in their junior year of high school) because few classes were available for them to take in their senior year. Others spent the next year enrolled at a community college where they took college courses that would be beneficial to them.

Advocates for meeting the needs of gifted and talented children carry the burden of convincing localities to allocate funds for the education of gifted children within the community or to expand such services. They must make their case for such additional services to school districts that are often already financially strapped. However, even with the current tight budgets, most districts use some process to identify gifted students and offer some services for these students in their districts.

Identifying Gifted Students

Identifying gifted students is not as simple a task as it may seem. Certainly the nature of the services available will partially determine a district's identification procedures (Nevo, 1994). If services are directed toward leadership or mathematical talent then procedures will aim to identify these types of giftedness. Districts must also decide whether their identification procedures should be inclusive or exclusive (Tuttle et al., 1988). An *exclusive* identification procedure is one which assures that every child admitted to a program for gifted children is indeed gifted. The district is then sure that all its services devoted to the needs of gifted pupils are being directed toward children who are definitely considered gifted. Using a stringent criteria, such as the top 2 percent, some gifted students may not receive services but the district can be certain that all the students receiving such services are gifted. An *inclusive* identification approach assures that every gifted child is identified, although some students who may not be gifted may receive services meant for gifted students. The criteria tends to be more flexible.

Procedures for identifying gifted and talented students must be fair and equitable if they are to serve students well and garner community support. Richert (1991; 1985) argues that all procedures for identifying gifted and talented students should meet the following standards:

- *Advocacy*: The identification process should be designed so that it will be in the best interests of all students.
- *Defensibility*: The procedures should be based upon research in the area of education for gifted children.
- *Equity*: The identification procedure should not overlook minority students or students with disabilities who often fail to gain acceptance into such programs.
- *Pluralism*: The definition of giftedness should be broad enough to identify many areas of giftedness.
- *Comprehensiveness*: As many gifted students should be identified and served as possible.
- *Pragmatism*: Whenever possible, procedures should allow for modification and use a number of different sources of information.

Unfortunately, many districts do not follow such policies, adopting narrow definitions of giftedness, collecting many sources of information but not using them, or using procedures that may place students from minority groups or students with disabilities at a distinct disadvantage (Richert, 1991).

Intelligence Tests and Tests of Cognitive Ability

Almost every process designed to identify intellectually gifted students uses intelligence tests or some standardized tests. It seems logical to use these tests, since on the surface they appear objective and in keeping with the average person's ideas about giftedness. A district may typically give a group test of intelligence or cognitive ability and use as the cutoff some score, be it 120, 130, or 140. After this, perhaps other sources of information are collected and may or may not be used. However, some gifted students will not score above these cutoffs, and as noted in the discussion of mental retardation in Chapter 4, major problems plague these intelligence tests and the question of their bias still lingers.

When testing for giftedness, other difficulties with intelligence testing beyond those described in earlier chapters can be raised. One could make the case that intelligence tests measure a type of conforming reasoning that may place students who are very original in their thinking at a disadvantage. This problem is especially apparent with group tests of intelligence which are so frequently used as screening instruments. For instance, if you were confronted with this analogy, how would you answer it?

Miami is to Heat as Chicago is to _____ .

Perhaps you would answer cold or wind. However, for a sports fan an equally correct answer is Bulls. The Heat is the National Basketball franchise in Miami, while the Bulls is the franchise in Chicago. Those students who may not think in a standard manner may score poorly and remain undiscovered. Group tests also do not work for people who are not motivated. If young students do not care how they do on the tests, they may not try very hard (Kaplan, 1986). The tests are also highly verbal and may identify only those who are already doing well (Davis & Rimm, 1989). The definition of giftedness offered at the beginning of the chapter uses the term *potential*, but intelligence tests may not show the potential of students as well as people might expect. Speed is also a factor on group intelligence tests, and a bright student who may not be very fast may suffer. Because these verbal tests are in English, some Hispanic and Asian youngsters may also be at a disadvantage (see Chapter 9).

When administering an individualized intelligence test such as the WISC-III or Stanford-Binet (fourth ed.), the psychologist may question the student and give credit for unusual, relevant responses. The expense of giving individualized intelligence tests is high enough that they are not used extensively with gifted children. Instead, group intelligence tests of some sort are often used as screening instruments. Unfortunately, they are not as valid or reliable as individual intelligence tests (Davis & Rimm, 1994). Group intelligence tests fail to identify many students who score above 125 on individual intelligence tests.

Achievement Tests

Some school districts include achievement test results in their criteria for identifying intellectually gifted students. Although a relationship exists between how someone performs on achievement tests, such as the Iowa Tests of Basic Skills or the Metropolitan Achievement Tests, and scores on intelligence tests, these tests may be most useful for identifying students with specific academic talents. Intellectually gifted children are not equally gifted in every area.

Unfortunately, these tests share some of the problems of group intelligence tests. They are highly verbal, depend upon the motivation of the child, and test how the child is presently functioning. They do not measure what the child is capable of doing in the future.

In addition, a rather unusual problem arises when using achievement tests. If a district would like to use a criterion of providing services for the top 5 percent of all students in the district, the coordinator may identify those who score in the 95th percentile on an achievement test. However, these achievement tests are meant to be used on the general population. They are not as accurate at the very top or the very bottom. The difference in one answer on a question can be very meaningful at the very top, and the tests may not really be a good way of differentiating between students at that level (Davis & Rimm, 1989). One answer for this problem is for promising students to take higher-level tests. This advanced testing is frequently done in mathematics.

Teacher Nominations

Clearly, additional information besides intelligence and achievement is necessary. The most common type of "additional" information provided during the assessment process is teacher nominations. Teachers who deal with these students on an everyday basis know the students and can identify some talents. Some teacher nominations may be informal, in the manner of a short descriptive letter, while some may involve checklists and rating scales.

Unfortunately, some evidence shows that teacher nominations are not always objective or correct. If one looks at the characteristics of gifted children discussed earlier, including originality, risk taking, and rebelliousness, one realizes these are not attributes always valued very highly by teachers. Recent research evidence, though, shows that teachers can be effective evaluators of giftedness (Bracy, 1994; Gagne, 1994). This is especially true when teachers are given training in what to look for (Richert, 1991). If not given such training, teachers may look for behavior such as neatness, punctuality, and cooperation. These are fine behaviors which may be found in some gifted students but may not be found in many others (Tuttle et al., 1988).

Parent Nominations

Parents offer another source of information. Although some people may think that parents are too biased to be taken seriously as sources of information, this assumption is not true (Tuttle et al., 1988). Parents are more realistic than most people think, and they do know something about their children's interests or aptitudes that even teachers may not know. For example, one set of parents recognized that their young child showed the ability to concentrate for hours on projects, to make things in a manner different than instructions indicated, and to show a great deal of attention to detail—behaviors that were not shown in class because the class offered no projects that could demonstrate the child's strengths. Parents may serve as sources of information about hobbies, special accomplishments and other characteristics that may not be noticeable to others. This additional source of information may be especially important in identifying the student with creative abilities, a problem that will be discussed in the next chapter. Of course, parent expectations can also pose possible problems. Parents may have to be reminded that not all students will be admitted to the program.

Peer Nominations and Self-Nominations

Peer nominations are growing in popularity as some districts seek to widen their identification process (Gagne, 1989). Students may be asked to list other students who they consider have exceptional ability in an area. Students tend to agree with each other concerning the intellectual and physical aptitudes of their peers, and show lesser agreement on creative aptitudes (Gagne, Begin, & Talbot, 1993). When using peer nominations, efforts must be made to examine the contents and carefully identify which talents are being assessed, refrain from adding together nominations for different abilities, and check for inter-judge agreement and for possible bias (Gagne, 1989).

Students may also, in some schools, submit self-nominations. In addition, people in charge of clubs or after-school activities can be encouraged to nominate children they believe are gifted.

Merely looking at scores on intelligence tests or achievement tests is obviously not sufficient. Evaluators need to have and use multiple sources of information.

The Process of Identification

The most common identification procedures involve one of four general approaches: cutoff scores, two-stage screening, pools, or a matrix of several scores (Tuttle et al., 1988). The *cutoff score approach* involves using an arbitrary cutoff in intelligence or achievement tests for inclusion into a gifted program. This strategy will omit many who do not score well on such tests and has been prohibited in some places. A *two-stage approach* involves a cutoff score which is somewhat lower than the arbitrary cutoff approach. From this larger group of children, other sources of information, such as teacher or parent recommendations are used. This method can be defended somewhat as fairer, but the initial criterion is still based upon one test.

The *pool or areas of assessment method* involves selecting several areas that reflect the desired characteristics of students admitted to the gifted program. Sources of information may include standardized tests, teacher nominations, achievement tests, parent recommendations, and others. Acceptable scores are set and to be selected the student must qualify in a preestablished number of areas. This approach may also incorporate a method for reconsideration of those students on the borderline.

The *matrix approach* is similar to the areas of assessment approach but is more quantitative in that a student is given a score for each area, the areas are weighted, and a total score is derived for each student. A cutoff for acceptance is used. The numbers are given as percentile ranks, and the more subjective information gained from teachers and parents is reviewed by a panel of educators and ranked by this panel. A reconsideration of children on the borderline may be built into the system.

Using both a standardized instrument *and* a cutoff is always a more secure way to identify gifted students. However, the use of intelligence tests to discover intellectual giftedness is a flawed use of an imperfect tool. Due to background or disability, some students who are gifted may not score well on such tests. Children with disabilities, who underachieve or who are members of some minority groups may be placed at a disadvantage if these tests are used as the sole criterion for identification.

No one denies that children who score very high on intelligence tests should be identified as gifted. However, districts should go beyond this. One of the most positive trends in the identification of gifted students is the collection of data by a variety of means and the emerging understanding that intelligence tests should not be used as the sole selection criterion (Richert, 1991). A system that involves acquiring and using information from a variety of sources may be more difficult to use, but its outcome is fairer and more likely to conform with the criteria for adequate identification procedures mentioned earlier.

Services for Gifted Students

Many different services are available for gifted students and these vary widely by district. These services can usually be placed under two large categories: acceleration and enrichment.

Acceleration

One method of meeting the needs of gifted students is through acceleration. **Acceleration** involves programs in which students complete courses of study in less time or at a younger age than usual (Reynolds & Birch, 1988). Acceleration can be accomplished in many ways. Early admission to school is one. Youngsters who are ready may start kindergarten early. Skipping is another alternative. Students who are especially gifted may skip a grade. Special accelerated classes is another possibility. Students may do two years of work in one. Years ago, in New York a program called special progress, or SP, allowed gifted students to complete seventh and eighth grade in one year. The idea of a student doing two years in one in a particular subject is sometimes called telescoping. Telescoping is especially prominent in mathematics. Early college enrollment and advanced placement are other options. For example, some students may wish to accelerate their courses and graduate early from high school. In other cases, dual attendance can be useful. That is, a student may attend both a high school and a college, taking courses in each and receiving credit in both high school and college (Pendarvis, Howley, & Howley, 1990). Students may also take advanced courses in high school that count for college credit. Many colleges accept credit from high schools where students have taken a college level course and then taken an examination. If the examination is passed at a particular level, the student is given college credit (see Schulz & Turnbull, 1991).

Acceleration certainly makes sense. After all, if a student can work at a higher level, why not do so? Why allow students to be bored by work they find unchallenging? Other advantages to acceleration can be realized by gifted students. Today, gifted students will probably require advanced graduate work, and they may find that without acceleration they do not finish their schooling until well into their mid-twenties. Saving some time makes sense since it will allow them to start their careers earlier. In addition, many gifted children have older friends.

Some forms of acceleration have not been popular. While advanced placement courses are allowed, skipping, telescoping, and early entrance are resisted by most school districts. A number of arguments are made against acceleration. First, some argue that these children may not fit in socially and may experience difficulty with interpersonal relationships. Second, some worry that by accelerating the student, gaps will be left in the student's knowledge base. Third, some argue that gifted children may burn out if accelerated. One objection specific to early entrance into kindergarten is the fear that children may not have the maturity, psychomotor skills, or physical endurance of their older peers (Schiever & Maker, 1991).

Each of these objections can be countered. No evidence exists for the supposition that gifted students will burn out. The risk of burnout, if it does exist, is not as great as the risk from lack of challenge, boredom, underachievement, and nonuse of ability (Compton, 1982). A risk of creating gaps in knowledge may exist, but this risk can be avoided by carefully evaluating the student to be certain the pupil is ready for acceleration. In addition, gifted students usually learn fairly quickly and can often fill in the gaps easily. No evidence that accelerated students exhibit any deficits in knowledge has been offered (Feldhusen, Proctor, & Black, 1986).

The possible problems created by early admission to kindergarten can be reduced by using appropriate screening procedures that will determine whether the

Acceleration:
A major division of services for gifted children in which a gifted student skips a grade or a particular unit or in which material is presented much more quickly than it would be for an average student.

THOUGHT QUESTION

5. Why are so many districts against acceleration programs, despite the fact that the research shows them to be beneficial?

child is ready for kindergarten (Fox & Washington, 1985). Tests of readiness in a number of areas may be used. Good screening procedures will offer early admission to those who are obviously ready and will deny such admission to those who are not mature enough. Some students will probably be on the borderline, and the decision in these cases will have to be made on a case-by-case basis.

People, though, are most concerned about the "social problems," about accelerated students fitting in. The story goes that students will not fit in, will not be able to function in the world comprised of average people, may not be socially accepted, and that their self-concepts will suffer because they will be placed among older students who are more mature (Swiatek & Benbow, 1991). No evidence exists that these children have social problems (Maker, 1987; Clark, 1988). Accelerated students are relatively popular, involved, and accepted.

In fact, not one study exists showing that acceleration is harmful to social or emotional development (Benbow, 1991). The only negative finding is that some decline in self-concept may occur but the interpretation of this finding is controversial. Some studies show that when children are accelerated, or even if placed in enrichment programs, some initial decline in self-concept takes place. Does this indicate a problem? Probably not, since this may be interpreted as an indication of greater realism on the part of the student rather than any problem with the self-concept (Richardson & Benbow, 1990).

Swiatek and Benbow (1991) followed highly gifted math students for ten years comparing those who had entered college early and those who did not. Few differences between the groups on academic or psychosocial variables appeared. Both reported splendid academic achievements and high personal satisfaction both with school and their own personal development. The academic performance of those who accelerated was slightly higher, and the researchers found no gender differences. When accelerated college students were compared on the basis of personal adjustment at the beginning and end of the academic year, no

There is no evidence of social difficulties among gifted children who are accelerated.

significant problems were found. However, those who were more troubled or had family problems did not fair as well as those who did not (Cornell, Callahan, & Lloyd, 1991). A study of the social, emotional, and behavioral adjustment of gifted accelerated students and average eighth-grade students found that the accelerated students showed levels of emotional adjustment and feelings of acceptance by others that were actually higher than those of the average students. Students who entered school early or skipped grades did not report unusual social isolation and had fewer serious behavioral problems than average students (Sayler & Brookshire, 1993). In another study, no evidence of burnout was found in a group of highly accelerated mathematics students (Kolitch & Brody, 1992).

Some studies have even found advantages in personal and academic growth comparing women who were early entrants with those gifted students who did not accelerate (Cornell et al., 1991). Studies of accelerated individuals show improved motivation, confidence and better scholarship, a reduction in lazy thinking, and better work habits (Schiever & Maker, 1991). When Janos (1987) compared the 19 youngest college students in Terman's classic sample with other college students of the same intelligence on career progress, academic success, and psychosocial adjustment, the younger college students earned higher grades, more academic honors, and participated in more extracurricular activities. They graduated and entered professions earlier and, at least at the beginning of their careers, were rated as higher achievers. No differences in psychosocial adjustment were found.

Students who are not gifted may elect to use acceleration to finish their schooling earlier. An enterprising high school student who goes to summer school to advance or who takes extra subjects (nine classes instead of eight in high school) may graduate in three or three-and-one-half years. The same can also be done in college. Although acceleration is considered here as an option and a desirable one for many gifted individuals, it can be chosen by others.

Acceleration is not a panacea, though. Students who skip a grade may find themselves in a higher level class but still not challenged by the curriculum. It may turn out to be "no more than the same curriculum but sooner and/or faster" (Schiever & Maker, 1991, p. 101). It may not offer additional content at a higher level. The studies noted do not demonstrate that acceleration is always desirable, but they do show that it is a viable option. Children should not be accelerated against their will, but when done properly, it is a sound option.

SCENARIO

3 There is no doubt that Kim is bright. She knows her math well and is advanced. She is very good in her other subjects but math is her best. She is in the ninth grade and is ready for calculus. Her parents believe that she should be placed in the senior level calculus class even though she is a "young" ninth grader. The math chairperson agrees that she is an excellent student but believes that she will not fit in and should not be accelerated. Rather the chairperson argues that she will help the honors class teacher give her special work. Her parents are still not satisfied and want her accelerated. In your opinion, under the circumstances should Kim be accelerated?

Enrichment

Enrichment involves offering a more in-depth, more varied educational experience and requires adding to or modifying the usual curriculum (Schiever & Maker, 1991). Enrichment activities do not require students to skip grades or accomplish anything earlier than usual. Enrichment can be implemented in a number of ways. It may involve Saturday classes, after school seminars, and special programs during the school day in which the student is placed with other gifted students in a different classroom and exposed to special, challenging activities (Feldhusen, 1991). The curriculum may involve projects, abstract work, and advanced problem solving, and should follow student interest. To be considered enrichment, any work must be qualitatively different from the regular curriculum, not just more work. Doing an extra book report or ten more math examples is not enrichment. More work does not make it enriched work (Clark, 1988). Special summer institutes can be quite successful. Some gifted students attend special summer institutes in which they live in residence halls at a university and attend classes taught by expert teachers for six or seven hours each day. Special recreation, tours, seminars, and other activities complement the curriculum. Student reaction to these experiences is very positive, praising the challenging course of study and the opportunity to make friends. Many say that they have gained increased confidence in their own abilities (Enersen, 1993).

One of the more interesting approaches to enrichment is Joseph Renzulli's Schoolwide Enrichment Triad Model (Renzulli & Reis, 1991). This approach is based upon Renzulli's triad model of giftedness. First, Renzulli believes that instead of merely identifying the top 3 percent, that a larger pool of about 15 percent or even 20 percent should be identified. Renzulli's model envisions three different types of enriched experience. Type 1 enrichment consists of general exploration and is designed to expose students to new and exciting topics and ideas not covered in the regular curriculum. This exposure is carried out through speakers, field trips, demonstrations, displays, and learning centers. Type 2 enrichment is aimed at promoting thinking, creativity, and problem solving, as well as sensitivity and appreciation. It emphasizes skills such as note taking, drawing conclusions, using reference skills, and improving communication. Both Type 1 and Type 2 enrichment are open to the whole pool. Type 3 enrichment involves investigation into real problems and is the highest form of the experience. The participants answer a research question by acting as professionals. They identify the problem, learn the process and the methodology of inquiry, and obtain the resources necessary to suggest solutions. This activity is not just an "academic" exercise, but may involve actually solving a particular problem, inventing something, or answering some scientific question. The finished products are shown to an audience, local legislators, or people who may use them. Outstanding work may be published.

Renzulli's gifted program differs in another way. It adopts a revolving door attitude. That is, students not in the talent pool who show some sparks of interest or commitment to an area are identified by teachers trained to do so and receive appropriate services that allow them to explore their interest, as long as it continues, with the aid of a teacher. The numbers of children that are served depend only on the resources of the school.

One of the most interesting aspects of this model of enrichment is that Types 1 and 2 are open to so many more students than conventional systems. This greater inclusiveness ensures better acceptance of the program by the community that sometimes wants to know why their children do not receive enrichment (Renzulli & Reis, 1991; Reis, 1989).

The Schoolwide Enrichment Triad Model has been implemented in schools around the world with many different populations and has been field tested and evaluated. In a review of the research, Renzulli and Reis (1994) found that programs based upon this model were positively viewed by the faculty and administration, creating more staff involvement and providing more incentives for students to strive for higher goals. These programs were effective in encouraging creativity and task commitment and producing high quality work.

Giving an intellectually gifted child twenty problems to solve instead of fifteen is not enrichment.

SCENARIO

4 You are a teacher of a regular American history class in junior high school and have a student who is very interested in the subject. Rolly has finished his project and written assignment in a few days and the quality of the work is excellent. He seems to know everything in the text and has read widely, especially in some areas such as the Civil War. He seems bored by the class. The school has no gifted social studies class, and so he must remain in your class. What could you do to enrich the subject matter?

IN THE CLASSROOM   Enriching the Curriculum

Teachers often want to enrich their lessons, challenging students to think and achieve. Just increasing the amount of work assigned is not enrichment. The following suggestions may help.

1. All gifted students must acquire basic skills with no gaps.	**Why?** One criticism of acceleration programs is the possibility of gaps. Being aware of the possibility and monitoring student progress can eliminate the problem.
2. Students should be encouraged to move ahead in the standard curriculum as rapidly as they can. Advanced books and materials should be available.	**Why?** School systems often pay only lip service to the idea that children should be allowed to advance at their own rate. Students should not be told that all students must be reading the same book at the same time.
3. Allow students to follow their interests, which may be connected in a tangential way to the	**Why?** Allowing students to follow their interests enhances motivation.

curriculum, through reports and projects.	
4. Show how various areas are connected.	**Why?** Many gifted students see connections between different areas, and teachers may encourage this integration.
5. Use independent study to maintain student interest.	**Why?** When students know the work assigned, independent study may allow students to study areas of particular interest.
6. Allow substitution of assignments.	**Why?** Substituting a different assignment for the regular assignment is appropriate as long as the teacher has evidence that the student has learned the skills necessary to succeed at the regular assignment (Delisle, 1992).
7. Use pretests to identify who knows the work before it is taught.	**Why?** If gifted students know the material before it is taught, they will be bored. Giving a pretest allows the teacher to identify students and provide enriched individual or small group work.
8. Incentives must be given for careful work. Telling students that if they get all the examples correct (or one wrong) in the first ten problems, they do not have to do the rest is one way of reducing this problem.	**Why?** Gifted students may not always be careful about their work.
9. Students should be encouraged to carry class discussions and projects into the wider realm of school or community action. This may involve projects that have some community value. For example, a student may have done a study in ecology that is presented to the legislature for action.	**Why?** Some school work is abstract and divorced from reality. Performing special work that may have an impact on the child's environment can be a useful motivational technique.

10. Help gifted students find outside activities that may promote learning, such as special summer programs or after-school activities.	**Why?** Special programs can provide the extra instruction necessary to promote the child's talents and abilities.
11. Help parents realize it is acceptable not to know the answers to their children's questions, that their children may not be gifted in every area, and that their children may choose intellectual pursuits over other activities.	**Why?** Parents of gifted children need to understand that it is acceptable for them not to know all the answers and find ways to help their children find their own answers. They may also have difficulty accepting their children's preference for intellectual pursuits over other activities (Keirouz, 1990). Teachers can help parents understand the needs and preferences of their children.
12. Include questions that force students to think, "What would happen if . . .," in lessons.	**Why?** Special questions and activities for students who are gifted or especially interested in an area promote thinking and learning.

Delivering Services to Gifted Students

Just as controversial as what type of services should be offered to gifted students is the manner in which the services should be delivered. Should gifted students be placed in their own classes, or simply taken out of class once or twice a week and, together with other gifted students, be exposed to a special curriculum? The advantages and disadvantages of each are found in Table 10.1.

Are Special Classes Better Than In-Class Programs?

Methodological difficulties abound when comparing special class attendance to in-class services for gifted children. Simply measuring the achievement or personal growth of children in both programs and making some sort of decision would not necessarily provide accurate data. One would have to be able to randomly assign children to each of these types of programs, which is not possible. A number of studies, although imperfect, seek to answer this question. Goldring (1990) analyzed 23 studies that sought to answer the question of which delivery method is best. Gifted students in special classrooms achieved more than gifted students in the regular classrooms, but benefits of being in a special class,

TABLE 10.1   **Service Delivery Models**

Many service delivery models are available. Each has its own advantages and disadvantages.

	ADVANTAGES	DISADVANTAGES
Special School	1. Offers a high level of peer support for students since all students are gifted. 2. Reduces feelings of being isolated. 3. Uses curriculum specifically designed to meet educational need. 4. Provides faculty which is likely to be prepared and committed to educating gifted children. 5. More likely to offer advanced courses at the high school level leading to college credit. 6. Meets the need for fast-paced, advanced curriculum more easily. 7. Allows the student opportunities to interact with peers of similar ability levels.	1. Does not provide the opportunity to interact with other nongifted children because of the segregation of special schools. 2. May encourage children to specialize too early in their lives. 3. May intensify competition. 4. May be very expensive to attend.
Special Class	1. Uses curriculum specifically designed to meet educational need. 2. Promotes interaction with other gifted children. 3. Allows for group work at high level due to the presence of other gifted students. 4. Meets the need for fast-paced, advanced curriculum more easily. 5. Allows an opportunity for interaction with broad range of other students since they remain in the neighborhood school.	1. Segregates students considered gifted. 2. May expect students who are gifted in one area to be gifted in many areas. 3. Prevents other students from having the experience of being exposed to these bright students because gifted students are not in regular classes.

depended upon the subject. The largest effects were in science and social studies with smaller effects in reading, mathematics, and writing. No significant differences in general self-concept or creativity were found. The higher the grade, the stronger the advantages for special classes. Therefore, special classes for gifted students would seem more important in middle and high school than elementary school. Students in those special classes, taught by teachers who had received special training to teach gifted students, did much better than students in special classes where the teacher did not receive such training. Reviews of the research find advantages for special classes whether enriched or accelerated (Kulik & Kulik, 1992; 1982). These students outperform those in regular classes. The reason may be that programs that require the most substantial changes in curriculum seem to produce the most positive effects, and special classes seem to require the greatest curricular adjustment.

One could make the case that the more complex and specialized the work, the more a special class would seem best. However, suggestions that gifted children

TABLE 10.1　*Continued*

	ADVANTAGES	**DISADVANTAGES**
Pull-out Program	1. Allows for both homogeneous grouping in special programs and heterogeneous grouping in regular classrooms. 2. Does not interfere with regular class work. If teachers are familiar with pull-out programs they can allow students to catch up with any work they may miss. 3. Permits teachers involved in the program to go well beyond what is done in the regular classrooms since students are taught their usual work in their regular classrooms. 4. Provides flexibility. 5. Receives more public support than other programs.	1. Is of dubious value if work in pull-out program is not tied to anything being learned in the regular classroom. 2. Presents logistic problems if students need to be bussed to other locations. 3. Fails to provide enough time to accomplish major projects. 4. May inadequately meet the needs of students if, as some authorities believe, pull-out program is simply a compromise.
Regular Classroom	1. Follows inclusion efforts that indicate gifted students should be taught in the regular classroom. 2. Provides a stimulating challenge to teachers who do have the ability to provide an appropriate educational experience for gifted children. 3. Eliminates need for labeling children. 4. Improves the intellectual level of the classes when gifted students remain in classes. 5. Enhances interaction of students of all ability levels.	1. Groups students by age, which has nothing to do with learning. 2. Uses vocabulary that may be at an inappropriate or unchallenging level for gifted students. 3. Uses texts that may be too limited in range and complexity. 4. May not meet the different and special needs of gifted students through regular classroom teaching.

Sources include Borland, 1989; Clark, 1992; Sapon-Shevin, 1992.

in special classes are more creative or have a better self-concept do not ring true.

Some drawbacks to special class placement for gifted students have been noted. For instance, some researchers find that the removal of very bright students may lead to a disadvantage for those nongifted children who do not have the benefit of the example of gifted children who may add new ideas to the class (Reynolds & Birch, 1988). While the full-time, self-contained class may be better for gifted students, this form of education will probably not be implemented by many schools due to budgetary constraints and concerns about exclusiveness and elitism (Feldhusen, 1991).

Although full-time special classes may not be a politically viable alternative for many districts, what of weekly classes for gifted students? Using such a pull-out system, gifted students meet at a certain time (for example, every Wednesday morning) and receive special lessons. In some districts, all gifted students from the schools in the district are bussed to one school in which all the education for gifted children occurs. Here, they receive enrichment. Of course, significant administrative problems can arise as students miss some of the work in their classes and must make it up.

The pull-out delivery system has the advantage of requiring only a few specially trained teachers and leaves gifted children in the regular classroom while still giving them some enrichment. The program is also highly visible to the community (Clark, 1988) and it brings gifted and talented students together for social and intellectual pursuits. Some authorities have criticized this method of service delivery, however (Cox, Daniels, & Boston, 1985). Pull-out programs do not satisfy the individual needs of students and they may even discourage regular classroom teachers from doing anything for gifted children since "they are in the Wednesday morning program" (Treffinger, 1991). Sometimes, the activities consist of nothing more than fun and games and little real problem-solving instruction goes on. In addition, what is learned is often not connected to the curriculum and the regular teacher has little idea of what is going on.

If the teacher is trained, the material taught in the special program integrated with the curriculum, and something of real value presented, the pull-out delivery system can be somewhat useful (Renzulli, 1987). Vaughn and colleagues (1991) analyzed the research on pull-out programs and found small or medium positive effects in the areas of academic achievement and critical and creative thinking. No adverse effects on self-concept were found. If they are done with care, especially for small school districts with limited resources, they can be useful.

Mentorships, Tutorials, and Internships

Some modes of delivery do not focus on the group but rather on the individual. Mentorship is one. A mentor is an older expert or gifted person who is a role model and informal teacher. The mentor may hold a position in a scientific lab or hospital in which the student can observe or assist. Mentorship programs have been shown to have a positive impact on gifted students' development of skills and aspirations. In one such program, gifted high school students were paired with a mentor in the area of special interest. These students were prepared in the school for their mentorship experiences. The mentorship program lasted for about 14 weeks with students implementing their learning plan created during the preparation phase of the program. Each student spent eight hours per week working on a project, observing the mentor in work situations, and exploring special interests within the field. Group discussions were also held. Results of the program showed that mentors had an especially positive effect in the area of vocational planning. Some students exposed to the lifestyle of the mentor decided to enter the field while others did not. The program had significant personal and academic benefits as well (Beck, 1989).

Tutorials have a more formal instructional role in which an experienced individual may tutor a younger gifted student. Internship is a third possibility. It is a formal arrangement in which a set of experiences in a work setting is given. Students may possibly intern at a laboratory or other work place (Fox & Washington, 1985).

No single program delivery method is acceptable to everyone. Although the research certainly favors homogeneous grouped classrooms, this arrangement may not be politically possible within the school or community. Services delivered in other ways including enrichment within the regular classroom and special weekly programs are possible, but it is much more difficult to make them academically useful. Much of the success of an enrichment program, though, as with any other program, depends upon the training and interest of the teacher. The teacher in a pull-out program should be well trained. Regular classroom teachers who deal with gifted students should receive in-service training or even a college course that would alert the teacher to the characteristics of gifted children, challenge any negative attitudes toward gifted students, and help the classroom teacher develop skills in enrichment.

Special Academic Ability

The federal definition of giftedness includes not only general intellectual ability but specific academic aptitude as well. This part of the definition is sometimes forgotten, especially in elementary school. Elementary school programs are often more general programs meant for broad academic aptitude. In secondary schools, a gifted student is more likely to be in one or two honors or advanced placement classes and in regular classes in other subjects. However, proceeding from regular classes to honors classes in many schools may not be easy. Although theoretically possible, most honor and nonhonor students are tracked. In one suburban district, a student had to be selected in sixth grade for honors mathematics. After that, the regular and honors groups were no longer covering the same material, and the student could not ever be considered for honors mathematics again.

Although children with high intelligence scores tend to do well in most subjects and on most tests of academic achievement and aptitude, their standardized test scores in specific areas may show a great deal more variability. A child with a 130 intelligence score may do exceptionally well in English and social studies and, although above average in mathematics, may not be gifted in that subject. In fact, among gifted children, intelligence score is not a good predictor of narrow aptitudes. Children with IQs of 130 are as likely to have high aptitude scores in specific areas as children with IQs of 160 (Pendarvis et al., 1990). Although scores on both verbal and mathematics tests are correlated, a number of talented students have fairly large discrepancies between verbal and math aptitudes. Some gifted students may have only an average aptitude in mathematics, and some mathematically gifted students may not do as well on tests of verbal abilities (Gordon, 1995). In fact, tests of mathematics aptitude correlate only moderately with general intelligence, probably because the former emphasizes conceptual knowledge and reasoning skills (Pendarvis et al., 1990). Educators should, therefore, look for exceptional ability in a particular subject not only in those who are above the cutoff of intelligence but in the general population of students.

One way to discover an exceptional ability is to look at divergent scores on achievement tests. If an individual consistently shows exceptional scores on math or social studies achievement tests, the child may be gifted in this area, even though the intelligence score may or may not be above the cutoff point. Some districts use a Specific Academic Aptitude Model in which acceleration and enrichment are provided on a subject-by-subject basis. Special mathematics classes are frequently offered, but literature, writing, science, and art and music are also commonly found. Students are screened and identified on the basis of achievement tests in the subject area. Previously earned grades in that subject and teacher recommendations are also given consideration. Students are usually referred to as talented rather than as generally gifted (Eby & Smutny, 1990).

Most students are not poor in one subject and very gifted in another. Such a pattern is relatively rare, but it is not unheard of.

Mathematical Ability

Perhaps the area in which measuring instruments other than intelligence tests are used most often is mathematics. The Study of Mathematically Precocious Youth (SMPY) was founded by Julian Stanley, in 1971, at Johns Hopkins University to help these gifted students achieve. SMPY is essentially a talent search. Students who score at or above the 97th percentile on various achievement tests in participating school districts are asked to take the Scholastic Aptitude Test (SAT) in the seventh grade. Interestingly enough, these students score high on the SAT math even though they have not yet taken classes that would allow them to solve these problems. It shows their superior reasoning ability (Benbow, 1991). Benbow and Minor (1986) found, in a follow-up study of about 2,000 seventh- and eighth-graders who qualified for this special program in mathematics on the basis of SAT scores, that SAT mathematics scores obtained in junior high school were strongly associated with science achievement in high school for both boys and girls. The talent search has been expanded to include verbal skills as well (Cohn, 1990).

Students who do well on the SAT are permitted to participate in special summer seminars and are helped in their school planning. These students benefit from the SMPY program, and studies show they are more advanced in their education than nonparticipants (Stanley & Benbow, 1986). When someone does very well in the SAT at this age, the result is a clear message to everyone that the child has superior abilities in the area (Cohn, 1990).

Based upon the research in the area, some conclusions are possible. Most of the time, children who show superior intelligence scores will show superior test scores in various academic areas. However, even though they may score above average, their abilities will also vary. Although not a common occurrence, an individual who shows a particular talent in an academic area may possibly not test out well on intelligence tests. Often talent searches have been used to discover youths who show special ability; the SAT is most commonly used to discover ability in mathematics. Gifted children should not be expected to score the same in every area of academia. Therefore, services for gifted children should be open to the student who does not score above the IQ cutoff but who may have special talent in a particular subject. Enrichment for this individual who may easily be overlooked is especially important.

SCENARIO

5 Mrs. Calhoun is a seventh-grade teacher. She has been told that two students in her science class are gifted and that she has the responsibility of meeting their needs through enrichment. She claims that she does this through special assignments. She gives each student much more homework. Instead of doing five questions, they are assigned ten—two of these questions are special "additional questions" that are difficult. She asks what else is she supposed to do? Being her chairperson, you would like to help her in this area. What would you suggest and how would you evaluate her enrichment activities?

Gifted Children in Adulthood

Generally, gifted children do quite well in adulthood. Terman's work, described earlier, certainly shows that gifted children achieve well in adulthood. They were successful in their professional lives, and their social and emotional development in adulthood were certainly quite good. The women in Terman's studies fared well also; two-thirds finished college during the Depression. Although fewer pursued careers than is the case today, they did serve as community leaders and often excelled in unpaid situations (Schuster, 1990).

Schuster (1990) reviewed four longitudinal follow-ups of gifted women born in 1910, 1920s–1930s, and 1940s. A greater proportion of women in the later cohorts followed careers. Those women in the 1940 cohort consistently reported more fulfillment of potential, life satisfaction, and self-perceived competence than those in the earlier cohorts. More recent longitudinal studies of gifted and talented women also find that they attained more than earlier groups of women (Hollinger & Fleming, 1992). Tomlinson-Keasey and Little (1990) tried to isolate factors other than cognitive skills that predicted adult achievements and personal adjustment. Personal adjustment had one very important predictor for both men and women and that was the harmony that existed in the family of origin. These gifted adults continued their close relationships with their family. The factors that predicted intellectual achievements were parents' education and intellectual determination. Parental education is an indicator of the family's socioeconomic status, and educated parents can usually provide an atmosphere that promotes academic achievement. Intellectual determination during childhood, the other factor in intellectual achievement, translates into high aspiration levels and an appreciation of intellectual and cognitive matters later in life. Sociability in childhood, on the other hand, did not predict adult adjustment for either men or women. In fact, sociability was negatively related to maintaining intellectual skills, and this finding held for both males and females. Children who were popular and socially oriented were less likely to maintain their intellectual skills in adulthood, whereas less popular children were more likely to do so. Perhaps the ability to work alone is important. Perhaps some intellectually gifted children look for excellence in interpersonal matters, not attending as much to their intellectual abilities.

Most of the gifted adults in these studies have succeeded in the personal and professional areas of their lives. This result is to be expected judging from Terman's research. The unanswered question that requires more research involves the differential effects on these people of receiving educational services for gifted children. In other words, how well do gifted people who have received various special services fare in later life compared with gifted people who may not have received such help? In answering that question, such research must control for family variables, including parental interest.

THOUGHT QUESTION

6. How would you measure the success of programs for gifted children?

The Future

It is easy to be discouraged about the lack of progress in providing special services for gifted students. However, as Reis (1989) notes, some advocates tend to lose sight of what has been accomplished when confronted with the work that still has to be done. Although interest in educating gifted children waxes and wanes, progress in the area is clearly visible. Most states now have offices for gifted education in their state education departments, and some interest on the part of the federal government exists.

The public's misconception of the educational opportunities for gifted children is one problem; another is the difficulties in encouraging people to consider education for gifted children as a priority when the need for other types of special education services is so much more visible. The arguments for such programs do not get much sympathy. The fact that many gifted children are not achieving up to their capabilities is countered by the fact that most gifted children "make it through school" and that the same lack of achievement could be said of other groups. Many average students do not work up to their potential. The idea that gifted children are an important resource is difficult to sell to the public in the cost-conscious 1990s.

Yet, many valid arguments exist for serving the special needs of gifted children, and the programs need not be overly expensive. The cost of acceleration is not great. For example, early entrance does not cost the district anything since these students would be entering anyway. Joint programs with colleges are not expensive; advanced placement programs do not really require much financial backing; and many other accelerated programs are cost effective and efficient educational tools.

In the area of enrichment, many of the opportunities outside of the classroom do require extra money, especially pull-out programs, but can be defended because they are not overly expensive and should accomplish something that can be measured. The argument for special schools for gifted students, staffed by experts in educating gifted children, while reasonable, will certainly not be accepted by school districts with strained resources. Some large cities may have such specialized high schools, but smaller districts will have to agree to create such regional schools for gifted children. This may be difficult. Any movement toward such educational opportunities at this point probably would have to be privately run and financed. Perhaps in the distant future, state governments with federal help may establish such centers. Advocates for gifted children would like to see the development of special educational centers for gifted students, but the arguments in favor of these centers have not as yet led to any general planning for their operation.

Renzulli's conception of offering enrichment programs that are open to a greater percentage of students is one way to overcome the reluctance of the general public to support education for gifted children. It has the benefit of expanding such educational opportunities to many more qualified students. Enrichment within the regular class is more difficult and requires some teacher training, but also is very cost effective.

Academically gifted students require special services if they are to develop their talents. Before this occurs, though, misunderstandings about what education of gifted students means and what it can accomplish must be corrected. However, such programs and services are in the spirit of creating an educational system in which every child's talents and abilities can be developed to the fullest extent possible.

 **Stretching the Limits**

Three students sit at a computer trying to find the smallest natural number with three factors. The students are gifted sixth grade students involved in a program that uses computers as tools for solving mathematical problems (Hersberger & Wheatley, 1989).

At another table, students are using a computer with a modem to access a database in order to find information on gene splicing. Still another group of students is communicating through the computer with a group of students in another state. They are working on a joint ecology project.

The computer can certainly be a useful tool in the education of gifted students. Gifted students may use word-processing, database, and spreadsheet programs. In one junior high school, an integrated program that contains all three programs is used. Each gifted student is required to use the programs in a creative manner. Often, students use the word processor for poems or words for a song, databases to create files on topics of interest, and spreadsheets for budgets or recipes (Eby & Smutny, 1990).

The computer can also be used in an instructional capacity, allowing gifted students to complete their work in a shorter period of time. This tutorial function may enable students to learn by themselves and save sufficient time to go on to more involved work, allowing for enrichment or acceleration.

Another very meaningful use of the computer in the education of gifted children is as a tool for teaching critical thinking and problem solving. For example, computers can generate a graph, and students can vary the value of x and y. Rules for solving problems in mathematics can be applied to business problems given to students to solve (Pogrow, 1985). Some programs present students with a set of tools and a problem and ask them to solve it (Dale, 1993). More than one way to solve these problems is usually possible, and students may be asked to come up with alternative approaches to the problem.

One difficulty that often arises in the education of gifted children is their desire to work on more advanced problems and become experienced with environments that may be either difficult to create or just too expensive. The use of computerized simulations and games allow for the effective presentation of problems to students and provide opportunities for students to try to solve problems, many of which are realistic but cannot be practically presented in the classroom in any other manner. Consider the student learning about the flow of blood in the human body, the food chain in a pond, the life cycle of a frog, or cell division (Harty, Kloosterman, & Matkin, 1988). Computer simulations allow students to view a graphic action sequence and to alter particular variables and see what happens.

Computer simulations also allow students to perform experiments that cannot be done in the classroom, to apply their knowledge interactively to a problem scenario, and to see graphically the results of changing elements of a situation. These simulation labs may be invaluable; such "dry labs" allow students to work on laboratory exercises that would not be feasible for practical reasons (Pogrow, 1985). Obviously, computer simulations will not take the place of all labs, since the physical setup of labs and actual hands-on experience are of value. But, because students do not have to set up the experiment and pour the chemicals they can participate in more labs (Vockell, 1987). Students can also run these computer-simulated experiments several times, investigating different hypotheses.

Through the use of computer simulations, students can become involved in various activities that otherwise would be impossible. For example, students can fly a plane or manage a nuclear reactor (Dale, 1993). Such simulations encourage students to develop their own interests.

Games may also be useful in the education of gifted children. Most people think of computer games in terms of a child blasting alien ships from outer space seeking to conquer Earth. Yet, games are a great source of intellectual challenge for gifted and talented children (Hamlett, 1984). Computer games can develop logical thinking, organization, and planning skills (Dale, 1993). In one game, students must use almanacs and travel guides to find thieves that go from place to place to avoid arrest (Brownell, 1987). The Carmen Sandiego software "Where in the USA . . .," "Where in Europe . . .," "Where in the World . . .," "Where in Time . . ." promotes research skills as students attempt to find Carmen and her gang. Computer games have been created for many subjects, including language, mathematics, logic, physics, chemistry, biology, economics, business, medicine, and geology (Tolman & Allred, 1987).

Computer simulations may be used for demonstration purposes by teachers as well. For instance, a teacher may show the class how things change when temperature and pressure are altered in an experiment. Used in this way, the computer simulation becomes a part of the daily lesson and an aid in presenting new material to a class.

Electronic telecommunications can also be quite useful in the education of gifted children. Gifted children can use a computer with a modem to plug into various databases allowing them to research areas of interest. They may also, through the use of electronic mail systems, discuss and solve problems with other gifted children in other areas of the world.

Computer programming is also sometimes a part of the education of some gifted children. Although some gifted children will enter the computer field itself, most will not. Therefore, the selection of programming languages should be based upon the students' interests and needs.

Different languages may be useful for different students (Dale, 1993). The language becomes a tool for use in solving problems in the child's area of interest.

One of the most interesting uses for computer technology is the exploration of artificial intelligence, a branch of computer science that uses the computer to solve problems that require knowledge, intuition, or imagination (Lindsey, 1993). The individual using the computer may program all the conditions in an environment, provide the computer with abilities and data, and then specify the tasks it is to perform. The results may be observed. Students can then test scientific theories and hypotheses.

These uses for the computer are not unique to the education of gifted students. Indeed, all students should learn to use word-processing programs, databases, and spreadsheets. Many students enjoy the idea of working on problem-solving activities, and simulations are motivating to many students. In fact, software is not usually specifically designed for the gifted population (Dale, 1993).

Judging which software would be especially useful for gifted children is not easy, since gifted children are such a heterogeneous population with different interests and abilities. Ability and interest, not age, should dictate the use of particular programs. Dale (1993) suggests that programs used in the education of gifted students should be flexible, support the interests of the students, allow many elements to be altered and modified, and give students maximum control. Naturally, such programs should also encourage creativity and intellectual development.

Gifted children can use the computer as a tool to foster their intellectual and problem-solving abilities. Programs can take the student beyond the classroom, allowing for experiences that would be impossible to create in the classroom. Computer software can allow students to develop their own solutions to problems and try them out. Good computer software can help expand the gifted student's horizons and help the teacher meet the special needs of these students.

S U M M A R Y

1. The federal government defines a gifted child as any child who either has demonstrated or seems to have the potential for high capabilities in general intellectual functioning, specific academic areas, creative or productive thinking, leadership, or the visual and performing arts.

2. The studies by Lewis Terman, who followed a number of gifted children throughout their lives served to reduce the stereotypes of gifted people. He found that gifted people do well socially, academically, and emotionally.

3. Intellectually gifted children are quick learners, original, independent, and self-confident. Gifted elementary school children are well accepted, but the acceptance of gifted children in secondary school is still a controversial matter. They are more persistent and have superior cognitive skills including concentration and memory.

4. The term *genius* has yet to be defined. Studies show that some children are very precocious—that is, they do things much earlier than other children. They are often successful but no more

than other gifted children. These children require an educational experience that the average school may have difficulty providing. They may benefit from university programs and other special programs.

5. Community opposition to special educational programs for gifted children is common because some people believe gifted children will succeed anyway, will look down on others, and that the programs are costly. Each assumption is false. Many gifted children underachieve; they do not look down on others; and many programs for gifted children are not overly expensive. Some people argue that providing special classes for gifted students is not in the spirit of the inclusion movement.

6. States are not required by federal law to provide any special education for gifted children, but many states have laws encouraging such programs.

7. Identification programs should be fair to all, based upon a defensible logic and research, should be broad enough to encompass different areas of giftedness, should identify as many gifted children as possible, and should use many sources of information in the identification program as possible.

8. A number of different approaches to identification are used. Standardized testing, specific tests of achievement, teacher, peer, and parent nominations and self-nominations are used.

9. Services for gifted children fall under two categories: acceleration and enrichment. Acceleration involves skipping a grade, taking two years of instruction in one year, or early entrance. The evidence does not indicate that children who are ready for such programs are harmed by them. Enrichment involves going over and beyond the usual course work. Enrichment activities require a more varied, richer educational experience, not just more work.

10. According to the evidence, gifted students in their own classes do better than in regular classes, at least in some areas. This result is especially true in secondary schools. Others argue that removing very bright students from other students injures the other students. Budgetary concerns are also an issue. Pull-out programs in which gifted students receive special services once or twice a week in special classes yield small-to-medium positive effects. Mentorships, tutorials, and internships may also be appropriate for gifted students.

11. Some students have a particularly advanced ability in a certain subject. These students also require special programs.

12. Studies on gifted children in adulthood show that they are generally successful and well adjusted. The long-term effects of educational programs on gifted people have been difficult to determine.

Creativity and Talent

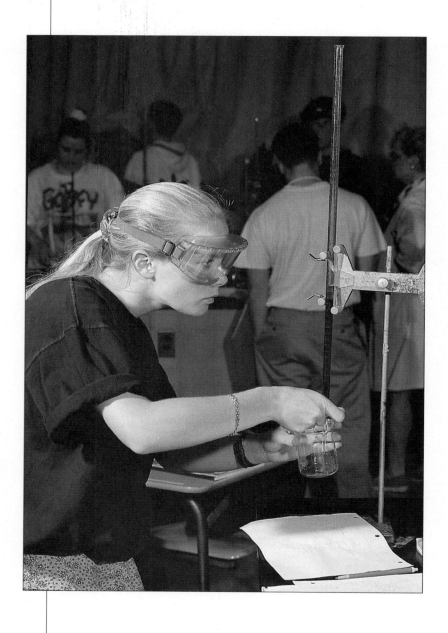

TRUE-FALSE STATEMENTS

See below for the correct answers.

1. Creativity may be accurately measured by a good, standardized intelligence test.
2. Expert evaluation of talent in art and music is as objective as the written tests used to measure other forms of giftedness.
3. People who are talented often first view their area of specialty as fun.
4. Most successful talented children who have fulfilled their potential do so in spite of their parents' lack of interest and encouragement.
5. As children who are talented develop their abilities, they tend to narrow their focus on these abilities rather than place attention in other areas.
6. Most adults who are the top ten achievers in their field were recognized as child prodigies.
7. Group leaders are usually more intelligent than the people they are leading.
8. Gifted students who underachieve usually evaluate themselves as superior and have very positive self-concepts.
9. Underachieving students often see the school curriculum as boring and irrelevant.
10. By definition, students with disabilities cannot be considered gifted.
11. Children from minority groups are underrepresented in programs for gifted and talented youth.

Answers to True-False Statements

1. False. See page 419.
2. False. See page 422.
3. True.
4. False. See page 427.
5. True.
6. False. See page 429.
7. True.
8. False. See page 435.
9. True.
10. False. See page 438.
11. True.

Taking Me by Surprise

When I first began teaching, I was assigned to teach an eighth grade social studies curriculum on urban studies, which included, among other things, a detailed look at the many facets of urban life—culture, housing, health care, education, and the environment. After teaching these elements individually, I combined them into a project. I divided the students into groups and asked each group to design a city that would provide adequate services for the population. The students were to use their imaginations, draw their plans, and write a group report that would define their ideas. They were also required to describe their designs to other students in the class.

The students seemed pleased at the prospect of designing their ideal city, and I offered guidelines and discussed possible ways of approaching the task. One student, John, asked if he could do it by himself. I hesitated, but the look on his face made me believe that he was serious about it.

When the time came for John to turn in his report, I had no idea what to expect. John had done some work in class—just as the groups were doing—mostly sketches, diagrams, and some reading. I was unprepared for his final product, which contained a diagram that measured five feet by four feet, with three acetate overlays and a report about a quarter-inch thick.

I was astounded. John's project was not only a work of art, it was conceptually superior to anything I had seen. John had limited the population density of each neighborhood by making certain that all types of housing existed. Each neighborhood had its own park system and each park had a different theme, such as pirate rides or a fairy tale motif. John had strategically placed ambulances in each neighborhood so that they would not have far to travel. He had designed a bus system and worked out the stops so that by taking no more than two buses a person could get from any one part of the city to any other part. The overlays showed these systems.

John was an average student who hardly ever participated in class. If called upon, he answered the question but that was all. He never elaborated and never asked any questions. His scholastic average was somewhere around 75. He was reading a bit lower than grade level, and an intelligence test showed his intelligence to lie within the average range.

I arranged a meeting with his mother, who described her son as quiet. His mother was pleased that her son's project was so well received. I asked John's mother about her son's work, and she told me that she thought the project was nice but that John was always doing things like that. During the summer, John had earned a couple of hundred dollars, which he had converted to pennies. After cleaning each penny, he constructed a large elephant-shaped bank from these pennies. For another project he had cut up old carpets from which he designed a scene from the Middle Ages of two knights fighting while a crowd, including kings and other royalty, watched. Here was a student with an average school record that did not mirror what obviously were a number of superior abilities and creativity.

I have often thought about John and wondered how many other students like him go through our schools without having their talents noticed. Chapter 10 discussed the challenges of identifying and educating students who are gifted in the intellectual and academic areas. This chapter will investigate other forms of gift-edness mentioned in the federal definition, including creativity, the arts, and leadership ability.

This chapter will also discuss some specific populations that are not identified as gifted nor offered special services for their giftedness in both the intellectual and creative areas as often as they should be. These include gifted children who underachieve, individuals with disabilities, children who are members of particular minority groups, and, in some circumstances, women.

Creativity

When asked to name people they think are creative, most students usually mention people in the arts or a very creative scientist such as Albert Einstein. Creativity is often viewed in terms of musicians or artists or mental geniuses who seemingly have made quantum leaps in contributing to humanity's ability to understand the world. Yet, this conception of creativity is too narrow. Most people would agree that John was creative, not only because his artwork was excellent but also because his conceptions were novel.

Defining Creativity

Defining creativity has never been an easy task. **Creativity** involves a "person's producing a novel response that solves the problem at hand" (Weisberg, 1986, p. 4). To be creative the response cannot be simply a repetition of something an individual saw or heard. Also, it must be appropriate; that is, it must solve the problem it is designed to solve. If a student hopes to solve the problem of increasing the efficiency of a kite, throwing a baseball at the kite may be novel, but it will not solve the problem.

The most popular way of looking at creativity is as a type of thinking. Guilford (1967) differentiated between two kinds of thinking: convergent and divergent. **Convergent thinking** involves arriving at an answer when given a particular set of facts and is the type of thinking measured by intelligence tests. **Divergent thinking** involves the ability to see new relationships between things or to see things in a new way that is still appropriate to the situation.

One test of creativity was developed by E. Paul Torrance and is called the **Torrance Tests of Creative Thinking (TTCT)**. The test measures creativity by considering four criteria: (1) *fluency*, the production of a large number of ideas, (2) *flexibility*, the ability to produce a variety of ideas, (3) *elaboration*, the development and embellishment of the ideas, and (4) *originality*, the production of ideas that aren't obvious (Hennessey & Amabile, 1987). Figure 11.1 shows some questions that illustrate the TTCT. Sometimes a test measuring just one of these criteria—ideational fluency, the production of a large number of ideas—is used by itself because it is highly correlated with other factors, such as originality and flexibility, but is easier to work with (Kogan, 1983).

Creativity:
The production of a novel response that appropriately solves a given problem.

Convergent thinking:
A type of thinking in which people solve problems by integrating information in a logical manner.

Divergent thinking:
A type of thinking marked by the ability to see new but still appropriate relationships between things in a given situation.

Torrance Tests of Creative Thinking (TTCT):
A test of creativity that measures fluency, flexibility, ability to elaborate, and originality of a person's thinking.

FIGURE 11.1   Problems from the Torrance Tests of Creative Thinking Try these sample problems testing creative thinking.

Source: E. Paul Torrance, *The Journal of Creative Behavior*, 1968, 2(3) with permission from the publisher, The Creative Education Foundation, Buffalo, N.Y. Copyright © 1968.

Problem 1   List all of the questions you can think of concerning the figure shown below. Ask all of the questions you need to know about what is happening. Do not ask questions that can be answered just by looking at the drawing. (Give yourself three minutes to list your questions.)

Problem 2   Suppose that all humans were born with six fingers on each hand instead of five. List all the consequences of implications that you can think of. (Give yourself three minutes.)

Problem 3   List as many white, edible things as you can in three minutes.

Problem 4   List all the words that you can think of in response to mother. (Give yourself three minutes.)

Problem 5   List all the uses that you can think of for a brick. (Give yourself three minutes.)

THOUGHT QUESTION

1. Why is creative thinking in childhood unrelated to such thinking in adulthood?

Not everyone is satisfied with the idea that creativity is solely a type of thinking or is the same as divergent thinking (Mansfield, Bussen, & Krepelka, 1978). Some consider this a rather narrow definition and point to evidence showing divergent thinking in childhood as not highly correlated with creative activities in adulthood (Feldhusen & Clinkenbeard, 1987).

Some see divergent thinking as one, but only one, of the components of creative activity. Along with divergent thinking other components include content knowledge, the ability to communicate, and the ability to critically analyze (Keating, 1980). Content knowledge is important because one would have difficulty thinking creatively if one did not understand the area in which creativity takes place. Communication skills are required in the broad sense, since an idea must be communicated to others. Even though the element of critical analysis has rarely been identified with creativity, it is an integral part of the process. If an individual has 15 ideas about what could occur and what should be done to solve a problem, how should that person proceed? A judgment needs to be made so that some avenues can be explored and others left behind. Critical analysis allows one to follow the most promising approach.

Looking at these conceptions of creativity, one can see that a fair estimate of a child's creativity cannot be obtained by just measuring intelligence. Districts that simply use intelligence scores and academic achievement as criteria identifying giftedness are doing students like John a disservice. In reality, the relationship between intelligence and creativity is hardly simple. Studies show that people with low intelligence scores do indeed show low creativity, but once an average intelligence score is in evidence, little relationship is found between intelligence and creativity (Hennessey & Amabile, 1987). Intelligence tests, then, are poor indicators of creativity. People tend to think only of pioneers who open new frontiers of knowledge as creative. However, creative performance can be found in many people if the atmosphere encourages creativity.

Encouraging Creativity

A number of professionally developed packages aim at improving divergent thinking. For example, the Purdue Creativity Program consists of 28 audio tapes and a set of printed exercises to accompany each tape. The tapes consist of two parts; a three- or four-minute presentation designed to teach a principle or idea for improving creative thinking and an eight- or ten-minute story about a famous American pioneer. The exercises consist of problems or questions designed to provide practice in creative thinking in areas measured by the TTCT (Feldhusen, Treffinger, & Bahlke, 1970).

Other programs teach particular techniques such as the use of brainstorming, in which students are encouraged to generate as many ideas as possible. These programs seek to encourage students to solve problems and to develop positive

One way to encourage creativity is to have students actually do something instead of just talking about it.

attitudes toward creative thinking. Some studies show these programs to be effective, but do not demonstrate whether the effects are sufficiently generalizable to real-world situations (Mansfield, Bussen, & Krepelka, 1978).

Most teachers, though, do not use professional programs to encourage creativity in the classroom. Instead, they may offer students opportunities to show their creative abilities and develop them within the regular curriculum. This task can be accomplished in a number of ways, such as asking students to consider what would happen in a given set of circumstances or requesting students to solve a problem in a novel manner (see In the Classroom below).

IN THE CLASSROOM   Encouraging Creativity

Students will not show their creative abilities unless they are given the opportunity to do so and the atmosphere of the classroom encourages creative thought and expression. Some general suggestions for encouraging creativity include the following:

1. Use divergent questions whenever possible.	**Why?** Convergent questions call for a limited number of correct answers; for example, "What is a figure with three sides called?" Asking divergent questions that have a number of possible correct answers requires students to engage in more thought (Montague, 1987). For example, "What are some similarities between baseball and football?" or "What conditions led to war in the colonies?" require more thought. "What if . . ." questions are also useful.
2. Provide an opportunity for creative expression. Encourage students to express themselves and to figure out new ways to accomplish some task.	**Why?** Some children receive little or no encouragement or opportunity to create. Asking questions in an open-ended manner or offering challenges in a lesson may create an opportunity for students to express themselves.
3. Allow students to try new things without fear of failure.	**Why?** Often students are afraid that everything will be graded, so they choose the safe alternative. If students are to be "daring" in their thoughts, they must feel that doing so will not adversely affect their grades.

4. Allow children to work together to create something.	**Why?** Some students like to work alone to solve a problem, while others prefer to work in groups.
5. Allow students to brainstorm solutions to problems; that is, allow students to suggest a wide range of solutions to a problem without fear of being criticized. Later, each possibility is evaluated.	**Why?** Brainstorming generates many different solutions to a problem encouraging students to be creative.
6. Encourage disagreement and constructive dissent.	**Why?** The toleration of dissent and disagreement generates an atmosphere of free expression and creativity.
7. Model creativity. If adults show creativity, children may follow the lead.	**Why?** Research shows that when creativity is modeled, students do not imitate the model's exact words or actions but rather learn to use their own imagination (Navarick, 1979).
8. Give students things to do not just to read.	**Why?** Many students enjoy working with their hands or "doing something." Projects and invention can be made part of certain units.
9. Encourage students to think in terms of invention.	**Why?** Students sometimes believe that everything has already been invented. Borton (1986) suggests that encouraging invention is possible if teachers (a) explain what an invention is; (b) convince children that invention is possible; (c) focus on improvement by asking children to consider how something could be changed to make it more useful; (d) look for a problem that needs solving while stressing reality over science fiction; and (e) encourage imagination.
10. Fight the conventional wisdom that creativity is for the few.	**Why?** Some students believe that if they are not intellectually gifted, they are not creative. Creativity is not the sole domain of brilliant or very talented people.

Creating Creativity

A number of conclusions are clear from the literature on creativity. First, although creativity has been linked to divergent thinking, it is not the only element in the creative process. Knowledge of subject matter and critical thinking are also important. Second, parents and teachers can increase divergent thinking in the home and classroom (Feldhusen & Clinkenbeard, 1987). Third, creativity is found in all areas of life; no one can relate creativity solely to one field, such as the arts or to "geniuses." Last, children will not show creativity unless they are challenged in areas in which they can bring their talents to the forefront. The idea that creative children will be creative in everything is incorrect. If creative children are to be identified, professionals will have to do more than merely give an intelligence test or look at those with the highest grades. Children will have to be given the opportunity to show their creative abilities so that those abilities may be identified and developed.

The Arts

THOUGHT QUESTION

2. By definition, would you consider all works of music and art creative?

When giftedness is discussed, children with artistic or musical talent immediately come to mind. A walk through any art museum or a night at the theater is sufficient to convince anyone that artistic and musical talent is certainly a province of giftedness. It should also convince anyone that its evaluation is quite subjective. No truly objective test is available to determine artistic or musical performance, although some objective tests may be used to determine one's knowledge of music and art. Talent is all in the eyes (or ears) of the beholders, who in this area are likely to be experts in the field.

Consider this problem. A teacher with expertise in music is asked to admit four violinists out of the ten that are auditioning for admission to a special school. They appear one by one to play a solo behind a screen (to prevent any prejudice from entering the decision). They are all excellent and have obviously had superior training. The expert must decide who should receive advanced education based upon experience and preferences.

Subjectivity may well enter into the decision. The judge may or may not like the violinist's style. The expert may or may not be favorably disposed toward the violinist's interpretation of the musical piece. Although the judge may strive to be fair and just, artistic preferences enter the picture.

The identification and training of talented children in music, art, dance, and drama are somewhat different. For example, musical talent can be divided into playing an instrument, understanding the structure of music, and composing. They do not necessarily go together. Some great performers do not understand music very well, and some competent musicians cannot compose music (see Pendarvis, Howley, & Howley, 1990). Therefore, musical training should not be thought of solely in terms of performance. Another problem arises. While it is true that many schools offer some elementary musical training where students can learn the basics of playing an instrument, limitations to what any public school can offer talented students is apparent. Most of the time, parents must search out private instruction and use their own resources. This makes it more difficult for children living in poverty to receive the necessary training in this area, or even to compete for a scholarship.

SCENARIO

1 Cal's father, Lee, has always been interested in music. He was a professional musician for a while, but never was able to make it a real career. He spends quite a bit of time with his son encouraging him to play the piano. For his part, Cal enjoys his father's attention and is doing well. Lee believes that if he spends enough time with his son and gives him the best lessons, Cal will become a superior musician. Lee claims that if you put 10,000 hours into anything you can become great at it. In your opinion, is Lee correct in his thinking and actions? Will it help Cal become a professional musician?

In the area of art and sculpture, no "real" performance takes place. The finished work is viewed, but the artist is free to change the work until it meets with the artist's satisfaction.

The third area of artistic giftedness is dance, which always involves performance. Although choreography is a talent, it is usually done by older dancers and teachers. Young dancers who are considered talented are expected to perform. Dancers must have both musical and superior physical abilities.

The last type of artistic talent is acting. The goal of great actors and actresses is to convince an audience that they are the character they are playing. Many schools offer some training in drama and theater, and groups of students may put on plays.

By the time students are involved in the arts in the secondary school, some have already had quite a bit of training. The real question is whether artistic talent can be predicted early enough to help children develop their talents. The most commonly used early sign of musical talent is absolute pitch, which is the ability to accurately identify a particular note that is played (Pendarvis et al., 1990). Some standardized tests can also be used to select musically talented students, such as the Wing Tests of Musical Intelligence and the Gordon Music Aptitude Profile. These tests measure musicality but not performance ability. Performance ability is always determined by auditions, which are judged by experts.

The determination of talent in art is difficult due to definitional problems. Age-related precocity in drawing skills is one possible early determinant. An individual who can draw a house and a person may have talent; however, drawing is not the only important aspect to being an artist as any walk through a museum of modern art will doubtless show. Educators in the field do not agree on the skills that comprise artistic talent, so testing is not really possible. Often, classroom teacher nominations, an analysis of one's portfolio, peer and self-nominations, interviews, art teacher nominations and a host of other criteria may be used to admit

Most people consider artists to be creative, but scientists and business people can also be creative.

an individual to a special art program. Art and music programs in the school are often run as enrichment programs.

Schools generally have few programs for either dance or drama. Although many schools have some opportunities for acting in plays, little systematic focus is offered for this area of talent. Some private acting schools do exist, making private instruction possible. Acting is sometimes offered as a mini-course or as an elective in some high schools.

Most dancers make their decision to enter the field fairly early and, by their teen years, are spending many hours in dance studios receiving training. In the area of dance, males may have an especially serious problem. Although dancing requires great physical skill, it is often subject to gender stereotyping. In fact, male dancers often describe themselves as less confident and have more internal conflict than female dancers. Males who show this talent may need special encouragement. Private schools are the rule, although there are a few large cities with public institutions devoted to the arts including dancing. For example, New York City's High School of the Performing Arts, now part of Fiorello LaGuardia High School of Music and Arts and the Performing Arts, helps educate promising musicians and dancers (Levy & Meek, 1992). Again, since much of the training is private, there is often a problem with financial resources.

One interesting approach to identifying dance and musical ability is found in the Talent Beyond Words Program (Kay & Subotnik, 1994). All third- through fifth-grade children in two public schools in New York City were given seven lessons on the essential skills in dance or music and taught by professionals. These skills stressed many different dance and music forms. Teachers were trained by professionals to serve as judges of dance or music auditions. Every week, each child was rated on the child's response to the lesson including skills, motivation, and creativity. Students who were identified as having talent took part in a concentrated after-school curriculum over the next three years. These students gained self-esteem, their school attendance improved, they showed increased enthusiasm for the arts and, of course, their skill level improved.

Children with artistic talents may feel isolated and out of touch with their peers and experiences in schools. Much of their effort, time, and attention may be focused on their area of talent. Their interests may not be the same as their peers. Most schools are not really set up to enhance and develop these areas to their fullest extent, even though some effort is expended, especially in the music area.

SCENARIO

2 Carla has always been interested in art. She draws well and is very involved in all forms of artistic expression. In fact, she doesn't really enjoy any other courses. Her parents understand her passion and encourage her interests, but they have two concerns. First, her interests are narrow and she shows interest in nothing else. Second, her friendships are few and also rather narrow. Her few friends are also interested in art. If you were her parents, would her interests and friendships cause you concern? If they do, how would you deal with the difficulty?

 **Technology and the Arts**

School art shows have changed. Years ago, anyone attending an art show would likely view paintings and drawings of different kinds, some photographs, and maybe sculpture. Today, along with these works, a person visiting a high school show may also see art that uses computer graphics, animation, and multimedia technology, as well as view student-made films.

Technology is influencing artistic and musical expression in many ways and allowing students gifted and talented in the arts to further develop their talents. Many high schools now offer specialized courses in different types of artistic expression: painting classes, sculpting classes, photography classes, and special classes on computer graphics and television production sometimes called TV journalism.

Computer graphics allows students to create art using various computer programs. Some of these programs such as Kid Pix are appropriate for young children, offering drawing tools for young children such as a pencil or a paintbrush and many different color paints. Different types of effects may be created. Other programs are designed for older students, offering more alternatives and allowing high school students to create professional-looking projects. On a different level, college students who are interested in architecture and engineering use various CAD (computer-aided design) software which allows students to use the computer to design houses and machinery (Dale, 1993).

Video arts have become especially popular in school (McWilliams & Hillegass, 1989). In some schools, students produce their own news programs and public service announcements, which are then shown within the school and to visitors. Students involved in these endeavors learn to plan, divide roles, and conduct research into the various issues they are covering (Reese, 1991). They learn technical skills, such as lighting, editing, and special effects (Kaplan, 1995). Sometimes, awards may be given out for the best one-minute public service announcements on such issues as drug use, drinking and driving, or other important topics.

The creation of multimedia programs is also possible if the equipment is available. These programs integrate music, voice, text, animation, and live-action video (Dale, 1993). Some useful equipment would be a laser videodisc for access to slides and films, VCR player for recording live action, a cassette player, digital scanner, and CD-ROM. Specialized software is required for the computer to control the equipment and produce the interactive productions (Dale, 1993). The more equipment the greater the flexibility and variety of effects possible. The multimedia environment allows children to be creative and produce presentations that are both educationally valuable and visually appealing.

Technology has also entered the music world. Music synthesizers making use of computer technology can accurately reproduce the sound of almost any instrument and can create original sounds (Brownell, 1987). A MIDI (musical instrument digital interface) permits a transfer of data between a synthesizer and a computer allowing the computer to assist the musician to compose, record, edit, and even print music (Winsor, 1992).

Programs are available on every level from beginner to expert that allow students to create music or listen to it and experiment with composition and even harmony (Male, 1994). The Bank Street MusicWriter program is like a word-processing program for music. It can be used to compose and practice music (Dale, 1993). The KidsTime program contains KidsNotes, which allows children to play notes on a keyboard shown on the monitor using a mouse. As the song is played, the musical notes are written on the bottom of the screen. Some prerecorded songs are available and student compositions can be stored (Lewis, 1994). Technology is also useful in the dance area. Different dance routines can be recorded on videotape and then played back to allow students to improve particular steps.

Four important points about technology and the arts need to be emphasized. First, technology offers artistically talented students both a new tool for expression as well as new forms of expression. Students can compose music and draw using computer technology. At the same time, technology can allow for the creation of new artforms such as the video arts and interactive displays.

Teachers of the arts need to be aware of its potential. At the Savannah College of Art and Design, many high school and college art teachers receive an education in computer skills useful in the art world. Teachers are taught to demonstrate color theory on the computer, to create graphics using computer programs, and to produce animation (Hawkins, 1992). These are new areas of art, which add to a rich artistic experience.

Second, many of these artistic endeavors allow for a greater integration of art and other subjects. For example, if a group of students is making a video about recycling, they might need to research the scientific, legal, and economic aspects of the issue. In this manner, other subjects are brought in and students are encouraged to apply what they are learning in their subjects to their artistic experience.

Third, the use of computer graphics, multimedia presentations, video arts, and computerized music programs opens up new areas of possible giftedness. Students may be especially talented in these artistic areas and less so in the more traditional areas. The use of technology also allows those students gifted in particular subjects, such as science or social studies, to create

presentations to show their projects to their fellow students in a more interesting manner. It also opens the possibility for a partnership, a team effort between students who may be gifted in science or social studies and those gifted in the arts.

Fourth, the use of technology in the arts can help motivate students. The possibility of producing a finished product using technologically advanced effects can motivate students to conduct research, learn to work in groups effectively, and integrate what they have learned in many subjects in order to produce quality work.

Naturally, what students can do is bounded by both the hardware and software available in this area in their schools. For example, students producing a news story for a television journalism class may find that they cannot obtain a particular special effect or font for lettering because the machines or software available are not capable of doing so (Kaplan, 1995). These limitations can also be a learning experience; students may creatively seek ways of obtaining the effects they want within the limits provided. In addition, students may become active in suggesting particular hardware and software packages that they believe are needed in order to create the programs they want.

Technology has much to offer artistically gifted students, and these students require a basic understanding of the computer as well as a specific knowledge of its use in the areas of interest. Arts programs in schools should be alert to the possibility that a child may be gifted in computer graphics or video arts just as a child may be a gifted artist or sculptor. Technology opens up many new opportunities in the area of artistic expression, and students are often excited about using computers to express themselves. Schools that integrate the use of technology into their art programs offer students new ways to express themselves that were not even dreamed of a generation ago.

How Does Talent Develop?

The dictionary defines talent as "any natural faculty, ability, or power. A special superior ability in art, mechanics, learning, etc." (*Webster's New Twentieth Century Dictionary of the English Language*, 1974). Most people believe that talent is something an individual is simply born with, which will develop despite any barriers. The question of whether talent has genetic roots and the extent of any genetic contribution is controversial. The second part of the statement, that children will develop their talent under any circumstances is not in keeping with the research in the field.

The most important study ever performed on the development of talent was conducted by Benjamin Bloom (1985). Bloom selected people from four distinct areas of talent. The first included the athletic or psychomotor fields; swimmers and tennis players were selected. The second involved the artistic areas; pianists and sculptors were selected. The third area studied included people with high cognitive abilities; mathematicians and research neurologists were used. The fourth area, interpersonal relations, could not be followed because Bloom and his colleagues could not find adequate criteria to decide who was exceptionally gifted in this area.

The research team first identified the top 25 people in each field with the help of multiple criteria. For example, the swimmers were selected because they earned a place on an Olympic swimming team; the pianists were all finalists in major competitions; and the mathematicians were all winners of major awards. After identifying these talented individuals, extensive interviews were conducted with these people, their parents, and sometimes teachers. Bloom wanted to identify the developmental and educational process that encouraged these talented people to succeed.

Bloom and colleagues found that no matter how much ability was initially found, talented individuals had to negotiate a long and intensive process of education and training in order to reach their goal. The talented individuals in all fields initially viewed the behaviors indicative of talent as basically play and fun. This stage was followed by a long sequence of educational and learning activities that involved higher and higher standards and an increased concentration on the area of talent. These children progressed from local, general teachers to more specific learning experiences with expert teachers. They progressed from play to a hobby to a combination of work and play to a lifelong career. Researchers found similarities in the home environments of these children. Their families emphasized the importance of doing one's best at all times and working hard. At first, this standard was applied to all areas of life and later concentrated mostly on the area of special talent. Parents strongly encouraged their children's development in these areas and gave less support to other possible activities and fields. Some sacrifice was also involved. Some parents were forced to spend a significant percentage of their resources for special teachers and for transportation to and from activities. These children shared household chores and responsibilities and always did them before going to play. Self-control and self-discipline were developed during childhood. Often these children came from homes in which there was originally an interest in sports, music, or intellectual activity.

No matter how much initial ability is present, the development of talent involves years of intensive preparation.

The education of these children in the early years seemed to be determined more by circumstances than personal choice. The child was exposed to something and made rapid progress in the first years. Often an excellent teacher made the field interesting; however, parental approval, rewards, and recognition were important. In the first period of formal instruction, motivation and effort counted far more than did particular gifts or special qualities.

As the child developed, the situation clearly demanded a more expert teacher. This teacher taught outstanding talent in the field and required perfection from students. The expert teacher was more demanding and the child showed increasing commitment. Although parents were still involved at this point, they did not monitor practice as much as in the early years. Precision and accuracy became most important. As the child continued to be educated, the amount of time spent on practice and in the field increased substantially, and the amount of time placed in other areas decreased.

Some chance elements operate in talent development. For example, many children had tried other pursuits before settling on their choice. The availability of facilities, such as tennis courts, musical instruments, or swimming pools, also had an effect in determining the development of talent.

Contrary to what might be expected, the overwhelming majority of these children were *not* regarded as child prodigies. Of the 120 individuals in the study, only a few were regarded as child prodigies by parents or teachers. Only a small number, 10 percent or less, had progressed far enough by 11 or 12 years of age to make any prediction about their future ascendance in the field as adults.

Bloom argues that the development of talent requires certain types of environmental support, special experiences, excellent teaching, and encouragement at each stage of development. No matter what the quality of initial gifts, each child experienced years of supervision, teaching, and practice. The general qualities of these achievers were strong interest and commitment to a particular field, a desire to reach a high level of attainment, and willingness to put in a great deal of time and effort. These individuals were able to learn rapidly and well.

Bloom notes that for certain areas such as sports, additional qualities such as motor coordination, speed of reflexes, and hand-eye coordination may be inborn and make certain skills easier to learn. However, Bloom does not emphasize the genetic aspects of talent at all. Even if these gifts are genetic, children had to be trained to reach their potential. In addition, dedication, attitude, and motivation were just as important.

One criticism of Bloom's approach is that anyone reading it carefully can argue that talent involves an interaction among various environmental agents. The impression is that almost anyone with certain attitudes and work habits may attain greatness. However, this position is difficult to argue because people are not blank slates. Certain aptitudes make it easier to learn certain skills, and genetic factors may influence one's abilities in a particular area (Gagne, 1991).

The extent to which genetic influences play a part in talent is still questionable. Whether or not talent is innate, everyone agrees that the development of talent requires hard work, a supportive atmosphere, and excellent teaching and training. It requires persistence and the willingness to devote oneself to a dream. In reviewing the research, one will note that very few of the experts in Bloom's study showed their talents extremely early and forced their way into the consciousness of the parents. They first received some training and then showed their talents. The rapid progress, reinforcement, and willingness of parents and sometimes teachers to encourage them were truly important.

Certainly some gifted children will show their talents very early. Gagne (1991) gives the example of Greg Louganis, the Olympic and world champion diver, who at 18 months of age accompanied his mother to his older sister's dance recital and showed a great sense of balance and precocious mastery of muscular control by performing gymnastic moves.

Although the ideal situation would be to recognize talent early so that children could receive the type of education that would allow them to fulfill their promise, the research suggests that many gifted children will not spontaneously show their gifts. Only after exposure to training do many children learn the skills easily, show rapid advancement, and continue to become more and more interested in their special areas. This development will only happen with outside help and encouragement, making the practice of exposing children to many areas in order to determine their strengths and talents a reasonable one.

THOUGHT QUESTION

4. *Why are most people who have done exceptionally well in their fields not child prodigies?*

THOUGHT QUESTION

5. *Is talent or giftedness in the arts determined by genetic or environmental factors (or both)?*

SCENARIO

3 Jennie is 4 years old and seems to love music. She toots on horns and plays drums with an amazing degree of rhythm. She seems genuinely interested in band instruments and knows the words to songs. Her parents feel that she may be musically gifted and would like to know how they can tell if she is gifted. What would be the best course for them to take?

Leadership

Terman argued that the leadership of the future would be found in those identified as gifted. Most general definitions of giftedness include the quality of leadership. However, the definition of giftedness in leadership is a problem. No accepted definition exists, increasing the intensity of the debate over which approach to leadership education is best.

One approach is to define leadership as "a set of skills that enables a group to reach its goals, to maintain itself with mutual satisfaction, and to adapt to environmental change; and that allow the individuals within the group to attain self-fulfillment" (Clark, 1988, p. 526). Studies often attempt to list the traits, characteristics, and skills of leaders (Davis & Rimm, 1994). Research shows that motivation to excel, originality, judgment, sociability, aggressiveness, generosity, and scholarly and physical prowess are some of the characteristics (Pendarvis et al., 1990). Leaders are more intelligent than the group members they are leading, can make decisions; can deal with abstract concepts and planning; have a sense of direction; are flexible and loyal; show self-confidence, perseverance, enthusiasm; and have the ability to communicate (Clark, 1988). Renzulli (1983) formulated a unique rating scale that can be used to evaluate leadership. It uses the following criteria:

1. A leader carries responsibility well and can be counted on to do what has been promised.
2. A leader is self-confident with both age mates and adults; seems comfortable when showing personal work to the class.
3. A leader is well liked.
4. A leader is cooperative, avoids bickering, and is generally easy to get along with.
5. A leader can express himself or herself clearly.
6. A leader adapts to new situations; is flexible in thought and action and is not disturbed when the usual routine is changed.
7. A leader enjoys being around other people.
8. A leader tends to dominate; usually directs activities.
9. A leader participates in most school social activities; can be counted on to be there (in Davis & Rimm, 1994, pp. 179-180).

These characteristics are general, but serve as a conceptual model. They may seem to read like a characteristic list of gifted students in general; indeed, some similarities do exist. However, the intelligence of leaders needs only to be somewhat higher than the members of the group they are leading, and their intelligence is not always in the gifted range (Pendarvis et al., 1990). Leaders of average groups of children have intelligence scores in the 115–130 range. Some schools simply give leadership training to all gifted children, but since most schools only consider giftedness in the academic realm, a problem may arise. Although these academically gifted children will certainly enter high-status fields, whether they become leaders cannot be predicted from academic ability (Baird, 1985). Terman's ideas that academically gifted children are all future leaders is doubtful and is certainly not true of gifted children with superior divergent thinking ability. Torrance (1962) found that the most highly creative thinkers were often ignored or even highly criticized by other group members. To be leaders, creative people must develop superior organization and interpersonal skill.

Unfortunately, these general characteristics of leaders are difficult to use in the identification process. Identification of leadership skill is mostly subjective and presents a formidable identification problem.

One problem in the determination of leadership is personality differences based on gender and ethnic membership. In elementary school, male leadership depends on verbal assertiveness and females on success at school tasks. Usually these boys are above average in athletic and physical prowess. Often women only show leadership when they are encouraged to do so and may not in groups in which they must compete with males. Gilligan and colleagues (1990) argue that women often have a different view of leadership and may seek consensus rather than compete in mixed groups. This tendency may be due to the contradictions in society in which women are often praised for being more passive and caring for others and in which a woman who is "aggressive" and ambitious may not be seen positively.

Leadership in various ethnic groups is likely to differ because leaders must be able to communicate and mirror their followers' ideas and feelings. Generally, leaders mirror the dominant values of the group they are leading, and these values may not be the same values as the dominant society. For instance, one group values individual achievement and aggressiveness while another group within the society values consensus, cooperation, and group achievement.

Whether a child's future leadership status can be predicted from studies of personality traits is questionable (Pendarvis et al., 1990). Perhaps the greatest problem in identifying leadership, though, is the desire of schools to identify only those leaders that seem to conform to our idea of the "All American" child. The class president and the leader of an academically talented group often show conforming values. Many emerging leaders may not show these values and represent positions that challenge the local power structure. Students who are not the most intellectually gifted but show leadership ability are often not even considered for a leadership program.

Clearly, then, identification of leaders must be performed not only within the school environment but also within the community. Students who show leadership in scouting, community groups, recreational facilities, and in religious groups must be considered. In fact, leadership in extracurricular activities is more predictive of adult leadership than academic achievement (Stodgill, 1974).

Although not every student with leadership qualities will show them in school, some do; and teachers can be asked who leads in the classroom and who other students look to for leadership. Observations by teachers can be a valuable source

THOUGHT QUESTION

6. *Do male and female leaders differ in methods and personality?*

Some leadership skills can be taught, although most schools do not have leadership training programs.

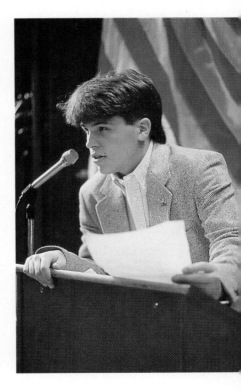

THOUGHT
QUESTION

7. Can leadership be taught or is it a personal skill that you either have or don't have?

of information. A combination of self, peer, and teacher nominations is useful. In one study, self-nomination was the most powerful predictor of leadership ability (Friedman, Friedman, & Van Dyke, 1984).

Can leadership skills be taught? Some leadership skills involve knowledge of parliamentary procedure and how to run a meeting, and certainly these skills can be taught. To be a good leader does not mean completely memorizing Roberts Rules of Order. However, some idea of the purpose behind committee meetings and how to run these meetings in order to make progress is important.

Another possibility is teaching techniques that would allow leaders to harness the creative abilities of the group. For example, brainstorming, techniques to build consensus, techniques to encourage participation, and ways of organizing groups are skills that can be taught. Leadership training programs may include training in group dynamics, communication skills, decision-making skills, planning, and values clarification (Karnes & Chauvin, 1986). Leadership, though, is more than a group of skills. Personal qualities such as being able to inspire confidence and abilities such as controlling one's own feelings are less amenable to training (Reynolds & Birch, 1988). Little evidence is available at the present time showing whether they can be taught.

Perhaps the most widely used leadership training program is the two-part Leadership Studies Program (Karnes & Chavins, 1986; Karnes, Meriweather, & D'Lio, 1987). This program is sometimes used in upper elementary school and secondary school. The first part of the program involves giving students the Leadership Skills Inventory (LSI), which measures student leadership ability in nine areas:

1. Fundamentals of leadership.
2. Written communication skills.
3. Speech communication skills.
4. Values clarification.
5. Decision-making skills.
6. Group dynamics skills.
7. Problem-solving skills.
8. Personal development skills.
9. Planning skills.

This assessment instrument demonstrates the strengths and weaknesses of the child. The second part involves using the Leadership Skills Activities Handbook, which contains a number of activities to strengthen the student's abilities in these areas. At the end of the program, a Plan for Leadership is developed. This involves statements of goals, objectives, activities to meet objectives, time lines, resource persons, and evaluation. When this program was followed by a group of children in grades 6 through 11, significant improvements on all scales of the LSI were found (Karnes et al., 1987).

Most schools do not have any leadership training programs. Classroom teachers, however, are often in a position to offer leadership positions to students. Too often, they choose as leaders students who are conforming and liked by the teacher. In addition, teachers do not give leadership and power very easily. Most teachers dominate the classroom, talk most of the time, and do not encourage students to ask many questions (Kaplan, 1990).

When leadership is assigned to students, female students and students from minority groups should be well represented. Some leadership training has focused just on women. The Program for Exceptionally Gifted Girls at Mary Baldwin College is a program that stresses advanced academic work in a nurturing context for developing leadership among young women. This program encourages gifted females to work together on various aspects of learning and helps develop leadership abilities. This strategy can also be used prior to adolescence so that girls learn the strengths they possess before the socialization pressure to hide them in puberty takes hold (Feldhusen, Van Tassel-Baska, & Seeley, 1989).

The area of leadership training is difficult to summarize. The few schools that offer such programs often confuse leadership with academic giftedness. They are not the same. Some children with leadership ability will not be included, but many students without such leadership ability will be placed into these programs if academic excellence is a criterion. Since objective methods of evaluation in this area are questionable, placement would probably best be based on a combination of parent, peer, self, and teacher nominations along with some investigation of outside leadership activities.

In addition, leadership training programs are difficult to assess. Leadership training may be desirable if it improves students' decision-making skills, communication abilities, and knowledge of group dynamics. No one can predict whether these children will become tomorrow's adult leaders, but those who show promise deserve an opportunity to develop their special skills.

When leadership positions are being assigned, teachers should be certain that people from all groups are represented.

SCENARIO

4

Taylor is a student who seems to dominate everyone around him. He is often chosen as the spokesperson and is very good at demolishing arguments. He is also opinionated, strong willed, and often tactless. He is a bit of a rebel and, although he may cause some difficulty with some teachers, he is well liked.

One of the teachers in the school would like to start a leadership training course but since Taylor is not in the gifted program the teacher has some doubt as to whether he should be included. What criteria for admittance to the course should this teacher use and what should these students be taught?

Underrepresented Groups in the Education of Gifted Children

Being identified as gifted and receiving appropriate services can make a difference in the development of a child's talents. However, according to a report issued by the U.S. Department of Education, certain groups are not identified as being gifted as often as they should be (see Sklaroff, 1993). Four groups noted in this report are underachieving youth, children with disabilities, youth from certain minority groups, and women.

The Underachieving Gifted Student

Mark is an eighth grader. Despite a tested intelligence score of 135 and doing very well on standardized reading tests, Mark's grades fall in the 70s. He is frequently disruptive, talks incessantly, and does only the minimum amount of work.

Linda is a sixth grader who is disorganized. She passes her subjects but does not offer anything more than a memorized version of the material. She tests at a very high intelligence level but does not function at that level in school.

If you were a teacher speaking to Mark's and Linda's parents would you label them underachievers? Many definitions for the term *underachiever* exist, but all of them have in common a significant discrepancy between intelligence or standardized tested abilities and performance in class (Feldhusen, 1989). A number of different conceptions of underachievement among gifted students can be found in the literature and these vary greatly; no single agreed-upon definition exists at the present time (Dowdall & Colangelo, 1982). Teachers often view underachieving gifted students as lazy, uninterested, and bored, and always as capable of better work. Underachievers are a concern in the area of gifted education because the definition of giftedness includes potential as well as performance.

Many patterns of underachievement exist. For example, Tannenbaum (1983) suggests that one type of underachiever does so because of overestimated intellectual abilities; another because the student lacks a particular aptitude; a third because the child does not have the necessary drive, mental health, or personal supports; a fourth type lacks proper nurturance at home or at school; and the fifth type underachieves through a series of distractions and misfortunes beyond anyone's control. These five factors serve as links between potential and fulfillment.

Various studies of gifted underachievers have identified some elements in common, but no single pattern has been found. Whitmore (1980) suggested that some children may be aggressive and act out by seeking negative attention, while others may withdraw. After reviewing a number of studies on underachieving gifted students, Clark (1988) suggested that gifted underachievers most often have a low self-concept and evaluate themselves negatively. They may believe that they are rejected by family or feel that their parents are dissatisfied with them. They often take no responsibility for their actions and externalize conflicts and problems. In a study of underachieving gifted children in elementary school, Laffoon and colleagues (1989) found that these students show a general distrust of adults, do not like school or teachers, and choose companions with similar attitudes. They seem rebellious, have weak motivation for academic achievement, and have poor study habits and lack skills. Their homework is often done poorly and is not complete. They are less persistent, show lack of self-discipline, are impulsive, show poor adjustment, and feel restricted.

Colangelo and colleagues (1993) compared two groups of gifted students who had scored above the 95th percentile on the American College Board Testing Program (ACT). One group had a grade point average of 3.75 or better on a 4.00 scale while the other group of high scoring adolescents had grade point averages of less than 2.25 (about a C). The investigators found that gifted underachievers were not necessarily from poverty or at-risk backgrounds. Although fewer gifted underachievers were satisfied with school, guidance services, and their educational experiences as a whole, the differences were notable but not overwhelming. For example, 52 percent of the underachieving gifted students were satisfied with high school instruction while 68 percent of the high achieving gifted students were pleased with it. About 45 percent of the underachieving gifted students were satisfied with guidance services compared with about 52 percent for the highly achieving gifted students. About 62 percent of all underachieving gifted students rated their overall education good or excellent (17 percent excellent, 44.5 percent good) while 81 percent of the gifted achievers rated their experience in school as either excellent or good (38.8 percent as excellent and 42.2 percent as good). Gifted high achievers had many more out-of-class accomplishments in community services, athletics, music, and other areas. Many gifted underachievers had solid future plans and resisted help in this area. They did not want to be involved in honors or independent study but did show a willingness to receive help in the area of study skills. Some studies find that these gifted underachievers are rebellious, but this study failed to find high rebelliousness in these students.

Underachieving gifted students generally do poorly when compared to gifted achievers in the areas of maturity, emotional adjustment, social adjustment, personality characteristics, self-concept, motivation, and conflict with the environment (Janos & Robinson, 1985). Davis and Rimm (1994) argue that the most important characteristic is poor self-esteem, which is at the root of the problem. The low self-esteem produces such behavior as academic avoidance, which in turn produces poor study habits and disciplinary problems. Gifted underachievers may avoid effort by telling others that school is irrelevant. They see no reason to study useless material. They also say they can do it if they want to. This avoidance protects them from admitting a lack of confidence or feared lack of ability. If they studied and did not do well, this result would confirm the possible shortcomings to themselves. The low grades become consistent with the low self-concept and low self-confidence. The picture of gifted underachieving students, then, is one of a poorly motivated student, who sometimes feels restricted and restless, who has poor study habits and a low sense of self-esteem.

Help for the Gifted Underachiever

Gifted underachieving students are not failing in school. They are usually bright enough or talented enough to pass the courses. They work below their capacity but may seem satisfied by their grades. Motivation, then, is a problem.

The most common strategy for countering underachievement in gifted children is counseling. Although some studies find that counseling has been successful in improving the academic performance of gifted underachieving students, many studies have not shown this to be an effective strategy (Clark, 1988). Some group counseling or counseling that involves the family may help some students, but again the results are not encouraging.

Some experts advocate using noncompetitive learning strategies, such as mastery learning. In mastery learning, standards of performance are high and constant but students are given a flexible amount of time to achieve such standards. Other such strategies include the use of cooperative learning strategies as well as contracts in which students and their teachers formulate realistic goals that the student can reach (Covington, 1984). All these strategies strengthen a student's perception of the importance of effort and promote realistic goal setting.

Rimm (1986) suggests a six-part strategy in the TRIFOCAL model including assessment, communication, changing expectations, role model identification, correction of deficiencies, and modifications of reinforcements. The first two steps, assessment and communication are relatively easy to understand. Changing expectations is more difficult. In this step, parents and teachers must give specific descriptions of strengths and alter students' expectations of themselves. Positive parental expectations are crucial, and sibling competition must be reduced. The most critical step is the discovery of a model for identification. Many of these children do not have good relationships with fathers. Underachieving children may be matched with an achieving person who serves as a model. The characteristics of the models include nurturance, same gender, similarities in background if possible, openness to sharing problems, willingness to give time, and a sense of accomplishment. Correcting skill deficiencies is important as well. The model must reinforce the independent work of the child and emphasize the relationship between effort and achievement. Last, modifications of reinforcements must occur and the child must be reinforced for good work.

Acceleration strategies may be used as part of the TRIFOCAL model. Parents and teachers often have objections to acceleration, and specifically to accelerating students who are gifted but underachieving. However, if students' intelligence or achievement test scores are quite high, subject or grade skipping places underachieving gifted students in more demanding academic environments that can sometimes motivate the student to improve academic performance (Rimm & Lovance, 1992). A program of acceleration and some counseling successfully improved student achievement for underachieving gifted students, especially if the underachievement was due to a boring and nonchallenging curriculum (Rimm & Lovance, 1992). Many of the teachers and parents found an adjustment period for these accelerated children lasting about one quarter to one semester, although most children did not describe early adjustment difficulties. Not all gifted underachieving students would be helped by such plans. Students with high intelligence scores but major skill deficits, those unwilling to take on the challenge of acceleration and those whose underachievement seems to be due to difficult home situations are not good candidates for acceleration.

In another approach, Emerick (1992) studied gifted students who had been underachieving and then, without extra help, began to achieve. One aspect that stood out was the integration of personal interests into the school work and out-of-school experiences. When students perceived a relationship between their own interests and learning experiences, they were motivated to achieve.

Alternative schools may be an answer for some, and such schooling should start earlier than high school, at least during the middle school stage. School-sponsored community service is also possible to add meaning to school (Feldhusen, 1989). Improvement of self-esteem, though, is most important.

The population of gifted underachieving students provides a great challenge for educators. The tendency is not to identify these students as gifted and deliver services to these students since their performance in the classroom is weak but passing. However, these students need special services if they are to develop their abilities (Emerick, 1992).

THOUGHT QUESTION

8. *Should bright children who are underachieving be placed in classes for gifted students ahead of children who are not as gifted as shown on intelligence tests but are doing well in school?*

SCENARIO

5 Donna is a classic underachieving student. She scores in the gifted intelligence range but is barely achieving an 80 percent average and does no more work than she has to. She often talks in class and does not follow directions. She feels school is boring and unchallenging. Her teachers believe that if the school work is that easy she should be getting As instead of high Cs and low Bs. Donna's parents were divorced a few years ago, and her mother has not had an easy time of it. Donna has a good relationship with her father whom she sees on weekends. Her mother punished her for her poor grades, but it did not help. Her father lectured her but again to no avail. Her counselor would like to place her in the school's gifted program but has met with some resistance on the part of the staff, since she is not doing even B work in some major classes. If you were Donna's counselor what would you do? If you were asked to develop a program for students like Donna in secondary school, what sort of program would you develop?

The Gifted Child with a Disability

What do Beethoven, Franklin Roosevelt, Helen Keller, Vincent Van Gogh, Albert Einstein, and Thomas Edison have in common? Of course, each of these people added much to civilization through their unique talents. What most people fail to realize is that each had a disability (Karnes & Johnson, 1991).

The child with a disability receives many services that focus on that disability. The child's lack of sight, hearing difficulties, motor problems, or communication problems are the center of concern. Often the need for treatment of the disability emphasizes the difficulty rather than the child's strengths. For example, consider a child with cerebral palsy. This child may need extensive physical therapy and speech therapy, which may be where the emphasis is placed. The child's unique talents may not be discovered or developed because of this emphasis on remediating the disability.

It is estimated that 2 percent of all children with disabilities are gifted (Whitmore & Maker, 1985). Some authorities argue that a 5 percent cutoff is probably more realistic (Davis & Rimm, 1994). Whatever the percentage of children with disabilities who are gifted, the need remains to identify them and provide appropriate educational services.

Identifying the Child with a Disability Who Is Gifted

Identifying children with disabilities who are gifted is not an easy task. As noted, professionals tend to concentrate on their disabilities rather than their talents. In addition, their disability may get in the way of recognizing their talents. For example, a student with a hearing impairment may not have excellent verbal skills, a student with a learning disability may show an uneven profile. Consider a young student named Roy from a poor home who had a learning disability. Although his intelligence score was in the bright-average range, the subtests showed many variations. He had great strengths in vocabulary, information, and the ability to abstract, but he was reading well below grade (Perino & Perino, 1981).

Many obstacles prevent identifying children with disabilities who are gifted (Whitmore & Maker, 1985). First, most people believe that persons with disabilities score below average in every area. This assumption is, of course, not true. Second, many students experience developmental delays especially in the verbal area, an area very much involved in evaluation criteria for identifying students as gifted. Third, as noted previously, often the strengths of these children are overlooked while professionals focus on the disability. Finally, the children with disabilities frequently do not have an opportunity to show their superior abilities.

Identification can be improved first by being aware of the possibility that some children with disabilities are gifted and by seeking them out. Special testing procedures are required, especially the use of nonverbal measures of ability such as the Raven's Progressive Matrices test or the performance subtests of the WISC-IV (Feldhusen et al., 1989).

Educating special education teachers as to the characteristics of gifted children can also help improve identification of these children. Most teachers trained to work with children with disabilities do not have much background in education for gifted children. Teacher nominations do not usually work well with identification of the child with a disability who is gifted, but if teachers are given training, they may be helpful. Peer and self-nominations are useful. Some advocate comparing the child with a disability to other children with the same disability to determine how well they are compensating for the disability and offering special educational services for gifted children to these students (Davis & Rimm, 1994).

People with disabilities can also be gifted. Franklin Roosevelt, elected president of the United States four times, is an example. Since so much emphasis is placed on a person's disability, such children may fail to be identified as being gifted.

Enabling Gifted Children with Disabilities

Children with disabilities who are gifted should be seen first as gifted and then as children who need extra help in showing these gifts or talents. As in all cases of working with individuals with disabilities, reducing the effects of the disability is crucial to success. For example, providing the necessary tools—sign interpreters for students with hearing impairments, access to computers with word-processing programs for students with learning disabilities, and other methods that compensate for the disability—may be required.

Some special considerations, though, are important in the case of gifted children with disabilities. First, gifted children usually have good self-concepts, but this generalization is not necessarily true if they also have a disability. Often these students feel less capable and less worthy. Helping to improve the self-concepts of these students is a primary goal.

Often one-to-one attention is necessary for these students to develop their talents, but dependence becomes a problem. Dependence is an undesirable trait and limits motivation and achievement. Disabled children who are gifted must be encouraged to develop intrinsic motivation and work independently. Communication with experts in the field may be required because most schools do not have much experience in dealing with these children. One last area of interest is internships. Internship programs involve experience and hands-on work and are especially successful in helping children with disabilities who are gifted to achieve (Cox, Daniels, & Boston, 1985).

One successful program model is the RAPYHT project, which stands for Retrieval and Acceleration of Promising Young Handicapped Talent. This program helps teachers and parents to identify and program for gifted and talented preschoolers with mild to moderate disabilities. It includes general programming, involving a series of classroom activities meant to bring out creativity and problem solving abilities, identification using a parent checklist, talent programming, parent involvement in the process, interagency collaboration, transitional procedures, and evaluation (Karnes & Johnson, 1991).

Identification is the first step in helping children with disabilities who are gifted obtain the special services they need. As is the case for all children, in order to identify these children, the school must provide an opportunity for children to show their talents by exposing children to different activities. Identification of various talents may require the use of special measuring and evaluation instruments. Finally, although programming depends upon the disability, some additional attention to both self-concept enhancement and social integration in the classroom is necessary.

Gifted Children from Minority Groups

African-American, Latino, and Native American children are not identified as gifted as often as their numbers in the general population indicate they should be (Chinn & Hughes, 1987; Ford & Harris, 1990; Smith, LeRose, & Clasen, 1991). One can reasonably assume that giftedness is found in the same proportion in each ethnic and racial group. The same percentage, then, of students from minority groups should be identified as gifted and receive special services designed to develop their talents. However, the figures prove otherwise. Approximately 30 percent of the public school system is composed of minority group students but only

Minority group students are under-identified as being intellectually gifted, but new procedures will reduce this problem.

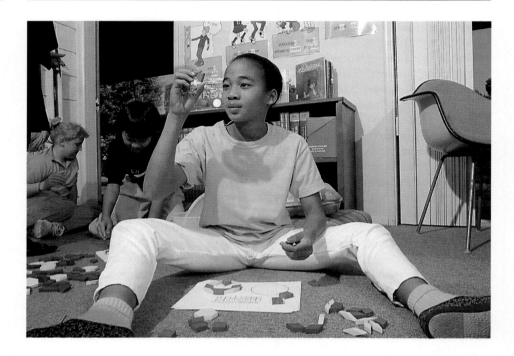

20 percent of the children in gifted programs are minority group members (Alamprese, Erlanger, & Brigham, 1989).

The fact that students from these groups are not identified as gifted in proportion to their numbers is the source of much concern. A number of factors contribute to the difficulties of identifying children from certain minority groups as gifted. Frequently, children from these groups live in poverty and the pervading effects of poverty may contribute to a reduction of scores on standardized instruments. Low socioeconomic status undoubtedly plays a role in how even the most highly intelligent minority group students achieve (Van Tassel-Baska & Willis, 1987). A significant relationship exists between economic disadvantage and SAT scores across ethnic groups (Van Tassel-Baska & Willis, 1987). Some definitions of giftedness depend upon standardized tests that may be inadequate for measuring intellectual ability in children from some minority groups (Clasen, Middleton, & Connell, 1994). Some argue that standardized tests have a built-in cultural bias, which limits their usefulness (see Chapter 4). Others argue that cultural differences may cause teachers and other referral agents not to identify a student from these groups as gifted. Still others point to the difficulty of identifying students as gifted whose primary language is not English (Barkan & Bernal, 1991). An overreliance on standardized tests may not identify gifted children whose primary language is other than English. Finally, in an attempt to widen the screening and identification process, some schools have encouraged parent nominations. Although Caucasian, Hispanic, and African-American parents all agree on the characteristics of gifted children, the parents of African-American and Hispanic-American children are much less likely to participate in the referral process (Scott et al., 1992).

On the other hand, differences may exist in the meaning of giftedness for some minority groups (Baldwin, 1991). Some Native American cultures do not emphasize individual achievement, and patterns of communication between people may differ. Kirschenbaum (1988) recommended that when dealing with Native American populations, especially children living on reservations, a search for superior aesthetic abilities, acquired skills, tribal/cultural understanding, and personal human qualities is most important. An inventory is available for use in identifying gifted Navaho children.

Being identified as gifted and receiving special services makes quite a bit of difference, too. In Racine, Wisconsin, students in the top 9 percent of the Caucasian, Hispanic-American, and African-American children tested before kindergarten were identified as gifted. Half the students who tested gifted were placed in the gifted program and half in the regular program. Twelve years later, a follow-up found that none of the minority students placed in the gifted program dropped out while 45 percent of the gifted children placed in regular classes dropped out (Smith et al., 1991).

Identification, then, is a key. Many suggestions concerning ways to identify minority group gifted children have been made. Some advocate the use of nontraditional measures to recognize cultural characteristics that may affect the identification process (Van Tassel-Baska, 1989). Teachers and parents need to focus on the student's strengths in nonacademic areas, especially creativity and psychomotor skills. Programs to address problems in motivation are needed as well. Baldwin (1991) suggests that giftedness includes cognitive, creative, psychosocial, and psychomotor gifts, although admittedly good measuring instruments are really not available. The assumption is that giftedness can be expressed in a variety of behaviors, and one is no more important than another. This line of thinking is well in keeping with Gardner's theory of multiple intelligences. A child who is gifted in one area may not be gifted in another, and the total picture is important to planning. The greatest challenge, though, is identifying the gifted minority group student with great academic potential who, at the moment, may not test above the district's cutoff for gifted children.

When dealing with minority populations, more subjective assessment is desirable, and the search should probably include superior potential rather than performance (Scruggs & Cohen, 1983). Although both are included in the definition, often performance is used as the only criterion. In addition, since cultural bias is possible both in intelligence tests and some achievement tests, other nontraditional assessments may be beneficial. The use of teacher nominations in identification of the gifted minority group student is complicated by the partiality of some teachers to those students who speak middle-class English and are easy to deal with in the classroom. However, an experienced teacher who is aware of the culture will be able to add comments of value.

Over the years, a number of different identification procedures have been tried with some success. For example, if the criteria used in a district is heavily weighted toward test scores and rigid cutoffs, minority students may be at some disadvantage; therefore, the cutoff should be more flexible. This rigidity can be eased after an initial screening if the percentage of minority group youth identified as gifted is too low for the district. Another alternative is to include more checklists tapping parent and teacher feedback and focus not only on academic skills but use of expressive speech, originality of ideas in problem solving, and skills in other areas. Another alternative is to select a percentage from every school within the district thus assuming that the percentage of gifted children in each school is the same. Since students from minority groups may be found more often in one

THOUGHT QUESTION

9. *Should cutoffs for admittance into classes for gifted children always be uniform for everyone or should one's membership in a group that is underrepresented be taken into account?*

school within the district due to housing patterns, this would ensure better districtwide participation by minority students.

Some professionally designed scales are available for use in identification as well. On one checklist, teachers are asked to look for characteristics of creativity in culturally different urban children living in poverty. The list of behaviors was generated by 36 teachers and based upon observed original behavior shown in a wide variety of situations (Swenson, 1978). Also available for use is the Baldwin Identification Matrix, which uses both objective and subjective evaluations to help identify such youth. Clasen and colleagues (1994) formulated special tests of problem solving and drawing to identify students who were exceptional problem solvers or had artistic talent. The researchers used very practical rather than abstract problems to test problem-solving ability and asked students to draw items that were common to all cultures in order to identify children who had artistic talent. These instruments were successful in identifying a similar percentage of majority and minority gifted children in the sixth grade.

Relatively little is written about what programs work for the gifted youth from minority groups, especially if they come from poverty backgrounds (Van Tassel-Baska, 1989). The services offered to gifted minority students are generally similar to those found in schools for nonminority gifted students. To encourage gifted minority students to succeed, though, increased parental involvement, use of experiential hands-on learning approaches, use of activities that allow for self-expression, and helpful participation of mentors and role models are recommended methods (Feldhusen, 1989).

The most crucial point is that gifted children are present in each culture and they may be overlooked. The exact procedures that should be used to identify gifted students differ with the minority group and must take into consideration the culture, language abilities, and attitudes toward giftedness in each cultural group.

SCENARIO

6 You are a teacher in a school in which roughly 40 percent of the student body is African-American and Hispanic-American. The school provides reasonable services for gifted students in many areas but you notice that fewer minority group students are found in these programs, and only one child with a disability is identified as gifted. The identification process is based mostly on scores on a test of cognitive ability and teacher recommendations. The committee is concerned about this situation and asks you how to improve the identification process in the academic, arts, and leadership areas. What recommendations would you make?

Women as a Special Group in Gifted Education

Anyone looking at a gifted and talented high school English or foreign language class would certainly wonder why gifted women should be considered as needing special attention. However, walk past a room in which physics or chemistry or some other honors science or mathematics course is being taught and the concern is more easily understood. Female students do not take as many advanced science or mathematics courses and are not identified as gifted in these areas as often as male students (Sadker & Sadker, 1994). Questions also arise about the school experiences of gifted female students and the vocational choices they make. Gifted women need special attention if their talents in these areas are to be developed.

Gifted Females in School

Girls typically outperform boys in elementary school on achievement tests, and gifted girls tend to show their giftedness before gifted boys (Kerr, 1991). They often have very high aspirations and fantasize about being astronauts, ambassadors, and professionals (Kerr, 1985). Girls may, in fact, have an advantage over boys in elementary school. The atmosphere of elementary school is feminine, with its great percentage of female teachers and its emphasis on obedience and activities that require fine motor coordination. Boys and girls experience school in different ways, and both male and female teachers value the stereotyped feminine traits of obedience and passivity rather than aggressiveness and independence (Etaugh & Hughes, 1975).

In secondary school, though, the situation changes. Girls' achievement levels slip. The gap between males and females closes rapidly in high school (Kaplan, 1990). Many girls' dreams of high achievement undergo a subtle change. Although both males and females lose intelligence points in adolescence, females lose more than males.

Statistics on how male and female students perform on college entrance examinations are instructive. Boys score much higher than girls on the PSAT. About 18,000 male students reach the highest PSAT categories, only 8,000 female students attain them. On the SAT, males outscore females on an average of 50 points on the mathematics section and 8 to 12 points on the verbal section (Gallagher & DeLisi, 1994; Sadker & Sadker, 1994). The Educational Testing Service recently made changes in the SAT including replacement of antonym questions with more sentence completions and reading passages, and allowing students to write in some of their own answers instead of selecting from multiple choice options. These changes may help female students to some extent. However, critics point out that while bias in question content is not blatant, questions on the SAT are more likely to deal with content of interest to males than females. Others point out that if the difference between males and females on SAT scores is based upon differential experiences in school, boys taking more high school math and science courses, for example, then these changes will not make much difference (Sadker & Sadker, 1994).

When Kerr and Colangelo (1988) investigated how students performed on the American College Testing (ACT) exam in the senior year of high school, 61 percent of students scoring above the 95th percentile were male, and 72 percent of students in the 99th percentile were male. Males outscore females at the highest levels on mathematics, science, and social studies but not in English. Females in the top 1 percent of National Merit Scholars maintain high career aspirations in adolescence, but until recently moderately gifted girls, those scoring in the top 5 percent on IQ and achievement tests, showed declining goals. This statistic may be changing. Among 12,330 girls scoring in the 95th percentile, about the same proportion of girls as boys, chose majors in premedicine, prelaw, and mathematics. Only in engineering was there a great difference.

The fact that males catch up and females lag in high school does not tell us anything about the reasons it happens. Theories abound but few real facts have been offered. Women have an achievement orientation equal to that of men. They are also as persistent as men. The evidence for self-esteem is mixed with some studies showing it to be very similar (Richmond-Abbott, 1983). Other studies show moderately higher levels of self-esteem in males (Robison-Awana, Kehle, & Jenson, 1986). Perhaps sex role orientation and expectations affect and sometimes limit academic plans and achievement. One study found that gifted boys are superior to average boys in academic and social self-concept but gifted girls are not similarly superior to nongifted girls (Kelly & Colangelo, 1984). In adolescence, then, although women still achieve well, their intelligence scores drop and they may begin to see their giftedness as less desirable. They often do not receive recognition for achievements, and they frequently attend less prestigious colleges than highly gifted boys. Their academic and vocational achievement compared to that of gifted males declines in adulthood (Kerr, 1985). Their salaries are less.

The barriers to gifted women's achievement, although fewer than years ago, are still present and can be found in the home, the society, and the school. In the home, socialization is often different for girls and boys. The traditional attitude is that males must prepare for upward achievement but females need not be as concerned (Perino & Perino, 1981). Not all families encourage their gifted female children to enter male-dominated fields or are as willing to pay for female children to attend the best schools as they are for their male children.

Schools may also share some of the blame. The school has been criticized for sexist practices in four main areas (Minuchin & Shapiro, 1983). These biases include teacher-student interactions, gender stereotypes in the curriculum, inequality in access to programs, and a lack of role models.

Differences exist in the way teachers interact with boys and girls. Teachers interact more with high-achieving boys than with high-achieving girls (Good, Sikes, & Brophy, 1973). When teachers attend to task-oriented activities in class, boys still receive more attention than girls (Fagot, 1977). In addition, when children demand attention, teachers respond to boys with instructions and girls with nurturance (Beal, 1994). Girls are also given more attention when physically close to teachers, while boys are given more attention when they are far away. Perhaps teachers expect good behavior from girls but feel that boys require encouragement. Male and female teachers are not very different in their views of student behavior. Perhaps these interactions reinforce physical proximity and conformity in girls and more task-oriented behavior in boys.

A study by the American Association of University Women (1992) found widespread discrimination from teachers, texts, and tests. Reviewing more than 1,000 articles, publications and hundreds of studies most from the 1980s, they concluded that teachers pay less attention to girls than boys; girls still lag in mathematics and science; and those who do well in the subjects still tend not to choose math and science careers. They also argue that some tests remain biased against girls, hurting their chances for scholarship, and some textbooks stereotype or ignore women. Even though girls get better grades, they are still shortchanged.

Sadker and Sadker (1985) observed teachers over a three-year period finding that teachers called on boys more often than girls, offered boys more detailed and constructive criticisms, and allowed boys to shout out answers but reprimanded girls for this practice. Two recent studies found that many teachers of mathematics and science ignore girls in favor of boys and the gap on science standardized tests may actually be widening, while the gap in math is narrowing. Those girls who do well do not continue. Teachers consistently underestimate their female students' abilities in mathematics (Kimball, 1989). Female students have less confidence in their math abilities, and with loss of confidence comes loss of performance (Junge & Dretzke, 1995). Boys get more detailed instruction on the correct approach. Girls are frequently told they are right or wrong and given the right answers. These differences are not deliberate, and even female teachers show these patterns (Kerr, 1991).

Differential teacher attitudes and behaviors may discourage female students from taking advanced science and mathematics courses. Simple training can improve teacher behavior. Teachers can learn to call on girls as often as boys, give girls informative responses, give girls praise and criticism in detail, reward girls' assertiveness in classroom, and resist over-helping by giving them answers (Kerr, 1991).

Not everyone agrees with the conclusion that girls are shortchanged. Some authorities argue that some of the research reviewed is questionable, that some research findings run contrary to their assertions, and that the strides in educational achievement made by women over the past few decades are disregarded (Schmidt, 1994). Others defend these conclusions.

If teachers view and treat girls and boys differently, do they identify more boys than girls as gifted? This question is not easy to answer, and the answer seems to depend upon the school. A study of referral patterns found great variability among schools with some showing a differential pattern of referral and others not showing such a pattern (Crombie, Bouffard-Bouchard, & Schneider, 1992). Generalizations, then, are difficult. Differences in gender enrollment in gifted programs may be due to a number of factors including differences in parental referrals, differences in performance on standardized tests, and even the refusal to enter such programs (Ebmier & Schmulbach, 1989). For example, gifted girls do not accept enrollment in accelerated programs as often as gifted boys do (Fox, Benbow, & Perkins, 1983; Terwilliger & Titus, 1995).

Mathematics and science books may also contribute to the perpetuation of traditional gender roles and subtly show girls that mathematics and science are not meant for them. A number of books are blatant not only in the narrative but also in their pictures. But bias does not have to be obvious, as when men are pictured as scientists and engineers and females are depicted as elementary school teachers and nurses. Some mathematics books give verbal problems that involve gender-stereotyped action sequences. Tom mixes chemicals or fixes his bicycle, while female names are used when something is being done to someone else. Evidence indicates that children are aware of the roles of the characters in the stories and especially remember if the gender role runs counter to expectation. Children, like adults, tend to resist change (Jennings, 1975).

In some cases, school personnel including teachers, administrators, and guidance counselors discourage girls from taking particular courses. A bright adolescent female may be advised not to take an advanced mathematics course because it's a waste of time. After all, what is she going to do with it anyway. This type of blatant sexism has been held up to public scrutiny and criticized, as it should be.

THOUGHT QUESTION

10. *In your school experience, do teachers treat male and female students differently? If your answer is yes, list the ways.*

Teachers seem to treat male and female students somewhat differently. Could such differential treatment affect these students' achievement later on?

THOUGHT QUESTION

11. What can be done to encourage gifted high school female students to follow careers in the sciences?

But such statements are probably less common than the subtle communication of expectations. In many schools and homes today, females are not actively restricted from these areas. They are simply not encouraged to take such courses (Sadker & Sadker, 1994). Females do not have to be actively dissuaded from achieving. Lack of encouragement produces similar results. For example, female students do not attend the computer room during lunch as often as males do. No one actively stops them from attending, but they do not come because some girls believe that computers and mathematics are not their domain. They must be encouraged to come to the computer room if they are to be familiar with computers (Sadker & Sadker, 1994).

Studies show that female students do not take as many science and mathematics courses in high school (Terwilliger & Titus, 1995). This reduced interest in science and mathematics may begin when students are in the middle school. Females do not think of science or mathematics as their "good" subjects as often as they did in elementary school, even though elementary school girls do well in these subjects and therefore have a history of success in science and math (Sadker & Sadker, 1994). By the time advanced courses in high school are to be chosen, a considerable gender difference is found. Girls take advanced biology, and boys choose physics and advanced chemistry. As girls proceed through high school, they see science and mathematics as less and less relevant to their futures.

Gifted Women and Vocational Choice

What types of vocational choices do gifted women make? Studies contradict each other in this area. Some studies show little difference in vocational choice between male and female students in high school (Kramer, 1986). Others show lower aspirations for females (Delisle, 1992). Women experience both internal and external barriers in making vocational decisions to enter fields in mathematics and the physical sciences. The external barriers include sexism, discrimination, and lack of role models. Some internal barriers include fear of being considered too bright and falling back onto very traditional societal roles (Delisle, 1992).

The picture, though, is not a simple one. Although women are still overrepresented in certain fields such as clerical and service positions, more women are entering what might be called nontraditional fields. A nontraditional field is one in which the overwhelming majority, more than two-thirds are workers of the opposite gender (Hayes, 1985). The trend for women to enter nontraditional fields can be analyzed in two ways. The first is pessimistic. For example, 85.4 percent of all elementary schoolteachers are female, as are 65 percent of retail sales workers. Women comprise 87.6 percent of the librarians, 95 percents of nurses, and 99 percent of secretaries (U.S. Department of Commerce, 1993). Most women are still opting to enter traditional fields, even if these fields are professional, such as teaching. Some change in the number of women who want to enter nontraditional fields is taking place, such as in the sciences, but it has been a relatively small change overall.

The other evaluation is more optimistic, seeing women as making substantial though uneven progress. In 1970, only 5 percent of lawyers were female; today, it is 21.4 percent. Some 20.4 percent of all physicians are female today, up from 10 percent in 1970. Women comprise 33.5 percent of computer scientists today compared with 13 percent in 1970. Today, 15.3 percent of architects are women, more than double the percentage in 1970; and the percentage of college and university professors has increased from 29 percent in 1970 to 40.9 percent today. In the area of business careers, the rise is also significant. In 1983, women held 32.4 percent of the executive, administrative, and managerial positions, while in 1992 women held 41.5 percent of the positions. More than one-third of the medical degrees and about 42 percent of the law degrees in 1990 were awarded to women (U.S. Department of Commerce, 1989; 1993). These figures show that women are entering these traditionally male-dominated fields in large numbers. Many of the women who enter nontraditional professional fields are gifted.

Many women, especially gifted women, may face problems in career planning that males do not. For example, men are socialized to accept the role of breadwinner, but women have developed a dual role as mother and worker, which often limits their career choices. Women are sometimes reluctant to enter careers in the sciences because they see problems combining family life and a career in this area (McLure & Piel, 1978). Although women are now entering nontraditional careers such as law and medicine, the woman entering chemistry, physics, and engineering is still a rarity.

In addition, even women with high grades and intellectual ability do not necessarily look toward higher-level positions (Church, 1983). While intelligence scores bear a reasonably close relationship to accomplishment among men, they have no relationship among women, with many women with intelligence scores above 120 occupied as housewives or office workers. Many are backups to men in power (Clark, 1988). Perhaps women's grades show women their ability but are not used to determine future plans; women are more influenced by other social and familial factors than men are.

Although asking how gifted females achieve in adulthood is an interesting research topic, studies are plagued by technical difficulties and are difficult to evaluate. Although most studies show that gifted women succeed, some authorities argue that based upon training and education, gifted females are underachieving (Reis, 1987). Because of the societal changes that have occurred, generalizations about women's achievements from studies conducted years ago are probably inaccurate. The cohort effect makes generational comparisons questionable. Gifted women born in the 1930s did not have the opportunities they do today. Differences as to the meaning of success also make interpretation difficult. Traditional studies of gifted women in adulthood often emphasize traditional achievement in terms of vocational achievement and may be stereotypically masculine. Studies also show that relational achievements are important to gifted women (Hollinger & Fleming, 1992).

When gifted women are questioned as to their concerns, women from cohorts ranging from 1910 through 1980 noted a lack of role models for gifted females, denial of giftedness, little organized mentoring and few networking skills, and poor guidance and counseling (Walker, Reis, & Leonard, 1992). Women, especially those who have talent in science and mathematics, require role models if they are to achieve. These role models may be able to show students how to combine a career in the sciences and a family, something female students consider very important. Female students must also be taught that giftedness and femininity are not mutually exclusive and that they can achieve interpersonally as well as academically. Mentoring programs may be useful, as students experience a relationship with a successful female scientist. Last, these bright students need counseling that will encourage them to continue to take math and science courses and enter careers in the physical sciences. School counselors are sometimes blamed for discouraging females from developing their potential. However, these students often have a sexist view of career choices before they are seen by counselors. In many instances, counselors of both sexes are less stereotyped in their views of work and gender roles than the females they are counseling (Hawley, 1982).

While concern about vocational choice is reasonable and elimination of the sometimes invisible barriers that negatively affect the achievement and career plans of gifted women is important, some politically correct view of how a woman should live should not be foisted on students. Too often, older stereotypes have been replaced by newer ones. For instance, one gifted female student felt rather guilty because she wanted to pursue a career in elementary school teaching. Her decision was not greeted with approval by her counselor, her teachers, and some friends who believed she could "do better." The goal should be to encourage women to enter the field of their choice unencumbered by artificial barriers, not to make the decision for them.

SCENARIO

7 Laura has the fifth highest grades in her high school. Her academic skills are excellent and she does very well in every major subject. Last week she announced that she wanted to be a nurse and enter the local college. The local college is good but Laura could attend a more prestigious school. In addition, both her parents, her counselor, and some of her teachers were very disappointed in her choice of major. While they believe that nursing is important, they believe that she could become a doctor or a medical researcher. Laura was surprised at their attitude and believes that she would enjoy a nursing career. In your opinion, should any attempt be made to change Laura's mind about her college or vocational choice?

 **THE CLASSROOM**   **Active Improvement**

A number of relatively simple changes can be accomplished both in the classroom and the home to help gifted females achieve.

1. Become aware of stereotyping both in communication and behavior and take special notice of placing students in gender stereotyped jobs, such as having boys do one thing and girls another.	**Why?** Statements such as "I need two strong boys to carry . . ." or "Girls are so artistic" are limiting (Shapiro, Kramer, & Hunerberg, 1981).
2. Target all groups for broadening gender roles, not just girls.	**Why?** If girls are targeted to help change their mathematics attitudes and nothing is done to change the attitudes of boys that mathematics is strictly a masculine domain, then gender role perceptions have not been expanded (Fennema, 1987).
3. Distribute leadership roles in the classroom equally.	**Why?** In some classes, boys may be chosen as leaders more often. Girls should receive equal experiences.
4. Show examples of stereotyping used in media and in school materials.	**Why?** Many students may not be aware of the sexist material in advertisements, such as those showing action-oriented toys meant only for males.
5. Be aware of expectations for students.	**Why?** Some teachers expect higher achievement in some areas from one gender than another, such as expecting boys to do well in mathematics and science and girls in English (Sadker & Sadker, 1994). This injures both boys and girls.
6. Review instructional materials for bias.	**Why?** Although many instructional materials have been improved in this regard, some bias may still exist.
7. Discuss successful women in the classroom. When discussing literature, science, or history, note nontraditional roles.	**Why?** Unfortunately, many classes minimize the contributions of great women in many areas of endeavor.

8. Look for gender-stereotyped practices in school such as girls taking cooking and boys taking shop.	**Why?** In order to discover children's talents, they need to be exposed to an activity first. If a child is not exposed to some activity because of gender, the child's talent may remain undiscovered.
9. Beware of tests that heavily favor science over language.	**Why?** These tests may not be balanced and hurt identification of gifted female students (Kerr, 1991).
10. Watch wording in questions that may involve sports and mechanics, which favor boys over girls. The same goes for questions that contain stereotyped feminine references.	**Why?** Some tests are not blatantly sexist but have a subtle bias that may affect one gender or the other.
11. Show role models for gifted women.	**Why?** A lack of role models, especially in the sciences, may reduce the expectations of gifted female students. Having successful women in nontraditional occupations come to class may increase student aspirations. Successful women who combine family and career are especially important.
12. Actively encourage female students to take science and mathematics courses and to participate in scientific endeavors.	**Why?** Active encouragement is necessary if gifted female students are to take their places in the sciences.
13. Actively sponsor mentorship programs.	**Why?** Such programs help introduce gifted females to people who have succeeded and help provide role models.

The Goal: Full Participation

Both this chapter and the previous one have repeatedly advocated the importance of broadening the definition of giftedness. Looking beyond intellectual giftedness is necessary if other forms of giftedness are to be identified and valued. It is also important to look at populations that have not been identified as gifted as often as their numbers indicate they should be. Members of some minority groups, children with disabilities, gifted children who underachieve, and in some cases, women, may need special identification procedures and some understanding of their unique needs. The idea is not to artificially include children from these groups who may not be gifted among the group of students identified as gifted just to be able to say that this percentage of gifted females and that percentage of gifted minority group students are involved. The purpose is to open up to all qualified students the benefits of special services for gifted students in order to better serve the entire school population.

S U M M A R Y

1. Creativity involves a novel response to solve a problem. Convergent thinking involves arriving at an answer when given a particular set of facts while divergent thinking involves the ability to see new but appropriate relationships between things. Creativity is sometimes measured by ideational fluency or the ability to produce a large number of ideas. Others believe creativity includes content knowledge, the ability to communicate, and the ability to analyze critically.

2. Measuring intelligence will not yield a fair estimate of creativity. Parents and teachers can encourage creativity, and some programs are commercially available to do the same.

3. Evaluating talent in the artistic, musical, dance, and drama areas is somewhat subjective. Often, experts rate talented students during an audition. Much of the training in the arts is done privately, which certainly places people living in poverty at a disadvantage. Self and peer nominations may also be helpful for suggesting who has talent.

4. Questions as to whether talent has genetic roots, and if it does, how much should be

attributed to genetics, remain largely unanswered. Studies of talented individuals show that they do not necessarily show their talents at an early age—although some certainly do—and that identification comes after being exposed to a particular activity. As children develop their talents, their focus often becomes narrower. The parents of these children emphasize doing the best one can and offer strong encouragement as a rule. Self-control and self-discipline are established in childhood.

5. Leadership is difficult to define but may include the ability to influence a group so that it reaches its goals and allows group participants to attain fulfillment. Leaders are more intelligent than the group they are leading but need not be intellectually gifted. Leadership in community and after-school activities is more predictive of adult leadership than is academic success. Training in group dynamics, communication, and decision-making skills may be helpful.

6. The term *underachievement* is used to describe situations in which students' abilities are

significantly greater than their achievements. Noncompetitive learning strategies may be effective and any strategy that strengthens the student's perception of the importance of effort may be helpful.

7. Between 2 and 5 percent of all students with disabilities are gifted. Their disability may get in the way of identifying them as gifted, especially since the educational focus is most often on the disability. Special testing programs are often required for identification. Gifted children with disabilities may require more encouragement since they generally do not have as positive a self-concept as other gifted children have.

8. Children from some minority groups are not identified as gifted as often as their numbers would indicate. Some reasons for the underidentification are the effects of poverty on achievement and cultural and linguistic differences. More subjective means of identification and more flexible cutoffs may help identify greater numbers of gifted minority group students.

9. Gifted female students do well in school, but evidence indicates that they are not reaching their potential. Although more women are entering nontraditional fields like medicine and law, women remain underrepresented in the physical sciences and engineering. Gifted females with mathematics and science aptitude need to be encouraged to enter these fields.

Hearing Impairment

HEARING IMPAIRMENT

TRUE-FALSE STATEMENTS

See below for the correct answers.

1. Hearing impairment is more common in children than adults.
2. Scientists have yet to verify the cause of most cases of profound hearing loss in children.
3. Only noise that is painful can cause permanent hearing loss.
4. Ninety percent of children with deafness have two parents who can hear.
5. Unfortunately, no one has discovered a way to test the auditory abilities of infants.
6. Most people with deafness are excellent at speech reading if they are sitting close enough to the speaker.
7. American Sign Language (ASL) is a manual language for deaf people with its own grammar.
8. Babies who are deaf babble in sign language if their parents use sign language to communicate.
9. American Sign Language is the most common language used in the education of children who are deaf in the United States.
10. More children who are deaf are attending private or public residential schools than ever before.
11. If a student with a hearing impairment has an interpreter, the teacher should ignore the interpreter and speak directly to the student.
12. Hearing aids essentially restore hearing in people whose auditory problems are not caused by nerve damage.

Answers to True-False Statements

1. False. See page 460.
2. True.
3. False. See page 462.
4. True.
5. False. See page 465.
6. False. See page 467.
7. True.
8. True.
9. False. See page 473.
10. False. See page 474.
11. True.
12. False. See page 486.

Simulating a Hearing Impairment

Place your hands over your ears tightly and ask a friend to talk to you in a moderately low voice. Now try reading your friend's lips. Your friend should speak normally. After a couple of minutes, repeat the gist of what you think was said. For a second exercise, try having a conversation with your friend on some simple topic in the same manner.

If you do these exercises properly, you may begin to appreciate what having a hearing impairment is like. Reading lips is not easy, and although you may improve with practice, even experienced speech-readers can understand at the most only about 50 percent of what they see. Because sounds in English are sometimes very similar to each other in physical production (viewed from the outside), a listener who is deaf can perceive only an estimated 30 to 40 percent of the sounds spoken by a speaker (Gallaudet College, 1975).

Hearing impairment is an invisible disability, and children with hearing impairments do not receive much sympathy (Coryell, Holcomb, & Scherer, 1992). The consequences of a hearing impairment are frequently quite serious for it too often leads to isolation. As Andrew Freeland puts it, "Blindness cuts people off from objects, deafness cuts people off from people" (1989, p. 1). Beethoven, who had a hearing impairment during adulthood, wrote, "Though endowed with a passionate and lively temperament and ever fond of the distractions offered by society, I was soon obliged to seclude myself and live in solitude" (Freeland, 1989, p. 1).

The public does not appreciate the many problems encountered by people with hearing impairments. Many people with severe auditory impairments have difficulty communicating with people who can hear. If a child has been born with a hearing impairment, the child may be significantly delayed in acquiring verbal language and experience speech problems (Nicholas, Geers, & Kozak, 1994). Children learn language by listening to and becoming actively involved in conversation. Children who cannot hear speech do not receive this stimulation and frequently develop difficulties communicating orally. The natural process by which speech is developed does not occur, and other ways to communicate must be used.

Most people with severe hearing impairments use sign language to communicate with the outside world. Since relatively few people who can hear understand sign language this limits the ability of people with hearing impairments to communicate with other people. Sometimes, the hearing parents of children who are deaf cannot communicate well with their own children, since children may have a greater knowledge of sign language than their parents do. Children with severe hearing impairments will spend a large part of their day interacting with people who do not know their language and who do not have much experience interacting with them. When hearing adults tried to communicate with children who were deaf by touch, gestures, and simple speech, they were successful only a little less than 50 percent of the time, compared with about 70 percent of the time with young children who could hear (Lederberg, 1984).

Children with severe hearing loss also find themselves limited in other ways, since people's daily lives are filled with sound. The ringing of the telephone, the cries of a baby, even the warning tone of a smoke alarm are lost. Today, the spotlight is on the use of technology to overcome some of these problems and, as we shall see, an amazing variety of devices can help people with auditory difficulties.

How We Hear

Before discussing hearing impairment some understanding of the structure of the auditory system and the process by which we hear is necessary (see Figure 12.1). The human auditory system is divided into three major divisions: the outer ear, the middle ear, and the inner ear. The outer ear consists of the pinna (the skin and cartilage attached to the side of the head) and the ear canal. The outer ear collects the sound.

The middle ear consists of the eardrum called the tympanic membrane, the ossicles made up of three tiny bones, and the eustachian tube that connects the throat and the middle ear. The eustachian tube allows air to flow into the middle ear, equalizes pressure, and drains off fluid. Sound causes the eardrum to vibrate. These vibrations are passed along to the three bones called the hammer, anvil, and stirrup, which conduct the sound. The middle ear converts sound energy into mechanical energy (Freeland, 1989).

The inner ear consists of the cochlea, the semicircular canals, and the endings of the auditory nerve. The cochlea converts mechanical energy into electrical impulses. The base of the cochlea and footplate of the stirrup meet at the oval window, which consists of tissue separating the middle ear and inner ear. The vibration of the footplate sets off a wave in the fluid-filled cochlea causing the hairlike projections inside the cochlea to move. These hairlike projections are in contact with nerve fibers and translate the motion into nerve impulses, which are then carried by the auditory nerve to the brain for processing (Rezen & Hausman, 1985). The semicircular canals do not affect hearing, but are responsible for balance.

Sound, itself, has a number of characteristics. The most important for our purposes are amplitude and frequency. **Amplitude** refers to the loudness of the sound and is measured in decibels. The **frequency** of the sound wave is the number of sound waves per second and is measured in hertz. Pitch is the psychological equivalent of frequency, and refers to a person's perception of how high or low a sound seems (Vergason, 1990).

Amplitude:
The loudness of the sound as measured in decibels.

Frequency:
The number of sound waves per second, measured in hertz.

Categorizing Hearing Impairments

Hearing impairments are usually categorized under three major headings: (1) the amount of hearing loss, (2) the part of the hearing apparatus that is affected, and (3) the age of onset of the loss.

FIGURE 12.1   Cross Section
Showing the Structure of the Ear

Source: Daniel D. Chiras. *Human Biology:
Health, Homeostasis, and the Environment.*
Copyright © 1991 by West Publishing
Company.

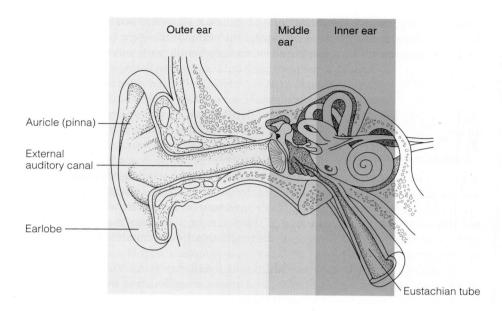

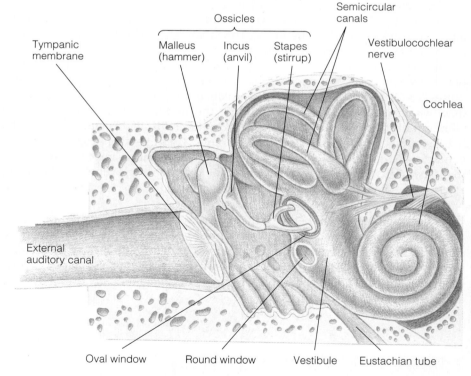

The Degree of Hearing Loss

Hearing impairment is a broad term that covers all degrees of hearing loss. According to the federal definition, deafness is a hearing impairment severe enough that the child is impaired in processing linguistic information through hearing, with or without amplification, which adversely affects educational performance. The term *hard of hearing* refers to a hearing impairment of lesser degree that adversely affects a child's educational performance (Bienenstock & Vernon, 1994). Children who are hard of hearing can use hearing aids to understand speech.

Degree of hearing loss is usually classified in terms of mild, moderate, severe, and profound. Mild loss (26–40 decibels or db) involves the loss of some sounds but not enough to affect most uses of hearing. Moderate loss (41–65 db) means that enough sounds are missed to affect a person's understanding and includes some speech sounds. Severe loss (66–95 db) means that many sounds are not heard including most speech sounds, while profound loss (95 db or more) means that almost all sounds are not heard (Martin, 1990).

These hearing loss ranges are not universally accepted. For example, Moores (1988) classifies the range of hearing losses in the following manner: mild hearing loss between 35–54 db (sometimes called level 1), moderate 55–69 db (level 2), severe 70–89 db (level 3), and profound 90 db and greater (level 4). The individual who is hard of hearing usually has a hearing loss between 35 and 69 db, while an individual who is considered deaf usually shows a hearing loss of greater than 70 db (Martin, 1990). Different states use different degrees of hearing loss in their classifications, and authorities differ about these ranges (Bienenstock & Vernon, 1994).

The Location of the Hearing Loss

A hearing impairment may be caused by difficulty anywhere in the auditory mechanism. A **conductive hearing loss** occurs when the sound is not conducted efficiently through the ear canal, ear drum, or the three bones in the middle ear. Conductive problems usually show themselves in an inability to hear sound of lower intensity (ASHA, 1992). A **sensorineural hearing loss** occurs when the inner ear or nerve pathways from the inner ear to the brain are damaged. This damage causes a reduction both in intensity of the sound heard and in the frequencies that can be processed. A **mixed hearing loss** occurs as a combination of the conductive and sensorineural types. Finally, a **central hearing loss** occurs when the auditory centers in the brain are injured.

The Age of Onset

The age at which a person experiences the auditory impairment is crucial to understanding the individual's functioning. The onset may occur during the prelingual or postlingual stage. The distinction is crucial. Children who have a **postlingual hearing loss**, or lose their hearing after age five or six, still have had the opportunity to develop reasonably mature speech patterns. A child with a **prelingual hearing loss**, on the other hand, who is born with a severe hearing impairment or becomes deaf due to an accident or illness before the age of three

Conductive hearing loss: A hearing loss due to difficulties in conducting sound through the ear canal, ear drum, and/or three bones in the middle ear.

Sensorineural hearing loss: A hearing loss due to damage to the inner ear or nerve pathways to the brain.

Mixed hearing loss: A hearing loss that is both conductive and sensorineural in origin.

Central hearing loss: A hearing loss due to damage to the auditory centers in the brain.

Postlingual hearing loss: A hearing loss that occurs after the child has learned basic language.

Prelingual hearing loss: A hearing loss that occurs before language is learned, commonly considered before the age of three years.

years, has not had these language experiences and has a more difficult time developing intelligible speech.

Prevalence

Prevalence figures for hearing loss vary widely depending upon the categories for degree of loss used, age of onset, ages of people surveyed, and method by which data is collected (NICD, 1987). About one baby in 1,000 is born with a profound hearing loss or deaf, or becomes so before the age of three years (NICD, 1987). If infants are included with moderate losses along with those with profound hearing impairments and deafness, the number may be as high as 1 in 750 (Ruppert & Buhrer, 1992).

In some populations, such as premature infants, the percentage with hearing impairment is greater and in the smallest infants—those weighing less than 1500 grams—between 9 and 17 percent may have a significant hearing impairment. Approximately 2,000–4,000 infants with profound hearing impairments are born each year. About 2 in every 100 persons under the age of 18 have a hearing impairment, although some studies give a higher prevalence and some a lower prevalence.

During the 1992–1993 school year, 60,896 children between the ages of 6 and 21 years received special education services due to auditory impairments. About 1.3 percent of all children being served by special education services are categorized as having auditory impairments (U.S. Department of Education, 1994).

The majority of school-aged children with mild to moderate hearing losses require little change in their schedules and relatively few services. Among children who have a hearing impairment and receive special services, 44 percent are diagnosed as having profound hearing loss, 23 percent have severe impairments, and the other 33 percent have less severe impairments (NICD, 1987). In most disability classifications, the majority of students receiving special education services have mild impairments. However, this is not the case with children with hearing impairments. Many children with mild hearing loss will not receive special education services, and the majority of children served in this category will have severe impairments.

Hearing impairment becomes much more common with age (Forbes et al., 1992; Schein, 1994). Many middle-aged people find that their hearing has worsened, and the incidence of hearing impairment rises sharply after age sixty. By the seventies, as many as 75 percent have some hearing impairment, and 15 percent of the people over sixty-five are deaf (Botwinick, 1984). An estimated 22 million Americans experience hearing loss (NICD, 1988). Of those, about 1.6 million Americans have severe or profound hearing loss or are deaf (Kabat, 1992).

One important and frequently overlooked demographic fact is the number of children with hearing impairments who are members of minority groups. In 1989, more than 35 percent of all hearing impaired students were members of minority groups. In some states such as California, Texas, and New York, the percentage was more than 50 percent (Schildroth, Rawlings, & Allen, 1991). Many come from

Most children without hearing impairments do not understand American Sign Language, making communication difficult.

poverty-filled environments and others may have a language other than English spoken in the home, making language acquisition of English an even more daunting task (Schildroth et al., 1991).

Causes of Hearing Impairment

Sometimes the cause of hearing impairments is easily found. For example, a buildup of wax in the ears and a blockage caused by a foreign object in the ear canal are relatively easy to spot and treat. Others, such as perforated eardrums (a hole in the eardrum) caused by injury, pressure changes, or infection can be repaired. Some congenital malformations in the middle ear may also be remedied by surgery.

By far, though, the most common cause of conduction problems is the very common disease called **otitis media**. Although it can occur at any age, it is most common in early childhood. Two-thirds of all preschoolers have had it at least once. Bacteria from upper respiratory infections spread to the middle ear through the eustachian tube. The tube is shorter and more horizontal in young children and permits fluids to build up rather than draining off, and the middle ear becomes swollen and painful. Although the infection is usually temporary if treated promptly and properly, it can become chronic and eventually lead to hearing loss. Some children are so prone to the disease that their ears will have to be drained and a small tube installed to help drainage in an operation called a tympanotomy.

Otitis media:
A middle ear infection that sometimes leads to hearing loss.

Two common causes of conductive hearing loss in adults are otosclerosis and presbycusis. Otosclerosis is a hereditary hearing problem in which an overgrowth of bone occurs in the middle ear. The stirrup may become fixed in place and this greatly reduces sound conduction. Surgery is required to fix this problem. Most common is presbycusis, which is a general term literally meaning "old hearing" and involves many changes in the auditory system; the bones become stiff and the eardrum thickens and becomes less flexible. Hearing aids may help remedy this condition.

Although a number of agents cause hearing problems, the largest single cause of profound hearing loss today is as it has been for over one hundred years; "cause unknown" accounts for as many as 30 percent of all cases of deafness. Only recently has much research looked into the genetic and medical causes of deafness (Moores, 1988). In addition, hearing impairments are often not diagnosed until the child is two years old or even older; and remembering an illness that occurred in the early stages of pregnancy is often difficult. When no obvious cause is found, the deafness may be attributed to genetics. More than 150 genetic disorders involve deafness in some way, either as the primary symptom or as one of a number of possible symptoms (Moores, 1988). About half of the "cause unknown" cases are thought to be due to genetic causation (NIH, 1982).

Hearing difficulties are also caused by infections or drugs. Years ago, the most common prenatal problem causing hearing disorders was rubella. Pregnant women rarely contract rubella today, because a vaccine is available. Other viruses

Excessive noise can affect
hearing ability.

during pregnancy are also related to hearing loss including cytomegalovirus
(CMV) and herpes simplex type 3, which affect the nervous system of newborns.

Other possible causes of hearing loss after birth include blows to the head, tumors, stroke, or accidents. Some illnesses such as meningitis cause hearing loss,
and certain medications can damage the hair cells inside the cochlea. Any person
taking medication who experiences a sudden change in hearing, ringing in the
ears, dizziness, or loss of balance should consult a doctor immediately.

The Special Case of Noise

Of all the possible environmental causes for hearing loss, noise has received the
most publicity. Noise can cause both temporary and permanent hearing loss. One
student told a class that her father who worked with construction machinery for
20 years did not realize that he had lost a part of his hearing. She had to raise her
voice in order for him to hear her at all, and the television set had to be very loud.

Of the approximately 22 million people in the United States with hearing impairments of all varieties, about 10 million are at least partially attributable to exposure to loud noises (NIH, 1990). Sound levels above 85 decibels are likely to
cause permanent loss after continued exposure. People whose jobs require exposure to noise should wear protective devices. Teenagers should be warned against
listening to very loud music. Many teenagers listen to music well above 85 decibels. Such sounds can produce irreversible hearing loss at any age and can cause
difficulty in understanding speech and tinnitus (ringing in the ears). Even very
loud sounds of short duration such as explosions or gunshots can produce immediate, severe, and even permanent hearing loss, but long-term exposure to less in-

**THOUGHT
QUESTION**

*1. Why do people have diffi-
culty convincing others
who always listen to very
loud music that it can
damage their hearing?*

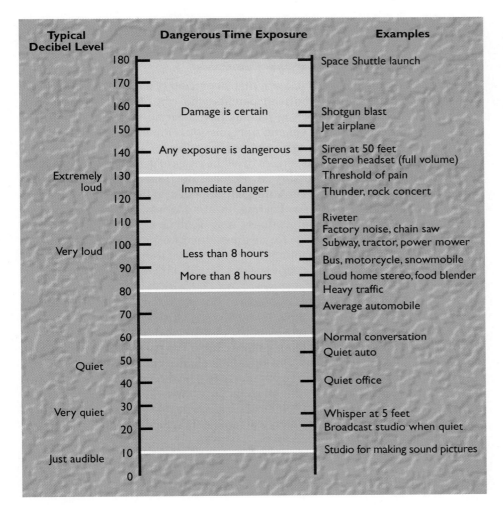

FIGURE 12.2   Decibel Ratings
The loudness of sound is
measured in decibels.

Source: Dennis Coon. *Introduction to
Psychology: Exploration and Application* Sixth
Edition. Copyright © 1992 by West Publishing
Company.

tense sounds take a gradual toll on one's hearing even without being aware of it. (Figure 12.2 shows the decibel ratings for many sounds.) More than 20 million Americans are exposed on a regular basis to such noise levels. People engaged in certain occupations in firefighting, law enforcement, military activities, construction and factory work, music, and farming are frequently exposed to such work-related noise. Some relatively common situations—listening to loud music, experiencing the noise from appliances, and operating machinery, such as lawn mowers—may sometimes fall into this category.

How does noise cause a hearing impairment? Loud sounds can damage all the structures of the ear but particularly the hair cells in the cochlea. Moderate exposure may initially cause temporary hearing loss, but repeated exposure causes a disruption of blood flow to the cochlea, which can damage a few scattered hair cells. With continuous exposure, the number of damaged hair cells increases, especially in the area responsible for high-frequency hearing.

Deaf Children and Their Deaf and Hearing Parents

People are usually surprised to learn that 90 percent of all children with severe hearing impairments are born to parents who can hear (Ritter-Brinton & Stewart, 1992). The reason hearing parents have hearing-impaired offspring is found in an understanding of genetic transmission. Dominant transmission requires the presence of only one gene and is responsible for about 10 percent of all childhood deafness and only 20 percent of all the cases of genetically caused deafness. Recessive transmission requires two genes (one from each parent) and can be transmitted by parents who carry the gene but have no hearing loss since they possess another gene for average hearing. In other words, two hearing people, each of whom have one gene for deafness, may produce a child with deafness. If both parents carry the same gene for deafness, their offspring have a 25 percent chance of having a hearing impairment. This recessive transmission is responsible for as much as 40 percent of early serious hearing loss in children and 80 percent of all genetically caused deafness.

Most genetically caused cases of deafness depend upon four or five different recessive genes that exist at different points on the chromosomes. The recessive nature of the genes is the reason two people who are deaf (even if the deafness is hereditary) are able to have children who can hear. The parents may be deaf due to defects in different gene pairs. Obviously, the chances of two deaf people having a hearing-impaired child are greater than if two hearing people marry, but two deaf people may also have offspring who can hear (Moores, 1988). Because transmission is usually recessive and genetically caused deafness may be the result of different sets of genes, most children who are deaf do have hearing parents and many deaf parents do have children who can hear.

Assessment of Hearing Problems

The sooner a child's hearing problem is diagnosed, the more likely that problems resulting from the hearing loss can be minimized. If an infant cannot hear well, much of what is said and auditory stimulation in general is reduced and perhaps distorted. Speaking is delayed and often poor. Yet, hearing impairments are often not discovered in infancy. Unless screening is conducted, the child who has a severe hearing impairment is not usually detected until 18 months of age or even older, even in infants at risk (Ruppert & Buhrer, 1992). This delay is unfortunate because children whose hearing loss is discovered and who receive help before 16 months of age develop speech and language skills far superior to those of children discovered later (McFarland & Simmons, 1980). The difference in the quality of speech and language of children who receive earlier help is the reason former Surgeon General of the United States, C. Everett Koop, issued a directive in 1989 stating that by the year 2000, our goal should be to identify a full 90 percent of all children with significant hearing impairment by one year of age.

Even later on in early childhood people may not be aware of a child's hearing problems, especially moderate or mild ones or ones that affect one ear. One professional couple discovered their child's hearing loss when they noticed that the

THOUGHT QUESTION

2. Why are 90 percent of deaf children born to hearing parents?

THOUGHT QUESTION

3. Why don't children with mild hearing impairments recognize that they cannot hear properly?

child picked up the telephone receiver with one hand and placed the receiver in the other hand before talking into the device.

If hearing loss is to be identified early, screening becomes particularly important. In some states screening is performed through a questionnaire that determines which children are most at risk for having or developing hearing problems. The risk category includes infants with family histories of hearing problems or genetic disorders associated with deafness, cranial abnormalities, low birth weight, bacterial meningitis, and the presence of a number of other risk factors. If the child falls into any risk category, the infant is then given special audiological tests.

Infants may be tested in a number of ways, but a relatively new method is called **auditory brainstem-evoked response (ABR)**. Electrodes are attached to the scalp, clicks of varying intensities are delivered through an earphone placed over the infant's ear, and brainwave activity is recorded. Estimates of hearing loss can be made by evaluating the brain wave patterns in response to the emitted sounds (Murray, 1988). Most children, though—80 percent in one study of more than 1,000 children—with hearing impairments are discovered through informal screening by parents and professionals when they notice delays in language development and lack of auditory response (Barringer et al., 1993).

Once a child can respond to a tone in a more voluntary manner, auditory testing becomes easier. Most school districts today conduct early screening for children as a way to satisfy the mandates of PL 94-142. Most commonly, schools use an **audiometer**, a machine that can transmit tones at various frequencies and intensities. Each ear is tested separately as the audiologist asks the person to raise a hand to indicate that a sound was heard. The results are plotted on a graph called an audiogram (see Figure 12.3). The pure tone audiometry test is a basic sensitivity test.

Other tests may localize a hearing problem. In a pure tone bone conduction test the audiologist places a tiny vibrator behind the ear or on the forehead, and the pure tone audiometry test is given. The vibrator bypasses both the outer ear and middle ear allowing the specialist to test the sensitivity of the inner ear.

Both of these tests measure pure tones, but in our daily life people are rarely exposed to pure tones like musical notes. In a speech reception or speech recognition threshold test, headphones are placed on the ears and the audiologist delivers words spoken at various intensities and frequencies through a tape recorder. The person is asked to repeat them. The words become more faint until the client must guess (Martin, 1990; Freeland, 1989). In another test called the speech detection threshold test (SDT), an individual's awareness of speech is measured and the audiologist seeks to discover the lowest level of intensity at which a person can detect the presence of speech and recognize it as such.

More involved tests are also available. For example, specific tests can diagnose the possible cause of a hearing problem by determining the reaction of the middle ear to changes in pressure, thereby determining the flexibility of the ear drum and abnormalities in the middle ear (Vergason, 1990).

Once a diagnosis of the hearing loss is made, the child may be evaluated for a hearing aid or other type of assistance. Such assistance is vital because hearing affects so many aspects of life. One important point to remember is that the child has always heard in a particular way, and the child assumes that type of hearing, whether impaired or not, is similar to what everyone else is experiencing. If hearing impairments are not discovered, adults and other children may think that a

Auditory brainstem-evoked response:
A method of detecting hearing loss in infants through an analysis of brain waves produced when sounds are delivered to the infant through earphones.

Audiometer:
A machine that transmits tones at various frequencies and intensities used to test auditory abilities.

Screening for auditory impairments often involves an audiometry examination.

FIGURE 12.3   Audiogram of Conductive Hearing Loss
This audiogram illustrates a mild to moderate hearing loss in both ears.

Source: Reprinted with the permission of Simon & Schuster from the Macmillan college text *Human Communication Disorders 4/E* by George Shames, Elizabeth Wiig, and Wayne Second. Copyright ©1994 by Macmillan College Publishing Company, Inc.

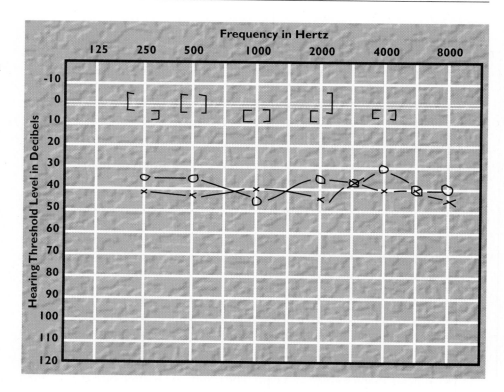

youngster who is ignoring a call is rude or even has a behavior disorder and that a child who is not doing well in school has mental retardation or doesn't try. The practice of testing the hearing of children who are considered to have mental retardation or a behavior disorder is recommended to determine whether auditory problems are involved.

Language Development Among Children with Severe Hearing Impairments

The language development of children with mild and even moderate hearing impairments is not controversial. These children often learn to speak in an intelligible manner and can process speech. They often require some speech therapy to improve pronunciation, but their integration into the regular school environment is not really debated. This assumption of integration is not the case for the child who has a prelingual profound hearing loss. Questions concerning the child's ability to communicate and appropriate schooling become contentious.

The most difficult question concerns what type of language training to give young children who are deaf or have severe hearing impairments. This area contains a number of alternatives (Bragg, 1994). Keep in mind, however, that 90 percent of these infants and young children will have hearing parents. Also consider the difficulties experienced by a hearing couple when told that their child is deaf.

They are often stunned. They must not only accept their child's deafness and deal with their feelings and disappointments, but also realize that they have an immediate decision to make concerning how they will communicate with the child. Should they learn sign language? Should they use some oral approach? If they decide to use sign language they will have to learn what is essentially another language. The decisions are difficult, and many parents lean heavily on the information offered to them by the professionals with whom they deal.

Children with serious hearing impairments face a number of communication challenges. They must communicate in some way with hearing people and also communicate with their peers who have hearing impairments. Three general approaches are most common. Each includes several subdivisions and has its advantages and disadvantages. First, manual systems involve the use of signs. Second, oral systems involve the use of residual hearing and speechreading. And last, total communication involves the use of all possible methods of communication. The controversy as to which is best produces a great deal of emotion on all sides and will continue into the future.

Oral Methods

Oral methods aim at encouraging children to receive and use language in the most conventional manner, without using sign language (MacDougall, 1991). Oralists want children who are deaf to use their residual hearing as best they can and combine it with other methods of oral communication.

One such method is speechreading. Actually, the term *speechreading* is both the newer and more accurate term for what was once called lipreading. Lipreading implies that the observer simply watches the movements of the mouth, while speechreading involves the use of gestures, facial expressions, and eye and body movements for greater comprehension (Carmen, 1983).

Speechreading is very difficult. Only about 30 to 40 percent of speech information is available through lip movements (Gatty, 1987). People who are deaf have to be good guessers and fill in the blanks using context and gestures (Rodda & Grove, 1987). Speechreading is also difficult because of the 30 to 40 percent of the sounds visible on the lips half of them are confusing because they look alike. Try to sit in front of a mirror and say "I made the bed" and "I baked the bread" (Mango, 1981). They look very similar. Do the same and say "kite," "height," and "night." Can you tell them apart?

Consider the problem for a speechreader who is trying to decipher the speaker's statements when the words are spoken quickly, sentences are not always completed, and the speaker may be partially turned away. Such variables as glare, the distance from the speaker, the angle of view, and many other variables affect speechreading ability. The best speechreaders are those who have become hearing impaired after they have acquired linguistic knowledge, have good residual hearing and good visual recognition, and are willing to make the guesses necessary. Even with so many problems, some people become very good speechreaders, especially if they can use their residual hearing effectively, but many, perhaps most, do not (NICD, 1989). Deaf children who speechread typically read only a small fraction of the words spoken (Vernon & Kohl, 1970). Even so, this does not mean that they cannot become skilled (Moores, 1988). Unfortunately, there has been a lack of interest in speechreading recently and not much improvement in teaching the skill.

Cued speech:
A system of communication in which eight hand shapes in four possible positions are used and offer added information to speechreading.

An adjunct to speechreading is called **cued speech**, a system of communication in which eight hand shapes in four possible positions give added information to speech that can be seen on the lips. The hand signals are cues that communicate the differences between sounds that look alike on the lips such as /p/, /b/, and /m/. The cues tell the individual the sound that is being uttered and takes some of the guesswork out of speechreading (Rodda & Grove, 1987).

Manual Methods

All manual methods of communication involve the use of signs. A number of sign languages are used in the United States.

American Sign Language

American Sign Language (ASL) is a recognized language (Freedman, 1994). Other countries have their own sign languages. It is not signed English (which is another way of signing). It has a grammar of its own and differs from English. For example, English contains some pronouns that indicate gender such as "he." ASL pronouns by themselves do not signify gender and only when a person sees where the sign is directed does gender become obvious. English has specific pronoun forms for grammatical purposes such as "She gave *him* the ticket." In ASL, the same sign is used for subjects and objects. English does not have a way of indicating if the object of the communication is within visual distance of the speaker. For example, if he has an apple, is the "he" here or somewhere else? In ASL the placement of the pronoun "he" tells us if he present or not (TRIPOD, 1992).

Three elements comprise a sign: the position of the hands, the way the hands are configured, and the movement of the hands to different positions (Moores, 1988). It is the dominant method of communication among people who are deaf

American Sign Language is a language with a special grammar of its own.

and is considered one of the more important elements in belonging to the deaf community.

Parents who are deaf and who use ASL note that their children produce signs as early as five months of age (Bates, O'Connell, & Shore, 1987). These are manual babbles and do not have any more meaning than a hearing child's babbles, although parents interpret their children's babbles.

When deaf parents of deaf infants use ASL with their children, their young children learn the signs naturally and without much artificial formal education and in a way that is similar to the way hearing children learn spoken language (Goldin-Meadow, 1991). For hearing parents of deaf children the situation is different, for these parents do not know ASL and must learn it first if they choose this option.

Manually Coded English

Another manual approach to communication is Manually Coded English (MCE) in which signs are used in English word order. A number of such communication systems are available, for example Seeing Essential English, Signing Exact English, Signed English, and Pidgin Sign Language (PSE). PSE uses signs from American Sign Language in English word order and can include some aspects of ASL grammar to denote plurals and the location of subjects. Pidgin Sign English is actually neither English nor ASL but combines elements of both. Manually Coded English provides a word-by-word translation of every word in English, including markers that signal inflections (Mayer & Lowenbraun, 1990).

Fingerspelling

Each letter in English also has a corresponding sign, allowing people to spell out words (see Figure 12.4). Theoretically, conversations can be entirely fingerspelled, but it would take too long to communicate a thought. Fingerspelling, though, is useful for technical words that either do not have a sign or the sign is not known to one of the participants in the conversation. It also can be used to indicate the names of places and people.

Total Communication

Today, **total communication** or the use of all possible methods of communication has become most popular. Total communication means the combination of an oral method and use of signs (Minnett, Clark, & Wilson, 1994). The child receives information through speechreading, amplification of signals using a hearing aid if practicable, and manual languages (Moores, 1988). Total communication, though, is as much a philosophy as a mode of communication (NICD, 1989). The philosophy translates into a belief that children with hearing impairments have the right to communicate by whatever means is useful and beneficial. Simultaneous communication presents the child with the two forms of communication (manual and oral) at the same time and is the most common form of communication used in educational settings.

Children with severe hearing impairments often find themselves using different communication strategies in different situations. While ASL is used at lunch with friends who are deaf, simultaneous communication is used in the classroom; at other times some form of speechreading is used when communicating with hearing people who do not know how to sign (Stewart, 1992).

Total communication:
The use of all possible means of communicating, including speech, signing, and speechreading.

The Great Debate

What is the best way to teach communication skills to children who are deaf? Traditionally, the debate was between oral and manual advocates. Supporters of the oral approach argued that the use of residual hearing, speechreading, and speech itself reduces the disability, and that using signs adversely affects the development of these oral skills. Those who favor the manual approach argue that early use of signs allows for early communication and actually helps develop language skills (Kamfe & Turecheck, 1987).

Today, however, the debate is between those who advocate purely oral methods and those who advocate total communication, since few advocate solely a manual system. Before 1970 the oral method held sway, but two events precipitated a crisis (Moores, 1988). First, a number of studies found that students with severe hearing impairments were not doing well in school, and these students were essentially taught using oral methods. Second, studies showed that deaf children of deaf parents (a distinct minority in the deaf community) who were exposed to sign language early in life showed better academic achievement in school. The oral-only approach was questioned and, in a very short time, most schools switched to a total communication program (Moores, 1988). By the mid 1980s,

FIGURE 12.4   Individual Letters in Sign Language

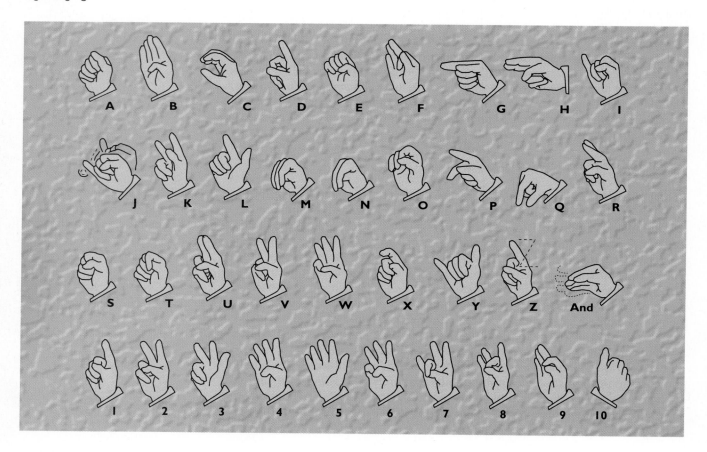

about 80 percent of all students with profound hearing loss and 75 percent of all students with severe hearing impairments were receiving instruction in signs with or without speech (Gallaudet Research Institute, 1985).

Although no one seriously questioned the fact that deaf children were not doing well in school (and still are not achieving well), the interpretation of the second point is controversial. The evidence that deaf children with deaf parents do better in school than deaf children of hearing parents has been confirmed by research and indeed most deaf parents use sign language with their children (Ritter-Brinton & Stewart, 1992). However, the conclusion that total communication is the best method for encouraging language acquisition for deaf children of hearing parents is still open to debate.

Deaf parents may find it easier to accept the hearing impairment of their child and already know sign language. Since most deaf children have hearing parents, educators must find the approach or approaches that are best for these children, instead of taking research from deaf children of deaf parents and assuming it can be generalized.

Conducting research into the effectiveness of various systems of communication is methodologically difficult. The variables are many, including parental acceptance of the hearing disability, the fact that many methods of communication may be used at various times, the richness of language used no matter what method is adopted, and the age of the child when deafness is discovered.

Brasel and Quigley (1977) compared the language abilities of deaf children who had deaf parents using a manually coded English system, deaf parents using ASL or some other sign language, hearing parents using oral methods with special training, and hearing parents using oral methods but with no training. The deaf children of parents who used the manually coded English system scored higher than all the other groups. Vernon and Kohl (1970) found an advantage for deaf children of deaf parents who used early manually coded English in a number of language areas compared with deaf children of hearing parents who used oral methods. This advantage occurred despite the fact that deaf children of hearing parents came from a higher socioeconomic environment and had more preschool experiences. Brasel and Quigley (1975) used four groups of deaf children including a manually coded English group whose deaf parents demonstrated good written English, a group including children of deaf parents who used ASL with a poor mastery of written English, an average oral group with deaf children of hearing parents who used no sign language and provided no special preschool experiences for their child, and a group of deaf children of hearing parents who received intensive oral training and a great deal of preschool experience. A number of important variables, such as socioeconomic status and age of onset were controlled. The manual groups with deaf parents performed significantly better than the two oral groups with hearing parents on all measures. Those using the manually coded English system scored the highest of all other groups.

A number of studies have emphasized the importance of manually coded English (Gardner & Zorfass, 1983). However, researchers do not yet agree that using a manually coded English system leads to better reading and writing scores (Mayer & Lowenbraun, 1990). These studies demonstrate that children of deaf parents who use manual communication do better than children of hearing parents who do not. The two groups of children; deaf children of deaf parents and deaf children of hearing parents differ in a number of ways including educational place-

THOUGHT QUESTION

4. *Why do deaf children of deaf parents do better in language and academic achievement compared to deaf children of hearing parents?*

THOUGHT QUESTION

5. *How would you design a study to determine which method of teaching language to children who are congenitally deaf is best?*

ment, degree of hearing loss, age of onset, intelligence, income level, and parental adjustment, among others. In addition, other researchers that have looked into the area come to different conclusions. For example, Jensema and Trybus (1978) placed children into signing and nonsigning groups whether or not parents were deaf and controlled for many variables including degree of hearing loss and family income. As you would expect, children with one or both parents hearing impaired tested better in comprehension, reading, and vocabulary than children with hearing parents. However, when comparing children based only on the method of communication used by parents, no significant relationship was found between method and reading skills. Families with two hearing-impaired parents did not speak much but used signs heavily; mixed families with one hearing and one hearing-impaired parent relied very heavily on speech and used little sign; and families of hearing parents ranked somewhere between the two groups in use of manual and oral communication. The two groups of families with at least one hearing-impaired parent used different methods of communication, and yet the children outperformed the children of hearing parents who ranked in-between in their use of manual and speech. The researchers argued that form did not matter.

Another study found the same lack of relationship between reading comprehension and method of communication, but uniformity of communication type used in the home and by the school was positively related to reading achievement (Morrison, 1982). Generally, studies seem to show that no matter what method of communication is used deaf children of deaf parents do better.

Just comparing methods ignores many factors including parental attitudes that relate to achievement and whether the language used at home and in school is rich or poor. Communication effectiveness may be more important than form. If this distinction is true, families may be more effective in their communication if they seek training in whatever system they choose in order to increase the effectiveness and complexity of the communication rather than concentrate on the form the family chooses (Ritter-Brinton & Stewart, 1992). What parents of deaf children need is an unbiased analysis of the various choices, including benefits and drawbacks of each system or combination of systems.

SCENARIO

1 You and your spouse have just been told that your infant has a profound hearing impairment. Both you and your spouse can hear well. You are both very upset and have a number of counseling sessions with experts in the field. You must find some way of communicating with the infant. Would you use sign language, an oral approach, or some combination and why?

Language Use in Schools

The large majority of schools today use simultaneous communication (Mayer & Lowebraun, 1990). However, teachers do not adhere strictly to the systems that they are using. They often do not sign in a grammatically correct manner (Kluwin, 1990). Teachers are often more involved with content than modeling correct grammar, although teachers improve with training. A large variation in signing accuracy is found, and in one study the average teacher accurately signed only 84 percent of the spoken words correctly (Mayer & Lowenbraun, 1990). Whereas English or ASL is often thought of as the primary languages for children with severe hearing impairments, it is Pidgin Signed English that is the most common method teachers use to sign, which is not recognized as a formal language at all (Stewart, 1992). Stewart argues that the lack of linguistic consistency in total communication classrooms and the lack of accountability for signing may be reasons for low English competence in children with deafness. A concern has been raised about the ability of teachers to speak and sign simultaneously as well as the absence of ASL in such programs.

The use of total communication has not proved to be a panacea, and recent research has cast doubts on whether children who are deaf can both speechread and interpret signs at the same time. Some authorities have questioned whether total communication really leads to better development of speech and language (Lynas, 1988). For example, Geers and colleagues (1984) compared deaf children from both oral-only and total communication programs. The results showed that those from oral communication programs used significantly better grammar. The children were tested in the mode of communication they were most comfortable. Some researchers claim that total communication programs have not lived up to expectations (Eagney, 1987).

Unfortunately, the research has not been all that successful in answering the question of which system works best either at home or at school, especially for deaf children of hearing parents. As noted earlier, just because deaf children of deaf parents do better and most deaf parents sign does not necessarily mean signing is the most desirable way to go for hearing parents who often must also learn ASL as a completely new language. On the other hand, little evidence indicates that the use of sign language interferes with learning other languages. Other factors besides the language system used may be just as important including acceptance of the child's hearing impairment, linguistic competence of parents, openness for reciprocal interaction with children, and perhaps even some continuity between home and school use of language. In addition, although studies sometimes show one type of communication method as better (such as total over oral or oral over total), the achievement of children who are deaf from various educational and communication backgrounds is still not equal to the academic achievement of their hearing peers (Wood, 1992). Children who are deaf generally do not do as well in school no matter which method or combination of methods is used.

Yet, despite difficulties some children with severe hearing impairments do succeed in school. More studies into the reasons why some children using oral methods and some children using manual methods succeed while other children in these same programs do not might be more useful. In other words, we need to answer the question of why some children from some schools and programs do so much better than others in the same programs (Wood, 1992).

Choices in Schooling

Most children with mild and moderate hearing losses are found in their neighborhood schools, and little controversy surrounds their placement or program of study while those who have more severe hearing impairments may be found in a number of settings. Some attend residential schools in which they live and study at the school and spend weekends at home. Others participate in a day-school program in which they daily attend a school for only children who are deaf. Others are educated in their neighborhood schools in self-contained classes and attend regular classes for physical education, art, and some academic classes. Others are fully included and attend all classes with children who can hear with the support of interpreters and tutors (NICD, 1987). The percentage of deaf students attending public and private residential schools as well as private day-schools for children who are deaf has decreased markedly and the percentage attending their neighborhood schools has increased (Moores, 1988).

The Strange Case of the Least Restrictive Environment

The trend towards including deaf students would seem to fit nicely into the ideal of the least restrictive environment and the philosophy of inclusion. After all, students who are deaf or have severe hearing impairments are being educated in an atmosphere in which they and their hearing peers can interact, which is more in keeping with the spirit of the law.

Although the law does not provide a formal definition of least restrictive environment, it is usually interpreted to mean placement in neighborhood schools with nondisabled peers. This interpretation has been used for deaf children as well (Stoefen-Fisher & Balk, 1992). But perhaps this environment is not the least restrictive in this case. Imagine yourself as a deaf person attending a regular public school, and you are the only deaf student in your classes. You do not speak especially well but are conversant in sign language. You use American Sign Language with your friends who are deaf and require an interpreter to understand your nonsigning teacher. You experience isolation, since none of the other students can sign. You must communicate through an interpreter and relatively few of your classmates have made any attempt to speak to you through the interpreter. Those who try to communicate with you find the communication barrier difficult to overcome.

This scenario has led some authorities to state that rather than leading to increased integration, including children who are deaf in regular classes leads to increased social isolation and leaves them unable to participate in many after-school activities. The isolation may result in a delayed development of emotional and social skills (Martens, 1989).

The meaning of least restrictive environment for children who are deaf is a controversial issue. In a government report, entitled "Toward Equality: Education of the Deaf," a recommendation was made that the Department of Education should refocus on the concept of least restrictive environment by emphasizing appropriateness over least restrictiveness (Commission on Education of the Deaf 1988). After hearing much testimony, the committee argued that the concept of least restrictive environment—if it means integration with hearing children—may not be appropriate for children who are deaf. After all, what is least restrictive about an environment in which you cannot communicate with other children? In

THOUGHT QUESTION

6. *In your opinion, what is the least restrictive environment for a deaf child?*

1992, the U.S. Office of Education announced that the least restrictive environment provisions when applied to deaf children should be interpreted to allow educational placements in a range of options, including residential schools (Delgado, 1993). This interpretation provides for more flexibility of the least restrictive provision than was previously the case.

The key to understanding the issue would be to discover how deaf children achieve academically and socially in different settings. Again, methodological complications make conducting such research difficult. Studies that have been conducted show that deaf children who attend regular classes with their hearing peers differ greatly from children who do not. Children with hearing impairments who are educated in the regular classroom tend to have less severe hearing problems, come from higher socioeconomic status families, have a later onset of deafness, use better speech patterns, and generally demonstrate better communication skills compared to those who are not recommended for education in the regular classroom (Stoefen-Fisher & Balk, 1992).

School Achievement of Children with Severe Hearing Impairments

One fact that is not disputed is that children who have severe hearing impairments or are deaf do not achieve well in the schools (Kamfe & Turecheck, 1987). They have significantly lower reading scores compared with their hearing peers (Kampfe & Turecheck, 1987; LaSasso, 1993). They arrive at elementary school with lower skills in language and this pattern continues (Brasel & Quigley, 1975; Spencer, Koester, & Meadow-Orlans, 1994). When Gregory and colleagues (1984) analyzed a group of high school seniors who were deaf and compared them to their hearing peers, the deaf seniors' motivation and achievement were significantly lower. Although children who are deaf have average abilities, their communication deficits cause them more difficulty in school. Those students with mild disorders usually do better than those with more severe disorders because they show a smaller language deficit (Davis et al., 1981). Two aspects of the family related to achievement are the emphasis on education and the family's adaptation to the child's deafness (Bodner-Johnson, 1985). Children do better if families actively support learning and assist their adolescents in getting into post-secondary education. Adaptation to deafness includes encouragement to try new things, improving communication, and emphasizing that people with hearing impairments can succeed (Schroedel, 1992).

Testing the intelligence level of children with severe auditory impairments is a definite concern. Verbal tests of intelligence do not work well and should not be used (Braden, 1992). Children with severe auditory impairments score higher on nonverbal tests, and special norms for people with severe hearing impairments are available for at least five intelligence tests including the WISC (Wechsler Intelligence Scale for Children). The distribution of intelligence in the deaf community appears to be quite similar to the distribution of intelligence in the hearing community. Therefore, if their progress in reading lags it is not due to any native inability, but rather because of the speech/language/hearing impediment and the lack of an appropriate teaching and learning environment.

From an academic viewpoint, studies show that students with hearing impairments who attend school with their hearing peers do better than those who do not (Bunch, 1994; Holt, 1994). In a survey of 1,465 children and youth with hearing

The meaning of the "least restrictive environment" is not clear for children with serious hearing impairments who may not be able to communicate well with other children.

impairments, those who were integrated showed higher levels of achievement in reading and math. Integrated students with profound hearing loss outperformed nonintegrated students with such a hearing loss. This finding held true even when degree of loss, age of onset, additional disability status, and ethnicity were controlled (Allen & Osborn, 1984). A study of 215 high school students, matched on hearing loss, social adjustment, and other factors, found that integrated students achieved significantly higher than students in self-contained classrooms (Kluwin & Moores, 1985). When Zweibel and Allen (1988) compared children with hearing impairments in special schools, those in special classes, and children attending class in regular classes, those taught in the regular classes performed better on standardized tests. Even so, these students did not do as well as their hearing peers.

The research on social development is not as clear (Bunch, 1994). Most studies show that not much social integration occurs in regular classrooms, and the social isolation of deaf children a major problem (Stinson & Lang, 1994; Gjerdingen & Manning, 1991). By its very nature, deafness is associated with isolation (Rendon, 1992). Children who are more linguistically proficient are more likely to interact with peers (Antia, 1985). Hearing and deaf children do not initiate many interactions with each other, but rather interact mostly in response to others (Raimondo & Maxwell, 1987).

The pattern may not start immediately but the isolation grows with age. Observations of hearing and deaf students in preschool find that deaf children have both an interest in and make attempts to interact even though they lack language skills (Minnett et al., 1994). Deaf initiators are more persistent than hearing peers,

THOUGHT QUESTION

7. *How can we better integrate children with serious hearing impairments into the social fabric of the school?*

Many children with severe hearing disabilities use interpreters to function in regular classrooms.

but are not very effective in gaining responses from hearing children (Vandell & George, 1981). Despite these young children's desire to communicate, their language problems and the inability of hearing children to understand them isolates deaf youngsters. The hearing youngsters do not adjust their strategies but keep using vocalizations without any gestures or the use of any other means to communicate. This failure leads to rejection and isolation and increases with age (McCauley, Kennedy, & Bruinincks, 1976).

The isolation is not just a problem for those who are not succeeding in school. In a study of outstanding deaf students who spent their school day totally in the regular classroom, partially in the regular classroom, and attending residential schools, the students who were identified as excellent were still isolated. Few students showed the combination of social confidence and close relationships with parents. The best adjusted were those who attended residential schools and had deaf parents, perhaps because they experienced fewer communication problems. But, as the authors suggest, these attributes did not guarantee a desirable situation as many did not have good relationships with their parents. In addition, their superior intelligence and language skills sometimes set them apart from even their deaf classmates. They attributed their isolation to communication problems. Other studies suggest that the social benefits of integrated classrooms are not what was hoped. Children with hearing impairments and their hearing peers are not interacting (Stoefen-Fisher & Balk, 1992).

SCENARIO

2 You are the parents of a child with congenital deafness who is now six years old and ready for first grade. Your child signs and tries to communicate with hearing children with both some success and some failure. You and your spouse must decide whether to send your child to a public school where an interpreter will be provided or a private dayschool only for deaf children. What factors would influence your decision?

The research points to the need to provide special attention to communication and social interaction. This special attention may include active intervention in two different areas. First, activities that promote social interaction must be built into lessons. Such activities may include cooperative learning, group projects, and peer tutoring. Children can be teamed using a buddy system to work on projects and achieve goals together. Second, some attention to the social skills of children with hearing impairments as well as hearing children in the classroom may also be necessary. Some children lack social skills in such areas as turn taking, initiating interaction, and generally interacting with others. A number of social skills training programs have successfully helped children with hearing impairments improve their social interaction. One program involved making students aware of target behaviors, such as turn taking; direct instruction; prompting the behavior; reinforcement for performing the target behavior; modeling; and feedback to increase a number of social behaviors. This multifaceted program was successful in improving turn-taking skills, initiating social interaction, and increasing instances of helping others and complimenting others in 12- and 13-year-old children who were deaf (Rasing & Duker, 1993).

SCENARIO

3 You are told that Kathy will be in your third grade class. Kathy has a profound hearing impairment and requires an interpreter. Kathy's parents, both of whom can hear, tell you that she is an intelligent child but her language development is not up to par. Her parents are even more concerned about her lack of friends in the class. She seems to have one friend who will not be in her class next year. Her parents are concerned because she is not really being integrated into the social structure of the class. They ask you to find out whether the other girl can be transferred to your class. In addition, they would like to know how to improve her interpersonal relationships next year. How would you respond?

Beethoven, who had a severe hearing impairment in adulthood, wrote about the isolation from society.

Even in college, isolation is common. Coryell and colleagues (1992) found little interaction between deaf and hearing students in a college environment where many deaf students were present. Friction was common. Negative attitudes toward students with hearing impairments were not unusual, and communication was limited. Sometimes, misunderstanding was the problem. One common means of getting attention is to tap the other person on the shoulder. Hearing people often perceived this action as an invasion of privacy and immaturity, which it was not. However, specific behaviors of individuals with hearing impairments contributed to the problem since often these students played stereos very loud or talked very loud late in the evening. On the positive side, some deaf students did manage to communicate with the hearing students and showed patience with beginning signers.

Rejection does not only occur at school but also in social activities. Hus (1979) studied school-aged children with hearing impairments who participated in a day camp with hearing children. These deaf children had been specially selected for superior language and social skills. Even so, little interaction occurred between the two groups, and the hearing children did not like their deaf peers.

The communication barrier is a serious one. Hearing children do not go out of their way to communicate. On the other side, Antia (1985) suggests that children with hearing impairments must learn the importance of greeting behaviors, extending and responding to invitations to join activities, and conversation skills such as asking questions about others' interests and responding to others, in order to overcome any difficulties they may have in this area due their isolation and lack of experience.

Hearing-impaired children may realize academic benefits in being educated in the regular classroom, but the social benefits are few and illusory. Clearly, if hearing-impaired students are to be integrated into the classroom, much more support will be required.

Teenagers with Hearing Impairments

If the childhood years for children with hearing impairments are often filled with communication problems and isolation, what is adolescence like? Loneliness is a large problem for all adolescents, and the social aspects of life including group acceptance and dating become paramount. One can easily imagine the difficulty of children with hearing impairments in hearing environments. During adolescence, deaf students in regular classrooms experience isolation from teachers and peers and lack support services required for participation in extra activities, which are often social (Murphy & Newton, 1987; Charlson, Strong, & Gold, 1987). Some believe this isolation is an argument for residential schools where adolescents with severe hearing impairments can be with others and will be more accepted, comfortable, and have greater access to school activities (Mertens, 1989). However, being away from families may be a problem, and research shows that adolescents with severe hearing disorders both in regular schools and residential settings are more prone than hearing students to boredom and depression, which are, again, related to loneliness and isolation (Watt & Davis, 1991). However, being with other deaf students does reduce the isolation somewhat.

Parents of children and adolescents with severe hearing impairments may cause an additional problem by being somewhat overprotective, and many parents have fostered a dependence that runs counter to most adolescents' striving for independence. Perhaps adolescents with hearing impairments must be told that many teens experience feelings of isolation and that even successful students often feel that way. They also require access to clubs and activities where they will meet other people, including some people with hearing impairments.

The Adjustment of People with Hearing Impairments

Numerous studies have investigated the social-emotional status of students with auditory impairments. Earlier studies and more recent studies differ in their conclusions. The isolation of people with severe hearing impairments, some psychologists argue, leads to some adjustment problems, most of which are not severe. Early studies concluded that immaturity, hyperactivity, and being egocentric are found more often in deaf children (Moores, 1988).

However, recently this negative view has been criticized for a number of reasons. First, few if any tests are standardized for individuals with severe hearing impairments, and using a test for hearing children with deaf children is improper. Second, many of the studies purporting to show poor adjustment have not differentiated between hearing-impaired children whose sole disability is an auditory one and those children with hearing impairments who have multiple disabilities. Many children with multiple disabilities have hearing impairments in addition to their other disabilities, and they more often show adjustment difficulties. Some characteristics, such as impulsivity, hyperactivity, and rigidity, attributed to people who have severe hearing impairments, are more likely to be found in those with multiple disabilities than in people whose sole problem is one of hearing.

When Meadow (1984) compared teachers' ratings of four groups of preschool children: deaf children with additional disabilities, deaf children without additional disabilities, hearing children with disabilities, and hearing children without disabilities, the deaf children without additional disabilities and the hearing children without disabilities were not significantly different and compared very favorably to the other two groups. Chess and Fernandez (1980) found that, with the exception of impulsivity, none of the other characteristics—hyperactivity, rigidity, and suspiciousness—could be found in a sample of children they followed from early childhood through adolescence as long as deafness was the only disability. Even the one significant characteristic, impulsivity, was found in only 20 percent of the sample.

IN THE CLASSROOM   Encouraging Full Participation for Students with Hearing Impairments

Teachers should be aware of children who do not seem to pay attention when called on, frequently lose their place, turn their head so a particular ear is toward the source of a sound, complain of discomfort in their ears, show delays in speech and language, turn the volume up on the television or radio, complain they cannot hear, or frequently ask the teach to repeat things (Stephens, Blackhurst, & Magliocca, 1982). In fact, a hearing assessment should be made for any child who is thought to have a learning disability, behavior disorder, or mental retardation to discover if a hearing loss is present and is connected to the problem or part of the cause.

The teacher who will be instructing a child with a hearing impairment can do many things to encourage the child's full participation in the class. Classroom adaptations for children with hearing impairments include the following:

1. If an interpreter is necessary, make certain you speak to the child, not to the interpreter. Tell other students they should do the same.	**Why?** Communication with children with hearing impairments should be direct. The interpreter is there only to translate what the teacher is saying to the child.
2. Introduce vocabulary and important terms ahead of time. Write them on the blackboard or give the students an outline.	**Why?** This gives the students an idea of what is going to be taught, making communication and learning easier.
3. Do not talk to the blackboard. If a child with a hearing disability	**Why?** Talking to the blackboard prevents students with hearing impair-

is trying to speechread, the results are disastrous. Try to remain stationary and watch for glare in the room.

ments from comprehending what the teacher is saying. Glare also makes speechreading difficult.

4. Use an overhead projector instead of the blackboard to increase the amount of time a teacher can spend looking at the students.

Why? Facing students makes it easier for students to speechread.

5. Use visual aids.

Why? Visual aids are useful since they communicate concepts and information visually and do not use the auditory channel.

6. Speak in your usual fashion and don't exaggerate lip movements, speech rate, or voice volume.

Why? Speaking this way is the best way to help students speechread.

7. Organize a system to help students with hearing impairments get classroom notes.

Why? Students with hearing impairments cannot take notes as they watch the teacher's lips or look at an interpreter. Have another student take notes and photocopy them for the student.

8. Seat students with severe auditory impairments between five and ten feet from the teacher.

Why? Close proximity to the teacher makes speechreading easier.

9. Encourage the child to ask for clarification whenever necessary. Rephrase the material, especially if the child is trying to speechread.

Why? When students feel secure enough to ask questions, the communication process is enhanced.

10. Encourage children with hearing impairments to express themselves.

Why? Children with hearing impairments may not feel part of the class and need encouragement to participate. Because they do not find communicating with the teacher or the class easy, they may not express their views. They need encouragement and to know that their teacher and classmates are interested in what they think and feel.

11. Watch for fatigue.	**Why?** Deaf children have a tendency to become fatigued, since their concentration needs to be total. Brief periods of rest may be required.
12. Make certain the child's hearing aid is working. Hearing aids should be check periodically.	**Why?** A student may not inform the teacher that the hearing aid is not working properly.
13. Obtain the child's attention before speaking. Face the person and maintain eye contact. Stand close to the person with no obstructions and stand in a well-lighted place. Background noises can be annoying, so try to limit them. Do not shout since this distorts sound, and use facial expressions and body language liberally.	**Why?** By following these simple instructions a child with a severe hearing impairment will be able to understand and to communicate more easily.
14. Use captioned films whenever possible.	**Why?** The use of captioning allows students who have severe hearing impairments to read the dialogue as it is spoken.
15. Question the student as you would any other student.	**Why?** The student with a hearing disability is an integral part of the class and should be treated that way.
16. Actively program social interaction that includes students with hearing impairments into classroom activities. Social skills training may also be necessary.	**Why?** Studies show that children with hearing impairments are often not socially involved in the classroom. Group work, cooperative learning, peer tutoring, buddy systems, and any other activities that promote communication and social interaction are helpful.

SCENARIO

4 Bill is a seventh grade student who has a severe hearing impairment. You are told that he can speechread and uses hearing aids. His speech is intelligible. He is reading on grade, and his work is good. What changes in the classroom and in classroom procedures would you make to accommodate Bill?

Postsecondary School Choices

The growth of postsecondary school options for students with hearing impairments is a great achievement. In 1960, a high school graduate with a severe hearing impairment had only two choices, Gallaudet University (at that time Gallaudet College) or attending an institution with no support services. Today, students with hearing impairments have access to postsecondary education on all levels (Moores, 1994). Today's options include vocational training programs and college and graduate school training. People with hearing impairments are served in a variety of settings ranging from programs serving only students with severe hearing impairments to integrated programs with many support services including sign interpreters.

Three major options are open to the deaf student who is looking for postsecondary education (American Council on Education, 1991). Deaf students who attend mainstream colleges can and frequently do succeed. They must, however, visit the college not only as hearing students do by investigating the basic programs and facilities but also determine just how responsive the college is to their needs.

One significant difference between elementary and high school on the one hand and college on the other is the responsibility for obtaining services. In elementary and secondary schools, the responsibility is clearly on the school district to identify and provide the services needed. In postsecondary education, the responsibility for obtaining help rests squarely with the student. If the student presents documentation that a disability exists, the college is legally bound to provide what is necessary according to Section 504 of the Rehabilitation Act of 1973 (PL 93-112). One will find widespread variation, though, in the services provided at different colleges.

A number of colleges have special programs for students with hearing impairments, and combine mainstream living and learning with programs aimed at meeting the needs of people with hearing impairments. The programs are regional in nature and funded by the federal government. These colleges offer faculties that are experienced in dealing with the needs of students with hearing impairments. Some teachers can sign, but all offer extensive technical support. Other schools not connected with the federal network may also offer special programs.

Two federally funded national academic institutions are available for people with severe hearing impairments. The first is Gallaudet University, where all classes are taught in sign. As a liberal arts school, it offers more than 40 undergraduate majors as well as graduate school. Many of its graduates become teachers and counselors. The National Technical Institute for the Deaf (NTID) is a college of the Rochester Institute of Technology (RIT) in Rochester, New York, and offers technical programs in business, computer science, engineering, and a number of other specialties. Qualified students may also take courses at any other college of RIT.

Vocational Issues

In the past, many people with hearing impairments worked in factories and had blue collar jobs. Vocational training often meant a type of apprenticeship or job training. Poor educational achievement, few active programs to help people with severe hearing impairments, and poor access to postsecondary education prevented most from participating fully and successfully in the economy at all levels.

Today, the entire situation is changing. Many of the manufacturing jobs have fled abroad, reducing manufacturing employment. The service industry has boomed, but many of these jobs pay poorly. The most common area of employment for deaf people is food service. Yet, at the same time, the growth of the computer industry has given a boost to employment opportunities for deaf people, and some are entering this industry. Construction and office work are also common. Higher service industry positions such as medical secretaries, physical and occupational therapists, registered nurses, and paralegals that have rarely been accessible have now been opened to people with hearing impairments.

However, service jobs in selling and those using information require a communications bridge. A potential double bias may occur when employers may not be willing to take the necessary steps to communicate and customers avoid the deaf individual. For instance, a college student who visits a deaf beautician was able to communicate what she wanted through pictures and gestures and simple phrasing. She was very satisfied with her beautician's skills. Many customers did not want to make the extra effort.

Although vocational training is certainly appropriate for some, entrance into the professions requires academic success. The high school graduation rates are lower for people with severe hearing loss and have not improved much over the past 15 years. About half of all deaf students graduate with a diploma from high school, and one in five deaf students leave high school with a certificate of attendance (Allen, Rawlings, & Schildroth, 1989).

High school completion and vocational training raise the important issue of transition. Transition programs must address not only the need for vocational and educational training but also the social and leisure areas, since isolation is such an important concern. The need for vocational planning is obvious. Evidence indicates that deaf individuals know less than their hearing peers about different types of occupations (Schroedel, 1992). They more frequently hold traditional attitudes about occupations and social roles. Parents of hearing-impaired teenagers often complain that their children require more vocational knowledge (Schroedel, 1992). Both families and schools must be active in providing deaf students with occupational information, and preparation for postsecondary employment should start early. In addition, schools must develop good relationships with state offices of vocational rehabilitation, which can often help with placement and financial aid (Schildroth et al., 1991). Evidence shows that students who complete postsecondary training successfully do find employment in their chosen fields and achieve (Bullis et al., 1995).

Studies find that about three-quarters of all deaf adolescents are engaged in some productive activity; about half enroll in postsecondary education of some type in the year following high school (Schildroth et al., 1991). Many work full or part time. The most common jobs are in food preparation, secretarial and office work, janitorial, and stock and freight handling (Schroedel, 1992).

The Americans with Disabilities Act will have an impact on the job opportunities available for people with hearing impairments. The prohibition against hiring practices that discriminate against people with disabilities, and the requirement that businesses make reasonable accommodations for employees who have disabilities, open up additional opportunities for people with hearing impairments (Marczely, 1993; McCrone, 1994).

Special Services for Deaf Students

If students with hearing impairments are to be integrated into the environment, they require special help especially in communication. Perhaps the most common form of assistance is interpreter services. The interpreter signs what the instructor is saying to the individual with a severe hearing impairment. The interpreter does not change what is said. The Registry of Interpreters for the Deaf maintains a list of interpreters in each state.

Students with severe hearing impairments also require notetakers and tutors (Wilson, 1981, Hurwitz, 1980). When someone else is taking notes, the student with a hearing impairment can pay strict attention to the interpreter or teacher. Notetakers, though, must be better students who understand the work, the meaning of what they are doing, and take excellent and complete notes. Finding such a student and perhaps training the student is somewhat less of a problem in the upper grades than the lower grades. The notetakers should be monitored by the teacher (Wilson, 1981).

Technology

The electronics revolution has affected the lives of people with hearing impairments more than on any other group of people with disabilities, allowing for a fuller and more satisfying life.

Hearing Aids

Hearing aids serve to amplify the sound. The modern hearing aid is smaller and more sophisticated due to the revolution in electronic technology. Many more people are capable of being helped by these devices, and 70 percent of all hearing aids are now worn entirely within the ear rather than outside the ear (Martin, 1990). Hearing aids do not restore hearing but can make soft sounds louder, which makes speech easier to comprehend. They may also allow people with hearing impairments to hear higher pitched sounds than they could without the devices. Amplification has its limits, and if soft sounds are amplified to the point at which they become audible to a hearing-impaired individual, others sounds might be so loud as to be intolerable. Amplification devices also do not help if a great deal of background noise is present or if distortion of sound is the problem (Rezen & Hausman, 1985).

Assistive Listening Devices

Assistive listening devices (ALD) are electronic systems that enable people with hearing impairments to hear in environments in which they may be sitting far away from the speaker or in which a great deal of added noise is present (Martin, 1990). A large lecture hall, religious services, or even a concert hall may prove difficult for people with hearing impairments. Assistive listening devices allow the speaker's voice to be picked up by the individual with a hearing impairment directly without having to travel through the air. For example, a person may be fitted with a behind-the-ear hearing aid that allows for direct input of radio transmissions; or a child may wear an FM radio receiver on the chest with a direct lead into the hearing aid amplifier. The teacher uses a lapel microphone that transmits an FM signal to the person's receiver. The teacher's words are transmitted directly to the child's ear at a great range. Many hearing aids have a "T" for telecoil setting on the controls that activates a coil, which responds to changing magnetic fields. (The wireless FM system just described may also use the "T" setting or a small headset or earphone.) This "T" setting allows the person to benefit from some alternative listening systems such as the induction loop system. In this system, wire is placed around an area be it a room or even a public building. The wire is connected to an amplifier and to the speaker's microphone; changes in the magnetic field are then picked up by the "T" setting in the hearing aid and changed to sound (Castle, 1988). Many telephones can be adapted to allow the "T" setting as well. Another system uses light energy in the form of infrared waves to carry the sound and requires special receivers to convert the light energy back into sound. This system offers much better sound quality (Martin, 1990; Castle, 1988).

Warning Devices

Imagine living by yourself and not being able to hear the phone ring, the door bell, or most importantly the fire or burglar alarm. Some instruments use a flash of light or even a strobe when the telephone or door bell rings or a baby cries. Lights that flash on and off are certainly useful in informing the person that the phone is ringing or the baby is crying. Other devices use vibrations rather than light. For example, a clock or a warning device may be connected to a vibrator so that the individual may be awakened during the night (Martin, 1990).

Using the Telephone

For some people who have hearing impairments, a relatively simple device that increases the volume on the telephone is sufficient. These devices are readily available. The user simply controls the amount of amplification (Castle, 1988). For

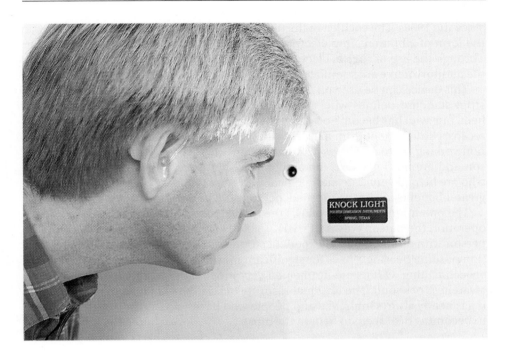

Many warning devices are available for people with hearing impairments.

A special communication device called a TDD, telecommunications device for the deaf, allows people with severe hearing disabilities to use the telephone.

those who are profoundly hearing impaired or deaf, a device called a TDD or telecommunication device for the deaf transmits typewritten messages over the telephone wires to another individual with a TDD (Rezen & Hausman, 1985). Some systems even produce a printout of the conversation. Many businesses, educational institutions, and governmental institutions have TDDs including fire and police departments. Telephone companies also have a service for people with severe hearing impairments who wish to communicate with people who do not have a TDD, a requirement under the Americans with Disabilities Act. Either the hearing or deaf person may call a special intermediary who is specially trained for the purpose and who then translates the hearing person's communication into a TDD or transmits the deaf person's TDD message orally to the hearing person (New York Relay Service, 1992).

Watching Television

Watching television and videos was once impossible for people who could not hear speech, but closed captioning has now brought thousands of hours of programs a year to people with severe hearing impairments. Closed captioning requires a special decoder attached to the television and allows the viewer to read the dialogue as it is captioned.

Cochlear Implants

So far, the technology discussed allows the individual to cope with the difficulties of living in a sound-filled world. A controversial surgery has raised the hope of reversing deafness in some people. The use of cochlear implants has been going on since the 1960s. The cochlea in the inner ear transforms the mechanical energy in the form of vibrations into electrical impulses that are fed to the auditory nerve. Through the use of special electrodes, the nerve fibers connecting the cochlea to the auditory nerve are stimulated.

This device can be used on only about 1 percent of all deaf people. Although no strict standard defines who is best helped, an implant candidate has typically been one who has become postlingually deaf, is an adult, has no residual hearing, receives little benefit from a hearing aid, and has a working auditory nerve and a nonworking cochlea. The psychological benefits vary greatly from person to person and are not related to the audiological benefits (Aplin, 1993). Some people who are helped very little audiologically are very satisfied; some who have gained greater benefits are not as satisfied, perhaps due to their initial expectations.

The operation frequently allows the individual to hear even though before the operation the person was deaf (NIH, 1988). However, the outcomes vary, and no person with an implant has experienced full restoration of hearing. The restoration of some hearing allows for significant improvements, often in the process of speechreading. Others are not helped very much, but most people welcome the awareness of sound. The National Institute of Health concluded that speechreading is nearly always improved and people who have acquired language skills prior to becoming deaf seem to benefit the most.

Dogs for Deaf People

Dogs that help people who have visual impairments are a relatively common sight. Their use with the people who have severe hearing impairments is relatively recent but makes sense. After all, not hearing a baby cry, the alarm clock ring, the oven buzz, or smoke alarm sound are problems. Some people who are deaf use specially trained dogs for these and other purposes. The dogs respond to hand signals and are taught to lead the owner to the source of the sound. They learn to respond to knocking at the door, doorbells, alarm clocks, smoke alarms, telephones, the sound of a baby crying, the person's name being called, and even oven buzzers. These dogs are classified according to their skills. Certified hearing dogs are trained to respond to these sounds. They have total public access rights to stores, restaurants, and public transportation. Other dogs are trained to respond to sounds but work only in the home and do not have legal access. These animals are meant for mostly younger deaf people (Rabat, 1992).

 **A Revolution in Living**

A person who is deaf is having a conversation with another individual who also has a severe hearing loss. They live two hundred miles away from each other. They are signing to each other using a video telephone. Each can watch the other and respond appropriately.

Another individual with an extensive hearing impairment is sitting in the classroom. As the teacher speaks, a machine turns the speech into text allowing the student to follow the lecture without having to watch an interpreter or speechread. The machine also saves the lecture as text so the student can read it over at a later time.

These two scenes may become commonplace in the future as communications technology for people who have extensive hearing impairments improves (Jensema, 1994). Some prototypes are presently available, which allow people to watch each other or that translate speech to text, but problems remain. For instance, the video telephone is technically possible today but will only be truly useful when copper wiring is replaced by fiber optics, a change that will take place. However, converting the 1.5 billion miles of telephone wire in the United States alone will be expensive and time consuming. Sending color video images through copper wiring is possible, but it would take a minute or so to send a single frame.

The future for speech recognition equipment is exciting. Machines capable of turning text to voice are now available, but despite great technological improvements a machine that will translate rapid conversations from voice to text in a practical manner without the need for any human interference or interpretation is still probably some years away (Jensema, 1994).

Technology continues to make an important contribution to the lives of people with hearing impairments especially in the areas of telecommunications devices, assistive listening devices, and captioning (Stuckless & Carroll, 1994). These technological innovations allow people with hearing impairments to become more independent as well as more involved in the world around them (Castle, 1994).

A number of technological innovations that help people with hearing impairments have been discussed in this chapter. Hearing aid technology has progressed to where they are now small and light. FM classroom amplification systems in which teachers wear wireless microphones that transmit the sound to children with hearing impairments who have wireless receivers allow students to hear the teacher without the always present background and classroom noise. Television captioning allows people with hearing impairments to watch a television program while the dialogue is presented as text on the screen. Technological aids serve as warning devices, for example, vibrators and strobe lights that are linked to special devices such as the front door bell, smoke alarms, or alarm clocks.

Modern technology is also used in the teaching process. For example, software is available that helps students learn to understand sign language and improve their speechreading abilities (see Kelly, 1993). Students can improve their skills using interactive video consisting of a videotape recorder or videodisc, a computer, and a video controller. Students can watch people sign on the computer and translate it into text by typing the sentence on the computer.

Students can also improve their reading and writing skills. Often, students with hearing impairments may use conventional software aimed at improving their vocabulary and grammar. Today, some special software packages are available, which are designed for people with severe hearing impairments and are programmed to provide students with feedback in such areas as spelling, capitalization, punctuation, and grammar based upon errors typically made by students with severe hearing impairments (Lewis, 1993).

Advances in the telecommunications area have reduced the isolation experienced by many people who have severe hearing impairments. The TDD (telecommunication device for the deaf) allows people with hearing impairments to communicate with each other. One individual with a TDD types a message that is converted into a form that can be carried over the telephone wires. The TDD on the receiving end converts it back into text. The conventional TDD, though, uses outdated technology and does not use standard computer language. It cannot help the person access electronic mail (E-mail), data bases, or bulletin boards (Davila, 1994). TDDs that use standard computer language are now available and allow people with hearing impairments access to computer-based communications technology. The TDD as it traditionally exists will be replaced by hybrid computers that perform the traditional TDD function and other communication functions. In fact, a computer chip is available that distinguishes between computer-sent messages, TDD messages, and voice communication, and routes calls to the correct device. The chips can even be automatically configured to handle each different type of call (Jensema, 1994).

Fax machines are becoming popular with people who have hearing impairments. The Fax machine allows transmission of graphic images from one point to another. Fax machines allow people with hearing impairments to communicate with businesses that do not have TDDs. The Fax machine supplements but does not replace the TDD.

Finally, the Americans with Disabilities Act requires all telephone companies to establish relay systems so that people with hearing impairments and a TDD can communicate with people who do not have a TDD. A person types a message on the TDD and an operator reads the message to the individual who does not have a TDD. The person wishing to respond tells the operator the message, which is then typed on a TDD and sent back to the sender of the message. In the future, new technology will allow people with hearing impairments to communicate with people without hearing impairments without the need for human intervention (Davila, 1994).

One thing is certain. The development of new technology to meet the needs of people with hearing impairments will continue (Davila, 1994). As it does, the isolation that surrounds so many people with extensive hearing impairments will be reduced. Options will be significantly increased making lives of people with hearing impairments more fulfilling and offering them many more opportunities to participate in every area of human endeavor.

Heather Whitestone, who has a severe hearing impairment, signs "I love you" to the crowd after winning the 1995 Miss America pageant.

Deaf Culture

Because of their isolation and distinct status, deaf people are sometimes seen as a cultural group. In fact, many people who are deaf see themselves as a distinct culture (Brubaker, 1994; Jones & Pullen, 1992). ASL is one way to identify oneself with the culture and is widely used in the group. As children who are deaf interact with others with hearing impairments, a cultural awareness and identity is established that enhances their self-concept (Innes, 1994). Since most deaf people have hearing parents, the language and culture are not transmitted from parent to child but from peers or deaf people who are adults to children. Social organizations for deaf people have been formed, and the idea of deaf people functioning as a distinct cultural group is now more accepted (Sorenson, 1991).

The Need for Answers

The environmental changes necessary to enable students with mild hearing loss to succeed in class and in society are relatively simple and straightforward. Many of these children can be helped with hearing aids and modifications in the classroom and home. Some modifications, including looking at the student when speaking, making certain hearing aids are working, providing the student with appropriate speech services, and helping students become involved socially within the classroom, can be easily accomplished.

When we turn to children with more severe hearing losses, this unanimity breaks down, and heated debates that have at times created more heat than light are common. Those who believe in total communication disagree strongly with those who believe in the more oral methods. Those who argue that children with hearing impairments require special schooling disagree strongly with those who believe that these students should be included and receive their education in the regular classroom. Unfortunately, the research does not present clear answers and one can readily criticize research on methodological grounds. Future research must answer two questions: First, how can students with severe hearing impairments develop their language and academic skills to the fullest extent? Second, how can teachers help to overcome the isolation that surrounds so many deaf people? Only if these two questions are answered can people with hearing impairments fully participate in society.

SUMMARY

1. The term *hearing impairment* covers all hearing loss. A person is deaf if the individual cannot understand speech even with a hearing aid. Degree of hearing loss—mild, moderate, severe, or profound—is often used in classification.

2. A conductive hearing loss occurs when sound is not carried efficiently through the outer and middle ear. A sensorineural loss occurs when the inner ear or the pathways to the brain are injured. A mixed hearing loss means that both conductive and sensorineural impairment is present; a central hearing loss is caused by a problem in the part of the brain that interprets the input from the auditory system.

3. Hearing impairments are considered prelingual if they occur before the age of three and postlingual if they occur after that age. A congenital hearing loss is one that is present at birth.

4. The largest cause of profound hearing loss is still labeled "unknown" and accounts for more than 30 percent of cases. The most common cause of conductive hearing problems is otitis media, a condition in which fluid builds up in the middle ear reducing the bones' ability to conduct the sound. Hearing loss at birth may be due to genetic factors or to a virus transmitted prenatally. Trauma, accidents, and some illnesses may also cause hearing loss, as may excessive noise.

6. Ninety percent of all deaf children are born to hearing parents. Although the chances are greater for having a deaf child if two deaf people marry, deaf parents most often have offspring who can hear.

7. Early diagnosis of hearing impairments is vital to the development of the child. Infants can be tested using auditory brainstem-evoked response (ABR). As children mature, many other tests can be used to diagnose hearing difficulties.

8. Oral methods of communication involve the use of residual hearing and speechreading. Speechreading is difficult because so many sounds look the same. Cued speech, which involves a set of hand gestures to add information to what is being said, may be used. Manual methods involve the use of sign language. American Sign Language (ASL) is a language with a grammar of its own. In Manually Signed English the word signs of ASL are used in English word order. In Pidgin Signed English some of the grammatical constructions of ASL are also used. Each letter in English also has a hand sign allowing for communication through fingerspelling. Total communication involves the use of all methods of communication including signs, speech, and speechreading.

9. Most educational programs use a total communication approach. The best way to teach communication skills to deaf children of hearing parents is still open to question.

10. Some children with profound hearing impairments attend residential schools where they live and study; others attend special day schools; others are educated in self-contained classrooms, while still others are educated in regular classrooms with the support of interpreters and tutors. Some question remains as to what the concept of "least restrictive environment" means for children with severe hearing impairments who may be isolated and find it difficult to participate in many extracurricular activities due to the communications barrier.

11. Some students with hearing impairments attend colleges with some support services, some attend colleges with special programs, while others attend special colleges for deaf individuals. Gallaudet University is the only liberal arts school for deaf people in the United States. The National Technical Institute for the Deaf is a college within the Rochester Institute of Technology, which prepares people with severe hearing disorders for careers in technical and scientific areas.

12. Special educational services for people with severe hearing impairments include interpreters and note takers. Technological improvements, such as assistive listening devices, closed captioning, and telecommunications devices, allow people with hearing impairments to live more satisfying lives.

Visual Impairment

TRUE-FALSE STATEMENTS

See below for the correct answers.

1. A person who has 20/20 vision has perfect vision.
2. People who are legally blind can see nothing in their environment.
3. Visual impairment is the second most common exceptionality in children.
4. A detailed analysis of visual functioning cannot be conducted before a child is two years of age.
5. Infants who are blind smile less than sighted infants.
6. An individual who is blind and shows such behaviors as poking at the eye repeatedly most probably has mental retardation as well as a visual impairment.
7. Most children with severe visual impairments are educated in regular classrooms rather than residential or special day schools.
8. Children with visual impairments usually require little, if any, modification in the content of what is being taught.
9. Teachers should not decrease the quantity of work required of a child with a visual impairment since the child should learn to do what other children can do.
10. Fewer people who are blind can read Braille today than 40 years ago.
11. People who are blind have a better sense of hearing and touch than sighted people.
12. The majority of people with severe visual impairments use a dog guide.

Answers to True-False Statements
1. False. See page 499.
2. False. See page 499.
3. False. See page 500.
4. False. See page 502.
5. True.
6. False. See page 506.
7. False.
8. True.
9. False. See page 516.
10. True.
11. False. See page 525.
12. False. See page 526.

The Not-So-Obvious Effects of Visual Impairment

Walk into an unfamiliar room and look around. Spend less than a minute trying to gather all the information possible and have someone ask you such questions as: "What is next to the desk?" "What color is the floor tile?" "How many people are in the room?" "Who is the person standing next to the couch?" "How many chairs are in the room?" "How are the chairs arranged?"

You will have no difficulty answering these questions. You take in the entire picture using your sense of vision. You understand the spatial relationships among items in the room, their shapes and sizes. You easily describe the people. A person with a severe visual impairment, though, could not answer some of these questions without help and would take quite a bit of time to answer other questions. It is very difficult, sometimes impossible, for people with severe visual impairments to gain an understanding of their entire environment. They must reconstruct the whole using bits and pieces they obtain mostly using other senses.

Sighted people react to blindness on an emotional level. People with visual impairments are perhaps the most patronized group in society. They are often seen as helpless and in need of constant protection, or as pitiful individuals in need of constant care. This stereotype perpetuates the idea that people who are blind cannot become independent (Verplanken, Meijnders, & Van de Wege, 1994; Sardegna & Paul, 1991). On the other hand, people with severe visual impairments are sometimes perceived as heroic, overcoming all odds to achieve a fulfilling lifestyle. The general public also holds a number of misconceptions about blindness, believing that people who are blind develop other senses that are more acute, have special musical talent, or possess a sixth sense for avoiding obstacles.

Visual impairment affects learning both in and out of the classroom. Some learning requires formal effort and study, such as remembering the capitals of the 50 states and is usually accomplished through regular classroom instruction. Incidental learning, on the other hand, takes place without much direct instruction or effort. Knowing how to pick up a spoon, how to cut with a knife, or that the spoon is to the right of the plate are casually learned without much instruction. Knowing what styles are in, that the tail of a dog may be long or short, or that people smile when they laugh are examples of such incidental learning. Children with severe visual impairments do not pick up as much incidental learning as their sighted peers. They cannot observe these relatively simple things in their environment and must find other ways to learn about them.

An estimated 90–95 percent of our perceptions are visual in origin (Hatlen & Curry, 1987). Although this figure is impossible to validate empirically, sighted infants and children obviously receive most of their information from their visual sense (Hatlen & Curry, 1987). People do not think twice about saying, "Look over here," "Did you see that . . . ?" or "Stop when the light turns red."

Without the benefit of vision, children must learn both spatial and material concepts differently. For instance, consider how sighted children learn geometric figures such as squares, circles, and rectangles. After seeing a rectangle, the child may be asked to find others in the environment. The child casually *looks* around the kitchen, the library, or the school and comes up with many examples. Each time, the child is impressed by the different colors, positions, and sizes of the rec-

THOUGHT QUESTION

1. Why do people seem to react to blindness so much more emotionally than to other disabilities?

tangles. The child who cannot see well must learn this concept differently. The concept of a rectangle may be taught both tactilely and through verbal description. Incidental learning and generalization, however, are much more difficult without the benefit of adequate vision. The concept must be specifically taught in different contexts with different sizes of rectangles.

In the social realm, consider having a conversation with a friend. In addition to voice quality and inflection, gestures and facial expressions are used. But children who have been blind from birth have never seen these gestures and expressions and may not produce them. Eye contact is difficult when a person cannot see the other person's eyes. A number of studies show that sighted people conversing with people with severe visual impairments often experience difficulties in communication due to lack of eye contact (Fichten et al., 1991).

One can easily understand the obvious difficulties a child with a visual impairment faces. These examples, though, point out some of the less apparent learning and social problems faced by children with severe visual impairments. Too often, the extent to which visual impairment affects learning is not truly understood, and so the needs of these children are not met. These problems arise not through a denial of the challenges they face nor through a desire to discriminate against them, but through a lack of understanding of the nature of their experience.

The Workings of the Eye

The eye works much like a camera (see Figure 13.1). Light first passes through the transparent covering of the eye called the cornea and enters the eye through the opening in the iris called the pupil. The iris, which is the colored portion of the eye, enlarges or becomes smaller depending upon the lighting, thus controlling the amount of light entering through the pupil. The light then strikes the lens, which changes shape to permit the eye to focus on the object. The lens thickens when focusing on near objects and becomes thinner for distant objects. The visual image then reaches the retina at the back of the eye. The image projected on the retina is upside down since the light crisscrosses while going through the cornea. Over 100 million specialized cells called rods and cones are present on the retina (Bailey & Hall, 1990). The rods function in poor illumination producing black and white vision, while the cones operate under conditions of good illumination and are responsible for color vision. These cells relay signals to the nerve cells that generate electrical signals sent along the optic nerve to the brain for interpretation. At the very center of the retina is the macula, a special area used in looking at fine details and differentiating colors. The fovea is the central portion of the macula and responds to the finest detail. The brain re-inverts the image so that we perceive it as right-side up and then interprets what we see (National Society to Prevent Blindness, 1992).

Defining Visual Impairment

Visual impairment is rather common but most times correctable. Many children require glasses or contact lenses to improve their **visual acuity**, the ability to see objects at particular distances. The five most common visual problems in children

Visual acuity:
The ability to see objects at particular distances.

FIGURE 13.1   Structures of the eye

Source: Daniel D. Chiras. *Human Biology: Health, Homeostasis, and the Environment.* Copyright © 1995 by West Publishing Company.

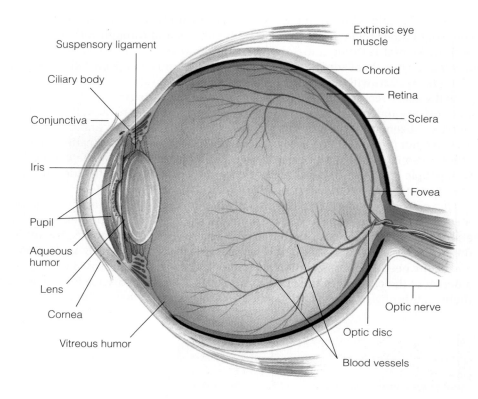

are myopia (nearsightedness), hyperopia (farsightedness), astigmatism, amblyopia (lazy eye), and strabismus (cross-eye).

- *Myopia*: In myopia, the eyeball is too long for normal focusing and distant images are blurred.
- *Hyperopia*: If the eyeball is too short for normal focusing, the images of near objects may be blurred.
- *Astigmatism*: Astigmatism results from an irregular shape in the surface of the cornea. The surface is steeper in one direction and flatter in another instead of being perfectly spherical in shape. This irregular shape results in an unevenly focused image on the retina and causes blurred vision and eyestrain (Bailey & Hall, 1990).
- *Amblyopia*: Children with amblyopia, or lazy eye, do not see through the eye clearly even though it is not diseased and corrective lenses are being used. It frequently occurs among children who have a different amount of hyperopia or myopia in one eye than in the other or who have one eye directed away from the object seen by the other eye (strabismus). Amblyopia is treated by patching the stronger eye, and sometimes by stimulating the "lazy eye" (Tavernier, 1993).
- *Strabismus*: Strabismus occurs when one eye does not aim directly toward an object of interest at which the other eye is aimed (National Society to Prevent Blindness, 1991). The eyes are not aligned properly toward the object. The eye may be directed inward, outward, upward, or downward. If not corrected, functional blindness in one eye may result as the brain suppresses the

unwanted image. Surgery is often performed after a period of time during which the "good" eye is covered to build up vision in the other eye.

These five visual problems can be corrected when discovered and treated promptly and effectively. Proper screening is important. If they are not discovered, the child will not receive the type of visual stimulation necessary for optimal development and efficient learning. In a school situation, the results can be devastating. A child who does not see the blackboard or a book comfortably is likely to fall behind. A child who sees everything blurred will not be able to read effectively. At times, children, especially teenagers, will refuse to wear corrective lenses preferring not to see the board rather than wear them. The advent of reasonably priced contact lenses reduces this problem, but teachers should be aware of the fact that some students who need glasses will not wear them.

Children with these relatively common visual impairments are not considered eligible for special education services, since their vision can be restored to a reasonable level and they can read regular print. They do not require changes in curriculum or teaching methodology. Children with visual impairments are eligible for special education if their vision cannot be corrected to a particular level of acuity or if their field of vision is severely limited.

Almost everyone is familiar with the Snellen chart. A person stands at a distance of 20 feet and is asked to read the letters on the chart. The letters get smaller and smaller with each line. Average vision is considered 20/20, meaning that the person can see at 20 feet what most people can see at that distance. **Legal blindness** is considered a visual acuity of 20/200 vision in the better eye, even with correction. Legal blindness means that a child has 10 percent or less of average vision (National Federation of the Blind, 1991). Many people may be surprised to learn that people with legal blindness can still see something. To be considered legally blind, the world does not have to be completely dark. Children who have **partial sight** have vision that falls between 20/70 and 20/200 in the better eye, with correction.

A person may have 20/20 eyesight and still be legally blind. Some people have such poor peripheral vision that they see as if looking through a keyhole. If a child's entire field of vision is less than 20 degrees, the child is also considered legally blind (Ashcroft & Zambone-Ashley, 1980).

The overwhelming percentage of people with visual impairments have at least some sight. In fact, over 75 percent of the people who have legal blindness have some sight (Sardegna & Paul, 1991). More than 90 percent of all people with serious visual disabilities have usable residual vision (Tavernier, 1993). This residual vision is of great importance today; children who have serious visual impairments are taught to use their remaining vision to the utmost.

Not all authorities use the term *blindness* in the same way. The American Foundation for the Blind recommends that the term *blind* be used only to describe the vision of those people who have no usable sight at all, and that the terms *visually impaired*, *low vision*, and *partially sighted* be used to describe the vision of people with some usable vision (Sardegna & Otis, 1991).

These acuity-based definitions are not very useful for educators. First, they do not deal with near-point vision—the ability to see very close as one would when reading. Second, although visual acuity is a valuable piece of information, it does not really indicate how effectively children may use their vision. A child with poor

Legal blindness:
A visual acuity of 20/200 vision or less in the better eye, even with correction, or a reduction of the visual field to less than 20 degrees.

Partial sight:
Visual acuity that falls between 20/70 and 20/200 in the better eye, with correction.

Low vision:
The educational definition that refers to the inability to read a newspaper at a reasonable viewing distance even with correction.

Blind:
The educational definition that refers to the need to learn through braille or some other nonvisual medium.

Braille:
A system of touch reading and writing in which raised dots represent the letters of the alphabet.

visual acuity may be more skilled in using residual vision than a visually impaired child with better acuity. In addition, a child with better vision may have some difficulty that interferes with neural processing of the image (Padula & Spungin, 1983). In the educational realm, visual impairment is described by the functional loss of vision rather than visual acuity itself. Finally, individual differences in visual problems, such as tolerance for glare, may affect visual functioning.

Due to these limitations, educational definitions are sometimes offered. For instance, the term **low vision** in the educational realm is used to describe any visual impairment, not only poor distance vision, that results in an inability to read a newspaper at a reasonable viewing distance even with correction. Generally, children with low vision can use their vision with various aids for many school learning activities including reading, but may need to use tactile materials to supplement printed material (Barraga & Erin, 1992). Students who are considered **blind** learn via braille or some other nonvisual media (NICHCY, 1992). **Braille** is a system of touch reading and writing in which raised dots represent the letters of the alphabet. In other words, they must be educated through tactile or sensory channels other than vision, although some perception of light may be useful for orientation and mobility (Scholl, 1986). Students with visual impairments are a heterogeneous group who only share one common characteristic: a visual impairment serious enough to require modification of the educational program (Scholl, 1987).

A Low-Prevalence Exceptionality

Visual impairment is a low-prevalence exceptionality. In the 1992–1993 school year, 23,811 children with visual impairments received services in special education programs, a reduction from the 38,000 served during the 1976–1977 school year (U.S. Department of Education, 1994). Severe visual impairment or blindness occurs at the rate of 1.5 per 1,000 for people under the age of 17. The rate increases with age and is much greater in old age. The rate for people aged 65–74 years is 59 per 1,000 and for those 75–84 years, 118.4 per 1,000 (Nelson & Dimitrova, 1993). Visual impairment, then, is more a condition of the elderly than of the young (Nixon, 1994). In fact, 60 percent of the people who are blind are over 65 years of age and 30 percent are between ages 18 and 64 years (Ryan, 1992). About 4.3 million Americans of all ages have visual impairments (Nelson & Dimitrova, 1993). Children with visual impairments comprise about 0.5 percent of all the students served by special education services (U.S. Department of Education, 1994).

These figures may underestimate the number of children who actually have serious visual impairments (Kelley & Wedding, 1995). Many children with multiple disabilities have visual impairments. An estimated 75–85 percent of all people with multiple disabilities are blind or partially sighted (Tavernier, 1993). For example, between 25 and 50 percent of children with cerebral palsy have visual problems that affect the educational process (Barraga & Erin, 1992). Children with neurological impairment and heart problems may also have visual difficulties (Ferrell et al., 1990). Medical improvements have allowed many premature infants with disabilities to survive adding to the number of children with visual impairments. Many of these children with visual impairments may be classified under different headings.

Even taking the increase in premature infants with visual impairments into consideration, visual impairment is not common among children, and most teachers have little experience with children who cannot see well. Teachers will proceed through their entire careers teaching many children diagnosed as having learning disabilities but only one or two students categorized as having visual impairments.

Causes of Visual Impairment in Children

The three most common causes of visual impairment in children are (1) inherited congenital disorders, (2) problems associated with prenatal development and prematurity, and (3) accidents.

Approximately 3,000 genetic diseases have been identified to date, 30 percent of which cause some visual problems. Genetic disease is the major cause of blindness in children birth through six years of age (Sardegna & Paul, 1991). **Retinitis pigmentosa** is a group of inherited disorders that cause progressive degeneration of the retina and vision loss (Kelly & Vergason, 1985). The earliest symptom is difficulty seeing at night, followed by a reduction in peripheral vision, which leaves only a small central portion of the visual field untouched. People describe it as looking through a long tunnel. Occasionally this vision may also diminish. The rate and extent of progression are variable (RP Foundation, 1989). Recently, scientists have discovered the gene for one form of this disease, which has opened up new areas of research and hopefully treatment (Altman, 1990). **Macular degeneration** is a genetic disorder appearing at birth or up to age six years. The macula, the center of the retina where the sharpest vision occurs is destroyed. Vision blurs and central vision may completely disappear leaving some peripheral vision. Presently, macular degeneration has no cure, but laser treatments may sometimes help (Sardegna & Paul, 1991).

Difficulties due to disease during pregnancy can also result in visual problems for the child. Years ago, rubella was a prime cause of such difficulties (Kaplan, 1991). The development of a vaccine to prevent rubella has dramatically reduced rubella-related visual problems to a point where they are quite rare. Fetuses exposed to gonorrhea are often premature and may be blind. The standard practice of placing a solution containing an antibiotic in the infant's eyes at birth is to protect against blindness in case the mother has gonorrhea. In many hospitals erythromycin or tetracycline may be used. Erythromycin also combats chlamydia, an infection that also can cause blindness in newborns (Simkin, Whalleny, & Keppler, 1984). Antibiotics treat these diseases successfully.

Premature infants often require special care to survive. Years ago, a condition called **retinopathy of prematurity** was common among premature babies given too much oxygen and was a major cause of blindness. Although better ways of helping premature infants have been developed, this condition still occurs, and the number of children with retinopathy of prematurity may be increasing as medical advancements allow doctors to save very small babies who once had no chance of survival (Ferrell et al., 1990). Often, these children have other disabilities as well.

Retinitis pigmentosa:
A group of inherited disorders that cause progressive degeneration of the retina and vision loss.

Macular degeneration:
A degeneration of the central portion of the retina, which causes visual loss.

Retinopathy of prematurity:
A condition of blindness resulting from an oversupply of oxygen, most often administered to premature infants.

Accidents and injuries also cause eye damage. In 1991, 270,615 Americans suffered eye injuries due to accidents, and more than 72,000 were children under the age of 15 years. These accidents are caused by toys that are inappropriate such as pellet guns; cigarettes, cigars and related products; and general household cleaners. Sports injuries have become a greater concern over the years. An estimated 35,000 sports-related eye injuries occur each year (National Society to Prevent Blindness, 1988). Ninety percent of all eye injuries can be prevented (National Society to Prevent Blindness, 1993). Better safety procedures, such as the use of protective eyewear for sports, can prevent accidents.

Assessing Visual Functioning

Most people can remember being screened for visual acuity probably through the use of the Snellen chart or a related type of instrument. Regular visual examinations may begin with a brief history in which parents and others will tell the doctor what they observe about the child's visual functioning. This inquiry is followed by an evaluation of the ability to see both near and far, of refractive error, of visual movement and tracking and the ability to coordinate both eyes, and of pupil dilation. This is followed by an examination of the internal workings of the eye (Best, 1992; Geruschat, 1990).

Such evaluations are much easier to conduct with children who can cooperate and answer questions. The chief difficulty is evaluating visual problems in children who are too young to respond helpfully or have an additional disability that prevents active cooperation. Evaluating the visual abilities of very young children with suspected problems is a complicated and imprecise procedure (Bishop, 1990). Sometimes the appearance of the eye is sufficient to identify the nature of the problem. But often, this is an insufficient analysis and various tests must be used.

Very young children cannot verbally describe what they see. They may not realize they have a visual problem, since they have always seen the world in a particular way and may not understand that the world does not appear to others in the blurred fashion in which they see it. Other children with multiple disabilities may show delayed motor development, may not look where told or shown, or may not react in the usual manner making visual assessment difficult.

Despite these problems, a number of ways of assessing the vision of young children exist. For preschoolers, a variation of the Snellen chart may include outlines of common objects rather than letters. Children may be asked either to name the object or to match it with an object on a card given to them. Another variation on this theme is to show children a set of miniature toys, a small doll, chair, or whatever and hold it about three meters from the children and ask them to name it or match it with a set that is close to them (Best, 1992).

Infants can be tested in a different way using preferential looking behavior (Rosenberg & Hertz, 1990). Young children prefer to look at patterns rather than a blank screen. A series of cards with stripes are shown to a child at the same time as a blank card. If the child consistently looks at the striped card, the child can see the pattern. The stripes are varied as to thickness and contrast and therefore a

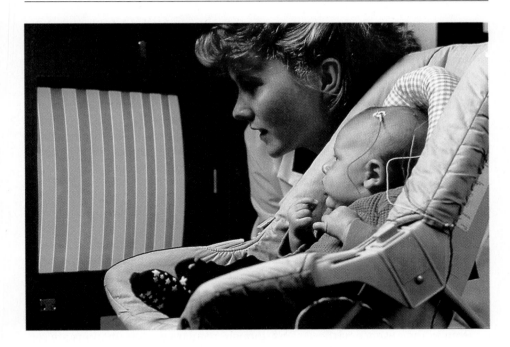

There are many techniques for assessing the vision of very young children. Here, an infant's vision is being assessed using a preferential looking technique.

threshold at which the infant does not see a pattern can be found. An acuity score can be obtained.

At six months, children may be screened using the roller ball test. The child is seated on the floor and a small white ball is rolled along the field of vision about three meters away. The child is expected to fixate on the ball when it stops. If the infant cannot, a visual problem may be present.

Recently, some experimentation has been conducted using visual-evoked response to diagnose eye problems (Morse & Trief, 1985). Electrodes that pick up the electrical activity in the occipital cortex, the region of the brain that interprets visual signals, are placed on the head of the young child and various visual stimuli are used to evaluate different aspects of the child's visual processing.

When severe impairments are suspected, tests that monitor awareness of light itself may be used. Various intensities of light may be shown until a response is produced. The nature of the response, attention to the stimulus, and the ability to track may be tested (Bishop, 1990).

Evaluators must differentiate between what the child can see and how the child uses the visual system. The clinical examination most often answers the question of what a child under ideal conditions can see. Educators are more interested in how the child is using the visual system. The results from various medical examinations are often poor predictors of functional performance. Only a limited relationship exists between visual acuity and visual performance (Geruschat, 1990).

Visual effectiveness is based upon three factors: visual capacity, what can actually be seen; visual attention, what is looked at; and visual processing, what sense is made of the visual world (Blanksby, 1991). Visual capacity is composed of acuity, visual field, and ocular movements. Visual attention involves alertness, the ability to develop and maintain an optimum level of sensitivity to stimuli, the selection of information, and the ability to shift attention. Visual processing involves making sense of the world and interpreting the visual patterns. Specific tools, such as the VAP-CAP, the Visual Assessment Procedure–Capacity, Attention, and Processing, can measure all three capabilities (Blanksby & Langford, 1993).

Most children who are blind have their disability discovered quickly. These infants show obvious signs, such as lack of focusing and a developmental delay in reaching. The discovery of partial sightedness is more difficult and often occurs much later. But discovery through screening and assessment is vital since the development of the remaining vision is so important. The earlier the impairment is discovered, the earlier treatment and training can be implemented in order to avoid the detrimental developmental effects of visual impairment.

Signs of Visual Problems in Children

Both parents and teachers must be alert to the possible signs that a child has a vision problem. Once a difficulty is discovered, it can either be rectified or, when necessary, a different learning environment created to match the visual abilities of the child. Table 13.1 lists the warning signs of possible visual difficulties, which can be placed under three different categories: behavior, appearance, and complaints (National Society to Prevent Blindness, 1991).

Even in the absence of these signs, though, regular eye examinations are recommended since some problems have no obvious signs or symptoms.

Developmental Concerns

Vision is intimately associated with development and the experiences that promote development. The child with average vision can follow objects in the environment, gaze at mother's face, learn about facial expressions, become fascinated by the movement of things in the environment, and form concepts about color, shape, and texture easily. The child who has a severe visual impairment cannot do these things and is at risk for developmental delay in the intellectual, emotional, and social areas of life.

One of the most common findings for infants who have severe visual impairments is that their development is delayed. Although not all children who are blind will show significant delays, most will (Padula & Sprungin, 1983).

The experiences of children who are blind are limited because they are not attracted to objects in their visual field. Babies who are blind are late in their reaching for noise-making objects and their independent exploration of the environment (Adelson & Fraiberg, 1974). Without adequate vision, they do not receive visual feedback, and observation learning cannot occur. Children may lack the motivation to explore their surroundings (O'Donnell & Livingston, 1991). Infants who are blind show significant delays in their motor milestones involving locomotion (Fraiberg, 1977).

When Ferrell and colleagues (1990) examined the development of young children with severe visual impairments they confirmed that visually impaired infants reached motor and visual motor milestones later, but still found them at the lower part of the average range. Infants who had other disabilities in addition to

TABLE 13.1　　**Warning Signs of Visual Impairment**

Behavior
Rubs eyes excessively
Shuts or covers one eye
Tilts head or thrusts head forward
Has difficulty with reading or other close-up work; holds objects close to eyes
Blinks more than usual or is irritable when doing close-up work
Is unable to see distant things clearly
Squints eyelids together or frowns

Appearance
Crossed eyes
Red-rimmed, encrusted, or swollen eyelids
Inflamed or watery eyes
Recurring infections on eyelids

Complaints
Itching, burning, or scratchy eyes
Cannot see well
Dizziness, headaches, or nausea following close-up work
Blurred or double vision

National Society to Prevent Blindness

their visual impairments were slower than children whose sole disability was a visual impairment and did not achieve these milestones in the average range. With the exception of a few abilities, such as searching for a dropped toy and picking up small pieces of food, children whose sole disability was visual impairment were not as slow in developing most skills as previously thought. Although degree of visual impairment was a factor affecting the amount of delay experienced, degree of visual impairment did not always predict the extent of the delays. Some children are better than others in using their residual vision, and their physical abilities and intelligence affect development. In addition, the environment provided for the infant is an important factor (Padula & Sprungin, 1983).

The early relationship between parent and child may also be adversely affected by the existence of a visual impairment (Dote-Kwan, 1995). One of the major tasks in the first two years is the establishment of a warm relationship, which is dependent upon attachment to caregivers (Kaplan, 1991). The child's disability may affect the moment-to-moment interaction between infant and parent known as **synchrony**. The basic pattern of communication may be altered. For example, an infant's smile reinforces the parent for whatever the parent has been doing, perhaps vocalizing to the child. Infants who are blind smile less than their sighted peers. Mothers are frequently disturbed by the absence of gaze from their infants (Fraiberg, 1977). These differences may negatively influence parent-child interactions. Parents of infants with visual impairments are less likely to talk and hold their infants than are parents of sighted children.

Children's behavior may also affect their early relationship with other children. Children with severe visual impairments often show self-stimulatory behavior called **blindisms**. These consist of rocking, rubbing, pressing or poking the eyes or staring at light, repetitive hand or finger movements, or head rocking or nodding

Synchrony:
The coordination between infant and caregiver in which each can respond to the subtle verbal and nonverbal cues of the other.

Blindisms:
Self-stimulatory behaviors such as eye-pressing, which are sometimes found in children who are blind.

(Brambring & Troster, 1992). Sighted peers may be confused by the child who shows these behaviors and avoid or withdraw from the child. The child also appears passive and does not relate to the environment when showing these movements (Lenhardt, 1990). People may incorrectly interpret these behaviors as signs of mental retardation or emotional disturbance and avoid children showing these behaviors.

Interpersonal relationships are also negatively affected by the lack of feedback received from other people through gestures and facial expressions. In everyday conversations, gestures are used to emphasize ideas. People gain valuable information from watching the gestures of others. Establishing and maintaining eye contact, frowning, smiling, winking, and nodding add to the richness of communication. Children who have severe visual impairments from birth or early childhood often do not know how to communicate on this level. On the other hand, sighted people frequently use auditory cues to enhance communication when they cannot see the other person, such as during a telephone conversation. They do not often do this in face-to-face interactions, which might be helpful for communication with people who are blind (Fichten et al., 1991; Erwin, 1993).

When people with visual impairments converse with each other, they compensate for the lack of visual cues by asking for additional information. In order to facilitate interactions with sighted peers, children with visual impairments learn to send visual signals such as nods and facial expressions. At the same time, sighted people must learn to give expanded explanations and use a greater variety of auditory signals when conversing with a person who has a visual impairment.

Despite these problems, some studies find no differences in social skills between people with and without visual impairments (Kemp & Rutter, 1982). More similarities in the communication of blind and sighted people can be found than differences. Still, some young people with visual impairments do show difficulties in some verbal and nonverbal components of social skills, including the use of gestures, posture, and smiling, and ask fewer open-ended questions (Fichten et al., 1991). In addition, visual impairment is a social challenge because children gain much knowledge about each other including clothing, hairstyles, and ways to act through visual scans, which are not available to children who have a visual impairment.

Children who are blind must also learn a set of skills that includes knowledge of when and how to ask for assistance (Erin, Dignan, & Brown, 1991). Significantly fewer interactions take place between sighted and nonsighted children than between sighted individuals in the same class (Hoben & Lindstrom, 1980). Children who are blind show more dependency and submissiveness than sighted children, although the pattern is not always clear. Rickelman and Blaylock (1983) noted that 57 percent of the responses of children who are blind to interpersonal interactions consisted of passive or withdrawn behaviors.

When teachers, parents of children with visual impairments, and children with visual impairments were asked to rank 70 possible variables in the order of what was most important to success in becoming fully functioning members of regular classes, the most important variable was considered teacher flexibility and acceptance by the regular classroom teacher. The second most important variable was peer interaction and acceptance, and the third was the social skills of the child with a visual impairment.

THOUGHT QUESTION

2. If submissiveness and dependence are problems with children who have visual impairments, what can be done to reduce the dependence?

Early Intervention

From this analysis of how visual impairment can affect the individual, two important points clearly stand out. First, visual impairment can lead to some difficulties in social interaction with parents and peers. Second, visual impairment can affect learning opportunities. Early intervention, then, is required if the child's development is to be optimized. Such early intervention emphasizes both working with parents and early childhood education.

Intervention may begin very early in infancy if the infant is known to have a severe visual impairment. Visual stimulation programs are effective (Tavernier, 1993). In one study, 15 infants with severe visual impairments were exposed to a program of visual stimulation while another 14 were not. The stimuli consisted of slides of patterns and facial drawings. The parents were lent a projector and a slide timer, a number of slides, and a screen. The slide show of 100 slides took about six minutes and was presented five days a week to the child for a year. The experimental group receiving the visual stimulation exhibited significant improvement in visual functioning compared to the control group (Leguire et al., 1992).

Parent education is required because the usual patterns of parent-infant communication are altered. Parents of children with severe visual impairments tend to care for the child's physical needs and otherwise leave the child alone (Friedman, 1989). In some programs, parents are taught by specially trained educators how to stimulate their children using touch and sound (Barraga & Erin, 1992). For example, parents must learn that tactile stroking and cuddling are absolutely necessary. The parent cannot wait for eye contact as a clue to the child's needs and respond to it. Toys must have different types of texture allowing a rich tactile experience, and many should make sounds. As the child grows, parents of children who are blind use more commands than are used with sighted children and do not involve the child in family conversation that often refers to visual objects or experiences. The child is exposed to conversation from others that is not personally involving. Some of these children develop imitative or even echolalic speech where they simply echo what they have heard around them.

One early program called the Parent and Toddler Training Program (PATT) demonstrates what can be done to maximize the development of children who are blind from birth and improve family functioning (Klein et al., 1988). The goals of the program are to enhance the social responsiveness of the children, develop an adequate education program for parents, and initiate interventions to improve the quality of family life and decrease stress.

PATT families participate in a two-hour weekly program over six months. After an initial assessment, a social worker and child development professionals discuss developmental concerns with the parents and ways to enhance the infant's development as well as communication techniques and problem solving. Information, training, and support are offered. The curriculum covers general development and developmental differences between sighted children and children with visual impairments and ways to stimulate and maximize development.

Discussions of social and emotional development cover early interactions with the infants, attitudes, and providing opportunities for social interaction. Parents are taught to identify the infant's cues and respond appropriately. Enhancing the

Visual experiences promote attachment. When a child is born with a severe visual impairment, parents must use the other senses to promote attachment.

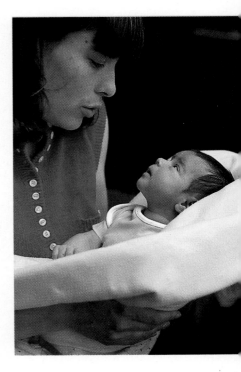

child's development focuses on both parents. A variety of physical and infant stimulation techniques and play skills are taught. Parents learn how to teach children to wind up a toy, drink from a cup, and feed themselves, and to provide tactile, kinesthetic, and auditory stimulation.

Behavior management techniques are also taught. For example, one child showed considerable eye pressing. After calculating a baseline, parents were told to use positive reinforcement and contingent hand restraint. Each time the toddler pressed his eyes the parents gave a loud verbal cue, "Stop," and restrained the toddler's hands in front of him for 30 seconds. Parents gave positive reinforcement in the form of verbal praise when the child engaged in appropriate activities. After a week, the eye pressing behavior was significantly reduced.

Finally, attention is focused on family relationships, feelings such as anxiety, grief, and depression, and improving communication among family members. The program is quite successful, and such programs have been instituted in various communities.

Other programs attempt to integrate children with visual impairments and their sighted peers very early. In one such program, parents and young children with and without visual impairments were included in a model play group in which children interact with each other, learning play and social skills (Friedman, 1989). Studies show developmental gains for children with visual impairments in integrated preschool programs and comparable gains for sighted children (Odom, DeKlyen, & Jenkins, 1984). Attitudinal changes on the part of the sighted children involved with children with visual impairment at the preschool age appear to be long lasting (Esposito & Reed, 1986). In other words, the integration helped the children with visual impairments and the extra attention necessary to integrate these children and adaptations in curriculum did not detract from the gains made by sighted children. The curriculum of the preschool, which emphasizes social skills, language development, the development of motor skills, cognitive skills, a positive self-concept, and healthy attitudes, are common to both the curricula for sighted children and children with visual impairments (Erin, 1993).

Preschool teachers already have excellent knowledge of general child development. The adaptations required for teaching children with visual impairments are not so much in curriculum but in the teaching methods used. Because children with visual impairments must make extensive use of other senses, teachers and parents must learn to "bring the world to them" through hands-on experience and concrete teaching of concepts, such as little and big, under and over, in and out, behind and ahead, basic shapes, and numbers (National Federation of the Blind, 1991). Parents are accustomed to helping their children become familiar with new places, and a few preliminary visits to the preschool for orientation purposes are desirable. The child will learn landmarks, for example, where the heat register and the wall clock are.

Early intervention is critical to later success in all developmental areas. Providing appropriate play environments designed to promote movement and exploration, and adapting materials for the use of children with visual impairments are not difficult to do (Schneekloth, 1989). Specialized training is also possible. Young children can learn to use some of the adaptive devices such as magnifiers and the long cane (Skellenger & Hill, 1991). Specially trained teachers instruct the children on positioning, localizing, scanning, tracking, and focusing. Children are taught to position themselves in the best place to see an object and to avoid glare. Localizing involves scanning for the clock on the wall which appears blurry and then to use a monocular device to see it clearly. A skill such as locating a small object by first associating its position with a larger object can be taught as can techniques for tracking and focusing (Cowan & Shepler, 1990).

SCENARIO

1 An agency that provides support services for young children with disabilities calls you and asks whether you would help integrate preschoolers with disabilities into a university preschool. Some of these youngsters have visual impairments. This attempt will be the first in the area, and they would like to do everything possible to make it a success. What steps would you take to increase your chances of successful integration?

Placement

The overwhelming majority—about 81 percent of school-age children with visual impairments and no additional disability—attend neighborhood schools and 61 percent are educated in the regular classroom for at least part of the day (U.S. Department of Education, 1994). The recent trend toward educating children with multiple disabilities in regular classes means that even more children with visual impairments will be educated in regular classrooms.

Naturally, this integration has meant a reduction in the number of children in special schools for children with visual impairments, which are often residential. While this trend may continue, not everyone is happy with it. Some argue that residential and special day schools remain a valid choice for some (Bina, 1993).

Just what role should residential and day schools play in the education of children with visual impairments is a controversial question. With the emphasis first on mainstreaming and now on inclusion, this question takes on special significance. Some argue that local schools cannot meet the needs for mobility training, braille, and learning to use technology for this population of students (Hatlen, 1993). Taking students out of the regular class and, sometimes, the neighborhood school is required if students are to develop skills necessary for success. Residential and day schools offer specialized training in mobility, orientation, and other skills in an environment adapted to the needs of children with visual disabilities, where teachers are specially trained to provide educational services. They offer children the opportunity to meet others with such disabilities. On the other hand, the limitations of a separate education, including the lack of opportunity to interact with their sighted peers still remains. Most experts do not believe that residential or day schools are best for everyone but argue that residential schools are a viable option for some students (see Erin, 1993).

Residential and day schools face a challenge if they are to survive. They have the expertise and knowledge about children with visual impairments that public schools do not, which places them in an excellent position to help meet the needs of these students (Stenehjem, 1993). Many experts, though, believe that these schools must now identify unmet needs of children with visual impairments and develop programs to meet these needs (Geruschat, 1993). These special schools become a community resource, cooperating rather than competing with the neighborhood school. For example, short-term placements of one week to one school year, may provide the training necessary for students with severe visual impairments to function in the community (MacCuspie et al., 1993). Cooperative placements in which children spend part of their day in a neighborhood school and part in a specialized setting are possible, depending upon practical concerns such as the distances to be travelled. Some residential schools have developed programs in conjunction with local schools in which residential schools furnish assistance in disability-specific skills and actively consult with the regular and special education staff to help design environments to meet the needs of the children as they attend neighborhood schools (Koehler & Loftin, 1993). Other schools have more actively reached into the community to provide services to students and their parents in many areas of concern (Miller, 1993). For example, they may offer direct instruction in skills, itinerant services in local schools, and technical assistance. Residential schools are an important resource and are changing in an attempt to meet the needs of students with visual impairments who are now more likely to be educated in regular classrooms. The residential school must enter a partnership with local schools and offer a variety of services to help students with visual impairments succeed in school and work (Stenehjem, 1993).

Service Delivery

A number of service delivery models are in use today for children with visual impairments. An itinerant teacher may travel to the school and work with a child as well as providing special modifications to the instructional program. This teacher may visit the school two or three days a week and provide the special equipment necessary, train the child in the use of special equipment, and consult with the regular classroom teacher. Such a model is most effective for students who are self-directed and independent and least effective for students who lack academic skills.

The teacher consultant is a special educator who advises regular classroom teachers, aides, and other school personnel in methods that will meet the student's needs. The consultant's duties are consultative rather than instructive. This method is least effective for children who require intensive skills training. It provides the least amount of instructional time to children with visual impairments, and some have questioned its effectiveness with this population (Head, 1990). It is increasingly being used, however, especially in rural areas.

The resource room is also used extensively. It provides specialized skills instruction and testing services. For example, teachers are encouraged to send their tests to the resource room where students with visual impairments can receive oral testing and additional time to take the tests—two modifications that are impossible in a 43-minute class session where other students might be disrupted by speech and questions.

Adaptation in the Classroom

A teacher of a child with a visual impairment must answer two major questions. First, what environmental changes and aids are required to allow this child to function in the classroom? Second, what modifications are required in the presentation of the work?

Environmental Modifications

Modifying the environment depends upon the teacher's understanding of the individual child's needs. The teacher must therefore gather as much information as possible regarding the visual functioning of the child. If the child has peripheral vision, then seating the child on the side of the classroom where the child may see the teacher without turning the head may be in order. If the child is bothered by glare, some adjustment to the lighting may be required. The child with a visual impairment may require some additional orientation to the room; showing the child around will help the child learn the landmarks in the classroom. If any physical changes are made to the room, such as altering chair arrangements, the student needs not only to be informed but to be physically shown the changes. Making certain obstacles are removed from the path is also important.

Modifications in Presentation

Teaching children with visual impairments does not usually require much modification in content, depending, of course on the existence of other disabilities such as neurological impairment. In general, students with visual impairment can be expected to complete the curriculum for sighted children. They can participate in class discussions and complete most class assignments. Substitute assignments are only necessary when the original assignment relies heavily on visual abilities and no auditory translation is practical. For example, a teacher may be able to describe a painting in words, but the evaluation of artistic style is difficult under such circumstances.

The greater problem involves the need for considerable planning and cooperation from others in order to prepare materials. For example, tape recordings may be required, a large print book provided, or a reader may be needed on a regular basis.

Despite the fact that people typically take in so much of their information by visual means, most classrooms provide a range of auditory experiences. With the proper adaptations, a regular classroom can provide an environment in which children and adolescents with visual impairments can succeed.

Two elements of adapting presentation include teaching in a concrete manner and emphasizing auditory and tactile modes of presentation. Without concrete teaching a child who is blind may possess the vocabulary but lack the concept (National Federation of the Blind, 1991). Teachers must present a concept more fully and not leave gaps which children with vision may fill using visual experience. At the same time, tactile learning is possible perhaps through the use of models. For example, one child seemed to know all about birds and their habits.

When one was brought to class, the child was surprised to find that the bird could walk. The discussion of birds had provided incomplete knowledge. After examining the bird, petting it, and feeling it take a step, the child's concept was more completely developed.

Teachers must also be aware of the tendency to use visual references in their teaching. Often teachers will say something that requires visualization and not realize it. A statement, such as "Pick up the papers," or even pointing to something is inappropriate when communicating with children who have visual impairments (Fichten et al., 1991). This change in orientation may require some consciousness raising. For example, when writing on the blackboard, a verbal explanation is required. Often teachers will not do this because they rely on the child's vision to discover that the math example requires addition rather than subtraction. Students with a visual impairment may not be able to read what is written on the blackboard and may not always ask for verbal explanation. Therefore, the teacher must explain it without being specifically asked to do so.

The adaptations in the arts and physical activities take some thought and planning but are not difficult. In the arts and crafts area, play dough and sculpture are possibilities. Fine motor skills may be honed using beadstringing, block sets, and puzzles with textured pieces. Dramatic play and games involving brain teasers and riddles are possible. Balls with buzzers and ring toss with electronic batteries that give out a sound are possibilities (Association for the Care of Children's Health, 1986).

One last point about communication is in order. For some reason, people tend to raise their voices when speaking to students with visual impairments. A number of students who have visual impairments comment on this tendency. When communicating with students who have visual impairments, looking at the stu-

Students with visual impairments often note that teachers seem to forget their need for greater verbal explanation, and they are reluctant to continue asking questions.

dent and talking as one would with any other student is best. The one change is, as noted earlier, not to depend upon visual cues for communication and to use fuller auditory explanations. Gaining the students attention by calling the student's name rather than pointing or nodding is appropriate.

SCENARIO

2 Jerry is a sixth-grader who is legally blind. He does well in your class and you have a good relationship with him, but he requires a tremendous amount of reassurance and attention. He demands to be physically close to you and is always asking questions, some of which you believe he can answer by himself. He lacks self-confidence. You are concerned that his dependence on you is undesirable since it will reduce the interaction with others and will tend to make him unpopular. How would you reduce the dependency without injuring your relationship with Jerry?

These regular classroom adaptations are relatively easy. Yet, many students with visual impairments note that they are frequently placed at a disadvantage because teachers forget about these adaptations and return to inappropriate teaching strategies. Three major problems were suggested by adults who recalled their experiences as students with visual impairments in a neighborhood school (Freeman et al., 1991). First, teachers did not adequately understand the student's need for additional time, despite information that had been provided to them. Second, in the rush sometimes found in classrooms, teachers forgot about the presence of a student with a visual impairment and, for instance, used an overhead projector with transparencies without adequate verbal explanation. Students were reluctant to keep reminding the teachers or complaining about the inappropriate teaching methods. Third, materials required for them were often not received in time or not available. Sometimes they had to use alternative materials that did not match their needs, including earlier editions of books. The situation became somewhat more complicated in secondary school since having a different teacher for each subject required students to constantly remind each teacher of their special needs. This repeated prompting became tiresome and sometimes embarrassing, and many simply accepted the situation and did not offer feedback on the teacher's unwitting failure to meet their needs.

The problems cited by people with partial sight are often worse, because teachers have more difficulty understanding their needs. In addition, some students fake sight (Freeman et al., 1991). Some children with partial sight try to avoid the negative stereotypes of blindness and to pass as completely sighted. This pretense often leads to exhausting, ineffective, and sometimes dangerous situations. When a child is blind, the child and the parents have little choice but to accept the situation and try to deal with it. When children have low vision, though, the situation differs. They and their parents may not accept the situation as easily and children may not be willing to use special equipment.

THOUGHT QUESTION

3. *Why do regular classroom teachers working with students with visual impairments often regress to using inappropriate methods of communication and teaching?*

THOUGHT QUESTION

4. *Why are the problems of acceptance and achievement often more severe for children with low vision than for children who are blind?*

SCENARIO

3   Lisa, a sophomore high school transfer student, is legally blind. Many of the teachers in the school have never had any experience teaching children with visual impairments. The principal asks you to write five or six suggestions to help the other teachers meet Lisa's needs. What suggestions would you offer your colleagues?

Social Skills and Integration

The social integration of children with visual impairments into the regular classroom environment requires direct teacher involvement. Earlier, this chapter noted the nature of communication difficulties and the possible development of dependence and submissiveness. Children with visual impairments often show a dependence on adults, which is related to a lack of popularity for children with and without disabilities (O'Connor, 1975).

Some particular teacher behaviors improve social interaction in the classroom (Workman, 1986). The most important teacher behavior is describing the social environment, which includes what people are doing in relation to a particular activity such as, "Danny is the doctor." Direct prompts in the form of specific suggestions on ways to interact or roles to take, or perhaps a suggestion to share the toy with another child also encourage interaction. Third, suggestions for interaction given to another child or to some group at large, such as "Tell Jon about the assignment," can improve social interaction.

Children with visual impairments may need some training in social skills. Van Hasselt and colleagues (1983) gave social skills training to four unassertive adolescents who were blind. The researchers first determined the nature of the behaviors requiring modification, for example maintaining eye contact, requesting a new behavior from others, or communicative competence involving the tone of voice and the use of expressive gestures. Role playing and feedback were then used to teach students these skills and resulted in improved social skills for these adolescents.

Teachers, then, must be active in encouraging interaction between children with and without visual impairments. As Workman's study demonstrated, prompting students and describing what is going on can be of great assistance. Another possibility is including the student in activities that require working together with others, such as group projects.

SCENARIO

4   Carlos is a fifth grader who has a severe visual impairment. He has very good verbal communication skills and his sighted peers interact with him in class. However, outside during recess he sits by himself and is not involved with the other children. How can you improve the situation and involve Carlos in recess activities?

Parent-School Articulation

Close parent-school cooperation is valuable for all students, but is particularly important for students with visual impairments. Parents can demonstrate how a device the child needs should be used. In addition, when assignments are being given, some parental help may be required. The parent may need to read the assignment to the child and, if necessary, go to the library to obtain a large print book. Sometimes parents may have an idea for adapting an assignment because they have more experience working with the child.

 **THE CLASSROOM**   **Meeting the Classroom Needs of Children with Visual Impairments**

1. Allow students with visual impairments to sit where they find it most comfortable.	**Why?** Students may be very sensitive to glare and lighting. Sit children away from glare.
2. Encourage children to tell the teacher about environmental problems.	**Why?** Many students will not complain about environmental problems and instead endure the glare and other difficulties which hinder their learning. Encourage students to engage in dialogue on this problem.
3. Print rather than use script on the blackboard.	**Why?** Print is easier to see than script.
4. Allow the child to use a desk copy or make a carbon or photocopy.	**Why?** A child with a visual impairment cannot be permitted to stand close to the blackboard since the child may block the vision of others. Providing alternatives, such as desk copies, is more practical.
5. Read what is written from the blackboard.	**Why?** For students who cannot see notes on the blackboard, verbalizing them is useful.
6. Allow students with visual impairments more time to do their work but keep high standards.	**Why?** Children with visual impairments take somewhat longer to complete their work (Rapp & Rapp, 1992). These students experience difficulty in focusing, and they read at a slower rate.

7. Reduce the quantity of work assigned as an acceptable alternative, but continue to demand quality work.	**Why?** Because they often take longer to do their work, reducing the quantity of work, such as assigning 7 instead of 10 problems, is acceptable.
8. Use alternative testing formats when necessary (Schnaiberg, 1995).	**Why?** Examinations may have to be given orally in some cases. In others, more time must be permitted for test performance that truly reflects their learning.
9. Make certain assistive devices are being used.	**Why?** Studies show that low vision aids are underutilized both inside and outside the school (Kalloniatis & Johnston, 1994).
10. Leave enough time to locate and obtain large print books or to make tapes.	**Why?** Lessons are more effective if appropriate materials are available.
11. Do not use visual references when speaking to the child.	**Why?** Teachers often use such references that are not comprehensible to the child.
12. Explain concepts in greater detail.	**Why?** Most often, teachers supplement auditory with visual information. This practice will not be effective when teaching children with visual impairments.
13. Teach in a concrete manner and emphasize auditory and tactile means of learning.	**Why?** Students with visual impairments must use other senses besides vision to learn.
14. Describe the social environment for the child.	**Why?** Children with visual impairments require explanations of many of the social interactions that are occurring since they cannot see them.
15. Actively encourage social interaction.	**Why?** Students need encouragement to interact with others and sometimes direct instructions on interaction.
16. Beware of overprotection.	**Why?** Some teachers and parents overprotect children with visual impairments (McBroom & Tedder,

	1993; National Federation for the Blind, 1991). Although safety is an important concern, students must be allowed to try, and succeed or fail.
17. Promote independence by praising individual effort.	**Why?** Becoming independent is difficult, especially for children with visual impairments. Praising individual effort increases feelings of competence.

Recreation and Physical Education

Exercise is important for physical health as well as being a source of enjoyment. Studies differ as to the extent of cardiovascular fitness in children with visual impairments; some studies show an equivalence in cardiovascular functioning, and others show less fitness. Specific programs of regular aerobic exercise yield important gains in cardiovascular fitness for children with visual impairments (Blessing et al., 1993).

Although one may have difficulty imagining a child who is blind running on a track or ice skating, these and other activities are quite possible and, in fact, enjoyed by a number of children with visual impairments. A jogger with a visual impairment may be able to run on a track with high contrasting surfaces or a distinctive texture that differentiates it from the surrounding area. Sometimes, special ropes or metal guides are available that can line the outside of a small track. Also, a runner may hold the elbow of a sighted jogger or run while each holds the opposite ends of a stick between them.

Competitive games can also be enjoyed. Children and adolescents with visual impairments have participated in such track and field events as the triple jump, shot put, and long jump. Bicycling is possible on a tandem bike. Bowling requires an adaptation such as a portable bowling rail that is assembled and placed next to the alley as a guide. Skiing clubs and special programs for people with visual impairments are also available for both cross-country and alpine skiing. Cross-country skiing is fairly slow and follows the tracks made by others. With the help of a sighted guide and explicit instructions this activity is possible. Alpine skiing is faster and more dependent upon rapidly processing visual information. Skiers who are blind often wear tunics or shirts printed with "blind skier" to advise others of their presence. Communication between a sighted guide who indicates turns and directions is necessary.

Other sports such as ice skating, speed skating, and roller skating require a sighted guide. Swimming in lanes using ropes or an outside wall is popular. Horseshoes may be adapted by distinctive color or texture and the posts can also give out an auditory cue. Balls of all types can be adapted with inner buzzers or beepers that alert a player with a visual impairment to their position. In fact, goal

With the necessary adaptations, children with severe visual impairments can participate in many leisure-time activities.

ball is a game played exclusively by people with visual impairments. The idea is to roll a ball containing bells past the opposing team and into a goal net. Each team consists of three players who alternately roll and defend. The floor is marked with tape to accent the goals and boundaries (Sardegna & Paul, 1991).

Assistive Technology

One universally accepted principle for helping children with visual impairments is that they must learn to use their residual vision as much and as well as possible. Many children receive specialized training in this area. A number of low vision aids exist, which can be extremely helpful. These aids may be as simple as a magnifying glass or as technologically advanced as a talking computer.

Perhaps the most common and familiar aid is the magnifying glass which can range from simple to sophisticated. A loupe, or spectacle magnifier, is a convex lens that clips onto an eyeglass frame and is attached by a thin metal arm that swings down into position. More than one loupe can be simultaneously mounted on frames so people can work at different distances.

Telescopic devices increase distance vision and may be hand held or spectacle mounted. Reading telescopes improve intermediate distance vision when clipped or mounted on eyeglasses. Other lens systems may include filters to reduce glare or ease bright lights and prisms to adjust the image to a different section of the retina and avoid blind spots. Electronic magnifying systems are available. For example, closed circuit television (CCTV) requires a camera and a television screen which allows an enlargement of print up to 60 times and displays the image on a

Closed circuit television, CCTV, magnifies print up to sixty times, giving people with visual impairments a chance to read.

screen. Information on the computer screen can be read out to the user through an installed speech synthesizer. The computer can interface with a device for printing braille so that computer users who prefer braille to auditory feedback may have a tactile display (Center for Special Education Technology, 1989).

Most students with substantial visual impairments require some modification of the visual materials used in the classroom. Substitutes for written material and some method of notetaking need to be worked out. For example, the standard textbook has a print size that may not be big enough, and children may not be able to take notes on regular paper. A great many substitutes are available.

For some, large print books are sufficient and often available. The American Printing House for the Blind and other agencies produce large print books. For other students, auditory substitutes such as talking books, readers, cassettes, or machines that can actually read print for the child are possibilities. Many community organizations and volunteer groups will record texts, articles, manuals, and classroom handouts for students. Cassettes can be used to record personal messages, notes, and lectures (Center for Special Education Technology, 1989). Paper with raised lines is also available so handwriting is possible. However, nothing takes the place of typing, and every student with a visual impairment needs to learn to use a typewriter or the equivalent word-processor, which has the letters raised on the keyboard as a guide.

One tactual device for reading is called the **optacon**. The optacon is a machine that converts print into tactual letter configurations that are read with the fingertips (Sardegna & Paul, 1991). A hand-held camera is scanned across each line of a text and a grid of 144 vibrating pins re-creates letters. The student uses the index finger to read a raised vibrating image of each letter. The machine is not easy to use and requires much practice and training, but it is portable and gives immediate access to printed material.

Many devices are used to magnify items allowing people with severe visual disabilities to see them.

Optacon:
A device that converts print into tactual letter configurations that are read with the fingertips.

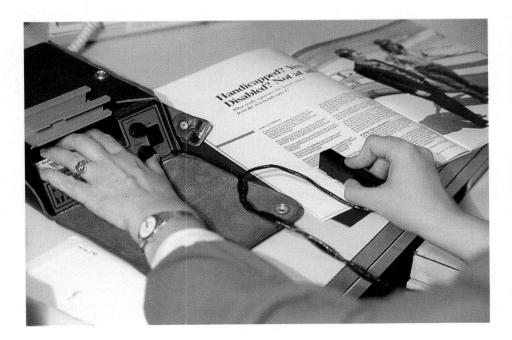

This device is a machine that converts print into tactile letter configurations.

Kurzweil Reading Machine:
A machine that converts print into sound.

The **Kurzweil Reading Machine** is a machine that converts print into sound. The user places the page to be read onto the machine and the machine reads the material out verbally. The user may control the speed of the reading or have the machine repeat the words. The machine can read almost any typed print style. This machine is expensive, but some colleges have them and allow not only students to use them but people in the general community who may benefit from them.

SCENARIO

5 Tina is a fourth-grade student who has partial sight. She has very thick glasses and uses a variety of low vision aids. The problem is that she does not always use them when they are appropriate. You feel that this lack of use causes some educational problems. How would you encourage her to use her visual aids?

This student is using a machine which converts print into synthesized speech.

ON-LINE   Being Blind in a Reading World

For the next two days, write down every time you read something. You may be surprised at the amount of incidental reading you do. Most people do not realize how much they use their ability to read in the course of a day. Of course, people often pick up books or magazines to read. But reading goes well beyond this. Scanning the ingredients on the can when shopping, looking at the telephone bill, reading the information on the computer monitor, and watching the signs when driving are just a few of the activities that require reading skills. Reading is such an integral part of life that most people take it for granted.

The lack of being able to read print of regular size as well as see graphical images on a screen creates difficulties for people with visual impairments. Numerous technological innovations have been developed and continue to be developed that enable people with visual impairments to read.

Technological assistance for reading can be divided into two categories. First, print can be magnified to a level that allows the reader to see the material. Second, print can be transformed into a different medium, such as sound or touch. Technological innovations have succeeded in doing both, but many challenges remain.

Most people with visual impairments have some residual vision and can take advantage of enlarged print. Enlarging print can be accomplished in many ways, through closed circuit television systems or various magnifying devices that use special hardware, software, or both (Ruconich, 1984). Some systems allow the user to magnify any portion of the screen desired as if one was running a magnifying lens over the screen around the cursor (Blenkhorn, 1994).

Closed-circuit television (CCTV) systems are popular. They use either a stand or hand-held camera, which projects a magnified image onto a television set. CCTV can be used to magnify print materials in every form including labels on packages or medicine, as well as to magnify any object the individual might want to see (Uslan, 1993). The cameras can be lightweight, some as light as seven ounces, and are a bit larger than a pack of cigarettes. The system itself is easily portable and can be used wherever a television set is present.

Reading machines of various types are also available. These machines convert the text on the monitor to a different modality. Text may be inputted using a braille keyboard and special software or hardware. The user has a choice of output. Text may be converted to braille or into synthesized speech. The text can also be stored for further use. The braille output may be produced on special printers that use braille paper or through paperless braille systems in which retractable pins are used to form braille characters (Sardegna & Paul, 1991). The optacon can also be used, as information is passed through the vibrating tactile display representing printed letters. Synthesized speech is a popular alternative. Translation to synthesized speech is especially important for those people who do not know braille, find braille too slow, or want an alternative to braille.

These reading machines use what are called computer-based optical character recognition (OCR) systems, and all have limitations on what types of fonts they can recognize (Converso & Hocek, 1990). New systems allow for greater control over all phases of the reading process. Using what is called intelligent character recognition (ICR) some machines can now recognize thousands of typefaces and styles (Dixon & Mandelbaum, 1990). Some companies are now experimenting with machines that can read handwriting. Some machines can read different languages and offer a variety of storage features (Random Access, 1993a). Use of these machines takes some training; the user must be able to use a keypad for adjusting volume, voice, and speech rate as well as for placing the document correctly so the page can be scanned (Hole & Holt, 1994).

Computer technology also allows people with visual impairments to become more efficient in their writing. Some programs translate from braille to print and print to braille, permitting people with visual impairments to share information with other people (Sardegna & Paul, 1991). One area of considerable importance to students is notetaking. A survey of college students with visual impairments found the use of laptop computers for notetaking purposes a popular option. Later, the stored notes are transformed into sound, visual, or tactual output. For example, some students used printouts with large fonts on special paper, often pink or blue, that reduced glare. Others printed their notes in braille or used a speech synthesizer. Students also use these computer setups to explore many different kinds of software and these experiences familiarize students with the use of the computer, which is often an important step toward later being able to use computers in the work place (Todd, 1992). One important element in students' successful use of computers was convenient access to computer facilities during both day and evening hours.

Most people with visual impairments find newspaper access difficult if not impossible. Some newspapers are published in large print but do not offer the entire text, and sometimes short tape-recorded versions are available but frequently long after the newspaper has been published. Access to newspapers may be gained in other ways. Radio reading services are available in some areas in which access to local newspapers, periodicals, and other materials is provided over the radio by readers on a special broadcast band (Dixon & Mandelbaum, 1990). A computerized newspaper service has begun in Sweden. During the night the newspaper is broadcast using an FM channel to a receiver attached to a computer's hard disk. The hard disk stores the material, and the individual uses a voice synthesizer to read the newspaper (Hjelmquist, Jansson, & Torell, 1990; Random Access, 1993b). Today, a service is available in which an individual accesses a subscriber service over the telephone and signals from a touch tone phone keypad what articles or sections the subscriber wishes to hear (Dixon & Mandelbaum, 1990). This service allows more flexibility since the subscriber does not have to wait for a regularly scheduled broadcast. For example, the person may want to have part of the sports section read at 7 A.M. and not wait for the broadcast of that section at 9 A.M.

Reading and writing are certainly important elements in everyday life, both inside and outside of school. Many new technological innovations, though, rely much more heavily on visual rather than auditory channels. For example, computers create visual displays of both text and graphics. The graphic presentations are used more and more to display concepts and information. New products are being introduced that allow people to complete chores more efficiently and independently. For example, the fax machine allows people to send facsimiles over the telephone wires, and many businesses now use fax machines extensively. Some restaurants allow people to fax their orders and then either pick them up or have them delivered at a specific time. Some modern telephones offer information in a visual manner on a computer-like screen, and some automatic ticketing machines at airports and rail stations allow people to insert a credit card, answer questions, and purchase plane or rail tickets without the need to stand on long lines. The automatic teller machine (ATM) is certainly popular, allowing people access to their money at any time of the day or night. Such machines rely on people to place their credit cards into a slot, answer questions and remove the card and the money (Schreier, 1990).

These systems combined with the increased emphasis on reading place many people with severe visual impairments at a disadvantage. For example, the use of computer graphics, which are not accessible for people with visual impairments, has certainly increased. Although people with visual impairments can make telephone calls, the information presented on screens on the top of the machine is difficult for people with visual impairments to read. Automatic teller machines require a person to use a keypad and access a screen filled with information (Schreier, 1990).

Technology that allows people with visual impairments access to these systems is available and will soon be incorporated into these systems. Telephone systems with visual displays can be produced with the ability to show large characters on demand and synthesized speech when required. Automatic ticketing machines may use synthesized speech to guide the purchaser, and some additional coding on the credit card may allow the machine to go into this auditory mode. Automated teller machines may also use synthesized speech to allow access as well as large print. Fax technology may also create some difficulties, mostly because some faxes are handwritten. A service is available in some parts of the country in which an individual may transmit the fax that the user has received to a central station where a sighted individual can then read it back (Gerrey, Brabyn, & Crandall, 1990).

Research on making graphics accessible is ongoing. One possibility is to interpret the graphics using optical character recognition (OCR) software, which can recognize the graphic and present the information using synthesized speech or braille. Another possibility is to develop software and hardware systems that convert the graphics on the monitor into a tactile display (Schreier, 1990). Such systems are still in their infancy but hold promise for the future.

The need to recognize graphics goes beyond the desirability of allowing people with visual impairments to understand and create graphs and pictures. Many computer programs are designed to use a graphical user interface (GUI). This involves the use of an icon or simple graphic rather than a typed word command to control a program. The person simply places the mouse over the icon and selects the operation desired. The use of these interfaces reduces the number of keystrokes. These simplified icons can create difficulties for people with visual impairments. New software has been developed, which interprets icons so the person with a visual impairment can use them (Boyd, Boyd, & Vanderheiden, 1990). Software is available that can recognize these icons and use nonvisual ways to communicate them to the user. Since icons are frequently found in the same place, people with visual impairments can learn to find them when desired. Voice-directed commands that orally tell the computer what to do are available today. The computer user simply tells the computer what operation to perform and the computer executes the task. These voice-activated systems are still relatively simple at the present time but will become more complex in the future.

Another significant area of most people's lives is television viewing. The audio portion is certainly available to people with a visual impairment but television is a visual medium. The person with a visual impairment may hear the dialogue but be unable to truly appreciate what is going on. This disadvantage is partially solved by using a descriptive video service, which allows a second narrative to be added. A second audio channel describes the key visual elements during gaps in the dialogue (Cronin & King, 1990).

The future of technology for people with visual impairments is exciting. Machines that translate print into auditory or tactual information will become more portable, offer more options, and have fewer limitations. The development of new technology will challenge the technical and creative abilities of scientists, allowing people with visual impairments access to the many activities in life that sighted people take for granted.

The Controversy Surrounding Braille

Braille is a physical communication system used by people who are blind. Raised dots on a page represent the letters of the alphabet. An arrangement of six dots comprises a braille cell. The dots can be arranged into 63 different patterns (American Foundation for the Blind, 1987). There are two levels of braille. Grade 1 Braille is similar to print with each letter written out in braille. It is rarely used today because it is very bulky. Grade 2 Braille is more like shorthand. Symbols or signs are used to represent frequently used words or combinations of letters. Braille is taught by special experts in the field.

Writing with braille is accomplished with a Perkins Brailler or a slate and stylist. A Perkins Brailler is a braille typewriter in which six keys—one for each of the dots on the braille cell—exist. An individual presses the keys together making an embossed print on the page. It is quite heavy but is most commonly used. A slate and stylus is composed of two rectangular metal plates hinged at one end. The upper plate has rows of small, open windows and directly underneath each window on the bottom plate is an indentation of a complete braille cell. A sheet of braille paper is placed between the two metal plates and a stylus, a short metal prong fastened to a handle, is held in the palm. The writer presses the stylus down and it pushes the paper against the corresponding indentation of the braille cell dot on the bottom plate. A raised dot is formed on the reverse side of the paper (Sardegna & Paul, 1991). A slate and stylist is lighter but requires more skill. Braille is useful for individuals with severe visual disabilities, but very few sighted people know how to read it. Therefore, producing printed copy is important and devices are now available which interface the Perkins Brailler with a computer printer so that regular print is available.

Today, controversy surrounds the teaching of braille. The percentage of people with severe visual impairments who can read braille has been declining since the 1950s due to the increased dependence on technology. In 1955, 50 percent of all people with severe visual impairments knew braille, while in 1989 only 12 percent did (De Witt, 1991).

Some advocates of braille claim that most blind people are functionally illiterate since they cannot use braille and must depend too much upon technology. They want teaching braille made mandatory, and legislation has been introduced in some states to do so. Proponents argue that technology and magnification devices are useful, but many students cannot read print unless it is enlarged requiring very bulky and sophisticated computer equipment. Children who do not know braille cannot take their own notes. However, such notetaking is possible with a slate and stylus which is easily portable. In addition, even with sophisticated equipment, some children are still able to read only about 10 words per minute while their sighted classmates read 200–300 words per minute. Although reading braille is slower than reading print, it is faster than 10 words per minute. Others with progressive visual disorders who can see now will lose their remaining vision in the future and should be prepared.

Other experts claim that making braille mandatory is counterproductive, inappropriate, and perhaps even harmful. They argue that it is wasteful for people with low vision. In addition, many children who are blind also have other disabilities, sometimes including severe mental retardation, neurological problems, and physical disabilities that make reading braille difficult if not impossible. Trying to teach braille would use up valuable instructional time that could be devoted to other pursuits (Viadero, 1989). Another problem is that people who are legally blind may still have peripheral vision, such as tunnel vision, and be able to read some print.

Some states have passed legislation requiring all children who are legally blind to be taught braille while others have defeated these proposals. Still other states have made arrangements to encourage braille teaching but have not mandated it and offer guidelines as to when it should be taught. An IEP may, indeed, contain a braille requirement.

Braille is a touch reading system. A reduction in the percentage of blind people who can use braille has occurred and there is a movement to encourage the learning of braille.

Providing Special Services

Professionals specially trained to teach children with visual impairments are required in at least four different areas: daily living skills instruction, orientation and mobility training, the teaching of specialized technology and braille, and training of residual vision (Head, 1990). Independent living skills are required if the individual is to become self-supporting. Sighted children learn how to dress, groom, cook, clean, shop, and make repairs in part by watching others. Children with visual impairments need specialized instruction in these areas. Most of the time, the parents of children who are blind are sighted and must learn ways to help their children develop these skills with the help of professionals.

Orientation and Mobility Skills

Basic travel skills are required if the individual is to become independent. These travel skills are divided into two categories. The first is **orientation** or the use of the remaining senses to establish one's position and relationships to other objects in the environment. The second is the actual movement or **mobility** from place to place as desired (American Foundation for the Blind, 1983). Getting around the classroom is a simple matter for most students, but not for children with a visual disability. Children who are blind may also lose orientation easily. If a child with sight wants to take something from a cubbyhole, it is a simple task. However, a student who is blind may be disoriented and be an inch away and not able to negotiate the situation. It is frightening to lose one's orientation. Instruction in orientation and mobility (travel) skills is required even if modifications in the school classroom are made.

Such factors as the person's motivation, the nature of the visual impairment, the presence of another disability, age, general health, and concept development skills all affect the extent to which a person masters orientation and mobility skills. The use of residual vision is emphasized. A person who can see a foot ahead has some means of perceiving objects. A person who can see forms and shapes has important cues.

An individual who is congenitally blind (blind since birth) must learn to use other senses besides vision to negotiate the environment. An individual who has become blind after birth, especially if the blindness occurred after early childhood, may have some visual memories that aid in understanding concepts. Still, every individual with a severe visual disability must use other senses for orientation and mobility. A common misconception is that people who are blind have better senses of hearing, touch, or smell. The other senses do not become more acute or more sensitive, but people who are blind may depend upon them more and develop their ability to interpret what they hear to a greater extent. For people with visual impairments, hearing provides important information necessary for identification, direction, and distance, information that a sighted person may not recognize. Individuals who are blind learn to use hearing to identify, discriminate, and select from among sounds, to localize them using sound reflection and echo location.

Orientation skills involve learning different ways to discover where one is in the environment. One way is to use landmarks, which are specific places that let people know where they are, such as a table against the living room wall or the teacher's desk in the front of the room near the window. Shorelines are the edges formed where two surfaces meet such as the rug and the floor or the door and the wall. Children are trained to use the back of their hands or the cane to follow a shoreline. The concept of squaring off is also taught. This involves lining oneself up in relation to a particular object to determine its direction or location. A person sitting at a desk may touch the desk to determine that it is directly in front, knowing that the door is therefore at a 45-degree angle to the right. At a street cor-

Orientation:
The use of the remaining senses to establish one's position and relationship to other objects in the environment.

Mobility:
The ability to move from place to place as desired.

Dog guides are allowed in restaurants and other public facilities.

ner the individual feels the edge of the curb with the cane and squares off to cross straight ahead.

The most common travel aid for people with visual impairments is the long cane or prescription cane. The cane is made of aluminum or fiberglass with a shaft about one-half inch in diameter. The cane is individually matched to the user's height, length of stride, and comfort level. The user moves the cane in an arc in front of the body, ensuring a safe space for the next step. Although it may sound easy, only with proper training and practice can a cane be used effectively. The cane gives a great deal of information about the environment but nothing concerning overhanging obstacles.

Perhaps the most famous mobility aid is the dog. Dog guides provide a means of travel and companionship. Several breeds of dogs can be trained, but Shepherds, Golden Retrievers, and Labrador Retrievers are most common. They undergo intensive training before being matched with their master. The dog is taught basic commands such as "sit," "stay," "left," "right," and "forward," and to respond appropriately to curbs, pedestrians, and traffic. The dog is also taught to protect the master from low hanging obstacles. The dog learns to cope with heavy traffic, crowds, and deal with elevators and revolving doors. The dog also learns intelligent disobedience, which means refusing a command like "forward" when it recognizes danger, such as a car approaching.

The person who is blind and the dog train together for about a month and become a team. Only about 1 percent of all blind people actually use a dog. To qualify, a person must be between 16 and 55 years of age (with a few exceptions), be in good health, have good hearing and average intelligence, and be emotionally stable enough to work with a dog and be responsible for its welfare. The person must also be totally blind without any useful vision. Young children may lack the maturity and the elderly the strength to deal with the dog.

Sometimes a sighted companion is the only real option for helping an individual who is blind travel from place to place. Even the person with a long cane or dog guide will prefer to take the arm of a sighted companion occasionally, especially in crowded or demanding circumstances such as a department store, a theater, or a busy intersection. In fact, proper use of a sighted guide is often the first lesson in mobility training. When walking with a sighted person, the person who is blind walks about a half a step behind, firmly holding the sighted person's arm just above the elbow. The person can then feel and easily follow the guide's movements. Some people who are blind encounter well-meaning sighted people who grab their arms and propel them dangerously ahead into the lane of traffic. For this reason, people who are blind are also taught ways of breaking the sighted person's grip.

Orientation and mobility specialists have traditionally worked with children who are blind. Today, some attention is directed at giving children with low vision some training as well (Smith, De l'aunne, & Geruschat, 1992).

Employment

The employment situation for people with visual impairments is deplorable. The unemployment rates reach as high as 70 percent (Sardegna & Paul, 1991).

In a 14-year followup of children who were blind, only 39 percent were employed, which is lower than the employment rate for people who have hearing impairments or who have physical disabilities (Freeman et al., 1991).

The need for improvements in rehabilitation, transition services, and job placement is obvious. Rehabilitation programs provide training and support in many areas of importance, including medical and vocational diagnostic services, home management skills, orientation and mobility skills, transportation, braille instruction, and adaptive aids. Successful transition programs require strong family support, competent teachers who can inspire, training in vocational skills, entry-level work experience, cooperative employers, and cooperation among various agencies responsible for the education of people with visual impairments (Ehrsten & Izzo, 1988).

The Americans with Disabilities Act requires employers to provide certain aids for people with visual impairments. For example, raised letters on elevator control panels and a computer interface for verbalizing what is on the computer screen are required. The adaptations for blind employees are not unusually difficult and may include talking calculators, tape recording notes, or typing notes on a braille typewriter. For some individuals with visual impairments, supportive employment services are also recommended (Hanley-Maxwell et al., 1990).

When asked, people with visual impairments stressed that they were not receiving adequate help in developing job search strategies, in obtaining information on career opportunities, and in buying assistive devices (Wolffe, Roessler, & Schriner, 1992). Many felt their career development needs were not being met. In their longitudinal study, Freeman and colleagues note that they "saw many blind people who clearly could be working (and usually wanted to) but were receiving disability pensions instead. These participants seemed to have the requisite social and intellectual skills plus sufficient motivation" (1989, p. 368). They argue that the high rate of unemployment is the result of inadequate services and poor attitudes on behalf of employers. If people with visual impairments are ever to be fully integrated into society, the unemployment rate must be addressed through preemployment programs that sharpen skills and a change in employer willingness to employ people with visual impairments (Ryder & Kawalec, 1995).

THOUGHT QUESTION

6. *Why is the employment picture so much worse for people with visual impairments than for people with other disabilities?*

Three Considerations

Three important areas stand out clearly in improving the quality of life for people who have visual impairments. First, children with visual impairments must be identified early and their parents given help to learn how to meet their children's special needs. Parents can learn new ways to stimulate their children. They can learn to communicate through words and touch and to deliberately introduce children to their environment instead of waiting for the child to reach out.

Second, individuals with severe visual impairments must learn self-help skills in order to become independent. They are often socially isolated and have parents who are apt to be restrictive. Dependence, passivity, and the lack of initiative may be the result (Jan, Freeman, & Scott, 1977). People are often presented with stories in the media showing how people who are blind lead fully independent lives, but this picture is too optimistic. Not all people with serious visual impairments get the opportunity to learn the skills needed to become independent. The most important skill—the ability to travel—requires mobility training by skilled professionals.

Third, people who are blind or have partial sight require some special consideration in their learning environments. These adaptations are not difficult, but require the teacher to keep them in mind. Unfortunately, many well-meaning teachers eventually forget the special needs of children with visual impairments and slip back into teaching methods that place these children at a disadvantage.

Visual impairment is a serious disability, but adverse developmental and academic effects are not inevitable. With early intervention, appropriate self-help skill training, and classroom aids, people with visual impairments can lead independent and satisfying lives within society.

S U M M A R Y

1. People with severe visual impairments have difficulty constructing a whole out of the parts or learning things incidentally through observation learning.

2. Legal blindness is defined as a visual acuity of 20/200 in the better eye with correction or a vision spanning less than 20 degrees of the visual field. Partial sight involves vision of 20/70 to 20/200 in the better eye with correction. Seventy-five percent of all people who are legally blind have some sight. Educational definitions are based upon visual functioning. People with low vision cannot read a newspaper at a reasonable distance with correction and require special devices to help them read and do school work. A student who is blind must use tactile means to read and learn, although some light perception may be present.

3. Visual impairment is a low-prevalence exceptionality among children. The rate of visual impairment rises sharply in old age. Many children with multiple disabilities have visual impairments.

4. The three most common causes of visual impairment in children are (1) inherited congenital disorders, (2) problems associated with prenatal development including disease and prematurity, and (3) accidents. The most common genetic disorders causing blindness are retinitis pigmentosa and macular degeneration.

5. Visual examinations can be performed even on infants and young children. Infants are tested using a preferential looking test based on the idea that children would rather look at something than a blank card. Variations of the Snellen chart using objects rather than letters or a matching test can be used for young children. Visual-evoked response in which electrodes are attached to the skull, a visual stimulus delivered, and the brain wave pattern in the occipital lobe of the brain analyzed is helpful.

6. Infants born blind show developmental delays. The extent of these delays is variable. Sometimes, parents of children with severe visual impairments do not interact with their children in ways that optimize their development. In addition, these children are not able to read gestures or facial expressions of others making communication more difficult.

7. Some children with serious visual impairments show communication problems. These children do not experience as many social interactions with their peers as sighted children. They show more submissiveness and

dependency than sighted children in their interactions, although the evidence is not unanimous in this regard.

8. Early intervention programs focus on delivering visual stimulation and showing parents how to establish and maintain a stimulating environment, as well as ways to improve the parent-child interaction.

9. Most children with visual impairments are educated in regular classes. Some argue that residential and day schools are still needed to meet the special needs of these students.

10. Many relatively simple classroom adaptations are effective in helping children with visual impairments. These children can participate in physical education and recreation through the use of special adaptations.

11. Children are helped to use their residual vision to the maximum extent possible through magnifiers of various types. Technological improvements such as computers fitted with speech synthesizers and "talking calculators" enable students to do their assignments. Closed circuit television allows for enlargement of print up to 60 times. Large print books are available as well. The optacon is a device that converts print into tactual letter configurations for reading, and the Kurzweil Reading Machine translates print into sound.

12. Braille is a system of touch reading and writing in which raised dots represent the letters of the alphabet. Today, only 12 percent of all people who are blind can read braille. A number of people support a movement to require the teaching of braille to all students with severe visual impairments. The requirement has been fought by others who argue it is not always appropriate.

13. At least four areas require specially trained experts: daily living skills instruction, orientation and mobility training, the teaching of specialized technology and braille, and training of residual vision.

14. The rate of unemployment for the visually impaired population is very high. Better rehabilitation services are needed. The Americans with Disabilities Act, which prohibits discrimination in hiring and requires accommodations, will help people with visual impairments succeed in the workforce.

Orthopedic Disabilities and Health Impairments

ORTHOPEDIC DISABILITIES AND HEALTH IMPAIRMENTS

Transcendence: Good or Bad?
Physical Disabilities and Health Impairments
Orthopedic Disabilities
Physical Disability and the Self-Concept

Classroom Concerns
■ On-Line: The Computer as Lifeline
The Child Whose Health Is Impaired
The Child with a Health Problem in School
■ In the Classroom: Helping Children with
Orthopedic and Health Impairments Succeed
A Hopeful Future
Summary

TRUE-FALSE STATEMENTS

See below for the correct answers.

1. Most children with cerebral palsy do not require special educational services.
2. People with orthopedic disabilities are often called the invisible disabled population, because they go unnoticed by the general population.
3. Little can be done to reduce the severity of paralysis caused by spinal cord injuries.
4. The most common educational problem associated with chronic illness is excessive absence from school.
5. As children mature, compliance with a medical regimen improves.
6. Most people with epilepsy can control their seizures using medication.
7. People with epilepsy are not allowed to drive.
8. Most children diagnosed as having cancer show major depression and other forms of psychopathology years after successful treatment.
9. Pediatric AIDS leads to significant neurological damage and intellectual deterioration.
10. Young children believe many things are contagious that really aren't contagious, such as toothaches.

Answers to True-False Statements
1. False. See page 533.
2. False. See page 534.
3. False. See page 540.
4. True.
5. False. See page 548.
6. True.
7. False. See page 554.
8. False. See page 551.
9. True.
10. True.

Transcendence: Good or Bad?

When New York Jets' defensive end Dennis Byrd was injured in a football game in 1992 and partially paralyzed, millions of sports fans followed his treatment and recovery (Cimini, 1992). Many people, especially in the New York metropolitan area, learned more about spinal cord injuries in the course of a few days than they had learned in their entire lives. Each news conference was heavily covered and the media extensively reported the strategy of the team of doctors working with him, as well as the new and sometimes experimental treatments used. His miraculous recovery, exemplified by his walk onto the playing field to the ovation of the fans before a game the next season, was as emotional a moment as any in sports.

Jim Abbott, a major league baseball player who has pitched for such teams as the California Angels, New York Yankees, and Chicago White Sox wears his glove on his right arm and quickly switches it to his left after he delivers the pitch because he does not have a right hand. He has been a successful pitcher in both leagues.

The media stresses the possibility of overcoming or transcending physical disability more than any other disability. People read about a ten-year-old, David, born with no arms or legs but with only a six inch, three-toed limb and many

The football injury and subsequent recovery of Dennis Byrd led to an increase in public awareness of, and interest in, spinal cord injuries.

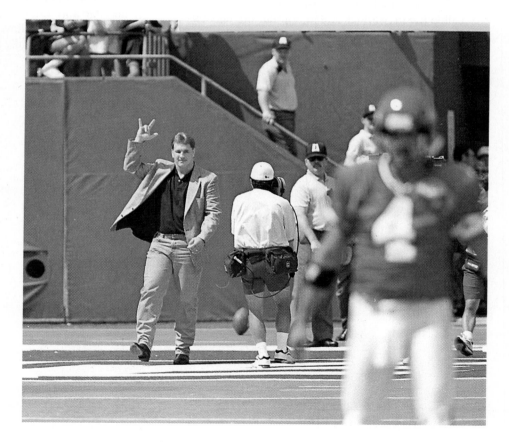

health problems. David is a well-adjusted popular child in his elementary school who makes honor roll and has high ambitions and a loving family (Grant, 1989). In the health area, people read about individuals who have survived cancer in childhood, or historical figures such as Theodore Roosevelt who were quite sick as children, and through hard work and physical training overcame their problems and achieved.

This emphasis on transcending a disability has both a positive and a negative side. The public certainly applauds the accomplishments of those who work so hard to achieve. The publicity accorded the disability helps galvanize public support for research and treatment. On the other hand, many people cannot transcend their disability, which raises the question of whether we are creating unreasonable expectations. Perhaps it would be better if the typical achiever with a disability is depicted in the news media, not just the super-achieving person (National Easter Seal Society, 1991).

Physical Disabilities and Health Impairments

The Individuals with Disabilities Education Act (IDEA) divides the classification of physical and health problems into two categories for the purpose of special education: orthopedic disabilities and health impairments (Mann, 1987a). **Orthopedic disabilities** refer to disabilities caused by physical impairments related to bones, joints, and muscles. According to the IDEA, a child is in need of special education assistance if the child's "orthopedic impairment adversely affects the child's educational performance" (Section 300.5). Conditions leading to such impairments include congenital malformations or the absence of a limb at birth, impairments caused by disease, and impairments from other causes, such as cerebral palsy.

The other general category, called "other health impaired," is defined as children having limited strength, vitality, or alertness, due to chronic or acute health problems such as a heart condition, tuberculosis, rheumatic fever, epilepsy, nephritis, asthma, sickle-cell anemia, hemophilia, or diabetes, which adversely affects a child's educational performance (Section 300.5).

Children with these disorders are not automatically considered to have a disability according to the IDEA. Notice that for both definitions, the disability must adversely affect the child's educational performance. Some conditions by their very nature will almost always permit such a classification. For example, about 95 percent of all children with cerebral palsy require special education. On the other hand, such conditions as asthma and epilepsy may or may not affect the child's educational performance. Unaffected performance is one reason why so many more children have chronic health disorders than are accorded special education services.

Prevalence

Health-related disabilities have a low prevalence. During the 1992–1993 school year, 52,921 children were classified as having orthopedic impairments, and 66,054 children were categorized as having "other health impairments" (U.S.

THOUGHT QUESTION

1. *What effect does publicizing the accomplishments of those people with disabilities who super-achieve have on the public's attitudes toward people with disabilities?*

Orthopedic disabilities: Disabilities caused by impairments to the bones, joints, or muscles.

There are many people with physical impairments who have succeeded, such as Jim Abbott, here shown pitching for the New York Yankees. These people can act as role models, but whether every person with such a disability can transcend it is questionable.

Department of Education, 1994). About 0.12 percent of the general student population have an orthopedic disability and 0.13 percent a health impairment that affects their school performance.

Beware of Generalizations

When discussing groups of children with specific disabilities, one can usually describe aspects of their cognitive and social functioning in general terms, while always reminding oneself of individual differences. This type of generalization is not the case with physical and health impairments. Various conditions differ greatly from each other. For example, the challenges faced by a child with cerebral palsy differ greatly from those faced by a child with epilepsy. The challenges of coping with leukemia are different than the challenges of a child dealing with diabetes. In addition, people with the same disorder may show a variety of symptoms, and with some conditions the severity of the disorder may vary. A child with epilepsy may have an occasional seizure or a number of seizures each day; a child with cerebral palsy may be gifted or have mental retardation. For these reasons, generalizations are difficult to make. Although the general problems of children who have orthopedic disabilities or health impairments can be discussed, generalizations as to their functioning are difficult to defend.

Orthopedic Disabilities

When asked to think of a person with a disability, many people conjure up the mental picture of a person in a wheelchair. One of the most prominent features of people with orthopedic disabilities is their visibility. A person can hardly *not* notice another person using a wheelchair or other mobility aid. Before the individual who has a physical disability has said one word, stereotypes held by the nondisabled individual usually enter the picture.

Orthopedic disabilities can result from a variety of causes. Some disabilities are present at birth (congenital), while others may be due to accidents that occur after birth. The most common causes of orthopedic disability are cerebral palsy, spina bifida, and spinal cord injuries.

Cerebral Palsy

Cerebral palsy:
A condition characterized by a disturbance in voluntary movement caused by damage to the brain.

Cerebral palsy (CP) is a condition characterized by a disturbance in voluntary movement caused by damage to the brain (Jones, 1987). It is actually a catchall term for a variety of disorders that affect the child's movement, balance, and posture (Gersh, 1991a). The damage is not found in the muscles or the spinal cord, but in some region of the brain. Depending upon the severity and location of the damage, other medical problems and educational difficulties may be present (Gersh, 1991a).

The symptoms of cerebral palsy vary widely. Some people with cerebral palsy speak clearly, others do not; some need braces, others wheelchairs for mobility.

The incidence of cerebral palsy is about 1.5–2 cases per 1,000 live births (Pope & Tarlov, 1991). Children with cerebral palsy comprise the largest category of children in programs for people with orthopedic disabilities, representing between 30 and 40 percent of all children in these programs (Jones, 1987).

Cerebral palsy is classified according to the location of the motor problems, type of muscular involvement, and its severity. For example, **monoplegia** involves motor limitations of one extremity, **hemiplegia** two extremities on the same side. **Diplegia** involves motor limitations of the legs with some involvement of the arms. **Paraplegia** describes motor limitations of both legs and **triplegia**, of three extremities. **Double hemiplegia** greatly affects motor limitations of the arms with less effect on the legs. **Quadriplegia** is motor limitations of all four extremities. These categories are also used for other conditions that cause paralysis.

Classifications in terms of muscular involvement include spasticity, athetosis, ataxia, tremor, or rigidity. The most common type of cerebral palsy, occurring in 40–60 percent of all cases, is spasticity. With spasticity, the movements are not smooth, and a loss of voluntary control occurs. It may affect any or all limbs. A flexing of the arms and fingers may be characteristic, or when the legs are involved, a scissoring movement of the legs may be observed (Jones, 1987). The child has difficulties with relaxed, slow movements and may knock over a glass when reaching for it (Cratty, 1986).

Athetoid cerebral palsy is the diagnosis in about 15–20 percent of those affected by the condition. It is characterized by involuntary writhing movements, especially in the fingers and wrist. These children make large, irregular twisting motions and facial grimaces. Problems in controlling the lips and tongue are common. These movements cease during sleep unlike the child with spastic cerebral palsy.

Ataxia is less common. It is characterized by a lack of coordination and a poor sense of balance. The eyes are also uncoordinated and the child exhibits a stumbling, lurching gait (Jones, 1987).

Rigidity and tremor types of cerebral palsy are rare. In rigidity, the muscles are stiff, and a rigid posture is maintained. Convulsions are common. In tremor, one extremity (usually one hand or arm) exhibits involuntary movements. Along with ataxia, these types comprise about 8 percent of all the cases. A mixed type that also occurs is a combination of the other types, with one type predominating, and is found in about 30 percent of all cases (Jones, 1987). As noted, cerebral palsy is also described in terms of its severity: mild, moderate, severe, or profound.

Besides difficulties in mobility and muscle control, children with cerebral palsy may show intellectual difficulties, medical problems such as seizures, and speech difficulties. Professionals have experienced difficulty in measuring the intelligence of children with cerebral palsy because some cannot speak well or manipulate objects. An estimated 25 percent of children with CP show mental retardation (Gersh, 1991b). Other studies have found somewhat higher figures for incidence (Nelson & Ellenberg, 1986). A reduction in the number of children with cerebral palsy considered to have mental retardation may have occurred due to early intervention programs and technological advances, which allow children to better demonstrate their intelligence (Blacklin, 1991).

Many children with cerebral palsy experience seizures. The figures vary from 25–35 percent (Jones, 1987) to 50 percent (Gersh, 1991a). As many as 70 percent have speech impairments (Jones, 1987). Other difficulties include learning prob-

Monoplegia:
Motor limitations of one extremity.

Hemiplegia:
Motor limitations of two extremities on the same side.

Diplegia:
Motor limitations of both legs with some limitation in the arms.

Paraplegia:
Motor limitations of both legs.

Triplegia:
Motor limitations of three extremities.

Double hemiplegia:
Motor limitations of the arms with less limitation of the legs.

Quadriplegia:
Motor limitations of four extremities.

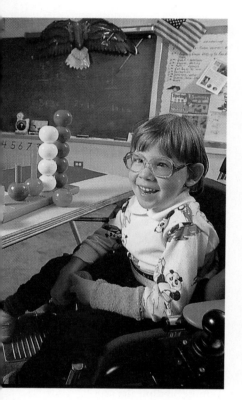

Children with cerebral palsy experience a variety of motor, and sometimes cognitive, difficulties. There are a number of different types of cerebral palsy.

THOUGHT QUESTION

2. *Cerebral palsy is a condition not a disease. Why do advocates for children with cerebral palsy respond so negatively to having it called a disease?*

lems, attention-deficit/hyperactivity disorder, and visual and hearing impairments. Many children with cerebral palsy, then, have multiple disabilities. However, no relationship necessarily exists between the extent of physical impairment and intellectual performance. Some individuals with severe motor involvement may be gifted (Lewis & Doorlag, 1987).

The causes of cerebral palsy are many and varied. They include an illness during the mother's pregnancy, lack of oxygen supply to the brain before or after birth, intrauterine infection, bleeding in the brain, malnutrition, metabolic disorders, maternal use of drugs in pregnancy, exposure to toxic substances, accidents, and lead poisoning. Certain diseases, such as meningitis and encephalitis, may lead to cerebral palsy as well. About 85 percent of all cases are congenital (Jones, 1987). Not too long ago, many professionals believed that difficult labors and too little oxygen at birth or shortly after were responsible for most cases of cerebral palsy. Although some cases (estimated at fewer than 10 percent) are caused in this manner, these factors are no longer thought to be the cause of most cases of cerebral palsy (Fink, 1986). While infants experiencing asphyxia are at risk for both cerebral palsy and mental retardation, only half of these infants ever develop any neurological abnormalities. On the other hand, about two-thirds of the infants who later show cerebral palsy do not show any neurological symptoms when examined a few minutes after birth. Cerebral palsy and other severe neurological problems may more often be caused by infections and biochemical conditions than by birth-related events.

In summary, little is certain about the prenatal and perinatal causes of cerebral palsy (Nelson & Ellenberg, 1986). While severe and prolonged fetal asphyxia is an identifiable cause of cerebral palsy, most children who develop the condition show no signs of asphyxia at birth; and for most children with cerebral palsy, no single cause can be identified (Fink, 1986; National Institute of Child Health and Human Development, 1986). Some experts flatly state that "we probably do not know what causes most cases of cerebral palsy" (Nelson & Ellenberg, 1986, p. 85).

The professional intervention required by children with cerebral palsy provides a good example of the team approach. Many of these children will work with a number of experts in different areas. A physical therapist treats problems with movement and posture, trying to help the child stand with proper body alignment, develop better balance, and improve gross motor coordination. Specially designed equipment is available, such as special supports for the foot or ankle or special seats. An occupational therapist helps the child deal with sensory, motor, and perceptual problems that may interfere with daily living skills, such as feeding and dressing. Receiving such therapy in the first few years is often critical to being able to perform these common everyday tasks on one's own. Because speech impairments are common, the services of a speech-language therapist are also beneficial (Foltz, DeGangi, & Lewis, 1991).

Children with cerebral palsy benefit from early intervention programs (Jarrett, 1991). Most of these programs are centered on the family, with professionals working with parents to achieve specific goals. As the child gets older, the services vary. Many people with cerebral palsy can attain a degree of independence, but may need assistance in certain daily living skills. The services required in the school depend, of course, on the child's individual needs.

Technological improvements help many of these children. Voice-activated computers and various mobility aids that can be engineered to allow maximum control of the environment greatly improve their lives (NICHCY, 1993). Electric wheelchairs, adaptive devices for improving handwriting, special seating and transfer equipment, and telecommunication instruments allow the individual to control the physical environment at home.

One problem in the education of some children with cerebral palsy is their lack of contact with their nondisabled peers. The various therapies required are time-consuming, and children with cerebral palsy spend much time in special centers. Children with cerebral palsy need to play with other children. Engaging in common childhood activities is therapeutic for these children and helps them develop their motor and social skills (Bleck, 1979).

SCENARIO

1 Enid has cerebral palsy. She is a student in your third-grade class and is doing regular class work. Her motor movements are poorly coordinated, but she can walk. Her speech, although somewhat difficult to comprehend, can be understood. She has told her parents that few children talk to her or play with her. What can you do to improve the child's integration into the class? Can her parents do anything to improve the situation?

Spina Bifida

Spina bifida, or open spine, is a defect in the spinal column resulting from the failure of the spine to close during the first month of pregnancy (Spina Bifida Association of America, 1992). It is a defect of the neural tube, an early prenatal structure that evolves into the brain and spinal cord (National Institutes of Health, 1986). There are three types of spina bifida. Spina bifida occulta occurs when an opening in one or more of the vertebrae of the spinal column exists without any damage to the spinal cord. Many Americans, an estimated 20 percent, may have this form of spina bifida, but because any symptoms are rare, few even know they have it (Moore & Persaud, 1993). Meningocele spina bifida occurs when the meninges or protective covering around the cord forms a sac called the meningocele and pushes through the opening in the vertebrae. Since the spinal cord remains intact, this defect can usually be repaired with little or no permanent damage. The third and most severe type of spina bifida is called myelomeningocele in which a portion of the spinal cord itself protrudes through the back. In some cases tissues and nerves are exposed, while in other cases the sacs are covered with skin. Only 4 percent of all children with difficulties due to spina bifida have the meningocele form, while 96 percent have the myelomeningocele form. Often the terms *spina bifida* and *myelomeningocele* are used interchangeably (NICHCY, 1991).

In the United States, 1 to 2 out of every 1,000 newborns have spina bifida (USDHHS, 1986). Spina bifida can be detected before birth through ultrasound imaging and by the test for alpha-fetoprotein (AFP), a chemical in the blood of pregnant women (Clark & DeVore, 1989). The causes of spina bifida remain a mystery, although both genetic and environmental factors may interact to cause the condition.

Spina bifida:
A defect in the spinal column resulting from the failure of the spine to close during the first month of pregnancy and leading to paralysis, loss of sensation in the limbs, and bowel and bladder incontinence due to nerve damage.

Physical and occupational therapists help people maximize their physical abilities.

Spina bifida may result in paralysis, loss of sensation in the limbs, and bowel and bladder incontinence due to nerve damage. In addition, hydrocephalus (an accumulation of fluid in the brain) occurs in 70–90 percent of all cases (March of Dimes, 1992). This condition is often treated by placing a functional shunt in the brain, which drains the fluid off and prevents brain damage.

Most people have never heard of spina bifida, because 25 years ago, more than 90 percent of all children born with spina bifida died within a few years of birth. Those children who survived often had severe mental retardation and were institutionalized. Today, 90 percent of all children with spina bifida live an average life span and most score in the average range of intelligence (Spina Bifida Association of America, 1992b). Medical advances in surgery and various mechanical aids for mobility have improved the lives of these children greatly, and most are educated in regular classrooms.

Children with spina bifida may require a procedure called clean intermittent catheterization (CIC) in order to attend school. In the 1984 case of *Irving Independent School District v. Tatro*, the Supreme Court ruled that catheterization was considered a related health service covered under the law. In the case, an eight-year-old girl born with spina bifida required catheterization every 3 or 4 hours. The Court stated that it was the school's responsibility to provide this service (Rothstein, 1995). CIC is a relatively simple procedure that can be performed by a nonmedical person with a little training or the school nurse. Many older children can perform it themselves, but younger children need help.

The presence of a shunt may lead to problems for students with spina bifida in the regular classroom. The shunt, which drains fluid from the brain, is not visible, but if it malfunctions, the teacher may be the first person to notice since a shunt malfunction leads to changes in the child's behavior and physical functioning. The changes differ with the child. Some experience headaches, some a pain in the neck area. Sometimes these changes involve loss of appetite, nausea, and drowsiness. Some children with spina bifida who have had hydrocephalus may experience difficulties in attention, language, reading, and mathematics (NICHCY, 1991). Children with spina bifida may also show motor or sensory problems. Some children require braces, others crutches, and still others a wheelchair for mobility. Sensory deficits can be serious; for instance, these children may not realize they are developing frostbite to their toes in cold weather or suffering a floor burn. The difficulties caused by the disorder may vary from mild to severe.

Many children with spina bifida can do well in school since most have average intelligence. Their special physical needs can be accommodated, allowing many of them to experience considerable academic success.

Spinal Cord Injuries

The type of injury Dennis Byrd of the Jets received was a spinal cord injury. About 225,000 people in the United States have experienced spinal cord injuries. Approximately 7,700 new cases occur each year (NARIC, 1990). The result of many spinal cord injuries is paralysis. The location of the injury on the spinal cord determines the severity of the impairment. About one-half of spinal cord injuries result in quadriplegia. People with quadriplegia require assistance with personal care routines. But with the aid of computers and other technological innovations, they are able to communicate with the outside world. One gunshot victim who can only move his eyes and mouth operates a computer that responds to voice

Much specially designed equipment is available for children with physical disabilities.

commands. Using electronic mail he corresponds with people all over the world. The computer brings him news stories and allows him to play games. He also works as a programmer for a governmental agency (Quittner, 1994). About 95 percent of all people with paraplegia, on the other hand, achieve independence in self-care activities and mobility in a wheelchair.

Spinal cord injuries are characterized by extent of the neurological injury. Complete injuries result in complete loss of sensation and motor control. People with incomplete lesions retain some sensation and motor control with the degree of impairment depending upon the extent of the lesion. About one-half the spinal cord injuries are complete lesions.

Older adolescents and young adults are at the highest risk for spinal cord injuries (Walker, 1991). Motor vehicle crashes account for 30–60 percent of all spinal cord injuries. Other important causes are firearms and sport injuries. Injuries sustained during diving are the cause of two-thirds of the sports-related spinal cord injuries.

One way to reduce spinal cord accidents is to protect passengers in cars more fully, reduce traffic accidents through more rigorous enforcement of drunk driving laws, and stress driving safety. Still another method is to require helmets while bicycling. A suggestion for the required inclusion of a safety helmet with each new bicycle purchased has even been made (Dannenberg & Vernick, 1993). Reducing the availability of firearms and improving sports equipment will also reduce such injuries.

For many years, the field of spinal cord injuries attracted little research. Since neurons in the central nervous system do not regenerate, the erroneous assumption was that little could be done for these individuals. However, two areas of great interest are the research breakthroughs in possible nerve regeneration and the discovery of medications that seem to reduce injury right after the accident (Walker, 1991).

Some evidence shows that nerves in the central nervous system that do not regenerate under usual circumstances may have the latent ability to do so if chemicals that stimulate this activity are present (Barinaga, 1991). In addition, in the future, experts in the field hope that grafting techniques may help regenerate nerves and tissue (Zinman, 1990). The use of new medications which minimize paralysis in some patients, reduce damage, and add muscle strength and sensation if administered within hours of the injury offer new hope to people with spinal cord injuries (Travis, 1992).

On a different level, the need for rehabilitation is obvious. Try to imagine what it would be like to have to learn how to feed yourself all over again or how to dress or bathe. Most people who experience a spinal cord injury must work very hard to regain the ability to perform daily functions and activities we all take for granted. Even though frustration at the beginning of rehabilitation is common, many individuals with spinal cord injury lead active lives.

SCENARIO

2

Jason uses a wheelchair for mobility. He is looking forward to being in a regular school and classroom. Specifically, what steps should be taken by the school and the teacher to ensure that the school is accessible?

Physical Disability and the Self-Concept

How well do people with physical disabilities adjust? How do they see themselves? The first question is easily answered. Evidence indicates that children with orthopedic disabilities do not differ qualitatively in adjustment from other children (Lewandowski & Cruickshank 1980). They also do not show significant emotional maladjustment as a group.

But what of their self-concept? Studies show that children with orthopedic disabilities usually describe themselves realistically and positively. Their chief problem lies in the field of interpersonal relations, where the prejudice and discomfort of others—sometimes combined with their own lack of experience and social involvement—can lead to difficulties.

Problems in self-concept or interpersonal relations do not exclusively depend upon the type and severity of the person's disability. Certainly, the loss of both legs is more significant than the loss of one's little finger. But the closeness of the physical deficit to the core of the individual's personality is a vital factor (Kaplan, 1986). People who define themselves in terms of playing the piano will find the loss of a finger catastrophic. A person who leads an athletic life may find the need to use a brace most distressing. The effect of a disability on a person's self-concept also depends on the feedback the person receives from others. If the individual is labeled "handicapped" and receives feedback accordingly, personal strengths and abilities may never be developed.

Accessibility

The most significant advancement for people who have orthopedic disabilities is the reduction of architectural barriers for those who use wheelchairs. Many public establishments have facilities that are accessible for people who use mobility aids; however, one cannot truly appreciate the frustration of people with orthopedic disabilities caused by inaccessibility unless one has experienced such barriers. People rarely think about a curb or a step, yet these obstacles may be insurmountable to a person using a wheelchair.

To appreciate the frustration of architectural barriers, one student used a wheelchair for a day. She wheeled herself from her apartment in the city to some stores a few blocks away. She noticed that people changed expressions when they approached her, and she had to crane her neck to look at the people passing in the street. The doors of some of the stores were too narrow, and the aisles were difficult to wheel through. She even encountered difficulty with slanted curbs. One curb was so difficult that she kept sliding down. The car in the nearest lane, filled with teenagers, waited impatiently for her to negotiate it. She got tired of trying, and to their surprise got up out of the wheelchair and pushed it up on the curb. Their expressions, as you can imagine, were of astonishment (Kaplan, 1986).

Section 504 of the Rehabilitation Act of 1973 requires that programs be accessible to students with disabilities (West et al., 1993). All new public buildings are built to be accessible, and many older ones have been modified to allow access for people with physical disabilities. The Americans with Disabilities Act (ADA) will certainly improve access to facilities by requiring changes to make them accessible. The ADA incorporates Section 504 requirements and extends them into the private sector.

Making the world and especially the school accessible is an important concern. Special parking for people with disabilities allows them easier use of the facilities. Within the facility, doors need to be wide enough to allow passage of a wheelchair, wheelchair ramps need to be available, and toilet cubicles should be built wide enough to accommodate people with wheelchairs and contain handrails placed for easy mobility from wheelchair to toilet. Another recommended change is non-slip floor coverings for people using crutches.

The key concept for improving the lives of people with physical disabilities is accessibility. Removing architectural barriers is an important step toward allowing people with physical disabilities to participate in everyday activities.

Classroom Concerns

Some children with orthopedic disabilities will require a different curriculum, especially if they also experience cognitive problems. However, many do not require content change if they have average intellectual ability (Kaplan, 1990). Teachers are sometimes concerned about the inclusion of children with physical disabilities. They are troubled about their responsibilities, about having to spend more time with children with orthopedic disabilities and of being overloaded by administrative duties and paperwork. Teachers working with younger students are concerned about any medical responsibilities they may have. These concerns decrease when teachers have experience teaching these children (Frith & Edwards, 1981).

Teachers do spend more time with children with orthopedic disabilities, but not much more. Brulle and colleagues (1983) investigated the time spent with students with physical disabilities by high school teachers in a suburban Chicago high school. These children had a variety of disabilities including mild hemiplegic cerebral palsy, severe quadriplegic cerebral palsy, and muscular dystrophy. Teachers did spend more time assisting these students, about 1.5 minutes per child per 50-minute period. Some children required more time, up to 5 minutes, while others less. This extra time requirement does not seem excessive, but the authors caution that placing two, three, or four students with such disabilities in the same classroom may not be advisable because the extra time multiplied rapidly. In addition, the equipment used by the students in these schools promoted maximum independence. Other programs may not offer the necessary resources, such as sophisticated computers and voice synthesizers.

Assistive Equipment

The role of technology in improving the lives of children with physical disabilities is an important one. Assistive technology is specialized hardware and software used by students with disabilities to increase their ability to participate in learning and daily living and to function as independently as possible. Many types of assistive equipment are available. For example, some mechanical and nonmechanical toys have been modified so that children with motor difficulties can use them.

Children with disabilities who require a wheelchair for mobility should not be isolated from their classmates.

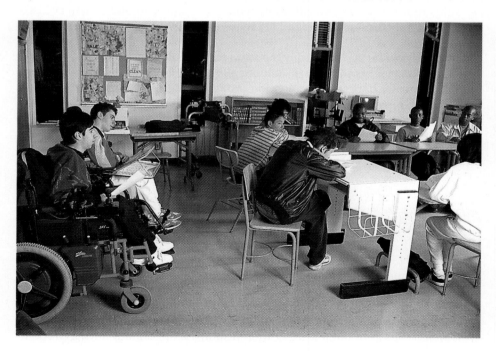

Powered and nonpowered wheelchairs and motorized scooters improve mobility. Communication aids include mechanical and often electronic communication devices that increase a student's ability to use language and participate in daily activities. Environmental controls can be altered to allow people with limited motor abilities to turn on lights, use the television, play video games, and adjust the thermostat. Last, personal computers have revolutionized the area of learning and daily living. These computers can be used for recreation, communication, vocational training, and other activities. Alternative keyboards and keyguards are available so that a person with limited motor skill may input information. Computers may also be voice controlled (Center for Special Education Technology, 1991).

The regular classroom teacher may communicate with parents and perhaps the physical therapist to better understand how the adaptive equipment is best used. The teacher is in an excellent position to monitor the child's use of assistive technology and communicate to parents any difficulties the child may be having.

The Computer as Lifeline

David's life was forever changed after an automobile accident. The 17-year-old high school junior had some limited use of his arms and hands, but his movements were not smooth and motor control was difficult. He required a wheelchair for mobility and a van to travel to and from school. Often, he could not go where he wanted because he was dependent on others for transportation. He would find himself frustrated and isolated. He was bored, sometimes depressed, and did not feel in control of his life. He experienced a dependence on others that he found difficult to accept.

Some adaptations allowed him to pursue some interests. His motorized wheelchair gave him access to many places, and he could turn appliances on and off using a number of environmental controls specially suited to his needs. However, the feelings of isolation remained.

The major change in David's life came when he was introduced to Internet by a teacher in his high school. Internet is a collection of many smaller networks which can all exchange information. It offers information and services to hundreds of thousands of computer users (Pliskin,

1995). The subscriber accesses the system and opens a new world of information. David has learned of other students who have his disability and shares information with them. He leaves messages on an E-mail system and sometimes receives 20 messages a day. He uses the system to access job opportunities for the summer. He also uses the system for leisure activities and tracks his favorite teams as well as reading announcements of forthcoming activities in a number of areas. David also uses the computer for classroom assignments. David calls his computer his emotional lifeline.

Technology has certainly changed the lives of people with physical disabilities, allowing them to perform daily activities they would not be able to do without help. Some helpful adaptations are relatively simple. For example, David uses a telephone with a large keypad because his motor control is not very good. Other people with physical disabilities may require different adaptations. For example, combs with long handles are available for people with limited arm movements and a special cuff for people who have difficulty holding forks or spoons. Velcro fasteners are easier to use than buttons or zippers and several companies offer clothing adapted to the needs of people using wheelchairs.

Many daily activities that people without physical disabilities take for granted—such as locking doors, turning on lights, and opening doors—can be difficult. Interfaces that allow a switch to be thrown turning on a light, the door to be opened by pressing a button, or a page of a book to be turned at the touch of a pad allow more independence for people with physical disabilities (Esposito & Campbell, 1993). David uses a master environmental control unit, which allows him to operate a number of electronic appliances. These control units and input devices differ in the types of signals they use (Lewis, 1993). Most people are familiar with them. Radio signals are used to control automatic garage door openers, and infrared signals control various functions on the television and the video cassette recorder. A controller of some type is available for most home appliances.

Some input strategy is needed as well. When using the television remote control, people press their selection on a keypad. Some people with physical disabilities can do the same, but other people may need alternative methods that are readily available. Some people may require larger keys (as David does), while others may need to use special switches designed to meet their individual needs. The type and location of the switch depends upon the individual's needs and capabilities. For example, a switch may be designed to take advantage of just about any consistent, voluntary movement an individual can make. An individual may use almost any part of the body to turn a pressure sensitive switch on and off or a head pointer may be adapted. Switches may be mounted to be used with the arm, head, or leg (Esposito & Campbell, 1993). Voice-activated systems are also available today, which allow the individual to use verbal commands to activate

control devices. Some systems allow for control of many devices using voice commands and one master controller. The ability to control these appliances means increased independence.

Access to a computer also increases independence for many people with physical disabilities. The first step in accessing a computer is to design a work area that allows for the best use of the computer. Modifications of the environment are necessary. Some of these adaptations include placing computers on tables that can be adjusted for height, mounting the monitor on the adjustable arm, and accommodating a wheelchair.

In order to use the computer, the individual must be able to turn it on, insert and remove discs, and input information into the computer. Devices are available that allow the individual to switch the computer on using a variety of different switching devices and other switches may work peripherals such as printers. Special devices are also available for loading and removing disks.

After the computer is turned on, some way to input information is required. The primary obstacle for children with physical disabilities is often the keyboard (Esposito & Campbell, 1993). Some people with physical disabilities cannot use the standard keyboard. For instance, an individual may not have control of the hands and fingers for keyboarding. A number of adapted keyboards are available. Two hardware devices commonly used are keyguards and keylocks. Keyguards are placed on top of the standard keyboard to increase the separation between keys, which prevents them from being activated by extraneous motion. Keylocks hold down one key while another is pressed to access some function, which is a difficult task for some people (Lewis, 1993). Some software is available that allows a key to be depressed for a longer period of time before being accepted by the computer. Many programs use the mouse to access functions and the speed and sensitivity of the mouse can also be modified.

For some people, the standard keyboard is inappropriate, but special provisions can be made to allow access. For example, an array of commands may appear on the bottom of the screen and the user may make selections by pressing the switch when the desired function is highlighted. Some pointing devices are cordless. The user may wear a small reflector on the headband, hat, or headset. As the individual moves the head a sensor points to a function menu and activates the desired command. Head movements can also control the cursor on the screen (Esposito & Campbell, 1993).

Voice input is available and becoming more sophisticated (Bristow et al., 1990). Voice input devices do not require a keyboard. A person speaks into a recognition device that transforms the verbalizations into information that the computer can understand. Each user must "train" the unit to recognize the voice. One of the most sophisticated systems uses a speech recognition board and software capable of understanding 25,000 common words, with room for adding 5,000 words of special need. A backup dictionary of 80,000 words is also available.

Training is easy. The user speaks a word into the microphone and the computer displays a list of likely words on the monitor, highlighting one. If the word is correct, the user continues to speak. If it is not the user selects another word on the list or dictates the correct spelling. The speaker must pause about one-quarter second between words. Many users can attain a speed of 30 to 40 words a minute (Lewis, 1993).

The computer has opened up new vistas for people with physical disabilities. For instance, one individual with muscular dystrophy and severe limitations in muscular movement earns a living by doing word processing and page layouts. He uses a specially adapted computer and joystick and types with one finger by pointing to letters on the screen. He runs his desktop publishing business from his apartment and uses a modem to transmit designs and layouts to a printing company (Sussman, 1994). Computer-assisted drafting and computer-assisted manufacturing use a mouse to move the cursor, which is possible for many people with physical disabilities. When it is not, other systems for moving the cursor, some described previously, are available.

Many programs including word processing, bookkeeping, and accounting can be accessed through voice input. One interesting writing program uses a feature called predictive spelling. When a person using a mouse begins to select letters from a display, the program guesses which word the writer might be forming and displays the five most likely words in a small window for the individual to choose. The program also adds punctuation and spacing where appropriate.

David uses his computer for recreation as well. Computer games of strategy, memory, and logic are favorites. Some programs allow children with physical disabilities to be creative. For instance, they may write music on the computer and generate their own compositions. The music may be played back, edited, and saved. People with physical disabilities often find that the use of the computer can provide a sense of autonomy and improve the individual's self-concept (Rushakoff & Lombardino, 1983).

The computer can be liberating. The Americans with Disabilities Act requires that reasonable accommodations be made to allow people to work, which may include working part or all of the day in the home for some people (Quittner, 1994). Although the potential for the computer and other electronic aids to help people with physical impairments live a more fulfilling life is great, some warn that isolation could again occur (see Quittner, 1994). After all, technology could become a tool to isolate the individual with a disability from the place of employment and the opportunity to meet other people. For some people who really cannot leave the house easily because they are on respirators or find movement very difficult, working at home is a blessing. But the number of such individuals is quite small (Sussman, 1994). Another concern is the cost of such adaptations, which can run quite high. Not every individual can afford an electronic page tuner or master controller.

Technological advances will continue and will allow people with physical disabilities to live more satisfying lives. People with physical disabilities who use computers find a world of social, academic, recreational, and vocational opportunities opening up to them. The computer provides the opportunity for them to remain productive and involved in the world around them.

Classroom Adaptations

Often, the child's motor limitations mean that activities must be specifically adapted to the child's abilities. Children with limited motor skills can do surprisingly well in a variety of activities if they have assistive technology and adapted materials. For example, a child with quadriplegia can draw or paint with a brush or pen in the mouth or on a head band. Games such as brain teasers, riddles, and other mental games can be played. Some board games, where the child can affect action by verbal means, are also effective.

In the area of language, audiovisual aids and electric page-turning devices are useful. Keeping rhythm to music with head movements, listening, and singing are possibilities (Association for the Care of Children's Health, 1988). Specific activity adaptations can be used for children with virtually every type of motor limitation.

Students with physical disabilities can be integrated into the regular classroom, but sometimes younger nondisabled students experience some apprehension and avoid them. In order to reduce this apprehension, a teacher may give students in the class information about the disabled student's condition, stressing that these students are no different except that they cannot walk, run, or perform some other purposeful motor acts. Sometimes films are available for this purpose. A teacher also needs to give attention to social integration. Again, the buddy system and group or cooperative learning strategies may help.

Beyond High School

People with orthopedic disabilities often rate their college experience as positive. In one study, West and colleagues (1993) surveyed college and university students with disabilities to determine level of satisfaction with accessibility, special services, and accommodations. Students expressed general satisfaction with their education and the services, but most had encountered barriers. The most frequent and frustrating barriers were a lack of understanding and cooperation from administrators, faculty, staff, and other students; a lack of adaptive technology aids; and some inaccessibility in buildings and grounds. However, many students were encouraged by the improvements made during their stay at the school.

Although many people with orthopedic disabilities complete college and enter the labor market, discrimination and misunderstanding are frequent occur-

THOUGHT QUESTION

3. How could a teacher deal with her third graders who are afraid of a child with some type of disability?

rences. Many people who are successful rely on personal networking, emphasize the benefit of early vocational rehabilitation and family support, and consider personal determination very important. Availability of transportation is also vital as is accessibility (Liebert, Lutsky, & Gottlieb, 1990). Still, many people with such disabilities who can work do not, and the unemployment rate is about twice as high as in the general population. Obviously, the areas of vocational preparation and reducing discrimination have room for much improvement.

The Child Whose Health Is Impaired

Many illnesses and health-related conditions can impair a child's functioning; fortunately most of these illnesses are rare. The overwhelming majority of children in developed countries do not have disabling physical illnesses. Of course, children, especially young children, are sometimes ill. Most experience **acute illnesses**, which make a sudden appearance, run their course, and disappear with complete recovery in a relatively short time. **Chronic illnesses,** such as diabetes and cancer, are ongoing in nature (Kaplan, 1993). Both acute and chronic illnesses are covered under the "other health related" category in IDEA, but most serious health-related problems arise from chronic diseases or conditions. In this section, a representative group of illnesses and conditions will be discussed, including asthma, diabetes mellitus, childhood cancer, epilepsy, traumatic brain injury, muscular dystrophy, sickle-cell anemia, cystic fibrosis, and AIDS.

Acute illness:
An illness with a sudden onset, which runs its course and usually results in a complete recovery.

Chronic illness:
Illnesses that are continuous or recurring and of long duration.

Common Problems of Children with Health Impairments

Considering the number of illnesses and the variability in symptoms, one must ask what these children could possibly have in common. Although generalizations concerning their functioning are difficult to make, these children share many common experiences. Their illnesses affect many aspects of their lives and the effects cannot be understood solely in terms of pain, hospitalization, and some daily medical regimen. Having a chronic illness such as diabetes or asthma may have profound psychological and social effects on children's lives. Although individual differences are important, and milder forms of diseases produce fewer problems than more severe forms, some of the major difficulties are discussed in the following sections.

Absence from School

Children with chronic illnesses are often absent from school, which is the most frequent problem from an educational point of view. A relationship generally exists between high rates of absence and low academic performance (Kovacs, Goldston, & Iyengar, 1992). These absences may occur once or twice a week, or the child may be absent for a week at a time. In either instance, the child may fall behind and, even with some tutoring, may be unable to catch up. In addition, such absences do not allow for the usual development of social relationships within the school and community.

Time Spent Alone

Many children with chronic illnesses spend a greater portion of their time alone (Wicks-Nelson & Israel, 1991). Some of this time is due to the illness itself, and some of it is because of a fear of reoccurrence of the health crisis.

Reduced Physical Activity

Children with chronic illnesses sometimes have limitations on their physical activities (Midence, 1994). For example, a child with asthma may not be allowed to participate in activities that include running or physical exertion, which may contribute to limited social development.

Psychological Unpredictability

Chronic conditions often flare up unpredictably. The child seems to be doing well and suddenly an attack or some manifestation of the illness occurs. This unpredictability can cause much anxiety and stress. Sometimes children with chronic illnesses develop an external locus of control, believing that they are not in control of the situation.

Being Different

Children with chronic health impairments often feel different from other children. Their lives may necessarily focus on their medical treatment. One teenager found that her day focused on decisions related to her treatment for cancer and, despite the interest of her friends, she felt separate and out of the mainstream.

Uncertain Long-Term Outcome

Often uncertainty is the only prognosis about the long-term outcome for these diseases. Children may not really know what the nature of their future may be or if they even have a future.

Everyday Medical Regimen

Many children with health problems are reminded of their disease each day in their regular medical regimen, which may include medication, medical monitoring, and various other strategies. These necessary treatments are constant reminders of their illness and sometimes interrupt their plans, even though they are often efficiently performed. In addition, children are frequently not compliant with the regimen. Compliance with a medical regimen is a greater problem among adolescents than younger children because parents have more responsibility with the routines of younger children (Tebbi et al., 1988). Adolescents, with their great need to fit in and not to be different, may let their medical regimen slip. Compliance is enhanced when both the child and parent clearly understand who is responsible for administering medications and when the responsible individual understands exactly what is necessary. Counseling may be required in cases where noncompliance is a continuing problem.

School nurses are specifically identified by many states as the agents responsible for dispensing medication and providing medical services for children who require them. Sometimes, paraprofessionals may be trained to do so, but they are legally under the direction of the school nurse (Sandberg, 1993). The New York state guidelines for dispensing medication are found in Table 14.1.

THOUGHT QUESTION

4. Why is compliance with a required medical regimen such a frequent problem among teenagers?

Effects of Medication

Often, the medications required for the child with a chronic disease may have unpleasant side effects. These side effects may involve cognitive and behavioral changes.

Asthma

Asthma is a common childhood chronic disorder affecting about 38 of every 1,000 children. It affects as many as 15 percent of boys and 11 percent of girls by age 15 years (Kohen, 1987). An estimated 2.7 million children and adolescents below the age of 18 years have asthma (Smith, 1992). Asthma is a disorder that involves the hyperresponsiveness of the upper respiratory tract to varying stimuli, resulting in the narrowing of air passages and problems with air exchange (Wicks-Nelson & Israel, 1991). The symptoms are attacks of wheezing and shortness of breath.

Some children with milder forms do outgrow the problem, but those with more severe problems often carry some respiratory problems into adulthood. A person can die from asthma, but the mortality rate has decreased over the past 20 years due to better treatment and preventive therapy (Kohen, 1987).

Asthma:
A disorder involving hyperresponsiveness of the upper respiratory tract to varying stimuli, resulting in the narrowing of air passages and problems with air exchange and causing difficulty in breathing.

TABLE 14.1   **Guidelines for Administering Medication**

(In February 1992, the New York State Education Department changed guidelines for administering medication in schools. Following is a summary of some procedures. For complete guidelines, contact your school district office.)

Medication must be administered by, or be under the supervision of, school nursing personnel.

If a person other than a licensed school health care professional has been delegated the task and is administering the medication, that person should:

    Be under the supervision of the school nursing personnel in the school setting

    Be able and willing to administer and record medications properly

    Be able to observe, evaluate, and report the student's reaction to medication, including expected or adverse reactions

    Have the proper training annually in the procedure

    Have the training documented, signed, filed, and reviewed periodically

A written statement from the parent or guardian requesting administration of medication in school as ordered by the licensed prescriber is required.

The parent or guardian must assume responsibility for having medication delivered directly to the health office in a properly labeled original container.

Medication is to be stored in a locked cabinet or separate locked drawer in the health office.

Medication requiring refrigeration should be refrigerated in a secure area.

New York Teacher, September 6, 1993.

The cause of asthma is not definitively known, but some ideas have surfaced (Wicks-Nelson & Israel, 1991). It may begin when some agent produces a hypersensitivity of the air passages. Once this hypersensitivity occurs, the child then begins to respond to a variety of irritants in the same manner. Anxiety, itself, may accompany this reaction, and fear of possible attacks may contribute to the probability and intensity of the attack. The underlying reason for the original hypersensitivity may never be known, but the secondary set of factors or triggers are often well established. Almost anything can be an irritant; however, the most common irritants are dust, humidity, exercise, and certain foods. Repeated respiratory infection may also play a role in the development of asthma. Respiratory infections can set off an attack or increase the severity of an attack.

Major improvements in medical therapy have led to better management of asthma. About 70 percent of the adults who have had asthma as children and received treatment are considerably improved or even free from attacks 20 years later (Wicks-Nelson & Israel, 1991). The treatment includes medication, avoidance of infection, avoidance of irritants, and better emergency care. Psychological help centers on reducing anxiety and taking control of the situation. To reduce anxiety, people with asthma may use relaxation and mental imagery. A child may learn to relax and imagine being on the beach, comfortably swimming and breathing easily. In one case, a child was often awakened at night with coughing spells. She became frightened, and lost sleep and the anxiety that she experienced affected her performance in school. After being taught relaxation and mental imagery techniques, her condition improved greatly.

Teachers may frequently find that children with asthma present two major challenges. First, eliminating or reducing exposure to known irritants in the classroom is sometimes possible. Second, absences can become a problem. If the

Children with asthma experience shortness of breath. The avoidance of infection and irritants is recommended.

child's asthma is well controlled, absence should not be much of a factor (Wilmott, Kolski, & Burg, 1984). However, if it is not well controlled, then absences will be relatively frequent. In addition, a conference with a doctor and parent should be held so that the teacher knows what to do if the child experiences an asthma attack.

SCENARIO

3 Janine has asthma. A few times in the recent past, she required emergency help, but Janine can handle most problems herself. The problem is that she is kept out of school by her well-meaning parents if she shows any difficulty such as a slight cold or does not feel perfectly healthy. Her attendance is poor; she has been absent at least one day almost every week of the semester. Sometimes she is out for more than a day each week. Her medical records do not show the need for such care, but the parents are frightened of a minor problem turning into a major or life-threatening asthmatic attack. Janine is falling further behind. What, if anything, should the school do in such a situation?

Diabetes Mellitus

Diabetes mellitus is a chronic metabolic disorder in which the body cannot properly convert glucose into usable energy (Bishop, 1994). The pancreas secretes insulin which plays an important part in this process. When insulin is not produced or not enough insulin is produced, diabetes is the result. Two types of diabetes exist (Whitney, Cataldo, & Rolfes, 1994). Type 1—often called juvenile diabetes or insulin-dependent diabetes—begins in childhood or adolescence and is caused by a complete inability of the pancreas to secrete insulin. It affects 1.8 of every 1,000 children (Wicks-Nelson & Israel, 1991). Type 2 diabetes, sometimes called late onset, involves insufficient insulin production or the inability of the body to use the insulin secreted and is commonly found in older people (Sarafino, 1994).

> **Diabetes mellitus:**
> A chronic metabolic disease characterized by poor blood glucose regulation and utilization, caused by insufficient or relatively ineffective insulin.

The symptoms of diabetes are great thirst, increased urination, and fatigue. If not controlled, a child can go into a coma and die. The actual cause of the disorder is not known. Some authorities believe it has a genetic base, others that it is partially caused by a virus, and still others believe it is an autoimmune disease.

To truly appreciate the challenges of managing the disease, some understanding of the medical regimen is required. This regimen includes regular injections of insulin, regular blood testing, avoidance of sugar, watching what one eats, taking special care of injuries, and many other precautions. People with the disease must be aware of their subjective feelings when their bodies have too little sugar due to too much insulin (hypoglycemia) or too much sugar due to insufficient insulin, called ketoacidosis (Lyen, 1984). Ketoacidosis may also be caused by infection or emotional stress.

Many children with chronic disorders can look forward to periods in which they are symptom-free and may be able to modify their medical regimen. This re-

This adolescent is performing her own blood glucose test, the results of which will affect the choices she makes during the day. Unfortunately, compliance with medical procedures is often wanting in adolescents with health problems.

prieve is not the case for children with diabetes who must monitor their insulin levels and take injections daily. Sometimes children exhibit major compliance problems with doctors' instructions. Young children will probably not be able to handle the regular testing and injections by themselves, but adolescents may be able to do so. Sometimes inaccuracy in reading the test results occurs. Unfortunately, some adolescents falsify the results of their blood testing because they do not want to change their behaviors or routines. Compliance is not an all-or-nothing situation. An adolescent may adhere to one particular part of the regimen and not another (Johnson et al., 1986). Everyone concerned needs to learn about the disease and the importance of the regimen to control it. In addition, counseling may help in dealing with the feelings that underlie the question of "why me?" and the tendency to minimize the seriousness of the disease and to rationalize the lack of compliance.

Children with diabetes have an average range of intelligence, but often show specific skill deficits (Hagen et al., 1990). The earlier the onset of the disease the more difficulties experienced in school. Some children with diabetes do not use efficient strategies to organize and recall information (Hagen et al., 1990). In addition, a small but progressive decline may be apparent in school grades and verbal intelligence during the school years, while an increase in nonverbal intelligence is the rule (Kovacs, Goldston, & Iyengar, 1992). More children with diabetes are poor readers than children without diabetes. At the same time, children who have poor control of their diabetes are more likely to be poor readers than children with good control of their disorder (Gath, Smith & Baum, 1980). Perhaps the self-control necessary to follow the regimen is good training for school. Whether these difficulties are due to the diabetes itself, the rate of absenteeism, or some other factor is unknown.

Children with diabetes do not show any more adjustment problems in school than children without diabetes. At home, though, fewer are considered well adjusted by their mothers, and more stress may be evident in the home (Lyen, 1984).

Teachers should be sensitive to signs that the child is hypoglycemic or going into ketoacidosis. Some symptoms of hypoglycemia include inattentiveness, sweating, dizziness, and drowsiness. A child with diabetes usually carries some form of sugar to counter a hypoglycemic episode. Signs of ketoacidosis include excessive thirst, nausea, and abdominal pains (Lyen, 1984). One last point is important. Although teachers do not have the sole responsibility to look after the

SCENARIO

4 John is a popular 15-year-old with a case of juvenile diabetes. He has had the disease for some time and has been taught everything necessary about the management of his condition. Yet, in recent months his compliance with the medical regimen has been poor, and his parents are very concerned. His attitude toward both diet and blood testing is casual, and he is not taking care of himself. His schoolwork seems to be suffering as well. If his parents asked you for advice, what would you tell them?

child's diet, teachers should have some idea of dietary restrictions so they do not give the child a wrong food and they can encourage the child to keep the diet.

Epilepsy and Other Seizure Disorders

Epilepsy is a condition in which recurrent electrical discharges in the brain disturb the usual functioning of the nervous system and produce seizures (Dreifuss, 1988). These seizures may involve a loss of consciousness and/or temporary changes in behavior depending upon which area of the brain is affected by the electrical discharges.

There are many types of seizures. *Generalized seizures* are those in which the entire brain is affected and a loss of consciousness occurs. There are four types of generalized seizures. In absence seizures (also called petit mal seizures), the child stares blankly and sometimes may blink or jerk repetitively. Objects may drop from the person's hands, and some mild involuntary movements may occur. This seizure ends rapidly, lasting only a few seconds. If absence seizures are frequent, the child may miss work or be seen as daydreaming. In myoclonic seizures, a sudden jerk occurs in one muscle group. It may be severe enough to throw the child to the ground. These seizures are often progressive, becoming more severe with time. In an atonic or drop attack, a sudden slumping of the body is due to a loss of muscle tone. Atonic seizures are rare, severe, and progressive. They may even lead to facial and head injuries. Last, is tonic-clonic seizures (grand mal seizures), during which the child falls to the ground and the body becomes rigid (tonic phase) and then jerks (the clonic phase). The seizure may last several seconds to several minutes. The child may then fall into a deep sleep or appear confused.

Partial seizures affect particular areas of the brain. A child having a simple partial seizure will remain conscious, but a body part, perhaps a leg may jerk. This seizing may spread to other parts of the same side. Complex partial seizures are similar to simple partial seizures except for a decreased awareness and, sometimes, a loss of consciousness. Repetitive motor actions in which unusual but purposeful activities such as pulling something, fumbling with something, or lip smacking can be observed (Dreifuss, 1988). Sometimes, these seizures are misinterpreted by adults as signs of substance abuse (Potolicchio, 1992).

Not all seizures are caused by epilepsy. Young children and adolescents may have convulsions from fever, an imbalance of body fluids, and from alcohol or drug withdrawal (NICHCY, 1993b). A single seizure does not automatically mean that the child has epilepsy.

About 2.5 million children and adolescents in the United States have epilepsy or other seizure disorders (Hauser & Hesdorffer, 1990a). Of the 300,000 new cases yearly, about 40 percent are diagnosed in children under the age of 18 years (Hauser & Hesdorffer, 1990b). The seriousness of epilepsy varies. Some cases are mild, while other cases may be quite severe (Hermann & Whitman, 1992).

Although many children with epilepsy may show minimal or even no difficulties in social or cognitive functioning, children with seizure disorders are at an increased risk of both behavioral and learning problems (Seidenberg & Berent, 1992). A discrepancy between academic performance and ability is often present. The process of learning may be disrupted by the effects of the seizures, medications taken to counter the epilepsy, cognitive difficulties of the child, or by people in the school environment who do not understand the disability or do not sup-

Epilepsy:
A condition in which recurrent electrical discharges in the brain disturb the usual functioning of the nervous system and cause seizures.

port the child (McLin, 1992). Sometimes, the seizures themselves may interfere with school performance. For example, children with absence seizures may miss work (NICHCY, 1993b). Perhaps the epilepsy itself, which is a basic disturbance in neural functioning, may cause underlying disturbances that affect cognitive abilities such as attention (Seidenberg & Berent, 1992). An increased risk of behavioral problems is present when comparing the population of children with epilepsy to children with other chronic medical problems, but the mechanisms are not understood (Seidenberg & Berent, 1992).

People with epilepsy are fearful about having a seizure, especially in public, and are under stress (Pianta & Lothman, 1994). They are more likely to have an external locus of control compared to other chronically ill children, as well as higher rates of depression (Hermann & Whitman, 1992). They have often been denied their civil rights, and job discrimination is a problem (Witt, 1992). The ADA prohibits discrimination if the applicant is qualified. The unemployment rate for people with seizure disorders is substantially higher than for the general population, and many who do find work are underemployed (McLin, 1992).

This discrimination is due to a misunderstanding of the disorder and its control. About 80 percent of the cases are well controlled through medication, although figures differ (Reisner, 1988). The medications are effective but do have side effects, which, again, may interfere with learning (Dodrill & Matthews, 1992). The effects depend upon the medication, the dosage, and individual factors. The most common side effect is some decrease in speed of response (Dodrill & Matthews, 1992). Some children outgrow the disorder as they mature (Potolicchio, 1992; Dreifuss, 1988).

People whose epilepsy is controlled through medication can engage in almost all activities. Some people go many years without having a seizure. Most states require a seizure-free period of varying lengths of time in order to have a driver's license (usually 6 to 12 months, but it varies) (Kaplan & Moore, 1988).

Most children with epilepsy are educated in regular classrooms, but the services they require differ greatly from child to child. The possible effects of the medication, especially if it results in slower response times, may require the teacher to place less emphasis on speed or adapt lessons and tests. In addition, teachers should be told what to do in case of a seizure. Those who have learning problems require special help directed at their problems (Diamond et al., 1988). In other words, some children with epilepsy whose condition is under control may need little additional attention, but much understanding. Other children with epilepsy may experience cognitive problems due to the disorder or the medication and may need extra help to catch up. Still others may have serious learning disabilities and experience significant developmental delays and require even more assistance. Few generalizations can be made.

Children with epilepsy must also deal with the psychological and social aspects of the condition, including public misconceptions about the disorder. They must deal with their fear of seizures, fear of the loss of self-control, as well as compliance with medication and its side effects (NICHCY, 1993b). The public fear of the disorder and unnecessary stigma attached to it require some educational consideration so that the next generation will understand the disorder and not ostracize or discriminate against people with epilepsy. If a child has missed school because of a seizure or had a seizure in class, the student may be embarrassed and avoid others. The teacher's kind remark welcoming the child back may be helpful (Chee & Clancy, 1984).

THOUGHT QUESTION

5. *Some people argue that teachers need not be told if a child has epilepsy that is being controlled because the chance of a seizure is slight and the teacher may act differently towards that child. Others claim that the teacher is a professional who should be informed. Should the teacher be informed when a student has epilepsy?*

SCENARIO

5 Jack had a seizure in class last week and has been out since that day. It was the first time in a number of years that he'd had a seizure in public. He is embarrassed and does not wish to return to the same sixth grade class. He claims that he will not be accepted. He wishes to change schools, and if he cannot do this at least change classes. If you were his parent what would you do? If Jack returned to the class, would you as a teacher say anything to the class or Jack?

Traumatic Brain Injury

About 2.2 of every 1,000 children each year experience traumatic brain injury (TBI). These brain injuries may be mild, moderate, or severe. Traumatic brain injury is one of the largest contributors to death and disability among children and adolescents in the United States (Martin, 1988a). Of the approximately 500,000 cases of traumatic brain injury reported each year, about 50,000 die. Many of the 450,000 who survive experience physical, cognitive, and behavioral difficulties (Prigatano, 1992). About one-third of all children who are unconscious for more than one week have intelligence scores less than 70; shorter periods of unconsciousness often lead to difficulties as well. In 1990, PL 101-476 made traumatic brain injury (TBI) a distinct diagnostic category (U.S. Department of Education, 1993). Some children with TBI may be diagnosed as having learning disabilities or served under the diagnosis of "other health impaired" (Bigler, 1987). Some experts argue that as many as 20 percent of all children diagnosed as having learning disabilities may have had a prior brain injury (Spivak, 1986).

The most common cause of TBI is motor vehicle crashes, accounting for one-third to one-half of all new cases. Falls cause 20–30 percent of total incidence. Violence, including gunshots and blows to the head, is also an important cause.

The majority of people with traumatic brain injury have mild injuries, and little is really known about the consequences of these injuries. Often, they report persistent headaches as well as other physical symptoms and some changes in behavior. The most comprehensive study of such mild injuries found that of 424 people examined three months after injury, 78 percent complained of persistent headaches, 50 percent had memory difficulties, and 34 percent who were employed prior to the accident had not yet returned to work (Rimel et al., 1981).

The consequences of moderate and severe traumatic brain injury are more thoroughly researched. Between 70,000 and 90,000 individuals sustain moderate to severe traumatic brain injuries each year, which result in disabling conditions. No two people with TBI show identical patterns of abilities and impairments (Deaton, 1987). Some people become unresponsive or are in permanent comas; others experience severe cognitive problems in attention, memory, language, and general intellectual performance. Physical, motoric, behavioral, cognitive, and interpersonal changes occur (Telzrow, 1987).

About 5 percent of all children with TBI have seizures; that figure increases to about 40 percent for children who have severe head injuries (see Mira & Tyler, 1991). Many children with TBI report persistent headaches. Whatever obvious motor problems exist right after the injury may improve quickly, but difficulties with complex and fine movements may remain. Speed of movement and task completion is often noticeably slower than it was prior to the injury (Mira & Tyler, 1991). Fatigue may be an important problem and sometimes balance or physical abilities are affected (Mira & Tyler, 1991).

Communications and language difficulties may exist (Bigler, 1988). Many of the more severe impairments—such as lack of speech, which may be present right after the injury—may subside, but some difficulties often remain, which still seriously affect learning, communication, and interpersonal relationships (Marquardt, Stoll, & Sussman, 1988). Although even in severe cases of TBI, lack of speech is found in less than 10 percent of the cases; problems in articulation, slow rates of speech, and minimal variation in pitch may be shown (Ylvisaker, 1993). Most children with TBI eventually produce grammatically correct sentences and understand everyday language in nonstressful situations. However, subtle problems in auditory processing and sentence construction are common. Children with TBI show difficulty using language in the classroom and in social interactions (Marquardt et al., 1988). They have difficulty retrieving the right word, and written language is often impaired, especially in younger children (Ylvisaker, 1993).

Students with TBI may show more difficulties in the classroom in language than they do on standardized clinical tests. The more demanding the situation, the greater the likelihood of these language difficulties being manifested. Vocabulary usually remains reasonably good, but a decline may occur. Children with TBI may not gain vocabulary words at an age-appropriate rate due to absences or learning difficulties (Cooper & Flowers, 1987). Academic problems are relatively common with decline in reading comprehension and arithmetic (Mira & Tyler, 1991).

Cognitive impairments vary but may become serious impediments to learning. Children with TBI may show a poor attention span, and their ability to divide their attention is impaired (Wood, 1988). Memory difficulties are also common (Glisky & Schacter, 1988). Nearly half of all children with TBI show verbal memory impairments of varying severity (Ewing-Cobbs & Fletcher, 1987). Other cognitive problems in concept formation, organization of sensory inputs, dealing with complex instructions, organizing verbal and written information, and flexibility in thinking may appear (Mira & Tyler, 1991). Children with TBI may have difficulty retrieving information and may be more distractible (Martin, 1988a).

Emotional disturbances and personality changes, including depression, irritability, agitation, difficulties in controlling anger, and withdrawal have also been noted (Prigatano, 1992). The more severe the trauma, the more likely the child will be to show behavioral difficulties (Deaton, 1987). Some children with TBI have difficulties adapting to small shifts in classroom routine and may be irritable and impulsive (Deaton, 1987). On the other hand, some children may withdraw (Lezak & O'Brien, 1988).

The possible long-term consequences of TBI, then, can be serious. The extent of the long-term injury depends on many factors including the extent of the lesion, the location of the lesion, the child's age at injury, and the static or progressive nature of the damage (Obrzut & Hynd, 1987). Children with TBI present a challenge for teachers and the school in general as well as the family.

Children with TBI differ from other children entitled to special education services in a number of important ways. First, the vast majority of these children will not have required special education services before the injury, meaning that their parents and family members have had little opportunity to understand the special education process (Martin, 1988b). A child who was functioning at grade level with few problems suddenly requires special care and special services in the schools. Parents of children with TBI are less likely to be able to deal with the special education process and system effectively than parents of other children needing special services who have gradually learned how to work within the system (Martin, 1988b).

In addition, the parents of a child with TBI may have just seen their child through a very trying and emotionally difficult time immediately after the accident when the child was unconscious or in a coma. They now see the improvement and have a tendency to misjudge the severity of the remaining difficulties (Lezak & O'Brien, 1988).

The assessment of a child with TBI will require the participation of many outside experts, including neurologists and physical therapists who are not aware of how schools are run or necessarily acquainted with the professionals within the school environment. These professionals must be involved and invited to IEP meetings (Martin, 1988b). For most children receiving special education services, observations by school personnel precede the process of evaluation. This prior observation is not the case in TBI. Finally, the experience of returning to school is difficult. Often, children with TBI are given home instruction before returning to school. Children may fall behind during this period. The question of when the child is ready to return to school is difficult to answer, but generally the child should display a sustained attention to work for 30 minutes, tolerate multiple stimuli that will be found in a classroom, respond to instruction, and interact with others (Mira & Tyler, 1991).

Students with TBI return to school to their teachers and peers who will probably see changes in their behavior and intellectual functioning. The child may not be able to handle some situations as well as the child did prior to the accident (Martin, 1988a). The early support received during the crisis situation may begin to decline (Mira & Tyler, 1991). The child may be treated differently and experience some avoidance or rejection.

Traditionally, children with TBI were served in hospital settings and private facilities. With the passage of new laws such as the Individuals with Disabilities Education Act, many more children will receive special services in their neighborhood schools, most of which have no experience dealing with children with TBI (Wiederholt, 1987).

Since the impairments and abilities of these children vary widely, the school-related needs of these children will also vary widely. All staff must be informed of how the injury has affected and will continue to affect the child's functioning (Mira & Tyler, 1991). As in all cases, the programming will depend upon the individual needs and abilities of the children. However, generally, children with TBI may experience fatigue and so their most challenging classes should be scheduled in the morning when they are more likely to be alert. Children may need more breaks and giving them an extra set of books to keep at home so that they do not have to carry them back and forth is a thoughtful gesture. The child with TBI may need special physical education and the help of another student to travel from class to class. Since many students with TBI will have difficulty with speed-related learning, allowing untimed tests is helpful. Since division of attention may be a problem, having another student take notes on carbon paper, photocopying notes, or allowing the use of a tape recorder permits the student with TBI to pay strict attention to the lesson. Although frequent assessments are always beneficial for children receiving special services, they are even more important for children with TBI who have complicated cognitive and communicative profiles that change over time (Ylvisaker, 1993).

In addition, some children will show behavioral difficulties, and the strategies discussed in Chapter 7 may be useful. The school psychologist and outside experts aware of the child's abilities and difficulties may be helpful in designing an appropriate behavior modification program if one is needed. One last point may be helpful. Transition from home study to school may require a transition team. In the first months, children with TBI may be easily confused and disoriented. A transition team may help welcome the student back and make whatever changes are required for the child to adjust to school.

Schools also have some responsibility to prevent head injuries. Students must be made aware of the risk of head injury due to not wearing helmets during bicycling or failure to wear seatbelts. Many programs try to reduce risk-taking behavior. The THINK FIRST program founded by the American Association for Neurological Surgeons and the Congress of Neurological Surgeons is a basic educational curriculum discussing vulnerability to injury and the consequences of risk taking. An 18-minute film, called "Harm's Way," addresses risk taking, discusses TBI and spinal cord injury, and stresses decision making as part of the program. Presentations by health care professionals and people who have experienced such injuries are also made. After presentations of these programs, knowledge increases substantially but only minimal changes in behavior occur (Englander et al., 1993). More effective ways to change risk-taking behavior are required.

The management of head injuries and the chance for some recovery has greatly improved (Bigler, 1987). The difficulties experienced by children with TBI can be substantial, but with good communication among professionals and parents, the special needs of these students can be met.

Cystic Fibrosis

Cystic fibrosis:
A severe genetic disease marked by digestive and respiratory problems.

Cystic fibrosis (CF) is a recessive genetic disease of the glands that produce mucus, saliva, and sweat. It affects many organs, including the lungs, liver, and pancreas. A person with cystic fibrosis has a low resistance to respiratory diseases and a tendency to dehydrate because of an excessive amount of salt in the sweat. New antibiotics have increased the life expectancy of individuals with this disorder. Between 70 and 80 percent survive to at least age 20 years if excellent medical treatment is received. In fact, one-third of the more than 15,000 patients listed in the registry of the North American National Cystic Fibrosis Foundation are older than 21 years (Colten, 1990). At this point, there is no cure. Cystic fibrosis is responsible for more deaths than any other genetic disease in the United States today.

Some of the recent research into this disorder is nothing short of sensational. Scientists have actually cured cystic fibrosis cells in the laboratory by inserting a healthy version of the gene that causes the disease (Angier, 1990a). The researchers used a genetically engineered virus to place good copies of the gene into cells taken from the respiratory tract and pancreas of cystic fibrosis patients. When this occurred, the cells became healthier and their functioning improved. This process is called gene therapy. A number of genetic diseases may be conquered using this type of therapy, which has already been used successfully on a rare genetic disorder in which children do not have the ability to fight off any disease (Angier, 1990b).

Treatment for cystic fibrosis is continuous and hospitalization during periods of crisis can be expected. Researchers estimate that the disease occurs in one out of every 2,000 births. About 1 in 20–30 people is a carrier (Reed, 1975). Today, a test is available, which can detect most carriers of the disease (Beaudet, 1990).

Children with CF demonstrate average intelligence and academic achievement. Often, school attendance becomes worse with age and periods of hospitalization are common, so procedures for allowing children to catch up are instituted. A chronic cough and a frail appearance may cause other children to avoid children with cystic fibrosis causing interpersonal difficulties. The class needs important information about CF and to realize that the disease is not contagious (Wilmott, Burroughs, & Beele, 1984).

Sickle Cell Anemia

Sickle cell anemia is an inherited defect in the structure of red blood cells. The child with sickle cell anemia, especially during periods of physical exertion or low oxygen, experiences considerable pain. Although many people with sickle cell anemia do not change their everyday routines, people with severe cases may experience heart and kidney problems (Fogel, 1984). Periods of crisis requiring hospitalization are not unusual. Many types of crisis may occur, but the most common involves an attack of pain mainly in the bones and joints of the hands and feet, arms and legs, back and chest (in older children), or abdomen. This pain occurs because small blood vessels are blocked by the sickle-shaped red blood cells and the cells become starved for oxygen. The pain may be mild or severe (Kim, Gaston, & Fithian, 1984). Resistance to disease is decreased, and the health of the child with sickle cell anemia is usually poor. The seriousness of the disorder varies. One student with sickle cell anemia may find that observing some simple precautions against overexertion sufficient, while another may have a school record showing many absences and periods of hospitalization.

Approximately 1 in 10 African-Americans is a carrier, and carrier status can be determined by a simple blood test. On the average, 1 marriage out of every 100 between African-Americans has the potential for producing a child who will have sickle cell anemia. At present, antibiotics and improved medical treatment can help alleviate the symptoms, but some children with severe cases of the disorder die in childhood (March of Dimes, 1986). Recently, a medication called hydroxyurea was found to significantly reduce the number of crises and hospital admissions for people with sickle cell anemia (Lane, 1995). Although the medication is only useful for a relatively small percentage of people, it is the first medication ever found that can prevent some of the crises experienced by people with sickle cell anemia.

Sickle cell anemia:
A genetic disorder marked by a defect in the structure of red blood cells.

The red blood cells of children with sickle cell anemia show the sickled shape. Small blood vessels are blocked by the sickle-shaped blood cells.

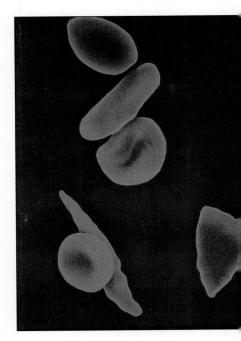

Since the effects of the disease are variable, their impact on the child's school career is difficult to determine. Except for about 6 percent of children with sickle cell who suffer stroke, these children have average intelligence (Kim et al., 1984). However, children with sickle cell anemia often do not do well in school, most likely due to absences. A child may have a good year and be absent very little followed by a year of frequent absences. Sometimes, these children experience difficulty catching up and require a great deal of encouragement and positive reinforcement to keep trying.

Muscular Dystrophy

Muscular dystrophy:
A disorder causing irreversible and progressive weakening of all the muscles.

Muscular dystrophy (MD) is a disease causing irreversible and progressive weakening of all the muscles (Bleck, 1979). It starts with weakness and ends with a total destruction of muscle tissue and death (Kolata, 1986). Muscle cells are replaced with fat cells and fibrous tissue (Cratty, 1986). Of a number of different kinds of muscular dystrophy, Duchenne's muscular dystrophy is the most common. Duchenne's muscular dystrophy is a sex-linked disorder. Its incidence is 279 per 1,000,000 male births. Some females, though, may also show it. It is often diagnosed at about age four years when the child is slow at walking and clumsy. Early signs also include running with an awkward flat-footed gait, tiptoeing, and swaying due to weakness (Cratty, 1986).

Management programs emphasize mobility training using mobility aids and wheelchairs. Children with MD show decreased school achievement as the disease progresses (Karagan, 1979; Bleck, 1979).

The child with muscular dystrophy has a limited amount of energy; any unnecessary activities, such as extended bus rides that might fatigue the child, should be avoided (Chee & Packer, 1984). The child's most important subjects should be scheduled early in the day to minimize the possibility of fatigue. Since these children often require wheelchairs for mobility, accessibility is important. If a child cannot take notes, a volunteer notetaker should be sought, and the use of a tape recorder encouraged. Many of the suggestions for dealing with children with orthopedic impairments discussed earlier will help these children as well.

Recent discoveries point to the potential long-term cure of the disorder. An essential protein called dystrophin is lost during the disease and replacing it may be possible (Thompson, 1992). The strategy is to inject healthy muscle cells into the sick children's muscles. Animal experiments suggest that the inserted cells, called myoblasts, will fuse to the diseased muscles and restore their healthy functioning by producing the dystrophin that is lost when the mutated gene neutralizes the dystrophin gene (Thompson, 1992; Hoffman, 1991). Although the gene for the disease has been identified and researchers are optimistic, a cure may be years away (Kolata, 1986).

Cancer

At one time, a diagnosis of cancer in a child was a death sentence. But this has changed. Now, more than 40,000 adults, most young adults, have survived childhood cancer. For example, 30 years ago a child diagnosed with the most common form of cancer, lymphocytic leukemia, was given only months to live (Balter, 1992). Today, about two-thirds live at least five years after diagnosis. Half the children with bone cancer survive five or more years, and Wilms' tumor of the kidney affecting mostly toddlers is now curable in 82 percent of cases. According to the National Cancer Institute, 63 percent of all young cancer patients survive at least five years or more after being diagnosed, a tremendous improvement over the 40 percent rate in the early 1970s. By the year 2000, an estimated one of every 1,000 Americans between the ages of 20 and 29 will be a cancer survivor (Monmany, Levy-Spira, & Hager, 1988).

Many children with cancer experience difficult medical treatments, which may lead to disfigurement, isolation from friends, and pain and suffering. All have uncertainties about the future and, when in remission, a fear that the cancer will recur. Many show anger and irritation, decreased academic performance, and some minor adjustment problems (Kvist et al., 1991). About 15 percent of the survivors require treatment for depression. Fritz and colleagues (1988) studied the psychological effects of childhood cancer on children and adolescents who had successfully completed treatment at least two years earlier. The children were diagnosed at an average age of 9.7 years. Chemotherapy and surgery were the most common treatments. Some had physical impairments from amputations or other permanent physical changes stemming from surgery. Three-quarters reported no limitations at school or work, and 21 percent reported only minor limitations. Thirty-one percent needed to attend to a residual physical problem at least once a day with medication or exercise. Two-thirds reported no physical interference in their daily living.

Of those still in school, 10 percent said their academic functioning had improved as a survivor, 32 percent said it was worse, and for the majority, 58 percent, it had remained unchanged. Twenty percent enjoyed school more as survivors and 30 percent enjoyed it less. Twenty-eight percent felt they had become less active. One-fifth had become more gregarious and socially involved as survivors, 57 percent unchanged, and 23 percent less sociable. Six percent were measured as significantly depressed and 14 percent as borderline depressed. Twenty-five percent received a global adjustment rating of excellent, 36 percent rated good, 26 percent average, 6 percent marginal, and 8 percent poor.

Two factors that seem most important to better functioning and adjustment are communication with the school during treatment and peer support. The need for direct communication between family and school concerning work-related help due to absences should be addressed.

The results of this and other studies show that the global adjustment of these children is good and that serious emotional, academic, or social problems are relatively rare. Cancer survivors are at increased risk for some psychological problems, especially depression and anxiety (Rait et al., 1988). Serious psychopathology is uncommon. However, some evidence indicates that children with cancer are less likely to try new activities, to verbalize, and are more passive, self-conscious, and easily embarrassed (see Ross, 1984). They do not express emotions very freely. Therefore, although serious psychopathology is relatively rare, some adjustment problems do occur, and these children must cope with a difficult situation.

Some conclusions are possible from these studies. First, most children with cancer show more stability than change, although some may improve or show declines in academic and social functioning. Second, a major factor in helping these children is direct communication between the family and the school. These children will be absent from school during their treatments and need help to catch up. Most teachers show a willingness to accommodate absences and make time for special needs (Fryer et al., 1989). Third, although major psychological problems are relatively rare, some problems including the need to adjust to the physical changes and emotional challenges presented by the disease and treatment do occur. The experience of finding out that one has cancer, the uncertainty about one's future, and the adjustments required necessitate counseling and understanding from peers and teachers.

The ability to give this understanding depends upon the feelings and attitudes of both professionals and students. Students may react poorly to the changes in the child's appearance. Faculty may feel uncomfortable (Ross, 1984). Sometimes teachers believe that the child cannot participate in certain activities. This limitation is often not the case, and a conference with the doctor and parent is needed to discuss what the student can and cannot do.

SCENARIO

6 Pat has been treated for cancer. She looks thin and haggard and has other physical difficulties as well as being more quiet than at the beginning of the year. The other children in your second-grade class avoid her and seem to be frightened. What would you do to better integrate Pat into the class and reduce her isolation?

Acquired Immune Deficiency Syndrome (AIDS)

Approximately 10,000 children in the United States have HIV infections, with 1,750 new cases discovered each year (Altman, 1995). The prognosis for these children is not good. However, new treatments may improve their chances of survival and some will attend school. Although AIDS is certainly found in every ethnic and socioeconomic level, low-income urban women and children are disproportionately involved, and a significant number of affected children are African-American and Hispanic (Capell et al., 1992; Hutchings, 1988). An estimated 1 in 2,200 infants born each year in the United States is infected with HIV (Onorato, Gwinn, & Dondero, 1994). The overwhelming majority of new cases of pediatric AIDS are caused by transmission of the virus prenatally or at birth (Oxtoby, 1994). AIDS may also be transmitted through breast milk if the mother is HIV positive (Landau-Stanton & Clements, 1993). Some adolescents, especially those with hemophilia, may have been infected through tainted blood. Today transfusions of tainted blood are a less likely occurrence because of better monitoring of the blood supply. Other adolescents may be infected through the use of shared needles or sexual contact with an infected individual.

Three questions concern the schooling of these children. First, should they attend a public school? Second, what is the effect of the disease on the child and the child's schooling? Third, what type of education is needed both to reduce the spread of the disease and to conquer the fear and prejudice against people with AIDS?

Children with AIDS have a legal right to schooling and generally do not present a danger to others (Savage, Mayfield, & Cook, 1993). Courts have not allowed schools to exclude children with HIV (Gostin, 1992). The Americans with Disabilities Act makes the exclusion of children with HIV in all schools including nursery schools illegal (Savage et al., 1993). Specific decisions on placement should be made on a case-by-case basis, but generally children who test HIV positive can be educated with other children safely (Chanock & Simonds, 1994).

Teachers, though, need to take precautions. Many school districts have issued specific instructions for handling bleeding and other possible sources of infection. These procedures are implemented whether or not the child is HIV positive as a precaution for all concerned.

The second question, that of the effects of the disease on children, yields a rather pessimistic assessment at this point. Since AIDS affects the immune system, children are more likely to be ill and out of school frequently. A great deal of evidence shows that the AIDS virus leads to significant neurological damage and intellectual deterioration (Griepp, Landau-Stanton, & Clements, 1993; Culliton, 1989). Children with AIDS show clear signs of dementia (Barnes, 1986). In adults, dementia is usually found at a late stage of AIDS, while in children it occurs early. These children manifest developmental delays that progressively worsen. For example, in the language area, a child may stop using words that the child once knew well. Intellectual decline is common with losses in demonstrated intelligence. Some children who were doing well in school now are not.

The treatment for children with AIDS is a source of controversy at the present time. AZT (zidovudine) is commonly used with adults to control the virus (Balis & Poplack, 1994; Sands et al., 1993), and evidence indicates that giving AZT to HIV positive women during pregnancy prevents the prenatal transmission of AIDS in many cases (Boyer et al., 1994). It has been used with children with some evidence showing that AZT may reverse the cognitive decline (Pizzo & Wilfert, 1994; Hutchings, 1988), however, AZT does not cure the disease, and these children eventually die. Its toxicity also limits its usefulness.

Lately, its use with children with HIV was opened to question when a preliminary report from a major study found that AZT alone was not effective and caused high rates of adverse side effects. Research continues on the effects of another medication, didanosine (ddI), and the combined approach using ddI and AZT (Altman, 1995). At this writing, a new government-sponsored forum is being scheduled to discuss how to treat HIV-infected children.

AIDS Education

As research continues to try to discover a cure and better ways of helping people with AIDS, educators have the responsibility of educating all children about AIDS. Two reasons support such education. First, children need to be educated so that they will not engage in behaviors that statistically place them at risk for getting AIDS, such as the use of shared IV needles and engaging in high-risk sex (Fisher, Fisher, & Rye, 1995). Second, some education is required to reduce the isolation and rejection of both children and adults who have AIDS.

How much do teens know about AIDS? Early studies in the 1980s showed relatively poor knowledge of AIDS, but more recent studies find that adolescents do know something about AIDS. Generally, teens appear now to have a moderate knowledge of AIDS, although some specifics appear to be missing (Kaplan, 1993).

Even when students know the facts, however, they do not always alter their behavior. Frequently, whatever changes they make may be ineffective. Studies vary widely on the use of condoms by adolescents; fewer appear to use condoms with secondary partners than with primary partners (Lustig, 1994). Condom use doubled among sexually active teenage males between 1979 and 1988 but has leveled off since then, and only a slight majority of 17-to-19 year-olds report using a condom the last time they had sexual intercourse (*CQ Researcher*, 1993).

When juniors and seniors in college were surveyed, their knowledge of AIDS was considered good, but only about one-third noted that they had made some changes in their sexual behavior, mostly in the area of becoming more selective (Roscoe & Kruger, 1990). Of course, the lack of change may also indicate that some of these teens are already engaging in safer sexual practices. The goals of many AIDS programs include convincing students to delay sexual intercourse, reduce the number of sexual partners, and use condoms if sexually active.

AIDS education is now mandated in most states, and the Surgeon General advocates that it begin by 9 or 10 years of age (Flax, 1987). One question, though, is how explicit it should be. For example, many people advocate emphasizing abstinence (Viadero, 1987). Others believe the school should teach about the use of condoms, which provide some protection. Should the emphasis be placed on explicit teaching of the sexual techniques that are most and least likely to cause contact with the AIDS virus, or should it simply be placed on abstinence as the only "certain" way to prevent the spread of AIDS?

AIDS education programs must offer students the facts and discuss prevention, including sexual abstinence and fidelity, as well as the use of condoms and careful selection of sex partners, and the dangers of using needles and syringes. It must deal with knowledge, attitudes, and behavior. Taking responsibility for one's own health and the health of others are values that must be addressed. AIDS education is a necessary part of the curriculum, but more research is needed to discover the most effective approach to changing attitudes and behavior in this area. It must also aim at reducing the unwarranted discrimination against people with AIDS who are frequently denied their civil rights out of ignorance.

The Child with a Health Problem in School

There is no substitute for knowledge about these illnesses. Unfortunately, many teachers complain that they do not have adequate knowledge about working with children who have chronic health problems (Johnson, Lubker, & Fowler, 1988). When Lynch and colleagues (1992) interviewed parents of children with chronic health problems in 100 school districts in California, the results were both encouraging and discouraging. Parents reported few barriers and were pleased with the educational programs and services that their children had received. Eighty-eight percent reported being very satisfied or generally satisfied. Seventy-six percent reported no difficulty in obtaining educational services, and 70 percent reported services had been available usually or most of the time. The greatest barrier the parents cited, however, was lack of public and staff awareness. The personnel in the districts concurred. Simply stated, both parents and school personnel agree that professionals are not well informed about chronic diseases and their classroom implications.

When asked about the problems these children experience in school, educators cited absences first, followed by falling behind in school, lack of interaction with peers, the fact that some schools cannot meet these children's needs, and problems in social adjustment. Parents' responses were somewhat different. Many of their responses (a little less than half) focused on the specific problems associated with the individual illness, such as restrictions on child's activities, exercise, diet, mobility, and the side effects of treatment. Many also mentioned feeling different from other children and the constant medical procedures they endure, some of which are painful. Other comments dealt with social and emotional issues, such as extreme embarrassment caused by side effects of treatment, loss of hair or dramatic changes in weight. Parents highlighted the pervasiveness of the illness in their child's life. The greatest concerns when returning to school after a bout with the illness was being behind and not being accepted. Their advice to teachers was to treat the child as they would any other child, become better informed about the illness, communicate with parents on a regular basis, remain hopeful, build the child's confidence and self-esteem, and be sensitive to the needs of the entire family. Parents also acknowledged some very positive experiences with teachers.

The primary way teachers learn about a disease is through the child's parents. A conference with the parents may be in order to deal with issues including changes in classroom procedures, ways of helping the child keep up with academic assignments during periods of absence, and whether any monitoring of changes is required by the teacher, which may indicate a change in the disease's course. Knowing what problems can arise and what to do if some crisis occurs adds to the teacher's sense of security as well as the student's. For example, knowing what to do if the child has a seizure helps ease everyone's stress.

One major problem that arises over and over again is that of absences. Families and teachers need to develop a method of getting work to the child on a regular basis when the child is ill. A smooth system, which may include sending the work to a guidance counselor and having a parent pick up the work at a specific time and return the student's work for correction, makes it much easier for everyone involved. A notetaker or tape of a lesson may be required as well.

Integrating the Student: The Question of Stigma

Many children with physical or health impairments are not well integrated into the school community. This "segregation" occurs even when there is no other disability present, such as mental retardation or behavior disorders. Active rejection may be the problem in some cases, but avoidance is more common. Two questions beg answers here. First, why do students reject or avoid children who have physical disabilities or health impairments? And second, what can be done to integrate these children into the class?

Often a stigma is attached to physical disabilities and health impairments. Historically, people with epilepsy have been stigmatized in terms of madness and spirit possession. Even today, people with epilepsy experience prejudice due to a misunderstanding of the disorder (Schneider, 1988). People with AIDS are also often rejected and stigmatized.

Some studies have reported that orthopedic disabilities and health impairments often cause some nondisabled people anxiety and discomfort (Fine & Asch, 1988). Perhaps people are threatened by the appearance of others who differ

THOUGHT QUESTION

6. *Why do people without disabilities often feel uncomfortable interacting with people who have orthopedic disabilities or obvious health problems?*

in physical appearance. On the other hand, people with disabilities may remind nondisabled people of the perilousness of life and they identify with the disabled person (Hahn, 1988). This anxiety may translate into a condescending attitude.

Makas (1988) found that people with and without physical disabilities have different ideas of what positive attitudes toward people with disabilities are. A scale to measure attitudes toward people with disabilities was administered to a group of adults with disabilities, a group of nondisabled adults identified by the disabled adults as having positive attitudes toward disabled people, and a general group of nondisabled people. Interesting differences were noted between the first two groups and the general group. For example, both the group of people with disabilities and those with positive attitudes toward people with disabilities disagreed with the idea that people with disabilities should be granted special concessions, such as not having to pay income taxes, overlooking conduct because of a disability, or not trying to win a game when competing with an individual with a physical disability. The general group of nondisabled people were more likely to feel that people with disabilities should be given extra privileges. The same disagreement was found on the issue of the personality of people who have disabilities. The group of people with disabilities and those with positive attitudes were more likely to reject ideas that people with disabilities are generally easier to get along with or that they seldom get angry or are especially courageous than were nondisabled people in the general group.

For respondents with disabilities, a positive attitude means either dispensing with the special category of disability or developing attitudes that help them secure their civil and social rights. For the general population of nondisabled respondents, positive attitudes reflect trying to be nice, helpful, and ultimately place the person with a disability in a needy situation. Nondisabled people may be perceived by people with disabilities as expressing negative attitudes when in fact the nondisabled persons are trying hard to express what they consider positive attitudes. Makas offers two examples. In the first, a person loses a game on purpose in order to make the individual with a disability feel better. In the second, a nondisabled person tells a newly hired individual with a disability that he is glad to work with him since he has always found people with disabilities to be pleasant and cheerful.

This study, and others like it, lead to the conclusion that people need education. Most people with disabilities do not want special treatment or to be perceived as having any special characteristics. Yet, the misunderstanding of the nondisabled population does not come out of malice, but out of a genuine lack of knowledge. An exchange of information between the people with disabilities and the general public is clearly needed. Better communication will place both at ease during interactions. Second, people of all ages need to understand the nature of the conditions discussed in this chapter. With children, the fear of contagion would be an important issue to address, especially with children who may not have sophisticated ideas about the cause of the physical problem. Children's ideas about illness change as they grow and develop, and become more accurate as they mature (Schvaneveldt, Lindauer, & Young, 1990).

Kister and Patterson (1980) examined preschoolers, kindergartners, and second- and fourth-grade children's views about contagion and the causes of illness. A cold was used as an example of a contagious disease, a toothache for a noncontagious disease, and a scraped knee for an accident. Children were asked: "If a boy your age went to school one day, and the girl sitting next to him had (the ailment), would he have to be careful so he wouldn't catch (the ailment) from her?"

Almost all the children understood that some ailments were contagious, but the younger children overextended the concept to include both noncontagious illness and accidents. Ten of 15 preschoolers believed that scraped knees, toothaches, or headaches were contagious, while only 1 of the 15 fourth graders overextended the concept. The younger children also believed in the concept of immanent justice for both illness and accident. In other words, people get sick or injured because they did something wrong. When children were told that a boy misbehaved and later caught a cold, many preschoolers believed that one caused the other. Children were more likely to use the immanent justice argument to understand illness than misfortune. Many preschoolers believe that someone had to do something wrong to die, or that the child may have caused the death by being unpleasant or disobedient.

During middle childhood, children become more logical but their understanding is limited to concrete principles. They understand that a germ makes someone ill but do not understand the underlying mechanism of why this happens. At about the age of 11 or 12 years, children begin to understand the mechanisms of illness and logically explain cause and effect.

A study of children's knowledge of AIDS found that knowledge increased with age. Still, mistakes were great. Some third graders believed you could contract AIDS from toilet seats or people's clothing, and many third graders believed that cigarettes caused the disease. This study did not find an immanent justice mentality, though (Schvaneveldt et al., 1990).

The teacher as well as the media (most young children get their information about AIDS and other health problems from the media) have a responsibility to educate children about disabilities. The fact that people cannot catch muscular dystrophy or epilepsy, that they can like or dislike a person with a disability because of who that person is, as well as understanding that it is acceptable to ask questions can be taught. At the same time, educating children in ways to reduce their chances of getting AIDS can be accomplished without ostracizing those children and adults who have the disease. Finally, the teacher is a model and must act the role. If the teacher interacts easily with the child with a physical disability or health problem, other children may follow the teacher's lead.

 **THE CLASSROOM**   **Helping Children with Orthopedic and Health Impairments Succeed**

Although children with orthopedic and health impairments present varied profiles of abilities and impairments, certain general suggestions for meeting the needs of this diverse group of children can be presented.

1. Obtain as much information about the orthopedic or health impairment as possible.	**Why?** This suggestion is always logical, but when trying to meet the needs of children with orthopedic and health impairments, it is an absolute necessity. Teachers often do not have extensive experience working with these children.

2. Learn the signs of a child experiencing side effects of medication or that indicate the condition is worsening.	**Why?** Different conditions and medications have different warning signs attached to them, and the teacher is in an excellent position of discovering a bad reaction to a medication or a decline in functioning before it is shown in other circumstances.
3. Analyze the classroom and school for barriers to access.	**Why?** The removal of barriers for access is a responsibility of the professional staff. Asking children who use wheelchairs about any environmental problems they may encounter is reasonable.
4. Make adequate provision for note taking in the classroom, if necessary.	**Why?** Some children will require taping or a class member to take notes. A smooth system makes it easier for everyone.
5. Make adequate provision for making up work and sending assignments home.	**Why?** Absences are frequently a problem with children with orthopedic and health problems and working out some method of getting the work to students is necessary.
6. Frequent communication with parents is required.	**Why?** Children with orthopedic and health problems may have medications changed or show changes in their conditions. Parents must be informed of changes in behavior or academic functioning.
7. Answer student questions about orthopedic or health impairments.	**Why?** Young students may be worried about contagion or may not know how to communicate with their peers who have impairments.
8. Students with orthopedic and health impairments need to be actively integrated into the social fabric of the classroom.	**Why?** These students are sometimes avoided by others. Teachers can help students become comfortable with children with disabilities by using the buddy system, a circle of friends, or group work.
9. Do not place students using wheelchairs in the back of the room.	**Why?** Often students using wheelchairs are physically separated from other students because they may

	need more room. Altering the space between the aisles and seating students with wheelchairs with other students is best.
10. Adapt lessons and tests as needed to adjust for lack of speed.	**Why?** The adaptations necessary depend upon the child's abilities. Many children may need few if any changes in curriculum. Some will have difficulty with responses that require speed. Altering the testing situation is appropriate.
11. Know what to do in an emergency.	**Why?** Some children with orthopedic and health impairments may experience crises. Asking the school nurse and the child's parents what crises, if any, might occur and learning what to do in case of a crisis can increase a teacher's sense of confidence.
12. If a child is absent for a period of time, have other students write or call the student.	**Why?** Children may be absent for some time and encouraging other students to write or call makes the student feel part of the class. The teacher also should be in constant contact with the family.

A Hopeful Future

Despite the physical and psychological pain, the frustration, and the barriers that exist, children with orthopedic and physical impairments have a brighter future than ever before. In the long range, new medications, medical procedures, and genetic engineering hold out the hope not only for improvement but for actual cure in some cases. In the present, better medical care, advanced technology, and the removal of barriers are positive steps toward improving the lives of these children. In a study of college students with disabilities, many students noted a marked improvement in the environment during their four years at the institutions (West et al., 1993). With the Americans with Disabilities Act and public opinion on their side, the removal of barriers to greater integration into society is not just a hope but may be a reality.

On the other hand, two areas of concern must be addressed. The first is the continuing lack of information and misinformation that the public and many school professionals have concerning orthopedic and health impairments. In many studies of the experiences of these children, other people's lack of understanding and knowledge about these conditions stands out as major complaints (Lynch et al., 1992; West et al., 1993). Second, the employment situation for people with these disabilities demands more attention. Discrimination is a great concern. Many people with orthopedic and health disabilities who can work encounter difficulty finding employment commensurate with their skills. Their unemployment rate is higher than the general population (Liebert et al., 1990). Expanding vocational rehabilitation services, ensuring transportation to and from the job, and improving the skills of individuals with disabilities may reduce this problem.

Perhaps the two problems are closely connected, and information and awareness will decrease the prejudice and help reduce the unemployment rate. Even with these problems and concerns, the future for children with health and orthopedic conditions is brighter than it has ever been and should continue to improve.

S U M M A R Y

1. The Individuals with Disabilities Education Act (IDEA) divides the classification of physical and health problems into two categories for the purpose of special education: orthopedic disabilities and health impairment. Health and orthopedic impairment are low prevalence exceptionalities.

2. Cerebral palsy (CP) is a condition characterized by varying degrees of disturbance of voluntary movements caused by damage to the brain. A significant percentage of children with cerebral palsy have intellectual, medical, and speech problems. A team of experts is usually needed to improve mobility and help the children become as independent as possible.

3. Spina bifida or open spine is a defect in the spinal column resulting from the failure of the embryo's spine to close during the first month of pregnancy. Spina bifida (myelomeningocele) may result in paralysis and loss of sensation in the limbs. Bowel and bladder incontinence may also occur. Most children with spina bifida have average intelligence. Many children with spina bifida require catheterization which, according to law, must be provided within the school as needed.

4. Spinal cord injuries often result in paralysis. Motor vehicle accidents are the most common cause; firearms and sports injuries are also leading causes. Recent improvements in medical care, including the development of new medications, have raised hope that the paralysis resulting from spinal cord injury can be reduced.

5. Children with health impairments that affect their school performance are more frequently absent, spend more time alone, are more likely to have reduced physical activities, are often anxious about having an attack of the disease, are not certain about their future, and must endure a daily medical regimen.

6. Asthma is a common problem in children, but when it is severe and recurring it may interfere with school performance. Knowing what to do during an attack, avoiding irritants, and helping students catch up on missed work are contributions a teacher can make in the management of the condition.

7. Children with diabetes must endure a constant vigilance involving testing and daily insulin injections. Teachers need to understand the symptoms that indicate the disease is not being

SUMMARY

managed properly and show sensitivity to the child's health needs and dietary requirements.

8. Epilepsy is a central nervous system condition characterized by periodic seizures. While some children with epilepsy do not have learning problems, they are at greater risk of cognitive difficulties as a group. Most cases can be controlled through medication.

9. Some children experience traumatic brain injury (TBI), most often from accidents. The outcomes are variable, but moderate and severe TBI often lead to cognitive difficulties and behavioral changes.

10. Cystic fibrosis (CF) is a recessive genetic disease of the glands that produce mucus, saliva, and sweat. A person with cystic fibrosis has a low resistance to respiratory diseases and a tendency to dehydrate because of an excessive amount of salt in the sweat. Absences due to periods of illness create learning problems.

11. sickle cell anemia is an inherited defect in the structure of red blood cells. The child with sickle cell anemia, especially during periods of physical exertion or low oxygen, experiences considerable pain. The severity varies.

12. Muscular dystrophy (MD) is a disease that causes progressive muscle weakness and eventually death due to destruction of muscle tissue. Of the various types of muscular dystrophy, the most common is Duchenne's muscular dystrophy.

13. Recent advances in treatment offer more hope than ever for children with childhood cancer. Some children show reduced academic achievement and some adjustment problems, but most do not show major psychological disorders. These children must adjust to a difficult and often painful treatment regimen.

14. Children with AIDS have the right to attend public school. As the disease progresses, neurological damage and intellectual decline occurs. The medical treatment of children with AIDS is controversial at this time.

15. Studies show that teenagers have a moderate knowledge of AIDS but do not change their behavior in ways that would effectively reduce the likelihood of contracting the AIDS virus. AIDS education must be developmentally appropriate.

Autism

TRUE-FALSE STATEMENTS

See below for the correct answers.

1. Autism is the most serious behavior disorder of childhood.
2. Most children with autism develop mature language but at a much later age than other children.
3. The most common behavioral problems of children with autism are noncompliance and temper tantrums.
4. Children with autism generally do well on tests of rote memory.
5. Children diagnosed as having autism usually test in the average range on individual intelligence tests.
6. Autism is one of the least common disabilities.
7. Autism is caused mostly by poor parenting practices, such as distant parents interacting with their children in a formal, cold manner.
8. Most programs that have helped children with autism use a psychoanalytic (Freudian) framework.
9. Young elementary school children can be taught to reinforce and prompt children with autism to improve the social skills of autistic children.

Answers to True-False Statements
1. True.
2. False. See page 574.
3. True.
4. True.
5. False. See page 575.
6. True.
7. False. See page 577.
8. False. See page 581.
9. True.

Autism: The Most Severe Childhood Behavior Disorder

Michael is six years old. He rocks back and forth, twirling the wheels of a toy car. His only communication is the occasional imitation of what someone else has just said. He resists being held and sometimes scratches himself until he bleeds.

Autism:

A pervasive developmental disorder characterized by a lack of social responsiveness, serious deficits in communication abilities, perceptual problems, and developmental delays.

Michael has **autism**, a pervasive developmental disorder in which the child shows qualitative impairments in social interaction and communication, as well as marked deficits in behavior (Olley, 1992). Besides the serious social and language impairments, other symptoms may include mental retardation, uneven cognitive development, abnormal motor behavior, unusual responses to sensory stimulation such as overreaction to sound, abnormal sleeping and eating habits and self-injury. It is the most severe behavior disorder of childhood (Lee & Gotlib, 1994).

Both the symptoms and severity of the behaviors shown by children with autism vary considerably, and the definition encompasses children whose specific behaviors differ greatly from each other (Harris, Gill, & Alessandri, 1991). In fact, some authorities claim that a better term than autism would be autistic syndrome since the variability is so great (Powers, 1992). Autism is a very serious pervasive disorder with a dramatic impact on every area of functioning. Children who cannot communicate effectively, whose emotional attachments are limited, and whose behavior may involve self-injury, tantrums, aggressiveness, or self-stimulation will affect everyone around them (Harris et al., 1991).

Until 1990, children with autism were eligible for services under the category of "other health impaired". Then, with the passage of Public Law 101-476, the Individuals with Disabilities Education Act (IDEA), it was accorded its own separate category (NICHCY, 1993).

Characteristics of Children with Autism

A number of characteristics distinguish children with autism from other children. The most prominent are lack of response to other people, difficulties in language development, the early onset of the disorder, and various forms of unusual behavior (Jones, 1988). These unusual behaviors may include self-injurious behavior, aggressive behavior toward others, and very stereotyped and rigid behaviors, such as eating only one food, or spinning the wheels of a car for hours in the same way (Winerop, 1994). Children with autism show an inability to relate to others. They do not make eye contact and resist being hugged. They prefer objects to people (Handleman, 1992).

They also show language deficits. Between 50 and 60 percent of all children with autism do not develop speech or language skills. Those who develop some language show abnormalities, such as echolalia, echoing or parroting the phrases of others. Echoing what they have heard may happen immediately following a person's statement or be delayed. Children with autism also show pronominal reversal, in which they confuse pronouns, using "you" instead of "I." Some have difficulty naming objects and may use incorrect speech inflections, such as ending statements with a question-like rise in tone and show unusual facial expressions and gestures (Comer, 1995).

The behavioral problems shown by these children are sometimes extreme. Some are aggressive toward others and destructive, while others engage in self-injury like hitting their heads against a wall or scratching. The most common behavioral problems, though, are tantrums and noncompliance (Olley, 1992). Other children show withdrawal and do not show tantrums. These children are less likely to be identified early. Children with autism have little interaction with parents and attachment does not take place.

Cognitive and information-processing difficulties are also present. They do not grasp concepts, and their learning is delayed (Romanczyk, Ekdahl, & Lockshin, 1992). They are attracted by repetition and may play with keys on a ring in the same manner for hours. They show no interest in age-appropriate toys.

Children with autism seem to select a part of a stimulus and maintain attention to this part (Powers, 1992). This is called **overselectivity** (Handleman, 1992). An expert in the field, Ivar Lovaas, argues that this characteristic is an important part of the syndrome. For example, an apple has a certain shape, color, taste, and texture. If a person only attended to the color, the individual could easily confuse it with a tomato (Lovaas et al., 1971). These children also show difficulties in generalizing what they have learned in one situation to another. They may function well in one store and not in another.

Children with autism score unevenly on subtests of the Wechsler Intelligence Scale for Children (WISC), performing poorly on subtests measuring verbal abstractions or skills and well on subtests involving visual-spatial or rote memory (*Psychosomatic Medicine*, 1993).

The intelligence of these children varies, with about 75 percent testing in the range of mental retardation (Rutter & Schopler, 1987). Yet, caution must be used when interpreting intelligence tests with children diagnosed as having autism, as for all children with disabilities, especially severe disabilities. The children's numerous impairments may affect their ability to answer questions or show intelligence. Generally, the more intelligent the child with autism the better the prognosis (Jones, 1988). The social functioning of people with autism in adulthood is correlated with verbal intelligence.

Children with autism also show significant delays in developing self-help skills. They become toilet-trained late and are delayed in their ability to dress themselves. As they age, the delays become more noticeable and the gaps between their chronological age and developmental level increase (Handleman, 1992).

These children generally do not develop a "theory of mind" (Happé, 1994; Leslie, 1987). That is, they do not show any understanding of the mental states or beliefs of others. They do not respond in a way that would allow anyone to believe they understand how others are feeling or thinking.

Autistic behavior is shown early in life. Autism is usually diagnosed when the child is between 18 and 24 months old (Olley, 1992). Parents, though, often reflect on the child's earliest behavior and identify specific behavior patterns that were of concern, such as an infant who was extremely quiet or fussy, who was under- and overresponsive to stimuli and neither showed eye contact nor responsiveness.

As noted earlier, children with autism differ widely from each other (Smith, Chung, & Vostanis, 1994). Not only do they differ in the severity of their

Overselectivity:
The phenomenon in which children with autism select a part of the stimulus and maintain their attention to the part rather than the whole stimulus.

THOUGHT QUESTION

1. Should children diagnosed as having autism be given regular individualized intelligence tests? If not, how would you measure their intellectual ability?

impairments, but some children with autism will show one set of behaviors and another a different set. Unfortunately, attempts at classifying subtypes have not yet been successful, but this may reflect the existing knowledge base, and ultimately subtypes may be found (Eaves, Ho, & Eaves, 1994; Szatmari, 1992). This variability in symptoms is reflected in the DSM-IV's diagnostic criteria (see Table 15.1). Of the groups of symptoms noted, a child does not have to show all symptoms to be considered to have an autistic disorder.

TABLE 15.1   **Diagnostic Criteria for Autistic Disorder**

A. A total of six (or more) items from (1), (2), and (3), with at least two from (1), and one each from (2) and (3):

(1) qualitative impairment in social interaction, as manifested by at least two of the following:

    (a) marked impairment in the use of multiple nonverbal behaviors such as eye-to-eye gaze, facial expression, body postures, and gestures to regulate social interaction

    (b) failure to develop peer relationships appropriate to developmental level

    (c) a lack of spontaneous seeking to share enjoyment, interests, or achievements with other people (e.g., by a lack of showing, bringing, or pointing out objects of interest)

    (d) lack of social or emotional reciprocity

(2) qualitative impairments in communication as manifested by at least one of the following:

    (a) delay in, or total lack of, the development of spoken language (not accompanied by an attempt to compensate through alternative modes of communication such as gesture or mime)

    (b) in individuals with adequate speech, marked impairment in the ability to initiate or sustain a conversation with others

    (c) stereotyped and repetitive use of language or idiosyncratic language

    (d) lack of varied, spontaneous make-believe play or social imitative play appropriate to developmental level

(3) restricted repetitive and stereotyped patterns of behavior, interests, and activities, as manifested by at least one of the following:

    (a) encompassing preoccupation with one or more stereotyped and restricted patterns of interest that is abnormal either in intensity or focus

    (b) apparently inflexible adherence to specific, nonfunctional routines or rituals

    (c) stereotyped and repetitive motor mannerisms (e.g., hand or finger flapping or twisting, or complex whole-body movements)

    (d) persistent preoccupation with parts of objects

B. Delays or abnormal functioning in at least one of the following areas, with onset prior to age 3 years: (1) social interaction, (2) language as used in social communication, or (3) symbolic or imaginative play.

C. The disturbance is not better accounted for by Rett's Disorder or Childhood Disintegrative Disorder.

American Psychiatric Association: *Diagnostic and Statistical Manual of Mental Disorders, Fourth Edition.* Washington, D.C.: American Psychiatric Association, 1994.

Why Discuss Autism?

Children diagnosed as having autism, then, show an impressive variety of serious impairments, and the next question is why autism is even being discussed here. Not many years ago, few people would even have mentioned the possibility that children with autism could be integrated into the regular classroom, although such integration did occur in nursery schools in Toronto, Canada, as far back as 1956 (see Lovatt, 1962). The prognosis was, and still is, relatively poor, and the behavior of these children is so unusual and difficult to control that mainstreaming or inclusion would not be considered an option for the overwhelming majority.

Much has changed. New methods of treatment and new understandings of the condition have brought some hope to families of children with autism. However, science is not yet at a stage of understanding that is sophisticated enough to provide psychologists with a standard treatment to bring these children from a state of showing autistic behavior to a state at which their behavior allows them to be educated in regular classrooms in every case, or even the great majority of cases. At the present time, the percentage of children with autism who are educated in the regular classroom is still rather small, although 50 percent of the graduates of certain programs can be educated in regular classes (Lovaas, Smith, & McEachin, 1989). In addition, the psychological treatments for these children are controversial. In fact, the technique sometimes used to encourage communication is one of the most controversial areas of treatment in all psychology.

Prevalence

Autism is rare, with a prevalence of 4 or 5 per 10,000 births (Harris et al., 1991). About 3 of 4 children affected are boys (Olley, 1992). When females have the disorder, they tend to be more seriously affected with lower intelligence scores and greater problems in cognition and language (Konstantareas, Homatidis, & Busch, 1989).

During the 1992–1993 school year, 15,527 children diagnosed with autism received special education services. Children diagnosed as having autism comprise about 0.3 percent of all the children receiving special education help (U.S. Department of Education, 1994).

What Causes Autism?

In the past, some psychologists believed that autism was caused by cold, distant parents. When a child was diagnosed as having autism, parents experienced unnecessary guilt. Absolutely *no* credible evidence has been presented that autism is caused by parenting practices (Wenar, 1994; Tsai & Ghaziuddin, 1992). This idea is a most destructive one, not only because it is incorrect, but because all successful treatment programs require active parental participation. A highly defensive parent is not going to be an effective agent of intervention (Powell, Hecimovic, & Christensen, 1992).

Today, the medical community accepts that organic factors are the cause of autism (Baker et al., 1994; Lee & Gotlib, 1994). There is evidence that a genetic link to autism exists (*Psychosomatic Medicine*, 1993). In one study, 21 same-sex children with autism who were twins were tested. Four of the eleven identical twins (sharing the same genetic endowment) were also diagnosed as having autism, but none of the fraternal twins shared autism (Fostein & Rutter, 1978). In other studies, the rate at which both identical twins have autism (the concordance rate), is even higher (Ritvo, Freeman, & Mason-Brothers, 1985). When autism is not found in the nonautistic identical twin, severe cognitive problems are still evident.

A relationship also exists between complications during pregnancy and delivery and autism. Perhaps injuries to the brain occur (Tsai & Ghaziuddin, 1992). Unfortunately, research linking these problems to autism are based upon correlational evidence, and cause and effect statements cannot be made.

Perhaps the best conclusion is that, although occasional cases are associated with medical disorders, most cases are genetically caused (Fostein & Rutter, 1988). The mode of transmission is uncertain, and more than one specific genetic form may exist (*Psychosomatic Medicine*, 1993).

The search for biological causes has led to a number of studies using various brain-scanning devices. These scans often show some structural abnormalities, but no single structural difference is common to all. PET scans, which can yield a graphic view of metabolic processes, blood volume, and blood flow in the brain, show elevated use of glucose and some other unusual findings, but again, none common to all. The same occurs with electroencephalograms (EEG), where irregularities in brain waves are plentiful but no one irregularity is common to all (Tsai & Ghaziuddin, 1992). Studies of neurochemistry show increased levels of the neurotransmitter serotonin and some possible role for the neurotransmitter dopamine. In fact, drugs that block dopamine receptors reduce some of the symptoms. Still, the research focusing on the specific physiological causes of the disorder is still in its infancy, and although positive findings may occur in the future, the precise cause of autism is, at present, unknown.

The Effects of Autism on the Family

A child with autism affects the family in many ways. Some families adjust better than others, and the challenges change with the age of the child. Stress is often a problem. The families of children with autism report more stress than families of children with mental retardation or those caring for children with chronic illnesses (Harris et al., 1991). Mothers are somewhat more affected by the stress than fathers (Bristol, 1984). The amount of time needed to help the child, the isolation from others, and the need for constant treatment can be exhausting.

Yet, studies of these family's marital adjustment show that it is good; parents show levels of marital adjustment similar to those demonstrated by other happily married couples (Koegel et al., 1982). Although raising a child with as severe a disorder as autism is certainly stressful, marriages can remain stable and happy.

Parent Training

Parents of children with autism need training if they are to cope with the challenges of raising a child with such a severe disorder. Parent training emphasizes three areas. First, the training program presents the most accurate information to parents concerning the nature of the disorder. Second, parents are taught behavioral strategies to counter the aggressiveness, tantrums, and noncompliance (Bristol & Schopler, 1983). If children continue to throw tantrums or remain destructive, the chances of integration are minimized. Parents must also learn ways of teaching their children such skills as dressing, eating, and bathing if these children are ever to be integrated into the classroom. Third, social support is emphasized. This social support comes from the spouse, other family members, parents of other children with autism, and professionals.

Mothers of autistic children experiencing the least stress are mothers with the greatest social support, especially from spouses and relatives (Bristol, 1984). For example, one child with autism did not sleep much at night. A parent had to watch him since the child was destructive. Both parents usually stayed up, each supporting the other, but the exhaustion was a telling sign and they needed some help to continue. Other types of support include financial aid, flexibility in treatment, special babysitting services, and professionals who will coordinate services (Powell et al., 1992). Research shows that parent training works (Howlin, 1981). Effective parent training is a major factor in reducing stress (Harris et al., 1991).

Parents of autistic children need help to learn behavioral techniques useful for dealing with the behaviors of autistic children.

Treatment for Autism

Until very recently, the prognosis for children with autism was quite pessimistic. An estimated 4 in 6 children with autism continued to have severe impairments into adulthood and were not employable; 1 in 6 made a fair recovery; and only 1 in 6 made a good enough recovery to be considered truly functional (Comer, 1995). The higher the intelligence score and the better the language skills, the more positive was the outcome.

The pessimistic outlook is slowly changing, however. A number of programs using intensive educational efforts begun early in childhood and based upon solid research evidence have been very effective. Perhaps the study by Lovaas (1987), though, is the best example.

Lovaas chose children independently diagnosed as having autism and whose average age was less than 4 years. Nineteen subjects were assigned to an intensive training group and 19 to a mini-training control group or another group consisting of children with autism who received no training. Before the training, the children were quite similar.

Children in the experimental, intensive training group worked for 2 years with specially trained student therapists and their parents for more than 40 hours a week on a one-to-one basis. Operant conditioning techniques were used. Behavioral deficits were first targeted and behavior improved. Aggression and self-stimulation were treated by ignoring the inappropriate behavior, use of timeout procedures, instituting more acceptable substitutes, and other procedures. After

Promising new programs entail the use of trained student therapists who spend considerable time with each autistic child.

that, language use, and teaching children the necessary behaviors to function in a preschool setting were emphasized. Next, the staff focused on emotional expression, preacademic skills, and learning through observation. Children in the mini-training group received the same treatment but with 10 hours per week of one-to-one interaction.

The results of the training were nothing short of spectacular. Forty-seven percent of the children in the intensive experimental group achieved average intelligence and were able to be educated with other children versus 2 percent of children in the other groups. Nine of the 19 children completed first grade successfully. Of the 10 who did not, 8 had aphasia (see Chapter 6). At age thirteen, 8 of the 19 experimental children could not be distinguished from their nondisabled classmates on many age-related measures (Lovaas et al., 1989). Although the study has been criticized methodologically (Schopler, Short, & Mesibov, 1989), its results are a hopeful sign that positive intervention strategies can be successfully used.

Other extremely intensive programs also work, so no single method is successful. For example, project LEAP was able to claim that one-half of the children were educated in regular classes without special services (Powers, 1992).

Programs that are successful share many commonalities (Powers, 1992; Berkell, 1992). They all use a behavioral framework and task analysis, target specific behaviors, use specific reinforcers, and engage in simple direct teaching. They heavily involve and train parents. The programs feature one-to-one attention and most begin intervention with the child at about age three. The programs also plan for generalization so the home, school, and community are involved. The curriculum emphasizes social and cognitive skills training and integrates these children with children without disabilities as much as possible. The personnel who work for so many hours with these children are specially trained.

A number of specific behavioral methods are used. For example, in the area of language, the child is first rewarded with food for any verbalization (Lovaas & Newsom, 1976). Then the reinforcer is only delivered when the response immediately follows the therapist's prompt. Reward is then given for closer and closer approximations of the verbalization that the therapist is making, and finally, the therapist introduces other dissimilar sounds and reinforces only correct responses. Speech sounds, words, and phrases are programmed so that the child gradually acquires language. Again, tremendous time, effort, and patience are required. Children with autism or mental retardation need to be specially prompted. Sometimes a verbal prompt may be sufficient, while at other times the child may physically be moved through the activity.

Facilitated Communication

The most spirited debate in the field centers on a particular method of communication. Children diagnosed as having autism have serious language deficiencies, and if they are to function in school and society they must communicate in one way or another. Some behavioral methods involving reinforcing the utterances of these children and demanding closer and closer approximations to real words to obtain the reinforcer have been used. Lately, though, a different approach has been advocated, and one that has pitted professional against professional.

Ivar Lovaas's research shows that with considerable support and intensive training, some children with autism can make spectacular progress.

Dear Mom:

Do you mind if two of my friends at school style my hair next week? Kathleen and Molly will put some interesting things in my hair like a pony tail and curl the bangs up in the air. They are nice friends that have been teaching me how to dance and all about music and their tapes. They tell me about the things they do at home and together I wish I could tell them about my life. We do some sharing when we play games but its not the same as real friends. It is so hard for me to develop normal friends since I can't laugh and talk about clothes I wear and boys I like or the concerts I've been to. so I wish I was not autistic. Wish I could do all the things that the other kids do. I guess I'm getting closer to normal but I am still so far away Please keep pushing me forward. I need your support and strength. Getting the most out of life and producing the most good is my goal. I want to be an active member of society and just not get dragged down by my handicap I love you mom.

Maggie (Maggie is a pseudonym) (Biklen et al., 1992, p. 1).

This was written by a 13-year-old student diagnosed as having autism who can speak only a few phrases and often echoes what she hears. She used a controversial technique called facilitated communication.

Facilitated communication was pioneered in the United States by Douglas Biklen and consists of a facilitator who supports the arm of the child while the

Facilitated communication:
A controversial technique for improving the communication abilities of children with severe disorders in which physical assistance is provided to individuals to allow them to more readily spell out words on a typewriter or other device.

child types thoughts on a keyboard. Facilitated communication is based upon the idea that using gestures is a more promising approach than modeling verbal language. It includes a number of steps.

First, the communicator types with one index finger, with hand-over-hand or hand-at-the-wrist support and then independently or with just a touch to the elbow or shoulder. Over time, the communicator progresses from structured work, such as fill in the blanks exercises and multiple choice activities to open-ended typed conversational text (Biklen et al., 1992). The key is the trainer or facilitator supporting the children's hands or arms as the child types on a typewriter (Spake, 1992).

The crux of the controversy is how to validate the use of the technique. Are these really the thoughts of the child, or is the facilitator influencing the typed communication? Other controversies are somewhat more theoretical and deal with trying to explain the processes involved.

Proponents offer a number of qualitative studies using observations, interviews, and videotapes as evidence for its effectiveness (Biklen & Duchar, 1994; Biklen et al., 1992; Biklen & Schubert, 1991). Testimonies of parents and some facilitators note the incredible improvements in children's communication skills. For example, 12-year-old Rusty, who used facilitated communication, was only typing his name and answering simple questions. His mother asked, as she always did, if there was anything he wanted to say. She expected him not to respond, but instead he typed "want yes rusty hewants to kewaqq ftre to kikll that dog." The language is indistinct, but the message that Rusty wanted to get rid of Frisky, the family pet, was clear. This statement proved to his parents that this was Rusty typing. He was simply angry at the dog (Spake, 1992, p. 44).

In another case, pioneer researcher Rosemary Crossley (1992) discusses the case of a teenager assessed as having autism and intellectual impairments with disjointed and echolalic speech. The teenager started using a keyboard with her mother holding her hand to help her achieve index finger isolation. The principal at the school thought her mother was doing the typing. Gradually, as the child's skills improved she was typing with her mother's arm around her waist for emotional support. Her principal, seeing this behavior, allowed a move to a local secondary school where she is in the tenth grade and typing without physical contact (Crossley & Remmington-Gurney, 1992).

Biklen notes that children with autism using this technique type unique errors, produce phonetic spellings, type phrases or sentences that are unusual and would not be expected, and type things not familiar to the facilitator and thereby reveal their true personalities. For example, Maggie wrote, "I can now tell people how intelligent I am inside. I can express the plans that I can even though I don't always get what I want. I can tell people my dreams and goals in life. . . . I can tell people what I like and dislike. I am me and everyone can love me because I am a good and valuable person" (Biklen, 1992, p. 21).

Facilitated communication has another side, though. Many authorities do not believe that the communication belongs to the individuals with autism. The children require support at the hand or wrist, making it difficult to observe whether they are moving on their own. Others type messages that are inconsistent with their own speech and above what professionals believe are their abilities. Others type with some facilitators and not at all with others, and some reveal deep personal feelings that are not reflected in their manner and behavior.

THOUGHT QUESTION

2. *Is qualitative evidence sufficient to advocate facilitated communication or are quantitative, controlled studies also needed?*

In addition, even supporters note that facilitators often misinterpret communication and give more support than is necessary or desirable. For example, when a teacher asked a child why he was agitated the child typed "sometimes i run out of joy." The instructor believed the boy's profound poetic notions until she found out that he always calmed himself by twirling a bottle of dishwashing liquid around (Crossley & Remmington-Gurney, 1992, p. 75). In addition, although people may assume that everything a child with autism types is true, these children do make up stories. Facilitators sometimes need to be reminded not to overreact to improbable information and not to take all communication literally.

This overreaction to what is communicated has led to some serious problems. When a child with autism noted in graphic terms that she was being sexually abused, the question of how to treat her communication came to the forefront. What should be done? Is it a fantasy or a lie, or is the child being abused? Facilitated communication can provide an outlet for resentment and anger. On the other hand, some of the cases may be valid. Even though discerning the truth is difficult, much of what a child communicates has to be questioned. For example, children from primarily Spanish or Hindi speaking homes have typed complaints of sexual abuse in perfect English (Seligmann & Chideya, 1992). These complaints of abuse are not rare, but to date only a few of the allegations have led to charges; however, even unsubstantiated claims cause tremendous damage. Parents accused with no other evidence besides the allegations of abuse made during facilitated communication sessions have faced the scorn of their neighbors, the expense of hiring lawyers, and the emotional devastation of being falsely accused (Green & Shane, 1994).

Many detractors point to the high degree of physical intervention provided by the facilitator even when the person with autism has sufficient motor skills to select the letters independently. They also complain about the need for a facilitator's strong belief in the efficacy of the technique for it to work. Sometimes, the facilitators have not been willing to have the process assessed independently (Prior & Cummins, 1992).

Some argue that when true objectivity is achieved in testing, evidence that the communication is coming from the facilitator is found (Prior & Cummins, 1992). In fact, controlled research has not produced evidence of independent communication from clients who do not usually communicate when the facilitator cannot be aware of the response asked of the client (Cabay, 1994; Green & Shane, 1994). For example, Wheeler and colleagues (1993) assessed the effectiveness of facilitated communication with 12 people with autism and 9 staff members who worked with them to provide facilitated communication. All the participants in the study were considered skilled in facilitated communication.

A physical setting was constructed that allowed the children with autism to see a card with a picture of a common item that each child knew (see Figure 15.1). In one condition, the child was presented with a stimulus card and the facilitator could not see the stimulus card. The child was asked to identify the picture through facilitated communication. In a second condition, the child was presented with a stimulus and the facilitator was not allowed to engage in physical contact, although verbal prompts could be used. In the third and most interesting condition, half the time the facilitator was shown the same card and half the time the facilitator was shown a different card than the one the child saw.

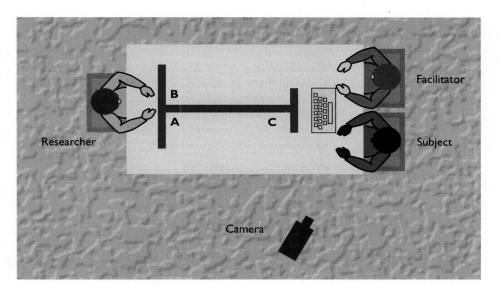

FIGURE 15.1   Materials and setting for Wheeler and colleagues' study of facilitated communication.

"An Experimental Assessment of Facilitated Communication," by D.L. Wheeler, J.W. Jacobson, R.A. Paglieri, and A.A. Schwartz, 1993, 31, p. 52. Reprinted by permission of The American Association on Mental Retardation.

The results showed that facilitated communication was not effective. In the first condition, only two of the possible 120 responses were even partially correct. In the second condition, none of the responses were correct. In the third condition in which sometimes the facilitators were shown the same card and sometimes a different card, results showed that the individuals with autism were being influenced and their responses sometimes controlled by the facilitators. When both the facilitators and the person with autism were shown the same card, the child identified the item correctly a little less than a quarter of the time. When the individual with autism and the facilitator were shown different cards, the individual with autism identified none of the cards, but about 20 percent of the time the person with autism typed what the facilitator saw! This was interpreted by the researchers as evidence that the facilitators were influencing the children. Even though the researchers note that no evidence exists that this facilitator influence is either purposeful or intentional, the influence is present.

Other questions concerning facilitated communication are also raised. If the technique does work, how can psychologists and educators determine which communications are the client's and which are the facilitator's? In addition, why is some physical contact necessary even after so many clients' ability to communicate has been established? Full independence is rarely achieved. Questions are also raised about the sophisticated level of dialogue shown via assisted communication. One client produced impressive communication with the facilitator, but without the facilitator could not produce a sentence that could be understood.

Still, it would be incorrect to suggest that because excesses sometimes creep into the way the method is used, it should completely be abandoned. The real problem comes from the lack of confirming evidence from controlled studies. Skeptics argue that conclusions cannot be drawn because of the strength and nature of the proofs offered. They claim that even subtle nonverbal cues including physical support cues may influence the children. The emotional involvement communicated may also be important.

THOUGHT QUESTION

3. *Would you use facilitated communication with a child who is diagnosed as having autism?*

A third perspective takes the middle ground. Its proponents argue that something is happening, but it is so far indefinable (Silliman, 1992).

Is facilitated communication a wonderful new tool that can unlock the innermost secrets of children with autism and other disabilities? Or is it a poorly designed technique with the potential for great injury to the family? The line is drawn and the challenge is clear. Unfortunately, neither proponents nor opponents can agree on how to validate the technique, and so the strong divisions in professional circles remain the rule. At the present time, no widely accepted answers to the questions posed exist, and professionals must await further developments in this area.

Children with Autism in the Classroom

To be included, children with autism must behave in an acceptable manner. If they show extreme symptoms, they cannot be integrated. Children with autistic symptoms are included only after they have already received individualized, intensive treatment and are considered ready for school. Even in Lovaas' very successful work, only about half were capable of being placed in the regular classroom. Still, this percentage represents a great improvement over the time when these children rarely if ever had the opportunity to interact with other children.

The regular classroom teacher who is educating a child with autism can expect that the child has had intensive treatment and will enter the educational setting with a team of experts ready to help. With early help, many behaviors that can adversely affect the classroom environment or require an inordinate amount of teacher time can be reduced or eliminated.

THOUGHT QUESTION

4. *If you were asked to be the regular classroom teacher for a child with autism, what questions would you ask and what requests would you make?*

As noted in Chapter 1, most arguments for full inclusion are made for children with mild and perhaps moderate impairments; however, a growing movement advocates the inclusion of children with severe disabilities in the regular classroom. Any decision on placement must be made on a case-by-case basis.

When dealing with a population that has so many serious difficulties, educators need to prepare the class as well as the child with autism. The class must understand the nature of the child's disability. Children with autism must learn to interact with other children and control their own destructive and self-injurious behavior.

Preschool Experiences

Children with autism have been successfully educated in regular preschools. However, programs that aim at improving the social functioning of the child as well as preparing the child for later education in regular classrooms must be based upon a judicious selection of children with autism with the abilities to succeed, sensitivity to the needs of all children, a well-trained staff, and programs that allow children to gradually enter an integrated classroom. Consider the organization of the Small Wonders class created in 1987 as an extension of the services offered by the Douglass Developmental Disabilities Center of Rutgers University in New Jersey. The program provides a preschool environment for both young-

Preschool programs for children with autism deal with improving skills necessary for later integration.

sters with autism and those without disabilities. Social integration is stressed with the hope of placing these children into regular kindergartens later on.

The Small Wonders class consists of six preschoolers with autism, eight children without disabilities, a special education teacher, three classroom assistants, and a clinical consultant. All the children with autism meet the DSM-IV criteria for the diagnosis and are specially selected for the preschool program.

The program consists of three classes: a prep class, a highly individualized program with a one-to-one structure throughout the school day; a segregated self-contained group-oriented program emphasizing individual skills as well as social and peer relations; and the Small Wonders integrated class. All the children in the integrated class have spent at least one year in either the prep class or segregated class. Programmed efforts in both classes focus on developing the necessary skills for children to make the transition to larger groups or integrated classes (Tomchek et al., 1992).

A careful look at the organization of this program shows why it is successful. Very practical and detailed steps are taken to ensure success. To make certain that the needs of all children in the program are satisfied, the staff remains sensitive to the needs of the children without disabilities and their parents. A balance is struck between the needs of both groups of children. For example, children with and without autism are encouraged to interact with each other, but opportunities for children without autism to choose friends among other nondisabled children and interact with them in age-appropriate activities are included.

In addition, the staff is well trained and sufficient for the task at hand. Planning and organization are strong, and the program allows children to graduate from a less integrated to a more integrated program when they are ready.

Inclusion in Elementary School

The integration of children with autism in kindergarten is a major decision. As has been noted so often, just placing children together does not ensure positive interaction. The behaviors of children with autism, even if the most disturbing behaviors are somewhat reduced at the time of placement in the regular classroom, can be very confusing for children without disabilities and avoidance is common. Attempts to improve interaction involve giving accurate information, structuring social interaction, and recruiting peers without disabilities as intervention agents.

Giving information in an age-appropriate manner is useful, although not sufficient to improve the social interaction among children who are and are not disabled (Wooten & Mesibov, 1986). Teachers also need to structure peer interaction through group activities (see Chapter 2), as well as to help children with autism improve their social behavior.

Sasso and colleagues (1985) demonstrated the need for adequate information-giving, structured activities, and social skills training in an interesting study of second and third graders. Students without disabilities were given information about various disabilities and individual differences in a 16-session program over a 9-week period.

Students participated in structured interactions using motor-skill games and music and art activities, which encouraged cooperation between children without disabilities and children with autism. In addition, some of the children with autism also received social skills training consisting of instruction in making eye contact, responding to greetings, and initiating greetings. For each skill, the social response was described, the response modeled, verbal reinforcement for approximations of the behavior given, and practice provided. The results showed that stu-

Some children with autism may be included in elementary school, especially if they have received intensive early training.

dents without disabilities who had both received information and participated in experiences with the children with autism had the most positive attitudes and made the greatest number of positive initiations toward the children with autism. Those initiations were most likely aimed at children with autism who had received social skills training. Other studies show that children with autism can be taught social skills and can learn to initiate social interactions during leisure activities with other children (Gaylord-Ross et al., 1984).

Peers can be trained to teach and reinforce appropriate social skills in their peers with autism (Brady et al., 1987). Under these controlled circumstances, the social skills of children with autism improve and general social interaction increases (Handlan & Bloom, 1993).

In another study of kindergarten children, giving information, structuring interactions, and prompting led to effective results. Peers were taught how to prompt and interact with children with autism through direct modeling and coaching (Handlan & Bloom, 1993). The modeling involved showing children without autism how to teach children with autism game-playing skills such as initiating a turn, rolling dice, operating game pieces, moving a marker in the correct sequence on the game board, and passing the game to the next child. Verbal reinforcement was modeled using specific praise with the child's name. For example, the teacher would say, "Good job, Joey, you waited your turn." The environment was structured to encourage interaction as well. The nondisabled children were willing and able to prompt and reinforce their peers with autism as long as an adult modeled what they were to do and reinforced their efforts. The students with autism experienced more social success if they had already mastered the skills of the game before playing it with another child.

SCENARIO

1 Donald is a child with autism placed in your third-grade class. He has come a long way since the time that he was first diagnosed. He sometimes shows some rocking and repetitive behaviors, but is progressing nicely. His verbal skills are developing, although he is still somewhat behind the other children. What could you do to improve Donald's growing verbal skills?

The Autism Mainstreaming Collaboration Model

If the inclusion of children with autism is to become a reality, attention to detail, sensitivity to everyone in the class, and preparation are needed. These qualities are shown in a general model for inclusion called the Autism Mainstreaming Collaboration Model (Simpson & Myles, 1993). The model is designed to support general educators who assume the primary teaching responsibility for children and youth with autism. The model emphasizes collaboration, shared responsibility, and shared decision-making among general educators, special educators, and support personnel.

The model is also based upon studies of general educators' attitudes, needs, and stated concerns. For instance, many studies show that teachers will agree to become the primary educators for children with autism if they are assured of training, support, and adequate resources. When Myles and Simpson (1989) asked teachers whether they would be willing to accept a student with a disability, 86 percent said yes if appropriate support and training were provided. Without such support 32 percent were willing.

Regular classroom teachers are willing to accept qualified students if they can rely on professionals from various disciplines to provide necessary intervention services. Therefore, the model provides for assistance from social workers, psychologists, speech pathologists, occupational therapists, and others as needed. Class size is reduced to allow for more individualized instruction. The relationship between the general educator and special service providers is one of collaboration in planning, and involves more than these professionals simply telling the teacher what should be done. Most teachers consider this collaboration absolutely necessary for effective inclusion (Myles & Simpson, 1989).

Additional planning time is given to permit teachers to individualize academic tasks and plan alternative or additional activities. Paraprofessionals are made available to assist students in practicing previously taught skills, to document student performance and progress, and to assist teachers with daily planning materials. Inservice training is also offered to teachers. Training and support, then, are the cornerstones of the program.

Everyone involved receives information. This information emphasizes human similarities and differences, characteristics of autism, and making friends with children who have autism. Children with autism receive the necessary training and attention, including direct skill instruction, peer-initiated interventions, and peer tutoring. The classroom teacher can expect full participation in decision making. This team approach requires adequate coordination.

Peer Tutoring

If students are to be trained to bring out the abilities of children with autism, one technique that should work is peer tutoring. In using peer tutoring, the first step is to identify children in general education with an interest in working and interacting with students with autism. Motivation and interest are most important, but these volunteers should also be chosen because they want to become friends with children with autism, as opposed to merely assuming a teaching role.

The tutors first learn about autism through age-appropriate materials. Such materials are available through many sources including the Autism Society of America. The tutors and tutees are then given an opportunity to get to know one another by engaging in structured but informal activities, such as various games. After two or three short sessions, peers are asked which students they want to tutor. Teacher and staff input is, of course, necessary but students' choices are given serious consideration.

The tutors are instructed in tutoring methods. The instruction revolves around the nature of the tutoring sessions, how to structure them, how to give directions, how to provide reinforcement, and how to manage unacceptable behavior. For example, the instructor may discuss how to tutor the child on math facts, model the activities for the tutor, and then provide opportunities for guided practice and even simulate the experience. Tutoring should be scheduled for a minimum of three times a week for 20–30 minutes. Adults should be available to supervise, respond to questions, handle problems, and deal with severe misbehavior if it occurs, as well as to reinforce tutors and tutees for their efforts.

Since the peer tutoring is designed to facilitate both academic and social development, participants are given time to play and socialize, so a 30-minute tutoring session may involve 20 minutes of tutoring and 10 minutes of play (Simpson, 1992).

 # Children with Autism and Computers: Unfinished Business

It would seem natural to use computers to help educate children with autism. After all, children with autism are fascinated by mechanical devices and might enjoy the types of activities that can be programmed on the computer. (Romanczyk, Ekdahl, & Lockshin, 1992). Indeed, computers have been used with children with autism in many ways for a number of years. They have been used to help develop communication abilities, as a teaching aid for new classroom material, and as a means to help children become more responsive to the environment.

The computer with voice output has been used to help children with severe and profound disabilities who do not speak (Durand, 1992). The computer can vocalize what is typed as well as present verbal challenges to the child. In one system, a computer sounds out the name of whatever letter the child types. Later, the computer can reverse the process and encourage the child to type the letter of a sound emitted from the computer. Only that letter's key will produce any response. Later, words are introduced and the computer may ask the student for particular words and accept only the correct letters spelled in the correct order. Finally, children are introduced to reading through typing answers to particular questions (Goodwin & Goodwin, 1969).

Colby (1973) designed a computer system to encourage children with autism to speak. A series of exploratory learning games were used. In the simplest, the computer vocalized the sound of any letter typed. In more complex activities, the computer generated complete sentences whenever a student touched a particular letter. The computer was programmed to occasionally omit a word in the sentence to encourage the child to generate the word. Using eight such exercises, 13 of 17 children with autism began to use speech to communicate with others.

Computers have also been used to help teach children with autism new concepts. A number of studies relate computer-aided instruction to improvements in attitude toward work (Panyan, 1984). Computer-based instruction allowed children without disabilities to use verbal prompts to help encourage their peers with autism to work on exercises presented on the computer. These prompts resulted in greater verbal interaction between students with autism and their peers without disabilities (Panyan, 1984).

Chen and Bernard-Opitz (1993) compared computer-aided instruction with personal instruction for four children with autism. The children were taught material related to memory, visual, and conceptual tasks. Students were videotaped at work with both the computer and the instructor. Motivation, general behavior and compliance, and learning rate were analyzed. Although each child reacted somewhat differently to the instruction, students showed more interest, greater motivation, and better behavior during computer-aided instruction. Two of the students began to take turns at the computer, which is a significant development in social behavior. Learning rate, though, was not affected.

Other studies also find that students with autism enjoy using the computer and may even prefer it to working with a human teacher.

Although some studies find advantages for computer-aided instruction on a measure of learning (Panyan, 1984), most do not (Romanczyk et al., 1992). Most do find improvements in behavior, attitude and motivation. For example, when children's performance on discriminating geometric shapes was studied, no differences in performance between computer-aided instruction and human instruction were found (Plienis & Romanczyk, 1985). This may still indicate some advantage for computer-aided instruction in some content areas since teachers often do not enjoy teaching simple, repetitive tasks. Students were also more disruptive with human teachers than when working with the computer. Other studies have also found that children are more enthusiastic and more compliant when using computer-aided instruction (see Chen & Bernard-Opitz, 1993).

Although the advantages in attitude, motivation, and behavior are often found, the actual situation may be more complicated. A complex relationship may exist among the type of task, task difficulty, and type of instructional method used. Children with autism are more disruptive working with teachers only when particular methods of instruction are being used. In addition, children with autism working with computers often omit material when the work becomes more difficult. Teachers do not allow as many omissions (Romanczyk et al., 1992). It may be that some of the findings on behavioral advantages may be due to the differences in the demands of computers and teachers.

Too often computers are viewed as drill and practice providers for children with autism. However, studies show that children with autism enjoy exploring the computer using programs such as LOGO. LOGO is a simple program which allows young children to create their own designs using a simple computer language. It does so by means of a turtle that leaves tracks on the computer screen when given specific, simple commands. For example, the command FORWARD 30 means that the turtle moves forward 30 steps. All commands are composed of very descriptive words (Brownell, 1987). One child with autism who was assumed to be deaf and was without speech uttered his first words while operating the LOGO turtle (Goldenberg, 1979). Children with autism who appear to be completely uninterested in their surroundings may become actively engaged in computer games (Geoffrion & Goldenberg, 1981).

One possible future use of the computer is to help children with autism overcome their overselectivity. Many children with autism are overselective, that is they focus on only one small aspect of a stimulus. Specific computer programs may help the child focus attention on the relevant cues of a stimulus, encouraging the children to make discriminations and reducing overselectivity (Chen & Bernard-Opitz, 1993).

The computer can serve as a tool to foster verbal competency, to teach material to children, to help children with autism explore their environment, and to help students overcome some of their cognitive and perceptual difficulties. The findings of increased motivation and interest and less misbehavior are significant. However, much unfinished business remains in applying the computer to the education of children with autism (Chen & Bernard-Opitz, 1993). Research is needed generally to find ways to improve computer programs so that they become more effective teaching tools for children with autism. Educators also must discover what tasks are best presented with the aid of the computer. Although there are reports of success in the use of computer technology, failures are also acknowledged. In addition, some potential for abuse of the technology is possible, such as using computers as electronic babysitters to keep children quiet (Romanczyk et al., 1992). Future research will lead to the development of improved computer programs to help children with autism develop their skills as well as determining the circumstances under which computer-aided instruction is of the greatest benefit to children with autism.

Children with Autism and the Classroom Teacher

Because of the rarity of the disorder and the fact that many children with the disorder are not presently educated in regular classes, teachers will not often be challenged to teach a child with autism. A child with autism receiving services in the regular classroom probably has had much contact with professionals. Therefore, much information about the child should be available. Learning about the child, the condition, and what has been done previously is a prerequisite to understanding the child's needs and developing appropriate programming strategies.

A team approach is an absolute necessity when educating a child with autism, as is paraprofessional help. Close collaboration among the various professionals responsible for the child's education and development has no substitute. If a behavior problem is exhibited, behavioral strategies designed by the special educator and the classroom teacher may be necessary. Some of these techniques are shown in Table 15.2. The collaborative model, discussed earlier, with its commitment to collaboration, its training of teachers, and its attention to everyone's needs, shows the most promise.

Children with autism must be prepared for their experience in an integrated classroom. Their classmates need to be given information about the disorder, engage in structured activities that encourage social interaction, and learn to play with and reinforce their peers with autism. With careful training and preparation, some children with autism can be successfully educated in the regular classroom and learn with their peers.

SCENARIO

2 You are asked to design a program that would successfully integrate a child diagnosed as having autism into your elementary school. This child has been undergoing intensive remediation for two or three years and is now judged ready for inclusion. Since this is the first child with autism to be educated in the school, the principal asks you to make recommendations for strategies that will be helpful in educating the child in the regular classroom. What suggestions would you make?

TABLE 15.2   **Behavior Management**

INTERVENTION	DESCRIPTION	USE
DRO (Differential Reinforcement of Other Behavior)	Reinforces the absence of the misbehavior following a specified interval of time.	Self-stimulation, noncompliance, throwing/grabbing
DRA (Differential Reinforcement of Appropriate Behavior)	Specifies an appropriate behavior to be increased by reinforcement. Child must be able to perform behavior.	Self-stimulation, noncompliance, throwing/grabbing
DRI (Differential Reinforcement of Incompatible Behavior)	A combination of DRO and DRA. Behavior is reinforced that is physically and functionally incompatible with the inappropriate behavior. Incompatible behavior must be educationally and socially relevant. Child must be able to perform behavior.	Self-stimulation noncompliance, throwing/grabbing
Time-out (Nonexclusionary; "sit and watch")	Child is removed from reinforcing events to another place in the room for a specified amount of time. He or she watches as teacher reinforces appropriate behavior in other children. Child must verbalize, if possible, why he or she was removed and what he or she must do upon return to room.	Noncompliance, aggressions, tantrums
Time-out (Exclusionary)	Child is removed from reinforcing events to a place outside the classroom for a specific amount of time. Child must verbalize, if possible, why he or she was removed and what he or she must do upon return to room.	Noncompliance, aggressions, tantrums
Extinction	The child will be completely ignored if she or he is engaged in an inappropriate behavior. There is no verbal or physical interaction with the child until child resumes some appropriate behavior.	Noncompliance, disruptive, inappropriate, attention-seeking behaviors
Overcorrection (Positive practice)	Child must complete a repetitive activity as a consequence.	Aggression, disruptive, inappropriate behaviors, self-stimulation, toileting accidents
Overcorrection (Restitutional)	Child must restore the environment to its original state or a state improved above and beyond state in which environment was before the disruption.	Disruptive behaviors (e.g., throwing, toileting accidents)

"Teaching Preschool Children with Autism and Their Normally Developing Peers: Meeting the Challenges of Integrated Education," by L.B. Tomchek, R. Gordon, M. Arnold, J. Handleman, and S. Harris, 1992, *Focus on Autistic Behavior*, 7, pp. 1–17.

 **IN THE CLASSROOM**   **Including the Child with Autism in the Regular Classroom**

The inclusion of children with autism into the regular classroom is a new challenge for the teacher. Relatively few children with autism are educated in regular classrooms at the present time but more children will be in the future as early intervention procedures become even more effective. The following suggestions may be helpful in educating children with autism.

1. Teaching a child with autism should be seen as a team approach with many professionals helping the classroom teacher.	**Why?** The child with autism being educated in a regular class has probably been treated by many professionals who have extensive experience with the child. Their experiences and suggestions are of great help to the teacher. Regular consultations should be scheduled.
2. Learn everything possible about the child's development, behavior, and what services the child has received.	**Why?** Understanding the nature of the child's difficulties and what has been accomplished previously can serve as a beginning for designing a program that will enable the child to learn.
3. Try to foster an atmosphere of shared decision making with other professionals responsible for the child's progress.	**Why?** Successful models for integration of children with autism into regular classes show that shared decision making among all professionals leads to superior results.
4. Do not assume that children with autism have mental retardation.	**Why?** The serious behavioral and linguistic difficulties of these children may lead to the assumption that they have mental retardation. The meaning of intelligence tests for children with autism is subject to question.
5. Beware of even suggesting that parents have caused their children's difficulties.	**Why?** Blaming parents is counterproductive since parental help is so often required. However, in the case of autism, old discredited theories did suggest such a connection. Even though these ideas have been proven false, parental guilt may be present.
6. Prepare the class for the child with autism.	**Why?** Discussing the nature of autism and some behaviors, such as rocking, may help allay the concerns of other children in the class.

7. Actively encourage social interaction through buddy programs, game playing, team activities, and group activities.	**Why?** Even if the more severe behavior disturbances are reduced, some problems may remain which cause classmates to avoid children with autism. Some direct method of fostering social interaction is required.
8. Help the child with autism learn social skills.	**Why?** Studies show that children with autism who receive social skills training are more likely to interact with other children in the class.
9. Children without autism can learn to use prompts to teach children with autism skills.	**Why?** Studies find that peers can be trained to prompt children with autism. Peers can teach children with autism how to play games, leading to better social interaction.
10. Support personnel including a paraprofessional are often required.	**Why?** Paraprofessionals can assist students in learning and practicing new skills. Their support gives the one-to-one attention these children may require.
11. Peer tutoring can be effective.	**Why?** Peer tutoring is one method of improving both interpersonal and academic skills.
12. Use positive behavioral strategies for modifying behavior, consulting professionals who may be of help. Such strategies must be in keeping with the legal and ethical guidelines established in the district and state.	**Why?** The professionals that comprise the team will have had experience modifying the child's behavior and will have a better idea of what will work.

The Future

Professionals have only begun to understand the mystery that is autism. New treatments, some of them controversial, will be forthcoming. The fact that some children with this disability can be educated in regular classes with early help shows the progress being made. For the first time, there is room for more than a little optimism, and parents of children with autism have a ray of hope that their children can be helped. Teachers who may be faced with the challenge of educating a child with autism have models available to them, which can make their job somewhat easier. However, the inclusion of such children must be seen as a team approach and the teacher must be provided with the training and support necessary to meet the needs of these challenging students.

SUMMARY

1. Children with autism show a lack of social behavior, severe language disabilities, and stereotyped behaviors such as rocking, and sometimes self-injurious behavior. It is the most severe behavior disorder of childhood.

2. Children diagnosed as having autism do not relate well to others, do not gaze at others, and resist being hugged. Their language development is severely impaired. They show learning problems and cognitive difficulties. Overselectivity involves focusing on only one element of a stimulus and not on the entire stimulus. Most children with autism are considered to have mental retardation, although testing the intelligence of children with these severe deficits may not be possible. Children with autism do not develop a theory of mind, that is, they do not show any understanding for the emotional states of others. The symptoms shown by these children differ as does the severity of the symptoms.

3. The prevalence of autism is four or five out of every 10,000 births. Three-quarters of all children with autism are boys.

4. Most authorities believe that autism is caused by organic factors. Some cases may be caused by complications at birth or before birth if the brain is injured.

5. Raising children with autism is stressful, but marriages involving these children are basically stable and happy. Parent training consists of information giving, mastering the use of behavioral strategies to reduce the incidence of behavior problems, and the creation of a network for social support.

6. A number of programs using intensive training in the preschool stage have been successful. Ivar Lovaas trained college students to act as therapists in a 40-hour-per-week, 52-week-a-year program for 2 years. The results showed dramatic improvements.

7. Facilitated communication is a technique for fostering communication in which a facilitator holds the arm or wrist of a child who then types out communication on a keyboard. The controversy involves the question of whether the child's thoughts or the facilitator's thoughts are being communicated. Although some qualitative evidence supports its use, controlled experimentation has to date failed to validate the technique.

8. Some children with autism have been successfully integrated into preschools. Such programs must have a well-trained staff, a highly organized structure, and consider the needs of all children. The model for effective inclusion of children with autism into the regular elementary classroom is based upon meeting the needs and concerns of the regular classroom teacher. A collaborative model is used with many professionals working in concert, in-service training is offered, the teacher participates in the decision-making process, and adequate time for planning is given. Providing information, structuring interactions, and training other children in the classroom to reinforce and prompt social behavior are effective ways to integrate children with autism into the regular classroom.

Severe and Multiple Disabilities

TRUE-FALSE STATEMENTS

See below for the correct answers.

1. The prevalence of children with severe and multiple disabilities is decreasing rapidly.
2. Children with severe disabilities learn more slowly and experience more difficulties generalizing what they have learned in one situation to a new situation than children without disabilities.
3. Most children with dual sensory impairments, those who are both deaf and blind, are educated in special schools.
4. Children with severe disabilities are more likely to be identified at or near birth than children with mild or moderate disabilities.
5. The causes of most cases of severe and multiple disability are genetic and medical rather than psychological.
6. Parents of children with severe disabilities are likely to take a present, one-day-at-a-time orientation compared to professionals who take a more futuristic orientation.
7. The percentage of children with multiple and severe disabilities educated in regular classes has increased sharply in the past 20 years.
8. Children with severe disabilities tend not to forget what they have learned as quickly as children without disabilities.
9. Most parents of children with severe disabilities want the schools to spend the largest amount of instructional time on academic areas.
10. People with severe disabilities cannot work in industrial settings because they cannot learn the required job skills.

Answers to True-False Statements
1. False. See page 601.
2. True.
3. True.
4. True.
5. True.
6. True.
7. True.
8. False. See page 616.
9. False. See page 628.
10. False. See page 634.

New Opportunities; New Challenges

Karen attended a special school staffed by experts in the field of special education for kindergarten, first, and second grade. Beginning in the third grade, Karen began attending a regular elementary school. She received the support services that she needed in the school. Now, in fifth grade, she attends a middle school in her district. Karen spends most of her day in classes with her nondisabled peers and receives some of her daily instruction in the community away from the school.

Karen was born with cerebral palsy and has mental retardation. Her physical disability prevents her from independently engaging in a number of daily activities. However, Karen enjoys partially participating in many activities. Karen cannot speak intelligibly and uses a communication board. She has also learned to operate her power wheelchair independently. Karen's teachers try to adapt materials and use technology so that she can control the environment and participate in many classroom activities. It is a challenge, but her parents see a steady improvement in her social skills and motivation to learn.

Not too long ago, the idea of children with severe and multiple disabilities attending school with their nondisabled peers was considered unrealistic. Today, the situation is changing. The inclusion movement advocates the integration of *all* children into the regular classroom, no matter how severe the disability (Stainback & Stainback, 1988). Some evidence indicates that such integration can occur successfully (Giangreco et al., 1993; Giangreco & Putnam, 1991).

Defining Severe Disabilities

The population of children with severe and multiple disabilities is quite heterogeneous. Some children have severe cognitive limitations, others extensive physical limitations, and still others combinations of physical, intellectual, sensory, and behavioral impairments. PL 94-142 defines severe disabilities in the following manner. Children considered to have severe disabilities are those who:

> because of the intensity of their physical, mental or emotional problems, need highly specialized educational, social, psychological, and medical services in order to maximize their full potential for useful and meaningful participation in society and for self-fulfillment.

The law defines multiple disabilities in terms of the presence of two or more serious disabling conditions, such as children who have dual sensory impairments (deaf-blindness), mental retardation and blindness, or cerebral palsy and deafness (see Haring et al., 1992).

The Association for Persons with Severe Handicaps (TASH) defines individuals with severe disabilities as:

> individuals of all ages who require extensive ongoing support in more than one major life activity in order to participate in integrated community settings and to enjoy a quality of life that is available to citizens with fewer or no disabilities. Support may be required for life activities such as mobility, communication, self-care, and learning as necessary for independent living, employment, and self-sufficiency (see Meyer, Peck, & Brown, 1991, p. 19).

Defining the severity of a particular disability by the level of support services required is currently advocated by the American Association on Mental Retardation (1992) (see also Chapter 4). For example, a child with mental retardation requiring pervasive supports would need supports characterized by constancy, high intensity, supports that are provided across environments and potentially of a life-sustaining nature.

Some discussion of children with severe disabilities has occurred in previous chapters, for example, those discussing mental retardation, physical disabilities, and autism. So why devote an entire chapter to the needs of this population? There are two reasons. First, the number of children with severe and multiple disabilities is small, so most professionals have very limited experience with this population. When discussing most disabilities such as mental retardation, the literature naturally focuses on milder forms in greater detail because so many more children have milder forms of the disability. The somewhat different needs of the far fewer children with more severe conditions are not the focus of these chapters. Second, although this population is heterogeneous, some similarities can be found in the challenges these children with severe disabilities present to educators.

There is a movement to define the severity of the disorder in terms of the supports required. Children with severe disabilities require intensive and pervasive supports.

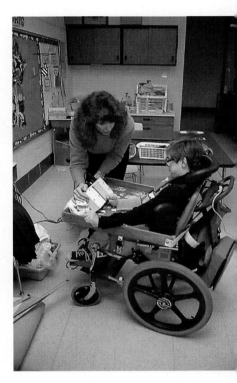

Prevalence and Incidence

Since severe disorders cut across diagnostic categories, prevalence and incidence figures are difficult to estimate. Snell (1987) estimates that about 0.05 percent of the population have severe and profound disabilities. Ludlow & Sobey (1984) estimate that between 0.1 and 1 percent of the population has a severe disability.

The prevalence figures used throughout this text are based upon the U.S. Department of Education's Report to Congress on the Implementation of the Individuals with Disabilities Education Act (1994). Data is reported in terms of the various categories of disability and is not collected or presented in terms of the severity of the condition or services required (Haring et al., 1992).

Data is reported, though, for multiple disabilities. During the 1992–1993 school year, 103,215 children with multiple disabilities were identified and received services. One specific category of multiple disability, dual sensory impairment (deaf-blindness), is listed separately and 1,425 children with this diagnosis between the ages of 6 and 21 years received services.

Evidence indicates a recent increase in the number of children with severe or multiple disabilities, as children who may not have survived years ago due to extreme prematurity or extensive medical problems are now saved by advancements in medicine (Alper, Schloss, & Schloss, 1994). Many of these children will have disabilities, some of them severe. In addition, the number of infants exposed prenatally to drugs is increasing, some of whom also have multiple or severe disabilities.

Areas of Concern

Painting a general portrait of the population of children with severe or multiple disabilities is difficult. Certainly, these children all have extensive impairments in a particular area of functioning. Some children with a severe disability in one area may have other disabilities that range from mild to moderate to severe and have other areas of functioning in which no disability is observed. For example, a child with mental retardation requiring pervasive support may also have physical limitations but no visual or auditory problems. A child with cerebral palsy may have visual difficulties but may not have intellectual deficits. The areas of possible impairment are as follows:

- *Intellectual deficits*: Difficulties in intellectual and cognitive functioning may be present and are the most common impairment for children with severe disabilities (Lyon & Lyon, 1991). Children may learn very slowly and show difficulties in abstraction and generalization. Many children with severe impairments show cognitive delays and do not easily acquire concepts and skills.
- *Communication impairments*: Some children with severe or multiple disabilities may be able to communicate relatively well, while others may not. Children with severe disabilities may require specially designed equipment to augment or enhance communication.
- *Developmental differences*: Children with severe disabilities usually develop their skills more slowly and may reach their developmental milestones, such as walking and talking, at much later ages.
- *Motor and physical impairments*: Children with severe or multiple disabilities may experience difficulties in movement or posture. They may use braces or wheelchairs.
- *Behavioral and emotional differences*: Some children with severe disabilities may demonstrate behavioral or emotional disturbances that may make their integration into the classroom more difficult. For example, a child who shows stereotypical movements such as rocking back and forth or engages in temper tantrums may be avoided by the other children. Behavioral impairments adversely affect interpersonal interactions and acceptance (Peck, Donaldson, & Pezzoli, 1990). They are often the focus of interventions using behavioral techniques to reduce the inappropriate behaviors.
- *Social behavior difficulties*: People with severe disabilities may demonstrate difficulty in developing social behaviors and in forming and maintaining relationships. Some of the difficulties may be associated with an intellectual or communication impairment, but the child's isolation and lack of opportunity to develop social skills also contribute to these difficulties.
- *Daily life skills*: Children with severe disabilities need support and direct instruction in such skills as brushing teeth, eating, dressing, and bathing. When children learn these skills, their independence is enhanced.
- *Sensory impairments*: Visual and auditory impairment may be present. Children who are both blind and deaf are considered to have dual sensory impairments.

Children with Dual Sensory Impairments

Children are considered to have **dual sensory impairments (deaf-blindness)** if they have both hearing and visual impairments that cause severe communication and education problems so they cannot be educated in special programs solely for children who are deaf or blind (*Federal Register*, 1977). Very few such children are completely without some residual vision, hearing, or both (Barrett, 1992). The population of children who are deaf and blind is extremely heterogeneous. Some children are born deaf and become blind later; some may be born blind and become deaf later in life; some are born deaf and blind; and still others may become deaf and blind later in life.

Each of these possibilities presents different challenges for parents and educators. A child who is born deaf and later becomes blind may have visual memories that help in orientation and differs from an individual who is born blind and becomes deaf later in life and can speak easily.

In the 1960s, an epidemic of rubella caused a dramatic increase in the incidence of children who had dual sensory impairments. But with the advent of the vaccine to prevent rubella, the most common cause of deaf-blindness is now Usher's syndrome, a genetic condition. Children with Usher's syndrome are born profoundly deaf and become blind later in life. The onset of the blindness is variable, often when the individual is a young adult (Barrett, 1992). Other causes of dual sensory impairments include meningitis, head trauma, various genetic conditions, toxicity due to mother's drug usage during pregnancy, and accidents. An estimated two-thirds of all children who have dual sensory impairments have other disabilities, such as neurological disorders, orthopedic problems, language and communication impairments, and medical problems (Zambone & Huebner, 1992).

Early intervention programs are available for parents who require training to help these children develop optimally. Parents must hold their children as much as possible and expose them to sound vibration by holding them near their chests and talking to them (Sardegna & Paul, 1991). When parents of children with dual sensory impairments were asked about what they wanted for their children, the need for a safe, comfortable, stable home was most important. Parents wanted their children to be productive with their time, engaging in meaningful activities and satisfying social interactions. Parents are most likely to support skill instruction if these skills are closely matched with goals parents want for their children (Giangreco et al., 1991).

The most important educational decision involves communication and language training. A total of 21 different methods of communication can be used with children who have dual sensory impairments. The choice of language modality depends upon an analysis of the child's residual hearing and vision, the child's educational history, the age at which the child became deaf and blind, and a number of other factors. For example, a child who became blind later but was deaf since birth may have developed the ability to use American Sign Language, just as an individual who was born blind but became deaf later might have been taught to use braille. Those who have enough hearing or become deaf after learning verbal language can often speak quite well.

A number of communication devices are available for those children who must communicate without the use of sound or sight. The alphabet glove is a thin

Dual sensory impairments (deaf-blindness): Children with both hearing and visual impairments that cause severe communication and education problems.

The TeleBraille machine allows children with dual sensory impairments to communicate with others. An individual types on the device and a braille message is received by the person with the dual sensory impairment, who may then reverse the process, with a typed message appearing to the other individual.

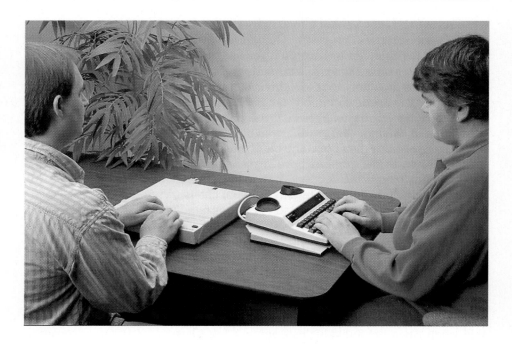

cotton glove printed with the letters of the alphabet at specific spots that are memorized by the wearer. The user or sighted person spells out words by touching the desired letters on the glove. The braille alphabet card is a pocketsize card that has both braille and printed letters on it. The user and sighted person spell out the word by touching the letters on the card. The TeleBraille machine is a modified TDD which provides a braille input and output. The TeleBraille can be used to communicate with standard TDDs over telephone lines or as an aid to communication for people with dual sensory impairments (Sardegna & Paul, 1991).

Children with dual sensory impairments are served in a variety of placements from residential schools to integrated classrooms with the support of specialists (Zambone & Huebner, 1992). Most, at the present time, are educated in special day and residential programs. A number of teaching methods are used but must be tailored to the individual's specific needs and abilities. When teachers of children with dual sensory impairments were sampled, the majority emphasized the need for repetition and practice of skills, guiding children through steps aimed at mastering a skill, using task analysis, using concrete objects in their teaching, and the importance of developing language and communication abilities through whatever communication method is most appropriate (Maxson et al., 1993).

People who are deaf *or* blind have many difficulties getting around and establishing interpersonal relationships. This task is even more difficult for children who have severe impairments both in sight and hearing. Most people who can see and hear have never met anyone who has dual sensory impairments and have no idea of the capabilities of this population.

Individuals with dual sensory impairments need substantial training and life-long support. They require interpreters, orientation and mobility services, help in transport, job restructuring, and individualized job training (Everson & Burwell, 1991). Many people have a difficult time understanding how people with such a disability can succeed, but some live relatively independent lives. For example, Linda is an adult with dual sensory impairment who after training found an apartment, learned to manage it, and began an internship in horticulture. She also cares for her six-year-old daughter (HKNC, 1993). Some people with dual sensory impairments can work in competitive employment settings such as restaurants, retail stores, and public libraries (Goetz et al., 1991).

The Helen Keller National Center for Deaf-Blind Youths and Adults (HKNC) is an agency that develops and coordinates programs for individuals who have dual sensory impairments. It was established by Congress in 1967 and consists of 10 regional offices and 31 affiliates, a national training team, and job placement services (HKNC, 1988). Recently the Center added services for elderly people who have dual sensory impairments and began a National Parent Network project and an internship program. The Center operates the National Technical Assistance Center (TAC), which funds demonstration projects for supported employment, community living, and parent and family services.

Screening, Evaluation, and Assessment for Children with Severe Disabilities

The screening, evaluation, and assessment of children with severe or multiple disabilities is fraught with difficulties. The nature of the disability may make common evaluation instruments less useful and, in some cases, impossible to use. A number of special challenges arise when children with severe disabilities are evaluated and assessed.

One such challenge is communication. Some evaluation instruments require a verbal response from the child. A child with a severe communication problem who cannot speak will have to signal in some other way. When a more involved answer is required, the difficulties become greater. Some children, though, cannot communicate effectively at all, making evaluation of many areas of functioning especially difficult.

The child's sensory and motor difficulties may also compromise the use of traditional assessment devices. Evaluators may have difficulties administering a test to a child with an auditory or visual impairment, especially if some cognitive impairment is also present.

Fatigue is still another factor. Some children with severe and multiple disabilities may fatigue easily and not be able to concentrate. Sometimes, this lack of stamina is caused by their medication and at other times by the impairment itself. The inability to concentrate and the fatigue factor make evaluation more difficult and time-consuming. Analyzing attentional abilities is, however, a part of the assessment process.

Last, maladaptive behaviors, including self-stimulation, noncompliance, and even resistance to the task itself, may interfere with the evaluation process.

Screening

Many children with severe or multiple disabilities do not proceed through a formal screening since their disabilities are obvious (Gaylord-Ross & Holvoet, 1985). These children are more likely than their peers with mild disabilities to be discovered early. Observations in the hospital and during infancy by both parents and professionals often are sufficient to recommend further evaluation.

Evaluation

The key to evaluating children with severe disabilities is to maximize their ability to respond and minimize the effects of the disabilities so the most accurate information is obtained. Certain characteristics of tests may make them more or less useful in evaluating this population (see Venn, 1994). For example, a test that allows for adaptable responses, such as signalling, is more useful than one that does not. An instrument that samples a wide spectrum of behaviors in which each subtest contains a number of items to test each behavior is most useful since the nature of the disability may make the use of some of the test items impossible. Flexible administration procedures are important, because children may need more time, and the test procedures may have to be adapted to the individual's abilities. Being able to award partial credit is also useful since a child may be able to complete only a part of an item.

Norm-referenced tests are not as useful in educational planning as criterion-referenced tests. Yet, norm-referenced tests, including intelligence tests are used much more frequently than criterion-referenced tests (Sigafoos, Cole, & McQuarter, 1987). The use of intelligence tests with children with severe and multiple disabilities is questionable. Few such tests have included students with severe disabilities in their norms. Intelligence tests are also less accurate at the extremes than in the middle. Most norm-referenced tests are not designed for children with severe disabilities who often have severe sensory, language, or motor impairments and are not standardized to allow the adaptations that are necessary for use with these children. Some intelligence tests, though, are specially designed to use with populations of children who cannot read or write and have difficulty listening or speaking. The Test of Nonverbal Intelligence-2 (TONI-2) measures intelligence and reasoning and requires the examiner to pantomime instructions. The child responds by pointing to the selected answers (Sweetland & Keyser, 1993).

Developmental scales are sometimes administered to children with severe disabilities. These scales yield information concerning the rate of a child's development of a particular skill. The developmental sequence is listed longitudinally, which offers information as to where the child is developmentally, what the next step might be, and theoretically, where to intervene. A child may be assessed on a particular skill and the behaviors that the child can and cannot perform determined.

The use of developmental scales for educational planning has been criticized. Children with severe disabilities may develop some skills in a different sequence. In addition, using these scales to pinpoint intervention can be inappropriate. As Linehan and colleagues note, "If developmental testing indicated that a child has not mastered sorting colors, stacking blocks or imitating animal sounds, these skills should not necessarily be targeted as IEP objectives" (Linehan, Brady, & Hwang, 1991, p. 147).

In a study of assessment practices with children with severe disabilities, Sigafoos and colleagues (1987) found that more than 40 percent of the tests administered involved students who were beyond the age range of the test employed. The use of scales designed for infants or young children with older children with severe disabilities is inappropriate. Last, sometimes developmental skills are viewed in the abstract rather than in terms of their function. Grasping is certainly an important motor skill, but it should be measured as a functional skill such as grasping a toothbrush. Developmental scales, then, are not as useful for this population.

Evaluation and assessment need not always rely on formal testing. Sometimes, a skill is directly evaluated; at other times, observation of the child in a natural situation or interviewing parents or teachers may be required (Brown & Snell, 1993). A child may be asked to point to a particular picture to see if the child can relate the word to the object. Of course, as in all testing, the examiner must be certain that the child understands the task and has the physical ability to signal. Such testing should be performed in the natural environment and during the time the skill would normally be used, if at all possible. For example, if skill in using utensils is to be assessed, the assessment should be conducted at meal time. Observations in both the home, classroom, and in other environments are valuable. The teacher and parents can report whether the student demonstrates a particular skill.

Today, many authorities recommend the use of ecological inventories that examine the environments in which children with severe disabilities will be present, what activities the child will engage in, and what skills are needed. Ecological inventories identify the skills needed for independent functioning in current and future environments (Linehan et al., 1991).

The importance of using an ecological rather than developmental approach as the basis for planning was demonstrated in a recent study. Eighty-four educators were randomly assigned to either a group that read a developmental assessment report with mental and developmental ages included or one which read an ecological assessment documenting observed competencies and needs in the daily environment. The educators reading the ecological assessment had significantly higher expectations for accomplishing IEP objectives (Linehan et al., 1991).

Causes of Severe and Multiple Disabilities

The causes of severe and multiple disabilities are thought to be mostly genetic and medical. For example, the most common causes of the most severe forms of mental retardation include genetic factors, infections, prenatal insults, trauma, poisoning, oxygen deprivation, metabolic and nutritional factors, and gross brain disease (Polloway & Patton, 1990). The causes of cerebral palsy are also physical in origin. Determining the cause of all cases of severe or multiple disabilities is not always possible. A severe disability may also be caused by more than one agent.

Although biological causation is prominent, environmental factors can increase or decrease the effects of the disability. The treatment the child receives, the attitudes of the parents, and numerous environmental factors operate to affect the child's functioning. If two children with identical conditions were present in a room, there is a good chance that one child would function much better than the other because caregiving, education, and other environmental factors affect the child's learning and functioning.

Family Adjustment

Not too many years ago, the family of a child diagnosed with a severe disability had few alternatives. Routinely, pediatricians would suggest institutionalization. Families could not hope for much community support. They faced a choice of either placing the child in a large institution with limited programs or keeping the child at home with relatively few community services available (Lyon & Lyon, 1991).

Today, the situation is different. Legislative progress and changes in attitudes allow for many more choices. Parents and professionals have joined together to demand basic rights and services for children with severe disabilities. Children are institutionalized much less often, and family and community-based services are available (Heal, Hanley, & Novak-Amado, 1988). Intervention services, especially for children with severe and multiple disabilities, begin early, because these children are more likely to be diagnosed in infancy (see Chapter 3).

The needs of families with severely disabled children are greater than those of families with children who have mild disabilities. Children with severe disabilities require a greater amount of attention, and a significant amount of time must be devoted to their physical care (Lyon & Lyon, 1991). Many of these children will need help to dress, bathe, and eat long after the age that other children learn these skills.

Parents also find it more difficult to coordinate the services their children need. A child with a mild disability may go to one specialist and a tutor. A child with a severe disability may have many appointments with therapists requiring more of the parents' time and resources. A child's medical problems may require various medical doctors, the child's sensory disabilities treatment from an ophthalmologist and audiologist, the child's physical disabilities help from occupational and physical therapists, the cognitive and language impairments access to speech and language therapists.

The family may also need greater emotional support and respite so they can continue to care for the child. Caring for a child with severe or multiple disabilities can be emotionally and psychologically exhausting. Direct family assistance is appreciated and involves home consultation, babysitting services, and respite care services (Bersani, 1987).

The impact of raising a child with a disability on parents and siblings was discussed in Chapter 2. Making generalizations is difficult; some families cope with the challenges better than others. Some have greater financial and emotional resources and extended families that offer more help than others. Generally, though, the amount of stress experienced by the family is related to the severity of the disability (Alper et al., 1994). However, so many other factors are at work that this generalization is not always the case.

Although the constant care needed by the child is taxing, the negative effects may be overstated (Lyon & Lyon, 1991). The presence of a child with a severe disability may affect the marriage, siblings, and extended family in various ways. The child's presence may strengthen or weaken the marriage, create greater sensitivity and appreciation in siblings, or contribute to adjustment problems, create parental satisfaction or dissatisfaction, and bring the extended family together or pull it apart (Turnbull & Morningstar, 1993). The presence of a child with a severe disability does not automatically affect siblings adversely. The self-concepts of adolescents with siblings with profound mental retardation do not differ from the self-concepts of adolescents with nondisabled siblings (Auletta & DeRosa, 1991). Many families establish patterns of care for the child where various people help in dressing and feeding. Early intervention services can improve the parent-child interaction and parental responsiveness leading to better parenting skills and the use of more effective management techniques (Fox & Westling, 1991).

Parents of children with severe or multiple disabilities may take a present, one-day-at-a-time orientation, which may contrast with the more longitudinal view of teachers. Such factors as the severity of the disability, multiplicity of disability, age, life expectancy, and parental beliefs about the child's future determine the family's willingness to engage in long-range planning (Giangreco et al., 1991).

Families of children with severe disabilities may have a difficult time obtaining services such as babysitting (Lyon & Lyon, 1991). Money is another problem. Adaptive clothing, vans, special furniture, toys, and other items are expensive and not always readily available (Turnbull & Morningstar, 1993).

The challenges faced by parents of children with severe or multiple disabilities are similar to, but greater than, those faced by parents of children with mild or moderate disabilities. These challenges change with the life cycle, and so new challenges come to the forefront as older challenges are met.

SCENARIO

1 A new state program is proposed, which will offer families with children with severe and multiple disabilities three weeks of state-financed care in a community residence, to permit the parents to go on vacations and trips. The parents may use the three weeks in any fashion they wish, for example, using one week in the winter and two in the summer. Advocates claim that parents of children with severe disabilities require time away from the stresses of raising a child with a severe disability and that if the family placed the child in an institution, permanent care would cost the taxpayers more. People who are against the program claim many people in poverty cannot afford vacations or babysitters either. Why single out one group for such a program? They also point out that it is costly, and the money could be spent in other ways directly affecting the child. As a citizen and a taxpayer in the community, what are your views on such a program?

Educational Alternatives

Traditionally, children with severe and multiple disabilities were educated in segregated schools and offered few programs. Many were institutionalized (Ferguson, Ferguson, & Bogdan, 1987). This situation is changing. The percentage of students with severe disabilities served in public schools has risen sharply over the past twenty years (Danielson & Bellamy, 1989). The percentage varies widely from state to state, however (Fredericks, 1987).

Three factors account for the change. First, legislation requiring education in the least restrictive environment and some court decisions give children with severe disabilities the right to be educated in regular schools and classrooms. The zero reject principle means that all students, regardless of the nature of the disability, are entitled to an education. In 1994, the New York State Board of Regents decided that school districts must first consider regular education classrooms as placements for all children. The new policy does not mandate placement in regular classrooms and keeps the full range of placement alternatives open (Sandberg, 1994). However, even the idea of considering placement in regular classrooms for all students shows the change.

Second, a change in philosophy has occurred. The concept of normalization, that education should take place in the most typical environment possible, adds impetus to the change (Wisniewski & Alper, 1994). When children with severe disabilities are included in the regular classroom, they are exposed to age mates who act as models. They experience a greater chance for meaningful social interaction. Regular classes are also age appropriate. In addition, much of the therapy and mobility training required by children with severe disabilities can take place in the regular classroom, although some will be provided elsewhere (Brown et al., 1991). Children with severe disabilities also receive increased opportunities for learning and practicing communication and social skills. Students without disabilities learn to appreciate human differences (Wisniewski & Alper, 1994).

Third, evidence from a number of studies of children with severe disabilities integrated into the neighborhood school environment and the regular classroom demonstrate the advantages of such placement (Kennedy & Itkonen, 1994). In one of the most interesting studies, Brinker & Thorpe (1984) found that students with severe disabilities placed in regular schools achieved more of their IEP goals than children who attended segregated schools. Two factors most important in predicting who would achieve were (1) functional level and (2) the degree of integration, measured by the amount of interaction between children with and without disabilities. Cole and Meyer (1991) found that children, with moderate to profound mental retardation whose mean age was 13.5 educated in integrated schools, progressed on a measure of social competence, while those in segregated schools regressed. The appropriateness and frequency of interactions and postschool adjustment in employment and community life are better when children are educated in integrated rather than segregated environments (McDonnell et al., 1991). Hunt and Farron-Davis (1992) compared the IEPs of students with severe disabilities attending a special class program and then switched to full-time membership in regular education classrooms. The IEPs were written by the same teachers. Significant differences existed in the quality of the IEP objectives with higher scores for full-time members of regular classes. Jenkins and colleagues (1985) found that the integration of children with disabilities did not adversely affect the education of children without disabilities. Some studies, in fact, find benefits for nondisabled students in this interaction. Students who participated in peer tutoring or a special friends program showed increased tolerance for other people and reduced fears of human differences (Helmstetter, Peck, & Giangreco, 1994; Peck et al., 1990).

Studies, then, show that children with severe disabilities achieve more and gain socially in a regular school environment and that the degree of integration is important. The models available to children with severe disabilities are often lacking in segregated schools, and the presence of and interaction with nondisabled peers provides appropriate peer models. The improvement may also be explained by the increased motivation when given opportunities to interact with others (Sailor, Gee, & Karasoff, 1993).

SCENARIO

2 Mr. and Mrs. Thomas are not certain that their eight-year-old child, Richard, should be educated in a regular class. Richard has mental retardation and a severe visual impairment. At times, he shows inappropriate behavior, such as rocking, as well. The Thomas' are fearful that the other children will tease him unmercifully and that he will be isolated. They also do not know whether he will benefit from this placement. You are the child's teacher next year, and the parents ask you for your evaluation of the situation. What would you say?

Integration Efforts

The inclusion of children with severe disabilities in the neighborhood school and regular classroom encounters a number of barriers and requires additional planning. As we have seen so often, just placing children with disabilities in a classroom does not ensure interaction will take place (Hilton & Liberty, 1992). It is a necessary but not sufficient condition for peer acceptance and social interaction (Evans et al., 1992). Children with severe disabilities often have communication and intellectual difficulties making participation in conversations difficult. In addition, some evidence indicates that social interaction between children with severe disabilities and their nondisabled peers may decline over the school year, if nothing is done to encourage it (Evans et al., 1992). During the first part of the semester, students are more likely to show assistance and attention, and interact in play and other situations. This attention declines, although the interactions that do occur are positive. Interpreting the reason for this decline in interaction is not easy. Perhaps the special attention that the child may have received is reduced somewhat, and now the child is being treated in a more natural way. However, perhaps the lack of communication skills and structured interaction cause the decline.

If children with severe disabilities are to be included successfully into the school and regular classroom, some leadership and commitment is required (Stainback & Stainback, 1988). Not every teacher, administrator, or parent must be intensely involved. Sometimes, a demonstration project is valuable in which professionals and parents who feel strongly about the benefits of educating children with severe disabilities in the regular classroom show that it can be accomplished. This commitment promotes wider acceptance and is a reasonable place to start. It also permits some experimentation with techniques, allowing successful ones to be used on a larger basis later on.

Some attention to the attitudes of everyone involved is required. Attitudes towards integration vary greatly. Negative attitudes are often based on a lack of training, lack of resources available to teachers, and inadequate knowledge of the best practices in the field, among other factors (Brinker & Thorpe, 1984). Generally, the more severe the disability is, the more negative the attitudes teachers have toward integration (Wisniewski & Alper, 1994).

Sometimes, people opposed to inclusive settings use the following arguments: (1) the children will be ridiculed and ostracized; (2) the education of children without disabilities will be hampered by the presence of children with such extensive needs; (3) too much additional instructional time will be required; and (4) the needs of the children with severe disabilities cannot be met within the general education program, sometimes due to lack of resources (Wisniewski & Alper, 1994).

Each of these can be disputed. Some children *without* disabilities are teased and ostracized, but this problem can be overcome. Evidence fails to show that the presence of children with disabilities adversely affects the education of others. If sufficient help is given, the additional instructional time is not great. Although the extent to which all the needs of the child with severe disabilities can be met in the regular classroom is still in question, some of their needs certainly can be met in such classrooms.

Teachers do not feel well prepared to teach children with severe disabilities. Even special educators have their doubts. In a survey of special educators, Izen and Brown (1991) found that many did not feel adequately trained by university teacher training programs to work with children with severe disabilities.

Attitudes change not only when accurate information concerning the needs of children with severe and multiple disabilities is given, but also when teachers have some experiences working with these children (Janney, 1995; Giangreco et al., 1993). Adequate in-service training is necessary as is the provision of adequate support services. These services are especially needed in the areas of teaching functional communication, applying appropriate behavior modification techniques, and identifying instructional needs and materials (Arick, Falco, & Brazeau, 1989). Advanced planning, sufficient preparation time, and in-service training are necessary to reduce resistance and change attitudes.

Some schools designate a person as a support facilitator who assists the regular classroom teacher with suggestions and sometimes provides hands-on help to adapt instruction to the needs of all members of the class. The support facilitator offers students direct instruction, helps students complete assignments, learn bus schedules, and practice social behaviors. Special educators can act in this role. In some cases, instead of just helping the child with a disability, the support facilitator may help any child in need of help within the classroom.

Another strategy is to develop a network of support. This network will serve as a way to structure interaction. The use of a circle of friends and buddy system lead to more social interactions (see Chapter 2). Cooperative learning groups and peer tutoring are successful in improving learning and promoting interaction with children with severe disabilities (Hunt et al., 1994; Wisnewski & Alper, 1994). When 158 teachers of students with moderate, severe, or profound disabilities were asked their ideas about facilitating friendships, they said they felt that friendships are most likely to develop when students are educated in regular classes for at least part of the day, information is presented, cooperative learning is used, peer tutoring is implemented, and social interaction skills taught (Hamre-Nietupski et al., 1993).

Promoting respect for individual differences can reduce prejudice and stereotyping. This is often accomplished by giving information about individual differences, reading about people with disabilities, and discussing the rights of all. Some criticism of just giving information or holding a special disabilities awareness week has surfaced (Hamre-Nietupski et al., 1989). These activities are not an integral component of the regular school experience. Although information-giving itself may be helpful, they are add-on programs and not part of a general educational program. Their peripheral status can be rectified through a procedure called curricular infusion. In this procedure, people without disabilities are provided not only with accurate information, but also given opportunities to actively learn about disabilities and interact with people with disabilities. These activities become a natural part of the curriculum of many subjects. Tables 16.1 and 16.2 show seventh-grade social studies and science infusion activities. Curricular infusion assures more participation on the part of the regular classroom teacher.

The benefits of inclusion do not mean that all children with severe disabilities should spend every minute of the school day in the regular classroom. As will be shown later in the chapter, many children need education outside the classroom, and some skills may be best taught in different environments.

Yet, even if some children with severe disabilities spend a substantial part of their day in a special classroom within the school or outside the school, opportunities for integration can be planned. Efforts can be made to be certain that children are visible throughout the school building. One student practiced using a walker in the halls. Within a short time, the nondisabled students became a cheering section rooting the child on. Other students with disabilities in the class delivered the daily attendance sheets to the main office. Within a short time, their classmates began to greet them. Children with disabilities were also integrated into some classes, such as music. A structured peer integration program was initiated, in which cooperative age-appropriate activities were emphasized, such as cooking and game playing.

THOUGHT QUESTION

1. *What are the strengths and weaknesses of using a special week designated as Disabilities Awareness Week to give information and structure interactions between children with and without disabilities?*

THOUGHT QUESTION

2. *Should all children with severe disabilities be educated in the regular classroom or are there certain circumstances in which such placement might be ill advised?*

SCENARIO

3 Kelly is a student in the second grade with multiple disabilities. She has central nervous system damage leading to seizures and cognitive impairments. She pays attention and enjoys being with people. Her teacher would like to include Kelly in the classroom activities as much as possible. Unfortunately, the other students do not go over to Kelly very much, and she does not seem to be able to initiate any conversation even though she can speak in an intelligible fashion. You are teaching a unit on different types of boats and how they float. Briefly describe ways of including Kelly in the classroom activities.

TABLE 16.1   **Seventh-Grade Social Studies Infusion Activities**

Unit: Awareness of Self and Others

A. Slide show on friendships was expanded to include slides of persons with disabilities interacting with friends.

B. Special educator conducted a presentation on friendships with students who have severe disabilities and encouraged volunteer partners.

Unit: Stereotyping

A. Guest speakers with disabilities

   1. Prior to the presentation, students were asked to describe the quality of life they expected regarding a person in a wheelchair who had attended a residential school for persons with disabilities.

   2. Presenter discussed his job (college professor), his living situation (married, family of four), and recreational interests (wheelchair basketball, 10K wheelchair racing, kayaking) and answered student questions.

   3. Students discussed how their views on the presenter's quality of life may have changed as a result of getting to know the presenter.

B. Alienation/prejudice toward group's activity

   1. 2/3 of the class was identified as the "in" group, 1/3 of the class as the "out" group.

   2. "In" group plans a party, participates in fun activity and receives a treat, while "out" group copies spelling words, writes a 100 word paragraph and completes worksheets.

   3. Large group discussion of feelings about being "in" or "out".

   4. Identification of groups in school who easily might be excluded/alienated (e.g. persons with disabilities).

   5. Discuss ways to increase the participation of students with severe disabilities in school and classroom activities.

   6. Students are given opportunities to volunteer to be partners to peers with severe disabilities.

Education and Training in Mental Retardation, 1989, p. 82. Reprinted by permission.

Community-Based Instruction

Children with severe disabilities learn more and develop better social skills when in contact with children without disabilities. This contact takes place in the regular classroom. However, many educators believe that much education and training must take place in the community, outside the classroom. If children with severe disabilities are to learn to use vending machines, buses, or order from a fast-food restaurant, community-based instruction (CBI) is necessary. Although some classroom simulations may be valuable, the problems in generalization that many of these students experience necessitates education in the community.

Elementary school students with severe disabilities receive most of their instruction in the classroom, with some community-based instruction perhaps once a week, learning domestic skills, or shopping in a supermarket. As the student progresses to the middle school and beyond, the proportion of time spent in community-based instruction increases to 50 percent and then later in high school to as much as 85 percent.

TABLE 16.2   **Seventh-Grade Science Infusion Activities**

Unit: Genetic/Environmental Influences on Development

A. Class discussion

  1. Genetic and environmental causes of disabilities

  2. Identification of similarities between disabled/nondisabled individuals

  3. Past (segregated) versus present (integrated) educational model

B. Teams debate segregated vs integrated education

  1. Four-person teams are formed.

  2. Teams visit integrated/segregated programs.

  3. Teams gather written information on integration/segregation.

  4. Guest speakers, one pro-integration, one pro-segregation, debate before the class.

  5. Teams debate before the class using previously gathered information.

C. Each student writes a position paper on integration/segregation.

D. All students visit students with severe disabilities to get to know them better.

Education and Training in Mental Retardation, 1989, p. 82. Reprinted by permission.

A problem arises as the amount of CBI increases while the amount of time spent in school decreases. Much attention is paid to social integration and the development of friendships in the school environment. As the amount of CBI increases, a reduction in these social interactions takes place, especially for secondary school students. Although professionals generally agree that CBI

Children with severe or multiple disabilities need community-based instruction in which they are taught important skills in the community, rather than in the classroom.

should increase with age, the proportion of time that students should spend in school or in CBI is controversial (Sailor et al., 1986). If too much time is spent in CBI then social interaction may be reduced.

In one program that combined CBI and interaction with classroom peers, children without disabilities were paired with children with mental retardation for trips to the grocery store (Beck et al., 1994). Prior to the trips, all students met to discuss the purposes of the trip. The trips lasted for 30–40 minutes, and the children without disabilities taking part in the program were rotated. Interactions between children with and without disabilities increased.

THOUGHT QUESTION

3. *Can you think of any ways to promote social interaction between children spending a large portion of their instructional time in community-based instruction and their nondisabled peers?*

Teaching Children with Severe and Multiple Disabilities

Because children with severe and multiple disabilities are a heterogeneous group, one has difficulties making generalizations about teaching strategies. Yet, some basic principles for teaching children with severe and multiple disabilities are based upon their learning characteristics. Generally, these children learn skills and concepts more slowly, forget more quickly, and have difficulties with generalization (Brown & Snell, 1993). They are likely to be significantly behind in their acquisition of skills and need direct instruction to master self-help skills.

An Attitude That All Children Can Learn

The first requirement for teaching children with severe or multiple disabilities is the attitude that *all* children can learn. A teacher who does not believe this may communicate negative expectations to the child with a disability and to all the other children in the classroom. The simple fact is that children with severe disabilities can and do learn, but not at the pace of children without disabilities or children with less severe disabilities (Brown & Snell, 1993).

Beware of Emphasizing Differences in Development

Any comparison between the learning rates of children with and without severe disabilities is likely to cause the teacher to focus on the performance deficits of children with severe disabilities. A norm-referenced approach is often used to discover that these children are far behind in many areas of development. However, this approach is not desirable. Rather, looking at what the child can do and what the child needs to know are more important.

Teaching Functional Skills

Functional skill:
A skill that is useful to the student in the daily routine and gives the child some control over the environment.

The education of children with severe and multiple disabilities is governed by the concept of a **functional skill**. A skill is functional if it is useful to the student and gives the child some control over the environment. Functional skills are those used frequently during an individual's daily routine and needed in the home, school, work, and community environments (Schleien, Green, & Heyne, 1993). The acquisition of functional skills allows an individual to perform as independently as possible in everyday settings. A decision on the functional nature of the skill to be taught is based upon an examination of the environments that the child is involved in today and what may be needed in the near future. In fact, functionality is a guideline for selecting IEP objectives (Brown & Snell, 1993).

In the classroom realm, the functionality of a particular skill is determined by agreement among all parties involved in the IEP. For example, being able to use the formula to change Fahrenheit to Centigrade and back again is not functional, but understanding the idea of hot and cold may be. Some skills in the communication area such as greeting others and responding are of a functional nature.

Teaching Functional Skills Not Often Taught in the Classroom
Many children with severe disabilities will require formal, direct instruction in basic communication and self-care skills. Some of these skills, such as bathing, are taught in the home. Others, such as some grooming skills, may be taught both at home and in school, although in privacy, while how to put on one's coat may be taught openly both at home and in the classroom. These skills are not usually taught in school. One challenge of educating children with severe disabilities is how to teach some self-care skills in primarily academic classrooms.

A number of alternatives are available (Hamre-Nietupski, McDonald, & Nietupski, 1992). First, partial assistance may be provided by a peer in the context of class activities. When a child could not put on boots easily, the child was taught to ask a nondisabled peer for assistance. The peer encouraged the young student to be independent on the easier steps.

A second strategy is to look for "down times" in the classroom, times between classroom activities or prior to or just after lunch and teach these skills at that time.

A third solution is to provide parallel instruction while peers participate in academic work. While students are working on math problems, a skill like matching coins can be taught. Especially in elementary school, some children without disabilities may require functional training as well. A last alternative is to remove a child for a short period of time for specialized instruction.

Partial Participation

Most children with severe and multiple disabilities will not be able to fully participate in every aspect of the educational program. A particular physical or cognitive skill may not be present and may be very difficult or impossible to teach. It also may not be the best use of limited instructional time to focus on that skill. The principle of **partial participation** (see Chapter 1) states that some individuals with severe disabilities may not be able to perform a particular activity independently, but can participate partially in many activities (Baumgart et al., 1982). It enables those students who might never be able to acquire a full enough repertoire of skills to participate completely in the activity to learn enough to participate partially (Ferguson & Baumgart, 1991). This ensures active participation in a variety of activities.

THOUGHT QUESTION

4. *What criteria would you use to determine whether to include a particular skill in the IEP of a student with severe disabilities?*

Partial participation: The principle that some individuals with severe disabilities may not be able to perform an activity with complete independence, but can participate at least partially in most activities.

Age Appropriateness

Children with severe disabilities are sometimes so far behind their peers that it is tempting to place them with much younger children who may be doing similar work. Doing so is inappropriate and may interfere with social interaction and development. Children are best placed in a class with chronological age peers.

Choices and Environmental Control

Control over the environment means making choices and showing one's preferences. Incorporating opportunities for making choices in the classroom is one measure of a high-quality educational program for children with severe and multiple disabilities (Sigafoos & Dempsey, 1992). In everyday life, people signal "yes" and "no" and state preferences. People control their environments, seeking those experiences that they want and avoiding those they do not want (Shevin & Klein, 1984). People choose among activities, choose whether to engage in a particular activity, choose when to terminate an activity, and choose with whom an activity will be performed.

Unfortunately, many children with severe disabilities are not afforded choices and do not experience control over their environments. This lack of control can lead to a state of learned helplessness where they simply give up trying. Communication of choice and preferences leads to an increase in personal autonomy and enhances self-worth (Houghton, Bronicki, & Guess, 1987). When children are allowed to make choices in social situations, children with severe disabilities show an increase in social interaction (Peck, 1985).

For children with severe disabilities to demonstrate choices and preferences, some method of communication must be established. Even for those who can signal their likes and dislikes, other people are continually telling them what to do, and they gain little practice in making choices. Children with severe disabilities need to be taught that they, too, can have some choices. This means they do not have to be passive recipients of the desires of others. Parents and teachers, then, should encourage children to make choices and participate in the decision-making process even if it takes somewhat longer.

THOUGHT QUESTION

5. *How can a teacher or parent encourage the use of choice in the classroom or home?*

Changing Inappropriate Behavior

Sometimes, inappropriate behavior and disruptive behavior may make it difficult to include the child. For example, a child who threw food, had little utensil use, and engaged in tantrums could not be allowed to eat in the cafeteria. The child ate in the classroom with two rotating classmate volunteers instead of in the cafeteria until the inappropriate behavior was controlled. Inappropriate and disruptive behavior in the classroom must be attended to because it interferes with learning and reduces acceptance and social interaction. When inappropriate behavior is noted, the teacher and special educator may adopt a number of strategies—many of which were discussed in Chapter 7—to reduce such behavior and increase socially acceptable behavior.

Emphasis on Social Interaction

One of the reasons for including children with severe disabilities in regular classrooms is to improve their social skills. Earlier in this chapter and throughout the text, many ways of accomplishing social integration were noted. When children interact, important learning occurs. Unfortunately, while nondisabled children in the class are working on one skill, the child with a severe disability is often working on something else, which is why partial participation, the use of cooperative learning activities, peer tutoring, buddy systems, and activities that structure social interaction into the daily routine of the classroom are so important.

Teaching in a Concrete Fashion

Much learning in the regular classroom is abstract, involving symbols and concepts not related to direct experience. Children with severe disabilities, especially those with cognitive impairments, have difficulties with abstract activities. Learning for children with severe disabilities occurs best when real and, if possible, tangible materials are involved. A real clock is more concrete than a picture of a clock, which is more concrete than a printed word (Brown et al., 1991).

 **Controlling the Environment**

We push the button on the remote control unit of the television set and the channel changes. We ring the doorbell and expect to hear a sound. We expect our actions to have an impact on the environment. We control our environments, changing them at our whim. We know that if we do not want the table in one corner, we can get up and move it. If we do not want the light on, we switch it off. We make thousands of choices every day of our lives. We decide what we want to do, who we want to do it with, and when we want to stop doing something. We decide to have coffee instead of tea, to call Henry instead of George.

People have a sense of control over their environments and their lives. This sense of control offers independence and a feeling of power and self-efficacy. We make many of our own decisions and carry them out without appreciating the importance of control and choices.

People with severe disabilities, though, often do not experience much control over their environment. Sometimes, their physical impairments may cause the difficulties, but as was noted in Chapter 14, technological innovations now permit more physical control over the environment. Using specially designed switches and keyboards, people with severe physical disabilities can now control computers, appliances, and household devices. When these physical disabilities, though, are combined with severe cognitive and communication impairments, understanding cause and effect and exercising control over the environment becomes more difficult.

Learning to control their environments and making their choices known are especially important for children with severe or multiple disabilities. Feeling in control increases independence and reduces learned helplessness. Augmentative and alternative communication systems, described in this chapter, allow for communication of choices for people who cannot easily communicate them verbally to others.

Understanding cause and effect, though, is central to being able to choose. One must first understand the relationship between doing, signalling, or saying something and what occurs in the environment. Some computer programs have been successful in teaching cause and effect. Cause and effect software requires a student to make a response that causes something to occur on the monitor. For example, a software program may require an individual to press a switch, touch a window, or press keys that produce some design, play music, or display an animated scene (Lewis, 1993). Of course, the response must be one the student can perform and the result something of interest to the student. Some of these programs generate game-like activities. In one, a fly may cross the screen and when a switch is pressed the frog's tongue captures the fly (Lewis, 1993).

After the student understands the cause and effect relationship, choice software is useful. In simple versions, the individual would be presented with two alternatives and asked to choose one. The individual may be given two boxes showing different objects; the student then touches the screen when the box surrounds the choice and hears the name of the object spoken.

Some programs require scanning in which a cursor or a box may highlight each alternative moving from one to the other until the student makes the selection, perhaps by hitting a switch or touching the monitor (Male, 1994). Perhaps a list of symbols is presented, and each is highlighted for a brief period of time. The student must press the switch when the desired symbol is found. This choice then results in a particular event, such as a story being told or a game being presented. Matching is an interesting activity that can be used with scanning. An image is presented, the computer highlights a number of choices until the identical image is shown, and the child must throw the switch. Once the technique of scanning is learned, a number of valuable educational programs may be used. Lessons can be delivered through the use of graphics and synthesized voices, and questions asked while the student using the scanning technique signals the answer.

An impressive method of giving people with severe and multiple disabilities some control over their environment was demonstrated using a sophisticated computer setup that allowed a woman with profound mental retardation and severe physical impairments to control various electrical devices using five verbalizations (Brown & Cavalier, 1992). The computer was programmed for voice-activated environmental control and so customized that it responded only when a match was made between the woman's vocal input and the stored voice templates. The word "four" activated videotapes telling classical stories, "move" activated the vibration message pad, "ray" activated the radio, and "bee" operated the videotape of three family segments. Finally, the word "off" deactivated any device operating.

The woman learned to use the words to activate and deactivate the devices. She also displayed considerable positive emotion when she was able to control these aspects of the environment and showed a preference for one activity (the videotape of the family) over the others. This study showed that people with severe mental retardation could understand cause and effect relationships necessary to successfully control voice-operated computer systems. She took great pleasure in performing these activities for both the people she lived with and for visitors. It also seemed to increase her desire to communicate new words and articulate new sounds. Her general behavior following the research was much more animated and attentive.

Most people take choice, preference, and control for granted. Through the use of technology, people with severe and multiple disabilities are now being afforded an opportunity to control some aspects of the environment. Their newfound freedom gives them more personal autonomy and dignity.

A General Framework for Teaching

Teaching children with severe disabilities involves a number of carefully planned steps. The following steps illustrate one way of organizing the learning experiences of children with severe or multiple disabilities and, indeed, for children with less severe disabilities:

1. *Assessment of environmental strengths and needs.* The first step is to assess what the child needs to know and be able to do, and the present state of the child's skills. An ecological assessment that looks at the interaction between the child and the environment is helpful for identifying strengths and weaknesses.

2. *Identify the target skill that requires instruction.* The skills to be taught are determined by the assessment. These skills are noted on the IEP and the regular classroom teacher and special education teacher can cooperate in identifying specific skills to be taught.

3. *Define the goals in a measurable manner.* The skills that are to be taught and the goals for achievement must be described in a manner that allows measurement. The goals must be observable, and the conditions under which the behaviors will be performed and the criteria for success noted. For example, "Given five napkins, Joy will fold them with 100% accuracy for three consecutive trials," gives all the necessary information. If counting is a skill to be taught, the goals may involve counting particular items in particular environments.

4. *Task analyze the skill.* **Task analysis** is the process of sequentially analyzing a skill into its teachable components (Moon & Inge, 1993). Each step consists of one observable behavior that is taught individually. Tasks are usually worded so they may be used as a prompt during instruction, such as "pick up the pitcher of milk."

    Although not all teaching is based upon task analysis, behaviors such as sweeping floors, cleaning tables, and making iced tea may require task analysis. Most skills—whether they involve daily routines, such as brushing one's teeth, or vocational skills such as putting together a bicycle brake—can be described in terms of discrete steps. This procedure, often used to teach skills to children with mental retardation, was discussed in Chapter 4. Task analysis involves identifying and defining the skill, performing the task and observing others to note the steps involved, and adapting steps if necessary.

5. *Analyze the skills required and adapt if necessary.* Sometimes a particular task requires a step that is difficult for a child to perform. The child may not have the physical skills. The principle of partial participation may be useful as it was with the young student who needed help in a couple of steps to put on boots but could do the rest. At times, a particular way around a particular step may be an option and adapting material or the sequence may be required.

6. *Use prompts and cues the student can understand.* Children with severe disabilities often need specific guidance to respond appropriately. A **prompt** is any event that helps to initiate a response (Kazdin, 1994). Behavior may be prompted in many ways. Some prompts are physical, for example, holding a

Task analysis:
The process of sequentially analyzing a skill into its teachable components.

Prompt:
A cue that initiates a response.

Task analysis is frequently used, as a skill is sequentially analyzed and children are taught one small part of the skill after another.

child's arm to assist the child to place a spoon in the mouth. Others are verbal, such as instructing a person to do something; others involve gestures such as pointing at something. Deciding which prompt to use depends upon the child's abilities and the nature of the task (Brown & Snell, 1993). Often, teachers invoke a strategy of using the least prompts (Test, Grossi, & Keul, 1988). The teacher progresses from the least amount of assistance, usually a verbal prompt, to the most intrusive, a physical prompt, until one produces the correct response (Brown & Snell, 1993).

Sometimes, more than one type of prompt is used. Schepis and colleagues (1987) taught a job skill of preparing envelopes for mailing, including stamping a return address, to people with profound mental retardation who could comply only with simple requests. Verbal instructions were provided to explain the sequence of behaviors, a visual prompt was provided if the individual did not show the correct behaviors and, finally, the individual was aided by being guided through the task with physical assistance, a physical prompt. These prompts were designed to increase the likelihood of correct performance. A creative use of prompting is shown in the use of verbal prompts delivered through recorded instructions on Walkman radios to teach adolescents to do their laundry, prepare food, and perform other necessary daily chores (Alberto et al., 1986).

The goal of any learning is to obtain the response in the absence of artificial prompts. This process usually involves fading the prompts. **Fading** is the gradual removal of a prompt. If the individual is learning a five-stage process, the learner may require five prompts at the beginning. As the child learns the task, fewer prompts are required. Achieving the final behavior

Fading:
The gradual removal of a prompt.

requires fading the prompts and reinforcing the correct responses as they occur.

One of the simplest ways of fading is to use a **time delay procedure**. In this procedure, teachers initially give the prompt immediately (zero second delay) after the instructional cue; but on successive trials, they delay giving the prompt for perhaps two, four, or six seconds in order to give the student a chance to perform the activity without an artificial prompt (Kaiser, 1993). For example, suppose a teacher shows a child six words and then says "point to the word *sandwich*" and gives a gestural prompt by pointing to the correct word. The teacher may shuffle the words and then give the instruction and allow a delay of perhaps six seconds for the answer to be given. Snell and colleagues (1989) taught three children with cerebral palsy and cognitive disabilities to brush their teeth. These students were taught the steps with physical prompts. During the first 10 trials of instruction, students received assistance immediately after the cue for the step was given. The time delay between stimulus and prompt was then increased as the trials continued. The students learned the skills and maintained them for 10 months.

7. *Provide feedback and reinforcement.* All children require feedback and reinforcement. Children with severe and multiple disabilities are accustomed to failing, and learned helplessness is a great problem. Feedback should be quick and positive. The nature of the reinforcer used depends upon the child's abilities and desires.

8. *Teach for generalization.* Children with severe disabilities often find generalization difficult, which is one reason for community-based instruction (Fox, 1989). Attention to generalization is necessary for all children, but especially for children with severe disabilities who may show more difficulty than others in this area.

One method to improve generalization, called general case instruction, emphasizes using examples and teaching in many environments so a child learns to perform skills across a wide range of settings and materials. Browder and Snell (1993) taught a twelve-year-old student to buy things in a convenience store. First, the types of stores in the area of the student's home that the student would use were located. The teacher then wrote a general task analysis, which could be applicable to any convenience store, and defined the stimulus and response variations that existed. Then the skill was taught and tested.

Another method of enhancing generalization is called the multiple exemplars method. In this technique, the desired situations are all listed, and children are taught a particular strategy that needs to be generalized in one situation after another until the child shows the ability to use the skill in all situations. For example, if there are five situations in which the child might need to generalize a skill, the skill is taught in situation one. The child is tested to see if the skill was generalized. If not, it is taught in the second situation and so on. The child is only taught the skill in the new situation if generalization did not occur.

9. *Evaluate progress.* Evaluating progress involves comparing the original goals to the child's present behavior after training. This step is important because if the child is not succeeding, some change in strategy is required.

Time delay procedure: A procedure in which the instructor initially delivers the prompt for a particular behavior immediately following the instructional cue but then delays giving the prompt on successive trials to give the learner a chance to respond.

What to Teach

What does the child with severe or multiple disabilities need to learn? As in every other case, the child's individual goals will be listed in the IEP. The curriculum is often organized into three major groups of skills (Ford et al., 1989). First, skills needed to function in the community, including those related to self-management, home living, recreation, leisure time pursuits, and vocational skills must be learned. Second, functional academics, including reading, writing, telling time, and using money are required. Third, skills that are embedded in most activities—for example, motor, communication, and social skills—are taught.

Communication Skills

Children with severe disabilities often have communication difficulties (Hedbring, 1995). Learning to communicate in some way is vital to the child's integration into society. Lack of communication negatively affects every area of functioning. If a child with a severe disability is to succeed in the regular classroom, the child must be able to communicate with fellow students and the teacher. Children need to communicate choices and preferences, ideas and feelings, as well as to respond to others.

Some children with severe disabilities can communicate well using short sentences; others may use phrases or single words. Some may not be able to speak at all and require various communication aids.

Augmentative and Alternative Communication

Augmentative and alternative communication (AAC): Systems of communication that facilitate communication for people with severe expressive and/or language disorders.

Many children with severe disabilities need to use **augmentative and alternative communication (AAC)**. An AAC facilitates communication for people with severe expressive and/or language disorders (ASHA, 1991). AAC systems fall into two categories, aided and unaided. An aided system requires some sort of device, such as a picture or a word board, a notebook, or a computerized aid. An unaided system is one based upon hand or body motions (Miller, 1993).

Unaided systems have the advantage of always being available and requiring no equipment. The most common AAC systems used with people with severe disabilities are unaided, including manually signed gestures (Soto et al., 1993). Sometimes, a gesture may be used with a vocalization, while at other times just pointing with one's finger is sufficient or holding one's hand up to signal "no." Many conventional gestures are easily understood by others.

Signing is another unaided system. As noted in Chapter 12, American Sign Language and various forms of signed English are commonly used by people with severe auditory impairments. Such signing can be useful for children with severe disabilities, but it requires somewhat sophisticated skills.

Aided systems vary according to the type of aid, the response mode used, and the symbol system displayed. These systems are created for the specific needs of the individual. A communication board consists of any flat surface that contains words, pictures, or symbols from which a student can make a selection. It may contain the vocabulary the child would need to ask and answer questions, make requests, and direct the actions of others. Most of the time, words or symbols are nouns, although some verbs may be included. Whether to use objects, photographs, line drawings, or words depends upon the cognitive abilities of the child. The child can signal the choice by either pointing or using an eye gaze (the child fixes the eyes on the choice) (Mervine, 1992). Some communication boards are single purpose displays, offering a number of symbols related to one activity, such as ordering food in a restaurant (Rothholz, Berkowitz, & Burberry, 1989). Multiple displays can be combined into a notebook or flip chart.

Often, teaching the child to use the board begins during an enjoyable activity, such as mealtime or a leisure time activity. Children may identify items they are using or be given choices that are delivered if the child signals. The child may also answer the question of what the child wishes to do next as communication increases (Mervine, 1992).

Initial training is often accomplished through modeling where the parent and teacher may point to the item and verbally name the item. Boards may initially be simple and increase with complexity as the child learns to use them.

Other aids are electronic. For example, a tape recorder with different messages, each accessible through individually tailored microswitches, can be useful. In one case, a child used an audible tone to signal for classroom attention. It was basically an audible electronic substitute for a raised hand (King, 1991). A recorded message can get a teacher's attention or ask a question in a store (Wacker et al., 1988).

The computer revolution raises some fascinating alternatives. The Touch Talker is a computer with a display monitor, a voice output, and a special overlapping keyboard that uses individually tailored symbols. The input mode can be fitted to the child's motor and sensory abilities. Output may be screen displays, printed copy, or synthesized speech. One child used a computer with a voice output to give "Simon Says" commands to classmates (Mirenda & Schuyler, 1988).

Children with severe disabilities can use computers if the input has been specially designed to their needs.

A child using an AAC system must be able to respond in some way. Pointing is the most common way to do so (Culp et al., 1986). A child uses a hand or fist to respond. A head pointer is also possible as is eye fixation. Another response mode is scanning in which the responses are presented in a series of choices until the desired message is reached and the choice signalled. In auditory human-aided scanning, the partner verbalizes a number of choices, as in "Do you want to . . ." and the child indicates the desired choices by responding only to the desired one using a head nod, eye blink, or some vocalization. Electronic scanning aids exist in which a light or marker systematically proceeds through a number of displayed messages until the desired one is reached. The child may use a switch of some sort to display the desired communication (Miller, 1993).

SCENARIO

4 Sandra is a sixth-grade student with multiple disabilities. She can make some verbalizations, say a few words, but cannot communicate orally very well. She uses communication boards. You will be her teacher next term and her parents ask you to help design a communication board or boards for use in the classroom. How would you go about doing so and what pictures, photographs, or line drawings would you include?

THOUGHT QUESTION

6. *How can a teacher encourage communication for a child who is used to having others predict the child's needs and provide them without communication?*

Types of Communication Needed

Teaching children with severe disabilities to communicate is often a difficult task. Children without severe disabilities learn language easily without much adult instruction through listening and participating (Kaplan, 1993). The typical channels for learning language may be compromised by the disabilities. In addition, children with severe disabilities may be used to having their needs recognized without any direct communication. For other children, their particular vocalization or movement may be familiar to the caregiver but not very useful in interactions with other people. Other children with severe disabilities are discouraged from communicating by the physical or cognitive effort it takes to do so. Children with severe disabilities need to be systematically taught to interact, which requires patience and planning (Siegel-Causey & Wetherby, 1993).

An assessment of the child's communication needs is often performed using an ecological inventory (Kaiser, 1993). The activities that require communication are identified. For each activity, general communication opportunities are listed and a potential teacher is identified. The communication abilities of the child are also assessed, and a plan of action formulated. For example, requesting and rejecting are important communication abilities in the home and school, as is the general social skill of greeting people, such as saying or indicating "hello." Another major area of content is conversation. Having a conversation means being able to initiate, continue, and terminate an interaction. These skills can be learned by some children with severe disabilities. Hunt and colleagues (1991) used topic-setting communication books to augment partially intelligible speech with three children with severe cognitive impairments in second through fourth grade. The children used these communication books to take turns in which the first partner chose a topic from the book and offered a question or comment on it. The second partner then gave an answer and asked a new question on the same or a different topic from the book. Peers were trained to refer to the communication book and to make comments or ask a question about pictures in the book and wait for a response from the child with a severe disability.

To teach communication skills, the teacher must develop a good relationship with the child and interact in areas in which the child shows an interest. The teacher must also increase both the opportunities and the need for the child to communicate by giving the child choices. Other people in the environment must be sensitized to the communication of children with severe disabilities so they can encourage such communication.

Some disturbing trends have appeared for children who learn how to communicate using AAC systems. First, the speaking partner typically dominates the conversation. The speaker communicates primarily to ask information, frequently repeating or rewording questions, and often without allowing time for the user to respond. The partner using the AAC system plays a passive, respondent role, initiating topics infrequently and often unsuccessfully, and using "yes" and "no" answers (Miller, 1993). Second, classroom personnel respond at a low rate to student-initiated choices (Houghton et al., 1987). This low response rate is especially evident when no formalized teaching is going on. Sometimes, the child's communications are not responded to by others. Perhaps the directness of the teaching process, the lack of spontaneity involved, and the difficulty using some of the communication aids cause these difficulties.

Traditionally, communication training for individuals with moderate and severe disabilities was scheduled in brief sessions isolated from the natural environment. Such teaching does not lead to generalization. Children learn language best when the communication results in immediate and potentially reinforcing consequences (Caro & Snell, 1989). In the ecological approach, the teacher carries out the communication skill training during routine class activities, such as during meal preparation, lunch time, and in transportation. Teachers and parents may model the use of AAC during conversations. A teacher may use a mini-board to comment that she likes ice cream and wait for the child to respond. The facilitator may then ask what the child likes.

Milieu teaching refers to language and communication procedures that are brief, positive in nature, and carried out in the natural environment as opportunities for teaching functional communication arise. The teacher arranges the environment to increase the likelihood that the child will need to communicate and may initiate communication (Kaiser, 1993). Language is, then, taught in naturally occurring contexts.

A number of strategies are used, such as time delay. At first, a teacher may point to some symbol or ask a question. As the child becomes better at communicating the teacher waits longer and longer before giving a prompt (Angelo & Goldstein, 1993). Praise or the assistance requested in the communication is given immediately following a communication.

Sometimes, a demand model is used in which the teacher verbally instructs the student to describe material, perhaps by saying, "Tell me what this is." If the student gives the proper response, the child is praised and given the material. If not, the teacher models the correct response and requires the student to imitate it (Kaiser, 1993; Caro & Snell, 1989). A missing item format may also encourage communication. During snack time, a child is only given two of three needed items, such as a cereal and a spoon without the milk, and the child has to request the missing item (Tirapelle & Cipani, 1992). If the request does not occur, the trainer uses the system of least prompts described earlier.

Functional Life Skills

Functional life skills are those skills people need in their everyday lives. Some functional life skills involve self-care such as brushing one's teeth, toileting, eating, and bathing, which are necessary for attaining a feeling of control and independence (Snell & Farlow, 1993). Living in the community requires functional life skills as well, including getting along with others, being able to get from place to place, and shopping (Lovett & Harris, 1987).

Parents consider these skills vital. Parents of 192 children with moderate to severe disabilities were surveyed to determine the percent of a typical school week that should be spent on functional life skills, academic skills, friendship-making skills, and other educational programs. The parents of children with severe disabilities expressed a preference for the greatest amount of time to be devoted to life skills; the next most important area involved friendship and social development, while the parents of children with moderate disabilities showed a preference for academic skills, then functional life skills, with friendship and social skills following in third place (Hamre-Nietupski, 1993).

Children with severe disabilities are often delayed in developing functional skills. They must be taught basic skills that other children may learn simply through observation or with a little direction. Less incidental learning takes place and extensive training is required to help children with severe disabilities acquire basic skills.

Some self-care skills can be taught in integrated settings; professionals may work with the child during times when the class activity may be inappropriate. Of the various ways to teach self-help skills, task analysis, modeling, and time delay are commonly used. For example, Spooner and colleagues (1989) taught first aid skills, including communicating the emergency and taking care of injuries to adolescents with severe disabilities. Training involved both group and individual instruction. The instructor first had a group discussion in which the whole task was modeled. Then each student practiced while receiving the least intrusive prompts with praise for the correct response on each step of the task-analyzed skill. Next, the student was tested on the task using no prompts, and the method was repeated daily until the skill was mastered.

In another program, four high school students with mental retardation were taught to use picture schedules to begin a series of behavioral tasks when they arrived at school each morning. When each had mastered the picture schedule, it was used again to prompt a group of behaviors at home. After the training, all students used the schedules at school and at home successfully (Irvine et al., 1992).

Leisure Skills

A full, satisfying life requires recreation. Unfortunately, this area has received little attention, and many children with severe disabilities have a great deal of "dead time" in which they have nothing to do (Schleien et al., 1993). During this time, inappropriate behavior is more likely to occur. Recreational skills increase independence, socialization, and friendship opportunities, improve motor and physical skills, and increase self-esteem.

The first step is to assess the individual's recreational needs and preferences. Such assessments emphasize what the child can and likes to do, not the limitations. Family members and others who know the child may offer suggestions based upon their experiences with the child. Communication of choices enters the picture. When children can communicate their choices of leisure time activities, their participation in activities increases (Dattilo & Rusch, 1985).

After determining the desired activities, the teacher will examine what skills the student has and what skills are lacking. Adapting the recreational activity when the participant cannot perform a step independently is especially important. The adaptations may involve modifying the material or equipment, the rules, skill level, or environment (Bernabe & Block, 1994). Adaptation of materials may involve adaptive switches or perhaps using soft rather than hard rubber balls. Changing the rules may allow a two-handed rather than one-handed dribble in basketball. Architectural barriers may be eliminated.

Studies and program evaluations show that children with severe disabilities can be taught leisure skills based upon what their same-aged peers without disabilities can do. After an initial assessment of skills, children with severe disabilities were taught such skills as throwing and catching Frisbees, playing games, and operating tape recorders (Horst et al., 1981). Children with moderate and severe disabilities were able to participate with their nondisabled peers in an integrated aerobic exercise program (Halle, Gabler-Halle, & Bemben, 1989).

People with severe disabilities can enjoy recreational activities if equipment is specially adapted to their needs.

Children with severe and multiple disabilities are sometimes included in school programs only to be segregated in summer programs. To enhance integration, special education programs may combine with community recreation programs (Hamre-Nietupski et al., 1992). In one effort, after selecting a site for the program and surveying an inventory of recreation services available to children without disabilities, community recreation agencies were approached and their support established. The program was publicized and special educators, parents, and community recreation staff met to plan the integrated activities. The children played with each other on the playground, listened to stories, sang songs, and participated in arts and crafts. Children regularly swam together, conversed, and played games. Some competitive activities such as softball were adapted by modifying materials and rules. Some of the adaptations are found in Table 16.3. Children without disabilities were prepared through brief discussions about the nature of the disabilities, communication abilities, and the children's likes and dislikes. Role play was used to develop the ability to communicate and interact. The program was implemented over six weeks and continued for three summers. Parents and children both with and without disabilities were pleased with the program, and some ongoing interactions between children with and without disabilities occurred.

TABLE 16.3   Sample Community Recreation Activities and Adaptations/Support Strategies

ACTIVITIES	ADAPTATIONS/SUPPORT STRATEGIES
1. Table games (e.g., "Yahtzee," "Uno")	• Substituted large foam dice for children who had difficulty seeing the dots on regular dice. • Games played in teams/pairs rather than individuals.
2. Crafts; plastic craft lace	• Adult assisted students in taping one end of plastic laces to work table. • Softer, thicker material, such as macrame cord, substituted for craft lace. • Students with and without disabilities worked on lacing in pairs.
3. Free play on playground equipment and in sandbox	• Adult brought toys preferred by students with disabilities with which nondisabled children might also play. • Adult assisted students in using equipment.
4. Softball	• Larger, softer ball used. • Larger bat used. • T-ball stand used for children in wheelchairs. • Nondisabled peers were "designated runners" for children with physical disabilities or pushed wheelchairs on the base paths.

Education and Training in Mental Retardation, 1992, p. 71. Reprinted by permission.

Functional Academics

Children with severe disabilities differ greatly in their academic needs. Some learn to read sentences, some read a few words. Some can use calculators, some cannot. Some can write their own names, others can write more. The extent of academic training depends upon student abilities, parental preferences, and current and future skill needs. Academic instruction must be functional, that is, be tied to needs in the present or immediate future. The progress is often slow, and children's needs and abilities must be carefully evaluated.

SCENARIO

5 As an elementary school teacher, you frequently find that children with disabilities are placed in your class. Most of these children have learning disabilities, although a child with mental retardation was placed in your class a few years ago. You are told that next year you will be instructing a student with multiple and severe disabilities. Arthur has cerebral palsy and mental retardation. He can speak some phrases, but people sometimes have difficulty understanding him. He needs a wheelchair for mobility. What steps would you take to ensure that his educational experience will be both pleasant and educationally valuable?

IN THE CLASSROOM — **Teaching Children with Severe or Multiple Disabilities in the Regular Classroom**

Children with severe or multiple disabilities are just beginning to be included into the regular classroom setting. The following suggestions may be helpful to teachers who may not have much experience teaching children with severe and multiple disabilities and may not know what to expect.

1. Discuss the IEP with parents and special educators.	**Why?** The modifications required for children with severe or multiple disabilities may be substantial. In addition, as in all cases, the classroom teachers should understand the goals noted on the IEP and the methods for meeting the challenges.
2. Introduce the student to others in the classroom.	**Why?** This may be the first time that the other children in the classroom have met a child with extensive disabilities and some apprehension may be present.

3. Become familiar with the child's mode of communication.	**Why?** Many children with severe and multiple disabilities use communication boards or other augmentative communication devices. Since communication is so important, becoming familiar with the child's mode of communication is vital to the child's success in the classroom.
4. Be aware of fatigue problems and possible side effects of medication taken by the child.	**Why?** The teacher is in an excellent position to observe the child. If the child tires easily, frequent rest periods may be needed. The side effects of medication should be reported to parents at once.
5. Special efforts to encourage interaction between the child with a severe disability and nondisabled peers must be maintained over the school year.	**Why?** Some teachers inaugurate a buddy or tutorial system at the beginning of the year and then as it shows success do little to maintain the system. Evidence indicates a decline in social interaction during the school year. Special efforts must be maintained if positive social interaction is to occur.
6. Consult with other professionals on the design and implementation of behavioral techniques to alter behavior.	**Why?** Some children with severe or multiple disabilities may show behaviors that must be altered using behavioral techniques. The school psychologist or other professional working with the child will help a teacher design a program which is effective and ethically acceptable.
7. Emphasize functional skills.	**Why?** Children with severe and multiple disabilities require instruction in skills which give the child some control over the environment. The teacher can receive help in deciding what skills are functional in the child's IEP and through consultation with other professionals.

8. Use partial participation.	**Why?** Children with multiple or severe disabilities may not be able to participate fully in every activity but often can participate in some way in most activities.
9. Make certain children with severe impairments interact with peers of similar chronological ages.	**Why?** Placement with younger children may not promote social development as much as interaction with children of the same age.
10. Allow children to make choices whenever possible.	**Why?** Many children with severe and multiple disabilities do not have the opportunity to make choices. People are always making choices for them. Whenever possible, teachers should allow children to make choices and gain experience in decision making.
11. Use tangible materials when possible.	**Why?** Children with severe and multiple disabilities frequently have difficulty with abstract concepts.
12. Use prompts when necessary.	**Why?** Children with severe and multiple disabilities may require prompting in order to perform some activities. These prompts must be individually suited to the children's abilities.
13. Do not depend on incidental learning.	**Why?** Children with severe and multiple disabilities often do not show much incidental learning. Basic skills must be specifically taught.
14. Teach generalization.	**Why?** Children with severe and multiple disabilities often have difficulties with generalization. Generalization can be accomplished using general case instruction or the multiple exemplars method.

Vocational Development

The transition from school to work is often very difficult for children with special needs. By law, each child must have an Individualized Transition Plan (ITP) by age 16 years, if not earlier. The ITP team includes the child and family, vocational education experts, vocational rehabilitation specialists, business and industry representatives, and representatives from sheltered workshops, a number of not-for-profit agencies, and the Social Security Administration. Job preparation requires both the skills necessary to do the job and those necessary to keep the job. Children with severe and multiple disabilities begin job training relatively early and much of the training is conducted in the community (Moon & Inge, 1993).

Families need accurate information about jobs in the community. Families may be encouraged to plan by viewing videotapes of individuals with severe disabilities who succeed at work, attending workshops where adult service providers make presentations, and touring job sites to talk with employers. They can communicate with others who have made the transition from school to work and learn about the possibilities and pitfalls encountered.

Some vocational preparation is school-based, but most training occurs in the community. A definite relationship has been found between successful job placement after graduation and having had community-based job training during the years students attend school (Hasazi et al., 1985). During the elementary school years, the emphasis is placed on learning basic skills such as eating, dressing, grooming and toileting, functional methods of communication, and mobility and social skills. Still, some career awareness may be possible with visits to various work sites. Some daily chores, such as preparing a snack and cleaning up, can be considered pre-vocational in nature. As the student matures, the community becomes the training site, often where the student will be working.

The vocational curriculum of the school cannot be divorced from the community in which the child lives. An assessment of the opportunities in the local labor market to determine the major employers, the types of employment available, and the types of employment obtained by individuals with disabilities is an important first step. A list of local businesses that might hire students with severe disabilities is composed and an analysis of what jobs may be available noted. For example, a hospital may have a number of jobs but perhaps only a few for which students with severe disabilities may realistically train, including food service, grounds maintenance, and clerical positions. Some job-related activities include labeling envelopes, folding letters, rolling silverware, folding towels, and certain janitorial services. The active participation of various business people is highly desirable. One definite problem is the lack of vocational opportunity in the community for people with the most severe disabilities. Even though some people with severe disabilities are participating successfully in the mainstream of the workforce, the number of such opportunities is limited (Rhodes et al., 1991).

The community-based vocational training may take place in the actual work environment, where skills are task analyzed and taught. Some people with severe disabilities may work in supported employment (see Chapter 4). Others work in sheltered workshops. The job depends upon the student's abilities and the opportunities available.

SCENARIO

6 Teresa is in secondary school. She has mental retardation and some motor skill problems. She is nearing 14 years of age, and her parents and teachers believe they should begin to look at possible vocational opportunities for her. Teresa likes to be with people and can communicate using a few words. She is easily frustrated, though, and sometimes cries and shakes when that occurs. What steps should be taken to help Teresa and her family prepare for the future?

How Far We've Come; How Far We Have to Go

A growing, but still limited, amount of research is available concerning teaching children with severe and multiple disabilities. Research has validated a number of practices. These methods are sometimes called best educational practices. When Williams and colleagues (1990) surveyed a number of experts in the field, nine best practices were noted (see Table 16.4). However, a gap appears between general acceptance of these practices and the level of implementation. More attention to implementing what is known is needed (Ayres et al., 1994).

Only recently have attempts been made to include children with severe or multiple disabilities in the regular classroom and society. Not all children with severe and multiple disabilities are best served by spending all their time in the regular classroom. Still, more and more children with severe and multiple disabilities will be based in the classroom in the future and will receive a large part of their education there.

If the level of support available today is compared to what was available 25 years ago, the progress is astounding. If the number of children with severe and multiple disabilities attending their regular school today is compared to the number 25 years ago, the trend is unmistakable. The attitudinal changes that have occurred in that time frame are certainly great. Significant progress has undoubtedly been made.

On the other hand, much remains to be done. More research is needed into teaching methods that work with children with severe and multiple disabilities. New ways of adapting the environment, of facilitating communication, and of teaching children with severe and multiple disabilities must be found. Although at this point society does not have the medical and educational knowledge to significantly reduce the performance and developmental differences between children with severe disabilities and other children, schooling can certainly produce meaningful outcomes (Ferguson & Baumgart, 1991).

A good beginning has been made, and more progress will occur in the future as we begin to accept the simple but powerful idea that all children have a right to develop their skills and abilities, no matter how extensive their disabilities.

TABLE 16.4   **Nine Best Practices**

1. *Age-appropriate placement in local public schools.*
   The placement of choice for all students (with and without handicaps) should be within chronologically age-appropriate regular classrooms in the student's local public schools.

2. *Integrated delivery of services.*
   IEPs and instructional programs should indicate the integration of instruction on education and related service goals into everyday school, home, and community activities. Related service providers should offer consultation and assistance to special and regular educators, parents, and others on developing, implementating, and integrating instruction on related service goals.

3. *Social integration.*
   Students with handicaps should have access to the same environments as nonhandicapped peers of similar chronological age. Primary goals of social integration should be to increase the number of integrated community and school environments and to improve the quality of interactions in those environments.

4. *Transition planning.*
   Transition planning should occur well in advance of major moves (e.g., early education/special education to elementary school, elementary to high school, high school to adult services). Transition objectives should be included in IEPs and reflect the input of significant parties affected by the transition.

5. *Community-based training.*
   Students should have the opportunity to acquire and demonstrate specific skills within appropriate community settings. Conditions and criteria of IEP goals and objectives should include performance in natural environments.

6. *Curricular expectations.*
   Curricula or curriculum guidelines should progress from no skills to adult functioning in all areas of integrated community life. A system for longitudinal monitoring of student progress should also be in place.

7. *Systematic data-based instruction.*
   Written schedules of daily activities, clearly defined objectives, reliably implemented instructional programs, and systematic data collection and analysis should be accepted procedure. Instructional decisions should be based upon documentation of students' progress.

8. *Home-school partnership.*
   Parents should have ongoing opportunities to participate in the development of their child's IEP and the delivery of educational and related services. A clearly delineated system for regularly communicating with parents can provide parents with information. Parental concerns should be reflected in IEP goals and objectives.

9. *Systematic program evaluation.*
   Educational and related services should be evaluated on a regular basis. Evaluations should actively involve the entire program staff and provide administrators and staff with information regarding the achievement of program goals; student progress; discrepancies needing remediation; directions for future programs change; and program impact upon students, their families, and the community.

Education and Training in Mental Retardation, 1990, p. 121. Reprinted by permission.

S U M M A R Y

1. Children with severe disabilities may show significant impairments in intellectual functioning, motor skills, communication, and sensory abilities as well as manifesting health problems, such as seizures. The Association for Persons with Severe Handicaps (TASH) defines a severe disability in terms of the intensity of supports required by the individual.

2. The number of children with severe or multiple disabilities is small, but is increasing.

3. Children are considered to have dual sensory impairments (deaf-blindness) if they have sufficient degrees of deafness and blindness so they cannot be educated solely in programs for either children with deafness or who are blind. Many methods of communication can be used depending upon the background of the children, their physical abilities, residual hearing and vision, and other factors. The Helen Keller National Center for Deaf-Blind Youths and Adults is an agency at the forefront of creating new programs for this population.

4. Children with severe or multiple disabilities are likely to be discovered early. Evaluation is difficult since the nature of the disabilities may make many commonly used instruments difficult or impossible to use. Norm-referenced tests yield information concerning how far the child is from the norms, but do not offer much help in educational planning. Ecological assessments are more useful for educational planning.

5. The causes of severe and multiple disabilities are mostly genetic and medical in nature, although the environment plays a significant part in determining the child's level of functioning.

6. The difficulties of caring for children with severe and multiple impairments are significant. These include the need to help children engage in self-care activities and coordinating the therapies required. The amount of stress is generally, but not always, related to the severity of the disorder.

7. The percentage of children with severe disabilities served in public schools is increasing. Studies show that children with severe disabilities do better socially and academically when integrated into the neighborhood school and regular classroom.

8. Community-based instruction is education in the community in which a functional skill is learned and practiced in the natural environment. It is especially important for children with severe disabilities who have difficulties generalizing skills. The amount of community-based instruction increases with the age of the child.

9. To teach children with severe or multiple disabilities effectively, an attitude that all children can learn must be taken. Teachers must consider what a child needs to learn to become as independent as possible, teach functional skills, and emphasize social skills. The principle of partial participation states that children with severe or multiple disabilities may not be able to participate entirely in many activities, but can participate to some extent in most activities. Children need to be placed in age-appropriate classrooms and have material presented in a concrete fashion. Giving the child choices and emphasizing communication are important factors in the education of the child.

10. A general framework for teaching children with severe or multiple disabilities involves using assessment, identifying the target skill to be taught, defining the goals in measurable fashion, task analyzing the skill, analyzing the skills involved and adapting the materials, deciding on prompting and fading strategies, giving feedback and reinforcement, attending to generalization, and measuring progress.

11. Children with severe disabilities often need help in communication. An augmentative and alternative communication system (AAC) facilitates communication for people with severe expressive and/or language disorders.

Communication skills are taught in the natural environment in the context of some daily activity.

12. Parents want daily living skills to be taught in school. In teaching these skills, task analysis is used with a time delay and modeling. Leisure skills are important to life satisfaction, and children with severe disabilities can participate in leisure time activities with children without disabilities if the environment is adapted.

13. Transition planning is required by law, and vocational training often starts early and is based in the community. With training, some people with severe or multiple disabilities can work in the community, some in supported employment and others in sheltered workshops.

References

Abromowitz, A.J., & O'Leary, G. (1991) Behavioral Interventions for the Classroom: Implications for Students with ADHD. *School Psychology Review* 20:220–234.

Achenbach, T.M., & Edelbrock, C. (1981) *Manual for the Child Behavior Checklist and Revised Child Behavior Profile*. Burlington, Vt.: University of Vermont.

Ackerman, G.L. (1993). A Congressional View of Youth Suicide. *American Psychologist* 48:183–185.

Adams, P.F., & Benson, V. (1990) Current Estimates from the National Health Interview Survey, 1989. *Vital and Health Statistics*, Series 10, no. 176 (DHHS Pub No Phs 90-1504). Hyattsville, Md.: National Center for Health Statistics.

Adelman, H.S. (1989) Beyond the Learning Mystique: An Interactional Perspective on Learning Disabilities. *Journal of Learning Disabilities* 22:301–305.

Adelman, H.S., (1992) L D: The Next 25 Years. *Journal of Learning Disabilities* 25:17–22.

Adelman, H.S. (1992) The Classification Problem in S. Stainback & W. Stainback (eds.) *Controversial Issues Confronting Special Education*. Needham Heights, Mass.: Allyn and Bacon 97–109.

Adelman, H.S., & Taylor, L. (1993) *Learning Problems and Learning Disabilities*. Belmont, Calif.: Brooks Cole.

Adelson, E., & Fraiberg, S. (1974) Gross Motor Development in Infants Blind from Birth. *Child Development* 45:114–126.

Affleck, J.Q., Edgar, E., Levine, P., & Kortering, L. (1990) Postschool Status of Students Classified as Mildly Mentally Retarded, Learning Disabled, or Nonhandicapped: Does It Get Better with Time? *Education and Training in Mental Retardation* 25:315–324.

Affleck, J.Q., Madge, S., Adams, A., & Lowenbraun, S. (1988) Integrated Classroom Versus Resource Model: Academic Viability and Effectiveness. *Exceptional Children* 54:339–348.

Ainsworth, S., & Fraser, J. (1986) *If Your Child Stutters*. Memphis, Tenn.: Speech Foundation of America.

Alamprese, J.A., Erlanger, W.J., & Brigham, N. (1989) *No Gifts Wasted: Effective Strategies for Educating Highly Able Disadvantaged Students in Math and Science* (vols. 1–2), Cosmos Corporation.

Alberto, P.A., Sharpton, W.R., Briggs, A., & Stright, M.H., (1986) Facilitating Task Acquisition through the Use of a Self-Operated Auditory Prompting System. *Journal of the Association for Persons with Severe Handicaps* 11:85–91.

Algozzine, B., Christenson, S., & Ysseldyke, J.E. (1982) An Analysis of the Incidence of Special Class Placement: The Masses Are Burgeoning. *The Journal of Special Education* 17:141–147.

Algozzine, B., Christenson, S., & Ysseldyke, J.E. (1982) Probabilities Associated with the Referral to Placement Process. *Teacher Education and Special Education* 5:19–23.

Algozzine, B., O'Shea, D.J., Stoddard, K., & Crews, W.B. (1988) Reading and Writing Competencies of Adolescents with Learning Disabilities. *Journal of Learning Disabilities* 21:154–160.

Allen, B.P. (1987) Youth Suicide. *Adolescence* 22:271–288.

Allen, B.P. (1994) *Personality Theories*. Needham, Mass: Allyn & Bacon.

Allen, D.A., & Affleck, G. (1985) Are We Stereotyping Parents? A Postscript to Blacher. *Mental Retardation* 23:200–202.

Allen, T., & Osborn, T. (1984) Academic Integration of Hearing-Impaired Students. *American Annals of the Deaf* 129:100–113.

Allen, T., Rawlings, B., & Schildroth, A. (1989) *Deaf Students and the School-To-Work Transition*, Baltimore, Md.: Paul H. Brookes.

Allison, P.D., & Furstenberg, F.F. (1989) How Marital Dissolution Affects Children: Variations by Age and Sex. *Developmental Psychology* 25:540–550.

Allport, G.W. (1954) *The Nature of Prejudice*. Reading, Mass.: Addison-Wesley.

Alper, S.K., Schloss, P.J., & Schloss, C.N. (1994) *Families of Students with Disabilities*, Boston: Allyn & Bacon.

Alperstein, G., Rappaport, C., & Flanigan, J.M., (1988) Health Problems of Homeless Children in New York City. *American Journal of Public Health* 78:1232–1233.

Altman, L.K. (January 25, 1990) Scientists Link a Defective Gene to a Leading Cause of Blindness. *New York Times*, A.18.

Altman, L.K. (Feb. 14, 1995). Children's AIDS Study Finds AZT Ineffective. *New York Times*, C13.

American Association of University Women (1992) *How Schools Shortchange Girls*, Washington, D.C.: AAUW Educational Foundation.

American Association on Mental Deficiency (1986) Position Statement on Aversive Therapy. *Mental Retardation* 25:118.

American Association on Mental Retardation (1992) *Mental Retardation: Definition, Classification, and Systems of Support*. Washington, D.C.: author.

American Association on Mental Retardation (1992) *Mental Retardation: Definition, Classification, and Systems of Supports* (9th ed.), Washington, D.C.: author

American Council on Education (1990) *Students Who Are Deaf or Hard of Hearing in Postsecondary Education*, Washington, D.C.: American Council on Education.

American Foundation for the Blind (1983) *How Does a Blind Person Get Around?* New York: author.

American Foundation for the Blind (1987) *Louis Braille*, New York: author.

American Home Economics Association (1986) Preventing Adolescent Pregnancy: Promising New Approaches. *Journal of Home Economics* 78:42–47.

American Medical Association Council on Scientific Affairs (AMA). (17 June 1992) Violence Against Women: Relevance for Medical Practitioners. *Journal of the American Medical Association*, 3185.

American Psychiatric Association (1993) *DSM-4 Draft Criteria*, Washington, D.C.: author.

American Psychiatric Association (1993) *Draft Criteria for DSM-IV*. Washington, D.C.: author.

American Psychiatric Association (1994) *Diagnostic and Statistical Manual of Mental Disorders*, 4th ed. (DSM-IV). Washington, D.C.: Author.

American Psychiatric Association (1994) *Diagnostic and Statistical Manual of Mental Disorders*, 4th ed. Washington, D.C.: American Psychiatric Association.

Anastasi, A. (1988) *Psychological Testing* 6th ed. New York: Macmillan.

Anderegg, M.L. (1995) personal communication.

Anderson, E.A., & Koblinsky, S.A. (1995) Homeless Policy: The Need to Speak to Families. *Family Relations* 44:13–18.

Anderson-Inman, L. (1986) Bridging the Gap: Student-Centered Strategies for Promoting the Transfer of Learning. *Exceptional Children* 52:562–572.

Anderson-Inman, L. (1987) Consistency of Performance across Classrooms: Instructional Materials versus Setting as Influencing Variables. *Journal of Special Education* 21:9–29.

Anderson, R., & Antonak, R.F. (1992) The Influence of Attitudes and Contact on Reactions to Persons with Physical and Speech Disabilities. *Rehabilitation Counseling Bulletin* 35:240–247.

Andrews, G., Craig, A., Feyer, A.M., Hoddinott, S., Howie, P., & Neilson, M. (1993) Stuttering: A Review of Research Findings and Theories Circa 1982. *Journal of Speech and Hearing Disorders* 48:226–246.

Andrews, G., Morris-Yates, A., Howie, P., & Martin, N. (1991) Genetic Factors in Stuttering Confirmed. *Archives of General Psychiatry* 48:1034–1035.

Andrews, G., Neilson, M., & Curlee, R. (1988) Stuttering. *JAMA* 260:1445ff.

Andrews, S.R., Blumenthal, J.B., Johnson, D.L., Kahn, A.J., Ferguson, C.J., Lasater, T.M., Malone, P.E., & Wallace, D.B. (1982) The Skills of Mothering: A Study of Parent-Child Developmental Centers. *Monographs of the Society for Research in Child Development* 47:6, serial number 198.

Angelo, D.H., & Goldstein, H. (1993) Effects of a Pragmatic Teaching Strategy for Requesting Information by Communication Board Users. *Journal of Speech and Hearing Disorders* 55:231–243.

Angier, N. (14 December 1990b) Gene-Treated Girl Is Raising Hopes. *New York Times*, A24.

Angier, N. (21 September 1990a) Team Cures Cells in Cystic Fibrosis by Gene Insertion. *New York Times*, 1ff.

Anthony, E.J. (1974) The Syndrome of the Psychologically Invulnerable Child. In E.J. Anthony & C. Koupernik (eds.), *The Child and His Family. 3. Children at Psychiatric Risk*. New York: Wiley.

Antia, S. (1985) Social Integration of Hearing-Impaired Children: Fact or Fiction? *Volta Review* 87:279–289.

Antia, S., & Kreimeyer, K. (1987) The Effect of Social Skill Training on the Peer Interaction of Preschool Hearing-Impaired Children. *Journal of the Division for Early Childhood* 11:206–216.

Antia, S., Kreimeyer, K.H., & Eldredge, N. (1993) Promoting Social Interaction Between Children with Hearing Impairments and Their Peers. *Exceptional Children* 60:262–275.

Antiles, A.J., & Trent, S.C. (1994) Overrepresentation of Minority Students in Special Education: A Continuing Debate. *The Journal of Special Education* 27: 410–437.

Antonak, R.F. (1981) Prediction of Attitudes Toward Disabled Persons. *Journal of General Psychology* 104:119–123.

Antonarakis, S.E. (28 March 1991) Parental Origin of the Extra Chromosome in Trisomy 21 as Indicated by Analysis of DNA Polymorphisms. Down Syndrome Collaborative Group. *New England Journal of Medicine* 324:872–876.

Apgar, V. (1953) A Proposal for a New Method of Evaluation of the Newborn Infant. *Current Researchers in Anesthesia and Analgesia* 32:260–267.

Apgar, V., Holdaday, D.A., James, L.S., Weisbrot, I.M., & Berien, C. (1958) Evaluation of the Newborn Infant: Second Report. *Journal of the American Psychological Association* 168:1985–1988.

Aphasia: Answers/Questions About Adult Aphasia. (1992) Rockville, Md.: American Speech-Language-Hearing Association.

Aplin, D.Y. (1993) Psychological Evaluation of Adults in a Cochlear Implant Program. *American Annals of the Deaf* 138:415–419.

Arfa, S., Fitzhugh-Bell, K., & Black, F.W. (1989) Neuropsychological Profiles of Children with Learning Disabilities and Children with Documented Brain Damage. *Journal of Learning Disabilities* 22:635–640.

Arick, J., Falco, R., & Brazeau, K. (1989) Prioritizing In-Service Needs for Educators of Students with Severe Handicaps in Heterogeneous Integrated Settings. *Journal of the Association of People with Severe Handicaps* 24:371–378.

Arnold, P., & Atkins, J. (1991) The Social and Emotional Adjustment of Hearing-Impaired Children Integrated in Primary Schools. *Educational Research* 33:223–229.

ASHA (1983) *Answers to Questions About Stuttering*. Rockville, Md.: American Speech-Language-Hearing Association.

ASHA (1991) Committee on Augmentative Communication: American Speech-Language-Hearing Association 33:8–12.

ASHA (1992) *Answers to Questions About Otitis Media, Hearing, and*

Language Development. Rockville, Md.: American Speech-Language-Hearing Association.

ASHA (1992) *Answers to Questions About Adult Aphasia.* Rockville, Md.: American Speech-Language-Hearing Association.

ASHA (1992) *Communication Disorders and Aging.* Rockville, Md.: American Speech-Language-Hearing Association.

ASHA (American Speech-Language-Hearing Association) (1992) *Hearing Impairment and the Audiologist,* Rockville, Md.

Ashcroft, S.C., & Zambone-Ashley, A.M. (1980) Mainstreaming Children with Visual Impairments. *Journal of Research and Development in Education* 13:22–36.

Association for Children with Special Needs (1988) *Activities for Children with Special Needs* (2d ed.), Washington, D.C.: author.

Association for the Care of Children's Health (1986) *Activities for Children with Special Needs,* Washington, D.C.: author.

Astone, N.M., & Upchurch, D.M. (1994) Forming a Family, Leaving School Early, and Earning a GED: A Racial and Cohort Comparison. *Journal of Marriage and the Family* 56: 759–772.

August, D.L. (May 1986) Bilingual Education Act, Title 2 of the Education Amendments of 1984. *Washington Report,* Washington Liaison Office of the Society for Research in Child Development.

Auletta, R., & DeRosa, A.P. (1991) Self-Concepts of Adolescent Siblings of Children with Mental Retardation. *Perceptual and Motor Skills* 73:211–214.

Aurelia, J.C. (1974) *Aphasia Therapy Manual.* Danville, Ill.: The Interstate Printers and Publishers.

Austin, A.B., & Draper, D.C. (1981) Peer Relationships of the Academically Gifted. A Review. *Gifted Child Quarterly* 25:129–133.

Axelrod, L. (1982) Social Perception in Learning Disabled Adolescents.

Journal of Learning Disabilities 15:610–613.

Axelrod, S. (1983) *Behavior Modification for the Classroom Teacher,* 2d ed. New York: McGraw Hill.

Ayllon, T., & Roberts, M.D. (1974) Eliminating Discipline Problems by Strengthening Academic Performance. *Journal of Applied Behavior Analysis* 7:71–76.

Ayres, B. J., Meyer, L. H., Erevelles, N., & Park-Lee, S. (1994) Easy for You to Say: Teacher Perspectives on Implementing Most Promising Practices. *Journal of the Association for Persons with Severe Handicaps* 19: 84–93.

Baca, L., & Cervantes, H. (eds.) (1989) *The Bilingual Special Education Interface.* Columbus, Ohio: Merrill.

Baca, L., & Harris, K.C. (Summer 1988) Teaching Migrant Exceptional Children. *Teaching Exceptional Children,* 32–35.

Badger, E., Burns, D., & Vietze, P. (1981) Maternal Risk Factors as Predictors of Developmental Outcome in Early Childhood. *Infant Mental Health Journal* 2:33–43.

Bagnato, S.J., & Neisworth, J.T. (1991) *Assessment for Early Intervention.* New York: The Guilford Press.

Bagnato, S.J., Neisworth, J.T., & Munson, S.M. (1993) Sensible Strategies for Assessment in Early Intervention. In D.M. Bryant & M.A. Graham (eds.) *Implementing Early Intervention.* New York: The Guilford Press, 148–157.

Bailey, I.L., & Hall, A. (1990) *Visual Impairment: An Overview,* New York: American Foundation for the Blind.

Baird, L.L. (1985) Do Grades and Tests Predict Adult Accomplishment? *Research in Higher Education* 23:3–85.

Baird, P.A., & Sadovnick, A.D. (1987) Life Expectancy in Down Syndrome. *Journal of Pediatrics* 49:110.

Baker, K.A., & de Kanter, A.A. (1981) *Effectiveness of Bilingual Education: A Review of the Literature.* Washington, D.C.: Office of Planning, Budget, and Evaluation.

Baker, P., Piven, J., Schwartz, S., & Patil, S. (1994) Brief Report: Duplication of

Chromosome 15q11–13 in Two Individuals with Autistic Disorder. *Journal of Autism and Developmental Disorders* 24: 529–535.

Baldwin, A.Y. (1991) Ethnic and Cultural Issues. In N. Colangelo & G.A. Davis (eds.), *Handbook of Gifted Education.* Needham Heights, Mass.: Allyn & Bacon, 416–428.

Balis, F. M., & Poplack, D. G., (1994) Drug development and Clinical Pharmacology of Antiretroviral Drugs. In P. A. Pizzo & C. M. Wilfert (eds.) *Pediatric AIDS* (2nd ed.). Baltimore: Williams & Wilkins, 625–651.

Balter, M. (19 June 1992) Studies Set to Test Competing Theories About Early Infection. *Science* 256:1633.

Bandura, A. (1986) *Social Foundations of Thought and Action: A Social Cognitive Theory.* Englewood Cliffs, N.J.: Prentice-Hall.

Bandura, A., Ross, D., & Ross, S.A. (1961) Transmission of Aggression through Imitation of Aggressive Models. *Journal of Abnormal and Social Psychology* 63:575–582.

Barach, C. (1983) *Help Me Say It.* New York: New American Library.

Barbetta, P.M., & Heron, T.E. (1991) Project Shine: Summer Home Instruction and Evaluation. *Intervention in School and Clinic* 26:276–281.

Barinaga, M. (1991) Challenging the "No New Neurons" Dogma. *Science* 255:1646.

Barkan, J.H., & Bernal, E.M. (1991) Gifted Education for Bilingual and Limited English Proficient Students. *Gifted Child Quarterly* 35:144–147.

Barkley, R.A. (1990) *Attention Deficit Hyperactivity Disorder.* New York: Guilford.

Barkley, R.A., Karlsson, J., Strzelecki, E., & Murphy, J.V. (1984) Effects of Age and Ritalin Dosage on the Mother-Child Interactions of Hyperactive Children. *Journal of Consulting and Clinical Psychology* 52:750–758.

Barnes, D.M. (1986) Brain Function Decline in Children with AIDS. *Science* 232:1196.

Barney, J., & Koford, J. (October 1986) Schools and Single Parents. *The Education Digest* 40–43.

Baroff, G.S. (1986) *Mental Retardation: Nature, Cause, and Management* (2d ed.). New York: Hemisphere.

Barraga, N.C., & Erin, J.N. (1992) *Visual Handicaps and Learning* (3d ed.), Austin, Tex.: Pro-Ed.

Barrett, S.S. (1992) Comprehensive Community-Based Services for Adults Who Are Deaf-Blind: Issue, Trends, and Services. *Journal of Visual Impairment & Blindness* 86:393–397.

Barringer, D.G., Strong, C.J., Blair, J.C., Clark, T.C., & Watkins, S. (1993) Screening Procedures Used to Identify Children with Hearing Loss. *American Annals of the Deaf* 138:420–426.

Bartoli, J.S. (1989) An Ecological Response to Coles's Interactivity Alternative. *Journal of Learning Disabilities* 22:292–298.

Bashir, A.S., & Scavuzzo, A. (1992) Children with Language Disorders: Natural History and Academic Success. *Journal of Learning Disabilities* 25:5–65.

Bassuk, E., & Rosenberg, L. (1988) Why Does Family Homelessness Occur? A Case-Control Study. *American Journal of Public Health* 78:783–787.

Bassuk, E., & Rubin, L. (1987) Homeless Children: A Neglected Population. *American Journal of Orthopsychiatry* 57:279–286.

Bassuk, E., Rubin, L., & Lauriat, A. (1986) Characteristics of Sheltered Homeless Families. *American Journal of Public Health* 76:1097–1100.

Bates, E., O'Connell, B., & Shore, C. (1987) Language and Communication in Infancy. In J.D. Osofsky (ed.), *Handbook of Infant Development* (2d ed.). New York: Wiley, 149–203.

Battle, J., & Blowers, T. (1982) A Longitudinal Comparative Study of the Self-Esteem of Students in Regular and Special Education Classes. *Journal of Learning Disabilities* 15:100–102.

Baumgart, D., Brown, L., Pumpian, I., Nisbet, J., Ford, A., Sweet, M., Messina, R., & Schroeder, J. (1982) Principle of Partial Participation and Individualized Adaptations in Education Programs for Severely Handicapped Students. *TASH Journal* 7:17–27.

Baumrind, D. (1994) The Social Context of Child Maltreatment. *Family Relations* 43: 360–368.

Bayley, N. (1969) *The Bayley Scales of Infant Development.* New York: Psychological Corporation.

Beal, C. R. (1994) Boys and Girls: The Development of Gender Roles. New York: McGraw Hill.

Beattie, S., Grise, P., & Algozzine, B. (1983) Effects of Test Modifications on the Minimum Competency Performance of Learning Disabled Students. *Exceptional Children* 49:75–77.

Beaudet, A.L. (1990) Cystic Fibrosis. *New England Journal of Medicine*, 2245–2247.

Bebout, L., & Arthur, B. (1992) Cross-Cultural Attitudes Toward Speech Disorders. *Journal of Speech and Hearing Research* 35:45–52.

Beck, A.T. (1967) *Depression: Clinical, Experimental, and Theoretical Aspects.* New York: Harper & Row.

Beck, A.T. (1974) The Development of Depression. In R. Friedman & M. Katz (eds.), *The Psychology of Depression: Contemporary Theory and Research.* Washington, D.C.: Winston, 3–30.

Beck, A.T. (1976) *Cognitive Therapy and the Emotional Disorders.* New York: International Universities Press.

Beck, F.W., Lindsey, J.D., & Frith, G.H. (1981) Effects of Self-Contained Special Class Placement on Intellectual Functioning of Learning Disabled Students. *Journal of Learning Disabilities* 14:280–282.

Beck, J., Broers, J., Hogue, E., Shipstead, J., & Kowlton, E. (1994) Strategies for Functional Community-Based Instruction and Inclusion for Children With Mental Retardation. *Teaching Exceptional Children* 44–48.

Beck, L. (1989) Mentorships: Benefits and Effects on Career Development. *Gifted Child Quarterly* 33:22–28.

Becker, J. V., Barham, J., Eron, L. D. & Chen, S. A. (1994) The Present Status and Future Directions for Psychological Research on Youth Violence. In L. D. Eron, J. H., Gentry, & P. Schlegel (eds.) *Reason to Hope: A Psychosocial Perspective on Violence and Youth.* Washington, D.C.: American Psychological Association, 435–447.

Beers, C., & Wehman, P. (1985) Play Skill Development. In M. Fallen & W. Umansky (eds.) *Young Children with Special Needs.* Columbus, Ohio: Merrill, 403–444.

Bell, R.Q. (1968) A Reinterpretation of the Direction of Effects in Socialization. *Psychological Review* 75:81–95.

Bell, R.Q. (1979) Parent, Child, and Reciprocal Influences. *American Psychologist* 34:821–827.

Bellack, L. (1986) *The Thematic Apperception Test, The Children's Apperception Test, and the Senior Apperception Technique in Clinical Use,* 4th ed. Orlando, Fl.: Academic Press.

Benavides, A. (1988) High Risk Predictors and Preferral Screening for Language Minority Students. In A.A. Ortiz & B.A. Ramirez (eds.), *Schools and the Culturally Diverse Exceptional Student: Promising Practices and Future Directions.* Reston, Va.: Council for Exceptional Children, 19–32.

Benbow, C.P. (1991) Mathematically Talented Children: Can Acceleration Meet Their Educational Needs? In N. Colangelo & G. Davis (ed.), *Handbook of Gifted Education.* Needham Heights: Mass.: Allyn & Bacon, 154–166.

Benbow, C.P., & Minor, L.L. (1986) Mathematically Talented Males and Females and Achievement in the High School Sciences. *American Educational Research Journal* 23:425–436.

Bender, W.N. (1986/1987) Effective Educational Practices in the Mainstream Setting: Recommended Model for Evaluation of Mainstream Teacher Classes. *The Journal of Special Education* 20:475–487.

Bender, W.N. (1987) Secondary Personality and Behavioral Problems in Adolescents with Learning Disabilities.

Journal of Learning Disabilities 20:280–285.

Bender, W.N. (1995) *Learning Disabilities* (2nd ed.) Needham Heights, Mass: Allyn & Bacon.

Bender, W.N., & Smith, J.K. (1990) Classroom Behavior of Children and Adolescents with Learning Disabilities. *Journal of Learning Disabilities* 23:298–305.

Benn, R. (1993) Conceptualizing Eligibility for Early Intervention Services. In D.M. Bryant & M.A. Graham (eds.) *Implementing Early Intervention.* New York: The Guilford Press, 18–46.

Berger, C.S., Sorensen, L., Gendler, B., & Fitzsimmons, J. (1990) Cocaine and Pregnancy: A Challenge for Health Care Providers. *Health and Social Work* 15:310–316.

Berger, E.P. (1995) *Parents as Partners in Education* (4th ed.). Englewood Cliffs, N.J.: Prentice Hall.

Berkell, D.E. (1992) Instructional Planning: Goals and Practice. In D.E. Berkell (ed.), *Autism: Identification, Education, and Treatment.* Hillsdale, N.J.: Erlbaum, 89–106.

Berko, F.G. (1992) The Americans With Disabilities Act of 1990. Albany, NY: Advocate for the Disabled.

Bernabe, E.A., & Block, M.E. (1994) Modifying Rules of a Regular Girls Softball League to Facilitate the Inclusion of a Child with Severe Disabilities. *Journal of the Association for Persons with Severe Handicaps* 19: 24–31.

Bernstein, M.E., & Morrison, M.E. (1992) Are We Ready for PL 99-457? *AAD* 137:7–15.

Berreuta-Clement, J.R., Schweinhart, L.J., Barnett, W.S., Epstein, A.S., & Weikart, D.P. (1984) *Changed Lives: The Effects of the Perry Preschool Program on Youths through Age 19.* Ypsilanti, Mich: High/Scope Press.

Berreuta-Clement, J.R., Schweinhart, L.J., Barnett, W.S., & Weikart, D.P. (1987) The Effects of Early Educational Intervention on Crime and Delinquency in Adolescence and Early Adulthood. In J.D. Burchard & S.N.

Burchard (eds.) *Primary Prevention of Psychopathology: Vol. 10. Prevention of Delinquent Behavior.* Newbury Park, Cal.: Sage, 220–240.

Bersani, H. (January 1987) Center Provides Timely Answers to Family Support Questions. *TASH Newsletter*, 4–5.

Besharov, D.J. (Fall 1989) Children of Crack. *Public Welfare*, 6–11.

Best, A.B. (1992) *Teaching Children with Visual Impairments*, Philadelphia, Pa.: Open University Press.

Best, J.B. (1986) *Cognitive Psychology.* St. Paul, Minn.: West Publishing Co.

Bienenstock, M.A., & Vernon, M. (1994) Classification by the States of Deaf and Hard of Hearing Students. *American Annals of the Deaf* 139:128–131.

Bigler, E.D. (1987) Acquired Cerebral Trauma: An Introduction to the Special Series. *Journal of Learning Disabilities* 20:454–457.

Bigler, E.D. (1988) Acquired Cerebral Trauma: Attention, Memory, and Language Disorders. *Journal of Learning Disabilities* 21:321–384.

Bigner, J.J. (1994) *Parent-Child Relations: An Introduction to Parenting* (4th ed.). New York: Macmillan.

Biklen, D., Corrigan, C., & Quick, D. (1989) Beyond Obligation. In D. Lipsky, & A Gartner (eds.) *Beyond Special Education.* Baltimore: Paul Brookes.

Biklen, D., & Duchan, J.F. (1994) "I Am Intelligent": The Social Construction of Mental Retardation. *The Journal of the Association for Persons with Severe Handicaps* 19: 173–185.

Biklen, D., Morton, M.W., Gold, D., Berrigan, C. & Swaminathan, S. (1992) Facilitated Communication: Implications for Individuals with Autism. *Topics in Language Disorders* 12:1–28.

Biklen, D., & Schubert, A. (1991) New Words: The Communication of Students with Autism. *Remedial and Special Education* 12:46–57.

Bina, M.J. (1993) Do Myths Associated with Schools for Students Who Are Blind Negatively Affect Placement Decisions? *Journal of Visual Impairment & Blindness* 87:213–215.

Birman, D. (1994) Acculturation and Human Diversity in a Multicultural Society. In E.J. Trickett, R.J. Watts, & D. Birman (eds.) *Human Diversity: Perspectives on People in Context.* San Francisco: Jossey-Bass Pub., 261–285.

Bishop, G.D. (1995) *Health Psychology: Integrating Mind and Body.* Needham, Mass.: Allyn & Bacon, Inc.

Bishop, V.E. (1990) Educational Placement Decision Making: An Ecological Model. *Journal of Visual Impairment & Blindness* 84:350–353.

Bishop, V.E. (1990) Evaluating Functional Vision in Infants and Young Children. In S.A. Aitken et al. (eds.), *Realities and Opportunities: Early Intervention with Visually Handicapped Children.* New York: American Foundation for the Blind, 47–55.

Bishop, V.E. (1991) Preschool Visually Impaired Children: A Demographic Study. *Journal of Visual Impairment & Blindness* 85:69–74.

Bjorklund, D.F. (1995) *Children's Thinking: Developmental Function and Individual Differences* (2nd ed.). Pacific Grove, Cal.: Brooks/Cole.

Blacher, J. (1984) *Severely Handicapped Young Children and Their Families.* Orlando, Fla.: Academic Press.

Blacher, J., Nihira, K., & Meyers, C.E. (1987) Characteristics of Home Environment of Families with Mentally Retarded Children: Comparison Across Levels of Retardation. *American Journal of Mental Deficiency* 91:313–320.

Blacher, J., & Turnbull, A.P. (1983) Are Parents Mainstreamed? A Survey of Parent Interactions in the Mainstreamed Preschool. *Education and Training of the Mentally Retarded* 18:10–16.

Black, J.L. (1986) AIDS: Preschool and School Issues. *Journal of School Health* 56:93–95.

Black, M.M. (1991) Early Intervention Services for Infants and Toddlers: A Focus on Families. *Journal of Clinical Child Psychology* 20:51–57.

Blacklin, J.S. (1991) Your Child's Development. In E. Geralis (ed.), *Children with Cerebral Palsy.* New York: Woodbine, 175–209.

Blankenship, C.S. (1985) Using Curriculum-Based Assessment Data to Make Instructional Decisions. *Exceptional Children* 51:233–238.

Blanksby, D.C. (1991) Visual Therapy: Theoretically Based Intervention for Visually Unresponsive or Inattentive Infants. *Journal of Visual Impairment & Blindness* 86:291–294.

Blanksby, D.C., & Langford, P.E. (1993). VAP-CAP: A Procedure to Assess the Visual Functioning of Young Visually Impaired Children. *Journal of Visual Impairment & Blindness* 87:46–49.

Blaske, D.M., Borduin, C.M., Henggeler, S.W., & Mann, B.J. (1989) Individual, Family, and Peer Characteristics of Adolescent Sex Offenders and Assaultive Offenders. *Developmental Psychology* 25:846–855.

Blau, T.H. (1991) *The Psychological Examination of the Child.* New York: Wiley.

Bleck, E.E. (March 1979) Integrating the Physically Handicapped Child. *Journal of School Health* 49:141–146.

Blenkhorn, P. (1994) Screen Transformations for Large-Character Access Systems. *Journal of Visual Impairment & Blindness* 88:213–220.

Blessing, D.L., McCrimmon, D., Stovall, J., & Williford, H.N. (1993) The Effects of Regular Exercise Programs for Visual Impaired and Sighted Children. *Journal of Visual Impairment & Blindness* 87:50–52.

Block, J.H., Block, J., & Gjerde, P.F. (1986) The Personality of Children Prior to Divorce: A Prospective Study. *Child Development* 57:827–840.

Bloodstein, O. (1987) *A Handbook of Stuttering.* Chicago: National Easter Seal Society for Crippled Children and Adults.

Bloom, B.S. (1985) *Developing Talent in Young Children,* New York: Ballantine Books.

Bloom, D.E. (September 1986) Women and Work. *American Demographics,* 25–30.

Bloom, D.T. (Winter 1991) Mainstreaming Remains the Goal. *Day Care and Early Education* 18:44–45.

Bodfish, J.W. (1992) Behavior Disorders Among the Institutionalized Mentally Retarded: Challenged People, Challenged Practices, Challenged Placement. *Behavioral Residential Treatment* 7:99–119.

Bodner-Johnson, B. (1985) Families that Work for the Hearing-Impaired Child. *Volta Review.*

Bohannon, J.N., & Stanowicz, L. (1988) The Issue of Negative Evidence: Adult Responses to Children's Language Errors. *Developmental Psychology* 24:684–689.

Bondy, E. (March/April 1984) Thinking about Thinking. *Childhood Education*: 234–238.

Borich, G.D. (1988) *Effective Teaching Methods.* Columbus, Ohio: Merrill.

Borland, J.H. (1989) *Planning and Implementing Programs for the Gifted,* New York: Teachers College, Columbia University.

Bornstein, P.H., & Quevillon, R.P. (1976) The Effects of Self-Instructional Package on Overactive Preschool Boys. *Journal of Applied Behavior Analysis* 9:179–188.

Borton, T. (1986) 8 Ways to Encourage Inventive Thinking. *Learning* 15:94–96.

Botwinick, J. (1984) *Aging and Behavior* (3d ed.), New York: Springer.

Boyd, L.H., Boyd, W.L., & Vanderheiden, G.C. (1990) The Graphical User Interface: Crisis, Danger, and Opportunity. *Journal of Visual Impairment & Blindness* 84:496–503.

Boyer, P.J., Dillon, M., Navaie, M., Deveikis, A., Keller, M., O'Rourke, S., & Bryson, Y.J. (June 22/29, 1994) Factors Predictive of Maternal-Fetal Transmission of HIV-1: Preliminary Analysis of Zidovudine Given During Pregnancy and/or Delivery. *JAMA* 271: 1925–1935.

Braaten, S., Kauffman, J.M., Braaten, B., Polsgrove, L., & Nelson, C.M. (1988) The Regular Education Initiative: Patent Medicine for Behavioral Disorders. *Exceptional Children* 55:21–27.

Bracey, G.W. (1994) Finding Gifted Kinds. *Phi Delta Kappan* 252–254.

Braden, J.P. (1992) Intellectual Assessment of Deaf and Hard-of-Hearing People: A Quantitative and Qualitative Research Synthesis. *School Psychology Review* 21:82–94.

Bradley, A. (15 May 1991) Newly Diverse Suburbs Facing City-Style Woes. *Education Week,* 1, 15ff.

Bradley, R.H., Whiteside, L., Mundfrom, D.J., Casey, P.H., Kelleher, K.J., & Pope, S.K. (1994) Early Indications of Resilience and Their Relation to Experiences in the Home Environments of Low Birthweight, Premature Children Living in Poverty. *Child Development* 65:346–360.

Brady, M.P., Shores, R.E., McEvoy, M.A., Ellis, D., & Fox, J.J. (1987) Increasing Social Interactions of Severely Handicapped Autistic Children. *Journal of Autism and Developmental Disorders* 17:375–391.

Brady, M.P., Swank, P.R., Taylor, R.D., & Freiberg, J. (May 1992) Teacher Interactions in Mainstream Social Studies and Science Classes. *Exceptional Children* 59:530–540.

Brady, M.P., Swank, P.R., Taylor, R.D., & Freiberg, J. (1992) Teacher Interactions Social Studies and Science Classes. *Exceptional Children* 58:530–540.

Brady, M.P., Swank, P.R., Taylor, R.D., & Freiberg, J. (1988) Teacher-Student Interactions in Middle School Mainstreamed Classes: Differences with Special and Regular Education Students. *Journal of Educational Research* 81:332–340.

Bragg, B. (1994) Culture, Language, and Deafness (Collectivism or Individualism). *Deaf American Monograph,* 15–16.

Brambring, M., & Troster, H. (1992) On the Stability of Stereotyped Behaviors in Blind Infants and Preschoolers. *Journal of Visual Impairment & Blindness* 86:105–110.

Branlinger, E. (1985) Mildly Mentally Retarded Secondary Students' Information about and Attitudes toward Sexuality and Sex Education. *Education and Training of the Mentally Retarded* 20:99–108.

Branlinger, E. (1988) Teachers' Perception of the Sexuality of Their Secondary Students with Mild Mental Retardation. *Education and Training in Mental Retardation* 23:24–37.

Brasel, K., & Quigley, S. (1975) *The Influence of Early Language and Communication Environments on the Development of Language in Deaf Children*, Urbana-Champaign, Ill.: University of Illinois, Institute for Research on Exceptional Children. Cited in Kampfe and Turecheck.

Brasel, K., & Quigley, S. (1977) The Influence of Certain Language and Community Environments in Early Childhood on the Development of Language in Deaf Individuals. *Journal of Speech and Hearing Research* 20:95–107.

Brickey, M., & Campbell, K. (1981) Fast Food Employment for Moderately and Mildly Retarded Adults. *Mental Retardation* 19:113–116.

Brier, N. (1986) The Mildly Retarded Adolescent: A Psychosocial Perspective. *Developmental and Behavioral Pediatrics* 7:320–323.

Brinker, R. P., & Thorpe, M.E. (1984) Integration of Severely Handicapped Students and the Proportion of IEP Objectives Achieved. *Exceptional Children* 51:168–175.

Bristol, M.M. (1984) Family Resources and Successful Adaptation to Autistic Children. In E. Schopler & G.B. Mesibov (eds.), *The Effects of Autism on the Family.* New York: Plenum, 289–310.

Bristol, M.M., & Schopler, E., (1983) Stress and Coping in Families of Autistic Adolescents. In E. Schopler & G.B. Mesibov (eds.), *Autism in Adolescents and Adults.* New York: Plenum, 251–278.

Bristow, D., Murphy, H., Pickering, G., & Raskind, M. (1990) Technology Reaching Out to Special Education Students. *Media & Methods* 26:38–40.

Brod, R.L., & McQuiston, J.M. (1983) American Indian Adult Education and Literacy: The First National Survey. *Journal of American Indian Education* 1:1–16.

Brody, G.H., & Forehand, R. (1988) Multiple Determinants of Parenting: Research Findings and Implications of the Divorce Process. In E.M. Hetherington & J.D. Arasteh (eds.), *Impact of Divorce, Single Parenting, and Stepparenting on Children.* Hillsdale, N.J.: Erlbaum, 135–155.

Bronfenbrenner, U. (1979) Contexts of Child Rearing: Problems and Prospects. *American Psychologist* 34:844–850.

Bronstein, P., Stoll, M.F., Clauson, J.A., Abrams, C.L., & Briones, M. (1994) Fathering After Separation or Divorce: Factors Predicting Children's Adjustment. *Family Relations* 43: 460–479.

Browder, D.M., & Snell, M.E. (1993) Daily Living and Community Skills. In M.E. Snell (ed.) *Instruction of Students with Severe Disabilities* (4th ed.). New York: Merrill, 480–525.

Browder, D.M., & Snell, M.E. (1993) Functional Academics. In M. E. Snell (ed.) *Instruction of Students with Severe Disabilities* (4th ed.). New York: Merrill, 442–480.

Brown, C. (11 October 1993) The Vanished Native Americans. *The Nation* 257:384–389.

Brown, C.C., & Cavalier, A.R. (1992) Voice Recognition Technology and Persons with Severe Mental Retardation and Severe Physical Impairment: Learning Response Differentiation and Affect. *Journal of Special Education Technology* 11:196–206.

Brown, F., & Snell, M. (1993) Meaningful Assessment. In M.A. Snell (ed.), *Instruction of Students with Severe Disabilities* (4th ed.). New York: Merrill, 61–93.

Brown, F.G. (1983) *Principles of Educational and Psychological Testing.* New York: Holt, Rinehart and Winston.

Brown, J.M., O'Keeffe, J., Sanders, S.H., & Baker, B. (1986) Developmental Changes in Children's Cognition to Stressful and Painful Situations. *Journal of Pediatric Psychology* 11:343–357.

Brown, L., Schwarz, P., Udvari-Solner, A., Kampschroer, E.F., Johnson, F., Jorgensen, J., & Gruenewald, L. (1991) How Much Time Should Students with Severe Intellectual Disabilities Spend in Regular Education Classrooms and Elsewhere? *Journal of the Association for Persons with Severe Handicaps* 16:39–47.

Brown, R. (1973) Development of the First Language in the Human Species. *American Psychologist* 28:97–106.

Brown, W.H., Ragland, E.U., & Fox, J.J. (1988) Effects of Group Socialization Procedures on the Social Behavior of Preschool Children. *Research in Developmental Disabilities* 9:359–376.

Browne, A., & Finkelhor, D. (1986) Impact of Child Sexual Abuse. *Psychological Bulletin* 99:66–77.

Brownell, G. (1987) *Computers and Teaching*, St. Paul, Minn.: West Publishing Co.

Browning, P., White, W., Nave, G., & Barkin, P. (1986) Interactive Video in the Classroom. *Education and Training in Mental Retardation* 21:85–92.

Brubaker, R.G. (1994) Acculturative Stress: A Useful Framework for Understanding the Experience of Deaf Americans. *Journal of Rehabilitation of the Deaf* 28: 1–15.

Brulle, A.R., Barton, L.E., Barton, C.L., & Wharton, D.L. (1983) A Comparison of Teacher Time Spent with Physically Handicapped and Able-Bodied Students. *Exceptional Children* 49:543–548.

Bryan, T. (1978) Social Relationships and Verbal Interactions of Learning Disabled Children. *Journal of Learning Disabilities* 11:58–66.

Bryan, T., Bay, M., & Donahue, M. (1988) Implications of the Learning Disabilities Definition for the Regular Education Initiative. *Journal of Learning Disabilities* 21:23–28.

Bryant, D.M., & Graham, M.A. (1993) Models of Service Delivery. In D.M. Bryant & M.A. Graham (eds.) *Implementing Early Intervention*. New York: The Guilford Press, 183–216.

Buchanan, M., & Wolf, J.S. (1986) A Comprehensive Study of Learning Disabled Adults. *Journal of Learning Disabilities* 19:34–38.

Bullis, M., Bull, B., Johnson, B., & Peters, D. (1995) The School-to-Community Transition Experiences of Hearing Young Adults and Young Adults Who Are Deaf. *The Journal of Special Education* 28: 405–423.

Bunch, G. (1994) Inclusion. *American Annals of the Deaf* 139:150–152.

Burlton-Bennet, J.A., & Robinson, V.M.J. (1987) A Single Subject Evaluation of the K-P Diet for Hyperkinesis. *Journal of Learning Disabilities* 20:331–335.

Burns, K., Chetnik, L., Burns, W., & Clark, R. (1991) Dyadic Disturbances in Cocaine-Abusing Mothers and Their Infants. *Journal of Clinical Psychology* 47:316–319.

Bushey, T., & Martin, R. (1988) Stuttering in Children's Literature. *Language, Speech, and Hearing Services in Schools* 19:235–250.

Butler, D.L. (1995) Promoting Strategic Learning by Postsecondary Students with Learning Disabilities. *Journal of Learning Disabilities* 28: 170–190.

Butler, J.W., Novy, D.M., Kagan, N., & Gates, G. (1994) An Investigation of Differences in Attitudes Between Suicidal and Nonsuicidal Student Ideators. *Adolescence* 29: 623–639.

Butler, R., & Marinow-Glassman, D. (1994) The Effects of Educational Placement and Grade Level on the Self-Perceptions of Low Achievers and Students with Learning Disabilities. *Journal of Learning Disabilities* 27:325–334.

Buzzelli, C.A., & File, N.K. (Fall 1991) Helping Children Learn About Disabilities: Part II. *Day Care and Early Education* 18:43–44.

Cabay, M. (1994) Brief Report: A controlled Evaluation of Facilitated Communication Using Open-Ended and Fill-in Questions. *Journal of Autism and Developmental Disorders* 24: 517–527.

Cahan, S., & Cohen, N. (1989) Age Versus Schooling Effects of Intelligence Development. *Child Development* 60:1239–1249.

Cain, L., Melcher, J., Johns, B., Ashmore, J., Callahan, C., Draper, I., Beveridge, P., & Weintraum, B. (1984) Reply to "A Nation at Risk." *Exceptional Children* 50:484–494.

Cairns, R.B., Cairns, B.D., Neckerman, H.J., Ferguson, L.L., & Gariepy, J.L. (1989) Growth and Aggression: 1. Childhood to Early Adolescence. *Developmental Psychology* 25:171–184.

Camara, K.A., & Resnick, G. (1989) Styles of Conflict Resolution and Cooperation between Divorced Parents: Effects on Child Behavior and Adjustment. *American Journal of Orthopsychiatry* 59:560–575.

Campbell, F.A., & Ramey, C.T. (1994) Effects of Early Intervention on Intellectual and Academic Achievement: A Follow-up Study of Children from Low-Income Families. *Child Development* 65:684–699.

Canavan, J.W. (1981) Sexual Child Abuse. In N.S. Ellerstein (ed.), *Child Abuse and Neglect: A Medical Reference*. New York: Wiley, 337–346.

Capell, F.J., Vugia, D.J., Mordaunt, V.L., Marelich, W.D., Ascher, M.S., Trachtenberg, A.I., Cunningham, G.C., Arnon, S.S., & Kizer, K.W. (1992) Distribution of HIV Type 1 Infection in Childbearing Women in California. *American Journal of Public Health* 82:254–256.

Carlberg, C., & Kavale, K. (1980) The Efficacy of Special Versus Regular Class Placement for Exceptional Children: A Meta-Analysis. *Journal of Special Education* 14:295–309.

Carlson, C.I. (1987) Helping Students Deal with Divorce-Related Issues. *Special Services in the Schools* 3:121–138.

Carlson, C.I. (1987) Social Interaction Goals and Strategies of Children with Learning Disabilities. *Journal of Learning Disabilities* 20:306–311.

Carmen, R. (1983) *Positive Solutions to Hearing Loss*, Englewood Cliffs, N.J.: Prentice-Hall.

Carnine, D.W., & Kameenui, E.J. (1990) The General Education Initiative and Children with Special Needs: A False Dilemma in the Face of True Problems. *Journal of Learning Disabilities* 23:141–144.

Caro, P., & Snell, M.P. (1989) Characteristics of Teaching Communication to People with Moderate and Severe Disabilities. *Education and Training in Mental Retardation* 24:63–75.

Carr, J. (1994) Annotation: Long Term Outcome for People with Down Syndrome. *Journal of Child Psychology and Psychiatry and Allied Disciplines* 35: 817–834.

Carroad, D.L. (1993) Interviews with Head Start Parents. *Children Today* 22: 14–20.

Carroll, D.W. (1994) *Psychology of Language*. Pacific Grover, Cal.: Brooks/Cole.

Cartledge, G., Stupay, D., & Kaczala, C. (1986) Social Skills and Social Perception of LD and Nonhandicapped Elementary School Students. *Learning Disabilities Quarterly* 9:226–234.

Carvajal, H.H., Hayes, J.E., Lackey, K.I., Rathke, M.L., Wiebe, D.A., & Weaver, K.A. (1993) Correlations between Scores on the Wechsler Intelligence Scale for Children-III and the General Purpose Abbreviated Battery of the Stanford-Binet IV. *Psychological Reports* 72:1167–1170.

Caspi, A., Elder, G.H., & Bem, D.J. (1987) Moving Against the World: Life-Course Patterns of Explosive Children. *Developmental Psychology* 23:308–313.

Castle, D.L. (1988) *Signaling and Assistive Listening Devices for Hearing-Impaired People*, Rochester, N.Y.: Rochester Institute of Technology.

Castle, D.L. (1994) Telecommunications Technologies Used by Employees Who Are Deaf. *Journal of Rehabilitation of the Deaf* 27: 1–8.

Casto, G., & Mastropieri, M.A. (1986) The Efficacy of Early Intervention Programs: A Meta-Analysis. *Exceptional Children* 52:417–424.

Cataldo, D.L. (September/October 1989) Networking with the Integrated Learning. *Media & Methods* 26:114.

Center, D.B., & Wascom, A.M. (1986) Teacher Perceptions of Social Behavior in Learning Disabled and Socially Normal Children and Youth. *Journal of Learning Disabilities* 19:420–425.

Center for Special Education Technology (1989) *Tech Use Guide: Using Computer Technology*, Reston, Va.: author.

Center for Special Education Technology (1991) *The Role of Occupational and Physical Therapists in Assistive Technology*, Reston, Va.: Council for Exceptional Children.

Chalfant, J.C. (1989) Learning Disabilities: Policy Issues and Promising Approaches. *American Psychologist* 44:392–398.

Chang, L., Morrissey, R.F., et al. (1995) Prevalence of Psychiatric Symptoms and Their Relation to Adjustment Among Chinese-American Youth. *Journal of the American Academy of Child and Adolescent Psychiatry* 34:91–100.

Chanock, S., & Simonds, R.J. (1994) Medical Issues Related to Provision of Care for HIV-Infected Children in Hospital, Home, Day Care, School, and Community. In P. A. Pizzo & C. M. Wilfert (eds.), *Pediatric AIDS* (2nd ed.). Baltimore: Williams & Wilkins, 889–906.

Chapman, J.W. (1988) Cognitive Motivational Characteristics and Academic Achievement of Learning Disabled Children: A Longitudinal Study. *Journal of Educational Psychology* 80:357–365.

Charlson, E., Strong, M., & Gold, R. (1987) How Successful Deaf Teenagers Experience and Cope with Isolation. *American Annals of the Deaf* 132:261–270.

Chasnoff, I.J. (1987) Perinatal Effects of Cocaine. *Contemporary Ob/Gyn*, 26 (March of Dimes reprint, entire issue).

Chasnoff, I.J., Burns, W.J., Schnoll, S.H., & Burns, K. (1985) Cocaine Use in Pregnancy. *New England Journal of Medicine* 315:305–307.

Chasnoff, I.J., Griffith, D.R., Freier, C., & Murray, J. (1992) Cocaine/Polydrug Use in Pregnancy: Two-Year Follow-Up. *Pediatrics* 89:284–289.

Chavkin, W., Kristal, A., Seabron, C., & Guiogli, P.E., (1987) Reproductive Experience of Women Living in Hotels for the Homeless in New York City. *New York State Journal of Medicine* 87:10–13.

Chee, C.M., & Clancy, R.R. (1984) Epilepsy. In J. Fithian (ed.), *Understanding the Child with a Chronic Illness in the Classroom.* Phoenix, Ariz.: Oryx Press, 57–79.

Chee, C.M., & Packer, R.J. (1984) The Muscular Dystrophies. In J. Fithian (ed.), *Understanding the Child with a Chronic Illness in the Classroom.* Phoenix, Ariz.: Oryx Press, 198–221.

Chen, S.H.A., & Bernard-Opitz, V. (1993) Comparison of Person and Computer-Assisted Instruction for Children with Autism. *Mental Retardation* 31:368–376.

Chernow, F.B., & Chernow, C. (1981) *Classroom Discipline and Control: 101 Practical Techniques*, New York: Parker.

Chess, S., & Fernandez, P. (1980) Do Deaf Children Have a Typical Personality? *Journal of the American Academy of Child Psychiatry* 19:654–664.

Chinn, P.C., & Hughes, S. (1987) Representation of Minority Students in Special Education Classes. *Remedial and Special Education* 8:41–46.

Church, A.G. (1983) Academic Achievement, Level of Occupational Plans, Delay of Gratification, Personal Control, and Self-Concepts for Males and Females in Introductory Anthropology. *Psychology: A Quarterly Journal of Human Behavior* 20:121–130.

Cimini, R. (3 December 1992) 7-Hour Success. *Newsday*, 166ff.

Clapp, G. (1988) *Child Study Research.* Lexington. Mass.: Heath.

Clarey, J.H., & Sanford, A. (1982) Female Career Preference and Androgyny. *Vocational Guidance Quarterly* 20:258–265.

Clarizio, H.F., & McCoy, G.F. (1983) *Behavior Disorders in Children,* 3rd ed. New York: Harper & Row.

Clark, B. (1988) *Growing Up Gifted* (3d ed.), Columbus, Ohio: Merrill.

Clark, B. (1992) The Need for a Range of Program Options for Gifted and Talented Students. In W. Stainback & S. Stainback (eds.), *Controversial Issues Confronting Special Education.* Boston: Allyn & Bacon, 55–68.

Clark, C. (September/October 1989) Distance Learning: A Spectrum of Opportunities. *Media & Methods* 26:22–27.

Clark, C.S. (15 January 1993) Child Sexual Abuse. *CQ Researcher* 3:38–44.

Clark, C.S. (1995) Parents and Schools. *CQ Researcher* 5: 49–69.

Clark, G.M. & Knowlton, H.E. (eds.) (1987) From School to Adult Living: A Forum on Issues and Trends. *Exceptional Children* 53:546–554.

Clark, S.L., & DeVore, G.R. (1989) Prenatal Diagnosis for Couples Who Would Not Consider Abortion. *Obstetrics and Gynecology* 73:1035–1037.

Clarke, A.M., & Clarke, A.D.B. (1986) Thirty Years of Child Psychology: A Selective Review. *Journal of Child Psychology and Psychiatry and Allied Disciplines* 27:719–759.

Clasen, D.R., Middleton, J.A., & Connell, T.J. (1994) Assessing Artistic and Problem-Solving Performance in Minority and Nonminority Students Using a Nontraditional Multidimensional Approach. *Gifted Child Quarterly*, 27–32.

Coates, R.D. (1989) The Regular Education Initiative and Opinions of Regular Classroom Teachers. *Journal of Learning Disabilities* 22:532–536.

Cochran, P.S., & Bull, G.L. (1993) Computers and Individuals with Speech and Language Disorders. In J.D. Lindsey (ed.), *Computers and Exceptional Individuals*, 2d ed., Austin, Tex.: Pro-Ed, 143–159.

Cohen, R., Duncan, M., & Cohen, S.L. (1994) Classroom Peer Relations of Children Participating in a Pull-Out Enrichment Program. *Gifted Child Quarterly* 38:33–37.

Cohen, S., Agosta, J., Cohen, J., & Warren, R. (1989) Supporting Families of Children with Severe Disabilities. *Journal of the Association for Persons with Severe Handicaps* 14:255–262.

Coie, J.D., & Dodge, K.A. (1988) Multiple Sources of Data on Social Behavior and Social Status in the School: A Cross-Age Comparison. *Child Development* 59:815–829.

Colangelo, N., & Brower, P. (1987) Gifted Youngsters and Their Siblings: Long-Term Impacts of Labeling on Their Academic and Personal Self-Concepts. *Roeper Review* 10:101–103.

Colangelo, N., & Kelly, K.R. (1983) A Study of Student, Parent, and Teacher Attitudes Towards Gifted Programs and Gifted Students. *Gifted Child Quarterly* 27:107–110.

Colangelo, N., Kerr, B., Christensen, P., & Maxey, J. (1993) A Comparison of Gifted Underachievers and Gifted High Achievers. *Gifted Child Quarterly* 37:155–160.

Colby, K.M. (1973) The Rationale for Computer-Based Treatment of Language Difficulties in Nonspeaking Autistic Children. *Journal of Autism and Childhood Schizophrenia* 3:254–260.

Cole, D.A. (1990) Relation of Social and Academic Competence to Depressive Symptoms in Childhood. *Journal of Abnormal Psychology* 99:422–429.

Cole, D.A. (1991) Preliminary Support for a Competency-Based Model of Depression in Children. *Journal of Abnormal Psychology* 100:181–190.

Cole, D.A., & Meyer, L.H. (1991) Social Integration and Severe Disabilities: A Longitudinal Analysis of Child Outcomes. *Journal of Special Education* 25:340–351.

Coleman, M.C. (1991) *Behavior Disorders* (2d ed.), Boston, Mass.: Allyn & Bacon.

Coleman, M.C. (1992) *Behavior Disorders: Theory and Practice,* 2d ed. Boston: Allyn & Bacon.

Coles, G.S. (1987) *The Learning Mystique: A Critical Look at "Learning Disabilities."* New York: Pantheon.

Coles, G.S. (1989) Excerpts From The Learning Mystique: A Critical Look at "Learning Disabilities." *Journal of Learning Disabilities* 22:276–284.

Coles, G.S. (1989b) LD Theory and a Tale from the Town of Chelm. *Journal of Learning Disabilities* 22:305–308.

Collier, V. (1989) How Long? A Synthesis of Research on Academic Achievement in a Second Language. *TESOL Quarterly* 23:509–531.

Colt, G.H. (September/October 1983) Suicide. *Harvard Magazine* 46–53, 63–66.

Colten, H.R. (1 February 1990) Screening for Cystic Fibrosis. *New England Journal of Medicine,* 328–329.

Comer, J.P. (1985) Empowering Black Children's Educational Environments. In H.P. McAdoo & U.L. McAdoo (eds.), *Black Children.* Beverly Hills, Calif.: Sage, 123–139.

Comer, R.J. (1992) *Abnormal Psychology.* New York: Freeman.

Commission on Education of the Deaf (1988) *Toward Equality: Education of the Deaf,* Washington, D.C.: U.S. Government Printing Office.

Communication Disorders and Aging (1992) Rockville, Md.: American Speech-Language-Hearing Association.

Compton, M.F. (1982) The Gifted Underachiever in Middle School. *Roeper Review* 4:23–25.

Condon, W.S., & Sander, L.W. (1974) Synchrony Demonstrated between Movements of the Neonate and Adult Speech. *Child Development* 65:456–462.

Conger, J.J., & Peterson, A.C. (1984) *Adolescence and Youth,* 3d ed. New York: Harper & Row.

Conners, F.A., & Detterman, D.K. (1987) Informative-Processing Correlates of Computer-Assisted Word Learning by Mentally Retarded Students. *American Journal of Mental Deficiency* 91:606–612.

Conroy, J.W., & Bradley, V.J. (1985) *The Pennhurst Longitudinal Study: A Report of Five Years of Research and Analysis.* Philadelphia: Temple University Developmental Disabilities Center.

Conte, R., & Andrews, J. (1993) Social Skills in the Context of Learning Disability Definitions: A Reply to Gresham and Elliott and Directions for the Future. *Journal of Learning Disabilities* 26:146–153.

Conti-Ramsden, G., & Dykins, J. (1991) Mother-Child Interactions with Language-Impaired Children and Their Siblings. *British Journal of Disorders of Communication* 26:337–354.

Converso, I., & Hocek, S. (1990) Optical Character Recognition. *Journal of Visual Impairment & Blindness* 84:507–509.

Cooper, J.A., & Flowers, C.R. (1987) Children with a History of Acquired Aphasia: Residual Language and Academic Impairment. *Journal of Speech and Hearing Disorders* 52:251–262.

Cornell, D.G. (1989) Child Adjustment and Parent Use of the Term "Gifted." *Gifted Child Quarterly* 33:59–64.

Cornell, D.G. (1990) High Ability Students Who Are Unpopular with Their Peers. *Gifted Child Quarterly* 34:155–160.

Cornell, D.G., Pelton, G.M., Bassin, L.E., Landrum, M., Ramsay, S.G., Cooley, M.R., Lynch, K.A., & Hamrick, E. (1990) Self-Concept and Peer Status Among Gifted Program Youth. *Journal of Educational Psychology* 82:456–463.

Coryell, J., Holcomb, T.K., & Scherer, M. (1992) Attitudes Towards Deafness: A Collegiate Perspective. *American Annals of the Deaf* 137:299–302.

Cosden, M.A., Gerber, M.M., Semmel, D.S., Goldman, S.R., & Semmel, M.I. (1987) Microcomputer Uses within Microeducational Environments. *Exceptional Children* 53:399–409.

Costa, A.L. (1984) Mediating the Metacognitive. *Educational Leadership* 42:57–67.

Cotler, S. (1986) Epidemiology and Outcome. In J.M. Reisman (ed.), *Behavior Disorders in Infants, Children, and Adolescents.* New York: Random House.

Council for Exceptional Children (1991) *Report of the CEC Advocacy and Governmental Relations Committee Regarding the New Proposed U.S. Federal Definition of Serious Emotional Disturbance.* Reston, Va.: Council for Exceptional Children.

Covington, M.V. (1984) The Self-Worth Theory of Achievement Motivation: Findings and Applications. *Elementary School Journal* 85:5–20.

Covington, M.V., Crutchfield, R.S., & Davies, L. (1966) *The Productive Thinking Program,* Berkeley: Education Innovation, Inc.

Cowan, C., & Shepler, R. (1990) Techniques for Teaching Young Children to Use Low Vision Devices. *Journal of Visual Impairment & Blindness* 84:419–421.

Cox, J., Daniels, N., & Boston, B.O. (1985) *Educating Able Learners: Programs and Promising Practices,* Austin, Texas: University of Texas Press.

CQ Researcher (8 May 1992) Seeking a Solution to Alcoholism 2:394.

CQ Researcher (14 May 1993) Preventing Teen Pregnancy 3:411–429.

Crapps, J.M., Langone, J., & Swaim, S. (1985) Quality and Quantity of Participation in Community Environments by Mentally Retarded Adults. *Education and Training in Mental Retardation* 20:123–129.

Cratty, B.J. (1986) *Perceptual and Motor Development in Infants and Children* (3d ed.), Englewood Cliffs, N.J.: Prentice-Hall.

Crawford, J. (25 March 1987) Bilingual Education Works, Study Finds. *Education Week,* 16.

Crombie, G., Bouffard-Bouchard, T., & Schneider, B.H. (1992) Gifted Programs: Gender Differences in Referral and Enrollment. *Gifted Child Quarterly* 36:213–214.

Cronin, B.J., & King, S.R. (1990) The Development of the Descriptive Video Service. *Journal of Visual Impairment & Blindness* 84:503–507.

Cross, D.R., & Paris, S.G. (1988) Developmental and Instructional Analyses of Children's Metacognition and Reading Comprehension. *Journal of Educational Psychology* 80:131–142.

Crossley, R., & Remington-Gurney, J. (1992) Getting the Words Out: Facilitated Communication Training. *Topics in Language Disorders* 12:29–45.

Cullinan, D., & Epstein, M.H. (1982) Behavior Disorders. In N.G. Haring (ed.), *Exceptional Children and Youth,* 3rd ed. Columbus, Ohio: Merrill, 207–239.

Culliton, B.J. (6 October 1989) AZT Reverses AIDS Dementia in Children. *Science* 246:21–23.

Culp, D., Abrosi, D., Berniger, T., & Mitchell, J. (1986) Augmentative Communication Aid Use—A Follow-Up Study. *Augmentative and Alternative Communication* 2:19–24.

Culp, R.E., Appelbaum, M.I., Osofsky, J.D., & Levy, J.A. (1988) Adolescent and Older Mothers: Comparison between Prenatal Maternal Variables and Newborn Interaction Measures. *Infant Behavior and Development* 11:353–362.

Culpepper, S. (Winter 1992) How to Recognize Handicaps in Preschoolers. Part I: Hearing, Vision, Motor, and Language Impairments. *Day Care and Early Education* 19:41–43.

Culpepper, S. (Spring 1993) How to Recognize Handicaps in Preschoolers: Part II: Cognitive and Emotional Exceptionalities. *Day Care and Early Education* 20:39–40.

Culton, G.L. (1986) Speech Disorders Among College Freshmen: A 13-Year-Survey. *Journal of Speech and Hearing Disorders* 51:3–8.

Cummins, J. (1989) A Theoretical Framework for Bilingual Special Education. *Exceptional Children* 56:111–119.

Dale, E.J. (1993) Computers and Gifted/Talented Individuals. In J.D. Linsey (eds.), *Computers and Exceptional Individuals.* Austin, Texas: Pro-Ed, 201–217.

Dale, P.S. (1976) *Language Development: Structure and Function,* 2d ed., Hinsdale, Ill.: Dryden.

Dana, R.H. (1993) *Multicultural Assessment Perspectives for Professional Psychology.* Boston: Allyn & Bacon.

Danielson, L.C., & Bellamy, G.T. (1989) State Variation in Placement of Children in Segregated Environments. *The Exceptional Child* 55:448–455.

Dannenberg, A.L., & Vernick, J.S. (1993) A Proposal for the Mandatory Inclusion of Helmets with New Children's Bicycles. *American Journal of Public Health* 83:644–646.

Darling, R.B. (1991a) Initial and Continuing Adaptation to the Birth of a Disabled Child. In M. Seligman (ed.) *The Family with a Handicapped Child,* 2d ed. Boston: Allyn & Bacon, 55–91.

Darling, R.B. (1991b) Parent-Professional Interaction: The Roots of Misunderstanding in M. Seligman (ed.) *The Family with a Handicapped Child,* 2d ed. Boston: Allyn & Bacon, 119–151.

Darlington, R.B., Royce, J.M., Snipper, A.S., Murray, W.H., & Lazar, I. (1980) Preschool Programs and the Later School Competence of Children from Low-Income Families. *Science* 208:202–204.

Dattilo, J., & Rusch, F.R. (1985) Leisure Participation for Persons with Severe Handicaps. *Journal of the Association for Persons with Severe Handicaps* 10:194–199.

Dauber, S.L., & Benbow, C.P. (1990) Aspects of Personality and Peer Relations of Extremely Talented Adolescents. *Gifted Child Quarterly* 34:10–14.

Davern, L., & Schnorr, R. (1991) Public Schools Welcome Students with Disabilities as Full Members. *Children Today* 20:21–25.

Davila, R.R. (1994) Technology and Full Participation for Children and Adults Who Are Deaf. *American Annals of the Deaf* 139:6–9.

Davis, G.A., & Rimm, S.B. (1989) *Education of the Gifted and Talented*, Englewood Cliffs, N.J.: Prentice-Hall.

Davis, G.A., & Rimm, S.B. (1994) *Education of the Gifted and Talented* (3rd ed.). Needham, Mass.: Allyn & Bacon.

Davis, J.M., Elfenbein, J., Schum, R., & Bentler, R.A. (1986) Effects of Mild and Moderate Hearing Impairments on Language, Educational, and Psychosocial Behavior of Children. *Journal of Speech and Hearing Disorders* 51:53–63.

Davis, J.M., Shepard, N.T., Stelmachowicz, P.G., & Gorga, M.P. (1981) Characteristics of Hearing-Impaired Children in the Public Schools. *Journal of Speech and Hearing Disorders* 25:130–143.

Davis, W.E. (1989) The Regular Education Initiative Debate: Its Promises and Problems. *Exceptional Children* 55:440–446.

Davison, G.C., & Neale, J.M. (1990) *Abnormal Psychology* (5th ed.). New York: Wiley.

Dean, A.L., Malik, M.M., Richards, W., & Stringer, S.A. (1986) Effects of Parental Maltreatment on Children's Conceptions of Interpersonal Relationships. *Developmental Psychology* 22:617–626.

Deaton, A.V. (1987) Behavioral Change Strategies for Children and Adolescents with Severe Brain Injury. *Journal of Learning Disabilities* 20:581–589.

Decker, S.N., & DeVries, J.C. (1980) Cognitive Abilities in Families with Reading Disabled Children. *Journal of Learning Disabilities* 13:517–522.

Delgado-Gaitan, C., & Trueba, H.T. (1985) Ethnographic Study of Participant Structures in Task Completion: Reinterpretation of "Handicaps" in Mexican Children. *Learning Disability Quarterly* 8:67–75.

Delgado, G.L. (1993) Outreach: The Resource of State Schools for the Deaf.

American Annals of the Deaf 138:411–414.

Delisle, J.R. (1992) *Guiding the Social and Emotional Development of Gifted Children*, New York: Longman.

Deno, S.L. (1985) Curriculum-Based Measurement: The Emerging Alternative. *Exceptional Children* 51:219–232.

Dettmer, P. (1993) Gifted Education: Window of Opportunity. *Gifted Child Quarterly* 37:92–94.

Dever, R.B. (1990) Defining Mental Retardation from an Instructional Perspective. *Mental Retardation* 28:147–153.

Dever, R.B. (1989) A Taxonomy of Community Living Skills. *Exceptional Children* 55:395–404.

de Villiers, J.G., & de Villiers, P.A. (1978) *Language Acquisition*. Cambridge, Mass.: Harvard University Press.

DeVine, R.A. (November 1980) Sexual Abuse of Children: An Overview of the Problem. In *Sexual Abuse of Children: Selected Readings*. Washington, D.C.: Department of Health and Human Services, Pub. 78–30161, 3–7.

De Witt, K. (12 May 1991). How Best to Teach the Blind: A Growing Battle Over Braille. *New York Times*, P1, 18.

Diamond, G.W. (1989) Developmental Problems in Children with HIV Infection. *Mental Retardation* 27:213–217.

Diamond, L., Anderson, S., Berk, H., & Smith, R. (1988) An Introduction to Special Education. In H. Reisner (ed.), *Children with Epilepsy*. New York: Woodbine, 147–172.

Diaz, R.M. (1985) Bilingual Cognitive Development: Addressing Three Gaps in Current Research. *Child Development* 56:1376–1388.

Dickerson, E.A., & Creedon, C.F. (1981) Self-Selection of Standards by Children: The Relative Effectiveness of Pupil-Selected and Teacher-Selected Standards of Performance. *Journal of Applied Behavior Analysis* 7:622.

Diener, C.I., & Dweck, C.S. (1978) Analysis of Learned Helplessness: Continuous Changes in Performance Strategy and Achievement Cognitions Follow-

ing Failure. *Journal of Personality and Social Psychology* 36:451–462.

Dinkmeyer, D., & Dinkmeyer, D., Jr. (1982) *Developing Understanding of Self and Others-Revised (DUSO)*. Circle Pines, Minn.: American Guidance Service.

Dixon, J.M., & Mandelbaum, J.B. (1990) Reading Through Technology: Evolving Methods and Opportunities for Print-Handicapped Individuals. *Journal of Visual Impairment & Blindness* 84:493–497.

Doberczak, T.M. et al. (1988) Neonatal Neurologic and Electroencephalophic Effects of Intrauterine Cocaine Exposure. *Journal of Pediatrics* 113:354–358.

Dodrill, C.B., & Matthews, C.G. (1992) The Role of Neuropsychology in the Assessment and Treatment of Persons with Epilepsy. *American Psychologist* 47:1139–1142.

Doherty, W.J., & Needle, P.H. (1991) Psychological Adjustment and Substance Use among Adolescents Before and After a Parental Divorce. *Child Development* 62:328–337.

Dollinger, S.J., Horn, J.L., & Boarini, D. (1988) Disturbed Sleep and Worries Among Learning Disabled Adolescents. *American Journal of Orthopsychiatry* 58:428–434.

Donnellan, A.M., & Mirenda, P.L. (1983) Issues Related to Professional Involvement with Families of Individuals with Autism and Other Severe Handicaps. *Journal of the Association for Persons with Severe Handicaps* 8:6–24.

Donnerstein, E., Slaby, R.G., & Eron, L.D. (1994) The Mass Media and Youth Aggression. In L.D. Eron, J.H., Gentry, & P. Schlegel (eds.) *Reason to Hope: A Psychosocial Perspective on Violence and Youth*. Washington, D.C.: American Psychological Association, 219–251.

Dornbusch, S.M., Carlsmith, J.M., Bushwall, S.J., Ritter, P.L., Leiderman, H., Hastof, A.H., & Gross, R.T. (1985) Single Parents, Extended Households, and the Control of Adolescents. *Child Development* 56:326–341.

Dote-Kwan, J. (1995) Impact of Mothers' Interactions on the Development of Their Young Visually Impaired Children. *Journal of Visual Impairment & Blindness* 89: 46–58.

Dowdall, C., & Colangelo, N. (1982) Underachieving Gifted Students: Review and Implications. *Gifted Child Quarterly* 26:179–184.

Drabman, R.S., & Thomas, M.H. (1975) Does TV Violence Breed Indifference? *Journal of Communication* 25:86–89.

Dreifuss, F.E. (1988) What Is Epilepsy? In H. Reisner (ed.), *Children with Epilepsy.* New York: Woodbine, 1–32.

Drew, C.J., Logan, D.R., & Hardman, M. (1992) *Mental Retardation: A Life Cycle Approach* (5th ed.). New York: Macmillan.

Drews, C.D., Yeargin-Allsopp, M., Decoufle, P., & Murphy, C. C. (1995) Variation in the Influence of Selected Sociodemographic Risk Factor Mental Retardation. *American Journal of Public Health* 85: 329–334.

Dubow, E.F., & Luster, T. (1990) Adjustment of Children Born to Teenage Mothers: The Contribution of Risk and Protective Factors. *Journal of Marriage and the Family* 52:393–404.

Dubow, E.F., & Tisak, J. (1989) The Relation between Stressful Life Events and Adjustment in Elementary School Children: The Role of Social Support and Social Problem-Solving Skills. *Child Development* 60:1412–1424.

Dudley-Marling, C., & Searle, D. (1988) Enriching Language Learning Environments for Students with Learning Disabilities. *Journal of Learning Disabilities* 21:140–143.

Duffelmeyer, F.A., & Baum, D.D., (1987) Reading Comprehension: Instruction vs. Practice. *Academic Therapy* 23:53–59.

Dullea, A. (12 October 1989) Opening the World to a Generation. *New York Times,* pp. C1, C6.

Duncan, G.J. (1991) The Economic Environment of Childhood. In A. C. Huston (ed.), *Children in Poverty.* New York: Cambridge University Press, 23–51.

Duncan, G.J., Brooks-Gunn, J., & Klebanov, P.K. (1994) Economic Deprivation and Early Childhood Development. *Child Development* 65:296–318.

Duran, R.P. (1989) Assessment and Instruction of At-Risk Hispanic Students. *Exceptional Children* 56:154–159.

Durand, V.M. (1992) New Directions in Educational Programming for Students with Autism. In D.E. Berkell (ed.) Autism: *Identification, Education, and Treatment.* Hillsdale, N.J.: Erlbaum, 273–295.

Durrer, J. (May/June 1992) Interactive Language Learning. *Media & Methods* 28:15–17.

Duwa, S.M., Wells, C., & Lalinde, P. (1993) Creating Family-Centered Programs and Policies. In D. M. Bryant & M. A. Graham (eds.) *Implementing Early Intervention.* New York: The Guilford Press, 92–124.

Dyson, L., Edgar, E., & Crnic, K. (1989) Psychological Predictors of Adjustment by Siblings of Disabled Children. *American Journal of Mental Retardation* 94:292–302.

Eagney, P. (1987) ASL? English? Which? Comparing Comprehension. *American Annals of the Deaf* 132:272–275.

Eastern, Paralyzed Veterans Association (1992) *Understanding the Americans with Disabilities Act.* New York: Author.

Eaves, L.C., Ho, H.H., & Eaves, D.M. (1994) Subtypes of Autism by Cluster Analysis. *Journal of Autism and Developmental Disabilities* 24: 3–22.

Ebel, R.L. (1977) *The Uses of Standardized Testing (Fastback 93).* Bloomington, Ind.: Phi Delta Kappa Educational Foundation.

Ebmeier, H., & Schmulbach, S. (1989) An Examination of the Selection Practices Used in the Talent Search Program. *Gifted Child Quarterly* 33:134–141.

Eby, J.W., & Smutny, J.F. (1990) *A Thoughtful Overview of Gifted Education,* White Plains, N.Y.: Longman.

The Economist (24 July 1993) Buffalo Sakes 328:25–26.

Edelman, M.W. (1985) The Sea Is So Wide and My Boat Is So Small: Problems Facing Black Children Today. In H.P. McAdoo & J.L. McAdoo (eds.), *Black Children.* Beverly Hills, Calif.: Sage, 72–85.

Eden-Piercy, G.V.S., Blacher, J.B., & Eyman, R.K. (1986) Exploring Parents' Reactions to Their Young Child with Severe Handicaps. *Mental Retardation* 24:285–291.

Edgar, E. (1987) Secondary Programs in Special Education: Are Many of Them Justifiable? *Exceptional Children* 53:555–561.

Education and Consolidation Act of 1981: PL 97-35, Section 582.

Egeland, B., Jacobovitz, D., & Sroufe, L.A. (1988) Breaking the Cycle of Abuse. *Child Development* 59:1080–1089.

Ehrsten, M.E., & Izzo, M.V. (1988) Special Needs Youth and Adults Need a Helping Hand. *Journal of Career Development* 15:53–64.

Elias, M.J. (1983) Improving the Coping Skills of Emotionally Disturbed Boys through Television-Based Social Problem Solving. *American Journal of Orthopsychiatry* 53:61–73.

Ellett, L. (1993) Instructional Practices in Mainstreamed Secondary Classrooms. *Journal of Learning Disabilities* 26:57–64.

Emerick, L.J. (1992) Academic Underachievement Among the Gifted: Students' Perceptions of Factors that Reverse the Pattern. *Gifted Child Quarterly* 36:140–146.

Emery, R.E. (1982) Interparental Conflict and the Children of Discord and Divorce. *Psychological Bulletin* 92:310–330.

Enersen, D.L. (1993) Summer Residential Programs: Academics and Beyond. *Gifted Child Quarterly* 37:169–176.

Englander, J., Cleary, S., O'Hare, P., Hall, K.M., & Lehmkuhl, L.D. (1993). Implementing and Evaluating Injury Prevention Programs. *Journal of Head Trauma Rehabilitation* 8:101–113.

Epstein, J.L., & Becker, H.J. (1982) Teachers' Reported Practices of Parent Involvement: Problems and Possibilities. *Elementary School Journal* 83:103–113.

Epstein, M.H., Bursuck, W., & Cullinan, D. (1985) Patterns of Behavior Problems Among the Learning Disabled Boys Aged 12–18, Girls Aged 6–11, and Girls Aged 12–18. *Journal of Learning Disabilities* 18:123–129.

Epstein, M.H., Singh, N.N., Luebke, J., & Stout, C.E. (1991) Psychopharmacological Intervention. II: Teacher Perceptions of Psychotropic Medication for Students with Learning Disabilities. *Journal of Learning Disabilities* 24:477–483.

Epstein, M.H., & Cullinan, D. (1987) Effective Social Skills Curricula for Behaviorally Disordered Students. *The Pointer* 31:21–24.

Erickson, M.T. (1992) *Behavior Disorders of Children and Adolescents*, 2d ed. Englewood Cliffs, N.J.: Prentice-Hall.

Erikson, E.H. (1963) *Childhood and Society*. New York: Norton.

Erin, J.N. (1993) Comment. *Journal of Visual Impairment & Blindness* 87:165–171.

Erin, J.N., Dignan, K., & Brown, P.A. (1991) Are Social Skills Teachable? A Review of the Literature. *Journal of Visual Impairment & Blindness* 85:58–61.

Eron, L.D., Walder, L.O., & Lefkowitz, M.M. (1971) *Learning of Aggression in Children*. Boston: Little, Brown.

Erwin, E.J. (1993) Social Participation of Young Children with Visual Impairments in Specialized and Integrated Environments. *Journal of Visual Impairment & Blindness* 87:138–142.

Erwin, P.G. (1994) Effectiveness of Social Skills Training with Children: A Meta-Analysis. *Counselling Psychological Quarterly*. 7: 305–311.

Esposito, B.G., & Reed, T.M. (1986) The Effects of Contact with Handicapped Persons on Young Children's Attitudes. *Exceptional Children* 53:224–229.

Esposito, L., & Campbell, P.H. (1993) Computers and Individuals with Severe and Physical Disabilities. In J.D. Lindsey (ed.), *Computers and Exceptional Individuals* (2d ed.). Austin, Tex.: Pro-Ed, 159–179.

Esterly, D.L., & Griffin, H.C. (1987) Preschool Programs for Children with Learning Disabilities. *Journal of Learning Disabilities* 20:571–573.

Etaugh, C., & Hughes, V. (1975) Teachers' Evaluations of Sex-Typed Behaviors in Children: The Role of Teacher Sex and School Setting. *Developmental Psychology* 11:394–395.

Evans, I. M., Salisbury, C.L., Palombaro, M.M., Berryman, J., & Hollowood, T.M. (1992) Peer Interactions and Social Acceptance of Elementary-Age Children with Severe Disabilities in an Inclusive School. *Journal of the Association for Persons with Severe Handicaps* 17:205–212.

Everson, J.M., & Burwell, J. (1991) Transition to Work: Addressing the Challenges of Deaf-Blindness. *Journal of Vocational Rehabilitation* 1:39–45.

Ewing-Cobbs, L., & Fletcher, J.M. (1987) Neuropsychological Assessment of Head Injury in Children. *Journal of Learning Disabilities* 20:526–535.

Eysenck, H.J. (1975) Crime as Destiny. *New Behaviour* 9:46–49.

Fagan, J., & Schur, D. (1993) Mothers of Children with Spina Bifida: Factors Related to Maternal Psychosocial Functioning. *American Journal of Orthopsychiatry* 63:146–152.

Fagot, B.I. (1977) Influence of Teacher Behavior in the Preschool. *Developmental Psychology* 9:198–206.

Fairbairn, D.M. (1987) The Art of Questioning Your Students. *The Clearing House* 61:19–22.

Farberow, N.L. (1985) Youth Suicide, A Summary. In L.L. Peck, N.L. Farberow, & R.E. Litman (eds.), *Youth Suicide*. New York: Springer, 191–205.

Fardig, D.B., Algozzine, S.E., Schwartz, S.E., Hensel, J.W., & Westling, D.C. (1985) Postsecondary Vocational Adjustment of Rural Mildly Retarded Students. *Exceptional Children* 52: 115–121.

Farnham-Diggory, S. (1992) *The Learning-Disabled Child*. Cambridge, Mass.: Harvard University Press.

Fazio, B.B., & Rieth, H.J. (1986) Characteristics of Preschool Handicapped Children's Microcomputer Use During Free-Choice Periods. *Journal of the Division for Early Childhood* 10:247–254.

FBI (1992) Uniform Crime Report. Washington, D.C.: U.S. Department of Justice.

Feagans, L. (1987) Learning Disabilities and Emotional/Behavioral Problems. In B.C. Epanchin & J.L. Paul (eds.) *Emotional Problems of Childhood and Adolescence*. Columbus, Ohio: Merrill, 340–357.

Federal Register. (1977) Education of Handicapped Children. U.S. Office of Education. *Federal Register* 42:65082–65085.

Federal Register (23 August 1977) 42478.

Federal Register (29 December 1977) Procedures for Evaluating Specific Learning Disabilities. Washington, D.C.: Department of Health, Education, and Welfare, 65083.

Federal Register (January 1981) Washington, D.C.: U.S. Government Printing Office.

Feingold, B.F. (1975) Hyperkinesis and Learning Disabilities Linked to Artificial Food Flavors and Colors. *American Journal of Nursing* 75:797–803.

Feinman-Nemser, S., & Floden, R.E. (1986) The Cultures of Teaching. In M.C. Wittrock (ed.) *Handbook of Research on Teaching*, 3d ed. New York: Macmillan 505–527.

Feldhusen, J.F. (1991) Saturday and Summer Programs. In N. Colangelo & G.A. Davis (eds.), *Handbook of Gifted Education*. Needham Heights, Mass.: Allyn & Bacon, 197–209.

Feldhusen, J.F. (March 1989) Synthesis of Research on Gifted Youth. *Educational Leadership*, 6–11.

Feldhusen, J.F., & Clinkenbeard, P.A. (1987) Creativity Instructional Materials: A Review of Research. *Journal of Creative Behavior* 20:1153–1182.

Feldhusen, J.F., Proctor, T.B., & Black, K.N. (1986) Guidelines for Grade Advancement of Precocious Children. *Roeper Review* 9:25–27.

Feldhusen, J.F., Treffinger, D.J., & Bahlke, S.J. (1970) Developing Creative Thinking: The Purdue Creativity Program. *Journal of Creative Behavior* 4:85–90.

Feldhusen, J., Van Tassel-Baska, J., & Seeley, K. (1989) *Excellence in Educating the Gifted*, Denver, Colo.: Love.

Feldman, D.H. (1993) Child Prodigies: A Distinctive Form of Giftedness. *Gifted Child Quarterly* 37:188–193.

Feldman, D.H. (1984) A Follow-Up of Subjects Scoring Above 180 IQ in Terman's "Genetic Studies of Genius." *Exceptional Children* 50:518–523.

Felice, M. (1986) Reflections on Caring for Indochinese Children and Youths. *Journal of Developmental and Behavioral Pediatrics* 7:124–128.

Fennema, E. (1987) Sex-Related Differences in Education: Myths, Realities, and Interventions. In V. Richardson-Koehler (ed.), *Educator's Handbook* New York: Longman, 329–348.

Ferguson, D.L., & Baumgart, D. (1991) Partial Participation Revisited. *Journal of the Association for Persons with Severe Handicaps* 16:217–227.

Ferguson, D.L., Ferguson, P.M., & Bogdan, R.C. (1987) If Mainstreaming Is the Answer, What Is the Question? In V. Richardson-Koehler (ed.), *Educators' Handbook*. New York: Longman, 394–419.

Fernald, A., & Simon, T. (1984) Expanded Intonation Contours in Mothers' Speech to Newborns. *Developmental Psychology* 20:104–113.

Ferrell, K.A., Trief, E., Dietz, S.J., Bonner, M.A., Cruz, D., Ford, E., & Stratton, J.M. (1990) Visually Impaired Infants Research Consortium (VIIRC): First-Year Results. *Journal of Visual Impairment & Blindness* 84:404–410.

Fewell, R.R. (1991) Parenting Moderately Handicapped Persons. In M. Seligman (ed.) *The Family with a Handi-*capped Child, 2d ed. Boston: Allyn & Bacon, 203–237.

Fichten, C.S., Judd, D., Tagalakis, V., Amsel, R., & Robillard, K. (1991) Communication Cues Used by People With and Without Visual Impairments in Daily Conversations and Dating. *Journal of Visual Impairment & Blindness* 85:371–377.

Fielding, J.E. (1985) Smoking: Health Effects and Control. *New England Journal of Medicine* 313:491–498.

Figueroa, R.A. (1989) Psychological Testing of Linguistic-Minority Students. *Exceptional Children* 56:145–154.

Figueroa, R.A., Fradd, S.H., & Correa, V.I. (1989) Bilingual Special Education and This Special Issue. *Exceptional Children* 56:174–179.

Fine, E. (1987) Are We Preparing Adolescents with Learning Disabilities to Cope With Social Issues? *Journal of Learning Disabilities* 20:633–634.

Fine, M., & Asch, A. (1988) Disability Beyond Stigma: Social Interaction, Discrimination, and Activism. *Journal of Social Issues* 44:3–21.

Fink, L. (May/June 1986) Pregnancy and Birth-Related Brain Disorders. *Children Today*, 26–27.

Fisher, W.A., Fisher, J.D., & Rye, B.J. (1995) Understanding and Promoting AIDS-Preventive Behavior: Insights from the Theory of Reasoned Action. *Health Psychology* 14: 255–264.

Flax, E. (24 June 1987) Koop Warns of an Explosion of AIDS Among Teenagers. *Education Week*, 3.

Flax, E. (Dec. 7, 1988) Rising Enrollment and Costs Threaten Special-Education Gains, Study Finds. *Education Week*, 6.

Flynn, J.M., Deering, W., Goldstein, M., & Rahbar, M.H. (1992) Electrophysiological Correlates of Dyslexic Subtypes. *Journal of Learning Disabilities* 25:133–141.

Fogel, A. (1984) *Infancy: Infant, Family and Society*. St. Paul, Minn.: West Publishing Co.

Foltz, L.C., DeGangi, G., & Lewis, D. (1991) Physical Therapy, Occupational Therapy, and Speech and Language Therapy. In E. Geralis (ed.), *Children with Cerebral Palsy*. New York: Woodbine, 209–261.

Forbes, W.F., Sturgeon, D., Hayward, L.M., Agwani, N., & Dobbins, P. (1992) Hearing Impairment in the Elderly and the Use of Assistive Listening Devices: Prevalences, Associations, and Evaluations. *International Journal of Technology and Aging* 8:39–61.

Ford, B.A. (1992) Multicultural Education Training for Special Educators Working with African-American Youth. *Exceptional Children* 58:107–113.

Ford, B.A. & Jones, C. (Summer 1990) Ethnic Feelings Book. *Teaching Exceptional Children*, 36–40.

Ford, D.Y., & Harris, J.J. (1990) On Discovering the Hidden Treasure of Gifted and Talented Black Children. *Roeper Review* 13:27–32.

Ford, L., Dineen, J., & Hall, J. (1984) Is There Life After Placement? *Education and Training of the Mentally Retarded* 9:291–296.

Ford, S., Schnott, R., Meyer, L., Davern, L., Black, J., & Dempsey, P. (1989) *The Syracuse Community-Referenced Curriculum Guide for Students with Moderate and Severe Disabilities*, Baltimore, Md.: Paul H. Brookes.

Fordham, S., & Ogbu, J.U. (1986) Black Students' School Success: Coping with the "Burden of Acting White." *Urban Review* 18:176–206.

Forehand, R., Middleton, K., & Long, N. (1987) Adolescent Functioning as a Consequence of Recent Parental Divorce and the Parent-Adolescent Relationship. *Journal of Applied Developmental Psychology* 8:305–315.

Forest, M., & Lusthaus, E. (1989) Promoting Educational Equality for All Students: Circles and Maps in S. Stainback, W. Stainback, & M. Forest (eds.) *Educating All Students in the Mainstream of Regular Education*. Baltimore, Md.: Brookes, 43–57.

Forest, M., & Lusthaus, E. (1990) Everyone Belongs with MAPS Action Planning System. *Teaching Exceptional Children*, 32–35.

Forgatch, M.S., Patterson, G.R., & Skinner, M.L. (1988) A Mediational Model for the Effect of Divorce on Antisocial Behavior in Boys. In E.M. Hetherington & J.D. Arasteh (eds.), *Impact of Divorced, Single Parenting, and Stepparenting on Children*. Hillsdale, N.J.: Erlbaum, 135–155.

Forman, E.A. (1988) The Effects of Social Support and School Placement on the Self-Concept of LD Students. *Learning Disabilities Quarterly* 11:114–124.

Forman, S.G. (1987) Affective and Social Education. In C.A. Maher & S.G. Forman (eds.), *A Behavioral Approach to Education of Children and Youth*. Hillsdale, N.J.: Erlbaum, 75–109.

Forness, S.R., & Kavale, K.A. (1988) Psychopharmacological Treatment: A Note on Classroom Effects. *Journal of Learning Disabilities* 21:144–147.

Foscarinis, M. (1991) The Politics of Homelessness: A Call to Action. *American Psychologist* 46:1232–1238.

Fost, D. (December 1991) American Indians in the 1990s. *American Demographics*, 26–33.

Fostein, S.E., & Rutter, M. (1978) A Twin Study of Individuals with Infantile Autism. In M. Rutter & E. Schopler (eds.), *Autism: A Reappraisal of Concepts and Treatment*. New York: Plenum.

Fourquerean, J.M., Meisgeier, C., Swank, P.R., & Williams, R.E. (1991) Correlates of Postsecondary Employment Outcomes for Young Adults with Learning Disabilities. *Journal of Learning Disabilities* 24:400–405.

Fowler, M. (September 1991), *Attention Deficit Disorder*. Washington, D.C.: National Information Center for Children and Youth with Disabilities.

Fox, C.L. (1989) Peer Acceptance of Learning Disabled Children in the Regular Classroom. *Exceptional Children* 56:50–59.

Fox, L. (1989) Peer Perceptions of Learning Disabled Children in the Regular Classroom. *Exceptional Children* 56:50–59.

Fox, L. (1989) Stimulus Generalization of Skills and Persons with Profound Mental Handicaps. *Education and Training in Mental Retardation* 24:219–227.

Fox, L., & Westling, D. (1991) A Preliminary Evaluation of Training Parents to Use Facilitative Strategies with Their Children with Profound Disabilities. *Journal of the Association for Persons with Severe Handicaps* 16:168–176.

Fox, L.H., Benbow, C.P., & Perkins, S. (1983) An Accelerated Mathematics Program for Girls: A Longitudinal Evaluation. In C.P. Benbow & J. Stanley (eds.), *Academic Precocity: Aspects of Its Development*. Baltimore, Md.: Johns-Hopkins University Press, 113–131.

Fox, L.H., & Washington, J. (1985) Programs for the Gifted and Talented: Past, Present, and Future in Intellectually Gifted Children. In F.D. Horowitz & M. O'Brien (eds.), *The Gifted and Talented: Developmental Perspectives*. Washington, D.C.: American Psychological Association, 197–223.

Fracasso, M.P., & Busch-Rossnagel, N.A. (1992) Parents and Children of Hispanic Origin. In M.E. Procidano & C.B. Fisher (eds.), *Contemporary Families*. New York: Columbia University Teachers College.

Fradd, S.H., & Correa, V.I. (1989) Hispanic Students at Risk: Do We Abdicate or Advocate? *Exceptional Children* 56:105–111.

Fraiberg, S. (1977) *Insights from the Blind*, New York: Basic Books.

Francis, H. (1975) *Language in Childhood: Form and Function in Language Development*. New York: St. Martin's Press.

Francis, P.L., Self, P.A., & Horowitz, F.D. (1987) The Behavioral Assessment of the Neonate: An Overview. In J.D. Osofsky (ed.) *Handbook of Infant Development*. New York: Wiley, 723–780.

Frankenberg, W., Dodds, J., Archers, P., Bresnick, B., Maschka, P., Edelman, N., & Shapiro, H. (1991) *Denver II*. Denver, Colo.: Denver Developmental Materials.

Frankenberger, W., & Fronzaglio, K. (1991) A Review of States' Criteria and Procedures for Identifying Children with Learning Disabilities. *Journal of Learning Disabilities* 24:495–500.

Franklin, M.E. (1992) Culturally Sensitive Instructional Practices for African-American Learners. *Exceptional Children* 59:115–123.

Fraser, W.I., & Rao, J.M. (1990) Recent Studies of Mentally Handicapped Young People's Behavior. *Journal of Child Psychology and Psychiatry and Allied Disciplines* 32:79–108.

Frederick-Dugan, A., Test, D.W., & Varn, L. (1991) Acquisition and Generalization of Purchasing Skills Using a Calculator by Students Who Are Mentally Retarded. *Education and Training in Mental Retardation* 26:381–387.

Fredericks, A.D. (December 1984) You've Got to Motivate Parents. *Early Years* 22ff.

Fredericks, B. (June 1987) Back to the Future: Integration Revisited. *The Association for Persons with Severe Handicaps Newsletter*, 1.

Freeland, A. (1989) *Deafness: The Facts*, Oxford: Oxford University Press.

Freedman, P. (1994) Counseling with Deaf Clients: The Need for Culturally and Linguistically Sensitive Interventions. *Journal of Rehabilitation of the Deaf* 27: 16–28.

Freeman, R.D., Goetz, E., Richards, D.P., & Groenveld, M. (1991) Definers of Negative Prediction: A 14-Year Follow-up Study of Legally Blind Children. *Journal of Visual Impairment & Blindness* 85:365–370.

Frey, K.S., Greenberg, M.T., & Fewell, R.R. (1989) Stress and Coping Among Parents of Handicapped Children: A Multidimensional Approach. *American Journal of Mental Retardation* 94:240–249.

Friedman, C.T. (1989) Integrating Infants. *Exceptional Parent* 19:52–57.

Friedman, H.S., Tucker, J.S., Schwartz, J.E., Tomlinson-Keasey, C., Martin,

L.R., Wingard, D.L., & Criqui, M.H. (1995) Psychosocial and Behavioral Predictors of Longevity. *The American Psychologist* 50: 69–78.

Friedman, P., Friedman, R., & Van Dyke, M. (1984) Identifying the Leadership Gifted: Self, Peer, or Teacher Nominations? *Roeper Review* 7:91–94.

Friedrich, W.N., & Boriskin, J.A. (1976) The Role of the Child in Abuse: A Review of the Literature. *American Journal of Orthopsychiatry* 46:27–38.

Frith, G.H., & Edwards, R. (1981) Misconceptions of Regular Classroom Teachers About Physically Handicapped Students. *Exceptional Children* 48:182–184.

Fritz, G.K., Williams, J.R., & Ameslan, M. (1988) After Treatment Ends: Psychosocial Sequelae in Pediatric Cancer Survivors. *American Journal of Orthopsychiatry* 58:552–561.

Frostig et al. (1963) *The Marianne Frostig Developmental Test of Visual Perception* (1963, Standardization). Palo Alto, Calif.: Consulting Psychologists Press.

Frostig, M. (1972) Visual Perception, Integrative Functions, and Academic Learning. *Journal of Learning Disabilities* 5:5–15.

Fryer, L.L., Saylor, C.F., Finch, A.J., & Smith, K. (1989) Helping the Child with Cancer: What School Personnel Want to Know. *Psychological Reports* 65:563–566.

Fuchs, D., & Fuchs, L.S. (1989) Effects of Examiner Familiarity on Black, Caucasian, and Hispanic Children: A Meta-Analysis. *Exceptional Children* 55:303–308.

Fuchs, D., & Fuchs, L.S. (1994) Inclusive Schools Movement and the Radicalization of Special Education Reform. *Exceptional Children* 60:294–309.

Fuchs, D., Fuchs, L.S., Benowitz, S., & Barringer, K. (1987) Norm-Referenced Tests: Are They Valid for Use with Handicapped Students? *Exceptional Children* 53:263–271.

Fuchs, D., Fuchs, L.S., Dailey, A.M., & Power, M.H. (1985) The Effect of Examiners' Experience on Handicapped Children's Test Performance. *Journal of Educational Research* 114:37–46.

Fuchs, L.S., Fuchs, D., Hamlett, C.L., Phillips, N.B., & Bentz, J. (1994) Classwide Curriculum-Based Measurement: Helping General Educators Meet the Challenge of Student Diversity. *Exceptional Children* 60:518–537.

Fuchs, L.S., Fuchs, D., & Stecker, P.M. (1989) Effects of Curriculum-Based Measurement on Teachers' Instructional Planning. *Journal of Learning Disabilities* 22:51–59.

Fugate, D.J., Clarizio, H.F., & Phillips, S.E. (1993) Referral-to-Placement Ratio: A Finding in Need of Reassessment? *Journal of Learning Disabilities* 26:413–416.

Furlong, M., & Yanagida, E. (1985) Psychometric Factors Affecting Multidisciplinary Team Identification of Learning Disabled Children. *Learning Disability Quarterly* 8:37–44.

Gadow, K.D. (1983) Effects of Stimulant Drugs on Academic Hyperactive and Learning Disabled Children. *Journal of Learning Disabilities* 16:290–299.

Gagne, F. (1989) Peer Nominations as a Psychometric Instrument: Many Questions Asked But Few Answered. *Gifted Child Quarterly* 33:53–58.

Gagne, F. (1994) Are Teachers Really Poor Talent Detectors? Comments on Pegnato and Birch's (1959) Study of the Effectiveness and Efficiency of Various Identification Techniques. *Gifted Child Quarterly* 38: 124–126.

Gagne, F., Begin, J., & Talbot, L. (1993) How Well Do Peers Agree Among Themselves When Nominating the Gifted or Talented? *Gifted Children Quarterly* 37:39–45.

Gajar, A. (1992) Adults with Learning Disabilities: Current and Future Research Priorities. *Journal of Learning Disabilities* 25:507–519.

Galaburda, A.M. (1989) Learning Disability: Biological, Societal, or Both? A Response to Gerald Coles. *Journal of Learning Disabilities* 22:278–283.

Galaburda, A.M., LeMay, M., Kemper, T.L. & Geschwind, N. (1978) Right-Left Asymmetries in the Brain. *Science* 199:852–856.

Galaburda, A.M., Sherman, G.F., Rosen, G.D., Aboitz, F., & Geschwind, N. (1985) Developmental Dyslexia: Four Consecutive Cases with Cortical Anomalies. *Annals of Neurology* 18:222–233.

Gallagher, A.M., & De Lisi, R. (1994) Gender Differences in Scholastic Aptitude Test Mathematics Problem Solving Among High-Ability Students. *Journal of Educational Psychology* 86: 204–211.

Gallagher, J.J. (1993) Policy Designed for Diversity: New Initiatives for Children with Disabilities. In D.M. Bryant & M.A. Graham (eds.) *Implementing Early Intervention.* New York: The Guilford Press, 336–351.

Gallaudet College (1975) *Deafness Briefs: Information on Deaf Adults,* Washington, D.C.: Gallaudet College.

Gallaudet Research Institute (1985) *Gallaudet Research Institute Newsletter* (J. Harkins, ed.), Washington, D.C.: Gallaudet University Press.

Galloway, J.P. (1990) Policy Issues for Learning Disability Computer Integration. *Journal of Learning Disabilities* 23:331–334, 338.

Garbarino, J., Guttman, E., & Seeley, J. (1986) *The Psychologically Battered Child: Strategies for Identification, Assessment, and Intervention.* San Francisco: Jossey-Bass.

Garber, H.L. (1988) *The Milwaukee Project: Preventing Mental Retardation in Children at Risk.* Washington, D.C.: American Association on Mental Retardation.

Garber, H., & Heber, F. (1976) The Milwaukee Project: Implications of the Effectiveness of Early Intervention in Preventing Mental Retardation. In P. Mittler (ed.) *Research to Practice in Mental Retardation: Care and Intervention,* vol. 1, Baltimore, Md.: University Park Press.

Garcia-Co, C., Hoffman, J., & Oh, W. (1987) The Social Ecology of Early Parenting of Caucasian Adolescent Mothers. *Child Development* 58:955–964.

Garcia, J., & Pugh, S.L. (November 1992) Multicultural Education in Teacher Preparation Programs. *Phi Delta Kappan*, 214–219.

Gardner, H. (1987a) The Theory of Multiple Intelligences. *Annals of Dyslexia* 37:19–35.

Gardner, H. (1987b) Beyond the IQ: Education and Human Development. *Harvard Educational Review* 57:187–193.

Gardner, H. (1983) *Frames of Mind*. New York: Basic Books.

Gardner, H. (1993) *Multiple Intelligences: The Theory in Practice*. New York: Basic Books.

Gardner, J.E., & Bates, P. (1991) Attitudes and Attributions on Use of Microcomputers by Students Who Are Mentally Retarded. *Education and Training in Mental Retardation* 26:98–107.

Gardner, J., & Zorfass, J. (1983) From Sign to Speech: The Language Development of a Hearing Impaired Child. *American Annals of the Deaf* 126:417–421.

Garland, A.F., & Zigler, E. (1993). Adolescent Suicide Prevention: Current Research and Social Policy Implications.

Garmezy, N. (1982) Research in Clinical Psychology: Serving the Future Hour. In I. Kendall & J.N. Butcher (eds.), *Handbook of Research Methods in Clinical Psychology* New York: Wiley, 677–690.

Garmezy, N. (1985) Stress Resistant Children: The Search for Protective Factors. In J. Stevenson (ed.), *Recent Research in Developmental Psychopathology*. Oxford: Pergamon Press.

Garner, R. (1992) Self-Regulated Learning, Strategy Shifts, and Shared Expertise: Reactions to Palincsar and Klenk. *Journal of Learning Disabilities* 25:226–229.

Gartner, A., & Lipsky, D.K. (1987) Beyond Special Education: Toward a Quality System for All Students. *Harvard Educational Review* 57:367–395.

Gaskins, R.W. (1988) The Missing Ingredients: Time on Task, Direct Instruction and Writing. *The Reading Teacher* 41:750–755.

Gath, A., Smith, M.A., & Baum, J.D. (1980) Emotional, Behavioral, and Educational Disorders in Diabetic Children. *Archives of Diseases in Childhood* 55:371–375.

Gatty, J. (1987) The Oral Approach: A Professional Point of View. In *Choices in Deafness*, Washington, D.C.: Woodbine House, 57–64.

Gaylord-Ross, R., & Haring, T. (1987) Social Interaction Research for Adolescents with Severe Handicaps. *Behavior Disorders* 12:264–275.

Gaylord-Ross, R.J., Forte, J., Storey, K., Gaylord-Ross, C., & Jameson, D. (1987) Community-Referenced Instruction in Technological Work Settings. *Exceptional Children* 54:112–120.

Gaylord-Ross, R.J., Haring, T.G., Breen, C., & Pitts-Conway, V. (1984) The Training and Generalization of Social Interaction Skills with Autistic Children. *Journal of Applied Behavior Analysis* 17:229–247.

Gaylord-Ross, R.J., & Holvoet, J. (1985) *Strategies for Educating Students with Severe Handicaps*, Boston: Little Brown.

Geers, A., Moog, J., & Schick, B. (1984) Acquisition of Spoken and Signed English by Profoundly Deaf Children. *Journal of Speech and Hearing Disorders* 49:378–388.

Geoffrion, L.D., & Goldenberg, E.P. (1981) Computer-Based Exploratory Learning Systems for Communication-Handicapped Children. *Journal of Special Education* 15:325–332.

George, N.L., & Lewis, T.J. (Winter 1991) EASE: Exit Assistance for Special Educators—Helping Students Make the Transition. *Teaching Exceptional Children* 34–39.

Gerber, P.J., Ginsberg, R., & Reiff, H.B. (1992) Identifying Alterable Patterns in Employment Success for Highly Successful Adults with Learning Disabilities. *Journal of Learning Disabilities* 25:475–487.

Gerber, P.J., Schneiders, C.A., Paradise, L.V., Reiff, H.B., Ginsberg, R.J., & Popp, P.A. (1990) Persisting Problems of Adults with Learning Disabilities: Self-Reported Comparisons from Their School-Age and Adult Years. *Journal of Learning Disabilities* 23:569–573.

Gerrey, W., Brabyn, J., & Crandall, W. (1990) The Use of Fax Technology to Address the Reading Needs of Blind and Visually Impaired Persons. *Journal of Visual Impairment & Blindness* 84:509–513.

Gersh, E.S. (1991a) What Is Cerebral Palsy? In E. Geralis (ed.) *Children with Cerebral Palsy*. New York: Woodbine, 57–91.

Gersh, E.S. (1991b) Medical Concerns and Treatment. In E. Geralis (ed.), *Children with Cerebral Palsy*. New York: Woodbine, 57–91.

Gerstein, R., & Woodward, J. (1994) The Language-Minority Student and Special Education: Issues, Trends, and Paradoxes. *Exceptional Children* 61:310–322.

Gersten, R., Crowell, F., & Bellamy, T. (1986) Spillover Effects: Impact of Vocational Training on the Lives of Severely Mentally Retarded Clients. *American Journal of Mental Deficiency* 90:501–506.

Geruschat, D.R. (1990) Functional Vision for Infants and Young Children: Assessment and Reporting. In S.A. Aitken et al. (eds.), *Realities and Opportunities: Early Intervention with Visually Handicapped Children*. New York: American Foundation for the Blind, 55–61.

Geruschat, D.R. (1993) Guest Editorial. *Journal of Visual Impairment & Blindness* 87:163–165.

Gewirtzman, R., & Fodor, I. (1987) The Homeless Child at School: From Welfare Hotel to Classroom. *Child Welfare* 66:237–245.

Giangreco, M.F., Cloninger, C.J., Mueller, P.H., Yuan, S., & Ashworth, S. (1991) Perspectives of Parents Whose Children Have Dual Sensory Impairments. *Journal of the Association for Persons with Severe Handicaps* 16:14–24.

Giangreco, M.F., Dennis, R., Cloninger, C., Edelman, S., & Schattman, R. (1993) "I've Counted Jon": Transformational Experiences of Teachers Educating Students with Disabilities. *Exceptional Children* 59:359–372.

Giangreco, M.F., & Putnam, J.W. (1991) Supporting the Education of Students with Severe Disabilities in Regular Education Environments. In L.H. Meyer, C.A. Peck, & L. Brown (eds.), *Critical Issues in the Lives of People with Severe Disabilities*. Baltimore, Md.: Paul H. Brookes, 245–271.

Gibbs, D.P., & Cooper, E.B. (1989) Prevalence of Communication Disorders in Students with Learning Disabilities. *Journal of Learning Disabilities* 22:60–63.

Gies-Zaborowski, J., & Silverman, F.H. (1986) Documenting the Impact of a Mild Dysarthria on Peer Perception. *Language, Speech, and Hearing Services in Schools* 17:143.

Gifted and Talented Children's Act of 1978: PL 95-561, Section 902.

Gikling, E.E., & Thompson, V.P. (1985) A Personal View of Curriculum-Based Assessment. *Exceptional Children* 52:205–218.

Gil, D.G. (1970) *Violence Against Children: Physical Child Abuse in the United States*. Cambridge, Mass.: Harvard University Press.

Gilligan, C., Lyons, N.P., & Hanmer, T.J. (eds.) (1990) *Making Connections: The Relational Worlds of Adolescent Girls at Emma Willard School*. Cambridge, Mass.: Harvard University Press.

Gispert, M., Wheeler, K., Marsh, L., & Davis, M.S. (1985) Suicidal Adolescents: Factors in Evaluations. *Adolescence* 20:753–762.

Gjerdingen, D., & Manning, F.D. (1991) Adolescents with Profound Hearing Impairments in Mainstream Education: The Clarke Model. *Volta Review* 93:139–148.

Glazer, S. (May 14, 1994) Preventing Teen Pregnancy. *CQ Researcher*, 411–429.

Gleason, J.B. (1985) *The Development Language*. Columbus, Ohio: Merrill.

Glisky, E.L., & Schacter, D.L. (1988) Acquisition of Domain-Specific Knowledge in Patients with Organic Memory Disorders. *Journal of Learning Disabilities* 21:333–340.

Goetz, L., Lee, M., Johnston, S., & Gaylord-Ross, R. (1991) Employment of Persons with Dual Sensory Impairments: Strategies for Inclusion. *Journal of the Association for Persons with Severe Handicaps* 16:131–139.

Gold, M. (1973) Research on the Vocational Habilitation of the Retarded: The Present and the Future. In N. Ellis (ed.) *International Review of Research in Mental Retardation*. New York: Academic Press.

Goldenberg, E.F. (1979) *Special Technology For Special Children*, Baltimore: University Park Press.

Goldfield, B.A., & Reznick, J.S. (1989) Early Lexical Acquisition: Rate, Content, and the Vocabulary Spurt. *Journal of Child Language* 17:171–183.

Goldiamond, I. (1976) Self-Reinforcement. *Journal of Applied Behavior Analysis* 9:509–514.

Goldin-Meadow, S. (7 April 1991) Deaf Children Are Able to Create Their Own Sign Language. *New York Times*, 18.

Goldman, S.R., & Pellegrino, J.W. (1987) Information Processing and Educational Microcomputer Technology: Where Do We Go from Here? *Journal of Learning Disabilities* 20:144–154.

Goldring, E.B. (1990) Assessing the Status of Information on Classroom Organizational Frameworks for Gifted Students. *Journal of Educational Research* 83:313–326.

Goleman, D. (1995, March 7) 75 Years Later, Study Still Tracking Genius. *New York Times*, C1, C9.

Good, R.H., & Salvia, J. (1988) Curriculum Bias in Published Norm-Referenced Reading Tests: Demonstrable Effects. *School Psychology Review* 17:51–60.

Good, T.L., Sikes, J.N., & Brophy, J.E. (1973) Effects of Teacher Sex and Student Sex in Classroom Interaction. *Journal of Educational Psychology* 65:74–87.

Goodglass, H., & Kaplan, E. (1983) *The Assessment of Aphasia and Related Disorders*, 2d ed. Philadelphia: Lea & Febiger.

Goodwin, M.S., & Goodwin, T.C. (1969) In a Dark Mirror. *Mental Hygiene* 53:550–563.

Gopnick, A., & Meltzoff, A. (1987) The Development of Categorization in the Second Year and Its Relation to Other Cognitive and Linguistic Developments. *Child Development* 58:1523–1531.

Gostin, L. (1992) The AIDS Litigation Project: A National Review of Court and Human Rights Commission Decisions on Discrimination. In E. Fee & D.M. Fox (eds.), *AIDS: The Making of a Chronic Disease*. Berkeley, Cal.: University of California Press: 144–170.

Gowen, J., Johnson-Martin, N., Goldman, B., & Appelbaum, M. (1989) Feelings of Depression and Parenting Competence of Mothers of Handicapped and Nonhandicapped Infants: A Longitudinal Study. *American Journal on Mental Retardation* 94:259–271.

Graham, M.A., & Bryant, D.M. (1993) Characteristics of Quality, Effective Service Delivery Systems for Children with Special Needs. In D.M. Bryant & M.A. Graham (eds.) *Implementing Early Intervention*. New York: The Guilford Press, 233–253.

Grant, J., & Semmes, P. (1983) A Rationale for LOGO for Hearing-Impaired Preschoolers. *American Annals of the Deaf* 128:564–569.

Grant, M. (15 May 1989) When the Spirit Takes Wing. *People*, 31, 51–57.

Gray, S.W., & Klaus, R.A. (1970) The Early Training Project: A Seventh Year Report. *Child Development* 51:908–924.

Graziano, A.M., DeGiovanni, I.S., & Garcia, K.A. (1979) Behavioral Treatment of Children's Fears: A Review. *Psychological Bulletin* 86:804–830.

Green, A.H., Gaines, R.W., & Sandgrund, A. (1974) Child Abuse: Pathological Syndrome of Family Reaction. *American Journal of Psychiatry* 131:882–886.

Green, G., & Shane, H.C. (1994) Science, Reason, and Facilitated Communication. *The Journal of the Association for Persons with Severe Handicaps* 19: 151–172.

Greenwood, C.R., Dinwiddie, G., Bailey, V., Carta, J.J., Dorsey, D., Kohler, F.W., Nelson, C., Rotholz, D., & Schulte, D. (1987) Field Replication of Classwide Peer Tutoring. *Journal of Applied Behavior Analysis* 20:151–160.

Gregorchik, L.A. (1992) The Cocaine-Exposed Children Are Here. *Phi Delta Kappan*, 709–711.

Gregory, J.F., Shanahan, T., & Walberg, H. (1986) A Profile of Learning Disabled Twelfth-Graders in Regular Classes. *Learning Disabilities Quarterly* 9:33–42.

Gregory, J.F., Shanahan, T., & Walberg, H.J. (1984) Mainstreamed Hearing-Impaired High School Seniors: A Re-Analysis of a National Survey. *American Annals of the Deaf* 129:11–16.

Gresham, F.M. (1982) Misguided Mainstreaming: A Case for Social Skills Training with Handicapped Children. *Exceptional Children* 48:422–433.

Gresham, F.M. (1984) Social Skills and Self-Efficacy for Exceptional Children. *Exceptional Children* 51:253–261.

Gresham, F.M., & Elliott, S.N. (1989) Social Skills Deficits as a Primary Learning Disability. *Journal of Learning Disabilities* 22:120–124.

Griepp, A., Landau-Stanton, J., & Clements, C.D. (1993) The Neuropsychiatric Aspects of HIV Infection and Patient Care. In J. Landau-Stanton & C.D. Clements and Associates (eds.) *AIDS Health and Mental Health: A Primary Sourcebook*. New York: Brunner/Mazel, 192–213.

Griffith, D.R. (September 1992) Prenatal Exposure to Cocaine and Other Drugs: Developmental and Educational Prognoses. *Phi Delta Kappan*, 30–34.

Grossberg, I.N., & Cornell, D.G. (1988) Relationship between Personality Adjustment and High Intelligence: Terman versus Hollingworth. *Exceptional Children* 55:266–272.

Grossman, F.K. (1972) *Brothers and Sisters of Retarded Children*. Syracuse, N.Y.: Syracuse University Press.

Grossman, H.J. (ed.) (1983) *Classifications in Mental Retardation*. Washington, D.C.: American Association on Mental Deficiency.

Guddemi, M. (Fall 1990) Play and Learning for the Special Child. *Day Care and Early Education* 18:39–40.

Guerra, N.G., & Slaby, R. (1990) Cognitive Mediators of Aggression in Adolescent Offenders: 2. Intervention. *Developmental Psychology* 26:269–277.

Guerra, N.G., Tolan, P.H., & Hammond, W.R. (1994) Prevention and Treatment of Adolescent Violence. In L.D. Eron, J.H., Gentry, & P. Schlegel (eds.) *Reason to Hope: A Psychosocial Perspective on Violence and Youth*. Washington, D.C.: American Psychological Association, 383–405.

Guilford, J.P. (1967) *The Nature of Human Intelligence*, New York: McGraw-Hill.

Guralnick, M.J. (1990) Social Competence and Early Intervention. *Journal of Early Intervention* 14:3–14.

Guralnick, M.J., & Bricker, D. (1987) The Effectiveness of Early Intervention for Children with Cognitive and General Developmental Delays. In M.J. Guralnick & F.C. Bennett (eds.) *The Effectiveness of Early Intervention for At-Risk and Handicapped Children*. Orlando, Fla.: Academic, 115–173.

Guralnick, M.J., & Groom, J.M. (1988) Peer Interactions in Mainstreamed and Specialized Classrooms: A Comparative Analysis. *Exceptional Children* 54:415–425.

Guralnick, M.J., & Weinhouse, E.M. (1984) Peer-Related Social Interactions of Developmentally Delayed Children: Development and Characteristics. *Developmental Psychology* 20:815–827.

Gutterman, E.M., O'Brien, J.D., & Young, J.G. (1987) Structured Diagnostic Interviews for Children and Adolescents: Current Status and Future Directions. *Journal of the American Academy of Child and Adolescent Psychiatry* 26:621–630.

Haager, D., & Vaughn, S. (1995) Parent, Teacher, Peer, and Self-Reports of the Social Competence of Students with Learning Disabilities. *Journal of Learning Disabilities* 28: 205–215, 231.

Hagen, J.W., Barclay, C.R., Anderson, B.J., Feeman, D.J., Segal, S.S., Bacon, G., & Goldstein, G.W. (1990) Intellectual Functioning and Strategy Use in Children with Insulin-Dependent Diabetes Mellitus. *Child Development* 61:1714–1728.

Hahn, H. (1988) The Politics of Physical Differences: Disability and Discrimination. *Journal of Social Issues* 44:39–47.

Haley, G.M.T. et al. (1985) Cognitive Bias and Depression in Psychiatrically Disturbed Children and Adolescents. *Journal of Consulting and Clinical Psychology* 53:535–537.

Halgren, D.W., & Clarizio, H.F. (1993) Categorical and Programming Changes in Special Education Services, *Exceptional Children* 59:547–555.

Hall, B.J.C. (1991) Attitudes of Fourth and Sixth Graders toward Peers with Mild Articulation Disorders. *Language, Speech, and Hearing Services in Schools* 22:334–340.

Hall, J.C., Stone, L., Walsh, M., Wager, D.W., Hakes, A.Z., & Graham, M.A. (1993) Predicting the Costs of Early Intervention. In D.M. Bryant & M.A.

Graham (eds.) *Implementing Early Intervention*. New York: The Guilford Press, 288–312.

Halle, J.W., Gabler-Halle, D., & Bemben, D.A. (1989) Effects of a Peer-Mediated Aerobic Conditioning Program on Fitness Measures with Children Who Have Moderate and Severe Disabilities. *Journal of the Association for Persons with Severe Handicaps* 14:33–47.

Hallenbeck, M.J., & McMaster, D. (Spring 1991) Disability Simulation for Regular Education Students. *Teaching Exceptional Children* 12–15.

Halpern, A.S. (1992) Transition: Old Wine in New Bottles. *Exceptional Children* 58:202–211.

Hamlett, C. (1984) Microcomputer Activities for Gifted Elementary Children. Alternatives to Programming. *Teaching Exceptional Children* 16:153–157.

Hammill, D.D. (1990) On Defining Learning Disabilities: An Emerging Consensus. *Journal of Learning Disabilities* 23:74–84.

Hamre-Nietupski, S. (1993) How Much Time Should Be Spent on Skill Instruction and Friendship Development? Preferences of Parents of Students with Moderate and Severe/Profound Disabilities. *Education and Training in Mental Retardation* 28:220–231.

Hamre-Nietupski, S., Ayres, B., Nietupski, J., Savage, M., Mitchell, B., & Bramman, H. (1989) Enhancing Integration of Students with Severe Disabilities Through Curricular Infusion: A General/Special Educator Partnership. *Education and Training in Mental Retardation*, 78–89.

Hamre-Nietupski, S., Hendrickson, J., Nietupski, J., & Sasson, G. (1993a) Perception of Teachers of Students with Moderate, Severe, or Profound Disabilities on Facilitating Friendships with Nondisabled Peers. *Education and Training in Mental Retardation* 28:111–127.

Hamre-Nietupski, S., McDonald, J., & Nietupski, J. (1992) Integrating Elementary Students with Multiple Disabilities into Supported Regular Classes: Challenges and Solutions. *Teaching Exceptional Children* 24:6–9.

Hamre-Nietupski, S., Nietupski, J., Krajewski, L., Moravec, J., Riehle, R., McDonald, J., Sensor, K., & Cantine-Stull, P. (1992) Enhancing Integration During the Summer. Combined Educational and Community Recreation Options for Students with Severe Disabilities. *Education and Training in Mental Retardation* 27:68–78.

Handlan, S., & Bloom, L.A. (1993) The Effect of Educational Curricula and Modeling/Coaching on the Interactions of Kindergarten Children with Their Peers with Autism. *Focus on Autistic Behavior* 8:1–11.

Handleman, J.S. (1992) Assessment for Curriculum Planning. In D.E. Berkell (ed.), *Autism: Identification, Education, and Treatment*. Hillsdale, N.J.: Erlbaum, 77–88.

Hanley, T.V. (1995/1994) The Need for Technological Advances in Assessment Related to National Educational Reform. *Exceptional Children* 61: 222–229.

Hanley-Maxwell, C., Griffin, S., Szymanski, E.M., & Godley, S.H. (1990) Supported and Time-Limited Transitional Employment Services. *Journal of Visual Impairment & Blindness* 84:160–164.

Hanline, M.F., & Galant, K. (1993) Strategies for Creating Inclusive Early Childhood Settings. In D.M. Bryant & M.A. Graham (eds.) *Implementing Early Intervention*. New York: The Guilford Press, 216–233.

Hanline, M.F., & Halvorsen, A. (1989) Parent Perceptions of the Integration Transition Process: Overcoming Artificial Barriers. *Exceptional Children* 55:487–492.

Hanline, M F., & Hanson, M.J. (1989) Integration Considerations for Infants and Toddlers with Multiple Disabilities. *Journal of the Association for Persons with Severe Handicaps (JASH)* 14:178–183.

Hansen, J.B., & Feldhusen, J.F. (1994) Comparison of Trained and Untrained Teachers of Gifted Students. *Gifted Child Quarterly* 38: 115–123.

Happe, F.G.E. (1994) An Advanced Test of Theory of Mind: Understanding of Story Characters' Thoughts and Feelings by Able Autistic, Mentally Handicapped, and Normal Children and Adults. *Journal of Autism and Developmental Disorders* 24: 129–155.

Hardy, J.B., Welcher, D.W., Mellits, E.D., & Kagan, J. (1976) Pitfalls in the Measurement of Intelligence: Are Standardized Intelligence Tests Valid for Measuring the Intellectual Potential of Urban Children? *Journal of Psychology* 94:43–51.

Haring, K., Farron-Davis, F., Goetz, L., Karasoff, P., & Sailor, & Zeph, L. (1992) LRE and the Placement of Students with Severe Disabilities. *Journal of the Association for Persons with Severe Handicaps* 17:145–153.

Harper, J.A. (1987) Preventive Preschool Programming That Works. *Phi Delta Kappan* 69:81–82.

Harris, S.L., Gill, M.J. & Alessandri, M. (1991) The Family with an Autistic Child. In M. Seligman (ed.), *The Family with a Handicapped Child* (2d ed.). Needham Heights. Mass.: Allyn & Bacon, 269–294.

Harry, B. (1992a) Making Sense of Disability: Low-Income, Puerto Rican Parents' Theories of the Problem. *Exceptional Children* 59:27–40.

Harry, B. (1992b) Restructuring the Participation of African-American Parents in Special Education. *Exceptional Children* 59:123–132.

Hart, S.R., & Brassard, M.R. (1987) A Major Threat to Children's Mental Health: Psychological Maltreatment. *American Psychologist* 42:160–166.

Harter, S. (1986) Processes Underlying the Construction, Maintenance, and Enhancement of the Self-Concept in Children. In J. Suls & A.G. Greenwald (eds.), *Psychological Perspectives on the Self*, vol. 3. Hillsdale, N.J.: Erlbaum, 139–181.

Hartup, W.W. (1983) Peer Reactions. In P.H. Mussen (ed.) *Handbook of Child Psychology: Socialization, Personality, and Social Development*, vol. 4, 4th ed. New York: Wiley, 103–197.

Harty, H., Kloosterman, P., & Matkin, J. (Summer 1988) Computer Applications for Elementary Science Teaching and Learning. *Journal of Computers in Mathematics and Science Teaching*, 26–29.

Hasazi, S.B., Gordon, L.R., Roe, C.A., Fink, K., Hull, M., & Salembier, G. (1985) A Statewide Follow-up on Post High School Employment and Residential Status of Students Labeled "Mentally Retarded." *Education and Training in Mental Retardation* 14:222–234.

Hasbrouck, J.M. (1992) FAMC Intensive Stuttering Treatment Program: Ten Years of Implementation. *Military Medicine* 157:5, 244–247.

Haskins, R. (1989) Beyond Metaphor: The Efficacy of Early Childhood Education. *American Psychologist* 44:274–282.

Hatcher, P.J., Hulme, C., & Ellis, A.W. (1994) Ameliorating Early Reading Failure by Integrating the Teaching of Reading and Phonological Skills: The Phonological Linkage Hypothesis. *Child Development* 65: 41–58.

Hatlen, P.H. (1993) A Personal Odyssey on Schools for Blind Children. *Journal of Visual Impairment & Blindness* 87:171–174.

Hatlen, P.H., & Curry, S.A. (1987) In Support of Specialized Programs for Blind and Visually Impaired Children: The Impact of Vision Loss on Learning. *Journal of Visual Impairment & Blindness* 81:7–13.

Haugland, S. (Spring 1993). Are Computers an Important Learning Resource? *Day Care and Early Education* 20:30–31.

Haugland, S. (Winter 1991). Tapping a Source of Rich Learning Potential. *Day Care and Early Education* 18:42–43.

Hauser, W.A., & Hesdorffer, D.C. (1990a) *Epilepsy: Frequency, Causes, and Consequences*, Landover, Md.: Epilepsy Foundation of America.

Hauser, W.A., & Hesdorffer, D.C. (1990b) *Facts About Epilepsy*, Landover, Md.: Epilepsy Foundation of America.

Hausman, B., & Hammen, C. (1993) Parenting in Homeless Families: The Double Crisis. *American Journal of Orthopsychiatry* 63: 358–368.

Hawkins, B. (1992) Art & Technology. *Media & Methods* 28:39.

Hawley, P. (1982) The State of the Art of Counseling High School Girls. Ford Foundation Faculty Fellowship for Research on Womens' Role in Society Project No. 675P (June 1975). Cited in P. Hawley, B. Even, Work and Sex Role Attitudes in Relation to Education and Other Characteristics. *Vocational Guidance Quarterly* 31:101–109.

Hayes, R. (1985) Men's Decisions to Enter or Avoid Nontraditional Occupations. *Career Development Quarterly* 32:37–48.

Hazzard, A. (1983) Children's Experience with Knowledge of, and Attitude Toward Disabled Persons. *Journal of Special Education* 17:131–139.

Head, D. (1990) Educational Deficit: An Inappropriate Service Criterion for Children with Visual Impairments. *Journal of Visual Impairment & Blindness* 84:207–211.

Heal, L.W., Hanley, J.I., & Novak-Amado, A.R. (1988) *Integration of Developmentally Disabled Individuals into the Community*, Baltimore, Md.: Paul H. Brookes.

Hebberler, K.M., Smith, B.J., & Block, T.L. (1991) A History of Legislation for the Early Intervention of Children with Handicaps. *Exceptional Children* 58:104–112.

Hedbring, C. (1995) Computers and Autistic Learners: An Evolving Technology. *Australian Journal of Human Communication Disorders* 13: 169–192.

Hedin, D. (1987) Expanding the Use of Corr-Age Peer Tutoring. *The Clearing House* 39–41.

Heflin, L.J., & Rudy, K. (1991) *Homeless and in Need of Special Education*. Reston, Va.: Council for Exceptional Children.

Hegde, M.N. (1995) *Introduction to Communication Disorders* (2nd ed.). Austin, Texas: Pro-Ed.

Helen Keller National Center for Deaf Blind Youths and Adults (HKNC) (1988) *Annual Report to Congress*, author.

Helen Keller National Center for Deaf-Blind Youths and Adults (HKNC) (1993) *Share Helen Keller's Vision*, author.

Helms, J.E. (1992) Why Is There No Study of Cultural Equivalence in Standardized Cognitive Testing. *American Psychologist* 47:1083–1102.

Helmstetter, E., Peck, C.A., & Giangreco, M.F. (1994) Outcomes of Interactions with Peers with Moderate or Severe Disabilities: A Statewide Survey of High School Students. *The Journal of the Association for Persons with Severe Handicaps* 19: 263–276

Henderson, S., Hesketh, B., & Tuffin, K. (1988) A Test of Gottfreson's Circumscription. *Journal of Vocational Behavior* 32:37–48.

Henggeler, S.W., Rodick, J.D., Bordvin, C.M., Hanson, C.L., Watson, S.M., & Urey, J.R. (1986) Multisystemic Treatment of Juvenile Offenders: Effects on Adolescent Behavior and Family Interaction. *Developmental Psychology* 22:132–141.

Hennessey, B.A., & Amabile, T.M. (1987) *Creativity and Learning*, Washington, D.C.: National Education Association.

Hennessy, K.D., Robideau, G.J., Cicchetti, D., & Cummings, E.M. (1994) Responses of Physically Abused and Nonabused Children to Different Forms of Interadult Anger. *Child Development* 65: 815–828.

Henry, T. (6 January 1994) Violence in Schools Grows More Severe. *U.S.A. Today*, D1.

Herbert, J.T., & Ishikawa, T. (1991) Employment-Related Interpersonal Competence among Workers with Mental Retardation. *Vocational Evaluation and Work Adjustment Bulletin* 87–94.

Herbert, W. (15 March 1993) Scientists Find Hereditary Form of Dyslexia. *Science News* 123:180.

Herman, S.E. (1991) Use and Impact of a Cash Subsidy Program. *Mental Retardation* 29:253–258.

Hermann, B., & Whitman, S. (1992) Psychopathology in Epilepsy. *American Psychologist* 47:1134–1138.

Hernandez, H. (1989) *Multicultural Education: A Teacher's Guide to Content and Process,* New York: Merrill.

Herrenkohl, E.C., Herrenkohl, R.C., & Egolf, B. (1994) Resilient Early School-Age Children from Maltreating Homes: Outcomes in Late Adolescence. *American Journal of Orthopsychiatry* 64:301–309.

Hersberger, J., & Wheatley, G. (1989) Computers and Gifted Students: An Effective Mathematics Program. *Gifted Children Quarterly* 33:106–109.

Hess, R.D., & Camara, K.A. (1979) Postdivorce Family Relationships as Mediating Variables in the Consequences of Divorce for Children. *Journal of Social Issues* 35:4.

Hetherington, E.M. (1972) Effects of Father Absence on Personality: Development in Adolescent Daughters. *Developmental Psychology* 7:313–321.

Hetherington, E.M. (1979) Divorce: A Child's Perspective. *American Psychologist* 34:851–859.

Hetherington, E.M., Cox, M., & Cox, R. (1976) Divorced Fathers. *Family Coordinator* 25:417–428.

Hetherington, E.M., Stanley-Hagan, M., & Anderson, E.R. (1989) Marital Transitions. *American Psychologist* 44:303–312.

Heyman, W.B. (1990) The Self-Perception of a Learning Disability and Its Relationship to Academic Self-Concept and Self-Esteem. *Journal of Learning Disabilities* 23:472–475.

Hickson, L., Blackson, L.S., & Reis, E.M. (1995) *Mental Retardation.* Needham Heights, Mass: Allyn & Bacon.

Higgins, K., & Boone, R. (1990) Hypertext Computer Study Guides and the Social Studies Achievement of Students with Learning Disabilities, Remedial Students, and Regular Education Students. *Journal of Learning Disabilities* 23:529–540.

Hill, J.L. (1990) Mainstreaming Visually Impaired Children: The Need for Modifications. *Journal of Visual Impairment and Blindness* 84:354–360.

Hilliard, A.G. (1980) Cultural Diversity and Special Education. *Exceptional Children* 46:584–588.

Hilton, A., & Liberty, K. (1992) The Challenge of Ensuring Educational Gains for Students with Severe disabilities Who Are Placed in More Integrated Settings. *Education and Training in Mental Retardation* 27:167–175.

Hirst, M.A. (1983) Young People with Disabilities: What Happens After 16? *Child Care, Health and Development* 9:273–284.

Hjelmquist, E., Jansson, B., & Torell, G. (1990) Computer-Oriented Technology for Blind Readers. *Journal of Visual Impairment & Blindness* 84:210–215.

Hoben, M., & Lindstrom, V. (1980) Evidence of Isolation in the Mainstream. *Journal of Visual Impairment & Blindness* 74:289–292.

Hoberman, H.M., & Garfinkel, B.D. (1988) Completed Suicide in Children and Adolescents. *Journal of the American Academy of Child and Adolescent Psychiatry* 27:689–695.

Hochman, D. (1995) Department Chairperson, Early Childhood Education Department, Suffolk Community College, personal communication.

Hoffman, F.J., Sheldon, K.L., Minskoff, E.H., Sautter, S.W., Steidle, E.F., Baker, D.P., Bailey, M.B., & Echols, L.D. (1987) Needs of Learning Disabled Adults. *Journal of Learning Disabilities* 20:43–52.

Hoffman, M. (6 December 1991) Putting New Muscle into Gene Therapy. *Science* 254:1455–1456.

Hoge, R.D., & McSheffrey, R. (1991) An Investigation of Self-Concept in Gifted Children. *Exceptional Children* 57:238–245.

Holder, H.B., & Kirkpatrick, S.W. (1991) Interpretation of Emotion from Facial Expressions in Children With and Without Learning Disabilities. *Journal of Learning Disabilities* 24:170–177.

Hole, W.C., & Holt, C. (1994) A Training Program in Assistive Technology for Library Patrons. *Journal of Visual Impairment & Blindness* 88:278–279.

Holland, A.L., Swindell, C.S., & Reinmuth, O.M. (1990) Aphasia and Related Adult Disorders. In G.H. Shames & E.H. Wiig (eds.), *Human Communication Disorders,* 3d ed. Columbus, Ohio: Merrill, 424–462.

Hollinger, C.L., & Fleming, E.S. (1992) A Longitudinal Examination of Life Choices of Gifted and Talented Young Women. *Gifted Children Quarterly* 36:207–212.

Hollingworth, L. (1942) *Children Above 180 IQ,* New York: World Book Company.

Holt, J. (1994) Classroom Attributes and Achievement Test Scores for Deaf and Hard of Hearing Students. *American Annals of the Deaf* 139: 430–437.

Horne, M.D., & Ricciardo, J.L. (1988) Hierarchy of Response to Handicaps. *Psychological Reports* 62:83–86.

Horst, G., Wehman, P., Hill, J.W., & Bailey, C. (1981) Developing Age-Appropriate Leisure Skills in Severely Handicapped Adolescents. *Teaching Exceptional Children* 14:11–16.

Houck, C.K., & Billingsley, B. (1989) Written Expression of Students With and Without Learning Disabilities: Differences Across the Grades. *Journal of Learning Disabilities* 22:561–567, 572.

Houghton, J., Bronicki, B., & Guess, D. (1987) Opportunities to Express Preferences and Make Choices among Students with Severe Disabilities in Classroom Settings. *Journal of the Association for Persons with Severe Handicaps* 12:18–27.

Householder, J., Hatcher, R., Burns, W., & Chasnoff, I. (1982) Infants Born to Narcotic-Addicted Mothers. *Psychological Bulletin* 2:453–468.

Houston, W.R., Clift, R.T., Freiberg, H.J., & Warner, A.R. (1988) *Touch the Future: Teach!* St. Paul, Minn.: West Publishing Co.

Howlin, P.A. (1981) The Effectiveness of Operant Language Training with Autistic Children. *Journal of Autism and Developmental Disorders.*

Huang, L.H. (1989) Southeast Asian Refugee Children and Adolescents. In J.T. Gibbs & L.H. Huang (eds.), *Children of Color.* San Francisco: Jossey-Bass, 278–321.

Hueffner, D.S. (1988) The Consulting Teacher Model: Risks and Opportunities. *Exceptional Children* 54:403–414.

Huesman, L.R., Eron, L.D., Lefkowitz, M.M., & Walder, L.O. (1984) Stability of Aggression over Time and Generations. *Developmental Psychology* 20:1120–1134.

Huesman, L.R., Lagerspetz, K., & Eron, L.D. (1984) Intervening Variables in TV Violence-Aggression: Evidence from Two Countries. *Developmental Psychology* 20:746–776.

Human Resources Center. (1988) *How to Succeed in College: A Handbook for Students with Learning Disabilities.* Albertson, N.Y.: Vocational Rehabilitation Services Division, The National Center on Employment and Disability, Human Resources Center.

Hunt, P., Alwell, M., & Goetz, L. (1991) Interacting with Peers Through Conversation Turntaking with a Communication Book Adaptation. *Augmentative and Alternative Communication* 7:117–126.

Hunt, P., & Farron-Davis, F. (1992) A Preliminary Investigation of IEP Quality and Content Associated with Placement in General Education Versus Special Education Classes. *Journal of the Association for People with Severe Handicaps* 17:247–253.

Hunt, P., Staub, D., Alwell, M., & Goetz, L. (1994) Achievement by All Students within the Context of Cooperative Learning Groups. *Journal of the Association for Persons with Severe Handicaps* 19: 290–301.

Huntington, D.D., & Bender, W.N. (1993) Adolescents with Learning Disabilities at Risk? Emotional Well Being, Depression, and Suicide. *Journal of Learning Disabilities* 26:159–166.

Hurford, D.P., Schauf, J.D., Bunce, L., Blaich, T., & Moore, K. (1994) Early Identification of Children at Risk for Reading Disabilities. *Journal of Learning Disabilities* 27:371–382.

Hurwitz, T.A. (1980) *The Tutor/Notetaker as a Support Service for Hearing-Impaired Students: Overview of the NTID Tutor/Notetaker Program,* Rochester, N.Y.: National Technical Institute for the Deaf.

Hus, Y. (1979) The Socialization Process of Hearing Impaired Children in a Summer Day Camp. *Volta Review* 81:146–156.

Huston, A.C. (1983) Sex Typing. In E.M. Hetherington (ed.), *Handbook of Child Psychology* (4th ed.) vol. 4. New York: Wiley, 387–469.

Huston, A.C. (1991) Children in Poverty: Developmental and Policy Issues. In A. C. Huston (ed.), *Children in Poverty.* New York: Cambridge University Press, 1–23.

Huston, A.C., McLoyd, V.C., & Coll, G.C. (1994) Children and Poverty: Issues in Contemporary Research. *Child Development* 65:275–282.

Hutchings, J.J. (May/June 1988) Pediatric AIDS: An Overview. *Children Today,* 4–7.

Hynd, G.W., & Semrud-Clikeman, M. (1989) Dyslexia and Brain Morphology. *Psychological Bulletin* 106:447–482.

Hynd, G., Marshall, R., & Gonzalez, J. (1991) Learning Disabilities and Presumed Central Nervous System Dysfunction. *Learning Disabilities Quarterly* 14:283–295.

Iacono, T.A., & Miller, J.F. (1989) Can Microcomputers Be Used to Teach Communication Skills to Students with Mental Retardation? *Education and Training in Mental Retardation* 24:32–44.

Infant Health and Development Program. (1990) Enhancing the Outcomes of Low Birth Weight, Premature Infants: A Multisite Randomized Trial. *Journal of the American Medical Association* 263:3035–3042.

Inge, K.J., Banks, D., Wehman, P., Hill, J., & Shafer, M.S. (1988) Quality of Life for Individuals Who Are Labeled Mentally Retarded: Evaluating Competitive Employment Versus Sheltered Workshop Employment. *Education and Training in Mental Retardation* 697–104.

Inger, M. (1993) Getting Hispanic Parents Involved. *Education Digest* 58:32–34.

Ingham, R.J. (1990) Stuttering: Recent Trends in Research and Treatment. In H. Winitz (ed.) *Human Communication and Its Disorders: A Review—1990.* Norwood, N.J.: Ablex Pub. Corporation.

Innes, J.J. (1994) Full Inclusion and the Deaf Student: A Deaf Consumer's Review of the Issue. *American Annals of the Deaf* 139:152–156.

Irvine, A.B., Singer, G.H., Erickson, A.M., & Stahlberg, D. (1992) A Coordinated Program to Transfer Self-Management Skills from School to Home. *Education and Training in Mental Retardation* 27:241–254.

Isenberg, J., & Quisenberry, N.L. (February 1988) Play: A Necessity for All Children. *Childhood Education* 138–145.

Izen, C.L., & Brown, F. (1991) Education and Treatment Needs of Students with Profound Multiple Handicapping and Medically Fragile Conditions: A Survey of Teachers' Perceptions. *Journal of the Association for Persons with Severe Handicaps* 16:94–103.

Jackson, S.C., Robey, L., Watjus, M., & Chadwick, E. (Fall 1991) Play for All Children: The Toy Library Solution. *Childhood Education* 27–31.

Jacobson, S.W., Jacobson, J.L., Sokol, R.J., Martier, S.S., & Ager, J.W. (1993) Prenatal Alcohol Exposure and Infant Information Processing Ability. *Child Development* 64:1706–1722.

Jambor, M. (Summer 1990) Welcoming the Child with Special Needs. *Day Care and Early Education* 17:40–41.

Jan, J.E., Freeman, R.D., & Scott, E.P. (1977) *Visual Impairment in Children and Adolescents*, New York: Grune and Stratton.

Janney, R.E., Snell, M.E., Beers, M.K., & Raynes, M. (1995) Integrating Students With Moderate and Severe Disabilities Intro General Education Classes. *Exceptional Children* 61: 425–439.

Janos, P.M. (1987) A Fifty-Year Follow-up of Terman's Youngest College Students and IQ-Matched Agemates. *Gifted Child Quarterly* 31:55–58.

Janos, P.M., Fung, H.C., & Robinson, N.M. (1985) Self-Concepts, Self-Esteem, and Peer Relations Among Gifted Children Who Feel "Different." *Gifted Child Quarterly* 29:78–82.

Janos, P.M., & Robinson, N.M. (1985) Psychosocial Development in Intellectually Gifted Children. In F.D. Horowitz & M. O'Brien (eds.), *The Gifted and Talented: Developmental Perspectives*. Washington, D.C.: American Psychological Association, 149–197.

Jarrett, M.H. (1991) Early Intervention and Special Education. In E. Geralis (ed.), *Children with Cerebral Palsy*. New York: Woodbine, 261–296.

Jarvis, P.A., & Justice, E.M. (1992) Social Sensitivity in Adolescents and Adults with Learning Disabilities. *Adolescence* 27:977–988.

Jenkins, J.R., & Heinen, A. (1989) Students' Preferences for Service Delivery: Pull-Out, In-Class, or Integrated Models. *Exceptional Children* 55:516–523.

Jenkins, J.R., Odom, S.L., & Speltz, M.L. (1989) Effects of Social Integration on Preschool Children with Handicaps. *Exceptional Children* 55:415–428.

Jenkins, J.R., Speltz, M.L., & Odom, S.L. (1985) Integrating Normal and Handicapped Preschoolers: Effects on Child Development and Social Interaction. *Exceptional Children* 52:7–18.

Jennings, S. (1975) Effects of Sex Typing in Children's Stories on Preference and Recall. *Child Development* 46:220–223.

Jensema, C.J. (1994) Telecommunications for the Deaf. *American Annals of the Deaf*, Special Issue, 139:22–27.

Jensema, C., & Trybus, K. (1978) *Communication Patterns and Educational Achievement of Hearing Impaired Students* (Series T,2) Washington, D.C.: Gallaudet University, Office of Demographic Studies. Cited in Ritter-Brinton.

Johnson, A. (1987) Attitudes Toward Mainstreaming: Implications for Inservice Training and Teaching the Handicapped. *Education* 107:229–233.

Johnson, J.A. (1981) The Etiology of Hyperactivity. *Exceptional Children* 47:348–354.

Johnson, J.E., & Yawkey, T.D. (1988) Play and Integration. In T.D. Yawkey & J.E. Johnson (eds.) *Integrative Processes and Socialization*. Hillsdale, N.J.: Erlbaum, 97–119.

Johnson, M.P., Lubker, B.B., & Fowler, M.G. (1988) Teacher Needs Assessment for the Educational Management of Children with Chronic Illnesses. *Journal of School Health* 58:232–235.

Johnson, R.T., & Johnson, D.W. (1981) Building Friendships Between Handicapped and Nonhandicapped Students: Effects of Cooperative and Individualistic Instruction. *American Education Research Journal* 18:415–423.

Johnson, S.B., Silverstein, J., Rosenbloom, A., Carter, R., & Cunningham, W. (1986) Assessing Daily Management in Childhood Diabetes. *Health Psychology* 5:545–564.

Jones, C.S. (1987) Cerebral Palsy. In C.E. Reynolds (ed.), *Encyclopedia of Special Education*. New York: Wiley, 293–296.

Jones, J.M., Levine, I.S., & Rosenberg, A.A. (1991) Homelessness Research, Services, and Social Policy. *American Psychologist* 46:1109–1111.

Jones, K.M., Torgesen, J.K., & Sexton, M.A. (1987) Using Computer-Guided Practice to Increase Decoding Fluency in Learning Disabled Children: A Study Using the Hint and Hunt 1 Program. *Journal of Learning Disabilities* 20:122–127.

Jones, L., & Pullen, G. (1992) Cultural Differences: Deaf and Hearing Researchers Working Together. *Disability, Handicap & Society* 7:189–196.

Jones, M.B. (January/February 1988) Autism: The Child Within. *Rutgers Magazine*, 10–14.

Judy, J.E., Alexander, P.A., Kulikowich, J.M., & Wilson, V.L. (1988) Effects of Two Instructional Approaches and Peer Tutoring on Gifted and Nongifted Sixth-Grade Students' Analogy Performance. *Reading Research Quarterly* 23:236–256.

Junge, M.E., & Dretzke, B.J. (1995) Mathematical Self-Efficacy Gender Differences in Gifted/Talented Adolescents. *Gifted Child Quarterly* 39: 22–28.

Juntune, J. (1982) Myth: The Gifted Constitute a Single Homogeneous Group! *Gifted Child Quarterly* 26:9–10.

Kahane, J., & Mayo, R. (1989) The Need for Aggressive Pursuit of Healthy Childhood Voices. *Language, Speech, and Hearing Services in Schools* 20:102–107.

Kail, C.J., Downs, J.C., & Black, D.D. (1988) Social Skills in the School Curriculum: A Systematic Approach. *NASSP Bulletin* 72:107–110.

Kaiser, A.P. (1993) Functional Language. In M.E. Snell (ed.), *Instruction of Students with Severe Disabilities* (4th ed.). New York: Merrill, 348–372.

Kalloniatis, M., & Johnston, A.W. (1994) Visual Environmental Adaptation Problems of Partially Sighted Children. *Journal of Visual Impairment & Blindness* 88:234–243.

Kampfe, C.M., & Turecheck, A.G. (1987) Reading Achievement of Prelingually Deaf Students and Its Relationship to Parental Method of Communication: A Review of the Literature. *American Annals of the Deaf* 132:11–15.

Kanfer, F.H., Karoly, P., & Newman, A. (1975) Reduction of Children's Fear of the Dark by Competence-Related and Situational Threat-Related Verbal Cues. *Journal of Consulting and Clinical Psychology* 43:251–258.

Kaplan, J. (1994) Personal Communication. New York.

Kaplan, J.E. & Moore, R.J. Jr. (1988) Legal Rights and Hurdles. In H. Reisner (ed.), *Children with Epilepsy*, New York: Woodbine, 173–203.

Kaplan, P.S. (1990) *Educational Psychology for Tomorrow's Teacher*, St. Paul, Minn.: West Publishing Co.

Kaplan, P.S. (1991) *A Child's Odyssey*, 2d ed. St. Paul, Minn.: West Publishing Co.

Kaplan, P.S. (1993) *The Human Odyssey*, 2d ed. St. Paul, Minn.: West Publishing Co.

Karagan, N.J. (1979) Intellectual Functioning in Duchenne Muscular Dystrophy: A Review. *Psychological Bulletin* 86:250–259.

Karnes, F.A., & Chauvin, J. (1986) The Leadership Skills: Fostering the Forgotten Dimension of Giftedness. *G/C/T* 9:22–23.

Karnes, F.A., Meriweather, S., & D'Lio, V. (1987) The Effectiveness of the Leadership Studies Program. *Roeper Review* 9:238–241.

Karnes, M.B., & Johnson, L.J. (1991) Gifted Handicapped. In N. Colangelo & G.A. Davis (eds.), *Handbook of Gifted Education*. Needham Heights, Mass.: Allyn & Bacon, 428–441.

Kaslow, N.J., Rehm, L.P., & Siegel, A.W. (1984) Social-Cognitive and Cognitive Correlates of Depression in Children. *Journal of Abnormal Child Psychology* 12: 605–620.

Kaslow, N.J., Tanenbaum, R.L., Abramson, L.Y., Peterson, C., & Seligman, M.E.P. (1983) Problem-Solving Deficits and Depressive Symptoms Among Children. *Journal of Abnormal Child Psychology* 11:497–502.

Kauffman, J.M. (1989) *Characteristics of Children with Behavior Disorders*, 4th ed. Columbus, Ohio: Merrill.

Kauffman, J.M., Gerber, M.M., & Semmel, M.I. (1988) Arguable Assumptions Underlying the Regular Education Initiative. *Journal of Learning Disabilities* 21:6–11.

Kaufman, A.S., Kamphaus, R.W., & Kaufman, N.L. (1985) The Kaufman Assessment Battery for Children (K-ABC). In C.S. Newmark (ed.) *Major Psychological Assessment Instruments.* Boston: Allyn and Bacon, 249–277.

Kaufman, J., & Zigler, E. (1987) Do Abused Children Become Abusive Parents. *American Journal of Orthopsychiatry* 57:186–192.

Kavale, K., & Forness, S.R. (1984) A Meta-Analysis of the Validity of Wechsler Scale Profiles and Recategorizations: Patterns or Parodies? *Learning Disabilities Quarterly* 7:136–156.

Kay, S.I., & Subotnik, R.F. (1994) Talent Beyond Words: Unveiling Spatial, Expressive, Kinesthetic, and Musical Talent in Young Children. *Gifted Child Quarterly* 38:70–74.

Kazak, A.E., & Marvin, R.S. (1984) Differences, Difficulties, and Adaptation: Stress and Social Networks in Families with a Handicapped Child. *Family Relations* 33:67–77.

Kazdin, A.E. (1989) Developmental Psychopathology: Current Research, Issues, and Directions. *American Psychologist* 44:180–187.

Kazdin, A.E. (1994) *Behavior Modification in Applied Settings*, Belmont, Calif.: Brooks/Cole.

Kazdin, A.E. (1994) *Behavior Modification in Applied Settings*. Belmont, Cal.: Wadsworth.

Kazdin, A.E. (1994) Interventions for Aggressive and Antisocial Children. In L.D. Eron, J.H., Gentry, & P. Schlegel (eds.) *Reason to Hope: A Psychosocial Perspective on Violence and Youth.* Washington, D.C.: American Psychological Association, 341–383.

Keating, D.P. (1980) Four Faces of Creativity: The Continuing Plight of the Intellectually Underserved. *Gifted Child Quarterly* 24:56–61.

Keefe, C.H. (1988) Social Skills: A Basic Subject. *Academic Therapy* 23:367–373.

Keirouz, K.S. (1990) Concerns of Parents of Gifted Children: A Research Review. *Gifted Child Quarterly* 34:56–63.

Keller, C.E., & Hallahan, D.P. (1987) *Learning Disabilities: Issues and Instructional Interventions.* Washington, D.C.: National Education Association.

Kelley, P., & Wedding, J.A. (1995) Medications Used by Students with Visual and Multiple Impairments: Implications for Teachers. *Journal of Visual Impairment & Blindness* 89: 38–45.

Kelley, S.D.M., & Lambert, S.S. (1992) Family Support in Rehabilitation: A Review of the Research, 1980–1990. *Rehabilitation Counseling Review* 36:98–119.

Kelly, J.A., & Drabman, R.S. (1977) Generalizing Response Suppression of Self-Injurious Behavior Through an Overcorrection Punishment Procedure: A Case Study. *Behavior Therapy* 8:468–472.

Kelly, J.B., & Wallerstein, J.S. (1976) The Effects of Parental Divorce: Experience of the Child in Early Latency. *American Journal of Orthopsychiatry* 46:20–33.

Kelly, K.R., & Colangelo, N. (1984) Academic and Social Self-Concepts of Gifted, General, and Special Students. *Exceptional Children* 51:551–554.

Kelly, L.J., & Vergason, G.A. (1985) *Dictionary of Special Education and Rehabilitation* (2d ed.), Denver: Love.

Kelly, R.R. (1993) Computers and Individuals with Sensory Impairments. In J.D. Lindsey (ed.), *Computers and Exceptional Individuals* (2d ed.). Austin, Tex.: Pro-Ed, 179–200.

Kemp, N.J., & Rutter, D.R. (1982) Cuelessness and the Content and Style of Conversation. *British Journal of Social Psychology* 21:43–49.

Kennedy, C.H., & Itkonen, T. (1994) Some Effects of Regular Class Participation on the Social Contacts and Social Networks of High School Students with Severe Disabilities. *The Journal of the Association for Persons with Severe Handicaps* 19: 1–10.

Kerachsky, S., & Halpern, A.S. (1987) Findings from the STETS Transitional Employment Demonstration. *Exceptional Children* 53:515–522.

Kerr, B. (1985) *Smart Girls, Gifted Women*, Columbus, Ohio: Ohio Psychology Press.

Kerr, B. (1991) Educating Gifted Girls. In N. Colangelo & G.A. Davis (eds.),

Handbook of Gifted Education. Needham Heights, Mass.: Allyn & Bacon, 402–416.

Kerr, B.A., & Colangelo, N. (1988) The College Plans of Academically Talented Students. *Journal of Counseling and Development* 67:42–48.

Kerr, B., Colangelo, N., & Gaeth, (1988) Gifted Adolescents' Attitudes Toward Their Giftedness. *Gifted Children Quarterly* 32:245–247.

Kerr, M.M., Nelson, C.M., & Lambert, D.L. (1987) *Helping Adolescents with Learning and Behavior Problems,* Columbus, Ohio: Merrill.

Kessler, J.W. (1988) *Psychopathology of Childhood* 2d ed. Englewood Cliffs, N.J.: Prentice-Hall.

Kilborn, P.T. (2 January 1990) For the Retarded, Independence in Real Jobs. *The New York Times* pp. A1–A15.

Kim, H.C., Gaston, G., & Fithian, J. (1984) sickle-cell Anemia. In J. Fithian (ed.), *Understanding the Child with a Chronic Illness in the Classroom.* Phoenix, Ariz.: Oryx Press, 180–197.

Kimball, M. (1989) A New Perspective on Women's Math Achievement. *Psychological Bulletin* 105:198–214.

King, N.J., & Ollendick, T.H. (1989) Children's Anxiety and Phobic Disorders in School Settings: Classification, Assessment, and Intervention Issues. *Review of Educational Research* 59:431–470.

King, T.W. (1991) A Signalling Device for Non-Oral Communicators. *Language, Speech, and Hearing Services in Schools* 22:277–282.

Kirk, S.A., McCarthy, J.J., & Kirk, W.D. (1968) *Illinois Test of Psycholinguistic Abilities,* rev. ed. Urbana: University of Illinois Press.

Kirschenbaum, R. (1988) Methods for Identifying the Gifted and Talented. *Journal for the Education of the Gifted* 11:53–63.

Kister, M.C., & Patterson, C.B. (1980) Children's Conceptions of the Causes of Illness: Understanding of Contagion and Use of Immanent Justice. *Child Development* 51:839–846.

Kistner, J., Haskett, M., White, K., & Robbins, F. (1987) Perceived Competence and Self-Worth of LD and Normally Achieving Students. *Learning Disabilities Quarterly* 10:37–44.

Kitano, H.H.L., & Daniels, R. (1988) *Asian Americans: Emerging Minorities.*, Englewood Cliffs, N.J.: Prentice-Hall.

Klein, B., Van Hasselt, V.B., Trefelner, M., Sandstrom, D.J., & Brandt-Snyder, P. (1988) The Parent and Toddler Training Project for Visually Impaired and Blind Multihandicapped Children. *Journal of Visual Impairment & Blindness* 82:59–64.

Klein, N., & Sheehan, R. (1987) Staff Development: A Key Issue in Meeting the Needs of Young Handicapped Children in Day Care Settings. *Topics in Early Childhood Special Education* 7:13–27.

Klerman, L.V. (1991a) The Association between Adolescent Parenting and Childhood Poverty. In A.C. Huston (ed.), *Children in Poverty.* New York: Cambridge University Press, 79–105.

Klerman, L.V. (1991b) The Health of Poor Children: Problems and Programs. In A.C. Huston (ed.), *Children in Poverty.* New York: Cambridge University Press, 136–158.

Klimoski, R., & Palmer, S.N. (1995) The ADA and the Hiring Process in Organizations. In S.M. Bruyere & J. O'Keeffe (eds.) *Implications of the Americans with Disabilities Act for Psychology.* New York: American Psychological Association and Springer Pub. Co. 37–85.

Kline, R.B., Snyder, J., Guilmette, S., & Castellanos, M. (1993) External Validity of the Profile Variability Index for the K-ABC, Stanford-Binet, and WISC-R: Another Cul-de-Sac. *Journal of Learning Disabilities* 26:557–567.

Kluwin, T. (ed.) (1990) *The Affective Costs of Mainstreaming,* Progress Report no. 4, Washington, D.C.: Gallaudet Research Institute.

Kluwin, T.N. (1993) Cumulative Effects of Mainstreaming on the Achieve-

ment of Deaf Adolescents. *Exceptional Children* 60:73–81.

Kluwin, T.N., & Moores, D.F. (1985) The Effects of Integration on the Mathematics Achievement of Hearing-Impaired Adolescents. *Exceptional Children* 52:153–160.

Knight, C.J., Peterson, R.L., & McGuire, B. (May 1982) Cooperative Learning: A New Approach to an Old Idea. *Teaching Exceptional Children* 233–238.

Knitzer, J., & Aber, L. (1995) Young Children in Poverty: Facing the Facts. *American Journal of Orthopsychiatry* 65: 174–176.

Knowlton, H.E., & Clark, G.M. (1987) Transition Issues for the 1990s. *Exceptional Children* 53:562–563.

Kobayashi-Winata, H., & Power, T.G. (1989) Child Rearing and Compliance: Japanese and American Families in Houston. *Journal of Cross-Cultural Psychology* 10:333–356.

Koegel, R.L., Schreibman, L., Britten, K.R., Burke, J.C., & O'Neill, R.E. (1982) A Comparison of Parent Training to Direct Child Treatment. In R.L. Koegel, A. Rincover, & A.L. Egel (eds.), *Educating and Understanding Autistic Children* San Diego, Calif.: College Hill, 260–279.

Koehler, W.S., & Loftin, M.M. (1993) Full-Service Utilization Through an Existing Orientation: A New Model for Residential Schools. *Journal of Visual Impairment & Blindness* 87:199–201.

Koeske, G.F., & Koeske, R.D. (1990) The Buffering Effect of Social Support on Parental Stress. *American Journal of Orthopsychiatry* 58:440–451.

Kogan, M.D., Alexander, G.R., Kotelchuck, M., Nagey, D.A., & Jack, B.W. (1994) Comparing Mothers' Reports on the Content of Prenatal Care Received with Recommended National Guidelines for Care. *Public Health Reports* 109: 637–647.

Kogan, N. (1983) Stylistic Variation in Childhood and Adolescence: Creativity, Metaphor, and Cognitive Style. In P.H. Mussen (ed.), *Handbook of Child*

Psychology (3d ed.) New York: Mc-Graw-Hill.

Kohen, D.P. (March/April 1987) Childhood Asthma. *Children Today*, 6–10.

Kolata, G. (5 December 1989). Understanding Down Syndrome: A Chromosome Holds the Key. *New York Times*, p. C3.

Kolata, G. (7 November 1986) Two Disease-Causing Genes Found. *Science* 234:669–670.

Kolitch, E.R., & Brody, L.E. (1992) Mathematics Acceleration of Highly Talented Students: An Evaluation. *Gifted Children Quarterly* 36:78–85.

Kondratas, A. (1991) Ending Homelessness: Policy Challenges. *American Psychologist* 46:1226–1232.

Konopasek, D.E. (1990) Priests on My Shoulder. In R.B. Rutherford, Jr. & S.A. DiGangi (eds.) *Severe Behavior Disorders of Children and Youth*, 13:11–17. Reston, Va.: Council for Children with Behavioral Disorders.

Konstantareas, M.M., Homatidis, S., & Busch, J. (1989) Cognitive, Communication, and Social Differences Between Autistic Boys and Girls. *Journal of Applied Developmental Psychology*, 10:411–424.

Korkman, M., & Pesonen, A.E. (1994) A Comparison of Neuropsychological Test Profiles of Children with Attention Deficit Hyperactivity Disorder and/or Learning Disorder. *Journal of Learning Disabilities* 27:383–392.

Kosslyn, S.M., & Koenig, O. (1992) *Wet Mind: The New Cognitive Neuroscience*. New York: The Free Press.

Kovacs, M., Goldston, D., & Iyengar, S. (1992) Intellectual Development and Academic Performance of Children with Insulin-Dependent Diabetes Mellitus: A Longitudinal Study. *Developmental Psychology* 28:676–685.

Kraaimaat, F.W., Janssen, P., & Rien, V.D.B. (1991) Social Anxiety and Stuttering. *Perceptual and Motor Skills* 72:766–771.

Kramer, L.R. (1986) Career Awareness and Personal Development: A Naturalistic Study of Gifted Adolescent Girls' Concerns. *Adolescence* 21:123–131.

Kramer, R.A., Allen, L, & Gergen, P.J. (1995) Health and Social Characteristics and Children's Cognitive Functioning: Results from a National Cohort. *American Journal of Public Health* 85: 312–318.

Kramer, R.A., LaRue, A., & Gergen, P.J. (1995) Health and Social Characteristics and Children's Cognitive Functioning: Results from a National Cohort. *American Journal of Public Health* 85: 312–318.

Krauthammer, C. (6 August 1990) The Tribalization of America. *Washington Post*, A-11.

Kulik, J., & Kulik, C. (1982) Effects of Ability Grouping on Secondary School Students. *American Educational Research Journal* 19:415[n]428.

Kulik, J., & Kulik, C. (1984) Effects of Accelerated Instruction on Students. *Review of Educational Research* 54:409–425.

Kulik, J., & Kulik, C. (1992) Meta-Analytic Findings on Grouping. *Gifted Children Quarterly* 36:73–78.

Kurdek, L.A. (1981) An Integrative Perspective on Children's Divorce Adjustment. *American Psychologist* 36:856–866.

Kvist, S.B.M., Rajantie, J., Kvist, M., & Siimes, M.A. (1991) Aggression: The Dominant Psychological Response in Children with Malignant Disease. *Psychological Reports* 68:1139–1150.

Laborde, P.R., & Seligman, M. (1991) Counseling Parents with Children with Disabilities: Rationale and Strategies. In M. Seligman (ed.) *The Family with a Handicapped Child*. Boston: Allyn & Bacon, 337–369.

Ladd, G. (1981) Social Skills and Peer Acceptance. Effects of a Social Learning Method for Training Verbal Social Skills. *Child Development* 52:171–178.

Laffoon, K.S., Jenkins-Friedman, R., & Tollefson, N. (1989) Causal Attributions of Underachieving Gifted, Achieving Gifted, and Non-Gifted Students. *Journal for the Education of the Gifted* 13:4–21.

LaFramboise, T.D., & Low, K.G. (1989) American Indian Children and Adolescents. In *Children of Color: Psychological Interventions with Minority Youth*. San Francisco: Jossey-Bass, 114–148.

Lajoie, S.P., & Shore, B.M. (1981) Three Myths: The Over-Representation of the Gifted Among Dropouts, Delinquents, and Suicides. *Gifted Child Quarterly* 25:138–141.

Lalas, J., & Wilson, T. (March/April 1993) New Technologies for ESL Students. *Media & Methods* 29:18–21.

Lamb, M.E., & Meyer, D.J. (1991) Fathers of Children with Special Needs. In M. Seligman (ed.) *The Family with a Handicapped Child*, 2d ed. Boston: Allyn & Bacon, 151–180.

Lambiotte, J.G., Dansereau, D.F., O'Donnell, A.M., Hall, R.H., & Rachlin, T.R. (1987) Manipulating Cooperative Scripts for Teaching and Learning. *Journal of Educational Psychology* 79:424–431.

Landau-Stanton, J., & Clements, C.D. and Associates (1993) *AIDS Health and Mental Health: A Primary Sourcebook*, New York: Brunner/Mazel.

Landesman-Dwyer, S. (1981) Living in the Community. *American Journal of Mental Deficiency* 86:223–234.

Landesman-Dwyer, S., & Emanuel, I. (1979) Smoking During Pregnancy. In J. Belsky (ed.) *In the Beginning*. New York: Columbia University Press, 1982, 37–42.

Larrivee, B. (1986) Effective Teaching for Mainstreamed Students Is Effective Teaching for All Students. *Teacher Education and Special Education* 9:172–179.

Larson, B.L., & Roberts, B.B. (1986) The Computer as a Catalyst for Mutual Support and Empowerment Among Learning Disabled Students. *Journal of Learning Disabilities* 19:52–55.

Larson, J. (1992) Understanding Stepfamilies. *American Demographics*, 36–42.

Larson, K.A., & Hammill, D.D. (1975) The Relationship of Selected Visual-Perceptual Abilities to School Learning. *Journal of Special Education* 9:281–291.

LaSasso, C.J. (1993) Reading Comprehension of Deaf Readers. *American Annals of the Deaf* 138:435–441.

Lass, N.J., Ruscello, D.M., Bradshaw, K.H., & Blankenship, B.L. (1991) Adolescents' Perceptions of Normal and Voice-Disordered Children. *Journal of Communication Disorders* 24:267–274.

Last, C.G. (1992) Anxiety Disorders in Childhood and Adolescence. In W.M. Reynolds (ed.), *Internalizing Disorders in Children and Adolescents*. New York: Wiley, 61–107.

Last, C.G., Francis, G., Hersen, M., Kazdin, A.E., & Strauss, C.C. (1987) Separation Anxiety and School Phobia: A Comparison Using DSM-III Criteria. *American Journal of Psychiatry* 144:653–657.

Lawrence, P.A. (1988) Basic Strategies for Mainstream Integration. *Academic Therapy* 23:349–355.

Lawton, M. (10 April 1991). More Than a Third of Teens Surveyed Say They Have Contemplated Suicide. *Education Week* 5.

Lazar, I., Darlington, R., Murray, H., Royce, J., & Snipper, A.S. (1982) Lasting Effects of Early Education: A Report from the Consortium for Longitudinal Studies. *Monographs of the Society for Research in Child Development* 47:2–3, serial number 195.

Lederberg, A.R. (1984) Interaction Between Deaf Preschoolers and Unfamiliar Hearing Adults. *Child Development* 55:598–606.

Lee, C.M., & Gotlib, I.H. (1994) Mental Illness and the Family. In L. L'Abate (ed.), *Handbook of Developmental Family Psychology and Psychopathology*. New York: Wiley, 243–264.

Lee, P.R., & Stewart, F.H. (1995) Editorial: Failing to Prevent Unintended Pregnancy Is Costly. *American Journal of Public Health* 85: 479–480.

Lee, V.L., Brooks-Gunn, J.L., & Schnur, E. (1988) Does Head Start Work? A One-Year Follow-Up Comparison of Disadvantaged Children Attending Head Start, No Preschool, and Other Preschool Programs. *Developmental Psychology* 24:210–223.

Leguire, L.E., Fellows, R.R., Rogers, G.I., Bremer, D.L., & Fillman, R.D. (1992) The CCH Vision Stimulation Program for Infants with Low Vision: Preliminary Results. *Journal of Visual Impairment & Blindness* 86:33–36.

Lehman, E.B., & Erdwins, C.J. (1981) The Social and Emotional Adjustment of Young, Intellectually Gifted Children. *Gifted Child Quarterly* 25:134–137.

Leister, C., Koonce, D., & Nisbet, S. (Winter 1993). Best Practices for Preschool Programs: An Update on Inclusive Settings. *Day Care and Early Education* 20:9–12.

Lenneberg, E.H. (1967) *Biological Foundations of Language*. New York: Wiley.

Leon, G.R., Kendall, P.C., & Garber, J. (1980) Depression in Children: Parent, Teacher, and Child Perspectives. *Journal of Abnormal Child Psychology* 8:221–235.

Leonard, L. (1990) Language Disorders in Preschool Children. In G.H. Shames & E.H. Wiig (eds.), *Human Communication Disorders,* 3d ed. Columbus, Ohio: Merrill, 159–193.

Leonard, L. (1994) Language Disorders in Preschool Children. In G.H. Shames, E.H. Wiig & W.A. Secord (eds.) *Human Communication Disorders* (4th ed.). New York: Macmillan, 35–82.

Lepper, M.R., & Gurtner, J.L. (1989) Children and Computers: Approaching the Twenty-First Century. *American Psychologist* 44:170–179.

Lequerica, M. (1993) Stress in Immigrant Families with Handicapped Children: A Child Advocacy Approach. *American Journal of Orthopsychiatry* 63:545–552.

Lerner, J. (1988) *Learning Disabilities*. Boston, Mass.: Houghton-Mifflin.

Leslie, A. (1987) Pretense and Representation: The Origins of "Theory of Mind." *Psychological Review* 94:412–426.

Lester, B.M., Corwin, J.J., Sepkowski, C., Seifer, R., Peucker, M., McClaughlin, S., & Golub, H.L. (1991) Neurobehavioral Syndromes in Cocaine-Exposed Newborn Infants. *Child Development* 53:687–692.

Lester, B.M., & Dreher, M. (1989) Effects of Marijuana Use During Pregnancy on Newborn Cry. *Child Development* 60:765–771.

Levin, E.K., Zigmond, N., & Birch, J.W. (1985) A Follow-Up Study of 52 Learning Disabled Adolescents. *Journal of Learning Disabilities* 18:2–7.

Levy, C., & Meek, L. (1992) Performing Arts: An Example of Excellence in Vocational Arts Education. *The Journal of Physical Education, Recreation & Dance* 63: 36–39.

Levy, J.M., Jessop, D.J., Rimmerman, A., & Levy, P.H. (1992) Attitudes of Fortune 500 Corporate Executives toward the Employability of Persons with Severe Disabilities: A National Study. *Mental Retardation* 30:67–75.

Lewandowski, L.J., & Cruickshank, W.M. (1980) Psychological Development of Crippled Children and Youth. In W.M. Cruickshank (ed.), *Psychology of Exceptional Children and Youth* (4th ed.). Englewood Cliffs, N.J.: Prentice-Hall, 345–381.

Lewinsohn, P.M. (1974) A Behavioral Approach to Depression. In R.J. Friedman & M.M. Katz (eds.) *The Psychology of Depression: Contemporary Theory and Research*. Washington, D.C.: Winston-Wiley.

Lewinsohn, P.M., & Graf, M. (1973) Pleasant Activities and Depression. *Journal of Consulting and Clinical Psychology* 41:261–268.

Lewinsohn, P.M., & Libet, J. (1972) Pleasant Events, Activity Schedules, and Depression. *Journal of Abnormal Psychology* 79:294.

Lewis, B.A., & Freebairn, L. (1992) Residual Effects of Preschool Phonology Disorders in Grade School, Adolescence, and Adulthood. *Journal of Speech and Hearing Research* 35:819–831.

Lewis, M.E. (March/April 1991) Using Videodiscs in ESL and LEP Classes. *Media & Methods* 27:24.

Lewis, R.B. (1993) *Special Education Technology*, Pacific Groves, Calif.: Brooks/Cole.

Lewis, R.B. (1994) *Special Education Technology*, Pacific Grove, Calif.: Brooks/Cole.

Lewis, R.B., & Doorlag, D.H. (1987) *Teaching Special Students in the Mainstream*, 2d ed. Columbus, Ohio: Merrill.

Lewis, R.G., & Ho, M.K. (1979) Social Work with Native Americans. *Social Work* 20:379–392.

Leyser, Y., & Gottlieb, J. (1980) Improving the Social Status of Rejected Pupils. *Exceptional Children* 46:459–461.

Lezak, M.D., & O'Brien, K.P. (1988) Longitudinal Study of Emotional, Social, and Physical Changes After Traumatic Brain Injury. *Journal of Learning Disabilities* 21:436–463.

Lieberman, L.M. (1981) The LD Adolescent . . . When Do You Stop? *Journal of Learning Disabilities* 14:425–426.

Lieberman, L.M. (1991) Preserving Special Education . . . For Those Who Need It. In S. Stainback & W. Stainback (eds.) *Controversial Issues Confronting Special Education*. Needham Heights, Mass.: Allyn and Bacon, 13–27.

Liebert, D., Lutsky, L., & Gottlieb, A. (1990) Postsecondary Experiences of Young Adults with Severe Physical Disabilities. *Exceptional Children* 56:56–62.

Liebert, R.M., & Sprafkin, J. (1988) *The Early Window: Effects of Television on Children and Youth*, 3rd ed. New York: Pergamon Press.

Lilly, M.S. (1986) The Relationship between General and Specific Education: A New Face on an Old Issue. *Counterpoint* 6:10.

Lilly, M.S. (1992) Labeling: A Tired, Overworked, Yet Unresolved Issue in Special Education. In S. Stainback & W. Stainback (eds.) *Controversial Issues Confronting Special Education*. Needham Heights, Mass.: Allyn and Bacon, 85–97.

Lindsey, J.D. (1993) Computer Terms. In J.D. Linsey (ed.), *Computers and Ex-ceptional Individuals* (2d ed.). Austin, Texas: Pro-Ed, 337–349.

Linehan, S.A., Brady, M.P., & Hwang, C. (1991) Ecological Versus Developmental Assessment: Influences on Instructional Expectations. *Journal of the Association for Persons with Severe Handicaps* 16:146–153.

Lipsky, D.K., & Gartner, A. (1991) Achieving Full Inclusion: Placing the Student at the Center of Educational Reform. In S. Stainback & W. Stainback (eds.) *Controversial Issues Confronting Special Education*. Needham Heights, Mass.: Allyn and Bacon, 3–13.

Locke, J.L. (1983) Clinical Phonology: The Explanation and Treatment of Speech Sound Disorders. *Journal of Speech and Hearing Disorders* 48:339–341.

Loeb, R.C., & Jay, G. (1987) Self-Concept in Gifted Children: Differential Impact in Boys and Girls. *Gifted Child Quarterly* 31:9–14.

Longo, D.C., & Bond, L. (1984) Families of the Handicapped Child: Research and Practice. *Family Relations* 33:57–65.

Longstreth, L.E. (1981) Revisiting Skeel's Final Study: A Critique. *Developmental Psychology* 17:620–625.

Losen, S.M., & Diament, B. (1978) *Parent Conferences in the Schools*, Boston: Allyn & Bacon.

Lovaas, O.I. (1987) Behavioral Treatment and Normal Educational and Intellectual Functioning in Young Autistic Children. *Journal of Consulting and Clinical Psychology* 55:3–9.

Lovaas, O.I., & Newsom, C.D. (1976) Behavior Modification with Psychotic Children. In H. Leitenbery (ed.), *Handbook of Behavior Modification and Behavior Therapy*. Englewood Cliffs, N.J.: Prentice-Hall.

Lovaas, O.I., Schreibman, L., Koegel, R.L., & Rehm, R. (1971) Selective Responding by Autistic Children to Multiple Sensory Input. *Journal of Abnormal Psychology* 77:211–222.

Lovaas, O.I., Smith, T., & McEachin, J.J. (1989) Clarifying Comments on the Young Autism Study: Replay to Schopler, Short, and Mesibov. *Journal of Consulting and Clinical Psychology* 57:165–167.

Lovatt, M. (1962) Autistic Children in a Day Nursery. *Exceptional Children* 29:103–108.

Lovett, D.L., & Harris, M.B. (1987) Important Skills for Adults with Mental Retardation: The Client's Point of View. *Mental Retardation* 25:351–356.

Lovett, M.W., Borden, S.L., DeLuca, T., Lacerenza, L., Benson, N.J., & Brackstone, D. (1994) Treating the Core Deficits of Developmental Dyslexia: Evidence of Transfer of Learning After Phonologically-and Strategy-Based Reading Training Programs. *Developmental Psychology* 30: 805–822.

Lovitt, T.C. (1989) *Introduction to Learning Disabilities*. Boston: Allyn & Bacon.

Ludlow, B.L. (1982) *Teaching the Learning Disabled*. Bloomington, Ind.: Phi Delta Kappa.

Ludlow, B.L., & Sobey, R. (1984) *The School's Role in Educating Severely Handicapped Students*, Bloomington, Ind.: Phi Delta Kappan Educational Foundation.

Lustig, S.R. (1994) The AIDS Prevention Magic Show: Avoiding the Tragic with Magic. *Public Health Reports* 109:162–167.

Lyen, K.R. (1984) Juvenile Diabetes. In J. Fithian (ed.), *Understanding the Child with a Chronic Illness in the Classroom*. Phoenix, Ariz.: Oryx Press, 40–56.

Lynas, W. (1988) Sign Systems in Special Education: Some Experiences of Their Use with Deaf Children. *Children, Language Teaching and Therapy* 4:251–270.

Lynch, E.W., Lewis, R.B., & Murphy, D.S. (1992) Educational Services for Children with Chronic Illnesses: Perspectives of Educators and Families. *Exceptional Children* 59:210–220.

Lynch, E.W., & Stein, R.C. (1987) Parent Participation by Ethnicity: A Comparison of Hispanic, Black, and Anglo Families. *Exceptional Children* 54:105–111.

Lyon, M.A. (1995) A Comparison Between WISC-III and WISC-R Scores for Learning Disabilities Reevaluations. *Journal of Learning Disabilities* 28: 253–255.

Lyon, S.R., & Lyon, G.A. (1991) Collaboration with Families of Persons with Severe Disabilities. In M. Seligman (ed.) *The Family with a Handicapped Child*, 2d ed. Boston: Allyn & Bacon, 237–262.

Maag, J.W., & Behrens, J.T. (1989) Depression and Cognitive Self-Statements of Learning Disabled and Seriously Emotionally Disturbed Adolescents. *Journal of Special Education* 23:17–27.

Maag, J.W., & Howell, K.W. (1991) Serving Troubled Youth or A Troubled Society? *Exceptional Children* 57:74–76.

MacArthur, C.A., & Schneiderman, B. (1986) Learning Disabled Students' Difficulties in Learning To Use a Word Processor: Implications for Instruction and Software Evaluation. *Journal of Learning Disabilities* 19:248–253.

MacCuspie, P.A., Harmer, D., McConnell, J., Fricker, J., & Johnson, J. (1993) Short-Term Placements: A Crucial Role for Residential Schools. *Journal of Visual Impairment & Blindness* 87:193–199.

MacDougall, J.C. (1991) Current Issues in Deafness: A Psychological Perspective. *Canadian Psychology* 32:612–627.

MacKinnon, D. (1978) *In Search of Human Effectiveness*, Buffalo, N.Y.: Creative Education Foundation.

Macmillan, D.L., Jones, R.L., & Olia, G.F. (1974) The Mentally Retarded Label: A Theoretical Analysis and Review of Research. *American Journal of Mental Deficiency* 79:241–261.

Madden, N.A., & Slavin, R.E. (1983) Mainstreaming Students with Mild Handicaps: Academic and Social Outcomes. *Review of Educational Research* 53:519–569.

Maddox, C.D., Scheiber, L.M., & Bass, J.E. (1982) Self-Concept and Social Distance in Gifted Children. *Gifted Child Quarterly* 26:77–81.

Madge, S., Affleck, J., & Lowenbraun, S. (1990) Social Effects of Integrated Classrooms and Resource Room/Regular Class Placements on Elementary Students with Learning Disabilities. *Journal of Learning Disabilities* 23:440–445.

Madison, C.L., & Gerlitz, D.M. (1991) Children's Perceptions of Lisping and Nonlisping Female Peers. *Child Study Journal* 21:277–284.

Maheady, L., Sacca, M.K., & Harper, G.F. (1988) Classwide Peer Tutoring with Mildly Handicapped High School Students. *Exceptional Children* 55:52–59.

Makas, E. (1988) Positive Attitudes Towards Disabled People: Disabled and Nondisabled Persons' Perspective. *Journal of Social Issues* 44:49–63.

Maker, C.J. (1987) Gifted and Talented. In V. Richardson-Koehler (ed.), *Educators' Handbook: A Research Perspective*. New York: Longman, 420–457.

Maker, J. (1986) Developing Scope and Sequence in Curriculum. *Gifted Child Quarterly* 30:151–158.

Male, M. (1993) *Technology for Inclusion*, Boston: Allyn & Bacon.

Male, M. (1994) *Technology for Inclusion*, Boston: Allyn & Bacon.

Malott, R.W., Whaley, D.L., & Malott, M.E. (1993) *Elementary Principles of Behavior* (2d ed.), Englewood Cliff, N.J.: Prentice Hall.

Manaster, G.J., Chan, J.C., Watt, C., & Wiehe, J. (1994) Gifted Adolescents' Attitudes Toward Their Giftedness: A Partial Replication. *Gifted Child Quarterly* 38: 176–178.

Mandell, C.J., & Fiscus, E. (1981) *Understanding Exceptional People*. St. Paul, Minn.: West Publishing Co.

Mandell, C.J., & Gold, V. (1984) *Teaching Handicapped Students*. St. Paul, Minn.: West Publishing Co.

Mandell, C.J., & Mandell, S.L. (1989) *Computers in Education Today*, St. Paul, Minn.: West Publishing Co.

Mango, K. (1991) *Hearing Loss*, New York: Franklin Watts.

Mann, L. (1987a) Health Impairments. In C.R. Reynolds (ed.), *Encyclopedia of Special Education*. New York: Wiley, 765–766.

Mann, L. (1987b) Orthopedic Impairment. In C.R. Reynolds (ed.), *Encyclopedia of Special Education*. New York: Wiley, 1134–1135.

Mann, V.A. (1989) The Learning Mystique: A Fair Appraisal, A Fruitful New Direction? *Journal of Learning Disabilities* 22:283–286.

Manning, M.L. (Jan. 1986) How Teachers Can Help the Child Nobody Likes. *Education Digest* 49–51.

Mansfield, R.S., Bussen, T.V., & Krepelka, E.J. (1978) The Effectiveness of Creativity Training. *Review of Educational Research* 48:517–536.

Marcenko, M.O., & Meyers, J.C. (1991) Mothers of Children with Developmental Disabilities. *Family Relations* 40:186–190.

March of Dimes (1986) *Sickle Cell Anemia*, Public Health Education Information Sheet: Genetic Series.

March of Dimes (1987A) *Down Syndrome*. Public Health Education Information Sheet: Genetic Series.

March of Dimes (1987B) *Congenital AIDS*. Public Health Information Sheet.

March of Dimes (1990) personal communication.

March of Dimes (1992) *Spina Bifida*, White Plains, N.Y.: March of Dimes.

Marczely, B. (1993) The Americans With Disabilities Act: Confronting the Shortcomings of Section 504 in Public Education. *West's Education Law Reporter* 78:199–207.

Margolis, H., & McGettigan, J. (1988) Managing Resistance to Instructional Modifications to Mainstreamed Environments. *Remedial and Special Education* 9:15–21.

Marland, S. (1972) *Education of the Gifted and Talented: Report to the Congress of the United States by the U.S. Commissioner of Education*, Washington, D.C.: U.S. Government Printing Office.

Marquardt, T.P., Stoll, J., & Sussman, H. (1988) Disorders of Communication in Acquired Cerebral Trauma. *Journal of Learning Disabilities* 21:340–352.

Martens, D.M. (1989) Social Experiences of Hearing-Impaired High School Youth. *American Annals of the Deaf* 134:15–19.

Martin, D.A. (1988a) Children and Adolescents with Traumatic Brain Injury: Impact on the Family. *Journal of Learning Disabilities* 21:464–470.

Martin, F.N. (1990) Hearing and Hearing Disorders. In G.H. Shames & E.H. Wiig (ed.), *Human Communication Disorders: An Introduction* (3d ed.). Columbus, Ohio: Merrill, 350–393.

Martin, H. (1978) A Child-Oriented Approach to Prevention of Abuse. In A.W. Franklin (ed.), *Child Abuse: Prediction, Prevention and Follow-Up.* London: Churchill-Livingston, 9–20.

Martin, R. (1988b) Legal Challenges in Educating Traumatic Brain Injured Students. *Journal of Learning Disabilities* 21:471–475, 485.

Martin, S.L., Ramey, C.T., & Ramey, S. (1990) The Prevention of Intellectual Impairment in Children of Impoverished Families: Findings of a Randomized Trial of Educational Day Care. *American Journal of Public Health* 80:844–847.

Marston, D. (1987–1988) The Effectiveness of Special Education: A Time Series Analysis of Reading Performance in Regular and Special Education Settings. *Journal of Special Education* 21:13–26.

Marston, D., & Magnusson, D. (1985) Implementing Curriculum-Based Measurement in Special and Regular Education Settings. *Exceptional Children* 51:266–276.

Mason, J.O. (1993) The Dimensions of an Epidemic of Violence. *Public Health Reports* 108: 1–4.

Massachusetts Eye and Ear Infirmary (1992) *Physician's Report: Understanding Voice and Its Disorders.* Boston, Mass.: Massachusetts Eye and Ear Infirmary.

Matheny, A.P., Dolan, A.B., & Wilson, R.S. (1976) Twins with Academic Learning Problems: Antecedent Characteris-

tics. *American Journal of Orthopsychiatry* 46:464–469.

Matthews, R.M., Whang, P.L., & Fawcett, S.B. (1982) Behavioral Assessment of Occupational Skills of Learning Disabled Adolescents. *Journal of Learning Disabilities* 15:38–41.

Matson, J.L., Sadowski, C., Matese, M., & Benavidez, D. (1993) Empirical Study of Mental Health Professionals' Knowledge and Attitudes Towards the Concept of Age Appropriateness. *Mental Retardation* 31:540–545.

Maxson, B.J., Tedder, N.E., Marmion, S., & Lamb, A.M. (1993) The Education of Youths Who Are Deaf-Blind: Learning Tasks and Teaching Methods. *Journal of Visual Impairment & Blindness* 87:259–262.

Mayer, P., & Lowenbraun, S. (1990) Total Communication Use Among Elementary Teachers of Hearing-Impaired Children. *American Annals of the Deaf* 135:257–263.

Mayes, L.C., Granger, R.H., Bornstein, M.H., & Zuckerman, B. (1992) The Problem of Prenatal Cocaine Exposure: A Rush to Judgment. *JAMA* 267:406–408.

McBride, B.A. (1990) The Effects of a Parent Education/Play Group Program on Father Involvement in Child Rearing. *Family Relations* 39:250–256.

McBroom, L. W., & Tedder, N.E. (1993) Transitional Services for Youths Who Are Visually Impaired. *Journal of Visual Impairment & Blindness* 87:69–72.

McCabe, M.P. (1993) Sex Education Programs for People with Mental Retardation. *Mental Retardation* 31:377–387.

McCaughrin, W.B., Ellis, W.K., Rusch, F.R., & Heal, L.W. (1993) Cost-Effectiveness of Supported Employment. *Mental Retardation* 31:41–48.

McCauley, K. (1992) Preventing Child Abuse through the Schools. *Children Today.* Washington, D.C.: Administration for Children and Families, Department of Health & Human Services, 21:8–11.

McCauley, R., Kennedy, P., & Bruincks, R. (1976) Behavioral Interactions of Hearing-Impaired Children in Regu-

lar Classrooms. *Journal of Special Education* 10:277–284.

McClaren, J., & Bryson, S.E. (1987) Review of Recent Epidemiological Studies of Mental Retardation: Prevalence, Associated Disorders, and Etiology. *American Journal on Mental Retardation* 92:243–254.

McClure, G.T., & Piel, E. (1978) College-Bound Girls and Science Careers: Perception of Barriers and Facilitating Factors. *Journal of Vocational Behavior* 12:172–183.

McConnell, B.B. (1981) Individualized Bilingual Instruction: A Validated Program Model Effective with Bilingual Handicapped Children. Cited in L. Baca & K.C. Harris (1988) Teaching Migrant Exceptional Children. *Teaching Exceptional Children*, 32–35.

McCrone, W.P. (1994) A Two-Year Report Card on Title I of the Americans with Disabilities Act: Implications for Rehabilitation Counseling with Deaf People. *Journal of Rehabilitation of the Deaf* 28:1–20.

McCubbin, M.A., & Huang, S.T.T. (1989) Family Strengths in the Care of Handicapped Children: Targets for Intervention. *Family Relations* 38:436–443.

McDonnell, A.P., & Hardman, M.L. (1989) The Desegregation of America's Special Schools: Strategies for Change. *Journal of the Association for Persons with Severe Handicaps* 14:68–74.

McDonnell, J., Hardman, M., Hightower, J., & Kiefer-O'Donnell, R. (1991) Variables Associated with In-School and After-School Integration of Secondary Students with Severe Disabilities. *Education and Training in Mental Retardation* 26:243–255.

McFarland, W.B., & Simmons, F.B. (1980) The Importance of Early Intervention with Severe Childhood Deafness. *Pediatric Annual* 9:13.

McGinnis, E., & Arnold, G. (1984) Skillstreaming the Elementary School Child. Champaign, Ill.: Research Press Company.

McGinnis, E., & Arnold, G. (1990) Skillstreaming in Early Childhood. Champaign, Ill.: Research Press Company.

McIntosh, R., Vaughn, S., & Zaragoza, N. (1991) A Review of Social Interventions for Students with Learning Disabilities. *Journal of Learning Disabilities* 24:451–457.

McKimmey, M.A. (1993) Play and Its Relationship to Language Development. *Children Today* 22: 14–16.

McKinney, J.D., & Fegans, L. (Summer 1984) Academic and Behavioral Characteristics of Learning Disabled Children and Average Achievers: Longitudinal Studies. *Learning Disabilities Quarterly* 7:251–255.

McKinney, J.D., & Hocutt, A.M. (1988) The Need for Policy Analysis in Evaluating the Regular Education Initiative. *Journal of Learning Disabilities* 21:12–18.

McLanahan, S.S., Astone, N.M., & Marks, N.F. (1991) The Role of Mother-Only Families in Reproducing Poverty. In A.C. Huston (ed.), *Children in Poverty*. New York: Cambridge University Press, 51–79.

McLaughlin, B. (1977) Second-Language Learning in Children. *Psychological Bulletin* 84:438–459.

McLaughlin, B. (1978) *Second-Language Acquisition in Childhood*, Hillsdale, N.J.: Erlbaum.

McLeskey, J., & Grizzle, K.L. (1992) Grade Retention Rates Among Students with Learning Disabilities. *Exceptional Children* 58:548–554.

McLeskey, J., & Pacchiano, D. (1994) Mainstreaming Students with Learning Disabilities. *Exceptional Children* 60:508–517.

McLeskey, J., & Waldron, N.L. (1991) Identifying Students with Learning Disabilities: The Effects of Implementing Statewide Guidelines. *Journal of Learning Disabilities* 24:501–507.

McLeskey, J., Waldron, N.L., & Wornhoff, S.A. (1990) Factors Influencing the Identification of Black and White Students with Learning Disabilities. *Journal of Learning Disabilities* 23:362–366.

McLin, W.M. (1992) Introduction to Issues in Psychology and Epilepsy. *American Psychologist* 47:1124–1125.

McLoyd, V.C., & Wilson, L. (1991) The Strain of Living Poor: Parenting, Social Support, and Child Mental Health. In A.C. Huston (ed.), *Children in Poverty*. New York: Cambridge University Press, 105–136.

McWilliams, C., & Hillegass, J. (1989) Student Produced Film, TV, and Video. *Media & Methods* 28:34–37.

Meadow, K. (1984) Social Adjustment of Preschool Children: Deaf and Hearing With and Without Other Handicaps. *Topics in Early Childhood Special Education* 3:4, 27–40.

Meichenbaum, D., & Goodman, J. (1971) Training Impulsive Children to Talk to Themselves. *Journal of Abnormal Psychology* 77:115–126.

Meisels, S.J. (1989) Meeting the Mandate of Public Law 99-457: Early Childhood Intervention in the Nineties. *American Journal of Orthopsychiatry* 59:451–460.

Melton, G.B., & Davidson, H.A. (1987) Child Protection and Society: When Should the State Intervene? *American Psychologist* 42:172–176.

Mercer, C.D. (1986) Learning Disabilities. In N.G. Haring & L. McCormick (eds.) *Exceptional Children and Youth* 4th ed. Columbus, Ohio: Merrill, 119–153.

Mercer, C.D., Hughes, C., & Mercer, A.R. (1985) Learning Disabilities Definitions Used by State Education Departments. *Learning Disabilities Quarterly* 8:45–55.

Mercer, C.D., King-Sears, P., & Mercer, A.R. (1990) Learning Disabilities Definitions and Criteria Used by State Education Departments. *Learning Disabilities Quarterly* 13:141–152.

Mercer, J., & Lewis, J. (1981) *System of Multicultural Pluralistic Assessment*. New York: Psychological Corporation.

Mergendoller, J.R., & Marchman, V.A. (1987) Friends and Associates. In V. Richardson-Koehler (ed.) *Educator's Handbook*. New York: Longman, 297–329.

Mertens, D.M. (1989) Social Experiences of Hearing-Impaired High School Youth. *American Annals of the Deaf* 134:15–19.

Mervine, P.L. (July/August 1992) "Mini" Communication Boards. *Exceptional Parent*, 22–25.

Metcoff, J., Coistiloe, P., Crosby, W.M., Sandstread, H.H., & Milne, D., (1989) Smoking in Pregnancy: Relation of Birth Weight to Maternal Plasma Carotene and Cholesterol Levels. *Obstetrics and Gynecology* 302:302–308.

Meyer, L.H., Peck, C.A., & Brown, L. (1991) *Critical Issues in the Lives of People With Severe Disabilities*, Baltimore, Md.: Paul H. Brookes.

Michaelson, C. (November 1, 1993) State Revising Draft Policy on Inclusion. *New York Teacher*, 3.

Midence, K. (1994) The Effects of Chronic Illness on Children and Their Families: An Overview. *Genetic, Social, and General Psychology Monographs* 120: 309–326.

Milburn, N., & D'Ercole, A. (1991) Homeless Women, Children, and Families. *American Psychologist* 46:1159–1160.

Miller, A. (1986) Performance Impairment After Failure: Mechanism and Sex Differences. *Journal of Educational Psychology* 78:486–491.

Miller, C. (1993) A Model for Outreach Technical Assistance. *Journal of Visual Impairment & Blindness* 87:201–204.

Miller, J.M. (1993) Augmentative and Alternative Communication. In M.E. Snell (ed.), *Instruction of Students with Severe Disabilities* (4th ed.). New York: Merrill, 319–347.

Miller-Jones, D. (1989) Culture and Testing. *American Psychologist* 44:360–367.

Minnett, A., Clark, K., & Wilson, G. (1994) Play Behavior and Communication between Deaf and Hard of Hearing Children and Their Hearing Peers in an Integrated Preschool. *American Annals of the Deaf* 139: 420–429.

Minskoff, E.H., Sautter, S.W., Hoffmann, F.J., & Hawks, R. (1987) Employer Attitudes Toward Hiring the Learning Disabled. *Journal of Learning Disabilities* 20:53–57.

Minskoff, E.H., Sautter, S.W., Steidle, E.F., & Hoffmann, J.F. (1989) A Homogeneous Group of Persons with Learning Disabilities: Adults with Severe Learning Disabilities in Vocational Rehabilitation. *Journal of Learning Disabilities* 22:537–543.

Minuchin, P.P., & Shapiro, E.K. (1983) The School as a Context for Social Development. In E.M. Hetherington (ed.), *Handbook of Child Psychology: Socialization, Personality, and Social Development*, vol. 4. New York: Wiley, 197–275.

Mira, M.P., & Tyler, J.S. (1991) Students with Traumatic Brain Injury: Making the Transition from Hospital to School. *Focus on Exceptional Children* 23:1–12.

Mirenda, P., & Schuyler, A. (1988) Augmenting Communication for Persons with Autism: Issues and Strategies. *Topics in Language Disorders* 9:24–43.

Moffitt, T.E. (1990) Juvenile Delinquency and Attention Deficit Disorder: Boys' Developmental Trajectories from Age 13 to Age 15. *Child Development* 61:893–910.

Mokros, J.R., & Russell, S.J. (1986) Learner-Centered Software: A Survey of Microcomputer Use with Special Needs Students. *Journal of Learning Disabilities* 19:185–189.

Moles, O.C. (November 1982) Synthesis of Recent Research on Parent Participation in Children's Education. *Educational Leadership* 44–47.

Molnar, J.M., Rath, W.R., & Klein, T.P. (1990) Constantly Compromised: The Impact of Homelessness on Children. *Journal of Social Issues* 46:109–124.

Montague, E.J. (1987) *Foundations of Secondary Classroom Instruction*, Columbus, Ohio: Merrill.

Montague, M. (1992) The Effects of Cognitive and Metacognitive Strategy Instruction on the Mathematical Problem Solving of Middle School Students with Learning Disabilities. *Journal of Learning Disabilities* 25:230–248.

Montague, M., & Bos, C. (1986) The Effect of Cognitive Strategy Training on Verbal Math Problem-Solving Performance of Learning Disabled Adolescents. *Journal of Learning Disabilities* 19:26–33.

Montgomery, M.S. (1994) Self-Concept and Children with Learning Disabilities: Observer-Child Concordance Across Six Context-Dependent Domains. *Journal of Learning Disabilities* 27:254–262.

Monmany, T., Levy-Spira, E., & Hager, M. (18 July 1988) Young Survivors in a Deadly War. *Newsweek*, 50–51.

Moon, M.S., & Inge, K. (1993) Vocational Preparation and Transition. In M.E. Snell (ed.), *Instruction of Students with Severe Disabilities* (4th ed.). New York: Merrill, 556–588.

Moore, G.P., & Hicks, D.M. (1994) Voice Disorders. In G.H. Shames, E.H. Wiig & W.A. Secord (eds.) *Human Communication Disorders* (4th ed.). New York: Macmillan, 292–335.

Moore, G.P. (1990) Voice Disorders. In G.H. Shames & E.H. Wiig (eds.), *Human Communication Disorders*, 3d ed. Columbus, Ohio: Merrill, 266–306.

Moore, K.L., & Persaud, T.V.N. (1993) *Before We Are Born*. Philadelphia: W.B. Saunders.

Moores, D.F. (1988) *Educating the Deaf* (3d ed.), Boston: Houghton Mifflin.

Moores, D.F. (1994) Postsecondary Education: A Success Story. *American Annals of the Deaf* 139:75.

Morgan, D., & York, M.E. (January 1981) Ideas for Mainstreaming Young Children. *Young Children* 36:22–23.

Morgan, R.L., Morre, S.C., McSweyn, C.A., & Salzberg, C.L. (1992) Transition from School to Work: Views of Secondary Special Educators. *Education and Training in Mental Retardation* 27:315–323.

Morine-Dershimer, G., & Beyerbach, B. (1987) Moving Right Along. . . . , In V. Richardson-Koehler (ed.), *Educators' Handbook*. New York: Longman, 207–233.

Morris, L., Warren, C.W., & Aral, S.O. (1993) Measuring Adolescent Sexual Behaviors and Related Health Outcomes. *Public Health Reports* 108:31–37.

Morris, M., & Levenberger, J. (1990) A Report of Cognitive, Academic, and Linguistic Profiles of College Students with and without Learning Disabilities. *Journal of Learning Disabilities* 23:355–360.

Morris, R.J., & Kratochwill, T.R. (1987) Dealing with Fear and Anxiety in the School Setting: Behavioral Approaches to Treatment. *Special Services in the Schools* 3:53–68.

Morrison, G.S. (1991) *Early Childhood Education Today*, 5th ed. New York: Merrill.

Morrison, M.M. (1982) Investigation of Variables Associated with the Reading Abilities of Eighty-Nine Secondary Deaf Students. Cited in C.M. Kampfe & A.G. Turecheck (1987) Reading Achievement of Prelingually Deaf Students and Its Relationship to Parental Method of Communication: A Review of the Literature. *American Annals of the Deaf* 127:11–15.

Morrow, R.D. (Nov 1987) Cultural Differences—Be Aware! *Academic Therapy* 23:143–149.

Morse, A., & Trief, E. (1985) Diagnosis and Evaluation of Visual Dysfunction in Premature Infants with Low Birth Weight. *Journal of Visual Impairment & Blindness* 79:248–251.

Moskowitz, C. (1988) Strategies for Mainstreamed Students. *Academic Therapy* 23:541–547.

Mueser, K.T., Valenti-Hein, D., & Yarnold, P.R. (1987) Dating Skills Groups for the Developmentally Disabled. *Behavior Modification* 11:200–228.

Munro, J.D. (1986) Epidemiology and the Extent of Mental Retardation. *Psychiatric Clinics of North America* 9:591–624.

Munson, S.M. (1986/1987) Regular Education Teacher Modifications for Mainstreamed Mildly Handicapped Students. *Journal of Special Education* 20:489–502.

Murphy, A., Paeschel, S., Duffy, T., & Brady, E. (1976) Meeting with Brothers and Sisters of Children with Down's Syndrome. *Children Today* 5:20–23.

Murphy, J.S., & Newton, B.J. (1987) Loneliness and the Mainstreamed Hearing-Impaired College Student. *American Annals of the Deaf* 132:21–35.

Murphy, V., & Hicks-Stewart, K. (1991) Learning Disabilities and Attention Deficit Hyperactivity Disorder: An Interactional Perspective. *Journal of Learning Disabilities* 24:386–388.

Murray, A.D. (1988) Newborn Auditory Brainstem-Evoked Responses (ABRs): Prenatal and Contemporary Correlates. *Child Development* 52:71–82.

Myles, B.S., & Simpson, R.L. (1989) Regular Educators' Modification Preferences for Mainstreaming Mildly Handicapped Children. *Journal of Special Education* 22:479–489.

Naeye, R.L., & Peters, E.C. (1984) Mental Development of Children Whose Mothers Smoked During Pregnancy. *Obstetrics and Gynecology* 64:601–607.

Naglieri, J.A., & Reardon, S.M. (1993) Traditional IQ Is Irrelevant to Learning Disabilities—Intelligence Is Not. *Journal of Learning Disabilities* 26:127–133.

NARIC (National Rehabilitation Information Center). (August 15, 1993) The Americans with Disabilities Act (ADA). A NARIC Resource Guide.

National Captioning Institute (1992) 1992 Brings Even More Captioned Programming from NCI. *Caption*, Falls Church, Va.: National Captioning Institute.

National Center for Education Statistics. (1992) *Digest of Education Statistics, 1992.* Washington, D.C.: Author.

National Center for Education Statistics. (1992) *Digest of Education Statistics, 1992.* Washington, D.C.: National Center for Educational Statistics, Table 50, p. 64.

National Center for Health Statistics (1990) Births, Marriages, Divorces, and Deaths for 1988. Monthly Vital Statistics Report, 38, no. 12, DHHS Pub no. (PHS) 90-1120.

National Commission on Excellence in Education (1983) *A Nation At Risk*, Washington, D.C.: author.

National Committee for Prevention of Child Abuse (NCPCA) (1994) *Current Trends in Child Abuse Reporting and Fatalities: The Results of the 1993 Annual Fifty-State Survey.* Chicago: NCPCA.

National Easter Seal Society (1991) *Awareness Is the First Step Toward Change*, Chicago, Ill.: National Easter Seal Society.

National Federation of the Blind (1991) *The Blind Child in the Regular Preschool Program*, Baltimore, Md.: author.

National Information Center for Children and Youth with Disabilities (NICHCY) (1993) *Emotional Disturbance.* Washington, D.C.: NICHCY.

National Information Center for Children and Youth with Disabilities (1992) *Visual Impairment*, Washington, D.C.: NICHCY.

National Institute of Child Health and Human Development (1986) *Prenatal and Perinatal Factors Associated with Brain Disorders*, Washington, D.C.: NICHD.

National Institute of Health (4 May 1988) *National Institutes of Health Consensus Development Conference Statement on Cochlear Implants*, Washington, D.C.: U.S. Department of Health and Human Services.

National Institute of Health (22–24 January 1990) *Noise and Hearing Loss (Consensus Statement from the NIH Consensus Development Conference)* vol. 8, no. 1, Bethesda, Md.: U.S. Department of Health and Human Services.

National Institute of Health (NIH) (1982) *Hearing Loss: Hope Through Research*, Bethesda, Md.: National Institutes of Health, NIH Pub no. 82-157.

National Institutes of Health (1986) *Spina Bifida*, Washington, D.C.: U.S. Dept. of Health and Human Services.

National Joint Committee on Learning Disabilities. (1988) Letter to NJCLD member organizations.

National Joint Committee on Learning Disabilities. (1993) Providing Appropriate Education for Students with Learning Disabilities in Regular Education Classrooms. *Journal of Learning Disabilities* 26:330–332.

National Joint Committee on Learning Disabilities, 1993, January. *A Reaction to "Full Inclusion": A Reaffirmation of the Right of Students with Learning Disabilities to a Continuum of Services*, author.

National Rehabilitation Information Center (December 1990) *Spinal Cord Injury: A NARIC Resource Guide for People with SCI and Their Families*, Washington, D.C.: NARIC.

National Society to Prevent Blindness (1988) *Don't Play Games with Your Eyes*, Schaumburg, Ill.: author.

National Society to Prevent Blindness (1989) *Major Causes of Vision Impairment in Adults.* Schaumburg, Il.: National Society to Prevent Blindness.

National Society to Prevent Blindness (1991) *Signs of Possible Eye Trouble in Children*, Schaumburg, Ill.: author.

National Society to Prevent Blindness (1992) *The Eye and How We See*, Schaumburg, Ill.: author.

National Society to Prevent Blindness (Summer 1993) Research Update. *Prevent Blindness News*, 2.

Navarick, D.J. (1979) *Principles of Learning: From Laboratory to Field*, Reading, Mass.: Addison-Wesley.

Nazarro, J.N. (ed.) (1981) *Culturally Diverse Exceptional Children.* Reston, Va.: Council for Exceptional Children.

NEA (1982) *Productive Relationships: Parent-School-Teacher*, Washington, D.C.: National Education Association.

Neiger, B.L., & Hopkins, R.W. (1988) Adolescent Suicide: Character Traits of High-Risk Teenagers. *Adolescence* 23:469–475.

Nelson, C.M. (1987) Behavioral Interventions: What Works and What Doesn't. *The Pointer*, 31:45–50.

Nelson, C.M., Center, D.B., Rutherford, R.B. Jr., & Walker, H.M. (1991) Serving Troubled Youth in a Troubled Society: A Replay to Maag and Howell. *Exceptional Children* 57:77–79.

Nelson, C.M., Rutherford, R.B. Jr., Center, D.B., & Walker, H.M. (1991) Do Public Schools Have an Obligation to

Serve Troubled Children and Youth? *Exceptional Children* 57:406–415.

Nelson, F.L. (1987) Evaluation of a Youth Suicide School Program. *Adolescence* 22:813–825.

Nelson, J.R., Smith, D.J., & Dodd, J.M. (1994) The Effects of Learning Strategy Instruction on the Completion of Job Applications by Students with Learning Disabilities. *Journal of Learning Disabilities* 27:104–110.

Nelson, K.A., & Dimitrova, E. (1993) Severe Visual Impairment in the United States and in Each State, 1990. *Journal of Visual Impairment & Blindness* 87:80–85.

Nelson, K.B., & Ellenberg, J.H. (1986) Antecedents of Cerebral Palsy. *New England Journal of Medicine* 315:81–86.

Neuspiel, D.R., & Hamel, S.C. (1991) Cocaine and Infant Behavior. *Developmental and Behavioral Pediatrics* 12:55–64.

Nevo, B. (1994) Definitions, Ideologies, and Hypotheses in Gifted Education. *Gifted Child Quarterly* 38: 184–186.

New York Regional Direction Center. (1988) *Helping the Preschool Child Who "Stutters."* New York: Regional Direction Center.

New York Relay Service (1992) *How Deaf People and Hearing People Can Talk by Telephone*, New York: AT&T.

New York State Department of Education (March 1982) *Alternative Testing Techniques for Children with Handicapping Conditions*. Albany, N.Y.: New York State Department of Education.

New York Times (15 September 1989) 14.

New York Times (July 23, 1993) Family's Battle to Put Child in Regular Classroom. *New York Times*, B5.

Newsday (12 March 1991) New Face of America, 10.

NICD (National Information Center on Deafness) (1987) *Educating Deaf Children: An Introduction*, Washington, D.C.: Gallaudet University.

NICD (National Information Center on Deafness) (1988) *The National Information Center on Deafness*, Washington, D.C.: Gallaudet University, no. 91-340-152.

NICD (National Information Center on Deafness) (1989) *Deafness: A Fact Sheet*, Washington, D.C.: Gallaudet.

NICHCY (1988) *Early Intervention for Children Birth Through 2 Years*, Washington, D.C.: NICHCY, News Digest #10.

NICHCY (1991) *Spina Bifida*, Washington, D.C.: National Information Center for Children and Youth with Disabilities.

NICHCY (1993) *Epilepsy*, Washington, D.C.: National Information Center for Children and Youth with Disabilities.

NICHCY (1993b) *Cerebral Palsy*, Washington, D.C.: National Information Center for Children and Youth with Disabilities.

NICHCY. (February 1990) *Individualized Education Programs*. Washington, D.C.: NICHCY.

NICHCY. (March 1993). Transition Services in the IEP. Washington, D.C.: NICHCY.

NICHCY (May 1992). *A Parent's Guide: Accessing Programs for Infants, Toddlers, and Preschoolers with Disabilities*, Washington, D.C.: Author.

NICHCY (National Information Center for Children and Youth with Disabilities) (1991) *General Information About Speech and Language Disorders*, Fact Sheet Number 11, Washington, D.C.: NICHCY.

NICHCY (National Information Center for Children and Youth with Disabilities) (1993) *Autism: Fact Sheet*, Washington, D.C.: author.

NICHCY (National Information Center for Children and Youth with Disabilities) (1993) *Mental Retardation*. Washington, D.C., NICHCY.

NICHCY. (September 1991) *Options After High School for Youth with Disabilities*. Washington, D.C.: NICHCY.

Nicholas, Geers, & Kozak (1994) Development of Communicative Function in Young Hearing-Impaired and Normally Hearing Children. *The Volta Review* 96: 113–135

Nietupski, S., McDonald, J. & Nietupski, J. (1992) Integrating Elementary Students with Multiple Disabilities into Supported Regular Classrooms. *Teaching Exceptional Children* 24:6–9.

Nihira, K., Foster, R., Shellhaas, M., & Leland, H. (1974) *AAMD Adaptive Behavior Scale* (rev. ed.). Washington, D.C.: American Association on Mental Deficiency.

Nippold, M.A., Schwarz, I.E., & Lewis, M. (1992) Analyzing the Potential Benefit of Microcomputer Use for Teaching Figurative Language. *American Journal of Speech-Language Pathology*. 1:36–43.

Nixon, H.L. (1994) Looking Sociologically at Family Coping with Visual Impairment. *Journal of Visual Impairment & Blindness* 87: 329–337.

Noh, S., Dumas, J.E., Wolf, L.C., & Fisman, S.N. (1989) Delineating Sources of Stress in Parents of Exceptional Children. *Family Relations* 38:456–461.

Nolen-Hoeksema, S., Girgus, J.S., & Seligman, M.E.P. (1992) Predictors and Consequences of Childhood Depressive Symptoms: A Five-Year Longitudinal Study. *Journal of Abnormal Psychology* 101:405–422.

Oakland, T., Shermis, M.D., & Coleman, M. (1990) Teacher Perceptions of Differences Among Elementary Students With and Without Learning Disabilities in Referred Samples. *Journal of Learning Disabilities* 23:499–504.

Obrzut, J.E., & Hynd, G.W. (1987) Cognitive Dysfunction and Psychoeducational Assessment in Individuals with Acquired Brain Injury. *Journal of Learning Disabilities*, 20:596–602.

O'Connor, L., & Schery, T.K. (1986) A Comparison of Microcomputer-Assisted and Traditional Language Therapy for Developing Communication Skills in Nonoral Toddlers. *Journal of Speech and Hearing Disorders* 51:356–361.

O'Connor, M. (1975) The Nursery School Environment. *Developmental Psychology*, 11:556–561.

O'Keeffe, J. (1995) Disability, Discrimination, and the Americans with Disabilities Act. In S.M. Bruyere & J. O'Keeffe (eds.) *Implications of the*

Americans with Disabilities Act for Psychology. New York: American Psychological Association and Springer Pub. Co. 1–15.

Odom, S.L., DeKlyen, M., & Jenkins, J.R. (1984) Integrating Handicapped and Nonhandicapped Preschoolers: Developmental Impact on Nonhandicapped Children. *Exceptional Children* 51:41–48.

Odom, S.L., McConnell, S.R. & Chandler, L.K. (1993) Acceptability and Feasibility of Classroom-Based Social Interaction Interventions for Young Children with Disabilities. *Exceptional Children* 60:226–236.

Odom, S.L. & Warren, S.F. (1988) Early Childhood Special Education in the Year 2000. *Journal of the Division for Early Childhood* 12:263–273.

O'Donnell, J.A., & Andersen, D.G. (1978) Factors Influencing Choice of Major and Career of Capable Women. *Vocational Guidance Journal* 26:214–222.

O'Donnell, L.M., & Livingston, R.L. (1991) Active Exploration of the Environment by Young Children with Low Vision: A Review of the Literature. *Journal of Visual Impairment & Blindness* 85:287–291.

Ogbu, J.U. (1978) *Minority Education and Caste,* New York: Academic Press.

Ogbu, J.U. (1981) Origins of Human Competence: A Cultural-Ecological Perspective. *Child Development* 52:413–429.

Ogbu, J.U. (1992) Understanding Cultural Diversity and Learning. *Educational Researcher* 21:5–14.

Ohanian, S. (November 1990). PL 94-142: Mainstream or Quicksand? *Phi Delta Kappan* 217–222.

O'Hare, W.P., & Frey, W.H. (September 1992) Booming, Suburban and Black. *American Demographics,* 30–38.

Okolo, C.M. (1993) Computers and Individuals with Mild Disabilities. In J.D. Lindsey (ed.) *Computers and Exceptional Individuals,* 2d ed. Austin, Tex.: Pro-Ed, 111–143.

Olion, L., & Gillis-Olion, M. (1984) Assessing Culturally Diverse Exceptional Children. *Early Childhood Develop-*

ment and Care, United Kingdom: Science Publishers, Inc.

Olley, J.G. (1992) Autism: Historical Overview, Definition, and Characteristics. In D.E. Berkell (ed.), *Autism: Identification, Education, and Treatment.* Hillsdale. N.J.: Erlbaum, 3–21.

Olness, K.N. (1986) Reflections on Caring for Indochinese Children and Youth. *Journal of Developmental and Behavioral Pediatrics* 7:129–130.

Olswang, L.B. (1991) Intervention Issues for Toddlers with Specific Language Impairments. *Topics in Language Disorders* 11:69–86.

Olweus, D. (1982) Development of Stable Aggressive Reaction Patterns in Males. In R. Blanchard & C. Blanchard (eds.), *Advances in the Study of Aggression,* vol. 1. New York: Academic Press.

Onorato, I.M., Gwinn, M., & Dondero, T.J. (1994) Applications of Data from the CDC Family of Surveys. *Public Health Reports* 109:204–212.

Onslow, M., & Ingham, R.J. (1987) Speech Quality Measurement and the Management of Stuttering. *Journal of Speech and Hearing Disorders* 52:1–17.

Orgain, L.S. (1993) Using Local Media to Educate Young Woman About FAS and FAE. *Public Health Reports* 108:171.

Ortiz, A. (1986) Characteristics of Limited English Proficient Hispanic Students Served in Programs for the Learning Disabled: Implications for Policy and Practice (Part 2). *Bilingual Special Educational Newsletter,* 4:1–5, cited in R.A. Figueroa, Psychological Testing of Linguistic Minority Students: Knowledge Gaps and Regulations. *Exceptional Children* 56:145–152.

Ortiz, A.A., & Garcia, S.B. (1988) A Prereferral Process for Preventing Inappropriate Referrals of Hispanic Students to Special Education. In A.A. Ortiz & B.A. Ramirez (eds.), *Schools and the Culturally Diverse Exceptional Student: Promising Practices and Future*

Directions. Reston, Va.: Council for Exceptional Children, 6–19.

Ortiz, A.A., & Polyzoi, E. (1988) Language Assessment of Hispanic Learning Disabled and Speech and Language Handicapped Students: Research in Progress. In A.A. Ortiz & B.A. Ramirez (eds.), *Schools and the Culturally Diverse Exceptional Student: Promising Practices and Future Directions.* Reston, Va.: Council for Exceptional Children, 32–45.

Ortiz, A.A., & Yates, J.R. (1988) Characteristics of Learning Disabled, Mentally Retarded, and Speech-Language Handicapped Hispanic Students at Initial Evaluation and Reevaluation. In A.A. Ortiz & B.A. Ramirez (eds.), *Schools and the Culturally Diverse Exceptional Student: Promising Practices and Future Directions.* Reston, Va.: Council for Exceptional Children, 50–62.

Osborne, A.G. (May 1992) Legal Standards for an Appropriate Education in the Post-Rowley Era. *Exceptional Children* 58:488–494.

Osborne, J.K., & Byrnes, D.A. (1990) Identifying Gifted and Talented Students in an Alternative Learning Center. *Gifted Child Quarterly* 34:143–146.

Owens, R.E. (1988) *Language Development,* 2d ed. Columbus, Ohio: Merrill.

Owens, R.E. (1990) Development of Communication, Language, and Speech. In G.H. Shames & E.H. Wiig (eds.) *Human Communication Disorders,* 3d ed. Columbus, Ohio: Merrill, 30–74.

Owens, R.E. (1992) *Language Development: An Introduction* (3rd ed.). New York: Macmillan

Owens, R.E. (1994) Development of Communication, Language, and Speech. In G.H. Shames, E.H. Wiig & W.A. Secord (eds.) *Human Communication Disorders* (4th ed.). New York: Macmillan, 36–82.

Owings, R.A., Petersen, G.A., Bransford, J.D., Morris, C.D., & Stein, B.S. (1980) Spontaneous Monitoring and Regulations of Learning: A Comparison of

Successful and Less Successful Fifth Graders. *Journal of Educational Psychology* 72:250–256.

Oxtoby, M.J. (1994) Vertically Acquired HIV Infection in the United States. In P.A. Pizzo & C.M. Wilfert (eds.) *Pediatric AIDS* (2nd ed.). Baltimore: Williams & Wilkins, 3–21.

Paden, E.P., Novak, M.A., & Beiter, A.L. (1987) Predictors of Phonologic Inadequacy in Young Children Prone to Otitis Media. *Journal of Speech and Hearing Disorders* 52:232–242.

Padilla, A.M., Lindholm, K.J., Chen, A., Duran, R., Hakuta, K., Lambert, W., & Tucker, G.R. (1991) The English-Only Movement: Myths, Reality, and Implications for Psychology. *American Psychologist* 46:120–131.

Padula, W.V., & Spungin, S.J. (March 1983) The Visually Handicapped Child. *The Bridge*, 20–22.

Page, E.G. (1972) Miracle in Milwaukee: Raising the IQ. *Educational Researcher* 15:8–16.

Page, E.G., & Grandon, G.M. (1981) Massive Intervention and Child Intelligence: The Milwaukee Project in Critical Perspective. *Journal of Special Education* 15:239–256.

Pagnano, C.W., & Burch, J.W. (1959) Locating Gifted Children in Junior High Schools: A Comparison of Methods. *Exceptional Children* 25:300–304.

Palfrey, J.S., Walker, D.K., Butler, J.A., & Singer, J.D. (1989) Patterns of Response in Families of Chronically Disabled Children: An Assessment in Five Metropolitan School Districts. *American Journal of Orthopsychiatry* 59:94–104.

Palincsar, A.S. (1986) The Role of Dialogue in Providing Scaffolded Instruction. *Educational Psychologist* 21:73–98.

Palincsar, A.S., & Brown, A.L. (1984) The Reciprocal Teaching of Comprehension-Fostering and Comprehension-Monitoring Activities. *Cognition and Instruction* 1:117–175.

Palincsar, A.S., & Klenk, L. (1992) Fostering Literacy Learning in Supportive Contexts. *Journal of Learning Disabilities* 25:211–225, 229.

Pambacker, M. (1992) Some Common Myths about Voice Therapy. *Language, Speech, and Hearing Services in Schools* 23:12–19.

Pang, V.O. (1994) Why Do We Need This Class? Multicultural Education for Teachers. *Phi Delta Kappan* 289–292.

Panyan, M. (1984) Computer Technology for Autistic Students. *Journal of Developmental Disorders* 14:375–382.

Parette, H.P., Jr., & Van Biervliet, A. (1991) School-Age Children with Disabilities: Technology Implications for Counselors. *Elementary School Guidance & Counseling* 25:182–193.

Paris, S.G., & Myers, M. (1981) Comprehension Monitoring: Memory and Study Strategies of Good and Poor Readers. *Journal of Reading Behavior* 13:5–22.

Paris, S.G., & Oka, E.R. (1986) Children's Reading Strategies, Metacognition and Motivation. *Developmental Review* 6:22–56.

Parke, R.D., & Collmer, C.W. (1975) Child Abuse: An Interdisciplinary Analysis. In E.M. Hetherington (ed.), *Review of Child Development Research*, vol. 5. Chicago: University of Chicago Press.

Parke, R.D., & Slaby, R.G. (1983) The Development of Aggression. In E.M. Hetherington (ed.), *Handbook of Child Psychology: Socialization, Personality, and Social Development*, 4th ed. New York: Wiley, 547–643.

Patterson, G.R. (1986) Performance Models for Antisocial Boys. *American Psychologist* 41:432–444.

Patterson, G.R., & Capaldi, D.M. (1990) A Mediational Model for Boys' Depressed Mood. In J. Rolf et al. (eds.), *Risk and Protective Factors in the Development of Psychopathology*. New York: Cambridge University Press, 141–164.

Patton, J., Payne, J., & Beirne-Smith, M. (1990) *Mental Retardation* (3d ed.). Columbus, Ohio: Merrill.

Patton, J.R., & Polloway, E.A. (1992) Learning Disabilities: The Challenges of Adulthood. *Journal of Learning Disabilities* 25:410–415.

Pearman, E.L., Barnhart, M.W., Huang, A.M., & Mellblom, C. (1992) Educating All Students in School: Attitudes and Beliefs About Inclusion. *Education and Training in Mental Retardation* 27:176–182.

Peck, C. (1985) Increasing Opportunities for Social Control by Children with Autism and Severe Handicaps: Effects of Student Behavior and Perceived Classroom Climate. *Journal of the Association for Persons with Severe Handicaps* 10:183–193.

Peck, C.A., Donaldson, J., & Pezzoli, M. (1990) Some Benefits Nonhandicapped Adolescents Perceive for Themselves from Their Social Relationships with Peers Who Have Severe Handicaps. *Journal of the Association for Persons with Severe Handicaps* 15:241–249.

Peck, C.A., Hayden, L., Wandschneider, M., Peterson, K., & Richards, S. (1989) Development of Integrated Preschools: A Qualitative Inquiry into Sources of Resistance among Parents, Administrator, and Teachers. *Journal of Early Intervention* 13:353–364.

Pendarvis, E.D., Howley, A.A., & Howley, C.B. (1990) *The Abilities of Gifted Children*, Englewood Cliffs, N.J.: Prentice Hall.

Penner, S.G. (1987) Parental Responses to Grammatical and Ungrammatical Child Utterances. *Child Development* 58:376–384.

Pepper, F.C. (1976) Teaching the American Indian Child in Mainstream Settings. In R.L. Jones (ed.), *Mainstreaming and the Minority Child*. Reston, Va.: Council for Exceptional Children.

Percival, F., & Ellington, H. (1988) *A Handbook of Educational Technology* (2d ed.). London: Kogan Page.

Perino, S.C., & Perino, J. (1981) *Parenting the Gifted*, New York: R.R. Bowker and Company.

Perlmutter, B.F., Crocker, J., Corray, D., & Garstecki, D. (1983) Sociometric Status and Related Personality Characteristics of Mainstreamed Learning Disabled Adolescents. *Learning Disabilities Quarterly* 6:20–30.

Petersen, C.I., & Warnsby, E. (1993) *Education Digest* 48:22–26.

Petti, M. (1987) Educational Implications of the Nonverbal WISC-R. *Academic Therapy* 23:177–181.

Petti, M. (1988) Educational Implications of the Verbal WISC-R. *Academic Therapy* 23:279–283.

Pfeifer, C.R. (1986) *The Suicidal Child.* New York: Guilford.

Pfeiffer, S.I. (1992) Psychology and Mental Retardation: Emerging Research and Practice Opportunities. *Professional Psychology: Research and Practice* 23:239–243.

Phares, E.J. (1988) *Clinical Psychology,* 3d ed. Chicago: The Dorsey Press.

Pianta, R.C., & Lothman, D.J. (1994) Predicting Behavior Problems in Children with Epilepsy: Child Factors, Disease Factors, Family Stress, and Child-Mother Interactions. *Child Development* 65: 1415–1429

Pickens, J., & McNaughton, S. (1988) Peer Tutoring of Comprehension Strategies. *Educational Psychology* 8:67–80.

Pizzo, P.A., & Wilfert, C.M. (1994) Antiretroviral Treatment for Children with HIV Infection. In P.A. Pizzo & C.M. Wilfert (eds.) *Pediatric AIDS* (2nd ed.). Baltimore: Williams & Wilkins, 651–689.

Plienis, A., & Romanczyk, R.G. (1985) Analysis of Performance, Behavior, and Predictors for Severely Disturbed Children: A Comparison of Adult Versus Computer Instruction. *Analysis and Intervention in Developmental Disabilities* 5:345–356.

Pliskin, S. (1994) Personal Communication: Computer Consultant.

Plomin, R., DeFries, J.C., & McClearn, G.E. (1990) *Behavioral Genetics: A Primer* (2d ed.). New York: Freeman.

Podell, D.M., Tournaki-Rein, N., & Lin, A. (1992) Automatization of Mathematics Skills via Computer-Assisted Instruction among Students with Mild Mental Handicaps. *Education and Training in Mental Retardation* 27:200–206.

Pogrow, S. (1985) Using Computers to Teach Problem-Solving Skills. *NAASP Bulletin* 69:47–54.

Polloway, E.A., & Patton, J.R. (1990) Biological Causes of Mental Retardation. In J.R. Patton, M. Beirne-Smith, & J.S. Payne (eds.) *Mental Retardation* (3d ed.). Columbus, Ohio: Merrill, 117–161.

Polloway, E.A., Schewel, R., & Patton, J.R. (1992) Learning Disabilities in Adulthood: Personal Perspectives. *Journal of Learning Disabilities* 25:520–522.

Polloway, E.A., & Smith, J.D. (1983) Changes in Mild Mental Retardation: Population, Programs, and Perspectives. *Exceptional Children* 50:149–159.

Pope, A.M., & Tarlov, A.R. (eds.) (1991) *Disability in America: Toward a National Agenda for Prevention* (Committee on a National Agenda for the Prevention of Disabilities, Institute of Medicine), Washington, D.C.: National Academy Press.

Poplin, M.S., & Wright, P. (1983) *Learning Disabilities Quarterly* 6:367–171.

Porter, R.P. (17 May 1990) Tongue-Tied by Bilingual Education. *Newsday,* 36.

Portes, P.R., Haas, R., & Brown, J.H. (1991) Predicting Children's Adjustment to Divorce. *Journal of Divorce* 15:87–103.

Portes, P.R., Howell, S.C., Brown, J.H., Eichenberger, S., & Mas, C.A. (1992) Family Functions and Children's Postdivorce Adjustment. *American Journal of Orthopsychiatry* 62:613–617.

Potolicchio, S. (February 1992) Understanding Epilepsy. *NEA Today* 10:13.

Powell, C., & Grantham-McGregor, S. (1989) Home Visiting of Varying Frequency and Child Development. *Pediatrics* 84:157–164.

Powell, T.H., Hecimovic, A., & Christensen, L. (1992) Meeting the Unique Needs of Families. In D.E. Berkell (ed.), *Autism: Identification, Educa-tion, and Treatment.* Hillsdale, N.J.: Erlbaum, 187–225.

Powers, M.D. (1992) Early Intervention for Children with Autism. In D.E. Berkell (ed.), *Autism: Identification, Education, and Treatment.* Hillsdale, N.J.: Erlbaum, 225–252.

Prater, L.P. (1992) Early Pregnancy and Academic Achievement of African-American Youth. *Exceptional Children* 59:141–150.

Presbie, R.J., & Brown, P.L. (1985) *Behavior Modification,* 2d ed. Washington, D.C.: NEA Professional Library.

Price, H.B. (November 1992) Multiculturalism: Myths and Realities. *Phi Delta Kappan,* 208–213.

Price, R.H., Cowen, E.L., Lorion, R.P., & Ramos-McKay, J. (1989) The Search for Effective Prevention Programs: What We Learned Along the Way. *American Journal of Orthopsychiatry* 59:49–58.

Prigatano, G.P. (1992) Personality Disturbances Associated with Traumatic Brain Injury. *Journal of Consulting and Clinical Psychology* 60:360–368.

Prinz, P.M., Nelson, K.E., & Stedt, J.D. (1982) Early Reading in Young Deaf Children Using Microcomputer Technology. *American Annals of the Deaf* 127:519–525.

Prior, M., & Cummins, R. (1992) Questions About Facilitated Communication and Autism. *Journal of Autism and Developmental Disorders* 22:331–338.

Psychological Corporation. (1993) *The Bayley Scales of Infant Development,* 2d ed. San Antonio, Tex.: Author.

Psychosomatic Medicine (1993) The Biology of Autism. (editorial). *Psychosomatic Medicine* 23:7–11.

Public Health Service (March/April 1993) More Indians Smoke, PHS Study Shows. *Public Health Reports,* 108:262.

Puig-Antioch, J., & Weston, B. (1983) The Diagnosis and Treatment of Major Depressive Disorder in Childhood. *Annual Review of Medicine* 34:231–245.

Putnam, J.W., Rynders, J.E., Johnson, R.T., & Johnson, D.W. (1989) Collaborative Skill Instruction for Promoting Positive Interactions Between Mentally Handicapped and Nonhandicapped Children. *Exceptional Children* 52:57–62.

Quay, H.C. (1986) Classification. In H.C. Quay & J.S. Werry (eds.), *Psychopathological Disorders of Childhood*, 3d ed. New York: Wiley.

Quittner, J. (12 November 1994) How Technology Is Enabling the Disabled. *Newsday*, 57, 60–61.

Rabat, R.G. (1992) *Dogs for the Deaf*, Central Point, Ore.: Dogs for the Deaf.

Radke-Yarrow, M., & Sherman, T. (1991) Hard Growing: Children Who Survive. In J. Rolf et al. (eds.), *Risk and Protective Factors in the Development of Psychopathology*. New York: Cambridge University Press, 97–120.

Rafferty, Y., & Rollins, N. (1990) Homeless Children: Educational Challenges for the 1990s. Cited in L.J. Heflin & K. Rudy, *Homeless and in Need of Special Education*. Reston, Va.: The Council for Exceptional Children.

Rafferty, Y., & Shinn, M. (1991) The Impact of Homelessness on Children. *American Psychologist* 46:1170–1179.

Raimondo, D., & Maxwell, M. (1987) The Modes of Communication Used in Junior and Senior High School Classrooms by Hearing-Impaired Students and Their Teachers and Peers. *Volta Review* 89:263–275.

Rait, D.S., Jacobsen, P.B., Lederberg, M.S., & Holland, J.C. (1988) Characteristics of Psychiatric Consultations in a Pediatric Center. *American Journal of Psychiatry* 145:363–364.

Ramey, C.T., & Ramey, S.L. (1992) Effective Early Intervention. *Mental Retardation*. 30:337–345.

Ramey, C.T., & Ramey, S.L. (1992) Effective Early Intervention. *Mental Retardation* 50:337–345.

Ramey, C.T., & Ramey, S.L. (1992) Effective Early Intervention. *Mental Retardation* 50:180–187.

Ramirez, B.A. (1988) Culturally and Linguistically Diverse Children. *Teaching Exceptional Children* 20:45.

Ramirez, B.A., & Johnson, M.J. (1988) American Indian Exceptional Children: Improved Practices and Policy. In A.A. Ortiz & B.A. Ramirez (eds.), *Schools and the Culturally Diverse Exceptional Student: Promising Practices and Future Directions*. Reston, Va.: Council for Exceptional Children, 128–139.

Ramirez, J.D. (1992) Executive Summary. *Bilingual Research Journal* 16:1–62.

Ramos-Ford, V., & Gardner, H. (1991) Giftedness from a Multiple Intelligence Model. In N. Colangelo & G.A. Davis (eds.), *Handbook of Gifted Education*. Needham Heights, Mass.: Allyn & Bacon, 55–65.

Random Access (April 1993a) *Journal of Visual Impairment & Blindness* 87:118.

Random Access (September 1993b) *Journal of Visual Impairment & Blindness* 87:276.

Rapp, D.W., & Rapp, A.J. (1992) A Survey of the Current Status of Visually Impaired Students in Secondary Mathematics. *Journal of Visual Impairment & Blindness* 86:115–117.

Rapport, M.D., Murphy, A., & Bailey, J.S. (1978) The Effects of a Response Cost Treatment Tactic on Hyperactive Children. *Journal of School Psychology* 18:98–110.

Raschke, D., Dedrick, C., Strathe, M., Yoder, M., & Kirkland, G. (1988) Cross-Age Tutorials and Attitudes of Kindergartners Toward Older Students. *The Teacher Educator* 23:10–18.

Rasing, E.J., & Duker, P.C. (1993) Acquisition and Generalization of Social Behaviors in Language-Disabled Deaf Children. *American Annals of the Deaf* 138:362–369.

Rausch, F.R., & Phelps, A. (1987) Secondary Special Education and Transition from School to Work: A National Priority. *Exceptional Children* 53:487–493.

Raviv, D., & Stone, C.A. (1991) Individual Differences in the Self-Image of Adolescents with Learning Disabilities: The Roles of Severity, Time of Diagnosis, and Parental Perceptions. *Journal of Learning Disability* 24:602–607.

Raybould, T. (1984) Precision Teaching. In D. Fontana (ed.) *Behaviorism and Learning Theory in Education*. Edinburgh, Scotland: Scottish Academic Press, 43–75.

Raynes, M., Snell, M., & Sailor, W. (December 1991) A Fresh Look at Categorical Programs for Children with Special Needs. *Phi Delta Kappan* 326–331.

Recognizing Communication Disorders (1992) Memphis, Tenn.: SFA.

Reed, E. (1975) Genetic Anomalies in Development. In E.M. Hetherington, S. Scarr-Salapatek, & G.M. Siegel (eds.), *Review of Child Development Research* (vol. 4). Chicago: University of Chicago Press.

Reese, P. (1991) Words of Wisdom for a Good Video Presentation. *Media & Methods* 28:54.

Reis, S. (1989) Reflections on Policy Affecting the Education of Gifted and Talented Students: Past and Future Perspectives. *American Psychologist* 44:399–409.

Reis, S.M., & Westberg, K.L. (1994) The Impact of Staff Development on Teachers' Ability to Modify Curriculum for Gifted and Talented Students. *Gifted Child Quarterly* 38: 127–135.

Reis, S.M. (1987) We Can't Change What We Don't Recognize: Understanding the Special Needs of Gifted Females. *Gifted Child Quarterly* 31:83–88.

Reisner, G. (1988) Adjusting to Your Child's Epilepsy. In H. Reisner (ed.), *Children with Epilepsy*. New York: Woodbine, 41–56.

Rendon, M.E. (1992) Deaf Culture and Alcohol and Substance Abuse. *Journal of Substance Abuse Treatment* 9:103–110.

Renzulli, J.S. (1983) Rating the Behavioral Characteristics of Superior Students. *G/C/T*, 30–35

Renzulli, J.S., & Hartman, R.K. (1971) Scale for Rating the Behavioral Characteristics of Superior Students. *Exceptional Children* 38:243–248.

Renzulli, J.S., & Reis, S.M. (1994) Research Related to Schoolwide Enrichment Triad Model. *Gifted Child Quarterly* 38:7–20.

Renzulli, J.S., & Reis, S.M. (1991) The Schoolwide Enrichment Model: A Comprehensive Plan for the Development of Creative Productivity. In N. Colangelo & G.A.Davis (eds.), *Handbook of Gifted Education.* Needham Heights, Mass.: Allyn & Bacon, 111–142.

Reschly, D., & Lamprecht, M. (September 1979) Expectancy Effects of Labels: Fact or Artifact? *Exceptional Children* 46:55–58.

Rescorla, L., Parker, R., & Stolley, P. (1991) Ability, Achievement, and Adjustment in Homeless Children. *American Journal of Orthopsychiatry* 6:210–220.

Resnick, T.J., & Rapin, I. (1991) Language Disorders in Childhood. *Psychiatric Annals* 21:709–716.

Reynolds, A.J. (1995) Effects of a Preschool Plus Follow-On Intervention for Children at Risk. *Developmental Psychology* 30: 787–804.

Reynolds, M.C., & Birch, J.W. (1988) *Adaptive Mainstreaming,* 3d ed. New York: Longman.

Reynolds, M.C., Wang, M.C., & Walberg, H.J. (1987) The Necessary Restructuring of Special and Regular Education. *Exceptional Children* 53:391–398.

Rezen, S.V., & Hausman, C. (1985) *Coping with Hearing Loss,* New York: Dembner Books.

Rhodes, L., Sandow, D., Mank, D., Buckley, J., & Albin, J. (1991) Expanding the Role of Employers in Supported Employment. *Journal of the Association for Persons With Severe Handicaps* 16:213–217.

Rice, M.L., Sell, M.A., & Hadley, P.A. (1991) Social Interactions of Speech-and-Language-Impaired Children. *Journal of Speech and Hearing Research* 34:1299–1307.

Rich, H.L., & Ross, S. (1989) Students' Time on Learning Tasks in Special Education. *Exceptional Children* 55:508–515.

Richardson, T.M., & Benbow, C.P. (1990) Long-Term Effects of Acceleration on the Social-Emotional Adjustment of Mathematically Precocious Youths. *Journal of Educational Psychology* 82:464–470.

Richert, E.S. (1981) Media Mirrors of the Gifted: E. Susan Richert's Review of the Film *Simon. Gifted Child Quarterly* 25:3–4.

Richert, E.S. (1991) Rampant Problems and Promising Practices in Identification. In N. Colangelo & G.A. Davis (eds.), *Handbook of Gifted Education.* Needham Heights, Mass.: Allyn & Bacon, 81–97.

Richert, S. (1985) Identification of Gifted Children in the United States: The Need for Pluralistic Assessment. *Roeper Review* 8:68–72.

Richmond-Abbott, M. (1983) *Masculine and Feminine,* Reading, Mass.: Addison-Wesley.

Richmond, J., & Ayoub, C.C. (1993) Evolution of Early Intervention Philosophy. In D.M. Bryant & M.A. Graham (eds.) *Implementing Early Intervention.* New York: The Guilford Press, 1–18.

Rickelman, B.L., & Blaylock, J.N. (1983) Behaviors of Sighted Individuals Perceived by Blind Persons as Hindrances to Self-Reliance in Blind Persons. *Journal of Visual Impairment & Blindness* 77:8–11.

Rieber, R.W. (1981) Phonatory and Resonatory Problems: Functional Voice Disorders. In R. W. Rieber (ed.), *Communication Disorders.* New York: Plenum, 259–275.

Rimel, R.W., Giordani, B., Barth, J.T., Boll, T.J., & Jane, A. (1981) Disability Caused by Minor Head Injury. *Neurosurgery* 9:221–228.

Rimm, S. (1986) *Underachievement Syndrome: Causes and Cures,* Watertown, Wis.: Apple Publishing.

Rimm, S.B., & Lovance, K.J. (1992) The Use of Subject and Grade Skipping for the Prevention and Reversal of Underachievement. *Gifted Child Quarterly* 36:100–105.

Rist, M.C. (January 1990) "Crack Babies" in School. *American School Board Journal,* 19–24.

Ritter-Brinton, K., & Stewart, D. (1992) Hearing Parents and Deaf Children. *American Annals of the Deaf* 137:85–91.

Ritvo, E.R., Freeman, B.J., Mason-Brothers, A., Mo, A. & Ritvo, A.M. (1985) Concordance for the Syndrome of Autism in 40 Pairs of Afflicted Twins. *American Journal of Psychiatry* 142:74–77.

Roberts, C., & Zubrick, S. (1993) Factors Influencing the Social Status of Children with Mild Academic Disabilities in Regular Classrooms. *Exceptional Children* 59:192–202.

Robertson, M.J. (1991) Homeless Women with Children. *American Psychologist* 46:1198–1204.

Robertson, P.E., Bhate, S.R., & Bhate, M.S. (1991) AIDS: Education and Adults with a Mental Handicap. *Journal of Mental Deficiency Research* 35:475–480.

Robin, A. (1976) The Turtle Technique: An Extended Case Study of Self-Control in the Classroom. *Psychology in the Schools* 13:449–453.

Robison-Awana, P., Kehle, T.J., & Jenson, W.R. (1986) But What About Girls? Adolescent Self-Esteem and Sex Role Perceptions as a Function of Academic Achievement. *Journal of Educational Psychology* 78:179–183.

Robinson, P.W., Newby, T.J., & Ganzell, S.L. (1981) A Token System for a Class of Underachieving Hyperactive Children. *Journal of Applied Behavior Analysis* 14:307–315.

Rodda, M., & Grove, C. (1987) *Language, Cognition, and Deafness,* Hillsdale, N.J.: Erlbaum.

Roedell, W. (1984) Vulnerabilities of Highly Gifted Children. *Roeper Review* 6:127–130.

Romanczyk, R.G., Ekdahl, M., & Lockshin, S.B. (1992) Perspectives on Research in Autism: Current Trends and Future Directions. In D.E. Berkell (ed.), *Autism: Identification, Education, and Treatment.* Hillsdale, N.J.: Erlbaum, 21–53.

Rondal, J.A. (1988) Language Development in Down's Syndrome: A Life-Span Perspective. *International Journal of Behavioral Development* 11:21–36.

Roscoe, B., & Kruger, T.L. (1990) AIDS: Late Adolescents' Knowledge and Its Influence on Sexual Behavior. *Adolescence* 25:39–46.

Rose, D.F., & Smith, B.J. (May 1993) Preschool Mainstreaming: Attitude Barriers and Strategies for Addressing Them. *Young Children* 59–62.

Rose, R.J., & Ditto, W.B. (1983) A Developmental-Genetic Analysis of Common Fears from Early Adolescence to Early Adulthood. *Child Development* 54:361–368.

Rosegant, T. (1985) Using the Computer as a Tool for Learning to Read and Write. *Journal of Learning Disabilities* 18:113–115.

Rosenberg, A.A., Solarz, A.L., & Bailey, W.A. (1991) Psychology and Homelessness: A Public Policy and Advocacy Agenda. *American Psychologist* 46:1239–1244.

Rosenberg, J., & Hertz, B.G. (1990) Preferential Looking Acuity in Multiple-Handicapped Children. In S.A. Aitken et al. (eds.), *Realities and Opportunities: Early Intervention with Visually Handicapped Infants and Children.* New York: American Foundation for the Blind, 55–61.

Rosenberg, M., Wilson, R., Maheady, L., & Sindelar, P.T. (1992) *Educating Students with Behavior Disorders.* Boston: Allyn & Bacon.

Rosenberg, M.S. (1987) New Dimensions for Research on the Psychological Maltreatment of Children. *American Psychologist* 42:166–172.

Rosenberger, P.B. (16 January 1992) Dyslexia: Is It a Disease? *New England Journal of Medicine* 326:192–193.

Rosenhan, D.L., & Seligman, M.E.P. (1995) *Abnormal Psychology* (3rd ed.). New York: Norton. also after trying on page 273

Rosenthal, E. (4 February 1990) When a Pregnant Woman Drinks. *New York Times: Science Times*, C1, C10.

Rosenthal, E. (4 February 1990). When a Pregnant Woman Drinks. *New York Times Magazine,* pp. 30–32ff.

Ross, A., & Parker, M. (1980) Academic and Social Self-Concepts of the Academically Gifted. *Exceptional Children* 47:7–10.

Ross, D.M., & Ross, S.A. (1976) *Hyperactivity: Research, Theory, and Action.* New York: Wiley.

Ross, J.W. (1984) The Child with Cancer in School. In J. Fithian (ed.), *Understanding the Child with a Chronic Illness in the Classroom.* Phoenix, Ariz.: Oryx Press, 152–164.

Rothenberg, J.J. (1990) An Outcome Study of an Early Intervention for Specific Learning Disabilities. *Journal of Learning Disabilities* 23:317–319.

Rothholz, D., Berkowitz, S., & Burberry, J. (1989) Functionality of Two Modes of Communication in the Community by Students with Developmental Disabilities: A Comparison of Signing and Communication Books. *Journal of the Association for Persons with Severe Handicaps* 14:227–233.

Rothstein, L.F. (1990) *Special Education Law.* White Plains, N.Y.: Longman.

Rothstein, L.F. (1995) *Special Education Law* (2nd ed.). White Plains, N.Y.: Longman.

Rotter, J.C., & Robinson, E.H. (1982) *Parent-Teacher Conferencing,* Washington, D.C.: National Education Association.

Rotter, J.C., Robinson, E.H., & Fey, M.A. (1987) *Parent-Teacher Conferencing,* 2d ed. Washington, D.C.: National Education Association.

Rourke, B.P. (1989) Coles's Learning Mystique: The Good, the Bad, and the Irrelevant. *Journal of Learning Disabilities* 22:274–278.

Rowe, M.B. (1986) Wait Time: Slowing Down May Be a Way of Speeding Up. *Journal of Teacher Education* 37:43–50.

Rowitz, L. (1989) Trends in Mental Retardation. *Mental Retardation* iii–vi.

Rowitz, L. (1988) The Forgotten Ones: Adolescence and Mental Retardation. *Mental Retardation* 26:115–117.

RP Foundation (1989) *Retinitis Pigmentosa,* Baltimore, Md.: author.

Rubin, K.H., & Howe, N. (1986) Social Play and Perspective Taking. In G. Fein & M. Rivkin (eds.) *The Young Child at Play: Reviews of Research,* vol. 4. Washington, D.C.: National Association for the Education of Young Children, 113–125.

Rubin, R.A., & Balow, B. (1978) Prevalence of Teacher Identified Behavior Problems: A Longitudinal Study. *Exceptional Children* 45:102–111.

Ruconich, S. (1984) Evaluating Microcomputer Access Technology for Use by Visually Impaired Students. *Education and the Visually Handicapped* 15:119–125.

Ruiz, N.T. (1989) An Optimal Learning Environment for Rosemary. *Exceptional Children* 56:130–144.

Ruppert, E.S., & Buhrer, K. (1992) Ohio's Infant Hearing Screening and Assessment Program. *Clinical Pediatrics* 31:19–22.

Rusalem, H., & Malikin, D. (1976) *Contemporary Vocational Rehabilitation.* New York: New York University Press.

Rush, A.J., Weisenburger, J., & Eaves, G. (1986) Do Thinking Patterns Predict Depressive Symptoms? *Cognitive Therapy and Research* 10:225–236.

Rushakoff, G.E., & Lombardino, L.J. (1983) Comprehensive Microcomputer Applications for Severely Physically Handicapped Children. *Teaching Exceptional Children,* 18–22.

Russell, S.C., & Williams, E.U. (1988) Homeless Handicapped Children: A Special Education Perspective. *Children's Environments Quarterly* 5:3–7.

Rust, J.O., & Miller, L.S. (1978) Using a Control Group To Evaluate a Resource Room Program. *Psychology in the Schools* 15:503–506.

Rutter, M. (1985) Resilience in the Face of Adversity: Protective Factors and Resistance to Psychiatric Disorder. *British Journal of Psychiatry* 147:598–616.

Rutter, M. (1980) School Influences on Children's Behavior and Development. The 1979 Kenneth Blackfan Lecture, Children's Hospital Medical Center, Boston. *Pediatrics* 65:208–220.

Rutter, M. (1990) Psychosocial Resilience and Protective Mechanisms. In J. Rolf et al. (eds.), *Risk and Protective Factors in the Development of Psychopathology*. New York: Cambridge University Press, 181–215.

Rutter, M., & Schopler, E. (1987) Autism and Pervasive Developmental Disorders: Concepts and Diagnostic Issues. *Journal of Autism and Developmental Disorders* 17:159–165.

Ryan, B.P. (1992) Articulation, Language, Rate, and Fluency Characteristics of Stuttering and Nonstuttering Preschool Children. *Journal of Speech and Hearing Research* 35:333–342.

Ryan, B.P., & Van Kirk, B. (1974) The Establishment, Transfer, and Maintenance of Fluent Speech in 50 Stutterers Using DAF and Operant Procedures. *Journal of Speech and Hearing Disorders* 39:3–10.

Ryan, E.B., Short, E.J., & Weed, K.A. (1986) The Role of Cognitive Strategy Training in Improving the Academic Performance of Learning Disabled Children. *Journal of Learning Disabilities* 19:521–529.

Ryan, F.J. (Feb 1994) Will Multiculturalism Undercut Student Individuality? *Education Digest*, 26–28.

Ryan, G.H. (1992) *Persons with Disabilities and You: A Resource Manual on Disabilities*, Springfield, Ill.: Department of Human Services and Office of the Secretary of State.

Ryder, B.E., & Kawalec, E.S. (1995) A Job-Seeking Skills Program for Persons Who Are Blind or Visual Impaired. *Journal of Visual Impairment & Blindness* 88: 107–111

Sabornie, E.J., & Kauffman, J.M. (1986) Social Acceptance of Learning Disabled Adolescents. *Learning Disabilities Quarterly* 9:55–60.

Sadker, M., & Sadker, D. (1985) Sexism in the Schoolroom in the '80s. *Psychology Today* 19:54–57.

Sadker, M., & Sadker, D. (1994) *Failing at Fairness: How America's Schools Cheat Girls*, New York: Macmillan.

Sailor, W., Gee, K., & Karasoff, P. (1993) Full Inclusion and School Restructuring. In M. E. Snell (ed.), *Instruction of Students with Severe Disabilities*. New York: Merrill, 1–23.

Sailor, W., Halvorsen, A., Anderson, J., Goetz, L., Gee, K., Doering, K., & Hunt, P. (1986) Community Intensive Instruction. In R. Horner, L. Meyer, & B. Fredericks (eds.), *Education of Learners with Severe Handicaps*. Baltimore, Md.: Paul H. Brookes, 251–288.

Saint-Laurent, L., & Lessard, J.C. (1991) Comparison of Three Educational Programs for Students with Moderate Mental Retardation Integrated in Regular Schools. *Education and Training in Mental Retardation* 9:370–379.

Salend, S.J. (Winter 1990) A Migrant Education Guide for Special Educators. *Teaching Exceptional Children*, 18–21.

Salend, S.J. (1994) *Effective Mainstreaming: Creating Inclusive Classrooms*, 2d ed. New York: Macmillan.

Salend, S.J., & Taylor, L. (1993) Working with Families: A Cross-Cultural Perspective. *Remedial and Special Education* 14:25–32, 39.

Salend, S.J., & Washin, B. (1988) Team-Assisted Individualization with Handicapped Adjudicated Youth. *Exceptional Children* 55:174–180.

Salisbury, D.F. (December 1988) When Is a Computer Better Than Flashcards? *Educational Technology*, 26–32.

Salt, R. (1991) Child Support in Context: Comments on Rettig, Christensen, and Dahl. *Family Relations* 40:175–178.

Salvesen, K.A., & Undheim, J.O. (1994) Screening for Learning Disabilities with Teacher Rating Scales. *Journal of Learning Disabilities* 27:60–66.

Salzinger, S., Feldman, R.S., Hammer, M., & Rosario, M. (1993) The Effects of Physical Abuse on Children's Social Relationships. *Child Development* 64:169–187.

Sameroff, A., Seifer, R., Barocas, R., Zax, M., & Greenspan, S. (1987) Intelligence Quotient Scores of 4-Year-Old Children: Social-Environmental Risk Factors. *Pediatrics* 79:343–350.

Sampson, P.D., Bookstein, F.L., Barr, H.M., & Stressguth, A.P. (1994) Prenatal Alcohol Exposure, Birthweight, and Measures of Child Size from Birth to Age 14 Years. *American Journal of Public Health* 84: 1421–1428.

Sandberg, B. (6 September 1993) Reading, Writing, and Medicating. *New York Teacher*, 15.

Sandberg, B. (30 May 1994) State Commits to Range of Placements. *New York Teacher* 35:3.

Sandberg, B., & Michaelson, C. (October 18, 1993) This Is a Sham: Parents, Educators Speak Out. *New York Teacher* 2–3.

Sandberg, L.D. (1982) Attitudes of Nonhandicapped Elementary School Students Toward School-Aged Trainable Mentally Retarded Students. *Education and Training of the Mentally Retarded* 17:30–34.

Sande, M.A., Carpenter, C.C.J., Cobbs, C.G., Holmes, K.K., & Sanford, J.P. (December 1, 1993) Antiretroviral Therapy for Adult HIV-Infected Patients: Recommendations From a State-of-the-Art Conference. *JAMA* 270: 2583–2590.

Sander, E. (1972) When Are Speech Sounds Learned? *Journal of Speech and Hearing Disorders* 37:55–63.

Sander, E. (1989) Arguments against the Aggressive Pursuit of Voice Therapy for Children. *Language, Speech, and Hearing Services in Schools* 20:94–101.

Sapon-Shevin, M. (1992) Including All Children and Their Gifts within Regular Classrooms. In W. Stainback & S. Stainback (eds.), *Controversial Issues Confronting Special Education*. Boston: Allyn & Bacon, 69–81.

Sarafino, E.P. (1979) An Estimate of Nationwide Incidence of Sexual Offenses Against Children. *Child Welfare*, 127–135.

Sarafino, E.P. (1994) *Health Psychology*. New York: Wiley.

Sardegna, J., and Paul, T.O. (1991) *The Encyclopedia of Blindness and Visual Impairment*, Austin, Tex.: Facts on File.

Sasso, G.M., Simpson, R.L., & Novak, C.G. (1985) Procedures for Facilitating Integration of Autistic Children in Public School Settings. *Analysis and Intervention in Developmental Disabilities* 5:233–246.

Sattler, J.M. (1988) *Assessment of Children* (3d ed.). San Diego: Jerome M. Sattler. Cited in C.R. Smith (1991), *Learning Disabilities* (2d ed.). Boston: Allyn & Bacon.

Sautter, R.C. (November 1992) Crack: Healing the Children. *Phi Delta Kappan* (Kappan Special Report) K1-K12.

Savage, S., Mayfield, P., & Cook, M. (1993) Questions About Serving Children with HIV/AIDS. *Day Care and Early Education* 3:10–12.

Sayler, M.F., & Brookshire, W.K. (1993) Social, Emotional, and Behavioral Adjustment of Accelerated Students, Students in Gifted Classes, and Regular Students in Eighth Grade. *Gifted Child Quarterly* 37:150–154.

Scarr, S. (1981) *Race, Social Class, and Individual Differences in I.Q.* Hillsdale. N.J.: Erlbaum.

Scarr, S. (1986) How Plastic Are We? *Contemporary Psychology* 31:565–567.

Schappert, S.M. (1992) *Office Visits for Otitis Media: United States, 1975–1990.* Washington, D.C.: U.S. Department of Health and Human Services, no. 214.

Schein, J.D. (1994) Deafness in Canada and the United States. *Deaf American Monograph*, 93–99.

Schell, G.C. (1981) The Young Handicapped Child: A Family Perspective. *Topics in Early Childhood Special Education* 1:21–27.

Schepis, M.M., Reid, D.H., & Fitzgerald, J.R. (1987) Group Instruction with Profoundly Retarded Persons: Acquisition, Generalization, and Maintenance of a Remunerative Work Skill. *Journal of Applied Behavior Analysis* 21:97–102.

Scherling, D. (1994) Prenatal Cocaine Exposure and Childhood Psychopathology: A Developmental Analysis. *American Journal of Orthopsychiatry* 64:9–19.

Schery, K.S. (1985) Correlates of Language Development in Language-Disordered Children. *Journal of Speech and Hearing Disorders* 50:73–83.

Schiever, S.W., & Maker, C.J. (1991) Enrichment and Acceleration: An Overview and New Directions. In N. Colangelo & G. Davis (ed.), *Handbook of Gifted Education.* Needham Heights: Mass.: Allyn & Bacon, 99–111.

Schildroth, A., Rawlings, B., & Allen, T. (1991) Deaf Students in Transition: Education and Employment Issues for Deaf Adolescents. *Volta Review* 93:41–53.

Schleien, S.J., Green, F.P., & Heyne, L.A. (1993) Integrated Community Recreation. In M.E. Snell (ed.), *Instruction of Students with Severe Disabilities* (4th ed.). New York: Merrill, 526–556.

Schlesinger, A.M. (Jan. 7, 1994) Does Multicultural Education Contribute to Racial Tensions? *CQ Researcher* 4: 17–18.

Schloss, P.J., Espin, C.A., Smith, M.A., & Suffolk, D.R. (1987) Developing Assertiveness During Employment Interviews with Young Adults Who Stutter. *Journal of Speech and Hearing Disorders* 52:30–36.

Schmidt, P. (Feb. 8, 1995) Considerable Movement In and Out of Poverty Tracked. *Education Week*, p3.

Schmidt, P. (May 11, 1994) "Anti-Achievement Attitude" Among African-Americans Challenged. *Education Week*, 10–11.

Schmidt, P. (September, 1994) Idea of "Gender Gap" under Attack. *Education Week*, 1 & 16.

Schnaiberg, L. (1995, Feb. 8) Demise of Records-Transfer System for Migrant Students Causes Concern. *Education Week*, 20.

Schnaiberg, L. (1995, May 17) Rhetoric Outstrips Reality in Assessing Special-Needs Students. *Education Week*, 6–7.

Schneekloth, L. (1989) Play Environments for Visually Impaired Children. *Journal of Visual Impairment & Blindness* 83:196–201.

Schneider, B.H., Clegg, M.R., Byrne, B.M., Ledingham, J.E., & Crombie, G. (1989) Social Relations of Gifted Children as a Function of Age and School Program. *Journal of Educational Psychology* 81:48–56.

Schneider, E.W., & Bennion, J.L. (1981) *The Instructional Media Library: Videodiscs*, Englewood Cliffs, N.J.: Educational Technology Publications.

Schneider, J.W. (1988) Disability as Moral Experience: Epilepsy and Self in Routine Relationships. *Journal of Social Issues* 44:63–78.

Schneidman, E.S., Farberow, N.L., & Litman, R.E. (1970) *The Psychology of Suicide.* New York: Science House.

Scholl, G.T. (1987) Appropriate Education for Visually Handicapped Students. *Teaching Exceptional Children*, 33–36.

Schopler, E., Short, A., & Mesibov, G. (1989) Relation of Behavioral Treatment to "Normal Functioning." Comment on Lovaas. *Journal of Consulting and Clinical Psychology* 57:162–164.

Schreier, E.M. (1990) The Future of Access Technology for Blind and Visually Impaired People. *Journal of Visual Impairment & Blindness* 84:520–523.

Schriberg, L.D., Kwiatkowski, J., & Snyder, T. (1989) Tabletop Versus Microcomputer-Assisted Speech Management: Stabilization Phase. *Journal of Speech and Hearing Disorders* 54:233–248.

Schroedel, J. (1992) Helping Adolescents and Young Adults Who Are Deaf Make Career Decisions. *Volta Review* 93:37–46.

Schulz, J.B., Carpenter, C.D., & Turnbull, A.P. (1991) *Mainstreaming Exceptional Students*, Boston: Allyn & Bacon.

Schumaker, J.B., & Hazel, J.S. (1984a) Social Skills Assessment and Training for the Learning Disabled; Who's on First and What's on Second? Part One. *Journal of Learning Disabilities* 17:422–431.

Schumaker, J.B., & Hazel, J.S. (1984b) Social Skills Assessment and Training for the Learning Disabled: Who's on First and What's on Second? Part

Two. *Journal of Learning Disabilities* 17:492–499.

Schumaker, J.B., Hazel, J.S., Sherman, J.A., & Sheldon, J.C. (1982) Social Skill Performances of Learning Disabled, Non-Learning Disabled, and Delinquent Adolescents. *Learning Disabilities Quarterly* 5:388–397.

Schuster, D.T. (1990) Fulfillment of Potential, Life Satisfaction, and Competence: Comparing Four Cohorts of Gifted Women at Midlife. *Journal of Educational Psychology* 82:471–478.

Schvaneveldt, J.D., Lindauer, S.L.K., & Young, M.H. (1990) Children's Understanding of AIDS: A Developmental Viewpoint. *Family Relations* 39:330–335.

Schwartz, R.G. (1994) Phonological Disorders. In G.H. Shames, E.H. Wiig & W.A. Secord (eds.) *Human Communication Disorders* (4th ed.). New York: Macmillan, 250–292.

Schwartzberg, N.S. (1991) Stut-t-t-t-tering. *Parents* 155–158.

Schweinhart, L.J., & Weikert, D.P. (1980) Young Children Grow Up: The Effects of the Perry Preschool Program on Youth Through Age 15. *Monographs of the High Scope Educational Research Foundation* no. 7.

Schweinhart, L.J., & Weikert, D.P. (1981) Effects of the Perry Preschool Program on Youths Through Age 15. *Journal of the Division of Early Childhood* 4:29–39.

Scott, M.E. (1988) Learning Strategies Can Help. *Teaching Exceptional Children*, 30–34.

Scott, M.S., Perou, R., Urbano, R., Hogan, A., & Gold, S. (1992) The Identification of Giftedness: A Comparison of White, Hispanic and Black Families. *Gifted Child Quarterly* 36:131–140.

Scruggs, T.E., & Cohen, S.J. (1983) A University-Based Summer Program for a Highly Able But Poorly Achieving Indian Child. *Gifted Child Quarterly* 27:90–93.

Sears, R.R., Maccoby, E.E., & Levin, H. (1957) *Patterns of Child Rearing*. New York: Harper & Row.

Segal, N.L. (1990) The Importance of Twin Studies for Individual Differences Research. *Journal of Counseling and Development* 66:612–622.

Segalowitz, N.S. (1981) Issues in the Cross-Cultural Study of Bilingual Development. In H.C. Triandis & A. Heron (eds.), *Handbook of Cross-Cultural Psychology* (vol. 4) Boston: Allyn and Bacon, 55–93.

Seidenberg, M., & Berent, S. (1992) Childhood Epilepsy and the Role of Psychology. *American Psychologist* 47:1130–1133.

Seider, R.A., Gladstien, K.L., & Kidd, K.K. (1983) Recovery and Persistence of Stuttering Among Relatives of Stutterers. *Journal of Speech and Hearing Disorders* 48:409–414.

Seitz, V., & Apfel, N.H. (1994) Parent-Focused Intervention: Diffusion of Effects on Siblings. *Child Development* 65:666–677.

Seitz, V., & Apfel, N.H. (1994) Effects of a School for Pregnant Students on the Incidence of Low-Birthweight Deliveries. *Child Development* 65:666–676.

Seligman, J., with Chideya, F. (21 September 1992) Horror Story or Big Hoax. *Newsweek*, 75.

Seligman, M. (1985) Handicapped Children and Their Families. *Journal of Counseling and Development* 64:274–276.

Seligman, M. (1991a) Family Systems and Beyond: Conceptual Issues. In M. Seligman (ed.) *The Family with a Handicapped Child*, 2d ed. Boston: Allyn & Bacon, 27–51.

Seligman, M. (1991b) Siblings of Disabled Brothers and Sisters. In M. Seligman (ed.) *The Family with a Handicapped Child*, 2d ed. Boston: Allyn & Bacon, 181–198.

Seligman, M.E., Peterson, C., Kaslow, N.J., Tanenbaum, R.L., Alloy, L.B., & Abramson, L.Y. (1984) Attributional Style and Depressive Symptoms Among Children. *Journal of Abnormal Psychology* 93:235–238.

Seligman, M.E.P. (1975) *Helplessness: On Depression, Development, and Death*. San Francisco: Freeman.

Seltzer, M.M. (1984) Correlates of Community Opposition to Community Residences for Mentally Retarded Persons. *American Journal of Mental Deficiency* 89:1–8.

Semmel, M.I., Abernathy, T.V., Butera, G., & Lesar, S. (September 1991). Teacher Perceptions of the Regular Education Initiative. *Exceptional Children* 55:9–21.

SFA (Stuttering Foundation of America) (1992) *Did You Know? (Fact Sheet)*. Memphis, Tenn.: Stuttering Foundation of America.

SFA (Stuttering Foundation of America) (1992) *National Stuttering Awareness Week*. Memphis, Tenn.: Stuttering Foundation of America.

Shade, D.D. (Fall 1991) Integrating Computers into the Curriculum. *Day Care and Early Education* 18:45–47.

Shafii, M., Carrigan, S., Whittinghill, J.R., & Derrick, S. (1985) A Psychological Autopsy of Completed Suicide in Children and Adolescents. *American Journal of Psychiatry* 142:1061–1064.

Shafrir, U., & Siegel, L.S. (1994) Subtypes of Learning Disabilities in Adolescents and Adults. *Journal of Learning Disabilities* 27:123–134.

Shames, G.H. (1990) Disorders of Fluency. In G.H. Shames & E.H. Wiig (eds.), *Human Communication Disorders*, 3d ed. Columbus, Ohio: Merrill, 306–350.

Shames, G.H., & Wiig, E.H. (1990) *Human Communication Disorders*, 3d ed. Columbus, Ohio: Merrill.

Shanker, A. (October 18, 1993) A Rush to Inclusion. *New York Teacher* 8.

Shapiro, E.S. (1988) Preventing Academic Failure. *School Psychology Review* 17:601–613.

Shapiro, E.S., & Derr, T.F. (1987) An Examination of Overlap between Reading Curricula and Standardized Achievement Tests. *Journal of Special Education* 21:59–67.

Shapiro, J., Kramer, S., & Hunerberg, C. (1981) *Equal Their Chances: Children's Activities for Non-Sexist Learning*, Englewood Cliffs, N.J.: Prentice-Hall.

Shatz, M. (1983) Communication. In P.H. Mussen (ed.) *Handbook of Child*

Psychology, 4th ed. New York: Wiley, 841–891.

Shevin, M., & Klein, N.K. (1984) The Importance of Choice-Making Skills for Students with Severe Disabilities. *Journal of the Association for Persons with Severe Handicaps* 9:159–166.

Shinn, M., Knickman, J.R., & Weitzman, B.C. (1991) Social Relationships and Vulnerability to Becoming Homeless among Poor Families. *American Psychologist* 46:1180–1187.

Shonkoff, J.P., & Hauser-Cram, P. (1987) Early Intervention for Disabled Infants and Their Families: A Quantitative Analysis. *Pediatrics* 80:650–658.

Shonkoff, J.P., Hauser-Cram, P., Krauss, M.W., & Upshur, C.C. (1992) Development of Infants with Disabilities and Their Families. *Monographs of the Society for Research in Child Development* vol. 57.

Shriner, J., & Salvia, J. (1988) Chronic Noncorrespondence Between Elementary Math Curricula and Arithmetic Tests. *Exceptional Children* 54:240–248.

Siegel-Causey, E., & Wetherby, A. (1993) Nonsymbolic Communication. In M.E. Snell (ed.), *Instruction of Students with Severe Disabilities* (4th ed.). New York: Merrill, 290–319.

Siegel, L.J., & Senna, J.J. (1988) *Juvenile Delinquency*, 3d ed. St. Paul, Minn.: West Publishing Co.

Siegel, M.A., & Misselt, A.L. (1984) Adaptive Feedback and Review Paradigm for Computer-Based Drills. *Journal of Educational Psychology* 76:310–318.

Siegel, S., & Gaylord-Ross, R. (1991) Factors Associated with Employment Success Among Youths with Learning Disabilities. *Journal of Learning Disabilities* 24:40–47.

Sigafoos, J., Cole, D.A., & McQuarter, R.J. (1987) Current Practices in the Assessment of Students with Severe Handicaps. *Journal of the Association for Persons with Severe Handicaps* 12:264–273.

Sigafoos, J., & Dempsey, R. (1992) Assessing Choice Making Among Children with Multiple Disabilities.

Journal of Applied Behavior Analysis 25:747–755.

Sigmon, S.B. (1989) Reaction to Excerpts from the Learning Mystique: A Rational Appeal for Change. *Journal of Learning Disabilities* 22:298–301.

Silliman, E.R. (1992) Three Perspectives of Facilitated Communication: Unexpected Literacy, Clever Hands, or Enigma. *Topics in Language Disorders* 12:60–68.

Silver, L.B. (1987) The "Magic Cure": A Review of the Current Controversial Approaches for Treating Learning Disabilities. *Journal of Learning Disabilities* 20:498–504.

Silver, L.B. (1990) Attention Deficit Hyperactivity Disorder: Is It a Learning Disability or a Related Disorder? *Journal of Learning Disabilities* 23:394–397.

Silver, L.B. (1991) The Regular Education Initiative: A Deja Vu Remembered with Sadness and Concern. *Journal of Learning Disabilities* 24:389–390.

Silverman, F.H., & Paulus, P.G. (1989) Peer Reactions to Teenagers Who Substitute /w/ for /r/. *Language, Speech, and Hearing Services in Schools* 20:219–221.

Silverman, F.H. (1995) *Speech, Language, and Hearing Disorders*. Needham, Mass.: Allyn & Bacon.

Simkin, P., Whalleny, J., & Keppler, A. (1984) *Pregnancy, Childbirth, and the Newborn*, Deephaven, Minn.: Meadowbrook Books.

Simons, M., Whitbeck, L.B., Conger, R.D., & Chyi-in, W. (1991) Intergenerational Transmission of Harsh Parenting. *Developmental Psychology* 27:159–172.

Simpson, R.L., (1992) Peer Tutoring and Students with Autism. *Focus on Autistic Behavior* 7:16–18.

Simpson, R.L., & Myles, B.S. (1993) Successful Integration of Children with Autism in Mainstreamed Settings. *Focus on Autistic Behavior* 7:1–13.

Simpson, R.L., & Sasso, G.M. (1992) Full Inclusion of Students with Autism in General Education Settings: Values

Versus Science. *Focus on Autistic Behavior* 7:1–13.

Sindelar, P.T., & Deno, S.L. (1978) The Effectiveness of Resource Programming. *Journal of Special Education* 12:17–28.

Sinott-Oswald, M., Gliner, J.A., & Spencer, K.C. (1991) Supported and Sheltered Employment: Quality of Life Issues among Workers with Disabilities. *Education and Training in Mental Retardation* 9:388–397.

Siperstein, G.N. (1992) Social Competence: An Important Construct in Mental Retardation. *American Journal on Mental Retardation* 96:iii–vi.

Skeels, H.M. (1966) Adult Status of Children with Contrasting Early Life Experiences: A Follow-Up Study. *Monographs of the Society for Research in Child Development* 31:3.

Skellenger, A.C., & Hill, E.W. (1991) Current Practices and Considerations Regarding Long Cane Instruction with Preschool Children. *Journal of Visual Impairment & Blindness* 85:101–104.

Sklaroff, S. (November 10, 1993) "Quiet Crisis" Seen Hampering Gifted Students. *Education Week*, 5.

Slavin, R.E. (1994) *A Practical Guide to Cooperative Learning*, Boston: Allyn & Bacon.

Slavin, R.E. (1984) Students Motivating Students to Excel: Cooperative Incentives, Cooperative Tasks, and Student Achievement. *Elementary School Journal* 85:53–63.

Slavin, R.E., Madden, N.A., & Leavey, M. (1984) Effects of Cooperative Learning and Individualized Instruction on Mainstreamed Students. *Exceptional Children* 50:434–443.

Sleeter, C.E. (March 1993) Multicultural Education: Five Views. *Education Digest*, 53–57.

Slonim, M.B. (1991) *Children, Culture, and Ethnicity*, New York: Garland Pub. Co.

Smith, A.J., De l'aunne, W., & Geruschat, D.R. (1992) Low Vision Mobility Problems: Perceptions of O&M Specialists and Persons with Low Vision. *Journal of Visual Impairment & Blindness* 86:58–62.

Smith, B., Chung, M.C., & Vastanis, P. (1994) The Path to Care in Autism: Is It Better Now? *Journal of Autism and Developmental Disorders* 24: 551–565.

Smith, C.R. (1991) *Learning Disabilities*, 2d ed. Boston: Allyn and Bacon.

Smith, D.D. (1989) *Teaching Students with Learning and Behavior Problems*, 2d ed. Englewood Cliffs, N.J.: Prentice-Hall.

Smith, E.J. (1977) Counseling Black Individuals: Some Stereotypes. *Personnel and Guidance Journal* 55:390–396.

Smith, J., LeRose, B., & Clasen, R. (1991) Underrepresentation of Minority Students in Gifted Programs. Yes! It Matters. *Gifted Child Quarterly* 35:81–83.

Smith, S. (November/December 1992) Profile of Chronically Ill Children. *Public Health Reports*, 13–14.

Smith, S.L. (March/April 1988) Preparing the Learning Disabled Adolescent for Adulthood. *Children Today* 17:4–8.

Snell, M. (1987) *Systematic Instruction of Persons with Severe Handicaps* (3d ed.), Columbus, Ohio: Merrill.

Snell, M.E., & Farlow, L.J. (1993) Self-Care Skills. In M.E. Snell (ed.), *Instruction of Students with Severe Disabilities* (4th ed.). New York: Merrill, 380–442.

Snell, M.E., Lewis, A.P., & Houghton, A. (1989) Acquisition and Maintenance of Toothbrushing Skills by Students with Cerebral Palsy and Mental Retardation. *Journal of the Association for Persons with Severe Handicaps* 14:216–226.

Solomons, H.C., & Elardo, R. (1989) Bite Injuries at a Day Care Center. *Early Childhood Research Quarterly* 4:89–96.

Sonnenschein, P. (1981) Parents and Professionals: An Uneasy Relationship. *Teaching Exceptional Children* 62–65.

Soodak, L.C. & Podell, D.M. (1994) Teachers' Thinking About Difficult-To-Teach Students. *Journal of Educational Research* 88: 44–52.

Sorenson, D.A. (1991) Facilitating Responsible Behavior in Deaf Children. *Journal of the American Deafness and Rehabilitation Association* 25:1–7.

Soto, G., Belfiore, P.J., Schlosser, R.W., & Haynes, C. (1993) Teaching Specific Requests: A Comparative Analysis on Skill Acquisition and Preference Using Two Augmentative and Alternative Communication Aids. *Education and Training in Mental Retardation* 28:169–178.

Sowa, C.J., & Burks, H.M. (1983) Comparison of Cognitive Restructuring and Contingency-Based Instructional Models for Alleviation of Learned Helplessness. *Journal of Instructional Psychology* 10:186–191.

Spafford, C.S., & Grosser, G.S. (1993) The Social Misperception Syndrome in Children with Learning Disabilities: Social Causes Versus Neurological Variables. *Journal of Learning Disabilities* 26:178–189.

Spake, A. (November 1992) Autistic Children Are Breaking Through. *Education Digest*, 41–45.

Sparrow, S., Balla, D., & Cicchetti, D. (1984) *Vineland Adaptive Behavior Scales*. Circle Pines, Minn.: Am Guid Serv.

Spencer, P., Koester, L.S., & Meadow-Orlans, K. (1994) Communicative Interactions of Deaf and Hearing Children in a Day Care Center. *American Annals of the Deaf* 139: 512–518.

Spina Bifida Association of America (1992a) *Frequently Asked Questions About Spina Bifida*, Rockville, Md.: Spina Bifida Association of America.

Spina Bifida Association of America (1992b) *Spina Bifida: What the Teacher Needs to Know*, Rockville, Md.: Spina Bifida Association of America.

Spivak, M.P. (1986) Advocacy and Legislative Action for Head Injured Children and Their Families. *Journal of Head Trauma Rehabilitation* 1:41–47.

Spivey, K. (1992) The Superstar Who Couldn't Speak. *Reader's Digest* 141:49–50.

Spooner, F., Stem, B., & Test, D.W. (1989) Teaching First Aid Skills to Adolescents Who Are Moderately Mentally Handicapped. *Education and Training in Mental Retardation* 24:341–351.

Sprafkin, J., & Gadow, K.D. (1986) Television Viewing Habits of Emotionally Disturbed, Learning Disabled, and Mentally Retarded Children. *Journal of Applied Developmental Psychology* 7:45–59.

Sprafkin, J., & Gadow, K.D. (1987) An Observational Study of Emotionally Disturbed and Learning Disabled Children in School Settings. *Journal of Abnormal Child Psychology* 15:393–408.

Sprafkin, J., Gadow, K.D., & Abelman, R. (1992) *Television and the Exceptional Child: A Forgotten Audience*. Hillsdale, N.J.: Erlbaum.

Sprafkin, J., Gadow, K.D., & Dussault, M. (1986) Reality Perceptions of Television: A Preliminary Comparison of Emotionally Disturbed and Nonhandicapped Children. *American Journal of Orthopsychiatry* 56:147–152.

Sprafkin, J., Kelly, E., & Gadow, K.D. (1987) Reality Perceptions of Television: A Comparison of Emotionally Disturbed, Learning Disabled, and Nonhandicapped Children. *Journal of Developmental and Behavioral Pediatrics* 8:149–153.

Sprafkin, J., & Rubinstein, E.A. (1982) Using Television to Improve the Social Behavior of Institutionalized Children. *Prevention in Human Services* 2:107–114.

Sprafkin, J., Watkins, L.T., & Gadow, K.D. (1990) Efficacy of Television Literacy Curriculum for Emotionally Disturbed and Learning Disabled Children. *Journal of Applied Developmental Psychology* 11:225–244.

Spreen, O., & Haaf, R.G. (1986) Empirically Derived Learning Disability Subtypes: A Replications Attempt and Longitudinal Patterns over 15 years. *Journal of Learning Disabilities* 19:170–180.

Sprigle, J.E., & Schaefer, L. (1985) Longitudinal Evaluation of the Effects of Two Compensatory Preschool Programs on Fourth through Sixth Grade Students. *Developmental Psychology* 17:835–858.

SRCD (Society for Research in Child Development) (1991) *U.S. Children and Their Families: Current Conditions and Recent Trends* (1989) Washington, D.C.: SRCD.

Stainback, S., & Stainback, W. (1988) Educating Students with Severe Disabilities. *Teaching Exceptional Children,* 16–19.

Stainback, S., & Stainback, W. (1991) Schools as Inclusive Communities. In S. Stainback & W. Stainback (eds.) *Controversial Issues Confronting Special Education.* Needham Heights, Mass.: Allyn and Bacon, 27–45.

Stainback, W., & Stainback, S. (1984) A Rationale for the Merger of Special and Regular Education. *Exceptional Children* 51:102–111.

Stainback, W., Stainback, S. & Wilkinson, A. (1992) Encouraging Peer Supports and Friendships. *Teaching Exceptional Children* 24:6–11.

Stanford, L.D., & Hynd, G.W. (1994) Congruence of Behavioral Symptomatology in Children with ADD/H, ADD/WO, and Learning Disabilities. *Journal of Learning Disabilities* 27:243–253.

Stanley, J.C. (1991) An Academic Model for Educating the Mathematically Talented. *Gifted Child Quarterly* 35:36–42.

Stanley, J.C., & Benbow, C.P. (1986) Extremely Young College Graduates: Evidence of Their Success. *College and University* 58:361–371.

Stanovich, K.E. (1989) Learning Disabilities in Broader Context. *Journal of Learning Disabilities* 22:287–292.

Stanovich, K.E. (1994) Does Dyslexia Exist? *Journal of Child Psychology and Psychiatry and Allied Disciplines* 25: 575–579.

Stark, E., (May 1986) Friends Through It All. *Psychology Today*, 54–60.

Stark, K.D., Reynolds, W.M., & Kaslow, N.J. (1987) A Comparison of the Relative Efficacy of Self-Control Therapy and a Behavioral Problem-Solving Therapy for Depression in Children. *Journal of Abnormal Child Psychology* 15:91–113.

Statistical Abstract (1992) Washington, D.C.: U.S. Department of Commerce.

Statistical Abstract (1994) Washington, D.C.: U.S. Department of Commerce.

Staub, D., & Hunt, P. (1993) The Effects of Social Interaction Training on High School Peer Tutors of Schoolmates with Severe Disabilities. *Exceptional Children* 60:41–57.

Steinberg, L., Catalano, R., & Dooley, D., (1981) Economic Antecedent of Child Abuse. *Child Development* 52:975–985.

Steinberg, L., Dornbusch, S.M., & Brown, B.B. (1992) Ethnic Differences in Adolescent Achievement. *American Psychologist* 47:723–729.

Steiner, S., & Larson, V.L. (1991) Integrating Microcomputers into Language Intervention with Children. *Topics in Language Disorders* 11:18–30.

Stenehjem, D.O. (1993) Residential Schools: An Underutilized Resource. *Journal of Visual Impairment & Blindness* 87:211–213.

Stephens, T., Blackhurst, A., & Magliocca, L. (1982) *Teaching Mainstreamed Students*, New York: Wiley.

Stern, D.N., Spieker, S., & MacKain, K. (1982) Intonation Contours as Signals in Maternal Speech to Prelinguistic Infants. *Developmental Psychology* 18:727–736.

Sternberg, R.J. (1982) Lies We Live By: Misapplication of Tests in Identifying the Gifted. *Gifted Child Quarterly* 26:157–161.

Sternberg, R.J. (1991) Giftedness According to the Triarchic Theory of Human Intelligence. In N. Colangelo & G.A. Davis (eds.), *Handbook of Gifted Education.* Needham Heights, Mass.: Allyn & Bacon, 45–55.

Stevenson, H.W., Lee, S.Y. et al. (1990) Contexts of Achievement. *Monographs of the Society for Research in Child Development*, Serial no. 221.

Stevenson, R.E. (1973) *The Fetus and Newly Born Infant: Influences of the Prenatal Environment.* St. Louis, Mo.: C.V. Mosby.

Stewart, D.A. (1992) Initiating Reform in Total Communication Programs. *Journal of Special Education* 26:68–84.

Stinson, M.S., & Lang, H.G. (1994) Full Inclusion: A Path for Integration or Isolation. *American Annals of the Deaf* 139:156–159.

Stodgill, R. (1974) *Handbook of Leadership: A Survey of Theory and Research*, New York: Free Press.

Stoefen-Fisher, J.M., & Balk, J. (1992) Educational Programs for Children with Hearing Loss: Least Restrictive Environment. *Volta Review* 93:19–27.

Stone, W.L., & La Greca, A.M. (1990) The Social Status of Children with Learning Disabilities: A Reexamination. *Journal of Learning Disabilities* 23:32–37.

Stonge, J.H., & Tenhouse, C. (1990) *Educating Homeless Children: Issues and Answers.* Bloomington, Ind.: Phi Delta Kappa Educational Foundation.

Strain, P.S., & Smith, B.J. (1986) A Counter-Interpretation of Early Intervention Effects: A Response to Casto & Mastropieri. *Exceptional Children* 52:260–265.

Strauss, C.C. (1987) Anxiety. In M. Hersen & V.B. Van Hasselt (eds.), *Behavior Therapy with Children and Adolescents.* New York: Wiley, 109–136.

Streissguth, A.P., Martin, D.C., Barr, H.M., Sandman, B.M., Kirchner, G.L., & Darby, B.L. (1984) Intrauterine Alcohol and Nicotine Exposure: Attention and Reaction Time in Four-Year-Old Children. *Developmental Psychology* 20:534–542.

Strobino, D.M. (1987) *The Health and Medical Consequences of Adolescent Sexuality and Pregnancy: A Review of the Literature in Risking the Future*, vol. 2. Washington, D.C.: National Academy Press, 93–123.

Stuckless, E.R., & Carroll, J.K. (1994) National Priorities on Educational Applications of Technology for Deaf and Hard-of-Hearing Students. *American Annals of the Deaf*, Special Issue, 139:62–66.

Sue, D., Sue, D.W., & Sue, S. (1990) *Understanding Abnormal Behavior* (3d ed.). Boston: Houghton Mifflin.

Sue, S., & Okazai, S. (1990) Asian-American Educational Achievements: A Phenomenon in Search of an Explanation. *American Psychologist* 45:913–920.

Sugai, G. (1988) Educational Assessment of the Culturally Diverse and Behavior-Disordered Student: An Examination of Critical Effect. In A.A. Ortiz & B.A. Ramirez (eds.), *Schools and the Culturally Diverse Exceptional Student: Promising Practices and Future Directions.* Reston, Va.: Council for Exceptional Children, 63–76.

Sussman, V. (12 September 1994) Opening Doors to an Inaccessible World. *U.S. News and World Report*, 85.

Swanson, H.L. (1994) Short-Term Memory and Working Memory: Do Both Contribute to Our Understanding of Academic Achievement in Children and Adults with Learning Disabilities? *Journal of Learning Disabilities* 27:34–50.

Swanson, J.M., Cantwell, D., Lerner, M., McBurnett, K., & Hanna, G. (1991) Effects of Stimulant Medication on Learning in Children with ADHD. *Journal of Learning Disabilities* 24:219–230.

Sweetland, R.C., & Keyser, D.J. (1991) *Tests: A Comprehensive Reference for Assessments in Psychology, Education, and Business,* 3rd ed. Austin, Tex.: Pro-Ed.

Sweetland, R.C., & Keyser, D.J. (1993) *Tests: A Comprehensive Reference for Assessments in Psychology, Education, and Business,* Austin, Texas: Pro-Ed.

Swenson, E.V. (1978) Teacher-Assessment of Creative Behavior in Disadvantaged Children. *Gifted Child Quarterly* 22:338–343.

Swiatek, M.A., & Benbow, C.P. (1991) Ten-Year Longitudinal Follow-up of Ability-Matched Accelerated and Un-accelerated Gifted Students. *Journal of Educational Psychology* 83:528–538.

Swift, J.N., & Gooding, C.T. (1983) Interaction of Wait Time Feedback and Questioning Instruction on Middle School Science Teaching. *Journal of Research for Science Teaching* 20: 721–730.

Swindell, C.S., Holland, A.L., & Reinmuth, O.M. (1994) Aphasia and Related Adult Disorders. In Human Communication Disorders (4th ed.). New York: Macmillan, 521–560.

Szatmari, P. (1992) A Review of the DSM3-R Criteria for Autistic Disorder. *Journal of Autism and Developmental Disorders* 22:507–523.

Tannenbaum, A. (1983) *Gifted Children,* New York: MacMillan.

Tarver-Behring, S., Barkley, R.A., & Karlsson, J. (1985) The Mother-Child Interactions of Hyperactive Boys and Their Normal Siblings. *American Journal of Orthopsychiatry* 55:202–209.

TASH, (1986) Resolution on the Cessation of Intrusive Interventions. In L.H. Meyer, C.A. Peck, & L. Brown, *Critical Issues in the Lives of People with Severe Disabilities*, 1991. Baltimore, Md.: Paul H. Brookes, 550.

Tavernier, G.G.F. (1993) The Improvement of Vision by Vision Stimulation and Training: A Review of the Literature. *Journal of Visual Impairment & Blindness* 87:143–148.

Taylor, O.L., & Payne, K.T. (1994) Language and Communication Differences. In *Human Communication Disorders* (4th ed.). New York: Macmillan, 136–173.

Taylor, R.L. (1993) Instruments for the Screening, Evaluation, and Assessment of Infants and Toddlers. In D.M. Bryant & M.A. Graham (eds.) *Implementing Early Intervention.* New York: The Guilford Press, 157–183.

Taylor, S.J. (1988) Caught in the Continuum: A Critical Analysis of the Principle of the Least Restrictive Environment. *Journal of the Association for Persons with Severe Handicaps* 13:41–53.

Tebbi, C.K., Richards, M.E., Cummings, K.M., Zevon, M.A. & Mallon, J.C. (1988) The Role of Parent-Adolescent Concordance in Compliance with Cancer Chemotherapy. *Adolescence* 23:599–611.

Telzrow, C.F. (1987) Management of Academic and Educational Problems in Head Injury. *Journal of Learning Disabilities* 20:536–545.

Terman, L.M., (1925) *Mental and Physical Traits of 1,000 Gifted Children. Genetic Studies of Genius* (vol. 1), Stanford, Calif.: Stanford University Press.

Terman, L.M., & Oden, M.H. (1947) The Gifted Child Grows Up: Twenty-five Years' Follow-up of a Superior Group. *Genetic Studies of Genius* (vol. 5), Stanford, Calif.: Stanford University Press.

Terman, L.M., & Oden, M.H. (1959) The Gifted Group at Mid-Life: Thirty-Five Years' Follow-Up of the Superior Child. In L. Terman (ed.), *Genetic Studies of Genius,* (vol. 5). Stanford, Calif.: Stanford University Press.

Terwilliger, J.S., & Titus, J.C. (1995) Gender Differences in Attitudes and Attitude Changes Among Mathematically Talented Youth. *Gifted Child Quarterly* 39: 29–35.

Test, D.W., Grossi, T., & Keul, P. (1988) A Functional Analysis of the Acquisition and Maintenance of Janitorial Skills in a Competitive Work Setting. *Journal of the Association for Persons with Severe Handicaps* 13:1–7.

Thompson, L. (7 August 1992). Researchers Call for Time Out on Cell-Transplant Research. *Science* 257:738.

Thompson, R.A., Cicchetti, D., Lamb, M.E., & Malkin, C. (1985) Emotional Responses of Down's Syndrome and Normal Infants in the Strange Situation: The Organization of Affective Behavior in Infants. *Developmental Psychology* 21:828–842.

Thurston, L.P. (1989) Helping Parents Tutor Their Children: A Success Story. *Academic Therapy* 24:579–587.

Tirapelle, L., & Cipani, E. (1992) Developing Functional Requesting: Acquisition, Durability, and Generalizations of Effects. *Exceptional Children* 58:260–269.

Todd, N. (1992) The Use of Portable Computers: A Survey of Visually Impaired College Students. *Journal of*

Visual Impairment & Blindness 86:370–371.

Tolman, M.N., & Allred, R.A. (1987) *The Computer and Education*, Washington, D.C.: National Education Association.

Tomchek, L.B., Gordon, R., Arnold, M., Handleman, J., & Harris, S. (1992) Teaching Children with Autism and Their Normally Developing Peers: Meeting the Challenges of Integrated Education. *Focus on Autistic Behavior* 7:1–19.

Tomlinson-Keasey, C. & Little, T.D. (1990) Predicting Educational Attainment, Occupational Achievement, Intellectual Skill, and Personal Adjustment Among Gifted Men and Women. *Journal of Educational Psychology* 82:442–445.

Topping, K. (1987) Peer Tutored Pair Reading: Outcome Data from Ten Projects. *Educational Psychology* 7:133–145.

Toro, P.A., & Warren, M.G. (1991) Homelessness, Psychology, and Public Policy. *American Psychologist* 46:1205–1207.

Toro, P.A., Weissberg, R.P., Guare, J., & Liebenstein, N.L. (1990) A Comparison of Children With and Without Learning Disabilities on Social Problem-Solving Skill, School Behavior, and Family Background. *Journal of Learning Disabilities* 23:115–119.

Torrance, E.P. (1962) *Guiding Creative Talent*, Englewood Cliffs, N.J.: Prentice-Hall.

Tower, R.L. (1987) *How Schools Can Help Combat Child Abuse and Neglect* (2d ed.). Washington, D.C.: NEA Professional Library.

Travis, J. (October 9, 1992) New Optimism Blooms for Developing Treatments. *Science* 258:218–222.

Treaster, J.B. (25 January 1993) Drop in Youths' Cocaine Use May Reflect a Societal Shift. *New York Times*, A14.

Treffinger, D.J. (1982) Gifted Students, Regular Classrooms: Sixty Ingredients for a Better Blend. *Elementary School Journal* 82:267–273.

Treffinger, D.J. (1991) Future Goals and Directions. In N. Colangelo & G. Davis (eds.), *Handbook of Gifted Education* Needham Heights, Mass.: Allyn & Bacon, 439–450.

Trehub, S. (1973) Infants' Sensitivity to Vowel and Tonal Contrasts. *Developmental Psychology* 9:81–96.

Trickett, P.K., Aber, J.L., Carlson, V., & Cicchitti, D. (1991) Relationship of Socioeconomic Status to the Etiology and Development of Physical Child Abuse. *Developmental Psychology* 27:148–159.

Trickett, P.K., & Kuczynski, L. (1986) Children's Misbehaviors and Parental Discipline Strategies in Abusive and Non-Abusive Families. *Developmental Psychology* 24:270–277.

TRIPOD (Spring 1992) *Sense*, vol. 10, no. 1, Burbank, Calif.: Tripod, 6.

Tritt, S.G., & Esses, L.M. (1988) Psychosocial Adaptation of Siblings of Children with Chronic Medical Illness. *American Journal of Orthopsychiatry* 58:211–220.

Trupin, E.W., Gilchrist, L., Maiuro, R.D., & Fay, G. (1979) Social Skills Training for Learning-Disabled Children. In L.A. Hamelynck (ed.) *Behavioral Systems for the Developmentally Disabled: Institutional, Clinic and Community Environments.* New York: Brunner/Mazel.

Tsai, L.Y., & Ghaziuddin, M. (1992) Biomedical Research in Autism. In D.E. Berkell (ed.), *Autism: Identification, Education, and Treatment.* Hillsdale, N.J.: Erlbaum, 53–77.

Tucker, J.A. (1985) Curriculum-Based Assessment: An Introduction. *Exceptional Children* 52:199–204.

Tur-Kaspa, H. & Bryan, T. (1995) Teachers' Ratings of the Social Competence and School Adjustment of Students with LD in Elementary and Junior High School. *Journal of Learning Disabilities* 28: 44–52.

Turkel, S.B., & Podell, D.M. (1984) Computer-Assisted Learning for Mildly Handicapped Students. *Teaching Exceptional Children* 16:258–262.

Turnbull, A., & Morningstar, M.E. (1993) Family and Professional Intervention. In M.E. Snell (ed.), *Instruction of Students with Severe Disabilities* (4th ed.). New York: Merrill, 31–61.

Turnbull, A.P., & Turnbull, H.R. (1990) *Families, Professionals, and Exceptionality: A Special Partnership*, Columbus, Ohio: Merrill, 134–135.

Tuttle, F.B. (1989) *Gifted and Talented Students* (rev. ed.), Washington, D.C.: National Education Association.

Tuttle, F.B., Becker, L.A., & Sousa, J.A. (1988) *Characteristics and Identification of Gifted and Talented Students* (3d ed.). Washington, D.C.: NEA Publications.

United States Department of Education. (1990) *Twelfth Annual Report to Congress on the Implementation of the Education of the Handicapped Act.* Washington, D.C.: U.S. Department of Education, 23.

U.S. Bureau of Labor (1990) *Statistical Update.*

U.S. Bureau of the Census (March 1988) Poverty in the United States, 1986. *Current Population Reports*, P-60, no. 160, Washington, D.C.

U.S. Consumer Product Safety Commission (1991) *National Electronic Injury Surveillance System. Product Summary Report—Eye Injuries, 1991*, Washington, D.C.: National Society to Prevent Blindness.

U.S. Department of Commerce (1989) *Statistical Abstracts of the United States* (109th ed.), Washington, D.C.: U.S. Department of Commerce.

U.S. Department of Commerce (1993) *Statistical Abstracts of the United States* (113th ed.), Washington, D.C.: U.S. Department of Commerce.

U.S. Department of Education. (1987a) *What Works: Research on Teaching.* Washington, D.C.: U.S. Department of Education.

U.S. Department of Education. (1987b) *What Works: Schools that Work: Educating Disadvantaged Children.* Washington, D.C.: U.S. Department of Education.

U.S. Department of Education (1989) *Eleventh Annual Report to Congress on the Implementation of the Education of the Handicapped Act,* Washington, D.C.

U.S. Department of Education (1993) *Fifteenth Annual Report to Congress on the Implementation of the Education of the Handicapped Act.* Washington, D.C.: U.S. Department of Education.

U.S. Department of Education (1993) *To Assure the Free Appropriate Public Education of All Handicapped Children: Fifteenth Annual Report to Congress on the Implementation of the Education of the Handicapped Act.* Washington, D.C.: U.S. Department of Education.

U.S. Department of Education (1993) *To Assure the Free Appropriate Public Education of All Children with Disabilities: Fifteenth Annual Report to Congress on the Implementation of the Individuals with Disabilities Education Act.* Washington, D.C.: U.S. Department of Education.

U.S. Department of Education (1994) *Sixteenth Annual Report to Congress on the Implementation of the Individuals with Disabilities Education Act,* Washington, D.C.: U.S. Department of Education.

U.S. Department of Education (1994) *To Assure the Free Appropriate Public Education of All Children With Disabilities. Sixteenth Annual Report to Congress on the Implementation of the Individuals With Disabilities Act,* Washington, D.C.: U.S. Department of Education.

U.S. Department of Education (July 1993) *National Goals for Education,* Washington, D.C.: U.S. Department of Education.

U.S. Department of Health and Human Services (1983) *Age Page: Aging and Your Eyes,* Washington, D.C.: Public Health Service, National Institutes of Health, no. 1983-416-519.

U.S. Department of Health and Human Services (1986) *Spina Bifida,* Washington, D.C.: Public Health Service.

USDHHS (United States Department of Health and Human Services). (1988) *Developmental Speech and Language Disorders.* Bethesda, Md.: National Institutes of Health, NIH Pub. No. 88-2757.

Uslan, M.M. (1993) A Review of Two Low-Cost Closed-Circuit Television Systems. *Journal of Visual Impairment & Blindness* 87:310–313.

U.S. News and World Report (27 October 1986) Children Under Stress.

U.S. News & World Report (March 31, 1986) Educating the Melting Pot, 20–21.

Utley, C., Lowitzer, A., & Baumeister, A. (1987) A Comparison of the AAMD's Definitions, Eligibility Criteria, and Classification Schemes with State Department of Education Guidelines. *Education and Training in Mental Retardation* 5:35–43.

Vadasy, P.F., Fewell, R.R., Meyer, D.J., & Schell, G. (1984) Siblings of Handicapped Children: A Developmental Perspective on Family Interactions. *Family Relations* 33:155–167.

Vandell, D.L., & George, L.B. (1981) Social Interaction in Hearing and Deaf Preschoolers: Successes and Failures in Initiations. *Child Development* 52:627–635.

Van Hasselt, V.B., Hersey, M., Kazdin, A.E., Simon, J., & Mastanuono, A. (1983) Training Blind Adolescents in Social Skills. *Journal of Visual Impairment & Blindness* 77:199–203.

Van Oudenhoven, J.P., Van Berjum, G., & Swen-Koopmans, T. (1987) Effect of Cooperative and Shared Feedback on Spelling Achievement. *Journal of Educational Psychology* 79:92–94.

Van Riper, C. (1982) *The Nature of Stuttering.* Englewood Cliffs, N.J.: Prentice Hall.

VanTassel-Baska, J. (1989) Gifted Girls. In J. Feldhusen, J. Van Tassel-Baska, & K. Seeley (eds.), *Excellence in Educating the Gifted.* Denver, Colo.: Love Pub. Co., 53–70.

Van Tassel-Baska, J. & Willis, G. (1987) A Three-Year Study of the Effects of Low Income on SAT Scores Among the Academically Able. *Gifted Child Quarterly* 31:169–173.

Vaughn, S. (1985) Why Teach Social Skills to Learning Disabled Students? *Journal of Learning Disabilities* 18:588–591.

Vaughn, S., Haager, D., Hogan, A., & Kouzekanani, K. (1992) Self-Concept and Peer Acceptance in Students with LD: A Four-to-Five-Year Prospective Study. *Journal of Educational Psychology* 84:43–50.

Vaughn, S., Hogan, A., Kouzekanani, K., & Shapiro, S. (1990) Peer Acceptance, Self-Perception, and Social Skills of LD Students Prior to Identification. *Journal of Educational Psychology* 82:101–106.

Vaughn, S., Schumm, J.S., & Kouzekanani, K., (1993) What Do Students with Learning Disabilities Think When Their General Education Teachers Make Adaptations? *Journal of Learning Disabilities* 26:545–555.

Vaughn, S., Zaragoza, N., Hogan, A., & Walker, J. (1993) A Four-Year Longitudinal Investigation of the Social Skills and Behavior Problems of Students with Learning Disabilities. *Journal of Learning Disabilities* 26:404–412.

Vaughn, V.L., Feldhusen, J.F., & Asher, J.W. (1991). Meta-Analyses and Review of Research on Pull-Out Programs in Gifted Education. *Gifted Child Quarterly* 35:92–98.

Venn, J. (1994) *Assessment of Students with Special Needs.* New York: Merrill.

Venn, J. (1994) *Assessment of Students with Special Needs.* New York: Macmillan.

Ventura, S.J. (1994) Recent Trends in Teenage Childbearing in the United States. *Statistical Bulletin* 75: 10–17.

Vergason, G.A., & Anderegg, M.L. (1991) Preserving the Least Restrictive Environment. In S. Stainback & W. Stainback (eds.) *Controversial Issues Confronting Special Education.* Needham Heights, Mass.: Allyn and Bacon, 45–55.

Vernon, M., & Kohl, S.D. (1970) Effects of Manual Communication of Deaf Children's Educational Achievement, Linguistic Competence, Oral Skills, and Psychological Adjustment. *American Annals of the Deaf* 115:527–536.

Verplanken, B., Meijnders, A., & van de Wege, A. (1994) Emotion and Cognition: Attitudes Toward Persons Who Are Visually Impaired. *Journal of Visual Impairment & Blindness* 88:504–511

Viadero, D. (5 May 1993) Special Education Update. *Education Week* 10.

Viadero, D. (6 December 1989) Parents of Blind Children Lead Push to Make Braille Instruction Available. *Education Week*, P5, 9.

Viadero, D. (15 June 1987) Youth Actions Seen Unchanged by AIDS Scare. *Education Week*, 16.

Viadero, D. (28 January 1987) Panels to Develop Model Suicide Prevention Program for Schools. *Education Week*, 5.

Viadero, D. (August 3, 1988) "Least Restrictive" Class Found Cheapest for Handicapped. *Education Week*, 7.

Vickers, H.S. (1994) Young Children at Risk: Differences in Family Functioning. *Journal of Educational Research* 87: 262–271.

Vockell, E.L. (1987) The Computer and Academic Learning Time. *The Clearing House* 61:72–75.

Vockell, E.L., & Mihail, T. (1993) Instructional Principles Behind Computerized Instruction for Students with Exceptionalities. *Teaching Exceptional Children* 25:36–43.

Vockell, E.L., & Mihail, T. (1993) Instructional Principles Behind Computerized Instruction for Students with Exceptionalities. *Teaching Exceptional Children* 25:38–43.

Vogel, S.A. (1990) Gender Differences in Intelligence, Language, Visual-Motor Abilities, and Academic Achievement in Students with Learning Disabilities: A Review of the Literature. *Journal of Learning Disabilities* 23:44–51.

Volin, R.A. (1991) Microcomputer-Based Systems Providing Biofeedback of Voice and Speech Production. *Topics in Language Disorders* 11:65–79.

Volk, D., & Stahlman, J.I. (Spring 1994). "I Think Everybody Is Afraid of the Unknown": Early Childhood Teachers Prepare for Mainstreaming. *Day Care and Early Education* 21:13–17.

Vorhees, C.V., & Mollnow, E. (1987) Behavioral Teratogenesis: Long-Term Influences on Behavior from Early Exposure to Environmental Agents. In J.D. Osofsky (ed.), *Handbook of Infant Development*. New York: Wiley, 913–972.

Wacker, D., Wiggins, B., Fowler, M., & Berg, W. (1988) Training Students with Profound or Multiple Handicaps to Make Requests Via Microswitches. *Journal of Applied Behavior Analyses* 21:331–343.

Wahlstrom, J. (1990) Gene Map of Mental Retardation. *Journal of Mental Deficiency* 34:11–27.

Walberg, H.J. (Feb. 1990) Productive Teaching and Instruction: Assessing the Knowledge Base. *Phi Delta Kappan*, 470–478.

Walden, E.L., & Thompson, S.A. (1981) A Review of Some Alternative Approaches to Drug Management of Hyperactivity in Children. *Journal of Learning Disabilities* 4:213–217.

Walker, B.A., Reis, S.M., & Leonard, J.S. (1992) A Developmental Investigation of the Lives of Gifted Women. *Gifted Children Quarterly* 36:201–206.

Walker, D.K., Singer, J.D., Palfrey, J.S., Orza, M., Wenger, M., & Butler, J.A. (1988) Who Leaves and Who Stays in Special Education: A Two-Year Follow-up Study. *Exceptional Children* 54:393–402.

Walker, M.D. (1991) Acute Spinal-Cord Injury. *New England Journal of Medicine* 324:1885–1887.

Wallander, J.L., Varni, J.W., Babani, L., DeHaan, C.B., Wilcox, K.T., & Banis, H.T. (1989) The Social Environment and the Adaptation of Mothers of Physically Handicapped Children. *Journal of Pediatric Psychology* 14:371–387.

Wallerstein, J.S. (1983) Children of Divorce: The Psychological Tasks of the Child. *American Journal of Orthopsychiatry* 53:230–243.

Wallerstein, J.S. (1987) Children of Divorce: Report of a Ten-Year Follow-Up of Early Latency-Age Children. *American Journal of Orthopsychiatry* 57:199–211.

Wallerstein, J.S., Corbin, S.B., & Lewis, J.M., (1988) Children of Divorce: A 10-Year-Study. In E.M. Hetherington & J.D. Arasteh (eds.), *Impact of Divorce, Single Parenting, and Stepparenting on Children*. Hillsdale, N.J.: Erlbaum, 197–215.

Wallerstein, J.S., & Kelly, J. (1979) Divorce and Children. In J.D. Noshpitz (ed.), *Basic Handbook of Child Psychiatry*, vol. 4. New York: Basic Books, 339–347.

Wallinga, C., Paguio, L., & Skeen, P. (1987) When a Brother or Sister Is Ill. *Psychology Today* 42, 43.

Wanat, P.E. (1983) Social Skills: An Awareness Program with Learning Disabled Adolescents. *Journal of Learning Disabilities* 16:35–38.

Wang, M.C., Anderson, K.A., & Baum, P.J. (1985) *Toward an Empirical Data Base on Mainstreaming: A Research Synthesis of Program Implementation and Effects*, Pittsburgh: Learning Research and Development Center: University of Pittsburgh.

Wang, M.C., & Walberg, H.J. (1988) Four Fallacies of Segregation. *Exceptional Children* 55:128–137.

Ward, M.J. (1991) Self-Determination Revisited: Going Beyond Expectations. Washington, D.C.: NICHY Transition Summary, 2–7.

Waring, D., Johnson, D.W., Maruyama, G., & Johnson, R. (1985) Impact of Different Types of Cooperative Learning on Cross-Ethnic and Cross-Sex Relationships. *Journal of Educational Psychology* 77:53–59.

Warren, S.F., & Abbeduto, L. (1992) The Relation of Communication and Language Development to Mental Retardation. *American Journal on Mental Retardation* 97:125–130.

Warren, S.F. & Horn, E.M. (1987) Microcomputer Applications in Early Childhood Special Education: Problems and Possibilities. *Topics in Early Childhood Special Education* 7:72–84.

Warren, S.F., & Kaiser, A.P. (1986) Generalization of Treatment Effects by

Young Language-Delayed Children: A Longitudinal Analysis. *Journal of Speech and Hearing Disorders* 51:239–251.

Washington, V. (1985) Head Start: How Appropriate for Minority Families in the 1980s. *American Journal of Orthopsychiatry* 55:577–590.

Wasik, B.H., Ramey, C.T., Bryant, D.M., & Sparling, J.J. (1990) A Longitudinal Study of Two Early Intervention Strategies: Project CARE. *Child Development* 61:1682–1697.

Watson, M. (1977) *Mainstreaming.* Washington, D.C.: National Educational Association.

Watt, J., & Davis, F. (1991) The Prevalence of Boredom Proneness and Depression Among Profoundly Deaf Residential School Adolescents. *American Annals of the Deaf* 136:409–413.

Webster's New Twentieth Century Unabridged Dictionary of the English Language (1974), s.v. "talent."

Wechsler, D. (1991) *Manual for the Wechsler Intelligence Scale for Children III.* San Antonio, Tex.: Psychological Corp.

Weinberg, R.A. (1979) Early Childhood Education and Intervention: Establishing an American Tradition. *American Psychologist* 34:912–916.

Weinreb, L., & Buckner, J.C. (1993) Homeless Families: Program Responses and Public Policies. *American Journal of Orthopsychiatry* 63:400–408.

Weisberg, R.W. (1986) *Creativity: Genius and Other Myths,* New York: Freeman.

Weiss, C.D., & Lillywhite, H.S. (1976) *Communication Disorders: A Handbook for Prevention and Early Intervention.* St. Louis: Mosby.

Weiss, G. (1990) Hyperactivity in Childhood. *New England Journal of Medicine* 323:1413–1414.

Wenar, C. (1994) *Developmental Psychopathology,* 3d ed. New York: McGraw Hill.

Wenkart, R.D. (1993) The Americans With Disabilities Act and Its Impact on Public Education. *West's Education Law Reporter* 82:291–302.

Werner, E.E. (November 1984) Resilient Children. *Young Children,* 686–692.

Werner, E.E., & Smith, R.S. (1982) *Vulnerable But Invincible: A Study of Resilient Children.* New York: McGraw-Hill.

Wertlieb, D., Weigel, C., & Feldstein, M. (1989) Stressful Experiences, Temperament, and Social Support: Impact on Children's Behavior Symptoms. *Journal of Applied Developmental Psychology* 10:487–505.

Wertlieb, D., Weigel, C., Springer, T., & Feldstein, M. (1987) Temperament as a Moderator of Children's Stressful Experiences. *American Journal of Orthopsychiatry* 57:234–245.

West, M., Kregel, J., Getzel, E.E., Zhu, M., Ipsen, S.M., & Martin, E.D. (1993) Beyond Section 504: Satisfaction and Empowerment of Students with Disabilities in Higher Education. *Exceptional Children* 59:456–467.

Westinghouse Learning Corporation (June 1969) *The Impact of Head Start: An Evaluation of Effects of Head Start on Children's Cognitive and Affective Development.* Executive Summary, Ohio University. Report to the Office of Economic Opportunity. Washington, D.C.: Clearinghouse for Federal Scientific and Technical Information (EDO93497).

Weyant, J.M. (1986) *Applied Social Psychology,* New York: Oxford University Press.

Whalen, C.K., & Henker, B. (1991) Social Impact of Stimulant Treatment for Hyperactive Children. *Journal of Learning Disabilities* 24:231–241.

Whalen, H., Henker, B., Buhrmester, D., Hinshaw, S.P., Huber, A., & Laski, K. (1989) Does Stimulant Medication Improve the Peer Status of Hyperactive Children? *Journal of Consulting and Clinical Psychology* 57:545–549.

Wheeler, D.L., Jacobson, J.W., Paglieri, R.A., & Schwartz, A.A. (1993) An Experimental Assessment of Facilitated Communication. *Mental Retardation* 31:49–61.

White, K.R., Bush, D., & Casto, G. (1986) Let the Past Be Prologue: Learning from Previous Reviews of Early Inter-

vention Efficacy Research. *Journal of Special Education* 19:417–428.

Whitman, B., Accordo, P., Boyert, M., & Kendagor, R. (1990) Homelessness and Cognitive Performance in Children: A Possible Link. *Social Work* 35:516–519.

Whitmore, J. (1980) *Giftedness, Conflict, and Underachievement,* Boston: Allyn & Bacon.

Whitmore, J., & Maker, J. (1985) *Intellectual Giftedness in Disabled Persons,* Rockville, Md.: Aspen.

Whitmore, J.R. (1980) *Giftedness, Conflict, and Underachievement,* Boston: Allyn & Bacon.

Whitney, E.N., Cataldo, C.B., & Rolfes, S.R. (1994) *Understanding Normal and Clinical Nutrition.* St. Paul, Minn.: West Publishing Co.

Whitehurst, G.J., Fischel, J.E., Lonigan, C.J., Valdez-Menchaca, M.C., Arnold, D.S., & Smith, M. (1991) Treatment of Early Expressive Language Delay: If, When, and How. *Topics in Language Disorders* 11:55–68.

Whurr, R., Lorch, M.P., & Nye, C. (1992) A Meta-Analysis of Studies Carried Out Between 1946 and 1988 Concerned with the Efficacy of Speech and Language Therapy Treatment for Aphasic Patients. *European Journal of Disorders of Communication* 27:1–17.

Wicks-Nelson, R., & Israel, A.C. (1991) *Behavior Disorders of Childhood* (2d ed.), Englewood Cliffs, N.J.: Prentice-Hall.

Wiebe, J.H. (1993) The Software Domain. In J.D. Lindsay (ed.), *Computers and Exceptional Individuals* (2d ed.). Austin, Tex.: Pro-Ed, 45–65.

Wiederholt, J.L. (1987) A Preface to the Special Series on Acquired Cerebral Trauma. *Journal of Learning Disabilities* 20:452–453.

Wierson, M., Forehand, R., Fauber, R., & McCombs, A., (1989) Buffering Young Male Adolescents Against Negative Parental Divorce Influences: The Role of Good Parent-Adolescent Relations. *Child Study Journal* 19:101–115.

Wiig, E.H. (1990) Language Disabilities in School-Age Children. In G.H. Shames & E.H. Wiig (eds.), *Human*

Communication. Columbus, Ohio: Merrill, 196–218.

Wikler, L.M. (1981) Chronic Stresses in Families of Mentally Retarded Children. *Family Relations* 30:281–288.

Wikler, L.M. (1986) Periodic Stresses of Families of Older Mentally Retarded Children: An Exploratory Study. *American Journal of Mental Deficiency* 90:703–706.

Wikler, L.M., Wasow, M., & Hatfield, E. (1981) Chronic Sorrow Revisited: Attitudes of Parents and Professionals About Adjustment to Mental Retardation. *American Journal of Orthopsychiatry* 51:63–70.

Wilchesky, M., & Reynolds, T. (1986) The Socially Deficient LD Child in Context: A Systems Approach to Assessment and Treatment. *Journal of Learning Disabilities* 19:411–415.

Will, M. (1986) Educating Children with Learning Problems: A Shared Responsibility. *Exceptional Children* 52:411–415.

Will, M. (November 1986) *Educating Students with Learning Disabilities.* Washington, D.C.: U.S. Department of Education, Office of Special Education and Rehabilitative Services.

Williams, B.L. (1975) The Bitch-100: A Culture-Specific Test. *Journal of Afro-American Issues* 3:103–116.

Williams, M. (1987) Aphasia. In R.L. Gregory (ed.), *The Oxford Companion to The Mind.* Oxford, England: Oxford University Press, 31–33.

Williams, W., Fox, T.J., Thousand, J., & Fox, W. (1990) Level of Acceptance and Implementation of Best Practices in the Education of Students with Severe Handicaps in Vermont. *Education and Training in Mental Retardation* 25:120–131.

Willig, A.E. (1985) A Meta-Analysis of Selected Studies on the Effectiveness of Bilingual Education. *Review of Educational Research* 55:269–317.

Wilmott, R., Burroughs, B.R., & Beele, D. (1984) Cystic Fibrosis. In J. Fithian (ed.), *Understanding the Child with a Chronic Illness in the Classroom.* Phoenix, Ariz.: Oryx Press, 114–134.

Wilmott, R., Kolski, G., & Burg, I. (1984) Asthma. In J. Fithian (ed.), *Understanding the Child with a Chronic Illness in the Classroom.* Phoenix, Ariz.: Oryx Press, 1–13.

Wilson, G.T., O'Leary, K.D., & Nathan, P. (1992) *Journal of Abnormal Psychology.* Englewood Cliffs, N.J.: Prentice-Hall.

Wilson, J., Blacher, J., & Baker, B.L. (1989) Siblings of Children with Severe Handicaps. *Mental Retardation* 27:167–173.

Wilson, J.J. (1981) Notetaking: A Necessary Support Service for Hearing-Impaired Students. *Teaching Exceptional Children,* 38–40.

Wilson, J.Q., & Herrnstein, R.J. (1985) *Crime and Human Nature.* New York: Simon & Schuster.

Winerop, M. (9 February 1994) In School. *New York Times,* B20.

Winick, B.J. (1995) The Side Effects of Incompetency Labeling and the Implications for Mental Health Law. *Psychology, Public Policy, and Law* 1:6–42.

Winkler, K.J. (November 1990) Proponents of "Multicultural" Humanities Research Call for a Critical Look at Its Achievements. *Chronicle of Higher Education* 28:A-5.

Winsor, P. (1992) Computer Applications in Music. In G. G. Bitter (ed.) *Macmillan Encyclopedia of Computers.* New York: Macmillan Publishing Company, 691–697.

Winter, S.W. (1994/1995) Diversity: A Program for All Children. *Childhood Education* 70: 91–95.

Winterling, V., Gast, D.L., Wolery, M., & Farmer, J.A. (1992) Teaching Safety Skills to High School Students with Moderate Disabilities. *Journal of Applied Behavior Analysis* 25:217–227.

Winters, R.L., Patterson, R., & Schontz, W. (1989) Visual Persistence and Adult Dyslexia. *Journal of Learning Disabilities* 22:641–645.

Wisdom, C.S. (1989) Does Violence Beget Violence? A Critical Examination of the Literature. *Psychological Bulletin* 106:3–28.

Wisniewski, L., & Alper, S. (1994) Including Students with Severe Disabilities in General Education Settings. *Remedial and Special Education* 15:4–13.

Witt, M.A. (1992) *Job Strategies for People with Disabilities,* Princeton, N.J.: Peterson's Guides.

Wolffe, K.E., Roessler, R.T., & Schriner, K.F. (1992) Employment Concerns of People with Blindness or Visual Impairments. *Journal of Visual Impairment & Blindness* 86:185–187.

Womack, S.T. (1989) Modes of Instruction. *The Clearing House* 62:205–210.

Wong, B.Y.L. (1992) On Cognitive Process-Based Instruction: An Introduction. *Journal of Learning Disabilities* 25:150–152, 172.

Wood, D. (1992) Total Communication in the Education of Deaf Children. *Developmental Medicine and Child Neurology* 34:266–269.

Wood, R.L. (1988) Attention Disorders in Brain Injury Rehabilitation. *Journal of Learning Disabilities* 21:327–333.

Wooten, M., & Mesibov, G.B. (1986) Social Skills Training for Elementary School Autistic Children with Normal Peers. In E. Schopler & G.B. Mesibov (eds.), *Social Behavior in Autism.* New York: Plenum, 305–319.

Workman, S.H. (1986) Teachers' Verbalizations and the Social Interaction of Blind Preschoolers. *Journal of Visual Impairment & Blindness* 80:532–534

Worsnop, R.L. (1991) Teenage Suicide. *CQ Researcher* 1:371–391.

Wrightman, M.J. (1991) Criteria for Placement Decisions with Cocaine-Exposed Infants. *Child Welfare* 70:653–663.

Wurtele, S.K., & Miller-Perrin, C.L. (1987a) Sexual Abuse Prevention: Are School Programs Harmful? *Journal of School Health* 57:228–231.

Wurtele, S.K., & Miller-Perrin (1987b) Harmful Effects of School-Based Sexual Abuse Prevention Programs? Reassure the Parents. In C.C. Tower, *How Schools Can Help Combat Child Abuse and Neglect* (2d ed.). Washington, D.C.: NEA Library, 146–153.

Yairi, E. (1983) The Onset of Stuttering in Two- And Three-Year-Old Children: A Preliminary Report. *Journal of Speech and Hearing Disorders* 48:171–177.

Yauman, B.E. (1980) Special Education Placement and the Self-Concepts of Elementary-School Age Children. *Learning Disabilities Quarterly* 3:30–35.

Ylvisaker, M. (1993) Communication Outcome in Children and Adolescents with Traumatic Brain Injury. *Neuropsychological Rehabilitation* 3:367–387.

York, J., Vandercook, T., MacDonald, C.M., Heise-Neff, C., & Caughey, E. (1992) Feedback about Integrating Middle-School Students with Severe Disabilities in General Education Classes. *Exceptional Children* 58:244–258.

Young, K.R. (1987) Future Directions in Social Skills Training, or Where Should We Be Going and Why? *The Special Educator* 7:1–3.

Youngman, G., & Sadongei, M. (1974) Counseling the American Indian Child. In D.R. Atkinson, G. Morten, & D.W. Sue (eds.), *Counseling American Minorities* (1979). Dubuque, Iowa: Brown, 59–64.

Zabin, L.S., Hirsch, M.B., Smith, E.A., Street, R., & Hardy, J.B. (1986) Evaluation of a Pregnancy Program for Urban Teenagers. *Family Planning Perspective* 11:119–126.

Zambone, A.M., & Huebner, K.M. (1992) Services for Children and Youths Who Are Deaf-Blind: An Overview. *Journal of Visual Impairment and Blindness* 86:287–290.

Zemlin, W.R. (1990) Anatomy and Physiology of Speech. In G.H. Shames & E.H. Wiig (eds.), *Human Communication Disorders*, 3d ed. Columbus, Ohio: Merrill, 74–126.

Zigler, E. (1992) Early Childhood Intervention: A Promising Preventative for Juvenile Delinquency. *American Psychologist* 47:997–1006.

Zigler, E., & Berman, W. (1983) Discerning the Future of Early Childhood Intervention. *American Psychologist* 38:894–907.

Zigler, E., & Hodapp, R.M. (1991) Behavioral Functioning in Individuals with Mental Retardation. *Annual Review of Psychology* 42:29–50.

Zigler, E., Taussig, C., & Black, K. (1992) Early Childhood Intervention: A Promising Preventative for Juvenile Delinquency. *American Psychologist* 47:997–1006.

Zigler, E.F. (1995) Meeting the Needs of Children in Poverty. *American Journal of Orthopsychiatry* 65: 6–9.

Zigmond, N., Levin, E., & Laurie, T.E. (1985) Managing the Mainstream: An Analysis of Teacher Attitudes and Student Performance in Mainstream High School Programs. *Journal of Learning Disabilities* 18:535–541.

Zigmond, N., & Thornton, H. (1985) Follow-up of Postsecondary Age Learning Disabled Graduates and Drop-outs. *Learning Disabilities Research* 1:50–55.

Zill, N., & Schoeborn, C.A. (1990) *Health of Our Nation's Children: Developmental, Learning and Emotional Problems. United States, 1988*, Advance Data, no. 190. Hyattsville, Md.: National Center for Health Statistics.

Zinman, D. (22 May 1990) Spinal Cord Injury. *Newsday*, 6ff.

Zuckerman, B. et al. (1989) Effects of Maternal Marijuana and Cocaine Use on Fetal Growth. *New England Journal of Medicine* 320:762–768.

Zuckerman, B., & Frank, D.A. (1992) "Crack Kids": Not Broken. *Pediatrics* 89:337–339.

Zweibel, A., & Allen, T. (1988) Mathematics Achievement of Hearing-Impaired Students in Different Educational Settings: A Cross-Cultural Perspective. *Volta Review* 90:287–293.

Glossary

acceleration A major division of services for gifted children in which a gifted student skips a grade or a particular unit or in which material is presented much more quickly than it would be for an average student.

acculturation The transfer of culture from one ethnic group to another.

alternate response training A self-control procedure in which students are taught to use responses that either interfere with or replace an undesirable response.

amplitude The loudness of the sound as measured in decibels.

Apgar Scoring System A relatively simple system used on infants at birth that gives a gross measure of infant survivability.

aphasia A loss of language or disruption of language due to brain injury.

articulation The ability to utter specific sounds required for communication.

articulation (phonological) disorder A speech disorder in which speech sounds are mispronounced.

assessment The ongoing procedures used to gather information concerning the needs of the child and the services necessary. It requires gathering information about the present level of performance, identifying objectives, and measuring progress.

Attention-deficit/hyperactivity disorder (ADHD) A diagnostic classification in the DSM-IV system involving a number of symptoms including inattention, impulsivity, and hyperactivity.

audiometer A machine that transmits tones at various frequencies and intensities used to test auditory abilities.

auditory brainstem-evoked response A method of detecting hearing loss in infants through an analysis of brain waves produced when sounds are delivered to the infant through earphones.

augmentative and alternative communication (AAC) Systems of communication that facilitate communication for people with severe expressive and/or language disorders.

autism A pervasive developmental disorder characterized by a lack of social responsiveness, serious deficits in communication abilities, perceptual problems, and developmental delays.

babbling Verbal production of vowel and consonant sounds strung together and often repeated.

behavior modification The use of the principles of learning theory to change behavior.

blind The educational definition that refers to the need to learn through braille or some other nonvisual medium.

blindisms Self-stimulatory behaviors such as eye-pressing, which are sometimes found in children who are blind.

braille A system of touch reading and writing in which raised dots represent the letters of the alphabet.

central hearing loss A hearing loss due to damage to the auditory centers in the brain.

cerebral palsy A condition characterized by a disturbance in voluntary movement caused by damage to the brain.

child abuse A general term used to denote an injury intentionally perpetrated on a child.

child neglect A term used to describe a situation in which the care and supervision of a child is insufficient or improper.

children with exceptional needs Children whose intellectual, emotional, or physical performance differs significantly from the average expected for their peer and cultural group so that special services are required for the child to develop adequately or learn well.

cohort effect The effect of living in a particular generation or historical time period.

communication The process of sharing information including facts, desires, and feelings.

conductive hearing loss A hearing loss due to difficulties in conducting sound through the ear canal, ear drum, and/or three bones in the middle ear.

conduct disorder A disorder marked by aggressive behavior and continuous violation of the basic rights of others.

convergent thinking A type of thinking in which people solve problems by integrating information in a logical manner.

cooperative learning Learning strategies that require two or more students to work together to reach some academic goal.

creativity The production of a novel response that appropriately solves a given problem.

criterion-referenced tests Tests in which student scores are compared to a particular criterion or absolute standard.

cued speech A system of communication in which eight hand shapes in four possible positions are used and offer added information to speechreading.

curriculum-based assessment (CBA) Assessment of a student's progress which is tied directly to the curriculum used to teach the child.

diplegia Motor limitations of both legs with some limitation in the arms.

direct instruction A type of instructional method especially useful for teaching a body of information that includes setting clear goals, presenting a sequence of well-organized assignments, explaining material to students, presenting examples, asking frequent questions, and giving frequent practice in what the students have learned.

disability A total or partial behavioral, mental, physical, or sensory loss of functioning.

divergent thinking A type of thinking marked by the ability to see new but still appropriate relationships between things in a given situation.

double hemiplegia Motor limitations of the arms with less limitation of the legs.

Down syndrome A chromosomal disorder leading to a distinct physical appearance and mental retardation of varying degree.

dual sensory impairments (deaf-blindness) Children with both hearing and visual impairments that cause severe communication and education problems.

early intervention A systematic effort to assist young children between the ages of birth and three years and their families. Programs attempt to enhance development, minimize potential developmental delays, remediate existing problems, and improve overall family functioning.

ecological assessment A type of assessment that seeks to understand the ongoing relationship between the child and the environment.

evaluation The determination of the child's eligibility for receiving special services.

external locus of control The belief that one is at the mercy of other people or fate.

externalizing behaviors A collection of behaviors that includes fighting, disobedience, and destructiveness.

extinction Withholding a reinforcer that is maintaining a particular behavior.

extinction burst The increase in the frequency of the undesirable

behavior that sometimes occurs when extinction procedures are initially implemented.

facilitated communication A controversial technique for improving the communication abilities of children with severe disorders in which physical assistance is provided to individuals to allow them to more readily spell out words on a typewriter or other device.

fading The gradual removal of a prompt or reinforcer.

fetal alcohol effect An umbrella term used to describe injury to the child caused by the mother's alcohol consumption during pregnancy, which is somewhat less pronounced than fetal alcohol syndrome.

fetal alcohol syndrome A number of characteristics—including mental retardation, facial abnormalities, growth defects, and poor coordination—caused by maternal alcohol consumption during pregnancy.

frequency The number of sound waves per second, measured in hertz.

functional skill A skill that is useful to the student in the daily routine and gives the child some control over the environment.

grammar A general term that refers to the total linguistic knowledge of phonology, morphology, syntax, and semantics.

handicap The difficulty an individual experiences in adjusting to the environment; the term used in connection with an environmental restriction.

hemiplegia Motor limitations of two extremities on the same side.

holophrase One word used to stand for an entire thought.

incidence The number of new cases of a condition within a particular time period, usually one year.

inclusion (full inclusion) A movement advocating that all services for

children with disabilities be delivered in the regular classroom.

Individualized Education Program (IEP) A written statement of the educational program specifically designed to meet a child's special needs.

Individualized Family Service Plan (IFSP) A plan describing the child's developmental level, family functioning, major outcomes, services the child will receive, and transition support for young children with disabilities and their families.

internal locus of control The belief that one is in control of one's own fate.

internalizing behaviors A collection of behaviors that includes anxiety, withdrawal, and depression.

isolated developmental dysphasias Language disorders involving delayed or deviant language in the absence of any other disability.

Kurzweil Reading Machine A machine that converts print into sound.

language Any system of arbitrary symbols with agreed-upon meanings.

language disorders Difficulties involving poor grammar, delayed language, or the proper use of words.

learned helplessness The learned inability to overcome obstacles that involves the belief that one cannot do anything to improve one's lot.

legal blindness A visual acuity of 20/200 vision or less in the better eye, even with correction, or a reduction of the visual field to less than 20 degrees.

lekotek (play library) A center in which children with disabilities can borrow specially adapted toys, games, and other material.

low vision The educational definition that refers to the inability to read a newspaper at a reasonable viewing distance even with correction.

macular degeneration A degeneration of the central portion of the retina, which causes visual loss.

mainstreaming The placement of children with disabilities in the regular classroom.

mental age The age at which an individual is functioning.

mental retardation A term referring to subaverage intellectual functioning which exists with impairments in adaptive behavior and occurs before a person is 18 years of age.

metacognition The conscious monitoring and regulation of the way people approach and solve a problem or challenge.

metamemory People's knowledge of their own memory processes.

mixed hearing loss A hearing loss that is both conductive and sensorineural in origin.

mobility The ability to move from place to place as desired.

monoplegia Motor limitations of one extremity.

morphology The study of the patterns of word formation in a particular language.

multicultural education A general term referring to a multidisciplinary approach to education aimed at teaching students about the cultural heritage of various groups and the many contributions each group makes to society.

normal curve A bell-shaped distribution in which scores occur symmetrically about the mean, and the mean and median are the same. It is very useful for understanding the distribution of many human traits.

norm-referenced tests Standardized tests in which the score of the test taker is compared to the scores of other students who took the test when it was developed.

oppositional defiant disorder A disorder in which children defy rules, show anger and resentment, and often lose their tempers, but show limited aggressiveness and do not usually violate the rights of others.

optacon A device that converts print into tactual letter configurations that are read with the fingertips.

orientation The use of the remaining senses to establish one's position and relationship to other objects in the environment.

orthopedic disabilities Disabilities primarily related to skeletal, spinal, or joint disease.

otitis media A middle ear infection that sometimes leads to hearing loss.

overselectivity The phenomenon in which children with autism select a part of the stimulus and maintain their attention to the part rather than the whole stimulus.

paraplegia Motor limitations of both legs.

partial participation The principle that some individuals with severe disabilities may not be able to perform an activity with complete independence, but can participate at least partially in most activities.

partial sight Visual acuity that falls between 20/70 and 20/200 in the better eye, with correction.

phobia A persistent and irrational fear of a specific object, activity, or situation.

phonation The ability to vocalize sounds.

phonology The study of the sounds of language, the rules for combining the sounds to make words, and the stress and intonation patterns of the language.

plasticity The extent to which an individual can be molded by environmental influence.

postlingual hearing loss A hearing loss that occurs after the child has learned basic language.

pragmatics The study of how people use language in various contexts.

precision teaching A systematic procedure using continuous and direct recording of behavior.

prelingual hearing loss A hearing loss that occurs before language is learned, commonly considered before the age of three years.

prevalence The total number of cases that exist within a particular population at a given time.

prompt A cue that initiates a response.

quadriplegia Motor limitations of four extremities.

reciprocal interaction The process by which an organism constantly affects and is affected by the environment.

reciprocal teaching An approach to teaching reading strategies that involves summarizing, question generating, clarifying, and predicting, and requires students and teacher to enter into a dialogue for discussing the meaning of a written passage.

Regular Education Initiative (REI) A movement in education to merge special education and general education.

reinforcer Any event that increases the likelihood the behavior that preceded it will reoccur.

resonance The quality of the voice.

response cost A punishment procedure in which a positive reinforcer is lost if an undesirable behavior is exhibited.

retinitis pigmentosa A group of inherited disorders that cause progressive degeneration of the retina and vision loss.

retinopathy of prematurity A condition of blindness resulting from an oversupply of oxygen, most often administered to premature infants.

reverse mainstreaming A program implemented in preschools for children with disabilities in which some children without disabilities are admitted in order to promote interaction between children with and without disabilities.

rhythm The rate and timing of speech.

screening Activities used to identify children in need of further evaluation or assessment.

self-determination The ability to make one's own decisions and choices.

self-reinforcement A process in which students reinforce themselves for desired behaviors.

semantics The study of the meaning of words.

sensorineural hearing loss A hearing loss due to damage to the inner ear or nerve pathways to the brain.

social competence The ability of young children to successfully select and carry out their interpersonal goals.

speech disorders Difficulties involving the physical reproduction of speech.

stress resistant (resilient) children Children who do not appear to be negatively affected by stress and are able to cope with stressful environments. The adjustment of these children during adolescence and adulthood is surprisingly good.

supported employment A program emphasizing placement of individuals with disabilities in competitive employment with a job coach.

synchrony The coordination between infant and caregiver in which each can respond to the subtle verbal and nonverbal cues of the other.

syndrome A collection of symptoms that are found together.

syntax The rules for combining words to make sentences.

systematic desensitization A behavioral technique for reducing anxiety, which involves progressive relaxation followed by the gradual introduction of the feared stimulus.

task analysis The process of breaking down tasks into the smallest elements in their proper sequence.

telegraphic speech Sentences in which only the basic words necessary to communicate meaning are used, which leaves out helping words such as "a" or "to."

teratogen Any agent that causes birth defects.

Theory of Multiple Intelligences A conception of intelligence advanced by Howard Gardner, who argues that there are seven different types of intelligence.

time delay procedure A procedure in which the instructor initially delivers the prompt for a particular behavior immediately following the instructional cue but then delays giving the prompt on successive trials to give the learner a chance to respond.

time-out A punishment procedure in which access to positive reinforcement is withdrawn for a brief time period if a serious behavior infraction occurs.

token economy (token reinforcement system) A system of reinforcement in which students receive a token (such as a star) for performing the desired behavior and can either use it immediately or save it and add it to previously earned tokens to "purchase" reinforcers.

Torrance Tests of Creative Thinking (TTCT) A test of creativity that measures fluency, flexibility, ability to elaborate, and originality of a person's thinking.

total communication The use of all possible means of communicating, including speech, signing, and speechreading.

triplegia Motor limitations of three extremities.

visual acuity The ability to see objects at particular distances.

voice disorder A speech disorder involving the quality of the vocalizations.

Index

Photo Credits